JACQUIE B

Vestments & Altar Hangings

Individually designed & created Stoles, Chasubles, Copes, Altar Cloths, Banners, Falls & Sculptures.

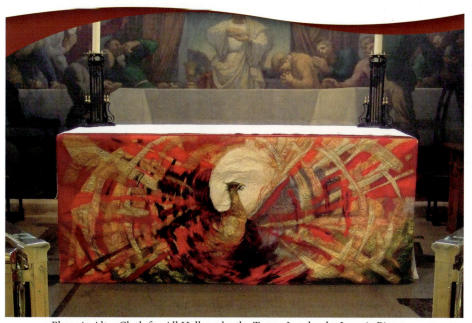

Phoenix Altar Cloth for All Hallows by the Tower, London by Jacquie Binns.

Web Page	www.JacquieBinns.com
Email	JB@JacquieBinns.com
Tel	020 8874 0895

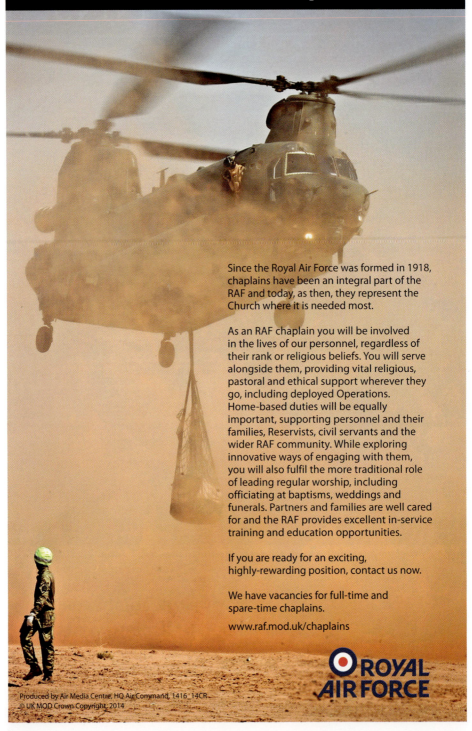

Could You Be Their Chaplain?

Since the Royal Air Force was formed in 1918, chaplains have been an integral part of the RAF and today, as then, they represent the Church where it is needed most.

As an RAF chaplain you will be involved in the lives of our personnel, regardless of their rank or religious beliefs. You will serve alongside them, providing vital religious, pastoral and ethical support wherever they go, including deployed Operations. Home-based duties will be equally important, supporting personnel and their families, Reservists, civil servants and the wider RAF community. While exploring innovative ways of engaging with them, you will also fulfil the more traditional role of leading regular worship, including officiating at baptisms, weddings and funerals. Partners and families are well cared for and the RAF provides excellent in-service training and education opportunities.

If you are ready for an exciting, highly-rewarding position, contact us now.

We have vacancies for full-time and spare-time chaplains.

www.raf.mod.uk/chaplains

ROYAL AIR FORCE

Produced by Air Media Centre, HQ Air Command, 1416_14CR
© UK MOD Crown Copyright 2014

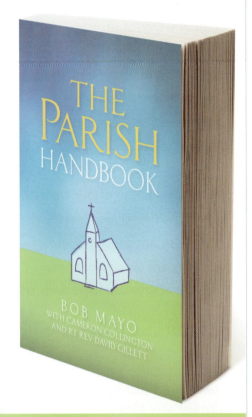

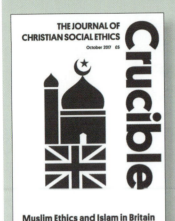
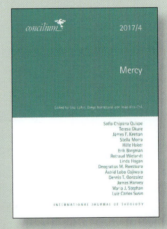

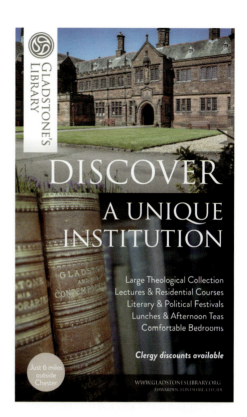

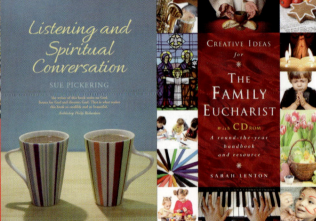

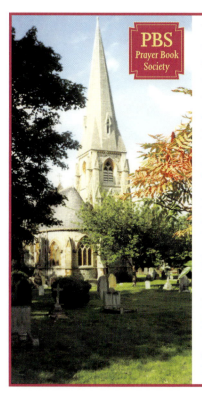

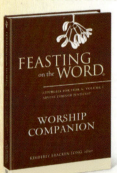

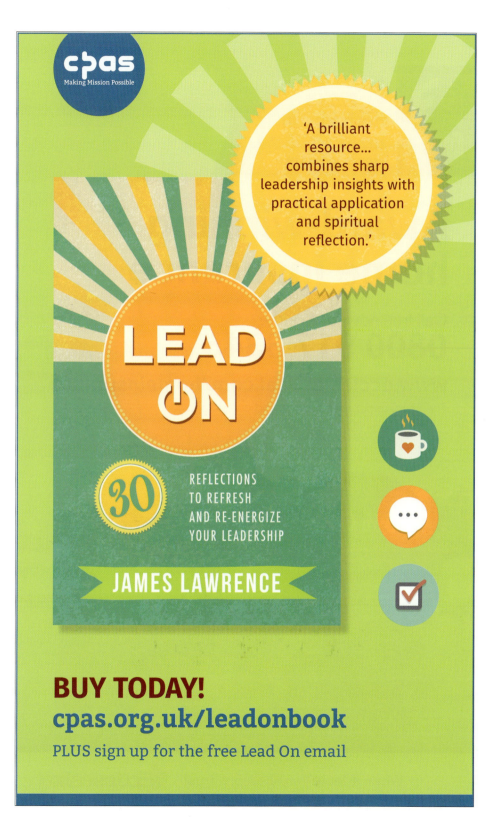

ROYAL NAVY CHAPLAIN:
PARISH MINISTRY ON A GLOBAL SCALE

Every pastor acts as friend and adviser to their community. You'll do it in unique environments all over the world.

Serve full-time or in the Reserves, committing to just three years and enjoying a career where no two days are the same.

Join the Royal Navy

Search: RN Chaplain
Call: 0345 607 5555
Email: navycnr-chaplain@mod.uk

ROYAL
NAVY

THE CHURCH OF ENGLAND

YEAR BOOK

2018

133RD EDITION

A directory of local and national
structures and organizations
and the Churches and Provinces
of the Anglican Communion

SINCE 1883

CHURCH HOUSE
PUBLISHING

Church House Publishing, Church House, Great Smith Street, London SW1P 3AZ

ISBN 978–0–7151–1130–7

ISSN 0069 3987

Typeset by RefineCatch Ltd, Bungay, Suffolk

Printed by Ashford Colour Press, Gosport, Hants

The Church of England Year Book

The official Year Book of the Church of England

133rd edition © The Archbishops' Council 2018

Contents

WELCOME TO THE 2018 CHURCH OF ENGLAND YEAR BOOK

Welcome to the 133rd Edition of *The Church of England Year Book* – the first edition of which appeared in 1883. This 2018 volume represents the latest information (as at October 2017) found in the new database that is also used to compile the online version of the *Year Book*. The Year Book online subscription service can be accessed via **www.crockford.org.uk/yearbook**.

The *Year Book* is the official directory of local and national structures and organizations of the Church of England and the Churches and Provinces of the Anglican and Porvoo Communions. Both the print and online editions of the Year Book are designed to work in tandem with its sister publication *Crockford's Clerical Directory*, providing readers of both publications with access to an enhanced range of data on individuals, dioceses, cathedrals and other institutions. For example, online *Year Book* 'Who's Who' profiles for members of the clergy also provide access to their *Crockford* biography to those with a valid subscription. There are obvious advantages to the online edition – not least the ability to update data more frequently – but the new system has been developed since June 2016 to provide data for an annual print edition in line with continuing demand.

This is the second edition to use the refreshed design and structure introduced for 2017, featuring:

- **A clearer page design** We have taken the opportunity to refresh the page design, mirroring the current design of *Crockford*.
- **A single, detailed Table of Contents** is now offered – making it easier to see what each part contains in one place, rather than, as before, in seven different places across the book.
- **Diocese name provided on the sidebar** on the relevant pages in Part 1, so that the relevant pages can be located more quickly in this most frequently used section of the book.
- **Removal of abbreviations** in the Who's Who section in particular, making each entry easier to read without reference to a key. Only qualifications and honours are now shown in their abbreviated form. Where abbreviated forms are used (for clerical titles, for example), the Year Book now endeavours to follow the same conventions as *Crockford*.
- **Fewer, clearer sections** – the previous 'General' section contained a somewhat eclectic and unpredictable range of information and was, as a result, not as widely used as those sections with a clearer purpose and focus. Hence, in this edition, material previously found in the General section has either been re-allocated (to 'National' or 'Other Organizations' as relevant) or has been omitted, particularly where it is freely available online, often via the free 'Listings' section of the Crockford and Year Book website (see www.crockford.org.uk/ listings).

We would encourage readers to let us know if you have any feedback or suggestions of other improvements you would like us to consider for the book and/or website editions.

Finally, we would like to express our continued thanks to all those who have helped us in compiling this edition by providing us with updates and information, without which production of such a reference work would be impossible.

E-mail: **yearbook@churchofengland.org**

CALENDAR 2018–19

According to the Calendar, Lectionary and Collects authorized pursuant to Canon B 2 of the Canons of the Church of England for use until further resolution of the General Synod of the Church of England.

Key
BOLD UPPER CASE – Principal Feasts and other Principal Holy Days
Bold Roman – Sundays and Festivals
Roman – Lesser Festivals
Small Italic – Commemorations
Italic – Other Observances

JANUARY 2018 (Year B)
1 **The Naming and Circumcision of Jesus**
2 Basil the Great and Gregory of Nazianzus, bishops, teachers of the faith, 379 and 389
Seraphim, monk of Sarov, spiritual guide, 1833
Vedanayagam Samuel Azariah, bishop, evangelist, 1945
6 **THE EPIPHANY**
7 **The Baptism of Christ** – *The First Sunday of Epiphany*
10 *William Laud, Archbishop of Canterbury, 1645*
11 *Mary Slessor, missionary in West Africa, 1915*
12 Aelred of Hexham, Abbot of Rievaulx, 1167
Benedict Biscop, Abbot of Wearmouth, scholar, 689
13 Hilary, Bishop of Poitiers, teacher of the faith, 367
Kentigern (Mungo), missionary bishop, 603
George Fox, founder of the Society of Friends (Quakers), 1691
14 **The Second Sunday of Epiphany**
17 Antony of Egypt, hermit, abbot, 356
Charles Gore, bishop, founder of the Community of the Resurrection, 1932
18–25 Week of Prayer for Christian Unity
18 *Amy Carmichael, founder of the Dohnavur Fellowship, spiritual writer, 1951*
19 Wulfstan, Bishop of Worcester, 1095
20 *Richard Rolle of Hampole, spiritual writer, 1349*
21 **The Third Sunday of Epiphany**
22 *Vincent of Saragossa, deacon, first Martyr of Spain, 304*
24 Francis de Sales, Bishop of Geneva, teacher of the faith, 1622
25 **The Conversion of Paul**
26 Timothy and Titus, companions of Paul
28 **The Fourth Sunday of Epiphany**
30 Charles, king and martyr, 1649
31 *John Bosco, priest, founder of the Salesian Teaching Order, 1888*

FEBRUARY
1 *Brigid, Abbess of Kildare, c.525*
2 **THE PRESENTATION OF CHRIST IN THE TEMPLE** (Candlemas)
3 Anskar, Archbishop of Hamburg, missionary in Denmark and Sweden, 865
4 **The Second Sunday before Lent**
6 *Martyrs of Japan, 1597*
Accession of Queen Elizabeth II, 1952
10 *Scholastica, sister of Benedict, Abbess of Plombariola, c.543*
11 **The Sunday next before Lent**
14 **ASH WEDNESDAY**
15 *Sigfrid, bishop, Apostle of Sweden, 1045*
Thomas Bray, priest, founder of SPCK and SPG, 1730
17 Janani Luwum, Archbishop of Uganda, martyr, 1977
18 **The First Sunday of Lent**
23 Polycarp, Bishop of Smyrna, martyr, c.155
25 **The Second Sunday of Lent**
27 George Herbert, priest, poet, 1633

MARCH
1 David, Bishop of Menevia, Patron of Wales, c.601
2 Chad, Bishop of Lichfield, missionary, 672
4 **The Third Sunday of Lent**
7 Perpetua, Felicity and companions, martyrs at Carthage, 203
8 Edward King, Bishop of Lincoln, 1910
Felix, bishop, Apostle to the East Angles, 647
Geoffrey Studdert Kennedy, priest, poet, 1929
11 **The Fourth Sunday of Lent** – *Mothering Sunday*
17 Patrick, bishop, missionary, patron of Ireland, c.460
18 **The Fifth Sunday of Lent**
19 **Joseph of Nazareth**
20 Cuthbert, Bishop of Lindisfarne, missionary, 68
21 Thomas Cranmer, Archbishop of Canterbury, Reformation martyr, 1556
24 *Walter Hilton of Thurgarton, Augustinian canon, mystic, 1396*
Paul Couturier, priest, ecumenist, 1953
Oscar Romero, Archbishop of San Salvador, martyr, 1980
25 **Palm Sunday**
26 Monday of Holy Week
27 Tuesday of Holy Week
28 Wednesday of Holy Week
29 **MAUNDY THURSDAY**
30 **GOOD FRIDAY**
31 Easter Eve

APRIL
1 **EASTER DAY**
2 Monday of Easter Week
3 Tuesday of Easter Week
4 Wednesday of Easter Week
5 Thursday of Easter Week
6 Friday of Easter Week
7 Saturday of Easter Week
8 **The Second Sunday of Easter**
9 **THE ANNUNCIATION OF OUR LORD TO THE BLESSED VIRGIN MARY**
10 William Law, priest, spiritual writer, 1761
William of Ockham, friar, philosopher, teacher of the faith, 1347
11 *George Augustus Selwyn, first Bishop of New Zealand, 1878*
15 **The Third Sunday of Easter**
16 *Isabella Gilmore, Deaconess, 1923*
19 Alphege, Archbishop of Canterbury, martyr, 1012
21 Anselm, Abbot of Le Bec, Archbishop of Canterbury, teacher of the faith, 1109
22 **The Fourth Sunday of Easter**
23 **George, martyr, patron of England, c.304**
24 *Mellitus, Bishop of London, first Bishop at St Paul's, 624*
The Seven Martyrs of the Melanesian Brotherhood, Solomon Islands, 2003
25 **Mark the Evangelist**
27 *Christina Rossetti, poet, 1894*
28 *Peter Chanel, missionary in the South Pacific, martyr, 1841*
29 **The Fifth Sunday of Easter**
30 *Pandita Mary Ramabai, translator of the Scriptures, 1922*

MAY
1 **Philip and James, Apostles**
2 Athanasius, Bishop of Alexandria, teacher of the faith, 373
4 **English saints and martyrs of the Reformation Era**
6 **The Sixth Sunday of Easter**
8 Julian of Norwich, spiritual writer, c.1417
10 **ASCENSION DAY**
12 *Gregory Dix, priest, monk. scholar, 1952*
13 **The Seventh Sunday of Easter**
14 **Matthias the Apostle**
16 *Caroline Chisholm, social reformer, 1877*
19 Dunstan, Archbishop of Canterbury, restorer of monastic life, 988
20 **PENTECOST**
21 *Helena, protector of the Holy Places, 330*
24 *John and Charles Wesley, evangelists, hymn writers, 1791 and 1788*
25 The Venerable Bede, monk, scholar, historian, 735
Aldhelm, Bishop of Sherborne, 709
26 Augustine, first Archbishop of Canterbury, 605
John Calvin, reformer 1564
Philip Neri, founder of the Oratorians, spiritual guide, 1595
27 **TRINITY SUNDAY**

28 *Lanfranc, Prior of Le Bec, archbishop, scholar, 1089*
30 Josephine Butler, social reformer, 1906
Joan of Arc, visionary, 1431
Apolo Kivebulaya, priest, evangelist in Central Africa, 1933
31 **Day of Thanksgiving for the Institution of Holy Communion (Corpus Christi)**

JUNE
1 **The Visit of the Blessed Virgin Mary to Elizabeth**
3 **The First Sunday after Trinity**
4 *Petroc, Abbot of Padstow, 6th century*
5 Boniface (Wynfrith) of Crediton, bishop, Apostle of Germany, martyr, 754
6 *Ini Kapuria, founder of the Melanesian Brotherhood, 1945*
8 Thomas Ken, Bishop of Bath and Wells, nonjuror, hymn writer, 1711
9 Columba, Abbot of Iona, missionary, 597
Ephrem of Syria, deacon, hymn writer, teacher of the faith, 373
10 **The Second Sunday after Trinity**
11 **Barnabas the Apostle**
14 *Richard Baxter, puritan divine, 1691*
15 *Evelyn Underhill, Spiritual Writer, 1941*
16 Richard, Bishop of Chichester, 1253
Joseph Butler, Bishop of Durham, philosopher, 1752
17 **The Third Sunday after Trinity**
18 *Bernard Mizeki, Apostle of the MaShona, martyr, 1896*
19 *Sundar Singh, sadhu (holy man), evangelist, teacher of the faith, 1929*
22 Alban, first martyr of Britain, c.250
23 Etheldreda, Abbess of Ely, c.678
24 **The Birth of John the Baptist** – *The Fourth Sunday after Trinity*
27 *Cyril, bishop, teacher of the faith, 444*
28 Iranaeus, Bishop of Lyons, teacher of the faith, c.200
29 **Peter and Paul, Apostles *or* Peter the Apostle**

JULY
1 **The Fifth Sunday after Trinity**
3 **Thomas the Apostle**
6 *Thomas More, scholar, and John Fisher, Bishop of Rochester, Reformation martyrs, 1535*
8 **The Sixth Sunday after Trinity**
11 Benedict of Nursia, abbot, Father of Western Monasticism, c.550
14 John Keble, priest, Tractarian, poet, 1866
15 **The Seventh Sunday after Trinity**
16 *Osmund, Bishop of Salisbury, 1099*
18 *Elizabeth Ferard, deaconess, founder of the Community of St Andrew, 1883*
19 Gregory, bishop and his sister Macrina, deaconess, teachers of the faith, c.394 and c.379
20 *Margaret of Antioch, martyr, 4th century*
Bartolomé de las Casas, Apostle to the Indies, 1566
22 **Mary Magdalene** – *The Eighth Sunday after Trinity*
23 *Bridget of Sweden, Abbess of Vadstena, 1373*

25 James the Apostle
26 Anne and Joachim, parents of the Blessed Virgin Mary
27 *Brooke Foss Westcott, Bishop of Durham, teacher of the faith, 1901*
29 **The Ninth Sunday after Trinity**
30 William Wilberforce, social reformer, Olaudah Equiano and Thomas Clarkson, anti-slavery campaigners, 1833, 1797 and 1846
31 *Ignatius Loyola, founder of the Society of Jesus, 1556*

AUGUST
4 *Jean-Baptiste Vianney, Curé d'Ars, spiritual guide, 1859*
5 **The Tenth Sunday after Trinity**
6 **The Transfiguration of Our Lord**
7 *John Mason Neale, priest, hymn writer, 1866*
8 Dominic, priest, founder of the Order of Preachers, 1221
9 Mary Sumner, founder of the Mothers' Union, 1921
10 Laurence, deacon at Rome, martyr, 258
11 Clare of Assisi, founder of the Minoresses (Poor Clares), 1253
   John Henry Newman, priest, Tractarian, 1890
12 **The Eleventh Sunday after Trinity**
13 Jeremy Taylor, bishop, teacher of the faith, 1667
   Florence Nightingale, nurse, social reformer, 1910
   Octavia Hill, social reformer, 1912
14 *Maximilian Kolbe, friar, martyr, 1941*
15 **The Blessed Virgin Mary**
19 **The Twelfth Sunday after Trinity**
20 Bernard, Abbot of Clairvaux, teacher of the faith, 1153
   William and Catherine Booth, Founders of the Salvation Army, 1912 and 1890
24 **Bartholomew the Apostle**
26 **The Thirteenth Sunday after Trinity**
27 Monica, mother of Augustine of Hippo, 387
28 Augustine, bishop, teacher of the faith, 430
29 Beheading of John the Baptist
30 John Bunyan, spiritual writer, 1688
31 Aidan, Bishop of Lindisfarne, missionary, 651

SEPTEMBER
1 *Giles of Provence, hermit, c.710*
2 **The Fourteenth Sunday after Trinity**
3 Gregory the Great, Bishop of Rome, teacher of the faith, 604
4 *Birinus, Bishop of Dorchester, Apostle of Wessex, 650*
6 *Allen Gardiner, missionary, founder of the South American Missionary Society, 1851*
8 The Birth of the Blessed Virgin Mary
9 **The Fifteenth Sunday after Trinity**
13 John Chrysostom, bishop, teacher of the faith, 407
14 **Holy Cross Day**
15 Cyprian, Bishop of Carthage, martyr, 258
16 **The Sixteenth Sunday after Trinity**
17 Hildegard, Abbess of Bingen, visionary, 1179

19 *Theodore of Tarsus, Archbishop of Canterbury, 690*
20 John Coleridge Patteson, first Bishop of Melanesia, and companions, martyrs, 1871
21 **Matthew, Apostle and Evangelist**
23 **The Seventeenth Sunday after Trinity**
25 Lancelot Andrewes, Bishop of Winchester, spiritual writer, 1626
   Sergei of Radonezh, monastic reformer, teacher of the faith, 1392
26 *Wilson Carlile, founder of the Church Army, 1942*
27 Vincent de Paul, founder of the Lazarists, 1660
29 **Michael and All Angels**
30 **The Eighteenth Sunday after Trinity**

OCTOBER
1 *Remigius, Bishop of Rheims, Apostle of the Franks, 533*
   Anthony Ashley Cooper, Earl of Shaftesbury, social reformer, 1885
3 *George Bell, bishop, ecumenist, peacemaker, 1958*
4 Francis of Assisi, friar, deacon, founder of the Friars Minor, 1226
6 William Tyndale, translator, Reformation martyr, 1536
7 **The Nineteenth Sunday after Trinity**
9 *Denys, bishop, and companions, martyrs, c.250*
   Robert Grosseteste, bishop, philosopher, scientist, 1253
10 Paulinus, bishop, missionary, 644
   Thomas Traherne, poet, spiritual writer, 1674
11 *Ethelburga, Abbess of Barking, 675*
   James the Deacon, companion of Paulinus, 7th cent.
12 Wilfrid of Ripon, bishop, missionary, 709
   Elizabeth Fry, prison reformer, 1845
   Edith Cavell, nurse, 1915
13 Edward the Confessor, King of England, 1066
14 **The Twentieth Sunday after Trinity**
15 Teresa of Avila, teacher of the faith, 1582
16 *Nicholas Ridley and Hugh Latimer, bishops, martyrs, 1555*
17 Ignatius, Bishop of Antioch, martyr, c.107
18 **Luke the Evangelist**
19 Henry Martyn, translator, missionary in India and Persia, 1812
21 **The Twenty-first Sunday after Trinity**
25 *Crispin and Crispian, martyrs at Rome, c.287*
26 Alfred, King of the West Saxons, scholar, 899
   Cedd, Abbot of Lastingham, Bishop of the East Saxons, 664
28 **Simon and Jude, Apostles** – *The Last Sunday after Trinity (Bible Sunday)*
31 *Martin Luther, reformer, 1546*

NOVEMBER
1 **ALL SAINTS' DAY**
2 Commemoration of the Faithful Departed (All Souls' Day)
3 Richard Hooker, priest, Anglican apologist, teacher of the faith, 1600
   Martin of Porres, friar, 1639
4 **The Fourth Sunday before Advent**
6 *Leonard, hermit, 6th cent.*
   William Temple, archbishop, teacher of the faith, 1944

7 Willibrord, bishop, Apostle of Frisia, 739
8 Saints and Martyrs of England
9 *Margery Kempe, mystic, c.1440*
10 Leo the Great, Bishop of Rome, teacher of the faith, 461
11 **The Third Sunday before Advent** – *Remembrance Sunday*
13 Charles Simeon, priest, evangelical divine, 1836
14 *Samuel Seabury, first Anglican Bishop in North America, 1796*
16 Margaret, Queen of Scotland, philanthropist, reformer of the Church, 1093
Edmund Rich of Abingdon, Archbishop of Canterbury, 1240
17 Hugh, Bishop of Lincoln, 1200
18 **The Second Sunday before Advent**
19 Hilda, Abbess of Whitby, 680
Mechtild, béguine of Magdeburg, mystic, 1280
20 Edmund, King of the East Angles, martyr, 870
Priscilla Lydia Sellon, a restorer of the religious life in the Church of England, 1876
22 *Cecilia, martyr at Rome, c.230*
23 Clement, Bishop of Rome, martyr, c.100
25 **Christ the King** – *The Sunday next before Advent*
29 *Day of Intercession and Thanksgiving for the Missionary Work of the Church*
30 **Andrew the Apostle**

DECEMBER
1 *Charles de Foucauld, hermit in the Sahara, 1916*
2 **The First Sunday of Advent (Year C)**
3 *Francis Xavier, missionary, Apostle of the Indies, 1552*
4 *John of Damascus, monk, teacher of the faith, c.749*
Nicholas Ferrar, deacon, founder of the Little Gidding Community, 1637
6 Nicholas, bishop, c.326
7 Ambrose, Bishop of Milan, teacher of the faith, 397
8 The Conception of the Blessed Virgin Mary
9 **The Second Sunday of Advent**
13 Lucy, martyr at Syracuse, 304
Samuel Johnson, moralist, 178
14 John of the Cross, poet, teacher of the faith, 1591
16 **The Third Sunday of Advent**
17 *O Sapientia*
Eglantyne Jebb, social reformer, founder of 'Save The Children', 1928
23 **The Fourth Sunday of Advent**
24 **Christmas Eve**
25 **CHRISTMAS DAY**
26 **Stephen, deacon, first martyr**
27 **John, Apostle and Evangelist**
28 **The Holy Innocents**
29 Thomas Becket, Archbishop of Canterbury, martyr, 1170

30 **The First Sunday of Christmas**
31 *John Wyclif, Reformer, 1384*

JANUARY 2019
1 **The Naming and Circumcision of Jesus**
2 Basil the Great and Gregory of Nazianzus, bishops, teachers of the faith, 379 and 389
Seraphim, monk, spiritual guide, 1833
Vedanayagam Samuel Azariah, bishop, evangelist, 1945
6 **THE EPIPHANY**
10 *William Laud, archbishop, 1645*
11 *Mary Slessor, missionary in West Africa, 1915*
12 Aelred of Hexham, Abbot of Rievaulx, 1167
Benedict Biscop, Abbot of Wearmouth, scholar, 689
13 **The Baptism of Christ** – *The Second Sunday of Epiphany*
17 Antony of Egypt, hermit, abbot, 356
Charles Gore, bishop, founder of the Community of the Resurrection, 1932
18–25 *Week of Prayer for Christian Unity*
18 *Amy Carmichael, founder of the Dohnavur Fellowship, spiritual writer, 1951*
19 Wulfstan, Bishop of Worcester, 1095
20 **The Third Sunday of Epiphany**
21 Agnes, child martyr at Rome, 304
22 *Vincent of Saragossa, deacon, first Martyr of Spain, 304*
24 Francis de Sales, Bishop of Geneva, teacher of the faith, 1622
25 **The Conversion of Paul**
26 Timothy and Titus, companions of Paul
27 **The Fourth Sunday of Epiphany**
28 Thomas Aquinas, priest, philosopher, teacher of the faith, 1274
30 Charles, king and martyr, 1649
31 *John Bosco, priest, founder of the Salesian Teaching Order, 1888*

Other Dates

6 February	Accession Day
11 February	Racial Justice Sunday
11 February	Unemployment Sunday
2 March	Women's World Day of Prayer
22 April	Vocations Sunday
6 May	Godparents' Sunday
10 May	'Thy Kingdom Come' until 20 May
13 May	Christian Aid Week until 19 May
1 July	Day of Prayer for Vocations to Religious Life
8 July	Sea Sunday
9 September	Education Sunday
7 October	Animal Welfare Sunday
14 October	Hospital Sunday
14 October	Prisons Sunday
24 October	United Nations Day
1 December	World AIDS Day
9 December	Human Rights Day

Dioceses and Cathedrals

PART 1

DIOCESE OF BATH AND WELLS

Founded in 909. Somerset; north Somerset; Bath; north-east Somerset; a few parishes in Dorset.

Population 947,000   Area 1,610 sq m
Full-time Stipendiary Parochial Clergy 195   Benefices 178
Parishes 463   Churches 560
www.bathandwells.org.uk
Overseas link dioceses: Luapula, Lusaka, Central Zambia, Northern Zambia and Eastern Zambia

BISHOP (78th)
The Rt Revd Peter Hancock, The Palace, Wells BA5 2PD   *T:* 01749 672341
                                    F: 01749 679355
            E: bishop@bathwells.anglican.org

BISHOP'S STAFF
Bishops' Senior Chaplain and Adviser Preb Stephen Lynas, The Palace, Wells BA5 2PD
                    T: 01749 672341 (office)
                                    F: 01749 679355
        E: chaplain@bathwells.anglican.org

SUFFRAGAN BISHOP
TAUNTON The Rt Revd Ruth Worsley, The Palace, Wells BA5 2PD   *T:* 01749 672341
                                    M: 07917 693285
    E: bishop.taunton@bathwells.anglican.org

ASSISTANT BISHOPS
The Rt Revd William Persson, Ryalls Cottage, Burton St Marnhull, Sturminster Newton DT10 1PS   *T:* 01258 820452
The Rt Revd Paul Barber, Hillside, 41 Somerton Road, Street BA16 0DR   *T:* 01458 442916
The Rt Revd Barry Rogerson, Flat 2, 30 Albert Road, Clevedon BS21 7RR   *T:* 01275 541964
        E: barry.rogerson@blueyonder.co.uk
The Rt Revd Roger Sainsbury, Abbey Lodge, Battery Lane, Portishead BS20 7JD
                    T: 01275 847082
            E: bishoproger@talktalk.net
The Rt Revd John Perry, 8 The Firs, Bath BA2 5ED   *T:* 01225 833987
            E: jperry8@btinternet.com
The Rt Revd George Cassidy, Darch House, 17 St Andrew Road, Stogursey, Bridgwater TA5 1TE   *T:* 01278 732625
        E: georgecassidy123@btinternet.com

CATHEDRAL CHURCH OF ST ANDREW IN WELLS
Dean The Very Revd Dr John Davies, The Dean's Lodging, 25 The Liberty, Wells BA5 2SZ   *T:* 01749 677888
    E: deanchaptersec@wellscathedral.uk.net
Canons Residentiary
Chancellor Canon Andrew Featherstone, 8 The Liberty, Wells BA5 2SU   *T:* 01749 679587
    E: chancellorofwellscathedral@gmail.com

Precentor Canon Nicholas Jepson-Biddle, 4 The Liberty, Wells BA5 2SU   *T:* 01749 673489
            E: nicklb@hotmail.co.uk
Treasurer Preb Dr Graham Dodds, 2 The Liberty, Wells BA5 2SU   *T:* 01749 670607
                                    F: 01749 674240
    E: graham.dodds@bathwells.anglican.org
Archdeacon The Ven Anne Gell, 6 The Liberty, Wells BA5 2SU   *T:* 01749 685147
        E: adwells@bathwells.anglican.org
Lay Members
Preb Dr Alan Kerbery, Cathedral Offices, Chain Gate, Cathedral Green, Wells BA5 2UE
Preb Dr Alison Perham (*Same Address*)
Preb Dr Tim Wilson (*Same Address*)
Cathedral Administrator Mrs Jackie Croft, Cathedral Offices, Chain Gate, Cathedral Green, Wells BA5 2UE   *T:* 01749 674483
                                    F: 01749 832210
    E: administrator@wellscathedral.uk.net
Registrar Mr Roland Callaby, Diocesan Registry, 14 Market Place, Wells BA5 2RE
                    T: 01749 674747
                                    F: 01749 834060
    E: roland.callaby@harris-harris.co.uk
Cathedral Organist Mr Matthew Owens, Cathedral Offices, Chain Gate, Cathedral Green, Wells BA5 2UE   *T:* 01749 674483
                                    F: 01749 832210
    E: musicoffice@wellscathedral.uk.net

ARCHDEACONS
WELLS The Ven Anne Gell, 6 The Liberty, Wells BA5 2SU   *T:* 01749 685147
        E: adwells@bathwells.anglican.org
BATH The Ven Dr Adrian Youings, The Rectory, Wild Oak Lane, Trull, Taunton TA3 7JT
                    T: 01823 253518
        E: adrianyouings@btinternet.com
TAUNTON The Ven Simon Hill, 2 Monkton Heights, West Monkton, Taunton TA2 8LU
                    T: 01823 413315
        E: adtaunton@bathwells.anglican.org

MEMBERS OF THE HOUSE OF CLERGY OF THE GENERAL SYNOD
Proctors for Clergy
Preb Stephen Lynas

The Revd Susan Margaret Rose
The Revd James Dudley-Smith
The Revd Susan Caroline Ralph

MEMBERS OF THE HOUSE OF LAITY OF THE GENERAL SYNOD

Mr James Edward Cary
Ms Christina Murray Baron
Mr Timothy Charles Hind
Mrs Jennifer Ann Humphreys
Mrs Kathryn Louise Slader Tucker

DIOCESAN OFFICERS

Diocesan Secretary Mr Nick May, Diocesan Office, The Old Deanery, Wells BA5 2UG
                    T: 01749 685109
                    F: 01749 674240
    E: nick.may@bathwells.anglican.org
Chancellor of Diocese The Rt Worshipful Timothy Briden, 1 Temple Gardens, Temple, London EC4Y 9BB   *T:* 020 7797 8300
                 F: 020 7707 8308
        E: into@lambchambers.co.uk
Registrar of Diocese and Bishop's Legal Secretary Mr Roland Callaby, Diocesan Registry, 14 Market Place, Wells BA5 2RE   *T:* 01749 674747
                 F: 01749 834060
    E: roland.callaby@harris-harris.co.uk

DIOCESAN ORGANIZATIONS

Diocesan Office The Old Deanery, Wells BA5 2UG   *T:* 01749 670777
                 F: 01749 674240
    E: general@bathwells.anglican.org
      W: www.bathandwells.org.uk

ADMINISTRATION

Diocesan Synod (Chair, House of Clergy) The Revd Jane Haslam, The Rectory, Cliff Road, North Petherton TA6 6NY   *T:* 01278 662429
    E: revjane.haslam@hotmail.co.uk
(Chair, House of Laity) Mrs Mary Masters, Edgarley Farmhouse, Edgarley, Glastonbury BA6 8LE   *T:* 01458 832332
      E: mm.edgarley@gmail.com
(Secretary) Mr Nick May, Diocesan Office, The Old Deanery, Wells BA5 2UG
                    T: 01749 685109
                    F: 01749 674240
    E: nick.may@bathwells.anglican.org
Board of Finance (Chair) Mr Harry Musselwhite, Highfields, 207 Bailbrook Lane, Bath BA1 7AB
                    T: 01225 858913
  E: harry.musselwhite@btopenworld.com
(Secretary) Mr Nick May, Diocesan Office, The Old Deanery, Wells BA5 2UG
                    T: 01749 685109
                    F: 01749 674240
    E: nick.may@bathwells.anglican.org

Finance Group Mr Nick May (*As above*)
Board of Patronage Mr Peter Evans (*Same Address & Fax*)   *T:* 01749 670777
    E: peter.evans@bathwells.anglican.org
Mission and Pastoral Committee Mr Peter Evans (*As above*)
(Designated Officer) Mr Peter Evans (*As above*)
(Assistant Diocesan Secretary) Mr Peter Evans (*As above*)
(Accountant/Head of Finance) Imogen Taylor (*Same Address, Tel & Fax*)
    E: imogen.taylor@bathwells.anglican.org
(Property Officer) Mrs Alison Walker (*Same Address, Tel & Fax*)
    E: ali.walker@bathwells.anglican.org
(Diocesan Surveyor) Mr Paul Toseland (*Same Address, Tel & Fax*)
    E: paul.toseland@bathwells.anglican.org

BISHOP'S LITURGY GROUP

Chair The Revd Robin Lodge, St Andrew's Vicarage, 118 Kingston Road, Taunton TA2 7SR   *T:* 01823 352471
    E: robin.lodge1@btinternet.com

CHURCH BUILDINGS

Advisory Committee for the Care of Churches (Chairman) Mr Chris Hyldon, Mill Stream Barn, Martin Street, Baltonsborough, Glastonbury BA6 8QT   *T:* 01458 851641
    E: chrishyldon@hotmail.com
(Secretary) Mr Roland Callaby, Diocesan Registry, 14 Market Place, Wells BA5 2RE
                    T: 01749 674747
                    F: 01749 834060
    E: roland.callaby@harris-harris.co.uk
(Assistant Secretary) Mrs Sarah Davis, Diocesan Registry
    E: sarah.davis@harris-harris.co.uk
Association of Change Ringers The Revd Tim Hawkings, The Rectory, Cheddar Road, Axbridge BS26 2DL   *T:* 01934 732261
    E: revhawkings@google-mail.com

DIOCESAN RECORD OFFICE

Somerset County Record Office, Somerset Heritage Centre, Brunel Way, Langford Mead, Norton Fitzwarren, Taunton TA2 6SF
                    T: 01823 278805
                    F: 01823 325402
    E: archives@somerset.gov.uk

DIOCESAN RESOURCE CENTRE

The Old Deanery, Wells BA5 2UG
                    T: 01749 685129
                    F: 01749 674240
    E: resourcecentre@bathwells.anglican.org

BATH & WELLS

EDUCATION

Board of Education (*Diocesan Director of Education*) Mrs Theresa Gale, Diocesan Office, The Old Deanery, Wells BA5 2UG
T: 01749 670777
F: 01749 674240
E: theresa.gale@bathwells.anglican.org
(*School Improvement Advisers*) Mrs Pauline Dodds (*Same Address, Tel & Fax*)
E: pauline.dodds@bathwells.anglican.org
Mr David Williams (*Same Address*)
T: 01749 670777
01749 674240
E: david.williams@bathwells.anglican.org
(*School Development Adviser*) Ms Natalie Paull (*Same Address*)
T: 01749 670777
F: 01749 674240
E: natalie.paull@bathwells.anglican.org
(*School Organization Team Leader*) Mrs Suzanne McDonald (*Same Address, Tel & Fax*)
E: suzanne.mcdonald@
bathwells.anglican.org
(*Parish Adviser for Young People*) Mr Tony Cook (*Same Address, Tel & Fax*)
E: tony.cook@bathwells.anglican.org
(*Parish Adviser for Children*) Mrs Jane Tibbs (*Same Address, Tel & Fax*)
E: jane.tibbs@bathwells.anglican.org
(*Safeguarding Adviser*) Ms Glenys Armstrong (*Same Address, Tel & Fax*)
E: glenys.armstrong@
bathwells.anglican.org

MINISTRY FORUM

Chair The Rt Revd Ruth Worsley, The Palace, Wells BA5 2PD
T: 01749 672341
M: 07917 693285
E: bishop.taunton@bathwells.anglican.org
Principal of the School of Formation Preb Dr Graham Dodds, 2 The Liberty, Wells BA5 2SU
T: 01749 670607
F: 01749 674240
E: graham.dodds@bathwells.anglican.org
Director of Continuing Ministerial Development Vacancy
Education for Discipleship Officer The Revd Jennifer Cole, Diocesan Office, The Old Deanery, Wells BA5 2UG
T: 01749 670777
F: 01749 674240
E: jennifer.cole@bathwells.anglican.org
Diocesan Director of Vocations The Revd Sue Rose (*Same Address, Tel & Fax*)
E: sue.rose@bathwells.anglican.org
Adviser in Prayer and Spirituality The Revd Jane Eastell, Meadowside, Wild Oak Lane, Trull, Taunton TA3 7JT
T: 01823 321069
E: jane.eastell@bathwells.anglican.org
Adviser in Care and Counselling of the Clergy and their Families Mrs Sue Yabsley, Prometheus Therapy Centre, Foundry Cottage, Foundry Road, Taunton TA1 1JJ
T: 01823 251915
E: sue.yabsley@bathwells.anglican.org

Chaplain to the Deaf Mrs Pamela Grottick, 9 Chestnut Close, Baltonsborough, Glastonbury BA6 8PH
T: 01458 851401
E: pamg@wpci.org.uk
Warden of Readers The Ven Simon Hill, 2 Monkton Heights, West Monkton, Taunton TA2 8LU
T: 01823 413315
E: adtaunton@bathwells.anglican.org
Director of Reader Studies Preb Dr Graham Dodds, 2 The Liberty, Wells BA5 2SU
T: 01749 670607
F: 01749 674240
E: graham.dodds@bathwells.anglican.org
Dean of Women Clergy Preb Paula Hollingsworth, Diocesan Office, The Old Deanery, Wells BA5 2UG (*Same Fax*)
T: 01749 670777
E: paula.hollingsworth@
bathwells.anglican.org

MISSION FORUM

Chairman Vacancy
Executive Officer/Diocesan Missioner Canon Roger Medley, Diocesan Office, The Old Deanery, Wells BA5 2UG
T: 01749 670777
F: 01749 674240
E: roger.medley@bathwells.anglican.org
Social Justice and Environment Adviser Mr David Maggs (*Same Address, Tel & Fax*)
E: david.maggs@bathwells.anglican.org
World Mission Adviser and Executive Secretary Zambia Link Mrs Jenny Humphreys (*Same Address, Tel & Fax*)
E: jenny.humphreys@bathwells.anglican.org
Rural Life Adviser Mr Rob Walrond, The Wagon House, Pitney, Langport TA10 9AP
T: 01458 253002
E: rob.walrond@hotmail.com
Healing Adviser The Revd Matthew Thomson, The Vicarage, Station Road, Congresbury, Bristol BS49 5DX
T: 01934 833126
E: revmattthomson@hotmail.com
Renewal Adviser The Revd Keith Powell, Homefields House, Paynes Lane, Othery, Bridgwater TA7 0QB
T: 01823 698619
E: jill.powell3@google-mail.com

PRESS AND PUBLICATIONS

Diocesan Communications Manager Miss Gillian Buzzard, Diocesan Office, The Old Deanery, Wells BA5 2UG
T: 01749 670777
F: 01749 674240
M: 07848 028798
E: gillian.buzzard@bathwells.anglican.org
Diocesan Communications Officer Mr James Butterworth (*Same Address, Tel & Fax*)
E: james.butterworth@
bathwells.anglican.org
Editor of Directory/Database Manager Mr Christopher Roome (*Same Address*)
T: 01749 685130
E: chris.roome@bathwells.anglican.org

RETREAT HOUSE
Abbey House, Glastonbury   *T:* 01458 831112
                             F: 01458 831893
              E: director@abbeyhouse.org

STEWARDSHIP GROUP
Chair Vacancy
Stewardship Adviser Mr Andrew Rainsford,
Diocesan Office, The Old Deanery, Wells BA5
2UG   *T:* 01749 670777
                             F: 01749 674240
     E: andrew.rainsford@bathwells.anglican.org

WIDOWS' OFFICER
The Revd Chris Hare, Cuckoo Hill, 61
Packsaddle Way, Frome BA11 2RW
                             T: 01373 469788
                   E: cshare@hotmail.co.uk

RURAL DEANS
ARCHDEACONRY OF BATH
Bath Richard Graham Wilson, The Rectory,
Watery Lane, Bath BA2 1RL
                             T: 01225 421438
              E: richard@stmichaelstwerton.com
Chew Magna Stephen Aragorn M'caw, 68 Park
Road, Keynsham, Bristol BS31 1DE
                             T: 0117 986 4437
                   E: samcaw@talk21.com
Locking Lydia Dorothy Ann Avery, The
Vicarage, Winscombe Hill, Winscombe BS25
1DE   *T:* 01934 843164
                   E: ldavery@btinternet.com
Midsomer Norton Christopher David North,
The Rectory, The Street, Chilcompton,
Radstock BA3 4HN   *T:* 01761 232219
                E: c.north123@btinternet.com
Portishead Noel Antony Hector, The Rectory,
All Saints' Lane, Clevedon BS21 6AU
                             T: 01275 873257
              E: eastcleveub@blueyonder.co.uk

ARCHDEACONRY OF TAUNTON
Crewkerne Jonathan Richard Morris, The
Rectory, New Street, North Perrott, Crewkerne
TA18 7ST   *T:* 01460 72356
                   E: jonbea@cooptel.net

Exmoor Caroline Susan Ralph, The Rectory,
Church Lane, Carhampton, Minehead TA24
6NT   *E:* caroline@249ralph.eclipse.co.uk
Ilminster Nigel Anthony Done, 21 Higher
Beacon, Ilminster TA19 9AJ   *T:* 01460 250802
                   E: nigel.done@btinternet.com
Quantock Benjamin Robert Glanville Flenley,
Shardloes, Staple Lane, West Quantoxhead,
Taunton TA4 4DE   *T:* 01984 631190
                E: flenbenley@btinternet.com
Sedgemoor Christopher David Keys, The
Vicarage, Church Lane, Weston Zoyland,
Bridgwater TA7 0EP   *T:* 01278 691098
                   E: chris.keys@me.com
Taunton Vacancy
Tone Matthew John Tregenza, The Rectory,
Church Street, Bishops Lydeard, Taunton TA4
3AT   *T:* 01823 432935
              E: matthew.tregenza@gmail.com

ARCHDEACONRY OF WELLS
Axbridge Sharon Margaret Joan Crossman,
The Vicarage, 81A Church Street, Highbridge
TA9 3HS   *T:* 01278 789290
              E: sharon.crossman@btopenworld.com
Bruton and Cary Elizabeth Anne Mortimer,
The Vicarage, Church Street, Castle Cary BA7
7EJ   *T:* 01963 351615
                   E: fr.liz@talktalk.net
Frome Graham Anthony Owen, Holy Trinity
Vicarage, Orchard Street, Frome BA11 3BX
                             T: 01373 462586
              E: graham-owen@hotmail.co.uk
Glastonbury David John Lamont MacGeoch,
The Vicarage, 24 Wells Road, Glastonbury
BA6 9DJ   *T:* 01458 834281
              E: all@macgeoch.fsnet.co.uk
Ivelchester Bruce Stephen Faulkner, 3 The
Paddocks, West Street, Ilchester, Yeovil BA22
8PS   *T:* 01935 849441
                   E: bsfaulkner1@aol.com
Shepton Mallet Tobias Charles Osmond, The
Vicarage, 94 St Thomas Street, Wells BA5 2UZ
                             T: 01749 672193
                   E: tobieosmond@gmail.com
Yeovil James Dudley-Smith, The Rectory, 41
The Park, Yeovil BA20 1DG   *T:* 01935 475352
                   E: jamesds@tesco.net

DIOCESE OF BIRMINGHAM

Founded in 1905. Birmingham; Sandwell, except for an area in the north in the diocese of Lichfield; Solihull, except for an area in the east in the diocese of Coventry; an area of Warwickshire; a few parishes in Worcestershire.

Population 1,564,000   Area 290 sq m
Full-time Stipendiary Parochial Clergy 147   Benefices 140
Parishes 151   Churches 184
www.cofebirmingham.com
Overseas link dioceses: Lake Malawi, Southern Malawi, Northern Malawi & Upper Shire

BISHOP (9th)
The Rt Revd David Andrew Urquhart, Bishop's Croft, Old Church Road, Harborne, Birmingham B17 0BG   *T:* 0121 427 1163
E: bishop@cofebirmingham.com

BISHOP'S STAFF
Bishop's Chaplain The Revd Kate Stowe, East Wing, Bishop's Croft, Old Church Road, Harborne, Birmingham B17 0BE
T: 0121 427 1163 (office)
E: bishopschaplain@cofebirmingham.com

SUFFRAGAN BISHOP
ASTON The Rt Revd Anne Hollinghurst, The Church of England, 1 Colmore Row, Birmingham B3 2BJ   *T:* 0121 426 0400
E: bishopofaston@cofebirmingham.com

ASSISTANT BISHOPS
The Rt Revd Maurice Walker Sinclair, 55 Selly Wick Drive, Selly Park, Birmingham B29 7JQ
T: 0121 471 2617
E: mauricewsinclair@blueyonder.co.uk
The Rt Revd Mark Santer, 81 Clarence Road, Moseley, Birmingham B13 9UH
T: 0121 441 2194
The Rt Revd Iraj Mottadeheh, 2 Highland Road, Newport TF10 7AE   *T:* 01952 813615
The Rt Revd Roderick Thomas, 28 St John's Meadow, Blindley Heath, Lingfield RH7 6JU
T: 01342 834140
E: admin@bishopofmaidstone.org
The Rt Revd Jonathan Goodall, Tree Tops, The Mount, Caversham, Reading RG4 7RE
T: 0118 948 1038
E: office@ebbsfleet.org.uk

CATHEDRAL CHURCH OF ST PHILIP
Dean The Very Revd Matt Thompson, Birmingham Cathedral, Colmore Row, Birmingham B3 2QB   *T:* 0121 262 1840
F: 0121 262 1869
E: dean@birminghamcathedral.com

Canons Residentiary
Canon Missioner The Revd Canon Nigel Hand, 12 Nursery Drive, Handsworth, Birmingham B20 2SW   *T:* 0121 262 1840
E: canonmissioner@birminghamcathedral.com
Canon Precentor The Revd Canon Andrew Lythall, Birmingham Cathedral, Colmore Row, Birmingham B3 2QB (*Same Tel*)
F: 0121 262 1869
E: canonliturgist@birminghamcathedral.com

Other Staff
Chief Executive Anna Pitt, Birmingham Cathedral, Colmore Row, Birmingham B3 2QB   *T:* 0121 262 1840
F: 0121 262 1869
E: anna.pitt@birminghamcathedral.com
Acting Head of Music Mr David Hardie (*Same Address, Tel & Fax*)
E: david.hardie@birminghamcathedral.com

ARCHDEACONS
ASTON The Ven Simon Heathfield, The Church of England, 1 Colmore Row, Birmingham B3 2BJ   *T:* 0121 426 0400
E: simonh@cofebirmingham.com
BIRMINGHAM The Ven Hayward Osborne, The Church of England, 1 Colmore Row, Birmingham B3 2BJ   *T:* 0121 426 0441
E: archdeaconofbham@cofebirmingham.com

MEMBERS OF THE HOUSE OF CLERGY OF THE GENERAL SYNOD
Proctors for Clergy
The Revd Canon Catherine Grylls
The Ven Simon Heathfield
The Revd Canon Priscilla White

MEMBERS OF THE HOUSE OF LAITY OF THE GENERAL SYNOD
Mr Ben Franks
Dr Rachel Jepson
Mr Geoffrey Shuttleworth

DIOCESAN OFFICERS

Diocesan Secretary Mr Andrew Halstead, The Church of England, 1 Colmore Row, Birmingham B3 2BJ   T: 0121 426 0401
          E: andrewh@cofebirmingham.com
Chancellor of Diocese Mr Mark Powell, c/o Diocesan Registrar, Shakespeare Martineau, 1 Colmore Square, Birmingham B4 6AA
Registrar of Diocese and Bishop's Legal Secretary Mrs Vicki Simpson, Diocesan Registry, Shakespeare Martineau, 1 Colmore Square, Birmingham B4 6AA   T: 0121 214 1247
          E: registry@shma.co.uk
Property Director Mr Daniel Mayes, The Church of England, 1 Colmore Row, Birmingham B3 2BJ   T: 0121 426 0409
          E: danielm@cofebirmingham.com

DIOCESAN ORGANIZATIONS

Diocesan Office The Church of England, 1 Colmore Row, Birmingham B3 2BJ
          T: 0121 426 0400
          W: www.cofebirmingham.com

ADMINISTRATION

Diocesan Synod (*Chair, House of Clergy*) The Revd Canon Martin Stephenson, 33 Paradise Lane, Hall Green, Birmingham B28 0DY
          T: 0121 777 1935
          E: martin.stephenson@cantab.net
(*Chair, House of Laity*) Mr Steven Skakel, The Church of England, 1 Colmore Row, Birmingham B3 2BJ   T: 0121 426 0400
          E: stevenskakel@gmail.com
(*Secretary*) Mr Andrew Halstead (*Same Address*)
          T: 0121 426 0401
          E: andrewh@cofebirmingham.com
Board of Finance (*Chair*) Mr Phil Nunnerley
(*Secretary*) Mr Andrew Halstead, The Church of England, 1 Colmore Row, Birmingham B3 2BJ   T: 0121 426 0401
          E: andrewh@cofebirmingham.com
Parsonages Committee Mr Andrew Halstead (*As above*)
Diocesan Trustees (*Secretary*) Mr Andrew Halstead (*As above*)
Pastoral Committee Mr Andrew Halstead (*As above*)
(*Designated Officer*) Mr Hugh Carslake, Shakespeare Martineau, 1 Colmore Square, Birmingham B4 6AA   T: 0121 214 0486
          E: hugh.carslake@shma.co.uk

CHRISTIAN STEWARDSHIP

Stewardship Support Mrs Amanda Homer, The Church of England, 1 Colmore Row, Birmingham B3 2BJ   T: 0121 426 0414
          E: amandah@cofebirmingham.com

CHURCH BUILDINGS

Advisory Committee for the Care of Churches (*Chair*) Mr Phil Nunnerley
(*Secretary*) Mr Adrian Mann, The Church of England, 1 Colmore Row, Birmingham B3 2BJ
          T: 0121 426 0400
          E: adrianm@cofebirmingham.com

CHURCHES AND INDUSTRY GROUP BIRMINGHAM

Industrial Chaplain (CIGB) (*Industrial Chaplain CIGB*) The Revd Peter Sellick, The Church of England, 1 Colmore Row, Birmingham B3 2BJ
          T: 0121 426 0425
          E: peters@cofebirmingham.com

COMMUNITY PROJECTS COMMITTEE

Chair The Revd Nigel Traynor, 1162 Tyburn Road, Pype Hayes, Birmingham B24 0TB
          T: 0121 373 3534
          E: revnigel@yahoo.co.uk

COMMUNITY REGENERATION

Director Mr Fred Rattley, c/o Balsall Heath Church Centre, 100 Mary Street, Birmingham B12 9JU   T: 0121 426 0442
          E: fredr@cofebirmingham.com

DIOCESAN RECORD OFFICES

Birmingham Archives and Heritage Library of Birmingham, Centenary Square, Broad Street, Birmingham B1 2ND
          T: 0121 242 4242
          E: enquiries@libraryofbirmingham.com
Warwick County Record Office Priory Park, Cape Road, Warwick CV34 4JS
Archive and Historic Environment Manager Mrs Sam Collenette   T: 01926 738959
          E: recordoffice@warwickshire.gov.uk
Sandwell Council Community History and Archives Service Smethwick Library, High Street, Smethwick, Warley, West Midlands B66 1AA   T: 0121 558 2561
          E: archives_service@sandwell.gov.uk

EDUCATION

Diocesan Director of Education Mrs Sarah Smith, The Church of England, 1 Colmore Row, Birmingham B3 2BJ   T: 0121 426 0400
          E: sarahs@cofebirmingham.com
Assistant Director of Education The Revd Peter French (*Same Address & Tel*)   F: 0121 428 1114
          E: peterf@cofebirmingham.com
RE Adviser Mrs Jill Stolberg (*Same Address, Tel & Fax*)   E: jills@cofebirmingham.com

HEALTHCARE CHAPLAINCIES
Bishop's Adviser The Ven Hayward Osborne, The Church of England, 1 Colmore Row, Birmingham B3 2BJ   *T:* 0121 426 0441
  E: archdeaconofbham@cofebirmingham.com

LITURGICAL
Bishop's Liturgical Advisory Committee Chair The Revd Canon Peter Babington, Parish Office, St Francis Centre, Sycamore Road, Bournville, Birmingham B30 2AA
                          T: 0121 472 7215
            E: pgbabington@gmail.com

MINISTRIES
Director of Ministry The Revd Canon Mark Pryce, The Church of England, 1 Colmore Row, Birmingham B3 2BJ   *T:* 0121 426 0400
            E: markp@cofebirmingham.com
Diocesan Director of Ordinands Vacancy
Bishop's Adviser for Lay Adult Education and Training The Revd Liz Howlett, The Church of England, 1 Colmore Row, Birmingham B3 2BJ
                          T: 0121 426 0400
              E: lizh@cofebirmingham.com
Diocesan Music Advisor Mr Mick Perrier (*Same Address & Tel*)
          E: mick@mperrier.freeserve.co.uk
Readers' Board (*Secretary*) Mr Michael Lynch, 57 Fairholme Road, Hodge Hill, Birmingham B36 8HN   *T:* 0121 242 0534
        E: mike4jeannie@blueyonder.co.uk

MISSION AND EVANGELISM
Chair The Rt Revd Anne Hollinghurst, The Church of England, 1 Colmore Row, Birmingham B3 2BJ   *T:* 0121 426 0400
      E: bishopofaston@cofebirmingham.com
Director of Mission The Revd Rhiannon King (*Same Address*)   *T:* 0121 426 0420
                          M: 07595 880584
          E: rhiannonk@cofebirmingham.com
Director of Mission Learning and Development Canon Dr Paula Gooder (*Same Address*)
                          T: 0121 426 0400
            E: paulag@cofebirmingham.com
Growing Younger Directors Ms Ruth Hassall (*Same Address & Tel*)
            E: ruthh@cofebirmingham.com
Ms Liz Dumain (*Same Address & Tel*)
              E: lizd@cofebirmingham.com
Bishop's Ecumenical Adviser The Revd Nick Parker, The Vicarage, High Street, Coleshill B46 3BP   *T:* 01675 462188
        E: nickthevicparker@outlook.com
Bishop's Rural Adviser The Revd Stephen Banks, The Vicarage, 132 Main Road, Austrey, Atherstone CV9 3EB   *T:* 01827 839022
      E: stephenbanks132@btinternet.com

Bishop's Adviser for the Environment The Revd Patrick Gerard, The Rectory, Church Lane, Lapworth, Solihull B94 5NX
                          T: 01564 782098
                E: patrick@gerard.net
Bishop's Adviser for New Religious Movements The Revd Paul Cudby, The Vicarage, Vicarage Hill, Tanworth-in-Arden, Solihull B94 5EB
                          T: 01564 742565
              E: paul@logos.myzen.co.uk
Malawi Partnership Officer The Revd Paul Bracher, The Vicarage, Hallmoor Road, Kitts Green, Birmingham B33 9QY
                          T: 0121 783 2319
        E: malawiofficer@cofebirmingham.com

PRESS AND PUBLICATIONS
Bishop's Advisor for Communications Mr Steve Squires, The Church of England, 1 Colmore Row, Birmingham B3 2BJ   *T:* 0121 426 0438
                          M: 07973 173195
            E: steves@cofebirmingham.com
Visual Storyteller (Filmmaker/Designer) Mr Ben Poffley (*Same Address*)   *M:* 07828 179988
            E: benp@cofebirmingham.com
Written Storyteller (Copywriting/Press) Ms Fiona Handscomb (*Same Address*)   *T:* 07392 196920
Editor of Contact Management System Mr Ben Franks (*Same Address*)   *T:* 0121 426 0446
            E: benf@cofebirmingham.com
Communications and Press Office Mrs Cara Butowski   *T:* 0121 426 0439
            E: carab@cofebirmingham.com

RETIREMENT OFFICERS
The Revd Barbara Fletcher, 231 Abbey Road, Smethwick B67 5NN   *T:* 0121 429 9354
                          M: 07972 627510
              E: bfletcher@talktalk.net
The Revd Canon Rob Morris, 61 Oxford Street, Stirchly, Birmingham B30 2LH
                          T: 0121 247 0355
                E: morrisrob4@aol.com

AREA DEANS
ARCHDEACONRY OF ASTON
Aston Nigel Martin Arthur Traynor, St Mary's Vicarage, 1162 Tyburn Road, Birmingham B24 0TB   *T:* 0121 373 3534
                  E: nigelt6@msn.com
Coleshill Stuart Conway Carter, The Vicarage, Lanchester Way, Castle Bromwich, Birmingham B36 9JG   *T:* 0121 218 6118
            E: stuwecarter@btinternet.com
Polesworth Jane Louise Claridge Shaw, The Vicarage, 1 Church Road, Dosthill, Tamworth B77 1LU   *T:* 01827 281349
              E: louiseshaw6@yahoo.co.uk

Solihull Toby Nicholas Crowe, Elmdon Rectory, 86 Tanhouse Farm Road, Solihull B92 9EY
T: 0121 743 6336
E: toby.crowe@rocketmail.com
Sutton Coldfield David Adrian Leahy, The Vicarage, 26 All Saints Drive, Sutton Coldfield B74 4AG
T: 0121 308 5315
E: revaleahy@gmail.com
Yardley and Bordesley Andrew Timothy Bullock, The Vicarage, 34 Dudley Park Road, Acocks Green, Birmingham B27 6QR
T: 0121 706 9764
E: andrewbullock2@blueyonder.co.uk

ARCHDEACONRY OF BIRMINGHAM
Central Birmingham Ian Harper, St John's Vicarage, Darnley Road, Birmingham B16 8TF
T: 0121 454 0973
E: harper-i1@sky.com
Edgbaston Nicholas John Cuthbert Tucker, The Vicarage, 1B Arthur Road, Birmingham B15 2UW
E: nick@hellotuckers.com

Handsworth Philip Calvert, St Mark's Clergy House, Bandywood Crescent, Birmingham B44 9JX
T: 0121 360 7288
E: frphilipcalvert@aol.com
King's Norton Robert Steven Fieldson, The Vicarage, 8 Cofton Church Lane, Barnt Green, Birmingham B45 8PT
T: 0121 445 1269
E: rob@fieldson.co.uk
Moseley Quentin David Warbrick, The Vicarage, 4 Vicarage Road, Kings Heath, Birmingham B14 7RA
T: 0121 444 0260
E: davidwarbrick@btinternet.com
Shirley Timothy Duncan Hill-Brown, 54 Glendon Way, Dorridge, Solihull B93 8SY
T: 01564 772472
E: duncan@ukonline.co.uk
Warley Debra Buckley, The Vicarage, 93A Church Road, Smethwick B67 6EE
T: 0121 558 1763
E: debbuckley@phonecoop.coop

DIOCESE OF BLACKBURN

Founded in 1926. Lancashire, except for areas in the east in the diocese of Bradford and in the south in the dioceses of Liverpool and Manchester; a few parishes in Wigan.

Population 1,341,000   Area 930 sq m
Full-time Stipendiary Parochial Clergy 158   Benefices 177
Parishes 237   Churches 272
Overseas link dioceses: Free State (South Africa), Braunschweig (Germany)
(Evangelical Lutheran Landeskirche)

BISHOP (8th)
The Rt Revd Julian Henderson, Bishop's House, Ribchester Road, Clayton-le-Dale, Blackburn BB1 9EF   *T:* 01254 248234
        F: 01254 246668
        E: bishop@bishopofblackburn.org.uk

BISHOP'S STAFF
Bishop's Secretary Mrs Sue Taylor, Bishop's House, Ribchester Road, Clayton-le-Dale, Blackburn BB1 9EF   *T:* 01254 248234
        F: 01254 246668
        E: secretary@bishopofblackburn.org.uk
Assistant Secretary Mrs Jill Ghafoor

SUFFRAGAN BISHOPS
BURNLEY The Rt Revd Philip J. North, Dean House, 449 Padiham Road, Burnley BB12 6TE
        T: 01282 479300
        E: bishop.burnley@blackburn.anglican.org
LANCASTER Vacancy

ASSISTANT BISHOP
The Rt Revd Cyril Ashton, Charis, 17c Quernmore Road, Lancaster LA1 3EB
        T: 01524 848684
        E: bpcg.ashton@btinternet.com

CATHEDRAL CHURCH OF ST MARY THE VIRGIN
Dean The Very Revd Peter Howell-Jones, The Deanery, Cathedral Close, Blackburn BB1 5AA
        M: 07435 969256
        E: dean@blackburncathedral.co.uk
Canons Residentiary The Revd Canon Andrew Horsfall, Cathedral Offices, Blackburn BB1 5AA   *T:* 01254 277430
        E: andrew.horsfall@
        blackburncathedral.co.uk
Sacrist The Revd Canon Andrew Hindley, 3 Cathedral Close, Blackburn BB1 5AA
        T: 01254 690080
E: andrew.hindley@blackburncathedral.co.uk

Other Staff
Director of Music Mr Samuel Hudson, 2 Cathedral Close, Blackburn BB1 5AA
        T: 01254 675639
        E: samuel.hudson@blackburncathedral.co.uk

ARCHDEACONS
BLACKBURN The Ven Mark Ireland, 19 Clarence Park, Blackburn BB2 7FA
        E: mark.ireland@blackburn.anglican.org
LANCASTER The Ven Michael Everitt, 6 Eton Park, Fulwood, Preston PR2 9NL
        T: 01772 700337
        E: michael.everitt@blackburn.anglican.org

MEMBERS OF THE HOUSE OF CLERGY OF THE GENERAL SYNOD
Proctors for Clergy
The Revd Paul Benfield
The Ven Michael Everitt
The Revd Canon Fleur Green
The Revd Alistair McHaffie
The Revd Christopher Newlands

MEMBERS OF THE HOUSE OF LAITY OF THE GENERAL SYNOD
Mr Stephen Boyall
Mrs Vivienne Goddard
Mrs Carolyn Johnson
Mrs Rosemary Lyon
Mrs Jacqueline Stamper
Mrs Susan Witts

DIOCESAN OFFICERS
Diocesan Secretary Canon Graeme Pollard, Diocesan Offices, Clayton House, Walker Office Park, Blackburn BB1 2QE
        T: 01254 503070
        E: graeme.pollard@blackburn.anglican.org
Chancellor of Diocese His Honour Judge John Bullimore, The Rectory, 5 Snowgate Head, Norn Lane, New Mill, Nr Huddersfield HD9 7HD   *T:* 01484 521025

Registrar of Diocese and Bishop's Legal Secretary
Mr Stephen Crossley, Darwen House, Walker
Business Park, Blackburn BB1 2QW
                                        T: 01254 686245
                              E: registry@napthens.co.uk

DIOCESAN ORGANIZATIONS
Diocesan Office Clayton House, Walker Office
Park, Blackburn BB1 2QE   *T:* 01254 503070

ADMINISTRATION
Diocesan Synod (Chairman, House of Clergy) The
Revd Canon Dr Simon Cox, All Hallows
Rectory, 86 All Hallows Road, Bispham,
Blackpool FY2 0AY   *T:* 01253 351886
                              E: drsjcox@yahoo.co.uk
(Chairman, House of Laity) Mr Robert Collins,
16 Edinburgh Close, Leyland PR25 4UT
(Secretary) Canon Graeme Pollard, Diocesan
Offices, Clayton House, Walker Office Park,
Blackburn BB1 2QE   *T:* 01254 503070
        E: graeme.pollard@blackburn.anglican.org
Board of Finance (Chairman) Canon John Dell,
66 Moseley Road, Burnley BB11 2RF
(Secretary) Canon Graeme Pollard, Diocesan
Offices, Clayton House, Walker Office Park,
Blackburn BB1 2QE   *T:* 01254 503070
        E: graeme.pollard@blackburn.anglican.org
Property Committee (Chairman) The Revd
Canon Andrew Sage
(Secretary) Canon Graeme Pollard, Diocesan
Offices, Clayton House, Walker Office Park,
Blackburn BB1 2QE   *T:* 01254 503070
        E: graeme.pollard@blackburn.anglican.org
Mission and Pastoral Committee Mrs Elaine
Hargreaves *(Same Address & Tel)*
(Designated Officer) Mr Stephen Crossley,
Darwen House, Walker Business Park,
Blackburn BB1 2QW   *T:* 01254 686245
                              E: registry@napthens.co.uk

CHURCH BUILDINGS
*Advisory Committee for the Care of Churches
(Chairman)* Mr John Tillotson, Bonds Farm,
Horns Lane, Goosnargh, Preston PR3 2NE
                                        T: 01772 783436
(Secretary) Mrs Christine Ellis, Diocesan
Offices, Clayton House, Walker Office Park,
Blackburn BB1 2QE   *T:* 01254 503074
        E: christine.ellis@blackburn.anglican.org

DIOCESAN RECORD OFFICES
Lancashire Archives and Record Office, Bow
Lane, Preston PR1 8ND   *T:* 01772 533039
            E: record.office@lancashire.gov.uk
Diocesan Registry, Napthens LLP, Greenbank
Court, Challenge Way, Greenbank Business
Park, Blackburn BB1 5QB   *T:* 01254 686244
                              E: registry@napthens.co.uk

DISCIPLESHIP AND MINISTRY
Director of Ordinands The Revd Dr John Darch,
24 Bosburn Drive, Mellor Brook, Blackburn
BB2 7PA   *T:* 01254 813544
Director of Ministry The Revd Canon Dr Susan
Penfold, Diocesan Offices, Clayton House,
Walker Office Park, Blackburn BB1 2QE
                                        T: 01254 503070
        E: sue.penfold@blackburn.anglican.org
Director of IME 1–4 The Revd Dr John Darch
(Same Tel)
Adviser in Women's Ministry The Revd Canon
Fleur Green, The Rectory, 2 St Peter's Close,
Darwen BB3 2EA   *T:* 01254 702411
                              E: chauntry1@live.co.uk
Mothers' Union Mrs Enid Nutland, 33 Catforth
Avenue, Marton, Blackpool FY4 4SF
*(Discipleship and Lay Ministry Development
Officer)* Mrs Mandy Stanton, Diocesan Offices,
Clayton House, Walker Office Park, Blackburn
BB1 2QE   *T:* 01254 503070

EDUCATION
Board of Education (Director) Mr Stephen
Whittaker, Diocesan Offices, Clayton House,
Walker Office Park, Blackburn BB1 2QE
                                        T: 01254 503070
        E: stephen.whittaker@blackburn.anglican.org
(Schools' Adviser) Mrs Lisa Horobin *(Same
Address & Tel)*
        E: lisa.horobin@blackburn.anglican.org
(Diocesan Youth Officer) Mr Ben Green *(Same
Address)*   *T:* 01254 503407
        E: ben.green@blackburn.anglican.org
(Children's Work Adviser) Mrs Susan Witts
(Same Address)   *T:* 01254 503070
        E: susan.witts@blackburn.anglican.org

LITURGICAL
Chairman Vacancy
Secretary The Revd Michael Gisbourne, St
Thomas' Vicarage, Church Street, Garstang,
Preston PR3 1PA   *T:* 01995 602162
        E: michael.gisbourne@phonecoop.coop

PARISH MISSION SUPPORT
Department Leader The Revd Canon David
Banbury, Diocesan Offices, Clayton House,
Walker Office Park, Blackburn BB1 2QE
                                        T: 01254 503070
        E: david.banbury@blackburn.anglican.org
Social Responsibility Lead Officer The Revd
Canon Ed Saville *(Same Address & Tel)*
        E: ed.saville@blackburn.anglican.org

PRESS AND PUBLICATIONS
Diocesan Communications Manager Mr Ronnie
Semley, Diocesan Offices, Clayton House,
Walker Office Park, Blackburn BB1 2QE
                                        T: 01254 503070
        E: ronnie.semley@blackburn.anglican.org

AREA DEANS
ARCHDEACONRY OF BLACKBURN
Accrington Ian Peter Enticott, St Paul's Vicarage, Barnfield Street, Accrington BB5 2AQ   *T:* 01254 433590
          E: ian.enticott@dunelm.org.uk
Blackburn with Darwen Arun Andrew John, St James's Vicarage, Cromer Place, Blackburn BB1 8EL   *T:* 01254 51864
          E: ajohn419@btinternet.com
Burnley Mark Andrew Jones, The Vicarage, 1 Arbory Drive, Padiham, Burnley BB12 8JS
                        T: 01282 772442
          E: jones.padiham@btinternet.com
Chorley David Alun Arnold, St Paul's Vicarage, Railway Road, Adlington, Chorley PR6 9QZ
                        T: 07786 168261
          E: frdavidarnold@gmail.com
Leyland Marc Ali Morad Wolverson, St James's Vicarage, 201 Slater Lane, Leyland PR26 7SH
                        T: 01772 421034
          E: revmarc@mcb.net
Pendle Edward Andrew Saville, The Vicarage, 5 Reedley Farm Close, Reedley, Burnley BB10 2RB   *T:* 01282 613235
          E: ed.saville@blackburn.anglican.org
Whalley Colin Richard Penfold, St Bartholomew's Vicarage, Church Lane, Great Harwood, Blackburn BB6 7PU
                        T: 01254 884039
          E: colin@thepenfolds.org.uk

ARCHDEACONRY OF LANCASTER
Blackpool Simon John Cox, All Hallows Rectory, 86 All Hallows Road, Blackpool FY2 0AY   *T:* 01253 351886
          E: drsjcox@yahoo.co.uk
Garstang Andrew Wilfrid Wilkinson, The Vicarage, 6 Vicarage Lane, Churchtown, Preston PR3 0HW   *T:* 01995 602294
          E: awilkinson703@btinternet.com
Kirkham Adrian David Lyon, St Anne's Vicarage, 4 Oxford Road, Lytham St Annes FY8 2EA   *T:* 01253 722725
          E: david.lyon1955@googlemail.com
Lancaster and Morecambe Linda Macluskie, St John's Vicarage, 2 St John's Avenue, Morecambe LA3 1EU   *T:* 01524 411039
          E: linda.macluskie@virgin.net
Poulton Martin Philip Keighley, The Vicarage, 7 Vicarage Road, Poulton-le-Fylde FY6 7BE
                        T: 01253 883086
          E: martinkeighley@btconnect.com
Preston Shaun Baldwin, The Vicarage, 410 Garstang Road, Broughton, Preston PR3 5JB
                        T: 01772 862330
          E: shaunbaldwin64@hotmail.com
Tunstall Nancy Elisabeth Goodrich, The Vicarage, 117 Main Road, Bolton le Sands, Carnforth LA5 8DX   *T:* 01524 823106
          E: nancy@goodrich.myzen.co.uk

DIOCESE OF BRISTOL

Founded in 1542. Bristol; the southern two-thirds of South Gloucestershire; the northern quarter of Wiltshire, except for two parishes in the north, in the diocese of Gloucester; Swindon, except for a few parishes in the north, in the diocese of Gloucester, and in the south, in the diocese of Salisbury; a few parishes in Gloucestershire.

Population 1,019,000   Area 470 sq m
Full-time Stipendiary Parochial Clergy 103   Benefices 106
Parishes 166   Churches 202
Overseas link dioceses: Uganda

BISHOP
Vacancy

SUFFRAGAN BISHOP
SWINDON The Rt Revd Dr Lee Rayfield, Mark House, Field Rise, Swindon SN1 4HP
T: 01793 538654
F: 01793 525181
E: bishop.swindon@bristoldiocese.org

CATHEDRAL CHURCH OF THE HOLY AND UNDIVIDED TRINITY
Dean The Very Revd Dr David Michael Hoyle, The Deanery, 20 Charlotte Street, Bristol BS1 5PZ
T: 0117 926 2443
E: dean@bristol-cathedral.co.uk
Residentiary Canons
Canon Precentor The Revd Canon Nicola Stanley, 55 Salisbury Road, Bristol BS6 7AS
T: 0117 926 4879
E: canon.precentor@bristol-cathedral.co.uk
Canon Pastor The Revd Canon Dr Robert Bull, 41 Salisbury Road, Bristol BS6 7AR
T: 0117 909 8910
E: canon.pastor@bristol-cathedral.co.uk
Diocesan Canon The Revd Canon Derek Chedzey, Diocesan Office, 1st Floor, Hillside House, 1500 Parkway North, Newbrick Road, Stoke Gifford, Bristol BS34 8YU
T: 0117 906 0100
Canons
Capitular Canons Canon Anthony Brown
Canon Jon Cannon
Canon John Savage
Other Staff
Chapter Clerk Miss Wendy Matthews, Bristol Cathedral, Abbey Gatehouse, College Green Bristol BS1 5TJ
T: 0117 946 8172
E: wendy.matthews@bristol-cathedral.co.uk
Cathedral Organist Mr Mark Lee, Bristol Cathedral, Abbey Gatehouse, College Green, Bristol BS1 5TJ
T: 0117 946 8177
E: organist@bristol-cathedral.co.uk
Cathedral Chaplain The Revd Sarah Evans, Bristol Cathedral, College Green, Bristol BS1 5TJ

Canon Theologian The Revd Canon Professor Martin Gainsborough (*Same Address*)

ARCHDEACONS
BRISTOL The Ven Christine Froude, Diocesan Office, 1st Floor, Hillside House, 1500 Parkway North, Newbrick Road, Stoke Gifford, Bristol BS34 8YU
T: 0117 906 0100
E: christine.froude@bristoldiocese.org
MALMESBURY The Ven Christine Froude, Diocesan Office, 1st Floor, Hillside House, 1500 Parkway North, Newbrick Road, Stoke Gifford, Bristol BS34 8YU
T: 0117 906 0100
E: christine.froude@bristoldiocese.org

MEMBERS OF THE HOUSE OF CLERGY OF THE GENERAL SYNOD
Proctors for Clergy
The Revd Canon Professor Martin Gainsborough
The Revd Paul Jonathan Langham
The Revd Canon Mark Pilgrim

MEMBERS OF THE HOUSE OF LAITY OF THE GENERAL SYNOD
Mr Ian Yemm
Canon David Froude
Mr Edward Shaw

DIOCESAN OFFICERS
Diocesan Secretary Mr Oliver Home, Diocesan Office, 1st Floor, Hillside House, 1500 Parkway North, Newbrick Road, Stoke Gifford, Bristol BS34 8YU
T: 0117 906 0100
E: oliver.home@bristoldiocese.org
Chancellor of Diocese The Revd Justin Gau, 3 Pump Court, Temple, London EC4Y 7AJ
T: 020 7353 0711
Registrar of Diocese and Bishop's Legal Secretary Mr Roland Callaby, Harris and Harris, 14 Market Place, Wells BA5 2RE
T: 01749 674747
F: 01749 676585
E: roland.callaby@harris-harris.co.uk

DIOCESAN ORGANIZATIONS
Diocesan Office Diocesan Office, 1st Floor, Hillside House, 1500 Parkway North, Newbrick Road, Stoke Gifford, Bristol BS34 8YU
T: 0117 906 0100
E: any.name@bristoldiocese.org

ADMINISTRATION
Diocesan Synod (Chairman, House of Clergy) The Revd Canon Raymond Adams
(Chairman, House of Laity) Canon David Froude
Board of Finance (Chairman) Mr Andrew Lucas, c/o Diocesan Office, 1st Floor, Hillside House, 1500 Parkway North, Newbrick Road, Stoke Gifford, Bristol BS34 8YU T: 0117 906 0100
(Secretary) Mr Oliver Home, Diocesan Office, 1st Floor, Hillside House, 1500 Parkway North, Newbrick Road, Stoke Gifford, Bristol BS34 8YU T: 0117 906 0100
E: oliver.home@bristoldiocese.org
(Finance Manager) Mr Matthew Hall *(Same Address)* T: 0117 906 0100
Mission and Pastoral Committee Vacancy *(enquires to Head of Governance and Property)* Mrs Sally Moody *(Same Address & Tel)*
(Diocesan Electoral Registration Officer) Mr Graham Shaul *(Same Address & Tel)*
(Designated Officer) Mr Roland Callaby, Harris and Harris, 14 Market Place, Wells BA5 2RE
T: 01749 674747
F: 01749 676585
E: roland.callaby@harris-harris.co.uk
(Safeguarding Adviser) Adam Bond, Diocesan Office, 1st Floor, Hillside House, 1500 Parkway North, Newbrick Road, Stoke Gifford, Bristol BS34 8YU T: 0117 906 0100
E: adam.bond@bristoldiocese.org
(Safeguarding Case Worker) Nick Papuca *(Same Address)*
E: nick.papuca@bristol.diocese.org

ADVISER FOR MINISTERIAL SUPPORT
Ian Tomkins, Diocesan Office, 1st Floor, Hillside House, 1500 Parkway North, Newbrick Road, Stoke Gifford, Bristol BS34 8YU
T: 0117 906 0100

CHURCH BUILDINGS
Advisory Committee for the Care of Churches (Chairman) Mr Simon Pugh-Jones
(DAC Secretary) Mrs Janet Saxon, Harris and Harris, 14 Market Place, Wells BA5 2RE
T: 01749 674747
F: 01749 676585
E: janet.saxon@harris-harris.co.uk

CHURCH MINISTRY OF HEALING
Chairman Mrs Brenda Munden
M: 07909 696325
E: bestview28@gmail.com

DIOCESAN ECUMENICAL AND GLOBAL DEVELOPMENT
Diocesan Ecumenical and Global Development Officer The Revd Chris Dobson, Diocesan Office, 1st Floor, Hillside House, 1500 Parkway North, Newbrick Road, Stoke Gifford, Bristol BS34 8YU T: 0117 906 0100

DIOCESAN LAY MINISTERS' COUNCIL
Secretary Mrs Sue Farrance, 102 Jersey Avenue, Brislington, Bristol BS4 4QZ
T: 0117 971 1629
E: sue.farrance@blueyonder.co.uk

DIOCESAN RECORD OFFICES
Bristol Record Office, 'B' Bond, Smeaton Road, Bristol BS1 6XN
County Archivist Mr J. S. Williams
T: 0117 922 4224
Wiltshire and Swindon History Centre Cocklebury Road, Chippenham SN15 3QN
County Archivist Mr John Darcy
T: 01249 705500

DIOCESAN WORSHIP AND LITURGY COMMITTEE
Chairman Canon Gill Behenna, 1 Saxon Way, Bradley Stoke, Bristol BS32 9AR
T: 01454 202483
E: gillbehenna@me.com

EDUCATION
Board of Education (Director) Mr John Swainston, Diocesan Office, 1st Floor, Hillside House, 1500 Parkway North, Newbrick Road, Stoke Gifford, Bristol BS34 8YU
T: 0117 906 0100
E: john.swainston@bristoldiocese.org

MINISTRY DEVELOPMENT
Adviser for Ministry Development (DDO) The Revd Canon Derek Chedzey, Diocesan Office, 1st Floor, Hillside House, 1500 Parkway North, Newbrick Road, Stoke Gifford, Bristol BS34 8YU T: 0117 906 0100
Administrators Mr James Edmonds, Diocesan Office, 1st Floor, Hillside House, 1500 Parkway North, Newbrick Road, Stoke Gifford, Bristol BS34 8YU T: 0117 906 0100
Mrs Rachel Miller *(Same Address & Tel)*

PRESS, PUBLICITY AND PUBLICATIONS
Communications Officer and Press Officer Mr Ben Evans, Diocesan Office, 1st Floor, Hillside House, 1500 Parkway North, Newbrick Road, Stoke Gifford, Bristol BS34 8YU
T: 0117 906 0100
E: ben.evans@bristoldiocese.org

STRATEGY SUPPORT

Transition Manager Mr George Rendell, Diocesan Office, 1st Floor, Hillside House, 1500 Parkway North, Newbrick Road, Stoke Gifford, Bristol BS34 8YU   *T:* 0117 906 0100

AREA DEANS

ARCHDEACONRY OF BRISTOL

Bristol South Nicholas John Hay, St Paul's Vicarage, 2 Southville Road, Bristol BS3 1DG
T: 07534 249338
E: nickthevichay@googlemail.com
Bristol West Matthew David Ineson, St Mary's Vicarage, Mariner's Drive, Bristol BS9 1QJ
T: 07896 997604
E: matineson@blueyonder.co.uk
City Roderic Paul Symmons, Redland Vicarage, 151 Redland Road, Bristol BS6 6YE
T: 0117 946 4691
E: rod@redland.org.uk

ARCHDEACONRY OF MALMESBURY

Chippenham Sally Ann Violet Wheeler, The Vicarage, Church Lane, Marshfield, Chippenham SN14 8NT   *T:* 01225 892180
E: rjwheeler77@gmail.com
Kingswood and South Gloucestershire Simon Jones, 119 North Road, Stoke Gifford, Bristol BS34 8PE   *T:* 0117 979 1656
E: simon@stmichaelsbristol.org
North Wiltshire Christopher Paul Bryan, The Rectory, 1 Rectory Close, Stanton St Quintin, Chippenham SN14 6DT   *T:* 01666 837522
E: christopher.bryan123@btinternet.com
Swindon Clive David Deverell, 26 The Bramptons, Shaw, Swindon SN5 5SL
T: 01793 877111
E: clive.deverell@btinternet.com

DIOCESE OF CANTERBURY

Founded in 597. Kent east of the Medway, excluding the Medway Towns in the diocese of Rochester.

Population 1,128,000   Area 1,050 sq m
Full-time Stipendiary Parochial Clergy 128   Benefices 145
Parishes 263   hurches 361
Overseas link dioceses: Antananarivo, Antsiranana,
Toamasina, Mahajanga (Madagascar), Arras (Pas-de-Calais), Basel

ARCHBISHOP (105th)
The Most Revd and Rt Hon Justin Portal Welby, Old Palace, Canterbury CT1 2EE
T: 01227 459382
F: 020 7261 9836

BISHOPS' STAFF
Diocesan Chaplain The Revd Jennifer Corcoran
Hon Chaplains Canon Roger Martin, 'Kwetu', 23 Tanners Hill Gardens, Hythe CT21 5HY
T: 01303 237204
E: rogmartin@btinternet.com
The Ven John Barton, 7 The Spires, Canterbury CT2 8SD
T: 01227 379688
E: johnbarton@greenbee.net
PA Mrs Anne Neal, Old Palace, Canterbury CT1 2EE
T: 01227 459382
F: 01227 784985
PA Mrs Sue Bowles (*Same Address, Tel & Fax*)

SUFFRAGAN BISHOP
Bishop of Dover The Rt Revd Trevor Willmott, Old Palace, The Precincts, Canterbury CT1 2EE
T: 01227 459382
F: 01227 784985
E: trevorwillmott@bishcant.org

PROVINCIAL EPISCOPAL VISITORS
EBBSFLEET The Rt Revd Jonathan Goodall, Tree Tops, The Mount, Caversham, Reading RG4 7RE
T: 0118 948 1038
E: office@ebbsfleet.org.uk
RICHBOROUGH The Rt Revd Norman Banks, Parkside House, Abbey Mill Lane, St Albans AL3 4HE
T: 01727 836358
E: bishop@richborough.org.uk

ASSISTANT BISHOPS
The Rt Revd Michael Gear, 10 Acott Fields, Yalding, Maidstone ME18 6DQ
T: 01622 817388
E: bp_mikegear@yahoo.com
The Rt Revd Richard Llewellin, 15a The Precincts, Canterbury CT1 2EL
T: 01227 764645
E: rllewellin@clara.co.uk

The Rt Revd Anthony Michael Turnbull, 67 Strand Street, Sandwich CT13 9HN
T: 01304 611389
E: amichaelturnbull@yahoo.co.uk

CATHEDRAL AND METROPOLITICAL CHURCH OF CHRIST
Dean The Very Revd Dr Robert Willis, The Deanery, The Precincts, Canterbury CT1 2EP
T: 01227 865200 (office)
E: dean@canterbury-cathedral.org
Canons Residentiary
Canon Treasurer The Revd Canon Nicholas Papadopulos, 15 The Precincts, Canterbury CT1 2EL
T: 01227 865233
E: nick.papadopulos@canterbury-cathedral.org
Archdeacon The Ven Jo Kelly-Moore, The Archdeaconry, 29 The Precincts, Canterbury CT1 2EP
T: 01227 865238
F: 01227 785209
E: archdeacon@canterbury-cathedral.org
Canon Pastor The Revd Canon Clare Edwards, 22 The Precincts, Canterbury CT1 2EP
T: 01227 865227
E: canonclare@canterbury-cathedral.org
Other Staff
Precentor and Sacrist The Revd Max Kramer, 5 The Precincts, Canterbury CT1 2EE
T: 01227 865225
M: 07796 673081
E: max.kramer@canterbury-cathedral.org
Receiver General Commodore Martin Atherton
T: 01227 865212
E: martin.atherton@canterbury-cathedral.org
Cathedral Organist Dr David Flood, 6 The Precincts, Canterbury CT1 2EE
T: 01227 865242
E: david.flood@canterbury-cathedral.org

ARCHDEACONS
ASHFORD The Ven Darren Miller, The Archdeaconry, Pett Lane, Charing, Ashford TN27 0DC (from 1/1/18)
CANTERBURY The Ven Jo Kelly-Moore, The Archdeaconry, 29 The Precincts, Canterbury CT1 2EP
T: 01227 865238
E: archdeacon@canterbury-cathedral.org

MAIDSTONE The Ven Stephen Taylor, The Archdeaconry, 4 Redcliffe Lane, Penenden Heath, Maidstone ME14 2AG
T: 01622 200221
E: staylor@archdeaconmaid.org

MEMBERS OF THE HOUSE OF CLERGY OF THE GENERAL SYNOD
Proctors for Clergy
Vacancy
The Dean of Canterbury
The Revd Canon Clare Edwards
The Revd Barney De Berry

MEMBERS OF THE HOUSE OF LAITY OF THE GENERAL SYNOD
Mr David Kemp
Miss Judith Rigby
Canon Rosemary Walters

DIGNITARIES IN CONVOCATION
The Dean of Canterbury

DIOCESAN OFFICERS
Diocesan Secretary Mr Julian Hills, Diocesan House, Lady Wootton's Green, Canterbury CT1 1NQ
T: 01227 459401
F: 01227 787073
E: jhills@diocant.org
Commissary General Miss Morag Ellis, c/o The Registry, Minerva House, 5 Montague Close, London SE1 9BB
T: 020 7593 5000
Diocesan Registrar and Legal Adviser to the Diocese Mr Owen Carew-Jones, Minerva House, 5 Montague Close, London SE1 9BB
T: 020 7593 5110
F: 020 7593 5099
E: ocj@wslaw.co.uk

DIOCESAN ORGANIZATIONS
Diocesan Office Diocesan House, Lady Wootton's Green, Canterbury CT1 1NQ
T: 01227 459401
F: 01227 450964
E: reception@diocant.org

ADMINISTRATION (RESOURCE MANAGEMENT AND COMPLIANCE)
Diocesan Synod (Chairman, House of Clergy) The Revd Andy Bawtree, The Vicarage, 23 Lewisham Road, Dover CT17 0QG
(Chairman, House of Laity) Mr Phil Sibbald, c/o Diocesan House
(Secretary) Mr Julian Hills, Diocesan House, Lady Wootton's Green, Canterbury CT1 1NQ
T: 01227 459401
F: 01227 787073
E: jhills@diocant.org

Board of Finance (Chairman) Mr Raymond Harris
(Secretary) Mr Julian Hills, Diocesan House, Lady Wootton's Green, Canterbury CT1 1NQ
T: 01227 459401
F: 01227 787073
E: jhills@diocant.org
(Director of Finance) Mr Douglas Gibbs *(Same Address)*
(HR Adviser) Mrs Sarah Marsden *(Same Address)*
(Director of Property Services) Mr Christopher Robinson *(Same Address)*

CHILDREN, SCHOOLS AND YOUNG PEOPLE (Including the Board of Education)
Chairman Mr Alasdair Hogarth
Director of Education Mr Quentin Roper, Diocesan House, Lady Wootton's Green, Canterbury CT1 1NQ
Assistant Director of Education (School Effectiveness) Mrs Niki Paterson *(Same Address)*
Assistant Director of Education (Schools Organization) Ms Robin Ford, Diocesan House, Lady Wootton's Green, Canterbury CT1 1NQ
Children and Young People's (ChYPs) Ministry Adviser Mr Murray Wilkinson, Diocesan House, Lady Wootton's Green, Canterbury CT1 1NQ

CHURCH BUILDINGS
Diocesan Advisory Committee for the Care of Churches (Secretary) Mr Ian Dodd, Diocesan House, Lady Wootton's Green, Canterbury CT1 1NQ
(Chairman) Dr Richard Morrice, 3 Stafford Road, Tunbridge Wells TN25 4QZ

COMMUNICATIONS
Communications Director Mrs Anna Drew, Diocesan House, Lady Wootton's Green, Canterbury CT1 1NQ
IT Manager Mr Mark Binns *(Same Address)*
IT and Communications Assistant Mrs Marilyn Shrimpton *(Same Address)*

COMMUNITY AND PARTNERSHIPS
Chairman Ms Amanda Cottrell
T: 01580 240973
Community and Partnership Exec Officer and Rural Life Adviser The Revd Canon Caroline Pinchbeck, Diocesan House, Lady Wootton's Green, Canterbury CT1 1NQ

DIOCESAN RECORD OFFICES
Cathedral Archives and Library, The Precincts, Canterbury CT1 2EH
T: 01227 865330

Kent History Services, Kent History and Library Centre, James Whatman Way, Maidstone ME14 1LQ   *T:* 08458 247200
     E: historyandlibrarycentre@kent.gov.uk

LICENSED MINISTRY
Chair Mrs Caroline Spencer, Little Eggarton, Godmersham, Canterbury CT4 7DY
Director of Ordinands The Revd Joss Walker, Diocesan House, Lady Wootton's Green, Canterbury CT1 1NQ
Assistant Directors of Ordinands The Revd Andy Bawtree   *T:* 01304 822037
     E: rockabillyrev@hotmail.com
The Revd Denise Critchell, 3 Somerset Close, Whitstable CT5 4RA
The Revd Craig Hunt, St Mary Bredin Church, 59 Nunnery Fields, Canterbury CT1 3JN
The Revd Chris Lavender, The Rectory, Poplar Grove, Allington, Maidstone ME16 0DE
The Revd Sue Martin   *T:* 01227 360948
     E: revsuemartin@btinternet.com
The Revd Liz Reesch, 88 Albany Road, Sittingbournc ME10 1EL
The Revd Louise Seear, The Vicarage, Oak Walk, Hythe CT21 5DN
Ministry Development Officer Mr Neville Emslie, Diocesan House, Lady Wootton's Green, Canterbury CT1 1NQ
Association of Readers (Warden) The Revd Donald Lawton
Mr Nigel Collins, Diocesan House, Lady Wootton's Green, Canterbury CT1 1NQ
Clergy Retirement and Registration Officers (Ashford Archdeaconry) The Revd Canon Gilbert Spencer   *T:* 01233 501774
     E: gilbert_spencer@hotmail.com
(Canterbury Archdeaconry) The Revd Grahame Whittlesea   *T:* 01227 472536
     E: gandawhittlesea@tiscali.co.uk
(Maidstone Archdeaconry) The Revd Ron Gamble
     T: 01622 744455
     E: r-gamble@sky.com

LOCAL CHURCH DEVELOPMENT
Chairman The Revd Canon Andrew Sewell, St Paul's Vicarage, 130 Boxley Road, Maidstone ME14 2AH   *T:* 01622 691926
     E: andrew@asewell.plus.com
Mission and Growth Adviser The Revd Canon Steve Coneys, The Vicarage, 11 Kimberley Grove, Seasalter, Whitstable CT5 4AY
     T: 01227 276795
     E: steveconeys@btinternet.com
Mission and Ministry Executive Officer Mrs Emma Sivyer, Diocesan House, Lady Wootton's Green, Canterbury CT1 1NQ
Local Ministries and Growth Advisor The Revd Peter Ingrams *(Same Address)*
Children's Missioner Captain Graham Nunn
     T: 01622 672088
     E: gnunn@diocant.org

Stewardship and Funding Adviser Mrs Liz Mullins, Diocesan House, Lady Wootton's Green, Canterbury CT1 1NQ
Part-time Assistant Stewardship and Funding Adviser Mrs Charlotte McCaulay *(Same Address)*

AREA DEANS
ARCHDEACONRY OF ASHFORD
Ashford Timothy Charles Wilson, The Rectory, The Street, Great Chart, Ashford TN23 3AY
     T: 01233 620371
     E: tandcwilson@lineone.net
Dover Andrew James Bawtree, The Vicarage, 23 Lewisham Road, Dover CT17 0QG
     T: 01304 822037
     E: rockabillyrev@hotmail.com
Dover John Anthony Patrick Walker, St Mary's Vicarage, Taswell Street, Dover CT16 1SE
     T: 07980 692813
     E: johnwalker_uk@btinternet.com
Elham David John Adlington, St Peter's Vicarage, North Street, Folkestone CT19 6AL
     T: 01303 254472
     E: david.adlington@btinternet.com
Romney and Tenterden Lindsay John Hammond, The Vicarage, Church Road, Tenterden TN30 6AT   *T:* 01580 761591
     E: tentvic@gmail.com
Sandwich Seth William Cooper, Elizabeth House, 32 St Mary's Road, Walmer, Deal CT14 7QA   *T:* 01304 366605
     E: sethandjen@tinyworld.co.uk

ARCHDEACONRY OF CANTERBURY
Canterbury Kevin Maddy, The Rectory, St Stephen's Green, Canterbury CT2 7JU
     T: 07720 499403
     E: revkmaddy@gmail.com
East Bridge Vacancy
Reculver Anthony William Everett, Christ Church Vicarage, 38 Beltinge Road, Herne Bay CT6 6BU   *T:* 01227 374906
     E: anthony@fayland.freeserve.co.uk
Thanet Ian Andrew Jacobson, The Rectory, 2 Newington Road, Ramsgate CT11 0QT
     T: 01843 582672
     E: andrew.jacobson@waitrose.com
West Bridge Paul Ronald Ratcliff, The Vicarage, 3 Hambrook Close, Chilham, Canterbury CT4 8EJ   *T:* 01227 730235
     E: pr.ratcliff@googlemail.com

ARCHDEACONRY OF MAIDSTONE
Maidstone Andrew William Sewell, St Paul's Vicarage, 130 Boxley Road, Maidstone ME14 2AH   *T:* 01622 691926
     E: andrew@asewell.plus.com

North Downs Steven Philip Hughes, 4 Kings Acre, Downswood, Maidstone ME15 8UP
T: 07896 098272
E: steven.hughes24@btinternet.com
Ospringe Stephen Hunter Lillicrap, The Vicarage, 76 Station Road, Teynham, Sittingbourne ME9 9SN   *T:* 01795 522510
E: steve.lillicrap@btopenworld.com

Sittingbourne Michael Johann Resch, 88 Albany Road, Sittingbourne ME10 1EL
T: 01795 473393
E: mikeresch@me.com
Weald Ann Elizabeth Jane Pollington, The Vicarage, Waterloo Road, Cranbrook TN17 3JQ   *T:* 01580 388173
E: ann.pollington@btinternet.com

DIOCESE OF CARLISLE

Founded in 1133. Cumbria, except for small areas in the east, in the diocese of Newcastle.

Population 496,000   rea 2,570 sq m
Full-time Stipendiary Parochial Clergy 109   Benefices 118
Parishes 249   Churches 335
www.carlislediocese.org.uk
Overseas link dioceses: Zululand (South Africa),
Stavanger (Norway), Northern Argentina

BISHOP (67th)

The Rt Revd James Newcome, Bishop's House, Ambleside Road, Keswick CA12 4DD
T: 01768 773430
E: bishop.carlisle@carlislediocese.org.uk

BISHOP'S STAFF

Bishop's Chaplain The Revd Canon Cameron Butland, Bishop's House, Ambleside Road, Keswick CA12 4DD   *T:* 01768 773430 (office)
E: cameron.butland@carlislediocese.org.uk

SUFFRAGAN BISHOP

PENRITH The Rt Revd Robert Freeman, Holm Croft, 13 Castle Road, Kendal LA9 7AU
T: 01539 727836
E: bishop.penrith@carlislediocese.org.uk

ASSISTANT BISHOPS

The Rt Revd Ian Macdonald Griggs, Rookings, Patterdale, Penrith CA11 0NP
T: 01768 482064
E: ian.griggs@virgin.net
The Rt Revd George Lanyon Hacker, Keld House, Milburn, Penrith CA10 1TW
T: 01768 361506
E: bishhack@mypostoffice.co.uk
The Rt Revd Andrew Alexander Kenny Graham, Fell End, Butterwick, Penrith CA10 2QQ   *T:* 01931 713147
The Rt Revd Hewlett Thompson, Low Broomrigg, Warcop, Appleby CA16 6PT
T: 01768 341281
The Rt Revd Robert Hardy, Carleton House, Back Lane, Langwathby, Penrith CA10 1NB
T: 01768 881210
The Rt Revd John Richardson, The Old Rectory, Bewcastle, Carlisle CA6 6PS
T: 01697 748389
The Rt Revd Nigel McCulloch, Stonelea, 1 Head's Drive, Grange over Sands LA11 7DY
T: 01539 536018
The Rt Revd Cyril Ashton, Charis, 17c Quernmore Road, Lancaster LA1 3EB
T: 01524 848684
E: bpcg.ashton@btinternet.com

The Rt Revd Peter Ramsden, 4 Railway Cottages, Long Marton, Appleby CA16 6BY
T: 017683 61175
The Rt Revd James Bell, Stonecroft, Bolton, Appleby in Westmorland CA16 6AL
T: 01768 361649
E: j.h.bell@btopenworld.com
The Rt Revd Glyn Webster, Holy Trinity Rectory, Micklegate, York YO1 6LE
T: 01904 628155
E: office@seeofbeverley.org

CATHEDRAL CHURCH OF THE HOLY AND UNDIVIDED TRINITY

Dean The Very Revd Mark Christopher Boyling, The Deanery, The Abbey, Carlisle CA3 8TZ   *T:* 01228 523335
E: dean@carlislecathedral.org.uk
Canons Residentiary The Revd Canon Janet (Jan) Elizabeth Kearton, 3 The Abbey, Carlisle CA3 8TZ   *T:* 01228 521857
E: canonwarden@carlislecathedral.org.uk
The Revd Canon Michael Alan Manley, 1 The Abbey, Carlisle CA3 8TZ   *T:* 01228 542790
E: canonmissioner@carlislecathedral.org.uk
The Revd Canon Peter Clement, Church House, 19-24 Friargate, Penrith, Cumbria CA11 7XR   *T:* 01768 807777
M: 07823 415815
E: peter.clement@
cumbriachristianlearning.org.uk
Other Staff
Lay Canons Canon James Westoll, Kirkandrews Tower, Longtown, Carlisle CA6 5NF
Canon Alex Barbour, Castlehow Scar, via Shap, Penrith CA10 3LG
Canon Bryan Gray, The Chapel, Hunsonby, Penrith CA10 1PN
Director of Strategic Operations Ms Sharon Parr, Cathedral Office, 7 The Abbey, Carlisle CA3 8TZ   *T:* 01228 548151
Commercial and Administration Co-ordinator Mrs Wendy Murrell (*Same Address*)
T: 01228 548071
Director of Music Mr Mark Duthie, 6 The Abbey, Carlisle CA3 8TZ   *T:* 01228 529246
E: directorofmusic@carlislecathedral.org.uk

ARCHDEACONS

CARLISLE The Ven Lee Townend, The New Vicarage, Plumpton, Penrith CA11 9PA
T: 01768 807777
E: archdeacon.north@carlislediocese.org.uk
WESTMORLAND AND FURNESS The Ven Vernon Ross, The Vicarage, Windermere Road, Lindale, Grange-over-Sands LA11 6LB
T: 01539 534717
E: archdeacon.south@carlislediocese.org.uk
WEST CUMBERLAND The Ven Richard Pratt, 50 Stainburn Road, Workington CA14 1SN
T: 01900 66190
E: archdeacon.west@carlislediocese.org.uk

MEMBERS OF THE HOUSE OF CLERGY OF THE GENERAL SYNOD

Proctors for Clergy
The Revd Canon Ruth Crossley
The Revd Stewart Fyfe
The Revd Canon Cameron Butland

MEMBERS OF THE HOUSE OF LAITY OF THE GENERAL SYNOD

Dr Christopher Angus
Mrs Valerie Hallard
Mr Geoffrey Hine
Mr David Mills

DIOCESAN OFFICERS

Diocesan Secretary Mr Derek Hurton, Church House, 19-24 Friargate, Penrith, Cumbria CA11 7XR
T: 01768 807760
E: diocesan.secretary@carlislediocese.org.uk
Registrar of Diocese and Bishop's Legal Secretary Mrs Jane Lowdon, Sintons Solicitors, The Cube, Barrack Road, Newcastle-upon-Tyne NE4 6DB
T: 0191 226 7878
F: 0191 226 7852
E: jane.lowdon@sintons.co.uk

DIOCESAN ORGANIZATIONS

Diocesan Office Church House, 19-24 Friargate, Penrith, Cumbria CA11 7XR T: 01768 807777
F: 01768 868918
E: enquiries@carlislediocese.org.uk
W: www.carlislediocese.org.uk

ADMINISTRATION

Diocesan Synod (Chairman, House of Clergy) The Revd Canon Alan Bing, 15 Ford Park Crescent, Ulverston LA12 7JR
T: 01229 584331
E: alanbing@live.co.uk
(Chairman, House of Laity) Dr Christopher Angus, Burtholme East, Lanercost, Brampton CA8 2HH
T: 016977 41504
E: chris.angus@btinternet.com

(Secretary) Mr Derek Hurton, Church House, 19-24 Friargate, Penrith, Cumbria CA11 7XR
T: 01768 807760
E: diocesan.secretary@carlislediocese.org.uk
Board of Finance (Chairman) The Revd Canon Martin Jayne, 12 Longmeadow Lane, Natland, Kendal LA9 7QZ
T: 015395 60942
E: martjay@mac.com
(Secretary) Mr Derek Hurton, Church House, 19-24 Friargate, Penrith, Cumbria CA11 7XR
T: 01768 807760
E: diocesan.secretary@carlislediocese.org.uk
(Head of Finance) Mr Ric Jaques *(Same Address)*
T: 01768 807761
E: ric.jaques@carlislediocese.org.uk
(Property Manager) Mr Neal Andrews *(Same Address)*
T: 01768 807762
E: property@carlislediocese.org.uk
Pastoral Committee Mr Derek Hurton *(Same Address)*
T: 01768 807760
E: diocesan.secretary@carlislediocese.org.uk
(Designated Officer) Mrs Jane Lowdon, Sintons Solicitors, The Cube, Barrack Road, Newcastle-upon-Tyne NE4 6DB
T: 0191 226 7878
F. 0191 226 7852
E: jane.lowdon@sintons.co.uk

CHURCH BUILDINGS

Advisory Committee for the Care of Churches (Chairman) Miss Lilian Hopkins, Rodford House, 5 Lorne Terrace, Brampton CA8 1NS
(Secretary) Mrs Rosaleen Lane, Church House, 19-24 Friargate, Penrith, Cumbria CA11 7XR
T: 01768 807771
E: rosaleen.lane@carlislediocese.org.uk

CUMBRIA CHRISTIAN LEARNING

Director The Revd Canon Roger Latham, Church House, 19-24 Friargate, Penrith, Cumbria CA11 7XR
T: 01768 807765
E: roger.latham@cumbriachristianlearning.org.uk
Learning Development Team Leader The Revd Nicola Pennington
E: nicki.pennington@cumbriachristianlearning.org.uk
Principal, Initial Ministerial Training Dr Karl Moller, Church House, 19-24 Friargate, Penrith, Cumbria CA11 7XR T: 01768 807765
E: karl.moller@cumbriachristianlearning.org.uk
Vice-Principal, Initial Ministerial Education The Revd Allison Fenton
E: allison.fenton@cumbriachristianlearning.org.uk
Adviser for Women's Ministry The Revd Canon Ruth Crossley, The Vicarage, Market Place, Dalton in Furness LA15 8AZ
T: 01539 560233
E: ruth.crossley@carlislediocese.org.uk

DIOCESAN RECORD OFFICES

Cumbria Archive Centre and Local Studies Centre, Scotch Street, Whitehaven CA28 7NL
T: 01946 506420
E: whitehaven.archives@cumbria.gov.uk
Cumbria Archive Centre, Lady Gillford's House, Petteril Bank Road, Carlisle CA1 3AJ
T: 01228 227285
E: carlisle.archives@cumbria.gov.uk
Cumbria Archive Centre, County Offices, Kendal LA9 4RQ
T: 01539 713540
E: kendal.archives@cumbria.gov.uk
Cumbria Archive Centre and Local Studies Centre, 140 Duke St, Barrow-in-Furness LA14 1XW
T: 01229 407377
E: barrow.archives@cumbria.gov.uk

ECUMENICAL AFFAIRS

Diocesan Ecumenical Officer The Revd David Cooper, The Vicarage, 45 Church Hill, Arnside LA5 0DW
T: 01524 761319
E: revdavidcooper@btinternet.com
Churches Together in Cumbria (Ecumenical Development Officer) Ms Helen Boothroyd, 46 Oak Avenue, Bare, Morecambe LA4 6HS
T: 0750 393 1196
E: hbctic@tiscali.co.uk
Rural Officer The Revd Sarah Lunn, Rectory, Long Marton, Appleby in Westmorland CA16 6BN
T: 01768 361269
E: sarahlunn63@gmail.com

EDUCATION

Board of Education, Church House, 19-24 Friargate, Penrith, Cumbria CA11 7XR
T: 01768 807777
F: 01768 868918
E: education@carlislediocese.org.uk
Director of Education Mr Michael Mill, Church House, 19-24 Friargate, Penrith, Cumbria CA11 7XR
T: 01768 807766
E: director.education@carlislediocese.org.uk
Deputy Director of Education Mrs Deborah Smith (*Same Address*)
T: 01768 807767
E: deborah.smith@carlislediocese.org

ENVIRONMENT

Environment Adviser The Revd Prof Ian James, High Pasture, Crook Road, Kendal LA8 8LY
T: 01539 721841
E: dr.i.n.james@btinternet.com

PARTNERSHIP IN WORLD MISSION

World Mission Officer Vacancy

PRESS AND PUBLICATIONS

Communications Officer Mr Dave Roberts
T: 01768 807764
M: 07469153658
E: communications@carlislediocese.org.uk

Diocesan Directory Mrs Eleanor Scott, Church House, 19-24 Friargate, Penrith, Carlisle Cumbria
E: eleanor.scott@carlislediocese.org.uk

REACH TEAM

Chair The Rt Revd Robert Freeman, Holm Croft, 13 Castle Road, Kendal LA9 7AU
T: 01539 727836
E: bishop.penrith@carlislediocese.org.uk
Reach Team Assistant Mrs Vicki Grant (*Same Address & Tel*)
E: vicki.grant@carlislediocese.org.uk
Diocesan Evangelism Enabler The Revd Michael Talbot, Church House, 19-24 Friargate, Penrith, Cumbria CA11 7XR
E: mike.talbot@carlislediocese.org.uk
Diocesan Fresh Expressions Enabler Mr Richard Passmore (*Same Address*)
E: richard.passmore@carlislediocese.org.uk
Youth, Children and Family Evangelism Enabler Mrs Sarah Hulme (*Same Address*)
E: sarah.hulme@carlislediocese.org.uk
Mrs Emma Richardson (*Same Address*)
E: emma.richardson@carlislediocese.org.uk

RETIRED CLERGY AND WIDOWS

Retired Clergy and Widows Officer The Ven Penny Driver, 32 Priory Crescent, Kent's Bank, Grange over Sands LA11 7BL
E: pennydriver52@gmail.com

SOCIAL RESPONSIBILITY

Churches Social Action Network The Ven Richard Pratt, 50 Stainburn Road, Workington CA14 1SN
T: 01900 66190
E: archdeacon.west@carlislediocese.org.uk
Industrial Mission The Ven Richard Pratt (*As above*)

RURAL DEANS
ARCHDEACONRY OF CARLISLE

Appleby Stewart John Fyfe, The Vicarage, Morland, Penrith CA10 3AX
T: 01931 714620
E: stewart.fyfe@btinternet.com
Brampton Richard James Anthony Tulloch, St Martin's Vicarage, Main Street, Brampton CA8 1SH
T: 016977 41304
E: rjatulloch@gmail.com
Carlisle Nigel David Beer, The Vicarage, Dykes Terrace, Carlisle CA3 9AS
T: 01228 514600
E: rev.beer@hotmail.co.uk
Penrith David Gareth Sargent, The Rectory, 3 Lamley Gardens, Penrith CA11 9LR
T: 01768 863000
E: revdave.sargent@talk21.com

ARCHDEACONRY OF WEST CUMBERLAND

Calder Allen James Banks, 36 Basket Road, Whitehaven CA28 9AH
T: 01946 61470
E: allenbanks@btinternet.com

Derwent Charles Henry Hope, St John's Vicarage, Ambleside Road, Keswick CA12 4DN
T: 01768 775855
E: charleshope@btopenworld.com
Solway Timothy David Herbert, The Vicarage, King Street, Aspatria, Wigton CA7 3AL
T: 01697 322712
E: therbert@globalnet.co.uk

ARCHDEACONRY OF WESTMORLAND AND FURNESS
Barrow Gary Marshall Cregeen, The Rectory, 98 Roose Road, Barrow-in-Furness LA13 9RL
T: 01229 877367
E: gary@gandjcregeen.co.uk

Furness Alan Charles Bing, The Rectory, 15 Ford Park Crescent, Ulverston LA12 7JR
T: 01229 584331
E: alanbing@live.co.uk
Kendal Angela Whittaker, The Vicarage, Natland, Kendal LA9 7QQ   *T:* 01539 560355
E: a-awhittaker@tiscali.co.uk
Windermere David Mark Baty Wilmot, St Mary's Vicarage, Ambleside Road, Windermere LA23 1BA   *T:* 01539 443032
E: vicar@stmaryswindermere.co.uk

DIOCESE OF CHELMSFORD

Founded in 1914. Essex, except for a few parishes in the north, in the dioceses of Ely and St Edmundsbury and Ipswich; five East London boroughs north of the Thames; three parishes in south Cambridgeshire.

Population 3,176,000   Area 1,530 sq m
Full-time Stipendiary Parochial Clergy 332   Benefices 312
Parishes 468   Churches 579
Overseas link dioceses: Embu, Kirinyaga, Meru, Mbere and Marsabit (kenya); Trinidad and Tobago; Karlstad; Iasi (Romania)

BISHOP
The Rt Revd Stephen Cottrell, Bishopscourt, Margaretting, Ingatestone CM4 0HD
T: 01277 352001
F: 01277 355374
E: bishopscourt@chelmsford.anglican.org

BISHOP'S STAFF
Bishop's Chaplain The Revd Matthew Jonathan Simpkins, Bishopscourt, Margaretting, Ingatestone CM4 0HD   *T:* 01277 352001
F: 01277 355374
E: chaplain@chelmsford.anglican.org
Director of Communications and Bishop's Press Officer Ralph Meloy, Diocesan Office
T: 01245 294424
07654 382674 (pager)
E: rmeloy@chelmsford.anglican.org

PROVINCIAL EPISCOPAL VISITOR
Assistant Bishop and Provincial Episcopal Visitor The Rt Revd Norman Banks, Parkside House, Abbey Mill Lane, St Albans AL3 4HE
T: 01727 836358
E: bishop@richborough.org.uk

AREA BISHOPS
BRADWELL Vacancy
BARKING The Rt Revd Peter Hill, Barking Lodge, Verulam Avenue, London E17 8ES
T: 020 8509 7377
E: b.barking@chelmsford.anglican.org
COLCHESTER The Rt Revd Roger A. B. Morris, 1 Fitzwalter Road, Lexden, Colchester CO3 3SS
T: 01206 576648
E: b.colchester@chelmsford.anglican.org

ASSISTANT BISHOPS
The Rt Revd Dr Trevor Mwamba, 20 Sandringham Road, Barking, IG11 9AB
T: 020 8594 4513
E: stmags@tiscali.co.uk

The Rt Revd Charles Derek Bond, 52 Horn Brook, Saffron Walden, Essex CB11 3JW
T: 01799 521308
E: bondd@aol.com
The Rt Revd Roderick Thomas, 28 St John's Meadow, Blindley Heath, Lingfield RH7 6JU
T: 01342 834140
E: admin@bishopofmaidstone.org

CATHEDRAL CHURCH OF ST MARY THE VIRGIN, ST PETER AND ST CEDD
Dean The Very Revd Nicholas J. Henshall, Cathedral Office, 53 New Street, Chelmsford CM1 1TY   *T:* 01245 294489
F: 01245 294499
E: nicholas.henshall@chelmsfordcathedral.org.uk
Canons Residentiary
Vice-Dean The Revd Canon Ivor Moody, 4 Bishopscourt Gardens, Springfield, Chelmsford CM2 6AZ   *T:* 01245 294493 (office)
01245 267773 (home)
E: ivor.moody@chelmsford.anglican.org
Canon Theologian The Revd Canon Edward Carter, 2 Harlings Grove, Chelmsford, CM1 1YQ   *T:* 01245 294486
E: edward.carter@chelmsfordcathedral.org.uk
Canon Precentor The Revd Canon Simon Pothen, 1a Harlings Grove, Chelmsford, CM1 1YQ
T: 01245 294482 (office)
01245 491599 (home)
E: simon.pothen@chelmsfordcathedral.org.uk
Other Staff
Associate Priest The Revd Kate Moore, 33 Church Street, Witham, CM8 2JP
T: 01376 501128
E: kate.moore@chelmsfordcathedral.org.uk
Director of Operations Ruth Collin
T: 01245 294488 (office)
E: ruth.collin@chelmsfordcathedral.org.uk
Communications and Services Manager Clare Broome   *T:* 01245 294498
E: clare.broome@chelmsfordcathedral.org.uk

Organist and Master of the Choristers James
Davy, 1 Harlings Grove, Chelmsford, CM1
1YQ   *T:* 01245 252429 (office)
  E: james.davy@chelmsfordcathedral.org.uk
Assistant Organist and Director of Girls' Choir
Laurence Lyndon-Jones (*Same Tel*)
                    E: laurence.lydon-jones@
                    chelmsfordcathedral.org.uk
Youth Minister Tim Leeson
                    T: 01245 294483 (office)
  E: tim.leeson@chelmsfordcathedral.org.uk
Corporate Events Manager Julie Brown
                    T: 01245 294480 (office)
  E: julie.brown@chelmsfordcathedral.org.uk
Hon Associate Chaplain and Bishop's Chaplain
The Revd Leslie Rogers, Bishopscourt,
Margaretting, Ingatestone CM4 0HD
                    T: 01277 352001
                    F: 01277 355374
  E: chaplain@chelmsford.anglican.org
*Hon Associate Chaplain and Diocesan Director of
Ordinands* The Revd Canon Philip Need,
Diocesan Office   *T:* 01245 294421
  E: ddo@chelmsford.anglican.org

ARCHDEACONS
BARKING The Ven Dr John Perumbalath, 11
Bridgefields Close, Hornchurch, RM11 1GQ
                    T: 01708 474951
  E: a.barking@chelmsford.anglican.org
WEST HAM The Ven Elwin Cockett, 86
Aldersbrook Rd, Manor Park, London E12
5DH   *T:* 020 8989 8557
  E: a.westham@chelmsford.anglican.org
HARLOW The Ven Vanessa Herrick, Glebe
House, Church Lane, Sheering CM22 7NR
                    T: 01279 734524
  E: a.harlow@chelmsford.anglican.org
CHELMSFORD The Ven Elizabeth Snowden, The
Archdeacon's Lodge, 136 Broomfield Road,
Chelmsford CM1 1RN   *T:* 01245 258257
  E: a.chelmsford@chelmsford.anglican.org
SOUTHEND The Ven Mike Lodge, The
Archdeacon's Lodge, 459 Rayleigh Road,
Thundersley, Benfleet SS7 3TH
                    T: 01268 779345
  E: a.southend@chelmsford.anglican.org
COLCHESTER The Ven Annette Cooper, 63
Powers Hall End, 136 Broomfield Road,
Witham CM8 1NH   *T:* 01376 513130
  E: a.colchester@chelmsford.anglican.org
STANSTED The Ven Robin King, The House, The
Street, Bradwell, Braintree CM77 8EL

MEMBERS OF THE HOUSE OF CLERGY OF THE GENERAL SYNOD
Proctors for Clergy
The Ven Dr John Perumbalath
The Revd Canon Sally Lodge
The Revd Stuart Halstead
The Revd John Dunnett

The Revd Canon David Banting
The Revd Canon Jenny Tomlinson
The Revd Brenda Claire Wallace

MEMBERS OF THE HOUSE OF LAITY OF THE GENERAL SYNOD
Michelle Tackie
Canon Robert Hammond
Mrs Mary Durlacher
Isabel Adcock
Mrs Kathleen Playle
Mr Robert Edwards
Ann Colton

DIOCESAN OFFICERS
Chief Executive and Diocesan Secretary John
Ball, Diocesan Office   *T:* 01245 294409
                    E: jball@chelmsford.anglican.org
Registrar of Diocese and Bishop's Legal Secretary
Mr Aiden Hargreaves-Smith, Diocesan
Registry, 5 Montague Close, London SE1 9BB
                    T: 020 7593 5127
                    F: 020 7898 1166
  E: chelmsfordregistry@wslaw.co.uk

DIOCESAN ORGANIZATIONS
Diocesan Office 53 New Street, Chelmsford
CM1 1AT   *T:* 01245 294400
                    F: 01245 294477
  E: reception@chelmsford.anglican.org

ADMINISTRATION
Dioc Synod (*Chairman, House of Clergy*) The
Revd Louise Margaret Williams, The Rectory,
42 Church Road, Shoeburyness SS3 9EU
                    E: revlwilliams@aol.com
(*Chairman, House of Laity*) Canon Robert
Hammond, 12 Leigh Cliff Road, Leigh-on-Sea
SS9 1DJ   *T:* 01702 472611
(*Secretary*) John Ball, Diocesan Office
                    T: 01245 294409
                    E: jball@chelmsford.anglican.org
                    T: 01245 294400
Board of Finance (*Chairman*) Percy Lomax
                    T: 01245 294400
(*Company Secretary*) Margaret Essery, Diocesan
Office   *T:* 01245 294426
                    E: messery@chelmsford.anglican.org
(*Director of Development and Property*) Michael
Minta (*Same Address*)   *T:* 01245 294434
                    E: mminta@chelmsford.anglican.org
(*Legal Advisers to the Board of Finance*) Minerva
House, 5 Montague Close, London SE1 9BB
                    T: 020 7593 5000

CHURCH BUILDINGS
Advisory Committee for the Care of Churches
(*Chairman*) Mr Malcolm Woods, 33

Southchurch Hall Close, Southend-on-Sea SS1 2TE   T: 01702 618097
(*Secretary*) Sandra Turner, Diocesan Office
T: 01245 294413
E: dac@chelmsford.anglican.org

COMMUNICATIONS
Communications Director Ralph Meloy, Diocesan Office   T: 01245 294424
07654 382674 (pager)
E: rmeloy@chelmsford.anglican.org

DIOCESAN HOUSE OF RETREAT
The Street, Pleshey, Chelmsford CM3 1HA
T: 01245 237251
F: 01245 237594
General Manager Stewart McCredie
E: smcredie@chelmsford.anglican.org

DIOCESAN RECORD OFFICE
Essex Records Office, Wharf Rd, Chelmsford CM2 6YT   T: 01245 244644
E: ero.enquiry@essexcc.gov.uk

EDUCATION
Director of Education Tim Elbourne, Diocesan Office   T: 01245 294440
E: telbourne@chelmsford.anglican.org

MISSION AND MINISTRY
Dean of Mission and Ministry The Revd Canon Dr Roger Matthews, Diocesan Office
T: 01245 294455
E: rmatthews@chelmsford.anglican.org
Diocesan Director of Ordinands and NSM Officer The Revd Canon Philip Need (*Same Address*)
T: 01245 294421
E: ddo@chelmsford.anglican.org
Lay Development Adviser The Revd Elizabeth Jordan (*Same Address*)   T: 01245 294449
E: ejordan@chelmsford.anglican.org
Adviser for Women's Ministry The Revd Canon Jenny Tomlinson, 17 Borough Lane, Saffron Walden, CB11 4AG   T: 01799 500947
Interfaith Adviser The Ven Dr John Perumbalath, 11 Bridgefields Close, Hornchurch, RM11 1GQ
T: 01708 474951
E: a.barking@chelmsford.anglican.org

MISSION AND PASTORAL COMMITTEE
(*Chairman*) The Rt Revd Stephen Cottrell, Bishopscourt, Margaretting, Ingatestone CM4 0HD
(*Secretary*) Nathan Whitehead, Diocesan Office   T: 01245 294412
E: nwhitehead@chelmsford.anglican.org

OTHER COMMITTEES
Liturgical Committee (*Chairman*) Vacancy

SAFEGUARDING
Safeguarding Manager Amanda Goh, Diocesan Office   T: 01245 294457
E: safeguarding@chelmsford.anglican.org

RURAL DEANS
ARCHDEACONRY OF BARKING
Barking and Dagenham Martin John Court, The Vicarage, 7 Chadwell Heath Lane, Romford RM6 4LS   T: 020 8590 2391
E: martin_stchads@live.co.uk
Havering David Hallett Hague, Good Shepherd Vicarage, 97 Collier Row Lane, Romford RM5 3BA   T: 01708 753395
E: vicargs@thegoodshepherd.co.uk

ARCHDEACONRY OF CHELMSFORD
Brentwood Paul Stuart Hamilton, The Rectory, Thorndon Gate, Ingrave, Brentwood CM13 3RG   T: 01277 812452
E: psh@btinternet.com
Chelmsford North Thomas William Page, Ascension Vicarage, 57 Maltese Road, Chelmsford CM1 2PB   T: 01245 269906
E: frtom1@priest.com
Chelmsford South Andrew Taylor Griffiths, Galleywood Vicarage, 450 Beehive Lane, Chelmsford CM2 8RN   T: 01245 353922
E: agriffiths@chelmsford.anglican.org
Maldon and Dengie Mark Richard North, The Vicarage, 2A Church Road, Burnham-on-Crouch CM0 8DA   T: 01621 782071
E: frmarknorth@btinternet.com

ARCHDEACONRY OF COLCHESTER
Colchester Paul Richard Norrington, The Rectory, 21 Cambridge Road, Colchester CO3 3NS   T: 01206 563478
E: paul.nozzer@btinternet.com
Harwich Simon Alexander Heron, The Rectory, Church Hill, Lawford, Manningtree CO11 2JX   T: 01206 392659
E: simon.heron@mac.com
St Osyth Pauline Claire Michalak Scott, The Rectory, St Andrew's Close, Alresford, Colchester CO7 8BL   T: 07872 968323
E: pauline@pscott.eclipse.co.uk
Witham Sally Nicole Lodge, The Rectory, 7 Chipping Dell, Witham CM8 2JX
T: 07747 612817
E: sally.lodge@btinternet.com

ARCHDEACONRY OF HARLOW
Epping Forest and Ongar Joyce Mary Smith, 2 Takeley Close, Waltham Abbey EN9 1QH
T: 01992 733655
E: revdjoyces@sky.com

Harlow Martin John Harris, The Rectory, 43 Upper Park, Harlow CM20 1TW
T: 01279 411100
E: martin.harris@messages.co.uk

ARCHDEACONRY OF SOUTHEND
Basildon Jane Freeman, 8 Friern Walk, Wickford SS12 0HZ   *T:* 01268 734077
E: email@janefreeman.fsnet.co.uk
Hadleigh David St Clair Tudor, St Nicholas House, 210 Long Road, Canvey Island SS8 0JR
T: 01268 682586
E: dstudor@tiscali.co.uk
Rochford Richard William Jordan, The Rectory, Church Road, Rawreth, Wickford SS11 8SH
T: 01268 766565
E: rwjordan@gmx.com
Southend Jonathan Collis, The Vicarage, 86 Tyrone Road, Southend-on-Sea SS1 3HB
T: 01702 587597
E: jonathan.collis@cantab.net
Thurrock Darren Barlow, The Rectory, 10 High View Avenue, Grays RM17 6RU
T: 01375 377379
E: revbarlow@talktalk.net

ARCHDEACONRY OF STANSTED
Braintree Elizabeth Jane Bendrey, 265C London Road, Black Notley, Braintree CM77 8QQ   *T:* 01376 567971
E: bethbendrey@hotmail.co.uk

Dunmow Cecilia Mary Hawkes, Greenfields, Felsted, Dunmow CM6 3LF
T: 01371 856480
E: cilla@hawkesfarming.co.uk
Hinckford Jonathan David Lowe, The Vicarage, Church Street, Steeple Bumpstead, Haverhill CB9 7DG   *T:* 01440 731687
E: jonathan.lowe@worship.org.uk
Saffron Walden David Robert Tomlinson, The Rectory, 17 Borough Lane, Saffron Walden CB11 4AG   *T:* 01799 500947
E: rector@stmaryssaffronwalden.org

ARCHDEACONRY OF WEST HAM
Newham Jeremy Stuart Fraser, St Paul's Vicarage, 65 Maryland Road, London E15 1JL
T: 020 8534 1164
E: jeremy@fraserwireless.co.uk
Redbridge Marie Segal, St Andrew's Vicarage, St Andrew's Road, Ilford IG1 3PE
T: 020 8554 9791
E: segal.marie@btinternet.com
Waltham Forest Christine Mary Rablen, Leyton Vicarage, 4 Vicarage Road, London E10 5EA
T: 020 8558 5766
E: christinerablen@dsl.pipex.com

DIOCESE OF CHESTER

Founded in 1541. Cheshire; Wirral; Halton, south of the Mersey; Warrington, south of the Mersey; Trafford, except for an area in the north, in the diocese of Manchester; Stockport, except for a few parishes in the north, in the diocese of Manchester, and in the east, in the diocese of Derby; the eastern half of Tameside; a few parishes in Derbyshire, a few parishes in Manchester; a few parishes in Flintshire.

Population 1,630,000   Area 1,030 sq m
Full-time Stipendiary Parochial Clergy 223   Benefices 216
Parishes 268   Churches 343
Overseas link dioceses: Aru and Boga Congo, Melanesia

BISHOP (40th)

The Rt Revd Dr Peter Robert Forster, Bishop's House, Abbey Square, Chester CH1 2JD
T: 01244 350864
E: bpchester@chester.anglican.org

SUFFRAGAN BISHOPS

BIRKENHEAD The Rt Revd (Gordon) Keith Sinclair, Bishop's Lodge, 67 Bidston Road, Prenton CH43 6TR   *T:* 0151 652 2741
E: bpbirkenhead@chester.anglican.org
STOCKPORT The Rt Revd Elizabeth Jane Holden Lane, Bishop's Lodge, Back Lane, Dunham Town, Altrincham WA14 4SG
T: 0161 928 5611
E: bpstockport@chester.anglican.org

ASSISTANT BISHOPS

The Rt Revd Roderick Thomas, 28 St John's Meadow, Blindley Heath, Lingfield RH7 6JU
T: 01342 834140
E: admin@bishopofmaidstone.org
The Rt Revd William Alaha Pwaisiho, The Rectory, Church Lane, Gawsworth, Macclesfield SK11 9RJ   *T:* 01260 223201
The Rt Revd Colin Frederick Bazley, 121 Brackenwood Road, Higher Bebington, Wirral CH63 2LU   *T:* 0151 608 1193
The Rt Revd Geoffrey Turner, 23 Lang Lane, West Kirby, Wirral CH48 5HG
T: 0151 625 8504
The Rt Revd John Hayden, 45 Birkenhead Rd, Hoylake, Wirral CH47 5AF   *T:* 0151 632 0448
The Rt Revd Graham Dow, 34 Kimberley Ave, Romiley, SK6 4AB   *T:* 0161 494 9148
The Rt Revd Alan Winstanley, 11 Thorneycroft Way, Crewe, CW1 4FZ   *T:* 07774 314 534
The Rt Revd Glyn Webster, Holy Trinity Rectory, Micklegate, York YO1 6LE
T: 01904 628155
E: office@seeofbeverley.org

CATHEDRAL CHURCH OF CHRIST AND THE BLESSED VIRGIN MARY

Dean The Very Revd Professor Gordon Ferguson McPhate, Deanery, 7 Abbey St, Chester CH1 2JF   *T:* 01244 500971
E: dean@chestercathedral.com
Residentiary Canons
Canon Chancellor The Revd Canon Jane Brooke, 12 Abbey Square, Chester CH1 2HU
T: 01244 324756
Canon Precentor Canon Jeremy Dussek, 9 Abbey Street, Chester CH1 2JF
T: 01244 500967
E: precentor@chestercathedral.com
Other Staff
Lay Reader Mr Chris Jones, 12 Abbey Square, Chester, CH1 2HU   *T:* 01244 500952
E: chris.jones@chestercathedral.com
Executive Director Carolyn Bruce
T: 01244 500950
E: finance.director@chestercathedral.com
Director of Music Mr Philip Rushforth, 12 Abbey Square, Chester CH1 2HU
T: 01244 500974
E: philip.rushforth@chestercathedral.com
Cathedral Architect Mr Tony Barton (*Same Address*)

ARCHDEACONS

CHESTER The Ven Dr Michael Gilbertson, Church House, 5500 Daresbury Park, Daresbury, Warrington WA4 4GE
T: 01928 718834 ext 258
E: michael.gilbertson@chester.anglican.org
MACCLESFIELD The Ven Ian Bishop, Church House, 5500 Daresbury Park, Daresbury, Warrington WA4 4GE
T: 01928 718834 ext 258
E: ian.bishop@chester.anglican.org

MEMBERS OF THE HOUSE OF CLERGY OF THE GENERAL SYNOD
Proctors for Clergy
The Ven Dr Michael Gilbertson
The Revd Canon David Felix
The Revd Dr Robert Munro
The Revd Alison Cox
The Revd Canon Elaine Chegwin Hall
The Revd Jennifer Gillies

MEMBERS OF THE HOUSE OF LAITY OF THE GENERAL SYNOD
Mrs Lucinda Brewster
Mr Peter Hart
Dr Graham Campbell
Mr Jeremy Harris
Mr John Freeman
Miss Deborah Woods
Dr John Mason
Canon Elizabeth Renshaw

DIOCESAN OFFICERS
Diocesan Secretary Mr George Colville, Church House, 5500 Daresbury Park, Daresbury, Warrington WA4 4GE   T: 01928 718834
        E: george.colville@chester.anglican.org
Chancellor of Diocese His Honour Judge David Turner, c/o Friars, White Friars, Chester CH1 1XS
Registrar of Diocese and Bishop's Legal Secretary Mrs Helen McFall, Friars, White Friars, Chester CH1 1XS   T: 01244 321066
        F: 01244 312582
        E: helen.mcfall@cullimoredutton.co.uk

DIOCESAN ORGANIZATIONS
Diocesan Office Church House, 5500 Daresbury Park, Daresbury, Warrington WA4 4GE
        T: 01928 718834
        E: churchhouse@chester.anglican.org

ADMINISTRATION
Diocesan Synod (Vice-President, House of Clergy) The Revd Dr Robert Munro
(Vice-President, House of Laity) Dr John Mason
(Secretary) Mr George Colville, Church House, 5500 Daresbury Park, Daresbury, Warrington WA4 4GE   T: 01928 718834
        E: george.colville@chester.anglican.org
Board of Finance (Chairman) Mr Ian Scott-Dunn
(Secretary) Mr George Colville, Church House, 5500 Daresbury Park, Daresbury, Warrington WA4 4GE   T: 01928 718834
        E: george.colville@chester.anglican.org
(Diocesan Surveyor) Mr Peter Gowrley *(Same Address)*
(Head of Finance) Mr Nigel Strange *(Same Address)*
(Designated Officer and Director of HR) Liz Geddes *(Same Address)*

CHURCH BUILDINGS
Advisory Committee for the Care of Churches (Chairman) Prof Robert Munn
(DAC Sec) Mr Paul Broadhurst, Church House, 5500 Daresbury Park, Daresbury, Warrington WA4 4GE

DIOCESAN RECORD OFFICE
Cheshire Records Office, Duke St, Chester CH1 1RL   T: 01244 972574

EDUCATION
Director of Education Mr Jeff Turnbull, Church House, 5500 Daresbury Park, Daresbury, Warrington WA4 4GE
Children Vacancy
Youth Vacancy

MISSION AND MINISTRY
Director of Ministry The Revd Canon Dr Christopher Burkett, Church House, 5500 Daresbury Park, Daresbury, Warrington WA4 4GE
        E: christopher.burkett@chester.anglican.org
Director of Ordinands The Revd Magdalen Smith *(Same Address)*
        E: magdalen.smith@chester.anglican.org
Director of Studies for Ordinands The Revd Gary O'Neill, 10 Neston Close, Helsby WA6 0FH
        T: 01928 723327
        E: gary.oneill@chester.anglican.org
Bishop's Officer for NSMs The Revd Canon Prof Roger Yates, 3 Racecourse Park, Wilmslow SK9 5LU   T: 01625 520246
Bishop's Advisor for MDR The Revd Gary O'Neill, 10 Neston Close, Helsby WA6 0FH
        T: 01928 723327
        E: gary.oneill@chester.anglican.org
Diocesan Dean of Women in Ministry The Revd Alison Fulford, The Vicarage, The Green, Wrenbury, Nantwich CW5 8EY
        T: 01270 780742
        E: revalisonfulford@hotmail.co.uk
Director of Studies for Readers Liz Shercliff, Church House, 5500 Daresbury Park, Daresbury, Warrington WA4 4GE
        E: liz.shercliff@chester.anglican.org
Warden of Readers The Revd John Knowles, 15 Clare Avenue, Handforth, Wilmslow SK9 3EQ
        T: 01625 526531
        E: john.knowles@chester.anglican.org
Clergy Development Officer The Revd Canon David Herbert, Church House, 5500 Daresbury Park, Daresbury, Warrington WA4 4GE
        E: david.herbert@chester.anglican.org
Warden of Pastoral Workers The Revd Vivien Gisby, Weston Vicarage, 225 Heath Road South, Weston, Runcorn WA7 4LY
        T: 01928 573798
        E: vivien.gisby@chester.anglican.org

Director of Studies for Pastoral Workers The Revd Peter Mackriell, St Philip's Vicarage, Chester Road, Kelsall, Tarporley CW6 0SA
T: 01829 752639
E: peter.mackriell@chester.anglican.
Parish Development Team (*Parish Development Officer*) The Revd Richard Burton, Church House
E: richard.burton@chester.anglican.org
The Revd Ian Rumsey (*Same Address*)
E: ian.rumsey@chester.anglican.org
(*Adviser in Christian Giving*) Mr Martin Smith (*Same Address*)
E: martin.smith@chester.anglican.org
(*Diocesan Worship Adviser*) The Revd Andy Stinson   E: revandystinson@gmail.com

MISSIONARY AND ECUMENICAL
Partners in World Mission Mr John Freeman, Stable Court, 20A Leigh Way, Weaverham, Northwich CW8 3PR   T: 01606 852872
County Ecumenical Development Officer The Revd Andrew Taylor   T: 01270 780529
E: ceo.ctic@googlemail.com

PRESS AND PUBLICATIONS
Diocesan Director of Communications Mr Stephen Regan, Church House, 5500 Daresbury Park, Daresbury, Warrington WA4 4GE   T: 07764 615069 (mobile)
E: stephen.regan@chester.anglican.org
Design and Communications Officer Mr Stephen Freeman
E: stephen.freeman@chester.anglican.org

SOCIAL RESPONSIBILITY
Director of Social Responsibility Mrs Janice Mason, Church House, 5500 Daresbury Park, Daresbury, Warrington WA4 4GE
E: janice.mason@chester.anglican.org

RURAL DEANS
ARCHDEACONRY OF CHESTER
Birkenhead Ronald Edward Iveson, The Vicarage, 6 Statham Road, Prenton CH43 7XS
T: 0151 652 4852
E: roniveson@hotmail.com
Chester Paul Christopher Owen Dawson, 10 Lower Park Road, Chester CH4 7BB
T: 01244 675199
E: paulcodawson@outlook.com
Frodsham Peter Rugen, St John's House, Pike Lane, Kingsley, Frodsham WA6 8EH
T: 01928 787180
E: p.rugen@btinternet.com
Great Budworth Alec George Brown, The Vicarage, High Street, Great Budworth, Northwich CW9 6HF   T: 01606 891324
E: alecgbrown@gmail.com

Malpas Ian Arthan Davenport, The Rectory, Church Street, Malpas SY14 8PP
T: 01948 860922
E: malpas.iandavenport@live.co.uk
Middlewich Simon Mark Drew, The Rectory, Poplar Fell, Nantwich Road, Middlewich CW10 9HG   T: 01606 833440
E: revsdrew@btinternet.com
Wallasey Graham John Cousins, The Rectory, Dawpool Drive, Moreton, Wirral CH46 0PH
T: 0151 641 0303
E: rector@christchurchmoreton.org.uk
Wirral North Peter Michael Froggatt, The Vicarage, 87 Barnston Road, Heswall, Wirral CH61 1BW   T: 0151 648 1776
E: peter@froggatt.org.uk
Wirral South Elisabeth Ann Glover, The Vicarage, 29 Ferry Road, Eastham, Wirral CH62 0AJ   T: 0151 327 2182
E: beth.glover@tesco.net

ARCHDEACONRY OF MACCLESFIELD
Bowdon Gabrielle Clair Jaquiss, Ingersley, Belgrave Road, Bowdon, Altrincham WA14 2NZ   T: 0161 928 0717
E: clairjq@aol.com
Chadkirk Janet Elizabeth Parker, The Vicarage, 2 Vicarage Close, High Lane, Stockport SK6 8DL   T: 01663 764519
E: revjanetparker@btinternet.com
Cheadle Robert Speight Munro, The Rectory, 1 Depleach Road, Cheadle SK8 1DZ
T: 0161 428 3440
E: rob@munro.org.uk
Congleton David James Page, The Rectory, 2 Taxmere Close, Sandbach CW11 1WT
T: 01270 762415
E: vicar@stpeters-elworth.org.uk
Knutsford Ian Blay, The Rectory, Church Lane, Mobberley, Knutsford WA16 7RA
T: 01565 873218
E: ianblay@btinternet.com
Macclesfield Veronica Weldon Hydon, 6 Merlin Close, Macclesfield SK10 2AS
T: 01625 573162
E: vhydon@hotmail.com
Mottram Alison Clare Cox, The Vicarage, 2 Church Square, Dukinfield SK16 4PX
T: 0161 330 2783
E: alisoncox19@hotmail.com
Nantwich Helen Fiona Chantry, St James's Vicarage, 66 Heathfield Road, Audlem, Crewe CW3 0HG   T: 01270 811543
E: helenchantry@btopenworld.com
Stockport David Thomas Brewster, St Mark's Vicarage, 66 Berlin Road, Stockport SK3 9QF
T: 0161 480 5896
E: dtbrewster@talktalk.net
Stockport Diane Veronica Cookson, St Saviour's Vicarage, 22 St Saviour's Road, Great Moor, Stockport SK2 7QE   T: 0161 483 2633
E: st.saviours@virgin.net

Founded in 1070, formerly called Selsey (◌◌ 681). West Sussex, except for one parish in the north, in the diocese of Guildford; East Sussex, except for one parish in the north, in the diocese of Rochester; one parish in Kent.

Population 1,680,000   Area 1,450 sq m
Full-time Stipendiary Parochial Clergy 251   Benefices 275
Parishes 362   Churches 481
www.chichester.anglican.org
Overseas link dioceses: IDWAL (Inter-Diocesan West Africa Link)
Ghana, Sieraa Leone, Cameroon, Guinea (West Africa)

BISHOP (103rd)

The Rt Revd Dr Martin Warner, The Palace, Chichester PO19 1PY   *T:* 01243 782161
E: bishop@chichester.anglican.org

BISHOP'S STAFF

Senior Chaplain The Revd Canon Stephen Ferns, c/o The Palace, Chichester PO19 1PY (*Same Tel*)
E: stephen.ferns@chichester.anglican.org
Personal Assistant Margaret Gibson, The Palace, Chichester PO19 1PY   *T:* 01243 782161
E: margaret.gibson@chichester.anglican.org

SUFFRAGAN BISHOPS

HORSHAM The Rt Revd Mark Sowerby, Bishop's House, 21 Guildford Road, Horsham RH12 1LU   *T:* 01403 211139
E: bishop.horsham@chichester.anglican.org
Personal Assistant Tanya Leese, Bishop's House, 21 Guildford Road, Horsham RH12 1LU
    T: 01403 211139
E: tanya.leese@chichester.anglican.org
LEWES The Rt Revd Richard Jackson, Ebenezer House, Kingston Ridge, Lewes BN7 3JU
    T: 01273 472475
E: bishop.lewes@chichester.anglican.org
Personal Assistant Aimee O'Neil, Ebenezer House, Kingston Ridge, Lewes BN7 3JU
E: aimee.oneil@chichester.anglican.org

ASSISTANT BISHOPS

The Rt Revd Kenneth Barham, Rosewood, Canadia Road, Battle TN33 0LR
    T: 01424 773073
The Rt Revd Alan Chesters, The College of St Barnabas, Blackberry Lane, Lingfield RH7 6NJ
    T: 01342 872861
The Rt Revd Dr Laurence Green, 86 Belle Hill, Bexhill-on-Sea, TN40 2AP   *T:* 01424 217872
The Rt Revd Michael Langrish, 39 The Meadows, Walberton, Arundel BN18 0PB
    T: 01243 551704
The Rt Revd Christopher Morgan, 6 Wellington Court, Grand Avenue, Worthing BN11 5AB   *T:* 01903 246184

The Rt Revd Nicholas Reade, 5 Warnham Gardens, Cooden, Bexhill-on-Sea TN39 3SP
    T: 01424 842673
E: nicholas.reade@btinternet.com
The Rt Revd David Wilcox, 4 The Court, Hoo Gardens, Willingdon, Eastbourne BN20 9AX
    T: 01323 506108
The Rt Revd Peter Wheatley, 47 Sedlescombe Road South, St Leonards-on-Sea TN38 0TB
    T: 01424 424814
E: peter.wheatley@outlook.com

CATHEDRAL CHURCH OF THE HOLY TRINITY

Dean The Very Revd Stephen Waine
    T: 01243 812484 (office)
E: dean@chichestercathedral.org.uk
Residentiary Canons
Chancellor Canon Dr Anthony Cane, The Residentiary, 2 Canon Lane, Chichester PO19 1PX   *T:* 01243 813594
    F: 01243 812499
E: chancellor@chichestercathedral.org.uk
Precentor The Revd Canon Timothy Schofield, 4 Vicars' Close, Chichester PO19 1PT (*Same Fax*)   *T:* 01243 813589
E: precentor@chichestercathedral.org.uk
Treasurer The Revd Canon Stephen Ferns, c/o The Palace, Chichester PO19 1PY
    T: 01243 782161
E: stephen.ferns@chichester.anglican.org
Other Staff
The Communar and Executive Director (also Clerk to the Trustees and Administrator of St Mary's Almshouses) David Coulthard   *T:* 01243 812489
E: communar@chichestercathedral.org.uk
Cathedral Organist and Master of the Choristers Mr Charles Harrison
E: organist@chichestercathedral.org.uk

ARCHDEACONS

BRIGHTON AND LEWES The Ven Martin Lloyd Williams, 12 Walsingham Road, Hove BN3 4FF   *T:* 01273 425691
E: archbandl@chichester.anglican.org

CHICHESTER The Ven Douglas McKittrick, 2 Yorklands, Dyke Road Avenue, Hove BN3 6RW
T: 01273 505330
E: archchichester@chichester.anglican.org
HASTINGS The Ven Edward Dowler, Beechmount, Beacon Road, Crowborough TN6 1UQ
T: 01273 425040
E: archhastings@chichester.anglican.org
HORSHAM The Ven Fiona Windsor, 28 Langley Lane, Ifield, Crawley RH11 0NA
T: 01273 425048
E: archhorsham@chichester.anglican.org

MEMBERS OF THE HOUSE OF CLERGY OF THE GENERAL SYNOD
Proctors for Clergy
The Revd Canon Andrew Cornes
The Revd Canon Mark Gilbert
The Revd Canon Rebecca Swyer
The Ven Fiona Windsor
The Revd James Hollingsworth

MEMBERS OF THE HOUSE OF LAITY OF THE GENERAL SYNOD
Dr Graham Parr
Mrs Diane Kutar
Mrs Mary Nagel
Mrs Tina Nay
Mr Bradley Smith
Mr Jacob Vince
Mrs Andrea Williams

DIOCESAN OFFICERS
Diocesan Secretary Ms Gabrielle Higgins, Diocesan Church House, 211 New Church Road, Hove BN3 4ED
T: 01273 421021
F: 01273 421041
E: diocesan.secretary@chichester.anglican.org
Chancellor of Diocese Chancellor Mark Hill, Francis Taylor Building, Inner Temple, London EC4Y 7BY
T: 0207 353 8415
E: mark.hill@ftb.eu.com
Registrar of Diocese and Bishop's Legal Secretary Mr Matthew Chinery, Winckworth Sherwood LLP, Minerva House, 5 Montague Close, London SE1 9BB
T: 0207 593 5000
E: mchinery@wslaw.co.uk

DIOCESAN ORGANIZATIONS
Diocesan Office Diocesan Church House, 211 New Church Road, Hove BN3 4ED
T: 01273 421021
F: 01273 421041
E: enquiry@chichester.anglican.org
W: www.chichester.anglican.org

ADMINISTRATION
Diocesan Synod (Chairman, House of Clergy) The Revd Canon Mark Gilbert, The Rectory, Rectory Lane, Petworth GU28 0DB
T: 01798 839057
E: frmarkssc@msn.com
(Chairman, House of Laity) Dr Graham Parr
Diocesan Fund and Board of Finance (Incorporated) (Chairman) Mr John Booth
(Secretary) Ms Gabrielle Higgins, Diocesan Church House, 211 New Church Road, Hove BN3 4ED
T: 01273 421021
F: 01273 421041
E: diocesan.secretary@chichester.anglican.org

COMMUNICATIONS
Communications Officer Mrs Lisa Williamson, Diocesan Church House, 211 New Church Road, Hove BN3 4ED
T: 01273 425691
out of hours: 07775 022461
E: communications@chichester.anglican.org

DIOCESAN RECORD OFFICES
East Sussex (County Archivist) Mrs Elizabeth Hughes, The Keep, Woollards Way, Brighton BN1 9BP
T: 01273 482349
West Sussex (County Archivist) Mr R. Childs, County Records Office, County Hall, Chichester PO19 1RN
T: 01243 533911

DISCIPLESHIP AND MINISTRY
Director for Apostolic Life The Revd Canon Rebecca Swyer, Diocesan Church House, 211 New Church Road, Hove BN3 4ED
T: 01273 421021
E: rebecca.swyer@chichester.anglican.org
Administrative Coordinator Jessye Hodges
T: 01273 425011
E: jessye.hodges@chichester.anglican.org
Young Vocations Officer Robert Norbury
T: 01273 421021
E: robert.norbury@chichester.anglican.org
Continuing Ministerial Development Officer Tim Watson *(Same Tel)*
E: tim.watson@chichester.anglican.org
Parish Development Officer Rob Dillingham
T: 07341 564304
E: rob.dillingham@chichester.anglican.org
Adult Education and Training Officer Ruth Sowerby
T: 01273 425016
E: ruth.sowerby@chichester.anglican.org
Diocesan Director of Ordinands Lu Gale
T: 01273 425014
E: lu.gale@chichester.anglican.org
MDR Administrator Ruth McBrien
T: 07341564195
E: ruth.mcbrien@chichester.anglican.org

Diocesan Spirituality Adviser Andrew Mayes
T: 01323 892964
E: andrew.mayes@chichester.anglican.org
Strategy and Resources Adviser John Sherlock
T: 01273 425685
E: john.sherlock@chichester.anglican.org
Diocesan Youth Officer Dan Jenkins
T: 01273 425012
E: dan.jenkins@chichester.anglican.org
Children and Family Work Adviser Irene Smale
T: 01273 425013
E: irene.smale@chichester.anglican.org
Librarian and Coordinator for The Magnet Nicole Blakey   T: 01424 431489
E: nicole.blakey@chichester.anglican.org

EDUCATION DEPARTMENT
Director of Education Canon Dr Ann Holt, Diocesan Church House, 211 New Church Road, Hove BN3 4ED   T: 01273 425687
E: ann.holt@chichester.anglican.org
Assistant Director of Education Mr Martin Lloyd
E: martin.lloyd@chichester.anglican.org
Head of School Organization and Effectiveness Mrs Ruth Cumming
E: ruth.cumming@chichester.anglican.org
School Effectiveness Officer Ms Rosemary Black
E: rosemary.black@chichester.anglican.org
Capital Assets Programme Manager Mrs Sally Collins
E: sally.collins@chichester.anglican.org
Capital Assets Officer Mrs Heather Broadbent
E: heather.broadbent@chichester.anglican.org
Interim Chief Executive of DCAT Mr Martin Lloyd
E: martin.lloyd@chichester.anglican.org
Head of Finance and Operations Jill Scarfield
E: jscarfield@thediocese.co.uk

MISSION AND PASTORAL
Diocesan Advisory Committee for the Care of Churches(DAC) (*Chairman*) The Ven Philip Jones
(*Secretary*) Mrs Anna-Marie Pagano, Diocesan Church House, 211 New Church Road, Hove BN3 4ED   T: 01273 425690
E: anna-marie.pagano@chichester.anglican.org
(*Assistant Secretary*) Mr Giles Standing
T: 01273 425017
E: giles.standing@chichester.anglican.org
Diocesan Mission and Pastoral Committee (*Chairman*) The Rt Revd Dr Martin Warner, The Palace, Chichester PO19 1PY
(*Secretary*) Mrs Anna-Marie Pagano, Diocesan Church House, 211 New Church Road, Hove BN3 4ED   T: 01273 425690
E: anna-marie.pagano@chichester.anglican.org

(*Assistant Secretary*) Mr Giles Standing
T: 01273 425017
E: giles.standing@chichester.anglican.org

SAFEGUARDING
Safeguarding Advisor Colin Perkins, Diocesan Church House, 211 New Church Road, Hove BN3 4ED   T: 01273 425792
E: colin.perkins@chichester.anglican.org

RURAL DEANS
ARCHDEACONRY OF BRIGHTON AND LEWES
Brighton Andrew John Woodward, 10 Chesham Street, Brighton BN2 1NA
T: 01273 698601
E: thewoodys1@tiscali.co.uk
Hove Terence Stephen Stratford, The Vicarage, West Beach, Shoreham-by-Sea BN43 5LF
T: 07967 850160
E: terry.stratford@yahoo.co.uk
Lewes and Seaford Judith Anne Egar, 15 St Peter's Place, Lewes BN7 1YP

ARCHDEACONRY OF CHICHESTER
Arundel and Bognor Mark Jonathan Standen, The Rectory, Rectory Lane, Angmering, Littlehampton BN16 4JU   T: 01903 784979
E: standens@angmering.org.uk
Chichester James Anthony Tomkins Russell, The Rectory, Church Lane, Hunston, Chichester PO20 1AJ   T: 01243 782003
E: russell.j760@gmail.com
Westbourne Martin John Lane, The Vicarage, Bosham Lane, Bosham, Chichester PO18 8HX
T: 01243 573228
E: martinjlane@gmail.com
Worthing Helena Margareta Buqué, The Rectory, School Hill, Findon, Worthing BN14 0TR   T: 07504 333853
E: hbuque@wsgfl.org.uk

ARCHDEACONRY OF HASTINGS
Battle and Bexhill Jonathan Jeremy Frais, St Mark's Rectory, 11 Coverdale Avenue, Bexhill-on-Sea TN39 4TY   T: 01424 843733
E: frais@tiscali.co.uk
Dallington Marc Andrew Lloyd, Warbleton Rectory, Rookery Lane, Rushlake Green, Heathfield TN21 9QJ   T: 01435 830421
E: marc_lloyd@hotmail.com
Eastbourne David John Gillard, The Vicarage, 11 Baldwin Avenue, Eastbourne BN21 1UJ
T: 01323 649728
E: djgillard@tiscali.co.uk
Hastings Michael Stephen Coe, The Rectory, 9 St Matthew's Road, St Leonards-on-Sea TN38 0TN   T: 01424 430262
E: mikelisac@aol.com

Rotherfield James Morley Packman, The Rectory, Church Lane, Frant, Tunbridge Wells TN3 9DX   *T:* 01892 750638
E: jamespackman@ymail.com
Rye David Richard Frost, The Rectory, Gungarden, Rye TN31 7HH
T: 01797 222430
E: david@drfrost.org.uk
Uckfield Patrick Macbain, The Vicarage, Lewes Road, Danehill, Haywards Heath RH17 7ER
T: 01825 790269
E: pmacbain@hotmail.com

ARCHDEACONRY OF HORSHAM
Cuckfield Michael John Maine, The Vicarage, 5 Barrowfield, Cuckfield, Haywards Heath RH17 5ER   *T:* 01323 509528
E: michaeljmaine@btinternet.com
East Grinstead Julia Kathleen Peaty, 15 Overton Shaw, East Grinstead RH19 2HN
T: 01342 322386
E: julia@peaty.net

Horsham Guy Stevenson Bridgewater, The Vicarage, Causeway, Horsham RH12 1HE
T: 01403 272919
E: bridgewaters@tiscali.co.uk
Hurst Kevin Michael O'Brien, St John's Rectory, 68 Park Road, Burgess Hill RH15 8HG
T: 01444 232582
E: kevin-obrien@tiscali.co.uk
Midhurst Derek Brian Welsman, Northgate, Dodsley Grove, Easebourne, Midhurst GU29 9BE   *T:* 01730 812655
E: derekwelsman@btinternet.com
Petworth Mark Gilbert, St Wilfrid's House, 7 Durnford Close, Chichester PO19 3AG
T: 01243 783853
E: frmarkssc@msn.com
Storrington Kathryn Alison Windslow, The Rectory, Rectory Road, Storrington, Pulborough RH20 4EF   *T:* 01522 810246
E: kathryn.windslow@btinternet.com

Re-founded in 1918. Coventry; Warwickshire, except for small areas in the north, in the diocese of Birmingham, and south-west in the diocese of Gloucester, and one parish in the south, in the diocese of Oxford; an area of Solihull.

Population 867,000   Area 700 sq m
Full-time Stipendiary Parochial Clergy 101   Benefices 122
Parishes 203   Churches 242
www.coventry.anglican.org
Overseas link dioceses:

BISHOP
The Rt Revd Dr Christopher John Cocksworth, Bishop's House, 23 Davenport Road, Coventry CV5 6PW   T: 024 7667 2244
F: 024 7610 0535
E: bishop@bishop-coventry.org

BISHOP'S STAFF
Personal Assistant Christine Camfield, Bishop's House, 23 Davenport Road, Coventry CV5 6PW   T: 024 7667 2244
F: 024 7610 0535
E: christine.camfield@bishop-coventry.org
Secretary Mrs Elizabeth Egan (*Same Address, Tel & Fax*)
E: elizabeth.egan@bishop-coventry.org

SUFFRAGAN BISHOP
WARWICK The Rt Revd John Ronald Angus Stroyan, Warwick House, School Hill, Offchurch, Leamington Spa CV33 9AL
T: 01926 427465
E: bishop.warwick@covcofe.org
Personal Assistant Mrs Kerry Vanston-Rumney
E: kerry.rumney@covcofe.org

ASSISTANT BISHOPS
Bishop of Ebbsfleet The Rt Revd Jonathan Goodall, Tree Tops, The Mount, Caversham, Reading RG4 7RE   T: 0118 948 1038
E: office@ebbsfleet.org.uk
Honorary Assistant Bishop and Officer for Retired Clergy and Spouses The Rt Revd David Evans
E: bishopdrjevans@talktalk.net

CATHEDRAL CHURCH OF ST MICHAEL
Dean The Very Revd John Witcombe
T: 024 7652 1227
E: john.witcombe@coventrycathedral.org.uk
Canons Residentiary
Canon Pastor The Revd Canon Kathryn Fleming, Cathedral Offices, 1 Hill Top, Coventry CV1 5AB   T: 024 7652 1230
E: kathryn.fleming@coventrycathedral.org.uk

Canon Precentor and Sub Dean The Revd Canon Dr David Stone (*Same Address*)
T: 024 7652 1212
E: david.stone@coventrycathedral.org.uk
Canon for Reconciliation Ministry The Revd Canon Dr Sarah Hills (*Same Address*)
T: 024 7652 1200
E: sarah.hills@coventrycathedral.org.uk
Other Staff
Canon Theologian The Revd Canon Professor Ben Quash, Department of Theology and Religious Studies, King's College London, The Strand, London WC2R 2LS
T: 020 7848 2339/2073
Canon Professor Richard Farnell
T: 024 7652 1200
Canon John Mumford (*Same Tel*)
Clerk to the College of Canons Mr Roger Pascall, 1 The Quadrant, Coventry CV1 2DW
T: 024 7663 1212
Director of Music Mr Kerry Beaumont (*Same Address*)   T: 024 7652 1219
E: kerry.beaumont@coventrycathedral.org.uk

ARCHDEACONS
COVENTRY The Ven John Green, Cathedral and Diocesan Offices, 1 Hill Top, Coventry CV1 5AB   T: 024 7652 1337
E: john.green@covcofe.org
WARWICK The Ven Morris Rodham, Cathedral and Diocesan Offices, 1 Hill Top, Coventry CV1 5AB   T: 024 7652 1337
E: morris.rodham@covcofe.org

MEMBERS OF THE HOUSE OF CLERGY OF THE GENERAL SYNOD
Proctors for Clergy
The Revd Andrew Attwood
The Revd Charlotte Gale
The Revd Dr Mark Bratton

MEMBERS OF THE HOUSE OF LAITY OF THE GENERAL SYNOD
Mr Samuel Margrave
Dr Yvonne Warren
Mr Andrew Williams

DIOCESAN OFFICERS
Diocesan Secretary Ruth Marlow, Cathedral and Diocesan Offices, 1 Hill Top, Coventry CV1 5AB   T: 024 7652 1307
                                                                              F: 024 7652 1330
                        E: ruth.marlow@covcofe.org
Chancellor Mr Stephen Eyre, Manby Bowdler, Routh House, Hall Court, Hall Park Way, Telford TF3 4NJ   T: 01952 292129
Deputy Chancellor Glyn Samuel, St Phillip's Chambers, 55 Temple Row, Birmingham B2 5LS
Registrar of Diocese and Bishop's Legal Secretary Mrs Mary Allanson, Rotherham & Co, 8 The Quadrant, Coventry CV1 2EL
                                          T: 024 7622 7331

DIOCESAN ORGANIZATIONS
Diocesan Office 1 Hill Top, Coventry CV1 5AB
                                          T: 024 7652 1200
                                          F: 024 7652 1330
                        W: www.coventry.anglican.org

ADMINISTRATION
Diocesan Synod (Chairman, House of Clergy) Vacancy
(Chairman, House of Laity) Vacancy *(As above)*
(Diocesan Secretary) Canon Simon Lloyd, Cathedral and Diocesan Offices, 1 Hill Top, Coventry CV1 5AB   T: 024 7652 1307
                                                                              F: 024 7652 1330
                        E: simon.lloyd@covcofe.org
Board of Finance (Chairman) Canon Ian Francis, The Firs, Main St, Frankton, Rugby CV23 9NZ
                                          T: 01926 632918
                        E: ian2140@bitinternet.com
(Director of Finance) Mr David Oglethorpe
                        E: david.oglethorpe@covcofe.org
(Director of Operations) Mr Stephen Davenport
                        E: stephen.davenport@covcofe.org
(Director of Communications) The Revd Graeme Pringle, Cathedral and Diocesan Offices, 1 Hill Top, Coventry CV1 5AB T: 024 7652 1336
                        E: graeme.pringle@covcofe.org
(Senior Property Manager) Mrs Nicky Caunt *(Same Address)*   E: nicky.caunt@covcofe.org
(Secretary to the Diocesan Trustees) Mrs Mary Allanson, Rotherham & Co, 8 The Quadrant, Coventry CV1 2EL   T: 024 7622 7331
Diocesan Mission and Pastoral Committee Mr Stephen Davenport
                        E: stephen.davenport@covcofe.org
(Designated Officer) Mr Stephen Davenport *(As above)*
(Diocesan Website Editor) Anna Laycock
                        E: anna.laycock@covcofe.org

CHURCH BUILDINGS
DAC Secretary and Operations Team Supervisor Dr Will Jones, Cathedral and Diocesan Offices, 1 Hill Top, Coventry CV1 5AB
                                          T: 024 7652 1327
                        E: will.jones@covcofe.org

Church Buildings Development and Project Officer Dr Claire Strachan *(Same Address)*
                                          T: 024 7652 1353
                        E: claire.strachan@covcofe.org

DIOCESAN RECORD OFFICE
Warwickshire County Record Office, Priory Park, Cape Road, Warwick CV34 4JS
Archives and Historic Environment Manager
Mrs Sam Collenette   T: 01926 738959
                        E: recordoffice@warwickshire.gov.uk

EDUCATION
Diocesan Director Canon Linda Wainscot, The Benn Education Centre, Claremont Road, Rugby CV1 3LU   T: 01788 422800
                        E: linda.wainscot@covcofe.org

MINISTRY
Principal of the Diocesan Training Partnership The Revd Canon Dr Richard Cooke, Cathedral and Diocesan Offices, 1 Hill Top, Coventry CV1 5AB   T: 024 7652 1316
                        E: richard.cooke@covcofe.org
Discipleship and Mission Development Adviser Mrs Katherine Walakira *(Same Address)*
                                          T: 024 7652 1305
                        E: katherine.walakira@covcofe.org
Diocesan Director of Ordinands The Revd Canon Dr Richard Cooke *(Same Address)*
                                          T: 024 7652 1316
                        E: richard.cooke@covcofe.org
Diocesan Learning Adviser (Ministerial Development) The Revd Naomi Nixon *(Same Address)*   T: 024 7652 1304
                        E: naomi.nixon@covcofe.org
Assistant Learning Adviser The Revd Josephine Houghton *(Same Address)*   T: 024 7652 1301
                        E: josephine.houghton@covcofe.org
Diocesan Vocations Adviser (and Young Vocations Champion) The Revd Ellie Clack *(Same Address)*   T: 024 7652 1316
                        E: ellie.clack@covcofe.org
Healthy Churches Development Mentor The Revd Tim Mitchell *(Same Address)*
                                          M: 079496 821460
                        E: tim.mitchell@covcofe.org
Transforming Communities Together Officer Mrs Jet Jones *(Same Address)*   T: 024 7652 1344
                        E: jet.jones@covcofe.org
Warden of Readers Vacancy
Readers Secretary Mrs Helen Allred
                                          T: 024 7634 2377
                        E: helen.allread@btinternet.com
Officer for Retired Clergy and Spouses The Rt Revd David Evans
                        E: bishopdrjevans@talktalk.net

AREA DEANS
ARCHDEACONRY OF COVENTRY
Coventry East Clive Duncan Hogger, St Margaret's Vicarage, 18 South Avenue, Coventry CV2 4DR   *T:* 024 7665 1642
E: rev2b@tiscali.co.uk
Coventry North Vacancy
Coventry South Stephen Roy Burch, St James's Vicarage, 395 Tile Hill Lane, Coventry CV4 9DP   *T:* 024 7646 6262
E: vicar@stjamesfletch.org.uk
Kenilworth Mark Quinn Bratton, The Rectory, Meriden Road, Berkswell, Coventry CV7 7BE
T: 01676 533766
E: markbratton@berkswellchurch.org.uk
Nuneaton Francis Peter Seldon, Chilvers Coton Vicarage, Coventry Road, Nuneaton CV11 4NJ   *T:* 024 7638 3010
E: frank@allsaintscoton.org

Rugby Timothy David Cockell, The New Rectory, Pool Close, Rugby CV22 7RN
T: 01788 812613
E: tim.cockell@btopenworld.com

ARCHDEACONRY OF WARWICK
Alcester Vacancy
Fosse Vacancy
Shipston Jill Tucker, The Old House, Back Lane, Oxhill, Warwick CV35 0QN *T:* 01295 680663
E: revjill.tucker@tiscali.co.uk
Southam Martin Charles Green, The Vicarage, 1 Manor Road, Bishop's Itchington, Southam CV47 2QJ   *T:* 01926 613466
E: revmcg@kerrins.net
Warwick and Leamington Vacancy

DIOCESE OF DERBY

Founded in 1927. Derbyshire, except for a small area in the north, in the diocese of Chester; a small area of Stockport; a few parishes in Staffordshire.

Population 1,050,000   Area 990 sq m
Full-time Stipendiary Parochial Clergy 140   Benefices 148
Parishes 254   Churches 317
www.derby.anglican.org
Overseas link dioceses: Overseas link of Derbyshire Churches (Baptist, Methodist, URC and Anglican): Church of North India

BISHOP (7th)

The Rt Revd Dr Alastair Redfern, The Bishop's House, 6 King Street, Duffield, Derby DE56 4EU   *T:* 01332 840132
E: bishop@bishopofderby.org

SUFFRAGAN BISHOP

REPTON The Rt Revd Jan McFarlane, Repton House, 39 Hickton Road, Swanwick, Alfreton DE55 1AF   *T:* 01733 608696
E: bishopofrepton@derby.anglican.org

ASSISTANT BISHOPS

The Rt Revd Richard Inwood, 43 Whitecotes Park, Chesterfield S40 3RT   *T:* 01246 766288
E: richardinwood@btconnect.com
The Rt Revd Jack Nicholls, 75 Rowton Grange Road, Chapel-en-le-Frith, High Peak SK23 0LD   *T:* 01298 938249
E: jnseraphim@gmx.com

CATHEDRAL CHURCH OF ALL SAINTS

Dean The Very Revd Stephen Hance, Derby Cathedral Centre, 18-19 Iron Gate, Derby DE1 3GP   *T:* 01322 341201
E: dean@derbycathedral.org
Canons Residentiary
Canon Precentor The Revd Canon Chris Moorsom, Derby Cathedral Centre, 18–19 Iron Gate, Derby DE1 3GP   *T:* 01332 341201
E: precentor@derbycathedral.org
Canon Missioner The Revd Canon Dr Elizabeth Thomson (*Same Address & Tel*)
E: missioner@derbycathedral.org
Canon Chancellor The Revd Canon Dr Simon Taylor, Derby Church House, Full Street, Derby DE1 3DR   *T:* 01332 388650
E: simon.taylor@derby.anglican.org
Diocesan Canon The Revd Canon Dr Sue Jones, Derby Church House, Full Street, Derby DR1 3DR   *T:* 01322 388682
E: susan.jones@derby.anglican.org

Other Staff
Cathedral and University Chaplain The Revd Adam Dickens, University of Derby, Kedleston Road, Derby DE22 1GB
T: 01332 591878 (university)
E: a.dickens@derby.ac.uk
Lay Chapter Members Mr David Legh
Mrs Val Grahl
Canon Mark Titterton
Chapter Steward Mrs Rachel Morris, Derby Cathedral Centre, 18–19 Iron Gate, Derby DE1 3GP   *T:* 01332 341201
E: rachel@derbycathedral.org
Finance Officer Mr Peter Holdridge (*Same Address*)   *T:* 01322 341201
E: peterh@derbycathedral.org
Development Officer Dr Alex Rock (*Same Address & Tel*)   *E:* alex@derbycathedral.org
Director of Music and Organist Mr Hugh Morris (*Same Address*)   *T:* 01322 202231
E: hugh@derbycathedral.org
Assistant Director of Music Mr Edward Turner, Derby Cathedral Centre, 18-19 Iron Gate, Derby DE1 3GP (*Same Tel*)
E: edward@derbycathedral.org

ARCHDEACONS

DERBY The Ven Dr Christopher Cunliffe, Derby Church House, Full Street, Derby DE1 3DR
T: 01332 388676 (office)
E: archderby@derby.anglican.org
CHESTERFIELD The Ven Carol Coslett (from Spring 2018)

MEMBERS OF THE HOUSE OF CLERGY OF THE GENERAL SYNOD

Proctors for Clergy
The Revd Mark Broomhead
The Revd Julian Hollywell
The Revd Canon Dr Simon Taylor

MEMBERS OF THE HOUSE OF LAITY OF THE GENERAL SYNOD

Mrs Kat Alldread
Mrs Rachel Bell
Mrs Hannah Grivell

DIOCESAN OFFICERS

Diocesan Secretary and Chapter Steward Mrs Rachel Morris, Derby Cathedral Centre, 18–19 Iron Gate, Derby DE1 3GP   *T:* 01332 341201
          E: rachel@derbycathedral.org
Chancellor of Diocese His Honour Judge John W. M. Bullimore, 5 Snowgate Head, Horn Lane, New Mill, Holmfirth HD9 7DH
Registrar of Diocese and Bishop's Legal Secretary Mrs Nadine Waldron, Eddowes Waldron Solicitors, 12 St Peter's Churchyard, Derby DE1 1TZ   *T:* 01332 348484
                         E: nh@ewlaw.co.uk

DIOCESAN ORGANIZATIONS

Diocesan Office Derby Church House, 1 Full Street, Derby DE1 3DR   *T:* 01332 388650
          E: enquiries@derby.anglican.org
          W: www.derby.anglican.org

ADMINISTRATION

Diocesan Synod (*Chairman, House of Clergy*) The Revd Peter Davey, The Vicarage,, 197 Heanor Road, Ilkeston DE7 8TA   *T:* 0115 932 5670
          E: peterdavey@outlook.com
(*Chairman, House of Laity*) Mrs Christine McMullen, Montpelier Farm Cottage, Montpelier Place, Waterswallows Road, Buxton SK17 7EJ   *T:* 01298 73997
(*Secretary*) Vacancy
Board of Finance (*Chairman*) The Rt Revd Dr Alastair Redfern, The Bishop's House, 6 King Street, Duffield, Derby DE56 4EU
                         T: 01332 840132
          E: bishop@bishopofderby.org
(*Executive Chair*) Canon Mark Titterton
(*Secretary*) Vacancy
(*Head of Finance*) Andy Watts
                         T: 01322 388650
          E: andy.watts@derby.anglican.org
(*HR Director*) Adele Poulson
                         T: 01332 388650
          E: adele.poulson@derby.anglican.org
(*Head of Property*) Graham Webster
                         T: 01322 388650
          E: graham.webster@derby.anglican.org
(*Property Surveyor*) Clinton Walker, Church House, Full Street, Derby DE1 3DR (*Same Tel*)
          E: clinton.walker@derby.anglican.org
Mission and Pastoral Committee (*Secretary*) Mr Nigel Sherratt, Derby Church House, 1 Full Street, Derby DE1 3DR   *T:* 01332 388650
(*Designated Officer*) Mrs Nadine Waldron, Eddowes Waldron Solicitors, 12 St Peter's Churchyard, Derby DE1 1TZ *T:* 01332 348484
                         E: nh@ewlaw.co.uk

CHURCH BUILDINGS

Advisory Committee for the Care of Churches (*Chairman*) The Revd Canon Matt Barnes

(*Secretary*) Mr Nigel Sherratt, Derby Church House, 1 Full Street, Derby DE1 3DR
                         T: 01332 388650

DIOCESAN RECORD OFFICE

Derbyshire Record Office, County Offices, Matlock DE4 3AG
County Archivist
Ms Sarah Chubb   *T:* 01629 538347
          E: record.office@derbyshire.gov.uk

EDUCATION

Derby Church House, 1 Full St, Derby DE1 3DR   *T:* 01332 388660
Senior Administrator Netta Russell
          E: netta.russell@derby.anglican.org
Director David Channon
          E: david.channon@derby.anglican.org
Deputy Director and Schools Adviser Mrs Alison Brown
          E: alison.brown@derby.anglican.org
Children's Work Adviser Sarah Brown
          E: sarah.brown@derby.anglican.org
Youth Adviser Mr Alistair Langton
          E: alistair.langton@derby.anglican.org
Director of School Improvement Mark Mallender
          E: mark.mallender@derby.anglican.org

MISSION AND MINISTRY

Director of Mission and Ministry The Revd Canon Dr Susan Jones   *T:* 01332 388682
          E: susan.jones@derby.anglican.org
Diocesan Director of Vocations The Revd Canon Geraldine Pond   *T:* 01332 388692
          E: ddv@derby.anglican.org
Director of Curate Training The Revd Canon Dr Simon Taylor, Derby Church House, Full Street, Derby DE1 3DR   *T:* 01332 388650
          E: simon.taylor@derby.anglican.org
Diocesan Missioner The Revd Jason Kennedy
                         T: 01332 388691
          E: jason.kennedy@derby.anglican.org
Community Action Officer Ms Stella Collishaw
                         T: 01322 388685
          E: stella.collishaw@derby.anglican.org
Community Projects Development Officer Mr Gareth Greenwood   *T:* 01332 388690
          E: gareth.greenwood@derby.anglican.org
Lay Ministry Officer/Warden of Readers Canon Dr Esther Elliott   *T:* 01322 388674
          E: esther.elliot@derby.anglican.org
Fresh Expressions Officer Vacancy

PRESS AND COMMUNICATIONS

Communications Co-ordinator Lucy Harrison, Derby Church House, 1 Full Street, Derby DE1 3DR   *T:* 01332 388680
          E: communications@derby.anglican.org

RETIREMENT CHAPLAINCY
The Revd Michael Mookerji, 1 Plymouth Walk, Church Gresley, Swadlincote DE11 9GU　　　　　　　　　*T:* 01283 335582
　　　E: michael.mookerji@live.co.uk

RURAL DEANS
ARCHDEACONRY OF CHESTERFIELD
Alfreton Vacancy
Bakewell and Eyam Colin Graham Pearson, The Vicarage, 71 Manchester Road, Chapel-en-le-Frith, High Peak SK23 9TH
　　　　　　　　　T: 01298 812134
　　　E: colin2pearson@gmail.com
Bolsover and Staveley Helen Guest, The Rectory, Sheepcote Road, Killamarsh, Sheffield S21 1DU　　　　　　　*T:* 0114 248 2769
　　　E: revsguest@btinternet.com
Buxton Colin Graham Pearson, The Vicarage, 71 Manchester Road, Chapel-en-le-Frith, High Peak SK23 9TH　　　　*T:* 01298 812134
　　　E: colin2pearson@gmail.com
Chesterfield Karen Elizabeth Hamblin, 1 Whitecotes Lane, Chesterfield S40 3HJ
　　　　　　　　　T: 07432 705255
　　　E: andrew.hamblin1@virgin.net
Glossop Colin Graham Pearson, The Vicarage, 71 Manchester Road, Chapel-en-le-Frith, High Peak SK23 9TH　　　　*T:* 01298 812134
　　　E: colin2pearson@gmail.com
Wirksworth David Charles Truby, The Rectory, Coldwell Street, Wirksworth, Matlock DE4 4FB　　　　　　　*T:* 01629 824707
　　　E: david.truby@btinternet.com

ARCHDEACONRY OF DERBY
Ashbourne Vacancy
Derby North Julian Francis Hollywell, St Werburgh's Vicarage, Gascoigne Drive, Spondon, Derby DE21 7GL　*T:* 01332 673573
　　　　　E: fatherjulian@btinternet.com
Derby South Vacancy
Duffield Jonathan Michael Page, Christ Church Vicarage, Bridge Street, Belper DE56 1BA　　　　　　　*T:* 01773 824974
　　　E: vicar@christchurchbelper.co.uk
Erewash Peter James Davey, The Vicarage, 197 Heanor Road, Ilkeston DE7 8TA
　　　　　　　　　T: 0115 932 5670
　　　E: petedavey@outlook.com
Heanor Karen Padley, All Saints' Vicarage, 85 Ilkeston Road, Heanor DE75 7BP
　　　　　　　　　T: 01773 712097
　　　E: karen@hpadley.fsnet.co.uk
Longford Andrew Graham Murphie, The Vicarage, 28 Back Lane, Hilton, Derby DE65 5GJ　　　　　　　*T:* 01283 733433
　　　E: andymurphie@btinternet.com
Melbourne Anthony Luke, The Rectory, Rectory Gardens, Aston-on-Trent, Derby DE72 2AZ
　　　　　　　　　T: 01332 792658
　　　E: theramsrev@gmail.com
Repton Graham Piers Rutter, The Vicarage, Church Street, Swadlincote DE11 8LF
　　　　　　　　　T: 01283 214583
　　　E: gprutter@gmail.com

DIOCESE OF DURHAM

Founded in 635. Approximates Durham, except for an area in the south-west in the diocese of Leeds and Gateshead; South Tyneside; Sunderland; Hartlepool; Darlington and Stockton-on-Tees.

Population 1,484,000   Area 980 sq m
Full-time Stipendiary Parochial Clergy 145   Benefices 176
Parishes 212   Churches 268
Overseas link dioceses: Lesotho

BISHOP (74th)

The Rt Revd Paul Roger Butler, Bishop's Office, Auckland Castle, Bishop Auckland DL14 7NR
T: 01388 602576
E: bishop.of.durham@durham.anglican.org

BISHOP'S STAFF

Chaplain to the Bishop of Durham and Office Manager The Revd Canon Denise Dodd, Bishop's Office, Auckland Castle, Bishop Auckland DL14 7NR   *T:* 01388 602576
E: denise.dodd@durham.anglican.org

SUFFRAGAN BISHOP

JARROW The Rt Revd Mark Watts Bryant, Bishop's House, 25 Ivy Lane, Low Fell, Gateshead NE9 6QD   *T:* 0191 491 0917
E: bishop.of.jarrow@durham.anglican.org

ASSISTANT BISHOPS

The Rt Revd Dr Graham Kings, c/o SPCK, 36 Causton Street, London SW1P 4ST
T: 01865 787501
E: graham.kings@durham.ac.uk
The Rt Revd John Pritchard, 42 Bolton Avenue, Richmond, DL10 4BA   *T:* 01748 850854
E: johnlpritchard@btinternet.com
The Rt Revd Dr David Stancliffe, Butts House 15 The Butts, Stanhope, Bishop Auckland DL13 2UQ   *T:* 01388 526912
E: david.stancliffe@hotmail.com
The Rt Revd Glyn Hamilton Webster, Holy Trinity Rectory, Micklegate, York YO1 6LE
T: 01904 628155
E: office@seeofbeverley.org.uk

CATHEDRAL CHURCH OF CHRIST, BLESSED MARY THE VIRGIN AND ST CUTHBERT OF DURHAM

Dean The Very Revd Andrew Tremlett, The Deanery, The College, Durham DH1 3EQ
T: 0191 374 4586 (office)
E: dean@durhamcathedral.co.uk

Canons Residentiary
The Revd Canon Dr David Kennedy, 7 The College, Durham DH1 3EQ
T: 0191 375 0242 (home)
0191 374 4065 (office)
E: canon.precentor@durhamcathedral.co.uk
The Revd Canon Rosalind Brown, 6a The College, Durham DH1 3EQ
T: 0191 386 4266 ext. 235 (office)
E: nave.canon@durhamcathedral.co.uk
The Ven Ian Jagger, 15 The College, Durham DH1 3EQ   *T:* 0191 384 7534
E: archdeacon.of.durham@
durham.anglican.org
The Revd Canon Professor Simon Oliver, 14 The College, Durham DH1 3EQ
T: 0191 334 3942 (office)
E: simon.oliver@durhamcathedral.co.uk
The Revd Canon Sophie Jelley, 3 The College, Durham DH1 3EQ   *T:* 0191 374 6004 (office)
E: sophie.jelley@durham.anglican.org
Lay Members
Mr Ivor Stolliday, The Cathedral Office, The College, Durham DH1 3EH   *T:* 07968 943101
E: ivor.stolliday@durhamcathedral.co.uk
Mrs Cathy Barnes (*Same Address*)
T: 0191 536 4205
E: cpbarnes@sky.com
Other Staff
Chapter Clerk Canon Philip Davies, The Cathedral Office DH1 3EH   *T:* 0191 374 4064
E: philip.davies@durhamcathedral.co.uk
Cathedral Organist Mr Daniel Cook, 6 The College, Durham DH1 3EQ   *T:* 0191 386 4266
E: organist@durhamcathedral.co.uk

ARCHDEACONS

SUNDERLAND The Ven Stuart Bain, St Nicholas Vicarage, Hedworth Lane, Boldon Colliery NE35 9JA   *T:* 0191 536 2300
E: archdeacon.of.sunderland@
durham.anglican.org
DURHAM The Ven Ian Jagger, 15 The College, Durham DH1 3EQ   *T:* 0191 384 7534
E: archdeacon.of.durham@
durham.anglican.org
AUCKLAND The Ven Rick Simpson (from 11/2/18)

MEMBERS OF THE HOUSE OF CLERGY OF THE GENERAL SYNOD
Proctors for Clergy
The Revd Canon David Brooke
The Revd Canon Graeme Buttery
The Ven Ian Jagger
The Revd Bill Braviner
The Revd David Tolhurst

MEMBERS OF THE HOUSE OF LAITY OF THE GENERAL SYNOD
Dr Richard Goudie
Dr James Harrison
Mrs Helen Jones
Mrs Helen Smith

DIOCESAN OFFICERS
Diocesan Secretary Mr Andrew Thurston, Cuthbert House, Stonebridge, Durham DH1 3RY   T: 01388 660010
    E: diocesan.secretary@durham.anglican.org
Chancellor of Diocese (until 31/10/17) The Worshipful the Revd Canon Rupert Bursell, Diocesan Registry, Messrs Smith Roddam, 56 North Bondgate, Bishop Auckland DL14 7PG
                           T: 01388 603073
                           F: 01388 450483
Deputy Chancellor (until 13/1/18, Chancellor from 14/1/18) Mr Adrian Iles, Diocesan Registry, Messrs Smith Roddam, 56 North Bondgate, Bishop Auckland DL14 7PG (*Same Tel & Fax*)
Registrar of Diocese and Bishop's Legal Secretary Ms H. Monckton-Milnes (*Same Address, Tel & Fax*)
Deputy Registrar Mr D. Harris (*Same Address, Tel & Fax*)
Property Manager, Diocesan Surveyor Mr Mike Galley, Diocesan Office, Cuthbert House, Stonebridge, Durham DH1 3RY
                           T: 01388 660006
    E: mike.galley@durham.anglican.org
Finance Manager Mrs Clare Thompson (*Same Address*)   T: 01388 660014
    E: clare.thompson@durham.anglican.org
Parish Giving Champion Mr Nathan Bruce (*Same Address*)   T: 01388 660011
    E: nathan.bruce@durham.anglican.org

DIOCESAN ORGANIZATIONS
Diocesan Office Cuthbert House, Stonebridge, Durham DH1 3RY   T: 01388 604515
    E: diocesan.office@durham.anglican.org

ADMINISTRATION
Diocesan Synod (Chairman, House of Clergy) The Revd David Tomlinson
(*Chairman, House of Laity*) Mr Andrew Rogers, 19 Trentbrooke Avenue, Hartlepool, TS25 5JN
    E: energy.education@btconnect.com

(*Secretary*) Mr Andrew Thurston, Cuthbert House, Stonebridge, Durham DH1 3RY
                           T: 01388 660010
    E: diocesan.secretary@durham.anglican.org
Bishop's Council, Board of Finance, Mission and Pastoral Committee (Chair) The Rt Revd Paul Butler, Bishop of Durham, Bishop's Office, Auckland Castle, Bishop Auckland DL14 7NR
                           T: 020 8692 7449
    E: stpaulsdeptford@btinternet.com
(*Secretary*) Mr Andrew Thurston, Cuthbert House, Stonebridge, Durham DH1 3RY
                           T: 01388 660010
    E: diocesan.secretary@durham.anglican.org
Finance Group (Chair) Ms Margaret Vaughan, 36 Beechwood Road, Eaglescliffe, Stockton on Tees TS16 0AE   T: 01642 787173
    E: magsandtabs@hotmail.co.uk
(*Secretary*) Mr Andrew Thurston, Cuthbert House, Stonebridge, Durham DH1 3RY
                           T: 01388 660010
    E: diocesan.secretary@durham.anglican.org
Investment Committee (Chair) Ms Margaret Vaughan, Diocesan Office, Cuthbert House, Stonebridge, Durham DH1 3RY
(*Secretary*) Mr Andrew Thurston (*Same Address*)
                           T: 01388 660010
    E: diocesan.secretary@durham.anglican.org
Audit Committee (Chair) The Revd Christopher Pearson (*Same Address*)   T: 01388 604515
    E: revcwpearson@gmail.com
(*Secretary*) Mr Andrew Thurston, Cuthbert House, Stonebridge, Durham DH1 3RY
Church Buildings Panel (Chair) Mr Geoff Taylor, 14 Academy Gardens, Gainford, Darlington DL2 3EN   T: 01325 730379
    E: geoffandsue@academygardens.fsnet.co.uk
(*Secretary*) Vacancy
Closed Churches Uses Panel (Chair) The Ven Ian Jagger, 15 The College, Durham DH1 3EQ
                           T: 0191 384 7534
    E: archdeacon.of.durham@
                           durham.anglican.org
(*Secretary*) Vacancy
(*Designated Officer*) Mr Paul Stringer, Diocesan Office, Cuthbert House, Stonebridge, Durham DH1 3RY   T: 01388 660002
    E: paul.stringer@durham.anglican.org
(*Administrative Secretary*) Mr Paul Stringer (*As above*)
(*Office Manager*) Mrs Mandy Blackett (*Same Address*)   T: 01388 660010
    E: mandy.blackett@durham.anglican.org
(*Pensions Officer*) Canon Keith Woodhouse, 85 Baulkham Hills, Penshaw, Houghton le Spring DH4 7RZ   T: 0191 584 3977
                           F: 0191 584 3977
    E: keith.woodhouse@durham.anglican.org
(*Adviser in Women's Ministry*) The Revd Sue Pinnington, Rectory, 5 Lingfield, Houghton le Spring DH5 8QA   T: 0191 584 3487
    E: rectorstmichaels@icloud.com

CHURCH BUILDINGS
Advisory Committee for the Care of Churches (Chairman) Mrs Sandra Robertson, Diocesan Office, Cuthbert House, Stonebridge, Durham DH1 3RY   *T:* 01388 604515
                E: dacchair@durham.anglican.org
(Secretary) Vacancy

DIOCESAN RECORD OFFICE
Archives and Special Collections, University Library (Palace Green Section), University of Durham, Palace Green, Durham DH1 3RN
                                T: 0191 334 2972
                E: pg.library@durham.ac.uk
County Record Office, County Hall, Durham DH1 5UL   *T:* 03000 267619
                E: record.office@durham.gov.uk
Archivist
Mr Andrew Gray   *T:* 0191 334 2972
                E: pg.library@durham.ac.uk
                        (for diocesan records)

EDUCATION
Director of Education for Durham and Newcastle Mr Paul Rickeard, Church House, St John's Terrace, North Shields NE29 6HS
                                T: 0191 270 4163
        E: paul.rickeard@drmnewcanglican.org
Assistant Director (Legal and Governance) Ms Liane Atkin *(Same Address)*   *T:* 0191 270 4164
                E: liane.atkin@drmnewcanglican.org
Assistant Directors (School Effectiveness) Miss Anne Vernon *(Same Address)*   *T:* 0191 270 4135
        E: anne.vernon@drmnewcanglican.org
Mrs Jo Warner, Church House, St John's Terrace, North Shields NE29 6HS
                                T: 0191 270 4162
        E: jo.warner@drmnewc.anglican.org
Bursar Mrs Eileen Bell, Church House, St John's Terrace, North Shields NE29 6HS
                                T: 0191 270 4141
        E: eileen.bell@drmnewcanglican.org
RE Advisors Miss Caroline Weir, Church House, St John's Terrace, North Shields NE29 6HS   *T:* 0191 270 4124
        E: caroline.weir@drmnewcanglican.org
Mrs Margaret Gibson *(Same Address & Tel)*
        E: margaret.gibson@drmnewcanglican.org

MISSION AND MINISTRY SUPPORT TEAM
Director of Mission, Discipleship and Ministry The Revd Canon Sophie Jelley, Cuthbert House, Stonebridge, Durham DH1 3RY
T: 0191 374 6004 (office)
        E: sophie.jelley@durham.anglican.org
Adviser in Pastoral Care and Counselling Mr Tony Wright   *T:* 07746 846317
                E: tony.wright@durham.anglican.org
Leader in Youth Mission and Ministry Mr Andy Harris   *T:* 0191 374 6008
        E: andy.harris@durham.anglican.org

Children's Ministry Adviser Mrs Sharon Pritchard   *T:* 0191 374 6019
        E: sharon.pritchard@durham.anglican.org
Liturgical Committee Chairman The Revd Canon Dr David Kennedy, 7 The College, Durham DH1 3EQ   *T:* 0191 375 0242 (home)
                        0191 374 4065 (office)
        E: canon.precentor@durhamcathedral.co.uk
Local Church Growth and Development Adviser (Missioner) The Revd Canon Judy Hirst
                                T: 0191 374 6014
        E: judy.hirst@durham.anglican.org
Generous Giving Project Officer (until 4/18) Mrs Rachael Phillips   *T:* 0191 374 6016
        E: rachael.phillips@durham.anglican.org
Warden of Reader Ministry The Rt Revd Mark Watts Bryant, Bishop's House, 25 Ivy Lane, Low Fell, Gateshead NE9 6QD
                                T: 0191 491 0917
        E: bishop.of.jarrow@durham.anglican.org
Archdeaconry Sub-wardens of Reader Ministry (Sunderland Archdeaconry) Mrs Hilary Avent, 19 Brookside, Houghton le Spring, DH5 9NW
                                T: 07870 501629
                E: hilary.avent@yahoo.co.uk
Archdeaconry Sub-wardens of Reader Ministry (Durham Archdeaconry) Mr Tony Holden, 27 Middridge Road, Langley Park, Durham DH7 9FH   *T:* 0191 373 2715
                E: tony.holden@dsl.pipex.com
Archdeaconry Sub-wardens of Reader Ministry (Auckland Archdeaconry) Mrs Hylda Hopper, 3 Dorchester Court, Marlborough Drive, Darlington DL1 5YD   *T:* 01325 460999
                        E: hyldahopper@aol.com

PRESS
Communications Adviser Mr Keith Blundy, Aegies Associates   *T:* 01325 301220
        E: pr@aegies.com or communications@
                        durham.anglican.org

AREA DEANS
ARCHDEACONRY OF AUCKLAND
Auckland Vacancy
Barnard Castle Alec James Harding, The Vicarage, Parson's Lonnen, Barnard Castle DL12 8ST   *T:* 01833 637018
        E: alec.harding@durham.anglican.org
Darlington David James Railton, The Vicarage, 104 Blackwell Lane, Darlington DL3 8QQ
                                T: 01332 843017
                E: davidrailton@gmail.com
Stanhope Vincent Thompson Fenton, The Rectory, 14 Hartside Close, Crook DL15 9NH
                                T: 01388 760939
        E: vincent.fenton@durham.anglican.org
Stockton Paul Stewart David Neville, The Vicarage, 76 Fairfield Road, Stockton-on-Tees TS19 7BP   *T:* 01642 640863
                        E: prevnev@gmail.com

ARCHDEACONRY OF DURHAM
Durham Vacancy
Easington Frances Jane Grieve, The Rectory, 107 Front Street, Cockfield, Bishop Auckland DL13 5AA   *T:* 01388 718447
    E: jane.grieve@durham.anglican.org
Hartlepool Janet Burbury, The Vicarage, Hart, Hartlepool TS27 3AP   *T:* 01429 262340
    E: janetb_231@hotmail.co.uk
Lanchester Heather Murray, Moorfield Collierley Vicarage, Bourne Terrace, Stanley DH9 8QS   *T:* 01207 284760
    E: revheather@btinternet.com
Sedgefield Vacancy

ARCHDEACONRY OF SUNDERLAND
Chester-le-Street David Charles Glover, 27 Wroxton, Washington NE38 7NU
    T: 0191 418 7911
    E: htcwashington@tiscali.co.uk

Gateshead Dorothy Margaret Snowball, 2 Oval Park View, Felling, Gateshead NE10 9DS
    T: 0191 469 5059
    E: dorothysnowball@btinternet.com
Gateshead West Thomas Edward Glover, St Paul's Rectory, Scotland Head, Blaydon-on-Tyne NE21 6PL   *T:* 0191 414 3165
    E: rectorofwinlaton@gmail.com
Houghton Le Spring Vacancy
Jarrow Vernon John Cuthbert, The Vicarage, 5 Sunderland Road, Cleadon, Sunderland SR6 7UR   *T:* 0191 536 7147
    E: vicar@cleadonallsaints.org
Wearmouth David Tolhurst, St Matthew's Vicarage, Silksworth Road, New Silksworth, Sunderland SR3 2AA   *T:* 0191 523 9932
    E: revtolhurst@btinternet.com

DURHAM

DIOCESE OF ELY

Founded in 1109. Cambridgeshire, except for an area in the north-west, in the diocese of Peterborough, and three parishes in the south, in the diocese of Chelmsford; the wester quarter of Norfolk; one parish in Bedfordshire.

Population 764,000   Area 1,530 sq m
Full-time Stipendiary Parochial Clergy 125   Benefices 161
Parishes 309   Churches 332
Overseas link dioceses: Vellore (Church of South India) (Ecumenical), Nordkirche (Germany) and Kigali (Church of the Province of Rwanda)

BISHOP (68th)
The Rt Revd Stephen Conway, The Bishop's House, Ely CB7 4DW   *T:* 01353 662749
E: bishop@elydiocese.org

BISHOP'S STAFF
Senior Chaplain to the Bishop of Ely The Revd Dr Hannah Cleugh (*Same Address & Tel*)
E: hannah.cleugh@elydiocese.org
Executive PA to the Bishop of Ely Mrs Carol Lawrie, The Bishop's House, Ely CB7 4DW
T: 01353 662749
E: bishoppa@elydiocese.org
Assistant Secretary Mrs Grazyna Karwoska-Budd

SUFFRAGAN BISHOP
HUNTINGDON The Rt Revd Dr David Thomson, 14 Lynn Road, Ely CB6 1DA
Bishop's Secretary Mrs Jo Godfrey (*Same Address*)   *T:* 01353 662137
F: 01353 669357
E: bishop.huntingdon@elydiocese.org

CATHEDRAL CHURCH OF THE HOLY AND UNDIVIDED TRINITY
Dean The Very Revd Mark Bonney, The Chapter Office, The College, Ely CB7 4DL
Canons Residentiary
The Revd Canon Dr Vicky Johnson, The Chapter House, The College, Ely CB7 4DL
T: 01353 660316
The Revd Canon Jessica Martin (*Same Address*)   *T:* 01353 667735
Canon Precentor The Revd Canon Dr James Garrard, The Chapter House, The College, Ely CB7 4DL
Other Staff
Administrator and Chapter Clerk Mr Stephen Bourne, The Chapter House, The College, Ely CB7 4DL   *T:* 01353 667735
Director of Music Mr Paul Trepte (*Same Address*)
T: 01353 660336

ARCHDEACONS
CAMBRIDGE The Ven Dr Alexander Hughes, St Botolph's Rectory, 1a Summerfield, Cambridge CB3 9HE   *T:* 01353 652719
E: archdeacon.cambridge@elydiocese.org
HUNTINGDON AND WISBECH The Ven Hugh McCurdy, Whitgift House, The College, Ely CB7 4DL   *T:* 01353 652709
E: archdeacon.handw@elydiocese.org

MEMBERS OF THE HOUSE OF CLERGY OF THE GENERAL SYNOD
Proctors for Clergy
The Ven Hugh McCurdy
The Revd Canon Mike Booker
The Revd Canon Nick Moir
The Revd Simon Talbott

MEMBERS OF THE HOUSE OF LAITY OF THE GENERAL SYNOD
Canon Janet Perrett
Mr Francis Spufford
Mr Richard Morgan

DIOCESAN OFFICERS
Diocesan Secretary Mr Paul Evans, Bishop Woodford House, Barton Road, Ely CB7 4DX
T: 01353 652701
01353 652702 (direct line)
E: paul.evans@elydiocese.org
Chancellor of Diocese The Hon Judge Leonard
Registrar of Diocese Mr Howard Dellar, 1 The Sanctuary, Westminster, London SW1P 3JT
T: 020 7222 5381
F: 020 7222 7502

DIOCESAN ORGANIZATIONS
Diocesan Office Bishop Woodford House, Barton Road, Ely CB7 4DX   *T:* 01353 652701
E: office@elydiocese.org

ADMINISTRATION
Diocesan Synod (*Chairman, House of Clergy*) The Revd Wendy Thomson, The Vicarage, Church Lane, Chatteris, Cambs PE16 6JA
E: wendy@chatteris.org
(*Chairman, House of Laity*) Canon Janet Perrett, 38 Beachampstead Road, Great Staughton, PE19 5DX *E:* jrperrett@talktalk.net
(*Secretary*) Mr Paul Evans, Bishop Woodford House, Barton Road, Ely CB7 4DX
T: 01353 652701
01353 652702 (direct line)
E: paul.evans@elydiocese.org
(*Assistant Diocesan Secretary Pastoral*) Miss Frances Godden
Finance Committee (*Chairman*) The Revd Canon Brian Atling, Blue Cedars, Common Lane, Hemingford Abbots, Huntingdon PE28 9AW *T:* 01480 493975
(*Secretary*) Mr Paul Evans, Bishop Woodford House, Barton Road, Ely CB7 4DX
T: 01353 652701
01353 652702 (direct line)
E: paul.cvans@clydiocese.org
(*Diocesan Accountant*) Mrs Lorraine Orbell
(*Property Manager*) Mrs Stella Green, Diocesan Office, Bishop Woodford House, Barton Road, Ely CB7 4DX
Board of Patronage (*Secretary*) Miss Frances Godden
(*Designated Officer*) Mr Paul Evans, Bishop Woodford House, Barton Road, Ely CB7 4DX
T: 01353 652701
01353 652702 (direct line)
E: paul.evans@elydiocese.org

CHURCH BUILDINGS
Diocesan Advisory Committee for the Care of Churches (*Secretary*) Miss Frances Godden
Archdeaconry of Cambridge Church Music Society (*Secretary*) Mrs Suzanne Barton, 239 Lichfield Road, Cambridge, CB1 3SH *T:* 01223 505764
E: suzanne_barton@yahoo.com
Ely RSCM Committee (*Secretary*) Mr Ken Diffey
T: 01480 458846
E: diffey@homecall.co.uk

DIOCESAN RECORD OFFICES
Huntingdonshire Archives Huntingdonshire Archives, Princes Street, Huntingdon PE29 3PA
(*Collections Archivist*) Mr Richard Anderson
T: 01480 372738
Norfolk Record Office Norfolk Record Office, The Archive Centre, Martineau Lane, Norwich NR1 2DQ
(*County Archivist*) Mr Gary Tuson
T: 01603 222599
Wisbech and Fenland Museum Wisbech and Fenland Museum, Museum Square, Wisbech PE13 1ES

(*Assistant Curator*) Mr J. R. Bell
T: 01945 583817
Cambridgeshire Archives Cambridgeshire Archives, Shire Hall, Castle Hill, Cambridge CB3 0AP
(*Collections Archivist*) Mr Richard Anderson
T: 01223 699487/699399

EDUCATION
E: cathy.priestley@elydiocese.org
W: http://www:elydiocese.org/education
Diocesan Board of Education (*Secretary*) Mr Andrew Read, Diocesan Office, Bishop Woodford House, Barton Road, Ely CB7 4DX
(*Director of Education*) Mr Andrew Read (*As above*)
(*Deputy Director of Education Schools Effectiveness*) Vacancy
(*Assistant Director of Education and RE Adviser Schools*) Dr Shirley Hall, Diocesan Office, Bishop Woodford House, Barton Road, Ely CB7 4DX
(*Schools Buildings and Finance Officer*) Vacancy

LITURGICAL COMMITTEE
Secretary Canon Simon Kershaw, 5 Sharp Close, St Ives PE27 6UN *T:* 01480 381471
E: simon@kershaw.org.uk

MINISTRY
Director of Ministry The Revd Canon Linda Church, Diocesan Office, Bishop Woodford House, Barton Road, Ely CB7 4DX
T: 01353 652733
Diocesan Director of Ordinands The Revd Anna Matthews *T:* 01353 652730
Reader Ministry Contact The Revd Canon Linda Church, Diocesan Office, Bishop Woodford House, Barton Road, Ely CB7 4DX
T: 01353 652733
Readers' Board (*Chair*) Mr Roger Cresswell, 8 Bishop's Way, Buckden, St Neots, Cambs PE19 5TZ *T:* 01480 811425
E: roger.cresswell@talktalk.net
(*Warden*) Mr Stephen Mashford, 7a Haggis Gap, Fulbourn, Cambridge CB21 5HD
T: 01223 882163
E: sandjmashford@aol.com

MISSION AND ECUMENICAL
Director of Mission The Revd Peter Wood
T: 01353 652723
Youth Adviser Mrs Rachael Heffer, Diocesan Office, Bishop Woodford House, Barton Rd, Ely CB7 4DX
Children's Adviser Mrs Debbie Hill (*Same Address*) *T:* 01353 652714
Fresh Expression of Church and Young Adults Adviser The Revd Ed Olsworth-Peter, Dioc Office

Social Justice Co-ordinator The Revd Jes Salt, Diocesan Office, Bishop Woodford House, Barton Rd, Ely CB7 4DX
Council for Mission (Chair) The Ven Hugh McCurdy, Whitgift House, The College, Ely CB7 4DL   *T:* 01353 652709
          E: archdeacon.handw@elydiocese.org
Diocesan Ecumenical Officer The Revd Sarah Gower, Christ Church House, 1 Benstead, Orton Goldhay, Peterborough PE2 5JJ
          T: 01733 394411
          E: sarahcgower@btinternet.com

PRESS AND PUBLICATIONS
Head of Communications Mr James Owen, Diocesan Office, Bishop Woodford House, Barton Road, Ely CB7 4DX   *T:* 01353 652728

SOCIAL RESPONSIBILITY
Cambridgeshire Deaf Association (Ely Dioc Association for the Deaf) Mr Andy Palmer, 8 Romsey Terrace, Cambridge, CB1 3NH
          T: 01223 246237
          F: 01223 411701
          E: office@cambsdeaf.org
Mothers' Union (President) Mrs Susan Baker, Diocesan Office, Bishop Woodford House, Barton Road, Ely CB7 4DX   *T:* 01353 652718

RURAL AND AREA DEANS
ARCHDEACONRY OF CAMBRIDGE
Bourn Vacancy
Cambridge North David James Maher, The Good Shepherd Vicarage, 51 Highworth Avenue, Cambridge CB4 2BQ
          T: 01223 363342
          E: vicar@churchofthegoodshepherd.co.uk
Cambridge South Robert Michael Mackley, The Vicarage, 1B Summerfield, Cambridge CB3 9HE   *T:* 01223 356641
          E: vicar@lsm.org.uk

Fordham and Quy Susan Jane Giles, The Vicarage, 86 High Street, Bottisham, Cambridge CB5 9BA   *T:* 01223 812726
          E: suethevic@btinternet.com
Granta Simon John Talbott, The Vicarage, 12 Church Street, Great Shelford, Cambridge CB22 5EL   *T:* 01223 847068
          E: s.talbott@virgin.net
North Stowe Neil James Blandford-Baker, The Vicarage, 9A Church Street, Histon, Cambridge CB24 9EP   *T:* 01223 233456
          E: jamesbb@btinternet.com
Shingay Felicity Anne Couch, The Rectory, Fishers Lane, Orwell, Royston SG8 5QX
          T: 01223 207212
          E: fcouch@btinternet.com

ARCHDEACONRY OF HUNTINGDON AND WISBECH
Ely John Howard Robson, St George's Vicarage, 30 Church Lane, Littleport, Ely CB6 1PS
          T: 01353 864695
          E: therevhoward@btinternet.com
Fincham and Feltwell William Spencer Dwerryhouse Burke, The Rectory, High Street, Fincham, King's Lynn PE33 9EL
          E: wsdburke@outlook.com
Huntingdon Edwood Brian Atling, Blue Cedars, 70 Common Lane, Hemingford Abbots, Huntingdon PE28 9AW   *T:* 01480 493975
          E: atling@btopenworld.com
March Andrew John Smith, St Peter's Rectory, 54 High Street, March PE15 9JR
          E: andrew.marchurch@gmail.com
St Ives Frederick James Kilner, 125 High Street, Somersham, Huntingdon PE28 3EN
          T: 01487 842864
          E: kilner@btinternet.com
St Neots Annette Susan Reed, The Vicarage, 24 St James's Road, Little Paxton, St Neots PE19 6QW   *T:* 01480 211048
          E: rev.reed@btinternet.com
Wisbech Lynn Marshland Matthew Laurence Bradbury, The Vicarage, Church Road, Wisbech St Mary, Wisbech PE13 4RN
          T: 01945 410814
          E: matthew.bradbury@ely.anglican.org

DIOCESE OF GIBRALTAR IN EUROPE

Founded 1980 by union of the Diocese of Gibraltar (founded 1842) and the (Fulham) Jurisdiction of North and Central Europe. Area, Europe, except Great Britain and Ireland; Morocco; Turkey; the Asian countries of the former Soviet Union.

Population   Area sq m
Full-time Stipendiary Parochial Clergy 159   Benefices
Parishes   Churches 295
Overseas link dioceses:

BISHOP OF GIBRALTAR IN EUROPE (4th)
The Rt Revd Dr Robert Innes, 47 rue Capitaine Crespel, B-1050 Ixelles, Belgium
T: 0032 (0)2 213 7480
E: bishop.europe@churchofengland.org

BISHOP'S STAFF
Bishop's Commissary and Chaplain The Ven Meurig Williams, 47 rue Capitaine Crespel, B-1050 Ixelles, Belgium   *T:* 0032 (0)2 213 7480
E: meurig.williams@churchofengland.org

SUFFRAGAN BISHOP
IN EUROPE The Rt Revd Dr David Hamid, 14 Tufton Street, London SW1P 3QZ
T: 020 7898 1160
F: 020 7898 1166
E: david.hamid@churchofengland.org
Bishop's Chaplain and PA The Revd Deacon Frances Hiller

ASSISTANT BISHOPS
The Rt Revd Norman Banks, Parkside House, Abbey Mill Lane, St Albans AL3 4HE
T: 01727 836358
E: bishop@richborough.org.uk
The Rt Revd Michael Colclough, 12 Grosvenor Court, Sloane Square, London SW1X 9PF
T: 020 3612 3135
E: michaeljcolclough@gmail.com
The Rt Revd John Flack, The Rectory, 38 West Street, Easton-on-the-Hill, Stamford PE9 3LS
T: 01733 202767
01780 753091
M: 07810 714056
E: johnflack67@yahoo.com
The Rt Revd Richard Garrard, 26 Carol Close, Stoke Holy Cross, Norwich NR14 8NN
T: 01508 494165
E: garrard.r.a@btinternet.com
The Rt Revd Edward Holland, 37 Parfrey Street, London W6 9EW   *T:* 020 8746 3636
E: ed.holland@uwclub.net

The Rt Revd Michael Manktelow, 14 Little London, Chichester, Chichester PO19 1NZ
T: 01243 531096
The Rt Revd Nicholas Reade, 5 Warnham Gardens, Cooden, Bexhill-on-Sea TN39 3SP
T: 01424 842673
E: nicholas.reade@btinternet.com
The Rt Revd Dr Harald Rein, Willadingweg 39, CH-3006 Bern, Switzerland
T: 00 41 31 351 35 30
E: bischof@christkatholisch.ch
The Rt Revd José Jorge Tavares de Pina Cabral, Secretaria Diocesano, Apartado 392, P-4431-905 Vila Nova de Gaia, Portugal
T: 00 351 22 375 4018
E: bispopinacabral@igreja-lusitana.org
The Rt Revd David Stancliffe, 15 The Butts, Stanhope, Bishop Auckland, Durham DL13 2UQ   *T:* 01388 526912
E: david.stancliffe@hotmail.com
The Rt Revd David Smith, 34 Cedar Glade, Dunnington, York YO19 5QZ
T: 01904 481225
E: david@djmhs.force9.co.uk
The Rt Revd Dr Stephen Venner, 81 King Harry Lane, St Albans AL3 4AS
T: 07980 743628
E: stephen@venner.org.uk
The Rt Revd Pierre Whalon, American Cathedral, 23 Avenue George V, 75008 Paris, France   *T:* 00 33 1 53 23 84 00 (Cathedral)
00 33 1 47 20 02 23 (Direct)
F: 00 33 1 47 23 95 30 (Cathedral)
E: office@tec-europe.org
The Rt Revd Michael Turnbull, 67 Strand Street, Sandwich CT13 9HN   *T:* 01304 611389
E: amichaelturnbull@yahoo.co.uk

CATHEDRAL CHURCH OF THE HOLY TRINITY, GIBRALTAR
Dean The Very Revd Dr John Paddock, 41 Jumpers Buildings, Rosia Road, Gibraltar
T: 00 350 200 78377 (Deanery)
F: 00 350 200 78463
E: deangib@gibraltar.gi

PRO-CATHEDRAL OF ST PAUL, VALLETTA, MALTA

Chancellor The Revd Canon Simon Godfrey, Chancellor's Lodge, St Paul's Anglican Pro-Cathedral, Independence Square, Valletta VLT12, Malta   *T:* 00 356 21 22 57 14
F: 00 356 21 22 58 67
E: anglican@onvol.net
simonhmgodfrey@googlemail.com

PRO-CATHEDRAL OF THE HOLY TRINITY, BRUSSELS, BELGIUM

Chancellor The Ven Dr Paul Vrolijk, Pro-Cathedral of the Holy Trinity, 29 rue Capitaine Crespel, B-1050 Ixelles, Belgium
T: 00 32 2 289 0921
F: 00 32 2 511 10 28
E: paul.vrolijk@europe.anglican.org

ARCHDEACONS

THE EASTERN ARCHDEACONRY The Ven Colin Williams, Montgolfier-Allee 8, 60486 Frankfurt am Main, Germany
T: 0049 (0)151 257 03461
E: e: colin.williams@europe.anglican.org
NORTH WEST EUROPE The Ven Dr Paul Vrolijk, Pro-Cathedral of the Holy Trinity, 29 rue Capitaine Crespel, B-1050 Ixelles, Belgium
T: 00 32 2 289 0921
E: paul.vrolijk@europe.anglican.org
FRANCE The Ven Meurig Williams, 47 rue Capitaine Crespel, B-1050 Ixelles, Belgium
T: 0032 (0)2 213 7480
E: meurig.williams@churchofengland.org
GIBRALTAR The Ven Geoffrey Johnston, 29 Little Fellows, Milford, Belper DE56 0RY
T: 00 44 (0)750 739 1297
E: geoff.johnston@europe.anglican.org
ITALY AND MALTA The Ven Vickie Lela Sims, via Solferino 17, 20121 Milano, Italy
T: 00 39 02 655 2258
E: allsaintspriest@hotmail.com
GERMANY AND NORTHERN EUROPE The Ven Colin Williams, Montgolfier-Allee 8, 60486 Frankfurt am Main, Germany
T: 0049 (0)151 257 03461
E: e: colin.williams@europe.anglican.org
SWITZERLAND The Ven Adele Kelham, Lindenstrasse 4, CH 5303, Wurenlingen, Switzerland   *T:* 00 41 21 312 65 63
E: kelham@bluewin.ch

MEMBERS OF THE HOUSE OF CLERGY OF THE GENERAL SYNOD

Proctors for Clergy
The Revd Canon Debbie Flach
The Revd Tuomas Mäkipää
Reverend Giles Williams

MEMBERS OF THE HOUSE OF LAITY OF THE GENERAL SYNOD

Mrs Madeleine Holmes
Mr Tjeerd Bijl
Mr David Coulston

DIOCESAN OFFICERS

Diocesan Secretary Mr Adrian Mumford, Diocesan Office, 14 Tufton Street, London SW1P 3QZ
Chancellor of Diocese Chancellor Mark Hill, Francis Taylor Building, Inner Temple, London EC4Y 7BY   *T:* 0207 353 8415
E: mark.hill@ftb.eu.com
Registrar of Diocese and Bishop's Legal Secretary Mr Aiden Hargreaves-Smith, Diocesan Registry, 5 Montague Close, London SE1 9BB
T: 020 7593 5127
F: 020 7898 1166
E: chelmsfordregistry@wslaw.co.uk

DIOCESAN ORGANIZATIONS

Diocesan Office 14 Tufton Street, London SW1P 3QZ   *T:* 020 7898 1155
F: 020 7898 1166
E: bron.panter@churchofengland.org

ADMINISTRATION

Dioc Synod (Lay Vice-President) Vacancy
(Secretary) Mr Adrian Mumford, Diocesan Office, 14 Tufton Street, London SW1P 3QZ
Board of Finance (Chairman) Mr Michael Hart, Diocesan Office, 14 Tufton St, London SW1P 3QZ
(Secretary) Mr Adrian Mumford, Diocesan Office, 14 Tufton Street, London SW1P 3QZ

ARCHBISHOP'S APOKRISARIOI AND REPRESENTATIVES

To the Holy See The Rt Revd David Moxon, The Anglican Centre in Rome, Palazzo Doria Pamphilj, Piazza del Collegio Romano 2 00186 Rome, Italy   *T:* 39 06 678 0302
F: 39 06 678 0674
E: director@anglicancentre.it
To the Patriarch of Romania, and the Patriarch of Bulgaria Vacancy
To the Archbishop of Athens and All Greece The Revd Canon Malcolm Bradshaw, c/o British Embassy, Ploutarchou 1, Athens 106 75
T: 00 30 210 721 4906 (home)
E: anglican@otenet.gr
To the Patriarch of Moscow and All Russia The Revd Clive Fairclough, Chaplain, The British Embassy Moscow, BFPO 5203, West End Road, Ruislip HA4 5EP   *T:* 007 495 629 0990
E: chaplain@standrewsmoscow.org
To the Patriarch of Serbia The Revd Robin Fox, St Mary's Anglican Church, Visegradska 23, 11000 Belgrade, Serbia *T:* 00 381 11 3232 948
E: robin.fox@sbb.co.rs

CHURCH BUILDINGS
Faculty Committee (Secretary) Mr Adrian Mumford, Diocesan Office, 14 Tufton Street, London SW1P 3QZ

DIOCESAN RECORD OFFICE
London Metropolitan Archives, 40 Northampton Road, London EC1R 0HB
T: 020 7332 3820
E: ask.lma@cityoflondon.gov.uk

ENVIRONMENT
Environmental Officer The Revd Elizabeth Bussmann, Spiezgaessli 5, 3703 Aeschi bei Spiez, Switzerland
T: 0041 336 550 211 / +41 795 309 445
E: mebussmann-morton@bluewin.ch

LITURGY
The Revd Dr Ben Gordon-Taylor, College of the Resurrection, Stocks Bank Road, Mirfield WF14 0BW, UK   *T:* 0044 (0)1924 490441
E: bgordon-taylor@mirfield.org.uk

MEDITERRANEAN MISSIONS TO SEAMEN
Administrator Mr Adrian Mumford, Diocesan Office, 14 Tufton Street, London SW1P 3QZ

MINISTRY AND TRAINING
Warden of Readers The Rt Revd Dr David Hamid, 14 Tufton Street, London SW1P 3QZ
T: 020 7898 1160
F: 020 7898 1166
E: david.hamid@churchofengland.org
Director of Ordinands The Revd Canon William Gulliford, Diocesan Office, 14 Tufton St, London SW1P 3QZ
E: william.gulliford@london.anglican.org
william.gulliford@london.anglican.org
Director of Training The Revd Ulla Monberg, Borgmester Jensens Allé 92th, 2100 Copenhagen, Denmark   *T:* 00 45 3526 0660
E: ulla.monberg@churchofengland.org

PRESS AND PUBLICATIONS
Press and Communications Officer The Revd Paul Needle, Diocesan Office, 14 Tufton Street, London SW1P 3QZ
T: 07712 463806 (mobile)
E: paul.needle@churchofengland.org
Editor of 'The European Anglican' The Revd Paul Needle (*As above*)

Transferred to Exeter in 1050, formerly at Crediton in 909. Devon, except for one parish in the south-east, in the diocese of Salisbury, and one parish in the west, in the diocese of Truro; Plymouth; Torbay.

Population 1,177,000   Area 2,570 sq m
Full-time Stipendiary Parochial Clergy 199   Benefices 160
Parishes 491   Churches 603
Overseas link dioceses: Cyprus and the Gulf; Thika (Kenya)

BISHOP (71st)
The Rt Revd Robert Atwell, Bishop's Office, The Palace Gatehouse, Palace Gate, Exeter EX1 1HX   *T:* 01392 272362
          E: bishop.of.exeter@exeter.anglican.org

BISHOP'S STAFF
Episcopal Vicar and Chaplain The Revd Preb Graham Stones, The Palace Gatehouse, Palace Gate, Exeter EX1 1HX   *T:* 01392 272362
          E: bishop's.chaplain@exeter.anglican.org
Executive Assistant Mrs Justine Tear, Bishop's Office, The Palace Gatehouse, Palace Gate, Exeter EX1 1HX (*Same Tel*)
          E: justine.tear@exeter.anglican.org
Administrative Secretary Mrs Claire Sherlock, Bishop's Office, The Palace Gatehouse, Palace Gate, Exeter EX1 1HX (*Same Tel*)
          E: claire.sherlock@exeter.anglican.org

SUFFRAGAN BISHOPS
CREDITON The Rt Revd Dame Sarah Mullally, 32 The Avenue, Tiverton, Devon EX16 4HW
          T: 01884 250002
          E: bishop.of.crediton@exeter.anglican.org
PLYMOUTH The Rt Revd Nicholas McKinnel, 108 Molesworth Road, Stoke, Plymouth PL3 4AQ   *T:* 01752 500059
          E: bishop.of.plymouth@exeter.anglican.org

ASSISTANT BISHOPS
The Rt Revd Richard Hawkins, 3 Westbrook Close, Whipton, Exeter EX4 8BS
          T: 01392 462622
The Rt Revd Martin Shaw, 11 Russell Terrace, Exeter, EX4 4HX   *T:* 01392 663511
          E: amartinshaw@gmail.com

CATHEDRAL CHURCH OF ST PETER
Dean The Very Revd Dr Jonathan Greener, The Deanery, 10 Cathedral Close, Exeter EX1 1EZ
          T: 01392 273509 (Office)
          E: dean@exeter-cathedral.org.uk
Canons Residentiary
Precentor Vacancy, 12 Cathedral Close, Exeter EX1 1EZ   *T:* 01392 259329
          E: precentor@exeter-cathedral.org.uk

Treasurer and Pastor Canon Ian Morter, 9 Cathedral Close, Exeter, EX1 1EZ
          T: 01392 285987 (Office)
          01392 758172 (Home)
          E: pastor@exeter-cathedral.org.uk
SSM Residentiary Canon The Revd Canon Dr John Searle, Belle Isle Lodge, Belle Isle Drive, Exeter EX2 4RY   *T:* 01392 432153
          E: j.f.searle@btinternet.com
Canons
Chapter Canons Mr Clive Cohen
Dame Suzi Leather
Mr Jonathan Harris
Other Staff
Managing Director Mr Alasdair Cameron
          T: 01392 285977
          E: alastair.cameron@
          exeter-cathedral.org.uk
Clerk of Works Mr Christopher Sampson
          T: 01392 285971
          E: clerkofworks@exeter-cathedral.org.uk
Liturgy and Music Department
          T: 01392 285984
          E: liturgy@exeter-cathedral.org.uk
Director of Music Mr Timothy Noon (*Same Tel*)
          E: music@exeter-cathedral.org.uk
Assistant Director of Music Mr David Davies, Flat 4 Closter Garth, Exeter, EX1 1JS
          T: 01392 270761 (Office)
          01392 270877 (Home)
          E: adom@exeter-cathedral.org.uk
Cathedral Development Director Mr Paul Courtney, Cathedral Development Office, 1 The Cloisters, Exeter EX1 1HS
          T: 01392 285974
          E: developmentdirector@
          exeter-cathedral.org.uk
Head of Visitor Services Catherine Escott
          T: 01392 285983
          E: visitors@exeter-cathedral.org.uk

ARCHDEACONS
EXETER The Ven Christopher Futcher, Emmanuel House, Station Road, Ide, Exeter EX2 9RS   *T:* 01392 425577
          E: archdeacon.of.exeter@exeter.anglican.org

TOTNES The Ven Douglas Dettmer, Blue Hills, Bradley Road, Bovey Tracey, Newton Abbot TQ13 9EU　　　　　　　T: 01626 832064
　　E: archdeacon.of.totnes@exeter.anglican.org
BARNSTAPLE The Ven Dr Mark Butchers, Stage Cross, Sanders Lane, Bishops Tawton, Barnstaple EX32 0BE　　　T: 01271 375475
　　　　　E: archdeacon.of.barnstaple@
　　　　　　　　　　　　exeter.anglican.org
PLYMOUTH The Ven Ian Chandler, St Mark's House, 46a Cambridge Road, Ford, Plymouth PL2 1PU　　　　　　　T: 01752 202401
　　　　　E: archdeacon.of.plymouth@
　　　　　　　　　　　　exeter.anglican.org

MEMBERS OF THE HOUSE OF CLERGY OF THE GENERAL SYNOD
Proctors for Clergy
The Ven Douglas Dettmer
The Revd Graham Hamilton

MEMBERS OF THE HOUSE OF LAITY OF THE GENERAL SYNOD
Mrs Anne Foreman
Miss Emma Forward
Dr Samuel Robinson
Dr Jack Shelley

DIOCESAN OFFICERS
Diocesan Secretary Mr Stephen Hancock, The Old Deanery, The Cloisters, Exeter EX1 1HS
　　　　　　　　　　　T: 01392 294927
　　E: stephen.hancock@exeter.anglican.org
Chancellor of Diocese The Honourable Sir Andrew McFarlane, Royal Courts of Justice, Strand, London WC2A 2LL
　　　　　　　　　　　T: 020 7947 6008
Deputy Chancellor of Diocese Mr Gregory Percy Jones, Francis Taylor Building, Inner Temple, London EC4Y 7BY　　　T: 020 7353 8415
Registrar of Diocese and Bishop's Legal Secretary Mr Martin Follett, Michelmores, Woodwater House, Pynes Hill, Exeter EX2 5WR
　　　　　　　　　　　T: 01392 687421
　　　　　　　　　　　F: 01392 360563
　　E: martin.follett@michelmores.com
Deputy Registrars Mr James Baker
Mr Simon Barnett

DIOCESAN ORGANIZATIONS
Diocesan Office The Old Deanery, The Cloisters, Exeter EX1 1HS

ADMINISTRATION
Diocesan Synod (*Chairman, House of Clergy*) The Revd Preb Michael Partridge, The Rectory, 9 Church Hill, Pinhoe, Exeter EX4 9ER
　　　　　　　　　　　T: 01392 466257
　　E: mike.partridge@exeter.anglican.org

(*Secretary, House of Clergy*) The Revd Guy Chave-Cox, St Paul's Vicarage, Old Sticklepath Hill, Barnstaple EX31 2BG　　T: 01271 344400
　　　　E: vicar@barnstaple-st-paul.org.uk
(*Chairman, House of Laity*) Mrs Marguerite Shapland, Bartley House, 21 Church Street, Braunton EX33 2EL　　　T: 01271 814082
　　　　　E: m.shapland07@btinternet.com
(*Secretary, House of Laity*) Mr Graham Lea, 2 Thornyville Close, Oreston, Plymouth PL9 7LE　　　　　　　　　T: 01752 403392

BISHOP'S RETIRED CLERGY OFFICERS
Barnstaple Archdeaconry (*All Deaneries*) The Revd Sarah Wood　　　　T: 01271 812730
　　　　　E: revjswood@hotmail.co.uk
Exeter Archdeaconry (*Aylesbeare Deanery*) The Revd Chris Cant　　　　T: 01395 488178
　　　　　E: chriscant@tiscali.co.uk
(*Cadbury and Christianity Deaneries*) The Revd David Francis　　　　T: 01363 776066
　　　　　E: stowrector@yahoo.co.uk
The Revd Jenny Francis (*Same Tel*)
　　　　　E: jennyfrancis1@btinternet.com
(*Tiverton and Cullompton Deanery*) The Revd Christopher Rowley　　　T: 01884 799011
　　　　E: christopherrowley@uwclub.net
(*Honiton and Ottery Deaneries*) The Revd David Scrace　　　　　　T: 01395 445591
　　　　　E: d.scrace@btopenworld.com
(*Kenn Deanery*) Vacancy
Plymouth Archdeaconry (*All deaneries*) The Revd Ian Provost　　E: ian.provost17@gmail.com
Totnes Archdeaconry (*Moreton and Newton Abbot and Ipplepen Deaneries*) The Revd Preb John Good　　　　　　　T: 01626 873181
　　　　　E: johngood1549@outlook.com
(*Okehampton, Totnes and Woodleigh Deaneries*) The Revd George Day　　　T: 01364 643912
　　　　　E: rev@georgeday.plus.com
(*Torbay Deanery*) The Revd Dr Charles Doidge
　　　　　　　　　　　T: 01803 690548
　　　　　E: charlesdoidge@talktalk.net

CHURCH AND SOCIETY
Director Mr Martyn Goss, The Old Deanery, The Cloisters, Exeter EX1 1HS
　　　　　　　　　　　T: 01392 294924
　　　　　　　　　　　F: 01392 499594
　　　　E: martyn.goss@exeter.anglican.org
Social Responsibility Officer Miss Sally Farrant (*Same Address*)　　　　T: 01392 294918
　　　　E: sally.farrant@exeter.anglican.org

CHURCH BUILDINGS
Diocesan Advisory Committee for the Care of Churches (*Chairman*) Mr Frank Eul
(*Secretary*) Mrs Louise Bartlett, The Old Deanery　　　　　　T: 01392 294944
　　　　E: louise.bartlett@exeter.anglican.org

Church Buildings Strategy Committee (Secretary)
Miss Charlotte Vickers   *T:* 01392 294934
    E: charlotte.vickers@exeter.anglican.org

COMMUNICATIONS
Director of Communications Mrs Rebecca
Paveley   *T:* 01392 294905
    E: rebecca.paveley@exeter.anglican.org
Publications Officer The Revd Nicky Davies
                              T: 01392 294915
    E: nicky.davies@exeter.anglican.org
Digital Media Officer Mr John Moxon
                              T: 01392 294904
    E: john.moxon@exeter.anglican.org
The Church of England, Devon (Diocesan News)
                              T: 01392 294905
    E: communications@exeter.anglican.org

DIOCESAN BOARD OF EDUCATION
Diocesan Director of Education John Searson,
The Old Deanery   *T:* 01392 294950
    E: john.searson@exeter.anglican.org
Deputy Director of Education Vacancy
*Diocesan Education Advisers (Governance,
Admissions and School Organization)* Mrs
Christina Mabin   *T:* 01392 294939
    E: christina.mabin@exeter.anglican.org
(Christian Distinctiveness and SACRES) Mr Ed
Pawson   *T:* 01392 294943
    E: ed.pawson@exeter.anglican.org
(Projects and Vulnerable Pupils) Mrs Tatiana
Wilson   *T:* 01392 294941
    E: tatiana.wilson@exeter.anglican.org
(HE, FE and School Chaplaincy) The Revd Cate
Edmonds   *T:* 01392 294933
    E: cate.edmonds@exeter.anglican.org
*Diocesan Education Officers (Training and Traded
Services)* Fran Bradley   *T:* 01392 294921
    E: fran.bradley@exeter.anglican.org
(Compliance Communication and EDBE Support)
Sarah Owen   *T:* 01392 294938
    E: sarah.owen@exeter.anglican.org
(Schools Project Manager) Charlotte Weston
                              T: 07876 541561
    E: charlotte.weston@exeter.anglican.org
*Administration (Website Content and General
Office Administration)* Vacancy
*St Christopher's Multi-Academy Trust (Central
Operations Administrator)* Jo Wilkey
                              T: 01392 241576
    E: office@stchristophersmat.org
(Chief Executive Officer) Jo Evans

DIOCESAN RECORDS OFFICE
Devon Heritage Centre, Great Moor House,
Bittern Road, Sowton Industrial Estate, Exeter
EX2 7NL
Archivist
Mr John Draisey   *T:* 01392 384253
    E: devrec@devon.gov.uk

MISCELLANEOUS ORGANIZATIONS
*Clergy Widows' and Widowers' Officers
(Barnstaple Archdeaconry) (All deaneries)* The
Revd Sarah Wood   *T:* 01271 812730
    E: revjswood@hotmail.co.uk
*Clergy Widows' and Widowers' Officers (Exeter
Archdeaconry) (All deaneries except Kenn
Deanery)* The Revd Tony Mortimer, 97
Egremont Road, Exmouth, EX8 1SA
                              T: 01395 271390
    E: tpmortimer@googlemail.com
Mrs Pauline Mortimer *(Same Tel & email)*
(Kenn Deanery) Vacancy
*Clergy Widows' and Widowers' Officers
(Plymouth Archdeaconry) (All deaneries)* The
Revd Ian Provost
    E: ian.provost17@gmail.com
*Clergy Widows' and Widowers' Officers (Totnes
Archdeaconry) (Moreton and Newton Abbot and
Ipplepen Deaneries)* The Revd Preb John Good
                              T: 01626 873181
    E: johngood1549@outlook.com
(Okehampton, Totnes and Woodleigh Deaneries)
The Revd George Day   *T:* 01364 643912
    E: rev@georgeday.plus.com
(Torbay Deanery) The Revd Dr Charles Doidge
                              T: 01803 690548
    E: charlesdoidge@talktalk.net

MISSION AND MINISTRY
Director The Revd Preb Philip Sourbut, The Old
Deanery, The Cloisters, Exeter EX1 1HS
                              T: 01392 294903
    E: philip.sourbut@exeter.anglican.org
Diocesan Mission Enabler The Revd Barry
Dugmore   *T:* 01392 294920
    E: barry.dugmore@exeter.anglican.org
Mission Community Development Officer
Vacancy
Director of Ordinands The Revd Preb Becky
Totterdell, The Palace Gatehouse, Palace Gate,
Exeter EX1 1HX   *T:* 01392 477702
    E: ddo@exeter.anglican.org
DDO Administrator The Revd Canon Andrew
Godsall, The Old Deanery, The Cloisters,
Exeter EX1 1HS *(Same Tel)*
    E: andrew.godsall@exeter.anglican.org
Dean for Women in Ministry The Revd Preb
Kathy Roberts, The Rectory, Black Torrington,
Beaworthy EX21 5PU   *T:* 01409 231279
    E: robertskm8@aol.com
Warden of Readers The Ven Christopher
Futcher, Emmanuel House, Station Road, Ide,
Exeter EX2 9RS   *T:* 01392 425577
    E: archdeacon.of.exeter@exeter.anglican.org
Readers' Administrator Hannah Cross
                              T: 01392 294911
    E: hannah.cross@exeter.anglican.org
Co-ordinator Spiritual Direction The Revd Helen
Bays, 14 Stockton Hill, Dawlish, EX7 9LP
                              T: 07722 106632
    E: spiritual.direction@exeter.anglican.org

EXETER

Diocesan Children's Work Adviser Miss Katherine Lyddon   *T:* 01392 294936
        E: katherine.lyddon@exeter.anglican.org
Diocesan Youth Work Adviser Mr Paul Reisbach
        T: 01392 294932
        E: paul.reisbach@exeter.anglican.org
Diocesan Youth Church Adviser The Revd James Grier   *E:* james.grier@exeter.anglican.org
Diocesan Consultant for Worship and Music Mr Andrew Maries   *T:* 01884 34389
        E: andrew.maries@exeter.anglican.org
Ministry of Healing and Deliverance The Ven John Rawlings   *T:* 01404 43404
        E: rawlings1@btinternet.com
County Ecumenical Officer The Revd Sue Macbeth
        E: churchestogetherdevon@gmail.com
Cyprus and the Gulf Link (*Chairman*) The Ven Christopher Futcher, Emmanuel House, Station Road, Ide, Exeter EX2 9RS
        T: 01392 425577
        E: archdeacon.of.exeter@exeter.anglican.org
Thika Link (*Parish links*) Mrs Jane Inwood
        T. 01647 252519
        E: thika.link@exeter.anglican.org
(*Mission Resources Adviser*) Mrs Katie Stevenson   *T:* 01392 294960
        E: katie.stevenson@exeter.anglican.org
(*Administrator*) Vacancy

SAFEGUARDING TEAM
Diocesan Safeguarding Adviser Vacancy
Assistant Safeguarding Adviser Vacancy
DBS Co-ordinator Mr Phill Parker
        T: 01392 294969
        E: dbs@exeter.anglican.org

SUPPORT SERVICES
Diocesan Secretary Mr Stephen Hancock, The Old Deanery, The Cloisters, Exeter EX1 1HS
        T: 01392 294927
        E: stephen.hancock@exeter.anglican.org
Assistant Diocesan Secretary Dr Ed Moffatt (*Same Address*)   *T:* 01392 294928
        F: 01392 499594
        E: ed.moffatt@exeter.anglican.org
Board of Finance (*Chairman*) Mr Giles Frampton (*Same Address*)
        E: giles.frampton@exeter.anglican.org
(*Director of Finance*) Mr Neil Williams (*Same Address*)   *T:* 01392 272686
        F: 01392 499594
        E: neil.williams@exeter.anglican.org
(*Finance Manager*) Mrs Michelle Clark (*Same Address*)   *T:* 01392 294926
        E: michelle.clark@exeter.anglican.org
(*Trusts*) Mrs Serena Nott (*Same Address*)
        T: 01392 294949
        E: trusts@exeter.anglican.org

(*Director of Property and Parsonages Committee Secretary*) Mr Graham Davies (*Same Address*)
        T: 01392 294954
        F: 01392 499594
        E: graham.davies@exeter.anglican.org
(*Diocesan Surveyors*) Mr Peter Stanton (*Same Address & Fax*)   *T:* 01392 294952
        E: peter.stanton@exeter.anglican.org
Mr Mark Lewis (*Same Address, Tel & Fax*)
        E: mark.lewis@exeter.anglican.org
Mr Graham Davies (*Same Address, Tel & Fax*)
        E: graham.davies@exeter.anglican.org
Mission and Pastoral Committee (*Secretary*) Mr Alistair Sutherland   *T:* 01392 294910
        E: alistair.sutherland@exeter.anglican.org
Board of Patronage (*Chairman*) Mrs Shirley-Ann Williams, 2 Katherine's Lane, Ridgeway, Ottery St Mary EX11 1FB   *T:* 01404 811064
(*Designated Officer under the Patronage Benefices Measure*) Mr Alistair Sutherland
        T: 01392 294910
        E: alistair.sutherland@exeter.anglican.org
(*Director of Human Resources*) Miss Catherine Allen, The Old Deanery, The Cloisters, Exeter EX1 1HS   *T:* 01392 345908
        E: catherine.allen@exeter.anglican.org

RURAL DEANS
ARCHDEACONRY OF BARNSTAPLE
Barnstaple Giles Anthony Beaumont Kingsmith, The Vicarage, Springfield Road, Woolacombe EX34 7BX   *T:* 01271 870467
        E: gkingsmith53@gmail.com
Hartland Penelope Jane Dobbin, 1 Riverside Close, Bideford EX39 2RX   *T:* 01237 477264
        E: penelopedobbin@outlook.com
Holsworthy Jane Eleanor Lucas, The Rectory, Ashwater, Beaworthy EX21 5EZ
        T: 01409 211205
        E: jane.e.lucas@btinternet.com
Shirwell Shaun O'Rourke, The Rectory, Barnstaple Hill, Swimbridge, Barnstaple EX32 0PH   *T:* 01271 830950
        E: revd.shaun@gmail.com
South Molton Adrian Mosedale Wells, The Vicarage, The Square, Witheridge, Tiverton EX16 8AE   *T:* 01884 861383
        E: vicaradrian@btinternet.com
Torrington Susanna Metz, The Rectory, Petrockstow, Okehampton EX20 3HQ
        T: 01837 810621
        E: susanna.metz@yahoo.com

ARCHDEACONRY OF EXETER
Aylesbeare James Benjamin Balfour Hutchings, The Rectory, 1 Maer Road, Exmouth EX8 2DA
        T: 01395 225212
        E: hutchingsjames@sky.com
Cadbury Nigel Guthrie, The Rectory, Church Street, Crediton EX17 2AQ   *T:* 01363 772669
        E: rev.guthrie@btinternet.com

Christianity Robin Howard Spenser Eastoe, The Rectory, 10 Victoria Park Road, Exeter EX2 4NT   *T:* 01392 677150
                    E: theeastoes@btinternet.com
Honiton Jeremy Charles Trew, The Vicarage, Colyford Road, Seaton EX12 2DF
                    T: 01297 20391
                    E: jeremytrew@hotmail.com
Kenn Martin Robert Wood, The Rectory, Church Lane, Cheriton Bishop, Exeter EX6 6HY   *T:* 01647 24119
                    E: revwood163@gmail.com
Ottery Mark Ward, The Vicarage, Newton Poppleford, Sidmouth EX10 0HB
                    T: 01395 568390
                    E: revmarkward@btinternet.com
Tiverton and Cullompton Simon George Guy Talbot, The Rectory, Old Village, Willand, Cullompton EX15 2RH   *T:* 01752 245813
                    E: simon@thetalbots.org.uk

ARCHDEACONRY OF PLYMOUTH

Ivybridge Anne Christine Legge, The Rectory, 8 Court Road, Newton Ferrers, Plymouth PL8 1DL   *T:* 01752 873192
                    E: annelegge@live.com
Plymouth City David Brian Michael Gill, The Vicarage, 53 Whitson Cross Lane, Tamerton Foliot, Plymouth PL5 4NT   *T:* 01752 771033
                    E: david@dbmg.freeserve.co.uk

Tavistock Nicholas Charles Law, The Rectory, Bere Alston, Yelverton PL20 7HH
                    T: 01822 840229
                    E: nick123law@gmail.com

ARCHDEACONRY OF TOTNES

Moreton Simon George Franklin, The Rectory, 3 Grays Meadow, Moretonhampstead, Newton Abbot TQ13 8NB   *T:* 01647 441413
                    E: safranklin@btinternet.com
Newton Abbot and Ipplepen Alan White, Flat 3, 7 Courtenay Road, Newton Abbot TQ12 1HP
                    T: 01626 332451
                    E: revalan.white@btopenworld.com
Okehampton Nicholas Patrick Weldon, The Rectory, Essington Close, North Tawton EX20 2EX   *T:* 01837 880183
                    E: npweldon@gmail.com
Torbay Roger John Carlton, The Vicarage, Palace Place, Paignton TQ3 3AQ
                    T: 01803 551866
                    E: roger.carlton@btinternet.com
Totnes Julian Charles Ould, The Rectory, Northgate, Totnes TQ9 5NX
                    T: 01803 862104
                    E: julian@totnesrectory.co.uk
Woodleigh Jacqueline Margaret Taylor, Dodbrooke Rectory, Church Street, Kingsbridge TQ7 1NW   *T:* 07812 589461
                    E: jtaylor808@btinternet.com

DIOCESE OF GLOUCESTER

Founded in 1541. Gloucestershire except for a few parishes in the north, in the diocese of Worcester; a few parishes in the south, in the diocese of Bristol, and one parish in the east, in the diocese of Oxford; in the northern third of South Gloucestershire; two parishes in Wiltshire; a small area in south-west Warwickshire; a few parishes in the souther part of Worcestershire.

Population 663,000   Area 1,130 sq m
Full-time Stipendiary Parochial Clergy 118   Benefices 94
Parishes 301   Churches 385
www.gloucester.anglican.org
Overseas link dioceses:

BISHOP (41st)

The Rt Revd Rachel Treweek, 2 College Green, Gloucester GL1 2LR   *T:* 01452 410022 ext 270
E: bgloucester@glosdioc.org.uk
Home address: Bishopscourt, Pitt Street, Gloucester GL1 2BQ

BISHOP'S STAFF

Bishop's Chaplain The Revd David Gardiner
Bishop's Secretary Mrs Diane Best, The Bishop of Gloucester's Office, 2 College Green, Gloucester GL1 2LR
T: 01452 410022 ext 270
E: dbest@glosdioc.org.uk

SUFFRAGAN BISHOP

TEWKESBURY The Rt Revd Robert Springett, Bishop's House, 3 Hill Road, Gloucester GL4 6ST   *T:* 01452 489456
E: btewkesbury@glosdioc.org.uk

ASSISTANT BISHOPS

The Rt Revd David Jennings, Laurel Cottage, East End, Northleach, Cheltenham GL54 3ET
T: 01451 860743
The Rt Revd Robert Evens, 30 Highland Road, Charlton Kings, Cheltenham GL53 9LT
T: 01242 251411
The Rt Revd Anthony Priddis, Round Oak Cottage, Bridstow, Ross-on-Wye HR9 6QJ
T: 01989 218503
The Rt Revd Christopher Hill, Hillview, Westend, Ruardean, Gloucester GL17 9TP
T: 01594 541831

CATHEDRAL CHURCH OF ST PETER AND THE HOLY AND INDIVISIBLE TRINITY

Dean The Very Revd Stephen Lake, The Deanery, 1 Miller's Green, Gloucester GL1 2BP   *T:* 01452 508217
E: dean@gloucestercathedral.org.uk

Canons Residentiary
Canon Chancellor The Revd Canon Celia Thomson, 3 Miller's Green, Gloucester GL1 2BN   *T:* 01452 415824
E: celia.thomson@gloucestercathedral.org.uk
Residentiary Canons The Ven Jackie Searle, 2 College Green, Gloucester GL1 2LR
T: 01452 835594
E: archdglos@glosdioc.org.uk
The Revd Canon Nikki Arthy, The Rectory, Hempsted, Gloucester GL2 5LW
T: 01452 523808
E: nikkiarthy@btinternet.com
The Revd Canon Andrew Braddock, 4 College Green, Gloucester GL1 2LR
T: 01452 835549
E: abraddock@glosdioc.org.uk
Director of Congregational Development and Canon Precentor The Revd Canon Richard Mitchell, c/o The Cathedral Office, 2 College Green, Gloucester GL1 2BN
T: 01452 332785
E: richard.mitchell@gloucestercathedral.org

Other Staff
Chief Operating Officer Emily Shepherd, The Cathedral Office, 2 College Green, Gloucester GL1 2LX   *T:* 01452 508216
E: emily.shepherd@gloucestercathedral.org.uk
Director of Music Mr Adrian Partington, 7 Miller's Green, Gloucester GL1 2BN
T: 01452 229819
E: adrian.partington@gloucestercathedral.org.uk
Assistant Director of Music Mr Jonathan Hope, 8a College Green, Gloucester GL1 2LX
T: 01452 874964
E: jonathan.hope@gloucestercathedral.org.uk
Singing Development Leader Nia Llewelyn Jones, The Cathedral Office, 2 College Green, Gloucester GL1 2LX   *T:* 01452 508212
E: nia.jones@gloucestercathedral.org.uk

Music Department Manager Mrs Helen Sims
(*Same Address & Tel*)
E: helen.sims@gloucestercathedral.org.uk
Executive PA Mrs Fiona Price, The Cathedral
Office, 12 College Green, Gloucester GL1 2LX
T: 01452 528095
F: 01452 300469
E: fiona.price@gloucestercathedral.org.uk

ARCHDEACONS

CHELTENHAM The Ven Philip John Andrew, 8
Grace Gardens, Cheltenham GL51 6QE
T: 01452 835594
E: archdchelt@glosdioc.org.uk
GLOUCESTER The Ven Jackie Searle, 2 College
Green, Gloucester GL1 2LR   T: 01452 835594
E: archdglos@glosdioc.org.uk

MEMBERS OF THE HOUSE OF CLERGY OF THE GENERAL SYNOD

Proctors for Clergy
The Revd Canon Dr Tudor Griffiths
The Revd Canon Richard Mitchell
The Ven Jackie Searle

MEMBERS OF THE HOUSE OF LAITY OF THE GENERAL SYNOD

Mrs Corinne Aldis
Dr William Belcher
Mr Martin Kingston
Mrs Margaret Sheather

DIOCESAN OFFICERS

Diocesan Secretary Canon Benjamin Preece
Smith, Church House, College Green,
Gloucester GL1 2LY
T: 01452 410022 ext. 236
E: bpreecesmith@glosdioc.org.uk
Chancellor of Diocese The Worshipful June
Rodgers, Gloucester Diocesan Registry, Veale
Wasbrough Vizards, Orchard Court, Orchard
Lane, Bristol BS1 5WS   T: 01173 145680
Registrar of Diocese Mr Jos Moule, Gloucester
Diocesan Regristry, Veale Wasbrough Vizards,
Narrow Quay House, Narrow Quay, Bristol BS1
5WS   T: 01179 252020
E: gloucesterregistry@vwv.co.uk

DIOCESAN ORGANIZATIONS

Diocesan Office Church House, College Green,
Gloucester GL1 2LY   T: 01452 410022
E: church.house@glosdioc.org.uk
W: www.gloucester.anglican.org

ADMINISTRATION

Diocesan Synod (*Chair of the House of Clergy*)
The Revd Canon Richard Mitchell, c/o The

Cathedral Office, 2 College Green, Gloucester
GL1 2BN   T: 01452 332785
E: richard.mitchell@
gloucestercathedral.org
(*Chair of the House of Laity*) Mrs Karen
Czapiewski, Low Wood, Ewen, Cirencester
GL7 6BU   T: 01285 770255
E: karen.czapiewski@btinternet.com
(*Secretary*) Canon Benjamin Preece Smith,
Church House, College Green, Gloucester GL1
2LY   T: 01452 410022 ext. 236
E: bpreecesmith@glosdioc.org.uk
Board of Finance (*Chair*) Mr Colin Rank, The
Old Forge, Kemble, Cirencester GL7 6AA
T: 01285 770491
(*Secretary*) Canon Benjamin Preece Smith,
Church House, College Green, Gloucester GL1
2LY   T: 01452 410022 ext. 236
E: bpreecesmith@glosdioc.org.uk
Resources Committee (*Secretary*) Mrs Judith
Knight, Diocesan Office, Church House,
College Green, Gloucester GL1 2LY
T: 04452 410022 ext. 258
E: jknight@glosdioc.org.uk
Pastoral Committee (*Secretary*) Canon Benjamin
Preece Smith, Church House, College Green,
Gloucester GL1 2LY
T: 01452 410022 ext. 236
E: bpreecesmith@glosdioc.org.uk
Board of Patronage (*Secretary*) Vacancy
Trust (*Secretary*) Canon Benjamin Preece Smith,
Church House, College Green, Gloucester GL1
2LY   T: 01452 410022 ext. 236
E: bpreecesmith@glosdioc.org.uk
Glebe Committee (*Secretary*) Canon Benjamin
Preece Smith (*As above*)
Mrs Paula Taylor (*Same Address*)
T: 01452 410022 ext. 229
E: ptaylor@glosdioc.org.uk
(*Head of HR and Safeguarding*) Mrs Judith
Knight, Diocesan Office, Church House,
College Green, Gloucester GL1 2LY
T: 04452 410022 ext. 258
E: jknight@glosdioc.org.uk

BISHOP'S WORSHIP, PRAYER AND SPIRITUALITY GROUP

Chair The Revd Canon Rob Axford
T: 01453 842175
E: rob@robaxford.plus.com
Secretary Mrs Iona Bird   T: 01452 835551
E: ibird@glosdioc.org.uk

CHURCH BUILDINGS

*Advisory Committee on Faculties and Care of
Churches* (*Chairman*) Mr Henry Russel, Ley
Mary Farmhouse, Windrush, Burford, Oxon
OX18 4TS   T: 01451 844477
(*Secretary*) Mrs Natalie Fenner, Diocesan
Office, Church House, College Green,
Gloucester GL1 2LY

GLOUCESTER

COMMUNICATIONS

Head of Communications Mrs Lucy Taylor, Diocesan Office, Church House, College Green, Gloucester GL1 2LY
　　　　　　　T: 01452 410022 ext. 250
　　　　　　　M: 07811 174125
　　　　　　　E: ltaylor@glosdioc.org.uk
Senior Communications Officers Mrs Katherine Clamp (*Same Address*)
　　　　　　　T: 01452 410022 ext. 291
　　　　　　　E: kclamp@glosdioc.org.uk
Mr Sam Cavender (*Same Address*)
　　　　　　　T: 01452 410022 Ext. 275
　　　　　　　E: scavender@glosdioc.org.uk

DIOCESAN RECORD OFFICE

Gloucestershire Archives, Clarence Row, Alvin Street, Gloucester GL1 3DW
Diocesan Archivist Ms Heather Forbes
　　　　　　　T: 01452 425295
　　　　　　　E: archives@gloucestershire.gov.uk

DIOCESAN RESOURCE CENTRE

Manager Mrs Hannah Hauxwell, 9 College Green, Gloucester GL1 2LX
　　　　　　　T: 01452 835559
　　　　　　　E: hhauxwell@glosdioc.org.uk

EDUCATION DEPARTMENT

Director of Education Mrs Rachel Howie, 4 College Green, Gloucester GL1 2LR
　　　　　　　T: 01452 41002 ext. 272
　　　　　　　E: rhowie@glosdioc.org.uk
Strategic Lead for Governance Mrs Linda Rolfe (*Same Address*)　*T:* 01452 410022 ext. 239
　　　　　　　E: lrolfe@glosdioc.org.uk
Strategic Lead for Buildings Mr Rob Stephens (*Same Address*)　*T:* 01452 410022 ext. 242
　　　　　　　E: rstephens@glosdioc.org.uk

MISSION AND MINISTRY

Director of the Department of Mission and Ministry The Revd Canon Andrew Braddock, 4 College Green, Gloucester GL1 2LR
　　　　　　　T: 01452 835549
　　　　　　　E: abraddock@glosdioc.org.uk
Director of Ordinands and Curate Training The Revd Ian Bussell, 4 College Green, Gloucester GL1 2LR　　　*T:* 01452 835545
Associate Director of Ordinands The Revd David Runcorn (*Same Address*)　*T:* 01452 835548
　　　　　　　E: druncorn@glosdioc.org.uk
Mission and Evangelism Officer The Revd Cate Williams (*Same Address*)　*T:* 01452 835543
Young People and Families Officer The Revd Joanne Wetherall　　*T:* 01452 835552
Warden of Readers The Revd David Runcorn (*Same Address*)　*T:* 01452 835582
　　　　　　　E: druncorn@glosdioc.org.uk

Self Supporting Ministry Officer The Revd Dr Nick Fisher (*Same Address*)　*T:* 01451 861195
　　　　　　　E: nick@5fishers.co.uk
Effective Ministry and Vocations Officer The Revd Pauline Godfrey (*Same Address*)
　　　　　　　T: 01452 835548
　　　　　　　E: pgodfrey@glosdioc.org.uk
Diocesan Ecumenical Officer The Revd Jacqui Hyde　　　　　　*T:* 01242 234955
　　　　　　　E: jacqui@clanhyde.me.uk
Civil Protection Liaison Officer The Revd Peter Cheesman　　　*T:* 01452 740533
　　　　　　　E: peter@the-cheesman.net
Chaplain to the Deaf and Hard of Hearing Community The Revd Steve Morris
　　　　　　　T: 01452 610450
　　　　　　　E: spadework@fsmail.net
Accord Mrs Victoria Braddock
　　　　　　　T: 01452 835546
　　　　　　　E: accordcourses@glosdioc.org.uk
Interfaith Advisor The Revd Simon Howell
　　　　　　　T: 01453 350387
　　　　　　　E: revsimonhowell@blueyonder.co.uk
Link Officer with the Committee for Minority Anglican Concerns The Revd Frances Quist
　　　　　　　E: francesquist@btinternet.com

AREA DEANS
ARCHDEACONRY OF CHELTENHAM

Cheltenham Nicholas Duff Davies, The Rectory, 80 Painswick Road, Cheltenham GL50 2EU
　　　　　　　T: 01242 321268
　　　　　　　E: nickduffdavies@gmail.com
Cirencester Howard Neil Gilbert, The Parsonage, 32 Watermoor Road, Cirencester GL7 1JR　　　　　*T:* 01285 885109
　　　　　　　E: father.howard@gmail.com
North Cotswold Katrina Ruth Scott, The Rectory, Copse Hill Road, Lower Slaughter, Cheltenham GL54 2HY　　*T:* 07799 065987
　　　　　　　E: krgscott@hotmail.com
Tewkesbury and Winchcombe Malcolm Allen, The Rectory, 4 Church Approach, Bishops Cleeve, Cheltenham GL52 8NG
　　　　　　　T: 01242 677851
　　　　　　　E: malc.rector@gmail.com

ARCHDEACONRY OF GLOUCESTER

Forest South Christopher Willis Maclay, St James's Vicarage, Coleford Road, Bream, Lydney GL15 6ES　　　*T:* 01594 368558
　　　　　　　E: chris.maclay@gmail.com
Gloucester City Janet Dorothy Faull, St Barnabas' Vicarage, 200 Reservoir Road, Gloucester GL4 6SB　　*T:* 07986 650459
　　　　　　　E: janetfaull@btinternet.com
Severn Vale Simon Ion Vincent Mason, The Rectory, 43 Court Road, Newent GL18 1SY
　　　　　　　T: 01531 820248
　　　　　　　E: mason.simon@ntlworld.com

Stroud Michael Richard Guy Smith, The Vicarage, 3 Vicarage Gardens, Nailsworth, Stroud GL6 0QS   *T:* 07840 260182
E: mike.davica@sky.com

Wotton David John Russell, The Rectory, 75 High Street, Wickwar, Wotton-under-Edge GL12 8NP   *T:* 01454 294267
E: davidrussell@gmx.com

DIOCESE OF GUILDFORD

Founded in 1927. The western two-thirds of Surrey south of the Thames, except for a small area in the north-east, in the diocese of Southwark; areas of north-east Hampshire; a few parishes in Greater London; one parish in West Sussex.

Population 1,052,000   Area 530 sq m
Full-time Stipendiary Parochial Clergy 177   Benefices 139
Parishes 162   Churches 212
Overseas link dioceses: IDWAL (Inter-Diocesan West Africa Link) Nigeria

BISHOP (9th)
The Rt Revd Andrew Watson, Willow Grange, Woking Road, Guildford GU4 7QS
T: 01483 590500
F: 01483 590501
E: bishop.guildford@cofeguildford.org.uk

BISHOP'S STAFF
Bishop's Chaplain The Revd Roland Olliff
E: roland.oliff@cofeguildford.org.uk
Bishop's Personal Assistant Mary Morris
E: mary.morris@cofeguildford.org.uk

SUFFRAGAN BISHOP
DORKING The Rt Revd Dr Jo Bailey Wells
Bishop's Personal Assistant Muriel Mulvany, Dayspring, 13 Pilgrim's Way, Guildford GU4 8AD
T: 01483 570829
F: 01483 567268
E: muriel.mulvany@cofeguildford.org.uk

CATHEDRAL CHURCH OF THE HOLY SPIRIT
Dean The Very Revd Dianna Gwilliams
T: 01483 547861 (office)
E: dean@guildford-cathedral.org
Canons Residentiary
Sub Dean The Ven Stuart Beake, Holly Hocks Barn, Holly Hocks Cottage, Hyde Street, Bramley, Guildford GU5 0HB
T: 01483 893981
E: stuart.beake@guildford-cathedral.org.uk
Canon Residentiary and University Chaplain The Revd Canon Dr Andrew Bishop, 6 Cathedral Close, Guildford GU2 7TL   *T:* 07891 994069
E: a.bishop@surrey.ac.uk
Canon Residentiary The Revd Canon Dr Julie Gittoes, 4 Cathedral Close, Guildford GU2 7TL   *T:* 07702 151173
E: julie@guildford-cathedral.org
Canon Liturgist (from 5/11/17) The Revd Canon Dr Paul Smith, 3 Cathedral Close, Guildford GU2 7TL   *T:* 01483 547865
E: paul.smith@guildford-cathedral.org

Other Staff
Dean's Personal Assistant Miss Emma Law
T: 01483 547862 (office)
E: deanspa@guildford-cathedral.org
Director of Operations Mr Matt O'Grady
T: 01483 547864
E: dops@guildford-cathedral.org
Cathedral Organist and Master of the Choristers Mrs Katherine Dienes-Williams, 5 Cathedral Close, Guildford GU2 7TL   *T:* 01483 54/866
E: organist@guildford-cathedral.org

ARCHDEACONS
SURREY The Ven Paul Davies (from 10/12/17)
DORKING The Ven Paul Bryer, Church House, 20 Alan Turing Road, Guildford GU2 7YF
T: 01483 790352
E: paul.bryer@cofeguildford.org.uk

MEMBERS OF THE HOUSE OF CLERGY OF THE GENERAL SYNOD
Proctors for Clergy
Vacancy
The Rt Revd Andrew Watson
The Ven Paul Bryer
The Revd Canon Robert Cotton
The Revd Cathy Blair

MEMBERS OF THE HOUSE OF LAITY OF THE GENERAL SYNOD
Vacancy
Canon Peter Bruinvels
Mrs Carolyn Graham
Mr James Lee

DIGNITARIES IN CONVOCATION
The Rt Revd Andrew Watson

DIOCESAN OFFICERS
Diocesan Secretary Mr Peter Coles, Church House, 20 Alan Turing Road, Guildford GU2 7YF
T: 01483 790300
F: 01483 790333
E: diocesan.secretary@cofeguildford.org.uk

Chancellor of Diocese Mr Andrew Jordan, 11 Fairlawn Avenue, Chiswick, London W4 5EF
Registrar of Diocese and Bishop's Legal Secretary Mr Howard Dellar, 1 The Sanctuary, Westminster, London SW1P 3JT
T: 020 7222 5381
F: 020 7222 7502
Deputy Registrars Susan Newell
Ian Blaney

DIOCESAN ORGANIZATIONS
Diocesan Office Church House, 20 Alan Turing Road, Guildford GU2 7YF   T: 01483 790300
F: 01483 790333

ADMINISTRATION
Diocesan Synod (President) The Rt Revd Andrew Watson
(Vice-President, House of Clergy) The Revd Cathy Blair, St Paul's Vicarage, Pembroke Road, Woking GU22 7ED   T: 01483 850489
E: cathy@stpaulswoking.org.uk
(Vice-President, House of Laity) Mrs Anne Martin, 8 Woodberry Close, Chiddingfold GU8 4SF   T: 01428 683854
(Secretary) Mr Peter Coles, Church House, 20 Alan Turing Road, Guildford GU2 7YF
T: 01483 790300
F: 01483 790333
E: diocesan.secretary@cofeguildford.org.uk
(Deputy Secretary) Mr Nick Edmonds *(Same Address)*   T: 01483 790303
E: nick.edmonds@cofeguildford.org.uk
Board of Finance (Chairman) Mr Nigel Lewis *(Same Address)*
(Accountant) Mr Malcolm Twigger-Ross, Old Alresford Place, Alresford SO24 9DH
T: 01962 737336
E: malcolm.twigger-ross@cofeguildford.org.uk
Pastoral Committee Mrs Wendy Harris, Church House, 20 Alan Turing Road, Guildford GU2 7YF   E: wendy.harris@cofeguildford.org.uk
(Designated Officer) Mr Howard Dellar, 1 The Sanctuary, Westminster, London SW1P 3JT
T: 020 7222 5381
F: 020 7222 7502

CHURCH BUILDINGS
Advisory Committee for the Care of Churches (Chairman) Mr John Alpass, Church House, 20 Alan Turing Road, Guildford GU2 7YF
(Secretary) Mrs Wendy Harris *(Same Address)*
E: wendy.harris@cofeguildford.org.uk

COMMUNICATIONS
Director of Communications Mr Nick Edmonds, Church House, 20 Alan Turing Road, Guildford GU2 7YF   T: 01483 790303
E: nick.edmonds@cofeguildford.org.uk

Media Officers Kate Jamieson
T: 01483 790345
David Green *(Same Tel)*
Editors of Diocesan Newspaper Kate Jamieson
T: 01483 790347
E: editorial@cofeguildford.org.uk
David Green *(Same Tel & email)*
Information and Web Administrator Mrs Mary Peters   T: 01483 790355
out of hours emergency no: 07500 042769
E: mary.peters@cofeguildford.org

COMMUNITIES ENGAGEMENT
Interim Director Jo Cookes, Church House, 20 Alan Turing Road, Guildford GU2 7YF
E: jo.cookes@cofeguildford.org.uk
Church and Community Adviser Tony Oakden *(Same Address)*   T: 01483 790325
E: tony.oakden@cofeguildford.org.uk
Health and Wellbeing Adviser Suzette Jones *(Same Address)*   T: 01483 790335
E: suzette.jones@cofeguildford.org.uk
Sensory Inclusion Adviser Tracey Wade *(Same Address)*   T: 01483 790327
E: tracey.wade@cofeguildford.org.uk
Surrey Faith Links Kauser Akhtar *(Same Address & Tel)*   E: kauser.akhtar@cofeguildford.org.uk
Bishop's Adviser for Hospital Chaplaincy The Revd Canon Judith Allford
E: jallford@btinternet.com

DIOCESAN RECORD OFFICE
Surrey History Centre, 130 Goldsworth Rd, Woking GU2 1ND
Team Leader, Heritage Public Services Mr Julian Pooley
Special Collections Archivist Di Stiff
T: 01483 518737

DISCIPLESHIP, VOCATION AND MINISTRY
Director of Discipleship, Vocation and Ministry and Co-Chair South Central Regional Training Partnership The Revd Canon Dr Hazel Whitehead, Church House, Alan Turing Road, Guildford GU2 7YF   T: 01483 790307
E: hazel.whitehead@cofeguildford.org.uk
Director of Ordinands, Vocations and IME 4–7 The Revd William Challis, Church House, 20 Alan Turing Road, Guildford GU2 7YF
T: 01483 790322
E: william.challis@cofeguildford.org.uk
Local Ministry Programme (Principal) The Revd Dr Steve Summers *(Same Address)*
T: 01483 790319
E: steve.summers@cofeguildford.co.uk
(Warden of Licensed Lay Ministers) Mrs Gertrud Sollars, 6 Overbrook, Godalming GU7 1LX
E: wardenoffilms@cofeguildford.org

(*Senior Tutor for Pastoral Assistants' Foundation Training*) Mrs Sue Lawrence, Church House, 20 Alan Turing Road, Guildford GU2 7YF
T: 01483 790321
E: sue.lawrence@cofeguildford.org.uk
(*CMD Tutors for Pastoral Assistants*) The Revd Canon Maggie Marsh *T:* 01483 790300
E: maggie.marsh@cofeguildford.org.uk
The Revd Christine White
E: christine.white@cofeguildford.org.uk
(*Vocations Officer*) The Revd Laurence Gamlen
T: 01483 790300
E: laurence.gamlen@cofeguildford.org.uk
(*Assessing the End of Curacy Officer*) The Revd Barbara Steele-Perkins (*Same Tel*)
E: barbara.steeleperkins@cofeguildford.org.uk
Readers' Board (*Registrar*) Dr Stephen Linton, 18 Bridgefield, Farnham, GU9 8AN
T: 01252 715209
E: registrarofllms@cofeguildford.org.uk
(*Adult Discipleship and Development Adviser*) The Revd Matt Prior *T:* 01483 790309
E: matt.prior@cofeguildford.org.uk
(*Diocesan Spiritual Growth Facilitator*) The Revd Sarah Hutton
E: sarah.hutton@cofeguildford.org.uk
(*Spiritual Direction Co-ordinator*) The Revd Canon Andrew Tuck
E: andrew.tuck@cofeguildford.org.uk

EDUCATION
Diocesan Education Centre, Stag Hill, Guildford GU2 7UP *T:* 01483 450423
F: 01483 450424
Director of Education and Secretary, Diocesan Board of Education Stephen Green
E: stephen.green@guildford.org.uk
Schools Officer RE, Spiritual Development and Christian Distinctiveness of Church Schools Mrs Jane Whittington
School Estates Officer Mr David Hallam
Further Education Adviser Vacancy
Centre Manager/PA to Director Mrs Sarah Tickner
Deputy Director of Education – Schools Mr Michael Hall

PARISH DEVELOPMENT AND EVANGELISM
Director The Revd Alan Hulme, Diocesan Education Centre, Stag Hill, Guildford GU2 7UP *T:* 01483 484921
E: alan.hulme@cofeguildford.org.uk
Stewardship Adviser Mrs Juliet Evans (*Same Address*) *T:* 01483 484923
E: juliet.evans@cofeguildford.org.uk
Local Mission Adviser Preb Stephen Cox (*Same Address*) *T:* 01483 484922
E: stephen.cox@cofeguildford.org.uk
Youth Ministry Adviser Mr David Welch (*Same Address*) *T:* 01483 484908
E: david.welch@cofeguildford.org.uk

Children and Families Ministry Adviser Mrs Alison Hendy (*Same Address*)
T: 01483 484910
E: alison.hendy@cofeguildford.org.uk
Healing Adviser The Revd Elizabeth Knifton
E: eknifton@acornchristian.org
World Mission Adviser The Revd Andrew Wheeler
E: andrew.wheeler@st-saviours.org.uk
Nigeria Link Officer The Revd David Minns
E: dkminns@btinternet.com
Sports Ministry Adviser The Revd Clive Potter, The Vicarage, Milford Heath Road, Milford GU8 5BX *T:* 01483 414710
E: milfordvicarage@gmail.com
Church Heritage and Tourism Adviser Vacancy

RETIRED CLERGY MINISTER
The Revd Canon John Salter, 7 Aldershot Road, Guildford GU2 8AE
T: 01483 511165
E: j.salter@btinternet.com

RURAL DEANS
ARCHDEACONRY OF DORKING
Dorking Alan Charles Jonas, The Vicarage, Guildford Road, Westcott, Dorking RH4 3QB
T: 01306 885309
E: alchasjonas@aol.com
Emly Phillip Thomas Johnson, All Saints' Vicarage, 1 Chestnut Avenue, Esher KT10 8JL
T: 020 8398 9685
E: vicar@allsaintschurchweston.org.uk
Epsom Desmond Carl Williamson, St Mark's Vicarage, St Mark's Road, Epsom KT18 5RD
T: 01737 353011
E: deswilliamson@tiscali.co.uk
Leatherhead Alan David Jenkins, The Rectory, 2A Fife Way, Bookham, Leatherhead KT23 3PH *T:* 01372 452405
E: alan.jenkins@stnicolasbookham.org.uk
Runnymede Sandra Christine Faccini, 50 Slade Road, Ottershaw, Chertsey KT16 0HZ
T: 01932 873160
E: sandra@faccinis.freeserve.co.uk
Woking Peter James Harwood, Christ Church Vicarage, 10 Russetts Close, Woking GU21 4BH *T:* 01483 762100
E: peter.harwood@christchurchwoking.org

ARCHDEACONRY OF SURREY
Aldershot George Peter Howgill Newton, 2 Cranmore Lane, Aldershot GU11 3AS
T: 01252 320618
E: g@gjsk.prestel.co.uk
Cranleigh Deborah Mary Sellin, The Vicarage, The Street, Wonersh, Guildford GU5 0PG
T: 01483 890453
E: d.sellin@ntlworld.com

Farnham Jane Louise Walker, The Vicarage, The Street, Frensham, Farnham GU10 3DT
T: 01252 792137
E: revjanewalker@gmail.com

Godalming Clive Geoffrey Potter, The New Vicarage, Milford Heath, Milford, Godalming GU8 5BX
T: 01483 414710
E: milfordvicarage@gmail.com

Guildford Nicholas Jolyon Williams, Christ Church Vicarage, 25 Waterden Road, Guildford GU1 2AZ
T: 01483 568870
E: nick@christchurchguildford.com

Surrey Heath Vacancy

DIOCESE OF HEREFORD

Founded in 676. Herefordshire; the southern half of Shropshire; a few parishes in Powys and Monmouthshire.

Population 326,000   Area 1,650 sq m
Full-time Stipendiary Parochial Clergy 85   Benefices 86
Parishes 340   Churches 403
Overseas link dioceses: Masasi and Tanga with Zanzibar,
Dar es Salaam (Tanzania), Kirchenkreis of Nurnberg

BISHOP
The Rt Revd Richard M. C. Frith, The Bishop's House, The Palace, Hereford HR4 9BN
T: 01432 271355
E: bishop@hereford.anglican.org

BISHOP'S STAFF
Chaplain to the Bishop of Hereford Preb Brian Chave
T: 01432 271355
E: b.chave@hereford.anglican.org
PA to the Bishop of Hereford Mrs Susan Lawson (*Same Tel*)
E: s.lawson@hereford.anglican.org
Secretary to the Bishop of Hereford Mrs Gail James (*Same Tel*)
E: g.james@hereford.anglican.org

SUFFRAGAN BISHOP
LUDLOW The Rt Revd Alistair J. Magowan, Bishop's House, Corvedale Road, Craven Arms, Shropshire SY7 9BT   T: 01588 673571
F: 01588 673571
E: office@bishopofludlow.co.uk
PA to the Bishop of Ludlow Mrs Joanne Gibbon (*Same Tel & email*)

HONORARY ASSISTANT BISHOPS
The Rt Revd Michael Bourke, The Maltings, Little Stretton SY6 6AP   T: 01694 722910
E: steamtrainhouse@yahoo.co.uk
The Rt Revd Robert Paterson, Cedar House, 63 Greenhill, Evesham WR11 4LX
T: 01386 247105
E: mar.erskine@me.com
The Rt Revd Michael Westall, Oak House, Kingstone, Hereford   T: 01981 250259
E: michaelwestall39@gmail.com

CATHEDRAL CHURCH OF THE BLESSED VIRGIN MARY AND ST ETHELBERT
Dean The Very Revd Michael Tavinor, The Deanery, College Cloisters, Hereford HR1 2NG   T: 01432 374203
E: dean@herefordcathedral.org

Canons Residentiary
Chancellor The Revd Canon Christopher Pullin, 2 Cathedral Close, Hereford HR1 2NG
T: 01432 374273
E: chancellor@herefordcathedral.org
Precentor The Revd Canon Andrew Piper, 1 Cathedral Close, Hereford HR1 2NG
T: 01432 374200
E: precentor@herefordcathedral.org
Minor Canon
Cathedral Chaplain The Revd Preb Pam Row, 6 Gorsty Lane, Hereford HR1 1UL
T: 01432 842867
E: pam.row@herefordcathedral.org
Other Staff
Additional Members Canon Richard Price, Cathedral Office, 5 College Cloisters, Hereford HR1 2NG
Canon Gordon Powell (*Same Address*)
Canon Barbara Gratton (*Same Address*)
Chapter Clerk and Chief Executive Glyn Morgan (*Same Address*)   T: 01432 374201
E: glyn.morgan@herefordcathedral.org
Director of Music Mr Geraint Bowen, 7 College Cloisters, Hereford HR1 2NG
T: 01432 374238
E: organist@herefordcathedral.org
Assistant Director of Music Mr Peter Dyke, 1a Cathedral Close, Hereford HR1 2NG
T: 01432 374272
E: peter.dyke@herefordcathedral.org

ARCHDEACONS
HEREFORD The Ven Paddy Benson, Diocesan Office, The Palace, Hereford HR4 9BL
T: 01432 373316
E: archdeacon@hereford.anglican.org
LUDLOW The Rt Revd Alistair J. Magowan, Bishop's House, Corvedale Road, Craven Arms, Shropshire SY7 9BT   T: 01588 673571
E: office@bishopofludlow.co.uk

MEMBERS OF THE HOUSE OF CLERGY OF THE GENERAL SYNOD
Proctors for Clergy
The Revd Laura Dalton

The Revd Preb Simon Cawdell
The Revd Neil Patterson

MEMBERS OF THE HOUSE OF LAITY OF THE GENERAL SYNOD
Wendy Coombey
Dr Martin Elcock
Elizabeth Bird

DIOCESAN OFFICERS
Diocesan Secretary Mr Sam Pratley, Diocesan Office, The Palace, Hereford HR4 9BL
T: 01432 373300
F: 01432 352952
E: s.pratley@hereford.anglican.org
Chancellor of Diocese Chancellor R. Kaye, c/o Hereford Diocesan Registry, 1 The Sanctuary, London SW1P 3JT   *T:* 020 7222 5381
Registrar of Diocese and Bishop's Legal Secretary Mr Howard Dellar, 1 The Sanctuary, Westminster, London SW1P 3JT (*Same Tel*)
F: 020 7222 7502
Diocesan Surveyor Mr Mike Williams, The Diocesan Office, The Palace, Herefod HR4 9BL   *T:* 01432 373300/301

DIOCESAN ORGANIZATIONS
Diocesan Office The Palace, Hereford HR4 9BL
T: 01432 373300
F: 01432 352952
E: diooffice@hereford.anglican.org

ADMINISTRATION
Diocesan Synod (*Chairman, House of Clergy*) The Revd Preb S. H. Cawdell, The Rectory, 16 East Castle Street, Bridgnorth, Shropshire WV16 4AL   *T:* 01746 761573
(*Chairman, House of Laity*) Vacancy
(*Secretary*) Mr Sam Pratley, Diocesan Office, The Palace, Hereford HR4 9BL
T: 01432 373300
F: 01432 352952
E: s.pratley@hereford.anglican.org
Board of Finance (*Chairman*) The Revd J. Rogers (*Same Address & Tel*)
(*Secretary*) Mr Sam Pratley (*Same Address & Tel*)   *F:* 01432 352952
E: s.pratley@hereford.anglican.org
(*Director of Finance*) Mr Stephen Herbert (*Same Address*)
Benefice Buildings Committee Mr Stephen Challenger (*Same Address*)
Glebe Committee Mr Stephen Challenger (*As above*)
Board of Patronage Mr Sam Pratley (*Same Address*)
T: 01432 373300
F: 01432 352952
E: s.pratley@hereford.anglican.org

(*Designated Officer*) Mr Howard Dellar, 1 The Sanctuary, Westminster, London SW1P 3JT
T: 020 7222 5381
F: 020 7222 7502
Trusts Mr Sam Pratley, Diocesan Office, The Palace, Hereford HR4 9BL   *T:* 01432 373300
F: 01432 352952
E: s.pratley@hereford.anglican.org

BORDERLANDS RURAL CHAPLAINCY
Ecumenical Agricultural Chaplain David Gwatkin   *T:* 07531 676832

CHURCH BUILDINGS
Advisory Committee for the Care of Churches (*Chairman*) Mrs Joyce Marston, Diocesan Office, The Palace, Hereford HR4 9BL
(*Secretary*) Mr Stephen Challenger (*Same Address*)

COMMUNITY LINK DEVELOPMENT OFFICER
Christine Pepler, Diocesan Office (Ludlow), Units 8/9, The Business Quarter, Ludlow Eco Park, Sheet Road, Ludlow SY8 1FD   *T:* 01584 871077
E: c.pepler@hereford.anglican.org

COMMUNITY PARTNERSHIP AND FUNDING
Interfaith Officer Preb David Roberts, 14 Beaconsfield Park, The Sheet, Ludlow SY8 4LY
T: 01584 878568
E: dhroberts38@gmail.com
Community Partnership and Funding Officer Wendy Coombey, Diocesan Office (Ludlow), Units 8/9, The Business Quarter, Ludlow Eco Park, Sheet Road, Ludlow SY8 1FD
T: 01584 871088
E: w.coombey@hereford.anglican.org

DIOCESAN RECORD OFFICE
Shropshire Archives Castle Gates, Shrewsbury, SY1 2AQ   *T:* 0345 678 9096
Herefordshire Archives and Records Centre Fir Tree Lane, Rotherwas, Hereford HR2 6LA
T: 01432 260750

EDUCATION
Director of Education Mr Philip Sell, Diocesan Office (Ludlow), Units 8/9, The Business Quarter, Ludlow Eco Park, Sheet Road, Ludlow SY8 1FD
Children and Families Support Officer Mrs Lizzie Hackney   *T:* 01584 871078
E: cfso@hereford.anglican.org

LUDLOW MASCALL CENTRE
T: 01584 873882
F: 01584 877945

MINISTRY AND TRAINING
Diocesan Director of Vocations and Ordinands (DDVO) The Revd Neil Patterson, Diocesan Office (Ludlow), Units 8/9, The Business Quarter, Ludlow Eco Park, Sheet Road, Ludlow SY8 1FD   *T:* 01584 871080
          E: ddvo@hereford.anglican.org
Ministerial and Spiritual Development and Curate Training Officer The Revd Nicholas Helm (*Same Address*)   *T:* 01584 871082
Mission Support Officer The Revd Caroline Pascoe (*Same Address*)   *T:* 01584 871086
Local Ministry Officer The Revd Dr John Daniels (*Same Address*)   *T:* 01584 871081
Self-supporting Ministry Adviser The Revd Anne Lanyon-Hogg, 7 Lockyear Close, Colwall, Malvern WR13 6NR   *T:* 01684 541979
Dean of Women's Ministry The Revd Preb Jane Davies, The Vicarage, Lugwardine, Herefordshire HR1 4AE   *T:* 01432 850244
Readers' Association (*Warden*) The Revd Dr John Daniels, Diocesan Office (Ludlow), Units 8/9, The Business Quarter, Ludlow Eco Park, Sheet Road, Ludlow SY8 1FD
          T: 01584 871081
Clergy Widows'/Widowers' Officers The Revd Dr Chris Fletcher   *T:* 01432 273149
The Revd Nigella Tyson   *T:* 01568 760610

MISSIONARY AND ECUMENICAL
Ecumenical Committee (*Chairman*) The Very Revd Michael Tavinor, The Deanery, College Cloisters, Hereford HR1 2NG
          T: 01432 374203
          E: dean@herefordcathedral.org
Council for World Partnership and Development (*Chairman*) Vacancy

PRESS, PUBLICITY AND PUBLICATIONS
Communications Director Mrs Catherine Cashmore, Diocesan Office, The Palace, Hereford HR4 9BL   *T:* 01432 373342
          E: ccashmore@hereford.anglican.org

RETIRED CLERGY OFFICER
The Revd Preb Andrew Talbot-Ponsonby
          T: 01432 264725

RURAL DEANS
ARCHDEACONRY OF HEREFORD
Abbeydore Nicholas Gerard Lowton, Forest Mill, Craswall, Hereford HR2 0PW
          T: 01981 510675
          E: lowton.nicholas@virgin.net
Bromyard Clive Roger Evans, The Vicarage, 28 Church Lane, Bromyard HR7 4DZ
          T: 01885 788275
          E: cliver.evans@tiscali.co.uk
Hereford Christopher Kevin William Moore, The Rectory, Fownhope, Hereford HR1 4PS
          T: 01432 860365
          E: chris@cm5j.com
Kington and Weobley Stephen Hollinghurst, The Rectory, St David's Street, Presteigne LD8 2BP   *T:* 01544 267777
          E: revsteve.hollinghurst@gmail.com
Ledbury Robert Ward, The Rectory, Cradley, Malvern WR13 5LQ   *T:* 01886 880438
          E: frrob@wardmail.fslife.co.uk
Leominster Michael John Kneen, The Rectory, Church Street, Leominster HR6 8NH
          T: 01568 615709
          E: mjkneen@btinternet.com
Ross and Archenfield Mark Johnson, Becket House, Much Birch, Hereford HR2 8HT
          T: 01981 540390
          E: revmark100@yahoo.co.uk

ARCHDEACONRY OF LUDLOW
Bridgnorth Jeannetta Hermina Stokes, The Vicarage, Hallon, Worfield, Bridgnorth WV15 5JZ   *T:* 01746 716698
          E: jeannetta.stokes@btopenworld.com
Clun Forest Stephanie Ann Cecilia Fountain, The Vicarage, Church Lane, Bishops Castle SY9 5AF   *T:* 01588 638095
          E: stephaniefountain@yahoo.co.uk
Condover Richard Hugh Oldham Hill, The Rectory, Ashbrook Meadow, Carding Mill Valley, Church Stretton SY6 6JF
          T: 01694 722585
          E: richard.hill@strettonparish.org.uk
Ludlow William Ashley Buck, The Rectory, The Hurst, Cleobury Mortimer, Kidderminster DY14 8EG   *T:* 01299 270264
          E: ashley.astrolabe@virgin.net
Pontesbury Margaret Angela Jones, The Deanery, Main Road, Pontesbury, Shrewsbury SY5 0PS   *T:* 01743 792221
          E: magz.stgeorges@talktalk.net
Telford Severn Gorge Ian Stuart Naylor, The Rector's House, Paradise, Coalbrookdale, Telford TF8 7NR   *T:* 01952 433248
          E: iandjnaylor@hotmail.co.uk

Founded in 2014. West Yorkshire, Yorkshire Dales,
areas of Barnsley, east Lancashire and
south-western County Durham.

Population 2,723,000   Area 2,630 sq m
Full-time Stipendiary Parochial Clergy 335   Benefices 304
Parishes 462   Churches 613
Overseas link dioceses: Colombo and Kurunagala (Sri Lanka), Erfurt (Germany),
Faisalabad (Pakistan), Mara, Rorya and Tarime (Tanzania), Skara (Sweden),
South Western Virginia (USA), Sudan

DIOCESAN BISHOP (1st)
The Rt Revd Nicholas Baines, Hollin House,
Weetwood Avenue, Leeds LS16 5NG
   E: lyndsay.horsman@leeds.anglican.org

BISHOP'S STAFF
Bishop's Chaplain The Revd Lynn Thorius,
Hollin House, Weetwood Avenue, Leeds LS16
5NG   T: 0113 284 4304
   E: lynn.thorius@leeds.anglican.org

AREA BISHOPS
BRADFORD The Rt Revd Toby Howarth, 47
Kirkgate, Shipley BD18 3EH   T: 01274 407471
   E: bishop.toby@leeds.anglican.org
HUDDERSFIELD The Rt Revd Jonathan Gibbs, Sir
John Ramsden Court, Ground Floor,
University of Huddersfield, Huddersfield HD1
2AQ   T: 01484 471801
   E: bishop.jonathan@leeds.anglican.org
RICHMOND The Rt Revd Paul Slater, Church
House, 17-19 York Place, Leeds LS1 2EX
   T: 0113 284 4302
   E: bishop.paul@leeds.anglican.org
RIPON The Rt Revd Helen-Ann Hartley (from
4/2/18)
WAKEFIELD The Rt Revd Tony Robinson, Church
House, 1 South Parade, Wakefield WF1 1LP
   T: 01924 250781
   E: bishop.tony@leeds.anglican.org

ASSISTANT BISHOPS
The Rt Revd Dr Colin Buchanan, 21 The Drive,
Alwoodley, Leeds LS17 7QB
   T: 0113 267 7721
The Rt Revd Dr Tom Butler, Overtown Grange
Cottage, The Balk, Walton, Wakefield WF2
6JX   T: 01924 256018
   E: bishop.tom@leeds.anglican.org
The Rt Revd Clive Handford, Wayside, 1 The
Terrace, Kirkby Hill, Boroughbridge YO51
9DQ   T: 01423 325406
   E: gchandford@gmail.com

The Rt Revd Glyn Webster, Holy Trinity
Rectory, Micklegate, York YO1 6LE
   T: 01904 628155
   E: office@seeofbeverley.org
The Rt Revd Christopher Paul Edmondson, 16
Cavalier Drive, Apperley Bridge, Bradford
BD10 0UF   T: 01274 284031
   E: chris.edmondson@me.com

CATHEDRAL CHURCH OF ST PETER BRADFORD
Dean The Very Revd Jerry Lepine, The Deanery,
1 Cathedral Close, Bradford BD1 4EG
   T: 01274 777720 (Office)
   E: jerry.lepine@bradfordcathedral.org
Canons Residentiary
Canon Precentor The Revd Canon Paul
Maybury, 3 Cathedral Close, Bradford BD1
4EG   T: 01274 777720
   E: paul.maybury@bradfordcathedral.org
Canon for Mission and Pastoral Development The
Revd Canon Mandy Coutts, 2 Cathedral
Close, Bradford BD1 4EG (*Same Tel*)
   E: mandy.coutts@bradfordcathedral.org
Other Staff
Director of Strategic Development and Operations
Ms Amanda Anderson, Bradford Cathedral,
Stott Hill, Bradford BD1 4EH   T: 01274 777726
   E: amanda.anderson@bradfordcathedral.org
Education and Visitor Officer Mrs Gillian Davis,
(*Same Address*)   T: 01274 777734
   E: gillian.davis@bradfordcathedral.org
Director of Music Alexander Berry
Assistant Director of Music Jon Payne
Head Verger and Reader Mr Jon Howard,
Bradford Cathedral, Stott Hill, Bradford BD1
4EH   T: 01274 777724
   E: jon.howard@bradfordcathedral.org
PA to the Dean and Communications Officer Mrs
Sandra Howard (*Same Address*)
   T: 01274 777723
   E: sandra.howard@bradfordcathedral.org
Music Administrator Ann Foster
Director of Finance Simon Dennis

Safeguarding Officer The Revd Canon Mandy Coutts, 2 Cathedral Close, Bradford BD1 4EG
T: 01274 777720
E: mandy.coutts@bradfordcathedral.org
Assistant Safeguarding Officer Ms Amanda Anderson, Bradford Cathedral, Stott Hill, Bradford BD1 4EH   *T:* 01274 777726
E: amanda.anderson@bradfordcathedral.org

CATHEDRAL CHURCH OF ST PETER AND ST WILFRID, RIPON
Dean The Very Revd John Dobson, Minster House, Bedern Bank, Ripon HG4 1PE
T: 01765 602609
E: deanjohn@riponcathedral.org.uk
Canons Residentiary
Canon Precentor The Revd Canon Paul Greenwell, St Wilfrid's House, Minster Close, Ripon HG4 1QP   *T:* 01765 600211
E: canonpaul@riponcathedral.org.uk
The Revd Canon Barry Pyke, 16 Primrose Drive, Ripon HG4 1EY
E: canonbarry@riponcathedral.org.uk
The Revd Canon Ailsa Newby, St Peter's House, Minster Close, Ripon HG4 1QP
E: canonailsa@riponcathedral.org.uk
Other Staff
Dean's Secretary Mrs Judith Bustard
T: 01765 603462
E: judithbustard@riponcathedral.org.uk
Director of Operations Miss Julia Barker, Cathedral Office, Liberty Courthouse, Minster Road, Ripon HG4 1QS (*Same Tel*)
E: juliabarker@riponcathedral.org.uk
Director of Music Mr Andrew Bryden, c/o Ripon Cathedral, Ripon HG4 1QT   *T:* 01765 603496
E: andrewbryden@
riponcathedral.org.uk

CATHEDRAL CHURCH OF ALL SAINTS, WAKEFIELD
Dean Vacancy
Canons Residentiary
Canons Residentiary The Revd Canon Derek Walmsley, 14 Belgravia Road, Wakefield WF1 3JP   *T:* 01924 434451
E: derek.walmsley@leeds.anglican.org
Canon Precentor The Revd Canon Leah Vasey-Saunders, 3 Cathedral Close, Margaret Street, Wakefield WF1 2DP   *T:* 01924 373923
E: precentor@wakefield-cathedral.org.uk
Canon Librarian The Revd Canon Dr John Lawson, 7 Belgravia Road, St John's, Wakefield WF1 3JP   *T:* 01924 380182
E: john.lawson@leeds.anglican.org
Sub Dean and Canon Pastor The Revd Canon Tony Macpherson, 3 Cathedral Close, Margaret Street, Wakefield WF1 2DP
T: 07780 990354
E: canontonymac@gmail.com

Other Staff
Office Manager & Dean's PA Mr Neil Holland
T: 01924 373923
E: neil.holland@wakefield-cathedral.org.uk
Head Verger Mrs Julie Lovell
T: 01924 434486 (direct line)
Priest Vicar The Revd June Lawson
T: 07780 990354
E: jlawson@mirfield.org.uk
Community Learning Manager Tracey Yates
T: 01924 373923
E: tracey.yates@wakefield-cathedral.org.uk
Director of Music Mr Tom Moore, Cathedral Centre, 8–10 Westmorland Street, Wakefield WF1 1PJ
E: tom.moore@wakefield-cathedral.org.uk
Curate The Revd Tim Stevens
T: 01924 434488
E: tim.stevens@wakefield-cathedral.org

ARCHDEACONS
BRADFORD The Ven Andy Jolley, The Rectory, 13 Westview Grove, Keighley BD20 6JJ
E: andy.jolley@leedsanglican.org
RICHMOND AND CRAVEN The Ven Beverley Mason, 4 Appleby Way, Knaresborough HG5 9LX
E: archdeacon.richmondandcraven@
leeds.anglican.org
LEEDS The Ven Paul Nicholas Ayers, 2 Wike Ridge Avenue, Leeds LS17 9NL
T: 0113 269 0594
HALIFAX The Ven Dr Anne Dawtry, 2 Vicarage Gardens, Brighouse, Brighouse HD6 3HD
T: 01484 714553
E: archdeacon.halifax@leeds.anglican.org
PONTEFRACT The Ven Peter Townley, The Vicarage, Kirkthorpe, Wakefield WF1 5SZ
T: 01924 434459 (church house direct line)
E: archdeacon.pontefract@
leedsanglican.org

MEMBERS OF THE HOUSE OF CLERGY OF THE GENERAL SYNOD
Proctors for Clergy
The Ven Paul Nicholas Ayers
The Revd Paul Cartwright
The Revd Canon Jonathan Jackson Clark
The Revd Canon Robert Gerard Cooper
The Ven Dr Anne Frances Dawtry
The Revd Canon Kathryn Anne Fitzsimons
The Revd Canon Ruth Elizabeth Hind
The Revd Canon Joyce Rosemary Jones
The Revd Canon Margaret Anne McLean
The Revd Gary Richard Waddington

MEMBERS OF THE HOUSE OF LAITY OF THE GENERAL SYNOD
Mr David Ashton
Ms Alison Mary Fisher

Canon Malcolm Keith Halliday
Professor Joyce Margaret Hill
Mr Stephen William Hogg
Ms Camilla Mary Rose Holmes
Mrs Zahida Bibi Mallard
Dr Richard John Mantle
Mr Paul Neville

DIOCESAN OFFICERS
Joint Diocesan Secretaries Mrs Debbie Child, Church House, 17-19 York Place, Leeds LS1 2EX   *T:* 0113 353 0272
          E: debbie.child@leeds.anglican.org
Mr Ashley Ellis, Church House, 17-19 York Place, Leeds WF1 1LP   *T:* 0113 3630 229
          E: ashley.ellis@leeds.anglican.org
Chancellor of Diocese Chancellor Mark Hill, Francis Taylor Building, Inner Temple, London EC4Y 7BY   *T:* 0207 353 8415
          E: mark.hill@ftb.eu.com
Registrar of Diocese and Bishop's Legal Secretary Mr Peter William Foskett, Diocesan Registry, Yorkshire House, East Parade, Leeds LS1 5BD
          T: 0113 280 2000
          E: peter.foskett@lf-dt.com

DIOCESAN ORGANIZATIONS
Diocesan Office 17-19 York Place, Leeds LS1 2EX

ADMINISTRATION
Chair of Board of Finance The Rt Revd Dr Tom Butler, Overtown Grange Cottage, The Balk, Walton, Wakefield WF2 6JX   *T:* 01924 256018
          E: bishop.tom@leeds.anglican.org
Secretary of Board of Finance Mr Ashley Ellis, Church House, 17-19 York Place, Leeds WF1 1LP   *T:* 0113 3630 229
          E: ashley.ellis@leeds.anglican.org
Finance Manager Mr Shaun Birch, St Mary's Street, Leeds LS9 7DP
Mr Bryan Lewis (*Same Address*)
Property Manager and Diocesan Surveyor Mr David Meadows, Church House, 17-19 York Place, Leeds LS1 2EX
Mr Michael Lindley (*Same Address*)
Mr Kevin Smith (*Same Address*)
Secretary of Mission and Pastoral Committee Mrs Judith Calvert (*Same Address*)

CHILDREN, YOUNG PEOPLE AND FAMILIES
Children and Young People's Adviser Mr Steve Grasham, Steeton, Keighley BD20 6SE
          E: steve.grasham@leeds.anglican.org
Children and Young People's Development Worker Mrs Anne Carter   *T:* 01423 509859
          E: anne.carter@leeds.anglican.org

Mr Graham Richards   *T:* 01423 884000
          E: graham.richards@leeds.anglican.org
Under 5s Adviser Mrs Ellie Wilson, Church House, 17-19 York Place, Leeds LS1 2EX
          T: 0113 3530 235
          E: ellie.wilson@leeds.anglican.org
Youth Work Adviser Capt Canon Nic Sheppard, 7 Loxley Grove, Wetherby LS22 7YG
          T: 01937 585440
          E: nic.sheppard@leeds.anglican.org
11–18yrs Adviser and Huddersfield and Wakefield episcopal areas Children, Youth and Families Team co-ordinator Mrs Liz Morton, Church House, 17-19 York Place, Leeds LS1 2EX
          T: 0113 3530 237
          E: liz.morton@leeds.anglican.org

CHURCH BUILDINGS
Chair of Diocesan Advisory Committee The Revd Simon Cowling, The Rectory, Bolton Abbey, Skipton BD23 6AL   *T:* 01756 710326
          E: simon.cowling@leeds.anglican.org
Secretary Mrs Sylvia Johnston, Church House, 17-19 York Place, Leeds LS1 2EX

COMMUNICATIONS
Communications Officer Ms Alison Bogle
          T: 0113 2000 540
          E: alison.bogle@leeds.anglican.org
Ms Jane Bower   *T:* 01924 371802
          E: jane.bower@leeds.anglican.org
The Revd Canon John Carter
          T: 01423 530369
          E: john.carter@leeds.anglican.org
Website manager Mr David Brighton
          E: web@leeds.anglican.org
Website administrator Mrs Chris Freeman
          T: 01539 727836
          E: chris.freeman@leeds.anglican.org

DIOCESAN RECORD OFFICES
Wakefield Council Archives, Registry of Deeds, Newstead Road, Wakefield WF1 2DE
          T: 01924 305980
          E: wakefield@wyjs.org.uk
Bradford Metropolitan District Archives, Former Central Library, Princes Way, Bradford BD1 1NN   *E:* bradford@wyjs.org.uk
Calderdale Metropolitan District Archives, Central Library, Northgate House, Northgate, Halifax HX1 1UN   *T:* 01422 392636
          E: calderdale@wyjs.org.uk
Durham Record Office, County Hall, Durham DH1 5UL   *T:* 0191 386 4411
Kirklees Council Archives, Huddersfield Library and Art Gallery, Princess Alexandra Walk, Huddersfield HD1 2SU   *T:* 01484 221966
          E: kirklees@wyjs.org.uk
Lancashire County Archives, Bow Lane, Preston PR1 2RE   *T:* 01772 533039
          E: record.office@lancashire.gov.uk

Leeds District Archives, PO Box 5, Nepshaw Lane, Morley, Leeds LS27 0QP
T: 0113 393 9771
E: leeds@wyjs.org.uk
North Yorkshire County Record Office, County Hall, Northallerton DL7 8DF
T: 01609 777585
E: archives@northyorks.gov.uk

EDUCATION
Diocesan Director of Education Mr Richard Noake, Church House, 17-19 York Place, Leeds LS1 2EX
T: 0113 3530 245
M: 07903 326053
E: richard.noake@leeds.anglican.org

MINISTRY AND MISSION
Bishop's Adviser for Church Growth The Revd Canon Robin Gamble, The Vicarage, 470 Leeds Road, Thackley, Bradford BD10 9AA
T: 01274 419754
E: robinp.gamble@blueyonder.co.uk
Bishop's Officer The Revd Canon Denise Poole, 23 Leylands Lane, Heaton, Bradford BD9 5PX
T: 01274 401679
E: denise.poole@leeds.anglican.org
Diocesan Director of Ordinands and Vocations The Revd Canon Derek Walmsley, 14 Belgravia Road, Wakefield WF1 3JP   T: 01924 434451
E: derek.walmsley@leeds.anglican.org
Ecumenical Officer The Revd Glenn Coggins, The Vicarage, 1 Church Lane, East Ardsley, Wakefield WF3 2LJ   T: 01924 822184
E: glenn.coggins@ely.anglican.org
Environment Officer Mrs Jemima Parker
T: 01423 569121
E: jemima.parker@leeds.anglican.org
Fresh Expressions Adviser Mrs Karin Shaw
T: 01423 500087
E: karin.shaw@leeds.anglican.org
Rural Ministry Officers The Revd David Houlton, The Vicarage, Church Lane, Gargrave, Skipton BD23 3NQ
T: 01756 748468
E: david.houlton@parishes.leeds.anglican.org
Mr Andrew Ryland, 12 Linton Falls, Linton in Craven, Skipton BD23 6BQ
T: 07771 797073
E: andy.ryland@leeds.anglican.org
The Revd Canon James Allison
T: 01422 202292
E: canonallison@btinternet.com
Safeguarding Advisers Mrs Jenny Price, Church House, 17-19 York Place, Leeds LS1 2EX
T: 0113 3530 258
M: 07800 740001
E: jenny.price@leeds.anglican.org
Mrs Jenny Leccardi (*Same Address*)
T: 0113 3530 259
M: 07872 005189
E: jenny.leccardi@leeds.anglican.org

STEWARDSHIP, GIVING AND DEVELOPMENT
Development Officer The Revd Uell Kennedy, Steeton, Keighley BD20 6SE
E: uell.kennedy@leeds.anglican.org
Mrs Susan Rundle, Church House, 1 South Parade, Wakefield WF1 1LP
E: susan.rundle@leeds.anglican.org
Giving and Resources Adviser Mrs Jo Beacroft-Mitchell, Church House, 17-19 York Place, Leeds LS1 2EX
E: jo.beacroft-mitchell@leeds.anglican.org
Stewardship Adviser Mr Paul Winstanley (*Same Address*)   T: 0113 3530 216
E: paul.winstanley@leeds.anglican.org

TRAINING
CME The Revd Canon Stephen Kelly, The Vicarage, Woolley, Wakefield WF4 2JU
T: 01226 382550
E: stephen.kelly@leeds.anglican.org
The Revd Louise Taylor-Kenyon, The Vicarage, 21 Shires Lane, Embsay, Skipton BD23 6SB
T: 01756 798057
E: louise.taylor-kenyon@leeds.anglican.org
Director of Lay Training and Director of Clergy Training The Revd Andrew Tawn, Church House, 17-19 York Place, Leeds LS1 2EX
T: 0113 3530 284
E: andrew.tawn@leeds.anglican.org
Director of School of Ministry (Laity) The Revd Canon Steve Davie, 93 The Village, Holme, Holmfirth HD9 2QG   T: 01484 684973
E: steve.davie@leeds.anglican.org
Director of Training The Revd Canon Dr John Lawson, 7 Belgravia Road, Wakefield WF1 3JP
T: 01924 380182
E: john.lawson@leeds.anglican.org
IME Officer The Revd Canon Stephen Kelly, The Vicarage, Woolley, Wakefield WF4 2JU
T: 01226 382550
E: stephen.kelly@leeds.anglican.org
IME 4–7 The Revd Jill Perrett, The Rectory, Low Mill Lane, Addingham, Ilkley LS29 0QP
T: 01943 831382
E: jill.perrett@parishes.leeds.anglican.org
Urban Ministry Officer The Revd Martine Crabtree, St George's Vicarage, 23c Broadway, Lupset WF2 8AA   T: 01924 787801
E: martinecrabtree@aol.com
The Revd Tracy Ibbotson, Holy Cross Vicarage, The Mount, Airedale, Castleford WF10 3JN
T: 01977 553157
E: ibbotson457@btinternet.com
Urban Parish Support Officer Canon Kingsley Dowling, Wortley Vicarage, Dixon Lane Road, Leeds LS12 4RU   T: 0113 263 8867
E: kingsley.dowling@hotmail.co.uk
Wardens of Readers The Revd Adrian Cragg, 6 Vicarage Close, Wyke, Bradford BD12 8QW
T: 01274 676059
E: adrian.cragg@leeds.anglican.org

The Ven Dr Anne Dawtry, 2 Vicarage Gardens, Brighouse, Brighouse HD6 3HD
T: 01484 714553
E: archdeacon.halifax@leeds.anglican.org

RURAL DEANS
ARCHDEACONRY OF BRADFORD
Aire and Worth Sandra Rhys Benham, The Vicarage, Church Hill, Baildon, Shipley BD17 6NE
T: 01274 589005
E: sandrabenham@btinternet.com
Inner Bradford Alistair Thomas Helm, The Rectory, 63 St Paul's Road, Manningham, Bradford BD8 7LS
T: 01274 482495
E: alistair.helm@btinternet.com
Outer Bradford Vaughan Pollard, The Vicarage, Clayton Lane, Clayton, Bradford BD14 6AX
T: 01274 880373
E: admin@stjohnsclayton.org.uk
South Craven and Wharfedale Philip Charles Gray, St Margaret's Vicarage, Wells Road, Ilkley LS29 9JH
T: 01943 607015

ARCHDEACONRY OF HALIFAX
Almondbury Mark Timothy Paul Zammilt, The Rectory, 2 Westgate, Almondbury, Huddersfield HD5 8XE
T: 01980 653953
E: zammitparish@yahoo.co.uk
Birstall Paul Jeremy Knight, St Peter's Vicarage, King's Drive, Birstall, Batley WF17 9JJ
T: 01924 473715
E: vicar@stpetersbirstall.co.uk
Brighouse and Elland Marion Russell, 1 Vicarage Gardens, Rastrick, Brighouse HD6 3HD
T: 07717 606770
E: revd.marion@gmail.com
Calder Valley Martin Stanley Harrison Macdonald, Broad Head End, Cragg Vale, Hebden Bridge HX7 5RT
T: 01422 881543
E: mshmacdonald@gmail.com
Dewsbury Simon Andrew Cash, The Vicarage, 11 Poplar Close, Worksop S80 3BZ
T: 01909 472069
E: simon_cash@sky.com
Halifax Kathia Andree Shoesmith, The Vicarage, Pavement Lane, Bradshaw, Halifax HX2 9JJ
T: 01422 244330
E: reverend.kathia@outlook.com
Huddersfield Simon Alan Moor, 59 Lightridge Road, Fixby, Huddersfield HD2 2HF
T: 01484 767708
E: samoor@talktalk.net
Kirkburton Joyce Rosemary Jones, Oakfield, 206 Barnsley Road, Denby Dale, Huddersfield HD8 8TS
T: 01484 862350
E: joycerjones@aol.com

ARCHDEACONRY OF LEEDS
Allerton Kathryn Anne Fitzsimons, Epiphany Vicarage, 227 Beech Lane, Leeds LS9 6SW
T: 0113 225 6702
E: kathrynfitzsimons@hotmail.com
Armley Arani Sen, 22 Hill End Crescent, Leeds LS12 3PW
T: 0113 263 8788
E: revaranisen@gmail.com
Headingley Richard James Dimery, St James's Vicarage, 1_Scotland Close, Horsforth, Leeds LS18 5SG
T: 0113 228 2902
E: richard@dimery.com
Whitkirk Rosemarie Eveline Hayes, The Rectory, Church Lane, Kippax, Leeds LS25 7HF
T: 0113 286 2710
E: rosemariehayes@live.co.uk

ARCHDEACONRY OF PONTEFRACT
Barnsley Stephen Peter Race, 22 Elmwood Way, Barnsley S75 1EY
T: 01226 206276
E: stephen.race@leeds.anglican.org
Pontefract Robert Gerard Cooper, The Vicarage, 9 The Mount, Pontefract WF8 1NE
T: 01977 706803
E: robert_cooper@msn.com
Wakefield June Margaret Lawson, 7 Belgravia Road, Wakefield WF1 3JP
T: 01924 380182
E: june.lawson@leeds.anglican.org

ARCHDEACONRY OF RICHMOND AND CRAVEN
Bowland Vacancy
Ewecross Vacancy
Harrogate John Smith, St Robert's Vicarage, 21 Crimple Meadows, Pannal, Harrogate HG3 1EL
T: 01423 391514
E: jrs.smith@talktalk.net
Richmond Yvonne Susan Callaghan, The Vicarage, St Paul's Drive, Brompton on Swale, Richmond DL10 7HQ
T: 01748 811748
E: revyvonnecallaghan@esbb.co.uk
Ripon Darryl Christopher Hall, The New Vicarage, New Church Street, Pateley Bridge, Harrogate HG3 5LQ
T: 07792 419982
E: horlix@aol.com
Skipton Ruth Harris, Christ Church Vicarage, Carleton Road, Skipton BD23 2BE
T: 01756 793612
E: ruth.harris11@btinternet.com
Wensley Christopher Michael Alan Hepper, The Vicarage, I'Anson Close, Leyburn DL8 5LF
T: 01969 622251
E: revmichael@btinternet.com

DIOCESE OF LEICESTER

Founded in 1926. Leicestershire; one parish in Northamptonshire; one parish partly in Derbyshire; one parish partly in Warwickshire.

Population 1,037,000   Area 830 sq m
Full-time Stipendiary Parochial Clergy 120   Benefices 106
Parishes 243   Churches 314
www.leicester.anglican.org
Overseas link dioceses: Mouth Kilimanjaro and Kiteto (Tanzania)
and Trichy, Tanjore (India)

BISHOP
The Rt Revd Martyn Snow, 2 College Green, Gloucester GL1 2LR
T: 01452 410022 ext 228
E: bshptewk@glosdioc.org.uk

BISHOP'S STAFF
Bishop's Policy Advisor and Chaplain The Revd Adrian Jones Bishop's Lodge Annexe, 12 Springfield Road, Leicester LE2 3BD
T: 0116 270 3390
F: 0116 270 3288
E: adrian.jones@leccofe.org
Executive Assistant to the Bishop Mrs Rachel Radford (*Same Address*)   *T:* 0116 270 8985
E: rachel.radford@leccofe.org
Bishop's PA Mrs Melanie Freeman (*Same Address*)   *E:* melanie.freeman@leccofe.org

SUFFRAGAN BISHOP
LOUGHBOROUGH The Rt Revd Guli Francis-Dehqani (from 30/11/17)
E: bishop.loughborough@leccofe.org

CATHEDRAL CHURCH OF ST MARTIN
Dean The Very Revd David Monteith
T: 0116 261 5356
E: david.monteith@leccofe.org
Canons Residentiary
Canon Chancellor The Revd Canon Rosy Fairhurst   *T:* 0116 261 5345
E: rosy.fairhurst@leccofe.org
Canon Precentor The Revd Canon Dr Johannes Arens   *T:* 0116 261 5364
E: johannes.arens@leccofe.org
Canon Missioner The Revd Canon Karen Rooms   *T:* 0116 261 5389
E: karen.rooms@leccofe.org
Canon Pastor and Sub-Dean The Revd Canon Alison Adams   *T:* 0116 261 5333
E: alison.adams@leccofe.org
Other Staff
Curate The Revd Sunny George
E: sunny.george@leccofe.org

Cathedral Administrator Mr Jonathan Kerry, St Martins House, 7 Peacock Lane, Leicester LE1 5PZ   *T:* 0116 261 5326
E: jonathan.kerry@leccofe.org
Deputy Administrator Mrs Elisa Simmons
T: 0116 261 5368
E: elisa.simmons@leccofe.org
Development Officer Ms Claire Recordon
T: 0116 261 5344
*E. claire.recordon@leccofe.org
Director of Music Dr Christopher Ouvry-Johns
T: 0116 261 5374
E: chris.johns@leccofe.org
Assistant Director of Music Mr Simon Headley
T: 0116 261 5381
E: simon.headley@leccofe.org
Cathedral Solicitor Mr Trevor Kirkman, Latham & Co., Charnwood House, 2/4 Forest Road, Loughborough LE11 3NP
T: 01509 238822
F: 01509 238833
E: trevorkirkman@lathamlawyers.co.uk
Director, Leicester Cathedral Revealed The Revd Pete Hobson   *T:* 0116 261 5363
E: pete.hobson@leccofe.org

ARCHDEACONS
LEICESTER The Ven Timothy Stratford, St Martins House, 7 Peacock Lane, Leicester LE1 5PZ   *T:* 0116 261 5319
E: tim.stratford@leccofe.org
LOUGHBOROUGH The Ven Claire Wood, The Archdeaconry, 21 Church Road, Glenfield, Leicester LE3 8DP   *T:* 0116 261 5321
E: claire.wood@leccofe.org

MEMBERS OF THE HOUSE OF CLERGY OF THE GENERAL SYNOD
Proctors for Clergy
The Revd Alison Booker
The Ven Timothy Stratford
The Revd Barry Hill

MEMBERS OF THE HOUSE OF LAITY OF THE GENERAL SYNOD
Mr Jonathan Cryer
Canon Shayne Ardron
Miss Rhian Ainscough

DIOCESAN OFFICERS
Diocesan Secretary Mr Jonathan Kerry, St Martins House, 7 Peacock Lane, Leicester LE1 5PZ   *T:* 0116 261 5326
          E: jonathan.kerry@leccofe.org
Assistant Diocesan Secretary Mr Andrew Brockbank, Peartree, 11 Orchard Way, Wymeswold, Loughborough LE12 6SW
          T: 0116 261 5312
          E: andrew.brockbank@leccofe.org
PA to Diocesan Secretary Mrs Carol Gibbons, St Martins House, 7 Peacock Lane, Leicester LE1 5PZ   *T:* 0116 261 5326
          E: carol.gibbons@leccofe.org
Chancellor of Diocese Mark Blackett-Ord, 5 Stone Buildings, Lincoln's Inn, London WC2A 3XT   *T:* 020 7421 7510
          F: 020 7831 8102
Registrar of Diocese and Bishop's Legal Secretary Mr Trevor Kirkman, Latham & Co., Charnwood House, 2/4 Forest Road, Loughborough LE11 3NP   *T:* 01509 238822
          F: 01509 238833
          E: trevorkirkman@lathamlawyers.co.uk

DIOCESAN ORGANIZATIONS
Diocesan Office St Martins House, 7 Peacock Lane, Leicester LE1 5PZ   *T:* 0116 261 5200
          W: www.leicester.anglican.org

ADMINISTRATION
Director of Finance Mr John Orridge, St Martins House, 7 Peacock Lane, Leicester LE1 5PZ
          E: john.orridge@leccofe.org
Management Accountant Mrs Caroline Wademan (*Same Address*)
          E: caroline.wademan@covlec.org
Mr Jim Pullen (*Same Address*)
          E: jim.pullen@covlec.org
Accounts Assistant Mrs Karen Issitt (*Same Address*)   *E:* karen.issitt@leccofe.org
Senior Property Manager Mrs Nicky Caunt (*Same Address*)   *E:* nicky.caunt@covlec.org
Clergy Housing Officer Mrs Dinta Chauhan (*Same Address*)   *E:* dinta.chauhan@covlec.org
Property Officer Miss Lesley Whitwell (*Same Address*)   *E:* lesley.whitwell@covlec.org
IT Manager Mr Phil Ash (*Same Address*)
          E: phil.ash@covlec.org
Diocesan Synod (*Chair, House of Clergy*) The Revd Dr Peter Hooper, 23 Ferndale Drive, Ratby, Leicester LE6 0LH   *T:* 0116 239 4606
          E: peter@hoopers.orangehome.co.uk
(*Chair, House of Laity*) Prof David Wilson
          E: djwilson@dmu.ac.uk

Diocesan Synod and Bishop's Council (*Secretary*) Mr Jonathan Kerry, St Martins House, 7 Peacock Lane, Leicester LE1 5PZ
          T: 0116 261 5326
          E: jonathan.kerry@leccofe.org
Mission and Pastoral Committee Mr Jonathan Kerry (*As above*)
Board of Finance (*Chair*) Mr Stephen Barney, Peartree, 11 Orchard Way, Wymeswold, Loughborough LE12 6SW   *T:* 01509 881160
          E: stephen4747@live.co.uk
(*Secretary*) Mr Jonathan Kerry, St Martins House, 7 Peacock Lane, Leicester LE1 5PZ
          T: 0116 261 5326
          E: jonathan.kerry@leccofe.org
Finance Committee Mr Jonathan Kerry (*As above*)
Property and Glebe Committee Mr Andrew Brockbank, Peartree, 11 Orchard Way, Wymeswold, Loughborough LE12 6SW
          T: 0116 261 5312
          E: andrew.brockbank@leccofe.org
(*Designated Officer*) Mr Jonathan Kerry, St Martins House, 7 Peacock Lane, Leicester LE1 5PZ   *T:* 0116 261 5326
          E: jonathan.kerry@leccofe.org
(*Generous Giving Development Officer*) Mrs Sally Hayden (*Same Address*)   *T:* 0116 261 5339
          E: sally.hayden@covlec.org
(*Director of Parish Funding and Fundraising*) Mr Andrew Nutter (*Same Address*)
          T: 0116 261 5322
          E: andrew.nutter@leccofe.org
(*Parish Funding Director*) Mrs Maxine Johnson, Brook House, Stonton Road, Church Langton, Market Harborough LE16 7SZ
          T: 01858 545745
          E: mjohnson@resort-solutions.co.uk
(*Growth Fund Administrator*) Mr Luke Fogg
          T: 0116 261 5200
          E: luke.fogg@leccofe.org
(*Diocesan Safeguarding Adviser*) Ms Rachael Spiers, St Martins House, 7 Peacock Lane, Leicester LE1 5PZ   *T:* 0116 261 5341
          E: rachael.spiers@leccofe.org

CHURCH BUILDINGS
Advisory Committee for the Care of Churches (*Chair*) The Revd Richard Curtis, Vicarage, Oakham Road, Tilton on the Hill LE7 9LB
          T: 07855 746041
(*Secretary*) Mr Rupert Allen, St Martins House, 7 Peacock Lane, Leicester LE1 5PZ
          T: 0116 261 5332
          E: rupert.allen@leccofe.org

DIOCESAN RECORD OFFICE
Leicestershire Records Office, Long Street, Wigston, Leicester LE18 2AH
          T: 0116 257 1080
          F: 0116 257 1120

ECUMENICAL
Ecumenical Officer Mr Vic Allsop, Clematis Cottage, 14 Church Lane, Hoby, Melton Mowbray, Leics LE14 3DR

EDUCATION
Diocesan Board of Education (Director) Mrs Carolyn Lewis, St Martins House, 7 Peacock Lane, Leicester LE1 5PZ
E: carolyn.lewis@leccofe.org
(PA to the Director) Vacancy
(Chief Executive of LACT) Ian Jones
E: ian.jones@leccofe.org
(Finance/Business Manager for LACT) Ian Sharpe   *E:* ian.sharpe@leccofe.org
(Chair) Vacancy
(School Inspections and Conference/Training Manager) Mrs Helen Van Roose, St Martins House, 7 Peacock Lane, Leicester LE1 5PZ
E: helen.vanroose@leccofe.org
(School Support Officer) Mrs Kerry Miller *(Same Address)*   *E:* kerry.miller@leccofe.org
(Senior Education Officer – School Effectiveness) Mr Stephen Gleave *(Same Address)*
E: stephen.gleave@leccofe.org

INTERFAITH
Director of Interfaith Relations and of the St Philip's Centre for Study and Engagement in a Multi Faith Society The Revd Dr Tom Wilson, St Philip's Centre, 2a Stoughton Drive North, Leicester LE5 5UB   *T:* 0116 273 3459
E: director@stphilipscentre.co.uk

LITURGICAL
Chairman The Revd Richard Curtis, The Old Forge, 16 High Street, Desford, Leicester LE9 9JF
Secretary The Revd Alison Booker, The Vicarage, Gaulby Road, Billesdon, Leicester LE7 9AG   *T:* 0116 259 6321
E: abooker@leicester.anglican.org

MINISTRY
Director of Mission and Ministry Canon Dr Mike Harrison, St Martins House, 7 Peacock Lane, Leicester LE1 5PZ   *T:* 0116 261 5328
F: 0116 261 5220
E: mike.harrison@leccofe.org
Head of the School for Ministry The Revd Dr Stuart Burns *(Same Address)*
T: 0116 261 5354
E: stuart.burns@leccofe.org
Mission Enabler The Revd Barry Hill *(Same Address)*   *T:* 0116 261 5335
E: barry.hill@leccofe.org
Mission and Ministry Consultant The Revd Nicky McGinty *(Same Address)*
T: 0116 261 5348
E: nicky@njmcginty.co.uk

Youth Ministry Officer Mike Kelly *(Same Address)*   *T:* 0116 261 5342
E: mike.kelly@leccofe.org
Diocesan Director of Ordinands The Revd Canon Sue Field, 134 Valley Road, Loughborough LE11 3QA   *T:* 01509 234472
E: sue.field134@gmail.com
Children's and Families Officer Louise Warner, St Martins House, 7 Peacock Lane, Leicester LE1 5PZ   *T:* 0116 261 5313
E: louise.warner@leccofe.org
Officer for Non-Stipendiary Ministry The Revd Louise Corke, The Rectory, 58 Pymm Ley Lane, Groby, Leicester LE6 0GZ
T: 0116 231 3090
E: words.th@talktalk.net
Warden of Evangelists The Revd Keith Elliott, The Vicarage, Thorpe Acre Road, Loughborough LE11 4LF   *T:* 01509 211656
E: keith@astad.org
Warden of Readers The Revd Stephen Bailey, St Paul's House, Hamble Road, Oadby, Leicester LE2 4NX   *T:* 0116 271 0519
E: vicarstpauloadby@gmail.com
Reader Training Officer The Revd Dr Stuart Burns, St Paul's House, Hamble Road, Oadby, Leicester LE2 4NX
Pastoral Assistants Adviser The Revd Alison Booker, The Vicarage, Gaulby Road, Billesdon, Leicester LE7 9AG   *T:* 0116 259 6321
E: abooker@leicester.anglican.org
Director of Post-Ordination Training The Revd Canon Jane Curtis, Vicarage, Oakham Road, Tilton on the Hill LE7 9LB   *T:* 0116 2597244
E: jcurtis@leicester.anglican.org
Director of Women's Ministry The Revd Canon Jane Curtis *(As above)*

PRESS AND COMMUNICATIONS
Communications Officer Ms Liz Hudson, St Martins House, 7 Peacock Lane, Leicester LE1 5PZ   *T:* 0116 261 5302
M: 07943 387265
E: liz.hudson@leccofe.org
Editor of Diocesan Directory Ms Liz Hudson *(As above)*
Editor of 'In Shape' Ms Liz Hudson *(As above)*

RETIRED CLERGY AND WIDOWS OFFICER
Anthony Wessel, The Old Forge, 16 High Street, Desford, Leicester LE9 9JF
T: 01455 822404
F: 01455 823545
E: anthony.wessel@dial.pipex.com

SOCIAL RESPONSIBILITY
Rural Officer The Revd Dr Peter Hooper, 23 Ferndale Drive, Ratby, Leicester LE6 0LH
T: 0116 239 4606
E: peter@hoopers.orangehome.co.uk

LEICESTER

Environment Officers The Revd Andrew Quigley, The Vicarage, 49 Ashley Way, Market Harborough LE16 7XD   *T:* 01858 410253
        E: andrew@aquigley.wanadoo.co.uk
The Revd Canon Alison Adams
        T: 0116 261 5333
        E: alison.adams@leccofe.org

AREA DEANS
ARCHDEACONRY OF LEICESTER
City of Leicester Richard Vernon Worsfold, The Vicarage, 17 Westcotes Drive, Leicester LE3 0QT   *T:* 0116 223 2632
        E: rworsfold@virginmedia.com
Framland Peter George Hooper, 2 Church Lane, Asfordby, Melton Mowbray LE14 3RU
        T: 0116 239 4606
        E: peter@hoopers.orangehome.co.uk
Gartree First Deanery Jonathan Murray Barrett, The Vicarage, Thurnby, Leicester LE7 9PN
        T: 0116 241 2263
        E: jon316@thurnbychurch.com
Gartree Second Deanery Jonathan Murray Barrett, The Vicarage, Thurnby, Leicester LE7 9PN   *T:* 0116 241 2263
        E: jon316@thurnbychurch.com

Goscote Robert Michael Gladstone, The Vicarage, 128 Hallfields Lane, Rothley, Leicester LE7 7NG   *T:* 0116 230 2241
        E: rob.gladstone@btconnect.com

ARCHDEACONRY OF LOUGHBOROUGH
Akeley East Wendy Margaret Dalrymple, The Rectory, 69 Westfield Drive, Loughborough LE11 3QL   *T:* 01403 752320
        E: priestwendy@btinternet.com
Guthlaxton David Ernest Hebblewhite, The Vicarage, 102A Station Road, Countesthorpe, Leicester LE8 5TB   *T:* 0116 278 4442
        E: davidheb@talktalk.net
North West Leicestershire Vivien Margaret Elphick, The Vicarage, High Street, Measham, Swadlincote DE12 7HZ   *T:* 01530 270354
        E: vivien@rectorybarn.wanadoo.co.uk
Sparkenhoe East Tom Laurence Ringland, The Rectory, 6 Station Road, Kirby Muxloe, Leicester LE9 2EJ   *T:* 0116 238 6822
        E: tringland@aol.com
Sparkenhoe West Gary James Weston, 21 Windrush Drive, Hinckley LE10 0NY
        T: 01455 233552
        E: gary.weston@ukonline.co.uk

DIOCESE OF LICHFIELD

Founded in 664, formerly Mercia (656). Staffordshire, except for a few parishes in the south-east, in the dioceses of Birmingham and Derby; a few parishes in the south-west, in the diocese of Hereford; the northern half of Shropshire; Wolverhampton; Walsall; the northern half of Sandwell.

Population 2,141,000   Area 1,730 sq m
Full-time Stipendiary Parochial Clergy 255   Benefices 250
Parishes 427   Churches 562
Overseas link dioceses: W. Malaysia, Kuching, Singapore, Qu'Appelle (Canada), Mecklenburg, Matlosane

BISHOP (99th)

The Rt Revd Dr Michael Ipgrave

BISHOP'S STAFF

Bishop's Chaplain The Revd Dr Rebecca Lloyd
    E: rebecca.lloyd@lichfield.anglican.org
Bishop's PA Ms Diana Hill   *T:* 01543 306000
    E: diana.hill@lichfield.anglican.org
Bishop's Secretary Mrs Margaret Wilson (*Same Tel*)
    E: margaret.wilson@lichfield.anglican.org

AREA BISHOPS

SHREWSBURY The Rt Revd Mark Rylands, 68 London Road, Shrewsbury SY2 6PG
    T: 01743 235867
    F: 01743 243296
    E: bishop.shrewsbury@lichfield.anglican.org
STAFFORD The Rt Revd Geoff Annas, Ash Garth, Broughton Crescent, Barlaston, Stoke-on-Trent ST12 9DD   *T:* 01782 373308
    F: 01782 373705
    E: bishop.stafford@lichfield.anglican.org
WOLVERHAMPTON The Rt Revd Clive Gregory, 61 Richmond Road, Merridale, Wolverhampton WV3 9JH   *T:* 01902 824503
    F: 01902 824504
    E: bishop.wolverhampton@lichfield.anglican.org

CATHEDRAL CHURCH OF ST MARY AND ST CHAD

Dean The Very Revd Adrian Dorber, The Deanery, 16 The Close, Lichfield WS13 7LD
    T: 01543 306250 (Office)
    E: adrian.dorber@lichfield-cathedral.org
Canons Residentiary
Vice-Dean and Canon for Liturgy and Formation The Revd Canon Dr Anthony Moore, 24 The Close, Lichfield WS13 7LD   *T:* 01543 306148
    E: anthony.moore@lichfield-cathedral.org
Canon Precentor The Revd Canon Andrew Stead (*Same Address*)   *T:* 07932 703032
    E: andrew.stead@lichfield-cathedral.org

Canon Custos The Revd Canon Peter Holliday, c/o Chapter Office, 19a The Close, Lichfield WS13 7LD   *T:* 01543 434537
    E: peter.holliday@lichfield-cathedral.org
Canon Chancellor The Revd Canon Pat Hawkins, 23 The Close, Lichfield WS13 7LD
    T: 01543 306101 (office)
    E: pat.hawkins@lichfield-cathedral.org
Other Staff
Members of Chapter (contact via Chapter Office)
Mr Michael Diamond
Mr Mark Hope-Urwin
Miss Anne Parkhill
The Rt Revd Mark Rylands, 68 London Road, Shrewsbury SY2 6PG   *T:* 01743 235867
    F: 01743 243296
    E: bishop.shrewsbury@lichfield.anglican.org
Mr Paul Spicer
Executive Director Mr Simon Warburton, Chapter Office, 19a The Close, Lichfield WS13 7LD   *T:* 01543 306105
    E: simon.warburton@lichfield-cathedral.org
Director of Fundraising Helen Geary (*Same Address*)   *T:* 01543 306244
    E: helen.geary@lichfield-cathedral.org
Director of Music Mr Ben Lamb, 11 The Close, Lichfield WS13 7LD   *T:* 01543 306200
    E: ben.lamb@lichfield-cathedral.org
Assistant Director of Music, Organist, Director of Cathedral Chamber Choir Mr Martyn Rawles, Chapter Office, 19a The Close, Lichfield WS13 7LD   *T:* 01543 306201
    E: martyn.rawles@lichfield-cathedral.org
Schools and Learning Manager Mr Alex Nicholson-Ward (*Same Address*)
    T: 01543 306240
    E: education@lichfield-cathedral.org
Music and Liturgy Coordinator Mrs Theresa Willmore (*Same Address*)   *T:* 01543 306101
    E: theresa.willmore@lichfield-cathedral.org
PA to the Dean Mrs Kate Durrant, The Deanery Office, 16 The Close, Lichfield WS13 7LD
    T: 01543 306250
    E: kate.durrant@lichfield-cathedral.org

PA to the Canon Chancellor Mrs Theresa Willmore, Chapter Office, 19a The Close, Lichfield WS13 7LD			*T:* 01543 306101
E: theresa.willmore@lichfield-cathedral.org

ARCHDEACONS

LICHFIELD The Ven Simon Baker, 10 Mawgan Drive, Lichfield WS14 9SD			*T:* 01543 306145
E: archdeacon.lichfield@ lichfield.anglican.org
STOKE-ON-TRENT The Ven Matthew Parker, 39 The Brackens, Clayton, Newcastle-under-Lyme ST5 4JL			*T:* 01902 372622
E: archdeacon.salop@ lichfield.anglican.org
SALOP The Ven Paul Thomas, Archdeacon's House, Tong Vicarage, Shifnal TF11 8PW
T: 01902 372622
E: archdeacon.salop@lichfield.anglican.org
WALSALL The Ven Susan Weller, The Small Street Centre, 1a Small Street, Walsall WS1 3PR			*T:* 01922 707861
E: archdeacon.walsall@ lichfield.anglican.org

MEMBERS OF THE HOUSE OF CLERGY OF THE GENERAL SYNOD
Proctors for Clergy
The Revd Canon Pat Hawkins
The Revd Preb Brian Williams
The Revd Damian Feeney
The Revd Zoe Heming
The Revd Shaun Morris
The Revd Sarah Schofield

MEMBERS OF THE HOUSE OF LAITY OF THE GENERAL SYNOD
Mrs Penelope Allen
Mr Christopher Gill
Mr John Naylor
Dr Chik Kaw Tan
Mr Robin Whitehouse
Mr John Wilson

DIOCESAN OFFICERS
Diocesan Secretary Mrs Julie Jones, St Mary's House, The Close, Lichfield WS13 7LD
T: 01543 306030
F: 01543 306039
E: julie.jones@lichfield.anglican.org
Chancellor of Diocese Mr Stephen Eyre, Manby Bowdler, Routh House, Hall Court, Hall Park Way, Telford TF3 4NJ			*T:* 01952 292129
Diocesan Registrar and Bishop's Legal Secretary Mr Niall Blackie, Manby Bowdler LLP, Routh House, Hall Court, Hall Park Way, Telford TF3 4NJ (*Same Tel*)			*F:* 01952 291716
E: n.blackie@fbcmb.co.uk

DIOCESAN ORGANIZATIONS
Diocesan Office St Mary's House, The Close, Lichfield WS13 7LD

ADMINISTRATION
Chairman Mr John Naylor, St Mary's House, The Close, Lichfield WS13 7LD
Team Leader Mrs Julie Jones (*Same Address*)
T: 01543 306030
F: 01543 306039
E: julie.jones@lichfield.anglican.org
Finance Director Mr Jonathan R. L. Hill (*Same Address*)
(*Chairman, House of Clergy*) The Revd John Allan, Vicarage, Church Road, Alrewas, Burton-on-Trent DE13 7BT			*T:* 01283 790486
E: therevdjohnallan@ therevdjohnallan.plus.com
(*Chairman, House of Laity*) Mr John Wilson, 49 Oakhurst, Lichfield WS14 9AL
T: 01543 268678
E: charity.services@btclick.com
Benefice Buildings and Glebe Committee (*Secretary*) Mr Andrew Mason, St Mary's House, The Close, Lichfield WS13 7LD
(*Diocesan Surveyor*) Mr Charles Glenn (*Same Address*)
Trust (*Secretary*) Mrs Diane Holt (*Same Address*)
(*Designated Officer*) Mr Niall Blackie (*Same Address*)			*T:* 01952 292129
F: 01952 291716
E: n.blackie@fbcmb.co.uk
Safeguarding Officer Mrs Kim Hodgkins (*Same Address*)			*T:* 01543 306030
E: kim.hodgkins@lichfield.anglican.org
Mission and Pastoral Committee (*Secretary*) Miss Clare Spooner (*Same Address*)
E: clare.spooner@lichfield.anglican.org

CHURCH BUILDINGS
Advisory Committee for the Care of Churches (*Chairman*) The Ven John Hall, 16 Mill House Drive, Cheadle, Stoke-on-Trent ST10 1XL
T: 01538 750628
E: j.hall182@btinternet.com
(*Secretary*) Mrs Kristina Williamson, 27 Frederick Road, Sutton, Coldfield B73 5QW
T: 07805 772626
E: kristina.williamson@ lichfield.anglican.org

DIOCESAN RECORD OFFICES
Staffordshire Record Office, Eastgate Street, Stafford ST16 2LZ			*T:* 01785 278379
E: staffordshire.record.office@ staffordshire.gov.uk
Lichfield Record Office, The Library, The Friary, Lichfield WS13 6QG			*T:* 01543 510720
E: lichfield.record.office@ staffordshire.gov.uk

Shropshire Archives, Castle Gates, Shrewsbury
SY1 2AQ   *T:* 01743 255350
            E: archives@shropshire.gov.uk

ECUMENISM

Area Ecumenical Adviser (Black Country)
Vacancy
Area Ecumenical Adviser (Shropshire) Mrs
Veronica Fletcher, 67 Derwent Drive, Priorslee,
Telford TF2 9QR   *T:* 01952 299318
            E: veronica.fletcher@telford.gov.uk
Area Ecumenical Adviser (Staffordshire) The
Revd Graham Gittings, 21 Princetown Close,
Meir Park, Stoke-on-Trent ST3 7WN
                          T: 01782 388866
            E: graham.gittings77@btinternet.com

EDUCATION

Chair of Board of Education The Rt Revd Mark
Rylands, 68 London Road, Shrewsbury SY2
6PG   *T:* 01743 235867
                          F: 01743 243296
    E: bishop.shrewsbury@lichfield.anglican.org
Director of Education and Team Leader Mr Colin
Hopkins, St Mary's House, The Close, Lichfield
WS13 7LD   *T:* 01543 622440
        E: colin.hopkins@lichfield.anglican.org
Deputy Director of Education Mrs Claire Shaw,
St Mary's House, The Close, Lichfield WS13
7LD   *T:* 01543 622430
School Buildings Officer Mr Steve Rayner (*Same
Address*)   *T:* 01543 622341

MINISTRY

Director of Ministry The Revd Lesley Bentley, St
Mary's House, The Close, Lichfield WS13 7LD
                          T: 01543 306227 (Office)
                          01889 508066 (Home)
        E: lesley.bentley@lichfield.anglican.org
PA to Director of Ministry Miss Jodie Galley
(*Same Address*)   *T:* 01543 306227
        E: jodie.galley@lichfield.anglican.org
*Ministry Development Department Administrator
(with responsibility for Ministry Development
Review)* Mrs Jane Instone (*Same Address*)
                          T: 01543 306228
        E: jane.instone@lichfield.anglican.org
Director of Ordinands Mrs Angela Bruno (*Same
Address*)   *T:* 01543 306220 (office)
            E: ddo@lichfield.anglican.org
*PA to the Director of Ordinands and Vocations
Department* Mrs Angela Bruno (*As above*)
Vocational Education Officer The Revd Deborah
Sheridan, 45 High Grange, Lichfield WS13
7DU   *T:* 01543 264363
            E: d.sheridan@postman.org.uk
*Vocations and Ministry Development Officer for
Minority Ethnic Anglicans, Wolverhampton* The
Revd Pamela Daniel, 33 Reform Street, West
Bromwich B70 7PF   *T:* 0121 525 1985
            E: pamdaniel@hotmail.com

Director of Lay Development Dr Lindsey Hall,
St Mary's House   *T:* 01543 306225 (office)
        E: lindsey.hall@lichfield.anglican.org
*Lichfield Director of Reader Training / OLM Tutor,
The Queen's Foundation, Birmingham* The Revd
Pauline Shelton, St Mary's House, The Close,
Lichfield, Staffs WS13 7LD
                          T: 01543 306224 (office)
        E: pauline.shelton@lichfield.anglican.org
Local Ministry Scheme Administrator Ms Julia
Cunningham   *T:* 01543 306223
        E: julia.cunningham@lichfield.anglican.org
Warden of Readers The Ven Paul Thomas,
Archdeacon's House, Tong Vicarage, Shifnal
TF11 8PW   *T:* 01902 372622
        E: archdeacon.salop@lichfield.anglican.org
Bishop's Adviser for Pastoral Care and Wellbeing
The Revd Preb Jane Tillier, 10 Plantation Park,
Keele, Newcastle ST5 5NA
                          T: 01782 639720
        E: jane.tillier@lichfield.anglican.org

MISSION

Director of Mission The Revd George Fisher, The
Parish Mission Office, The Small Street Centre,
1a Small Street, Walsall WS1 3PR
                          T: 01922 707863 (Office)
                          01922 650063 (Home)
        E: george.fisher@lichfield.anglican.org
Director of World Mission The Revd Philip
Swan, The World Mission Office, The Small
Street Centre, 1a Small Street, Walsall WS1
3PR   *T:* 01922 707860 (office)
                          01902 621148 (Home)
        E: philip.swan@lichfield.anglican.org
Parish Mission Research Assistant Mr Richard
Barrett, The Parish Mission Office, The Small
Street Centre, 1a Small Street, Walsall WS1
3PR   *T:* 01922 707863 (office)
        E: richard.barrett@lichfield.anglican.org
PA to the Director of World Mission Mrs Susanna
Somerville, St Peter's House, Exchange Street,
Woverhampton WV1 1TS
Youth and Children's Adviser Mr Mark Hatcher,
Hillcroft, Stoney Lane, Endon, Stoke-on-Trent
ST9 9BX   *T:* 01782 502822
        E: mark.hatcher@lichfield.anglican.org
Spiritual Companions Co-ordinator The Revd
Christine Polhill, Little Hayes, Beaudesert
Park, Cannock Wood, Rugeley WS5 4JJ
                          T: 01543 674474
        E: christine@reflectiongardens.org.uk
Diocesan Schools Outreach Adviser Miss Libby
Leech, St Mary's House, The Close, Lichfield
WS13 7LD   *T:* 07891 290564
        E: libby.leech@lichfield.anglican.org
Youth and Vocations Enabler Mr Jon White, The
Small Street Centre, 1a Small Street, Walsall
WS1 3PR   *T:* 07792 498248
        E: jon.white@lichfield.anglican.org

TRANSFORMING COMMUNITIES

Transforming Communities Director The Revd David Primrose, Hill House, Vicarage Lane, Bednall, Stafford ST17 0SE   T: 01785 748976
Transforming Communities Assistant The Revd Ruth Brooker, The Small Street Centre, 1a Small Street, Walsall WS1 3PR
T: 01922 707864
E: ruth.brooker@lichfield.anglican.org

RURAL DEANS

ARCHDEACONRY OF LICHFIELD

Lichfield Margaret Mattocks, The Vicarage, Church Road, Burntwood, Walsall WS7 9EA
T: 01543 675014
E: margmattocks1@live.co.uk
Penkridge Gregory Howard Yerbury, The Rectory, New Road, Penkridge, Stafford ST19 5DN   T: 01785 714344
E: rector@stmichaelspenkridge.co.uk
Rugeley Simon Charles Davis, The Vicarage, Market Place, Abbots Bromley, Rugeley WS15 3BP   T: 01283 840242
E: revdsimon@davisfamily.waitrose.com
Tamworth Debra Anne Dyson, The Vicarage, Comberford Lane, Wigginton, Tamworth B79 9DT   T: 01827 690380
E: debdyson@btinternet.com

ARCHDEACONRY OF SALOP

Edgmond and Shifnal Keith Hodson, The Rectory, Beckbury, Shifnal TF11 9DG
T: 01952 750474
E: keithhodson@talk21.com
Ellesmere Vacancy
Hodnet Hywel Geraint Snook, The Vicarage, 1 Christ Church Copse, Christ Church Lane, Market Drayton TF9 1DY   T: 01630 652801
E: hywel.snook@tiscali.co.uk
Oswestry Adrian Richard Bailey, The Vicarage, Old Chirk Road, Gobowen, Oswestry SY11 3LL   T: 01691 661226
E: arb2@totalise.co.uk
Shrewsbury Mark Harold Salmon, Harlescott Vicarage, Meadow Farm Drive, Shrewsbury SY1 4NG   T: 01743 362883
E: mark.salmon@xalt.co.uk
Telford Timothy Storey, The Rectory, 20 Burlington Close, Dawley, Telford TF4 3TD
T: 01952 595915
E: revtimstorey@gmail.com
Wem and Whitchurch Adam Jonathan Barnett Clayton, The Rectory, Myddle, Shrewsbury SY4 3RX   T: 01939 291801
E: adam@ajbc.fsnet.co.uk
Wrockwardine David Andrew Ackroyd, The Vicarage, High Street, Cheswardine, Market Drayton TF9 2RS   T: 01630 661204
E: revandy320@btopenworld.com

ARCHDEACONRY OF STOKE-ON-TRENT

Alstonfield Michael John Evans, The Vicarage, Church Lane, Ipstones, Stoke-on-Trent ST10 2LF   T: 01538 266313
E: revdmjevans@btinternet.com
Cheadle Robert Speight Munro, The Rectory, 1 Depleach Road, Cheadle SK8 1DZ
T: 0161 428 3440
E: rob@munro.org.uk
Eccleshall Ian Ralph Cardinal, 11 Farrier Close, Stone ST15 8XP   T: 01785 812747
E: rector@stmichaelschurchstone.co.uk
Leek Brian Edward Statham, The Vicarage, Baddeley Green Lane, Stoke-on-Trent ST2 7EY
T: 01782 534062
E: brianstatham@aol.com
Newcastle Terence Bernard Bloor, 211 Basford Park Road, Newcastle ST5 0PG
T: 01782 619045
E: terry.bloor@btinternet.com
Stafford Philip Sharman Daniel, The Rectory, Stafford Road, Weston, Stafford ST18 0HX
T: 01889 271870
E: revpsdan@btinternet.com
Stoke Nigel William Reid Evans, The Rectory, 151 Werrington Road, Bucknall, Stoke-on-Trent ST2 9AQ   T: 01782 280667
E: nigelwrevans4@btinternet.com
Stoke North Nigel William Reid Evans, The Rectory, 151 Werrington Road, Bucknall, Stoke-on-Trent ST2 9AQ   T: 01782 280667
E: nigelwrevans4@btinternet.com
Stone Ian Ralph Cardinal, 11 Farrier Close, Stone ST15 8XP   T: 01785 812747
E: rector@stmichaelschurchstone.co.uk
Tutbury Michael Raymond Freeman, Horninglow Vicarage, 14 Rolleston Road, Burton-on-Trent DE13 0JZ   T: 01283 568613
E: cft-rfreeman@supanet.com
Uttoxeter Brian Stanley Peter Leathers, The New Vicarage, Limekiln Lane, Alton, Stoke-on-Trent ST10 4AR   T: 01538 702469
E: briantopsey@googlemail.com

ARCHDEACONRY OF WALSALL

Trysull Maureen Patricia Hobbs, The Vicarage, 20 Dartmouth Avenue, Pattingham, Wolverhampton WV6 7DP   T: 01902 700257
E: hobbsmaureen@yahoo.co.uk
Walsall Carl Anthoney St Aubyn Ramsay, The Vicarage, 39 Hall Lane, Pelsall, Walsall WS3 4JN   T: 01922 682098
E: spreeboy@talk21.com
Wednesbury Martin Michael Ennis, 26 View Point, Tividale, Oldbury B69 1UU
T: 01384 257888
E: frmennis@gmail.com
West Bromwich Ronald Anthony Farrell, Friar Park Vicarage, Freeman Road, Wednesbury WS10 0HJ   T: 0121 556 5823
E: father.ron@btinternet.com

West Bromwich Michael John Claridge, St Andrew's Vicarage, Oakwood Street, West Bromwich B70 9SN   *T:* 0121 553 1871
          E: mjclaridge@me.com
Wolverhampton David William Wright, The Rectory, 42 Park Road East, Wolverhampton WV1 4QA   *T:* 01902 423388
          E: david.wright@lichfield.anglican.org

Wulfrun Nicholas Edgar Watson, The Rectory, 9 Vicarage Road, Wednesfield, Wolverhampton WV11 1SB   *T:* 01902 731462
          E: newatson@btopenworld.com

DIOCESE OF LINCOLN

Founded in 1072, formerly Dorchester (◻◻ 886), formerly Leicester (◻◻ 680), originally Lindine (◻◻ 678). Lincolnshire; North East Lincolnshire; North Lincolnshire, except for an area in the west, in the dioces of Sheffield.

Population 1,071,000   Area 2,670 sq m
Full-time Stipendiary Parochial Clergy 160   Benefices 190
Parishes 492   Churches 627
www.lincoln.anglican.org
Overseas link dioceses: RC Diocese of Brugge, Harnosands (Sweden),
Tirunelveli (CSI), Tuticorin-Nazareth (CSI)

BISHOP (72nd)
The Rt Revd Christopher Lowson, The Old Palace, Lincoln LN2 1PU   T: 01522 504092
F: 01522 504051
E: bishop.lincoln@lincoln.anglican.org

BISHOP'S STAFF
Bishop's Chaplain The Revd Jayson Rhodes (from 10/11/17)
Bishop's Strategic Implementation Adviser The Revd David Dadswell   T: 01522 504062
E: bishops.strategy@lincoln.anglican.org

SUFFRAGAN BISHOPS
GRANTHAM The Rt Revd Dr Nicholas Chamberlain, The Old Palace, Lincoln LN2 1PU   T: 01552 504092
F: 01522 504051
E: bishop.grantham@lincoln.anglican.org
GRIMSBY The Rt Revd David Court (*Same Address, Tel & Fax*)
E: bishop.grimsby@lincoln.anglican.org

ASSISTANT BISHOPS
The Rt Revd Norman Banks, Parkside House, Abbey Mill Lane, St Albans AL3 4HE
T: 01727 836358
E: bishop@richborough.org.uk
The Rt Revd David Rossdale, Home Farm, East Keal, Spilsby PE23 4AY
The Rt Revd David Tustin, The Ashes, Tunnel Road, Wrawby DN20 8SF

CATHEDRAL CHURCH OF THE BLESSED VIRGIN MARY
Dean The Very Revd Christine Wilson, The Deanery, 11 Minster Yard, Lincoln LN2 1PJ
T: 01522 561630
E: dean@lincolncathedral.com
Canons Residentiary
Subdean The Revd Canon John Patrick, The Subdeanery, 18 Minster Yard, Lincoln LN2 1PY   T: 01522 561626
E: subdean@lincolncathedral.com

Precentor The Revd Canon Sal MacDougall
E: precentor@lincolncathedral.com
Other Staff
Interim Chapter Clerk Mr Will Harrison, Chapter Office, Lincoln Cathedral, Lincoln LN2 1PX   T: 01522 561604
E: chapterclerk@lincolncathedral.com
Director of Music and Organist and Master of the Choristers Mr Aric Prentice, Lincoln Minster School, Prior Building, Upper Lindum Street, Lincoln LN2 5RW   T: 01522 551300
E: aric.prentice@church-schools.com
Assistant Director of Music and Sub-Organist Mr Jeffrey Makinson, 2a Vicars Court, Lincoln LN2 1PT   T: 01522 561647
E: jeffreymakinson@aol.com
Organist Laureate Dr Colin Walsh, Graveley Place, 12 Minster Yard, Lincoln LN2 1PJ
T: 01522 561646
E: colinwalsh1@btinternet.com

ARCHDEACONS
STOW AND LINDSEY The Ven Mark John Steadman, Edward King House, The Old Palace, Lincoln LN2 1PU   T: 01522 504050
E: archdeacon.stow@lincoln.anglican.org
BOSTON The Ven Dr Justine Allain Chapman, Archdeacon's House, Castle Hill, Welbourn, Lincoln LN5 0NF   T: 01400 273335
E: archdeacon.boston@lincoln.anglican.org
LINCOLN The Ven Gavin Kirk, Edward King House, The Old Palace, Lincoln LN2 1PU
T: 01522 504039
E: archdeacon.lincoln@lincoln.anglican.org

MEMBERS OF THE HOUSE OF CLERGY OF THE GENERAL SYNOD
Proctors for Clergy
The Revd Alyson Buxton
The Ven Dr Justine Allain-Chapman
The Revd Martyn Andrew Nicholas Taylor

MEMBERS OF THE HOUSE OF LAITY OF THE GENERAL SYNOD
Mr Nigel Bacon
Mr Carl Fender

LINCOLN

Prof Muriel Robinson
Mrs Susan Slater

DIOCESAN OFFICERS
Diocesan Secretary Vacancy
    E: interim.diosec@lincoln.anglican.org
Deputy Diocesan Secretary Mr Will Harrison
(Same Address)   *T:* 01522 504033
    E: will.harrison@lincoln.anglican.org
Assistant Diocesan Secretary Mr David Mason
(Same Address)   *T:* 01522 504064
                          F: 01865 790470
    E: david.mason@lincoln.anglican.org
Chancellor of Diocese His Honour Judge Mark
Bishop, The Diocesan Registry, Roythornes
Solicitors,   Enterprise   Way,   Pinchbeck,
Spalding PE11 3YR
Registrar of Diocese and Bishop's Legal Secretary
Mrs Julie Robinson *(Same Address)*
                          T: 01775 842618
    E: julierobinson@roythornes.co.uk

DIOCESAN ORGANIZATIONS
Diocesan Office Edward King House, Minster
Yard, Lincoln LN2 1PU   *T:* 01522 504050
                          F: 01522 504051
    E: reception@lincoln.anglican.org
    W: www.lincoln.anglican.org

ADMINISTRATION
Diocesan Synod (Chairman, House of Clergy) The
Revd Canon Christopher Lilley
(Chairman, House of Laity) Mr Nigel Bacon
(Secretary) Mr Will Harrison, Edward King
House, Minster Yard, Lincoln LN2 1PU
                          T: 01522 504033
    E: will.harrison@lincoln.anglican.org
Bishop's Council (Chairman) The Rt Revd
Christopher Lowson
(Secretary) Mr Will Harrison, Edward King
House, Minster Yard, Lincoln LN2 1PU
                          T: 01522 504033
    E: will.harrison@lincoln.anglican.org
Board of Finance (Chairman) Mr James Birch
(Same Address)
Trusts Committee Mr Andrew Gosling *(Same
Address)*
Assets Committee Mrs Ann Treacy *(Same
Address)*
Investment Policy Committee Mrs Ann Treacy
(As above)
Glebe Committee Mr Andrew Gosling *(Same
Address)*
Parsonages and Properties Mr Nicholas Turner
(Same Address)
Board of Patronage Mr Steven Sleight *(Same
Address)*
(Designated Officer) Mrs Julie Robinson, The
Diocesan   Registry,   Roythornes   Solicitors,
Enterprise   Way,   Pinchbeck,   Spalding PE11
3YR   *T:* 01775 842618
    E: julierobinson@roythornes.co.uk

(Diocesan Electoral Registration Officer) Mr Will
Harrison, Edward King House, Minster Yard,
Lincoln LN2 1PU   *T:* 01522 504033
    E: will.harrison@lincoln.anglican.org

CHURCH BUILDINGS
*Advisory Committee for the Care of Churches
(Chairman)* The Revd Canon John Patrick, The
Subdeanery, 18 Minster Yard, Lincoln LN2
1PY   *T:* 01522 561626
    E: subdean@lincolncathedral.com
(Secretary) Mr Keith Halliday, Edward King
House, Minster Yard, Lincoln LN2 1PU
                          T: 01522 504046
(Church Buildings Officer) Mr Ben Stoker *(Same
Address)*
(Historic Churches Support Officer) Mr Matthew
Godfrey *(Same Address)*
(Closed Churches) Vacancy

DIOCESAN RECORD OFFICE
Lincolnshire Archives Office, St Rumbold
Street, Lincoln LN2 5AB   *T:* 01522 526204

EDUCATION
Director of Education Jacqueline Waters-
Dewhurst, Edward King House, Minster Yard,
Lincoln LN2 1PU   *T:* 01522 504010
    E: education@lincoln.anglican.org
Diocesan Board of Education (Chair) Prof Muriel
Robinson
    E: muriel.robinson@lincoln.anglican.org
(Deputy Director of Education) Mr Paul
Thompson, Edward King House, Minster Yard,
Lincoln LN2 1PU
(Diocesan Board of Education Business Manager)
Mrs Bridget Starling *(Same Address)*
(Schools Adviser) Mr David Clements *(Same
Address)*

LITURGICAL COMMITTEE
Chairman The Ven Gavin Kirk, Edward King
House, The Old Palace, Lincoln LN2 1PU
                          T: 01522 504039
    E: archdeacon.lincoln@lincoln.anglican.org

MINISTRY
Principal of EM3 The Revd Sally Myers, Edward
King House, Minster Yard, Lincoln LN2 1PU
                          T: 01522 504021
*Diocesan Director of Ordinands and Vocations
Adviser* The Revd Canon Dr Jeffrey Heskins
(Same Address)   *T:* 01522 504029
Adviser on Women's Ministry Vacancy
Ordinands' Grants Mrs Ann Treacy, Edward
King House, Minster Yard, Lincoln LN2 1PU
Warden of Readers The Revd Sally Buck
                          T: 01427 788251

Readers (Secretary) Mr J. Marshall, 73 Sentance Crescent, Kirton, Boston PE20 1XF
T: 01205 723097
Clergy Widows Officers Canon and Mrs Michael Boughton, 45 Albion Crescent, Lincoln LN1 1EB
T: 01522 569653
Clergy Retirement Officer The Ven Geoff Arrand

MISSION AND ECUMENICAL CONCERNS
Ecumenical Officer Vacancy
Churches Together in all Lincolnshire Vacancy
Lincolnshire Chaplaincy Services (Company No. 6491058) (Chair of Board and Chaplaincy Director) The Revd Canon Andrew Vaughan, Edward King House, Minster Yard, Lincoln LN2 1PU
T: 01522 528266
E: andrewvaughan@ntlworld.com
(Business Manager) Miss Alison McNish *(Same Address)*
T: 01522 504070
(Agricultural Chaplain) Canon Alan Robson, The Manse, 1 Manor Drive, Wragby, Market Rasen LN8 5SL
T: 01673 857871
(Work with Young People) Captain D. Rose, Edward King House, Minster Yard, Lincoln LN2 1PU
T: 01522 504066
(Parish Support and Youth Project Worker) Suzanne Starbuck *(Same Address)*

PRESS, PUBLICITY AND PUBLICATIONS
Communications Officers Miss Michelle Lees, Edward King House, Minster Yard, Lincoln LN2 1PU
T: 01522 504034
The Revd Adrian Smith *(Same Address & Tel)*

RURAL DEANS
ARCHDEACONRY OF BOSTON
Beltisloe Christopher John Atkinson, The Vicarage, Church Walk, Bourne PE10 9UQ
T: 01778 422412
E: chris_atk@yahoo.com
Elloe East Rosamund Joy Seal, The Vicarage, 5 Church Street, Holbeach, Spalding PE12 7LL
T: 01406 424989
E: rosamund@sealatmoulton.co.uk
Elloe West Philip Brent, The Rectory, 13 Church Street, Market Deeping, Peterborough PE6 8DA
T: 01778 342237
E: philip@candace.fsnet.co.uk
Grantham Christopher Paul Boland, The Vicarage, Edinburgh Road, Grantham NG31 9QZ
T: 01476 564781
E: cpboland@btinternet.com
Loveden Sonia Patricia Barron, The New Rectory, 6 Rectory Lane, Claypole, Newark NG23 5BH
T: 07800 583824
E: rectorclaypole5@gmail.com

Stamford Mark Warrick, All Saints' Vicarage, Casterton Road, Stamford PE9 2YL
T: 01780 756942
E: mark.warrick@stamfordallsaints.org.uk

ARCHDEACONRY OF LINCOLN
Calcewaithe and Candleshoe Terence Steele, The Vicarage, Glebe Rise, Burgh le Marsh, Skegness PE24 5BL
T: 01754 810216
E: father.terry@btclick.com
Christianity David John Osbourne, The Rectory, 2A St Helen's Avenue, Lincoln LN6 7RA
T: 01522 682026
E: david.osbourne@hotmail.co.uk
Graffoe Vacancy
Holland Paul Vincent Noble, The Rectory, Fishtoft Road, Skirbeck, Boston PE21 0DJ
T: 01205 362734
E: frpnoble@skirbeckrectory.freeserve.co.uk
Lafford Christine Pennock, The Rectory, All Saints' Close, Ruskington, Sleaford NG34 9FP
T: 01526 832463
E: revpennock77@btinternet.com
Louthesk Vacancy

ARCHDEACONRY OF STOW AND LINDSEY
Axholme, Isle of Jonathan William Thacker, St George's Vicarage, 87 Ferry Road, Scunthorpe DN15 8LY
T: 01724 843328
E: pajdog2017@gmail.com
Bolingbroke Peter Frederick Coates, The Vicarage, Church Street, Spilsby PE23 5DU
T: 01790 752526
E: peter.coates50@yahoo.com
Corringham Phillip Wain, Oaktree House, Padmoor Lane, Upton, Gainsborough DN21 5NH
T: 01427 613188
E: phillip.wain@btinternet.com
Grimsby and Cleethorpes Andrew Patrick Dodd, The Rectory, 49 Park Drive, Grimsby DN32 0EG
T: 01472 351815
E: andrew@vincerdodd.co.uk
Haverstoe Vacancy
Horncastle Mark Noel Holden, The Vicarage, Church Street, Wragby, Lincoln LN8 5RA
T: 01673 857825
E: wragbygroup@aol.com
Lawres Richard Henry Crossland, The Vicarage, 2 Vicarage Lane, Nettleham, Lincoln LN2 2RH
T: 01522 754752
E: rcrossland@voxhumana.co.uk
Manlake Jonathan William Thacker, St George's Vicarage, 87 Ferry Road, Scunthorpe DN15 8LY
T: 01724 843328
E: pajdog2017@gmail.com
West Wold Vacancy
Yarborough David Peter Rowett, The Vicarage, Beck Hill, Barton-upon-Humber DN18 5EY
T: 01652 632202
E: david.rowett@aol.com

DIOCESE OF LIVERPOOL

Founded in 1880. Liverpool; Sefton; Knowsley; St Helens; Wigan, except for areas in the north, in the diocese of Blackburn, and in the east, in the diocese of Manchester; Halton, north of the river Mersey; Warrington, north of the river Mersey; most of West Lancashire.

Population 1,596,000   Area 390 sq m
Full-time Stipendiary Parochial Clergy 179   Benefices 135
Parishes 199   Churches 241
www.liverpool.anglican.org
Overseas link dioceses: Virginia (USA)

BISHOP (8th)

The Rt Revd Paul Bayes, Bishop's Lodge, Woolton Park, Woolton, Liverpool L25 6DT

BISHOP'S STAFF

Bishop's Executive Assistant Nichola James, Bishop's Lodge, Woolton Park, Woolton, Liverpool L25 6DT   *T:* 0151 421 0831 (Office)
F: 0151 428 3055
E: bishopslodge@liverpool.anglican.org

SUFFRAGAN BISHOP

WARRINGTON The Rt Revd Richard Blackburn St James' House, 20 St James Road, Liverpool L1 7BY   *T:* 0151 705 2140
F: 0151 428 3055
E: bishopofwarrington@
liverpool.anglican.org
Bishop's Personal Assistant Mrs Nerys Cooke, (*Same Address and Tel*)
E: nerys.cooke@liverpool.anglican.org

ASSISTANT BISHOPS

The Rt Revd Cyril Ashton, Charis, 17c Quernmore Road, Lancaster LA1 3EB
T: 01524 848684
E: bpcg.ashton@btinternet.com
The Rt Revd Glyn Webster, Holy Trinity Rectory, Micklegate, York YO1 6LE
T: 01904 628155
E: office@seeofbeverley.org
The Rt Revd John Goddard, 39 Kearsley Avenue, Tarleton, Preston PR4 6BP
T: 01772 812532
E: john.goddard39@gmail.com
The Rt Revd Stephen Lowe, 2 Pen-y-Glyn, Bryn-y-Maen, Colwyn Bay LL28 5EW
T: 01492 533510
E: lowehulme@btinternet.com

CATHEDRAL CHURCH OF CHRIST

Dean
Vacancy

Canons Residentiary
Canon Precentor The Revd Canon Myles Davies   *T:* 0151 702 7203
E: myles.davies@liverpoolcathedral.org.uk
Vacancy
Director of the Joshua Centre for Pioneer Ministry The Revd Canon Richard White
T: 0151 702 7243
E: www.liverpool.anglican.org/joshua-centre
Canon for Discipleship The Revd Canon Paul Rattigan   *T:* 0151 702 7233
E: paul.rattigan@liverpoolcathedral.org.uk
Other Staff
Cathedral Curate The Revd Mohammed Eghtedarian   *T:* 0151 702 7278
E: mohammed.e@liverpoolcathedral.org.uk
Mission Pastor Mr Mike Prescott
T: 0151 702 7235
E: mike.prescott@liverpoolcathedral.org.uk
Chief Officer Mr Mike Eastwood, St James' House, 20 St James Road, Liverpool L1 7BY
T: 0151 705 2112
F: 0151 709 2885
E: mike.eastwood@liverpool.anglican.org
Director of Music Mr David Poulter
T: 0151 702 7291/7240
E: david.poulter@liverpoolcathedral.org.uk
Assistant Choral Director Mr Stephen Mannings   *T:* 0151 702 7234
Organist Titulaire Prof Dr Ian Tracey
E: ian.tracey@liverpoolcathedral.org.uk

ARCHDEACONS

LIVERPOOL The Vaen Mike McGurk, 445 Aigburth Road, Liverpool LI9 3PA
T: 0151 705 2154
E: mike.mcgurk@liverpool.anglican.org
KNOWSLEY AND SEFTON The Ven Peter Spiers, St James' House, St James Road, Liverpool L1 7BY   *T:* 0151 705 2159
E: pete.spiers@liverpool.anglican.org
WIGAN AND WEST LANCASHIRE The Ven Jennifer McKenzie, St James' House, St James Road, Liverpool L1 7BY   *T:* 0151 705 2154
E: jennifer.mckenzie@liverpool.anglican.org

ST HELENS AND WARRINGTON The Ven Roger Preece, St James' House, St James Road, Liverpool L1 7BY

T: 0151 705 2154

E: roger.preece@liverpool.anglican.org

MEMBERS OF THE HOUSE OF CLERGY OF THE GENERAL SYNOD
Proctors for Clergy
The Revd Sonya Doragh
The Revd Kate Wharton
The Ven Peter Spiers
The Revd Canon Paul Rattigan

MEMBERS OF THE HOUSE OF LAITY OF THE GENERAL SYNOD
Mr David Martlew
Mr Keith Cawdron
Mrs Debra Walker
Mr Christopher Pye
Canon Margaret Swinson

DIOCESAN OFFICERS
Diocesan Secretary Mr Mike Eastwood, St James' House, 20 St James Road, Liverpool L1 7BY   T: 0151 705 2112
F: 0151 709 2885
E: mike.eastwood@liverpool.anglican.org
Chancellor of Diocese Sir Mark Hedley
Registrar of Diocese and Bishop's Legal Secretary Mr Howard Dellar, 1 The Sanctuary, Westminster, London SW1P 3JT
T: 020 7222 5381
F: 020 7222 7502
Assistant Diocesan Secretary Stuart Haynes, St James' House, 20 St James Road, Liverpool L1 7BY   T: 0151 705 2150
M: 07534 218122
E: stuart.haynes@liverpool.anglican.org
Diocesan Secretary Assistant Brenda Edwards
T: 0151 705 2139
E: brenda.edwards@liverpool.anglican.org

DIOCESAN ORGANIZATIONS
Diocesan Office St James' House, 20 St James Road, Liverpool L1 7BY   T: 0151 709 9722
F: 0151 709 2885
W: www.liverpool.anglican.org

ADMINISTRATION
Diocesan Synod (*Chair, House of Clergy*) The Revd Canon Joan Matthews, 8 The Parchments, Newton-le-Willows, Warrington WA12 0DY   T: 01925 270795
E: revjoan@hotmail.com
(*Chair, House of Laity*) Mrs Debra Walker, Willow Lodge, Church Lane, Lydiate, Merseyside L31 4HL   T: 0151 520 2496
E: debrawalker@btinternet.com

(*Secretary*) Mr Mike Eastwood, St James' House, 20 St James Road, Liverpool L1 7BY
T: 0151 705 2112
F: 0151 709 2885
E: mike.eastwood@liverpool.anglican.org
(*Assistant Secretary*) Vacancy
Board of Finance (*Chair*) Mr David Greensmith, St James' House, 20 St James Road, Liverpool L1 7BY
(*Secretary*) Mr Mike Eastwood (*Same Address*)
T: 0151 705 2112
F: 0151 709 2885
E: mike.eastwood@
liverpool.anglican.org
Mission and Pastoral Committee (*Chair*) The Rt Revd Richard Blackburn (*Same Address*)
T: 0151 705 2140
F: 0151 428 3055
E: bishopofwarrington@
liverpool.anglican.org
(*Secretary*) Mrs Sandra Holmes
T: 0151 705 2142
E: sandra.holmes@liverpool.anglican.org
(*Bishop's Planning Officer*) The Revd David Burrows, St James' House, 20 St James Road, Liverpool L1 7BY
E: davidmacburrows@msn.com
(*Assistant Bishop's Planning Officer*) The Revd Robert Williams   E: robw49@tiscali.co.uk
Clergy Housing and Glebe Committee (*Chair*) Mr David Burgess, St James' House, 20 St James Road, Liverpool L1 7BY
(*Surveyor*) Mr Alan Gayner (*Same Address*)
(*Support*) Mrs Claire Evans (*Same Address*)
T: 0151 705 2129
E: claire.evans@liverpool.anglican.org
(*Human Resources Adviser*) Miss Sharon Townson   T: 0151 705 2143
E: sharon.townson@liverpool.anglican.org
(*Designated Officer*) The Revd David Burrows, St James' House, 20 St James Road, Liverpool L1 7BY   E: davidmacburrows@msn.com

CHURCH BUILDINGS
Advisory Committee for the Care of Churches (*Chair*) The Revd Canon Cllr Stephen Parish, 26 Leamington Close, Great Sankey, Warrington WA5 3PY   T: 01925 711830

CHURCH GROWTH TEAM
Director Canon Linda Jones, St James' House, 20 St James Road, Liverpool L1 7BY
T: 0151 705 2109
E: linda.jones@liverpool.anglican.org
Mission and Pastoral Officer Mrs Sandra Holmes   T: 0151 705 2142
E: sandra.holmes@liverpool.anglican.org
Children and Families Missioner Mrs Sue Mitchell   T: 0151 705 2167
E: sue.mitchell@liverpool.anglican.org

Youth and Families Officer Emma O'Hagan
T: 07934190616
E: emma.ohagan@liverpool.anglican.org
Diocesan Missioner Janice Hill
T: 07843972358
E: janice.hill@liverpool.anglican.org
Diocesan Ecumenical Adviser Canon Linda Jones, St James' House, 20 St James Road, Liverpool L1 7BY   T: 0151 705 2109
E: linda.jones@liverpool.anglican.org

CHURCHES TOGETHER IN THE MERSEYSIDE REGION
Ecumenical Co-ordinator The Revd Ian Smith, Quaker Meeting House, 22 School Lane, Liverpool L1 3BT   T: 0151 709 0125
E: office@ctmr.org.uk
Elizabeth Hachmoeller (*Same Address, Tel & email*)

COMMUNICATIONS
Director Stuart Haynes, St James' House, 20 St James Road, Liverpool L1 7BY
T: 0151 705 2150
M: 07534 218122
E: stuart.haynes@liverpool.anglican.org
Communications Manager Mrs Jude Knight (*Same Address*)   T: 0151 702 7230
E: jude.knight@liverpool.anglican.org
Communications Officer Mrs Sarah Doyle (*Same Address*)   T: 0151 705 2131
E: sarah.doyle@liverpool.anglican.org
Graphic Designer Michelle Evans (*Same Address*)   T: 0151 705 2114
E: michelle.evans@liverpool.anglican.org

DIOCESAN LITURGY AND WORSHIP FORUM
Chair The Revd Jeremy Fagan, 27 Shakespeare Avenue, Kirkby L32 9SH   T: 0151 547 2133
E: faganj@mac.com

DIOCESAN RECORD OFFICE
1 The Sanctuary, Westminster, London SW1P 3JT   T: 020 7222 5381
F: 020 7222 7502

The Lancashire Record Office, Bow Lane, Preston PR1 2RE

EDUCATION
Chair The Rt Revd Richard Blackburn, St James' House, 20 St James Road, Liverpool L1 7BY   T: 0151 705 2140
F: 0151 428 3055
E: bishopofwarrington@liverpool.anglican.org
Director of Education The Revd Richard Peers (*Same Address*)

Assistant Director Mr Stuart Harrison (*Same Address*)
Senior Diocesan Schools Adviser Mr David Thorpe (*Same Address*)
Diocesan Schools Adviser Mrs Joan Stein (*Same Address*)

JUSTICE, INCLUSION AND EXTERNAL RELATIONS
Director of Social Justice The Revd Canon Dr Ellen Loudon, St James' House, 20 St James Road, Liverpool L1 7BY   T: 0151 521 2113
E: ellen.loudon@liverpool.anglican.org
Departmental Chair Canon Professor Hilary Russell   E: hilaryerussell@gmail.com
Deputy Chair Vacancy
Disability Awareness Officer and Vulnerable Adults Advisor Sister Ruth Reed
E: ruth.reed@liverpool.anglican.org
Child Protection Adviser Mrs Su Foster
E: su.foster@liverpool.anglican.org
Domestic Abuse Adviser Mrs Helen Clarey
E: helen.clarey@talktalk.net
Chair, Anglican Partnerships and Links The Revd Canon Malcolm Rogers
E: malrogers@blueyonder.co.uk
Team Leader, Pastoral Services for the Deaf Community The Revd Dr Hannah Lewis
E: hannah.lewis@liverpool.anglican.org
Heritage Support Officer Mr Ian Simpson
T: 0151 705 2127
E: ian.simpson@liverpool.anglican.org
Development Officer (Together Liverpool) The Revd John Davis   T: 0151 705 2163
E: john.davis@togetherliverpool.org.uk
Church Credit Champions Network Co-ordinator Julia Webster   T: 0151 705 2204
E: julia.webster@togetherliverpool.org.uk
Chair, Arts and Culture Network The Revd Canon Dr Ellen Loudon, St James' House, 20 St James Road, Liverpool L1 7BY
T: 0151 521 2113
E: ellen.loudon@liverpool.anglican.org
Adviser on Elderly Person Issues Mrs Mary Kessler   E: marykessler@idnet.com

LEARNING AND STEWARDSHIP
Director The Revd Steve Pierce, St James' House, 20 St James Road, Liverpool L1 7BY
T: 0151 705 2120
E: steve.pierce@liverpool.anglican.org
Learning Managers Mrs Suzanne Matthews
The Revd Bob Banton
Director of Studies The Revd Peter Whittington
Vocations Officer Mrs Debbie Ellison
E: lifelonglearning@liverpool.anglican.org
Resources Officers Gordon Fath
Cath Gaskell
E: resources.team@liverpool.anglican.org

MINISTRY

Director of Vocations The Revd Simon Chesters, St James' House, 20 St James Street, Liverpool L1 7BY   *T:* 0151 705 2185
      E: simon.chesters@liverpool.anglican.org
Dean of Women's Ministry Vacancy
Readers' Association (Warden) (*Readers' Association Warden*) Mr Spen Webster
      E: spen.webster@liverpool.anglican.org

MISSION IN THE ECONOMY (MITE)

Team Coordinator Mike Prescott
      E: missionintheeconomy@hotmail.com

AREA DEANS
ARCHDEACONERY OF ST HELENS AND WARRINGTON

St Helens David Dean Eastwood, The Vicarage, 51A Rainford Road, Dentons Green, St Helens WA10 6BZ   *T:* 01744 27446
      E: davideastwood86@googlemail.com
Warrington Paul David Wilson, The Rectory, 129 Church Street, Warrington WA1 2TL
                  T: 01925 635020
      E: revpdwilson@aol.com
Widnes Janice Margaret Collier, The Vicarage, 2 Vicarage Close, Hale Village, Liverpool L24 4BH   *T:* 0151 425 3195
      E: janice.collier@hotmail.co.uk
Winwick Stephen Bernard Grey, St Thomas's Vicarage, Church Street, Garstang, Preston PR3 1PA   *T:* 01995 602192
      E: revstephengrey@gmail.com

ARCHDEACONRY OF KNOWSLEY AND SEFTON

Bootle Thomas Rich, Christ Church Vicarage, 1 Breeze Hill, Bootle L20 9EY
                  T: 0151 525 2565
      E: tom@richchurch.freeserve.co.uk

Huyton Andrew David Stott, St Luke's Vicarage, Princess Drive, Liverpool L14 8XG
                  T: 0151 259 8125
      E: andrew@stott401.fsnet.co.uk
North Meols Philip Charles Green, St John's Vicarage, Rufford Road, Southport PR9 8JH
                  T: 01704 227662
      E: revphilgreen@talktalk.net
Sefton Anne Elizabeth Taylor, St Peter's Vicarage, Cricket Path, Formby, Liverpool L37 7DP   *T:* 01704 872824
      E: revannetaylor@gmail.com

ARCHDEACONRY OF LIVERPOOL

Liverpool North Vacancy
Liverpool South Roland Harvey, St Michael's Vicarage, 49 Harbour Drive, Liverpool L19 8AB   *T:* 07817 901455
      E: rolandharvey68@gmail.com
Toxteth and Wavertree Elaine Jones, 29 Moel Famau View, Liverpool L17 7ET
                  T: 07787 550622
      E: joneselaine@hotmail.co.uk
Walton Vacancy
West Derby Emma Louise Williams, 28 Brookland Road West, Liverpool L13 3BQ
                  T: 0151 228 2426
      E: revdem1411@btinternet.com

ARCHDEACONRY OF WIGAN AND WEST LANCASHIRE

Ormskirk William Duncan Petty, 181 Ennerdale, Skelmersdale WN8 6AH
                  T: 01704 892444
      E: duncan@thepettys.freeserve.co.uk
Wigan Philip Gregory Anderson, St John's Vicarage, 2 Shelley Drive, Orrell, Wigan WN5 8HW   *T:* 01942 375209
      E: philipanderson@merseymail.com

DIOCESE OF LONDON

Founded in 314. The City of London; Greater London north of the Thames, except five East London boroughs in the diocese of Chelmsford, and an area in the north in the diocese of St Albans; Surrey north of the Thames; a small area of southern Hertfordshire.

Population 4,299,000   Area 280 sq m
Full-time Stipendiary Parochial Clergy 509   Benefices 408
Parishes 398   Churches 492
www.london.anglican.org
Overseas link dioceses: Niassa and Lebombo (Mozambique), Angola

BISHOP
Vacancy

BISHOP'S STAFF
Diary Assistant Frances Charlesworth
Personal Assistant Janet Laws

SUFFRAGAN BISHOPS
FULHAM The Rt Revd Jonathan Baker, Bishop of Fulham's Office, 5 St Andrew Street, London EC4A 3AF   *T:* 020 7932 1130
     E: bishop.fulham@london.anglican.org
ISLINGTON The Rt Revd Ric Thorpe, 26 Canonbury Park South, London N1 2FN
               T: 07776 204945
     E: bishop.islington@london.anglican.org

AREA BISHOPS
EDMONTON The Rt Revd Robert Wickham, 27 Thurlow Road, London NW3 5PP
               T: 020 3837 5250
     E: bishop.edmonton@london.anglican.org
▢▢▢▢▢▢▢▢ The Rt Revd Dr Graham Tomlin, Dial House, Riverside, Twickenham TW1 3DT
               T: 020 7932 1180
     E: bishop.kensington@london.anglican.org
STEPNEY The Rt Revd Adrian Newman, 63 Coborn Road, London E3 2DB
               T: 020 7932 1140
     E: bishop.stepney@london.anglican.org
WILLESDEN The Rt Revd Peter Broadbent, 173 Willesden Lane, London NW6 7YN
               T: 020 8451 0189
               F: 020 8451 4606
               M: 07957 144674
     E: bishop.willesden@btinternet.com

ASSISTANT BISHOPS
The Rt Revd Michael Colclough, 12 Grosvenor Court, Sloane Square, London SW1X 9PF
               T: 020 3612 3135
     E: michaeljcolclough@gmail.com

The Rt Revd Edward Holland, 37 Parfrey Street, London W6 9EW   *T:* 020 8746 3636
     E: ed.holland@uwclub.net
The Rt Revd Robert Ladds, St Peter's Mission House, Wapping Lane, London E1W 2RW
     E: episcopus@ntworld.com
The Most Revd Walter Makhulu, 16 Downside, 8–10 St John's Avenue, London SW15 2AE
               T: 020 8704 1220
     E: makhulu@btinternet.com
The Rt Revd Michael Marshall, 53 Oakley Gardens, Easton, London SW3 5QQ
               T: 020 7351 0928
     E: sebastian97@hotmail.co.uk
The Rt Revd Preb Sandy Millar, 37 Alde Lane, Aldeburgh IP15 5DZ   *T:* 01728 452926
     E: sandy.millar@techademic.net
The Rt Revd Stephen Platten, 73A Gloucester Place, London W1U 8JW
     E: stephen.platten@icloud.com
The Rt Revd Nigel Stock, Bishop at Lambeth, Lambeth Palace, London SE1 7JU
               T: 020 7898 1198
                   020 7898 1200
     E: nigel.stock@lambethpalace.org.uk
The Rt Revd Peter Wheatley, 47 Sedlescombe Road South, St Leonards-on-Sea TN38 0TB
               T: 01424 424814
     E: peter.wheatley@outlook.com
The Rt Revd and Rt Hon. Lord Harries of Pentregarth, 41 Melville Road, Barnes, London SW13 9RH   *T:* 020 8288 6053
     E: richard.d.harries@googlemail.com

CATHEDRAL CHURCH OF ST PAUL
Dean The Very Revd Dr David Ison, The Chapter House, St Paul's Churchyard, London EC4M 8AD   *T:* 020 7246 8360
     E: deanspa@stpaulscathedral.org.uk
Canons Residentiary
Chancellor Canon Mark Oakley, The Chapter House, St Paul's Churchyard, London EC4M 8AD   *T:* 020 7246 8378
     E: chancellor@stpaulscathedral.org.uk
Precentor Canon Michael Hampel (*Same Address*)   *T:* 020 7246 8304
     E: precentor@stpaulscathedral.org.uk

Canon Pastor Canon Tricia Hillas (*Same Address*) T: 020 7246 8378
E: pastor@stpaulscathedral.org.uk
Treasurer The Revd Canon Jonathan Brewster (*Same Address*) T: 020 3887 8867
E: treasurer@stpaulscathedral.org.uk
Canon Non-Residentiary The Ven Sheila Watson (*Same Address*)
E: vensheilawatson@gmail.com
Canons
Lay Canons Mr Gavin Ralston, The Chapter House, St Paul's Churchyard, London EC4M 8AD T: 020 7246 8350
E: gralston@stpaulscathedral.org.uk
Ms Pim Baxter OBE (*Same Address & Tel*)
E: pbaxter@stpaulscathedral.org.uk
Minor Canons
Succentor The Revd Rosemary Morton, The Chapter House, St Paul's Churchyard, London EC4M 8AD T: 020 7246 8338
E: succentor@stpaulscathedral.org.uk
Sacrist The Revd James Milne (*Same Address*)
T: 020 7246 8331
E: sacrist@stpaulscathedral.org.uk
Other Staff
Priest Vicar The Revd Helen O'Sullivan (*Same Address*) T: 020 7246 8323
E: chaplain@stpaulscathedral.org.uk
Headmaster of the School Mr Simon Larter-Evans, St Paul's Cathedral School, New Change, London EC4M 9AD T: 020 7248 5156
E: admissions@spcs.london.sch.uk
Registrar Ms Emma Davies, The Chapter House, St Paul's Churchyard, London EC4M 8AD T: 020 7246 8312
E: registrar@stpaulscathedral.org.uk
Dean's Virger Mr Charles Williams (*Same Address*) T: 020 7246 8320
E: deansvirger@stpaulscathedral.org.uk
Solicitor to the Foundation at St Paul's Cathedral Mr Owen Carew-Jones, Minerva House, 5 Montague Close, London SE1 9BB
T: 020 7593 5110
F: 020 7593 5099
E: ocj@wslaw.co.uk
Surveyor to the Fabric Mr Oliver Caroe, The Chapter House, St Paul's Churchyard, London EC4M 8AD T: 020 7246 8341
E: oliver@caroe.biz
Director of Music Mr Andrew Carwood (*Same Address*) T: 020 7236 6883
E: directorofmusic@stpaulscathedral.org.uk
Organist Mr Simon Johnson (*Same Address*)
T: 020 7246 8336
E: organist@stpaulscathedral.org.uk
Sub-Organist Vacancy (*Same Address*)
T: 020 7651 0897
E: suborganist@stpaulscathedral.org.uk

ARCHDEACONS

LONDON The Ven Luke Miller, The Old Deanery, Dean's Court, London EC4V 5AA
T: 020 7932 1133
E: archdeacon.london@london.anglican.org
TWO CITIES The Ven Rosemary Lain-Priestley, London Diocesan House, 36 Causton Street, London SW1P 4AU T: 020 3837 5225
E: archdeacon.twocities@
london.anglican.org
HACKNEY The Ven Liz Adekunle, c/o Christ Church Spitalfields, Fournier Street, London E1 6LY T: 020 3837 5232
E: archdeacon.hackney@
london.anglican.org
MIDDLESEX The Ven Stephan Welch, 98 Dukes Ave, London W4 2AF T: 020 8742 8308
E: archdeacon.middlesex@
london.anglican.org
HAMPSTEAD The Ven John Hawkins, London Diocesan House, 36 Causton Street, London SW1P 4AU T: 020 7932 1190
E: archdeacon.hampstead@
london.anglican.org
NORTHOLT The Ven Duncan Green, London Diocesan House, 36 Causton Street, London SW1P 4AU T: 020 7932 1274
E: archdeacon.northolt@
london.anglican.org

MEMBERS OF THE HOUSE OF CLERGY OF THE GENERAL SYNOD

Proctors for Clergy
The Revd Dr Sean Doherty
The Revd Dr Andrew Emerton
The Ven Luke Miller
The Revd Jane Morris
The Revd Preb Alan Moses
The Revd Bertrand Olivier
The Revd Dr Jason Roach
The Revd Charles Skrine
The Revd Christopher Smith
The Revd Sally Ann Hitchiner
The Revd Anne Helen Stevens

MEMBERS OF THE HOUSE OF LAITY OF THE GENERAL SYNOD

Mrs Enid Barron
Miss Susan Breen
Mr Andrew Brydon
Miss Deborah Buggs
Mrs Sarah Finch
Mr Aiden Hargreaves-Smith
Ms Josile Munro
Dr Lindsay Newcombe
Mr Clive Scowen
Dr Megan Warner
Mr Richard Wellings-Thomas

DIGNITARIES IN CONVOCATION
The Rt Revd Peter Broadbent

DIOCESAN OFFICERS
General Secretary and Chief Executive Mr Richard Gough, London Diocesan House, 36 Causton Street, London SW1P 4AU
T: 020 7932 1100
Chancellor of Diocese Chancellor The Worshipful Nigel Seed, Winckworth Sherwood, Minerva House, 5 Montague Close, London SE1 9BB
T: 020 7593 5110
F: 020 7248 3221
Registrar of Diocese and Bishop's Legal Secretary Mr Paul Morris (*Same Address, Tel & Fax*)
Official Principal of the Archdeaconry of Hackney His Honour David Smith, Beachcroft, Beach, Bitton, Bristol BS30 6NP
Official Principal of the Archdeaconry of Hampstead Ms Sheila Cameron, 2 Harcourt Building, Temple, London EC4Y 9DB
Official Principal of the Archdeaconry of Northolt Mr Paul Morris, Winckworth Sherwood, Minerva House, 5 Montague Close, London SE1 9BB
T: 020 7593 5110
F: 020 7248 3221

DIOCESAN ORGANIZATIONS
Diocesan Office London Diocesan House, 36 Causton Street, London SW1P 4AU
T: 020 7932 1100
F: 020 7932 1110
W: www.london.anglican.org

ADMINISTRATION
London Diocesan Fund (Diocesan Board of Finance) (Chair) Vacancy
(*Vice Chairs*) The Revd Preb Alan Moses, 7 Margaret Street, London W1W 8JG
T: 020 7636 1788
E: alanmoses111@gmail.com
Mr James Normand
Finance Committee Mr James Normand
Diocesan Synod (House of Clergy) The Revd Preb Alan Moses, 7 Margaret Street, London W1W 8JG
T: 020 7636 1788
E: alanmoses111@gmail.com
(*House of Laity*) Mr James Normand
Diocesan Board for Schools The Ven Luke Miller, The Old Deanery, Dean's Court, London EC4V 5AA
T: 020 7932 1133
E: archdeacon.london@london.anglican.org
Director of Finance and Operations Mr Richard Antcliffe
Director of Human Resources Colette Black
Director of Property Mr Michael Bye
Director of Development Edward Moody
Synodical Secretary Mrs Monica Bolley

Communications Manager Mr Robert Hargrave, 36 Causton Street, London SW1P 4AU
T: 020 7932 1227
E: robert.hargrave@london.anglican.org
Diocesan Advisory Committee (Chair) The Baroness Wilcox
(*Secretary*) Mr Geoffrey Hunter

DIOCESAN RECORD OFFICE
City of Westminster Archives Centre, 10 St Ann's Street, London SW1P 2DE
T: 020 7798 2180
E: archives@westminster.gov.uk

EDUC`ATION
Senior Chaplain for Higher Education The Revd Andrew Willson, Chaplaincy Centre, Imperial College, 10 Princes Gardens, London SW7 1NA
T: 020 7594 9600
E: a.willson@imperial.ac.uk
Director, London Diocesan Board for Schools Mr Inigo Woolf, London Diocesan House, 36 Causton Street, London SW1P 4AU
T: 020 7932 1165
E: inigo.woolf@london.anglican.org

ENVIRONMENT
Head of Environment and Sustainability Mr Brian Cuthbertson, 36 Causton Street, London SW1P 4AU
T: 020 7932 1229
E: brian.cuthbertson@london.anglican.org

LITURGICAL
Chairman The Very Revd Dr David Ison, The Chapter House, St Paul's Churchyard, London EC4M 8AD
T: 020 7246 8360
E: deanspa@stpaulscathedral.org.uk

MINISTRY
Director of Ministry, Warden of Licensed Lay Ministry The Revd Dr Neil Evans, 23 St Albans Avenue, London W4 5LL
T: 020 8987 7332
E: neil.evans@london.anglican.org
Vicar General to the London College of Bishops, Diocesan Director of Ordinands Preb Nick Mercer, The Old Deanery, Dean's Court, London EC4V 5AA
T: 020 7489 4274
E: nick.mercer@london.anglican.org
Two Cities (Area Director of Training and Development) The Revd Dr Neil Evans, 23 St Albans Avenue, London W4 5LL
T: 020 8987 7332
E: neil.evans@london.anglican.org
(*Dean of Women's Ministry*) The Ven Rosemary Lain-Priestley, London Diocesan House, 36 Causton Street, London SW1P 4AU
T: 020 3837 5225
E: archdeacon.twocities@london.anglican.org

Stepney (*Area Director of Training and Development*) The Revd Irena Edgcumbe, The Centre for Training and Development, St Anne's Community Hall, Hemsworth Street, London N1 5LF   T: 020 7033 3446
          E: irena.edgcumbe@london.anglican.org
(*Dean of Women's Ministry*) Vacancy
Kensington (*Area Director of Ministry*) The Revd Martin Breadmore, 207 London Road, Twickenham TW1 1EJ   T: 020 8891 0324
          E: martin.breadmore@london.anglican.org
(*Dean of Women's Ministry*) Vacancy
Edmonton (*Area Director of Training and Development*) Vacancy (*As above*)
Willesden (*Area Director of Training and Development*) The Revd Andrew Corsie, Holy Trinity Church, Suez Avenue, Perivale UB6 8LN   T: 020 8991 9571
          E: andrew.corsie@london.anglican.org
(*Dean of Women's Ministry*) The Revd Jane Manley, St Paul's Vicarage, Thurlstone Road, Ruislip Manor, Ruislip HA4 0BP
          T: 01895 633499
          E: jane.e.manley@btinternet.com

MISSION
Children's Ministry Adviser Sam Donoghue, London Diocesan House, 36 Causton Street, London SW1P 4AU   T: 020 7932 1255
          E: sam.donoghue@london.anglican.org
Diocesan Community Ministry Adviser Vacancy

PRESS AND COMMUNICATIONS
Press, Media and Public Affairs (*Communications Manager*) Mr Robert Hargrave, 36 Causton Street, London SW1P 4AU   T: 020 7932 1227
          E: robert.hargrave@london.anglican.org

AREA DEANS
ARCHDEACONRY OF CHARING CROSS
Westminster (Paddington) Paul Richard Thomas, St James's Vicarage, 6 Gloucester Terrace, London W2 3DD   T: 020 7262 1265
          E: vicar@stjamespaddington.org.uk
Westminster (St Margaret) Philip Anthony Edwin Chester, St Matthew's House, 20 Great Peter Street, London SW1P 2BU
          T: 020 7222 3704
          E: paec@stmw.org
Westminster (St Marylebone) Leslie Alan Moses, All Saints' Vicarage, 7 Margaret Street, London W1W 8JG   T: 020 7636 1788
          E: alan@moses.org.uk

ARCHDEACONRY OF HACKNEY
Hackney Rosémia Brown, 134 Rushmore Road, London E5 0EY   T: 020 8985 1750
          E: rosemia.brown@sky.com

Islington Jessica Suzanne Swift, 306B Amhurst Road, London N16 7UE   T: 020 7923 0114
          E: swift_jessica@hotmail.com
Tower Hamlets Andrew Rider, The Rectory, 2 Fournier Street, London E1 6QE
          T: 020 7247 0790
          E: arider@ccspitalfields.org

ARCHDEACONRY OF HAMPSTEAD
Barnet, Central Gregory Austin David Platten, 14 Oakleigh Park South, London N20 9JU
          T: 020 8445 0015
          E: gregory@priest.com
Barnet, West Paul Edward Berry, 1 Beulah Close, Edgware HA8 8SP   T: 020 8958 9730
          E: paul.berry@london.anglican.org
Camden, North (Hampstead) Jonathan George Frederick Kester, Emmanuel Vicarage, Lyncroft Gardens, London NW6 1JU
          T: 020 7435 1911
          E: frjonathan@mac.com
Camden, South (Holborn and St Pancras) Christopher Matthew Smith, St Alban's Clergy House, 18 Brooke Street, London EC1N 7RD
          T: 020 7405 1831
          E: fathercsmith@gmail.com
Enfield Stuart James Owen, All Saints' Vicarage, 43 All Saints' Close, London N9 9AT
          T: 020 8803 9199
          E: fr.stuart@gmail.com
Haringey, East Ian George Booth, The Rectory, 1A Selborne Road, London N22 7TL
          E: frianbooth@hotmail.com
Haringey, West Philip Henry Sudell, 163 Colney Hatch Lane, London N10 1HA
          T: 020 8883 7417
          E: philip.sudell@gracech.org.uk

ARCHDEACONRY OF LONDON
City Oliver Charles Milligan Ross, St Olave's Rectory, 8 Hart Street, London EC3R 7NB
          T: 020 7702 0244
          E: ocmross@mac.com

ARCHDEACONRY OF MIDDLESEX
Chelsea Emma Ruth Dinwiddy Smith, 29 Burnsall Street, London SW3 3SR
          T: 020 7351 7365
          E: emmasmith@chelseaparish.org
Hammersmith and Fulham Timothy James Stilwell, St Dionis' Vicarage, 18 Parson's Green, London SW6 4UH   T: 020 7731 1376
          E: tim@stdionis.org.uk
Hampton Joseph Barnaby Moffatt, The Vicarage, 11 Twickenham Road, Teddington TW11 8AQ   T: 020 8977 2767
          E: vicar@stmarywithstalban.org
Hounslow Richard Stephen Frank, 295 St Margarets Road, Twickenham TW1 1PN
          T: 020 8891 3504
          E: richardfrank@allsoulschurch.org.uk

Kensington Mark Ronald O'Donoghue, 20 South End Row, London W8 5BZ
T: 020 7795 6330
E: mark@christchurchkensington.com
Spelthorne Andrew Saville, The Vicarage, The Broadway, Laleham, Staines TW18 1SB
T: 01784 455524
E: andy@savilles.org.uk

ARCHDEACONRY OF NORTHOLT
Brent Graham Peter Noyce, 26 Ashburnham Road, London NW10 5SD   *T:* 020 8960 6211
E: graham@noycefamily.co.uk

Ealing Stephen Mark Newbold, St Stephen's Vicarage, Sherborne Gardens, London W13 8AQ
T: 020 8810 4929
E: vicar@ststephens-ealing.org
Harrow Ian Peter Dowsett, St Paul's Vicarage, Findon Close, Harrow HA2 8NJ
T: 020 8864 0362
E: irdowsett@talk21.com
Hillingdon Desmond Peter Banister, All Saints' Vicarage, Ryefield Avenue, Uxbridge UB10 9BT
T: 01895 239457
E: ppash@uk2.net

DIOCESE OF MANCHESTER

Founded in 1847. Manchester, except for a few parishes in the south, in the diocese of Chester; Salford; Bolton; Bury; Rochdale; Oldham; the western half of Tameside; an area of Wigan; an area of Trafford; an area of Stockport; an area of southern Lancashire.

Population 2,153,000   Area 420 sq m
Full-time Stipendiary Parochial Clergy 207   Benefices 181
Parishes 257   Churches 314
Overseas link dioceses: Lahore, Namibia, Tampere

BISHOP (11th)

The Rt Revd David Walker, Bishopscourt, Bury New Road, Salford M7 4LE
T: 0161 792 2096 (office)
F: 0161 792 6826
E: bishop@
bishopscourt.manchester.anglican.org

BISHOP'S STAFF

Bishop's Senior Chaplain The Revd Canon Dr Ian Jorysz, Bishopscourt, Bury New Road, Salford M7 4LE
E: chaplain@
bishopscourt.manchester.anglican.org

SUFFRAGAN BISHOPS

BOLTON The Rt Revd Mark Ashcroft, Bishop's Lodge, Walkden Road, Worsley, Manchester M28 2WH
T: 0161 790 8289
M: 07810 272020
MIDDLETON The Rt Revd Mark Davies, The Hollies, Manchester Road, Rochdale OL11 3QY
T: 01706 358550
F: 01706 354851
E: bishopmark@manchester.anglican.org

CATHEDRAL AND COLLEGIATE CHURCH OF ST MARY, ST DENYS AND ST GEORGE

Dean The Very Revd Rogers Govender, Manchester Cathedral, Victoria Street, Manchester M3 1SX
T: 0161 833 2220
F: 0161 839 6218
E: dean@manchestercathedral.org
Canons Residentiary
Sub Dean and Canon for Theology and Mission The Revd Canon David Holgate, 3 Booth Clibborn Court, Park Lane, Manchester M7 4PJ
T: 0161 833 2220
F: 0161 839 6218
E: canon.holgate@manchestercathedral.org
Canon Pastor The Revd Canon Marcia Wall, Manchester Cathedral, Victoria Street, Manchester M3 1SX (*Same Tel*)
E: canon.pastor@manchestercathedral.org

Archdeacon of Salford The Ven David Sharples (*Same Address & Tel*)
E: archsalford@manchester.anglican.org
Canons
Lay Members of Chapter Canon Philip Blinkhorn
Canon Dr Addy Lazz-Onyenobi
Mrs Jenny Curtis
Mr Nicholas Rank
Other Staff
Cathedral Chaplains The Revd Peter Bellamy-Knights
E: peter.bellamy-knights@
manchestercathedral.org
The Revd Canon Adrian Rhodes
E: office@manchestercathedral.org
Cathedral Administrator and Chapter Clerk Mr Stuart Shepherd, Manchester Cathedral, Victoria Street, Manchester M3 1SX
T: 0161 833 2220 (ext. 229)
E: cathedral.administrator@
manchestercathedral.org
Education Officer Mrs Pam Elliott (*Same Address*)
T: 0161 833 2220 (ext. 236)
E: pam.elliott@manchestercathedral.org
Organist and Master of the Choristers Mr Christopher Stokes (*Same Address*)
T: 0161 833 2220 (ext. 225)
E: christopher.stokes@
manchestercathedral.org
Sub-Organist Mr Geoffrey Woollatt (*Same Address*)
T: 0161 833 2220 (ext. 215)
E: geoffrey.woollatt@manchestercathedral.org
Dean's PA Mrs Alison Rowland (*Same Address*)
T: 0161 833 2220 (ext. 220)
E: alison.rowland@manchestercathedral.org
Communications and Marketing Officer Miss Joanne Hooper (*Same Address*)
T: 0161 833 2220 (ext. 221)
E: joanne.hooper@manchestercathedral.org
Worship and Music Administrator Miss Kerry Garner (*Same Address*)
T: 0161 833 2220 (ext. 238)
E: worship-music.admin@
manchestercathedral.org
Office Assistant Miss Natasha Price (*Same Address*)
T: 0161 833 2220 (ext. 235)
E: natasha.price@manchestercathedral.org

Head Verger Mr Derrick May (*Same Address*)
T: 0161 833 2220
E: derrick.may@manchestercathedral.org
Verger Mr Martin Taylor (*Same Address & Tel*)
E: martin.taylor@manchestercathedral.org
Cathedral Architect Mr John Prichard, Lloyd Evans Prichard, No 5 The Parsonage, Manchester M3 2HS   T: 0161 834 6251
E: john.prichard@lep-architects.co.uk
Cathedral Accountant Mr John Atherden, Manchester Cathedral, Victoria Street, Manchester M3 1SX
T: 0161 833 2220 (ext 234)
E: accountant@manchestercathedral.org
Finance Assistant Mrs Joanne Hodkin (*Same Address*)   T: 0161 833 2220 (ext. 224)
E: joanne.hodkin@manchestercathedral.org
Director of Fundraising and Development Mr Anthony O'Connor (*Same Address*)
T: 0161 833 2220 (ext. 233)
E: anthony.o'connor@
manchestercathedral.org
Logistics Officer Mr Peter Mellor (*Same Address*)   T: 0161 833 2220 (ext. 249)
E: peter.mellor@manchestercathedral.org
Visitor Services Manager Mrs Dympna Gould (*Same Address*)   T: 0161 833 2220 (ext. 227)
E: dympna.gould@manchestercathedral.org
Volunteer Programme Coordinators (Volition) Tony Maunder (*Same Address*)
T: 0161 833 2220 (ext. 242)
E: tony.maunder@manchestercathedral.org
John Emsley (*Same Address & Tel*)
E: john.emsley@manchestercathedral.org

ARCHDEACONS

MANCHESTER The Ven Karen Lund, 11 Moorgate Avenue, Manchester M20 1HE
T: 0161 448 1976
E: archmanchester@manchester.anglican.org
BOLTON The Ven David Bailey, 14 Springside Road, Bury BL9 5JE   T: 0161 761 6117
E: archbolton@btinternet.com
ROCHDALE The Ven Cherry Vann, 57 Melling Road, Oldham OL4 1PN   T: 0161 678 1454
E: archrochdale@manchester.anglican.org
SALFORD The Ven David Sharples, 2 The Walled Gardens, Ewhurst Avenue, Swinton M7 0FR
T: 0161 794 2331 / 0161 708 9366
E: archsalford@manchester.anglican.org

MEMBERS OF THE HOUSE OF CLERGY OF THE GENERAL SYNOD

Proctors for Clergy
Vacancy
The Revd Lisa Battye
The Revd Graham Hollowood
The Revd Canon Sharon Jones
The Revd Canon Andy Salmon
The Ven Cherry Vann

MEMBERS OF THE HOUSE OF LAITY OF THE GENERAL SYNOD

Mr Philip Geldard
Ms Margaret Parrett
The Worshipful Canon Geoffrey Tattersall QC
Mr Michael Heppleston
Canon Dr Adanna Lazz-Onyenobi
Canon Phillip Blinkhorn

DIOCESAN OFFICERS

Diocesan Secretary Canon Martin Miller, Diocesan Office, Church House, 90 Deansgate, Manchester M3 2GH   T: 0161 828 1412
F: 0161 828 1480
Chancellor of Diocese The Worshipful Canon Geoffrey Tattersall, Diocesan Registry, Church House, 90 Deansgate, Manchester M3 2GH
T: 0161 834 7545
Deputy Chancellor Ms C. Otton-Goulder (*Same Address & Tel*)
Registrar of Diocese and Bishop's Legal Secretary Mrs Jane Monks (*Same Address*)
T: 0161 839 0093
0161 834 7545
F: 0161 839 0093
Diocesan Surveyor Mr Darren Bamford, Diocesan Office, Church House, 90 Deansgate, Manchester M3 2GH   T: 0161 828 1417
F: 0161 828 1484

DIOCESAN ORGANIZATIONS

Diocesan Office Church House, 90 Deansgate, Manchester M3 2GH   T: 0161 828 1400
F: 0161 828 1480

ADMINISTRATION

Diocesan Synod (Chair, House of Clergy) Vacancy
(Chair, House of Laity) Mr Richard Lewis
Board of Finance (Chair) Canon Phillip Blinkhorn, 1 Blundell Close, Unsworth, Bury BL9 8LH   T: 0161 766 6301
(Secretary) Canon Martin Miller, Diocesan Office, Church House, 90 Deansgate, Manchester M3 2GH   T: 0161 828 1412
F: 0161 828 1480
(Head of Finance and IT) Mr David Weldon (*Same Address*)   T: 0161 828 1461
(Legal Secretary) Mrs Jane Monks, Diocesan Registry, Church House, 90 Deansgate, Manchester M3 2GH   T: 0161 839 0093
0161 834 7545
F: 0161 839 0093
Property Committee (Property Secretary) Mr Darren Bamford, Diocesan Office, Church House, 90 Deansgate, Manchester M3 2GH
T: 0161 828 1417
F: 0161 828 1484

Diocesan Office (*Chairman*) The Ven David Bailey, 14 Springside Road, Bury BL9 5JE
T: 0161 761 6117
F: 0161 763 7973
E: archbolton@btinternet.com
Mission and Pastoral Committee (*DMPC Secretary*) The Revd Alan Simpson, Diocesan Office, Church House, 90 Deansgate, Manchester M3 2GH
(*Chair*) The Rt Revd Mark Davies, The Hollies, Manchester Road, Rochdale OL11 3QY
T: 01706 358550
F: 01706 354851
E: bishopmark@manchester.anglican.org
(*Designated Officer*) Mrs Jane Monks, Diocesan Registry, Church House, 90 Deansgate, Manchester M3 2GH   T: 0161 839 0093
0161 834 7545
F: 0161 839 0093

CHURCH BUILDINGS
Advisory Committee for the Care of Churches (*Chair*) Mr John Walsh, 52 New Hall Lane, Heaton, Bolton BL1 5LW
(*DAC Secretary*) The Revd Alan Simpson, Diocesan Office, Church House, 90 Deansgate, Manchester M3 2GH

DIOCESAN RECORD OFFICE
The Central Library, St Peter's Square, Manchester M2 5PD   T: 0161 234 1980

EDUCATION
Board of Education (*Chair*) The Rt Revd Mark Davies, The Hollies, Manchester Road, Rochdale OL11 3QY   T: 01706 358550
F: 01706 354851
E: bishopmark@manchester.anglican.org
(*Director*) Canon Maurice Smith, Diocesan Office, Church House, 90 Deansgate, Manchester M3 2GH   T: 0161 828 1400
F: 0161 828 1484
(*Assistant Director of Education and School Improvement*) Mr Malcolm Finney (*Same Address*)
(*Assistant Director of Education: Schools Estate and Finance*) Mr Ian Tomkin (*Same Address*)
(*Children's Work Officer*) Vacancy
(*Youth Work Officer*) Miss Susie Mapledoram, Diocesan Office, Church House, 90 Deansgate, Manchester M3 2GH

MISSION AND MINISTRY
(*Director of Mission and Ministry*) The Revd Canon Peter Reiss, Diocesan Office, Church House, 90 Deansgate, Manchester M3 2GH
T: 0161 828 1400
Diocesan contact for environmental issues The Revd John Hughes (*Same Address*)

Transforming Communities Team Leader/ Mission Planning Officer Ms Alison Peacock (*Same Address*)
Parish Development Officer Mr Colin Barson (*Same Address*)
Healthy Churches Team Leader/ Local Ministry Officer The Revd Tim Evans
Heritage and Archdeaconry Resources Adviser Ms Heather Ford, Diocesan Office, Church House, 90 Deansgate, Manchester M3 2GH
Training Officer (CME and Laity) The Revd Julia Babb (*Same Address*)
Diocesan Director of Ordinands and OLM Officer The Ven David Sharples, 2 The Walled Gardens, Ewhurst Avenue, Swinton M7 0FR
T: 0161 794 2331 / 0161 708 9366
F: 0161 794 2411
E: archsalford@manchester.anglican.org

PRESS AND PUBLICATIONS
Editor of Diocesan Year Book / Editor of Diocesan Magazine / Communications and Events Manager Mrs Ann Mummery, Diocesan Office, Church House, 90 Deansgate, Manchester M3 2GH
T: 0161 828 1470
M: 07836 224444
E: amummery@manchester.anglican.org

RETIRED CLERGY
Retired Clergy and Widows Officer The Ven Alan Wolstencroft, The Bakehouse, 1 Latham Row, Bolton BL6 6QZ   T: 01204 469985
E: wolstencroftalan@gmail.com

AREA DEANS
ARCHDEACONRY OF BOLTON
Bolton Vincent Craig Whitworth, St Paul's Vicarage, Vicarage Lane, Halliwell, Bolton BL1 8BP   T: 01204 849079
E: vincentwhitworth@hotmail.com
Bury Simon David James Cook, All Saints' Vicarage, 10 Kirkburn View, Bury BL8 1DL
T: 0161 797 1595
E: simondjcook@aol.com
Deane Terence Paul Clark, Deane Rectory, 234 Wigan Road, Bolton BL3 5QE
T: 01204 61819
E: deanechurchoffice@btinternet.com
Radcliffe and Prestwich Alison Jane Hardy, Stand Rectory, 32 Church Lane, Whitefield, Manchester M45 7NF   T: 0161 766 2619
E: alisonhardy@fsmail.net
Rossendale Lynda Edith Maria Woodall, St John's Vicarage, Stud Brow, Facit, Rochdale OL12 8LU   T: 01706 878293
E: lyn.woodall@googlemail.com
Walmsley Nicholas John McKee, St Paul's Vicarage, Sweetloves Lane, Bolton BL1 7ET
T: 01204 304119
E: rev.nick@live.co.uk

ARCHDEACONRY OF MANCHESTER

Ardwick Craig Philip Smith, The Rectory, 42 Wellington Street, Manchester M18 8LJ
T: 0161 231 7401
Heaton Marcus Howard Maxwell, St John's Rectory, 15 Priestnall Road, Stockport SK4 3HR
T: 0161 442 1932
E: marcus.maxwell@ntlworld.com
Hulme Anthony William Hardy, St Edmund's Rectory, 1 Range Road, Manchester M16 8FS
T: 0161 226 4554
E: tonybillhardy@gmail.com
Stretford Alexander Honeyman Clephane, 306 Church Road, Urmston, Manchester M41 6JJ
T: 0161 747 8816
E: alexclephane@btinternet.com
Withington Stephen Michael Edwards, William Temple Vicarage, Robinswood Road, Manchester M22 0BU
T: 0161 437 3194
E: revdstephenedwards@yahoo.co.uk

ARCHDEACONRY OF ROCHDALE

Ashton-under-Lyne Philip Roger Dixon, St Stephen's Vicarage, 176 Stamford Road, Audenshaw, Manchester M34 5WW
T: 0161 370 1863
E: revrogerdixon@outlook.com

Heywood and Middleton Frances Clare Guite, St Martin's Vicarage, Vicarage Road North, Rochdale OL11 2TE
T: 01706 632353
E: francesguite@yahoo.co.uk
Oldham East Graham Hollowood, St Mark's Vicarage, 1 Skipton Street, Oldham OL8 2JF
T: 0161 624 4964
E: graham.hollowood@virgin.net
Oldham West David Roy Penny, St Matthew's Vicarage, Mill Brow, Chadderton, Oldham OL1 2RT
T: 0161 624 8600
E: revdpenny@btinternet.com
Rochdale Karen Louise Smeeton, 13 Brooklands Court, Rochdale OL11 4EJ
T: 07504 960446
E: therevdksmeeton@gmail.com

ARCHDEACONRY OF SALFORD

Eccles Karen Hopwood Owen, 8 Landrace Drive, Worsley, Manchester M28 1UY
T: 07964 663225
E: karen.h.owen@ntlworld.com
Leigh Julian John Hartley, St John's Vicarage, Mosley Common Road, Worsley, Manchester M28 1AN
T: 0161 790 2957
E: rev.hartley@hartley.me.uk
Salford Daniel John Ashworth Burton, The Rectory, 92 Fitzwarren Street, Salford M6 5RS
T: 0161 745 7608
E: ashworthburton@hotmail.com

Founded in 1882. Northumberland; Newcastle upon Tyne; North Tyneside; a small area of eastern Cumbria; four parishes in northern County Durham.

Population 818,000   Area 2,100 sq m
Full-time Stipendiary Parochial Clergy 116   Benefices 129
Parishes 170   Churches 237
www.newcastle.anglican.org
Overseas link dioceses: Winchester, More (Norway), Botswana (Africa)

BISHOP (12th)
The Rt Revd Christine Elizabeth Hardman, Bishop's House, 29 Moor Road South, Gosforth, Newcastle upon Tyne NE3 1PA
T: 0191 2852220
E: bishop@newcastle.anglican.org

BISHOP'S STAFF
Bishop's Chaplain Vacancy

SUFFRAGAN BISHOP
BERWICK The Rt Revd Mark Tanner, Berwick House, Longhirst Road, Pegswood, Morpeth NE61 6XF
T: 01670 519000
E: bishopofberwick@newcastle.anglican.org

PROVINCIAL EPISCOPAL VISITOR
BEVERLEY The Rt Revd Glyn Webster, Holy Trinity Rectory, Micklegate, York YO1 6LE
T: 01904 628155
E: office@seeofbeverley.org

HONORARY ASSISTANT BISHOPS
The Rt Revd John Packer, Devonshire House, Alma Place, Whitley Bay NE26 2EQ
T: 0191 2534321
The Rt Revd Stephen Pedley, The Blue House, Newbrough NE47 5AN   *T:* 01434 674238
The Rt Revd John Henry Richardson, Old Rectory, Bewcastle, Carlisle CA6 6PS
T: 01697 748389
The Rt Revd Stephen Platten, 73A Gloucester Place, London, W1U 8JW   *T:* 0207 2833121

CATHEDRAL CHURCH OF ST NICHOLAS
Dean The Very Revd Christopher Charles Dalliston, 26 Mitchell Avenue, Jesmond, Newcastle upon Tyne NE2 3LA (until 7/1/18)
T: 0191 2816554 / 0191 2321939
E: dean@stnicholascathedral.co.uk
Canons Residentiary The Ven Geoffrey Vincent Miller, 80 Moorside North, Newcastle upon Tyne NE4 9DU   *T:* 0191 2738245
E: g.miller@newcastle.anglican.org
The Revd Canon John Robert Sinclair, 16 Towers Avenue, Newcastle upon Tyne NE2 3QE   *T:* 0191 2810714
E: johnsinclair247@aol.com

The Revd Canon Steven Harvey, 2a Holly Avenue, Newcastle upon Tyne NE2 2PY
T: 0191 2815790
E: steven.harvey@stnicholascathedral.co.uk
The Revd Canon Clare MacLaren, 55 Queens Terrace, Newcastle upon Tyne NE2 2PL
T: 0191 2321939
E: clare.maclaren@stnicholascathedral.co.uk
Other Staff
Director of Music Mr Michael Stoddart
T: 01912 357551
E: michael.stoddart@stnicholascathedral.co.uk
Assistant Director of Music Mr Kris Thomsett
E: kris.thomsett@stnicholascathedral.co.uk
Operations Director Ms Kate Sussams
T: 0191 2321939
E: kate.sussams@stnicholascathedral.co.uk
Communications Officer Robyn Frame
T: 01912 321939
E: robin.frame@stnicholascathedral.co.uk
Cathedral Administration Officer Ms Elspeth Robertson, Cathedral House, 42/44 Mosley Street, Newcastle upon Tyne NE1 1DF
T: 0191 2357554
E: office@stnicholascathedral.co.uk
Finance Officer Mrs Neringa Baguckiene
T: 0191 2321939
E: neringa@stnicholascathedral.co.uk

ARCHDEACONS
NORTHUMBERLAND The Ven Geoffrey Vincent Miller, 80 Moorside North, Newcastle upon Tyne NE4 9DU   *T:* 0191 2738245
E: g.miller@newcastle.anglican.org
LINDISFARNE The Ven Peter John Alan Robinson, 4 Acomb Close, Morpeth NE61 2YH
T: 01670 503810
E: p.robinson@newcastle.anglican.org

MEMBERS OF THE HOUSE OF CLERGY OF THE GENERAL SYNOD
Proctors for Clergy
The Revd Catherine Pickford
The Revd Canon John Sinclair
Canon Dr Dagmar Winter

MEMBERS OF THE HOUSE OF LAITY OF THE GENERAL SYNOD
Miss Isabella McDonald-Booth
Canon Carol Wolstenholme
Dr John Appleby

DIOCESAN OFFICERS
Diocesan Secretary Canon Shane Waddle, Church House, St John's Terrace, North Shields NE29 6HS   *T:* 0191 2704114
M: 07775 037121
E: s.waddle@newcastle.anglican.org
Chancellor of Diocese Mr Euan Duff, Broad Chare Chambers, 33 Broad Chare, Newcastle upon Tyne NE1 3DQ   *T:* 0191 2320541
Registrar of Diocese and Bishop's Legal Secretary Mrs Jane Lowdon, Sintons Solicitors, The Cube, Barrack Road, Newcastle-upon-Tyne NE4 6DB   *T:* 0191 226 7878
F: 0191 226 7852
E: jane.lowdon@sintons.co.uk

DIOCESAN ORGANIZATIONS
Diocesan Office Church House, St John's Terrace, North Shields NE29 6HS
T: 0191 2704100
F: 0191 2704101
E: info@newcastle.anglican.org
W: www.newcastle.anglican.org

ADMINISTRATION
Diocesan Synod (*Chair, House of Clergy*) The Revd Canon John Robert Sinclair, 16 Towers Avenue, Newcastle upon Tyne NE2 3QE
T: 0191 2810714
E: johnsinclair247@aol.com
(*Chair, House of Laity*) Canon Carol Wolstenholme, Church House, St John's Terrace, North Shields NE29 6HS
T: 0191 2745144
E: cawol43@aol.com
(*Secretary*) Canon Shane Waddle (*Same Address*)   *T:* 0191 2704114
M: 07775 037121
E: s.waddle@newcastle.anglican.org
Board of Finance (*Chair*) Canon Simon Harper (*Same Address*)
(*Secretary*) Canon Shane Waddle (*Same Address*)   *T:* 0191 2704114
M: 07775 037121
E: s.waddle@newcastle.anglican.org
(*Accountant*) Mr Phillip Ambrose
(*Property Manager*) Mr Ian Beswick, Church House, St John's Terrace, North Shields NE29 6HS   *T:* 0191 270 4125
E: i.beswick@new
castle.anglican.org
Diocesan Society (*Chair*) Canon Gilfrid Baker-Cresswell (*Same Address*)
Mission and Pastoral Committee (*Chair*) The Revd Canon Paul Malcolm Scott

(*Secretary*) Mrs Carol Hepple, Church House, St John's Terrace, North Shields NE29 6HS
T: 0191 270 4120

ADVISERS
Adviser in Local Evangelism The Revd Canon John Sinclair, 16 Towers Avenue, Newcastle upon Tyne NE2 3QE   *T:* 0191 2819375
E: johnsinclair247@aol.com
Church and Church Society The Revd Dr Nicholas Buxton, The Vicarage, 3 Crossway, Newcastle upon Tyne NE2 3QH
T: 0191 2120181
E: buxton.nicholas@gmail.com
Ecumenical Officer The Revd Janet Appleby, 282 Wingrove Road North, Newcastle upon Tyne NE4 9EE   *T:* 0191 2750211
E: janeteappleby@yahoo.com
Inter-Faith and Ethnic Relations Adviser Mrs Lesley Hillary, Church House, St John's Terrace, North Shields NE29 6HS
T: 0191 2704148
E: l.hillary@new
castle.anglican.org
Partners Development Officer The Revd Frances Wilson (*Same Address*)   *T:* 0191 2704147
E: f.wilson@new
castle.anglican.org
Pastoral Care and Counselling Adviser The Revd Canon Peter Kenney, 7 Spring Gardens Court, North Shields NE29 0AN
T: 0191 2579512
E: peter.kenney5@btinternet.com
Rural Affairs Adviser The Revd Jonathan Mason
Spirituality and Spiritual Direction Adviser The Revd Lesley Chapman

CHURCH BUILDINGS
Advisory Committee for the Care of Churches (*Chair*) Canon Roger Styring, 6 Lealands, Lesbury, Alnwick NE66 3QN
(*Secretary*) Mrs Lucy Burfield, Church House, St John's Terrace, North Shields NE29 6HS
Closed Churches Committee Mrs Lucy Burfield (*As above*)

DIOCESAN RECORD OFFICE
Northumberland Collections Service, Woodhorn, Queen Elizabeth II Country Park, Ashington NE63 9YF   *T:* 01670 624455
E: collections@woodhorn.org.uk

DIOCESAN RESOURCE CENTRE
Karenza Passmore, Church House, St John's Terrace, North Shields NE29 6HS *T:* 0191 270 4161   *F:* 0191 2704101
E: k.passmore@resourcescentreonline.co.uk

DIOCESAN WIDOWS OFFICER
Mrs Marjorie Craig, 5 Springwell Meadow, Alnwick NE66 2NY   *T:* 01665 602806

EDUCATION

Chair of Newcastle Diocesan Education Board The Ven Peter Robinson, Church House, St John's Terrace, North Shields NE29 6HS
E: p.robinson@newcastle.anglican.org
Joint Education Team (Joint working with Diocese of Durham) (Director of Education) Mr Paul Rickeard (*Same Address*)   T: 0191 270 4163
E: paul.rickeard@drmnewcanglican.org
(PA to Director) Mrs Susie Taylor (*Same Address*)
(Assistant Directors of Education School Effectiveness) Miss Anne Vernon (*Same Address*)   T: 0191 270 4135
E: anne.vernon@drmnewcanglican.org
Mrs Jo Walker, Church House, St John's Terrace, North Shields NE29 6HS
(Assistant Director of Education Governance) Ms Liane Atkin, Church House, St John's Terrace, North Shields NE29 6HS   T: 0191 270 4164
E: liane.atkin@drmnewcanglican.org
(Bursar) Mrs Eileen Bell (*Same Address*)
T: 0191 270 4141
E: eileen.bell@drmnewcanglican.org
(Administrators) Mrs Lisa Padgett (*Same Address*)
Mrs Suzanne Keenan (*Same Address*)
(Religious Education Adviser) Mrs Margaret Gibson (*Same Address*)   T: 0191 270 4124
E: margaret.gibson@ drmnewcanglican.org

LITURGICAL

Secretary to the Worship and Liturgy Task Group Mrs Jacqueline Thompson, Bishop's House, 29 Moor Road South, Gosforth Newcastle upon Tyne   T: NE3 1PA
0191 2852220
E: jthompson@newcastle.anglican.org

MINISTRY AND TRAINING

Director of Ordinands Vacancy
Adviser for Retired Clergy The Revd Canon Colin Gough, 44 Tyelaw Meadows, Shilbottle, Alnwick NE66 2JJ   T: 01665 58110
E: canoncolin@gmail.com
Continuing Ministerial Development Adviser The Revd Catherine Pickford, Church House, St John's Terrace, North Shields NE29 6HS
Bishop's Adviser for Women's Ministry Canon Dr Dagmar Winter (*Same Address*)
Development Officer for Children's and Young People's Work Team Leader Mrs Judith Sadler (*Same Address*)
Diocesan Environment Officer The Revd Dr John Harrison
Lindisfarne Regional Training Partnership (Chair) The Ven Peter Robinson, Church House, St John's Terrace, North Shields NE29 6HS
E: p.robinson@newcastle.anglican.org
(Principal) Vacancy

(Director of Studies and Formational Tutor for Clergy IME 1–3) The Revd Dr David Bryan, Church House, St John's Terrace, North Shields NE29 6HS   T: 0191 270 4150
E: davidbryan@lindisfarnertp.org
(Formational Tutor for Clergy IME 4–7) The Revd Rick Simpson, The Rectory, Brancepeth, Durham DH7 8EL   T: 0191 380 0440
E: ricksimpson@lindisfarnertp.org
(Formational Tutor for Readers) The Revd Dr Michael Beck, Church House, St John's Terrace, North Shields NE29 6HS
T: 0191 270 4138
E: michaelbeck@lindisfarnertp.org
(Director of Discipleship Development) The Revd Jane Scott (*Same Address*)
(Administrator) Mrs Jenny Burton (*Same Address*)   T: 0191 270 4144
E: jennyburton@lindisfarnertp.org
Secretary, Association of Readers Dr Hilary Elder, 2 Dover Close, Bedlington NE22 6NN
T: 01670 824248
E: hilaryelder@talktalk.net
Retreat House (Warden) (Retreat House Warden) Jane Easterby, Shepherds Dene Retreat House, Riding Mill, Hexham NE44 6AF
T: 01434 682212
E: enquiry@shepherdsdene.co.uk
Sons of Clergy Society Mrs Marjorie Craig, 5 Springwell Meadow, Alnwick NE66 2NY
T: 01665 602806
Associate Director of Ordinands Dr Hilary Elder, Church House, St John's Terrace, North Shields NE29 6HS   T: 0191 270 4138
E: hilaryelder@lindisfarnertp.org
Lay Ministry Tutor Dr Melody Briggs (*Same Address*)   T: 0191 279 4138
E: melodybriggs@lindisfarnertp.org
Developing Discipleship Officer Dr Hilary Elder (*Same Address*)   T: 0191 270 4138
E: hilaryelder@lindisfarnertp.org

PRESS, PUBLICITY AND PUBLICATIONS

Development Officer for Communications Mr Roderick Stuart, Church House, St John's Terrace, North Shields NE29 6HS
T: 0191 270 4139
E: r.stuart@newcastle.anglican.org
Editor of 'Link' Mr Roderick Stuart (*As above*)
Editor of Diocesan Year Book Canon Shane Waddle, Church House, St John's Terrace, North Shields NE29 6HS   T: 0191 2704114
M: 07775 037121
E: s.waddle@newcastle.anglican.org

SAFEGUARDING

Diocesan Safeguarding Officer Ms Ruth Rogan, Church House, St John's Terrace, North Shields NE29 6HS   M: 07825 167016
E: r.rogan@newcastle.anglican.org

NEWCASTLE

STEWARDSHIP
Parish Giving Officer Mr Richard Gascoyne, Church House, St John's Terrace, North Shields NE29 6HS   *T:* 0191 2704136
    E: r.gascoyne@newcastle.anglican.org
Project Manager for Developing Stewardship Rachel Jobes, Church House, St John's Terrace, North Shields NE29 6HS   *T:* 0191 2704128
    E: r.jobes@newcastle.anglican.org

AREA DEANS
ARCHDEACONRY OF LINDISFARNE
Alnwick Paul Malcolm Scott, St Michael's Vicarage, Howling Lane, Alnwick NE66 1DH
    T: 01665 602184
    E: paulscott1957@btinternet.com
Bamburgh and Glendale Judith Rosalind Glover, The Vicarage, South Lane, North Sunderland, Seahouses NE68 7TU   *T:* 01665 720202
    E: judy@alwinton.net
Bellingham Stephen Graham Wilkinson, St Nicholas' Vicarage, 1 Cateran Way, Cramlington NE23 6EX   *T:* 01670 714271
    E: revd.steve.wilkinson@googlemail.com
Corbridge Vacancy
Hexham Jonathan Wingate Russell, The Rectory, 16 Forstersteads, Allendale, Hexham NE47 9AS   *T:* 01434 618607
    E: rector@allendalechurch.co.uk

Morpeth John Charles Park, Bothal Rectory, Longhirst Road, Pegswood, Morpeth NE61 6XF   *T:* 01670 510793
    E: john.park53@yahoo.co.uk
Norham George Robert Joseph Kelsey, The Vicarage, Church Lane, Norham, Berwick-upon-Tweed TD15 2LF   *T:* 01289 382325
    E: robert.josephkelsey@live.com

ARCHDEACONRY OF NORTHUMBERLAND
Bedlington Philip Geoffrey John Hughes, Seghill Vicarage, Mares Close, Seghill, Cramlington NE23 7EA   *T:* 0191 298 0925
    E: p.hughes.1@btinternet.com
Newcastle Central Mark Wroe, 13 Glastonbury Grove, Newcastle upon Tyne NE2 2HA
    T: 0191 240 1017
    E: mark@htj.org.uk
Newcastle East Martin Paul Lee, The Vicarage, 3 Station Road, Benton, Newcastle upon Tyne NE12 8AN   *T:* 0191 266 1921
    E: martinlee903@btinternet.com
Newcastle West Nicholas Peter Darby, St James and St Basil Vicarage, Wingrove Road North, Newcastle upon Tyne NE4 9EJ
    T: 0191 274 5078
    E: npdarby@gmail.com
Tynemouth Frances Mary Wilson, St Peter's Vicarage, The Quadrant, North Shields NE29 7JA   *E:* franceswilson59@gmail.com

Founded in 1094, formerly Thetford (☐☐ 1070), originally Dunwich (☐☐ 630) and Elmham (☐☐ 673). Norfolk, except for the western quarter in the diocese of Ely; an area of north-east Suffolk.

Population 905,000   Area 1,800 sq m
Full-time Stipendiary Parochial Clergy 170   Benefices 176
Parishes 555   Churches 639
Overseas link dioceses: Lulea (Sweden), Papua New Guinea

BISHOP (71st)

The Rt Revd Graham Richard James, Bishop's House, Norwich NR3 1SB   *T:* 01603 629001
E: bishop@dioceseofnorwich.org

BISHOP'S STAFF

Bishop's Chaplain The Revd Susanna Gunner
Bishop's PA Mrs Coralie Nichols, Bishop's House, Norwich NR3 1SB   *T:* 01603 629001
E: coralie.nichols@dioceseotnorwich.org

SUFFRAGAN BISHOPS

LYNN The Rt Revd Jonathan Meyrick, The Old Vicarage, Castle Acre, King's Lynn PE32 2AA
T: 01760 755553
E: bishoplynn@dioceseofnorwich.org
Suffragan Bishop's PA Mrs Ann Whittet (*Same Address*)
E: ann.whittet@dioceseofnorwich.org
THETFORD The Rt Revd Dr Alan Winton, Herfast House, 5 Vicar Street, Wymondham NR18 0PL
T: 01953 528010
E: bishop.thetford@dioceseofnorwich.org
Suffragan Bishop's PA Mr Graham Cossey (*Same Address & Tel*)
E: graham.cossey@dioceseofnorwich.org

ASSISTANT BISHOPS

The Rt Revd Norman Banks, Parkside House, Abbey Mill Lane, St Albans AL3 4HE
T: 01727 836358
E: bishop@richborough.org.uk
The Rt Revd Anthony Foottit, Ivy House, Whitwell St, Reepham NR10 4RA
T: 01603 870340
E: acfoottit@hotmail.com
The Rt Revd Peter Fox, Vicarage, Harwood Road, Norwich NR1 2NG   *T:* 01603 625679
E: peterandangiefox@yahoo.co.uk
The Rt Revd Richard Garrard, 26 Carol Close, Stoke Holy Cross, Norwich NR14 8NN
T: 01508 494165
E: garrard.r.a@btinternet.com
The Rt Revd David Gillett, 10 Burton Close, Diss IP22 4YJ   *T:* 01379 640309
E: dkgillett@btinternet.com

The Rt Revd David Leake, The Anchorage, Lower Common, East Runton, Cromer NR27 9PG   *T:* 01263 513536
E: david@leake8.wanadoo.co.uk
The Rt Revd Malcolm Menin, 32c Bracondale, Norwich NR1 2AN   *T:* 01603 627987
The Rt Revd Lindsay Urwin
E: lindsayurwin1@gmail.com
The Rt Revd Roderick Thomas, 28 St John's Meadow, Blindley Heath, Lingfield RH7 6JU
T: 01342 834140
E: admin@bishopofmaidstone.org

CATHEDRAL CHURCH OF THE HOLY AND UNDIVIDED TRINITY

Dean The Very Revd Jane Hedges, The Deanery, The Close, Norwich NR1 4EG
T: 01603 218308
E: dean@cathedral.org.uk
Canons Residentiary
Canon for Mission and Pastoral Care The Revd Canon Andy Bryant, 52 The Close, Norwich NR1 4EG   *T:* 01603 218331 (office)
E: canon.missionandpastoral@cathedral.org.uk
Precentor The Revd Canon Aidan Platten, 33 The Close, Norwich NR1 4DZ
T: 01603 218314
E: canonprecentor@cathedral.org.uk
Canon Librarian and Vice-Dean The Revd Canon Dr Peter Doll, 56 The Close, Norwich NR1 4EG   *T:* 01603 666758 (Home)
01603 218336 (Office)
E: canonlibrarian@cathedral.org.uk
Canon for Continuing Ministerial Development The Revd Canon Keith James, 25 The Close, Easton, Norwich NR1 4DZ   *T:* 01603 218300
E: canonforcmd@cathedral.org.uk
Other Staff
Chapter Steward Mr Neil Parsons, The Chapter Office, 65 The Close, Norwich NR1 4DH
T: 01603 218304
E: chaptersteward@cathedral.org.uk
Master of the Music Mr Ashley Grote (*Same Address*)   *T:* 01603 218319
E: masterofmusic@cathedral.org.uk
Sacrist Mr Roger Lee (*Same Address*)
T: 01603 218325
E: sacrist@cathedral.org.uk

ARCHDEACONS

NORWICH The Ven Karen Hutchinson, 31 Bracondale, Norwich NR1 2AT
T: 01603 620007
E: archdeacon.norwich@
dioceseofnorwich.org
NORFOLK The Ven Steven Betts, 8 Boulton Road, Thorpe St Andrew, Norwich NR7 0DF
T: 01603 559199
E: archdeacon.norfolk@
dioceseofnorwich.org.org
LYNN The Ven John Ashe, Holly Tree House, Whitwell Road, Sparham, Norwich NR9 5PN
T: 01362 688032
E: archdeacon.lynn@dioceseofnorwich.org

MEMBERS OF THE HOUSE OF CLERGY OF THE GENERAL SYNOD

Proctors for Clergy
The Very Revd Jane Hedges
The Revd Charles Read
The Revd Canon Howard Stoker
The Revd Patrick Richmond

MEMBERS OF THE HOUSE OF LAITY OF THE GENERAL SYNOD

Mr Robin Back
Mr Andrew Gray
Mrs Caroline Herbert

DIOCESAN OFFICERS

Diocesan Secretary Mr Richard Butler, Diocesan House, 109 Dereham Road, Easton, Norwich NR9 5ES
T: 01603 880853
E: richard.butler@dioceseofnorwich.org
Chancellor of Diocese Mrs Ruth Arlow, c/o Diocesan Registry, Batt Broadbent, 42-44 Castle Street, Salisbury SP1 3TX
T: 01722 411141
E: registry@salisbury.anglican.org
Registrar of Diocese and Bishop's Legal Secretary Mr Stuart Jones, Birketts LLP, Kingfisher House, 1 Gilders Way, Norwich NR3 1UB
T: 01603756501
E: stuart.jones@dioceseofnorwich.org

DIOCESAN ORGANIZATIONS

Diocesan Office Diocesan House, 109 Dereham Road, Easton, Norwich NR9 5ES
T: 01603 880853
E: diocesan.house@dioceseofnorwich.org

ADMINISTRATION

Diocesan Synod (*Chair, House of Clergy*) Canon Sally Theakston, The Rectory, Vicarage Meadows, Dereham NR19 1TW
T: 01362 693680
E: stheakston@aol.com

(*Chair, House of Laity*) Ms Vivienne Clifford-Jackson, 8 Badger Close, Mulbarton NR14 8NT
T: 01508 571346
E: vivienne@cliffordconsulting.org.uk
(*Designated Officer*) Mr Richard Butler, Diocesan House, 109 Dereham Road, Easton, Norwich NR9 5ES
T: 01603 880853
E: richard.butler@dioceseofnorwich.org
Board of Finance (*President*) The Rt Revd Graham Richard James, Bishop's House, Norwich NR3 1SB
T: 01603 629001
E: bishop@dioceseofnorwich.org
(*Chair*) Mr Bill Husselby, c/o Diocesan House, 109 Dereham Road, Easton, Norwich NR9 5ES
E: bill.husselby@cogent.co.uk
(*Secretary*) Mr Richard Butler, Diocesan House, 109 Dereham Road, Easton, Norwich NR9 5ES
T: 01603 880853
E: richard.butler@dioceseofnorwich.org
(*Director of Finance*) Miss Susan Bunting (*Same Address*)
T: 01603 882377
E: susan.bunting@dioceseofnorwich.org
Property Committee (*Chair*) Mark Little, c/o Diocesan House, 109 Dereham Road, Easton, Norwich NR9 5ES
E: mrlittle700@btinternet.com
(*Surveyor*) Mr Michael Marshall, Diocesan House, 109 Dereham Road, Easton, Norwich NR9 5ES
T: 01603 882364
E: michael.marshall@dioceseofnorwich.org
Board of Patronage (*Chair*) Mr David Pearson, 17 North Drive, Great Yarmouth NR30 4EQ
T: 01493 842623
(*Secretary*) Mrs Jennifer Vere, Southlands, Church Corner, North Lopham, Diss IP22 2LP
T: 01379 687679
E: jennyvere@btinternet.com
DAC (Diocesan Advisory Committee for the Care of Churches) (*Chair*) Mr Alan Kefford, c/o Diocesan House, 109 Dereham Road, Easton, Norwich NR9 5ES
E: akeff@aol.com
(*Secretary*) Mr Matthew McDade, Diocesan House, 109 Dereham Road, Easton, Norwich NR9 5ES
T: 01603 882350
E: matthew.mcdade@dioceseofnorwich.org

COMMUNICATIONS

(*Bishop's Press Officer*) Mrs Katherine Limbach, Diocesan House, 109 Dereham Road, Easton, Norwich NR9 5ES
T: 07818 422395
katherine.limbach@dioceseofnorwich.org
(*Marketing and Communications Manager*) Mr Gordon Darley (*Same Address*)
T: 01603 882349
E: gordon.darley@dioceseofnorwich.org

DIOCESAN RECORD OFFICE

Norfolk Record Office, Archive Centre, County Hall, Martineau Lane, Norwich NR1 2DO
T: 01603 222599

ECUMENICAL
Diocesan Ecumenical Officer Vacancy

EDUCATION
Board of Education (Chair) Canon Mark Allbrook, Diocesan House, 109 Dereham Road, Easton, Norwich NR9 5ES
    E: markallbrook@btconnect.com
(Director of Education) Paul Dunning *(Same Address)*   *T:* 01603 881352
    E: paul.dunning@dioceseofnorwich.org
Children, Youth and Families (Development Officer) Mr Jonathan Richardson *(Same Address)*   *T:* 01603 737215
    E: jonathan.richardson@
    `dioceseofnorwich.org
The Horstead Centre (Residential Activity Centre) (Manager) Josie Barnett, The Horstead Centre, Rectory Road, Horstead, Norwich NR12 7EP *(Same Tel)*
    E: josie.barnett@dioceseofnorwich.org

LITURGICAL
Chair of Liturgical Committee The Revd Charles Read   *T:* 01603 882331
    E: charles.read@dioceseofnorwich.org
(Social and Community Concerns Coordinator) Vacancy

MINISTRY
Discipleship and Ministry Forum (Chair) The Rt Revd Dr Alan Winton, Herfast House, 5 Vicar Street, Wymondham NR18 0PL
            T: 01953 528010
    E: bishop.thetford@dioceseofnorwich.org
(Bishop's Officer for Ordinands and Initial Training) The Revd David Foster, Diocesan House, 109 Dereham Road, Easton, Norwich NR9 5ES   *T:* 01603 882337
    E: david.foster@dioceseofnorwich.org
(Reader Training Coordinator) The Revd Charles Read   *T:* 01603 882331
    E: charles.read@dioceseofnorwich.org
(Continuing Ministerial Development Officer) The Revd Canon Keith James, Diocesan House, 109 Dereham Road, Easton, Norwich NR9 5ES
            T: 01603 882339
    E: keith.james@dioceseofnorwich.org
(Lay Development Officer) The Revd Dr Paul Overend *(Same Address)*   *T:* 01603 882336
    E: paul.overend@dioceseofnorwich.org
Readers' Committee (Chair and Warden of Readers) The Ven Karen Hutchinson, 31 Bracondale, Norwich NR1 2AT
            T: 01603 620007
    E: archdeacon.norwich@
    dioceseofnorwich.org
(Administrator to the Warden of Readers) Mrs Alison Steward, Holly Tree House, Whitwell Road, Sparham, Norwich NR9 5PN
    E: alison.steward@dioceseofnorwich.org

(Honorary Secretary) Mr John Hooper, 42 Norwich Road, Tacolneston NR16 1BY
            T: 01508 489050
    E: johnhooper66@btinternet.com

MISSION
The Rt Revd Dr Alan Winton, Herfast House, 5 Vicar Street, Wymondham NR18 0PL
            T: 01953 528010
    E: bishop.thetford@dioceseofnorwich.org

RETIREMENT OFFICER
Bishop's Officer for Retired Clergy and Widows The Revd Dr Andrew Sangster, 10 Harvey Lane, Norwich NR7 0BQ   *T:* 01603 437402
    E: asangster666@btinternet.com

TOURISM
Vacancy

URBAN AFFAIRS
Urban Affairs and Church Urban Fund Canon Peter Howard, St Francis Vicarage, Rider Haggard Road, Norwich NR7 9UQ
            T: 01603 702799
    E: plhoward@btinternet.com

RURAL DEANS
ARCHDEACONRY OF LYNN
Breckland Stuart Robert Nairn, The Rectory, Main Road, Narborough, King's Lynn PE32 1TE   *T:* 01760 338552
    E: nairn.nvgrectory@btinternet.com
Burnham and Walsingham Alan Bernard Elkins, 4 The Lawn, Fakenham NR21 8DT
            T: 01328 855075
    E: alanelkins@btinternet.com
Dereham in Mitford Mark Allan McCaghrey, The Vicarage, Back Lane, Mattishall, Dereham NR20 3PU   *T:* 01362 850971
    E: mmccaghrey@gmail.com
Heacham and Rising Jonathan Byam Valentine Riviere, The Rectory, Sandringham PE35 6EH
            T: 01485 540587
    E: rector.sandringham@gmail.com
Holt Jeremy Gordon Sykes, The Vicarage, 1 Grange Close, Briston, Melton Constable NR24 2LY   *T:* 01263 860280
    E: jeremy@sykes-uk.com
Holt Philip Gray Blamire, The Rectory, The Street, Weybourne, Holt NR25 7SY
            T: 01263 588268
    E: philgb@lineone.net
Ingworth Andrew Mark Beane, The Vicarage, Cawston Road, Aylsham, Norwich NR11 6NB
            T: 01263 732686
    E: andrew.beane@btinternet.com

Lynn James Alexander Nash, The Rectory, 47 Castle Rising Road, South Wootton, King's Lynn PE30 3JA   *T:* 01553 671381
          E: james.nash8@btopenworld.com
Repps Christian John Heycocks, The Vicarage, 10 North Street, Sheringham NR26 8LW
          T: 01263 822089
          E: rev.heycocks15@btinternet.com
Sparham Andrew Mark Beane, The Vicarage, Cawston Road, Aylsham, Norwich NR11 6NB
          T: 01263 732686
          E: andrew.beane@btinternet.com

ARCHDEACONRY OF NORFOLK
Blofield Vacancy
Depwade Heather Yvonne Wilcox, The Rectory, 8 Flowerpot Lane, Long Stratton, Norwich NR15 2TS   *T:* 07932 416233
          E: rev.heather@btconnect.com
Great Yarmouth John Michael Kinchin-Smith, The Old Vicarage, Duke Road, Gorleston, Great Yarmouth NR31 6LL   *T:* 01493 717739
          E: johnks1881@aol.com
Humbleyard Paul David Burr, The Vicarage, The Common, Swardeston, Norwich NR14 8EB   *T:* 01508 570550
          E: paul.burr@tiscali.co.uk
Loddon David Cadwaladr Owen, The Vicarage, 4 Market Place, Loddon, Norwich NR14 6EY
          T: 07837 800009
          E: david.chetvalley@gmail.com
Loddon Robert Hugh Parsonage, The Rectory, Rectory Lane, Poringland, Norwich NR14 7SL
          T: 01508 492215
          E: rector@poringland-benefice.org.uk

Lothingland Jeremy Simon Bishop, The Rectory, Rectory Road, Carlton Colville, Lowestoft NR33 8BB   *T:* 01502 565217
          E: jbishop771@aol.com
Redenhall Nigel Owen Tuffnell, The Rectory, 10 Swan Lane, Harleston IP20 9AN
          T: 01379 308905
          E: rector@7churches.org.uk
St Benet at Waxham and Tunstead Simon Peter Lawrence, The Rectory, Camping Field Lane, Stalham, Norwich NR12 9DT
          T: 01692 580250
          E: simon.stalham@btinternet.com
Thetford and Rockland Matthew Christopher Jackson, The Rectory, Surrogate Street, Attleborough NR17 2AW   *T:* 01953 453185
          E: therectory@me.com

ARCHDEACONRY OF NORWICH
Norwich East Darren Thomas Thornton, St Giles's Vicarage, 44 Heigham Road, Norwich NR2 3AU   *T:* 01603 623724
          E: d.thornton@uea.ac.uk
Norwich North Simon Colin Stokes, The Vicarage, 2 Wroxham Road, Norwich NR7 8TZ   *T:* 01603 426492
          E: simon@simonstokes.co.uk
Norwich South Ian Hugh Dyble, St Thomas's Vicarage, 77 Edinburgh Road, Norwich NR2 3RL   *T:* 01603 624390
          E: iandyble@live.co.uk

NORWICH

105

Founded in 1542. Oxfordshire; Berkshire; Buckinghamshire;
one parish in each of Hampshire and Hertfordshire.

Population 2,375,000   Area 2,210 sq m
Full-time Stipendiary Parochial Clergy 363   Benefices 289
Parishes 612   Churches 815
Overseas link dioceses: Vaxjo (Sweden), Kimberley and
Kuruman (South Africa), Nandyal (South India)

BISHOP
The Rt Revd Dr Steven John Lindsey Croft,
Church House Oxford, Langford Lane,
Kidlington OX5 1GF   T: 01865 208222
        E: bishopoxon@oxford.anglican.org

BISHOP'S STAFF
Bishop's Domestic Chaplain The Revd Paul
Cowan, Church House Oxford, Langford Lane,
Kidlington OX5 1GF   T: 01865 208200

PROVINCIAL EPISCOPAL VISITOR
EBBSFLEET The Rt Revd Jonathan Goodall, Tree
Tops, The Mount, Caversham, Reading RG4
7RE   T: 0118 948 1038
        E: office@ebbsfleet.org.uk

AREA BISHOPS
BUCKINGHAM The Rt Revd Dr Alan Wilson,
Sheridan, Grimms Hill, Great Missenden,
Bucks HP16 9BG   T: 01494 862173
        F: 01494 890508
        E: bishopbucks@oxford.anglican.org
DORCHESTER The Rt Revd Colin Fletcher,
Church House Oxford, Langford Lane,
Kidlington OX5 1GF T: 01865 208200 (Office)
        E: bishop.dorchester@
        oxford.anglican.org
READING The Rt Revd Andrew Proud, Bishop's
House, Tidmarsh Lane, Tidmarsh, Reading
RG8 8HA   T: 0118 984 1216
        F: 0118 984 1218
        E: bishopreading@oxford.anglican.org

ASSISTANT BISHOPS
The Rt Revd Keith Arnold, 9 Dinglederry,
Olney MK46 5ES   T: 01234 713044
The Rt Revd Bill Down, 54 Dark Lane, Witney
OX28 6LX   T: 01993 706615
The Rt Revd David Jennings, Laurel Cottage,
East End, Northleach, Cheltenham GL54 3ET
        T: 01451 860743
The Rt Revd James Johnson, St Helena, 28
Molyneux Drive, Bodicote, Banbury OX15
4AP   T: 01295 255357

The Rt Revd Peter Nott, Westcot House,
Westcot, Sparsholt, Wantage OX12 9QA
        T: 01235 751233
The Rt Revd Anthony Russell, Lye Hill House,
Holton, Oxford OX33 1QF   T: 01865 876415
The Rt Revd Henry Scriven, 16 East St Helens
Street, Abingdon, Oxford OX14 5EA
        T: 01235 536607
The Rt Revd Humphrey Southern, Ripon
College, Cuddesdon, Oxford OX44 9EX
The Rt Revd John Went, Latimer Rectory,
Latimer, Chesham HP5 1UA
        T: 01494 765586

CATHEDRAL CHURCH OF CHRIST
Dean The Very Revd Professor Martyn Percy,
The Deanery, Christ Church, Oxford OX1
1DP   T: 01865 276161
Residentiary Canons
Sub-Dean The Revd Canon Dr Edmund Newey,
Christ Church, Oxford OX1 1DP
        T: 01865 276278
        E: subdean@chch.ox.ac.uk
Diocesan Canon Precentor The Revd Dr Grant
Bayliss, Christ Church, Oxford, OX1 1DP
        T: 01865 276214
        E: grant.bayliss@chch.ox.ac.uk
Residentiary Canons The Revd Canon Professor
Nigel Biggar, Christ Church, Oxford OX1 1DP
        T: 01865 276219
        E: nigel.biggar@chch.ox.ac.uk
The Revd Canon Professor Sarah Foot (*Same
Address*)   T: 01865 286078
        E: sarah.foot@chch.ox.ac.uk
The Revd Canon Professor Graham Ward
(*Same Address*)   T: 01865 286334
        E: graham.ward@chch.ox.ac.uk
The Ven Martin Gorick (*Same Address*)
        T: 01865 276185
        E: martin.gorick@chch.ox.ac.uk
Canon Professor Carol Harrison (*Same
Address*)   T: 01865 276247
        E: carol.harrison@chch.ox.ac.uk
Other Staff
Cathedral Organist Canon Dr Stephen
Darlington, Christ Church, Oxford OX1 1DP
        T: 01865 276195
        E: stephen.darlington@chch.ox.ac.uk

Cathedral Registrar Mr John Briggs (*Same Address*)   *T:* 01865 286846
     E: john.briggs@chch.ox.ac.uk
Registrar and Canons' PA Mrs Izabela Hreska (*Same Address*)   *T:* 01865 276188
     E: izabela.hreska@chch.ox.ac.uk
Cathedral Office Manager Mrs Eileen Head (*Same Address*)   *T:* 01865 610935
     E: eileen.head@chch.ox.ac.uk
Dean's Verger Mr Matthew Power (*Same Address*)   *T:* 01865 286002/276154
     E: matthew.power@chch.ox.ac.uk
Canons' Verger and Sacristan Mr Matthew Ball (*Same Address*)   *T:* 01865 276154/286002
     E: matthew.ball@chch.ox.ac.uk
Cathedral Verger and Liturgy Assistant Mr David Bannister (*Same Address*)   *T:* 01865 276214
     E: david.bannister@chch.ox.ac.uk
Verger Mr Jim Godfrey (*Same Address*)
     T: 01865 286165
     E: jim.godfrey@chch.ox.ac.uk
Visitors Officer Ms Miranda Hockliffe (*Same Address & Tel*)
     F: miranda.hockliffe@chch.ox.ac.uk
Education Officer Mrs Jackie Holderness (*Same Address*)   *T:* 01865 286003
     E: jacqueline.holderness@chch.ox.ac.uk
Dean's PA Ms Rachel Perham
     T: 01865 276161
     F: 01865 276238
     E: rachel.perham@chch.ox.ac.uk

ARCHDEACONS

OXFORD The Ven Martin Gorick, Church House Oxford, Langford Lane, Kidlington OX5 1GF
     T: 01865 208200
     E: archdeacon.oxford@oxford.anglican.org
DORCHESTER The Ven Judy French, Church House Oxford, Langford Lane, Kidlington OX5 1GF   *T:* 01865 208245
     E: archdeacon.dorchester@
     oxford.anglican.org
BERKSHIRE The Ven Olivia Graham, Foxglove House, Love Lane, Donnington, Newbury RG14 2JG   *T:* 01865 208200 (office)
     E: archdber@oxford.anglican.org
BUCKINGHAM The Ven Guy Elsmore, Archdeacon's House, Stone, Aylesbury HP17 8RZ   *T:* 01865 208266
     E: archdeacon.buckingham@
     oxford.anglican.org

MEMBERS OF THE HOUSE OF CLERGY OF THE GENERAL SYNOD
Proctors for Clergy
The Revd Samuel Allberry
The Revd Dr Andrew Atherstone
The Revd Jonathan Beswick
The Revd Canon Susan Booys
The Revd Prof Mark Chapman
The Revd Canon Charlie Cleverly

The Revd Canon Rosie Harper
The Ven Martin Gorick

MEMBERS OF THE HOUSE OF LAITY OF THE GENERAL SYNOD
The Rt Hon Canon Sir Tony Baldry
Dr Andrew Bell
Mr Graham Caskie
Miss Prudence Dailey
Mrs Julie Dziegiel
Mr Gavin Oldham
Ms Jayne Ozanne
Mrs Kathryn Winrow

DIOCESAN OFFICERS
Diocesan Secretary Canon Rosemary Pearce, Church House Oxford, Langford Lane, Kidlington OX5 1GF   *T:* 01865 208200
     E: diosec@oxford.anglican.org
Chancellor of Diocese The Revd Alexander McGregor, Diocesan Registry, 16 Beaumont Street, Oxford OX1 2LZ   *T:* 01865 297200
     F: 01865 726274
     E: jrees@wslaw.co.uk
Deputy Chancellor Mr Christopher Rogers (*Same Address, Tel, Fax & email*)
Registrar of Diocese and Bishop's Legal Secretary The Revd Canon John Rees (*Same Address, Tel, Fax & email*)
Registrar of the Archdeaconries The Revd Canon John Rees (*As above*)

DIOCESAN ORGANIZATIONS
Diocesan Office Church House Oxford, Langford Lane, Kidlington OX5 1GF
     T: 01865 208200

ADMINISTRATION
Diocesan Synod (*Vice-President, House of Clergy*) The Revd Canon Susan Booys, Church House Oxford, Langford Lane, Kidlington OX5 1GF
     E: rector@dorchester-abbey.org.uk
(*Vice-President, House of Laity*) Mrs Judith Scott (*Same Address*)
     E: judithscott762@btinternet.com
(*Secretary*) Canon Rosemary Pearce (*Same Address*)   *T:* 01865 208200
     E: diosec@oxford.anglican.org
Board of Finance (*Chairman*) The Revd John Tattersall (*Same Address & Tel*)
     F: 01865 790470
     E: jhtatters@aol.com
(*Secretary*) Canon Rosemary Pearce (*Same Address & Tel*)   *E:* diosec@oxford.anglican.org
(*Director of Glebe and Buildings*) Mr David Mason (*Same Address*)   *T:* 01865 208230
     E: david.mason@oxford.anglican.org

(*Diocesan Trustees Oxford Ltd Trust Administrator*) Caroline Dyer, Church House Oxford, Langford Locks, Kidlington OX5 1GF
(*Pastoral Committee Secretary*) Petronella Spivey, Church House Oxford, Langford Lane, Kidlington OX5 1GF   T: 01865 208245
     E: petronella.spivey@oxford.anglican.org
(*Designated Officer*) The Revd Canon John Rees, Diocesan Registry, 16 Beaumont Street, Oxford OX1 2LZ   T: 01865 297200
          F: 01865 726274
     E: jrees@wslaw.co.uk
(*Electoral Roll Officer*) Petronella Spivey, Church House Oxford, Langford Lane, Kidlington OX5 1GF   T: 01865 208245
     E: petronella.spivey@oxford.anglican.org

CHURCH BUILDINGS
Advisory Committee for the Care of Churches (*Chairman until 31/12/17*) Mr Charles Baker
     E: charlesfbaker@btinternet.com
(*Chairman from 1/1/2018*) The Revd Canon Adrian Daffern
     E: adrian.daffern@oxford.anglican.org
(*Secretary*) Mrs Liz Kitch, Church House Oxford, Langford Lane, Kidlington OX5 1GF
          T: 01865 208243
     E: liz.kitch@oxford.anglican.org
Closed Churches Committee (*Secretary*) Petronella Spivey (*Same Address*)   T: 01865 208245
     E: petronella.spivey@oxford.anglican.org

COMMUNICATIONS
Director of Communications Mr Stephen Buckley   T: 01865 208224
          M: 07824 906839
     E: stephen.buckley@oxford.anglican.org
Editor of Diocesan Newspaper 'The Door' Miss Joanne Duckles (*Same Mobile*)
          T: 01865 208227
     E: joanne.duckles@oxford.anglican.org

DIOCESAN RECORD OFFICES
County Archivist, St Luke's Church, Temple Road, Cowley OX4 2EN   T: 01865 398200
     E: archives@oxfordshire.gov.uk
Berkshire Record Office, 9 Coley Ave, Reading RG1 6AF   T: 0118 901 5132
Buckinghamshire Record Office, County Hall, Aylesbury HP20 1UA   T: 01296 382587

EDUCATION
Acting Director of Education Mrs Fiona Craig, Church House Oxford, Langford Lane, Kidlington OX5 1GF   01865 208236
     E: fiona.craig@oxford.anglican.org

HUMAN RESOURCES
Director of Human Resources (including clergy HR) Mrs Poli Shajko, Church House

Oxford, Langford Lane, Kidlington OX5 1GF   T: 01865 208770
     E: poli.shajko@oxford.anglican.org
Safeguarding Adviser Mr John Nixson
          T: 01865 208290
     E: john.nixson@oxford.anglican.org

MISSION
Director Mr Andrew Anderson-Gear, Church House Oxford, Langford Lane, Kidlington OX5 1GF   T: 01865 208251
     E: andrew.anderson-gear@oxford.anglican.org
Deputy Director (Mission – Ministerial Formation) The Revd Dr David Heywood (*Same Address & Tel*)   E: david.heywood@oxford.anglican.org
Deputy Director (Social Responsibility) Ms Alison Webster (*Same Address*)   T: 01865 208213
     E: alison.webster@oxford.anglican.org
Parish Development Advisers (Buckingham) The Revd Gill Lovell   T: 01865 208256
     E: gill.lovell@oxford.anglican.org
(*Dorchester*) The Revd Preb Charles Chadwick
          T: 01865 208246
     E: charles.chadwick@oxford.anglican.org
(*Berkshire*) Vacancy
Diocesan Canon Precentor: Continuing Ministerial Development The Revd Dr Grant Bayliss, Christ Church, Oxford, OX1 1DP
          T: 01865 276214
     E: grant.bayliss@chch.ox.ac.uk
Children's Adviser Mrs Yvonne Morris, Church House Oxford, Langford Lane, Kidlington OX5 1GF   T: 01865 208255
     E: yvonne.morris@oxford.anglican.org
Youth Adviser Mr Ian Macdonald (*Same Address*)   T: 01865 208253
     E: ian.macdonald@oxford.anglican.org
Generous Giving Adviser Mr Jonathan Farnhill
          T: 01865 208757
     E: jonathan.farnhill@oxford.anglican.org
Parish Giving Scheme Adviser Vacancy
World Development Adviser Mrs Maranda St John Nicolle   E: maranda@ccow.org.uk
Deputy Warden of Readers and Director of Postgraduate Studies The Revd Dr Phillip Tovey, Church House Oxford, Langford Lane, Kidlington OX5 1GF   T: 01865 208212
     E: phillip.tovey@oxford.anglican.org
Director of Initial Ministerial Education (Part 2) The Revd Dr Beren Hartless (*Same Address*)
          T: 01865 208258
     E: beren.hartless@oxford.anglican.org
Local Ministry Training Co-ordinator The Revd Dr Phil Cooke   T: 01865 208282
     E: revphilcooke@gmail.com
Diocesan Director of Ordinands The Revd Caroline Windley, Church House Oxford, Langford Lane, Kidlington OX5 1GF
          T: 01865 208283
     E: caroline.windley@oxford.anglican.org

Area Directors of Ordinands (Dorchester) The Revd Jane Hemmings T: 01865 208249
  E: jane.hemmings@oxford.anglican.org
(Oxford and Berkshire) The Revd Nicholas Cheeseman, Church House Oxford, Langley Lane, Kidlington OX5 1GF (Same Tel)
  E: nicholas.cheeseman@oxford.anglican.org
(Buckingham) The Revd Caroline Windley, Church House Oxford, Langford Lane, Kidlington OX5 1GF T: 01865 208283
  E: caroline.windley@oxford.anglican.org
Vocation Network Chair The Revd Caroline Windley (As above)

MISSIONARY AND ECUMENICAL
Partnership in World Mission (Secretary) The Revd Canon Robert Teare, 29 Elizabeth Drive, Wantage OX12 9YA T: 01235 770966
  E: robertteare@googlemail.com

SOCIAL RESPONSIBILITY
Social Responsibility Adviser Ms Alison Webster, Church House Oxford, Langford Lane, Kidlington OX5 1GF T: 01865 208213
  E: alison.webster@oxford.anglican.org
PACT (Parents and Children Together) Council for Social Work Mrs Jan Fishwick, 7 Southern Court, South Street, Reading RG1 4QS T: 0118 938 7600 E: info@pactcharity.org
Council for the Deaf (Chairman) The Revd Tim Edge, 27 Burford Road, Witney OX28 6DP
  T: 01993 773438
  E: tim.edge@talk21.com

AREA DEANS
ARCHDEACONRY OF BERKSHIRE
Bracknell Darrell Dale Hannah, All Saints' Rectory, London Road, Ascot SL5 8DQ
  T: 01344 621200
  E: drddhannah@yahoo.co.uk
Bradfield Heather Christina Winifred Parbury, The Rectory, St James's Close, Pangbourne, Reading RG8 7AP T: 0118 984 2928
  E: parbury@btinternet.com
Bradfield William Henry Norbury Watts, The Vicarage, Pangbourne Road, Upper Basildon, Reading RG8 8LS T: 01491 671714
  E: revwillwatts@btinternet.com
Maidenhead and Windsor Margaret Kathleen Bird, 73 Alma Road, Windsor SL4 3HD
  T: 01753 315397
  E: margaret.bird@talktalk.net
Newbury Mark David Bennet, The Rectory, 2 Rectory Gardens, Thatcham RG19 3PR
  T: 01635 867342
  E: markbennet@btinternet.com
Reading Graeme Fancourt, The Vicarage, 50 London Road, Reading RG1 5AS
  T: 07824 452534
  E: fancourt@gmail.com

Sonning Julie Frances Ramsbottom, The Rectory, The Village, Finchampstead, Wokingham RG40 4JX T: 0118 973 6374
  E: julie.ramsbottom@talk21.com

ARCHDEACONRY OF BUCKINGHAM
Amersham Martin Jonathan Williams, The Rectory, Oxford Road, Gerrards Cross SL9 7DJ
  T: 01753 883301
  E: martin.williams@saintjames.org.uk
Amersham Timothy James Lincoln Harper, The Rectory, Church Street, Amersham HP7 0DB T: 01494 724426
  E: harpervic@yahoo.co.uk
Aylesbury David Gareth Williams, The Rectory, Church Lane, Princes Risborough HP27 9AW
  T: 01844 344784
  E: rector@stmarysrisborough.org.uk
Buckingham Rosamunde Mair Roberts, The Vicarage, Thornborough Road, Padbury, Buckingham MK18 2AH T: 01280 813162
  E: lenborough.vicar@gmail.com
Burnham Roderick John Cosh, The New Vicarage, Mill Street, Colnbrook, Slough SL3 0JJ T: 01753 681432
  E: rod@tommiez.com
Claydon David John Meakin, The Rectory, 1 Green Acres Close, Whitchurch, Aylesbury HP22 4JP T: 01296 641606
  E: d.meakin@btinternet.com
Milton Keynes Timothy Norwood, 3 Daubeney Gate, Shenley Church End, Milton Keynes MK5 6EH T: 01908 505812
  E: tim@thenorwoods.fsnet.co.uk
Mursley Vacancy
Newport Vacancy
Wendover Deiniol John Owen Kearley-Heywood, The Rectory, 140 Wycombe Road, Prestwood, Great Missenden HP16 0HJ
  T: 01494 866530
  E: rector@htprestwood.org.uk
Wycombe David Bull, The Rectory, The Causeway, Marlow SL7 2AA T: 01628 471650
  E: dave.bull@hotmail.com

ARCHDEACONRY OF DORCHESTER
Abingdon Vacancy
Aston and Cuddesdon Alan Garratt, The Rectory, 3 Fish Ponds Lane, Thame OX9 2BA
  T: 01844 212225
  E: alan.garratt@hotmail.co.uk
Bicester and Islip Stephen Robert Griffiths, 104 Camp Road, Upper Heyford, Bicester OX25 5AG T: 01869 233249
  E: steph78griff@hotmail.com
Chipping Norton Sally Ann Welch, The Vicarage, Church Lane, Charlbury, Chipping Norton OX7 3PX T: 01865 552890
  E: sally.welch@19a.org.uk

Deddington Jeffrey James West, St Mary's Centre, Horse Fair, Banbury OX16 0AA
T: 07766 198484
E: curate@stmaryschurch-banbury.org.uk
Henley Linda Jean Smith, The Vicarage, Reading Road, Woodcote RG8 0QX
T: 01491 680979
E: woodcotevicarage@btinternet.com
Vale of White Horse David Michael Williams, The Vicarage, Great Coxwell, Faringdon SN7 7NG
T: 01367 240665
E: davidwilliams24@btinternet.com
Wallingford David Rice, The Rectory, 22 Castle Street, Wallingford OX10 8DW
T: 01491 202188
E: david.rice5@ntlworld.com
Wantage Jason Paul St John Nicolle, The Rectory, Church End, Blewbury, Didcot OX11 9QH
T: 01235 850267
E: office@churnchurches.co.uk

Witney Toby Christopher Wright, Witney Rectory, 13 Station Lane, Witney OX28 4BB
T: 01993 704441
E: toby-wright@btconnect.com
Woodstock David Stuart Tyler, The Rectory, Swan Lane, Long Hanborough, Witney OX29 8BT
T: 01993 881270
E: revdavidtyler@googlemail.com

ARCHDEACONRY OF OXFORD
Cowley Timothy James Stead, The Vicarage, 46 Quarry Road, Headington, Oxford OX3 8NU
T: 01865 307939
E: tim_stead@btinternet.com
Oxford William Richard Donaldson, St Edmund Hall, Queens Lane, Oxford OX1 4AR
T: 01865 279021
E: w.r.donaldson@btinternet.com

DIOCESE OF PETERBOROUGH

Founded in 1541. Northamptonshire, except for one parish in the west in the diocese of Leicester; Rutland; Peterborough, except for an area in the south-east; one parish in Lincolnshire.

Population 910,000   Area 1,140 sq m
Full-time Stipendiary Parochial Clergy 148   Benefices 128
Parishes 349   Churches 381
www.peterborough-diocese.org.uk
Overseas link dioceses: Bungoma (Kenya), Seoul (Korea)

BISHOP (37th)
The Rt Revd Donald Spargo Allister, Bishop's Lodging, The Palace, Peterborough PE1 1YA
T: 01733 562492
E: bishop@peterborough-diocese.org.uk

BISHOP'S STAFF
Bishop's Chaplain The Revd Canon Tim Alban Jones, Bishop's Lodging, The Palace, Peterborough PE1 1YA   *T:* 01733 887014
E: tim.albanjones@peterborough-diocese.org.uk
Bishop's Personal Assistant Mrs Alex Tolley (*Same Address*)   *T:* 01733 887015
E: alex.tolley@peterborough-diocese.org.uk
Bishop's Secretary Mrs Cheryl Craggs (*Same Address*)   *T:* 01733 887037
E: cheryl.craggs@peterborough-diocese.org.uk

SUFFRAGAN BISHOP
BRIXWORTH The Rt Revd John Holbrook, Orchard Acre, 11 North Street, Northampton NN6 0DW   *T:* 01604 812328
E: bishop.brixworth@peterborough-diocese.org.uk

ASSISTANT BISHOP
The Rt Revd John Flack, The Rectory, 38 West Street, Easton-on-the-Hill, Stamford PE9 3LS
T: 01733 202767
01780 753091
M: 07810 714056
E: johnflack67@yahoo.com

CATHEDRAL CHURCH OF ST PETER, ST PAUL AND ST ANDREW
Dean The Very Revd Christopher Dalliston (from 20/1/18)
Canons Residentiary
Acting Dean The Revd Canon Tim Alban Jones

Precentor Revd Canon Bruce Ruddock, Precentor's Lodging, 14A Minster Precincts, Peterborough PE1 1XX   *T:* 01733 355310
E: bruce.ruddock@peterborough-cathedral.org.uk
Canon Missioner (from 21/1/18) The Revd Canon Sarah Brown
Canons Residentiary The Revd Canon Ian Black, 26 Minster Precincts, Peterborough PE1 1XZ   *T:* 01733 873064 (home)
E: canonianblack@btinternet.com
Other Staff
Lay Members of Chapter Mr John Henniker-Major, Linden House, Brook Lane, Great Easton, Market Harborough LE16 8SJ
T: 01604 608211 (Office)
01536 770320 (Home)
E: john.henniker-major@carterjonas.co.uk
His Honour Neil McKittrick, 41 Chisenhale, Orton Waterville, Peterborough PE2 5FP
T: 01733 237535
E: nam1492@btinternet.com
Mrs Maria Steele, 55 Thorpe Road, Thorpe Malso, Peterborough PE3 6AN
T: 07880 585624
E: mariasteele9@sky.com
Hon Treasurer Nickolas Robertson, The Old Rectory, Thorpe Malso, Kettering NN14 1JS
T: 01536 485305
E: nicholas.robertson@live.com
Chapter Administrator Mrs Maria Elsey, Cathedral Office, Minster Precincts, Peterborough PE1 1XS   *T:* 01733 355308
Director of Music Mr Steven Grahl, The Music Office, 28 Minster Precincts, Peterborough PE1 1XS   *T:* 01733 355318
E: music.director@peterborough-cathedral.org.uk

ARCHDEACONS
NORTHAMPTON The Ven Richard Ormston, Westbrook, 11 The Drive, Northampton NN1 4RZ   *T:* 01604 714015
E: archdeacon.northampton@peterborough-diocese.org.uk

OAKHAM The Ven Gordon Steele, The Diocesan Office, The Palace, Peterborough PE1 1YB
T: 01733 887017
E: archdeacon.oakham@peterborough-diocese.org.uk

MEMBERS OF THE HOUSE OF CLERGY OF THE GENERAL SYNOD
Proctors for Clergy
The Revd Mark Lucas
The Revd Stephen Trott

MEMBERS OF THE HOUSE OF LAITY OF THE GENERAL SYNOD
Dr Nigel Ashton
Canon Liz Holdsworth
Mr Andrew Presland

DIOCESAN OFFICERS
Diocesan Secretary Mr Andrew Roberts, Diocesan Office, The Palace, Peterborough PE1 1YB
T: 01733 887000
E: diosec@peterborough-diocese.org.uk
Assistant Diocesan Secretary Mr Howard Cattermole (*Same Address & Tel*)
Chancellor of Diocese Chancellor David Pittaway, c/o Diocesan Registrar, 35 Thorpe Road, Longthorpe, Peterborough PE3 6AG
Deputy Chancellor Chancellor George Pulman, Diocesan Registry, 53 New Street, Chelmsford CM1 1NE
T: 01245 259470
Registrar of Diocese and Bishop's Legal Secretary Miss Anna Spriggs, c/o Diocesan Registrar, 35 Thorpe Road, Longthorpe, Peterborough PE3 6AG
T: 01733 882800
E: anna.spriggs@hcsolicitors.co.uk

DIOCESAN ORGANIZATIONS
Diocesan Office The Palace, Peterborough PE1 1YB
T: 01733 887000
E: office@peterborough-diocese.org.uk
W: www.peterborough-diocese.org.uk

ADMINISTRATION
Diocesan Synod (*Vice-President, Clergy*) Canon Lee Francis-Dehqani, The Vicarage, Vicarage Road, Oakham LE15 6EG
T: 01572 722108
E: leet.fd@gmail.com
(*Vice-President, Laity*) Mr John MacMahon, 12 Westminster Croft, Brackley NN13 7ED
T: 01280 703791
E: j2macmahon@o2.co.uk
(*Secretary*) Mr Andrew Roberts, Diocesan Office, The Palace, Peterborough PE1 1YB
T: 01733 887000
E: diosec@peterborough-diocese.org.uk

Board of Finance (*Chairman*) Dr Paul Buckingham (*Same Address & Tel*)
E: paul.buckingham@yahoo.co.uk
(*Secretary*) Mr Andrew Roberts (*Same Address & Tel*)
E: diosec@peterborough-diocese.org.uk
Houses Committee (*Chairman*) Mr Robert Purser (*Same Address & Tel*)
(*Property Officer*) Mrs Sandra Allen (*Same Address*)
(*Safeguarding Officer*) Mr Garry Johnson (*Same Address*)
Mission and Pastoral Committee Mr Andrew Roberts (*Same Address*)
T: 01733 887000
E: diosec@peterborough-diocese.org.uk
Board of Patronage Mr Andrew Roberts (*As above*)
(*Designated Officer*) Mr Andrew Roberts (*As above*)

CHURCH BUILDINGS
Advisory Committee for the Care of Churches (*Chairman*) Mr John White, c/o DAC, Diocesan Office, The Palace, Peterborough PE1 1YB
T: 01733 887007
F: 01733 555271
E: dac@peterborough-diocese.org.uk

COMMUNICATIONS
Communications Officer Mrs Shelly Stevenson, Diocesan Office, The Palace, Peterborough PE1 1YB
T: 01733 887012
F: 01733 555271
E: communications@peterborough-diocese.org.uk

DIOCESAN RECORD OFFICES
Diocesan Record Office Wootton Park, Northampton, NN4 9BQ
(*County Archivist*) Miss Sarah Bridges
T: 01604 762129
E: archivist@northamptonshire.gov.uk
Leicestershire Record Office Leicestershire Record Office, Long Street, Wigston Magna, Leicester LE18 2AH
(*County Archivist*) Mr Carl Harrison
T: 0116 257 1080

EDUCATION
Board of Education (*Schools*) (*Director of Education Schools and Secretary*) Mrs Miranda Robinson, Bouverie Court, The Lakes, Bedford Road, Northampton NN4 7YD
T: 01604 887006
F: 01604 887077
E: education@peterborough-diocese.org.uk

(*Deputy Director of Education Schools*) Mr Peter Goringe (*Same Address, Tel & email*)

LITURGICAL
Liturgical Officer Vacancy

MINISTRY
Diocesan Vocations Adviser and Director of Ordinands The Revd Canon Steve Benoy, Bouverie Court, The Lakes, Bedford Road, Northampton NN4 7YD   T: 01604 887047
F: 01604 887077
Coordinator of Adult Education and Training Canon Liz Holdsworth (*Same Address & Fax*)
T: 01604 887042
E: liz.holdsworth@
peterborough-diocese.org.uk
Continuing Ministerial Education Officer The Revd Hannah Jeffery (*Same Address*)
T: 01604 887000
F: 01604 887077
E: hannah.jeffery@
peterborough-diocese.org.uk
Curates' Training Coordinator Vacancy
Self Supporting Ministry Officer The Revd Elizabeth Pelly, Home Farm, Wakefield Lodge, Potterspury, Towcester NN12 7QX
T: 01327 811218
F: 01327 811326
E: lulu.pelly@farming.co.uk
The Revd Jo Saunders, Mellstock, Bourne Road, Essendine, Stamford, Lincolnshire PE9 4LH   T: 01780 480479
E: revjosaunders@live.co.uk
Warden of Readers The Ven John Hall, 16 Mill House Drive, Cheadle, Stoke-on-Trent ST10 1XL   T: 01538 750628
E: j.hall182@btinternet.com
Warden of Pastoral Assistants The Revd David Kirby, Rectory, Church Way, Weston Favell, Northampton NN3 3BX   T: 01604 413218
E: kirbydg@gmail.com
Warden of Parish Evangelists The Revd Melvyn Pereira, 20 Ribble Close, Wellingborough NN8 5XJ   T: 01933 673437
E: melvyn.pereira@
gleneagleschurch.co.uk

MISSION
Diocesan Mission Enabler The Revd Miles Baker, Bouverie Court, The Lakes, Bedford Road, Northampton NN4 7YD   T: 01604 887043
F: 01604 887077
E: miles.baker@
peterborough-diocese.org.uk
Children's Missioner Mrs Rona Orme (*Same Address & Fax*)   T: 01604 887045
E: rona.orme@
peterborough-diocese.org.uk

Youth Officer (Interns) Mr Peter White (*Same Address & Fax*)   T: 01604 887044
E: peter.white@peterborough-diocese.org.uk
Mission in Society Officer Vacancy
Urban Priority Areas Link Officer and Church Urban Fund Officer Vacancy
Ecumenical Officer The Revd Sam Randall, Sundial House, 57 Main Street, Yarwell PE8 6PR   T: 01780 784684
E: sam.randall@peterbworough-diocese.org.uk
Hospital Chaplaincy Adviser Canon Lesley McCormack, Barnbrook, Water Lane, Chelveston, Wellingborough NN9 6SP
T: 01933 492609
E: lesley.mccormack@kgh.nhs.uk
Rural Officer Vacancy

RURAL DEANS
ARCHDEACONRY OF NORTHAMPTON
Brackley Simon Paul Dommett, The Rectory, Croughton Road, Aynho, Banbury OX17 3BD
T: 01869 810903
E: the.revd.simon@gmail.com
Brixworth Stephen Trott, The Rectory, Humfrey Lane, Boughton, Northampton NN2 8RQ
T: 01604 845655
E: strott@btinternet.com
Daventry Sarah Denner-Brown, The Rectory, 71 High Street, Braunston, Daventry NN11 7HS   T: 01788 890298
E: sarah@talkingdirect.co.uk
Northampton Beverley Jayne Hollins, The Vicarage, 29 Back Lane, Hardingstone, Northampton NN4 6BY   T: 01604 945818
E: beverley.hollins@gmail.com
Towcester Paul Douglas McLeod, The Vicarage, 24A High Street, Silverstone, Towcester NN12 8US   T: 01327 858101
E: revpaulmcleod@btinternet.com
Wellingborough Miranda Jane Hayes, The Vicarage, 7 High Street, Earls Barton, Northampton NN6 0JG   T: 01604 810447
E: mail@mirandahayes.org

ARCHDEACONRY OF OAKHAM
Corby Ian Austin Pullinger, St Columba's Vicarage, 157 Studfall Avenue, Corby NN17 1LG   T: 01536 400225
E: ianpullinger@btinternet.com
Higham Stephen Kenneth Prior, The Rectory, Rectory Road, Rushden NN10 0HA
T: 01933 312554
E: sprior@toucansurf.com
Kettering Hannah Mary Jeffery, 19 Rosemount Road, Kettering NN15 6EU   T: 01536 660415
E: revhj@outlook.com
Oundle Stephen Jeremy Webster, 2 Herons Wood Close, Oundle, Peterborough PE8 4HW
T: 01832 275631
E: stephen.webster@yahoo.co.uk

Peterborough Ian Christopher Black, 26 Minster Precincts, Peterborough PE1 1XZ
T: 01733 873064
E: canonianblack@btinternet.com

Rutland Lee Thomas Francis-Dehqani, The Vicarage, Vicarage Road, Oakham LE15 6EG
T: 01572 722108
E: leet.fd@gmail.com

DIOCESE OF PORTSMOUTH

Founded in 1927. The south-eastern third of Hampshire;
the Isle of Wight.

Population 784,000 Area 420 sq m
Full-time Stipendiary Parochial Clergy 96 Benefices 125
Parishes 140 Churches 170
Overseas link dioceses: IDWAL (Inter-Diocesan West Africa Link) Ghana,
Gambia, Liberia (West Africa)

BISHOP (9th)
The Rt Revd Christopher Foster, Bishopsgrove,
26 Osborn Road, Fareham PO16 7DQ
T: 01329 280247
E: bishop@portsmouth.anglican.org

BISHOP'S STAFF
Bishop's Chaplain The Revd Dr Richard Wyld
Administrative Secretary Rachel Houlberg
Bishop's PA Mrs Clare Jones

ASSISTANT BISHOPS
The Rt Revd Timothy Bavin, Alton Abbey,
Abbey Road, Beech, Alton GU34 4AP
T: 01420 562145
The Rt Revd Ian Brackley, 1 Bepton Down,
Petersfield GU31 4PR *T:* 01730 266465
E: ijbrackley@gmail.com
The Rt Revd Jonathan Frost, Bishop's House, St
Mary's Church Close, Southampton SO18 2ST
T: 023 8067 2684
E: bishop.jonathan@winchester.anglican.org
The Rt Revd John Hind, 1 Stanley Road,
Emsworth PO10 7BD *T:* 07768 081106
E: johnwhind@gmail.com
The Rt Revd Tim Thornton, Lambeth Palace,
London SE1 7JU *T:* 020 7898 1200
E: tim.thornton@lambethpalace.org.uk

CATHEDRAL CHURCH OF ST THOMAS OF CANTERBURY
Dean The Very Revd David Brindley, The
Deanery, 13 Pembroke Road, Portsmouth PO1
2NS *T:* 023 9289 2963
E: david.brindley@
portsmouthcathedral.org.uk
Canons Residentiary
Canon Precentor The Revd Canon Dr Jo
Spreadbury, 51 High Street, Old Portsmouth
PO1 2LU *T:* 023 9282 3300 ext 226 (office)
E: jo.spreadbury@
portsmouthcathedral.org.uk
Canon Chancellor The Revd Canon Peter
Leonard, 32 Woodville Drive, Pembroke Park,
Portsmouth PO1 2TG
T: 023 9282 3300 ext 229 (Office)
M: 07817 722219
E: peter.leonard@portsmouth.anglican.org

The Revd Canon Nick Ralph, First Floor,
Peninsular House, Wharf Road, Portsmouth
PO2 8HB *T:* 023 9289 9674 (office)
M: 07817 722219 (mobile)
E: nick.ralph@portsmouth.anglican.org
The Revd Canon Dr Anthony Rustell, 1
Pembroke Close, Old Portsmouth PO1 2NX
T: 023 9289 9654 (office)
E: anthony.rustell@portsmouth.anglican.org
Other Staff
*Cathedral Administrator, Chapter Clerk and
Clerk to Cathedral Council* Mr Peter Sanders,
Cathedral Offices, St Thomas's Street, Old
Portsmouth PO1 2HA
T: 023 9282 3300 ext 228 (office
E: peter.sanders@portsmouthcathedral.org.uk
Assistant Curate The Revd Dawn Banting (*Same
Address*)
Head Verger Malina Wyzykowska (*Same
Address*) *T:* 023 9289 2969
E: malina.wyzykowska@
portsmouthcathedral.org.uk
Cathedral Organist and Master of the Choristers
Dr David Price *T:* 023 9289 2961
E: david.price@portsmouthcathedral.org.uk
Cathedral Sub-Organist (until 31/12/17) Oliver
Hancock, Flat 1, Cathedral House, St Thomas's
Street, Old Portsmouth PO1 2HA
T: 023 9282 3300
E: oliver.hancock@
portsmouthcathedral.org.uk
Cathedral Sub-Organist (from 1/1/18) Sachin
Gunga (*Same Address & Tel*)
E: sachin.gunga@
portsmouthcathedral.org.uk
Personal Assistant Liz Snowball, Cathedral
Office, Cathedral House, 63–67 St Thomas's
Street, Old Portsmouth PO1 2HA
E: liz.snowball@portsmouthcathedral.org.uk

ARCHDEACONS
THE MEON The Ven Gavin Collins, Victoria
Lodge, 36 Osborn Road, Fareham PO16 7DS
T: 01329 608895
E: admeon@portsmouth.anglican.org
PORTSDOWN The Ven Dr Joanne Grenfell, 313
Havant Road, Farlington, Portsmouth PO6
1DD *T:* 023 9289 9650
E: adportsdown@portsmouth.anglican.org

THE ISLE OF WIGHT The Ven Peter Sutton, 5 The Boltons, Kite Hill, Wootton Bridge, Isle of Wight PO33 4PB   *T:* 01983 884432
            E: adiow@portsmouth.anglican.org

MEMBERS OF THE HOUSE OF CLERGY OF THE GENERAL SYNOD
Proctors for Clergy
The Revd Canon Peter Leonard
The Ven Gavin Collins
The Revd Canon Bob White

MEMBERS OF THE HOUSE OF LAITY OF THE GENERAL SYNOD
Canon Lucy Docherty
Mrs Emily Bagg
Mr Mark Emerton

DIOCESAN OFFICERS
Diocesan Secretary The Revd Wendy Kennedy, First Floor, Peninsular House, Wharf Road, Portsmouth PO2 8HB   *T:* 023 9289 9664
            E: wendy.kennedy@
            portsmouth.anglican.org
Deputy Diocesan Secretary Mrs Jenny Hollingsworth (*Same Address*)
            T: 023 9282 9664
            E: jenny.hollingsworth@
            portsmouth.anglican.org
PA to Diocesan and Deputy Diocesan Secretaries and DAC Secretaries Mr David Cain (*Same Tel*)
            E: executive.assistant@
            portsmouth.anglican.org
Miss Catherine Gray (*Same Tel & email*)
Chancellor of Diocese His Honour Judge Philip Waller, 49 Woodstock Road North, St Albans AL1 4QD   *T:* 01727 839668
            E: HHJ.Philip.Waller@eJudiciary.net
Registrar of Diocese and Bishop's Legal Secretary Miss Hilary Tyler, Messrs Brutton & Co., West End House, 288 West St, Fareham PO16 0A
            T: 01329 236171
            F: 01329 289915
            E: hilary.tyler@brutton.co.uk

DIOCESAN ORGANIZATIONS
Diocesan Office First Floor, Peninsular House, Wharf Road, Portsmouth PO2 8HB
            T: 023 9289 9650
            E: admin@portsmouth.anglican.org

ADMINISTRATION
Diocesan Synod (*Secretary*) The Revd Wendy Kennedy, First Floor, Peninsular House, Wharf Road, Portsmouth PO2 8HB   *T:* 023 9289 9664
            E: wendy.kennedy@
            portsmouth.anglican.org
(*Chairman House of Clergy*) The Revd Canon Bob White, St Mary's Vicarage, Fratton Road, Portsmouth PO1 5PA
            T: 023 9282 2990 (office)
            E: revrcwhite@aol.com

(*Chairman, House of Laity*) Vacancy
Bishop's Council/Board of Finance/Pastoral Committee (*Chairman*) The Rt Revd Christopher Foster, Bishopsgrove, 26 Osborn Road, Fareham PO16 7DQ
(*Secretary*) The Revd Wendy Kennedy, First Floor, Peninsular House, Wharf Road, Portsmouth PO2 8HB   *T:* 023 9289 9664
            E: wendy.kennedy@portsmouth.anglican.org

CHURCH BUILDINGS
Diocesan Advisory Committee for the Care of Churches (*Chair*) The Very Revd David Brindley, The Deanery, 13 Pembroke Road, Portsmouth PO1 2NS   *T:* 023 9289 2963
            E: david.brindley@
            portsmouthcathedral.org.uk
(*Secretary*) Miss Catherine Gray
            T: 023 9282 9664
            E: executive.assistant@
            portsmouth.anglican.org
Mr David Cain (*Same Tel & email*)
Closed Churches for Regular Worship Committee (*Chair*) The Revd Wendy Kennedy, First Floor, Peninsular House, Wharf Road, Portsmouth PO2 8HB   *T:* 023 9289 9664
            E: wendy.kennedy@portsmouth.anglican.org
(*Secretary*) Mrs Jenny Hollingsworth (*Same Address*)   *T:* 023 9282 9664
            E: jenny.hollingsworth@
            portsmouth.anglican.org

DIOCESAN RECORD OFFICES
Portsmouth History Centre Portsmouth History Centre, Central Library, Portsmouth PO1 2DX   *T:* 023 9268 8046
            E: portsmouthhistorycentre@
            portsmouth.gov.uk
Hampshire Record Office Hampshire Record Office, Sussex St, Winchester SO23 8TH
            T: 01962 846154
            F: 01962 878681
            E: enquiries.archives@hants.gov.uk
Isle of Wight County Record Office Isle of Wight County Record Office, 26 Hillside, Newport, Isle of Wight PO30 2EB
(*Archivist*) Mr R. Smout   *T:* 01983 823821
            E: record.office@iow.gov.uk

MINISTRY
Widows Officers (Mainland) The Revd Canon Peter Kelly, 16 Rosedale Close, Titchfield, Fareham PO14 4EL   *T:* 01329 849567
            E: peterkelly@swanmore.net

MISSION AND DISCIPLESHIP
Head of Department The Revd Canon Dr Anthony Rustell, 1 Pembroke Close, Old Portsmouth PO1 2NX
            T: 023 9289 9654 (office)
            E: anthony.rustell@portsmouth.anglican.org

Diocesan Director of Ordinands The Revd Belinda Davies, The Vicarage, 269 Hawthorn Crescent, Cosham PO6 2TL   *T:* 07881 787921
E: belinda.davies@portsmouth.anglican.org
Diocesan IME The Ven Peter Sutton, 5 The Boltons, Kite Hill, Wootton Bridge, Isle of Wight PO33 4PB   *T:* 01983 884432
E: adiow@portsmouth.anglican.org
Youth and Children's Work Adviser Ben Mizen, First Floor, Peninsular House, Wharf Road, Portsmouth PO2 8HB   *T:* 023 9289 9652
E: ben.mizen@portsmouth.anglican.org
Spirituality Adviser The Revd Dr Ruth Tuschling (*Same Address*)   *T:* 023 9289 9686
E: ruth.tuschling@portsmouth.anglican.org
Healing Advisor Dr David Pearson, 27 Livingstone Road, Southsea, PO5 1RS
T: 023 9275 3260
E: david.pearson@portsmouth.anglican.org
Stewardship Adviser Victoria James, Dioc Office   *T:* 023 9289 9655
E: victoria.james@portsmouth.anglican.org

MISSION AND EDUCATION
Director of Education, Portsmouth and Winchester The Revd Jeff Williams, First Floor, Peninsular House, Wharf Road, Portsmouth PO2 8HB
T: 023 9289 9680
E: jeff.williams@portsmouth.anglican.org
Head of Department The Revd Jeff Williams (*As above*)

MISSION AND RESOURCES
Head of Department Mrs Jenny Hollingsworth, First Floor, Peninsular House, Wharf Road, Portsmouth PO2 8HB   *T:* 023 9282 9664
E: jenny.hollingsworth@portsmouth.anglican.org
Diocesan Property Manager and Surveyor and Secretary to Property Committee Mr Chris Pride (*Same Address*)   *T:* 023 9289 9663
E: chris.pride@portsmouth.anglican.org
Synod and Office Support Manager Mrs Jane Dobbs (*Same Address*)   *T:* 023 9289 9661
E: jane.dobbs@portsmouth.anglican.org
Safeguarding Adviser Mr Ian Berry (*Same Address*)   *T:* 023 9289 9665
E: ian.berry@portsmouth.anglican.org

MISSION AND SOCIETY
Chair (appointed by the Bishop) The Revd Canon Bob White, St Mary's Vicarage, Fratton Road, Portsmouth PO1 5PA
T: 023 9282 2990 (office)
E: revrcwhite@aol.com
Head of Mission and Society Section and Social Responsibility Adviser The Revd Canon Nick Ralph, First Floor, Peninsular House, Wharf Road, Portsmouth PO2 8HB
T: 023 9289 9674 (office)
M: 07817 722219 (mobile)
E: nick.ralph@portsmouth.anglican.org

Chair of the Council for Social Responsibility Steering Group Canon Lucy Docherty, 33 Southampton Road, Fareham PO16 7DZ
M: 07952 780108
E: lucy@docherty1.co.uk
Interfaith Adviser The Revd Andy Marshall, Oasis Suite, Nuffield Centre, St Michael's Road, University of Portsmouth PO1 2ED
T: 023 9284 3030
Mental Health Adviser The Revd James Hair, Fareham and Gosport Adult Mental Health Service, 219 West Street, Fareham PO16 0ET
T: 01329 825231
E: James.Hair@southernhealth.nhs.uk
New Religious Movements Adviser Vacancy
Port Chaplain The Revd Philip Hiscock, 15 Winnham Drive, Fareham. PO16 8QF
T: 023 9234 6881
E: philip.hiscock@ntlworld.com
Porvoo Adviser Vacancy
Diocesan Rural Officer and Rural Affairs Adviser (Mainland) Vacancy
Rural Affairs Adviser (IOW) The Revd Canon Graham Morris, The Vicarage, 14 Argyll Street, Ryde, Isle of Wight PO33 3BZ
T: 01983 716435
E: revcanongraham@gmail.com
Urban Ministry Adviser The Revd Canon Bob White, St Mary's Vicarage, Fratton Road, Portsmouth PO1 5PA
T: 023 9282 2990 (office)
E: revrcwhite@aol.com
Chaplain to the Deaf and Hard of Hearing The Revd Robert Sanday, The Vicarage, Grange Road, Netley Abbey SO31 5FF
T: 023 8045 6778
E: robertsanday12@gmail.com
Communications Adviser Mr Neil Pugmire, First Floor, Peninsular House, Wharf Road, Portsmouth PO2 8HB   *T:* 023 9289 9673
E: neil.pugmire@portsmouth.anglican.org
Disability Adviser The Revd Robert Sanday, The Vicarage, Grange Road, Netley Abbey SO31 5FF   *T:* 023 8045 6778
E: robertsanday12@gmail.com
Environment Adviser Vacancy
Ecumenical Adviser Vacancy
Interdiocesan West Africa Link (Chair) The Revd Canon Graham Morris, The Vicarage, 14 Argyll Street, Ryde, Isle of Wight PO33 3BZ
T: 01983 716435
E: revcanongraham@gmail.com

AREA DEANS
ARCHDEACONRY OF PORTSDOWN
Havant Andrew Martin Wilson, Portsdown Vicarage, 1A London Road, Widley, Waterlooville PO7 5AT   *T:* 023 9237 5360
E: wilson@ntlworld.com
Havant Karina Beverley Green, St Alban's Vicarage, Martin Road, Havant PO9 5TE
T: 023 9307 6871
E: canonkarina@talktalk.net

Portsmouth Robert Charles White, St Mary's Vicarage, Fratton Road, Portsmouth PO1 5PA
T: 023 9282 2687
E: revrcwhite@gmail.com

ARCHDEACONRY OF THE ISLE OF WIGHT
Isle of Wight Alison Kerr, The Rectory, 69 Victoria Grove, East Cowes PO32 6DL
T: 01983 299930
E: rev.allie@hotmail.com

ARCHDEACONRY OF THE MEON
Bishop's Waltham Gregg Richard Mensingh, The Rectory, 46 High Street, Botley, Southampton SO30 2EA   *T:* 01489 796703
E: gregg.mensingh@gmail.com

Fareham Susan Allman, The Vicarage, 24 Frog Lane, Titchfield, Fareham PO14 4DU
T: 01329 842324
E: susanrev@hotmail.co.uk
Gosport Karen Irene Mitchell, St Matthew's Vicarage, 7 Duncton Way, Gosport PO13 0FD
T: 01329 829883
E: karen.mitchell@talk.talk.net
Petersfield Jane Ball, The Vicarage, Church Street, East Meon, Petersfield GU32 1NH
T: 01730 823618
E: jandjball@btinternet.com

DIOCESE OF ROCHESTER

Founded in 604. Kent west of the Medway; except for one parish in the south-west in the diocese of Chichester; the Medway Towns; the London boroughts of Bromley and Bexley, except for a few parishes in the diocese of Southwark; one parish in East Sussex.

Population 1,351,000   Area 540 sq m
Full-time Stipendiary Parochial Clergy 199   Benefices 184
Parishes 216   Churches 261
www.rochester.anglican.org
Overseas link dioceses: Estonia, Harare, Kondoa, Mpwapwa

BISHOP (106th)
The Rt Revd James Langstaff, Bishopscourt, St Margaret's Street, Rochester ME1 1TS
T: 01634 842721
E: bishopscourt@rochester.anglican.org

BISHOP'S STAFF
Chaplain The Revd Lindsay Llewellyn-MacDuff
T: 01634 814439
E: lindsay@rochester.anglican.org

SUFFRAGAN BISHOP
TONBRIDGE Vacancy

ASSISTANT BISHOPS
The Rt Revd Dr Michael Nazir-Ali, c/o 70 Wimpole Street, London W1G 8AX
T: 020 3327 1130
E: oxtrad@gmail.com
The Rt Revd Michael Turnbull, 67 Strand Street, Sandwich CT13 9HN
T: 01304 611389
E: amichaelturnbull@yahoo.co.uk
The Rt Revd Rod Thomas, 28 St John's Meadow, Blindley Heath, Lingfield RH7 6JU
T: 01342 834140
E: admin@bishopofmaidstone.org
The Rt Revd Norman Banks, Parkside House, Abbey Mill Lane, St Albans AL3 4HE
T: 01727 836358
E: bishop@richborough.org.uk
The Rt Revd Ken Sandy Edozie Okeke, 50 Essex Road, Longfield, Kent DA3 7QL
T: 01474 709627
E: kengozi8@yahoo.com

CATHEDRAL CHURCH OF CHRIST AND THE BLESSED VIRGIN MARY
Dean The Very Revd Dr Philip Hesketh, Chapter Office, Garth House, The Precinct, Rochester ME1 1SX
T: 01634 843366
F: 01634 401410

Canons Residentiary
Archdeacon The Ven Simon Burton-Jones, The Archdeaconry, The Precinct, Rochester ME1 1TG
T: 01634 560000 (office)
01634 813533 (Home)
E: archdeacon@rochestercathedral.org
Precentor The Revd Matthew Rushton, East Canonry, 2 Kings Orchard, Rochester ME1 1TG
E: matthew.rushton@rochestercathedral.org
Canon for Mission and Growth The Revd Canon Rachel Phillips, Prebendal House, 1 Kings Orchard, Rochester ME1 1TG
T: 01707 874126
Other Staff
Chapter Clerk – Executive Director Simon Lace, Chapter Office, Garth House, The Precinct, Rochester ME1 1SX
T: 01634 843366
E: chapterclerk@rochester.cathedral.org
Cathedral Organist and Director of Music Mr Scott Farrell, Garth House, The Precinct, Rochester ME1 1SX
T: 01634 810061
E: dom@rochestercathedral.org

ARCHDEACONS
BROMLEY AND BEXLEY The Ven Dr Paul Wright, The Archdeaconry, The Glebe, Chislehurst BR7 5PX
T: 020 8467 8743
E: archdeacon.bromley@rochester.anglican.org
ROCHESTER The Ven Simon Burton-Jones, The Archdeaconry, The Precinct, Rochester ME1 1TG
T: 01634 560000 (office)
E: archdeacon@rochestercathedral.org
TONBRIDGE The Ven Julie Conalty, c/o Diocesan Office, St Nicholas Church, Boley Hill, Rochester ME1 1SL
E: archdeacon.tonbridge@rochester.anglican.org

MEMBERS OF THE HOUSE OF CLERGY OF THE GENERAL SYNOD
Proctors for Clergy
The Revd Mark Barker
The Ven Julie Conalty
The Revd Canon Angus MacLeay
The Revd Rachel Wilson

MEMBERS OF THE HOUSE OF LAITY OF THE GENERAL SYNOD
Brig Ian Dobbie
Mr Philip French
Dr Mike Lawes
Mrs Angela Scott
Mr Martin Sewell

DIOCESAN OFFICERS
Diocesan Secretary Mr Geoff Marsh, St Nicholas Church, Boley Hill, Rochester ME1 1SL
T: 01634 560000
E: geoff.marsh@rochester.anglican.org
Chancellor of Diocese Mr John Gallagher, Hardwicke Building, New Square, Lincoln's Inn, London WC2A 3SB   *T:* 020 7242 2523
Registrar of Diocese and Bishop's Legal Secretary Mr Owen Carew-Jones, Minerva House, 5 Montague Close, London SE1 9BB
T: 020 7593 5110
F: 020 7593 5099
E: ocj@wslaw.co.uk

DIOCESAN ORGANIZATIONS
Diocesan Office St Nicholas Church, Boley Hill, Rochester ME1 1SL   *T:* 01634 560000
E: enquiries@rochester.anglican.org
W: www.rochester.anglican.org

ADMINISTRATION
Diocesan Synod (Chair, House of Clergy) The Revd Alyson Davie
E: alyson@stjohnsmeopham.co.uk
(Chair, House of Laity) Mr Philip French
E: philip.c.french@btinternet.com
(Secretary) Mr Geoff Marsh, St Nicholas Church, Boley Hill, Rochester ME1 1SL
T: 01634 560000
E: geoff.marsh@rochester.anglican.org
Board of Finance (Chair) Canon Judith Armitt
(Secretary) Mr Geoff Marsh, St Nicholas Church, Boley Hill, Rochester ME1 1SL
T: 01634 560000
E: geoff.marsh@rochester.anglican.org
(Assistant Diocesan Secretary Property) Mr Mark Trevett, Boley Hill, Rochester ME1 1SL
E: mark.trevett@rochester.anglican.org
(Director of Strategy and Implementation) Mr Matthew Girt *(Same Address)*
E: matthew.girt@rochester.anglican.org
(Finance Director) The Revd Richard Williams
E: richard.williams@rochester.anglican.org
Pastoral Committee Mrs Suzanne Rogers, Boley Hill, Rochester ME1 1SL
E: suzanne.rogers@rochester.anglican.org
Board of Patronage Miss Kayleigh Kidner
E: kayleigh.kidner@rochester.anglican.org
(Designated Officer) Mr Owen Carew-Jones, Minerva House, 5 Montague Close, London SE1 9BB   *T:* 020 7593 5110
F: 020 7593 5099
E: ocj@wslaw.co.uk

Trusts Mr Geoff Marsh, St Nicholas Church, Boley Hill, Rochester ME1 1SL
T: 01634 560000
E: geoff.marsh@rochester.anglican.org
(Stewardship Adviser) Mr Brian Pull *(Same Address)*   *E:* brian.pull@rochester.anglican.org

CHURCH BUILDINGS
Advisory Committee for the Care of Churches (Chair) Mr Derek Shilling, Ivy Bank, Shoreham Road, Otford, Sevenoaks TN14 5RP
T: 01959 522059
(DAC Secretary) Mrs Sarah Anderson, St Nicholas Church, Boley Hill, Rochester ME1 1SL   *E:* sarah.anderson@ rochester.anglican.org
(Closed Churches) Mr Geoff Marsh *(Same Address)*   *T:* 01634 560000
E: geoff.marsh@rochester.anglican.org

COMMUNICATIONS
Director Lindy Mackenzie, St Nicholas Church, Boley Hill, Rochester ME1 1SL
T: 01634 560000
M: 07901 670257
E: lindy.mackenzie@rochester.anglican.org
Communications Assistant Mrs Katerina Gerhardt *(Same Address & Tel)*
E: katerina.gerhardt@ rochester.anglican.org

DIOCESAN RECORD OFFICES
Bexley Local Studies and Archive Centre, Central Library Townley Rd, Bexleyheath DA6 7HJ   *T:* 020 8301 1545
E: archives@bexley.gov.uk
Medway Archives and Local Studies Centre, Gun Wharf, Dock Road, Chatham ME4 4TR
T: 01634 332714
E: malsc@medway.gov.uk
Kent History and Library Centre, James Whatman Way, Maidstone ME14 1LQ
T: 03000 413131
E: historyandlibrarycentre@kent.gov.uk
Bromley Local Studies and Archives, Central Library, High Street, Bromley, Kent BR1 1EX
T: 020 8460 9955
E: historic.collections@gll.org

EDUCATION
Board of Education (Acting Chair)
(Secretary and Director) Mr Alex Tear, St Nicholas Church, Boley Hill, Rochester ME1 1SL   *E:* alex.tear@rochester.anglican.org
(Deputy Director) Mr John Constanti *(Same Address)*
E: john.constanti@rochester.anglican.org
(Assistant Director Schools) Mrs Virginia Corbyn *(Same Address)*
E: virginia.corbyn@rochester.anglican.org

FORMATION AND MINISTRY

Director The Revd Canon Christopher Dench, St Nicholas Church, Boley Hill, Rochester ME1 1SL   *E:* chris.dench@rochester.anglican.org

Assistant Director The Revd Trevor Gerhardt (*Same Address*)
    E: trevor.gerhardt@rochester.anglican.org

Training Officer Mrs Alison Callway (*Same Address*)
    E: alison.callway@rochester.anglican.org

Director of Ordinands The Revd Pamela Ive
    E: pamelaive@btinternet.com

Warden of Lay Ministry Mrs Karen Senior, St Nicholas Church, Boley Hill, Rochester ME1 1SL   *E:* readers@rochester.anglican.org

Diocesan Co-ordinator of Spirituality The Revd Susanne Carlsson (*Same Address*)
    E: susanne.carlsson@rochester.anglican.org

Diocesan Vocations Adviser The Revd Canon Mark Griffin, St Luke's Vicarage, 30 Eardley Road, Sevenoaks TN13 1XT   *T:* 01732 452462
    E: revd.mark.griffin@talk21.com

MISSION AND COMMUNITY ENGAGEMENT

Director Vacancy

Interfaith Adviser The Ven Dr Paul Wright, The Archdeaconry, The Glebe, Chislehurst BR7 5PX   *T:* 020 8467 8743
    E: archdeacon.bromley@
    rochester.anglican.org

Diocesan Children's and Youth Work Adviser Mrs Cheryl Trice, St Nicholas Church, Boley Hill, Rochester ME1 1SL
    E: cheryl.trice@rochester.anglican.org

AREA DEANS

ARCHDEACONRY OF BROMLEY AND BEXLEY

Beckenham Robert Matthew Hinton, Christ Church Vicarage, 18 Court Downs Road, Beckenham BR3 6LR   *T:* 020 8650 3487
    E: revrobhinton@hotmail.com

Bromley Alan Keeler, St Mary's Vicarage, 74 London Lane, Bromley BR1 4HE
    T: 020 8460 1827
    E: alan.keeler@diocese-rochester.org

Erith Adam Julian David Foot, St John's Vicarage, Danson Lane, Welling DA16 2BQ
    T: 020 8303 1107
    E: adam.foot@diocese-rochester.org

Orpington John Tranter, The Rectory, Skibbs Lane, Orpington BR6 7RH   *T:* 01689 825749
    E: revjohnt@talktalk.net

Sidcup Philip Anthony Wells, The Vicarage, 1 Hurst Road, Sidcup DA15 9AE
    T: 020 8300 8231
    E: vicar@holytrinitylamorbey.org

ARCHDEACONRY OF ROCHESTER

Cobham James Arthur Fletcher, The Rectory, 3 St John's Lane, Hartley, Longfield DA3 8ET
    T: 01474 703819
    E: rector@fawkhamandhartley.org.uk

Dartford Kenneth William Clark, The Rectory, Church Road, Greenhithe DA9 9BE
    T: 01322 382076
    E: kenneth.clark@diocese-rochester.org

Gillingham Ann Richardson, Holy Trinity Vicarage, 2 Waltham Road, Gillingham ME8 6XQ   *T:* 01634 231690
    E: ann_r@btinternet.com

Gravesend Susan Comport Brewer, The Vicarage, 48 Old Road East, Gravesend DA12 1NR   *T:* 01474 352643
    E: suec@brewer86.plus.com

Rochester Vacancy

Strood Sharon Louise Copestake, The Vicarage, Galahad Avenue, Rochester ME2 2YS
    T: 01634 864348
    E: sharon.copestake@pipnjims.co.uk

ARCHDEACONRY OF TONBRIDGE

Malling Matthew Alexander John Buchan, The Rectory, 73 Rectory Lane North, Leybourne, West Malling ME19 5HD   *T:* 01732 842187
    E: frbuchan@frbuchan.force9.co.uk

Paddock Wood Bryan Thomas Knapp, The Vicarage, 169 Maidstone Road, Paddock Wood, Tonbridge TN12 6DZ
    T: 01892 833917
    E: bryan.knapp@diocese-rochester.org

Sevenoaks Vacancy

Shoreham Timothy Rex Hatwell, The Rectory, Bates Hill, Ightham, Sevenoaks TN15 9BG
    T: 07799 601546
    E: tim.hatwell@diocese-rochester.org

Tonbridge Mark Edward Brown, The Vicarage, Church Street, Tonbridge TN9 1HD
    T: 01732 770962
    E: mark@tonbridgeparishchurch.org.uk

Tunbridge Wells James Patrick Stewart, The Vicarage, 12 Shandon Close, Tunbridge Wells TN2 3RE   *T:* 01892 530687
    E: jpstewart4@googlemail.com

ROCHESTER

DIOCESE OF ST ALBANS

Founded in 1877. Hertfordshire, except for a small area in the south, in the diocese of London, and one parish in the west, in the diocese of Oxford; Bedfordshire, except for one parish in the north, in the diocese of Ely, and one parish in the west, in the diocese of Oxford; an area of Greater London.

Population 1,917,000   Area 1,120 sq m
Full-time Stipendiary Parochial Clergy 239   Benefices 193
Parishes 338   Churches 408
www.stalbans.anglican.org
Overseas link dioceses: Jamaica, Guyana, NE Caribbean and Aruba (West Indies)

BISHOP (10th)
The Rt Revd Dr Alan Gregory Clayton Smith, Abbey Gate House, Abbey Mill Lane, St Albans AL3 4HD   T: 01727 853305
                                           F: 01727 846715
          E: bishop@stalbans.anglican.org

BISHOP'S STAFF
Chaplain Capt Andrew Crooks
                              T: 01727 853305
          E: chaplain@stalbans.anglican.org
PA Mrs Rosamund Adlard
          E: radlard@stalbans.anglican.org
Administrative Secretary to the Bishop Mrs Deborah Hoare
          E: dhoare@stalbans.anglican.org

SUFFRAGAN BISHOPS
BEDFORD The Rt Revd Richard Atkinson, Bedford Road, Cardington MK44 3SS
                              T: 01234 831432
                              F: 01234 831484
     E: bishopbedford@stalbans.anglican.org
HERTFORD The Rt Revd Dr Michael Beasley, Bishopswood, 3 Stobarts Close, Knebworth SG3 6ND   T: 01438 817260
     E: bishophertford@stalbans.anglican.org

ASSISTANT BISHOPS
The Rt Revd Robin J. N. Smith, 7 Aysgarth Road, Redbourn, St Albans AL3 7PJ
The Rt Revd John Gladwin, The White House, 131A Marford Road, Wheathampstead, St Albans AL4 8NH   T: 01582 834223
The Rt Revd Norman Banks, Parkside House, Abbey Mill Lane, St Albans AL3 4HE
                              T: 01727 836358
          E: bishop@richborough.org.uk
The Rt Revd Dr Stephen Venner, 81 King Harry Lane, St Albans AL3 4AS   T: 07980 743628
          E: stephen@venner.org.uk

CATHEDRAL AND ABBEY CHURCH OF SAINT ALBAN
Dean The Very Revd Dr Jeffrey John, The Old Rectory, Sumpter Yard, St Albans AL1 1BY
                              T: 01727 890202
          E: dean@stalbanscathedral.org
Canons Residentiary
Canon Chancellor The Revd Canon Kevin Walton, 2 Sumpter Yard, St Albans AL1 1BY
                              T: 01727 890242
          E: canon@stalbanscathedral.org
Director of Mission The Revd Canon Tim Lomax
Director of Ministry and Ministry Development Officer The Revd Canon Dr Tim Bull, 43 Holywell Hill, St Albans AL1 1HE
                              T: 01727 841116
          E: dome@stalbans.anglican.org
Minor Canons
Youth Chaplain The Revd Sally Jones, 2 Dean Moore Close, St Albans AL1 1DW
Precentor The Revd Berkeley Zych, 1 Dean Moore Close, St Albans, AL1 1DW
Other Staff
Cathedral Administrator and Clerk to the Chapter Ms Heather Smith, The Chapter House, Sumpter Yard, St Albans AL1 1BY
                              T: 01727 890208
          E: admin@stalbanscathedral.org
Master of the Music Mr Andrew Lucas, 31 Abbey Mill Lane, St Albans, AL3 4HA
                              T: 01727 890245
          E: music@stalbanscathedral.org
Assistant Master of the Music and Director of the Abbey Girls Choir Mr Tom Winpenny, 34 Orchard Street, St Albans AL3 4HL *(Same Tel)*
          E: amom@stalbanscathedral.org
Cathedral Education Officer Steve Clarke, Education Centre, Sumpter Yard, St Albans AL1 1BY   T: 01727 890262
          E: education@stalbanscathedral.org
Cathedral Architect Ms Kelley Christ
Archaeological Consultant Prof Martin Biddle

ARCHDEACONS

ST ALBANS The Ven Jonathan Smith, 6 Sopwell Lane, St Albans AL1 1RR   *T:* 01727 847212
    E: archdstalbans@stalbans.anglican.org
BEDFORD The Ven Paul Hughes, 17 Lansdowne Road, Luton LU3 1EE   *T:* 01582 730722
    E: archdbedf@stalbans.anglican.org
HERTFORD The Ven Janet Mackenzie, Glebe House, St Mary's Lane, Hertingfordbury SG14 2LE   *T:* 01727 818159
    E: archdhert@stalbans.anglican.org

MEMBERS OF THE HOUSE OF CLERGY OF THE GENERAL SYNOD

Proctors for Clergy
The Revd Canon Dr Tim Bull
The Revd Will Gibbs
The Revd Kevin Goss
The Revd Peter Kay
The Revd Steve Wood

MEMBERS OF THE HOUSE OF LAITY OF THE GENERAL SYNOD

Mr Simon Baynes
Mr William Seddon
Canon Peter Adams
Mr Anthony Archer
Mr Tim Fleming

DIOCESAN OFFICERS

Diocesan Secretary Miss Susan Pope, Holywell Lodge, 41 Holywell Hill, St Albans AL1 1HE
    T: 01727 854532
    F: 01727 844469
    E: mail@stalbans.anglican.org
Chancellor of Diocese His Honour the Worshipful Roger G. Kaye (*Same Address*)
    T: 01727 865765
Registrar of Diocese and Bishop's Legal Secretary Mr Matthew Chinery, Winckworth Sherwood LLP, Minerva House, 5 Montague Close, London SE1 9BB   *T:* 0207 593 5000
    E: mchinery@wslaw.co.uk
Surveyor Mr Alastair Woodgate, c/o 41 Holywell Hill, St Albans AL1 1HE
    T: 01727 854516

DIOCESAN ORGANIZATIONS

Diocesan Office Holywell Lodge, 41 Holywell Hill, St Albans AL1 1HE   *T:* 01727 854532
    F: 01727 844469
    E: mail@stalbans.anglican.org
    W: www.stalbans.anglican.org

ADMINISTRATION

Diocesan Synod (*Chairman, House of Clergy*) The Revd Canon Jo Loveridge, All Saints Vicarage, Churchfields, Hertford SG13 8AE
    T: 01992 589147

(*Chairman, House of Laity*) Mr John Wallace
(*Secretary*) Miss Susan Pope, Holywell Lodge, 41 Holywell Hill, St Albans AL1 1HE
    T: 01727 854532
    F: 01727 844469
    E: mail@stalbans.anglican.org
Board of Finance (*Chairman*) Canon David Nye
(*Secretary*) Miss Susan Pope, Holywell Lodge, 41 Holywell Hill, St Albans AL1 1HE
    T: 01727 854532
    F: 01727 844469
    E: mail@stalbans.anglican.org
(*Financial Secretary*) Mr Martin Bishop (*Same Address*)
(*Estates Secretary*) Mrs Michèle Manders (*Same Address*)
Board of Patronage Mrs Emma Critchley (*Same Address*)
Mission and Pastoral Committee Mrs Emma Critchley (*As above*)
Trusts Mr Nigel Benger (*Same Address*)

CHURCH AND SOCIETY

Director of Mission The Revd Canon Tim Lomax
Church and Community Officer Mr Christopher Neilson   *T:* 01727 851748

CHURCH BUILDINGS

Advisory Committee for the Care of Churches (*Chairman*) Dr Christopher Green
(*Secretary*) Mrs Emma Critchley, Holywell Lodge, 41 Holywell Hill, St Albans AL1 1HE

DIOCESAN RECORD OFFICES

County Hall, Hertford, G13 8DE
    T: 01992 555105
County Hall, Bedford MK42 9AP
(*County Archivist*) Mr Kevin Ward (*Same Address*)   *T:* 01234 63222 ext 277

EDUCATION

Diocesan Education and Resources Centre Holywell Lodge, 41 Holywell Hill, St Albans AL1 1HE   *T:* 01727 854532
    F: 01727 844469
Director of Education Mr David Morton (*Same Address*)
Deputy Directors of Education Ms Lizzie Jeanes (*Same Address*)
Ms Charlotte Johnson (*Same Address*)
RE Adviser Mrs Jane Chipperton (*Same Address*)

MINISTRY

Director of Ordinands The Revd Dr Quentin Chandler

Ministerial Development Officer/Director of Ministry The Revd Canon Dr Tim Bull, 43 Holywell Hill, St Albans AL1 1HE
T: 01727 841116
E: dome@stalbans.anglican.org
Parish Development Officer The Revd Jeanette Gosney   *T:* 01727 818141
Officer for IME 4–7 The Revd James Webster
Reader Ministry Officer Ms Lauryn Awbrey
T: 01727 818154
Associate Director of Ordinands The Revd Emma Coley
Board of Readers' Work Mrs Margaret Tinsley, 145 The Ridgeway, St Albans AL4 9XA
T: 01727 859528
Mr Richard Osborn, 41 Tiverton Road, Potters Bar EN6 5HX   *T:* 01707 657491
Youth Officer Mr Dean Pusey, Holywell Lodge, 41 Holywell Hill, St Albans AL1 1HE
Children's Mission Enabler Mrs Margaret Pritchard Houston (*Same Address*)

MISSIONARY AND ECUMENICAL
Ecumenical Officers (*Bedford Archdeaconry*) The Revd Stephen Toze   *E:* s@steve777.plus.com
(*Hertford Archdeaconry*) The Revd Paul Seymour
E: revpaulseymour@btinternet.com
(*St Albans Archdeaconry*) Vacancy
Board for Church and Society (*Chairman*) The Rt Revd Dr Michael Beasley, Bishopswood, 3 Stobarts Close, Knebworth SG3 6ND
T: 01438 817260
E: bishophertford@stalbans.anglican.org
(*International Mission Council*) The Revd Ray Porter, 24 Bevington Way, Eynesbury, St Neots PE19 2HQ   *T:* 01480 211839
Workplace Matters Vacancy

PRESS AND PUBLICATIONS
Diocesan Communications Officer Mr Arun Kataria, Holywell Lodge, 41 Holywell Hill, St Albans AL1 1HE   *T:* 01727 818110
F: 01727 844469
E: comms@stalbans.anglican.org
Communications Assistant Mrs Claudia Ashley-Brown (*Same Address*)

STEWARDSHIP
Mission Resourcing Officer Mr Chris Wainman, Holywell Lodge, 41 Holywell Hill, St Albans AL1 1HE   *T:* 01727 854532

RURAL DEANS
ARCHDEACONRY OF BEDFORD
Ampthill and Shefford Lynda Klimas, The Rectory, Clophill Road, Maulden, Bedford MK45 2AA   *T:* 07896-182776
E: rev.l.klimas@btinternet.com

Bedford Richard Charles Hibbert, Christ Church Vicarage, 115 Denmark Street, Bedford MK40 3TJ   *T:* 01234 359342
E: vicar@ccbedford.org
Biggleswade Lindsay Charles Dew, 22 Angell's Meadow, Ashwell, Baldock SG7 5QS
T: 01462 743617
E: lindsay.dew@btinternet.com
Dunstable Bernard John Minton, St Barnabas' Vicarage, Vicarage Road, Leighton Buzzard LU7 2LP   *T:* 01525 372149
E: bernardminton@aol.com
Luton Vacancy
Sharnbrook Stephen John Liley, The Vicarage, Green Lane, Clapham, Bedford MK41 6ER
T: 01234 352814
E: the.lileys@ukgateway.net

ARCHDEACONRY OF HERTFORD
Barnet James Edmond Alexander Mustard, The Rectory, 136 Church Hill Road, Barnet EN4 8XD   *T:* 020 8368 3840
E: rector.eastbarnet@gmail.com
Bishop's Stortford Vacancy
Buntingford Kate Rebecca Peacock, The Vicarage, Great Hormead, Buntingford SG9 0NT   *T:* 01763 289258
E: kate.peacock@btopenworld.com
Cheshunt Charles Edward Cameron Hudson, The Vicarage, Churchfields, Broxbourne EN10 7AU   *T:* 01992 444117
E: bwparishoffice@btinternet.com
Hertford and Ware Joan Margaretha Holland Loveridge, All Saints' Vicarage, Churchfields, Hertford SG13 8AE   *T:* 01992 584899
E: jonloveridge@hotmail.com
Stevenage Christopher Edward Bunce, The Rectory, Cuttys Lane, Stevenage SG1 1UP
T: 07815 041852
E: cebunce@gmail.com
Welwyn Hatfield Jennifer Elizabeth Fennell, The Vicarage, 48 Parkway, Welwyn Garden City AL8 6HH   *T:* 01707 320960
E: jennyfennell@virginmedia.com

ARCHDEACONRY OF ST ALBANS
Berkhamsted Jonathan Andrew Gordon, St Mary's Rectory, 80 High Street, Northchurch, Berkhamsted HP4 3QW   *T:* 01442 871547
E: ebenezer@
jonathangordon.wanadoo.co.uk
Hemel Hempstead Elizabeth Mary Hood, The Vicarage, 14 Pancake Lane, Hemel Hempstead HP2 4NB   *T:* 01442 264860
E: lizziehood@aol.com
Hitchin Jane Frances Mainwaring, St Mark's Vicarage, St Mark's Close, Hitchin SG5 1UR
T: 01462 422862
E: jane@stmarks-hitchin.org.uk

Rickmansworth David Martin Hall, Christ Church Vicarage, Rickmansworth Road, Chorleywood, Rickmansworth WD3 5SG
T: 01923 282149
E: david.andmaryhall@tiscali.co.uk
St Albans Mark Andrew Slater, St Luke's Vicarage, 46 Cell Barnes Lane, St Albans AL1 5QJ *T:* 01727 865399
E: mark.slater@saint-lukes.co.uk

Watford David John Middlebrook, St Luke's Vicarage, Devereux Drive, Watford WD17 3DD *T:* 01923 231205
E: dmiddlebrook@btinternet.com
Wheathampstead Richard Mark Banham, The Rectory, Old Rectory Gardens, Wheathampstead, St Albans AL4 8AD
T: 01582 833144
E: richard@banham.org

DIOCESE OF ST EDMUNDSBURY AND IPSWICH

Founded in 1914. Suffolk, except for a small area in the north-east, in the diocese of Norwich; one parish in Essex.

Population 668,000   Area 1,430 sq m
Full-time Stipendiary Parochial Clergy 121   Benefices 125
Parishes 445   Churches 479
Overseas link dioceses: Hassalt (Belgium), Kagera (Tanzania)

BISHOP
The Rt Revd Martin Seeley, 4 Park Road, Ipswich IP1 3ST   *T:* 01473 252829
          E: bishops.office@cofesuffolk.org

BISHOP'S STAFF
Executive Assistant Mrs Susan Lowery, 4 Park Road, Ipswich IP1 3ST   *T:* 01473 252829
Bishop's Secretary Mrs Terry Atkins
Assistant Secretary Mrs Sally Fitch
          E: sally.fitch@cofesuffolk.org
Assistant Secretary Mrs Julia Venmore-Rowland
          E: julia.venmore-rowland@cofesuffolk.org

SUFFRAGAN BISHOP
DUNWICH The Rt Revd Mike Harrison, Robin Hall, Chapel Lane, Mendlesham, Stowmarket IP14 5SQ   *T:* 01473 252829
          E: bishop.mike@cofesuffolk.org

CATHEDRAL CHURCH OF ST JAMES AND ST EDMUND, BURY ST EDMUNDS
Dean
Vacancy
Canons Residentiary
Precentor The Revd Canon Philip Banks, 1 Abbey Precincts, Bury St Edmunds IP33 1RS
          T: 01284 748724
          E: precentor@stedscathedral.org
Sub-Dean and Canon Pastor The Revd Canon Matthew Vernon, 2 Abbey Precincts, Bury St Edmunds IP33 1RS   *T:* 01284 701472
          E: canon.pastor@stedscathedral.org
Other Staff
Head of Finance Mrs Elizabeth Gibson, Abbey House, Angel Hill, Bury St Edmunds IP33 1LS
          T: 01284 748727
          E: finance.manager@stedscathedral.org
Director of Music Mr James Thomas, Abbey House, Angel Hill, Bury St Edmunds IP33 1LS
          T: 01284 748379
          E: dom@stedscathedral.org
Assistant Director of Music Mr Dan Soper (*Same Address*)   *T:* 01284 748737
          E: adom@stedscathedral.org

PR Manager Mrs Sarah Friswell, Abbey House, Angel Hill, Bury St Edmunds IP33 1LS
          T: 01284 748726
          E: pr.manager@stedscathedral.org

ARCHDEACONS
IPSWICH Vacancy
SUDBURY The Ven David Jenkins, Sudbury Lodge, Stanningfield Road, Great Whelnetham, Bury St Edmunds IP30 0TL
          T: 01284 386942
          E: archdeacon.david@cofesuffolk.org
SUFFOLK The Ven Ian Morgan, The Archdeaconry, Church Road, Marlesford, Woodbridge IP13 0AT   *E:* archdeacon.ian@cofesuffolk.org

MEMBERS OF THE HOUSE OF CLERGY OF THE GENERAL SYNOD
Proctors for Clergy
The Revd Canon Jonathan Alderton-Ford
The Revd Andrew Dotchin
The Revd Christopher (Tiffer) Robinson

MEMBERS OF THE HOUSE OF LAITY OF THE GENERAL SYNOD
Canon Anthony Allwood
Mrs Karen Galloway
Mr David Lamming

DIOCESAN OFFICERS
Diocesan Secretary Anna Hughes, St Nicholas Centre, 4 Cutler Street, Ipswich IP1 1UQ
          T: 01473 298500
          01473 298501
          E: anna.hughes@cofesuffolk.org
Chancellor of Diocese Mr David Etherington, 20–32 Museum Street, Ipswich IP1 1HZ
Deputy Chancellor of Diocese His Honour Judge Anthony Leonard (*Same Address*)
Registrar of Diocese and Bishop's Legal Secretary Mr James Hall (*Same Address*)
          T: 01473 232300
          F: 01473 230524
          E: james-hall@birketts.co.uk

Deputy Registrar Mr Stuart Jones, Birketts LLP, Kingfisher House, 1 Gilders Way, Norwich NR3 1UB   *T:* 01603756501
      E: stuart.jones@dioceseofnorwich.org

DIOCESAN ORGANIZATIONS

Diocesan Office St Nicholas Centre, 4 Cutler Street, Ipswich IP1 1UQ   *T:* 01473 298500
      F: 01473 298501
      E: dbf@cofesuffolk.org

ADMINISTRATION

Diocesan Secretary Anna Hughes, St Nicholas Centre, 4 Cutler Street, Ipswich IP1 1UQ
      T: 01473 298500
      01473 298501
      E: anna.hughes@cofesuffolk.org
Director of Strategic Planning and Communications Mr Gavin Stone (*Same Address*)
      T: 01473 298522
      M: 07917 385843
      E: gavin.stone@cofesuffolk.org
Head of Stewardship and Generous Giving The Revd Canon Graham Hedger (*Same Address*)
Pastoral and DAC Secretary Mr James Halsall (*Same Address*)
Director of Finance Mr Gary Peverley (*Same Address*)   *T:* 01473 298575
      E: gary.peverley@cofesuffolk.org
Head of Property Dawn Gillett (*Same Address*)
      T: 01473 298507
      E: dawn.gillett@cofesuffolk.org
Designated Officer Diane Matthews (*Same Address*)   *T:* 01473 298504
      E: diane.matthews@cofesuffolk.org
Diocesan Synod (*Chairman, House of Clergy*) The Revd Canon Jonathan Alderton-Ford
(*Chairman, House of Laity*) Canon Michael Wilde
(*Secretary*) Anna Hughes, St Nicholas Centre, 4 Cutler Street, Ipswich IP1 1UQ
      T: 01473 298500
      01473 298501
      E: anna.hughes@cofesuffolk.org

CHURCH BUILDINGS

Advisory Committee for the Care of Churches (*Chairman*) The Rt Revd Graeme Paul Knowles, 102A Barons Road, Bury St Edmunds IP33 2LY   *T:* 01284 723823
(*Secretary*) Mr James Halsall, St Nicholas Centre, 4 Cutler Street, Ipswich IP1 1UQ

CLERGY RETIREMENT OFFICER

The Revd Ian Hooper, 26 Drake Close, Stowmarket IP14 1UP
      T: 01449 770179
      E: ianavrilhooper126@btinternet.com

COMMUNICATIONS

Director of Stretegic Planning and Communications Mr Gavin Stone, St Nicholas Centre, 4 Cutler Street, Ipswich IP1 1UQ   *T:* 01473 298522
      M: 07917 385843
      E: gavin.stone@cofesuffolk.org
Bishop's Press Officer John Howard (*Same Address*)   *T:* 07872 314653
      E: john.howard@cofesuffolk.org
Communications Manager Leonie Ryle (*Same Address*)   *T:* 01473 298546
      E: leonie.ryle@cofesuffolk.org

COUNSELLING

Adviser in Pastoral Care and Counselling Susannah Izzard, Corner House, Mill Lane, Barnby, Beccles NR34 7PX   *T:* 07702 571760
      E: susannah.izzard@cofesuffolk.org

DIOCESAN RECORD OFFICES

77 Raingate, St, Bury St Edmunds IP33 2AR
      T: 01284 352352 Ext 2352
Gatacre Rd, Ipswich, IP1 2LQ
      T: 01473 264541
The Central Library, Lowestoft, NR32 1DR
      T: 01502 405357

DIOCESAN WIDOWS OFFICER

Vacancy

MINISTRY

Diocesan Director of Mission and Ministry The Revd Dave Gardner, St Nicholas Centre, 4 Cutler Street, Ipswich IP1 1UQ
      T: 01473 298521
      E: dave.gardner@cofesuffolk.org
Diocesan Director of Ordinands and New Ministers The Revd Tim Jones, The Rectory, Ingham Road, West Stow, Bury St Edmunds IP28 6ET   *T:* 01284 729148
      E: tim.jones@cofesuffolk.org
Discipleship and Ministry Development Officer Miss Ruth Dennigan, St Nicholas Centre, 4 Cutler Street, Ipswich IP1 1UQ
      T: 01473 298503
      E: david.herrick@cofesuffolk.org
Vocations Adviser (Sudbury) Vacancy
Vocations Adviser (Suffolk) The Revd Betty Mockford, 10 Castle Brooks, Framlingham IP13 9SF   *T:* 01728 724193
Warden of Readers and Licensed Lay Ministers Officer The Rt Revd Mike Harrison, Robin Hall, Chapel Lane, Mendlesham, Stowmarket IP14 5SQ   *T:* 01473 252829
      E: bishop.mike@cofesuffolk.org

Diocesan Children's Officer and Cathedral Education Officer Mrs Helen Woodroffe, The Discovery Centre, St Edmundsbury Cathedral, Angel Hill, Bury St Edmunds IP33 1LS
T: 01284 748731
F: 01284 748731
E: helen@discoveryc.fsnet.co.uk

MISSION AND PUBLIC AFFAIRS

Agricultural Chaplain Sally Fogden, Meadow Farm, Sapiston, Bury St Edmunds IP31 1RX
T: 01359 268923
E: sallyfogden@tiscali.co.uk
Bishop's Ecumenical Adviser The Revd John Thackray, The Vicarage, 89 Blackhorse Lane, Ipswich IP1 2EF
T: 07780 613754
E: thereverendfather@hotmail.com
Bishop's Inter Faith Adviser The Revd Canon Charles Jenkin, The Vicarage, 18 Kingsfield Avenue, Ipswich IP1 3TA
T: 01473 289001
E: c.jenkin@tiscali.co.uk
Chaplain to the Deaf Community Vacancy

SCHOOLS

Diocesan Director of Education Mrs Jane Sheat, St Nicholas Centre, 4 Cutler Street, Ipswich IP1 1UQ
T: 01473 298570
E: jane.sheat@cofesuffolk.org
Deputy Diocesan Director of Education Vacancy
School Effectiveness Officer Mr Philip Knowles
T: 01473 298545
E: philip.knowles@cofesuffolk.org
Diocesan Schools Adviser Mrs Helen Matter, St Nicholas Centre, 4 Cutler Street, Ipswich IP1 1UQ
E: helen.matter@cofesuffolk.org

SPIRITUALITY

Diocesan Spiritual Director for Cursillo The Revd Chris Ramsey
E: revchrisramsey@googlemail.com
Lay Director for Cursillo Mrs Gwen Runnacles, The Bungalow, Church Hill, Burstall, Ipswich IP8 3DU
T: 01473 652494
E: gwen.runnacles@virgin.net

RURAL DEANS
ARCHDEACONRY OF IPSWICH

Bosmere Diane Ruth Williams, 10 Meadow View, Needham Market, Ipswich IP6 8RH
T: 01449 720316
E: diane.rev@btinternet.com
Colneys Andrew Steward Dotchin, The Rectory, 176 Fircroft Road, Ipswich IP1 6PS
T: 01473 741389
E: revdotchin@gmail.com
Hadleigh David St Clair Tudor, St Nicholas House, 210 Long Road, Canvey Island SS8 0JR
T: 01268 682586
E: dstudor@tiscali.co.uk

Ipswich Nicholas Steven Atkins, St Matthew's Rectory, 3 Portman Road, Ipswich IP1 2ES
T: 01473 251630
E: rector@smast.org.uk
Samford Liesbeth Oosterhof, The Rectory, Rectory Field, Chelmondiston, Ipswich IP9 1HY
T: 01473 781902
E: l.oosterhof@btinternet.com
Stowmarket Vacancy
Woodbridge Hilary Clare Sanders, The Rectory, St Michael's Close, Framlingham, Woodbridge IP13 9BJ
T: 01728 768875
E: revclaresanders@tiscali.co.uk

ARCHDEACONRY OF SUDBURY

Clare Stuart Mitchell, The Vicarage, 14 High Street, Clare, Sudbury CO10 8NY
T: 01787 278482
E: thevicarage8ny@btinternet.com
Ixworth David Harry Messer, The Rectory, 1 Old Rectory Gardens, Stanton, Bury St Edmunds IP31 2JH
E: davidharrymesser93@gmail.com
Lavenham Stephen Geoffrey Franklyn Earl, The Rectory, Church Street, Lavenham, Sudbury CO10 9SA
T: 01787 247244
E: earls2222@btinternet.com
Mildenhall John Christopher Hardy, The Rectory, 21 Hamilton Road, Newmarket CB8 0NY
T: 01638 660729
E: rector@stmarysandstagnesnewmarket.org.uk
Sudbury Simon David Gill, 5 Clermont Avenue, Sudbury CO10 1ZJ
T: 01787 375334
E: sallie.simon@tinyworld.co.uk
Thingoe Mark Newby Haworth, The Rectory, 59 Bennett Avenue, Bury St Edmunds IP33 3JJ
T: 01284 755374
E: father.mark@virgin.net

ARCHDEACONRY OF SUFFOLK

Hartismere Susan Ann Loxton, The Rectory, Doctors Lane, Stradbroke, Eye IP21 5HU
T: 01379 388493
E: revloxton@gmail.com
Hoxne Susan Ann Loxton, The Rectory, Doctors Lane, Stradbroke, Eye IP21 5HU
T: 01379 388493
E: revloxton@gmail.com
Loes Mark Sanders, The Rectory, Woodbridge Road, Grundisburgh, Woodbridge IP13 6UF
T: 01473 735182
E: mark@stedmundsbury.anglican.org
Saxmundham Christine Howick Redgrave, Aisthorpe, The Street, Darsham, Saxmundham IP17 3QA
T: 01728 667095
E: redgrave460@btinternet.com
Waveney and Blyth Simon John Pitcher, The Vicarage, Gardner Road, Southwold IP18 6HJ
T: 01502 722192
E: revsimon@talktalk.net

DIOCESE OF SALISBURY

Founded in 1075, formerly Sherborne (🕮 705) and Ramsbury
(🕮 909). Wiltshire, except for the norther quarter, in the
diocese of Bristol; Dorset, except for an area in the east, in the
diocese of Winchester; a small area of Hampshire,
a parish in Devon.

Population 948,000   Area 2,050 sq m
Full-time Stipendiary Parochial Clergy 193   Benefices 138
Parishes 442   Churches 570
www.salisbury.anglican.org
Overseas link dioceses: Episcopal Church of the Sudan, Evreux (France)

BISHOP (78th)
The Rt Revd Nicholas Holtam, South Canonry,
71 The Close, Salisbury SP1 2ER
T: 01722334031
F: 01722 413112
E: bishop.salisbury@salisbury.anglican.org

SUFFRAGAN BISHOPS
RAMSBURY The Rt Revd Edward Condry,
Diocesan Office, Church House, Crane Street,
Salisbury SP1 2QB   *T:* 01722 438662
F: 01722 411990
E: e.ramsbury@salisbury.anglican.org
SHERBORNE The Rt Revd Karen Gorham,
Sherborne Office, St Nicholas Church Centre,
30 Wareham Road, Corfe Mullen, Dorset
BH21 3LE   *T:* 01202 659427
E: bishop.sherborne@salisbury.anglican.org

CATHEDRAL CHURCH OF THE BLESSED VIRGIN MARY
Dean
Vacancy
Canons Residentiary
Acting Dean and Chancellor The Revd Canon
Edward Probert, Wyndham House, 65 The
Close, Salisbury SP1 2EN   *T:* 01722 555189
F: 01722 555109
E: chancellor@salcath.co.uk
Precentor The Revd Canon Tom Clammer,
Wyndham House, 65 The Close, Salisbury SP1
2EN   *T:* 01722 555125
F: 01722 555117
E: precentor@salcath.co.uk
Treasurer The Revd Canon Robert Titley,
Wyndham House, 65 The Close, Salisbury SP1
2EN   *T:* 01722 555186
F: 01722 555109
E: treasurer@salcath.co.uk
Other Staff
Vicar of the Close The Revd Canon Ian
Woodward, 68a The Close, Salisbury SP1 2ES
T: 01722 555192
E: voc@salcath.co.uk

Chapter Clerk Mrs Jacqueline Molnar, Chapter
Office, 6 The Close, Salisbury SP1 2EG
T: 01722 555105
F: 01722 555109
E: chapterclerk@salcath.co.uk
Visitors Department Jane Morgan, Wyndham
House, 65 The Close, Salisbury SP1 2EN
T: 01722 555120
F: 01722 555116
E: j.morgan@salcath.co.uk
Education Centre Mrs Susan Hayter, The
Gatehouse, The Close, Salisbury SP1 2EL
T: 01722 555180
E: education@salcath.co.uk
Director of Music Mr David Halls, Department
of Liturgy and Music, Wyndham House, 65
The Close, Salisbury SP1 2EN
T: 01722 555127
E: d.halls@salcath.co.uk

ARCHDEACONS
SHERBORNE The Ven Paul Taylor, Aldhelm
House, West Stafford, Dorchester DT2 8AB
T: 01202 659427
E: adsherborne@salisbury.anglican.org
DORSET The Ven Antony MacRow-Wood, 28
Merriefield Drive, Broadstone BH18 8BP
T: 01202 659427
E: addorset@salisbury.anglican.org
SARUM The Ven Alan Jeans, Herbert House, 118
Lower Road, Lower Bemerton SP2 9NW
T: 01722 438662
E: adsarum@salisbury.anglican.org
WILTS The Ven Susan Groom, Southbroom
House, London Road, Devizes SN10 1LT
T: 01722 438662
E: adwilts@salisbury.anglican.org

MEMBERS OF THE HOUSE OF CLERGY OF THE GENERAL SYNOD
Proctors for Clergy
The Revd Peter Breckwoldt
The Revd Canon Jane Charman
The Ven Alan Jeans
The Revd Christopher Tebbutt
The Revd Canon Thomas Woodhouse

MEMBERS OF THE HOUSE OF LAITY OF THE GENERAL SYNOD
Mr Paul Boyd-Lee
Miss Fenella Cannings-Jurd
Mrs Gillian de Berry
Mr Keith Leslie
Mrs Debrah McIsaac
Mr Richard Mervyn Jones

DIOCESAN OFFICERS
Diocesan Secretary Mrs Lucinda Herklots, Church House, Crane Street, Salisbury SP1 2QB   *T:* 01722 411922
F: 01722 411990
Chancellor of Diocese Mrs Ruth Arlow, c/o Diocesan Registry, Batt Broadbent, 42-44 Castle Street, Salisbury SP1 3TX
T: 01722 411141
E: registry@salisbury.anglican.org
Registrar of Diocese and Bishop's Legal Secretary Mrs Sue de Candole, Batt Broadbent, Minster Chambers, 42–44 Castle Street, Salisbury SP1 3TX *(Same Tel)*   *F:* 01722 411566
E: registry@battbroadbent.co.uk

DIOCESAN ORGANIZATIONS
Diocesan Office Church House, Crane Street, Salisbury SP1 2QB   *T:* 01722 411922
F: 01722 411990
E: enquiries@salisbury.anglican.org
W: www.salisbury.anglican.org

ADMINISTRATION
Diocesan Secretary Mrs Lucinda Herklots, Church House, Crane Street, Salisbury SP1 2QB   *T:* 01722 411922
F: 01722 411990
Deputy Diocesan Secretary Mr Stephen Dawson *(Same Address)*
Diocesan Synod (Chairman, House of Clergy) The Revd Canon Thomas Woodhouse, 17a Edward Road, Dorchester DT1 2HL   *T:* 01305 267944
(Chairman, House of Laity) Mrs Gillian Clarke, 7 Denewood Road, West Moors, Ferndown BH22 0LX   *T:* 01202 894913
E: gillianmaryclarke@hotmail.com
(Secretary) Mrs Lucinda Herklots, Church House, Crane Street, Salisbury SP1 2QB
T: 01722 411922
F: 01722 411990
Board of Finance (Chairman) Mr Nigel Salisbury, 48 The Close, Salisbury SP1 2EL
T: 01722 416186
(Secretary) Mrs Lucinda Herklots, Church House, Crane Street, Salisbury SP1 2QB
T: 01722 411922
F: 01722 411990
(Diocesan Accountant) Miss Liz Ashmead *(Same Address)*   *T:* 01722 411955

(Diocesan Surveyor) Mr Shawn Donneky *(Same Address)*   *T:* 01722 411933
Pastoral Committee (Secretary) Mrs Siobhan Forster *(Same Address)*
(Designated Officer) Mrs Sue de Candole, Batt Broadbent, Minster Chambers, 42–44 Castle Street, Salisbury SP1 3TX   *T:* 01722 411141
F: 01722 411566
E: registry@battbroadbent.co.uk

ADVISORY COMMITTEE FOR THE CARE OF CHURCHES
(Chairman) Vacancy
(Secretary) Mrs Sue Cannings, Church House, Crane Street, Salisbury SP1 2QB
T: 01722 438654
Re-Use of Closed Churches Working Group and Furnishings Officer Mr Simon Ferris *(Same Address)*   *T:* 01722 411933
Ringers' Association Mr Anthony Lovell-Wood, 11 Brook Close, Tisbury, Salisbury SP3 6PW
T: 01747 871121

DIOCESAN RECORD OFFICES
Diocesan Record Office and Wiltshire Parochial Records Diocesan Record Office and Wiltshire Parochial Records, Wiltshire and Swindon History Centre, Cocklebury Road, Chippenham SN15 3QN
T: 01249 705500 and ask for the Duty Archivist
Dorset History Centre Dorset History Centre, Bridport Road, Dorchester DT1 1RP
(County Archivist) Mr Hugh Jacques *(Same Address)*   *T:* 01305 250550
Hampshire Record Office Hampshire Record Office, Sussex Street, Winchester SO23 8TH
T: 01962 846154

EDUCATION
Director of Education Mrs Joy Tubbs, Diocesan Education Centre, Wilton SP2 0AG
T: 01722 428420
F: 01722 328010
Board of Education (Chairman) The Ven Antony MacRow-Wood, 28 Merriefield Drive, Broadstone BH18 8BP   *T:* 01202 659427
F: 01202 691418
E: addorset@salisbury.anglican.org
(Deputy Director of Education) Mr Giles Pugh, Diocesan Education Centre, The Avenue, Wilton SP2 0AG
(Finance) Mr Giles Pugh *(As above)*
(Buildings Officer) Mr Martyn Kemp *(Same Address)*
(Youth and Children's Officers) Youth and Children's Ministry Team, Diocesan Education Centre, The Avenue, Wilton SP2 0AG
T: 01722 428427

MINISTRY

Director of Learning for Discipleship and Ministry The Revd Canon Jane Charman, Church House, Crane Street, Salisbury SP1 2QB
T: 01722 411944
E: ldmt@salisbury.anglican.org
Vocations Co-ordinator The Revd Benny Hazlehurst (*Same Address*)
Co-ordinator for Initial Ministerial Education/ Director of Ordinands The Revd Charlie Allen (*Same Address*)
Discipleship Co-ordinator Sister Debbie Orris (*Same Address*)   *T:* 01722 411944
E: debbie.orris@salisbury.anglican.org
Co-ordinator for Ministry for Mission The Ven Alan Jeans, Herbert House, 118 Lower Road, Lower Bemerton SP2 9NW   *T:* 01722 438662
F: 01722 411990
E: adsarum@salisbury.anglican.org
Warden of Licensed Lay Ministers The Rt Revd Karen Gorham, Sherborne Office, St Nicholas Church Centre, 30 Wareham Road, Corfe Mullen, Dorset BH21 3LE   *T:* 01202 659427
E: bishop.sherborne@salisbury.anglican.org
Lay Pastoral Assistant Officer (Sarum) Vacancy
Lay Pastoral Assistant Officer (Wilts) Mrs Liz Giles   *T:* 01793 852643
Lay Pastoral Assistant Officer (Dorset) Mrs Penny Haigh   *T:* 01929 471768
Lay Pastoral Assistant Officer (Sherborne) Vacancy
Clergy Retirement Officer (Wilts) The Revd Ann Philp   *T:* 01722 555178
Clergy Retirement Officer (Dorset) Canon John Wood, 16 Dunnabridge Street, Dorchester, Dorset DT1 3TQ   *T:* 01305 268749
E: john.s.wood@btinternet.com

MISSION COUNCIL

Chairman The Ven Alan Jeans, Herbert House, 118 Lower Road, Lower Bemerton SP2 9NW
T: 01722 438662
F: 01722 411990
E: adsarum@salisbury.anglican.org
Secretary Miss Fiona Torrance, Church House, Crane Street, Salisbury SP1 2QB
T: 01722 411922

MISSIONARY AND ECUMENICAL

Mission and Stewardship Adviser (Dorset) Mr Ian Bromilow, The Old School, Hilton, Blandford Forum DT11 0DB   *T:* 01258 880044
Mission and Stewardship Adviser (Wiltshire) Mr John Kilbee, Downs View, Goatacre, Calne SN11 9HY   *T:* 01249760776
County Ecumenical Officer (Wiltshire) Vacancy
County Ecumenical Officer (Dorset) Mrs Katja Babei   *T:* 07500 984705
European Affairs Officer The Revd Canon Richard Franklin, Holy Trinity Vicarage, 7 Glebe Close, Weymouth DT44 9RL
T: 01305 760354

Chaplain to Travelling People The Revd Jonathan Herbert, The Friary, Hilfield, Dorchester DT2 7BE   *T:* 01300 341345
International Development and World Mission The Revd Canon Ian Woodward, 68a The Close, Salisbury SP1 2ES   *T:* 01722 555192
E: voc@salcath.co.uk

PRESS AND PUBLICATIONS

Director of Communications Mr Gerry Lynch, Church House, Crane Street, Salisbury SP1 2QB   *T:* 01722 438650
M: 07779 780739
E: comms@salisbury.anglican.org
Editor of E-Directory Mrs Miriam Longfoot (*Same Address*)   *T:* 01722 411922

SOCIAL JUSTICE

Social Justice Programme Manager Mr Colin Brady, 23 Bagber Farm Cottages, Milton Road, Milborne St Andrew, Blandford Forum DT11 0LB   *T:* 01258 839140
Officer for Rural Areas (Wiltshire) Vacancy
Officer for Rural Areas (Dorset) The Revd Canon Dr Jean Coates, Three Gables, Colesbrook, Gillingham, Dorset SP8 4HH   *T:* 01747 229168
Diocesan Environment Officer Mr David Morgan, 12 St John's Hill, Wimborne BH21 1DD   *T:* 01202 883504

RURAL DEANS
ARCHDEACONRY OF DORSET

Milton and Blandford Jonathan Paul Triffitt, The Vicarage, 31 Fruitfields Close, Devizes SN10 5JY   *T:* 01380 721441
E: jonathantriffitt@icloud.com
Poole Lucinda Jane Holt, The Rectory, 10 Poplar Close, Poole BH15 1LP
T: 01202 672694
E: revlucy@tiscali.co.uk
Purbeck Simon Francis Everett, The Rectory, 22 Worgret Road, Wareham BH20 4PN
T: 01747 811291
E: reveverett@btinternet.com
Wimborne Andrew John William Rowland, The Vicarage, 57 Glenwood Road, West Moors, Ferndown BH22 0EN   *T:* 01202 893197
E: ajwrowland@tiscali.co.uk

ARCHDEACONRY OF SARUM

Alderbury David Gary Bacon, The Rectory, Bramshaw, Lyndhurst SO43 7JF
T: 01794 390256
E: davidbramrec@aol.com
Chalke Mark Robert Wood, The Rectory, 27A West Street, Wilton, Salisbury SP2 0DL
T: 07770-305990
E: rectorwilton@gmail.com

Salisbury Paul Frank David Taylor, The Vicarage, 52 Park Lane, Salisbury SP1 3NP
T: 01722 333762
E: plaj.taylor52@btopenworld.com
Stonehenge Eleanor Jane Rance, The Rectory, Chapel Lane, Shrewton, Salisbury SP3 4BX
T: 01980 620580
E: reveleanorrance@gmail.com

ARCHDEACONRY OF SHERBORNE
Blackmore Vale Simon Paul Chambers, St James's Vicarage, 34 Tanyards Lane, Shaftesbury SP7 8HW   *T:* 01747 852193
E: simon@simonchambers.com
Dorchester Jonathan Trevor Lloyd Still, The Vicarage, 4 Back Lane, Cerne Abbas, Dorchester DT2 7JW   *T:* 01300 341251
E: cernevicar@gmail.com
Lyme Bay David Frederick Beresford Baldwin, The Rectory, 3 Clay Lane, Beaminster DT8 3BU   *T:* 01308 862150
E: revdavidbaldwin@gmail.com
Sherborne Vivian John Enever, The Rectory, Trent, Sherborne DT9 4SL   *T:* 01935 851118
E: trentrectory@gmail.com
Weymouth and Portland Timothy Ralph West, The Rectory, Sutton Road, Preston, Weymouth DT3 6BX   *T:* 01305 833142
E: team.rector@hotmail.co.uk

ARCHDEACONRY OF WILTS
Bradford Andrew Eric Evans, The Rectory, Ham Green, Holt, Trowbridge BA14 7PZ
T: 01225 782289
E: goodevansitsandrew@tiscali.co.uk
Calne Jane Darwent Curtis, St Bartholomew's Vicarage, Glebe Road, Royal Wootton Bassett, Swindon SN4 7DU
Devizes Paul Richardson, The Rectory, Brandon House, Potterne Road, Devizes SN10 5DD   *T:* 01380 829616
E: paul.richardson8@btinternet.com
Heytesbury Pauline Ann Reid, The Rectory, 6 Homefields, Longbridge Deverill, Warminster BA12 7DQ   *T:* 01638 508990
E: revpauline@btinternet.com
Marlborough Andrew Geoffrey Studdert-Kennedy, The Rectory, 1 Rawlingswell Lane, Marlborough SN8 1AU   *T:* 01672 514357
E: andrewsk1959@btinternet.com
Pewsey Gerald Edward Richard Osborne, Lawn Farm, Milton Lilbourne, Pewsey SN9 5LQ
T: 01672 563459
E: gerald.osborne@lawnfarm.co.uk

DIOCESE OF SHEFFIELD

Founded in 1914. Sheffield; Rotherham; Doncaster, except for a few parishes in the south-east, in the diocese of Southwell and Nottingham; an area of North Lincolnshire; an area of south-eastern Barnsley; a small area of the East Riding of Yorkshire.

Population 1,287,000   Area 610 sq m
Full-time Stipendiary Parochial Clergy 122   Benefices 149
Parishes 175   Churches 213
www.sheffield.anglican.org
Overseas link dioceses: Argentina, Hattingen Witten (Germany)

BISHOP

The Rt Revd Dr Pete Wilcox, Bishopscroft, Snaithing Lane, Sheffield S10 3LG
T: 0114 230 2170
E: bishop@sheffield.anglican.org

BISHOP'S STAFF

Domestic Chaplain The Revd Canon Geoffrey Harbord, Bishopscroft, Snaithing Lane, Sheffield S10 3LG
T: 0114 230 2170
F: 0114 263 0110
E: geoffrey.harbord@sheffield.anglican.org

SUFFRAGAN BISHOP

DONCASTER The Rt Revd Peter Burrows, Doncaster House, Church Lane, Fishlake, Doncaster DN7 5JW   *T:* 01302 846610
E: bishoppeter@bishopofdoncaster.org.uk

ASSISTANT BISHOPS

The Rt Revd Dr Tim Ellis, 8 Mason Grove, Sheffield S13 8LL   *T:* 07850 783756
E: fatherowl@gmail.com
The Rt Revd Glyn Webster, Holy Trinity Rectory, Micklegate, York YO1 6LE
T: 01904 628155
E: office@seeofbeverley.org
The Rt Revd Roderick Thomas, 28 St John's Meadow, Blindley Heath, Lingfield RH7 6JU
T: 01342 834140
E: admin@bishopofmaidstone.org

CATHEDRAL CHURCH OF ST PETER AND ST PAUL

Dean The Very Revd Peter Bradley, The Cathedral, Church Street, Sheffield S1 1HA
T: 0114 263 6061
E: dean@sheffield-cathedral.org.uk
Canons Residentiary
Vice Dean and Precentor The Revd Canon Christopher Burke   *T:* 0114 263 6066
E: christopher.burke@
sheffield-cathedral.org.uk
Canon Missioner The Revd Canon Keith Farrow   *T:* 0114 263 6065
E: keith.farrow@sheffield-cathedral.org.uk

Other Staff
Director of Music Thomas Corns, The Cathedral, Church Street, Sheffield S1 1HA
T: 0114 263 6069
E: musicians@sheffield-cathedral.org.uk
Assistant Director of Music Mr Joshua Hales *(Same email)*   *T:* 0114 263 6070
Cathedral Archer Project Manager Tim Renshaw, Church Street, Sheffield S1 1HA
T: 0114 321 2314
E: tim.renshaw@sheffield-cathedral.org.uk
Assistant Curate of Pioneer Ministry The Revd Dr Beth Keith   *T:* 0114 263 6062
E: beth.keith@sheffield-cathedral.org.uk
Director of Operations Mrs Fran Joel
T: 0114 263 6068
E: fran.joel@sheffield-cathedral.org.uk

ARCHDEACONS

SHEFFIELD AND ROTHERHAM The Ven Malcolm Chamberlain, 95–99 Effingham Street, Rotherham S65 1BL   *T:* 01709 309110
E: malcolm.chamberlain@
sheffield.anglican.org
DONCASTER The Ven Stephen Wilcockson, 95–99 Effingham Street, Rotherham S65 1BL
T: 01709 309110
E: steve.wilcockson@sheffield.anglican.org

MEMBERS OF THE HOUSE OF CLERGY OF THE GENERAL SYNOD

Proctors for Clergy
The Ven Malcolm Chamberlain
The Revd Canon Geoffrey Harbord
The Revd Eleanor Robertshaw

MEMBERS OF THE HOUSE OF LAITY OF THE GENERAL SYNOD

Canon Elizabeth Paver
Miss Jane Patterson
Canon Mark Russell

DIOCESAN OFFICERS

Diocesan Secretary Mrs Heidi Adcock, Church House, 95-99 Effingham Street, Rotherham S65 1BL   *T:* 01709 309117
E: heidi.adcock@sheffield.anglican.org

Chancellor of Diocese Her Honour Judge Sarah Singleton, Wake Smith Solicitors Ltd, No 1 Velocity, 2 Tenter Street, Sheffield S1 4BY
T: 0114 266 6660
Registrar of Diocese and Bishop's Legal Secretary Mr Andrew Vidler, Wake Smith Solicitors Ltd, No 1 Velocity, 2 Tenter Street, Sheffield SS1 4BY (*Same Tel*)
E: andrew.vidler@wake-smith.com

DIOCESAN ORGANIZATIONS

Diocesan Office Church House, 95–99 Effingham Street, Rotherham S65 1BL
T: 01709 309100
F: 01709 512550
E: reception@sheffield.anglican.org
W: www.sheffield.anglican.org

ADMINISTRATION
Diocesan Secretary Mrs Heidi Adcock, Church House, 95–99 Effingham Street, Rotherham S65 1BL
T: 01709 309117
E: heidi.adcock@sheffield.anglican.org
Director of Finance Mr Chun Tsang (*Same Address*)
T: 01709 309142
E: chun.tsang@sheffield.anglican.org
Diocesan Surveyor Fraser Andrews, Andrews Allen Associates, Gisborne House, 3 Gisborne Road, Ecclesall, Sheffield S11 7HA
T: 0114 2678248; 07803 905228
E: fraser.andrews@sheffield.anglican.org
Board of Finance (*Chair*) Mr Ian Walker, Church House, 95–99 Effingham Street, Rotherham S65 1BL
T: 01709 309 100
E: ian.walker@sheffield.anglican.org
Diocesan Mission and Pastoral Committee (*Chair*) The Rt Revd Peter Burrows, Doncaster House, Church Lane, Fishlake, Doncaster DN7 5JW
T: 01302 846610
E: bishoppeter@bishopofdoncaster.org.uk
(*Secretary*) Mrs Heidi Adcock, Church House, 95-99 Effingham Street, Rotherham S65 1BL
T: 01709 309117
E: heidi.adcock@sheffield.anglican.org
Redundant Churches Uses Committee (*Chair*) Vacancy
(*Secretary*) Vacancy (*As above*)
Board of Patronages (*Chair*) The Rt Revd Dr Pete Wilcox
(*Secretary*) Mrs Heidi Adcock, Church House, 95-99 Effingham Street, Rotherham S65 1BL
T: 01709 309117
E: heidi.adcock@sheffield.anglican.org
(*DAC Chair*) The Revd Canon Peter Ingram, The Vicarage, 80 Millhouses Lane, Sheffield S7 2HB
T: 0114 236 2838
(*DAC Secretary*) Dr Julie Banham, Diocesan Church House, 95–99 Effingham Street, Rotherham S65 1BL
T: 01709 309121
E: julie.banham@sheffield.anglican.org

(*Designated Officer*) The Revd Canon Geoffrey Harbord, Bishopscroft, Snaithing Lane, Sheffield S10 3LG
T: 0114 230 2170
F: 0114 263 0110
E: geoffrey.harbord@ sheffield.anglican.org
(*Communications Manager*) Miss LJ Buxton, Church House, 95–99 Effingham Street, Rotherham S65 1BL
DIOCESAN SYNOD (*Chair, House of Clergy*) The Revd Canon Ian Smith, Warmsworth Rectory, 187 Warmsworth Road, Doncaster DN4 0TW
T: 01302 853324
E: ian.smith@sheffield.anglican.org
(*Chair, House of Laity*) Dr Jackie Butcher
(*Secretary*) Mrs Heidi Adcock, Church House, 95–99 Effingham Street, Rotherham S65 1BL
T: 01709 309117
E: heidi.adcock@sheffield.anglican.org

CHURCH BUILDINGS
Advisory Committee for the Care of Churches (*Chair*) The Revd Canon Peter Ingram, The Vicarage, 80 Millhouses Lane, Sheffield S7 2HB
T: 0114 236 2838
(*Secretary*) Dr Julie Banham, Diocesan Church House, 95–99 Effingham Street, Rotherham S65 1BL
T: 01709 309121
E: julie.banham@sheffield.anglican.org

CHURCH TOURISM
Mrs Heidi Adcock, Church House, 95–99 Effingham Street, Rotherham S65 1BL
T: 01709 309117
E: heidi.adcock@sheffield.anglican.org

DIOCESAN RECORD OFFICES
Sheffield City Archives, 52 Shoreham St, Sheffield S1 4SP
T: 0114 273 4756
Doncaster Archives, King Edward Road, Balby, Doncaster DN4 0NA
T: 01302 859811

DIOCESAN SAFEGUARDING ADVISER
Linda Langthorne, Church House, 95–99 Effingham Street, Rotherham S65 1BL

EDUCATION
Diocesan Board of Education (*Chair*) The Rt Revd Peter Burrows, Doncaster House, Church Lane, Fishlake, Doncaster DN7 5JW
T: 01302 846610
E: bishoppeter@bishopofdoncaster.org.uk
(*Secretary*) Mr Huw Thomas, Church House, 95–99 Effingham Street, Rotherham S65 1BL
T: 01709 309123
E: huw.thomas@sheffield.anglican.org
(*Director of Education*) Mr Huw Thomas (*As above*)

FAITH AND JUSTICE
Chair The Ven Malcolm Chamberlain, Church House, 95–99 Effingham Street, Rotherham S65 1BL
T: 01709 309110
F: 01709 309107
E: malcolm.chamberlain@
sheffield.anglican.org
Director of Parish Support The Revd Canon Mark Cockayne (*Same Address*)
T: 01709 309132
E: mark.cockayne@sheffield.anglican.org
Bishop's Adviser on Black Concerns The Revd Anesia Cook, St Peter's Vicarage, 17 Ashland Road, Sheffield S7 1RH *T:* 0114 2509716
Bishop's Rural Adviser The Revd Keith Hale, Tankersley Rectory, 9 Chapel Road, Pilley, Barnsley S75 3AR *T:* 01226 744140

MINISTRY AND MISSION
Director of Formation for Ministry Dr Christine Gore, Church House, 95–99 Effingham Street, Rotherham S65 1BL *T:* 01709 309144
E: christine.gore@sheffield.anglican.org
Director of Parish Support The Revd Canon Mark Cockayne (*Same Address*)
T: 01709 309132
E: mark.cockayne@sheffield.anglican.org
Mission Development Adviser (Doncaster) The Revd Canon Mark Wigglesworth (*Same Address*) *T:* 01709 309130
E: mark.wigglesworth@sheffield.anglican.org
Mission Development Adviser (Sheffield and Rotherham) The Revd John Hibberd (*Same Address*) *T:* 01709 309134
E: john.hibberd@
sheffield.anglican.org
Children and Young People's Adviser Mr Mike North (*Same Address*) *T:* 01709 309146
E: mike.north@sheffield.anglican.org
Mission Partnership Development Worker Project Manager Mr Graham Millar (*Same Address*)
T: 01709 309143
E: graham.millar@sheffield.anglican.org
Centenary Project Leader Mrs Helen Cockayne (*Same Address*) *T:* 01709 309145
E: helen.cockayne@
sheffield.anglican.org
Director of Ordinands The Revd Stephen Hunter, Overhill, Townhead Road, Dore, Sheffield S17 3GE *T:* 0114 236 9978
Director of IME4–7 The Revd Tim Fletcher, The Vicarage, 214 Oldfield Road, Stannington, Sheffield S6 6DY *T:* 0114 2349247
Assistant POT Officers The Revd Gary Schofield, The Vicarage, Manor Road, Wales, Sheffield S26 5PD *T:* 01909 771 111
The Revd Jan Foden, The Vicarage, Stainforth Road, Barnby Dun, Doncaster DN3 1AA (NSM) *T:* 01302 882 835

Discipleship Development Officer The Revd Alan Isaacson, The Rectory, High Bradfield, Sheffield S6 6LG *T:* 0114 285 1225
Bishop's Adviser on Women in Ministry The Revd Abi Thompson, The Vicarage, 10 Clifton Crescent North, Rotherham S65 2AS
T: 01709 363 082
Bishop's Advisers on Spirituality The Revd Neil Bowler
The Revd Angie Lauener, 82 Pingle Road, Sheffield S7 2LL *T:* 0114 236 2188
Bishop's Adviser on Self Supporting Ministry Vacancy
Bishop's Adviser on Church Army Ministry The Revd Jane Truman, Wilson Carlile College of Evangelism, 50 Cavendish Street, Sheffield S3 7RZ *T:* 0114 209 6201
Warden of Readers Miss Imogen Clout, Ivy Bank, 327 Fulwood Road, Sheffield S10 3BJ
T: 0114 2686645
Readers' Board (Secretary) Miss Joan Robinson, 4 Kelvin Grove, Wombwell, Barnsley S73 0DL
Ecumenical Officer Vacancy

PRESS AND PUBLICATIONS
Communications Manager Miss LJ Buxton, Church House, 95–99 Effingham Street, Rotherham S65 1BL

AREA DEANS
ARCHDEACONRY OF DONCASTER
Adwick-le-Street Barbara Amanda Juliet Barraclough, Woodkirk Vicarage, 1168 Dewsbury Road, Dewsbury WF12 7JL
T: 01924 472375
E: amanda.barraclough1@btinternet.com
Doncaster Janice Margaret Foden, The Rectory, Church Street, Armthorpe, Doncaster DN3 3AD *T:* 07803 925083
E: janfoden@hotmail.com
Doncaster, West Neil Martyn Redeyoff, The Rectory, Rectory Lane, Finningley, Doncaster DN9 3DA *T:* 01302 770240
E: neilredeyoff1@btinternet.com
Doncaster, West Ian Smith, Warmsworth Rectory, 187 Warmsworth Road, Doncaster DN4 0TW *T:* 01302 853324
E: ian.smith@sheffield.anglican.org
Snaith and Hatfield Elizabeth Anne Turner-loisel, The Vicarage, 2 Vicarage Close, Hatfield, Doncaster DN7 6HN *T:* 01302 459110
E: revd.liz@gmail.com
Tankersley Keith John Edward Hale, The Rectory, 9 Chapel Road, Tankersley, Barnsley S75 3AR *T:* 01226 744140
E: revkeith.hale@virgin.net
Wath Andrew Robert Brewerton, The Vicarage, Highthorn Road, Kilnhurst, Mexborough S64 5TX *T:* 01709 589674
E: andy@brewerton.org

ARCHDEACONRY OF SHEFFIELD AND ROTHERHAM
Attercliffe Vacancy
Ecclesall Toby Kenton Hole, St Chad's Vicarage, 9 Linden Avenue, Sheffield S8 0GA
T: 0114 274 9302
E: toby.hole@gmail.com
Ecclesfield Alan Timothy Isaacson, The Rectory, High Bradfield, Bradfield, Sheffield S6 6LG
T: 0114 285 1225
E: alan.isaacson@sheffield.anglican.org

Hallam Vacancy
Laughton Frances Mary Eccleston, The Vicarage, 1 Barnfield Road, Sheffield S10 5TD
T: 0114 230 2531
E: frances.eccleston@sheffield.anglican.org
Rotherham Peter John Hughes, The Rectory, 5 Church Lane, Wickersley, Rotherham S66 1ES
T: 01709 543111
E: peter.j.hughes59@btinternet.com

DIOCESE OF SODOR AND MAN

Founded in 447. The Isle of Man.

Population 88,000   Area 220 sq m
Full-time Stipendiary Parochial Clergy 15   Benefices 14
Parishes 15   Churches 40
Overseas link dioceses: Cashel, Ferns and Ossory (Ireland)

BISHOP
The Rt Revd Peter Eagles, Thie yn Aspick, 4 The Falls, Douglas, Isle of Man IM4 4PZ
T: 01624 622108
E: bishop@sodorandman.im

BISHOP'S STAFF
Bishop's Chaplain (until 31/12/17) The Revd Canon Margaret Burrow, Thie yn Aspick, 4 The Falls, Douglas, Isle of Man IM4 4PZ
E: chaplain@sodorandman.im
Bishop's Secretary Mrs Lorna Cook
E: secretary@sodorandman.im

CATHEDRAL CHURCH OF ST GERMAN, PEEL
Dean The Very Revd Nigel Godfrey, The Deanery, Albany Road, Peel, Isle of Man IM5 1JS
T: 01624 844830
E: dean@sodorandman.im
Canons The Revd Canon Clive Burgess, St Peter's Rectory, Church Road, Onchan IM3 1BF
The Revd Canon John Coldwell, The Vicarage, 85 Ballanard Road, Douglas IM2 5HE
E: media@sodorandman.im
The Revd Canon Dr Joseph Heaton, Rushen Vicarage, Barracks Road, Port St Mary IM9 5LP
The Revd Canon Janice Ward, The Vicarage, Main Road, Crosby IM4 4BH

ARCHDEACON
The Ven Andrew Brown, St George's Vicarage, 16 Devonshire Road, Douglas, Isle of Man IM2 3RB
T: 01624 675430
E: archdeacon@sodorandman.im

MEMBERS OF THE HOUSE OF CLERGY OF THE GENERAL SYNOD
Proctors for Clergy
The Ven Andrew Brown

MEMBERS OF THE HOUSE OF LAITY OF THE GENERAL SYNOD
Mrs Susan Kennaugh

DIOCESAN OFFICERS
Vicar-General and Chancellor of Diocese The Worshipful Canon Geoffrey Tattersall, Byrom Street Chambers, 12 Byrom Street, Manchester, England M3 4PP
E: gftqc@hotmail.co.uk
Diocesan Registrar Mrs Louise Connacher, The Registry, Stamford House, Piccadilly, York YO1 9PP
T: 01904 623487
E: registrar@sodorandman.im
Diocesan Synod Secretary Mrs Michelle Barwood, 11 Glen Maye Park, Glen Maye, Isle of Man IM5 3AX
T: 01624 673477
E: synod@sodorandman.im

DIOCESAN ORGANIZATIONS
Diocesan Office c/o The Bishop's Office, Thie yn Aspick, 4 The Falls, Douglas, Isle of Man IM4 4PZ
T: 01624 622108
E: secretary@sodorandman.im

ADMINISTRATION
Diocesan Synod (Chairman, House of Clergy) The Revd Canon John Coldwell, The Vicarage, 85 Ballanard Road, Douglas IM2 5HE
E: media@sodorandman.im
(Chairman, House of Laity) Mr Stephen Hamer
E: shamer@aol.com
Board of Finance (Chairman) The Ven Andrew Brown, St George's Vicarage, 16 Devonshire Road, Douglas, Isle of Man IM2 3RB
T: 01624 675430
E: archdeacon@sodorandman.im
(Secretary) Mrs Michelle Barwood, 11 Glen Maye Park, Glen Maye, Isle of Man IM5 3AX
T: 01624 673477
E: synod@sodorandman.im
(Diocesan Treasurer) Mrs Lisa Johnson, 21 Brighton Terrace, Douglas, Isle of Man IM1 4AP
T: 01624 677512
E: treasurer@sodorandman.im

ARCHIVED DIOCESAN RECORDS
The Manx Museum Library, Kingswood Grove, Douglas, Isle of Man IM1 3LY
T: 01624 648000
Archivist Miss Wendy Thirkettle

CHAPLAINS

Bishop's Chaplain (until 31/12/17) The Revd Canon Margaret Burrow, Thie yn Aspick, 4 The Falls, Douglas, Isle of Man IM4 4PZ
E: chaplain@sodorandman.im
P.T.O. Ministers (lay and ordained) The Revd Leslie Lawrinson
Bishop's Visitors Dr Paul Bregazzi
Mrs Barbara Bregazzi
King William's College The Revd Erica Scott
IOM Prison, Jurby The Revd Brian Evans-Smith
Hospice Isle of Man Vacancy
The Isle of Man College The Revd Daniel Richards
IOM Constabulary (ecumenical) (IOM Constabulary ecumenical) The Revd Jo Dudley
Mothers' Union Mr Nigel Cretney
Noble's General Hospital The Revd Canon Philip Frear
Ramsey Cottage Hospital The Revd Brian Evans-Smith
The House of Keys Vacancy
Widows and Widowers of Public Ministers Mrs Brenda Willoughby

CHURCH BUILDINGS

Advisory Committee for the Care of Churches (Secretary) Mrs Michelle Barwood, 11 Glen Maye Park, Glen Maye, Isle of Man IM5 3AX
T: 01624 673477
E: synod@sodorandman.im

CHURCH COMMISSIONERS FOR THE ISLE OF MAN

Chair The Revd Canon Margaret Burrow, Thie yn Aspick, 4 The Falls, Douglas, Isle of Man IM4 4PZ   *E:* chaplain@sodorandman.im
Secretary Mrs Michelle Barwood, 11 Glen Maye Park, Glen Maye, Isle of Man IM5 3AX
T: 01624 673477
E: synod@sodorandman.im
Members The Ven Andrew Brown
The Revd Canon Clive Burgess
Mr Stephen Hamer
Mrs Susan Kennaugh
The Revd Canon John Coldwell
Mrs Jacqy Frear
Mr Julian Power
Mrs Susan Waring

COMMUNICATION

Media and Communications Officer The Revd Canon John Coldwell, The Vicarage, 85 Ballanard Road, Douglas IM2 5HE
E: media@sodorandman.im
Data Protection Officer Mr Charles Flynn
Manx Radio Canon Miss Judith Ley
Webmaster The Revd Canon John Coldwell, The Vicarage, 85 Ballanard Road, Douglas IM2 5HE   *E:* media@sodorandman.im

EDUCATION, FAMILIES, CHILDREN AND YOUNG PEOPLE

Children's Work Adviser Vacancy
Church School Liaison The Revd James McGowan
Mothers' Union President Mrs Patricia Costain
Youth Work Adviser Miss Ruth Walker
Safeguarding Officer The Revd Jo Dudley

MISSION AND CHURCH LIFE

Ecumenical Adviser Mr Howard Connell
Healing and Deliverance Adviser The Revd Canon Philip Frear
Leisure, Sport and Tourism Adviser The Very Revd Nigel Godfrey, The Deanery, Albany Road, Peel, Isle of Man IM5 1JS
T: 01624 844830
E: dean@sodorandman.im
Spiritual Life Adviser Miss Karen Garrett
World Mission Co-ordinators The Revd Canon Malcolm Convery
Mrs Valerie Convery
Christian Giving Adviser The Revd Diane Marchment
C.M.E.A.C. Link Vacancy

MISSION PARTNERSHIP LEADERS

North The Revd Chris Lowdon
South The Revd Canon Dr Joseph Heaton, Rushen Vicarage, Barracks Road, Port St Mary IM9 5LP
East The Revd Canon Clive Burgess, St Peter's Rectory, Church Road, Onchan IM3 1BF
West The Very Revd Nigel Godfrey, The Deanery, Albany Road, Peel, Isle of Man IM5 1JS   *T:* 01624 844830
E: dean@sodorandman.im

PUBLIC MINISTRY

Director of Vocation and Training (DDO) (Director of Vocation and Training DDO) The Very Revd Nigel Godfrey, The Deanery, Albany Road, Peel, Isle of Man IM5 1JS   *T:* 01624 844830
E: dean@sodorandman.im
Director of Studies IME 1–3 The Revd Canon Margaret Burrow, Thie yn Aspick, 4 The Falls, Douglas, Isle of Man IM4 4PZ
E: chaplain@sodorandman.im
Director of Ministerial Development (CMD & IME 4–7) (Director of Ministerial Development CMD & IME 4–7) Vacancy
Warden of Readers Mrs Margaret Galloway

SECTOR MINISTERS AND ADVISERS SOCIAL RESPONSIBILITY

Access and Disability Mr Guy Thompson
Church and Society Adviser Vacancy
Environment Advisers The Revd Brian Evans-Smith
Mrs Mary Evans-Smith
Rural Life Adviser Vacancy

DIOCESE OF SOUTHWARK

Founded in 1905. Greater London south of the Thames, except for most of the London Boroughs of Bromley and Bexley, in the diocese of Rochester, and a few parishes in the south-west, in the diocese of Guildford; the eastern third of Surrey.

Population 2,852,000   Area 320 sq m
Full-time Stipendiary Parochial Clergy 323   Benefices 256
Parishes 293   Churches 356
southwark.anglican.org
Overseas link dioceses: Manicaland, Central Zimbabwe,
Matabeleland, Masvingo (Zimbabwe)

BISHOP

The Rt Revd Christopher Chessun, Bishop's Office, Trinity House, 4 Chapel Court, Borough High Street, London SE1 1HW
T: 020 7939 9420
F: 0843 2906894
E: bishop.christopher@
southwark.anglican.org

BISHOP'S STAFF

Bishop's Chaplain The Revd Joshua Rey, Trinity House, 4 Chapel Court, Borough High Street, London SE1 1HW   *T:* 020 7939 9422
E: joshua.rey@southwark.anglican.org
Bishop's Personal Assistant Ms Winsome Thomas (*Same Address*)   *T:* 020 7939 9400
E: winsome.thomas@southwark.anglican.org
Bishop's Press Officer The Revd Canon Wendy Robins (*Same Address*)   *T:* 020 7939 9436
E: wendy.robins@southwark.anglican.org
Personal Assistant Mrs Penny Lochead (*Same Address*)   *T:* 020 7939 9400
E: penny.lochead@southwark.anglican.org

AREA BISHOPS

CROYDON The Rt Revd Jonathan Clark, Croydon Episcopal Area Office, St Matthew's House, 100 George Street, Croydon CR0 1PJ
T: 020 8256 9630
F: 020 8256 9631
E: bishop.jonathan@southwark.anglican.org
KINGSTON The Rt Revd Dr Richard Cheetham, Kingston Episcopal Area Office, 620 Kingston Road, Raynes Park, London SW20 8DN
T: 020 8545 2440
F: 020 8545 2441
E: bishop.richard@southwark.anglican.org
WOOLWICH The Rt Revd Karowei Dorgu, Trinity House, 4 Chapel Court, Borough High Street, London SE1 1HW   *T:* 020 7939 9400
E: bishop.karowei@southwark.anglican.org

ASSISTANT BISHOPS

The Rt Revd Dr David Atkinson, 6 Bynes Road, South Croydon CR2 0PR   *T:* 020 8406 0895
E: davidatkinson43@
virginmedia.com
The Rt Revd Jonathan Baker, Bishop of Fulham's Office, 5 St Andrew Street, London EC4A 3AF   *T:* 020 7932 1130
E: bishop.fulham@
london.anglican.org
The Rt Revd Michael Doe, 405 West Carriage House, Royal Carriage Mews, London SE18 6GA   *T:* 020 3259 3841
E: michaeldd@btinternet.com
The Rt Revd and Rt Hon. Lord Harries of Pentregarth, 41 Melville Road, Barnes, London SW19 9RH   *T:* 020 8288 6053
E: richard.d.harries@googlemail.com
The Rt Revd Dr Graham Kings, Mission Theologian to the Anglican Communion, 483b Southwark Park Road, London SE16 2JP
M: 07786 071677
E: graham.kings@durham.ac.uk
The Rt Revd Peter Selby, 57 Girton Road, London SE26 5DJ   *E:* peterselby@onetel.com
The Rt Revd Tim Thornton, Bishop at Lambeth, Lambeth Palace, London SE1 7JU
T: 020 7898 1198
020 7898 1200
E: tim.thornton@lambethpalace.org.uk
The Rt Revd Rod Thomas, 28 St John's Meadow, Blindley Heath, Lingfield RH7 6JU
T: 01342 834140
E: admin@bishopofmaidstone.org
The Rt Revd Peter Wheatley, 47 Sedlescombe Road South, St Leonards-on-Sea TN38 0TB
T: 01424 424814
E: peter.wheatley@outlook.com
The Rt Revd Stephen Platten, 73A Gloucester Place, London, W1 8JW   *T:* 020 7283 3121
The Rt Revd Precious Sontoye Omuku, 4 Litchfield Avenue, Morden SM4 5QS
T: 020 8640 7311
E: precious.omuku@yahoo.co.uk

CATHEDRAL AND COLLEGIATE CHURCH OF ST SAVIOUR AND ST MARY OVERIE

Dean The Very Revd Andrew Nunn, Cathedral Office, Montague Chambers, London Bridge, London SE1 9DA   *T:* 020 7367 6727 (Office)
020 7928 3336 (Home)
F: 020 7367 6725 (Office)
E: andrew.nunn@southwark.anglican.org

Canons Residentiary

Pastor and Sub Dean The Revd Canon Michael Rawson, Cathedral Office, Montague Chambers, London Bridge, London SE1 9DA
T: 020 7367 6706 (Office)
020 7820 3873 (Home)
E: michael.rawson@southwark.anglican.org

Precentor The Revd Canon Gilly Myers (*Same Address*)   *T:* 020 7367 6731 (Office)
020 7582 4442 (Home)
E: gilly.myers@southwark.anglican.org

Chancellor and Director of Ministerial Education The Revd Canon Dr Mandy Ford, Trinity House, 4 Chapel Court, Borough High Street, London SE1 1HW   *T:* 020 7939 9449
E: mandy.ford@southwark.anglican.org

Treasurer and Diocesan Director of Ordinands The Revd Canon Leanne Roberts (*Same Address*)   *T:* 020 7939 9458
E: leanne.roberts@southwark.anglican.org

Other Staff

Succentor The Revd Rachel Young, Cathedral Office, Montague Chambers, London Bridge, London SE1 9DA   *T:* 020 7967 6705
E: rachel.young@southwark.anglican.org

Priest Assistant The Revd Canon Wendy Robins, Bishop's Office, Trinity House, 4 Chapel Court, Borough High Street, London SE1 1HW   *T:* 020 7939 9436
E: wendy.robins@southwark.anglican.org

Cathedral Organist Mr Peter Wright, Cathedral Office, Montague Chambers, London Bridge, London SE1 9DA   *T:* 020 7367 6703
E: peter.wright@southwark.anglican.org

Comptroller Mr Matthew Knight (*Same Address*)   *T:* 020 7367 6726
E: matthew.knight@southwark.anglican.org

Education Officer Mrs Lisa Bewick, Cathedral Office   *T:* 020 7367 6715
E: edcentre@southwark.anglican.org

Assistant Curates The Revd Jessie Daniels-White, Cathedral Office, Montague Chambers, London Bridge, London SE1 9DA
T: 07899 928918
E: jessie.danielswhite@southwark.anglican.org

The Revd David Adamson (*Same Address*)
T: 020 3612 4687 (home)
E: daviddominic@stgeorge-themartyr.co.uk

ARCHDEACONS

SOUTHWARK The Ven Dr Jane Steen, Trinity House, 4 Chapel Court, Borough High Street, London SE1 1HW
E: jane.steen@southwark.anglican.org

LAMBETH The Ven Simon Gates, Kingston Episcopal Area Office, 620 Kingston Road, Raynes Park, London SW20 8DN
T: 020 8545 2440
E: simon.gates@southwark.anglican.org

REIGATE The Ven Moira Astin, St Matthew's House, 100 George Street, Croydon CR0 1PJ
T: 020 8256 9630
E: moira.astin@southwark.anglican.org

LEWISHAM AND GREENWICH The Ven Alastair Cutting, Trinity House, 4 Chapel Court, Borough High Street, London SE1 1HW
T: 020 7939 9408
E: alastair.cutting@southwark.anglican.org

WANDSWORTH The Ven John Kiddle, Kingston Episcopal Area Office, 620 Kingston Road, Raynes Park, London SW20 8DN
T: 020 8545 2440
E: john.kiddle@southwark.anglican.org

CROYDON The Ven Christopher Skilton, Croydon Episcopal Area Office, St Matthew's House, 100 George Street, Croydon CR0 1PJ
T: 020 8256 9630
E: chris.skilton@southwark.anglican.org

MEMBERS OF THE HOUSE OF CLERGY OF THE GENERAL SYNOD

Proctors for Clergy

The Revd Canon Simon Butler
The Revd Canon Giles Goddard
The Revd Timothy Goode
The Revd Canon Gary Jenkins
The Revd Dr Rosemarie Mallett
The Ven Dr Jane Steen

MEMBERS OF THE HOUSE OF LAITY OF THE GENERAL SYNOD

Mrs April Alexander
Mr Adrian Greenwood
Mr Thomas Hatton
Mr Carl Hughes
Capt Nicholas Lebey
Ms Caroline Myers
Mr Brian Wilson

DIOCESAN OFFICERS

Diocesan Secretary Ruth Martin, Trinity House, 4 Chapel Court, Borough High Street, London SE1 1HW   *T:* 020 7939 9400
F: 020 7939 9468
E: ruth.martin@southwark.anglican.org

Deputy Diocesan Secretary The Revd Canon Stephen Roberts (*Same Address, Tel & Fax*)
E: stephen.roberts@southwark.anglican.org

Chancellor of Diocese Mr Philip Petchey, Francis Taylor Building, Inner Temple, London EC4Y 7BY   *T:* 020 7353 8415
Registrar of Diocese and Bishop's Legal Secretary Mr Paul Morris, Minerva House, 5 Montague Close, London SE1 9BB   *T:* 020 7593 5084
F: 020 7593 5099

DIOCESAN ORGANIZATIONS

Diocesan Office Trinity House, 4 Chapel Court, Borough High Street, London SE1 1HW
T: 020 7939 9400
F: 020 7939 9468
E: trinity@southwark.anglican.org
W: southwark.anglican.org

ADMINISTRATION

Diocesan Synod (*Chair, House of Clergy*) The Revd Dr Rosemarie Mallett, c/o Diocesan Office, Trinity House, 4 Chapel Court, Borough High Street, London SE1 1HW
E: rosemarie.mallett@ southwark.anglican.org
(*Chair, House of Laity*) Mr Adrian Greenwood
(*Secretary*) Ruth Martin, Trinity House, 4 Chapel Court, Borough High Street, London SE1 1HW   *T:* 020 7939 9400
F: 020 7939 9468
E: ruth.martin@southwark.anglican.org
South London Church Fund and Diocesan Board of Finance (*Chair*) Mr Gerald Allison, Kingston Episcopal Area Office, London, Raynes Park, London SW20 8DN   *T:* 020 8545 2440
F: 020 8545 2441
E: simon.gates@southwark.anglican.org
Mr Gerald Allison
(*Secretary*) Ruth Martin, Trinity House, 4 Chapel Court, Borough High Street, London SE1 1HW   *T:* 020 7939 9400
F: 020 7939 9468
E: ruth.martin@southwark.anglican.org
Parsonages Board (*Chair*) The Ven Dr Jane Steen (*Same Address*)
E: jane.steen@southwark.anglican.org
(*Secretary*) Ruth Martin (*Same Address*)
T: 020 7939 9400
F: 020 7939 9468
E: ruth.martin@southwark.anglican.org
Mission and Pastoral Committee (*Chair*) The Ven Simon Gates, Kingston Episcopal Area Office, London, Raynes Park, London SW20 8DN
T: 020 8545 2440
F: 020 8545 2441
E: simon.gates@southwark.anglican.org
(*Secretary*) The Revd Canon Stephen Roberts, Trinity House, 4 Chapel Court, Borough High Street, London SE1 1HW   *T:* 020 7939 9400
F: 020 7939 9468
E: stephen.roberts@southwark.anglican.org

CHURCH BUILDINGS

Advisory Committee for the Care of Churches (*Chairman*) Mr Paul Parkinson, c/o Dioc Office (*Secretary*) The Revd Canon Stephen Roberts, Trinity House, 4 Chapel Court, Borough High Street, London SE1 1HW
T: 020 7939 9400
F: 020 7939 9468
E: stephen.roberts@southwark.anglican.org

COMMUNICATIONS

Director of Communications and Resources and Bishop's Press Officer The Revd Canon Wendy Robins, Bishop's Office, Trinity House, 4 Chapel Court, Borough High Street, London SE1 1HW   *T:* 020 7939 9436
E: wendy.robins@southwark.anglican.org
Communications Officer Mr Steve Harris, Diocesan Office, Trinity House, 4 Chapel Court, Borough High Street, London SE1 1HW   *T:* 020 7939 9437
E: steve.harris@southwark.anglican.org
Web Manager and Social Media Officer Daniel Stone   *T:* 020 7939 9439
E: daniel.stone@southwark.anglican.org

DIOCESAN RECORD OFFICES

London Metropolitan Archives, 40 Northampton Rd, London EC1R 0HB
T: 020 7332 3820
F: 020 7833 9136
Lewisham Local Studies and Archives Centre, Lewisham Library, 199–201 Lewisham High Street, London SE13 6LG   *T:* 020 8297 0682
F: 020 8297 1169
Bexley Local Studies and Archive Centre, Central Library, Townley Road, Bexleyheath DA6 7HJ   *T:* 020 8303 7777
Surrey History Centre, 130 Goldsworth Road, Woking GU21 6ND   *T:* 01483 518737
F: 01483 594595
London Borough of Sutton Local Studies Centre, St Nicholas Way, Sutton SM1 1EA
T: 020 8770 4747

DISCIPLESHIP AND MINISTRY

Director of Ministry and Discipleship The Revd Canon Dr Mandy Ford, Trinity House, 4 Chapel Court, Borough High Street, London SE1 1HW   *T:* 020 7939 9449
E: mandy.ford@southwark.anglican.org
Assistant Director of Discipleship and Training Vacancy

EDUCATION

Board of Education (*Director*) Canon Colin Powell, 48 Union Street, London SE1 1TD
T: 020 7234 9200
E: colin.powell@southwark.anglican.org

(*Assistant Director*) Dr Carol Jerwood (*Same Address*)   T: 020 7232 9200
                                        F: 020 7234 9801

MISSION AND EVANGELISM
Chair The Rt Revd Jonathan Clark, Croydon Episcopal Area Office, St Matthew's House, 100 George Street, Croydon CR0 1PJ
                                        T: 020 8256 9630
                                        F: 020 8256 9631
    E: bishop.jonathan@southwark.anglican.org
Canon Missioner and Director of Mission and Evangelism Vacancy
Mission Support Officer c/o Diocesan Office, Trinity House, 4 Chapel Court, Borough High Street, London SE1 1HW
Mission Action Planning Vanessa Elston, Trinity House, 4 Chapel Court, Borough High Street, London SE1 1HW   T: 020 7939 9473
    E: vanessa.elston@southwark.anglican.org
Dean of Fresh Expressions The Revd Canon Will Cookson, c/o Trinity House, 4 Chapel Court, Borough High Street, London SE1 1HW
    E: will.cookson@southwark.anglican.org
Consultant Adviser for Youth and Children's Work Hugh Ridsdill-Smith, Trinity House, 4 Chapel Court, Borough High Street, London SE1 1HW   T: 020 7939 9414
                        E: hugh.ridsdill-smith@
                        southwark.anglican.org

OTHER OFFICERS
Dean of Women's Ministry The Revd Anna Eltrungham   T: 020 8690 2499
Spiritual Formation Adviser Mr Chris Chapman, Diocesan Office, Trinity House, 4 Chapel Court, Borough High Street, London SE1 1HW   ·   T: 020 7939 9474
                        E: chris.chapman@
                        southwark.anglican.org
Retirement Officer The Revd Nicky Tredennick
                                        T: 01342 843570
                    E: rev.nicky@btinternet.com
Ecumenical Relations Group The Revd Peter William Hart   T: 020 8392 1425
                        E: pwhart1@aoi.com
Warden of Readers Nicole Burgum
                                        T: 020 8697 1391
    E: nicole.burgum@southwark.anglican.org

PUBLIC POLICY GROUP
Director of Justice, Peace and Integrity of Creation The Revd Dr Rosemarie Mallett, c/o Diocesan Office, Trinity House, 4 Chapel Court, Borough High Street, London SE1 1HW
                        E: rosemarie.mallett@
                        southwark.anglican.org
Public Policy Research Officer Theo Shaw (*Same Address*)
    E: theo.shaw@southwark.anglican.org

Adviser on Economic Development: The Revd Andrew Wakefield   T: 020 8542 6566
Environmental Officer Mrs Sue Mallinson, c/o Diocesan Office, Trinity House, 4 Chapel Court, Borough High Street, London SE1 1HW
Inter-faith Relations Co-ordinator Siriol Davies
                                        T: 020 7701 4854
                        E: sirioldavies@yahoo.co.uk

SAFEGUARDING
Diocesan Safeguarding Adviser Kate Singleton, c/o Diocesan Office, Trinity House, 4 Chapel Court, Borough High Street, London SE1 1HW   T: 020 7939 9400
    M: 07982 279713 (out of hours, or if unavailable on landline)
    E: kate.singleton@southwark.anglican.org
Assistant Safeguarding Advisers Steve Short (*Same Address, Tel & Mobile*)
    E: steve.short@southwark.anglican.org
Louise Vernon (*Same Address, Tel & Mobile*)
    E: louise.vernon@southwark.anglican.org

STEWARDSHIP
Director of Communications and Resources The Revd Canon Wendy Robins, Bishop's Office, Trinity House, 4 Chapel Court, Borough High Street, London SE1 1HW   T: 020 7939 9436
    E: wendy.robins@southwark.anglican.org
Parish Giving Communications Officer Gabby Parikh, Trinity House, 4 Chapel Court, Borough High Street, London SE1 1HW
                                        T: 020 7939 9438

VOCATIONS
Diocesan Director of Ordinands The Revd Canon Leanne Roberts, Trinity House, 4 Chapel Court, Borough High Street, London SE1 1HW   T: 020 7939 9458
    E: leanne.roberts@southwark.anglican.org
Assistant Diocesan Director of Ordinands The Revd Andrew Zihni   T: 020 7939 9472
    E: andrew.zihni@southwark.anglican.org
Diocesan Discipleship and Vocations Missioner Vacancy

AREA DEANS
ARCHDEACONRY OF CROYDON
Croydon Addington Jennifer Jane Elisabeth Rowley, St John's Rectory, Upper Selsdon Road, South Croydon CR2 8DD
                                        T: 07709 252692
                        E: jennyrowley@waitrose.com
Croydon Central William Frederick Warren, St Peter's Vicarage, 20 Haling Park Road, South Croydon CR2 6NE   T: 020 8688 4715
                    E: wfwarren2003@yahoo.co.uk
Croydon North Catherine Jane Tucker, The Vicarage, 115 St Saviour's Road, Croydon CR0 2XF   T: 020 8699 3466
                    E: curateperryhill@hotmail.co.uk

Croydon South Paul Carlton Roberts, The Rectory, 232 Coulsdon Road, Coulsdon CR5 1EA   *T:* 01737 552152
                E: rev.paul.c.roberts@gmail.com
Sutton Darren Noel Miller, The Rectory, 33 Mickleham Gardens, Cheam, Sutton SM3 8QJ   *T:* 020 8641 4664
                E: dnmiller@dandsmiller.me.uk

ARCHDEACONRY OF LAMBETH

Lambeth North Caroline Anne Clarke, 42 The Chase, London SW4 0NH   *T:* 020 7622 0765
                E: clarkecaroline@hotmail.com
Lambeth South David John Stephenson, All Saints' Vicarage, 165 Rosendale Road, London SE21 8LN   *T:* 020 8670 0826
                E: vicar@all-saints.org.uk
Merton Bruce Walter Rickards, 85A Toynbee Road, London SW20 8SJ   *T:* 020 8540 4150
                E: byrickards@btinternet.com

ARCHDEACONRY OF LEWISHAM AND GREENWICH

Charlton Kim William Hitch, St James's Rectory, 62 Kidbrooke Park Road, London SE3 0DU   *T:* 020 8856 3438
                E: k.w.hitch@btinternet.com
Deptford Peter James Farley-Moore, St John's Vicarage, St John's Vale, London SE8 4EA
                E: peter.stjohnsdeptford@gmail.com
Eltham and Mottingham Brett Ernest Ward, Holy Trinity Vicarage, 59 Southend Crescent, London SE9 2SD   *T:* 020 8850 1246
                E: fr.brett@ht-e.org.uk
Lewisham, East Stephen Philip Hall, 48 Lewisham Park, London SE13 6QZ
                        T: 020 8690 2682
                E: vicar@lewishamparish.com
Lewisham, West Michael Brooks, Holy Trinity Church, 4 Trinity Path, Sydenham SE26 4EA
                        T: 020 7771 3541
Plumstead Clive Richard Welham, The Vicarage, 42 Jago Close, London SE18 2TY
                        T: 020 8854 3395
                E: welhamclive@yahoo.co.uk

ARCHDEACONRY OF REIGATE

Tandridge (Acting) Kathryn Janet Percival, The Rectory, High Street, Limpsfield, Oxted RH8 0DG   *T:* 01883 722351
                E: kathryn.percival@blueyouder.co.uk
Reigate Andrew Thomas Cunnington, St Matthew's Vicarage, 27 Ridgeway Road, Redhill RH1 6PQ   *T:* 01737 761568
                E: andrew@stmatthews-redhill.org.uk

ARCHDEACONRY OF SOUTHWARK

Bermondsey Mark Richard Nicholls, St Mary's Rectory, 72A St Marychurch Street, London SE16 2JE   *T:* 07909 546659
                E: mmarini2001@aol.com
Camberwell Vacancy
Dulwich Susan Jane Height, 110 Fawnbrake Avenue, London SE24 0BZ
                        T: 07843 253700
                E: susan_height@yahoo.co.uk
Southwark and Newington Andrew Denis Paul Moughtin-Mumby, St Peter's Rectory, 12 Villa Street, London SE17 2EJ   *T:* 020 7703 3139
                E: rector@stpeterswalworth.org

ARCHDEACONRY OF WANDSWORTH

Battersea Richard Godfrey Taylor, The Vicarage, 8 Lavender Gardens, London SW11 1DL   *T:* 020 7223 5953
                E: fatboytaylor@gmail.com
Kingston Helen Mary Durant-Stevensen, 2 California Road, New Malden KT3 3RU
                        T: 020 8942 0544
                E: helends@ccnm.org
Richmond and Barnes Vacancy
Tooting Susan Elizabeth Mary Davis, 26 Abbotsleigh Road, London SW16 1SP
                        T: 020 8769 5117
                E: sue.clarke@kcl.ac.uk
Wandsworth Gregory Stephen Prior, Wandsworth Vicarage, 11 Rusholme Road, London SW15 3JX   *T:* 020 8788 7400
                E: greg@wandsworthparish.co.uk

DIOCESE OF SOUTHWELL AND NOTTINGHAM

Founded in 1884. Nottinghamshire; a few parishes
in South Yorkshire.

Population 1,140,000   Area 840 sq m
Full-time Stipendiary Parochial Clergy 109   Benefices 146
Parishes 244   Churches 300
www.southwell.anglican.org
Overseas link dioceses: Natal (South Africa)

BISHOP

The Rt Revd Paul Williams, c/o Jubilee House,
Westgate, Southwell NG25 0JH
T: 01636 817996
E: bishop@southwell.anglican.org

BISHOP'S STAFF

Interim Chaplain The Revd Tom Gillum
Personal Assistant Mrs Amy Jones

SUFFRAGAN BISHOP

SHERWOOD The Rt Revd Anthony Porter, Jubilee
House, Westgate, Southwell NG25 0JH
T: 01636 819133
E: bishopsherwood@southwell.anglican.org
Personal Assistant Mrs Jacky Bates

PROVINCIAL EPISCOPAL VISITOR

Beverley The Rt Revd Glyn Webster, Holy
Trinity Rectory, Micklegate, York YO1 6LE
T: 01904 628155
E: office@seeofbeverley.org

ASSISTANT BISHOPS

The Rt Revd John Finney, Greenacre, Crow
Lane, South Muskham, Newark NG23 6DZ
T: 01636 679791
The Rt Revd Richard Inwood, 43 Whitecotes
Park, Chesterfield S40 3RT   T: 01246 766288
E: richardinwood@btconnect.com
The Rt Revd Martyn Jarrett, 91 Beaumont
Rise, Worksop S80 1YG (*Same Tel*)
The Rt Revd Ronald Milner, 7 Crafts Way,
Southwell NG25 0BL   T: 01636 816256
The Rt Revd Roy Williamson, 30 Sidney Road,
Beeston, Nottingham NG9 1AN
T: 0115 925 4901

CATHEDRAL AND PARISH CHURCH OF
THE BLESSED VIRGIN MARY

Dean The Very Revd Nicola Sullivan, The
Residence, Vicars Court, Church Street,
Southwell NG25 0HP   T: 01636 817282
E: dean@southwellminster.org.uk

Canons Residentiary
Canon Chancellor The Revd Canon Nigel
Coates, 3 Vicars' Court, Southwell NG25 0HP
T: 01636 817296
E: nigelcoates@southwellminster.org.uk
Precentor Canon Jacqueline (Jacqui) D. Jones,
2 Vicars' Court, Southwell NG25 0HP
T: 01636 817295
E: jacquijones@southwellminster.org.uk
Other Staff
Chapter Clerk Mrs Caroline Jarvis, The Minster
Office, The Minster Centre, Church Street,
Southwell NG25 0HD   T: 01636 817285
E: chapterclerk@southwellminster.org.uk
Rector Chori Paul Proctor
Head Verger Mr Andrew Todd, The Vestry,
Southwell Cathedral   T: 01636 817290
E: vergers@southwellminster.org.uk

ARCHDEACONS

NEWARK The Ven David Picken, 22 Rufford
Road, Edwinstowe, Mansfield NG21 9HY
T: 01636 817206 (office)
E: archdeacon-newark@
southwell.anglican.org
NOTTINGHAM The Ven Sarah Clark, 4 Victoria
Crescent, Sherwood, Nottingham NG5 4DA
T: 01636 817206 (office)
E: archd-nottm@southwell.anglican.org

MEMBERS OF THE HOUSE OF CLERGY
OF THE GENERAL SYNOD

Proctors for Clergy
The Ven David Picken
The Revd Chris Hodder
The Revd Ian Paul

MEMBERS OF THE HOUSE OF LAITY OF
THE GENERAL SYNOD

Mrs Joan Beck
Mr Nick Harding
Mr Colin Slater
Ms Tracey Frances Byrne

DIOCESAN OFFICERS

Chief Executive Canon Nigel Spraggins, Jubilee House, Westgate, Southwell NG25 0JH
T: 01636 817206 (Office)
01636 816445 (Home)
F: 01636 815084
M: 07887 538682
E: ce@southwell.anglican.org
Executive Personal Assistant to the Chief Executive and Archdeacons Mrs Jo Padmore
T: 01636 817206
E: archdeaconspa@southwell.anglican.org
Chancellor of Diocese The Worshipful Mark Ockelton, Diocesan Office, Jubilee House, Westgate, Southwell NG25 0JH
T: 01636 917209
Deputy Chancellor Mrs Jacqueline Humphreys
Registrar of Diocese and Bishop's Legal Secretary Mrs Amanda Redgate
T: 01636 817209
E: amanda.redgate@southwell.anglican.org
Deputy Registrar Mr Charles George

DIOCESAN ORGANIZATIONS

Diocesan Office Jubilee House, Westgate, Southwell NG25 0JH
T: 01636 814331
E: mail@southwell.anglican.org
W: www.southwell.anglican.org

ADMINISTRATION

Diocesan Synod (Vice-president and Chair, House of Clergy) Vacancy
(Chair, House of Laity) Mr Michael Wilson
(Secretary) Canon Nigel Spraggins, Jubilee House, Westgate, Southwell NG25 0JH
T: 01636 817206 (Office)
01636 816445 (Home)
F: 01636 815084
M: 07887 538682
E: ce@southwell.anglican.org
Finance (Director of Finance) Mrs Rebecca Bowes
T: 01636 817202
E: rebecca.bowes@southwell.anglican.org

CARE OF CHURCHES

Advisory Committee for the Care of Churches (Chair) The Revd Bronwen Gamble, 2 Dobbin Close, Cropwell Bishop, Nottingham NG12 3GR
E: brongamble@hotmail.com
(DAC Secretary and GIS Manager) Mr Jonathan Pickett
T: 01636 817210
E: jonathan.pickett@southwell.anglican.org

CHAPLAIN TO RETIRED CLERGY/CLERGY WIDOWS OFFICER

The Revd Reginald Walton, 19 the Malsters, Newark NG24 4RU
T: 01636 659869
E: regwalton40@gmail.com

DIOCESAN RECORDS OFFICE

Nottinghamshire Archives, County House, Castle Meadow Rd, Nottingham NG1 1AG
Principal Archivist
Ms Ruth Imeson
T: 0115 950 4524

DISCIPLESHIP AND MINISTRY

Director, Discipleship and Ministry The Revd Canon Dr Richard Kellett, Diocesan Office, Jubilee House, Westgate, Southwell NG25 0JH
T: 01636 817231
E: richard.kellett@southwell.anglican.org
Vocations Adviser and Diocesan Director of Ordinands The Revd Sue Hemsley Halls *(Same Address)*
T: 01636 817212
E: suehh@southwell.anglican.org
Dean of Women's Ministry Vacancy
Ministry Development Adviser The Revd Jackie Johnson
T: 01636 817208
E: jackie.johnson@southwell.anglican.org
Warden of Readers Mr Christopher Perrett, Harvest Barn, Grassthorpe, Newark, Nottingham NG23 5QZ
T: 01636 822426
E: chris.perrett@southwell.anglican.org
Sport Ambassador Mr Rob Taylor
T: 07775 687682
E: rob.taylor@southwell.anglican.org
Principal of the School of Discipleship The Revd David Emerton, Diocesan Office, Jubilee House, Westgate, Southwell NG25 0JH
T: 01636 817232
E: david.emerton@southwell.anglican.org

EDUCATION

Diocesan Office, Jubilee House, Westgate, Southwell NG25 0JH
T: 01636 814504
(Education Department)
Director of Education Mrs Claire Meese *(Same Address)*
T: 01636 817238
Deputy Director (Schools) Mrs Samantha Dennis
T: 01636 817247
E: samantha.dennis@southwell.anglican.org
Assistant Director (Schools) Mrs Sheila Barker
T: 01636 817235
E: sheila.barker@southwell.anglican.org
Youth Ministry Adviser (Support and Partnerships) Mrs Angela Brymer
T: 07887 530751
E: youthministryadviser@southwell.anglican.org
Youth Ministry Adviser (Growth and Development) Mr David Keetley
T: 07720 511192
E: youthministryadviser2@southwell.anglican.org
Children's Ministry Adviser Mr Nick Harding
T: 01636 817234
E: nick@southwell.anglican.org

PARISH SUPPORT

Director of Parish Support Mr Fraser McNish
T: 01636 817244
E: fraser@southwell.anglican.org

Parish Support (Property) (Building Surveyor) Mr
Ian Greaves   *T:* 01636 817214

PARTNERSHIPS AND MISSION
Director, Partnerships and Mission The Revd
David McCoulough   *T:* 01636 817246
    E: davidmcc@southwell.anglican.org
Partnerships Officer The Revd Liam O'Boyle
                 T: 07860 507318
    E: liam.o'boyle@southwell.anglican.org
Partnerships Officer (Older People) Paul Howard
                 T: 07854 893270
    E: paul.howard@southwell.anglican.org
Chaplain to the Deaf Community The Revd
Susan Bloomfield
    E: susan.bloomfield@southwell.anglican.org
Workplace Chaplain The Revd Jo Tatum
                 T: 0115 846 5760
    E: jo.tatum@southwell.anglican.org

PRESS AND PUBLICATIONS
Director of Communications Richard Ellis,
Jubilee House, Westgate, Southwell NG25 0JH
    E: richard.ellis@southwell.anglican.org

AREA DEANS
ARCHDEACONRY OF NEWARK
Bassetlaw and Bawtry Jonathan Edward Tully
Strickland, The Vicarage, Martin Lane, Bawtry,
Doncaster DN10 6NJ   *T:* 01302 710298
    E: strickers@tesco.net
Mansfield Angela Fletcher, The Rectory,
Church Road, Warsop, Mansfield NG20 0SL
                 T: 01623 843290
    E: angela_fletcher43@hotmail.com

Newark and Southwell John Mark Arthur
Adams, The Vicarage, St John Street, Mansfield
NG18 1QH   *T:* 01623 660822
    E: revdmarkadams@gmail.com
Newstead Margaret Fiona Shouler, The
Vicarage, 58 Church Lane, Selston,
Nottingham NG16 6EW   *T:* 01773 813777
    E: fionashouler@hotmail.com

ARCHDEACONRY OF NOTTINGHAM
East Bingham Edana Bronwen Gamble,
The Rectory, 2 Dobbin Close, Cropwell
Bishop, Nottingham NG12 3GR
                 T: 0115 989 3172
    E: brongamble@hotmail.com
Gedling Anthony Richard Giles, The Vicarage,
12 Lingwood Lane, Woodborough,
Nottingham NG14 6DX   *T:* 0115 965 3727
    E: ant.dianne@btopenworld.com
Nottingham North Peter Alexander Huxtable,
The Vicarage, 61 Church Street, Stapleford,
Nottingham NG9 8GA   *T:* 0115 854 0196
    E: peter.hux@virginmedia.com
Nottingham South Stephen David Silvester, 37
Lyme Park, West Bridgford, Nottingham NG2
7TR   *T:* 0115 982 0407
    E: steve@stnics.org
West Bingham Mark Adrian Fraser, 10 Scafell
Close, West Bridgford, Nottingham NG2 6RJ
                 T: 07963 397688
    E: mark.fraser@tiscali.co.uk
West Bingham John William Bentham, 51
Chaworth Road, West Bridgford, Nottingham
NG2 7AE   *T:* 0115 846 1054
    E: john.bentham@nottingham.ac.uk

DIOCESE OF TRURO

Founded in 1877. Cornwall; the Isles of Scilly;
two parishes in Devon.

Population 557,000   Area 1,390 sq m
Full-time Stipendiary Parochial Clergy 88   Benefices 113
Parishes 217   Churches 306
Overseas link dioceses: Strangnas, Sweden

BISHOP
Vacancy

BISHOP'S STAFF
Bishop's Secretary Mrs Karen Madeley, Lis
Escop, Feock, Truro TR3 6QQ
E: office@truro.anglican.org
Bishop's Secretary Mrs Ruth Trinick (*Same
Address & email*)

SUFFRAGAN BISHOP
ST GERMANS The Rt Revd Chris Goldsmith, Lis
Escop, Feock, Truro TR3 6QQ
E: bishopofstgermans@truro.anglican.org

CATHEDRAL CHURCH OF THE BLESSED VIRGIN MARY IN TRURO
Dean The Very Revd Roger Bush
T: 01872 245006
Canons Residentiary
Chancellor The Revd Canon Alan Bashforth,
Cathedral Office, 14 St Mary's Street, Truro
TR1 2AF   *T:* 01872 276782
E: alan@trurocathedral.org.uk
Pastor The Revd Canon Lynda Barley (*Same
Address*)   *T:* 01872 245016
E: lynda@trurocathedral.org.uk
Precentor The Revd Canon Simon Griffiths, 14
St Mary's Street, Truro TR1 2AF
T: 01872 245003
E: simongriffiths@trurocathedral.org.uk
Canons
Chapter Canons Mrs Daphne Skinnard
Mrs Helen Davies
Other Staff
Director of Music Christopher Gray, Cathedral
Office, 14 St Mary's Street, Truro TR1 2AF
E: chris@trurocathedral.org.uk

ARCHDEACONS
CORNWALL The Ven Bill Stuart-White, 10 The
Hayes, Bodmin Road, Truro TR1 1FY *T:* 01872
242374
E: bill@truro.anglican.org

BODMIN The Ven Audrey Elkington, 4 Park
Drive, Bodmin PL31 2QF   *T:* 01208 892811
E: audrey@truro.anglican.org

MEMBERS OF THE HOUSE OF CLERGY OF THE GENERAL SYNOD
Proctors for Clergy
The Revd Canon Alan Bashforth
The Revd Andrew Yates
The Revd Canon Anne Brown

MEMBERS OF THE HOUSE OF LAITY OF THE GENERAL SYNOD
Mrs Susannah Leafe
Mrs Sheri Sturgess
Dr Mike Todd

DIOCESAN OFFICERS
Diocesan Secretary Mrs Esther Pollard, Church
House, Woodlands Court, Truro Business
Park, Threemilestone, Truro TR4 9NH
T: 01872 274351
E: esther.pollard@truro.anglican.org
Head of Church House Operations Kate Cortez
Assistant Diocesan Secretary Mrs Lesley Fusher
E: lesley.fusher@truro.anglican.org
Chancellor of Diocese The Rt Worshipful
Timothy Briden, Lamb Chambers, Lamb
Building, Temple, London EC4Y 7AS
T: 020 7797 8300
020 7707 8308
E: info@lambchambers.co.uk
Registrar of Diocese and Bishop's Legal Secretary
Mr Jos Moule, Truro Diocesan Registry, Veale
Wasbrough Vizards, Narrow Quay House,
Narrow Quay, Bristol BS1 4QA
T: 0117 314 5420
E: truroregistry@vwv.co.uk

DIOCESAN ORGANIZATIONS
Diocesan Office Church House, Woodlands
Court, Truro Business Park, Threemilestone,
Truro TR4 9NH   *T:* 01872 274351
E: info@truro.anglican.org

ADMINISTRATION

Diocesan Synod and Bishop's Council (Secretary)
Mrs Esther Pollard, Church House, Woodlands
Court, Truro Business Park, Threemilestone,
Truro TR4 9NH   T: 01872 274351
       E: esther.pollard@truro.anglican.org
Diocesan Synod (Chairman, House of Clergy) The
Revd Canon Alan Bashforth, Cathedral Office,
14 St Mary's Street, Truro TR1 2AF
                                     T: 01872 276782
       E: alan@trurocathedral.org.uk
(Chairman, House of Laity) Mrs Sheri Sturgess
Board of Finance (Chairman) Mr Mike Sturgess
(Secretary) Mrs Esther Pollard, Church House,
Woodlands Court, Truro Business Park,
Threemilestone, Truro TR4 9NH
                                     T: 01872 274351
       E: esther.pollard@truro.anglican.org
Parsonages Committee Mrs Esther Pollard *(As
above)*
Mission and Pastoral Committee Mrs Esther
Pollard *(As above)*
Glebe Committee Mrs Esther Pollard *(As above)*
Board of Patronage Dr Mike Todd
(Designated Officer) Mrs Esther Pollard, Church
House, Woodlands Court, Truro Business
Park, Threemilestone, Truro TR4 9NH
                                     T: 01872 274351
       E: esther.pollard@truro.anglican.org

CHURCH BUILDINGS

*Advisory Committee for the Care of Churches
(Chairman)* Dr John Kidman, Trepenal Barn,
Blisland, Bodmin PL30 4HS   T: 01208 821525
                                     E: john@tavas.co.uk
(Secretary) Mrs Clare Jones
Truro Diocesan Guild of Ringers (President) Mrs
Annie Holland   T: 01872 552407
                          E: president@tdgr.org.uk
(General Secretary) Mr Robert Perry, 11 Trevaylor
Close, Truro TR1 1RP   T: 01872 277117
Churches Uses Committee (Secretary) Mrs Katie
Wright

DIOCESAN RECORDS

Diocesan Records Officer Mr David Thomas,
County Hall, Truro TR1 3AY   T: 01872 323127
                          E: cro@cornwall.gov.uk

DIOCESAN RETIREMENT CHAPLAIN

The Revd Brian McQuillen, 7 Bonython Drive,
Grampound, Truro TR2 4RL   T: 01726 883184
       E: brianmcq.chap@btinternet.com

EDUCATION AND TRAINING

Director of Education and Discipleship The Revd
Simon Cade, Church House, Woodlands
Court, Truro Business Park, Threemilestone,
Truro TR4 9NH   T: 01872 247214
       E: simon.cade@truro.anglican.org

Director of Schools Mrs Jo Osborne *(Same
Address)*   T: 01872 247218
       E: jo.osborne@truro.anglican.org
*Project Officer, Youth Discipleship and Lay
Pastoral Training and Support* Mrs Sarah Welply
(Same Address)
       E: sarah.welply@truro.anglican.org
Discipleship Project Officer Mrs Shelley Porter,
4 Park Drive, Bodmin PL31 2QF
                                     T: 01208 892811
       E: shelley.porter@truro.anglican.org

MINISTRY

Director of Ministry Dr Jonathan Rowe, Church
House, Woodlands Court, Truro Business
Park, Threemilestone, Truro TR4 9NH
                                     T: 01872 274351
       E: jonathan.rowe@truro.anglican.org
Director of Ordinands The Revd Jane Vaughan-
Wilson, 4 Tolver Road, Penzance TR18 2AG
                                     T: 01736 351825
       E: jvaughanwi@hotmail.co.uk
*South-west Ministry Training Course (Acting
Principal)* Kim Mathers, South West Ministry
Training Course, Swanview Suite, Riverside
Centre,   13–14   Okehampton   Street,
St Thomas, Exeter EX4 1DU
                                     T: 01392 264403
Warden of Readers The Rt Revd Chris
Goldsmith, Lis Escop, Feock, Truro TR3 6QQ
       E: bishopofstgermans@truro.anglican.org
Deputy Warden of Readers The Revd Paul
Arthur, The Rectory, 16 Trelavour Road, St
Dennis, St Austell PL26 8AH
                                     T: 01726 822317
       E: kpaularthur@googlemail.com

MISSION FORUM

Chairman The Ven Bill Stuart-White, 10 The
Hayes, Bodmin Road, Truro TR1 1FY
                                     T: 01872 242374
       E: bill@truro.anglican.org
Diocesan Ecumenical Officer The Revd Elizabeth
Foot,   Nancledra   Vicarage,   Nancledra,
Penzance TR20 8LQ   T: 01736 741448
       E: guenolesenara@hotmail.co.uk
Evangelism Group The Revd Angela Butler, 22
Esplanade Road, Newquay   T: 01637 859238
       E: angelambutler@btinternet.com
World Church Committee Chairman The Ven
Bill Stuart-White, 10 The Hayes, Bodmin
Road, Truro TR1 1FY   T: 01872 242374
       E: bill@truro.anglican.org
Social Responsibility Officer The Revd Andrew
Yates, Church House, Woodlands Court,
Truro Business Park, Truro TR4 9NH
       E: andrew.yates@truro.anglican.org
Environment Core Group The Ven Bill Stuart-
White, 10 The Hayes, Bodmin Road, Truro
TR1 1FY   T: 01872 242374
       E: bill@truro.anglican.org

PRESS AND PUBLICATIONS

Head of Communications and Media Relations Kelly Rowe, Church House, Woodlands Court, Truro Business Park, Threemilestone, Truro TR4 9NH   *T:* 01872 274351
      E: kelly.rowe@truro.anglican.org
Editor of Diocesan News Leaflet Kelly Rowe (*As above*)
Editor of Online Diocesan Directory Mrs Lesley Fusher   *E:* lesley.fusher@truro.anglican.org

STEWARDSHIP

Parish Support Advisers Mrs Rebecca Evans, Church House, Woodlands Court, Truro Business Park, Threemilestone, Truro TR4 9NH   *T:* 01872 274351
      E: rebecca.evans@truro.anglican.org
Mrs Liz Wallace (*Same Address & Tel*)
      E: liz.wallace@truro.anglican.org

RURAL DEANS
ARCHDEACONRY OF BODMIN

Stratton Anthony Michael Windross, The Rectory, The Glebe, Week St Mary, Holsworth EX22 6UY   *T:* 01303 266217
      E: amwindross@btinternet.com
Trigg Major Audrey Anne Elkington, 4 Park Drive, Bodmin PL31 2QF   *T:* 01208 892811
      E: audrey@truro.anglican.org
Trigg Minor and Bodmin John Owen Hereward, 8 Winwell Field, Wadebridge PL27 6UJ
      E: johnhereward@hotmail.com

Wivelshire, East Christopher Mark Painter, Oaklands House, Albaston, Gunnislake PL18 9EZ   *T:* 0161 945 7876
      E: revchrispainter@gmail.com
Wivelshire, West Philip Paul Clayton Sharp, The Rectory, Barbican Road, Looe PL13 1NX
      T: 01503 263070
      E: ppsharp@tiscali.co.uk

ARCHDEACONRY OF CORNWALL

Carnmarth North Caspar James Barnard Bush, 2 The Old Orchard, Trewirgie Road, Redruth TR15 2SX   *T:* 01872 510044
      E: casparbush@gmail.com
Carnmarth South Geoffrey Kenneth Bennett, The Vicarage, Merry Mit Meadow, Budock Water, Falmouth TR11 5DW   *T:* 01326 376422
      E: g.k.bennett@amserve.net
Kerrier David George Miller, St Michael's Rectory, Church Lane, Helston TR13 8PF
      T: 01326 572516
      E: millerourrectory@googlemail.com
Penwith Vanda Sheila Rowe, The Rectory, Rectory Road, St Buryan, Penzance TR19 6BB
      T: 01980 610305
      E: canonvanda@gmail.com
Powder Vacancy
Pydar Hilary Lynn Samson, The Rectory, Penhale View, My Lords Road, Fraddon, St Columb TR9 6LX   *T:* 01726 860514
      E: hilarysamson@btinternet.com
St Austell Marion Lily Barrett, The Rectory, St Mewan Lane, St Mewan, St Austell PL26 7DP
      T: 01726 72679
      E: marionstmewan@btinternet.com

DIOCESE OF WINCHESTER

Founded in 676. Hampshire, except for the south-eastern quarter, in the diocese of Portsmouth, an area in the north-east, in the diocese of Guildford, a small area in the west, in the diocese of Salisbury, and one parish in the north, in the diocese of Oxford; an area of eastern Dorset; the Channel Islands.

Population 1,233,000   Area 1,130 sq m
Full-time Stipendiary Parochial Clergy 158   Benefices 141
Parishes 255   Churches 357
www.winchester.anglican.org
Overseas link dioceses: Province of Uganda, Province of Myanmar,
Provinces of Rwanda, Burundi and Republic of Congo (formerly Zaire)

BISHOP
The Rt Revd Timothy John Dakin, Wolvesey, Winchester SO23 9ND   *T:* 01962 854050
E: bishop.tim@winchester.anglican.org

BISHOP'S STAFF
Bishop's Chaplain The Revd Mat Phipps
E: mat.phipps@winchester.anglican.org

SUFFRAGAN BISHOPS
BASINGSTOKE The Rt Revd David Williams, Bishop's Lodge, Colden Lane, Old Alresford SO24 9DH   *T:* 01962 737330
E: bishop.david@winchester.anglican.org
SOUTHAMPTON The Rt Revd Dr Jonathan Frost, Bishop's House, St Mary's Church Close, Wessex Lane, Southampton SO18 2ST
T: 023 8055 3627
E: bishop.jonathan@winchester.anglican.org

ASSISTANT BISHOPS
The Rt Revd John Dennis, 7 Conifer Close, Winchester SO22 6SH   *T:* 01962 868881
The Rt Revd John Ellison, The Furrow, Evingar Road, Whitchurch RG28 7EU
T: 01256 892126
The Rt Revd Christopher Herbert, 1 Beacon Close, Boundstone, Farnham GU10 4PA
T: 01252 795600
The Rt Revd Henry Scriven, 16 East St Helens Street, Abingdon, Oxford OX14 5EA
T: 01235 536607
The Rt Revd Timothy Bavin, Alton Abbey, Abbey Road, Beech, Alton GU34 4AP
T: 01420 562145
The Rt Revd Trevor Willmott, Old Palace, The Precincts, Canterbury CT1 2EE
T: 01227 459382
F: 01227 784985
E: trevorwillmott@bishcant.org
The Rt Revd Dom Giles Hill, Alton Abbey, Abbey Road, Beech, Alton GU34 4AP
T: 01420 562145

CATHEDRAL CHURCH OF THE HOLY TRINITY, AND OF ST PETER, ST PAUL AND OF ST SWITHUN
Dean The Very Revd Catherine Ogle, 7A The Close, Winchester SO23 9LS
T: 0121 262 1840
E: coglcathome@aol.com
Canons Residentiary
The Revd Canon Sue Wallace, Cathedral Office, 9 The Close, Winchester SO23 9LS
T: 01962 857216
E: roland.riem@
winchester-cathedral.org.uk
The Revd Canon Roland Riem (*Same Address*)
Canon Principal The Revd Canon Mark Collinson (*Same Address*)   *T:* 01962 710985
E: mark.collinson@
winchester-cathedral.org
Canons
Lay Canons Mrs Annabelle Boyes, Cathedral Office, 9 The Close, Winchester SO23 9LS
T: 01962 857206
F: 01962 857201
E: annabelle.boyes@
winchester-cathedral.org.uk
Professor Lord Raymond Plant (*Same Address*)
T: 01962 857200
Mr George Medd (*Same Address & Tel*)
Mrs Debbie Thrower (*Same Address & Tel*)
Other Staff
Close Vicar The Revd Gregory Clifton-Smith, Cathedral Office, 9 The Close, Winchester SO23 9LS   *T:* 01962 857231
E: gregory.clifton-smith@winchester-cathedral.org.uk
Clerk at Law Mr Julian Hartwell (*Same Address*)   *T:* 01962 857200
Director of Music Mr Andrew Lumsden (*Same Address*)   *T:* 01962 857218
E: andrew.lumsden@
winchester-cathedral.org.uk
Assistant Director of Music Mr George Castle (*Same Address*)   *T:* 01962 857213
E: george.castle@
winchester-cathedral.org.uk

ARCHDEACONS

BOURNEMOUTH The Ven Dr Peter Rouch, Glebe House, 22 Bellflower Way, Chandlers Ford SO53 4HN   *T:* 023 8026 0955
          E: peter.rouch@winchester.anglican.org
WINCHESTER The Ven Richard Brand, 22 St John's Street, Winchester SO23 0HF
                    T: 01962 710960
          E: richard.brand@winchester.anglican.org

MEMBERS OF THE HOUSE OF CLERGY OF THE GENERAL SYNOD
Proctors for Clergy
The Rt Revd Timothy John Dakin
The Revd Andrew Micklefield
The Revd James Pitkin
The Ven Dr Peter Rouch
The Revd Dr Benjamin Sargent

MEMBERS OF THE HOUSE OF LAITY OF THE GENERAL SYNOD
Mr Simon Clift
Mrs Alison Coulter
Ms Jay Greene
Mrs Christine Fry
Mrs Lucy Moore
Mr Ian Le Marquand
Mr David Robilliard

DIGNITARIES IN CONVOCATION
The Rt Revd Timothy John Dakin

DIOCESAN OFFICERS
Chief Executive Mr Andrew Robinson, Old Alresford Place, Alresford SO24 9DH
                    T: 01962 737305
                    F: 01962 737358
     E: andrew.robinson@winchester.anglican.org
Registrar of Diocese Mrs Sue de Candole, Batt Broadbent, Minster Chambers, 42–44 Castle Street, Salisbury SP1 3TX   *T:* 01722 411141
                    F: 01722 411566
          E: registry@battbroadbent.co.uk

DIOCESAN ORGANIZATIONS
Diocesan Office Old Alresford Place, Alresford SO24 9DH   *T:* 01962 737300
                    F: 01962 737358
          W: www.winchester.anglican.org

ADMINISTRATION
Head of Operations and Chief of Staff Mr Colin Harbidge, Old Alresford Place, Alresford SO24 9DH   *T:* 01962 737307
     E: colin.harbidge@winchester.anglican.org
Head of Finance Mr Malcolm Twigger-Ross (*Same Address*)   *T:* 01962 737336

E: malcolm.twigger-ross@cofeguildford.org.uk
Head of Resource Development The Revd Anthony Smith (*Same Address*)
                    T: 01962 737342
     E: anthony.smith@winchester.anglican.org
Diocesan Synod (*Chairman, House of Clergy*) The Revd Andrew Micklefield
(*Chairman, House of Laity*) Mr Ian Newman, Meadow View, 15 Bowerwood Road, Fordingbridge SP6 1BL   *T:* 01425 653269
                    E: ian@innewman.co.uk
(*Secretary*) Mr Andrew Robinson, Old Alresford Place, Alresford SO24 9DH   *T:* 01962 737305
                    F: 01962 737358
     E: andrew.robinson@winchester.anglican.org
Board of Finance (*Chairman*) The Rt Revd Timothy John Dakin, Wolvesey, Winchester SO23 9ND   *T:* 01962 854050
     E: bishop.tim@winchester.anglican.org
Mission and Pastoral Committee (*Secretary*) (*Diocesan Records Officer/Parish Support Adviser*) Miss Jayne Tarry, Old Alresford Place, Alresford SO24 9DH   *T:* 01962 737348
     E: jayne.tarry@winchester.anglican.org
(*Editor of Diocesan Directory*) Miss Jayne Tarry (*As above*)

ADVISERS
Stewardship Adviser The Revd Gordon Randall, Old Alresford Place, Alresford SO24 9DH
                    T: 01962 737323
     E: gordon.randall@winchester.anglican.org
Head of Human Resources Ms Susan Beckett (*Same Address*)   *T:* 01962 737353
     E: susan.beckett@winchester.anglican.org
Diocesan Environmental Officer The Revd Gordon Randall (*Same Address*)
                    T: 01962 737323
     E: gordon.randall@winchester.anglican.org

CHURCH BUILDINGS
Head of DAC, Pastoral and Closed Churches Mrs Cath Roberts, Old Alresford Place
                    T: 01962 737306
               E: catherine.roberts@
                    winchester.anglican.org

CLERGY RETIREMENT OFFICERS
Archdeaconry of Bournemouth The Revd Canon Peter Doores   *T:* 01420 88794
          E: peter@doores.myzen.co.uk
Archdeaconry of Winchester The Revd Michael Kenning   *T:* 01256 87989
     E: michael.kenning@telorycoed.co.uk

CLERGY WIDOWS' AND WIDOWERS' OFFICER
The Revd Barry Kent   *T:* 01425 616670
          E: barrykent@minster.com

COMMUNICATIONS

Communications Officer Mr Ben Frankel, Luther Pendragon   *T:* 01962 737325
out of hours: 020 7618 9197
E: dioceseofwinchester@luther.co.uk

DIOCESAN RECORD OFFICES

Southampton City Record Office Southampton City Record Office, Civic Centre, Southampton SO14 7LY
(Archivist) Mrs Sue Woolgar
T: 023 8083 2251
E: city.archives@southampton.gov.uk
Hampshire Record Office Hampshire Record Office, Sussex Street, Winchester SO23 8TH
(Archivist) Janet Smith   *T:* 01962 846154
E: enquiries.archives@hants.gov.uk
Guernsey Island Archives Guernsey Island Archives, St Barnabas, Cornet Street, St Peter Port, Guernsey GY1 1LF   *T:* 01481 724512
F: 01481 715814
E: archives@gov.gg
Jersey Archive Service Jersey Archive Service, Clarence Rd, St Helier, Jersey JE2 4JY
(Archivist) Linda Romeril   *T:* 01534 833300
F: 01534 833301
E: archives@jerseyheritagetrust.org

DISCIPLESHIP AND MINISTRY (SCHOOL OF MISSION)

Canon Principal to School of Mission The Revd Canon Mark Collinson, Wolvesey, Winchester SO23 9ND   *T:* 01962 710985
E: mark.collinson@winchester.anglican.org
Vocations Adviser and Diocesan Director of Ordinands The Revd Dr Marcus Throup
T: 01962 710984
E: marcus.throup@winchester.anglican.org
Mission and Training Adviser Preb Paul Dunthorne   *T:* 01962 710980
E: paul.dunthorne@winchester.anglican.org
Evangelism, Church Growth and Fresh Expressions Adviser The Revd Phil Dykes, Wolvesey, Winchester SO23 9ND   *T:* 01962 710973
Diocesan Children and Families Adviser Mr Andy Saunders *(Same Address)*   *T:* 01962 710972
E: andy.saunders@winchester.anglican.org
Diocesan Youth Adviser Ms Sarah Long *(Same Address)*   *T:* 01962 710971
E: sarah.long@winchester.anglican.org

EDUCATION

Director of Education The Revd Jeff Williams, First Floor, Peninsular House, Wharf Road, Portsmouth PO2 8HB   *T:* 023 9289 9680
E: jeff.williams@portsmouth.anglican.org

SAFEGUARDING AND INCLUSION

Safeguarding Adviser Vacancy

AREA DEANS

ARCHDEACONRY OF BOURNEMOUTH

Bournemouth Jennifer Carol Nightingale, 13 Brackendale Road, Bournemouth BH8 9HY
T: 01202 533356
E: jennynightingale@sky.com
Christchurch Gary James Philbrick, The Rectory, 71 Church Street, Fordingbridge SP6 1BB   *T:* 01425 839622
E: gary.philbrick@dsl.pipex.com
Eastleigh Fiona Caroline Gibbs, 16 Elliot Rise, Hedge End, Southampton SO30 2RU
T: 01489 795443
E: revfigibbs@gmail.com
Lyndhurst Peter Brian Christopher Salisbury, The Vicarage, Grove Road, Lymington SO41 3RF   *T:* 01590 673847
E: peter@lymingtonchurch.org
Romsey Vacancy
Southampton Jane Judith Bakker, The Vicarage, 41 Station Road, Southampton SO19 8FN
T: 023 8044 8337
E: jjbakker@tiscali.co.uk

ARCHDEACONRY OF WINCHESTER

Alresford Graham Philip Bowkett, The Rectory, The Goodens, Cheriton, Alresford SO24 0QH
T: 01962 771226
E: rector@upperitchen.org
Alton Vacancy
Andover John Patrick Harkin, St Mary's Vicarage, Church Close, Andover SP10 1DP
T: 01264 362268
E: harkin12@btinternet.com
Basingstoke Richard John St Clair Harlow, The Rectory, The Green, Tadley RG26 3PB
T: 07875-969128
E: richard73harlow@aol.com
Odiham Marion Elizabeth de Quidt, The Vicarage, London Road, Hook RG27 9EG
T: 01372 209630
E: marion@stmarysfetcham.org.uk
Whitchurch Craig Laurence Marshall, The Vicarage, St Mary Bourne, Andover SP11 6AY
T: 01278 734777
E: craig785@btinternet.com
Winchester Karen Patricia Kousseff, 15 Long Barrow Close, South Wonston, Winchester SO21 3ED   *T:* 01962 885114
E: kkousseff@tiscali.co.uk

The Channel Islands

The Channel Islands were formerly part of the Diocese of Coutances, Normandy, but were transferred in 1499/1500 to the Diocese of Winchester by Papal Bull, confirmed in a letter from Henry VII to Thomas Langton, the Bishop of Winchester. After some years in which the Bishops of Coutances continued to exercise *de facto* jurisdiction over the Islands, the transfer to the Diocese of Winchester was put beyond doubt by a letter from Elizabeth I in 1568 and an Order in Council dated 11 March 1569. The Order in Council directed that Henry VII's letter should not henceforth be brought into question and that the Islands and the Diocese were 'perpetually united'. The physical remoteness of the Channel Islands meant that bishops from England did not visit the Islands until 1818, although improved communications and travel in recent times have enabled a more normal relationship between the Deaneries in the Islands and the Diocese. The Deans of Jersey and Guernsey are members of the Diocesan Synod and the Bishop's Council, and the Bishops of Winchester, Basingstoke and Southampton frequently minister in the Islands.

The Channel Islands fall under the Ordinary jurisdiction of the Bishop of Winchester. They are, however, unusual in a number of ways. Jersey has its own Canons, originally promulgated in 1623 and revised extensively in 2011, which recognize the Bishop of Winchester's Ordinary jurisdiction. Guernsey has no written Canons, but follows the English Canons closely. Measures of the General Synod do not automatically apply in the Channel Islands but may be applied, with or without variation, by a scheme made by the Bishop of Winchester under the Measure in accordance with the Channel Islands (Church Legislation) Measure 1931, following consultation with the Islands. In some limited circumstances (e.g. where a Measure affects the formularies of the Church of England) a Measure may be extended to the Channel Islands by express provision in the Measure itself.

The Deans of Jersey and Guernsey hold Commissary powers from the Bishop of Winchester and may institute, collate or license clergy in the Islands at the Bishop's request. They are also Commissioned as presidents of the Ecclesiastical Courts and may grant marriage licences, including special licences and faculties. The Guernsey Ecclesiastical Court retains its jurisdiction in matters concerning probate and may issue Letters of Administration in matters of personalty.

The Deans of Jersey and Guernsey are recognized in a number of ways in civic society by virtue of their office. The Dean of Jersey is an *ex officio* member of the States, the Island's Parliament, although he does not have a vote. The Dean of Guernsey is not a member of the States of Deliberation (the Island's Parliament) but he is a member of the States of Election which appoints Jurats to the Royal Court.

Since 1875 the Dean of Jersey has always been Rector of St Helier. The Dean of Guernsey has usually been Rector of the Town Church in St Peter Port, but this has not always been the case. In addition to the twelve ancient parishes in Jersey and ten in Guernsey which form the basis of local life and government, there are five newer congregations in Jersey and three in Guernsey.

The deaneries of Jersey and Guernsey are now under the episcopal supervision of the Bishop of Dover and administration has passed to the Diocese of Canterbury.

Dean of Jersey The Very Revd Mike Keirle, The Deanery, David Place, St Helier, Jersey CI JE2 4TE   *Tel:* 01534 720001
email: mrkeirle@cwgsg.net

Dean of Guernsey The Very Revd Timothy Barker, St Andrew's Rectory, Route de St Andre, St Andrew, Guernsey GY6 8XN
Tel: 01481 238568
email: deanofguernsey@gmail.com

Founded in 679. Worcestershire, except for a few parishes in the south, in the diocese of Gloucester, and in the north, in the diocese of Birmingham, Dudley; a few parishes in Wolverhampton, Sandwell and in northern Gloucestershire.

Population 883,000   Area 670 sq m
Full-time Stipendiary Parochial Clergy 110   Benefices 94
Parishes 169   Churches 276
Overseas link dioceses: Peru (Province of Southern Cone), Morogoro (Province of Tanzania) and Propstei Stendal-Magdeburg (EMD-EKD)

BISHOP (113th)
The Rt Revd John Geoffrey Inge, The Bishop's Office, The Old Palace, Worcester WR1 2JE
T: 01905 731599
F: 01905 739382
E: bishop.worcester@cofe-worcester.org.uk

SUFFRAGAN BISHOP
DUDLEY The Rt Revd Graham Usher, Bishop's House, Bishop's Walk, Cradley Heath B64 7RH
T: 0121 550 3407
F: 0121 550 7340
E: bishopsofficedudley@cofe-worcester.org.uk

ASSISTANT BISHOP
The Rt Revd Michael Hooper, 6 Avon Drive, Eckington, Pershore, Worcs WR10 3BU
T: 01386 751589
The Rt Revd Christopher Mayfield, Harwood House, 54 Primrose Crescent, Worcester WR5 3HT
T: 01905 764822
The Rt Revd Mark Santer, 81 Clarence Road, Moseley, Birmingham B13 9UH
T: 0121 441 2194
The Rt Revd Humphrey Taylor, 10 High Street, Honeybourne, Evesham WR10 7PQ
T: 01386 934846
The Rt Revd Anthony Priddis, Round Oak Cottage, Bridstow, Ross-on-Wye HR9 6QJ
T: 01989 218503
The Rt Revd Jonathan Goodall, Tree Tops, The Mount, Caversham, Reading RG4 7RE
T: 0118 948 1038
E: office@ebbsfleet.org.uk
The Rt Revd Robert Paterson, Cedar House, 63 Greenhill, Evesham WR11 4LX
T: 01386 247105
E: mar.erskine@me.com

CATHEDRAL CHURCH OF CHRIST AND THE BLESSED MARY THE VIRGIN OF WORCESTER
Dean The Very Revd Peter Gordon Atkinson, The Deanery, 10 College Green, Worcester WR1 2LH
T: 01905 732939
01905 732909 (office)
E: peteratkinson@worcestercathedral.org.uk

Canons Residentiary The Revd Canon Dr Alvyn Pettersen, 2 College Green, Worcester WR1 2LH
T: 01905 732942
E: alvynpettersen@worcestercathedral.org.uk
The Revd Canon Dr Georgina Byrne, 15B College Green, Worcester WR1 2LH
T: 01905 732900
E: georginabyrne@worcestercathedral.org.uk
The Revd Canon Dr Michael Brierley, 15A College Green, Worcester WR1 2LH
T: 01905 732940
E: michaelbrierley@worcestercathedral.org.uk

Canons
Lay Canons Mrs Vanessa Godfrey, Chapter Office, 8 College Yard, Worcester WR1 2LA
Dr David Bryer (Same Address)
Miss Anne Penn (Same Address)
Other Staff
Cathedral Steward Mrs Val Floy, Chapter Office, 8 College Yard, Worcester WR1 2LA
T: 01905 732907
E: valfloy@worcestercathedral.org.uk
Organist and Director of Music Dr Peter Nardone, 5A College Yard, Worcester WR1 2LA
T: 01905 732916
E: peternardone@worcestercathedral.org.uk

ARCHDEACONS
WORCESTER The Ven Robert Jones, The Archdeacon's House, Walker's Lane, Whittington, Worcester WR5 2RE
T: 01905 773301
E: kjones@cofe-worcester.org.uk
DUDLEY The Ven Nikki Groarke, 15 Worcester Road, Droitwich WR9 8AA   T: 01905 773301
E: kjones@cofe-worcester.org.uk

MEMBERS OF THE HOUSE OF CLERGY OF THE GENERAL SYNOD
Proctors for Clergy
The Revd Wyn Beynon
The Revd Dr Sarah Brush
The Ven Nikki Groarke

MEMBERS OF THE HOUSE OF LAITY OF THE GENERAL SYNOD
Mrs Susan Adeney
Ms Kashmir Garton
Mr Robin Lunn

DIOCESAN OFFICERS
Diocesan Secretary Mr Robert Higham, The Old Palace, Deansway, Worcester WR1 2JE
T: 01905 20537
Chancellor of Diocese The Worshipful Dr Charles Mynors
Registrar of Diocese and Bishop's Legal Secretary Mr Stuart Ness, Messrs Stallard, March & Edwards, 8 Sansome Walk, Worcester WR1 1LN
T: 01905 723561
F: 01905 723812
Deputy Diocesan Registrar Jack Smith (*Same Address*)
Diocesan Surveyor Mr Mark Wild, The Old Palace, Deansway, Worcester WR1 2JE
T: 01905 20537

DIOCESAN ORGANIZATIONS
Diocesan Office The Old Palace, Deansway, Worcester WR1 2JE
T: 01905 20537
F: 01905 612302

ADMINISTRATION
Diocesan Secretary Mr Robert Higham, The Old Palace, Deansway, Worcester WR1 2JE
T: 01905 20537
Assistant Diocesan Secretary (Finance) Mr Stephen Lindner (*Same Address*)
DAC Secretary Mr John Dentith (*Same Address*)
Diocesan Synod (*Chair, House of Clergy*) The Revd Wyn Beynon
(*Chair, House of Laity*) Dr Andew Quinn
Diocesan Board of Finance (*Chair of DBF*) Canon Alastair Findlay
(*Company Secretary*) Mr Robert Higham, The Old Palace, Deansway, Worcester WR1 2JE
T: 01905 20537
Diocesan Mission, Pastoral and Resources Committee (being the Diocesan Mission Pastoral Committee) (*Secretary*) Mr Robert Higham (*As above*)
Parsonages Committee (*Chair*) Mr Robert Pearce, c/o The Old Palace, Deansway, Worcester WR1 2JE
(*Secretary*) Mr Stephen Lindner, The Old Palace, Deansway, Worcester WR1 2JE
Investment and Glebe Committee (*Chair*) Mr Eric Wiles (*Same Address*)
(*Secretary*) Mr Stephen Lindner (*Same Address*)
(*Glebe Agent*) Mr Anthony Champion, Halls (Midlands) LLP, 1 Kings Court, Charles Hastings Way, Worcester WR5 1JR
T: 01905 728444

Mission & Pastoral Committee Mr Robert Higham, The Old Palace, Deansway, Worcester WR1 2JE
T: 01905 20537
Board of Patronage Mr Robert Higham (*As above*)
(*Designated Officer*) Mr Robert Higham (*As above*)
Diocesan Trustees Mr Stuart Ness, Messrs Stallard, March & Edwards, 8 Sansome Walk, Worcester WR1 1LN
T: 01905 723561
F: 01905 723812

CHURCH BUILDINGS
Advisory Committee for the Care of Churches (*Chair*) Mr Ian Stainburn, c/o The Old Palace, Deansway, Worcester WR1 2JE
(*Secretary*) Mr John Dentith, The Old Palace, Deansway, Worcester WR1 2JE
Change Ringers Association Mr D. Andrews

DIOCESAN RECORD OFFICES
County Archivist Adrian Gregson, The Hive, Sawmill Walk, The Butts, Worcester WR5 3PA
T: 01905 766530
F: 01905 766363
Dudley Archives and Local History Department Dudley Archives and Local History Department, Tipton Road, Dudley DY1 4SQ
(*Archivists*) Helen Donald
Robert Bennett
T: 01384 812770

EDUCATION
Board of Education (*Chair*) Mr Bryan Allbutt
T: 01905 452169
(*Director of Education*) Mrs Margaret James, The Old Palace, Deansway, Worcester WR1 2JE
E: mjames@cofe-worcester.org.uk

MISSION AND UNITY
Ecumenical Officer The Revd David Ryan, The Old Palace, Deansway, Worcester WR1 2JE

PRESS AND PUBLICATIONS
Diocesan Communications Officer and Bishop's Press Officer Samantha Setchell, The Old Palace, Deansway, Worcester WR1 2JE
T: 07852 302516
Editor of the Diocesan Directory Mrs Alison Vincent (*Same Address*)

RETIRED CLERGY
Deans of Retired Clergy The Revd Judith Liley, The Old Palace, Deansway, Worcester WR1 2JE
The Ven Chris Liley (*Same Address*)

SAFEGUARDING OFFICE
Diocesan Safeguarding Officer Mrs Hilary Higton, c/o The Old Palace, Deansway, Worcester WR1 2JE
T: 07495 060869
E: hhigton@cofe-worcester.org.uk

SOCIAL RESPONSIBILITY
Commission for Social Responsibility (Chairman)
The Revd Richard Clark

TRAINING AND MINISTRY
Director of Ministry and Discipleship The Revd
Canon Jonathan Kimber, The Old Palace,
Deansway, Worcester WR1 2JE
Diocesan Director of Ordinands and Vocation
The Revd John Fitzmaurice (*Same Address*)
Dean of Women's Ministry Vacancy
Children's Officer Mrs Emma Pettifer, The Old
Palace, Deansway, Worcester WR1 2JE
Youth Officer Mr Simon Hill (*Same Address*)
Calling Young Disciples Project Director The
Revd Ruth Walker (*Same Address*)
Mission Development Officers The Revd Doug
Chaplin (*Same Address*)
          E: dchaplin@cofe-worcester.org.uk
The Revd Phillip Jones, 7 Egremont Gardens,
Worcester WR4 0QH   *T:* 01905 755037
          E: phillip.jones@cofe-worcester.org.uk
Stewardship Officer The Revd Alison Maddocks,
The Palace, Deansway, Worcester WR1 2JE

RURAL DEANS
ARCHDEACONRY OF DUDLEY
Bromsgrove Paul Lawlor, The Vicarage, 219 St
George's Road, Redditch B98 8EE
          T: 01527 62375
          E: paul@pjlawlor.me.uk
Droitwich Sheila Kathryn Banyard, The
Rectory, 205 Worcester Road, Droitwich WR9
8AS   *T:* 01905 773134
          E: sk.banyard@virgin.net
Dudley Dominic Melville, 506 Bromsgrove
Road, Hunnington, Halesowen B62 0JJ
          T: 0121-550 7426
          E: domelville@orange.net

Kidderminster Hugh Anthony Burton, The
Rectory, 30 Leswell Street, Kidderminster
DY10 1RP   *T:* 01562 824490
          E: hugh.burton@kidderminstereast.org.uk
Kingswinford David James Hoskin, The
Vicarage, Maughan Street, Quarry Bank,
Brierley Hill DY5 2DN   *T:* 01384 565480
          E: davidhoskin@supanet.com
Stourbridge Andrew Keith Sillis, The Vicarage,
34 South Road, Stourbridge DY8 3YB
          T: 01562 884 155
          E: asillis@aol.com
Stourport Mark Turner, 14 Dunley Road,
Stourport-on-Severn DY13 0AX
          T: 01299 829557
          E: revmturner@tiscali.co.uk

ARCHDEACONRY OF WORCESTER
Evesham Richard James Gordon Thorniley,
The Rectory, Station Road, Harvington,
Evesham WR11 8NJ   *T:* 01386 870527
          E: richardgill@rthorniley.fsnet.co.uk
Malvern Vacancy
Martley and Worcester West David Royston
Sherwin, The Rectory, Martley, Worcester
WR6 6QA   *T:* 01886 888664
          E: davidwin56@aol.com
Pershore Susan Kathryn Renshaw, The
Vicarage, Drakes Bridge Road, Eckington,
Pershore WR10 3BN   *T:* 01386 750203
          E: canonsusan@btinternet.com
Upton Christopher Ashley Moss, The Vicarage,
Longdon, Tewkesbury GL20 6AT
          T: 01684 833256
          E: cmoss@holyplace.feeserve.co.uk
Worcester East Charles Leslie Thomas, The
Vicarage, Cranham Drive, Worcester WR4
9PA   *T:* 01905 754385
          E: revcharlesthomas@gmail.com

DIOCESE OF YORK

Founded in 627. York; East Riding of Yorkshire, except for an area in the south-west, in the diocese of Sheffield; Kingston-upon-Hull; Redcar and Cleveland; Middlesbrough; the eastern half of North Yorkshire; Stockton-on-Tees, south of the Tees; an area of Leeds.

Population 1,438,000   Area 2,670 sq m
Full-time Stipendiary Parochial Clergy 201   Benefices 245
Parishes 447   Churches 588
www.dioceseofyork.org.uk
Overseas link dioceses: Cape Town (South Africa), Mechelen-Brussels (Belgium)

ARCHBISHOP (97th)
The Most Revd and Rt Hon Dr Sentamu, Bishopthorpe Palace, Bishopthorpe, York YO23 2GE

BISHOP'S STAFF
Chief of Staff The Revd Malcolm Macnaughton
T: 01904 772362
E: malcolm.macnaughton@
archbishopofyork.org
Chaplain and Researcher The Revd Dr Daphne Green
E: daphne.green@archbishopofyork.org
Domestic Chaplain The Revd Richard Carew
E: richard.carew@archbishopofyork.org
Communications Officer Mrs Elizabeth Addy
E: elizabeth.addy@archbishopofyork.org

SUFFRAGAN BISHOPS
BEVERLEY The Rt Revd Glyn Webster, Holy Trinity Rectory, Micklegate, York YO1 6LE
T: 01904 628155
E: office@seeofbeverley.org
HULL The Rt Revd Alison White, Hullen House, Woodfield Lane, Hessle HU13 0ES
T: 01482 649019
F: 01482 647449
E: bishopofhull@yorkdiocese.org
SELBY The Rt Revd Dr John Bromilow Thomson, The Vicarage, York Road, Selby YO8 5JP
E: bishopofselby@yorkdiocese.org
WHITBY The Rt Revd Paul John Ferguson, 21 Thornton Road, Stainton, Middlesbrough TS8 9DS
T: 01642 593273
E: bishopofwhitby@yorkdiocese.org

ASSISTANT BISHOPS
The Rt Revd Nicholas Baines, Bishopscroft, Ashwell Road, Bradford BD9 4AU
The Rt Revd Gordon Bates, 19 Fernwood Close, Brompton, Northallerton DL6 2UX
T: 01609 761586
The Rt Revd Graham Cray, The Dovecote, Main Street, Kirby Misperton, Malton YO17 6XL
E: grahamcray@btconnect.com

The Rt Revd David Charles James, 7 Long Lane, Beverley HU17 0NH
T: 01482 871240
E: davidjames43@karoo.co.uk
The Rt Revd James Stuart Jones, c/o The Diocese of York, Amy Johnson Way, Clifton Moor, York YO30 4XT
T: 01904 699500
The Rt Revd David Smith, 34 Cedar Glade, Dunnington, York YO19 5QZ
T: 01904 481225
E: david@djmhs.force9.co.uk
The Rt Revd Martin Wallace, 28 Alexandra Court, Bridlington YO15 2LB
T: 01262 670265
E: mdw28@btinternet.com

CATHEDRAL CHURCH OF ST PETER
Dean The Very Revd Vivienne Faull, Church House, 10–14 Ogleforth, York YO1 7JN
T: 01904 557202 (office)
E: viviennef@yorkminster.org
Canons Residentiary
Precentor The Revd Canon Peter Moger, 2 Minster Court, York YO1 7JJ
T: 01904 557205 (office)
01904 557265 (home)
E: precentor@yorkminster.org
Canon Chancellor The Revd Canon Dr Christopher Collingwood, 3 Minster Court, York YO1 7JJ
T: 01904 557205 (Office)
01904 557267 (Home)
E: christopherc@yorkminster.org
Canon Pastor The Revd Canon Michael Smith, 4 Minster Yard, York YO1 7JD
T: 01904 557205 (office)
01904 557264 (Home)
E: michaels@yorkminster.org
Succentor Catriona Cumming, 2A Minster Court, York YO1 7JJ
E: catrionac@yorkminster.org
Canons
Lay Canons Canon Dr Andrew Green, c/o Church House, 10–14 Ogleforth, York YO1 7JN
E: andrewgreen@bpipoly.com
Canon Dr Julia Winkley (*Same Address*)
E: juleswinkley@gmail.com
Canon Neil Harkin (*Same Address*)
E: neil.harkin@what-group.co.uk

Canon Dr Richard Shephard (*Same Address*)
E: richardshep49@gmail.com
Other Staff
Chapter Steward Kathryn Blacker, Church
House, 10-14 Ogleforth, York YO1 7JN
T: 01904 557212
E: kathrynb@yorkminster.org
Director of Finance Eve Hartrick (*Same Address*)
T: 01904 559212
E: eveh@yorkminster.org
Superintendent of Works Paul Greene, The
Works Department, 4 Deangate, York YO1
7JA   T: 01904 559525
E: paulg@yorkminster.org
Communications Director Sharon Atkinson,
Church House, 10–14 Ogleforth, York YO1
7JN   T: 01904 557248
E: sharona@yorkminster.org
Director of Learning and Participation Richard
Butterfield (*Same Address*)   T: 01904 559543
E: richardb@yorkminster.org
Director of Music Mr Robert Sharpe (*Same
Address*)   T: 01904 557205
E: roberts@yorkminster.org
Human Resources Ruth Dunlop, Church House,
10-14 Ogleforth, York YO1 7JN
T: 01904 559212
E: ruthd@yorkminster.org
Headmaster Mr Alex Donaldson, The Minster
School, York YO1 7JP   T: 0844 939 0000
E: hm@yorkminster.org
Chapter Clerk Mr Andrew Oates, Church
House, 10–14 Ogleforth, York YO1 7JN
T: 01904 557210
E: chapterclerk@yorkminster.org
Minster Police Minster Police, York Minster,
York YO1 7HH   T: 01904 557222
E: police@yorkminster.org

ARCHDEACONS

YORK The Ven Sarah Bullock, 1 New Lane,
Huntington, York YO32 9NU
T: 01904 557222
E: adyk@yorkdiocese.org
THE EAST RIDING The Ven Andy Broom, Brimley
Lodge, 27 Molescroft Road, Beverley HU17
7DX   E: ader@yorkdiocese.org
CLEVELAND The Ven Samantha Rushton, 48
Langbaurgh Road, Hutton Rudby, Yarm TS15
0HL   T: 01642 706095
E: adcl@yorkdiocese.org

MEMBERS OF THE HOUSE OF CLERGY OF THE GENERAL SYNOD

Proctors for Clergy
The Ven Sarah Bullock
The Revd Jacqueline Doyle-Brett
The Revd Adam Gaunt
The Revd Paul Hutchinson
The Revd Rowan Williams

MEMBERS OF THE HOUSE OF LAITY OF THE GENERAL SYNOD

Canon Linda Ali
Mrs Heather Black
Mrs Rosalind Brewer
Miss Lucy Gorman
Dr Nick Land
Mr Mike Stallybrass

DIOCESAN OFFICERS

Diocesan Secretary Canon Peter Warry, The
Diocese of York, Amy Johnson Way, Clifton
Moor, York YO30 4XT   T: 01904 699500
F: 01904 699501
Chancellor of Diocese The Rt Worshipful Peter
Collier, c/o The Registry, Stamford House,
Piccadilly, York YO1 9PP
*Registrar of Diocese and Archbishop's Legal
Secretary* Mrs Caroline F. Mockford, The
Registry, Stamford House, Piccadilly, York YO1
9PP   T: 01904 623487
F: 01904 611458

DIOCESAN ORGANIZATIONS

Diocesan Office The Diocese of York, Amy
Johnson Way, Clifton Moor, York YO30 4XT
T: 01904 699500
F: 01904 699501
E: office@yorkdiocese.org
W: www.dioceseofyork.org.uk

ADMINISTRATION

Diocesan Synod (*Chairman, House of Clergy*) The
Revd Tim Robinson, The Vicarage, Baxtons
Road, Helmsley YO62 5HT   T: 01439 770983
E: revtimrobinson@gmail.com
(*Chairman, House of Laity*) Dr Nick Land, Low
Farm House, Ingleby Greenhow, Great Ayton,
Middlesbrough TS9 6RG
E: drnickland@aol.com
(*Secretary*) Canon Peter Warry, The Diocese of
York, Amy Johnson Way, Clifton Moor, York
YO30 4XT   T: 01904 699500
F: 01904 699501
(*Assistant Diocesan Secretary*) Ms Shirley Davies
(*Same Address*)
Board of Finance (*Chairman*) Mrs Maureen
Loffill (*Same Address*)
(*Secretary*) Mrs Catherine Evans (*Same Address*)
(*Finance Manager*) Mrs Catherine Evans (*As
above*)
(*Diocesan Surveyor and Estates Manager*) Mr
Graham Andrews (*Same Address*)
Pastoral and Mission Committee Ms Shirley
Davies (*Same Address*)
(*Designated Officer*) Canon Peter Warry (*Same
Address*)   T: 01904 699500
F: 01904 699501
Property Sub-Committee Mr Graham Andrews
(*Same Address*)

CHILDREN AND YOUTH

East Riding Adviser Jon Steel, 2 Appin Close, Bransholme, Hull HU7 5BB   *T:* 01482 828805
M: 07736 378051
York Adviser Vacancy
Cleveland Advisers The Revd and Mrs Andrew and Jo Bowden, Chapel House, Back Lane, West Lutton, Malton YO17 8TF
T: 07544 705064
E: andy@woldsvalley.plus.com

CHURCH BUILDINGS

Advisory Committee for the Care of Churches (*Chairman*) The Revd Canon John Weetman, The Abbey Vicarage, 31a Leeds Road, Selby YO8 4HX   *T:* 01757 705130
(*Secretary*) Ms Catherine Copp, The Diocese of York, Amy Johnson Way, Clifton Moor, York YO30 4XT
(*Church Buildings Adviser*) Mr Philip Thomas (*Same Address*)
Closed Churches Ms Shirley Davies (*Same Address*)

COMMUNICATIONS

Communications Officer Mr Martin Sheppard, The Diocese of York, Amy Johnson Way, Clifton Moor, York YO30 4XT
E: martin.sheppard@yorkdiocese.org

DIOCESAN RECORD OFFICES

Borthwick Institute of Historical Research The Borthwick Institute of Historical Research, University of York, Heslington, York YO10 5DD
(*Director and Diocesan Archivist*) Christopher C. Webb   *T:* 01904 321166
East Riding of Yorkshire Archive Office East Riding of Yorkshire Archive Office, County Hall, Beverley HU17 9BA
(*Archivist*) Mr Ian Mason (*Same Address*)
T: 01482 392790
E: ian.mason@eastriding.gov
North Yorkshire County Record Office North Yorkshire County Record Office, Malpas Road, Northallerton DL7 8PB
(*Acting County Archivist*) Mrs Judith A. Smeaton   *T:* 01609 777585
Cleveland County Archives Department Cleveland County Archives Department, Exchange House, 6 Marton Road, Middlesbrough TS1 1DB
(*Archivist*) Mr D. Tyrell   *T:* 01642 248321

ECUMENICAL ADVISERS

York Archdeaconry The Revd Andrew Clements, The Vicarage, 80 Osbaldwick Lane, York YO10 3AX   *T:* 01904 416763
E: andrew@ozmurt.freeserve.co.uk
East Riding Archdeaconry Vacancy
Cleveland Archdeaconry Canon Stella Vernon

EDUCATION

Diocesan Director of Education Mr Andrew Smith, The Diocese of York, Amy Johnson Way, Clifton Moor, York YO30 4XT
Deputy Director of Education Mrs Claire Graham-Brown
School Effectiveness Adviser Mrs Alison Smith
Education Adviser and Siams Manager Mrs Olivia Seymour
School Development Advisers Mrs Katherine Humpleby
Ms Helen Wren
Mrs Chelo Brooks, The Diocese of York, Amy Johnson Way, Clifton Moor, York YO30 4XT
E: chelo.brooks@yorkdiocese.org
School Buildings Officer Simon Quartermaine

LITURGICAL

York Diocesan Worship and Liturgical Group The Revd Canon Peter Moger, 2 Minster Court, York YO1 7JJ   *T:* 01904 557205 (office)
01904 557265 (home)
E: precentor@yorkminster.org

MINISTRY AND MISSION

Director of Training for Missional Ministry The Revd Dr Gavin Wakefield, The Diocese of York, Amy Johnson Way, Clifton Moor, York YO30 4XT   *T:* 01904 699504
E: gavin.wakefield@yorkdiocese.org
Director of York School of Ministry Mrs Lynn Comer (*Same Address & Tel*)
E: lynncomer@yorkdiocese.org
Diocesan Adviser on Vocations The Revd David Mann, 64 Strensall Road, Huntington, York YO32 9SH   *T:* 01904 768668
E: david.mann@yorkdiocese.org
Dean of Self Supporting Ministry The Revd Dr Julie Watson, 25 Fox Lane, Thorpe Willoughby, Selby YO8 9NA   *T:* 01757 703123
E: julie301watson@btinternet.com
Dean of Women's Ministry The Revd Canon Elaine Bielby, St Helen's Vicarage, Welton, Brough HU15 1ND   *T:* 01482 666677
E: ebielby@ebielby.karoo.co.uk
Warden of Readers The Ven Samantha Rushton, 48 Langbaurgh Road, Hutton Rudby, Yarm TS15 0HL   *T:* 01642 706095
F: 01642 706097
E: adcl@yorkdiocese.org

SAFEGUARDING

Safeguarding Adviser Julie O'Hara, The Diocese of York, Amy Johnson Way, Clifton Moor, York YO3 4XT
E: safeguarding@yorkdiocese.org
Independent Chair Dr Susan Proctor, The Diocese of York, Amy Johnson Way, Clifton Moor, York YO30 4XT

RURAL DEANS
ARCHDEACONRY OF CLEVELAND
Guisborough Rachel Elizabeth Harrison, St Peter's Vicarage, 66 Aske Road, Redcar TS10 2BP   *T:* 01642 489842
                    E: rachelhere@hotmail.com
Middlesbrough Dominic Paul Black, The Vicarage, James Street, North Ormesby, Middlesbrough TS3 6LD   *T:* 01642 271814
           E: dominic.black@trinitycentre.org
Mowbray Fiona Ruth Mayer-Jones, 27 Mowbray Road, Northallerton DL6 1QT
                    T: 07450 402953
                    E: fionaruth@gmail.com
Northern Ryedale Timothy James Robinson, The Vicarage, Baxtons Road, Helmsley, York YO62 5HT   *T:* 01439 770983
           E: tim.robinson123@btinternet.com
Stokesley William John Ford, The Rectory, 6 Westgate, Yarm TS15 9QT   *T:* 01642 964664
                    E: revjohnford@sky.com
Whitby Michael George Timothy Gobbett, The Rectory, Chubb Hill Road, Whitby YO21 1JP   *T:* 01740 620274
           E: michael.gobbett@btinternet.com

ARCHDEACONRY OF THE EAST RIDING
Beverley Richard Francis Parkinson, The Rectory, Main Street, Cherry Burton, Beverley HU17 7RF   *T:* 01964 503036
                    E: richard@poiema.co.uk
Bridlington Matthew Rupert Pollard, The Rectory, Church Green, Bridlington YO16 7JX   *T:* 01262 672221
           E: matthewrpollard@btinternet.com
Central and North Hull Timothy Martin Harley Boyns, All Saints' Vicarage, 4 Chestnut Avenue, Hessle HU13 0RH   *T:* 01482 648555
           E: timboyns@timboyns.karoo.co.uk
East Hull Timothy Martin Harley Boyns, All Saints' Vicarage, 4 Chestnut Avenue, Hessle HU13 0RH   *T:* 01482 648555
           E: timboyns@timboyns.karoo.co.uk
Harthill Jacqueline Anne Tonkin, Monument Lodge, Back Street, Langtoft, Driffield YO25 3TD   *T:* 01377 267321
           E: jacki.tonkin1@btinternet.com

Holderness, North Anne Margaret White, The Vicarage, Carlton Drive, Aldbrough, Hull HU11 4SF   *T:* 01964 527230
                    E: white.anne19@gmail.com
Holderness, South Susan Joy Walker, The Vicarage, Main Road, Thorngumbald, Hull HU12 9NA   *T:* 01964 601381
           E: susanwalkerfe@hotmail.co.uk
Howden Michael John Proctor, The Vicarage, 10 Station Road, South Cave, Brough HU15 2AA   *E:* revmikeproctor@gmail.com
Scarborough Michael John Leigh, St Mark's Vicarage, 77 Green Lane, Scarborough YO12 6HT   *T:* 01723 363205
                    E: mike@singingvicar.co.uk
West Hull Timothy Martin Harley Boyns, All Saints' Vicarage, 4 Chestnut Avenue, Hessle HU13 0RH   *T:* 01482 648555
           E: timboyns@timboyns.karoo.co.uk

ARCHDEACONRY OF YORK
Ainsty, New Geoffrey Robert Mumford, The Vicarage, 17 Sutor Close, Copmanthorpe, York YO23 3TX   *T:* 01904 707716
                    E: gmumford@btinternet.com
Derwent Nicholas William Randle Bird, The Rectory, 30 Church Street, Dunnington, York YO19 5PW   *T:* 01904 489349
                    E: frnick.bird@btinternet.com
Easingwold Elizabeth Claire Hassall, The Rectory, Church Hill, Crayke, York YO61 4TA
                    T: 01347 822809
                    E: revliz@trundlebug.co.uk
Selby Christopher Wilton, The Vicarage, 2 Sir John's Lane, Sherburn in Elmet, Leeds LS25 6BJ   *T:* 01977 682122
                    E: frwilton@aol.com
South Wold Rodney Nicholson, 96 Shipman Road, Market Weighton, York YO43 3RB
                    T: 01200 458019
                    E: rodnic03@gmail.com
Southern Ryedale Rachel Ann Hirst, The Vicarage, 80 Langton Road, Norton, Malton YO17 9AE   *T:* 01653 699222
           E: rachel.hirst40@googlemail.com
York Terence McDonough, The Vicarage, 1 Fulford Park, Fulford, York YO10 4QE
                    T: 01904 633261
                    E: tmcd@stoswalds.church

ROYAL PECULIARS, THE CHAPELS ROYAL, ETC.

Westminster Abbey

Description of Arms. Azure, a cross patonce between five martlets or; on a chief or France and England quarterly on a pale, between two roses, gules, seeded and barbed proper.

COLLEGIATE CHURCH OF ST PETER

The Collegiate Church of St Peter in Westminster, usually called Westminster Abbey, is a Royal Peculiar, and, as such, it is extra-provincial as well as extra-diocesan and comes directly under the personal jurisdiction of Her Majesty The Queen, who is the Visitor.

Throughout medieval times it was the Abbey Church of a great Benedictine Monastery, which was in existence at Westminster before the Norman Conquest. After the dissolution of the monastery in 1540 it became increasingly a great national shrine, where famous writers, poets, statesmen and leaders in the Church and State are buried. It is the Coronation Church, and in it also take place from time to time Royal weddings and many services on great occasions of a National or Commonwealth character. Daily, the Holy Communion is celebrated and Morning and Evening Prayers are said or sung.

THE VISITOR
The Sovereign

DEAN
The Very Revd Dr John R. Hall, The Deanery, Westminster SW1P 3PA   *T:* 020 7654 4801
F: 020 7654 4883
E: john.hall@westminster-abbey.org
W: www.westminster-abbey.org

CANONS OF WESTMINSTER
Sub-Dean and Canon Steward The Revd Canon Anthony Ball, 5 Little Cloister, London SW1P 3PL   *T:* 020 7654 4805
E: anthony.ball@westminster-abbey.org

Canon Theologian The Revd Prof Vernon P. White, 3 Little Cloister, London SW1P 3PL
T: 020 7654 4808
F: 020 7654 4811
E: vernon.white@westminster-abbey.org

Canon Treasurer and Almoner The Revd David Stanton, 1 Little Cloister, London SW1P 3PL
T: 020 7654 4804
F: 020 7654 4811
E: david.stanton@westminster-abbey.org

Rector of St Margaret's Church The Revd Jane Sinclair, 2 Little Cloister, London SW1P 3PL
T: 020 7654 4815
F: 020 7654 4811
E: jane.sinclair@westminster-abbey.org

MINOR CANONS
Precentor The Revd Christopher B. Stoltz, 6 Little Cloister, London SW1P 3PL
T: 020 7654 4855
E: christopher.stoltz@westminster-abbey.org

Sacrist The Revd Mark Birch, 6 Little Cloister, London SW1P 3PL   *T:* 020 7654 4850
E: mark.birch@westminster-abbey.org

CHAPLAIN
The Revd Jenny Petersen, The Chapter Office, 20 Dean's Yard, London SW1P 3PA
T: 020 7654 4850
E: jennifer.petersen@westminster-abbey.org

PRIESTS VICAR
The Revd Sarah Archer
The Revd Paul Bagott
The Revd Alan Boddy
The Revd Stephen Buckley
The Revd N. J. Bunker
The Revd Philip Chester
The Revd Chris Chivers
The Revd Jonathan Coore
The Revd Dominic Fenton
The Revd Ralph Godsall
The Rt Revd Jonathan Goodall
The Revd Alan Gyle
The Revd James Hawkey
The Revd Rose Hudson-Wilkin
The Rt Revd Josiah Idowu-Fearon
The Revd Laura Jørgensen
The Rt Revd Graeme Knowles
The Revd Michael Macey
The Revd Peter McGeary
The Revd Andrew Moughtin-Mumby
Preb Jonathan Osborne
The Revd Dr Fiona Stewart-Darling
The Very Revd Dr Victor Stock
The Revd Garry Swinton
The Revd Justin White
The Revd Gavin Williams

LAY OFFICERS

Receiver General and Chapter Clerk Sir Stephen Lamport KCVO DL, The Chapter Office, 20 Dean's Yard, London SW1P 3PA
T: 020 7654 4861
F: 020 7654 4914
E: stephen.lamport@westminster-abbey.org
W: www.westminster-abbey.org

Organist and Master of the Choristers Mr James O'Donnell (*Same Address*)   T: 020 7654 4854
E: music@westminster-abbey.org

Registrar Sir Stephen Lamport KCVO DL (*same address*)

Press and Communications Office (*Same Address*)
T: 020 7654 4923
E: press@westminster-abbey.org

Head of Communications Mr Duncan Jeffery (*Same Address*)   T: 020 7654 4888
F: 020 7654 4891
E: duncan.jeffery@westminster-abbey.org

Surveyor of the Fabric Mr Ptolemy Dean (*Same Address*)

Head of the Abbey Collection Dr Tony Trowles, The Muniment Room and Library, Westminster Abbey, London SW1P 3PL
T: 020 7654 4829
E: tony.trowles@westminster-abbey.org

Keeper of the Muniments Mr Matthew Payne (*Same Address*)   T: 020 7654 4829
E: matthew.payne@westminster-abbey.org

Headmaster of the Choir School Mr Jonathan Milton, Dean's Yard, London SW1P 3NY
T: 020 7654 4918
E: jonathan.milton@westminster-abbey.org

Legal Secretary Mr Christopher Vyse, The Chapter Office, 20 Dean's Yard, London SW1P 3PA   T: 020 7654 4885
E: chris.vyse@westminster-abbey.org

Auditor Mr Andrew McIntyre, Ernst & Young, 1 More London Place, London SE1 2AF
T: 020 7951 2068

Windsor

Description of Arms. The shield of St George, argent a cross gules, encircled by the Garter

THE QUEEN'S FREE CHAPEL OF ST GEORGE WITHIN HER CASTLE OF WINDSOR

A ROYAL PECULIAR

Founded by Edward III in 1348 and exempt from diocesan and provincial jurisdictions, the College of St George is a self-governing secular community of priests and laymen, the first duty of which is to celebrate Divine Service daily on behalf of the Sovereign, the Royal House and the Order of the Garter. Its present Chapel was founded by Edward IV in honour of Our Lady, St George and St Edward in 1475 and, with the cloisters and buildings annexed, is vested in the Dean and Canons. In it the Eucharist, Mattins and Evensong are sung or said daily and are open to all.

The Order of the Garter has its stalls and insignia in the Quire, where Knights and Ladies Companions are installed by the Sovereign. Beneath the Quire – the scene of many Royal funerals – are vaults in which lie the bodies of six monarchs. Elsewhere in the Chapel are the tombs of four others.

The College has its own school of 400 children, where it maintains twenty-four choristerships. It also awards an organ scholarship. A house for conferences has been established under the name of St George's House.

THE VISITOR
The Sovereign

DEAN
The Rt Revd David Conner KCVO, The Deanery, Windsor Castle, Windsor, Berkshire SL4 1NJ
T: 01753 865561

CANONS
Canon Precentor and Chaplain to the Great Park The Revd Canon Martin Poll, Chaplain's Lodge, Windsor Great Park, Windsor, Berkshire SL4 2HP   T: 01784 432434

Canon Treasurer and Warden, St George's House The Revd Canon Dr Hueston Finlay, 8 The Cloisters, Windsor Castle, Windsor, Berkshire SL4 1NJ   T: 01753 848887

Canon Steward The Revd Canon Dr Mark Powell, 6 The Cloisters, Windsor Castle, Windsor, Berkshire SL4 1NJ   T: 01753 848709

MINOR CANONS
Chaplain to St George's School The Revd Franklin Lee   T: 01753 848710

LAY OFFICERS
Chapter Clerk Miss Charlotte Manley LVO OBE, Chapter Office, 2 The Cloisters, Windsor Castle, Windsor, Berkshire SL4 1NJ
T: 01753 848888

Director of Music Mr James Vivian, 23 The Cloisters, Windsor Castle, Windsor, Berkshire SL4 1NJ   *T*: 01753 848747

Assistant Director of Music Mr Luke Bond, 3 The Cloisters, Windsor Castle, Windsor, Berkshire SL4 1NJ

Clerk of Accounts Mr Nick Grogan, 2 The Cloisters, Windsor Castle, Windsor, Berkshire SL4 1NJ   *T*: 01753 848720

Clerk of Works Mr Darren Cave, 11a The Cloisters, Windsor Castle, Windsor, Berkshire SL4 1NJ   *Tel*: 01753 848766

Archivist and Chapter Librarian Dr Clare Rider ⅲ, The Vicars' Hall Undercroft, Windsor Castle, Windsor, Berkshire SL4 1NJ   *T*: 01753 848724

Virger Mr Vaughn Wright, 22 Horseshoe Cloister, Windsor Castle, Windsor, Berkshire SL4 1NJ   *T*: 01753 848727

Head Master, St George's School Mr Christopher McDade, St George's School, Windsor Castle, Windsor, Berkshire SL4 1QF   *T*: 01753 865553

Domestic Chaplains to Her Majesty the Queen

Buckingham Palace The Revd Paul Wright
Windsor Castle The Dean of Windsor

Sandringham The Revd Jonathan Riviere

Chapels Royal

The Chapel Royal is the body of Clergy, Singers and Vestry Officers appointed to serve the spiritual needs of the Sovereign – in medieval days on Progresses through the Realm as well as upon the battlefields of Europe, as at Agincourt. Its ancient foundation is first century with the British Church: its latter day choral headquarters have been at St James's Palace since 1702 along with the Court of St James. Since 1312 the Chapel Royal has been governed by the Dean who, as the Ordinary, also exercises, along with the Sub-Dean, jurisdiction over the daughter establishments of Chapels Royal at the Tower of London and at Hampton Court Palace. Members of the public are welcome to attend Sunday and weekday services as advertised.

The Chapel Royal conducts the Service of Remembrance at the Cenotaph in Whitehall, with a Forces Chaplain in company, and combines with the choral establishment of the host abbey or cathedral on the occasion of Royal Maundy, under the governance of the Lord High Almoner and Sub-Almoner. Each Member of the College of thirty-six Chaplains to Her Majesty the Queen, headed by the Clerk and Deputy Clerk of the Closet, is required by Warrant to preach in the Chapel Royal once a year, and is visibly distinguished, along with the Chapel Royal, Forces and Mohawk Chaplains, by the wearing of a royal scarlet cassock.

Dean of the Chapels Royal
The Bishop of London

Sub-Dean
The Revd Paul Wright
Chapel Royal, St James's Palace, London SW1A 1BL   *T*: 020 7024 5576

CHAPEL ROYAL AND THE QUEEN'S CHAPEL, ST JAMES'S PALACE
Priests in Ordinary
The Revd Richard Bolton
The Revd William Whitcombe

Deputy Priests
The Revd Canon Prof Peter Galloway
The Revd Canon Roger Hall
The Revd Canon Anthony Howe
The Revd Canon Mark Oakley
Preb Jonathan Osborne
The Revd Dr Stephen Young

HAMPTON COURT PALACE
Chapel Royal, Hampton Court, East Molesey, Surrey KT8 9AU   *T*: 020 3166 6515

Chaplain
The Revd Canon Anthony Howe

HM TOWER OF LONDON
The Chaplain's Residence, London EC3N 4AP   *T*: 020 3166 6796
(includes the Chapels Royal of St John the Evangelist and St Peter ad Vincula)

Chaplain
Canon Roger Hall

THE ROYAL CHAPEL OF ALL SAINTS, WINDSOR GREAT PARK

This is a Private Chapel and the property of the Crown within the grounds of the Royal Lodge. Attendance is restricted to residents and employees of the Great Park.

Chaplain

The Ven Martin Poll, Chaplain's Lodge, Windsor Great Park, Windsor, Berkshire SL4 2HP   *T:* 01784 432434

College of Chaplains

The position of Royal Chaplain is a very ancient one. The College of Chaplains, the members of which as such must not be confused with the Priests in Ordinary, preach according to a Rota of Waits in the Chapels Royal. The College comprises the Clerk of the Closet (who presides), the Deputy Clerk of the Closet, and thirty-six Chaplains. When a vacancy in the list of chaplains occurs, the Private Secretary to Her Majesty the Queen asks the Clerk of the Closet to suggest possible names to Her Majesty. The duties of the Clerk of the Closet include the presentation of bishops to Her Majesty when they do homage before taking possession of the revenues of their Sees; and he also examines theological books whose authors desire to present copies to Her Majesty the Queen. He preaches annually in the Chapel Royal, St James's Palace.

CLERK OF THE CLOSET

The Rt Revd James Newcome (*Bishop of Carlisle*)

DEPUTY CLERK OF THE CLOSET

The Revd Paul Wright

CHAPLAINS TO HER MAJESTY THE QUEEN

The Revd Hugh Bearn
The Revd Mary Bide

The Revd Canon Georgina Byrne
The Revd Rupert Charkham
The Revd Canon Andrew Clitherow
Preb Kathleen Garlick
The Revd Canon Jeremy Haselock
The Revd Emma Ineson
The Revd Rose Hudson-Wilkin
The Revd Canon George Kovoor
The Revd Edward Lewis
Preb Paul Lockett
The Revd Canon Kevan McCormack
Preb Edward Mason
The Revd Canon Paul Miller
The Revd David Nicholson
The Ven William Noblett
The Revd Hugh Palmer
The Revd Canon Robin Pryce
The Revd Canon Geoffrey Ravalde
The Revd Canon John Rees
The Revd Jonathan Riviere
The Revd Canon Bruce Ruddock
The Revd Canon John Taylor
The Revd Canon Nicholas Thistlethwaite
The Revd Canon Anthony Shepherd

Extra Chaplains
The Revd Canon Anthony Caesar
The Revd John Robson
Preb William Scott

Royal Almonry

The Royal Almonry dispenses the Queen's charitable gifts and is responsible for the Royal Maundy Service each year, at which Her Majesty distributes Maundy money to as many men and as many women pensioners as the years of her own age.

HIGH ALMONER

The Rt Revd John Inge (*Bishop of Worcester*)

SUB-ALMONER

The Revd Paul Wright
Chapel Royal, St James's Palace, London SW1A 1BL

The Queen's Chapel of the Savoy

Savoy Hill, Strand, London WC2R 0DA
                    T: 020 7379 8088 (Chaplain) *or*
                    020 7836 7221 (Steward)
                    E: chapel@duchyoflancaster
                    W: www.royalchapelsavoy.org

CHAPEL OF THE ROYAL VICTORIAN ORDER

The Queen's Chapel of the Savoy was built as the principal chapel of a hospital for 'pouer, nedie people' founded by King Henry VII and finished in 1512 after his death. It is a private

Chapel of Her Majesty the Queen in right of her Duchy of Lancaster, and Her Majesty appoints the chaplain. It is, therefore, a 'free' Chapel not falling within any diocese or episcopal jurisdiction.

On the occasion of his Coronation in 1937, King George VI commanded that the chapel of the Savoy should become the chapel of the Royal Victorian Order, an honour in the personal gift of the Sovereign, and the Chaplain of the Queen's Chapel is ex officio Chaplain of the Order. An ante-chapel (now renamed the Lancaster Hall), chaplain's office and robing room were constructed in 1958 to provide additional accommodation.

A new three-manual Walker organ was presented to the Chapel by Her Majesty the Queen in 1965. Further work in 2011–12 included the installation of a new stained glass window to mark the Diamond Jubilee of the Queen's reign, an extension of the royal robing room, the creation of a new sunken courtyard on the north side of the Lancaster Hall, the construction of a new chaplain's study and an office for the Steward, and the development of new facilities for receptions.

Members of the public are welcome to attend services which are held on Sundays (11 am) and weekdays (except August and September) with the exception of those for special or official occasions. The Chapel has a particularly fine musical tradition with a choir of men and boys. The Chapel is normally open to the public between 1 October and 31 July from 9am to 4pm Monday to Thursday.

CHAPLAIN
The Revd Canon Prof Peter Galloway JP OBE

STEWARD
Sqn Ldr Thomas Leyland BSC RAF (rtd)

MASTER OF MUSIC
Mr Philip Berg MVO FRCO ARCM

CHAIRMAN OF THE COUNCIL
Mr Tim Crow

Royal Memorial Chapel Sandhurst

Camberley, Surrey GU15 4PQ
T: 01276 412543
F: 01276 412097

The Royal Memorial Chapel Sandhurst is the Chapel of the Royal Military Academy Sandhurst. It is also the Memorial Chapel of the officers of the British Army. The present building was erected after the First World War as a memorial to those trained at Sandhurst who gave their lives in that conflict. Their names are inscribed on the Chapel's pillars. A memorial book contains the names of all officers of the Commonwealth Armies who died in the Second World War, and a page of this book is turned at the beginning of principal services. A Book of Remembrance containing the names of all officers who have been killed in service since 1947 is kept in the South Africa Chapel.

The main Sunday service is at 1030. The forms of service include the *Book of Common* *Prayer, Common Worship*, and special services within the Academy's calendar. Services are open to the public, and passes may be obtained by contacting the Chapel Office.

SENIOR CHAPLAIN
The Revd David Crees

ASSISTANT CHAPLAIN
The Revd Chris Kellock CF

ORGANIST AND DIRECTOR OF MUSIC
Mr Peter Beaven

CONSTITUTION OF THE CHAPEL COUNCIL
Maj-Gen P. C. Marriot (*Chairman*); Canon J. R. B. Gough (*Deputy Chairman*); Maj J. M. Watkinson (*Secretary*); Maj-Gen Sir Simon Cooper; Maj Gen R. L. Kirkland; Brig M. Owen

The Royal Foundation of St Katharine

2 Butcher Row, London E14 8DS
T: 0300 111 1147
F: 0300 777 1147
E: info@rfsk.org.uk
W: www.rfsk.org.uk

St Katharine's, founded by Queen Matilda in 1147 originally adjacent to the Tower of London, is a charitable conference and retreat centre at Limehouse in East London, between the City and Canary Wharf. It serves the Church of England, other churches and charities, offering an attractive setting for day or residential group meetings, seminars or retreats. It is also an excellent place to stay for business or pleasure in London. There are excellent facilities with residential en suite accommodation for 44 people and a choice of 7 meeting rooms. Daily worship is held in the peaceful chapel.

Her Majesty Queen Elizabeth II is Patron of the Foundation.

MEMBERS OF THE COURT
The Revd John Tattersall (*Chairman*)
Mr David Swanney (*Treasurer*)
The Rt Revd and Rt Hon Richard Chartres (*Bishop of London*)
Mr Ian Graham

Mr Andrew Grigson
Mr Simon Martin
Sir Stephen Lamport
Mrs Elizabeth Marshall
Revd Mark Aitken (*Master*)

MASTER
The Revd Mark Aitken

Deans of Peculiars

The few present-day Deans of Peculiars are the residue of some 300 such office-holders in the medieval period, when the granting of 'peculiar' status, fully or partially exempting a jurisdiction from episcopal control, was commonly employed by popes and others to advance the interests of a particular institution, or limit the power of the bishops. Unlike the Royal Peculiars, the deaneries had little in common, and the privileges and duties of the individual posts ranged from nominal to significant. Most of the special provisions were brought to an end in the nineteenth century. But each Peculiar has interesting light to throw on a phase of Anglican or national history.

Dean of Battle
The Very Revd Canon Dr John Edmondson, The Deanery, Caldbec Hill, Battle, E. Sussex TN33 0JY
Tel and *F:* 01424 772693
E: dean@johnedmondson.org

Deans of Bocking
Vacancy, The Deanery, Bocking, Braintree, Essex CM7 5SR
T: 01376 324887 / 01376 553092 (Office)
The Very Revd Martin Thrower, The Deanery, Church Street, Hadleigh, Ipswich IP7 5DT
T: 01473 822218
E: martin.thrower@btinternet.com

Dean of Stamford
The Very Revd Mark Warrick (*Vicar of Stamford All Saints with St John the Baptist*), All Saints Vicarage, Casterton Road, Stamford PE9 2YL
T: 01780 756942
E: mark.warrick@stamfordallsaints.org.uk

Preachers at the Inns of Court

GRAY'S INN
The Rt Revd Michael Doe, 405 West Carriage House, Royal Carriage Mews, Royal Arsenal, Woolwich SE18 6GA   *T:* 020 3259 3841
E: Michael.Doe@graysinn.org.uk

LINCOLN'S INN
The Very Revd Derek Watson, 83 Winchester Street, London SW1V 4NU

THE TEMPLE
Master The Revd Robin Griffith-Jones, The Master's House, Temple, London EC4Y 7BB
T: 020 7353 8559
E: master@templechurch.com
Reader Revd A. H. Mead, 11 Dungarvan Avenue, London SW15 5QU
T: 020 8876 5833

National Structures

PART 2

ARCHBISHOPS' PERSONAL STAFF

Archbishop of Canterbury's Personal Staff

Chief of Staff & Strategy
Canon David Porter
    E: david.porter@lambethpalace.org.uk

Archbishop's Senior Personal Assistant
Jacqueline Balfour
    E: jacqueline.balfour@lambethpalace.org.uk

Archbishop's Diary Manager
Katherine Richards
    E: katherine.richards@lambethpalace.org.uk

Chaplain
The Revd Isabelle Hamley
    E: isabelle.hamley@lambethpalace.org.uk

Archbishop's Adviser for Evangelism and Witness
The Revd Canon Chris Russell
    E: chris.russell@lambethpalace.org.uk

Archbishop's Adviser for Reconciliation
Canon Dr Sarah Snyder

Director of Communications
Mrs Ailsa Anderson
    E: ailsa.anderson@lambethpalace.org.uk

Digital Communications Officer
Mr Chris Cox
    E: chris.cox@lambethpalace.org.uk

Correspondence Secretary and CDM Officer
Mr Andrew Nunn
    E: andrew.nunn@lambethpalace.org.uk

Archbishop's Adviser on Anglican Communion Affairs
The Rt Revd Anthony Poggo

Anglican Communion Liaison Officer
Miss Fiona Millican
    E: fiona.millican@lambethpalace.org.uk

Secretary for Inter Religious Affairs
The Revd Mark Poulson   T: 020 7898 1477
    E: mark.poulson@churchofengland.org

Finance Officer
Miss Rebecca Pashley
    E: rebecca.pashley@lambethpalace.org.uk

Steward
Mr Quentin Padgett
    E: quentin.padgett@lambethpalace.org.uk

Archbishop's Ecumenical Adviser
The Revd Dr William Adam
                            T: 020 7898 1474
    E: william.adam@lambethpalace.org.uk

Head of Media
Ruth Mawhinney
    E: ruth.mawhinney@lambethpalace.org.uk

Office
Lambeth Palace, London SE1 7JU
                            T: 020 7898 1200
                            F: 020 7401 9886
    W: www.archbishopofcanterbury.org

Archbishop of York's Personal Staff

Chief of Staff
The Revd Malcolm Macnaughton
                        T: 01904 772362
    E: malcolm.macnaughton@
        archbishopofyork.org

Chaplain/Researcher to the Archbishop
The Revd Dr Daphne Green
    E: daphne.green@archbishopofyork.org

Domestic Chaplain to the Archbishop
The Revd Richard Carew
    E: richard.carew@archbishopofyork.org

Adviser in Mission Strategy and Church Revitalisation
The Ven John Day   T: 07921406178
    E: john.day@archbishopofyork.org

Personal Assistant
Miss Alison Cundiff
    E: alison.cundiff@archbishopofyork.org

Palace and Events Manager
Frazer Tobin   T: 01904 772377
    E: frazer.tobin@archbishopofyork.org

Communications Office
Elizabeth Addy
    E: elizabeth.addy@archbishopofyork.org

THE GENERAL SYNOD OF THE CHURCH OF ENGLAND

The General Synod of the Church of England

Composition of the General Synod

	Canterbury	York	Either	Totals
House of Bishops				
Diocesan Bishops	30	12		42
Suffragan Bishops including the Bishop of Dover *ex officio* and Bishop to the Armed Forces	6	3	1	9 / 1
	36	15	1	52
House of Clergy				
Deans	3	2		5
Armed Forces Synod and Chaplain-General of Prisons			7	7
Elected Proctors and the Dean of Guernsey or Jersey	129	55		184
University Proctors	4	2		6
Religious Communities			2	2
Co-opted places (maximum)	3	2		5
	139	61	9	209

	Canterbury	York	Either	Totals
House of Laity				
Elected Laity	136	59		195
Religious Communities			2	2
Lay Armed Forces Services			3	3
Co-opted places (maximum)			5	5
			2	2
Ex officio	136	59	12	207
House of Bishops, House of Clergy or House of Laity				
Ex officio (Dean of the Arches, the two Vicars General, the Third Church Estates Commissioner, the Chairman of the Pensions Board and six Appointed Members of the Archbishops' Council)			11	11
Maximum totals	311	135	33	479

The General Synod consists of the Convocations of Canterbury and York, joined together in a House of Bishops and a House of Clergy, and having added to them a House of Laity.

The House of Bishops is made up of the Upper Houses of the Convocations of Canterbury and York. It consists of the archbishops and all other diocesan bishops and the Bishop of Dover and Bishop to the Forces as ex officio members, four bishops elected by and from the suffragan bishops (and certain other bishops) of the Province of Canterbury (other than the Bishop of Dover), three bishops elected by and from the suffragan bishops (and certain other bishops) of the Province of York, and any other bishops residing in either Province who are members of the Archbishops' Council.

The House of Clergy is made up of the Lower Houses of the Convocations of Canterbury and York. It consists of clergy (other than bishops) who have been elected, appointed or chosen in accordance with Canon H 2 and the rules made under it (including deans, proctors from the dioceses and university constituencies and clerical members of religious communities) together with ex officio members.

The House of Laity consists of members from each diocese of the two Provinces elected by lay members of the deanery synods (or annual meetings of the chaplaincies in the case of the Diocese in Europe) or chosen by and from the lay members of religious communities, together with ex officio members.

Representatives of other Churches, the Church of England Youth Council, and Deaf

Anglicans Together are invited to attend the Synod and under its Standing Orders enjoy speaking but not voting rights.

GENERAL SYNOD LEGISLATION, CONSTITUTION AND BUSINESS
For information on the past and present proceedings of the General Synod, see: https:// churchofengland.org/about-us/structures/general-synod/about-general-synod.aspx

OFFICE
Church House, Great Smith Street, London
SW1P 3AZ   *T:* 020 7898 1000
                 F: 020 7898 1369
       E: synod@churchofengland.org

DATES OF SESSIONS
For dates of sessions see:
       www.churchofengland.org/about-us/
      structure/general-synod/future-dates.aspx

OFFICERS OF THE GENERAL SYNOD
Presidents
The Most Revd and Rt Hon John Sentamu
The Most Revd and Rt Hon Justin Welby

Prolocutor of the Lower House of the Convocation of Canterbury
The Revd Canon Simon Butler

Prolocutor of the Lower House of the Convocation of York
The Ven Cherry Vann

Chair of the House of Laity
Canon Dr Jamie Harrison

Vice-Chair of the House of Laity
Canon Elizabeth Paver

Secretary General
Mr William Nye   *T:* 020 7898 1361
       E: william.nye@churchofengland.org

Clerk to the Synod
Dr Jacqui Philips   *T:* 020 7898 1385
       E: jacqui.philips@churchofengland.org

Chief Legal Adviser and Joint Registrar of the Provinces of Canterbury and York
Mr Stephen Slack

Deputy Legal Adviser
The Revd Alexander McGregor

Standing Counsel
Mr Christopher Packer

OFFICERS OF THE CONVOCATIONS
Synodical Secretary of the Convocation of Canterbury
The Revd Paul Benfield

Synodal Secretary of the Convocation of York
The Ven Alan Wolstencroft

NON-DIOCESAN MEMBERS
The following are non-diocesan members of General Synod:
The Rt Revd Tim Thornton

Suffragan Bishops in Convocation
Canterbury
The Rt Revd Jonathan Baker
The Rt Revd Pete Broadbent
The Rt Revd Dr Jonathan Frost
The Rt Revd Alistair Magowan
The Rt Revd Jonathan Meyrick
The Rt Revd Trevor Willmott

York
The Rt Revd Richard Blackburn
The Rt Revd Jonathan Gibbs
The Rt Revd Libby Lane
The Rt Revd Glyn Webster

Deans in Convocation
Canterbury
The Very Revd David Ison
The Very Revd Andrew Nunn
The Very Revd Jane Hedges

York
The Very Revd Peter Bradley
The Very Revd Rogers Govender

Armed Forces Synod
The Ven Jonathan Chaffey
Lt Col Jane Hunter
The Ven Clinton Langston
The Ven Ian Wheatley
Lt Gemma Winterton

University and Theological Education Institutions Representatives in Convocation
The Revd Dr Emma Ineson
The Revd Canon Judith Maltby
Vacancy

Representatives of Religious Communities in Convocation
Canterbury
Sister Anita Cook

York
The Revd Thomas Seville

Lay Representatives of Religious Communities
Sister Catherine Harvey

Ex officio Members of the House of Laity
Representatives who have been appointed to the Synod under its Standing Orders with speaking but not voting rights:

Dean of the Arches
The Rt Worshipful Charles George

Vicar-General of the Province of Canterbury
The Rt Worshipful Timothy Briden, 1 Temple
Gardens, Temple, London EC4Y 9BB
T: 020 7797 8300
F: 020 7707 8308
E: info@lambchambers.co.uk

Vicar-General of the Province of York
The Rt Worshipful Peter Collier, c/o The
Registry, Stamford House, Piccadilly, York YO1
9PP

First Church Estates Commissioner
Ms Loretta Minghella

Second Church Estates Commissioner
The Rt Hon Dame Caroline Spelman

Third Church Estates Commissioner
Mr Andrew Mackie

*Chairman of the Church of England Pensions
Board*
Dr Jonathan Spencer

Chairman of the Dioceses Commission
Canon Prof Michael Clarke

*Chaplain-General of Prisons and Archdeacon of
Prisons*
The Ven Michael Kavanagh

Ecumenical Representatives
Bishop Dr Joe Aldred
His Grace Bishop Angaelos
The Revd Philip Cooper
The Revd Prof Paul Fiddes
The Very Revd Dr Angus Morrison
The Very Revd ArchPriest Maxim Nikolsky
The Revd Canon John O'Toole
The Revd Andrew Prasland
The Revd Dr Roger Walton

*Church of England Youth Council
Representatives*
Annika Matthews
Edward Cox
Sarah Maxfield-Phillips

Deaf Anglicans Together Representatives
Mary Bucknall
Catherine Farmbrough
Sarah Tupling

Appointed Members of the Archbishops' Council
Mrs Mary Chapman
Mr Matthew Frost
The Revd Dr Rosalyn Murphy
Mr Mark Sheard
Canon Dr John Spence
Ms Rebecca Swinson

The House of Bishops

The House of Bishops meets separately from
sessions of the General Synod twice a year, in
private session. It has a special responsibility
for matters relating to doctrine and liturgy
under Article 7 of the Constitution of General
Synod. Its agendas nevertheless range more
widely, reflecting matters relating to the
exercise of episcope in the Church. Each year
the College of Bishops – consisting of all
diocesan and suffragan bishops – also meet, as
do diocesan bishops with the archbishops.

Chairman
The Most Revd and Rt Hon Justin Welby

Vice-Chairman
The Most Revd and Rt Hon John Sentamu

Secretary
Mr William Nye LVO   T: 020 7898 1361
E: william.nye@churchofengland.org

Theological Consultant
The Revd Canon Dr Jeremy Worthen
T: 020 7898 1488
E: jeremy.worthen@churchofengland.org

**THE STANDING COMMITTEE OF THE
HOUSE OF BISHOPS**
The Standing Committee consists of the
Archbishops of Canterbury and York and the
Bishops of Coventry, Dover, London, Rochester,
Sheffield and Willesden. In addition, one
female regional representative also attends.
The committee's principal role is to prepare the
agendas for the House's meetings, but it also
deals with other matters on the House's behalf.

Chairman
The Most Revd and Rt Hon John Sentamu

Secretary
Mr William Nye LVO   T: 020 7898 1361
E: william.nye@churchofengland.org

**DEVELOPMENT AND APPOINTMENTS
GROUP**

Chair
The Rt Revd Tim Thornton

Secretary
Mr Brad Cook   T: 020 7898 1878
E: brad.cook@churchofengland.org

The House of Clergy

Membership of the House of Clergy comprises the Lower House of the Convocation of Canterbury and the Lower House of the Convocation of York joined into one House.

The Standing Committee of the House of Clergy consists of the Standing Committee of the Lower House of the Canterbury Convocation (the Prolocutor, Pro-Prolocutors, elected members of the Archbishops' Council, and four elected members) and the Assessors of the York Convocation (the Prolocutor,

Deputy Prolocutors, elected members of the Archbishops' Council, and two elected assessors).

Joint Chairs
The Prolocutors of the Convocations

Secretary
Mr Jonathan Neil-Smith   *T:* 020 7898 1373
        E: jonathan.neil-smith@
        churchofengland.org

The House of Laity

The Standing Committee of the House of Laity consists of the Chair and Vice-Chair and the members elected by the House to the Archbishops' Council (2 members), the Business Committee (3 members) and the Appointments Committee (3 members).

Chair
Dr James Harrison

Vice-Chair
Canon Elizabeth Paver

Secretary
Mr Andrew Brown   *T:* 020 7898 1374
        E: andrewjbrown@churchofengland.org

Principal Committees

THE BUSINESS COMMITTEE
The Committee is responsible for organizing the business of the Synod, enabling it to fulfil its role as a legislative and deliberative body.

Chair
The Revd Canon Susan Booys

Secretary
Dr Jacqui Philips   *T:* 020 7898 1385
        E: jacqui.philips@churchofengland.org

Members
The Rt Revd Pete Broadbent
The Revd Canon Graeme Buttery
The Revd Preb Simon Cawdell
Mrs Anne Foreman
Canon Robert Hammond
The Revd Canon Joyce Jones
Mr Clive Scowen

The Legislative Committee
The Legislative Committee is a statutory committee, required by the Church of England Assembly (Powers) Act 1919 and the Constitution of the General Synod. It acts in accordance with the procedures prescribed by the 1919 Act in submitting Measures to Parliament for approval once they have received final approval by the General Synod.

Ex officio members
The Archbishop of Canterbury
The Archbishop of York

The Prolocutors of the Convocations
The Chair and Vice-Chair of the House of Laity
The Dean of the Arches
The Second Church Estates Commissioner

Elected members
The Revd Paul Benfield
Canon Peter Bruinvels
Mr Clive Scowen
The Rt Revd Dr Alan Smith
The Worshipful Canon Geoffrey Tattersall

Secretary
Mr Stephen Slack   *T:* 020 7898 1366
        E: stephen.slack@churchofengland.org

THE STANDING ORDERS COMMITTEE
The Committee keeps under review the procedures and Standing Orders of the General Synod.

Ex officio members
The Prolocutors of the Convocations
The Chair and Vice-Chair of the House of Laity

Appointed members
The Revd Preb Simon Cawdell
Mrs Mary Durlacher
The Revd Canon Sharon Jones
Mr David Robilliard
Mr Clive Scowen

Secretary
Mr Sion Hughes Carew
        E: sion.hughes-carew@churchofengland.org

PRINCIPAL COMMISSIONS

The Clergy Discipline Commission

The Clergy Discipline Commission is constituted under the Clergy Discipline Measure 2003. Under that Measure the Commission is required to give general advice to disciplinary tribunals, the courts of the Vicars-General, bishops and archbishops as to the penalties which are appropriate in particular circumstances; to issue codes of practice and general policy guidance to persons exercising functions in connection with clergy discipline; and to make annually to the General Synod through the House of Bishops a report on the exercise of its functions during the previous year.

Under the 2003 Measure the Commission is also required to compile and maintain 'provincial panels' of persons available for appointment as members of a disciplinary tribunal or a Vicar-General's Court for the purposes of dealing with cases under it, and to formulate guidance for the purposes of the 2003 Measure generally and to promulgate it in a Code of Practice approved by the Dean of the Arches and the General Synod.

The Commission also monitors the exercise of discipline, highlights and encourages best practice, and builds up casework experience in disciplinary matters.

Chair
The Rt Hon Lord Justice McFarlane

Deputy Chair
Sir Mark Hedley

Secretary
Mr Sion Hughes Carew
    E: sion.hughes-carew@churchofengland.org

MEMBERS
The Ven Moira Astin
The Rt Revd Nicholas Baines
Mr Martin Follett
Canon Dr Jamie Harrison
The Rt Revd Christopher Lowson
Mr David Mills
The Ven Jackie Searle
The Revd Canon John Sinclair
Canon Carol Wolstenholme

The Crown Nominations Commission

The Commission was established by the General Synod in February 1977. Its function is to consider vacancies in diocesan bishoprics in the Provinces of Canterbury and York, and candidates for appointments to them. At each meeting the Chair is taken by the Archbishop in whose Province the vacancy has arisen. The Commission agrees upon two names for nomination to the Prime Minister by the appropriate Archbishop or, in the case of the Archbishopric of Canterbury or York, by the chair of the Commission. The names submitted are given in an order of preference voted upon by the Commission. The Prime Minister accepts the first name and reverts to the second name should the first be unable to take up the post.

Secretary to the Commission
Canon Caroline Boddington, Church House, Great Smith Street, London SW1P 3AZ
                    T: 020 7898 1876/7
                    F: 020 7898 1899
                    E: caroline.boddington@
                        churchofengland.org

MEMBERS
Ex officio
The Most Revd and Rt Hon John Sentamu
The Most Revd and Rt Hon Justin Welby

Elected Members

Three members of the House of Clergy
The Revd John Dunnett
The Revd Canon Judith Maltby
The Very Revd Andrew Nunn

Three members of the House of Laity
Mrs April Alexander
Mr Aiden Hargreaves-Smith
Miss Jane Patterson

Six members of the Vacancy-in-See Committee of the diocese whose bishopric is to become, or has become, vacant

Ex officio non-voting members
Canon Caroline Boddington
Mr Edward Chaplin

The Dioceses Commission

A Dioceses Commission was set up in 1978 under the Dioceses Measure 1978. In 2008 it was replaced by a new body of the same name, established under the Dioceses, Pastoral and Mission Measure 2007. Part II of that Measure makes provision for such matters as the reorganization of diocesan boundaries, the creation and revival of suffragan sees, and the delegation of episcopal functions by diocesan bishops to suffragan and assistant bishops.

The Commission's duties are laid down by the Measure. Its primary duty is to keep under review the provincial and diocesan structure of the Church of England and in particular the size, boundaries and number of provinces; the size, boundaries and number of dioceses and their distribution between the provinces; the number and distribution of bishops and the arrangements for episcopal oversight. The Commission may make reorganization schemes either of its own volition or in response to proposals from diocesan bishops. Schemes require the approval of the diocesan synods concerned (other than in exceptional circumstances) and that of the General Synod. The Commission also gives advice on good practice regarding diocesan administration and responds to requests for advice on particular

issues. It comments on proposals to change the names of episcopal sees. Diocesan bishops are obliged to seek the views of the Commission if they propose to fill a vacant suffragan see.

Further information about the Commission and its work may be found on the Church of England website at:
www.churchofengland.org/about-us/structure/dioceses-commission

Chairman
Canon Prof Michael Clarke

Vice-Chair
The Revd Paul Benfield

Secretary
Mr Jonathan Neil-Smith   *T:* 020 7898 1373
E: jonathan.neil-smith@churchofengland.org

MEMBERS
Mr Anthony Archer
The Rt Revd Christopher Foster
Malcolm Halliday
The Revd Canon Geoffrey Harbord
Ruth Martin
The Rt Revd Dame Sarah Mullally
The Revd Dr Robert Munro
Canon Professor Hilary Russell

The Faith and Order Commission

The Faith and Order Commission consists of not more than sixteen persons appointed by the Archbishops. The Commission advises the Archbishops, House of Bishops and the Council for Christian Unity on matters of ecumenical, theological and doctrinal concern. The Commission also gives advice on occasion to the General Synod and acts as a theological resource for the Church of England as a whole.

Chairman
The Rt Revd Dr Christopher Cocksworth

Secretary
The Revd Canon Dr Jeremy Worthen
     T: 020 7898 1488
E: jeremy.worthen@churchofengland.org

MEMBERS
Professor Nicholas Adams
The Revd Canon Professor Loveday Alexander
The Rt Revd Donald Allister
The Revd Dr Andrew Atherstone
The Rt Revd Jonathan Baker
The Rt Revd Dr Tim Dakin
Professor Mike Higton
The Rt Revd Anne Hollinghurst
Dr Joshua Hordern
The Revd Dr Emma Ineson
The Rt Revd Dr Michael Ipgrave
The Revd Dr Rosalyn Murphy
The Revd Thomas Seville

The Fees Advisory Commission

The Fees Advisory Commission is constituted under Part II of the Ecclesiastical Fees Measure 1986, as amended. It makes recommendations as to certain fees to be paid to ecclesiastical judges, legal officers and others, and embodies

those recommendations in Orders which are laid before the General Synod for approval. If approved, the Orders take effect unless annulled by either House of Parliament, and are published as Statutory Instruments.

Chair
Mr John Alpass

Secretary
Mr Sion Hughes Carew
    E: sion.hughes-carew@
    churchofengland.org

Members
Mr Niall Blackie
Mrs Carolyn Graham
Mr Bill Husselby
The Revd Canon Joyce Jones
The Revd Canon John Rees
The Worshipful Canon Geoffrey Tattersall
The Revd Stephen Trott

The Legal Advisory Commission

The Commission gives legal opinions to the General Synod and to senior officers of the Church of England, including diocesan chancellors and registrars, upon questions generally affecting the Church of England and advises the General Synod upon the revision of ecclesiastical statutes, measures and canons when so requested. The Commission cannot accept requests for advice from private individuals or secular bodies and does not normally give opinions on contentious matters.

The opinions of the Commission and its predecessor, the Legal Board, on matters of general interest are published by Church House Publishing in a loose-leaf form under the title *Legal Opinions Concerning the Church of England.* The 8th edition was published in May 2007. Opinions issued by the Commission since that date can be accessed at http://www.churchofengland.org/about-us/structure/churchlawlegis/guidance

Chair
The Worshipful the Revd Canon Rupert Bursell

Secretary
The Revd Alexander McGregor
    T: 020 7898 1748
    E: alexander.mcgregor@
    churchofengland.org

Administrative Secretary
Mr Sion Hughes Carew
    E: sion.hughes-carew@churchofengland.org

MEMBERS
Ex officio members
The Rt Worshipful Timothy Briden
The Rt Worshipful Peter Collier
The Rt Worshipful Charles George
Ms Caroline Mockford
Mr Christopher Packer
The Revd Canon John Rees
Mr Stephen Slack

Appointed and co-opted members
The Worshipful Ruth Arlow
Mr Peter Beesley
The Revd Paul Benfield
The Ven Douglas Dettmer
The Worshipful Morag Ellis
Mr Peter Foskett
Miss Cordelia Hall
The Worshipful Mark Hill
His Honour Judge David Hodge
The Rt Revd Christopher Lowson
Prof David McClean
The Worshipful Dr Charles Mynors
Mr Robert Pearce
Mr Andrew Roberts

Office
The Legal Office, Church House, Great Smith Street, London SW1P 3AZ

The Legal Aid Commission

The Legal Aid Commission operates under the Church of England (Legal Aid) Measure 1994 and the Church of England (Legal Aid) Rules 1995, and administers the Legal Aid Fund which was originally set up under the Ecclesiastical Jurisdiction Measure 1963 and is continued by the 1994 Measure and the 1995 Rules.

Legal aid under the 1994 Measure may be granted at the discretion of the Commission, subject to various conditions, for certain types of proceedings before Ecclesiastical Courts and tribunals; details of eligibility for legal aid and the Commission's procedures, together with an application form for legal aid, are obtainable from the Secretary, on request, or at www.churchofengland.org/about-us/structure/churchlawlegis/clergydiscipline/legalaid.aspx

Chairman
His Honour Judge Andrew Rutherford

Secretary
Mr Stephen York   *T:* 020 7898 1703
     F: 020 7898 1718/1721
     E: stephen.york@churchofengland.org

MEMBERS
Isabel Adcock
The Revd Paul Benfield
Mrs Rosalind Brewer
The Revd Canon Geoffrey Harbord
Mr Aiden Hargreaves-Smith
Mrs Carolyn Johnson
The Revd Canon Joyce Jones
The Revd Canon Sally Lodge
The Rt Revd Alistair Magowan
The Ven Clive Mansell

NATIONAL STRUCTURES

The Liturgical Commission

In response to resolutions by the Convocations in October 1954, the Archbishops of Canterbury and York appointed a standing Liturgical Commission 'to consider questions of a liturgical character submitted to them from time to time by the Archbishops of Canterbury and York and to report thereon to the Archbishops'. In 1971 the Commission became a permanent Commission of the General Synod. Its functions are:

- to prepare forms of service at the request of the House of Bishops for submission to that House in the first instance;
- to advise on the experimental use of forms of service and the development of liturgy;
- to exchange information and advice on liturgical matters with other Churches both in the Anglican Communion and elsewhere;
- to promote the development and understanding of liturgy and its use in the Church.

Chair
The Rt Revd Robert Atwell

National Liturgy and Worship Adviser
Dr Matthew R. C. Salisbury
     T: 020 7898 1765
     E: matthew.salisbury@churchofengland.org

Administrative Secretary
     T: 020 7898 1376
Sue Moore   *T:* 020 7898 1376
     E: sue.moore@churchofengland.org

MEMBERS
The Revd Dr Andrew Atherstone
The Revd Philip Barnes
The Revd Mark Earey
The Rt Revd Richard Frith
Ms Kashmir Garton
The Revd Canon Dr Christopher Irvine
The Revd Canon Dr Simon Jones
Canon Simon Kershaw
The Revd George Lane
The Revd Fiona Mayer-Jones
Mrs Lucy Moore
Dr Bridget Nichols,
Canon Shayne Ardron
The Revd Canon Dr Jo Spreadbury
The Revd Canon Dr Samuel Wells

THE CONVOCATIONS OF CANTERBURY AND YORK

Members of the Convocations

CONSTITUTION

Each of the Convocations consists of two Houses, an Upper House and a Lower House. The Upper House consists of all the diocesan bishops in the Province, the Bishop of Dover (in the case of the Convocation of Canterbury), bishops elected by and from amongst suffragan bishops of the Province, and any other bishops residing in the Province who are members of the Archbishops' Council. The Archbishop presides. The Lower House comprises clergy (other than bishops) who have been elected, appointed or chosen in accordance with Canon H 2 and the rules made under it (including deans, proctors from the dioceses and university and theological education institution constituencies, and clerical members of religious communities) together with ex-officio members. The Prolocutor is the chair and spokesperson of the House.

Upper House	Canterbury	York	*Either Province*
Diocesan Bishops	30	12	-
Bishop of Dover	1	-	-
Bishop to the Forces	1	-	-
Elected Suffragan Bishops	5	4	-
	37	16	-

Lower House	Canterbury	York	*Either Province*
Deans	3	2	-
Dean of Jersey or Guernsey	1	-	-
Armed Services	3	-	-
Elected Proctors	128	55	-
Chaplain-General of Prisons	1	-	-
University and TEI Proctors	-	-	4
Religious	-	-	2
Co-opted Clergy	-	-	-
	136	57	6

ACTS AND PROCEEDINGS

For the Acts and Proceedings of the Convocations, readers are referred to The Chronicle of the Convocation of Canterbury and to the York Journal of Convocation. Back numbers are available from Wm Dawson & Sons Ltd, Cannon House, Folkestone, Kent.

Officers of the Convocations

Convocation of Canterbury
President
The Most Revd and Rt Hon Justin Welby

Prolocutor of the Lower House
The Revd Canon Simon Butler

Pro-Prolocutors
Preb Stephen Lynas
The Revd Jane Morris

Standing Committee of the Lower House
The Revd Canon Simon Butler
The Revd Preb Simon Cawdell
The Revd Zoe Heming
The Revd Julian Holywell

Preb Stephen Lynas
The Revd Jane Morris
The Revd Sarah Schofield
The Revd Stephen Trott

Registrar
Mr Stephen Slack   T: 020 7898 1366
          E: stephen.slack@churchofengland.org

Synodical Secretary, Actuary and Editor of the Chronicle of Convocation
The Revd Stephen Trott

Ostiarius
Mr Clive McCleester

Convocation of York
President
The Most Revd and Rt Hon Dr John Sentamu

Prolocutor of the Lower House
The Ven Cherry Vann

Deputy Prolocutors
The Ven Paul Ayers
The Revd Paul Benfield

Assessors (Standing Committee)
The Ven Paul Ayers
The Revd Paul Benfield
The Revd Paul Cartwright
The Revd Jacqueline Doyle-Brett

The Revd Canon Joyce Rosemary Jones
The Revd Ian Paul
The Ven Peter Spiers
The Ven Cherry Vann
The Revd Canon Dr Dagmar Winter

Registrar
Ms Caroline Mockford

Synodal Secretary and Treasurer and Editor of the Journal of Convocation
The Ven Alan Wolstencroft

Apparitor
Mr Alex Carberry

THE ARCHBISHOPS' COUNCIL

The Archbishops' Council

Charity Registration no: 1074857
Telephone: 020 7898 1000
Fax: 020 7898 1369

The objects of the Archbishops' Council under the National Institutions Measure 1998 are to 'co-ordinate, promote, aid and further the work and mission of the Church of England'. It aims to further its statutory object by:

- providing an informed Christian view in public debate.
- promoting the views of the Church of England to parliament and government.
- overseeing the delivery of services and support to dioceses and parishes.
- ensuring that policy and resources are considered together.

The Archbishops' Council works closely with the Offices of the Archbishops of Canterbury and York, the House of Bishops and the General Synod, the Church Commissioners and the Church of England Pensions Board. It is supported in its wide-ranging brief by the staff and members of its Divisions:

- Education
- Cathedral and Church Buildings – which includes the Church Buildings Council and the Cathedrals Fabric Commission for England
- Central Secretariat – which includes the Council for Christian Unity and Research and Statistics
- Church House Publishing
- Ministry
- Mission and Public Affairs – which includes the Committee for Minority Ethnic Anglican Concerns

The work of the Council is described in more detail in its annual report. Its mission is to support the Church in her worship of God and her preparation in:

- proclaiming the Good News of the kingdom
- teaching, baptizing and nurturing new believers;
- responding to human need by loving service;
- seeking to transform unjust structures in society; and

- striving to safeguard the integrity of creation and sustaining and renewing the life of the earth.

The Council's objectives are:

- To enhance the Church's mission by
  - promoting spiritual and numerical growth;
  - enabling and supporting the worshipping Church and encouraging and promoting new ways of being Church; and
  - engaging with social justice and environmental stewardship.
- To sustain and advance the Church's work in education, lifelong learning and discipleship;
- To enable the Church to select, train and resource the right people, both ordained and lay, to carry out public ministry and to encourage lay people in their vocation to the world; and
- To encourage the maintenance and development of the inherited fabric of Church buildings for worship and service to the community.

It engages on behalf of the Church with Government on a wide range of issues of concern to the Church of England and its mission to the nation.

Its programme of work for the new quinquennium, in collaboration with the House of Bishops, is set out in GS 1978 to GS 1981, Renewal and Reform. This seeks to build on the following three main themes set out by the Archbishop of Canterbury in his Presidential Address to General Synod in November 2010 and to:

- support the spiritual and numerical growth of the Church of England – including the growth of its capacity to serve the whole community of this country;
- re-shape the Church's ministry for the century coming, so as to make sure that there is a growing and sustainable Christian witness in every local community; and
- simplify the governance and structures of the Church of England in order to release energy for mission and evangelisation.

MEMBERS
Joint Presidents
The Most Revd and Rt Hon Dr John Sentamu
The Most Revd and Rt Hon Justin Welby

Officers of the General Synod
The Revd Canon Simon Butler
Canon Dr James Harrison
Canon Elizabeth Paver
The Ven Cherry Vann

Elected by the General Synod:
The Rt Revd Stephen Conway
The Rt Revd Dr Steven Croft
The Revd Ian Paul
Canon Mark Russell
The Revd Sarah Schofield

A Church Estates Commissioner
Ms Loretta Minghella

Appointed by the Archbishops
Mrs Mary Chapman
Mr Matthew Frost
The Revd Dr Rosalyn Murphy
Mrs Rebecca Salter
Canon John Spence

Staff
Secretary General
Mr William Nye   T: 020 7898 1361
        E: william.nye@churchofengland.org

Education/National Society
The Revd Nigel Genders   T: 020 7898 1500
        E: nigel.genders@churchofengland.org

Mission and Public Affairs
The Revd Canon Dr Malcolm Brown
                            T: 020 7898 1468
        E: malcolm.brown@churchofengland.org

Communications
Tashi Lassalle   T: 020 7898 1295
        E: tashi.lassalle@churchofengland.org

Cathedral and Church Buildings
Becky Clark   T: 020 7898 1887
        E: becky.clark@churchofengland.org

Ministry
The Ven Julian Hubbard   T: 020 7898 1390
        E: julian.hubbard@churchofengland.org

Human Resources
Hannah Foster   T: 020 7898 1565
        E: hannah.foster@churchofengland.org

Legal Adviser
Mr Stephen Slack   T: 020 7898 1366
        E: stephen.slack@churchofengland.org

Clerk to the Synod and Director of Central Secretariat
Dr Jacqui Philips   T: 020 7898 1385
        E: jacqui.philips@churchofengland.org

NATIONAL STRUCTURES

The Appointments Committee of the Church of England

A joint committee of the General Synod and the Archbishops' Council, the Appointments Committee is responsible for making appointments and/or recommendations on appointments to synodical and other bodies as the Archbishops, the Synod or the Archbishops' Council require. It published its guidelines for best practice in the making of such appointments in 2015 as GS Misc 1122, which can be downloaded from the Church of England website.

Chairman
Canon Margaret Swinson

Secretary
Mr Jonathan Neil-Smith   T: 020 7898 1373
        E: jonathan.neil-smith@
                churchofengland.org

Four members appointed by the Archbishops' Council
The Revd Dr Rosalyn Murphy
Canon Elizabeth Paver
Vacancies x 2

Seven elected Members
Canon Lucy Docherty
Mrs Sarah Finch
The Revd Canon Giles Goddard
The Rt Revd Julian Henderson
Dr Rachel Jepson
The Revd Mark Lucas
The Ven Dr John Perumbalath

Audit Committee

The Committee provides independent oversight of the Archbishops' Council's framework of corporate governance, risk management, and internal control. It oversees the discharge of the Council's responsibilities relating to financial statements, external and internal audit and internal control systems, and reports to the Council thereon with recommendations as appropriate.

Chair
Mr Stephen William Hogg

Secretary
Mr Aneil Jhumat   *T:* 020 7898 1658
                    E: aneil.jhumat@churchofengland.org

Membership
Debbie Buggs
Bethany Burrow
Simon Butler
Andrew Weatherill

Finance Committee

MEMBERS
Chair appointed by Archbishops' Council
Canon John Spence

Three members elected by the General Synod:
Mr Carl Hughes
The Revd Canon Andy Salmon
The Revd Canon Martyn Taylor

Three members appointed by the Archbishops' Council on the recommendation of the Appointments Committee:
The Ven Annette Cooper
Sandra Newton
Vacancy

Three members elected by the Inter-Diocesan Finance Forum:
Canon Michael Arlington
Mrs Lucinda Herklots
Canon Elizabeth Renshaw

Secretary
David White   *T:* 020 7898 1684
                    E: david.white@churchofengland.org

Terms of reference
- To advise the Archbishops' Council and the dioceses on all financial aspects of the Archbishops' Council's work, including its investment, stewardship and trustee responsibilities, on the effects of the public financial policy and on the overall financial needs and resources of the Church.
- To make recommendations to the Archbishops' Council as to its annual budget and on mechanisms for monitoring and controlling the expenditure of the Council.
- To consult with the dioceses on financial matters, and to make recommendations thereon as appropriate to the Archbishops' Council and the dioceses.
- To carry out such other work as may be entrusted to it by the Archbishops' Council.

Investment Committee

MEMBERS
Appointed by the Finance Committee

(Chair)
Canon Michael Arlington
Mr John Booth
Mrs Lucinda Herklots
Canon Emma Osborne
The Revd Glyn Owen
Canon John Spence

Secretary
David White   *T:* 020 7898 1684
                    E: david.white@churchofengland.org

Summary of Terms of Reference
Responsibility for setting investment policy lies with the Archbishops' Council with advice from its Finance Committee.

Within that policy, the Investment Committee has responsibility for implementing the investment strategy, and reporting regularly on progress. The Investment Committee's responsibilities include:

- to select and review the appointment of investment managers;
- to set the strategy for the Council's investment managers including setting performance objectives, investment guidelines and benchmarks to meet the investment policy set by Council;
- to decide the most appropriate investment strategy for each of the Council's charitable settlements.

Archbishops' Council: key working relationships

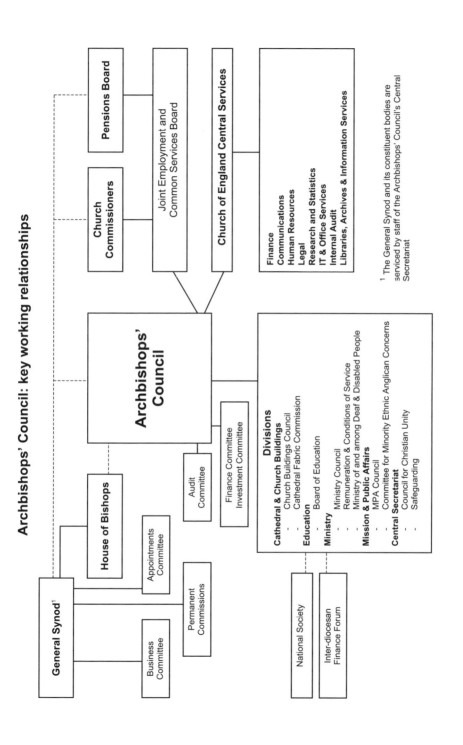

General Synod[1]

House of Bishops

Business Committee

Appointments Committee

Permanent Commissions

Archbishops' Council

Audit Committee

Finance Committee
Investment Committee

Church Commissioners

Pensions Board

Joint Employment and Common Services Board

Church of England Central Services

Finance
Communications
Human Resources
Legal
Research and Statistics
IT & Office Services
Internal Audit
Libraries, Archives & Information Services

Divisions

Cathedral & Church Buildings
- Church Buildings Council
- Cathedral Fabric Commission

Education
- Board of Education

Ministry
- Ministry Council
- Remuneration & Conditions of Service
- Ministry of and among Deaf & Disabled People

Mission & Public Affairs
- MPA Council
- Committee for Minority Ethnic Anglican Concerns

Central Secretariat
- Council for Christian Unity
- Safeguarding

National Society

Inter-diocesan Finance Forum

[1] The General Synod and its constituent bodies are serviced by staff of the Archbishops' Council's Central Secretariat

Central Secretariat

The Central Secretariat is the department which services the main governance bodies of the Church of England including the Archbishops' Council and all Bishops' meetings. The Central Secretariat also services a number of other boards and committees of General Synod, the House of Bishops and the Archbishops' Council such as the Council for Christian Unity, the Faith and Order Commission, the Dioceses and Liturgical Commissions, the Appointments Committee and the General Synod Business Committee.

The Clerk to the Synod is also the Director of the Central Secretariat, acts as Secretary to the Business Committee, supports the Secretary General with the staffing of episcopal meetings and provides advice and assistance as necessary to synodical bodies and members of Synod.

Clerk and Director
Clerk to the Synod and Director Central Secretariat
Dr Jacqui Philips   *T:* 020 7898 1385
    E: jacqui.philips@churchofengland.org

Synod Office
    W: www.churchofengland.org/about-us/
          structure/general-synod.aspx

Head of Governance Services and Outreach
Vacancy

Head of Events – General Synod and House of Bishops and Secretary to the House of Laity
Mr Andrew Brown   *T:* 020 7898 1374
    E: andrewjbrown@churchofengland.org

PA to Clerk to the Synod and Administrative Secretary
Miss Polly Dunn   *T:* 020 7898 1380
    E: polly.dunn@churchofengland.org.uk

Synod Office Executive Officers
Ms Casey Chick   *T:* 020 7898 1470
    E: casey.chick@churchofengland.org.uk
Vacancy

Dioceses and Liturgical Commissions
    W: www.churchofengland.org/about-us/
          structure/dioceses-commission.aspx
    W: www.churchofengland.org/
          prayer-worship/worship/the-liturgical-
          commission.aspx

Secretary: Dioceses Commission, House of Clergy, Standing Committee of the House of Clergy and Secretary to the Appointments Committee
Mr Jonathan Neil-Smith   *T:* 020 7898 1373
    E: jonathan.neil-smith@
          churchofengland.org

National Liturgy and Worship Adviser
Dr Matthew R. C. Salisbury   *T:* 020 7898 1765
    E: matthew.salisbury@churchofengland.org

Administrative Secretary to the Liturgical Commission; Secretary: Churches' Funerals Group
Sue Moore   *T:* 020 7898 1376
    E: sue.moore@churchofengland.org

Council for Christian Unity
Secretary for Ecumenical Relations and Theology
The Revd Canon Dr Jeremy Worthen
          T: 020 7898 1488
    E: jeremy.worthen@churchofengland.org

Archbishop's Ecumenical Advisor and Council for Christian Unity Ecumenical Officer
The Revd Dr William Adam
          T: 020 7898 1474
    E: william.adam@lambethpalace.org.uk

National Ecumenical Adviser
The Revd Dr Callan Slipper
          T: 020 7898 1479
    E: callan.slipper@churchofengland.org

Adviser for European Church Relations
The Revd Dr Matthias Grebe
    E: matthias.grebe@churchofengland.org

Research Officer, Faith and Order Commission
Amelia Sutcliffe
    E: amelia.sutcliffe@churchofengland.org

Assistant Secretary, Council for Christian Unity
Vacancy

Team Administrator, Council for Christian Unity
Angeline Leung   *T:* 020 7898 1473
    E: angeline.leung@churchofengland.org

National Safeguarding Team

The National Safeguarding Team (NST) works to build the strong foundations for a safer church. Their activities include developing national Safeguarding policy and practice guidance which is approved by the House of Bishops for implementation in the dioceses and all other Church organizations. The NST is also responsible for developing and implementing a national safeguarding training framework for the Church of England, developing robust quality assurance processes, including independent audits of dioceses, offering practice guidance on complex cross-diocese casework and liaising with other national stakeholders including other faith and secular organizations concerned with safeguarding children and vulnerable adults, including Government. The National Safeguarding Team sits within the Central Secretariat of the Church of England.

W: https://www.churchofengland.org/
clergy-office-holders/safeguarding-
children-vulnerable-adults.aspx

National Safeguarding Adviser – Child and Adult Protection for the Church of England
Graham Tilby   T: 020 7898 1330

National Safeguarding Policy Manager
Heather Reid   T: 0207 7898 1230
    E: heather.reid@churchofengland.org

Senior Casework Manager
Moira Murray   T: 020 7898 1477
    E: moira.murray@churchofengland.org

Provincial Caseworkers
Lambeth Palace
Caroline Venables
    E: caroline.venables@churchofengland.org

Bishopsthorpe
Anna Flower
    E: anna.flower@churchofengland.org

Safeguarding Training and Development Officer (on maternity leave)
Lisa Clarke   T: 0207 898 1009
    E: lisa.clarke@churchofengland.org

Safeguarding Training and Development Officer (maternity cover)
Andrea Watkins
    E: andrea.watkins@churchofengland.org

Executive Officer, Safeguarding
Hannah Sinclair
    E: hannahsinclair@churchofengland.org

The Council for Christian Unity

The Council was established as an advisory committee of the General Synod on 1 April 1991 to continue and develop the ecumenical work formerly undertaken by the Board for Mission and Unity. That Board, set up on 1 January 1972, had inherited the responsibilities of the Missionary and Ecumenical Council of the Church Assembly (MECCA) and the Church of England Council on Foreign Relations (CFR).

Secretary for Ecumenical Relations and Theology
The Revd Canon Dr Jeremy Worthen
                    T: 020 7898 1488
    E: jeremy.worthen@churchofengland.org

Assistant Secretary
Vacancy

Ecumenical Officer
The Revd Dr William Adam   T: 020 7898 1474
    E: william.adam@lambethpalace.org.uk

National Ecumenical Officer for England
The Revd Dr Callan Slipper   T: 020 7898 1479
    E: callan.slipper@churchofengland.org

Adviser for European Church Relations
The Revd Dr Matthias Grebe
    E: matthias.grebe@churchofengland.org

MEMBERS
Chairman
The Rt Revd Donald Allister

Membership Elected:
The Revd Dr Andrew Atherstone
Dr Rachel Jepson
Dr Lindsay Newcombe
Canon Elizabeth Paver

Appointed:
The Revd Prof Mark Chapman
Canon Elizabeth Paver
The Revd Dr Gavin Wakefield

FUNCTIONS OF THE COUNCIL (Adapted from the Constitution)

• To stimulate and encourage theological reflection in consultation with the Faith and Order Commission and to advise the Archbishops' Council and the General Synod on unity issues and proposals in the light of the Christian understanding of God's purposes for the world.
• To advise the House of Bishops on matters referred to it by the House.
• To foster ecumenical work in the Church nationally and in the dioceses.
• In conjunction with the Archbishops' Council to promote unity and ecumenical concerns in the work of all the Boards, Councils, Divisions, etc.
• In ecumenical concerns on behalf of the Archbishops' Council to be the principal link between the General Synod and
    • The Anglican Consultative Council;
    • individual provinces and dioceses of the Anglican Communion and the

United Churches incorporating former Anglican dioceses.
- On behalf of the Archbishops' Council to be the principal channel of communication between the General Synod and
- The World Council of Churches;
- The Conference of European Churches;
- Churches Together in Britain and Ireland;
- Churches Together in England;
- all other Christian Churches in the British Isles and abroad.
- To service committees and commissions engaged in ecumenical discussions with other Churches.

COMMITTEE FOR ROMAN CATHOLIC RELATIONS

The Committee for Roman Catholic Relations consists of not more than fifteen persons appointed by the Archbishops after consultation with the Council. This Committee promotes relations between the Church of England and the Roman Catholic Church in this country and it meets twice a year with the equivalent Roman Catholic body. The two bodies form the English Anglican Roman Catholic Committee.

Chairman
The Rt Revd Tim Thornton

MEISSEN COMMISSION – ANGLICAN COMMITTEE

The Meissen Commission (the Sponsoring Body for Church of England EKD Relations) was established in 1991 to oversee the implementation of the Meissen Declaration and encourage relationships with the Evangelical Church in Germany. It comprises Anglican and German committees.

Chairman
The Rt Revd Nicholas Baines

ECUMENICAL INSTRUMENTS

Contact is maintained with the World Council of Churches, the Conference of European Churches, Churches Together in Britain and Ireland, and Churches Together in England, where members and staff represent the Church of England at various levels. The Council is particularly concerned with helping the Church of England to relate effectively at every level to the ecumenical instruments.

PANELS OF THE CCU

The CCU has two subsidiary panels:

Methodist-Anglican Panel for Unity in Mission
Co-Chairman (Anglican)
Vacancy

Porvoo Panel
Chairman
The Rt Revd David Hamid

Ministry Division

MINISTRY COUNCIL
Chairman of Ministry Council
The Rt Revd Dr Steven Croft

Director of Ministry Division
The Ven Julian Hubbard   T: 020 7898 1390
     E: julian.hubbard@churchofengland.org

Functions of the Council
The functions of the Ministry Council shall be:

- To advise the Archbishops' Council and the House of Bishops on a strategy for the development of vocation to ministry and on a strategy for theological education and training.
- To encourage those in education and careers work throughout the Church in the provision of sustained programmes of vocational development and recruitment for accredited ministry, ordained and lay.
- To advise the House of Bishops on policy for the selection of candidates for accredited ministry, ordained and lay.

- To oversee and advise the work of staff in the arrangement of and participation in selection conferences.
- To oversee the training of bishops' selectors.
- To work in collaboration with Diocesan Directors of Ordinands and others as appropriate on policy and practice related to the selection and care of candidates for ministry.
- To scrutinise and validate programmes for those training under Bishops' Regulations, and to keep under review all forms of training for authorized ministry, ordained and lay, including Reader training.
- To advise the Archbishops' Council and the House of Bishops on policy concerning theological colleges and courses.
- To advise the Archbishops' Council and the House of Bishops on the financial aspects of theological education and training.
- To produce, in partnership with dioceses, a framework of national policy for the

deployment of all ministerial resources, ordained and lay, available to the Church by identifying trends in the numbers and composition of the Church's licensed ministries and advising on their implications for mission and ministry.
• To work in collaboration with ecumenical partners on matters within the Committee's terms of reference.

MEMBERS
Chair
The Revd Sonia Barron
The Revd Canon Professor Nigel Biggar
The Revd Canon Jane Charman
Mr John Craven
The Rt Revd Dr Steven Croft
Mrs Vivienne Goddard
The Rt Revd Christine Hardman
Canon John Spence
The Rt Revd David Walker
The Rt Revd Andrew Watson

MINISTRY DIVISION
Ministry Division supports the programme and administrative work of the Council in renewing discipleship and ministry, developing vocations and supporting the selection and formation of candidates for lay and ordained ministry.

Director
The Ven Julian Hubbard   T: 020 7898 1390
    E: julian.hubbard@churchofengland.org

Head of Discipleship and Vocation
Mrs Catherine Nancekievill
          T: 020 7898 1399
    E: catherine.nancekievill@
          churchofengland.org

Head of Formation
The Revd Dr Ian McIntosh   T: 020 7898 1897
    E: ian.mcintosh@churchofengland.org

Head of Ministry Development
Vacancy

Head of Resources
Mr Ian Barnetson   T: 020 7898 1392
    E: ian.barnetson@churchofengland.org

National Deaf Ministry Adviser
Canon Gill Behenna, 1 Saxon Way, Bradley Stoke, Bristol BS32 9AR   T: 01454 202483
    E: gillbehenna@me.com

National Disability Adviser
Mr Roy McCloughry   T: 07974 768935
          E: rkml@me.com

Selection Secretaries
The Revd Liz Boughton   T: 020 7898 1593
    E: liz.boughton@churchofengland.org

Mr Kevin Diamond   T: 020 7898 1402
    E: kevin.diamond@churchofengland.org
Miss Joy Gilliver   T: 020 7898 1439
    E: joy.gilliver@churchofengland.org
The Revd Hilary Ison   T: 020 7898 1424
    E: hilary.ison@churchofengland.org
The Revd Catherine Williams
          T: 020 7898 1395
    E: catherine.williams@churchofengland.org

Grants Officer
Dr Mark Hodge   T: 020 7898 1396
    E: mark.hodge@churchofengland.org

GRANTS FOR MINISTERIAL EDUCATION
Details about grants can be obtained on the Ministry pages of the Church of England website or from the Grants Officer.

GROUPS AND PANELS OF THE MINISTRY COUNCIL
The Council has the following working groups or panels.

Quality In Formation Panel
The Quality in Formation Panel is responsible for overseeing the transition to a single quality framework for inspection, validation, moderation and Reader moderation and to carry out the current process. The Panel also provides training and support or reviewers carrying out quality reviews.

Chair
Professor Michael Wright

Contact
The Revd Dr Ian McIntosh   T: 020 7898 1897
    E: ian.mcintosh@churchofengland.org

Finance Panel
The Finance Panel is responsible for advising the Ministry Council on all aspects of its financial responsibility regarding the cost of ordinands training funded from Central Church Funds. It prepares and administers the Training Budget, and advises on the financial support of candidates.

Chair
Mr John Craven

Head of Resources
Mr Ian Barnetson   T: 020 7898 1392
    E: ian.barnetson@churchofengland.org

Candidates Panel
The Candidates Panel advises sponsoring bishops on issues surrounding the training of individual candidates, including changes in the length of training; transferring candidates between institutions; candidates returning to training after an extended break; suitability of candidates for transferring of category of ministry; suitability of ministers from other

denominations to be ministers in the Church of England; candidates' potential to be theological educators.

Chair
The Rt Revd Mark Bryant

Contact
The Revd Dr Ian McIntosh   *T:* 020 7898 1897
   E: ian.mcintosh@churchofengland.org

Research Degrees Panel
The Research Degrees Panel gives permission and budgets for ordinands seen as potential theological educators to study for research degrees outside of Bishops' Regulations for Training as part of pre-ordination training.

Chair
The Revd Canon Judith Maltby
The Revd Dr Ian McIntosh   *T:* 020 7898 1897
   E: ian.mcintosh@churchofengland.org

Vocations Working Group
The Ordained Vocations Working Group aims to increase by 50 per cent the number of candidates coming into training for ordained stipendiary and self-supporting ministry by 2020 in the context of a growth in all vocations, and to attract a cohort that is missional, adaptable and collaborative and reflects our continued commitment to recruiting more diverse and younger ordinands.

Chair
Mrs Catherine Nancekievill
The Rt Revd Andrew Watson

COMMITTEE FOR MINISTRY OF AND AMONG DEAF AND DISABLED PEOPLE
We are CMDDP: a group of Deaf, disabled, hearing, differently abled and non-disabled people working together to help the Church of England fulfil its calling to be a sign of the radically inclusive kingdom of God for all people – without exception.

We are here to inspire the institution and local parishes to break down barriers, embracing and affirming the gifts of all people for the benefit of the whole Church. This involves taking seriously our legal obligations to make all 'reasonable adjustments' required by the Equality Act of 2010, and then going beyond this as a foretaste of the abundant welcome of Christ. We regard this as part of renewing and reforming the Church.

We are here to challenge the Church and model a counter-cultural vision where those considered as 'weaker members' are honoured and valued as agents of the Gospel of Jesus.

We are here to ensure the work of CMDDP is understood as essential to the mission of the Church of England, not an optional extra.

We are here to enable the church to be truly healthy and faithful to its witness of reflecting God's image, by empowering all people to participate and flourish equally.

Chair
The Rt Revd Nicholas Holtam

Members
Penny Beschizza
Mr Graham Caskie
Mrs Debbie Child
The Revd Professor Chris Cook
The Revd Zoe Heming
The Revd Alice Kemp
The Revd Dr Hannah Lewis
The Revd John Naude
The Revd Mark Smith
The Revd Professor John Swinton

National Disability Adviser
Mr Roy McCloughry   *T:* 07974 768935
   E: rkml@me.com

National Deaf Ministry Adviser
The Revd Canon Gill Behenna

Secretary
Patrick Shorrock

The Central Readers' Council

The Central Readers' Council (CRC) works to enhance the contribution of Readers to the overall ministry of the Church, and particularly to encourage the most effective integration with other forms of ministry, ordained and lay. It works in cooperation with the Ministry Division. CRC provides a forum for the exchange of ideas between dioceses on Reader matters and publishes a quarterly magazine, *The Reader*.

CRC is a registered charity, which derives its income mostly from capitation grants made by diocesan Readers' boards. It has its

origins in the revival of Reader ministry in the Church of England in 1866 and particularly in the Central Readers' Board, which was granted a constitution by the Archbishops in 1921. CRC today is the immediate successor to the Central Readers' Conference, under a new constitution adopted in 2002, and revised in 2007 and 2010 and again in 2017.

CRC has three representatives from each diocese, including the Warden and Secretary of Readers, and one representative from each of the Armed Forces. Any Reader appointed to a Ministry Division committee is ex officio a member of CRC. The annual general meeting is held in March or April each year.

Patron
HRH The Duke of Edinburgh

Presidents
The Most Revd and Rt Hon John Sentamu
The Most Revd and Rt Hon Justin Welby

Chair
The Rt Revd Martyn Snow

Vice-Chair
Mrs Gertrud Sollars

Secretary
Mr Andrew Walker   *T:* 07765 069534
              E: crcsec@btinternet.com

Associate Secretary
Ms Susanne Mitchell   *T:* 020 7898 1417
      E: susanne.mitchell@churchofengland.org

National Consultant for Reader Formation
Canon Rosemary Walters   *T:* 01227 768891
              E: ra.walters@btinternet.com

National Consultant for Reader CMD
Mrs Lynn Comer   *T:* 01904 699504
              E: lynncomer@yorkdiocese.org

Editor of 'The Reader'
Mrs Richenda Milton-Dawes
                    T: 01666 824029
              E: editor@cofereadermag.co.uk

MEMBERS
The CRC Executive Committee is elected for a five-year term co-terminous with General Synod. In addition to the Chair, Vice-Chair and all the officers listed above, the Committee consists of:

Two Wardens
The Ven Christopher Futcher
Mrs Karen Senior

Reader representatives
Mrs Kathleen Bradshaw
Miss Imogen Clout
Mrs Ruth Haldane
Mrs Angela Mirani

Treasurer
Mr Richard Havergal

NATIONAL STRUCTURES

MISSION AND PUBLIC AFFAIRS DIVISION
Mission and Public Affairs Council

Chair
Mr Mark Sheard

Vice-Chairs
The Rt Revd Dr Alan Smith (Bishop of St Albans)
The Rt Revd Jan McFarlane (Bishop of Repton)

Director
The Revd Canon Dr Malcolm Brown
T: 020 7898 1468
E: malcolm.brown@churchofengland.org

FUNCTIONS OF THE COUNCIL
The function of the MPA Council is to assist the Archbishops' Council and the other National Church Institutions in discharging their responsibility to support, promote and extend the mission, ministry and witness of the Church of England to the nation, and in particular:

- to ensure that the concerns and interests of the Church at national level, especially concerning moral and ethical issues, are represented authoritatively to national institutions including the government;
- to support the mission of the Church of England in its dioceses and parishes through creative initiatives, building strategic links and theological resources; and
- to be an advocate for, and to offer support to, areas of the Church of England's ministry, mission and witness which are at risk of being marginalized or which have not yet achieved their full potential.

In discharging this function, the particular responsibilities of the MPA Council shall include:

- the Church of England's engagement with social, political and environmental issues; community life and civil society; and its work for justice, peace and integrity of creation at local, national and international levels;
- mission and evangelism; the Church of England's responsibilities for world mission and development; inter religious affairs; and theological and missiological reflection on these topics;
- the Church of England's responsibility to confront the reality of racism in its own life and in society;
- the support of minority ethnic Christians in the Church of England and their contribution to its life and witness within and beyond the Church of England;

- support for Church of England chaplains in the public sector and elsewhere, especially in the field of spiritual, mental and physical health and healthcare.

Key relationships
The MPA Council shall:

- advise the Archbishops' Council, the General Synod and the House of Bishops on matters within the MPA Council's remit;
- work in partnerships with dioceses, Church of England networks and voluntary societies on matters within its remit;
- relate to the ecumenical instruments (Churches Together in England, Churches Together in Britain and Ireland), appropriate bodies in other Churches and denominations and the member Churches and structures of the Anglican Communion on issues relating to the Church of England's mission and role in public life;
- relate to parliament, government departments and voluntary bodies relevant to its work.

MEMBERS

Chair
Mr Mark Sheard

Vice Chairs
The Rt Revd Dr Alan Smith (Bishop of St Albans)
The Rt Revd Jan McFarlane (Bishop of Repton)

General Synod elected members:
Dr John Appleby
The Ven Malcolm Chamberlain
The Revd Dr Sean Doherty
The Revd Canon Dr Rosemarie Mallett
Ms Josile Munro
Ms Margaret Parrett

Appointed and co-opted members
The Revd Canon Dr Victoria Johnson
Vacancies x 3

STAFF
All staff are based in Church House, Westminster with the following exceptions: the office of the National Rural Officer is at the Arthur Rank Centre, Stoneleigh Park, Warwickshire CV8 2LZ; the National Inter-Faith Relations Adviser is based at Lambeth Palace and the Presence and Engagement National Programme Coordinator is based out of London.

Director
The Revd Canon Dr Malcolm Brown
T: 020 7898 1468
E: malcolm.brown@churchofengland.org

Parliamentary Secretary
Mr Richard Chapman   T: 020 7898 1438
E: richard.chapman@churchofengland.org

Deputy Parliamentary Secretary
Mr Simon Stanley   T: 020 7898 1478
E: simon.stanley@churchofengland.org

Adviser for Home Affairs, Marriage and Family Life
The Revd Martin Kettle   T: 020 7898 1531
E: martin.kettle@churchofengland.org

Adviser for International and Development Affairs
Dr Charles Reed   T: 020 7898 1533
E: charles.reed@churchofengland.org

Adviser for Medical Ethics, Health and Social Care Policy
The Revd Dr Brendan McCarthy
T: 020 7898 1523
E: brendan.maccarthy@churchofengland.org

Adviser for Economic and Social Affairs
Mr Tom Sefton   T: 020 7898 1446
E: tom.sefton@churchofengland.org

Adviser for Minority Ethnic Anglican Concerns
Dr Elizabeth Henry   T: 020 7898 1442
E: elizabeth.henry@churchofengland.org

Adviser for World Mission Policy
Canon Janice Price   T: 020 7898 1328
E: janice.price@churchofengland.org

Adviser for Mission Theology, Alternative Spiritualities and New Religious Movements
Dr Anne Richards
T: 020 7898 1444
E: anne.richards@churchofengland.org

Adviser for Inter-Faith Relations
The Revd Mark Poulson   T: 020 7898 1477
E: mark.poulson@churchofengland.org

Presence and Engagement National Programme Coordinator
Kat Brealey   T: 07951 671552
E: kat.brealey@churchofengland.org

National Rural Officer
Canon Dr Jill Hopkinson, The Arthur Rank Centre, Stoneleigh Park, Warwickshire CV8 2LZ   T: 024 7685 3073
F: 024 7669 6460
E: jill.hopkinson@churchofengland.org

Hospital Chaplaincies Administrator
Miss Mary Ingledew   T: 020 7898 1895
E: mary.ingledew@churchofengland.org

COMMITTEE FOR MINORITY ETHNIC ANGLICAN CONCERNS

The principal tasks of the Committee are to monitor and make recommendations about issues which arise or which ought to arise in the context of the work of the Archbishops' Council and its Divisions and of the General Synod itself, as far as they have policy implications for minority ethnic groups within the Church and the wider community; and to assist the Bishops and their dioceses in developing diocesan-wide strategies for combating racial bias within the Church and in society, encouraging them to make the problem of racism a priority concern in their programmes and to circulate the best analyses of racism, including theological analyses.

Chair
The Ven Dr John Perumbalath, 11 Bridgefields Close, Hornchurch, RM11 1GQ
T: 01708 474951
E: a.barking@chelmsford.anglican.org

Adviser for Minority Ethnic Concerns
Dr Elizabeth Henry   T: 020 7898 1442
E: elizabeth.henry@churchofengland.org

GROUPS AND PANELS OF THE MPA COUNCIL

The Council currently has the following working groups or panels. Those which are ecumenical or formally constituted with other agencies, are described in greater detail.

CofE World Mission and Anglican Communion Panel

The CofE World Mission and Anglican Communion Panel is a partnership between the General Synod and the World Mission Agencies of the Church of England drawing its members from the General Synod, the Mission Agencies, representatives of Diocesan Companion Links, Associate Members and our ecumenical partners. There are ten full partner Agencies: Church Army, the Church's Ministry among Jewish People (CMJ), Church Mission Society (CMS), Church Pastoral Aid Society (CPAS), Crosslinks, Intercontinental Church Society (ICS), The Mission to Seafarers, The Mothers' Union, the Society for Promoting Christian Knowledge (SPCK) and the United Society for Partnership in the Gospel (USPG). There are over 20 Associate Members.

Its main tasks are concerned with the Church of England's role in furthering partnership in mission within the Anglican Communion; supporting the work of Diocesan Companion Links; and with providing a central focus for the Church of England's World Mission Agencies. It has an advisory role in enabling English dioceses and General Synod to see their way more clearly towards their participation in world mission as members of the Anglican Communion and ecumenically.

Chair
The Rt Revd Andrew Watson (Bishop of Guildford)

Secretary
Canon Janice Price   *T:* 020 7898 1328
          E: janice.price@churchofengland.org

Mission Theology Advisory Group (MTAG)
The ecumenical Mission Theology Advisory Group is composed of nominees from the Mission and Public Affairs Division of the Archbishops' Council and the Trustees of Churches Together in Britain and Ireland (CTBI). It is concerned with the theology of mission as a resource for the churches' engagement with the world, and deals with theological issues referred to it by the participating bodies. MTAG also provides resources in the areas of spirituality, theology, reconciliation, evangelism and mission.

Co-Chair (with The Revd Prof John Drane)
The Rt Revd Dr Michael Ipgrave (Bishop of Lichfield)

Secretary
Dr Anne Richards   *T:* 020 7898 1444
          E: anne.richards@churchofengland.org

Rural Affairs Group
Primarily a consultative group, with the purpose to shape, envision and develop a programme of work and activities to support the mission and growth of the rural Church of England.

Chair
The Rt Revd Richard Frith (Bishop of Hereford)

Secretary
Canon Dr Jill Hopkinson, The Arthur Rank Centre, Stoneleigh Park, Warwickshire CV8 2LG   *T:* 024 7685 3073
          E: jill.hopkinson@churchofengland.org

Presence and Engagement Task Group
Presence and Engagement is the Church of England's national programme equipping Christians for mission and ministry in religiously diverse communities. More information, contacts and resources can be found at www.presenceandengagement.org.uk.

Chair
The Rt Revd Tony Robinson (Bishop of Wakefield)

Secretary
Kat Brealey   *T:* 07951 671552
          E: kat.brealey@churchofengland.org

Diocesan Inter-Faith Advisers
Bath and Wells
The Revd Simon Bale
          E-mail: sj_bale@icloud.com

Birmingham
Dr Andrew Smith
          E-mail: andrews@birmingham.anglican.org

Blackburn
Mr Andrew Pratt
          E-mail: andrewpratt1@btinternet.com

Bristol
The Revd Ed Davis
          E-mail: ed.davis@bristol.ac.uk

Canterbury
The Revd Steven Hughes
          E-mail: steven.hughes24@btinternet.com

Carlisle
The Revd Cameron Butland
          E-mail: cbsa03@gmail.com

Chelmsford
The Revd Julia Murphy
          E-mail: jmmurphy@essex.ac.uk

Chester
The Revd Roger Clarke
          E-mail: yficerdy@btopenworld.com

Chichester
Canon Dr Andrew Wingate
          E-mail: andrewwingate5@gmail.com

Derby
Mr Kevin Ball
          E-mail: k.h.ball@tinyworld.co.uk

Durham
The Revd Chris Howson
          E-mail: chaplain@sunderland.ac.uk

Exeter
The Revd Canon John Hall
          E-mail: jehall1949@icloud.com

Gloucester
The Revd Simon Howell
          E-mail: revsimonhowell@talktalk.net

Guildford
The Revd Andrew Bishop
          E-mail: andrew@guildford-cathedral.org

Hereford
The Revd David Roberts
          E-mail: dhroberts38@gmail.com

Leeds
Mr Richard Bennett
          E-mail: richard.bennett@
          faithfulneighbours.org.uk

Leicester
The Revd Dr Tom Wilson
          E-mail: director@stphilipscentre.co.uk

Lichfield
The Revd Ray Gaston
          E-mail: ray.gaston@lichfield.anglican.org

Lincoln
The Revd Mike Cooney
          E-mail: mike.cooney@btinternet.com

Liverpool
Mrs Nadine Daniel
                    E-mail: nadine.daniel@
                    liverpoolcathedral.org.uk

London (Edmonton)
The Revd James Walters
          E-mail: j.walters2@lse.ac.uk

London (Northolt)
The Ven Duncan Green
          E-mail: archdeacon.northolt@
                    london.anglican.org

London (Stepney)
The Revd Alan Green
          E-mail: alan.green@virgin.net

London (Willesden)
The Revd Laurence Hillel
                    E-mail: laurence.hillel@
                    londoninterfaith.org.uk

Manchester
The Revd Stephen Williams
          E-mail: saintgabriel@talktalk.net

Manchester (Oldham)
The Revd Philip Rawlings
          E-mail: philjr053@gmail.com

Newcastle
Mrs Lesley Hillary
          E-mail: l.hillary@newcastle.anglican.org

Norwich
The Rt Revd David Gillett
          E-mail: dkgillett@btinternet.com

Oxford
The Ven Martin Gorick
          E-mail: archdeacon.oxford@
                    oxford.anglican.org

Portsmouth
The Revd Andy Marshall
          E-mail: andy.marshall@port.ac.uk

Rochester
The Revd Richard Martin
          E-mail: ramartin@talktalk.net

St Albans
The Revd Bonnie Evans-Hills
          E-mail: bonnie.evans-hills@hotmail.co.uk

St Edmundsbury and Ipswich
The Revd Charles Jenkin
          E-mail: c.jenkin@tiscali.co.uk

Salisbury
The Revd Guy Wilkinson
          E-mail: guy@gwilkinson.org.uk

Sheffield
The Revd John Hibberd
          E-mail: john.hibberd@sheffield.anglican.org

Sodor and Man
The Revd James McGowan
          E-mail: revdjamesmcgowan@outlook.com

Southwark
Mrs Siriol Davies
          E-mail: siriol.davies@southwark.anglican.org

Southwark (Croydon)
The Revd Dr Jacob Devadson
          E-mail: 2revjacob@gmail.com

Southwell and Nottingham
The Revd David McColough
          E-mail: davidmcc@southwell.anglican.org

Truro
The Revd Jem Thorold
          E-mail: chaplain@truro.anglican.org

York
The Revd Dominic Black
          E-mail: dominic.black@trinitycentre.org

NATIONAL STRUCTURES

EDUCATION OFFICE
The Formation of People for the Transformation of the World

The Education Office promotes the mission of the Church of England through transformative lifelong education (statutory and voluntary) with a focus on wisdom for living and the spiritual, intellectual and emotional development that leads to the flourishing of every person.

The work of the Church of England Education Office is to:

• Offer a compelling vision for the purpose of lifelong education (both statutory and voluntary) in the mission of the Church of England

• Speak confidently on behalf of the Church in the public sphere, offering advocacy and challenge across the breadth of education issues for all ages.

• Engage with government departments to shape and respond to policy and practice to ensure that public debate recognizes the true value of education.

• Equip parishes, dioceses and schools to lead debate in their local context.

Governance

The Archbishops' Council and National Society have an Operating Framework which sets out how the two bodies work together to discharge their overlapping responsibilities in England effectively, so as to advance the mission of the Church of England, enhance the effectiveness of its work in education and among children and young people more generally and ensure that the work of the integrated staff team of the Education Office is resourced and communicated.

The Education Office operates in four main areas, with overall leadership provided by the Chief Education Officer.

1. Developing the Church's presence and witness in higher education by:

   • developing, implementing and monitoring policy for the Church of England in relation to higher education

   • stimulating and developing practical concern in student and university affairs – a concern both for the life of higher education institutions, their ethical, social, spiritual and religious concerns, and for the individuals who work and study in the sector

   • liaison and partnership with national bodies, including the Department for Business, Innovation, and Skills, the Higher Education Funding Council,

representative university groups, ecumenical and other faith bodies

   • supporting and developing the network of chaplains in higher education by providing training and ongoing communication.

2. In further education the key role is strategic support and development with the aim of developing the Church's presence and witness within FE colleges and the wider post-16 sector by:

   • engaging with the Government's programme of reform by monitoring policy and contributing to improvement strategies

   • increasing the Church's involvement through establishing and supporting chaplaincy and college/faith partnerships

   • helping to shape the sector's understanding of spiritual and moral development for staff and students, fostering shared human values and dialogue and promoting a more holistic educational experience for all students

   • working with a range of ecumenical and inter-faith partners

   • resourcing and supporting the growing number of chaplains in schools.

The Division is involved in the work of the eleven Universities founded as a direct result of the Church's role as first provider of mass schooling. All are highly diverse organizations which retain a commitment to teacher education alongside a wide portfolio of courses, including (for most) significant departments of theology and religious studies.

3. Informal learning and nurture of children and young people is guided by Going for Growth, the formally adopted framework for national work. Going for Growth provides three focuses of work at national level:

   • working towards every child and young person having a life-enhancing encounter with the Christian faith and the person of Jesus Christ

   • working for the transformation of communities, recognizing and enabling the capacity of children and young people to be the agents of change for themselves and for others

   • professional support and challenge of all those working with children and young people in the name of the church.

Areas of work flowing from Going for Growth include developing materials for parishes to help them listen to children and make changes; research and data to help identify successful mission activities with children and young people; integrating and strengthening the Church of England Youth Council within the work of the Church.

Support and development of the diocesan youth and children's officers is provided through training and ongoing communication, principally through the Going for Growth website and the Child in the Midst mailing.

4. Work with schools furthering the development and effectiveness of the Church's 4,700 academies, primary and secondary schools in the light of far-reaching changes to the education system in England. The ongoing work of the Education Office includes:

- The development of a Foundation for Educational Leadership to support and enhance the implementation of succession strategies
- increasing the number of Church of England schools especially through the Free School programme
- support to diocesan education teams in the development of academies
- enabling DBEs to grow their provision through professional support and guidance, releasing and accessing funds for new developments
- support for governors and employers of the school workforce
- identifying, disseminating and sharing the best practice
- revision and development of the nationally authorized framework for the denominational inspection of Anglican and Methodist schools, including the training and accreditation for inspectors
- sample contracts and associated policies for appointment of staff in church schools

- resourcing high quality Religious Education and collective worship, including developing a new scheme of work for Church schools in the teaching of Christianity and promotion of the Worship Workshop website
- monitoring the impact of legislation, capital programmes and the various programmes for expanding and changing the school system.

Chief Education Officer
The Revd Nigel Genders   T: 020 7898 1500
    E: nigel.genders@churchofengland.org

Head of School Policy
Ms Rowan Ferguson   T: 020 7898 1789
    E: rowan.ferguson@churchofengland.org

Christian character, RE and SIAMS Manager
Mr Derek Holloway   T: 020 7898 1490
    E: derek.holloway@churchofengland.org

Foundation Project Development Manager
Mr James Townsend   T: 020 7898 1515
    E: james.townsend@churchofengland.org

National Going for Growth (Children and Youth) Adviser
The Revd Mary Hawes   T: 020 7898 1504
    E: mary.hawes@churchofengland.org

National Adviser for Higher Education
Vacancy   T: 020 7898 1513
    E: garry.neave@churchofengland.org

National Further Education and post 16 Adviser
The Revd Garry Neave   T: 020 7898 1517
    E: garry.neave@churchofengland.org

Business and Support Manager
Mrs Cheryl Payne, Church House, Great Smith Street, London SW1P 3AZ   T: 020 7898 1501
    E: cheryl.payne@churchofengland.org

CATHEDRAL AND CHURCH BUILDINGS DIVISION

The Cathedral and Church Buildings Division is the national resource supporting the use, conservation and development of the Church of England's 42 cathedrals and 16,000 parish churches for worship, mission and community engagement. The Church of England has responsibility for 12,500 listed buildings (including 45 per cent of England's Grade I listed buildings and

three world heritage sites), while many churchyards are an important ecological resource.

We provide the secretariat for three statutory bodies: the Church Buildings Council (CBC), the Council's Statutory Advisory Committee (SAC) on Closed and Closing Churches and the Cathedrals Fabric Commission for England (CFCE).

We campaign on behalf of cathedral and church buildings, with the Government, Historic England and other heritage bodies to keep church buildings in their vision and to ensure church buildings' interests are taken into account.

We work strategically, ensuring that where national initiatives can make a significant difference we help add value to the work of cathedrals, dioceses and parishes. We are outward-looking and service-orientated. We develop new approaches to opening churches to their communities and create models that can be used across the country. Our campaigns raise awareness of conservation issues and threats to church buildings (such as the HS2 rail project or changes to national planning policy) and have been highly influential in lobbying the Government and other national bodies.

In 2015 we published the Report of the Church Buildings Review, which was accepted by Synod at its November meeting, and subsequently put out for wider consultation. This was the first comprehensive review for many years into national policy and resourcing put into church buildings. It was jointly commissioned by the Archbishops' Council and the Church Commissioners. The review group, chaired by the Bishop of Worcester, was set up as part of the Renewal and Reform programme. The review considered models for church custodianship, funding and care and brought to the fore the term 'festival church'. This is a proposal to keep churches open for worship and part of the community whilst removing some of the burdens legally required of parish churches.

The review also looked at the way church buildings are staffed from Church House and proposed a bringing together of the Archbishops' Council and Church Commissioners staff working in this area. This began in 2016 with the staff teams moving together in Church House. The report propose the establishment of a new Church Buildings Commission that will replace the Church Buildings Council and the Church Buildings Uses and Disposals Committee.

The new Faculty Jurisdiction Rules 2015 came into force on 1 January 2016. These have introduced a greater consistency of regulation across the dioceses, most especially by introducing new national lists of works that can be done without a faculty, replacing the previous diocesan de minimis lists.

During 2015 the number of diocese uses the online faculty system grew from the initial three pilot dioceses to twenty-two. There are a further eight dioceses signed up and the system is widely accepted nationally. Coupled with this the Church Heritage Record went live in 2015. This brings heritage information about church buildings into step with the national secular building online equivalents. Its particular benefit to parishes is that it works seamlessly with the online faculty system to populate the formulaic parts of faculty forms and to assist parishes with their Statements of Significance by providing a place to store and link to relevant information about the building and its history.

Our website Churchdays.co.uk uses data from the Church Heritage Record to present information to encourage tourist visits to church buildings. The site includes a searchable map showing churches and nearby attractions. It includes a simple encouragement to visit churches, an illustrated guide to key features of most buildings and a featured church section. Updated every month, featured churches articles draw attention to a themed group of features across several churches. These include the oldest churches, churches with good environmental credentials, pre-Raphaelite stained glass and many others.

ChurchCare (www.ChurchCare.co.uk) is the Division's website and name for the department's non-statutory functions. ChurchCare provides a comprehensive source of information for everyone involved in managing church and cathedral buildings and maintaining them for the enjoyment of future generations.

ChurchCare also includes Shrinking the Footprint, the Church's national campaign working with dioceses to reduce their carbon footprint by 80 per cent and raise awareness of environmental issues. Shrinking the Footprint is a cross-divisional campaign involving Cathedral and Church Buildings Division and Mission and Public Affairs. The Chairman of the Environmental Working Group is the Rt Revd Nicholas Holtam, Bishop of Salisbury.

Shrinking the Footprint hosted the organisation of the Pilgrimage to Paris, in partnership with Christian Aid, Tearfund and CAFOD. Forty pilgrims walked the 200 miles from London to Paris to press for an ambitious climate change agreement in the COP21 talks. In Paris the pilgrims were welcomed by Christiana Figueres of the United Nations, and the Bishop of Salisbury represented faith organizations in public conversation with President Hollande. Pressure from faith organizations was seen as key to the successful talks.

In 2015 Shrinking the Footprint achieved a stage one Heritage Lottery Fund grant for the Virtuous Circles project. Based on the church at Dulas in Herefordshire the project will introduce a pod for visitor accommodation into the nave of the church, whilst leaving the chancel for worship. The church is on key long-distance footpaths and is well placed for walker accommodation. The project will provide local employment and generate funds for the upkeep of the building.

A list of the Diocesan Environmental Officers can be found here: http://www.churchcare.co.uk/churches/church-buildings-council/who-s-who/deos/deo-contact-details

In 2016 Her Majesty the Queen celebrated her 90th birthday. In 2015 the Division spearheaded a campaign to encourage each church to hold a festival of some sort on the weekend of 10-12 June 2016. We brought together key groups in church celebration events (musicians, flower arrangers, bell ringers, education) to coordinate activity.

The policy underlying all our activities is to keep church buildings open, serving the worshipping community and wider society. Following the Division's involvement, the Diocese of Norwich is to launch a new Diocesan Trust to support rural churches with little or no community, which will assist with repairs and maintenance whilst enabling churches to stay open. The initiative is a new arm to the Division's Open and Sustainable Churches campaign which encourages congregations, dioceses and archdeacons to share their buildings and engage with community, cultural, and commercial groups, thereby gaining more financial and social capital to further mission and maintain the Church's priceless heritage. In addition we are carrying out further work on the important use of church buildings for social engagement and expanding guidance on ChurchCare on food banks, night shelters and community banks.

In 2015 the Division worked with the DCMS and National Heritage Memorial Fund on the Listed Places of Worship Roofs Grant Fund. In total this will release £55 million for essential works to roofs and rainwater goods, the two most important elements to keeping a building in good condition. The Division also raises funds for distribution to cathedrals and church buildings for the conservation of fabric and treasures in church buildings. Two funds, the Anglican Parish Churches Fund (charity number 1148066) and the English Cathedrals Fund (charity number 1148698) act as vehicles for charitable donations to support these programmes. Since 2000 we have distributed over £9 million for church buildings projects.

For more information on the work of the Division, see the ChurchCare Annual Review 2014 http://www.churchcare.co.uk/images/AnnualReview_2014_low_res_web.pdf which provides an update to the ChurchCare Impact Review 2013 http://www.churchcare.co.uk/images/Churchcare_Impact_Review_digital_15.05.13.pdf

ChurchCare is on Twitter @CofE_Churchcare and Facebook. Shrinking the Footprint is on Twitter @CofECampaign and Facebook. ChurchDays is on Twitter @ChurchDays

Lead Bishop on Cathedrals and Church Buildings
The Rt Revd Dr John Inge

Director
Becky Clark   T: 020 7898 1888
                         E: becky.clark@churchofengland.org

The Church Buildings Council

The Church Buildings Council (CBC) advises Chancellors and Diocesan Advisory Committees on faculty applications and clergy, churchwardens, architects and others responsible for church buildings on their care, use and development. It considers proposals that have a high impact on significant buildings, parts of buildings or their contents that are, or may become, the subject of faculty applications (e.g. the construction of church extensions, re-ordering schemes, the sale of church furnishings, the partial demolition of churches, the conservation of significant furnishings and related archaeological work). The CBC also acts on the Archbishops' Council's behalf in contacts with Government and in negotiations with professional bodies over church inspection and repair; it assists in the review of legislation relating to church buildings and their contents.

The CBC maintains contact with Diocesan Advisory Committees through regular circulation of information, by an annual meeting for Chairmen, Secretaries and other members, and by visits. The Chair of the CBC and Director of the Division have regular meetings with the Dean of the Arches and the Chair of the Ecclesiastical Judges Association and contribute to their biennial conferences.

The CBC's specialist committees offer expert advice on conservation matters. They consist of experts from leading institutions including the V&A, Royal Collection and Cambridge University.

Annually about 20 churches are closed nationally under the Mission and Pastoral Measure. The CBC, through its Statutory Advisory Committee, advises the Church Commissioners and the Churches Conservation Trust on the interest, quality and importance of closed and closing churches and their contents, and the alteration and conversion of churches for alternative use, working closely with government and local authorities of Church and State. The CBC provides Diocesan Mission and Pastoral Committees with detailed reports about the architectural and historic qualities of churches considering closure for regular worship which also include additional advice about ways the building could be adapted to stay in use in the parish system.

Chairman
The Rt Hon Canon Sir Tony Baldry

Vice Chairman
The Revd Canon Michael Ainsworth

Members
A list of current Church Building Council members can be found here:
http://www.churchcare.co.uk/images/
Churches/church-buildings-council.pdf

The Cathedrals Fabric Commission for England

The Cathedrals Fabric Commission for England (CFCE) acts as a planning authority to cathedrals, overseeing the Church's own system of controls under the Care of Cathedrals Measure 2011. Cathedral Chapters are required to get permission from the CFCE, or in some cases their own Fabric Advisory Committee, before implementing any proposals which would materially affect the character and heritage significance of a cathedral building, its setting, or archaeological remains within its precinct, or an object of artistic, archaeological, architectural or historic interest owned by the Chapter.

The Commission offers free, expert advice on the architecture, archaeology, conservation and history of cathedrals and their precincts, landscape and environment, publishes a range of guidance and advisory notes (available on www.ChurchCare.co.uk) and runs seminars and conferences for Fabric Advisory Committees and cathedral chapters and their professional advisers.

Chair
Dame Fiona Reynolds

Vice-Chair
Sir Paul Britton
Jennie Page

Members
For a list of members please visit http://churchcare.co.uk/cathedrals/cathedrals-fabric-commission-for-england

Staff of the Cathedral and Church Buildings Division

Director
Becky Clark   *T:* 020 7898 1888
          E: becky.clark@churchofengland.org

Senior Church Buildings Officer
Dr David Knight   *T:* 020 7898 1874
          E: david.knight@churchofengland.org

Major Project Officer
Dr Joseph Elders   *T:* 020 7898 1875
          E: joseph.elders@churchofengland.org

Head of Conservation
Janet Berry   *T:* 020 7898 1889
          E: janet.berry@churchofengland.org

Fundraising and Development Officer
Joseph Friedrich   *T:* 020 7898 1885
          E: joseph.friedrich@churchofengland.org

Cathedrals Officer
Anne Locke   *T:* 020 7898 1862
          E: anne.locke@churchofengland.org

Church Buildings Officers
Christina Emerson   *T:* 020 7898 1886
          E: christina.emerson@churchofengland.org
Lisa McIntyre   *T:* 020 7898 1864
          E: lisa.mcintyre@churchofengland.org

Church Buildings Officer, Closed Churches
Tom Ashley   *T:* 020 7898 1871
          E: thomas.ashley@churchofengland.org

Faculty Online Project Officer
Julie Patenaude   *T:* 020 7898 1860
          E: julie.patenaude@churchofengland.org

Conservation Grants Administrator
John Webster   *T:* 020 7898 1863
          E: john.webster@churchofengland.org

Environmental Policy Officer
Kirsten Firth   *T:* 020 7898 1865
          E: kirsten.firth@churchofengland.org

Honorary Librarians
Diana Coulter   *T:* 020 7898 1884
          E: diana.coulter@churchofengland.org
Sue Drury   *T:* 020 7898 1884
          E: sue.drury@churchofengland.org
Angela Horrocks   *T:* 020 7898 1884
          E: angela.horrocks@churchofengland.org

Church House Publishing

The Archbishops' Council publishes a range of print and digital resources to support the ministry and mission of the Church under its Church House Publishing imprint, with Hymns Ancient & Modern (HA&M) acting as its production and marketing arm under an agreement in place since 2009.

Publishing Manager
Dr Thomas Allain Chapman
        T: 020 7898 1450
        E: thomas.allain-chapman@
          churchofengland.org

General Enquiries   *T:* 01603 785923
        F: 01603 785915
     E: publishing@churchofengland.org

The Church of England Year Book
        E: yearbook@churchofengland.org

The Pilgrim Course
        E: pilgrim@churchofengland.org

Crockford's Clerical Directory
The Compiler, Crockford
Church House, Great Smith Street, London
SW1P 3AZ   *T:* 020 7898 1012
         F: 020 7898 1769
     E: crockford@churchofengland.org

NATIONAL STRUCTURES

Life Events

The Life Events team looks at how to help churches make the most of mission and ministry opportunities arising from contact with people at times of transition in their lives – weddings, baptism of a child and funerals. Through the approximately 5,500 services held each week throughout the Church of England, the Church encounters around 500,000 people who come as guests as well as the key participants at these services. The team provides research, resources and training to help parishes become confident in this core ministry.

Head of Life Events
The Revd Canon Dr Sandra Millar
        E: sandra.millar@churchofengland.org

Projects Officer
Suzanne Gray
        E: suzanne.gray@churchofengland.org

Weddings
www.yourchurchwedding.org is a very popular and successful website, viewed by nearly a million people each year. Work continues in encouraging local churches to be involved in local wedding fairs as well as engaging with Wedding Shows nationally. Resources to help parishes give good information and maintain contact with wedding couples are available through www.churchprinthub.org

Baptisms
Extensive and wide-ranging research with families and clergy has informed the development of resources to support church ministry to parents wanting to have children under 12 baptized. There is a website for parents, www.churchofenglandchristenings.org, and resources for churches which are available through www.churchsupporthub.org and www.churchprinthub.org.

Funerals
Research with bereaved people, funeral directors, and clergy has helped to shape the approach to funeral ministry. The Church of England is still the leading provider of funeral 'services' and Life Events works to help parishes hold conversations about death and dying, to build good pastoral and professional relationships, and to know more about changing cultural and practical trends around funerals. This work has resulted in a new funerals website, www.churchofenglandfunerals.org, as well as new resources for churches available via www.churchsupporthub.org and www.churchprinthub.org

Office
Church House, Great Smith Street, London
SW1P 3AZ

Renewal and Reform

Renewal and Reform is a body of work which seeks to provide a narrative of hope to the Church of England in the twenty-first century. It builds on the three goals articulated by General Synod in 2010 to:

- contribute as the national church to the common good
- facilitate the growth of the church in numbers and depth of discipleship
- re-imagine the church's ministry

Renewal and Reform seeks to build on the excellent work already taking place across the church to articulate a hopeful future for our churches and, more particularly, the communities we serve. The work is multi-faceted and incorporates a number of priorities based on a realistic assessment of where we are and how we might respond.

Programme Director
Mike Eastwood

Programme Manager
Dylan O'Sullivan

Office
Church House, Great Smith Street, London SW1P 3AZ   *T:* 020 7898 1011
W: https//www.churchofengland.org/ renewal-reform.aspx

CHURCH OF ENGLAND CENTRAL SERVICES

Finance and Resources

Finance and Resources is a shared service function providing six levels of support to the NCIs and wider Church generally:

1. The Finance Operations Section is responsible for processing, recording and maintaining the prime books of account, banking, payments, payroll (including Clergy Pay), management reporting, statutory financial reporting, budgeting and forecasting, securing assets and ensuring the bodies are legally compliant in terms of statutory reporting, tax and charity law.
2. The Financial Policy and Planning section provides financial analysis and advice to help inform management decisions across the NCIs and has a watching brief over the finances of the Church as a whole.
3. The SAP support team is responsible for managing the use of and controls within the NCIs SAP system.
4. The Research and Statistics team collaborates with all sectors of the national Church bodies to provide research and statistical information and services.
5. The Strategy and Development Unit advises on resource allocation, evaluating the effectiveness of spending plans and measuring impact.
6. The National Stewardship and Resources Officer supports parishes and dioceses in developing mechanisms for effective giving and manages the National Procurement team negotiating purchasing contracts which are available for parishes, cathedrals and dioceses to participate in.

Chief Finance and Operations Officer
Gareth Mostyn

Finance Operations
In addition to maintaining the key information systems the Finance Operations team covers Payroll, Treasury, Processing, Financial and Management Accounting and Tax.

Payroll Services
Pay every month over:

* 8,000 active clergy
* 800 staff in the NCIs and Pensions Board homes

* 18,000 pensioners based in the UK and overseas

Treasury
Handle the NCIs' non-investing bank activities, monitoring up to £30 million of balances and cash flow demands on a daily basis.

Accounts Payable
Process 35,000 suppliers' invoices every year, and maintain supplier master data on SAP.

Accounts Receivable
Process 75,000 invoices to customers and receipt of £720 million in payments every year and maintain customer master data on SAP.

Financial Accounting
We keep an eye on the data that ends up in the finance system, as a result of the work by the teams above. Once we are sure the data is complete and we have carried out all the necessary checks and balances, we produce statutory accounts for the three main NCIs, central service company and the four pension schemes, as well as around 30 other smaller entities. We are the main point of contact with external auditors.

Management Accounting
Provide regular management accounts for the three main NCIs and the central service company and develop and agree the annual budgets, involving total expenditure of £164 million.

Tax
Provide a tax strategy for the NCIs, ensuring existing and new activities account for tax correctly, whilst ensuring investments and other activities are structured in a way to ensure the NCIs can take advantage of the reliefs available to UK-based charities.

Director of Finance Operations
Joanna Woolcock   *T:* 020 7898 1677
          E: joanna.woolcock@churchofengland.org

FINANCIAL POLICY AND PLANNING
The Financial Policy Section provides financial analysis, information and advice to support decision-making. It has a key role in helping the National Church Institutions – the Archbishops' Council, Church Commissioners

201

and Pensions Board – and increasingly the monitoring and management of their finances. We aim to be forward-looking and thinking and act in a Business Partner role, working alongside others to help identify and evaluate options and manage financial risk.

In respect of wider Church finances it produces an annual consolidation of Church of England finances called the financial overview. It has developed financial information dashboards for dioceses to help their planning and arranges an annual Diocesan Finance Conference. It also worked with the Diocesan and Cathedrals Accounts Groups to develop new guidance for producing reports and accounts under the new accounting standards introduced in 2015.

The department provides the secretariat for the Council's Finance Committee which is responsible for the management of the Council's financial business and advice and coordination on financial matters over the Church as a whole, its Investment Committee and the Inter-Diocesan Finance Forum. The latter, which comprises three representatives of each diocese, provides a twice-yearly opportunity for consultation and discussion on issues of mutual interest including remuneration policy, conditions of service, pensions policy, the Council's budget and apportionment. It seeks to ensure that the General Synod is aware of the significant financial implications of proposals before decisions are taken and calculates and communicates the apportionment of the Council's budget to dioceses.

The section supports the work of the Church Commissioners' Assets Committee and its staff level Assets Management Group. Key roles include being the main point of contact with the Commissioners actuaries in the annual assessment of their pensions obligations and the capacity of the fund for other support to the Church, oversight of the production of coordinated investment performance statistics and financial forecasts in respect of income, cashflow and longer-term actuarial projection. It assists the Pensions Board in the financial management of the CHARM clergy retirement housing scheme and led the project which resulted in the Board issuing a £100 million listed bond in 2015.

Head of Financial Policy and Planning
David White   *T:* 020 7898 1684
    E: david.white@churchofengland.org

SAP SUPPORT TEAM
The SAP support team is responsible for managing the use of the NCIs SAP system, supporting the core modules of finance, real estate, purchasing, loans management and plant maintenance.

The SAP team provides a helpdesk service for the Archbishops' Council, Church Commissioners, Church of England Pensions Board and Church of England Central Services, dealing with technical changes to the system and user queries in relation to all modules.

Service Delivery Manager
Sarah Jowett   *T:* 020 7898 1600
    E: sarah.jowett@churchofengland.org

RESEARCH AND STATISTICS
See page 203.

STRATEGY AND DEVELOPMENT UNIT
The role of the Strategy and Development Unit is to undertake research, analysis and strategy development on behalf of the Church of England in respect of the resourcing of its ministry and mission (principally relating to those resources held at national level). One key part of the role is to ensure that the funds managed by the Church Commissioners are being used effectively to advance the spiritual and numerical growth of the Church. The other key part of the Unit's work is to provide support to diocesan senior leadership teams in developing their growth, change management and resource allocation strategies.

Director of Strategy and Development Unit
Philip James   *T:* 020 7898 1671
    E: philip.james@churchofengland.org

STEWARDSHIP AND RESOURCES
Through its Christian Stewardship Committee, the Archbishops' Council affirms the principles and practice of Christian stewardship as a part of discipleship. Stewardship advisers encourage church people to respond to God's love and generosity and resource God's mission through the Church by the discovery and use of human and financial resources. This is often focused on the giving of money – regularly, tax-effectively and in proportion to income.

Initiatives are promoted, support given and ideas exchanged between the diocesan members of the Christian stewardship network. There is a particular focus on identifying, documenting and resourcing elements of good practice, so that other dioceses and parishes can benefit from what is proven to be effective.

The team make available a national website to resource all those concerned with Christian giving, stewardship and parish finances: www.parishresources.org.uk. This contains a wide range of resources for parish-giving officers, treasurers, gift-aid secretaries and those who preach and teach on stewardship and generosity as well as issues relating to PCCs as charities, and other associated issues.

Through the Parish Buying initiative, all parts of the church are able to access national contracts which pool the Church's purchasing power. This not only aims to save money, but to save time and enable parishes and others to buy with confidence. This is supervised by a National Procurement Group, and can be accessed at www.parishbuying.org.uk.

Another way of exercising stewardship is for people to leave a gift in their wills. Each year parishes receive a total of about £50 million. Our Legacy and Funding Officer runs workshops for parishes and there is a specific website aimed at those considering leaving a gift to the Church: www.churchlegacy.org.uk. Workshops are also held to support those parishes who are running major capital campaigns.

National Stewardship and Resources Officer
John Preston   *T:* 020 7898 1540
                    E: john.preston@churchofengland.org

National Legacy and Funding Officer
Eleanor Stead   *T:* 020 7898 1564
                    E: eleanor.stead@churchofengland.org

Risk Management and Internal Audit Department

The Risk Management and Internal Audit Department provides internal audit services to the Church Commissioners, the Church of England Pensions Board, the Archbishops' Council and the other National Church Institutions.

The department carries out risk based internal audit assignments in accordance with the annual internal audit plan, approved by the Audit Committee, and also investigates particular issues that might arise from time to time.

The department coordinates and facilitates the risk management process and works with management to update operational and strategic risk registers. In addition, it provides consultancy support to managers on matters of governance, risk and internal control.

Director of Risk Management and
Internal Audit
Mr Aneil Jhumat   *T:* 020 7898 1658
                    E: aneil.jhumat@churchofengland.org

Research and Statistics

The Research and Statistics unit collects, analyses, and publishes data relating to a wide range of aspects of the Church of England. These include annual attendance and finance statistics, information about licensed ministers, and the activities of Cathedrals and chapels.

We use data from the national census and other government statistics to provide parish-level information for the Church of England's 12,500 parishes. Publications and data can be accessed at:
                https://www.churchofengland.org/
about-us/facts-stats/research-statistics.aspx

Head of Research and Statistics
Dr Bev Botting   *T:* 020 7898 1542
                    E: bev.botting@churchofengland.org

Senior Statistical Research Officers
Dr Ken Eames   *T:* 020 7898 1592
                    E: ken.eames@churchofengland.org

Louise McFerran   *T:* 020 7898 1546
                    E: louise.mcferran@churchofengland.org

Information Systems and Office Manager
Simeon Christian   *T:* 020 7898 1549
                    E: simeon.christian@churchofengland.org

Statistical Research Officers
Charlotte Hall   *T:* 020 7898 1591
                    E: charlotte.hall@churchofengland.org
Charlotte Sibtain   *T:* 020 7898 1594
                    E: charlotte.sibtain@churchofengland.org

Assistant Statistical Researcher
Sola Odunsi   *T:* 020 7898 1547
                    E: sola.odunsi@churchofengland.org

Mapping and Graphics Officers
Gwen Jones   *T:* 020 7898 1724
                    E: gwen.jones@churchofengland.org
Geraldine O'Donnell   *T:* 020 7898 1725
                    E: geraldine.odonnell@churchofengland.org

Information Technology Services

The IT Department has undergone a radical transformation. IT executes a mixture of on-premise, Cloud and third-party IT services, in an IT environment that utilizes the latest technologies. The IT function serves 600 staff in NCIs and NCIs co-located bodies and provides support to leverage IT effectively and adopt common solutions where practical. IT provides a broad range of services covering service desk, technical consultancy, architecture, desktops, platforms for hosting applications, websites and data, telephony, security, change management, business analysis, project support, training, procurement and systems administration.

Director of IT
Yasmin Thompson, Church House, Great Smith Street, London SW1P 3AZ
T: 020 7898 1640 or 07879021035

Libraries and Archives

The Record Centre, which is a central service operated by the Church Commissioners, houses the non-current records of the Church Commissioners, the Archbishops' Council, the Church of England Pensions Board, the General Synod and the National Society, together with those of some ecumenical bodies. Its main purposes are to provide records management advice and low-cost off-site storage for the business records of the Central Church Bodies as well as to preserve, develop and promote access to its archival and printed collections in support of the work of the Church and the wider public. Enquiries are welcome; archive material can be seen at our Reading Room by prior appointment.
Open: 1000–1600 hours Tues–Thurs
Closed Public Holidays

Office
Church of England Record Centre, 15 Galleywall Road, South Bermondsey, London SE16 3PB   T. 020 7898 1030
E: archives@churchofengland.org

Human Resources Department

The Human Resources (HR) department aims to facilitate the National Church Institutions (NCIs) and diocesan bishops in achieving their mission and business objectives by delivering efficient and cost-effective HR services, including support for recruitment, in relation to the 470 staff employed by the NCIs and the 141 staff of diocesan bishops. It also contracts with the Corporation of Church House for services in relation to their 33 staff.
How we do this in relation to the NCIs:

- Establishing a partnership culture and collaborative working between the employers and their people
- Creating a high-performance working environment where employees have role clarity and focus on delivery, learning and development
- Sustaining a diverse workforce and a fair and just workplace
- Maximizing opportunities for employees and the organizations through strategic resourcing, succession planning and talent management
- Engaging with our customers to assist their articulation and our understanding of their needs and expectations to facilitate the successful delivery of their service
- Promoting a safe and healthy working environment
- Enabling, with others (particularly diocesan HR Advisers), bishops and dioceses to better support and develop their parochial clergy.

STAFF
Director of Human Resources
Hannah Foster   T: 020 7898 1565
E: hannah.foster@churchofengland.org

Senior HR Manager
Miss Leann Dawson   T: 020 7898 1411
E: leann.dawson@churchofengland.org

HR Manager
Miss Kristal Clark   T: 020 7898 1747
E: kristal.clark@churchofengland.org

Secretary, Remuneration and Conditions of Service Committee
Ms Pavlina Wilkin   T: 020 7898 1651
E: pavlina.wilkin@churchofengland.org

Remuneration and Conditions of Service Committee

The Remuneration and Conditions of Service Committee meets four times a year and advises the Archbishops' Council and the House of Bishops on a strategy for ministry, with particular reference to the remuneration and conditions of service of those in authorized ministry. The Committee works in collaboration with dioceses, the Church Commissioners and the Church of England Pensions Board, and with ecumenical partners on the following matters:

- To produce, in partnership with dioceses, a framework of national policy for stipends and other related matters, and to advise dioceses as appropriate on such matters.
- To develop policy relating to pensions in collaboration with the Church of England Pensions Board and, where appropriate, the Church Commissioners.
- To promote, in partnership with dioceses, clear conditions of work for all licensed ministers.
- To make recommendations about the scope, structure and level of parochial fees.
- To monitor and advise in consultation with interested parties on sector and chaplaincy ministries within the total ministry of the Church.

- To work in collaboration with dioceses and, as far as possible, with ecumenical partners in the provision and development of continuing ministerial education for and review of accredited ministers, ordained and lay.
- To report regularly to the Archbishops' Council on its work.

Chair
The Rt Revd David Walker

MEMBERS
The Revd Dr Philip
Miss Imogen Clout
Canon David Froude
The Revd Mary Gregory
The Ven Ian Jagger
Sandra Newton
Miss Susan Pope
Canon Nigel Spraggins
Mr Brian Wilson

Secretary
Ms Pavlina Wilkin   *T:* 020 7898 1651
          E: pavlina.wilkin@churchofengland.org

Legal Office

The Legal Office of the National Institutions of the Church of England is responsible for providing legal advice and other services to the National Church Institutions. Its principal functions are:

- responsibility for the legislative programme of the General Synod;
- giving advice to the National Church Institutions and their respective committees and staff; and
- undertaking some transactional work for the National Church Institutions, especially the Church Commissioners and the Pensions Board.

Head of the Legal Office, Chief Legal Adviser to the Archbishops' Council, Registrar and Chief Legal Adviser to the General Synod and Official Solicitor to the Church Commissioners
Mr Stephen Slack   *T:* 020 7898 1366
          E: stephen.slack@churchofengland.org

Deputy Head of the Legal Office, Deputy Legal Adviser to the Archbishops' Council and the General Synod and Deputy Official Solicitor to the Church Commissioners
The Revd Alexander McGregor
          T: 020 7898 1748
          E: alexander.mcgregor@churchofengland.org

Legislative Counsel to the General Synod
Mr Christopher Packer

Office
Church House, Great Smith St, London SW1P 3AZ DX: 148403 WESTMINSTER 5
          F: 020 7898 1718/1721
          E: legal@churchofengland.org

NATIONAL STRUCTURES

Communications Office

Communication is central to the mission of the Church as a Christian presence in every community. The Communications Office provides media support and advice in a digital age to a wide range of people and organizations. The media team works across a broad portfolio and works closely with Church House Publishing (www.chpublishing.co.uk) and the Life Events team (www.churchofengland funerals.org, www.churchofengland christenings.org).

The Office serves all the National Church Institutions (including the Archbishops' Council, Church Commissioners and Pensions Board), the General Synod and the House of Bishops, and works closely with Lambeth and Bishopthorpe. It also supports and shares best practice with diocesan communicators around the country, working closely with them on national campaigns and issues and providing professional development opportunities.

The team operates a 24 hour media cover while working on a range of proactive good news stories about the Church. In the past few years, these have included the #justpray campaign and #churchlive weekly project, along with media work around safeguarding, education, cathedral and church buildings and a range of public affairs areas including the assisted dying bill. The office has developed a new training programme of communications and media courses and specialized media training for all bishops.

The Church of England website, www.churchofengland.org, is run by the team and continues to be the first port of call for many wanting to find out more about the Christian faith and the Church of England, with more than 2.3 million unique users last year. The popular Twitter feed @c_of_e has more than 56,000 followers.

Director of Communications
Tashi Lassalle
E: tashi.lassalle@churchofengland.org

Deputy Director of Communications
Rachel Harden
    E: rachel.harden@churchofengland.org

Deputy Director (Digital)
Adrian Harris
    E: adrian.harris@churchofengland.org

Head of Media Operations
John Bingham
    E: john.bingham@churchofengland.org

Senior Media Officers
Martha Linden
    E: martha.linden@churchofengland.org
Anna McCrum
    E: anna.mccrum@churchofengland.org

Media Officer
Ben Hollebon
    E: ben.hollebon@churchofengland.org

Digital Officer
Tallie Proud
    E: talitha.proud@churchofengland.org

Marketing Officer
Nardine Soloman
    E: nardine.soloman@churchofengland.org

Head of Finance Communications
Mark Arena
    E: mark.arena@churchofengland.org

Media and PR Officer (Finance)
Chris Le Marquand
    E: chris.lemarquand@churchofengland.org

Office
Church House, Great Smith Street, London SW1P 3AZ   *T:* 020 7898 1326

THE CHURCH COMMISSIONERS FOR ENGLAND

The Church Commissioners for England

Chairman
The Most Revd and Rt Hon Justin Welby

Secretary
Andrew Brown   *T:* 020 7898 1785
     E: andrew.brown@churchofengland.org

Chief Finance Officer for the National Church Institutions
Gareth Mostyn

Director of Investments
Mr Tom Joy   *T:* 020 7898 1115
     E: tom.joy@churchofengland.org

Pastoral and Closed Churches Secretary and Bishoprics and Cathedrals Secretary (Pastoral reorganization, closed churches, clergy housing and glebe)
Mr Paul Lewis   *T:* 020 7898 1741
     E: paul.lewis@churchofengland.org

Director of Libraries and Archives
Mr Declan Kelly, Church of England Record Centre, 15 Galleywall Road, South Bermondsey, London SE16 3PB
                                T: 020 7898 1432
     E: declan.kelly@churchofengland.org

FUNCTIONS
The Church Commissioners' main tasks are to manage their assets, and make money available in accordance with the duties laid upon them by Acts of Parliament and Measures of the General Synod and former Church Assembly, and to discharge other administrative duties entrusted to them.

These duties include financial support for mission and ministry in parishes, particularly in areas of need and opportunity, clergy pensions for service before 1998 and other legal commitments such as those in relation to bishops and cathedrals, and the administration of the legal framework for pastoral reorganization and settling the future of churches closed for worship.

CONSTITUTION
The Church Commissioners were formed on 1 April 1948, when Queen Anne's Bounty (1704) and the Ecclesiastical Commissioners (1836) were united.

The full body of Commissioners meets once a year to consider the Report and Accounts and the allocation of available money. The management of the Commissioners' affairs is shared between the Board of Governors, the Assets Committee, the Bishoprics and Cathedrals Committee, the Pastoral Committee, the Church Buildings (Uses and Disposals) Committee and the Audit and Risk Committee.

The National Institutions Measure 1998 created the Archbishops' Council, with consequential amendment to the Church Commissioners' functions and working relationships. The Measure also transferred their former function and powers as Central Stipends Authority to the Council on 1 January 1999.

As from 2010 the Church Commissioners are a registered charity and regulated by the Charity Commission.

CHARITABLE EXPENDITURE IN 2015
The Commissioners' charitable expenditure falls under two main headings:

- Provision of non-pensions support – £95.8 million in 2015 – to the Church including parish mission and ministry support of £47.5 million which was mainly targeted towards areas of greatest financial need.
- Payment of clergy pensions and pensions to their widows – £122.7 million in 2015. The Church of England Pensions Board authorizes pensions, but much of the money is provided and paid by the Church Commissioners. The Commissioners are responsible for pensions earned on service before 1 January 1998 and dioceses and parishes for pensions earned after that date.

MANAGEMENT OF ASSETS
The total return on the Commissioners' assets in 2015 was 8.2 per cent and their return over the last thirty years was 9.7 per cent (compared with an industry benchmark of 9 per cent).

MISSION AND PASTORAL MEASURE RESPONSIBILITIES
The Commissioners are responsible for preparing schemes for pastoral reorganization based on proposals put forward by Bishops under the Mission and Pastoral Measure 2011. This includes the consideration of

any representations made in response to consultation on draft schemes. Those making representations have the opportunity to address the relevant Commissioners' Committee.

The Commissioners also deal with objections to certain personage and glebe transactions.

CLOSED CHURCH BUILDINGS

The Mission and Pastoral Measure 2011 sets out the process for closing a church building which is no longer needed for public worship. The Commissioners will prepare a draft scheme to give effect to the proposals, consult locally and hear any representations received in respect of them.

The Commissioners also determine the future use of closed church buildings. Under the Measure, dioceses are charged with

seeking an alternative use for closed church buildings and the Commissioners determine the suitability of such uses, publishing draft schemes to enable their disposal and considering any representations.

Buildings of high heritage value for which no suitable alternative use can be found may be vested in the Churches Conservation Trust, an independent body jointly funded by the Church and State to care for such closed church buildings.

FURTHER INFORMATION

Further information is available in the Commissioners' Annual Report and Accounts, which is available free of charge from the Commissioners and via the Church of England website at https://www.churchofengland.org/about-us/structure/churchcommissioners/annual-reports.aspx

The Church Commissioners and Board of Governors

The Board of Governors transacts the functions and business of the Commissioners except where, by statute or through delegation by the Board, these are exercised by Committees. Except State office holders, all Church Commissioners are members of the Board of Governors.

Email: commissioners.enquiry@churchofengland.org

The Archbishops of Canterbury and York
The Most Revd and Rt Hon John Sentamu
The Most Revd and Rt Hon Justin Welby

First Church Estates Commissioner
Ms Loretta Minghella

Second Church Estates Commissioner
The Rt Hon Dame Caroline Spelman

Third Church Estates Commissioner
Mr Andrew Mackie

Four bishops elected by the House of Bishops of the General Synod
The Rt Revd Christopher Lowson
The Rt Revd David Walker
The Rt Revd Martin Warner

Two deans or provosts elected by all the deans and provosts
The Very Revd Jonathan Greener
The Very Revd Stephen Lake

Three clergy elected by the House of Clergy of the General Synod
The Revd Canon Bob Baker
The Revd Stephen Trott
Vacancy

Four lay persons elected by the House of Laity of the General Synod
Mrs April Alexander
Canon Peter Bruinvels
Mr Gavin Oldham
Mr Jacob Vince

Three persons nominated by Her Majesty the Queen
Mr Harry Hart
Mr Ian Watmore
Mr John Wythe

Three persons nominated by the Archbishops of Canterbury and of York acting jointly
Mr Jeremy Clack
Mr Mark Woolley
Vacancy

Three persons nominated by the Archbishops acting jointly after consultation with others including the Lord Mayors of the cities of London and York and the Vice-Chancellors of Oxford and Cambridge
Ms Poppy Allonby
Mr Graham Oldroyd
Mr Hywel Rees-Jones

Six State Office Holders
The First Lord of the Treasury
The Lord President of the Council
The Lord Chancellor
The Speaker of the House of Lords
The Secretary of State for Culture, Media and Sport
The Speaker of the House of Commons

Legal Department

Official Solicitor
Mr Stephen Slack   *T:* 020 7898 1366
     E: stephen.slack@churchofengland.org

Deputy Official Solicitor
The Revd Alexander McGregor
     T: 020 7898 1748
     E: alexander.mcgregor@churchofengland.org

Assets Committee

Exclusive responsibility for managing the Commissioners' assets, for investment policy and for advising the Board on the maximum amount of money available for distribution each year. The Committee is assisted by two sub-groups working on the Commissioners' stock exchange and property portfolios.

Chairman
Ms Loretta Minghella

Secretary
Andrew Brown   *T:* 020 7898 1785
     E: andrew.brown@churchofengland.org

Members
Ms Poppy Allonby
Canon Peter Bruinvels
Mr Harry Hart
Mr Graham Oldroyd
The Rt Revd David Walker
Mr Mark Woolley
Mr John Wythe

Audit and Risk Committee

Responsible for all matters relating to the audit of the Commissioners' accounts and related matters.

Chairman
Mr Hywel Rees-Jones

Secretary
Mr Aneil Jhumat   *T:* 020 7898 1658
     E: aneil.jhumat@churchofengland.org

Members
Ian Ailles
Mrs April Alexander
Mr Jeremy Clack
Mr Stephen East
Mr George Lynn
Mr Hywel Rees-Jones

Bishoprics and Cathedrals Committee

Responsible for the costs of episcopal administration, the provision and management of suitable housing for diocesan bishops, assisting by grants and loans with the housing of suffragan and assistant bishops, and some assistance in respect of cathedral clergy and lay staff.

Chairman
Mr Andrew Mackie

Secretary
Mr Paul Lewis   *T:* 020 7898 1741
     E: paul.lewis@churchofengland.org

Members
The Revd Mary Bide
The Rt Revd Peter Burrows
Mrs Rosemary Butler
The Very Revd Jonathan Greener
The Very Revd Stephen Lake
Mr Andrew Mackie
Canon Betty Renshaw
Mr Jacob Vince
The Revd Canon Marcia Wall
The Rt Revd Martin Warner

Mission and Pastoral Committee

Responsible for matters concerning pastoral reorganization, parsonages and glebe property.

Chairman
Mr Andrew Mackie

Secretary
Mr Paul Lewis   *T:* 020 7898 1741
                    E: paul.lewis@churchofengland.org

Members
The Revd Canon Bob Baker
Canon Peter Bruinvel

The Ven Penny Driver
The Revd Canon Stephen Evans
William Featherby
Mrs Julia Flack
The Very Revd Jonathan Greener
The Rt Revd Christopher Lowson
Mr Andrew Mackie
Miss Susan Pope
The Rt Revd Tim Thornton

Church Buildings (Uses and Disposals) Committee

Responsible for the Commissioners' work relating to closed church buildings.

The Commissioners draw no income from the State.

Chairman
Mr Andrew Mackie

Secretary
Mr Paul Lewis   *T:* 020 7898 1741
                    E: paul.lewis@churchofengland.org

Members
Mrs April Alexander
The Revd Canon Bob Baker
The Revd Canon Peter Cavanagh
Mrs Margaret Davies
Mr Andrew Mackie
Mr John Steel
The Revd Simon Talbott
The Revd Stephen Trott
Mr Ian Watmore

CHURCH OF ENGLAND PENSIONS BOARD

Pensions Board

The Church of England Pensions Board provides retirement services to those who have worked for or served the Church of England. These include the administration of various pension schemes for the stipendiary clergy and lay workers and the provision of retirement housing for retired clergy. In doing so, it assists over 38,000 people across over 450 Church-of-England-based employers.

VISION AND VALUES
The Board's vision is to deliver a professional, high-quality and efficient service to our customers, respecting their needs and the interests of those who fund it.

In our decision-making and operations we are guided by the following values:

- Excellence – we take pride in doing a good job.
- Integrity – we are trustworthy.
- Respect – we treat everyone with dignity.

PENSIONS
The Board administers three main pension schemes.

- The Church of England Funded Pension Scheme (CEFPS) provides pensions and other benefits for clergy and others in stipendiary ministry, for service from 1 January 1998. Benefits arising from service prior to 1998 are financed by the Church Commissioners. The CEFPS held assets of £1,654 million at the end of 2016. The next actuarial valuation will take place at the end of 2018.
- The Church Worker's Pension Fund (CWPF) is a centralized pension scheme for employers connected with the ministry and mission of the Church of England. At the end of 2016, it held assets of £509 million. The actuarial valuation as at 31 December 2016 will be completed by early 2018.
- The Church Administrators Pension Fund (CAPF) provides pensions and other benefits to the staff employed by the National Church Institutions. At the end of 2016, it held assets of £137 million. The next actuarial valuation will take place as at 31 December 2017.

RETIREMENT HOUSING
Around one in four clergy retiring from the stipendiary ministry seeks our assistance in the provision of retirement housing.

The purpose of the retirement housing scheme – the Church Housing Assistance for the Retired Ministry (CHARM) – is to assist those stipendiary clergy who have been unable to make their own provision for somewhere to live in retirement. CHARM is a discretionary facility and its operation is subsidized partly by the wider Church of England through Vote 5 of the Archbishops' Council's Budget. Property is available either to rent from the Board, or to purchase in partnership with the Board through a shared ownership scheme. In total, the Board assists around 2,000 retired clergy households with their housing needs.

Supported Housing
The Board maintains seven Christian retirement communities to house Church pensioners who want to live as independently as possible but with access to support services. At the centre of each community is the liturgical and spiritual life of the Church of England. As well as a self-contained flat, residents enjoy use of dining facilities, a library, communal grounds and a chapel.

PUBLICATIONS
The Board's Annual Report and Summary Report for 2016, together with various publications including information about the pension and housing schemes, are available to download from www.cepb.org.uk.The annual report is usually published each July.

Pensions Helpline T: 020 7898 1802
E: pensions@churchofengland.org

Housing Helpline T: 020 7898 1824
E-mail: housing@churchofengland.org

Chairman
Dr Jonathan Spencer

Chief Executive
Vacancy

Pensions Manager
Peter Dickinson   T: 020 7898 1810
    E: peter.dickinson@churchofengland.org

Head of Housing
Loraine Miller   T: 020 7898 1852
    E: loraine.miller@churchofengland.org

Customer Insight and Strategy Director
Linda Ferguson   T: 020 7898 1833
    E: linda.ferguson@churchofengland.org

Chief of Staff
Lee Marshall   T: 020 7898 1681
    E: lee.marshall@churchofengland.org

Chief Investment Officer
Pierre Jameson   T: 020 7898 1122
    E: pierre.jameson@churchofengland.org

MEMBERS
The 20 members of the Board represent a balance of skills and expertise and are drawn from a wide range of constituencies, as specified in the Church of England Pensions Regulations 1997.

Appointed Chair by the Archbishops with the approval of the General Synod
Dr Jonathan Spencer

Appointed by the Archbishops of Canterbury and York after consultation with the representatives of dioceses
Canon David Froude

Appointed by the Archbishops of Canterbury and York
Roger Mountford

Appointed by the Church Commissioners
Mr Jeremy Clack

Elected by the House of Bishops
The Rt Revd Dr Alan Wilson

Elected by the House of Clergy
The Revd Paul Benfield
The Revd Paul Boughton
The Revd Nigel Bourne
The Revd Canon David Stanton

Elected by the House of Laity
Jane Bisson
Roger Boulton
Canon Nicolete Fisher
Alan Fletcher
Canon Emma Osborne
Mr Brian Wilson

Elected by Members of the Church Workers Pension Fund
Ian Boothroyd
Ian Clark

Elected by Members of the Church Administrators Pension Fund
Maggie Rodger

Elected by the Employers participating in the Church Workers Pension Fund and Church Administrators Pension Fund
Richard Hubbard
Canon Sandra Newton

CO-OPTIONS
The Board has co-opted the following, who bring a particular expertise, to serve on its committees:

The Revd Richard Battersby
Simon Baynes
Matthew Beesley
Jeremy Gray
David Hunt
Peter Parker
Henrietta Podd
Ben Preece Smith
Jonathan Rodgers
The Revd Canon David Stanton

OTHER BOARDS, COUNCILS, COMMISSIONS, ETC OF THE CHURCH OF ENGLAND

The Churches Conservation Trust

The Churches Conservation Trust is the national charity protecting historic churches at risk. We've saved over 345 unique buildings which attract almost 2 million visitors a year. With our help and your support they are kept open, in use and free to all – living once again at the heart of their communities.

Our historic churches host occasional services as well as concerts, exhibitions, lectures, other events and in some instances commercial businesses. The Trust, which is a registered charity, depends upon statutory funding from the Church Commissioners (10.5 per cent), the Department for Culture, Media and Sport (20.7 per cent) and charitable grants, voluntary donations and earned income (69 per cent).

Chief Executive
Mr Crispin Truman, 4th Floor, Society Building, 8 All Saints Street, London N1 9RL
T: 0845 303 2760
F: 020 7841 0434
E: central@thecct.org.uk

Deputy Chief Executive and Director of Conservation
Ms Sarah Robinson

Director, West
Mr Colin Shearer

Director, North
Ms Rosi Lister

Director, South East
Mr Peter Aiers

Director of Development
Mr Anthony Bennett

Director of Resources
Mr Stuart Popple

Head of Regeneration
Mr Matthew McKeague

Head of Resources
Ms Tanya Bunney

BOARD OF TRUSTEES
The Revd Duncan Dormor
Lady Lucy French
Mr Simon Jenkins
Ms Beth McHattie
Ms Liz Peace
Mr Nick Thompson
Mr Humphrey Welfare
Mr Duncan Wilson

(Chairman)
Mr Loyd Grossman

(Deputy Chair)
Ms Jane Weeks

CCLA Investment Management Limited

CCLA Investment Management Limited (CCLA) is a specialist investment management company serving charities, churches and local authorities. It is the largest manager of charitable funds in the UK, by the number of individual investing charities. It aims to provide good quality investment management services at reasonable cost. It is the manager, registrar and administrator of the CBF Church of England Funds, the trustee of which is CBF Funds Trustee Limited and to which CCLA is accountable. Six Funds are offered to Church of England investors: the Investment Fund, a mixed fund invested mainly in equities, the UK Equity Fund, the Global Equity Income Fund, the Fixed Interest Securities Fund, the Deposit Fund and the Property Fund. CCLA also manages pooled charity funds and segregated charity portfolios.

CCLA is owned 54 per cent by the CBF Church of England Investment Fund, 22 per cent by the COIF Charities Investment Fund (part of which is non voting), 13 per cent by the Local Authorities Mutual Investment Trust and 11 per cent by the Executive Directors. CCLA is authorized and regulated by the Financial Conduct Authority (FCA) under the Financial Services and Markets Act 2000 (FSMA). Under the FSMA, the CBF, in its role as Trustee, is not considered to be operating the

Funds 'by way of business'. In consequence, it is not required to be regulated by the FCA. Deposits taken by The CBF Church of England Deposit Fund are exempted from the FSMA by virtue of the Financial Services and Markets Act (Exemption) Order 2001.

Company Registration No 2183088
    Authorized and regulated by the Financial Conduct Authority

Executive Directors
Chief Executive
Mr Michael Quicke
            E: michael.quicke@ccla.co.uk

Chief Investment Officer
Mr James Bevan   E: james.bevan@ccla.co.uk

Director of Market Development
Mr Andrew Robinson
            E: andrew.robinson@ccla.co.uk

Chief Operating Officer
Mr Adrian McMillan
            E: adrian.mcmillan@ccla.co.uk

Non Executive Directors
Mrs Rosie Norris
Mr Trevor Salmon
The Revd John Tattersall
Mr Richard Williams

(Chairman)
Mr Richard Horlick

Company Secretary
Mrs Jacqueline Fox

The CBF Church of England Funds

Established under the Church Funds Investment Measure 1958, these open-ended funds aim to meet most of the investment needs of a church trust and are used by diocesan boards of finance and trusts, cathedrals, diocesan boards of education, theological colleges, church schools and educational endowments, church societies and many PCCs.

INVESTMENT FUND
The Fund is suitable for all of a CofE charity's long-term funds where the charity is looking for a good level of distributions and long-term protection from inflation. The portfolio is an actively managed diversified portfolio of assets designed to help protect current and future beneficiaries from the effects of inflation. It will consist primarily of equities but will also include property, bonds, and other asset classes. It is managed in a risk-controlled way and like all the CBF Funds invests in line with Church ethical guidelines.

UK EQUITY FUND
The Fund is an actively managed portfolio of equities and suitable for the long-term funds of a CofE charity seeking exposure to UK equities.

FIXED INTEREST SECURITIES FUND
The portfolio is an actively managed portfolio of predominately sterling denominated fixed interest securities and is suitable for long-term funds seeking an income by investing in bonds.

DEPOSIT FUND
This money Fund is for cash balances which need to be available at short notice and with minimal risk of capital loss. Accounts in the Fund obtain a rate of interest close to money market rates even on small sums. Daily deposit and withdrawal facilities. The Fund is rated AAAf/S1 by Fitch Ratings.

PROPERTY FUND
Invests directly in UK commercial property. Fund is intended primarily for long-term investment. Month end share dealings but periods of notice may be imposed. The Fund provides a high level of income.

GLOBAL EQUITY INCOME FUND
The Fund is an actively managed diversified portfolio of global equities and is suitable for the long-term funds of any CofE charity seeking a high income from investing in global equities.

The Corporation of the Church House

The Corporation owns and maintains Church House, Westminster which is the administrative headquarters of the national institutions of the Church of England.

    The original Church House was built in the early 1890s as the Church's memorial of Queen Victoria's Jubilee, to be the administrative headquarters of the Church of England, and was replaced by the present building to a design by Sir Herbert Baker. The

foundation stone was laid in 1937 by Queen Mary and on 10 June 1940 King George VI, accompanied by the Queen, formally opened the new House and attended the first Session of the Church Assembly in the great circular hall. The building was almost immediately requisitioned by the Government and for the rest of the war became the alternative meeting place of both Houses of Parliament; the Lords sat in the Convocation Hall and the Commons in the Hoare Memorial Hall. Oak panels in these halls commemorate this use.

By October 1946 some administrative offices of the Church Assembly returned to Church House and the Church Assembly was able to return for its Autumn Session in 1950. The building is now the headquarters of the Archbishops' Council, the Church Commissioners and the Church of England Pensions Board, as well as being the venue for the General Synod in the spring and (if it meets) in the autumn. A large-scale refurbishment carried out in 2006 has provided sufficient open-plan office space to accommodate nearly all staff of the Central Church Institutions, who moved into Church House during the early part of 2007.

Church House has also become an important national centre for conferences and meetings, the income from which contributes significantly to the maintenance costs of the building.

The business of the Corporation is vested in its Council of nine (of whom three are nominated by the Appointments Committee, two are elected by the membership of the Corporation and four are co-opted by the Council).

Presidents
The Most Revd and Rt Hon Dr John Sentamu
The Most Revd and Rt Hon Justin Welby

Chairman of Council
Canon Dr Christina Baxter

Treasurer
David Barnett

Secretary
Chris Palmer, Church House, Great Smith Street, London SW1P 3AZ   *T:* 020 7898 1311
F: 020 7898 1321
E: chris.palmer@churchofengland.org

The National Society (Church of England and Church in Wales) for the Promoting of Education

The National Society is a Church of England and Church in Wales education service. It was founded by Royal Charter in 1811, with supplemental Charters in 1934, 1972, 1985, 1987, 1997 and 2015, to provide education for all, firmly based on the Christian Gospel and Anglican principles.

The Society was chiefly responsible for setting up, in cooperation with local clergy and others, the nationwide network of Church schools in England and Wales; it was also, through the Church colleges, a pioneer in teacher education. The original purpose of the Society was 'The Promotion of the Education of the Poor in the Principles of the Established Church'. The objects of the Society are now the promotion, encouragement and support of education in accordance with the principles of the Church of England, in England and in Wales and in any other part of the world where the Church of England or churches in communion with it may be at work.

The latest supplemental charter sets out the composition of the Council which is now formed of twelve trustees: The Chairman, Honorary Treasurer; three appointed by the Archbishops of Canterbury and York; two appointed by the Archbishop of Wales; three appointed by the Council's nominations committee and two elected from the General Synod.

Along with the Archbishops' Council, The National Society provides the governance for the Church of England's work in education

and operates primarily through the Education Office.

ARCHIVE MATERIAL
After over two centuries of close association with Church schools and colleges, the National Society has built up an impressive collection of documents in its archives. These include about 15,000 files of correspondence with schools throughout England and Wales founded in association with the National Society and many published works, including the Society's own. Access is available to bona fide researchers by appointment at the Church of England Record Centre.

Patron
Her Majesty The Queen

Co-Presidents
The Most Revd Barry Morgan
The Most Revd and Rt Hon Dr John Sentamu
The Most Revd and Rt Hon Justin Welby

Chairman of the Council
The Rt Revd Stephen Conway, The Bishop's House, Ely CB7 4DW   *T:* 01353 662749
E: bishop@elydiocese.org

Chief Officer
The Revd Nigel Genders   *T:* 020 7898 1500
E: nigel.genders@churchofengland.org

Honorary Treasurer
The Revd Canon Peter Ballard

THE ECCLESIASTICAL COURTS

The Ecclesiastical Courts & Disciplinary Tribunals

The Ecclesiastical Courts consist of (1) the Diocesan or Consistory Courts, (2) the Provincial Courts, and for both Provinces (3) the Court of Ecclesiastical Causes Reserved and, when required, (4) a Commission of Review. In certain faculty cases an appeal lies from the Provincial Courts to the Judicial Committee of the Privy Council. The jurisdiction of the Archdeacons' Courts is now confined to the visitations of archdeacons. The Ecclesiastical Courts are in the main now regulated by the Ecclesiastical Jurisdiction Measure 1963. The Court of Faculties is the Court of the Archbishop of Canterbury through which the legatine powers transferred to the Archbishop of Canterbury by the Ecclesiastical Licences Act 1533 are exercised.

The personnel of the Diocesan Courts is given in the diocesan lists. The personnel of the Court of Faculties and of the Provincial and some of the other Courts is as follows:

THE COURT OF ARCHES
Dean of the Arches
The Rt Worshipful Charles George

Registrar
The Revd Canon John Rees, Diocesan Registry, 16 Beaumont Street, Oxford OX1 2LZ
T: 01865 297200
F: 01865 726274
E: jrees@wslaw.co.uk

THE COURT OF THE VICAR-GENERAL OF THE PROVINCE OF CANTERBURY
Vicar-General
The Rt Worshipful Timothy Briden, 1 Temple Gardens, Temple, London EC4Y 9BB
T: 020 7797 8300
F: 020 7707 8308
E: info@lambchambers.co.uk

Registrar
The Revd Canon John Rees, Diocesan Registry, 16 Beaumont Street, Oxford OX1 2LZ
T: 01865 297200
F: 01865 726274
E: jrees@wslaw.co.uk

THE CHANCERY COURT OF YORK
Auditor
The Rt Worshipful Charles George

Registrar
Mr Lionel Lennox, The Provincial Registry, Stamford House, Piccadilly, York YO1 9PP
T: 01904 623487
F: 01904 561470
E: lpml@denisontill.com

THE COURT OF THE VICAR-GENERAL OF THE PROVINCE OF YORK
Vicar-General
The Rt Worshipful Peter Collier, c/o The Registry, Stamford House, Piccadilly, York YO1 9PP

Registrar
Mr Lionel Lennox, The Provincial Registry, Stamford House, Piccadilly, York YO1 9PP
T: 01904 623487
F: 01904 561470
E: lpml@denisontill.com

THE COURT OF ECCLESIASTICAL CAUSES RESERVED
Judges
(five vacancies)

Registrar for the Province of Canterbury
The Revd Canon John Rees, Diocesan Registry, 16 Beaumont Street, Oxford OX1 2LZ
T: 01865 297200
F: 01865 726274
E: jrees@wslaw.co.uk

Registrar for the Province of York
Mr Lionel Lennox, The Provincial Registry, Stamford House, Piccadilly, York YO1 9PP
T: 01904 623487
F: 01904 561470
E: lpml@denisontill.com

THE COURT OF FACULTIES
Master of the Faculties
The Rt Worshipful Charles George

Registrar
Mr Peter Beesley, 1 The Sanctuary, London SW1P 3JT
T: 020 7222 5381
F: 020 7222 7502
E: faculty.office@1Thesanctuary.com

DISCIPLINARY TRIBUNALS CONSTITUTED UNDER THE CLERGY DISCIPLINE MEASURE 2003

President of Tribunals
Rt Hon Lord Justice McFarlane

Deputy President of Tribunals
Sir Mark Hedley
c/o The Legal Office, Church House, Great Smith St, London SW1P 3AZ

'Legally qualified' members of the provincial panels of Canterbury and York (the same ten are appointed to each panel) from which the chair of a disciplinary tribunal will be appointed by the President of Tribunals if the President or Deputy President is not to chair the tribunal.

Chancellor Linda Box
His Honour the Worshipful Dr Rupert Bursell QC
Mr David Cheetham MBE
His Honour Judge Simon Grenfell
Canon Christopher Hodson
His Honour the Worshipful Roger Kaye QC
His Honour Judge John Lodge
Mr Geoffrey Tattersall QC
His Honour Judge David Turner QC
His Honour Judge Samuel Wiggs

Registrar of Tribunals for the Province of Canterbury Revd Canon John Rees (as above)
Registrar of Tribunals for the Province of York Mr Lionel Lennox (as above)
Designated Officer Mr Adrian Iles, The Legal Office, Church House, Great Smith St, London SW1P 3AZ

Appeal Panels

APPEAL PANEL CONSTITUTED UNDER SCHEDULE 4 MISSION AND PASTORAL MEASURE 2011
(Tribunals to settle compensation claims of clergy dispossessed under a Pastoral Scheme or Order)

Chair
The Dean of the Arches

Deputy Chairs
The Vicar-General of Canterbury
The Vicar-General of York

In addition to the Chair, a tribunal comprises three members of the Lower House of the relevant Province and one member of the House of Laity.

APPEAL PANEL CONSTITUTED UNDER STANDING ORDER 120(f)(i)
(Tribunals to hear appeals in internal General Synod elections)

House of Bishops
Panel members to be confirmed

House of Clergy
Panel members to be confirmed

House of Laity
Panel members to be confirmed

APPEAL PANEL APPOINTED PURSUANT TO RULE 44(8) OF THE CHURCH REPRESENTATION RULES AS AMENDED BY THE NATIONAL INSTITUTIONS MEASURE 1998 (SCHEDULE 5, PARAGRAPH 2(c))
(Tribunals to hear appeals in elections to the House of Laity of the General Synod)
The Dean of the Arches
The Vicar-General of Canterbury
The Vicar-General of York
Other panel members to be confirmed

Secretary Vacancy

APPEAL PANEL APPOINTED PURSUANT TO RULE 25(5) OF THE CLERGY REPRESENTATION RULES 1975 TO 2004
(Tribunals to hear appeals in elections to the Convocations)
The Dean of the Arches
The Vicar-General of Canterbury
The Vicar-General of York
Other panel members to be confirmed

Secretary Vacancy

Other Organizations

PART 3

Classified List of Organizations Included in this Section

Anglican Religious Communities
See pages 226–36

Animal Welfare
Anglican Society for the Welfare of Animals

Art, Architecture
Art and Christianity Enquiry
Art and Sacred Places
Christian Arts
Church Monuments Society
Ecclesiological Society
Friends of Friendless Churches
York Glaziers' Trust

Bell-ringing
Ancient Society of College Youths
Central Council of Church Bell Ringers
Society of Royal Cumberland Youths

Bible Study
BRF
Bible Society
Lord Wharton's Charity
SASRA
Scripture Union
SGM Lifewords (formerly Scripture Gift
  Mission International)
Summer Biblical Study in Cambridge

Blind People
Guild of Church Braillists
RNIB (Royal National Institute of Blind
  People)
St John's Guild

Church Buildings
Friends of Friendless Churches
Greater Churches Network
National Churches Trust
Marshall's Charity
Vergers, Church of England Guild of

Church Societies – General
Additional Curates Society
Affirming Catholicism
Association of English Cathedrals
Cathedral and Church Shops Association
Cathedral Libraries and Archives Association
Cathedrals Administration and Finance
  Association
Catholic Group in General Synod
Church of England Flower Arrangers
  Association
Church Society
Church Union
Churches' Advertising Network
Modern Church
Open Synod Group

Society for the Maintenance of the Faith
Society of the Faith (Inc)
Unitas – The Catholic League

Church Societies – Specific
Anglican Fellowship in Scouting and Guiding
Anglican Mainstream
Association of Diocesan Registry Clerks
  (Southern Province)
Baptismal Integrity
Christian Evidence Society
CHRISM
Church House Deaneries Group
Church of England Record Society
College of Readers
Community of Aidan and Hilda
Day One Christian Ministries
Diocesan Clergy Chairs' Forum
Ecumenical Society of the Blessed Virgin Mary
Forward in Faith
Foundation for Church Leadership
Guild of St Leonard
Guild of Servants of the Sanctuary
Reform
Royal Martyr Church Union
Society of King Charles the Martyr
Society of Mary
Third Province Movement

Clergy Associations
Anglo-Catholic Ordination Candidates' Fund
Association of Black Clergy
Association of Hospice and Palliative Care
  Chaplains
Association of Ordinands and Candidates for
  Ministry
College of Health Care Chaplains
English Clergy Association
Federation of Catholic Priests
Fellowship of Word and Spirit
Industrial Mission Association
Retired Clergy Association
Society of Catholic Priests
Society of Ordained Scientists
Society of the Holy Cross
Unite Clergy and Faith Workers
See also **Professional Groups**

Conference Centres
Sarum College
Ashburnham Place
Belsey Bridge Conference Centre
High Leigh Conference Centre
Lee Abbey

Consultancy
CTBI Christians Abroad
Grubb Institute
Living Stones

Coordinating Bodies
Church of England Evangelical Council
Churches' Funerals Group
Churches' Legislation Advisory Service
Evangelical Alliance
National Association of Diocesan Advisers for
    Women's Ministry
Religious Education Council of England and
    Wales
Universities and Colleges Christian Fellowship

Counselling
Anglican Pastoral Care
Lesbian and Gay Christian Movement
Relate
True Freedom Trust

Deaf People
Action on Hearing Loss (formerly RNID)
British Deaf Association
Deaf Anglicans Together
Deaf People, Royal Association for

Defence, Disarmament, Pacifism
Anglican Pacifist Fellowship
Commonwealth War Graves Commission
Council on Christian Approaches to Defence
    and Disarmament

Drama
Actors' Church Union
Radius

Ecumenism
Anglican and Eastern Churches Association
Anglican–Lutheran Society
Churches' Funeral Group
Fellowship of St Alban and St Sergius
International Ecumenical Fellowship
Nikaean Club
Nikaean Ecumenical Trust
Order of Christian Unity
Society of Archbishop Justus Ltd
Society of St Willibrord

Education
Archbishop's Examination in Theology
Association of Church College Trusts
Awareness Foundation
Christian Education
Culham St Gabriel's Trust
Lincoln Theological Institute
Mirfield Centre
RE Today Services
Religious Education Council of England and
    Wales
Royal Alexandra and Albert School
Royal Asylum of St Ann's Society
St George's College, Jerusalem
St Hild and St Bede Trust
SCALA (School Chaplains and Leaders
    Association)
Scripture Union

United Church Schools Trust
Woodard Corporation, the (Woodard Schools)
See also Theological Education Institutions,
    pages 238–9

Evangelism
Church Army
College of Evangelists
Fresh Expressions

Family
CARE
Family Action
Fellowship of St Nicholas
Mothers' Union
St Michael's Fellowship

Finance
Ecclesiastical Insurance Office PLC
Ecumenical Council for Corporate
    Responsibility
Number 1 Trust Fund

Grant-Making Bodies
All Saints Educational Trust
Bristol Clerical Education Society
Church of England Clergy Stipend Trust
Church Pastoral Aid Society Ministers in
    Training Fund
Cleaver Ordination Candidates' Fund
Culham St Gabriel's Trust
Elland Society Ordination Fund
Foundation of St Matthias
Hockerill Educational Foundation
Keswick Hall Trust Charity
Newton's Trust
Ordination Candidate Funds (General)
Pilgrim Trust
Queen Victoria Clergy Fund
Sarum St Michael Educational Charity
St Christopher's Educational Trust
St Luke's College Foundation
St Mary's College Trust
St Peter's Saltley Trust
The Revd Dr George Richards' Charity
See also **Welfare**

Health, Healing and Medicine
Acorn Christian Healing Foundation
Association of Hospice and Palliative Care
    Chaplains
Burrswood
Christian Healing Mission
Christian Medical Fellowship
College of Health Care Chaplains
Guild of Health and St Raphael
Guild of Pastoral Psychology
Harnhill Centre of Christian Healing
Hospice Movement
Pilsdon at Malling Community
Richmond Fellowship
St Luke's Healthcare for the Clergy
Together for Short Lives

Inter Faith, Religions
Council of Christians and Jews
INFORM
Inter Faith Network
World Congress of Faiths

Internet
COIN: Christians on the Internet
Society of Archbishop Justus Ltd

Libraries and Archives *see* pages 239–41

Marriage
Anglican Marriage Encounter
Broken Rites
Relate

Media
Church and Media Network
Church of England Newspaper
Church Times
CTVC
Mediawatch-UK
Office of Communications
Sandford St Martin Trust
World Association for Christian
   Communication

Ministry
CHRISM
Diaconal Association of the Church of
   England
Diakonia
Distinctive Diaconate
MODEM

Ministry, Women
Li Tim-Oi Foundation
WATCH

Mission
Aim International
Bible Society
Christian Witness to Israel
Church's Ministry Among Jewish People
Greenbelt Festivals
London City Mission
Mersey Mission to Seafarers, The
Mission to Seafarers, The
SASRA
Scripture Union
SGM Lifewords (formerly Scripture Gift
   Mission International)
Society for Promoting Christian Knowledge
Student Christian Movement
Trinitarian Bible Society
Universities and Colleges Christian
   Fellowship

Mission Overseas
All Nations Christian College
Church Mission Society
Crosslinks
Feed the Minds

Highbury Centre, The
Intercontinental Church Society
Interserve
Korean Mission Partnership
Leprosy Mission
Melanesian Mission
Mid-Africa Ministry
Mozambique and Angola Anglican
   Association (MANNA)
New England Company
OMF International (UK)
Overseas Bishoprics Fund
Oxford Mission
Papua New Guinea Church Partnership
Reader Missionary Studentship
   Association
Southern Africa Church Development Trust
Tearfund
USPG
World Vision

Music
Archbishops' Certificate in Church Music
Choir Benevolent Fund
Choir Schools Association
Church Music Society
Guild of Church Musicians
Hymn Society of Great Britain and Ireland
Jubilate Group
Morse-Boycott Bursary Fund
Plainsong and Medieval Music Society
Royal College of Organists
Royal School of Church Music

Overseas
Christian Aid
CTBI Christians Abroad
Farnham Castle International Briefing and
   Conference Centre
United Nations Association (UNA–UK)
Womenaid International
World Vision

Patronage Trusts *see* pages 242–3

Prayer, Meditation, Retreats
Archway
Association for Promoting Retreats
Confraternity of the Blessed Sacrament
Friends of Little Gidding
Guild of All Souls
Guild of St Leonard
Julian Meetings, The
Julian of Norwich, Friends of
Pilsdon at Malling Community
Retreat Association
Sarum College
Servants of Christ the King
Society of Retreat Conductors
Women's World Day of Prayer

Professional Groups
Actors' Church Union
Association of Christian Teachers

OTHER ORGANIZATIONS

Association of Christian Writers
Association of Ordinands and Candidates for
    Ministry
Christian Arts
Christians at Work
Christians in Library and Information Services
Church House Deaneries' Group
Church Schoolmasters' and School
    Mistresses' Benevolent Institution
Deans' Conference
Deans' Vergers' Conference
Ecclesiastical Law Society
Guild of Pastoral Psychology
Homes for Retired Clergy
Industrial Mission Association
National Association of Diocesan Advisers in
    Women's Ministry
Society of Retreat Conductors
Unite Clergy and Faith Workers
Vergers, Church of England Guild of
See also **Clergy Associations**

Publishing, Print Media
BRF
Feed the Minds
Rebecca Hussey's Book Charity
Scripture Union
Society for Promoting Christian Knowledge
Trinitarian Bible Society
See also **Media**

Renewal
Keswick Convention
Sharing of Ministries Abroad (SOMA)

Research
CARE
Centre for the Study of Christianity and
    Sexuality
Christian Research
Churches' Fellowship for Psychical and
    Spiritual Studies
Germinate: The Arthur Rank Centre
Latimer Trust
Rural Theology Association
St George's House, Windsor
Urban Theology Unit
William Temple Foundation

Rural Affairs
Germinate: The Arthur Rank Centre
Rural Theology Association

Scholarship and Science
Alcuin Club
Canterbury and York Society
Christian Evidence Society
Ecclesiastical Law Society
Faith and Thought
Henry Bradshaw Society
Latimer Trust
National Archives, The
Philip Usher Memorial Fund

Pusey House
Society for Liturgical Study
Society for Old Testament Study
Society of Ordained Scientists
Summer Biblical Study in Cambridge

Social Concern
Age UK
Changing Attitude
Christians on the Left (formerly the
    Christian Socialist Movement)
Church Housing Trust
Church Urban Fund
English Churches Housing Group
Lesbian and Gay Christian Movement
Livability
Mediawatch–UK
National Council for Social Concern
Order of Christian Unity
Pilsdon at Malling Community
St Pancras and Humanist Housing
    Association
Samaritans

Theological Education Institutions
see pages 238–9

Training
Anglican Marriage Encounter
Bridge Pastoral Foundation
Christian Education
Christians at Work
College of Preachers
Girls Friendly Society in England and Wales
Industrial Christian Fellowship
Paradox Ministries
RE Today Services
Student Christian Movement
William Temple Foundation

Travel, Pilgrimage
Accueil, Rencontre, Communauté UK
British Isles and Eire Airport Chaplains'
    Network
Cathedrals Plus
Journeying
Walsingham, Shrine of Our Lady of

Welfare
Almshouse Association
Beauchamp Community
Bromley and Sheppard's Colleges
Came's Charity for Clergymen's Widows
Catch 22 (formerly Rainer)
Church of England Soldiers', Sailors' and
    Airmen's Clubs
Church of England Soldiers', Sailors' and
    Airmen's Housing Association
Church Schoolmasters' and School
    Mistresses' Benevolent Institution
Church Welfare Association
College of St Barnabas

Community Housing and Therapy
Compassionate Friends, The
Corporation of the Sons of the Clergy
Diocesan Institutions of Chester, Manchester, Liverpool and Blackburn
Elizabeth Finn Care
Family Action
Frances Ashton Charity
Friends of the Clergy Corporation
Friends of the Elderly
Homes for Retired Clergy
Keychange
Langley House Trust
Livability
Pyncombe Charity
St Michael's Fellowship
Samaritans
Seamen's Friendly Society of St Paul
Smallwood Trust (formerly the Society for the Assistance of Ladies in Reduced Circumstances)
Society for the Relief of Poor Clergymen
Society of Mary and Martha
The Revd Dr George Richards' Charity
Together (formerly MACA – Mental After Care Association)
YMCA
Young Women's Trust

Worship
Alcuin Club
Praxis
Prayer Book Society

Youth
Accueil, Rencontre, Communauté UK
Barnardo's
Boys' Brigade
Campaigners England and Wales
Catch 22 (formerly Rainer)
Children's Society
Church Lads' and Church Girls' Brigade
Fellowship of St Nicholas
Frontier Youth Trust
Girlguiding UK
Girls' Brigade
Girls Friendly Society in England and Wales
Lee Abbey Household Communities
Lee Abbey International Students' Club
St Christopher's Fellowship
Scout Association
Shaftesbury Young People
Urban Saints (formerly Crusaders)
William Temple House

OTHER ORGANIZATIONS

RELIGIOUS COMMUNITIES

Anglican Religious Communities

The roots of the Religious Life can be traced back to the Early Church in Jerusalem, and the subsequent traditions such as the Benedictines, Franciscans, etc., were flourishing in England until the Reformation when all were suppressed.

Most Anglican Communities were founded in the nineteenth century as a result of the Oxford Movement. There are over eighty different Communities in the British Isles and throughout the Anglican Communion. Some are very small. Some have over 100 members worldwide.

Religious Communities are formed by men and women who feel called to seek God and live out their baptismal vows in a particular way under vows. There are some 400 Anglican men and women living this life in the United Kingdom.

PRAYER AND WORK

Each Community has its own history and character; some follow one of the traditional Rules, and others those written by more recent founders, but all have one thing in common: their daily life based on the work of prayer and living together centred in their Daily Office and the Eucharist. The work grows from the prayer, depending on the particular Community and the gifts of its members.

Some Communities are 'enclosed'. The members do not normally go out, but remain within the convent or monastery and its grounds, seeking and serving God through silence and prayer, study and work. Other Communities share the basic life of prayer and fellowship and are involved in a variety of work in society at large.

HOSPITALITY

Most Community houses offer a place where people can go for a time of Retreat, either alone or with a group, for a day, several days, or occasionally for longer periods of time. They offer a place of quiet to seek God, grow in prayer and find spiritual guidance.

THE CALLING

People who feel called to the Religious Life and who wish to apply to a Community need to be over 21. They normally need to be physically and psychologically robust. Academic qualifications are not essential. There is a training period of about three years before any vows are taken.

Those who are considering a vocation are advised to visit Community houses to experience their particular ethos: further information is available from the houses or general enquiries may be made to Anglican Religious Communities at the address below. Details of Communities may be found in *Anglican Religious Life*, published by Canterbury Press, or, in an abbreviated form, via the following web address: www.arcie.org.uk

Advisory Council on the Relations of Bishops and Religious Communities

This Council, to serve the two Provinces, is responsible to the Archbishops and the House of Bishops. Its functions are:

(1) to advise bishops upon (a) questions arising about the charters, constitutions and rule of existing Communities, (b) the establishment of new Communities, (c) matters referred to it by a diocesan bishop

(2) to advise existing Communities or their Visitors in any matters that they refer to it

(3) to give guidance to those who wish to form Communities.

The Chairman and Convenor of the Council must be a diocesan bishop appointed by the Archbishops of Canterbury and York. The Council consists of at least thirteen members, three of whom are nominated by the bishops and ten elected by the Communities. Up to five additional members may be co-opted.

Chairman
The Rt Revd David Walker, Bishop of Manchester

Three Bishops nominated by the House of Bishops :
The Rt Revd Tim Dakin, Bishop of Winchester
The Rt Revd Tony Robinson, Bishop of Wakefield
The Rt Revd Jonathan Clark, Bishop of Croydon

Members elected by the religious communities:
Sister Anita CSC
Sister Elizabeth Pio SSB
Sister Joyce CSF
Sister Mary Julian CHC
Sister Mary Stephen OSB
Sister Rosemary CHN

Father Peter Allan CR
Brother Damian SSF
Abbot Stuart Burns OSB

Co-opted members:
The Revd Canon Chris Neal
The Revd Ian Mobsby
Dr Peta Dunstan
The Revd Tim Watson

**Anglican Religious Communities
Committee Representative:**
Dom Simon Jarratt OSB

Conference of Religious Representative:
Abbot Richard Yeo OSB

Secretary of the Council:
Father Colin CSWG

Anglican Religious Communities in England

ARC is an umbrella body of all members of Anglican Religious Communities, Monks and Nuns, Brothers and Sisters living in community under vows of poverty, chastity and obedience. The communities range from large monastic houses to small groups of two or three brothers or sisters living and working in urban areas. It acts to support its members by encouraging cooperation and the exchange of ideas and experiences which are relevant to Religious Life. The ARC Committee has members elected from four constituent groups: Leaders, General Synod Representatives, Novice Guardians and Professed Religious. An annual conference is held. Contact: The Secretary, Anglican Religious Communities, Church House, Great Smith Street, London, SW1P 3AZ
E: info@arcie.org.uk

OTHER ORGANIZATIONS

Religious Communities (Men)

Benedictine Community of St Benedict's Priory
Founded in 1914.

- 1926–87 Nashdom Abbey
- 1987–2010 Elmore Abbey
- From 2010 St Benedict's Priory, Salisbury

Resident community four monks. Oblate confraternity of around 300. The community receives day guests. *Visitor* The Rt Revd Dominic Walker OGS *Conventual Prior* Dom Simon Jarratt OSB, 19a The Close, Salisbury, SP1 2EB   *E:* salisbury.priory@gmail.com

Community of Our Lady and St John
Founded in 1884. A community of Benedictine monks which undertakes retreats. Guest accommodation for 18 people. Other work includes the manufacture of altar wafers and incense. The Seamen's Friendly Society of St Paul is managed from the Abbey. Day conference facilities and residential groups welcome: contact the Guestmaster. *Visitor* The Rt Revd Michael Scott-Joynt *Abbot* The Rt Revd Dom Giles Hill OSB, Alton Abbey, Abbey Road, Alton, GU34 4AP   *T:* 01420 562145
E: giles@altonabbey.org.uk
W: www.altonabbey.org.uk

Community of the Glorious Ascension
Founded in 1960 – the brothers are based in Devon and continue the monastic pattern of a common life, prayer and worship, together with their work of hospitality and ministry. The Sisters have established a priory in the nearby village of Chillington. *Visitor* The Rt

Revd Richard Hawkins *Prior* Br Simon CGA, The Priory, 26 Helmers Way, Chillington, Kingsbridge, TQ7 2EZ   *T:* 01548 580127
E: ascensioncga@fsnet.com

Community of the Resurrection
Founded in 1892, it lives a monastic life, and undertakes and supports teaching, retreats, and other missionary and pastoral works.

Visitor The Rt Revd Graham James *Superior* Fr George Guiver CR, House of the Resurrection, Mirfield, WF14 0BN   *T:* 0194 494318
E: community@mirfield.org.uk
W: www.mirfield.org.uk

Theological College College of the Resurrection, Mirfield WF14 0BW   *Tel:* 01924 481900
Fax: 01924 492738
E: registrar@mirfield.org.uk
Web: http://college.mirfield.org.uk

The Mirfield Centre offers a programme of day and evening events and small conferences as well as offering a meeting place for about 50 people. *Address* Mirfield Centre, College of the Resurrection, Mirfield WF14 0BW
Tel: 01924 481920
Fax: 01924 492738
email: centre@mirfield.org.uk
Web: www.mirfieldcentre.org.uk

Company of Mission Priests
Founded in 1940. A society of apostolic life, a dispersed community of male priests of the Anglican Communion who, wishing to consecrate themselves wholly to the Church's mission, keep themselves free from the attachments of marriage and family, and

endeavour to encourage and strengthen one another by mutual prayer and fellowship, sharing the vision of St Vincent de Paul of a priesthood dedicated to service, and in association with the whole Vincentian family. *Visitor* The Rt Revd Martin Warner *Secretary* Fr Andrew Welsby *Warden* Fr Beresford Skelton CMP, St Giles Vicarage, Walsall Street, Willenhall, WV13 2ER

T: 01902 605722
E: andrew.welsby@hotmail.co.uk
W: www.missionpriests.com

Oratory of the Good Shepherd

Founded in 1913 at Cambridge University, the Oratory is a society of celibate priests and laymen of the Anglican Communion who are endeavouring, under the direction of the Rule, to live a life of devotion and service.

Members of the Oratory work in four provinces:

* Europe,
* Australia,
* North America and
* Southern Africa.

They are bound together by a common Rule and discipline. They do not normally live together in community but meet for Chapter and are resident regularly for an annual Oratory Retreat and for Provincial Chapter (annual) and General Chapter (triennial).

Members include bishops, parish priests, lecturers and missionaries. A two-year period of probation precedes profession, and after ten years of profession, life vows may be taken. The Rule of the Oratory requires celibacy, the daily offices, where possible daily Eucharist, and a regular account of spending and direction of life. In addition, 'Labour of the Mind' is a characteristic of the Oratory and members are expected to spend time in study.

Attached to the Oratory are Companions and Associates, lay, ordained, married and single, who keep a Rule of Life and are part of the Oratory family. *European Provincial* The Revd Peter Ford *Superior* The Revd Prof Peter Hibbert OGS, 2 Blossom Road, Erdington, Birmingham, B24 0UD *E:* phibbert@ogs.net

Society of St Francis, The

The Society comprises a First Order for men (Society of St Francis) and women (see Community of St Francis), called to the Franciscan life under the vows of poverty, chastity and obedience; a Second Order of enclosed sisters (see Community of St Clare); and the Third Order for ordained and lay people, pledged to the spirit of the vows (see Third Order, Society of St Francis).

The Brothers of the First Order, founded in 1921, live a life of community centred on prayer and engage in active work especially in the areas of the poor and underprivileged. The three large Friaries in this province (at Hilfield, Glasshampton and Alnmouth) have a ministry with guests and retreatants. The other centres of work are principally within a city context from which the brothers engage in various active ministries. Some work with educational institutions, conducting retreats and with parishes continues.

There are five Provinces: Europe, Province of the Divine Compassion, Papua New Guinea, the Solomon Islands, and the Americas.

Minister General Brother Clark Berge SSF, c/o San Damiano Friary, 573 Dolores Street, San Francisco, CA 94110, USA

Tel: (+1) 415 861 7951
E: clarke.berge@s-s-f.org

European Province

Minister Brother Benedict SSF, 25 Karnac Road, Leeds, LS8 5BL *Tel:* 0113 226 0647
email: ministerssf@franciscans.org.uk
Web: www.franciscans.org.uk

Assistant Minister Brother Philip Bartholomew SSF (Canning Town)
Bishop Protector Rt Revd Stephen Cottrell (*Bishop of Chelmsford*)

Houses
All SSF-UK houses can be emailed using [name of the house] ssf@franciscans.org.uk e.g. hilfieldssf@franciscans.org.uk

Friary of St Francis, *Alnmouth*, Alnwick, Northumberland, NE66 3NJ
Tel: 01665 830213/830660
Fax: 01665 830580

The Master's Lodge, 58 St Peter's Street, *Canterbury* CT1 2BE *Tel:* 01227 479364
St Anthony's Friary, Enslin Gardens, *Newcastle* upon Tyne NE6 3ST
St Mary at the Cross, *Glasshampton*, Shrawley, Worcester WR6 6TQ *Tel:* 01299 896345
Friary of St Francis, *Hilfield*, Dorchester, Dorset, DT2 7BE *Tel:* 01300 341345
Fax: 01300 341293
25 Karnac Road, *Leeds* LS8 5BL
Tel: 0113 226 0647

Religious Communities (Women)

Benedictine Community of St Mary's Abbey

We are a monastic community of women following the Rule of St Benedict. Our home is a Benedictine Abbey that flourished from c. 1090 to 1538. Our priorities are prayer, community life and hospitality to those who stay at our guest house and who wish to share in our worship and silence.

The newly developed St Benedict's Centre, opened in September 2016, offers a place for individuals and groups to study, meet and pray.   *Tel:* 07393 418727
E: bookings@stbenedictscentre.org

Visitor The Rt Revd Laurie Green *Abbess* Sister Mary David Best OSB, 52 Swan Street, West Malling, Kent, ME19 6JX   *T:* 01732 843309
W: www.mallingabbey.org

Community of All Hallows

Founded in 1855. Augustinian Visitation Rule. Guests, retreats and spiritual direction. Relocating from Ditchingham during the course of 2018 – further details to appear on website when known.

Work and Houses at Ditchingham:
The Convent (*as above*)
Lavinia House, Ditchingham
Guests, retreats and spiritual direction
Tel: 01986 892840

All Hallows House, Rouen Road, Norwich NR1 1QT   *Tel:* 01603 624738
Guests, retreats and spiritual direction

All Hallows Country Hospital and All Hallows Nursing Home: the hospital and nursing home have now been combined under the management of the All Hallows Health Care Trust.

Ditchingham Day Nursery: the childcare provision has transferred ownership and is now managed by The Benjamin Foundation.

Visitor The Rt Revd Graham James *Leaders* Sister Sheila and Sister Elizabeth CAH, All Hallows Convent, Bungay, Suffolk, NR35 2DT
T: 01986 892749
E: allhallowsconvent@btinternet.com
W: www.allhallows.org

Community of St Andrew

Founded in 1861. Full membership of the Community consists of professed sisters who are Deaconesses or Distinctive Deacons or Priests. Present number is five. The fundamental ministry is the offering of prayer and worship, evangelism and pastoral work now through retirement ministries.

The Community celebrated its 150th anniversary at St Andrewstide 2011 with the (private) publication of *The Deaconess Community of St Andrew 1861–2011*, 225pp and photos. The 150th anniversary of the reception of Deaconess Licence No.1 by Elizabeth Ferard, on 18 July 1862 was celebrated by members of the Deaconess Order of the Church of England at Lambeth Palace in July 2012. *Visitor* The Rt Revd Richard Chartres *Superior* The Revd Mother Lillian, St Mary's Convent and Nursing Home, Burlington Lane, Chiswick, W4 2QE
T: 020 8747 0001 (Mother Lillian)
01903 238017 (Sr Teresa)
E: teresajoan@btinternet.com

Community of St Clare

Founded in 1950 to be the Second Order of the Society of St Francis, we are a small community of women living a vowed, contemplative, enclosed life.

Like St Clare, our life/work is dependence on God in prayer. We pray for the whole world and in particular for our sisters and brothers after the example of Francis and Clare. We have a determination for a simple life, earning our living by the production of Communion wafers and by designing and printing greetings cards. We have a large garden where we grow vegetables, fruit and flowers and look after hens. We share our life in hospitality to those who visit or come to stay at the Old Parsonage, and all who wish may come to our chapel for the daily celebration of the Eucharist and four-fold Office. *Bishop Protector* The Rt Revd Stephen Cottrell *Abbess* Sister Damien OSC, St Mary's Convent, Freeland, Witney, OX29 8AJ   *T:* 01993 881225
E: damien@oscfreeland.co.uk
W: www.oscfreeland.org.uk

Community of St Francis

Founded in 1905, the sisters of the First Order of the Society of St Francis, in the European Province (now including a Region in South Korea) and in the Province of the Americas, seek to live the gospel for today through lives of prayer, study and work. Prayer, together and alone, with the Eucharist having a central place, is the heart of each house and each sister's life. Six sisters are priests, and three live the solitary life. Study nurtures each sister's spiritual life and enables and enriches ministries.

Work (voluntary or salaried) includes practical domestic tasks and a wide range of ministries. Currently these include hospitality, spiritual direction, leading retreats and quiet days, preaching, parish work and missions, cathedral chaplaincy, speaking and writing, administration, teaching computer skills, being a presence in poor urban areas, hospice chaplaincy, work with deaf and blind people, befriending and support of people with particular vulnerabilities, theological college chaplaincy, ministerial development and mentoring, making vestments and clerical wear, running an after school project for children, assisting in care for homeless people and providing a short-term residential facility for families of those with a life-threatening illness. In all this the sisters seek to follow Christ in the footsteps of Francis and Clare of Assisi, and in the spirit of humility, love and joy.

Minister General: Sister Helen Julian CSF
email: ministergeneralcsf@
franciscans.org.uk

European Province
Minister Provincial Sister Sue CSF, Southwark
Tel: 020 7928 7121
email: ministercsf@franciscans.org.uk
website http://www.franciscans.org.uk

Bishop Protector The Rt Rev'd Stephen Cottrell (Bishop of Chelmsford)
Houses St Alphege Clergy House, Pocock Street, London SE1 0BJ   *Tel:* 020 7898 8912
E: southwarkcsf@franciscans.org.uk

San Damiano, 38 Drury Street, Metheringham, Lincoln LN4 3EZ   *Tel:* 01526 321115
email: metheringhamcsf@
franciscans.org.uk

The Vicarage, 11 St Mary's Road, Plaistow, London E13 9AE   *Tel:* 020 8552 4019
E: plaistowcsf@franciscans.org.uk

St Francis House, 113 Gillott Road, Birmingham B16 0ET   *Tel:* 0121 454 8302
email: birminghamcsf@franciscans.org.uk

St Matthew's House, 25 Kamloops Crescent, Leicester LE1 2HX   *Tel:* 0116 253 9158
E: leicestercsf@franciscans.org.uk

Korean Region
44–23, Suryu-gil, Haepyeong-myeon, Gumi-si, Gyeongsangbukdo 730–872, Republic of Korea
Tel: 054 451 2317
E: csfkorea@gmail.com

Deputy Bishop Protector for Korean Region The Rt Revd Onesimus Park (*Bishop of Busan*)

Province of the Americas
Minister Provincial, Province of the Americas Sister Pamela Clare CSF, St Francis House, 3743 Cesar Chavez St, San Francisco CA 94110-4316 USA
E: pamelaclarecsf@aol.com
Web: www.communitystfrancis.org

Bishop Protector The Rt Revd Bevi Edna (Nedi) Rivera, (*Bishop of Eastern Oregon*)

Community of St John Baptist
Founded in 1852 to honour and worship Almighty God and to serve him in works of charity. Undertakes mission and parish work, group quiet days, private retreats and spiritual direction. *Visitor* The Rt Revd John Pritchard *Chaplain* The Very Revd Lister Tonge *Community Leader* Sr Jane Olive, Harriet Monsell House, Ripon College, Cuddesdon, Oxford, OX44 9EX   *T:* 01865 877400
E: enquiries@rcc.ac.uk
W: www.csjb.org.uk

Community of St John the Divine
The Community was founded in 1848. The underpinning of our life and work is a spirituality based on St John the Apostle of Love. Today, as we continue to welcome people to test their vocation in the Religious Life, we have considered the challenge of change. The small core group of the Community has become the centre for a growing circle of Associates who share much of our life.

Our vision is to be a centre of prayer within the diocese, to exercise a ministry of hospitality to individuals and groups, to offer a ministry of spiritual accompaniment and spiritual accompaniment. *Visitor* The Rt Revd David Urquhart *Leaders of the Community* Sister Christine CSJD and Sister Margaret Angela CSJD, St John's House, 113 Coleshill Road, Marston Green, Birmingham, B37 7HT
T: 0121 788 0391
E: csjdivine@btconnect.com
W: www.csjd.org.uk

Community of St Mary the Virgin
The Community of St Mary the Virgin (CSMV) was founded in 1848. We are called to respond to our vocation in the spirit of the Blessed Virgin Mary: 'Behold, I am the handmaid of the Lord. Let it be to me according to your word.' Our common life is centred in the worship of God through the Eucharist, the daily Office and personal prayer, from which all else flows. The strong musical tradition of CSMV continues to enrich our worship.

The work of the Community is inspired by Mary's words, 'Whatever He says to you, do it.' It may take the form of outgoing ministry in neighbourhood and parish or in living alongside those in inner city areas. For others, it will be expressed in hospitality, spiritual direction, preaching and retreat giving, or in creative work in studio and press. An extensive new area of mission has opened up for us since the launch of our interactive website in September 2009. In addition to a daily update, we offer weekly meditations and retreats on line. We are able to receive requests for prayer through our website, and we also stream all our Offices live.

The Community has had a share in the nurturing and training of a small indigenous Community in Madagascar, and continues to maintain links with the sisters there. The Community also lived and worked in India and South Africa for many years. Involvement with both these countries remains through 'Wantage Overseas'. Our links with South Africa are also maintained by groups of Oblates and Associates living there. There are larger groups of Oblates and Associates in England.

At St Mary's Convent there is a Guest Wing for those who wish to spend time in rest, retreat and silence within the setting of a religious community. *Visitor (Acting)* The Rt Revd Steven Croft (Bishop of Oxford) *Superior* Mother Winsome CSMV, St Mary's Convent, Challow Road, Wantage, OX12 9DJ
T: 01235 763141
E: srstella@csmv.co.uk
guestwing@csmv.co.uk
W: www.csmv.co.uk

Community of St Peter
Founded in 1861 for mission work and nursing. The Sisters are dispersed, but meet together at least monthly. The sisterhood is now five in number. Reverend Mother Lucy Clare lives at Church of England Supported Housing, Fosbrooke House, Flat 33, 8 Clifton Drive, Lytham FY8 5RQ. Her responsibility is to keep in touch with sisters regularly by e-mail or telephone or other modern technology. Sister Angela lives in Woking and works within St Columba's House retreat and conference centre. Sisters Margaret Paul, Rosamond and Georgina Ruth live at St Mary's Nursing Home and Convent, Burlington Lane, London W4 2QE. *Visitor* The Rt Revd David Walker *Superior* Mother Lucy Clare CSP, St Peter's Convent, c/o St Columba's House, Maybury Hill, Woking, GU22 8AB
T: 01483 750739
E: reverendmother@stpetersconvent.co.uk
W: stcolumbashouse.org.uk

Community of St Peter, Horbury
Benedictine in spirit. Undertakes a variety of pastoral ministries and retreat work. *Visitor* The Rt Revd Tony Robinson (Bishop of Wakefield). St Peter's Convent, 14 Spring End Road, Horbury, Wakefield, WF4 6DB
E: stpetersconvent@virginmedia.com

Community of the Companions of Jesus the Good Shepherd
Founded in 1920. Undertakes work with the elderly, lay and ordained ministry training, quiet days, retreats and spiritual direction. *Visitor* The Rt Revd Dominic Walker OGS

Superior Sister Ann Verena CJGS, Harriet Monsell House, Ripon College, Cuddesdon, Oxford, OX44 9EX 　　　*T:* 01865 877400
E: enquiries@rcc.ac.uk

Community of the Holy Cross
Founded in 1857 for mission work but later adopted the Rule of St Benedict. All the work, centred on the daily celebration of the Divine Office and the Eucharist, is done within the Enclosure.

The Sisters contribute articles on spirituality and Christian unity to various publications and disseminate these via their website and Facebook page. A variety of prayer and greeting cards are also produced by the Sisters. The Community provides for Quiet Days for individuals and groups, and there is limited residential accommodation for those wishing to make longer retreats. *Visitor* The Rt Revd Dr David Hope *Mother Superior* The Revd Mother Mary Luke CHC, Holy Cross Convent, Highfields, Nottingham Road, Costock, Loughborough, LE12 6XE 　　　*T:* 01509 852761
E: mother@holycrosschc.org.uk
sisters@holycrosschc.org.uk
W: www.holycrosschc.org.uk

Community of the Holy Name
Founded in 1865. Undertakes mission and retreat work. Guests received.

Branch Houses
64 Allexton Gardens, Welland Estate, Peterborough PE1 4UW 　*Tel:* 01733 352077

St John's Rectory, St John's Road, Longsight, Manchester M13 0WU 　　*Tel:* 0161 224 4336

Overseas
Lesotho Convent of the Holy Name, PO Box 22, Ficksburg 9730, RSA 　*Tel:* 00266 22400249

Zululand Convent of the Holy Name, P/B 806, Melmoth 3835, RSA 　　*Tel:* 00273 54502892

Visitor The Rt Revd John Inge *Superior* Sister Pauline Margaret CHN, Convent of the Holy Name, Morley Road, Oakwood, Derby, DE21 4QZ 　　　　　　　　*T:* 01332 671716
E: bursarsoffice@tiscali.co.uk
W: www.chnderby.org

Community of the Sacred Passion
Founded in 1911. An order which combines prayer and mission work in varying forms. In England the sisters continue their life of prayer at the Mother House and a house in Clapham. Their active work is a response to the needs of the people among whom they live and so keeps developing.

The Community withdrew from Tanzania in June 1991, leaving behind a community of more than ninety Tanzanian women known as the Community of St Mary. This community is still given support by CSP, as is the Kwamkono Polio Hostel which was founded by CSP. *Visitor* The Rt Revd Ian Brackley *Superior* Mother Philippa CSP, Convent of the Sacred Passion, 22 Buckingham Road, Shoreham-by-Sea, BN43 5UB

T: 01273 453807
E: communitysp@yahoo.co.uk

Community of the Sisters of the Church
Founded 1870 and has a modern rule, based on the original, expressing a life rooted in prayer and worship, which flows into an active ministry through hospitality, pastoral and social justice work, spiritual direction and counselling.

Other Houses in the UK
82 Ashley Road, St Paul's Bristol BS6 5NT
Tel: 0117 941 3268
10 Furness Road, West Harrow HA2 0RL
Tel: 020 8423 3780

Novitiate
St Gabriel's, 27a Dial Hill Rd, Clevedon, North Somerset BS21 7HL   *Tel:* 01275 544 471

Main Houses of Overseas Provinces
Sister Linda Mary CSC, Mother Superior and Australia Provincial, 29 Lika Drive, Kempsey, NSW 2440, Australia
send all correspondence to: PO Box 1105, Glebe, NSW2037, Australia
E: cscaust@hotmail.com

Sister Margaret CSC, Canadian Provincial CSC c/o Sr Margaret Hayward, 1003/6 John Street, Oakville, ON L6K 3T1
email: sistersofthechur ch@sympatico.ca

Sister Veronica CSC, Solomon Islands Provincial, Box 510, Honiara, Solomon Islands
email: veronica@ sistersofthechurch.org

Visitor The Rt Revd Christopher Chessun (Bishop of Southwark) *UK Provincial* Sister Aileen CSC, St Michael's Convent, Vicarage Way, Gerrards Cross, SL9 8AT
E: info@sistersofthechurch.org.uk
W: www.sistersofthechurch.org.uk

Community of the Sisters of the Love of God
A contemplative community with a strong monastic tradition founded in 1906, which seeks to witness to the priority of God and to respond to the love of God – God's love for us and our love for God. We believe that we are called to live a substantial degree of withdrawal, in order to give ourselves to a spiritual work of prayer which, beginning and ending in the praise and worship of God, is

essential for the peace and well-being of the world. Through offering our lives to God within the Community and through prayer and daily life together, we seek to deepen our relationship with Jesus Christ and one another.

The Community has always drawn upon the spirituality of Carmel; life and prayer in silence and solitude is an important dimension in our vocation. The Community also draws from other traditions, and our Rule is not specifically Carmelite. Another important ingredient is an emphasis on the centrality of Divine Office and Eucharist together in choir, inspired partly by the Benedictine way of life.

SLG Press publishes pamphlets on spirituality and prayer.

SLG Press, Convent of the Incarnation, Fairacres, Parker Street, Oxford OX4 1TB
Tel: 01865 241874
Fax: 01865 241889
E: editor@slgpress.co.uk
Web: www.slgpress.co.uk

Visitor The Rt Revd Michael Lewis *Reverend Mother* Sister Clare-Louise SLG, Convent of the Incarnation, Fairacres, Parker Street, Oxford, OX4 1TB   *T:* 01865 721301
E: sisters@slg.org.uk
guests@slg.org.uk (Guest Sister)
W: www.slg.org.uk

Edgware Abbey
The Community was founded by the Revd Henry Daniel Nihill and Mother Monica Skinner in 1866 in Shoreditch, London. Living under the Rule of St Benedict, the Community's primary objective is prayer at the heart of the Church through the offering of the Divine Office and Eucharist, and through the service of hospitality, especially in caring for the sick and poor as Christ Himself.

From the beginning, under the dedication of St Mary at the Cross, the vocation of the Community has been to stand with Mary, the Mother of Jesus beside those who suffer. The care given in those early days to the sick and poor and disabled children of the local area grew and developed through the years, and continues today in Henry Nihill House in the beautiful grounds of the abbey, providing high-quality care and nursing for disabled people and frail elderly people.

Edgware Abbey is seen as a haven of peace which enfolds many visitors. All are offered Benedictine hospitality with space for rest and renewal. The small comfortable guest wing provides short-stay accommodation and a small centre for Parish Group Quiet Days and

Meetings. All visitors are welcome to share in the Community's offering of the Divine Office and Eucharist, which remains central to its life.

Chapel Service times are subject to change: please check with Edgware Abbey. *Visitor* The Rt Revd Peter Wheatley *Abbess* Mother Mary Therese Zelent OSB, Anglican Benedictine Community of St Mary at the Cross, 94A Priory Field Drive, Edgware, HA8 9PU

T: 020 8958 7868
E: info@edgwareabbey.org.uk

Order of the Holy Paraclete
Founded in 1915 and based on the Rule of St Benedict. Main undertaking: prayer, pastoral work, retreats, conferences, missions and parish work.

Residential Conference Centre Sneaton Castle Centre, Whitby YO21 3QN

Tel: 01947 600051
Fax: 01947 603490
email: sneaton@globalnet.co.uk
Web: www.sneatoncastle.co.uk

Accommodation (100 beds) for large and small groups for parish activities, conferences and school visits. Day visits, including tea, talk and tours.

Branch Houses
St Oswald's Pastoral Centre, Woodlands Drive, Sleights, Whitby YO21 1RY

Tel: 01947 810496
Fax: 01947 810759
email: ohpstos@globalnet.co.uk

IGRs, retreats, parish groups, individual guests.

Work in York Minster
1 Minster Court, York YO1 7JJ

Tel: 01904 557276
E: sistersohp@googlemail.com

On the staff of Bishopthorpe Palace
3 Acaster Lane, Bishopthorpe YO23 2SA

Tel: 01904 777294
email: ohpbishopthorpe@
archbishopofyork.org

All Saints House, South Avenue, Dormanstown TS10 5LL

Tel: 01642 486424
email: sisteranita@btinternet.com

Work in parishes and schools.

Overseas
Convent of the Holy Spirit, PO Box AH 9375, Ahinsan, Kumasi, Ashanti, Ghana

Tel: 00233 242 203 432
E: abbaotoo498@yahoo.com

Eye clinic, pastoral work, craft and sewing. Anglican Sisters OHP, Resurrection House, PO Box 596, Sunyani, Brong Ahafo Ghana

Tel: 00233 243 7068
E: nyamebekyere2010@yahoo.com

Fostering vocations, Bishop's Secretary, wafer making, vocational school. *Visitor* The Most Revd John Sentamu *Prioress* Sister Carole, St Hilda's Priory, Sneaton Castle, Whitby, YO21 3QN

T: 01947 602079
ohppriorywhitby@btinternet.com
W: www.ohpwhitby.org

Sisters of Bethany
Founded in 1866 for hospitality, retreat work and prayer for Christian Unity. The Sisters are available for leading quiet days and retreats, as spiritual directors, and also to give talks on prayer. People are welcome to come individually or as groups to spend time in silence and prayer. It is possible to accommodate a few residential guests, or groups of up to 24 for the day. A reference is required for guests applying to stay for the first time. *Visitor* The Rt Revd Trevor Willmott *Superior* Mother Rita Elizabeth SSB, 7 Nelson Road, Southsea, PO5 2AR

T: 023 9283 3498
E: ssb@sistersofbethany.org.uk
W: www.sistersofbethany.org.uk

Sisters of Charity
Founded in 1869. The Rule is based on that of St Vincent de Paul. We assist as required in parish work and in intercessory prayer, and maintain a nursing home. Morning Prayer 9 am. Most convenient time to telephone 5.30–7.00 pm.

Branch Houses
St Vincent's Nursing Home, Plympton, Plymouth PL7 1NE   *Tel:* 01752 336205

Carmel, 7a Gress, Isle of Lewis HS2 0NB
Tel: 01851 820734

Visitor The Rt Revd Martin Shaw *Superior* The Revd Mother Elizabeth Mary SC, 83 Fore Street, Plympton, Plymouth, PL7 1NB

T: 01752 336112
E: plymptonsisters@gmail.com

Society of All Saints Sisters of the Poor
Founded in London 1851. Works of the Society:

St John's Residential Home for the Elderly, St Mary's Rd, Oxford OX4 1QE

Tel: 01865 247725
E: admin@st-johns-home.org

Guest House (single and twin accommodation available). Also meeting facilities for small groups, weekdays, daytime only. Enquiries regarding visits, private retreats and conferences welcomed. Telephone as shown above for All Saints' Convent.

The Society is associated with:
Helen and Douglas House; The Porch Steppin' Stone Centre. *Visitor* The Rt Revd Bill Ind *Community Leader* Sister Jane ASSP, All Saints Convent, 15A Magdalen Road, Oxford, OX4 1RW   *T:* 01865 249127
E: admin@socallss.co.uk
Guests' e-mail: guestsister@socallss.co.uk
W: asspoxford.org

Society of St Margaret
Founded in 1855 and undertakes nursing and parish work. Sisters available for spiritual guidance. A residential home for elderly retired ladies and nursing home for those needing full-time nursing care.

Branch House St Mary's Convent and Nursing Home, Burlington Lane, Chiswick, London W4 2QE (guest house for elderly ladies and nursing home for geriatric and disabled ladies)
Tel: 020 8994 4641
Fax: 020 8995 9796

Superior Sister Jennifer Anne SSM
Visitor The Rt Revd Martin Warner
Overseas St Margaret's Convent (*semi-autonomous*), 157 St Michael's Road, Polwatte, Colombo 3, Sri Lanka

A home for the aged and a retreat house.
Sister Superior Sister Chandrani SSM
Tel: 00 94 11 2320692
Visitor The Rt Revd Dhiloraj Canagasaby

Branch House
St John's Home, 133 Galle Road, Moratuwa, Sri Lanka (children's home)
Tel: 00 94 11 264530

Independent Convents of the Society of St Margaret
St Saviour's Priory, 18 Queensbridge Road, London E2 8NS
Leader Sister Judith SSM   *Tel:* 020 7739 6775
E: ssmpriory@aol.com

Priory of Our Lady, Bridewell Street, Walsingham, Norfolk NR22 6ED
Joint Leaders Sisters Mary Teresa SSM and Mary Angela SSM   *Tel:* 01328 820340

St Margaret's Convent, 50 Harden Hill Road, Box C, Duxbury MA 02331-0605, USA
Superior Sister Adele Marie SSM
Tel: 00 1 781 934 9477
E: ssmconvent@ssmbos.com

Visitor The Rt Revd Martin Warner *Superior* Sister Cynthia Clare SSM, Hooke Hall, 250 High Street, Uckfield, RN22 1EN   *T:* 01825 766808
E: egmotherssm@hotmail.com

Society of the Precious Blood
Founded in 1905 and based on the Rule of St Augustine. Contemplative and exists for the purpose of perpetual intercession for the Church and for the world. *Visitor* The Rt Revd Stephen Cottrell *Superior* The Revd Mother Victoria Mary SPB, Burnham Abbey, Lake End Road, Taplow, Maidenhead, SL6 0PW
E: burnhamabbey@btinternet.com
W: www.burnhamabbey.org

Society of the Sacred Cross
We are an Anglican contemplative community living a life of prayer, based on silence, solitude and learning to live together, under monastic vows. The Daily Offices and other times of shared and private prayer span each day, together with a common life which includes study, recreation and work in the house and grounds of the convent.

At the heart of the corporate life of the community is the Eucharist and the crucified and risen Lord is the focus of its life and the source of the power to live it. Our purpose is to pray, and to offer an environment of prayer and hospitality to guests, visitors, those on retreat, parishes and clergy.

We welcome people from all denominations and those who are simply seeking to widen their spiritual horizons. The Tymawr Community is at the centre of the family of The Society of the Sacred Cross – people who link in with our life through prayer, work and mutual support. Some commit to a personal rule of life to form a structure for a life of prayer in their own circumstances.

Our own dedication to a life of prayer includes praying for others and supporting the ministry of other Christians.

If you would like to visit us or to come for a quiet day, or longer, you would be very welcome. It is possible for men and women, married or single, to experience the contemplative life by living alongside the community and sharing in our work and prayer for periods longer than the usual guest stay. This has proved a very creative and worthwhile experience for many people. *Visitor* The Rt Revd Dominic Walker OGS, *Superior* Sister Gillian Mary SSC Tymawr Convent, Lydart, Monmouth, NP25 4RN
T: 01600 860244
E: tymawrconvent@btinternet.com
W: www.tymawrconvent.org

St Saviour's Priory
Autonomous convent of the Society of St Margaret, working as staff members (lay or

ordained) in various parishes, dance workshops, complementary therapy, with the homeless, etc.; retreats and individual spiritual direction. The Priory has a few guest rooms and facilities for individual private retreats as well as excellent facilities for small group meetings. *Visitor* The Rt Revd Jonathan Clark

Superior The Revd Sister Judith Blackburn SSM, St Saviour's Priory, 18 Queensbridge Road, London, E2 8NS
T: 020 7739 6775 (guest bookings)
020 7739 9976 (sisters)
E: ssmpriory@aol.com
W: www.stsaviourspriory.org.uk

Religious Communities (Mixed)

Benedictine Community at Mucknell Abbey
By a common life of prayer, manual work and study the Community tries to create an atmosphere of stillness and silence in which the Community and its guests are enabled to be open and receptive to the presence of God.

While the recitation of the Office and celebration of the Eucharist constitute the principal work of the Community, the ministry of hospitality, the care of the grounds (which comprise a large organic kitchen garden in 40 acres of orchard, meadow and woodland), and the income-generating crafts of incense-making, icon writing and block-mounting provide a variety of manual work for the members of the Community and those guests who wish to share in it.

The monastery seeks to be a place of encounter and reconciliation. The early concern of the Community was to pray for Christian unity, and the Community enjoys links with Baptist, Lutheran, Old Catholic, Orthodox and Roman Catholic communities, and is particularly committed to the furthering of the Covenant between the Church of England and the Methodist Church. This ecumenical concern has broadened to include dialogue with people of other faiths, particularly those with a monastic tradition, and those who are seeking a spiritual way, either within or outside an established religious tradition. *Visitor* The Rt Revd John Inge *Abbot* Brother Thomas Quin OSB, Mucknell Abbey, Mucknell Farm Lane, Stoulton, WR7 9RB   *T:* 01905 345900
E: abbot@mucknellabbey.org.uk

Community of St Anselm
Each year, the Archbishop of Canterbury invites Christians aged 20–35 from around the world to spend ten months in a radical Jesus-centred community of prayer, study and service in the wider community – all based at Lambeth Palace in London.

Members come from many different denominations, including Anglican, Roman Catholic, Methodist and Pentecostal. They may be resident, following a full-time programme of prayer, study and service to the wider community, or non-resident, pursuing their 'Year in God's Time' while keeping their own jobs and accommodation in and around London. The Archbishop of Canterbury serves as the Community's Abbot.

The Community of St Anselm is an Acknowledged Religious Community of the Church of England and a Registered Charity in England and Wales (no. 1161185). *Prior* The Revd Anders Litzell *Director of Community* Sister Sonia Béranger *Program Manager* Ms Christina Winn *Community Manager* Ms Estelle Kim Lin, Lambeth Palace, London, SE1 7JU   *T:* 020 7898 1210
E: stanselm@lambethpalace.org.uk
W: www.stanselm.org.uk

Community of the Servants of the Will of God
Founded in 1953 for men (clerical and lay). Women are now received also. Contemplative. Retreats and conferences. The Community has also founded a charitable trust for promoting the Christian tradition of contemplative life and prayer within the Church. *Visitor* The Rt Revd John Hind *Father Superior* The Revd Fr Colin CSWG, Monastery of the Holy Trinity, Crawley Down, Crawley, RH10 4LH
T: 01342 712074
E: brother.andrew@cswg.org.uk

Society of St Francis, Third Order
One of the three Orders of the Society of St Francis (see also Communities for Men and Communities for Women). The Third Order is made up of women and men, lay and ordained, single and married, seeking to live out Franciscan ideals in the ordinary walks of life. There are just under 2000 Tertiaries in the European Province; there are four other Provinces: Africa, the Americas, Asia Pacific (Australia with Papua New Guinea and East Asia) and Pacific (New Zealand and the Solomon Islands), *Minister General* Ken E. Norian TSF *Minister Provincial European Province* Averil E. Swanton, 11 The Grange, Fleming Way, Exeter, EX2 4SB   *T:* 01392 430355
E: ministertssf@tssf.org.uk
W: www.tssf.org.uk

Society of the Sacred Mission
A religious community engaged in educational, pastoral and missionary work. The Society is divided into provinces:

Province of Europe
Visitor The Rt Revd John Pritchard
Provincial Fr Colin Griffiths SSM
The Well, Newport Road, Willen MK15 9AA
Tel: 01908 300552
E: ssmeprovincial@gmail.com

Houses
St Antony's Priory, 74 Claypath, Durham DH1
1QT   *Tel:* 0191 384 3747
email: info@stantonyspriory.co.uk

The Well, Newport Rd, Willen MK15 9AA
Tel: 01908 242190
email: info@thewellatwillen.org.uk

1 Linford Lane, Milton Keynes, Bucks. MK15
9DL   *Tel:* 01908 663749

Australian Province
Visitor The Rt Revd Garry Weatherill (Bishop
of Ballarat)
Provincial Fr Christopher Myers SSM

St John's Priory, 14 St John's Street, Adelaide,
South Australia 5000
email: ssm.s.province@esc.net.au

Houses
St John's Priory, 14 St John's St, Adelaide,
S Australia 5000

Southern African Province
Visitor The Most Revd Thabo Makgoba
(Archbishop of Cape Town)
Provincial Fr Tanki Mofana SSM
St Stephen's, Mohale's Hoek, Lesotho
E: mofanatanki@yahoo.com

Houses
SSM Priory, PO Box 1579, Maseru 100, Lesotho,
Southern Africa   *E:* ssmaseru@tlmail.co.ls

Healing of Memories Institute
Fr Michael Lapsley
SSM House, 33 Elgin Rd, Syband Park, Cape
Town 7700, RSA   *E:* michaelssm@gmail
W: www.sacredmission.org

Conference Centres

Ashburnham Place
Ashburnham Place, Battle, TN33 9NF
T: 01424 892244
E: bookings@ashburnham.org.uk
W: www.ashburnham.org.uk

Belsey Bridge Conference Centre
Belsey Bridge Conference Centre, Ditchingham,
Bungay, NR35 2DZ   *T:* 01986 892133
E: belseybridge@cct.org.uk
W: www.cct.org.uk

Hayes Conference Centre
Hayes Conference Centre, Swanwick, DE55
1AU   *T:* 01773 526000
E: office@cct.org.uk
W: www.cct.org.uk

High Leigh Conference Centre
High Leigh Conference Centre, Lord Street,
Hoddesdon, EN11 8SG   *T:* 01992 463016
E: highleigh@cct.org.uk
W: www.cct.org.uk

Lee Abbey
Lee Abbey Fellowship, Lynton, EX35 6JJ
T: 0800 389 1189
E: publicity@leeabbey.org.uk
W: www.leeabbey.org.uk

Retreat Houses

**Abbey House (Bath and Wells Retreat
House)**
Chilkwell Street, Glastonbury, Somerset, BA6
8DH   *T:* 01458 831112

**All Hallows Convent (Norwich Diocese
Retreat House)**
Ditchingham, Bungay, NR35 2DT
T: 01986 892840

**Bishop Woodford House (Ely Diocese
Retreat House)**
Warden Peggie Banks, Barton Road, Ely,
Cambs., CB7 4DX   *T:* 01353 663039

**Carlisle Diocesan Conference and
Retreat Centre**
General Manager Jonathan Green, Rydal Hall,
Ambleside, Cumbria, LA22 9LX
T: 01539 432050
E: mail@rydalhall.org

Chester Diocesan Conference Centre
Director The Revd Jonathon Green, Foxhill
House and Woodlands, Tarvin Road,
Frodsham, WA6 6XB   *T:* 01928 733777
E: foxhill@chester.anglican.org
W: http://foxhillchester.co.uk

Community of St Peter (Wakefield Diocese Retreat House)
Horbury, W Yorks., WF4 6BB
T: 01924 272181

Diocesan House of Retreat (Chelmsford Diocese)
Warden The Revd Sheila Coughtrey, Pleshey, Chelmsford, Essex, CM3 1HA
T: 01245 237251

Epiphany House (Truro Diocese Retreat House)
Kenwyn, Church Road, Truro, Cornwall, TR1 3DR   *T:* 01872 272249

Holland House (Worcester Diocese Retreat House)
Warden Ian Spencer, Cropthorne, Pershore, WR10 3NB   *T:* 01386 860330
E: enquiries@hollandhouse.org

Horstead Centre (Norwich Diocese Retreat House)
Manager Mark Heybourne, Norwich, NR12 7EP   *T:* 01603 737215
01603 737674

House of Bethany (Guildford Diocese Retreat House)
7 Nelson Road, Southsea, Hants, PO5 2AR
T: 023 9283 3498

Launde Abbey (Leicester Diocese Retreat House)
Warden The Ven David Newman, East Norton, Leicestershire, LE7 9XB   *T:* 01572 717254
E: info@launde.org.uk
W: www.laundabbey.org.uk

Lichfield Diocesan Retreat and Conference Centre
Director Simon Hudson, Shallowford House, Stone, Staffs., ST15 0NZ   *T:* 01785 760233

Ludlow Conference Centre (Hereford Diocese Retreat House)
Lower Galdeford, Ludlow, Shropshire, SY8 1RZ   *T:* 01584 873882
E: info@ludlowconferencecentre.co.uk

Monastery of the Holy Trinity (Chichester Diocese Retreat House)
Crawley Down, Crawley, W Sussex, RH10 4LH
T: 01342 712074

Old Alresford Place (Winchester Diocese Retreat House)
Winchester Retreat and Conference Centre, Old Alresford, Hants., SO24 9DH
T: 01962 737360
E: ian.knight@winchester.anglican.org

Parcevall Hall (Bradford Diocese Retreat House)
Appletreewick, Skipton, N Yorks., BD23 6DG
T: 01756 720213

Retreat Association
Clare Charity Centre, Wycombe Road, Saunderton, Buckinghamshire, HP14 4BF
T: 01494 569056
E: info@retreats.org.uk
W: www.retreats.org.uk

Sacrista Prebend Retreat House (Southwell Diocese Retreat House)
4 Westgate, Southwell, Notts, NG25 0JH
T: 01636 816 833

Sarum College (Salisbury Diocese Retreat House)
19 The Close, Salisbury, SP1 2EE
T: 01722 424800
E: hospitality@sarum.ac.uk

Shepherd's Dene (Dioceses of Newcastle and Durham Retreat House)
Riding Mill, Northumberland, NE44 6AF
T: 01434 682212

Sneaton Castle Centre (York Diocese Retreat House)
Centre Manager Linda Antill, Whitby, N Yorks, YO21 3QN   *T:* 01947 600051
E: sneaton@globalnet.co.uk
W: www.sneatoncastle.co.uk

Society of St Francis (Salisbury Diocese Retreat House)
The Friary, Hilfield, Dorchester, DT2 7BE
T: 01300 341345

Southwark Diocese Retreat House
Wychcroft, Bletchingley, Redhill, Surrey, RH1 4NE   *T:* 01883 743041

St Columba's House (Guildford Diocese Retreat House)
Director Fr Owen Murphy, Maybury Hill, Woking, Surrey, GU22 8AB
T: 01483 766498

St Mary's Convent (Oxford Diocese Retreat House)
Wantage, OX12 9DJ   *T:* 01235 763141
01235 774075

St Oswald's Pastoral Centre (York Diocese Retreat House)
Woodlands Drive, Sleights, Whitby, N Yorks., YO21 1RY   *T:* 01947 810496

OTHER ORGANIZATIONS

The Community of Sisters of the Church (Southwark Diocese Retreat House)
St Michael's Convent, 56 Ham Common, Richmond, TW10 7JH   *T:* 020 8940 8711
020 8948 2502

The Royal Foundation of Saint Katharine Retreat and Conference Centre (London Diocese Retreat House)
Master The Revd Mark Aitken, 2 Butcher Row, London, E14 8DS   *T:* 0300 111 1147
E: master@rfsk.org.uk
W: http://rfsk.org

Whalley Abbey (Blackburn Diocese Retreat House)
Warden Canon Andrew Sage, Whalley, Clitheroe, Lancs., BB7 9SS   *T:* 01254 828400

Wydale Hall (York Diocese Retreat House)
York Diocesan Retreat and Conference Centre, Brompton-by-Sawdon, Scarborough, N Yorks., YO13 9DG   *T:* 01723 859270
E: admin@wydale.org
W: www.wyedale.org

Theological Education Institutes

All Saints Centre for Mission and Ministry (formerly SNWTP)
Aiken Hall, University of Chester, Crab Lane, Warrington WA2 0BD
Principal The Ven Dr John Applegate
Tel: 01925 534303
Email: snwtpprincipal@chester.ac.uk

Cranmer Hall (St John's College)
Durham DH1 3RJ
Warden The Revd Dr Philip Plyming
Tel: 0191 3343924
Fax: 0191 3343866
Email: enquiries@cranmerhall.com

College of the Resurrection
Stocks Bank Road, Mirfield WF14 0BW
Principal The Revd Fr Peter Allan
Tel: 01924 490441
Fax: 01924492738
Email: principal@mirfield.org.uk

Cumbria Christian Learning
Church House, 19-24 Friargate, Penrith CA11 7XR
Director The Revd Canon Roger Latham
Tel: 01768 807765
Email: admin@
cumbriachristianlearning.org.uk

Eastern Region Ministry Course
1A The Bounds, Lady Margaret Road, Cambridge CB3 0BJ
Principal The Revd Alexander Jensen
Tel: 01223 760444
Email: asj43@cam.ac.uk

Lincoln School of Theology
Edward King House, Minster Yard LN2 1PU
Principal The Revd Sally Myers
Tel: 01522 504050
Email: sally.myers@lincoln.anglican.org

Lindisfarne Regional Training Partnership
St John's Terrace, North Shields NE29 6HS
Principal The Revd Dr David Bryan
Tel: 0191 2704144
Email: davidbryan@lindisfarnertp.org

Local Ministry Programme: Guildford
Church House, 20 Alan Turing Road, Guildford GU2 7YF
Principal The Revd Dr Stephen Summers
Tel: 01483 790319
Email: steve.summers@
cofeguildford.org.uk

Oak Hill Theological College
Chase Side, Southgate, London N14 4PS
Acting Principal Dr Daniel Strange
Tel: 020 84490467
Fax: 020 84415996

Oxford Local Ministry Programme
Church House Oxford, Langford Lane, Kidlington OX5 1GF
Local Ministry Training Co-ordinator The Revd Dr Phil Cooke   *Tel:* 01865 208282
Fax: 01865 790470
Email: phil.cooke@oxford.anglican.org

The Queen's Foundation for Ecumenical Theological Education
Somerset Road, Edgbaston, Birmingham B15 2QH
Principal The Revd Canon Dr David Hewlett
Tel: 0121 4541527
Fax: 0121 4548171
Email: enquire@queens.ac.uk

Ridley Hall
Ridley Hall Road, Cambridge CB3 9HG
Principal The Revd Dr Michael Volland
Tel: 01223 741060
Fax: 01223 746581
Email: ridleypa@hermes.cam.ac.uk

Ripon College Cuddesdon (including Oxford Ministry Course and West of England Ministerial Training Course)
Oxford OX44 9EX
Principal The Rt Revd Humphrey Southern
Tel: 01865 874404
Fax: 01865 875431
Email: enquiries@rcc.ac.uk

St Augustine's College of Theology
52 Swan Street, West Malling ME19 6JX
Principal The Revd Dr Alan Gregory
Tel: 01732 252656
Email: office@staugustines.college.ac.uk

St Hild College
Stocks Bank Road, Mirfield WF14 0BW
Principal The Revd Canon Mark Powley
Tel: 01924 481924
Email: enquiries@sthild.org

St John's School of Mission
Chilwell Lane, Bramcote, Nottingham NG9 3DS
Principal The Revd Dr David Hilborn
Tel: 0115 9251114
Fax: 0115 9436438
Email: enquiries@stjohns-nottm.ac.uk

St Mellitus College (including NTMTC)
24 Collingham Road, London SW5 0LX
Dean The Revd Dr Andrew Emerton
Tel: 020 7052 0573
Email: info@stmellitus.ac.uk

St Stephen's House
16 Marston Street, Oxford OX4 1JX
Principal The Revd Canon Dr Robin Ward
Tel: 01865 613500
Fax: 01865 613513
Email: enquiries@ssho.ox.ac.uk

Sarum College
19 The Close, Salisbury SP1 2EE
Principal The Revd Canon Dr James Woodward
Tel: 01722 424820
Email: jww@sarum.ac.uk

South West Ministry Training Course
Riverside Church and Conference Centre, 13-14 Okehampton Road, St Thomas, Exeter EX4 1DU
Joint Principals Dr Jonathan Rowe and the Revd Preb Philip Sourbut
Tel: 01392 272544
Email: principal@SWMTC.org.uk

Trinity College
Stoke Hill, Bristol BS9 1JP
Principal The Revd Dr Emma Ineson
Tel: 0117 9682803
Fax: 0117 9687470
Email: principal@trinity-bris.ac.uk

Westcott House
Jesus Lane, Cambridge CB5 8BP
Principal The Revd Canon Christopher Chivers
Tel: 01223 741000
Fax: 01223 741002
Email: info@westcott.cam.ac.uk

Wycliffe Hall
54 Banbury Road, Oxford OX2 6PW
Dean The Revd Dr Justyn Terry
Tel: 01865 274200
Fax: 01865 274215
Email: enquiries@wycliffe.ox.ac.uk

OTHER ORGANIZATIONS

Libraries and Archives

Canterbury Cathedral Archives and Library
Library collections: 52,000 printed volumes, 15th century to present. The Howley-Harrison Collection (16,000 books and pamphlets) includes anti-slavery and Oxford Movement material. Also cathedral printed music, and scores of Canterbury Catch Club. Three parish libraries: Crundale, Elham and Preston-next-Wingham, in a Dr Bray cabinet. The collections include substantial holdings on national and local history, including the English Civil War, travel, botany, English and foreign literature.

Archive collections: 2km of collections of manuscripts and archives, 9th century to present, including the Dean and Chapter's archives; records of the Diocese of Canterbury; parish records; records of Canterbury City Council and other organizations, businesses, administrations and individuals in the Canterbury area.

Cathedral Librarian Mrs Karen Brayshaw *Cathedral Archivist* Mrs Cressida

Williams, The Precincts, Canterbury, Kent, CT1 2EH
T: 01227 865330 (Archives)
01227 865287 (Library)
E: archives@canterbury-cathedral.org
library@canterbury-cathedral.org

Crowther Library
30,000 volumes, 250 current periodicals. Successor to the Partnership House Mission Studies Library that incorporated the post-1945 collections of the former Church Missionary Society and United Society for the Propagation of the Gospel. Stock focuses on the work of the Church worldwide, missiology, history of mission, church history, African and Asian Christianity and interfaith relations. Also houses CMS's pre-1945 collection entitled the Max Warren Collection. Reference only. *Librarian* Ken Osborne, Church Mission Society, Watlington Road, Oxford, OX4 6BZ
T: 01865 787552
E: ken.osborne@cms-uk.org
W: www.cms-uk.org/heritage/default.htm

Durham Cathedral Library

Chapter Library of 375 medieval manuscripts from the 7th century onwards, including Northumbrian, Norman and scholastic material. 1000 post-medieval manuscripts. Manuscript and printed music dating from the 16th century to the early 19th century. Archival collections include historical collections for County Durham and the NE of England, with much of wider interest, formed by local antiquaries, during the 17th to 20th centuries. Printed books include 70 incunabula, around 30,000 books printed pre-1851 and modern, borrowable works on church history, local interest and the arts.

Archdeacon Sharp Library, owned by the Lord Crewe Trustees and administered by Durham Cathedral Library, contains around 15,000 modern theology books, most borrowable. Catalogue is available through the Durham University Library catalogue, at: https://library.dur.ac.uk/ *Canon Librarian* Canon Rosalind Brown *Head of Collections* Lisa di Tommaso, The College, Durham, DH1 3EH
T: 0191 386 2489
E: Library@durhamcathedral.co.uk

Exeter Cathedral Library and Archives

20,000 items (Library); 50,000 (Archives), Manuscripts include Exeter Book and Exon Domesday; special collections include cathedral manuscripts and archives, early printed books in medicine and science, Cook Collection (16th–19th c., early linguistics), printed tracts (mainly Civil War period), Harington Collection (16th–19th c., theology, ecclesiastical history, history).

An online catalogue of our collections is available via the website. Medical and scientific collections also catalogued in *Medicine and Science at Exeter Cathedral Library*, compiled by Peter W. Thomas (University of Exeter Press, 2003). See also *The Library and Archives of Exeter Cathedral*, by L. J. Lloyd and Audrey M. Erskine, 3rd edn (Exeter 2004). *Cathedral Librarian* Peter Thomas *Assistant Librarian* Stuart Macwilliam *Cathedral Archivist* Ellie Jones, c/o Cathedral Office, 1 The Cloisters, Exeter, EX1 1HS   *T:* 01392 421423
E: library@exeter-cathedral.org.uk
archive@exeter-cathedral. org.uk
W: www.exeter-cathedral.org.uk/
Admin/Library/html

Gladstone's Library

Extensive holdings in Theology and Religious Studies. Main subject areas include: contextual theologies, Christian doctrine, biblical studies, ethics, spirituality, liturgy, church history plus Islamic Collection, Liberal/ Radical Theology Archive, Bishop Moorman Franciscan Collection and excellent holdings in nineteenth-century history, art and

literature. Twenty-six bedrooms, four conference rooms and chapel. Subsidised rates for clergy and students. Bursaries and scholarships available. *Warden* The Revd Peter Francis, Church Lane, Hawarden, Flintshire, CH5 3DF   *T:* 01244 532350
E: enquiries@gladlib.org
W: www.gladstoneslibrary.org

Hereford Cathedral Library and Archives

The Library cares for the Mappa Mundi (c. 1300), Chained Library and All Saints' Chained Library. The collection includes 227 medieval manuscripts from the 8th to the early 16th centuries, over 3,000 pre-1801 printed books including 56 incunabula, 10,000 books published post-1800 (many borrowable) and manuscript and printed music (18th to 20th centuries). There are also 30,000 archives of the Dean and Chapter, dating from the 9th to 21st centuries. Photographic service available. *Librarian* Dr Rosemary Firman *Archivist* Dr Bethany Hamblen *Library and Archives Assistant* James North, Hereford Cathedral, Hereford, HR1 2NG   *T:* 01432 374225/6
E: library@herefordcathedral.org
W: www.herefordcathedral.org

Lambeth Palace Library

Main library for the history of the Church of England, open for public use since 1610. 200,000 printed books and pamphlets, 4,900 manuscripts 9th–20th centuries. Registers and correspondence of Archbishops of Canterbury 12th–20th centuries. Records of Province of Canterbury, the Faculty Office, Lambeth Conferences up to 1968, Bishops of London, and papers of churchmen, statesmen and organizations within the Church of England. Also holds the manuscripts and printed books earlier than 1850 from Sion College Library. *Librarian and Archivist* Giles Mandelbrote, London, SE1 7JU
T: 020 7898 1400
E: archives@churchofengland.org
W: www.lambethpalacelibrary.org

Pusey House Library and Archive

A theological library of 75,000 volumes specialising in Anglo-Catholicism, Patristics, Church history and liturgy. The archive contains extensive material on the Tractarians and the Oxford Movement; Anglo-Catholic societies and religious orders; papers of notable Anglicans. *Librarian* Anna James *Principal* The Revd Dr George Westhaver *Chaplain* The Revd Mark Stafford, St Giles, Oxford, OX1 3LZ   *T:* 01865 288024
E: pusey.librarian@stx.ox.ac.uk
W: http://www.puseyhouse.org.uk/
the-library-and-archive.html
http://www.puseyhouse.org.uk/
the-library-and-archive.html

Sarum College Library

Open: 0900–1700 Mon–Fri and some evenings during term time

Founded 1860. More than 40,000 volumes mostly on academic theology, church history, ethics and Christian spirituality. Rare book collection including 274 bound volumes of mainly 20th-century tracts, sermons, charges and letters. About 1000 volumes are added each year.

Fifty journals are taken, with back numbers available for reference use. Inter-library loan services offered. Internet and Wi-Fi. Archive of the Christian Socialist Movement. Catalogue accessible from the library homepage at the above web address. Accommodation available. Researchers and sabbaticals welcome. Quiet space. Coffee, tea and lunches may be purchased. There is also a bookshop selling academic theology books and church supplies.

Fees: £40 per annum for reading rights; £50 per annum for reading and borrowing rights; £5 per day or £10 per week for visitors (subject to revision)

Director of Learning Resources Jennifer Monds *Librarian* Jayne Downey, 19 The Close, Salisbury, SP1 2EE   *T:* 01722 424803
E: library@sarum.ac.uk
W: www.sarum.ac.uk/library

Sarum College Bookshop

Assistant Manager Emily Button
Tel: 01722 326899
email: bookshop@sarum.ac.uk
Web : www.sarumcollegebookshop.co.uk

Open: 0900–1645 Mon–Fri, 1000–1600 Sat, and Tues evenings during term time

Excellent selection of new and second-hand academic theology, church history, ethics, Christian spirituality, etc. Mail order facility. Out-of-print and hard-to-find title search facility. Church supplies and cards for all church events (ordination, confirmation, baptism, etc.) Clergy discount. Online shop – www.sarumcollegebookshop.co.uk

St Paul's Cathedral Library

Re-established after the Great Fire of 1666, the library is strong in theology, ecclesiastical history, and sermons, especially of the 17th and 18th centuries. Special collections include early printed Bibles; St Paul's Cross sermons; 19th-century tracts.

The archive of the Dean and Chapter is deposited at London Metropolitan Archives, 40 Northampton Road, London EC1R 0HB email: ask.lma@cityoflondon.gov.uk *Librarian* Mr Jo Wisdom, The Library, St Paul's Cathedral, London, EC4M 8AE   *T:* 020 7246 8345
E: library@stpaulscathedral.org.uk

United Society for the Propagation of the Gospel Library

Bodleian reader's ticket required – details at www.bodleian.ox.ac.uk/bodley/using-this-library/getting-a-readers-card

The Society's library to 1944 and archival material circa 1701–1965. Extensive collections from the 19th century, back holdings of missionary journals. *Archivist* Miss Lucy McCann, The Bodleian Library, Weston Library, Broad Street, Oxford, OX1 3BG
T: 01865 277150
E: specialcollections.enquiries@bodleian.ox.ac.uk
W: www.bodleian.ox. ac.uk/bodley/finding-resources/special

Westminster Abbey Library

Library and archives of the Dean and Chapter of Westminster. Library includes manuscripts, early printed books (16,000), and modern collections (5,000) concerned with the history of Westminster Abbey and associated subjects. Extensive archive of the medieval monastery and its estates together with post-Reformation Abbey records to the present day.

Open: 1000–1300, 1400–1645 hours Mon–Thurs; appointments required *Librarian* Dr Tony Trowles *Keeper of the Muniments* Mr Matthew Payne, Westminster Abbey Muniment Room and Library, London, SW1P 3PA
T: 020 7654 4830
E: library@westminster-abbey.org
W: www.westminster-abbey.org

York Minster Historic Collections

Library: 90,000 volumes. Theology; church history, art, architecture and stained glass; extensive collections of pre-1801 books; incunables; special collections of Yorkshire history and Yorkshire Civil War tracts.

Archives: music and photographic collections; Yorkshire topographical prints; archives of Dean and Chapter from medieval times; manuscripts.

Web: (Library catalogue) http://yorsearch.york.ac.uk/ (Guide to Historic Collections) http://www.yorkminster.org/treasures-and-collections/historic-collections.html

Open: 0900–1700 hours Mon–Fri for general use. Archive, Special Collections and artefacts by appointment only

Closed on public holidays

Collections: Cathedral and Parish Plate; Textiles; Historic Furnishings inc. ornaments, furniture and adornments; Monuments; Displaced Glass; Worked Stone; Archaeology; Treasures. *Librarian* Ms Sarah Griffin *Archivist* Mr Peter Young *Assistant Director of Collections and Learning* Miss Victoria Harrison, The Old Palace, Dean's Park, York, YO1 7JQ
T: 01904 557250
E: library@yorkminster.org

OTHER ORGANIZATIONS

Patronage Trusts

Church Pastoral Aid Society Patronage Trust	*Secretary* The Revd John Fisher CPAS, Unit 3, Sovereign Court One Sir William Lyons Road Coventry CV4 7EZ *Tel:* 0300 123 0780 extn 4387/4388 *email:* jfisher@cpas.org.uk/ patronage@cpas.org.uk	A Trust holding Rights of Presentation to a number of benefices. Administered by the Church Pastoral Aid Society.
Church Patronage Trust	*Secretary* Preb Charles Marnham 4 Chester Square London SW1W 9HH *Tel:* 020 7730 8889 *email:* charles@stmichaelschurch.org.uk *Web:* www.churchpatronagetrust.co.uk	A Trust holding the Rights of Presentation to a number of benefices. Evangelical tradition.
Church Society Trust	*Chairman* The Revd Dick Farr Ground Floor, Centre Block Hille Business Estate, 132 St Albans Road Watford WD24 4AE *Tel:* +44 (0)1923-255410 *email:* admin@churchsociety.org	Patron of more than 100 livings.
Church Trust Fund Trust	*Secretary* The Revd John Fisher CPAS, Unit 3, Sovereign Court One Sir William Lyons Road Coventry CV4 7EZ *Tel:* 0300 123 0780 extn 4387/4388 *email:* jfisher@ cpas.org.uk / patronage@cpas.org.uk	A Trust holding Rights of Presentation to a number of benefices. Administered by the Church Pastoral Aid Society.
Guild of All Souls	*General Secretary* David G. Llewelyn Morgan Guild of All Souls 2 St Andrew's Road Willesden Green London NW10 2QS *Tel:* 020 8459 3813 *Web:* www.guildofallsouls.org.uk	Patron of 41 livings of Catholic tradition.
Hulme Trustees	*Secretary* Mr Jonathan Shelmerdine Butcher and Barlow Solicitors 31 Middlewich Rd Sandbach Cheshire CW11 1HW *Tel:* 01270 762521	A Trust holding the Rights of Presentation to a number of benefices.
Hyndman's (Miss) Trustees	*Executive Officer* Mrs Ann Brown 6 Angerford Avenue Sheffield S8 9BG *Tel:* 0114 255 8522 *email:* ann.brown@hyndmans.org.uk *web:* www.hyndmans.org.uk	Patronage Trust. Varied churchmanship.

Intercontinental Church Society	Unit 11, Ensign Business Centre Westwood Way Westwood Business Park Coventry CV4 8JA *Tel:* 024 7646 3940 *Web:* www.ics-uk.org *email:* enquiries@ics-uk.org	ICS is an international Church of England mission agency to English-speakers who live, study, work or holiday abroad, in countries where English is not the main language. We do this by planting and growing international churches and by outreach to tourists through our seasonal chaplaincies.
Martyrs Memorial and Church of England Trust	*Secretary* The Revd John Fisher CPAS, Unit 3, Sovereign Court One Sir William Lyons Road Coventry CV4 7EZ *Tel:* 0300 123 0780 extn 4387/4388 *email:* jfisher@ cpas.org.uk / patronage@cpas.org.uk	A Trust holding Rights of Presentation to a number of benefices. Administered by the Church Pastoral Aid Society.
Peache Trustees	*Secretary* Canon Roger Salisbury 6 Church Street Widcombe Bath BA2 6AZ *Tel:* 01225 489076 *email:* patronage@btinternet.com	A Trust holding the Rights of Presentation to a number of benefices. Evangelical tradition.
Simeon's Trustees	*Executive Officer* Mrs Ann Brown 6 Angerford Ave Sheffield S8 9BG *Tel:* 0114 255 8522 *email:* ann.brown@simeons.org.uk *web:* www.simeons.org.uk	Holds and administers the patronage of those livings in the Church of England which belong to the Trust on the principles laid down in Charles Simeon's Charge.
Society for the Maintenance of the Faith	*President* Dr Brian Hanson *Secretary* The Revd John Hanks 20 Ogleforth, York YO1 7JG *Web:* www.smftrust.org.uk	Founded in 1873, the Society presents, or shares in the presentation of, priests to over 80 benefices. As well as its work as a patronage body the Society aims to promote Catholic teaching and practice in the Church of England at large.

OTHER ORGANIZATIONS

ORGANIZATIONS

Accueil, Rencontre, Communaute UK (ARC UK)

ARC UK is a charity that organizes summer projects in which young people from across Europe give guided tours in their native language to visitors to churches. In so doing we seek to turn tourists into pilgrims through devotional tours in which visitors have the chance to engage, question and wonder.

Our projects aim to enable churches in their ministry of welcome and education, ecumenical links and youth involvement. ARC UK is part of a network of associated organizations which organizes such projects throughout Europe. We are always interested to hear from those who might like to participate on one of our projects, or churches who might be interested in hosting a project.

We are supported in our work by our Patron, the Bishop of Southwark, the Rt Revd Christopher Chessun. *President* Sarah Morton *Secretary* Vacancy *Recruitment Officer* archukrecruit@googlemail.com *Treasurer* Rory Lamb   *E:* president.arcuk@gmail.com
W: www.encounterarc.org.uk

Acorn Christian Healing Foundation

Acorn Christian Healing Foundation delivers healing and wholeness to individuals and communities. Through training, service and resources we provide a safe and effective Christian context in which people can experience personal and community wholeness, through exploring the essential elements of Healing, Reconciliation and Listening, around the UK and at its Training and Retreat Centre in Bordon, Hampshire.

Established in 1983 by Bishop Morris Maddocks, Acorn has been at the forefront of providing people, regardless of their circumstances, background or life choices, with the opportunity to experience the 'shalom' – a life-encompassing peace – that is at the heart of the Christian message. Shalom impacts every area of a person's life – relationships, physical and spiritual wellbeing and emotional wholeness.

Acorn remains engaged in and committed to being a transformative agent in today's multifaceted society. Our training events are divided into three main pathways of learning: healing, reconciliation and listening. *Director* The Revd Wes Sutton *Chaplain* The Revd Elizabeth Knifton *Director of Operations* Elaine Gold *National Training Manager* Howard

Fleming, Whitehill Chase, High Street, Bordon, GU35 0AP   *T:* 01420 478121
E: info@acornchristian.org
W: www.acornchristian.org

Action on Hearing Loss (formerly the Royal National Institute for Deaf People)

Action on Hearing Loss is the largest charity representing the 9 million deaf and hard of hearing people in the UK. It offers a range of services for deaf and hard of hearing people, and provides information and support on all aspects of deafness, hearing loss and tinnitus. As a membership charity, it aims to achieve a radically better quality of life for deaf and hard of hearing people. Action on Hearing Loss's work involves campaigning and lobbying, providing services, training, products and equipment, and undertaking medical and technical research. It works throughout the UK. *Chairman* Mr James Strachan *Chief Executive* Dr John Low, 1–3 Highbury Station Road, London, N1 1SE
T: 0808 808 0123 (Voice)
0808 808 9000 (Textphone)
E: informationline@hearingloss.org.uk
W: www.rnid.org.uk

Actors' Church Union

Founded in 1899. Members and associates serve those engaged in the performing arts through their interest, their action – often in association with other related bodies – and their prayers. Additionally, more than two hundred honorary chaplains serve all members of the profession in theatres, studios and schools at home and overseas. As well as spiritual counsel and practical advice, material help is given when possible. Through the Children's Charity, for example, funds are available for theatrical parents facing difficulties with the costs of their children's education. *President* The Rt Revd Jack Nicholls *Senior Chaplain* The Revd Lindsay Meader, St Paul's Church, Bedford Street, Covent Garden, London, WC2E 9ED   *T:* 020 7240 0344
E: actorschurchunion@gmail.com
W: www.actorschurchunion.org

Additional Curates Society

Founded in 1837 to help maintain additional curates in poor and populous parishes and especially in new areas. The Society also fosters vocations to the priesthood. *General Secretary* The Revd Darren Smith *Chairman* Prebendary David Houlding *Vice Chairman* Mr

Andrew Roberts *Treasurer* Mrs Mary Bashford, Gordon Browning House, 8 Spitfire Road, Birmingham, B24 9PB   *T:* 0121 382 5533
E: info@additionalcurates.co.uk
W: www.additionalcurates.co.uk

Affirming Catholicism

A movement within the Church of England and the Anglican Communion, formed in 1990. 'The object of the Foundation shall be the advancement of education in the doctrines and the historical development of the Church of England and the Churches of the wider Anglican Communion, as held by those professing to stand within the catholic tradition' (extracted from the Trust Deed). Its purposes are:

- to promote theological thinking about the contemporary implications of Catholic faith and order;
- to further the spiritual growth and development of clergy and laity;
- to organize or support lectures, conferences and seminars; to publish or support books, tracts, journals and other educational material;
- and to provide resources for local groups meeting for purposes of study and discussion.

Chair The Revd Canon Dr Rosemarie Mallett *Administrator* Mark Perrett, St Mary's Parish Office, Stoke Newington Church Street, London, N19 9ES   *T:* 079 9185 1722
E: administrator@affirmingcatholicism.org.uk
W: www.affirmingcatholicism.org.uk

Age UK (formerly Age Concern England)

Age UK cares about all older people and believes later life should be fulfilling and enjoyable. For too many this is impossible. As the leading charitable movement in the UK concerned with ageing and older people, Age UK finds effective ways to change that situation.

Nationally, we take a lead role in campaigning, parliamentary work, policy analysis, research, specialist information and advice provision, publishing and training in the care of older people. Where possible we enable older people to solve problems themselves, providing as much or as little support as they need.

Locally, Age UK provides community-based services such as lunch clubs, day centres and home visiting. These services are made possible through the work of many thousands of volunteers. Innovative programmes promote healthier lifestyles and provide older people with opportunities to give the experience of a lifetime back to their communities. Age UK is dependent on donations and legacies. The helpline is open seven days a week from 8 am to 7 pm *Chief Executive* Mr Tom Wright CBE, Tavis House, 1–6 Tavistock Square, London, WC1H 9NA   *T:* 0800 169 8080
0800 169 2081 (helpline)
E: contact@ageuk.org.uk
W: www.ageuk.org.uk

AIM International

AIM International is the largest evangelical Christian mission agency with a purely African focus, working in more than twenty countries in Africa and ministering to the African diaspora living around the world. Founded in 1895, it has nearly a thousand mission partners working together to see Christ-centred churches established among all Africa's peoples. With a priority for church planting, AIM International is also involved in long- and short-term ministries of leadership training, education and healthcare. *International Director* Dr Luke Herrin *UK Director* The Revd Andrew Chard MA, AIM International, Halifax Place, Nottingham, NG1 1QN   *T:* 0115 983 8120
E: admin.eu@aimint.net
W: www.aimint.org

Alcuin Club

Founded in 1897 to promote the study of liturgy, the Alcuin Club has a long and proud record of publishing both works of scholarship and practical manuals. Publications include collections, tracts and a new series of liturgy guides designed to accompany Common Worship. It also publishes, in conjunction with GROW, a series of Joint Liturgical Studies which has won wide acclaim. Members pay an annual subscription and receive new titles on publication. *President* The Rt Revd Stephen Platten *Vice President* The Revd Canon Dr Donald Gray CBE *Chairman* The Revd Canon Christopher Irvine *Treasurer* Mr John Collins CBE, 5 Saffron St, Royston, Herts, SG8 9TR   *T:* 01763 248678
E: alcuinclub@gmail.com
W: www.alcuinclub.org.uk

All Nations Christian College

All Nations came into existence in 1971 following the merger of three Bible colleges. While interdenominational in character, around 20 per cent of its students are members of the Anglican Communion. The College exists to train students primarily for cross-cultural ministries. With up to 120 international students of about 30 nationalities, as well as a respected international team of tutors, the community studying and socializing life is vibrant and challenging.

Students can follow a ten-week (en route), one-year or two-year biblical and intercultural studies course with a profound missiological emphasis. In addition to the popular Cert HE, Dip HE and BA (Hons) programmes, there are now validated specialist pathways in the Arts, Leadership and Development Studies. The College also offers a thirteen-week online programme (en route explore) and a five-day short course for groups heading out on to short term mission trips (en route express). This can be accessed as a residential or on line course.

The All Nations Masters programme in Contemporary Mission Studies was the first to be taught in the UK and has attracted leaders from around the world. There are five exit awards to choose from: MA in Contemporary Mission Studies, MA in Development with Mission, MA in Leadership with Mission, MTh in Contextual Theology with Mission, MTh in Messianic Jewish Theology and Intercultural Studies. The College has a good mix of married and single students. There are number of facilities to help such as childcare on site, wifi access, multi-gym, sports ground and beautiful surroundings, to name a few. *For details of programmes, apply to the Admissions Registrar,* All Nations, Easneye, Ware, SG12 8LX

T: 01920 443500
E: info@allnations.ac.uk
W: www.allnations.ac.uk

All Saints Educational Trust

Home/EU applicants: personal scholarships for intending teachers in degree-level education and/or professional training, particularly teachers of religious education, home economics and other subjects; those studying dietetics, food and nutrition, and public health promotion. Postgraduate qualifications relevant to continuing professional development may be considered. Financial constraint must in all cases be demonstrated.

Not assisted: school pupils, students of coun-selling, engineering, law, medicine, ordination, social work, commercial hospitality.

Overseas applicants: scholarships for full-time, taught postgraduate study in the UK only (taught Masters programmes favoured; doctorates and PGCE programmes will not normally be funded).

Corporate awards: given for imaginative new projects that will support the classroom teacher and build up the profession, preference being given to those aimed at enhancing the Church's contribution to education. Member of the Association of Church College Trusts (see separate entry). *Clerk to the Trust* Mr K. D. Mitchell, Knightrider House, 30–32 Knightrider Street, London, EC4V 5JT

T: 020 7256 9360
020 7248 8380
E: clerk@aset.org.uk
W: www.aset.org.uk

Almshouse Association (National Association of Almshouses)

Supports 1,650 member almshouse charities in providing good quality housing for those in need, many of whom are elderly. This is achieved through advising on best practice in almshouse management as well as advising and lobbying on regulatory matters relating to almshouses. The Association also provides grants and loans to enable almshouse charities to carry out essential repairs and refurbishments to what, in many cases, are ancient, listed buildings. Its other key role is to promote and encourage new building of almshouses. A number of these almshouse trusts have Anglican chaplains or appoint Anglican clergy as Master or Custos of the foundation. *Chair* Mrs Elizabeth Fathi *Director* Mr Anthony De Ritter *Deputy Director* Mr Julian Marczak *Assistant Director* Mr Christopher Targowski, Billingbear Lodge, Maidenhead Road, Wokingham, RG40 5RU   *T:* 01344 452922
E: naa@almshouses.org
W: www.almshouses.org

Ancient Society of College Youths

Established 1637. An international bell-ringing society based in the City of London, the College Youths seeks to recruit leading ringers from any part of the world in which English style change-ringing is practised. Members are active in supporting ringing for church services throughout the world. The Society maintains a charitable fund for the maintenance of bells, fittings and towers of churches where it has a current or historic association. *Secretary* Mr David E. House, 28 Waldegrave Road, Brighton, Sussex, BN1 6GE

T: 01273 507077
07710 085403
E: secretary@ascy.org.uk
W: www.ascy.org.uk

Anglican and Eastern Churches Association

Founded in 1864 to promote mutual understanding of, and closer relations between, the Orthodox, Oriental and Anglican Churches. Patrons: the Archbishop of Canterbury and the Patriarch of Constantinople. *Presidents* The Lord Bishop of London and Archbishop Gregorios of Thyateira and Great Britain *Chairman* the Revd Dr William Taylor *General Secretary* Ms Janet Laws, c/o The Old Deanery, Dean's Court, London, EC4V 5AA

T: 020 7248 6233
E: janet.laws@btopenworld.com

Anglican Fellowship in Scouting and Guiding

Founded in 1983 at the request of Guiders, Scouters and clergy. Its aims are to support leaders and clergy in the religious aspect of

the Promise and Law and other training programmes in Scouting and Guiding, and to maintain links with other Guide/Scout religious guilds and fellowships in order to foster ecumenical understanding. The Anglican Fellowship is a national Scout 'Active Support Unit' and is recognized in a support role by the Guide Association, the Church of England and the Church in Wales. Membership is open to Scout Groups (which do not have to be church sponsored), individuals aged 18 years or over who are members of the Scout or Guiding movement, and others (e.g. clergy) who are sympathetic to the aims of Guiding or Scouting. *Chairman* Mrs June Davies *Vice-Chairman* Vacancy *Secretary* Miss Joan Taylor *Treasurer* Miss Sandra Bendall, 31 Loseley Road, Farncombe, Godalming, GU7 3RE   *T:* 01483 428876
E: nanniejune@btinternet.com
W: www.anglicanfellowship.org.uk

Anglican Mainstream

Anglican Mainstream is a movement of organizations, churches, dioceses and individuals within the Anglican Communion worldwide, dedicated to teaching and preserving the Scriptural truths on which the Anglican Church was founded. It seeks to nurture, support and provide a network for orthodox Anglicans throughout the Communion. It published *Repair the Tear* as a response to the Windsor Report and *God, Gays and the Church*. Its Marriage, Sex and Culture group seeks, through bi-annual conferences, to support Christian marriage as a calling. It has a website, www.anglican-mainstream.org, as an information resource for orthodox Anglicans. *Convenor* Dr Philip Giddings *Executive Secretary* The Revd Andrew Symes, 21 High Street, Eynsham, OX29 4HE
T: 01865 883388
E: office@anglican.mainstream.org
W: www.anglicanmainstream.org

Anglican Marriage Encounter

Anglican Marriage Encounter is a voluntary organization which offers residential programmes for married and engaged couples to review and deepen their relationship by developing a compelling vision for their marriage, and providing the communication skills to support this. *Lay Executive Couple* Nigel and Tracey Burt, Taliesin, 1 Chillerton, Netley Abbey, Southampton, SO31 5GU
T: 023 8056 1342
E: mail@marriageencounter.org.uk
W: www.marriageencounter.org.uk / www.engagedencounter.org.uk

Anglican Pacifist Fellowship

Founded in 1937. Members pledged to renounce war and all preparation to wage war and to work for the construction of Christian peace in the world. Quarterly newsletter *The Anglican Peacemaker*. *Chairperson* Nat Reuss *Hon Secretary* Dr Tony Kempster, 11 Weavers End, Hanslope, Milton Keynes, MK19 7PA
T: 01908 510642
E: ajkempster@aol.com
W: www.anglicanpeacemaker.org.uk

Anglican Pastoral Care (Association of Advisers in Pastoral Care and Counselling)

Aims to support the work of Bishops' and Diocesan Advisers in Pastoral Care and Counselling or their equivalents; to encourage the appointment of an adviser in every diocese and to promote good practice in pastoral care and counselling of those in ministry, within the structures of the Church of England. Full membership is open to Bishops' and Diocesan Advisers or their equivalents. Associate membership is open to those holding similar appointments in other denominations and those interested in furthering the work of the Association. Anglican Pastoral Care, 68 John Street, Hinckley, Leicestershire, LE10 1UY
W: www.pastoralcare.org.uk

Anglican Society for the Welfare of Animals

Founded in 1972 for the purpose of including the whole creation in the redemptive love of Christ and especially for prayer, study and action on behalf of animals. Registered Charity no. 1087270. Promotes Animal Welfare Sunday each October and offers a free information pack to all churches. *President* The Rt Revd Dominic Walker OGS *Chairman* The Revd Dr Helen Hall *Treasurer* Mrs Jenny White, PO Box 7193, Hook, RG27 8GT
T: 01252 843093
E: AngSocWelAnimals@aol.com
W: www.aswa.org.uk

Anglican–Lutheran Society

Founded in 1984 to pray for the unity of the Church and especially the Anglican and Lutheran Communions; to encourage opportunities for common worship, study, friendship and witness; to encourage a wider interest in and knowledge of the Anglican and Lutheran traditions and contemporary developments within them. The Society publishes a newsletter, *The Window*, and organizes conferences, lectures and other events. *Co-Presidents* The Very Revd Dr J. Arnold (Anglican); The Rt Revd J. Johannesdotter (Lutheran) *Co-Moderators* The Rt Revd Michael Ipgrave (Anglican); the Revd Dr Jaako Rusama (Lutheran), Rectory Farm, Rectory Road, Retford, DN22 7AY
T: 01601777 719200 (Secretary)
E: Dick@ccwatford.u-net.com
W: www.anglican-lutheran-society.org

Anglo-Catholic Ordination Candidates' Fund
Secretary Revd J. F. H. Shead SSC, 57 Kenworthy Rd, Braintree, CM7 1JJ   *T:* 01376 321783
E: j.shead@tiscali.co.uk

Archbishop's Examination in Theology
Until 2007 the Archbishop's Examination in Theology comprised the Diploma of Student in Theology (the Lambeth Diploma) and the Degree of Master of Arts (the Lambeth MA). The Lambeth Diploma was instituted in 1905 by Archbishop Randall Davidson. It provided an opportunity for women to study theology, principally so that they could teach religious education in schools and churches. It was then extended to both men and women and the means of study was either by thesis or examination. The Lambeth MA was inaugurated by Dr Runcie in 1990 in order to provide an opportunity for theological study at a more advanced level. In 2007 the Archbishop's Examination in Theology was revised and now offers the Lambeth MPhil research degree, with the opportunity to extend to a Lambeth PhD. (The Lambeth Diploma and Lambeth MA are no longer options.) *For more information about the MPhil/PhD research degrees please contact* Executive Assistant: Patronage and Awards, Archbishop's Examination in Theology, Lambeth Palace, London, SE1 7JU
E: ruth.ruse@lambethpalace.org.uk

Archway
Retreat and Conference House Wardens' Association. Promotes the use of retreat and conference houses as a vital contribution to the life and development of Church and community. Is available to advise trustees/ management committees and diocesan boards on issues concerning the running of retreat houses. *President* The Rt Revd Alison White, Bishop of Hull *Secretary* Janet Haynes *Administrator* Mr Jeff Witts, Norlands, Norwich Road Edgefield, Norfolk, NR24 2RL
T: 01263 587661
E: admin@archwardens.org.uk
W: www.archwaywardens.org.uk

Art and Christianity Enquiry (ACE)
ACE is the leading UK organization in the field of visual arts and religion. ACE offers stimulating educational projects and publications, advice, information and skills. The ACE awards for religious art, architecture and literature are given biennially. The quarterly journal *Art and Christianity* is available by membership; complimentary copy available on request. *Director* Laura Moffatt, 70 Cowcross Street, London, EC1M 6EJ   *T:* 020 3757 5492
E: enquiries@acetrust.org
W: www.acetrust.org

Art and Sacred Places (ASP)
ASP promotes interaction between religion and art, largely by siting specially commissioned contemporary art in sacred places. It engages new audiences by exploring the relationship between art and spirituality, encouraging debate and understanding. ASP's work is based on the conviction that art and religion share fundamental concerns and explore similar territory, albeit in significantly different ways. ASP's portfolio of projects includes inspirational permanent commissions, innovative temporary commissions and mutually beneficial interfaith projects. ASP was founded under the auspices of Bishop John Gladwin in 1999 and became a charity in 2001. Charity Registration no. 1086739. Enquiries welcome. *Chair* Stephen Tucker
E: stucker957@btinternet.com
W: www.artandsacredplaces.wordpress.com (blog); www.artandsacredplaces.org

Association for Promoting Retreats (APR)
The APR celebrated its centenary year in 2013, having been founded in 1913 to foster the growth of the spiritual life in the Anglican Communion by the practice of retreats. Welcomes as members all Christians in sympathy with this aim. Membership by subscription for individuals, parishes and retreat houses. The APR is one of the retreat groups which form the Retreat Association (see separate entry). *Administrator and Secretary* Mrs Demelza Henderson, 2 Brookfield Cottages, The Strand, Lympstone, Exmouth, EX8 5ES   *T:* 01395 272243
E: promoting.retreats@gmail.com
W: www.promotingretreats.org

Association of Black Clergy
Founded in 1982 to bring together the minority ethnic clergy and lay ministers of the Christian Church in the United Kingdom, to provide support for all minority ethnic clergy and lay ministers, to encourage good practice and challenge racism individually, institutionally and structurally in particular in the Christian Church in the United Kingdom and to promote theological education and training that is relevant to minority ethnic Christian leadership. *Chairman* Revd Jennifer Thomas *Vice-Chair* Revd Karowei Dorgu *Facilitators (South)* Revd Yvonne Clarke, Revd Charles Lawrence *Facilitator (North)* Very Revd Rogers Govender, Sherwood Park Vicarage, Sherwood Park Rd, Mitcham, CR4 1NJ   *T:* 020 8764 1258

Association of Christian Teachers
ACT is a non-denominational Christian membership organization which provides professional and spiritual support to Christians engaged in pre-school, primary, middle,

secondary, special, college and university education in England. ACT encourages Christians to apply their faith to their work and provides opportunities for them to share together in prayer and fellowship. ACT strives to influence policy makers, politicians, the media and the Church by speaking from a professionally well-informed standpoint with a loving, Christian voice on behalf of Christians working in education. *Director (Strategy)* Mr Clive Ireson *Office Manager* Mrs Carol Horne, Suite 7 Rowan House, 23 Billing Road, Northampton, NN1 5AT

T: 01604 632046
E: act@christians-in-education.org.uk
W: www.christians-in-education.org.uk

Association of Christian Writers

The Association of Christian Writers aims to encourage, equip and inspire its members to use their talents with integrity, and to produce excellent material which comes from a Christian world view. We hold two writers' days per year, and local writing groups meet regularly. We also produce a quarterly magazine for members. *Chair* Angela Hobday *Overseas Support and Vice-Chair* Marion Osgood *Administrator* Jane Brocklehurst *Treasurer* Brian Stevens,

E: admin@christianwriters.org.uk
W: www.christianwriters.org.uk

Association of Church College Trusts

In 1979 the Association of Church College Trusts was established as a loosely knit organization to facilitate an exchange of information and cooperation. It meets every six months.

The Church College Trusts were formed following the closure of their respective Colleges of Education. They are autonomous, answerable only to the Charity Commission; their financial management policies are such that they are required both to sponsor present work from their income and also to ensure that their capital is maintained at a level that can finance similar levels of work in the future. In the last 30 years they have been involved in helping individual teachers, students and others, sponsoring corporate projects in part or in total, and aiding school, college and church educational activities.

The individual Trusts are: All Saints Educational Trust, Culham St Gabriel's Trust, Foundation of St Matthias, Hockerill Educational Foundation, Keswick Hall Charity, St Christopher's Educational Trust, St Hild and St Bede Trust, St Luke's College Foundation, St Mary's College Trust, St Peter's Saltley Trust and Sarum St Michael Educational Charity (see separate entries). Please note that applications have to be made to the individual Trusts concerned and not centrally through the Association. *Secretary* Dr Mark Chater, 15 Norham Gardens, Oxford, OX2 6PY

T: 01865 284885
E: enquiries@csgt.org.uk
W: www.cstg.org.uk

Association of Diocesan Registry Clerks

The Association was established in 1999 to support and assist clerks and assistant staff in the furtherance of their professional roles in the diocesan and provincial registries and the Faculty Office of the Church of England by encouraging and sharing knowledge of ecclesiastical law, practice and procedures, imparting and exchanging information, and promoting discussion relevant to their roles. A day conference is organized for members, alternating biannually with a two-day residential conference; a lively group email correspondence provides an invaluable resource and a semi-regular newsletter keeps members informed. *President* The Right Worshipful Charles George QC, Dean of the Arches and Auditor *Chair* Mary Jamieson *Secretary* Cassi Errington *Treasurer* Liz Matthews, Sintons LLP, The Cube, Barrack Road, Newcastle-upon-Tyne, NE4 6DB

T: 0191 226 7878
E: mary.jamieson@sintons.co.uk
W: www.registryclerks.org

Association of English Cathedrals

Established in 1990 and authorized by the Administrative Chapters of the Anglican Cathedrals as their representative organization, the AEC deals with governmental agencies, the General Synod and its constituent bodies and the Churches' Legislation Advisory Service on behalf of the English cathedrals, provided only that it cannot commit any individual cathedral chapter to a specific decision. Membership consists of one representative of each Administrative Chapter. *Chairman* The Very Revd Adrian Dorber *Executive Director* Mrs Sarah King, PO Box 53506, London, SE19 1ZL

T: 07860 921419
E: sarah.king@englishcathedrals.co.uk
W: www.englishcathedrals.co.uk

Association of Hospice and Palliative Care Chaplains (AHPCC)

The AHPCC is the professional organization for health care chaplains whose primary role is to provide spiritual and religious care in hospices and other palliative care settings.

Hospice and Palliative Care Chaplains seek to work as members of a multidisciplinary team committed to providing holistic care. They have primary responsibility for the spiritual and religious care of patients, carers, staff and volunteers, regardless of faith or life stance. They provide an informed ethical, theological and pastoral resource for individuals and for their employing organizations, and offer training and pastoral support to staff. The AHPCC aims to identify and promote good practice, to provide support and training opportunities to its members, to collaborate with other palliative care professionals and to promote links with church bodies and faith communities.

The AHPCC offers information and advice about appointments, induction, and training courses, keeps members up to date with current issues by means of its website, and organizes a three-day conference and training event in May each year. The AHPCC is happy to liaise with religious bodies, training institutions and individuals interested to know more about palliative care chaplaincy. Many hospices offer placements and courses which form part of pre- and post-ordination training. The AHPCC monitors professional developments within the constituency of palliative care, and works to its own professional Standards, Competencies and Code of Conduct. It collaborates closely with other Chaplaincy bodies e.g. the College of Health Care Chaplains, the Scottish Association of Chaplains in Healthcare, and the UK Board for Healthcare Chaplaincy to further the professionalism of healthcare chaplaincy throughout the UK.

The membership fee is currently £35, and individuals interested in becoming members should consult the website for information. *President* Revd Judy Davies *Website Editor* Mike Rattenbury   *E:* president@ahpcc.org.uk
editor@ahpcc.org.uk
W: www.ahpcc.org.uk

Awareness Foundation
The Awareness Foundation is an international ecumenical institution committed to fostering community harmony through education.

The Foundation's teaching programme, the Awareness Course, is designed and written by Bishop Michael Marshall and Revd Nadim Nassar to educate Christians for life in the twenty-first century. Each course module is written from a Christian viewpoint, teaching Christians about their own faith and that of their neighbours, so that they can respect the differences and live in a diverse society without fear and without compromising their faith. The Course considers Islamic and Jewish perspectives to build an awareness of 'the other' and to go deeper into the Christian faith. It is designed to be taught in churches, parish halls or any appropriate space, and is suitable for regular or occasional churchgoers, Christians outside the Church, seekers and the undecided.

New courses are published each year. *President* Rt Revd Michael Marshall *Director* Revd Nadim Nassar *Chair of Trustees* Charles

Longbottom *Chief Executive Officer* Helen Carey, Holy Trinity Church, Sloane St, London, SW1X 9BZ
T: 020 7730 8830 (Office)
020 7259 0619 (Education)
E: tfcc@tfccinternational.com
W: www.tfccinternational.com

Baptismal Integrity (BI)
BI has four aims:

• to bring to an end the indiscriminate administration of infant baptism;
• to demonstrate that baptism is the sacrament instituted by Christ for those becoming members of the visible church;
• to seek the reform of the Canons and rules of the Church of England in line with the above stated aims;
• and to promote within the Church of England debate and review of the biblical, theological, pastoral and evangelistic aspects of Christian initiation.

BI affirms the propriety of baptizing the infants of practising Christian believers and also of deferring baptism until later years. It also affirms the relevance and value of the Service of Thanksgiving for the Gift of a Child. BI publishes its magazine *Update* at intervals. Membership is £10 per annum (or concession) – more information via website or Chairman. *President* The Rt Revd Colin Buchanan *Acting Chairman* The Revd Dr Clifford Owen *Secretary* The Revd Dr John Hartley *Membership Officer* The Revd David Perry, 11 Middle Garth Drive, South Cave, Brough, HU15 2AY
E: editorial@baptism.org.uk
W: www.baptism.org.uk

Barnardo's
Founded in 1866, Barnardo's is the UK's largest children's charity, whose inspiration and values derive from the Christian faith. It runs more than 400 projects nationwide and each year helps more than 100,000 children, young people and their families to overcome severe disadvantage.

Barnardo's believes in children and works with them over the long term to tackle the effects of disadvantage and to ensure they can fulfil their potential. Children are helped to address problems such as abuse, homelessness and poverty and to tackle the challenges of disability. Barnardo's also campaigns for better care for children and their families in the community and champions the rights of every child. The charity no longer runs orphanages and now concentrates on working with children and their families in the community. *President* HRH The Duchess of Cornwall *Chief Executive* Javed Khan,

Barnardo's, Tanners Lane, Barkingside, Ilford, IG6 1QG   T: 020 8550 8822
E: supportercare@barnardos.org.uk
W: www.barnardos.org.uk

Beauchamp Community
Situated near Malvern, we are a Christian Almshouse Charity providing unfurnished single and double flats for retired clergy and laity at reasonable cost. Aged from 60 years upwards, applicants should be in good health. Daily Eucharist in a caring community. Apply to the Administrator. *Warden* Mrs Lesley Lewis *Chaplain* Fr Roger Watson, Newland, Malvern, WR13 5AX   T: 01684 562100
E: bcomadmin@btconnect.com
W: www.beauchamp150.co.uk

Bible Reading Fellowship
At the heart of BRF's ministry is the desire to help people of all ages – children, adults and families – to explore Christianity and to grow in faith. We're passionate about helping people to engage with the Bible and prayer, and about resourcing Christian discipleship.

These aims are fulfilled through the following ministries and resources:

- Barnabas in Churches – visit www.barnabasinchurches.org.uk. Includes free resources to use with under 11s and much more.
- Barnabas in Schools – visit www.barnabasinschools.org.uk. Working with primary schools to help children and their teachers explore Christianity creatively.
- Bible Reading Notes – visit www.biblereadingnotes.org.uk. Four different series to choose from.
- Bible Reading Notes Resource Pack – visit www.biblereadingnotes.org.uk. Discover all you need to know about promoting daily reading notes in church.
- BRF publishing – visit www.brfonline.org.uk. Church resources, prayer and spirituality, group study books and more.
- Church accounts – receive discount off BRF's books to help you encourage reading in your church. Contact Rebecca Fillis on 01865 319714 to find out more.
- Faith in Homes – visit www.faithinhomes.org.uk. Helping churches to support families to develop faith in the home. Free ideas, resources and more.
- Electronic books – visit www.brfonline.org/ebooks. New BRF titles available for the Kindle.
- Foundations21 – visit www.foundations21.net. BRF's free online discipleship resource for groups and individuals.
- Messy Church – visit www.messychurch.org.uk. BRF's dynamic fresh expression of church based around welcome, crafts and art celebration, and eating together. Active in 14 countries.
- Who Let The Dads Out? – visit www.wholetthedadsout.org. A way of reaching dads and their young children in your community.

BRF is a registered charirty (no. 233280). *Chair of Trustees* Rt Revd Colin Fletcher, Bishop of Dorchester *Chief Executive* Mr Richard Fisher *Deputy Chief Executive* Mrs Karen Laister, 15 The Chambers, Vineyard, Abingdon, OX14 3FE
T: 01865 319700
E: enquiries@brf.org.uk
W: www.brf.org.uk

Bible Society
Bible Society is working towards a day when the Bible's life-changing message is shaping lives and communities everywhere. We aim to show how the Bible connects with life. We make Scriptures available where there are none. And we work with the Church to help it live out the Bible's message in its daily life and witness. *Chief Executive* Paul Williams *Executive Director of Charity* Paul Woolley *Executive Director of Finance* Julie Fletcher, Stonehill Green, Westlea, Swindon, SN5 7DG
T: 01793 418100
E: contactus@biblesociety.org.uk
W: www.biblesociety.org.uk

Boys' Brigade
Week by week the Boys' Brigade reaches out to children and young people, both girls and boys. We are passionate about partnering with churches to build bridges into local communities and engage a generation of children and young people with a message of hope rooted in Jesus. *Director for England* Eric Hudson, Felden Lodge, Felden Lane, Hemel Hempstead, HP3 0BL   T: 01442 231681
E: enquiries@boys-brigade.org.uk
W: www.boys-brigade.org.uk

Bridge Pastoral Foundation (formerly the Clinical Theology Association)
Founded in 1962. The core activity of the Association is seminars in pastoral care and pastoral counselling, which are directed by authorized tutors and widely available in the UK. Seminars are designed to promote self-awareness, which is needed for effective pastoral work, and to teach the theory and practice of pastoral counselling with reference to the assumptions, values and meanings of the Christian faith. Further information about Bridge Pastoral Foundation education and training may be obtained from the Administrator. 2 Gar Street, Winchester, SO23 8GQ   T: 01962 843040
E: admin@bridgepastoral.org.uk
W: www.bridgepastoral.org.uk

Bristol Clerical Education Society

Grants of up to £250 to ordinands and, occasionally, to clergy undertaking CME, for specific and practical needs. *Secretary* Mrs S. J. Clover, The Croft, Cox's Hill, Ashton Keynes Wiltshire, SN6 6NY   *T:* 01285 861199
E: sueclover.clover@googlemail.com

British Deaf Association

The British Deaf Association (BDA) is the largest national organization run by Deaf people with Deaf people. We represent the UK's Deaf community and campaign for the official recognition of British Sign Language (BSL). Our vision is 'Deaf people fully participating and contributing as equal and valued citizens in the wider society'. Our mission is to ensure a world in which the language, culture, community, diversity and heritage of Deaf people in the UK is respected and fully protected, ensuring that Deaf people can participate and contribute as equal and valued citizens in the wider society. This will be achieved through:

- improving the quality of life by empowering Deaf individuals and groups;
- enhancing freedom, equality and diversity;
- protecting and promoting BSL.

Patron HRH The Duke of York *Chair* Terry Riley *Chief Exec* David Buxyon, BDA Head Office, 18 Leather Lane, London, EC1N 7SU
T: 020 7405 0090
E: bda@bda.org.uk
W: www.bda.org.uk

British Isles and Eire Airport Chaplains' Network

The British Isles and Eire Airport Chaplains' Network meets twice a year for a day or two-day conference and is working towards seeing airport chaplaincy established at every international or regional airport in the UK and Ireland. In 2005 there were chaplaincies at 35 airports, with others being negotiated. Of these, full-time chaplains or chaplaincy teams are at: Heathrow, Gatwick, Manchester, Luton and East Midlands. All airport chaplains are on call and are pleased to be able to assist those travelling through airports in any way. They can be contacted via the airport information desk. Some airport chaplaincies have web pages on their particular airport websites; for a list of sites visit the address given below. *Coordinator* Revd Roy Monks *General Secretary* Vacancy, East Midlands Airport Chaplaincy Team, Chaplains' Office, East Midlands Airport, Castle Donington, Derby, DE74 2SA   *T:* 01332 818407 ext 6407
E: roy.monks@talk21.com
W: www.aoa.org.uk/ourmem/index.asp

Broken Rites

Formed in 1983, Broken Rites is an interdenominational and independent association for the divorced and separated spouses/partners of Anglican clergy, ministers and Church Army officers living in the United Kingdom, the Republic of Ireland and the geographical area covered by the Diocese in Europe. It welcomes the support of everyone who is in sympathy with its aims:

- to support one another with compassion, understanding and practical help where possible;
- to continue to draw the attention of the Churches to the problems of former clergy spouses/partners;
- and, while affirming the Christian ideal of lifelong marriage, to promote a more vivid awareness among Christian people of the increasing incidence of clergy marriage/ partnership breakdown.

Hon Secretary Sue Atack *Co-Chair* Margaret Wilkinson   *T:* 020 8650 2312
E: enquiry@brokenrites.org
W: www.brokenrites.org

Bromley and Sheppard's Colleges

Bromley College was founded in 1666 to provide houses for clergy widows and Sheppard's College in 1840 to provide houses for unmarried daughters of clergy widows who had lived with their mothers at Bromley College. Houses in both colleges have been converted into flats and widows/widowers of clergy, retired clergy and their spouses, divorced and separated spouses of clergy or retired clergy of the Church of England, the Church in Wales, the Scottish Episcopal Church or the Church of Ireland may now be admitted. Contact the Chaplain/Clerk to the Trustees. *Clerk and Chaplain* Revd Christopher Boulton, Chaplain's Office, Bromley and Sheppard's Colleges, London Road, Bromley, BR1 1PE   *T:* 020 8460 4712
E: bromleysheppardscolleges@btconnect.com
W: www.bromleycollege.org

Burrswood

Burrswood is a Christian hospital and place of healing founded in 1948 by Dorothy Kerin, who received a commission from God to 'heal the sick, comfort the sorrowing and give faith to the faithless'.

The Dorothy Kerin Trust is a registered charity, administered by a board of trustees and has:

- a non-surgical hospital with 40 beds for short-term inpatient care supported by an inter-disciplinary team of resident doctors, nurses, physiotherapists and counsellors;

- a church with resident chaplains, which is fully integrated within the hospital and has healing services open to the public twice a week;
- a guest/retreat house with single and twin rooms, sleeping 9;
- a physio- and hydrotherapy complex for inpatients and outpatients, and
- a medical and counselling outpatient facility.

Additional public facilities include a Christian bookshop and tea room on-site and a charity shop in nearby Crowborough. Profits from these trading operations go into Burrswood's 'Access to Care' bursary fund which assists financially disadvantaged patients to receive care. *Chief Executive Officer* John Ashelford *Senior Chaplain* Revd Christine Garrard *Senior Physician* Dr Paul Worthley, Groombridge, Tunbridge Wells, TN3 9PY
T: 01892 863637 (Enquiries)
01892 865988 (Admissions)
E: enquiries@burrswood.org.uk
W: www.burrswood.org.uk

Came's Charity for Clergymen's Widows
Founded to provide small annual grants to benefit clergy widows who are wanting. Apply to the Clerk. *The Clerk*, Worshipful Company of Cordwainers, Dunster Court Mincing Lane, London, EC3R 7AH   T: 020 7929 1121
E: office@cordwainers.org

Campaigners England and Wales, The
Founded 1922, The Campaigners England and Wales is a national youth movement working in partnership with local churches. The Campaigners England and Wales trains and resources local leaders, enabling them to operate an exciting and relevant relational and holistic programme of evangelism and Christian discipleship for boys and girls between 4 and 18. It is recognized by UK government education departments and is a member of the Evangelical Alliance. *Executive Director* Mr John Radcliffe *Resources Director* Mr Tony Etherington, 7 Frankpledge Road, Cheylesmore, Coventry, CV3 5GT
T: 0247 650 5758
W: www.campaignersew@weebly.com

Canterbury and York Society
Founded 1904 for the printing of bishops' registers and other ecclesiastical records. *Joint Presidents* The Archbishops of Canterbury and York *Chairman* Dr P. Zutshi *Secretary* Dr C. Fonge *Treasurer* Dr R. Hayes, c/o Borthwick Institute, University of York Heslington, York, YO10 5DD   E: charles.fonge@york.ac.uk
W: http://www.canterburyandyork.org

CARE (Christian Action Research and Education)
CARE is a registered charity seeking to combine practical caring initiatives, at national and community level, with public policy on social and ethical issues. CARE campaigns, provides resources, undertakes caring work and helps to bring Christian insight and experience to matters of public policy, education and practical caring initiatives, particularly on the behalf of the needy. *Chairman* Revd Lyndon Bowring *Chief Executive* Mrs Nola Leach *Director of Parliamentary Affairs* Dr Dan Boucher, 53 Romney St, London, SW1P 3RF
T: 020 7233 0455
08453 100 244 (supporter helpline)
E: mail@care.org.uk
W: www.care.org.uk

Catch 22 (formerly Rainer)
A national voluntary organization, founded in 1788, working primarily with young people at risk, through over 60 community-based projects, some in partnership with local authorities and other voluntary organizations. Particular services include leaving care projects and bail support schemes, accommodation and support to young people on release from young offender institutions or who are homeless, youth training and employment schemes. *Chief Exec* Chris Wright, Churchill House, 27 Bear Tree Street, London, EC1V 3AG
T: 020 7336 4800
E: information@catch-22.org.uk
W: www.catch-22.org.uk

Cathedral and Church Shops Association
The Association provides a forum for the exchange of information, and arranges an annual conference and trade fair for its members. We sponsor meetings of shop staff in several areas of the country each spring, giving advice and assistance for the setting up and running of church shops from experienced shop managers. Membership is open to any cathedral/church/abbey/religious house which is under sole control, or operated by a trading company for the sole benefit, of its chapter, parochial church council or religious house. *Chairman* Hugh Fearnall JP *Hon Secretary* Ann Waller, Stable Cottage, Aydon, Corbridge Northumberland, NE45 5PL
T: 07779 346150
W: www.cathedralandchurchshops.com

Cathedral Libraries and Archives Association
The CLAA supports the work of the cathedral and capitular libraries and archives in the Anglican churches of the United Kingdom and Ireland. It seeks to advance education by the promotion, preservation and protection of

those collections and provides a forum for cooperation and the exchange of information among those who care for them. *Chairman* Very Revd Peter Atkinson *Hon Secretary* Judith Curthoys *Hon Treasurer* Dr Michael Stansfield, c/o Archives and Special Collections, Durham University Library, Palace Green, Durham, DH1 3RN   *T:* 0191 334 2972
                E: m.m.n.stansfield@durham.ac.uk
                W: www.cathedrallibrariesandarchives.
                wordpress.com

Cathedrals Administration and Finance Association (CAFA)
In 1975 cathedral administrators and treasurers began, as a body, to exchange information on all matters touching on best practice and the most effective administration of the English Anglican cathedrals. The association now enjoys a valued link with the Association of English Cathedrals for which organization it undertakes research as needed. There is an annual conference and regular regional meetings. *Chairman* Vacancy *Treasurer* Mrs Caroline Robinson *Admin Secretary* Nicola Elliott, Church House, Great Smith St, London, SW1P 3NZ   *T:* 020 7898 1067
                E: nicola.elliott@churchofengland.org

Cathedrals Plus
Founded in 1981, Cathedrals Plus, formerly known as The Pilgrims' Association, provides a forum in which those responsible for the care and welcome of pilgrims, visitors and tourists to our cathedrals, abbeys, churches, shrines and chapels can meet and exchange ideas and experiences. It is also responsible for bringing together those in cathedrals and churches who deliver education outside the classroom both to schools and adults.

Originally a Trust, Cathedrals Plus is now a fully democratic institution governed by a Council of 15 members elected at the annual general meeting. Membership is both ecumenical and international, consisting of the great majority of Church of England cathedrals, four Roman Catholic cathedrals and several of the most visited parish churches, abbeys, priories and chapels from Anglican, Roman Catholic and Free Church denominations in England, Wales, the Republic of Ireland and Belgium.

Cathedrals Plus operates mainly through an annual conference and periodic newsletters and through its website. It is consulted regularly by government and VisitBritain on tourism and educational matters relating to cathedrals and churches and is currently absorbing the work of CPAL, Cathedrals as Partners in Adult Education, into its remit. *Chairman* Very Revd Charles Taylor *Secretary* Dr Paul Hammans *Hon Treasurer* Barry Palmer,

Snuffy Cottage, 3 Park Road, Southolt, Eye, IP23 7QW   *T:* 01728 628374
                E: secretary@cathedralsplus.org.uk
                W: www.cathedralsplus.org.uk

Catholic Group in General Synod
The Catholic Group consists of those on General Synod committed to the catholic, traditional and orthodox voice in the Church of England. It seeks to make a positive contribution to all debates and especially where Catholic faith and order are involved. It welcomes both the ARCIC discussions and dialogue with the Orthodox churches. The group maintains that ethical teaching which scripture and tradition have consistently upheld. *Chairman* Canon Simon Killwick *Secretary* Mrs Mary Nagel, Aldwick Vicarage, 25 Gossamer Lane, Bognor Regis, PO21 3AT
                T: 01243 262049
                E: mary@nagel.me.uk

Central Council of Church Bell Ringers
Founded in 1891, the Central Council of Church Bellringers' aims are:

- to promote the ringing of church bells;
- to represent the ringing exercise to the world at large;
- and to provide expert information and advice to ringers, church authorities and the general public on all matters relating to bells and bell-ringing.

President Mrs Kate Flavell *Hon Secretary* Mrs Mary Bone, 11 Bullfields, Sawbridgeworth, CM21 9DB   *T:* 01297 726159
                E: secretary@cccbr.org.uk
                W: www.cccbr.org.uk

Centre for the Study of Christianity and Sexuality
Launched in 1996, CSCS provides opportunities for issues of sexuality and gender identity to be discussed honestly and openly, and aims to help others in the churches to provide similar opportunities. CSCS is a unique, UK-based, ecumenical network specifically engaged in this task.

CSCS is associated with the international journal *Theology & Sexuality* and publishes *CSCS News* three times a year. It also organizes an annual conference. Patrons and Matron: The Rt Revd John Gladwin (formerly Bishop of Chelmsford), The Revd David Gamble (Chair of The Methodist Council), The Revd Roberta Rominger (former URC General Secretary). *Chair* Mr Martin Pendergast *Secretary* The Revd Canon Jane Fraser *Acting Treasurer* Mr Michael Egan *Newsletter Editor* Mr Anthony Woollard, PO Box 24632, London, E9 6XF
                E: info@christianityandsexuality.org
                W: www.christianityandsexuality.org

Changing Attitude

Working for lesbian, gay, bisexual and transgender affirmation within the Anglican Communion, Changing Attitude is a network of lesbian, gay, bisexual, transgendered and heterosexual members of Anglican churches founded in 1995

In England local groups meet regularly in eight dioceses to offer encouragement and support and provide educational and training resources. We have a network of contacts in over thirty-three dioceses and supporters in every English diocese. Changing Attitude has groups in Australia, Ireland, Kenya, New Zealand, Nigeria, Scotland and Wales. We work alongside Integrity USA and Canada and with many international groups and networks campaigning for equality. *Director* The Revd Colin Coward *Hon Administrator* Brenda Harrison, 6 Norney Bridge, Mill Rd Worton, Devizes, SN10 5SF   *T:* 01380 724908
07770 844302
E: ccmcoward@aol.com
W: www.changingattitude.org.uk

Children's Society, The

The Children's Society has helped change children's stories for over a century. We expose injustice and address hard truths, tackling child poverty and neglect head-on. We fight for change based on the experiences of every child we work with and the solid evidence we gather.

Through our campaigning, commitment and care, we are determined to give every child in this country the greatest possible chance in life. We transform children's lives by pressurizing central and local government to protect them, and we challenge attitudes that perpetuate harm and injustice. We are inspired by Christian values and work in close partnership with churches. In hard times, children are among the hardest hit. We don't just help them survive – we help them flourish. *Chair of Trustees* Rt Revd Tim Thornton, *Chief Executive Officer* Revd Matthew Reed, Edward Rudolf House, 69–85 Margery St, London, WC1X 0JL
T: 020 7841 4400 (Switchboard)
0845 300 1128 (Supporter Action Line)
E: supportercare@childrenssociety.org.uk
W: www.childrenssociety.org.uk

Choir Benevolent Fund

Founded in 1851. A registered Friendly Society for subscribing cathedral and collegiate lay clerks and organists. *Trustees* The Deans of St Paul's, Westminster and Windsor *Secretary* Mr Roland Tatnell, Foxearth Cottage, Frittenden, Cranbrook, TN17 2AU   *T:* 01580 712825

Choir Schools Association

Founded in 1918 to promote the welfare of children in cathedral, collegiate and parish church choir schools. In 1985 it set up a bursary trust to help children from low income families become choristers. *Chairman* Mr Tim Cannell *Administrator* Mrs Susan Rees, 39 Grange Close, Winchester, SO23 9ND
T: 01962 890530
E: info@choirschools.org.uk
W: www.choirschools.org.uk

CHRISM (CHRistians In Secular Ministry)

Formed in 1984, CHRISM is the national association for all Christians who see their secular employment as their primary Christian ministry and for those who support that vision. CHRISM welcomes members, both lay and ordained, from all Christian denominations, encourages them to be active within their own faith communities and to champion ministry in and through secular employment. A journal is published quarterly, as well as occasional papers. We hold an open annual conference and also a members' reflective weekend. *Secretary* The Revd Sue Cossey   *T:* 0117 957 4267
E: sue.cossey@yahoo.co.uk
W: www.chrism.org.uk

Christian Aid

Christian Aid is an agency of the British and Irish churches and as such is one of the largest church-related international relief and development agencies in Europe. It works largely in the developing world providing support wherever the need is greatest, irrespective of race or religion.

A substantial amount of its voluntary income is received through the annual Christian Aid Week collections led by churchgoers. It funds projects in more than 50 countries, standing by poor communities whether they are digging wells or fighting the consequences of debt, unfair trade or climate change, learning to read or articulating human rights abuses, healing the wounds of war or tackling the spread of preventable illnesses.

Money spent overseas is passed to local partner organizations as Christian Aid believes that poor communities are best placed to devise and run their own projects and solve their own problems. Channelling money in this way is seen as an effective and respectful way of giving poor people the means to help themselves. Prevention of the causes of poverty is better than cure, but Christian Aid remains active in emergencies, sending immediate help and capacity to cope with emergencies and disaster mitigation including food, shelter, medicine and transport when flood, famine, earthquake or war strike.

The agency's charitable work includes campaigning and education work in the UK and Ireland, which accounts for up to 11 per cent of its income. This is because Christian Aid believes it must also tackle the structures and systems that keep people poor. It puts great emphasis on the involvement of individuals to address the root causes of poverty and encourage action by politicians and international institutions that will lead to their removal. *Director* Vacancy *Chair of the Board* Dame Anne Owers, Inter-Church House, 35–41 Lower Marsh, London, SE1 7RL *T:* 020 7620 4444

> *E:* info@christian-aid.org.uk
> *W:* www.christian-aid.org.uk

Christian Arts

An association of artists, architects, designers, craftsmen and craftswomen all involved in the arts who are committed Christians and wish to explore and deepen the relationship between their faith and the arts. Its activities include holding exhibitions, study days and an annual conference. An illustrated magazine is published twice a year, with interim newsletters. Many members are available to accept commissions. Information may be found on the website detailed below.

> *E:* membershipsecretary@
> christianartists.org.uk.com
> *W:* www.christianartists.org.uk

Christian Education (incorporating International Bible Reading Association and RE Today Services)

Christian Education provides advice, resources and opportunities for teaching and learning in the school, the church and the family group, carrying forward the work of the National Christian Education Council and the Christian Education Movement. *Chief Executive* Peter Fishpool, Maranatha House, Unit 5, Northwood Close, Shrivenham, SN6 8HL

> *E:* membership secretary@christian.
> artists.org.uk
> *W:* www.christian.education

Christian Evidence Society

Founded in 1870, its principal object is 'to give instruction in evidences of Christianity'. Initially it produced tracts, sponsored lectures and arranged open-air work at Tower Hill and Hyde Park Corner. Later it organized annual Drawbridge Lectures by distinguished names. Nowadays its literature is on its website, available for free download by all and it sponsors broadcasts on Premier Radio. To mark the Darwin anniversary, in 2009 the Revd Professor Alister McGrath delivered a Drawbridge Lecture on 'Belief in God'. *President* The Archbishop of Canterbury *Chairman* Revd Prof Richard Burridge *Administrator*

Mr Christopher Garman, Springers, The Street, Coney Weston Bury St Edmunds, IP31 1HG

> *T:* 01359 221600
> *E:* admin@christianevidence.org
> *W:* www.christianevidencesociety.org.uk

Christian Healing Mission

The Christian Healing Mission (CHM) seeks to bring people into the presence of Jesus and to find the healing that flows from him. There are two main strands to the work: taking the exciting message of the person of Jesus the healer to as many churches and groups as possible and providing places where people can safely find Jesus and his healing touch.

The Mission has a non-residential healing centre in London and a number of link centres and churches throughout the country. It offers training for those who are, or wish to be, involved in prayer ministry. Although rooted in the Church of England, the CHM is keen to work with people and churches of all denominations. The Director is an Anglican priest with many years' experience of parish ministry and is also the Bishop of Kensington's Adviser for Healing. *Director* The Revd John Ryeland *Chaplain* The Revd Sarah Swift, 8 Cambridge Court, 210 Shepherds Bush Rd, London, W6 7NJ   *T:* 020 7603 8118

> *E:* chm@healingmission.org
> *W:* www.healingmission.org

Christian Medical Fellowship

CMF has four aims:

- Discipleship – to unite Christian doctors and medical students in Christ, and to encourage them to deepen their faith, live like Christ, and serve him obediently, particularly through acting competently and with compassion in their medical practice.
- Evangelism – to encourage Christian doctors and medical students to be witnesses for Christ among all those they meet.
- Mission – to mobilize and support all Christian doctors, medical students and other healthcare professionals, especially members, in serving Christ throughout the world.
- Values – to promote Christian values, especially in bioethics and healthcare, among doctors and medical students, in the Church and in society.

Chief Executive Dr Peter Saunders *Head of Communications* John Martin, 6 Marshalsea Rd, London, SE1 1HL   *T:* 020 7234 9660

> *E:* mail@cmf.org.uk
> *W:* www.cmf.org.uk

Christian Projects OCU

Christians from all denominations who care about Christian values in the family, medical ethics, Christian education and the media, and run an annual Schools Bible Project for secondary schools across Britain. *Chairman* Mrs Joanna Bogle DSG *Vice-Chairman* Lady Elizabeth Benyon, St Stephen's Vicarage, Cressingham Road, London, SE13 5AG

E: christianprojects@gmail.com
W: www.christianprojectsocu.org.uk

Christian Research

Christian Research is an authoritative voice on the Christian world and has been providing insight on the thoughts, views and opinions of the practising Christian community for over 20 years. Today we operate an online panel with over 5000 members, identifying long-term religious trends, as well as Christians' response to current affairs and topical issues.

Our Resonate panel is primed to help you. Although there were 33 million people stating they are Christians (over 59 per cent) in the UK 2011 Census – most of them are only traditionally or nominally Christian which makes our research panel incredibly relevant as it comprises those who are committed practising Christians and enables us to research and understand how their views and attitudes differ from the public as a whole. Stonehill Green, Westlea, Swindon, SN5 7DG

T: 01793 418 364
E: admin@christian-research.org
W: www.christian-research.org

Christian Witness to Israel

To a people of promise – the message of Messiah. Working alongside local churches, Christian Witness to Israel has been sharing the message of Messiah with the Jewish people for over 150 years. It is a non-denominational, international and evangelical organization with workers in seven countries worldwide.

We believe that the Jewish people's greatest need is to know Jesus their Messiah. In order to help meet this need, we provide appropriate literature and run an evangelistic website. We also host outreach events and provide training for Christians who wish to share the gospel with their Jewish friends, neighbours and colleagues. *General Secretary* Mr Mike Moore, 166 Main Rd, Sundridge, Sevenoaks, TN14 6EL

T: 01959 565955
E: comms@cwi.org.uk
W: www.cwi.org.uk

Christians at Work

Christians at Work seeks to encourage, support and equip Christian fellowship, evangelism and witness in the workplace. It does this by seeking to unite Christian men and women at work in order to promote a sense of unity in the gospel.

The organization produces resources, fact sheets and Bible study material, organizes conferences and seminars for local churches and coordinates a network of around 200 workplace groups and around 200 individual members committed to the extension of Christ's kingdom in the working world. It was founded in 1942 to:

- bring together Christians to pray and work for the extension of Christ's kingdom in the world of business and industry;
- encourage active evangelism and fellowship;
- provide information, literature and other facilities; and
- help Christians who stand alone in their place of work and to provide a means whereby young Christians starting work may be strengthened in their faith.

Director Revd Brian Allenby, Suite 10, Hubbway House, Bassington Lane, Cramlington Northumberland, NE23 8AD

T: 01670 700908
E: brianallenby@caw.uk.net
W: www.caw.uk.net

Christians in Library and Information Services

Constituted 1976 under the original name of Librarians' Christian Fellowship to provide opportunities for Christians working in library and information services to consider issues in their professions from a Christian standpoint, and to promote opportunities for presenting the Christian faith to people working in libraries and information services of all kinds. *Hon Secretary* Graham Hedges, 34 Thurlestone Ave, Ilford, IG3 9DU

T: 020 8599 1310
E: secretary@christianlis.org.uk
W: www.christianlis.org.uk

Christians on the Left (formerly the Christian Socialist Movement)

Christians on the Left seeks to be the Christian conscience of the Labour Party and a voice to churches on social and political issues. We have a tradition stretching back 150 years, believing that the teachings of Jesus – justice, equality and love for one another – are inextricably linked to the foundations and continuation of the Labour Party.

Newsletters and other articles are published throughout the year on our own website and through Christian and Mainstream Media. We also organize events, such as hustings for the leadership of the Labour Party, and have a presence at the Labour Conference, where we run fringe events with other major organizations, well-known journalists and prominent political figures. Details of membership rates are available on our website.

Director Dr Andy Flannagan *Chair* Jonathan Reynolds MP, PO Box 65108, London, SW1P 9PQ   *T:* 020 7783 1590
E: info@christiansontheleft.org.uk
W: Http://www.christiansontheleft.org.uk

Church and Media Network, The

The Church and Media Network supports, encourages and inspires Christians who work in, and with, the media through its three core services – themedianet, Day of Prayer for the Media and the CMN Annual Conference. The Charity is chaired by Steve Cox. Jenny Lee is the charity's brand new Network Development Manager, while Esther Kuku has recently been appointed as the Network's Content Producer to take responsibility for the Charity's communications. For further information, please visit www.themedianet.org

Church Army

Church Army is a mission-focused community of people who are committed to enabling and resourcing the church and its members to share the gospel. Our vision is for everyone, everywhere to encounter God's love and be empowered to transform their communities through faith shared in words and action. Everything we do is underpinned by our values: we are prayerful, expectant, risk-taking, generous, collaborative, accountable and unconditional.

Our evangelists and projects work across the British Isles and Ireland to share the good news of Jesus. We work in a variety of contexts and reach out to communities in ways that help them live life to the full as we seek to transform lives with the gospel. We work with the homeless, the marginalized, those battling addictions, young offenders and other marginalised groups. We serve communities, work with children and young people and help the shut-in elderly.

We are also committed to building new forms of Christian community to reach people who have little or no experience of church. We work tirelessly to live God's love with those whom we serve. *President* The Rt Revd and Rt Hon Lord Williams of Oystermouth *Chief Executive* Canon Mark Russell, Wilson Carlile Centre, 50 Cavendish Street, Sheffield, S3 7RZ   *T:* 0300 123 2113
E: comms@churcharmy.org
W: www.churcharmy.org/
http://twitter.com/churcharmy

Church House Deaneries' Group – The National Deaneries Network

Exists to stimulate local and national consideration of the developing role of the deanery, to encourage an informal network for the exchange of information about deanery thinking and deanery initiatives, and to promote the mission opportunities of deaneries. Every two years since 1988 it has held a national conference about deaneries. *Contact*, The Vicarage, Station Road, Benton, Newcastle upon Tyne, NE12 8AN
T: 0191 266 1921
E: secretary@chdg.org.uk
W: www.chdg.org.uk

Church Housing Trust

Church Housing Trust is committed to changing the lives of homeless people, providing the help and services they would otherwise be denied. Our principal objective is to raise funds to benefit homeless people and those in housing need, and in particular those cared for by Riverside ECHG (formerly English Churches Housing Group).

Our funds support residents in more than 80 projects throughout England, including hostels, women's refuges, projects for young people, supported housing for ex-Service people, accommodation for vulnerable young parents and children, specialist supported housing for people with drug, alcohol and mental health problems, and projects for ex offenders. Our funds help turn hostels into homes and prepare homeless people for independent living through life skills and education and training programmes.

Charity no. 802801.PO Box 50296, London, EC1P 1WF   *T:* 020 7269 1630
E: info@churchhousingtrust.org.uk
W: www.churchhousingtrust.org.uk

Church Lads' and Church Girls' Brigade

The Brigade is the Anglican Church's only uniformed youth organization, welcoming children and young people of all faiths and none, from ages 5 years to 21 years, engaging in 'fun, faith and friendship', equipping them to cope with the demands that society places upon them.

The Brigade creates a caring and safe environment in which friendships between young people, children and adults can be established; helping children and young people to grow in confidence, developing their individual skills and abilities to work together, showing concern for others and the environment, exploring their spirituality and developing moral values. Operating in four age groups: 5–7 years, 7–10 years, 10–13 years and 13–21 years, there are appropriate training and activity programmes for all leaders and members to be engaged in. *Patron* HM The Queen *President* The Archbishop of Canterbury *Governor* Anthony Baker *Brigade Chaplain* Rt Revd Jack Nicholls, National Headquarters, Saint Martin's House, 2 Barnsley Rd, Wath-Upon-Dearne, Rotherham, S63 6PY   *T:* 01709 876535
E: brigadesecretary@clcgb.org.uk
W: www.clcgb.org.uk

Church Mission Society

We are a community of people in mission who want the world to know Jesus. Founded in 1799 in the crucible of the anti-slavery movement, CMS has some 350 people currently serving through our mission programmes internationally, sharing Jesus and changing lives in Africa, Asia, Europe, the Middle East and Latin America.

The 2,500 members of the CMS mission community aspire to live a life shaped by God's mission wherever they are. CMS Pioneer Mission Leadership Training is a unique course for pioneer mission leaders working in many contexts, including those training to be ordained pioneer ministers in the Church of England.

CMS is committed to working in networks, especially with CMS Africa and AsiaCMS, and is a founder member of the Faith2Share mission movements network.

Registered Charity no. 1131655. Company no. 6985330. *Patron* The Archbishop of Canterbury *Episcopal Visitor* Rt Revd Dr Christopher Cocksworth, Bishop of Coventry *Chair of Trustees* John Ripley *Executive Leader* Revd Canon Philip Mounstephen, Watlington Rd, Oxford, OX4 6BZ

T: 01865 787 400 (Switchboard)
E: info@cms-uk.org
W: www.cms-uk.org

Church Monuments Society

Founded in 1979 to encourage the appreciation, study and conservation of monuments. The Society promotes a biennial symposium, excursions, study days, a twice-yearly newsletter and an annual refereed journal. It also offers a programme of visits to locations throughout the country, a series of occasional lectures and an opportunity for people to meet and exchange views on a subject which spans many disciplines. It is the only society to cover all periods and all types of monument, and is the sponsor of the National Ledger Stone Survey. *President* Dr Phillip G. Lindley *Secretary* Dr Amy L. Harris *Treasurer* Dr John Brown *Membership Secretary* Mr Clive Easter, c/o Society of Antiquaries of London, Burlington House, Piccadilly, London, W1J 0BE

T: 01752 773634 (Membership)
01837 851483 (Publicity)
E: churchmonuments@aol.com
W: www.churchmonumentssociety.org

Church Music Society

Founded in 1906, the society is a leading publisher of all types of Church music, and has consistently served the Church of England by this means. An annual lecture and other events for members pursue further aims of advancing knowledge of the art and science of Church music.

Although much of the society's focus is on music specifically for liturgy, CMS publications are also in world-wide use by choirs of all types for concerts, recitals and recordings. *Te Deum Laudamus*, a CD of CMS publications, is now available. Details of membership and activities are available from the Secretary. *President* The Dean of Hereford *Chairman* Mr Timothy Byram-Wigfield *Hon Secretary* Dr Simon Lindley, *T:* 0113 255 6143
E: cms@simonlindley.org.uk
W: www.church-music.org.uk

Church of England Clergy Stipend Trust

Founded 1952 to augment stipends of parochial clergy, normally through Diocesan Boards of Finance. *Chairman* Mr J. W. Parkinson FCA, 3 Bunhill Row, London, EC1Y 8YZ *T:* 020 7423 8000

Church of England Evangelical Council

Founded in 1960 to promote effective consultation between Anglican evangelical leaders, in order that the evangelical heritage, as expressed in the Basis of Faith, may be better applied to contemporary problems in church and nation. CEEC seeks to interact with and encourage diocesan evangelical fellowships, societies, and other groups working within the evangelical constituency, and is a channel for establishing and maintaining relationships with the Church of England as a whole, and with evangelicals in other churches. It acts as the English agent of the Evangelical Fellowship in the Anglican Communion. *President* The Rt Revd Julian Henderson *Chairman* The Revd Hugh Palmer *Secretary* Stephen Hofmeyer *Treasurer* The Revd George Curry,
T: 020 7580 3522
W: www.ceec.info

Church of England Flower Arrangers Association

The Church of England Flower Arrangers Association (CEFAA) was founded in 1981 to help and encourage all those who tend flowers in churches and link them in fellowship and friendship. It is open to all those baptized in the Christian faith. The aims are to expand interest in church flower arranging, to use talent to enrich places of worship and to support what theology and creation try to teach.

CEFAA is a voluntary charity whose constitution covers the work members do in churches, church buildings and at church events. The Association is not sponsored and is non-competitive.

Registered Charity no. 514372. *President* Revd Noel Michell *Chairman* Mrs Ada Fawthrop *Treasurer* Mrs Naomi Hadden *Secretary* Mr Roger Brown, 25B Church Road, Hale Village, Liverpool, L24 4AY *T:* 0151 425 2823
E: cefaa@btinternet.com
W: www.cefaa.org.uk

OTHER ORGANIZATIONS

259

Church of England Newspaper

A weekly newspaper which aims to provide a full, objective and lively coverage of Christian news from Britain and overseas. Contents include general features, book, music, film and art reviews, the latest clergy appointments and an ongoing focus on how the Church can improve its mission.

Goes to press on Tuesday; published Friday; deadline for advertisements 10.00am Monday; price £1.50 (annual subscription UK £75, Eur £95, Rest of world £115; Online £35; other rates on application).The Church of England Newspaper, 14 Great College Street, London, SW1P 3RX   *E:* cen@churchnewspaper.com
W: www.churchnewspaper.com

Church of England Record Society

Founded in 1991 with the object of promoting interest in and knowledge of the history of the Church of England from the sixteenth century onwards, the Society publishes primary material of national significance for Church history. It aims to produce one volume each year, set against an annual subscription of £25 (individuals), and £38 (institutions). *Hon Secretary* Dr Michael Snape, Dept of Modern History, University of Birmingham, Edgbaston, Birmingham, B15 2TT

E: m.f.snape@bham.ac.uk
W: www.coers.org

Church of England Soldiers', Sailors' and Airmen's Clubs (1891)

A registered charity which, since its foundation in 1891, has maintained clubs at home and abroad for HM Forces and their dependants, regardless of their beliefs. In 1974 CESSAC helped establish a separate sheltered housing association (CESSAHA) for ex-Service people and/or their families over the age of 60. The two organizations share an office and work together to manage further sheltered housing belonging to the Crown charity, Greenwich Hospital (for ex Naval Service personnel or widows/widowers). Donations always welcomed – details on their shared website www.cessaha.co.uk. *General Secretary* Cdr Patrick Keefe, CESSAC, 1 Shakespeare Terrace, 126 High St, Portsmouth, PO1 2RH

T: 023 9282 9319
E: patrick.keefe@cessaha.co.uk
W: cessaha.co.uk

Church of England Soldiers', Sailors' and Airmen's Housing Association Ltd (1972)

A charitable Housing Association, registered with the Homes and Communities Agency (L0104) to provide low-cost rented sheltered accommodation for over-60s ex-Service people and/or their families regardless of belief. Construction costs were provided partly by government grants, but donations are always welcome to help fund modernization – see the website shared with sister charity below. *Chief Exec* Cdr Patrick Keefe *Director of Housing* Gill Peckham, CESSA H. A., 1 Shakespeare Terrace, 126 High St, Portsmouth, PO1 2RH   *T:* 023 9282 9319
E: patrick.keefe@cessaha.co.uk
W: www.cessaha.co.uk

Church Pastoral Aid Society Ministers in Training Fund

The Church Pastoral Aid Society administers the Ministers in Training Fund. This fund gives grants to evangelical Anglican students for personal maintenance (not fees) who have been recommended for training for ordained ministry following a Bishop's Advisory Panel or an accredited lay ministry selection process and are facing financial difficulties. *Ministers in Training Administrator* Miss Joanna Coleman, Ministers in Training Fund, CPAS, Sovereign Court One (Unit 3), Sir Williams Lyons Road, Coventry, CV4 7EZ

T: 0300 123 0780 (ext. 4374)
E: jcoleman@cpas.org.uk
W: www.cpas.org.uk

Church Pastoral Aid Society Patronage Trust

A Trust holding Rights of Presentation to a number of benefices. Administered by the Church Pastoral Aid Society. *Secretary* The Revd John Fisher, CPAS, Unit 3, Sovereign Court One, Sir William Lyons Road, Coventry, CV4 7EZ   *T:* 0300 123 0780 extn 4387/4388
E: jfisher@cpas.org.uk
patronage@cpas.org.uk

Church Patronage Trust

A Trust holding the Rights of Presentation to a number of benefices. Evangelical tradition. *Secretary* Preb Charles Marnham, 4 Chester Square, London, SW1W 9HH

T: 020 7730 8889
E: charles@stmichaelschurch.org.uk
W: www.churchpatronagetrust.co.uk

Church Schoolmasters and School Mistresses' Benevolent Institution

Founded in 1857 to provide assistance for Church of England teachers in England and Wales in times of temporary affliction or misfortune, or upon retirement or permanent disablement, and assistance towards the maintenance and education of their orphans. The CSSBI runs Glen Arun Care Home which has a strong Christian ethos and is set in a semi-rural location. The home provides residential and nursing care accommodation. It has 35 single rooms where residents can benefit from 24 hour nursing care. *Patron* HM The Queen *President* The Bishop of London *Chairman* Miss Diana Bell *Patient Care Manager* Mrs Sue Green,

Glen Arun, 9 Athelstan Way, Horsham, RH13 6HA　　　　*T:* 01403 253881 (Admin)
01403 255749 (Nursing Office)
E: glenarun@hotmail.com

Church Society

Formed in 1950 by the amalgamation of the Church Association and National Church League, which was founded in 1835, the Church Society continues to seek to maintain the evangelical and reformed faith of the Church of England, based upon the authority of Holy Scripture (see Canon A 5) and the foundational doctrines of the Thirty-nine Articles and the Book of Common Prayer.

The Society publishes a journal, *Churchman*, and a quarterly magazine, *Crossway*. It also publishes books and booklets, and blogs on current issues in the CofE. It organizes conferences including the Junior Anglican Evangelical Conference. Patron of c. 120 parishes, administered through the Church Society Trust. *President* The Rt Revd Wallace Benn *Chairman* The Revd Paul Darlington, Ground Floor, Centre Block, Hille Business Estate, 132 St Albans Road, Watford, WD24 4AE　　　　　*T:* 01923 255410
E: admin@churchsociety.org
W: www.churchsociety.org

Church Society Trust

Patron of more than 100 livings. *Chairman* The Revd Dick Farr, Ground Floor, Centre Block, Hille Business Estate, 132 St Albans Road, Watford, WD24 4AE　　　　*T:* 01923 255410
E: admin@churchsociety.org

Church Times

Established 1863. The best-selling, award-winning independent weekly newspaper and website, reporting on the worldwide Christian Church and Anglicanism in particular. As well as its wide news coverage, the paper contains reflection on current affairs, general features, reviews of books, music and arts, a comprehensive gazette, and the biggest selection of church job advertisements.

Goes to press on Wednesday; published on Friday; advertisements to be placed on Friday for the following week; price £2.20; for subscription rates see website. 3rd Floor, Invicta House, 108–114 Golden Lane, London, EC1Y 0TG
T: 020 7776 1060
W: www.churchtimes.co.uk

Church Trust Fund Trust

A Trust holding Rights of Presentation to a number of benefices. Administered by the Church Pastoral Aid Society. *Secretary* The Revd John Fisher, CPAS, Unit 3, Sovereign Court One, Sir William Lyons Road, Coventry, CV4 7EZ　　　*T:* 0300 123 0780 extn 4387/4388
E: jfisher@cpas.org.uk
patronage@cpas.org.uk

Church Union

Founded in 1859 at the time of the Oxford Movement, to promote catholic faith and order, it continues this work today by providing support and encouragement to those lay people and priests who wish to see catholic faith, order, morals and spirituality maintained and upheld, and who wish to promote catholic unity. The Union publishes books and tracts and produces an in-house magazine, the *Church Observer*. *President* The Revd Prebendary David Houlding SSC *Chairman* The Revd Fr Darren Smith *Treasurer* The Revd Fr Martin Ennis *Membership Secretary* Additional Curates Society, 16 Commercial Street, Birmingham, B1 1RS
T: 0121 382 5533
E: secretary@churchunion.co.uk
W: www.churchunion.co.uk

Church Urban Fund

The Church Urban Fund (CUF) raises money to change lives in the poorest communities in England. Working with the Church of England, CUF's mission is to serve people of faith who put their faith into action in the community. Working in collaboration with dioceses and partner organizations, CUF funds faith-based social action in the most economically and socially deprived areas of England, but its support also extends to advocacy and practical advice, working to create sustainable, relevant and local solutions to deep-rooted issues.

The projects CUF partners with work in a broad range of areas, including community development, support for vulnerable and marginalized groups, housing and homeless, and interfaith dialogue. CUF is also closely involved in wider debate, both inside and outside the Church, representing faith-based social action and enabling the voices of faith communities and practitioners to be heard at a national level. Our vision is to see all local churches and Christians in England empowered to work to end poverty in their communities.

Established in 1987 following the landmark report *Faith in the City*, CUF has supported nearly 5,500 projects across England. Our experience over the last 25 years has been that a combination of money and capacity building is the best way to sustainably support projects. This explains CUF's shift from an endowed fund towards an active, fundraising foundation model. We are now a development organization that provides advice, money and guidance to local churches and activists who share our passion to see lives changed. This change marks an important stage in the charity's development and maturation. CUF's work has been made possible by the continuing support of individuals, parishes and dioceses, which have contributed to the Fund's work through time, money and prayers.

CUF is about Christians working together to tackle poverty, transforming the lives of society's poorest and most marginalized in England. We recognize the inherent worth of all human beings, made, as they are, in the image of God, and believe in an inclusive society that values each and every individual. We embrace and embody the Church's calling to respond to poverty in England. We want to see all Christians, in every church and every community, tackling the problem together through the giving of time, money, action and prayer. We believe that the most effective response to poverty happens at the local, personal level, from people working within the community and sensitive to its needs. With an established presence in every community in England, the Church is uniquely placed to deliver such a response, touching areas that other agencies simply cannot reach.

Many Christians, both clergy and lay people, are already building transformative relationships with the poor and vulnerable. Living sacrificially, they achieve miracles but they can often feel isolated in challenging circumstances. Nurturing them is part of CUF's work, but there is much more to be done. That's why we are moving from offering short-term funding to developing local partnerships with Anglican dioceses which will provide long-term, sustainable support. In partnership with dioceses throughout England, we are expanding our networks to reinforce the efforts of those working in deprived areas, by improving their access to resources, in the form of money, information and expertise.

While continuing to educate people about the problem of poverty in England, we need to share the many stories of lives being turned around and the once desperate being given back their future. We need the solidarity and commitment of Christians everywhere. Then, together, we can really tackle poverty in England. For further information on the resources available please visit our website. Church House, Great Smith Street, London, SW1P 3AZ

E: enquiries@cuf.org.uk
W: www.cuf.org.uk

Church Welfare Association (Incorporated)

Founded in 1851. Gives financial aid to Church projects assisting and supporting women and children in need of residential care and/or moral support. We can also support Day Care projects designed to assist and support women and children, particularly single-parent families. *Honorary Secretary*

Mrs Bridget Trump, Portway Place, The Portway Stratford sub Castle, Salisbury, SP1 3LD
E: secretary@churchwelfareassociation.org.uk
W: www.churchwelfareassociation.org.uk

Churches' Advertising Network (also known as ChurchAds.Net)

A professional group of Christians from all traditions cooperating to develop the professional use of advertising as part of the Churches' communication and outreach. CAN seeks free or low cost poster space and radio airtime from leading media owners, which it uses on behalf of the Churches. All members give their services free.

Charity Registration no. 1096868. *Chair* Mr F. Goodwin *Secretary & Treasurer* The Revd Tony Kinch *Asst Treasurer* Mrs Karen Gray *Trustee* Mr Michael Elms, The Methodist Centre, 24 School St, Wolverhampton, WV1 4LF   *T:* 01902 422100
E: churchads@methodist.fsnet.co.uk
W: www.churchads.org.uk

Churches' Fellowship for Psychical and Spiritual Studies

Founded in 1953 to study the psychic and spiritual and their relevance to Christian faith and life. *President* Dr Santha Bhattacharji *Chair* Mrs Davina Thomas *General Secretary* Mr Julian Drewett, The Rural Workshop, South Road, North Somercotes, Louth, LN11 7PT
T: 01507 358845
E: gensec@churchesfellowship.co.uk
W: www.churchesfellowship.co.uk

Churches' Funerals Group

The Churches' Group on Funeral Services at Cemeteries and Crematoria was formed as an advisory group in 1980 by the mainstream Churches in England and Wales to co-ordinate their policies in connection with the pastoral and administrative aspects of funeral services at cemeteries and crematoria, and to represent the Churches at national level in joint discussions with public and private organizations on any matters relating to ministry at such funerals. The Group keeps in close touch with the main organizations concerned with funeral provision and bereavement counselling. To reflect its involvement in the wider aspects of all concerned with funerals and death in our society, the Group shortened its working title in 2002 to 'The Churches' Funerals Group'.

Publications sponsored by the Group include *The Role of the Minister in Bereavement: Guidelines and Training Suggestions* (Church House Publishing, 1989); *Guidelines for Best Practice of Clergy at Funerals* (Church House Publishing, 1997); and two joint funeral service books (The Canterbury Press, Norwich), one for use in England (1986, 1994,

2001 and 2009), the other for use in Wales (1987). Three previous conference reports have been published: *The Role of a Minister at a Funeral* (1991), *Bereavement and Belief* (1993) and *Clergy and Cremation Today* (1995). An information leaflet entitled *Questions Commonly Asked about Funerals* (2nd edition, 2007) is also available free of charge from the Secretary. *Chairman* The Rt Revd James Langstaff, Bishop of Rochester *Secretary* Ms Sue Moore, Church House, Great Smith St, London, SW1P 3AZ   *T:* 020 7898 1376
E: enquiries@christianfunerals.org

Churches' Legislation Advisory Service
Founded in 1941 (as the Churches Main Committee), and first registered as a charity in 1966, CLAS exists to advance the religious and other charitable work of its member Churches by furthering their common interests in those secular issues (such as property matters, finance, tax and charitable status) which help underpin and deliver that work.
   Registered Charity No. 256303. *Chairman* Rt Revd Alastair Redfern *Secretary* Frank Cranmer, Church House, Great Smith St, London, SW1P 3AZ   *T:* 020 7222 1265
E: frank.cranmer@centrallobby.com
W: www.clas.org.uk

Churches Visitor and Tourism Association
A charitable ecumenical organization committed to promoting the daily openness of church buildings to visitors and tourists as a contributory component of the Church's mission, and to the significance of church buildings as places of worship, repositories of architectural heritage and locations for community engagement. In addition to its own resources CVTA, through its website, signposts organizations which specialize in offering literature and training in ministry to visitors and tourists. A newsletter is published approximately bi-monthly.
   Charity Registration No. 1101254. *Chair* Canon John D. Brown *Administrator* Mrs Carol Roast, c/o 556 Galleywood Road, Chelmsford, Essex, CM2 8BX   *T:* 01245 358185
E: canonjbrown@mac.com
W: www.cvta.org.uk

Cleaver Ordination Candidates' Fund
The Cleaver Ordination Candidates Fund exists for the support and encouragement of Anglican ordinands committed to a traditional Catholic understanding of the priesthood and episcopate, and to urge the importance of continuing sound theological learning among the clergy. Book grants are awarded to eligible ordinands, and applications may be considered from clergy in respect of university fees for post-graduate theological study. *Clerk to the*

Cleaver Trustees The Revd John Hanks, 20 Ogleforth, York YO1 7JG
E: clerk@cleaver.org.uk
W: www.cleaver.org.uk

CMJ UK
Founded in 1809 as the London Society for Promoting Christianity Among the Jews, to take the Christian gospel to Jewish people. *President* The Rt Revd David Evans *Chair* Wendy Scott *CEO* The Revd Alex Jacob, Eagle Lodge, Hexgreave Hall Business Park, Farnsfield, Notts, NG22 8LS   *T:* 01623 883960
E: enquiries@cmj.org.uk
W: www.cmj.org.uk

COIN: Christians on the Internet
An interdenominational group of Christians throughout Britain and Ireland working together since 1995 to advise, help and encourage the Church in its use of the Internet. It functions both as a group of individuals able to offer their particular expertise, and also, through email, as a lively online community discussing in depth a wide variety of issues affecting Christians, including specialist lists discussing Church of England issues and Common Worship. Further details of COIN and its activities can be found on its website. *Chair* Andrew Foulsham *Secretary* Jill Wright *Treasurer* The Revd Peter Muir *Membership Secretary* The Revd Alan Jesson
E: jill@woodchipcomputers.co.uk
W: www.coin.org.uk

College of Evangelists
The national College of Evangelists was founded in 1999 to support and give the accreditation of the Archbishops of Canterbury and York to evangelists in the Church of England. To be admitted as a member of the College, evangelists will be involved in active evangelistic ministry (not just training or teaching about evangelism) and will be operating nationally or regionally, beyond their diocesan boundaries. Potential candidates should contact their diocesan bishop in the first instance. *Chairman* The Rt Revd Martyn Snow *Enquiries to* Jenny Moorby, Bishop's Lodge, Springfield Road, Leicester, LE2 3BD
T: 0116 270 8985
E: jenamoorby@gmail.com

College of Health Care Chaplains
The College of Health Care Chaplains (CHCC) is the largest professional body representing chaplaincy within healthcare and an autonomous section of Unite the Union (Britain and Ireland's biggest trade union with 1.5 million memberships), which negotiates terms and conditions for all chaplains (irrespective of College membership) on a

national basis; members also receive professional support on employment issues.

Founded in 1992, the College is a multi-faith, interdenominational professional association open to all recognized health care chaplaincy staff, full-time and part-time, including voluntary and support workers, and others with an interest in health care chaplaincy. With around 800 members throughout the United Kingdom, it provides peer support, advice and fellowship for members nationally and in ten regional branches with a focus on professional development, good practice and training.

The College publishes two issues a year of *The Journal of Health and Social Care Chaplaincy* (available on subscription to non-members). The College exists to promote the professional standing of healthcare chaplaincy and that of its members both nationally and within health and social care organizations. 'We work as a part of the healthcare team to care for the whole person.' *President* The Revd Mark Burleigh *Vice-President* The Revd Gareth Rowlands *Registrar* The Revd William Sharpe, Unite Health Sector, 128 Theobald's Road, London, WC1X 8TN   *T:* 020 3371 2046
E: president@healthcarechaplains.org
W: www.healthcarechaplains.org

College of Preachers
An ecumenical network of preachers, ordained and lay, dedicated to preaching which is faithful and fresh, biblical and relevant, and to helping one another to develop preaching skills through seminars, conferences, a journal and guided study. *Chairman* Rt Revd Stephen Cottrell *Administrator* Miss Helen Skinner, 16 Exeter Road, West Bridgford, Nottingham, NG2 6FA
E: administrator@collegeofpreachers.co.uk
W: www.collegeofpreachers.co.uk

College of Readers
The College of Readers (CoR) is an independent membership organisation. Under the patronage of the Bishop of Ebbsfleet It provides fellowship and support for Readers (Licensed Lay Ministers) of the Anglican Communion in the British Isles, who subscribe to the authority of scripture, the grace of the sacraments and the traditional understanding of the ordained ministry of the bishop, priest and deacon. The College publishes a quarterly magazine, *Blue Scarf*, which keeps all members in touch. The opportunity for study and fellowship is provided through meetings arranged by the committee at various locations. *Chairman* Mr Barry Barnes *Registrar/Treasurer* Mrs Mary E. Snape, 1 Soames Crescent, Stoke-on-Trent, ST3 5UE
E: mary@college-of-readers.org.uk
W: htt::://www.college-of-readers.org.uk

College of St Barnabas
Set in idyllic Surrey countryside, the College is a residential community of retired Anglican clergy, including married couples and those who have been widowed. Admission is also open to Readers, licensed Church Workers and other practising Anglican communicants. There are facilities for visitors and guests, and occasional quiet days and private retreats can be accommodated.

Residents lead active, independent lives for as long as possible. There is a Nursing Wing providing domiciliary, residential and full nursing care for those who need it, to which direct admission is possible. This enables most residents to remain members of the College for the rest of their lives. Respite care for patients and/or carers can occasionally be offered here. Sheltered flats in the Cloisters all have separate sitting rooms, bedrooms and en suite facilities. There are two chapels, daily Eucharist and Evensong, three libraries, a well-equipped common room and refectory, a snooker table and a nine-hole putting green.

The College is easily accessible by road and is also next to Dormans Station on the line from London to East Grinstead. For further details or to arrange a preliminary visit, please see our website or contact the Warden. *Warden* Fr Howard Such *Bursar* Paul G. F. Wilkin, The College of St Barnabas, Blackberry Lane, Lingfield, RH7 6NJ   *T:* 01342 870260
E: warden@collegeofstbarnabas.com
W: www.st-barnabas.org.uk

Commonwealth War Graves Commission
Founded in 1917. Responsible for marking and maintaining in perpetuity the graves of those of Commonwealth Forces who fell in the 1914–18 and 1939–45 Wars and for commemorating by name on memorials those with no known grave. *President* HRH The Duke of Kent *Chairman* Secretary of State for Defence in the UK, 2 Marlow Rd, Maidenhead, Berkshire, SL6 7DX   *T:* 01628 507 138
E: legal@cwgc.org
W: www.cwgc.org

Community Housing and Therapy
CHT provides group and individual psychotherapy in residential settings to clients who are experiencing mental health and emotional difficulties. The care of each client is planned through an individual Care Plan which is reviewed every three to six months. Reviews are interdisciplinary and CHT therapists with social workers and psychiatrists, together with others, review progress and set goals together with the client. These goals focus on key areas in the life of each client, for example, housing needs, relationships, medication and re-training for work. *Chief Exec* Mr John Gale *Chief Operating*

Officer Ms Inma Vidana *Deputy Director, Clinical Services* Miss Beatriz Sanchez *Senior Managers* Mr Terry Saftis, Mrs Yin Ping Leung, 24/5–6 The Coda Centre, 189 Munster Rd, London, SW6 6AW   *T:* 020 7381 5888
0800 018 1261 (Freephone)
E: co@cht.org.uk
W: www.cht.org.uk

Community of Aidan and Hilda
A dispersed, ecumenical and international body of Christians who journey with God, and re-connect with the Spirit and the Scriptures, the saints and the streets, the seasons and the soil. The Community seeks to cradle a Christian spirituality for today which renews the Church and brings healing to fragmented people and communities. It welcomes people of all backgrounds and countries who wish to be wholly available to God the Holy Trinity, and to the way of Jesus as revealed in the Bible. In the earthing of that commitment members draw particular inspiration from Celtic saints such as Aidan and Hilda.

Members follow a Way of Life based on a rhythm of prayer and study, simplicity, care for creation, and mission, seeking to weave together the separated strands of Christianity. Each shares their journey with a spiritual companion known as a Soul Friend. The work of the Community is the work of each member and can be expressed individually and corporately in many ways, such as through link houses, churches, monastic experiments, and indigenous national branches. Its mother house and spirituality centre is The Open Gate, Holy Island, Berwick-upon-Tweed, TD15 2SD. *Guardians* The Revd Graham Booth, Mrs Penny Warren *Founding Guardian* The Revd Ray Simpson *Secretary* Carol Few *Retreat House Wardens* Kevin and Lesley Downham, The Open Gate, Holy Island, Berwick-upon-Tweed, TD15 2SD   *T:* 050 728 9505
E: aidanandhildacommunity@gmail.com
W: www.aidanandhilda.org

Compassionate Friends, The
The Compassionate Friends is an organization of bereaved parents, siblings and grandparents offering support and mutual understanding to others after the loss of a child, of any age, from any cause. We have a National Telephone Helpline, with calls taken only by bereaved parents, which is available for support and information 365 days a year. We also have a comprehensive website which includes a Members Forum which enables those who join up to speak electronically to others similarly bereaved.

Our helpline and website are the best ways to get contact us initially and we will then put you in touch with our local support volunteers, local groups, weekend gatherings and meetings, information leaflets, bereavement support publications and postal library. Support specifically for siblings is also available. Helpline hours: daily 10.00 am–4.00 pm and 7.00–10:00 pm.
T: 0845 123 2304 (Helpline)
E: helpline@tcf.org.uk
W: www.tcf.org.uk

Confraternity of the Blessed Sacrament
Founded in 1862 to honour Jesus Christ our Lord in the Blessed Sacrament; to make mutual eucharistic intercession and to encourage eucharistic devotion.

Registered Charity no. 1082897. *Superior-General* Revd Christopher Pearson *Secretary General* Canon Lawson Nagel, Aldwick Vicarage, 25 Gossamer Lane, Bognor Regis, PO21 3AT
T: 01243 262049
E: cbs@confraternity.org.uk
W: www.confraternity.org.uk

Council of Christians and Jews
Founded in 1942 to combat all forms of religious and racial intolerance, to promote mutual understanding and goodwill between Christians and Jews, and to foster cooperation in educational activities and in social and community service. Forty local branches in the UK.

Presidents: the Archbishop of Canterbury; the Cardinal Archbishop of Westminster; the Moderator of the Free Churches; the Moderator of the General Assembly of the Church of Scotland; the Archbishop of Thyateira and Great Britain; the Chief Rabbi of the United Hebrew Congregations of the Commonwealth; the Senior Rabbi to the Movement for Reform Judaism; the Spiritual Head, Spanish and Portuguese Jews' Congregation; the Chief Executive, Liberal Judaism. *Patron* HM The Queen *Chair* The Rt Revd Michael Ipgrave, Bishop of Lichfield *Director* Dr Jane Clements, Collaboration House, 77–79 Charlotte Street, London, W1T 4PW   *T:* 020 3515 3003
E: cjrelations@ccj.org.uk
W: www.ccj.org.uk

Council on Christian Approaches to Defence and Disarmament
CCADD was established in 1963 by the Rt Revd Robert Stopford, then Bishop of London, to study problems relating to defence and disarmament within a Christian context. The British Group of CCADD comprises Christians of different traditions, varying vocations and specializations and political views, with a range of responsibilities, governmental and non-governmental. CCADD seeks to bring an ethical viewpoint to bear on disarmament and arms control and related issues and to this end the British Group has always stressed the importance of dialogue between official and

non-official bodies. *President* The Rt Revd Lord Harries of Pentregarth *Chairman* Mr Brian Wicker *Admin Secretary* Mrs Liza Hamilton, 5 Cubitts Meadow, Buxton, Norwich, NR10 5EF
T: 07975 564623
E: ccadd@lineone.net
W: http://website.lineone.net/~ccadd

Crosslinks
Crosslinks is an international mission society with its roots in the Bible, working largely within the worldwide Anglican Communion. Our strapline is 'God's word to God's world'. Our business is making Christ known through the proclamation of the gospel and training those who will train others for gospel ministry. We do this by organizing gospel partnerships across cultural boundaries. *President* Mr David Mills *General Secretary* Revd Canon Andy Lines *Chairman* Revd James Poole, 251 Lewisham Way, London, SE4 1XF   T: 020 8691 6111
E: info@crosslinks.org
W: www.crosslinks.org

CTBI Christians Abroad
CTBI Christians Abroad is a project of Churches Together in Britain and Ireland. CTBI Christians Abroad provides self-funded opportunities for men and women of any age to work overseas in development or mission in Africa, Asia, South America and the Caribbean for short periods in projects associated with local Christian communities. Using a team of six experienced consultants CTBI Christians Abroad also provides, to national and local churches in Britain and Ireland, support and consultancy services to mission partners working overseas, to the personnel function of the church and to development projects overseas.

- For further information and travel, health and accident or medical insurance for overseas travellers, visit www.cabroad.org.uk
- For Volunteer opportunities contact David Brett, recruit@cabroad.org.uk
- For Consultancy services contact Colin South, support@cabroad.org.uk

c/o 22 Ebenezer Close, Witham, Essex, CM8 2HX   T: 03000 121 201
E: recruit@cabroad.org.uk
insurance@cabroad.org.uk
W: www.cabroad.org.uk

CTVC
Television, radio and new media production company founded by the British film pioneer, Lord Rank.

CTVC specializes in making documentaries on religious, ethical and moral issues. The company has produced documentaries for the BBC, Channel 4 and ITV as well as radio programmes for BBC Radio 3, 4 and the World Service. In the last few years CTVC has been awarded the prestigious Sandford St Martin religious broadcasting award. CTVC also hosts TrueTube, an award-winning website for secondary schools that provides interactive resources for films for RE, PSHE and Citizenship lessons.

Alongside filmmaking, CTVC also runs *Things Unseen*, a podcast with its own website engaging both people of faith and those who 'believe but don't belong'. CTVC has one of the largest film and tape archive of any independent production company in Britain, covering the hundreds of films and programmes we have made over the past 80 years. McBeath House, 310 Goswell Road, London, EC1V 7LW   T: 020 7940 8480
E: info@ctvc.co.uk
W: www.ctvc.co.uk and www.truetube.co.uk

Culham St Gabriel's Trust
Culham St Gabriel's is an endowed charitable trust dedicated to educational work in support of religious education (RE). We are committed to excellence in religious education for all learners. We support teachers by helping them to offer the best, high-quality learning experiences in RE and spiritual and moral development. We also support work that promotes the links between school ethos, values, leadership and school improvement.

Culham St Gabriel's is formed of the union of two church college trusts, Culham Educational Foundation and St Gabriel's Trust, both of which have shared a long-term commitment to supporting religious education. We provide individual and corporate grants to support research, development and innovation in RE in the UK.

We enable RE professionals to run an extensive programme of networks, conferences, professional development opportunities and websites for teachers of RE, supported by our national network of consultants and collaborative projects. Current collaboration includes a strategy on Research for RE, designed to improve research-practice links, and an emerging strategy to support leaders in the RE professional community.

We work with a wide range of other funders to ensure a coherent and system-wide approach to supporting RE and moving it forward. Our key partners are the Church of England Education Office, including the Foundation for Educational Leadership; the National Association of Teachers of RE (NATRE); and the RE Council (REC). *Director* Dr Mark Chater FRSA *Chair of Trustees* Dr Priscilla Chadwick FRSA, 62 Banbury Road, Oxford, OX2 6PN
T: 01865 612035
E: enquiries@cstg.org.uk
W: www.cstg.org.uk

Day One Christian Ministries

Day One Publications produces Christian books and cards, and Day One Prison Ministry works to supply prisons with evangelistic items free of charge. We now offer tours to Israel, Egypt, Greece and Turkey, with more places to follow. *Managing Director* Mr Mark Roberts, Ryelands Road, Leominster, HR6 8NZ
T: 01568 613740
E: sales@dayone.co.uk
W: www.dayone.co.uk

Deaf Anglicans Together (DAT)

(formerly National Deaf Church Conference) This is the members' organization for deaf people in the Church of England, and it welcomes members of other churches and hearing people as well. DAT provides fellowship and training through conferences and other events, and promotes British Sign Language and deaf culture by means of workshops and festivals, exploring the use of drama, storytelling. signed hymns and poems. DAT also acts as a forum for exploring relevant issues, and encourages the participation of deaf people in the structures of the Church. DAT has three representatives on General Synod and three representatives on the Committee for Ministry of and among Deaf and Disabled People (CMDDP). DAT also works closely with other organizations involved with deaf Christians, including Go! Sign (Christian Deaf Link UK), Signs of God and the Christian Interpreters Network. *Contact* Revd Bob Shrine, 7 Russell Hall Lane, Queensbury, Bradford, BD13 2AJ   *E:* deafanglicans@gmail.com
W: www.deafanglicanstogether.org

Deaf People, Royal Association for

RAD promotes the welfare and interests of deaf people, working with the Deaf Community, Deaf Clubs, deaf individuals and the parents of deaf children. Most of RAD's work is in London, Essex and the south-east of England. RAD is organized around the following services:

- Deaf Community Development;
- Advice and Advocacy;
- Learning Disability;
- Mental Health;
- Sign Language Interpreting;
- Training.

Chief Executive Dr Jan Sheldon, Century House South, Riverside Office Centre, North Station Road, Colchester, CO1 1RE   *T:* 0845 688 2525
0845 688 2527 (Text)
E: info@royaldeaf.org.uk
W: www.royaldeaf.org.uk

Deans' Conference

The Deans' Conference is the meeting together (three times annually) of those who preside over their Cathedral Chapters to reflect upon cathedral issues of particular concern to Deans in their public and cathedral roles. *Chairman* The Dean of Canterbury *Secretary* The Dean of Gloucester, Gloucester Cathedral, 12 College Green, Gloucester GL1 2LX   *T:* 01452 508217
E: dean@gloucestercathedral.org.uk

Deans' Vergers' Conference

Founded in 1989 to bring together Head Vergers who are employed in that capacity by a Dean and Chapter of the Church of England. The Conference enables members to communicate with one another, exchange and discuss ideas of common interest and to have regular contact with the Deans' Conference. The Head Vergers of the forty-two English cathedrals, Westminster Abbey and St George's Windsor are eligible for membership. *Chairman* Alex Carberry *Treasurer* Clive McCleester *Secretary* Glynn Usher, Head Verger and Sub-Sacrist, Bristol Cathedral, College Green, Bristol, BS1 5TJ
T: 0117 946 8179 (Direct)
0117 926 4879 (Cathedral Office)
E: glynn.usher@bristol-cathedral.co.uk

Diaconal Association of the Church of England

DACE is a professional association for diaconal ministers (deacons, accredited lay workers and Church Army officers) working in the Church of England, established in 1988 to succeed the Deaconess Committee and the Anglican Accredited Lay Workers Federation. Associate membership is also open to those who support diaconal ministry, and diaconal ministers working in other provinces in the UK.

DACE exists to promote the distinctive (permanent) diaconate and other diaconal ministries in the Church of England, support all nationally recognized diaconal ministers, and to consider the theological and practical implications of diaconal ministry within the total ministry of the Christian Church, in partnership with other agencies and denominations.

DACE is a member of the Diakonia World Federation of Diaconal Associations and Diaconal Communities, and a registered charity. *President* Revd David Rogers *Secretary* Revd Ann Wren *Treasurer* Revd Christopher Wren, St Peter's Bourne, 40 Oakleigh Park South, London, N20 9JN   *T:* 0208 4455 535
E: secretary@dace.org
W: www.dace.org

Diakonia

Founded in 1947 to link the various European deaconess associations, Diakonia is now a World Federation of Diaconal Associations. It concerns itself with the nature and task of Diakonia and encourages deaconesses, deacons, and lay people doing diaconal work.

Diakonia also furthers ecumenical relations between the diaconal associations in other countries. The Diaconal Association of the Church of England is a member. There is a Diakonia UK Liaison Group which also includes representatives from the Methodist Diaconal Order, the Church of Scotland Diaconate and the Deaconesses of the Presbyterian Church in Ireland. *Secretary* Sr Traude Leitenberger,

E: secretary@diakonia-world.org
W: www.diakonia-world.org

Diocesan Clergy Chairs' Forum

The Forum is a voluntary group, allowing the elected chairs of the houses of clergy in each diocese to share ideas and experience, to address together various issues affecting the Church of England, to offer mutual support, and to develop principles of best practice in fulfilling this role in each diocese. Guidelines for best practice have been agreed with the House of Bishops. *Chair* The Revd Preb Simon Cawdell *Hon. Secretary* The Revd Canon Steve Parish, 26 Leamington Close, Warrington, WA5 3PY   *T:* 01925 711830
E: bloovee@outlook.com

Diocesan Institutions of Chester, Manchester, Liverpool and Blackburn

For the relief of widows and orphans of clergymen who have officiated in their last sphere of duty in the Archdeaconries of Chester, Macclesfield, Manchester, Rochdale, Liverpool, Warrington or Blackburn. *Chair* Canon Michael S. Finlay, 40 Chatteris Park, Sandymoor, Cheshire, WA7 1XE
T: 01928 579354
E: finlay289@btinternet.com

Distinctive Diaconate

An unofficial Church of England centre which serves to promote the diaconate as one of the historic orders of the Church's ministry with manifold potential for ministry today. From 1981 to 2012 it produced *Distinctive Diaconate News,* and, from 1994–2012, *Distinctive News of Women in Ministry.*

A *History of the Community of St Andrew: 1861–2011* was produced for its sesquicentennial, 30 November 2012. A commemorative booklet, *Our 150th,* was prepared for the 150th anniversary of the Deaconess Order of the Church of England which was celebrated at Lambeth Palace in July 2012. Writings on the history of women's diaconate are in preparation. *Editor* The Revd Dr Sr Teresa CSA, 12 Ramsay Hall, 9–13 Byron Road, Worthing, BN11 3HN *T:* 01903 238017
E: teresajoan@btinternet.com

Ecclesiastical Insurance Group

Ecclesiastical is an independent UK-owned insurer and investment management organization that donates a significant proportion of its profits to charity. Ecclesiastical has been providing a range of personal insurances, financial advice and investment services for the Church and community for 130 years.

Today Ecclesiastical provides a range of personal insurances and financial services, including home insurance, savings and investments and funeral plans through their partner company. They also offer specialist commercial insurance for churches, church halls, charities, historic buildings, schools and care sector organizations.

Ecclesiastical is owned by a registered charity, Allchurches Trust, and is one of the UK's largest grant-making trusts. *Chairman* Mr John Hylands *Group Chief Executive* Mr Mark Hews, Beaufort House, Brunswick Road, Gloucester, GL1 1JZ   *T:* 0345 777 3322
E: information@ecclesiastical.com
W: www.ecclesiastical.com

Ecclesiastical Law Society

Founded in 1987 to promote the study of ecclesiastical law, through the education of office bearers and practitioners in the ecclesiastical courts, the enlargement of knowledge of ecclesiastical law among clergy and laity of the Anglican Communion, and assistance in matters of ecclesiastical law to the General Synod, Convocations, bishops and church dignitaries. It is open to all with an interest in ecclesiastical law. *President* Dr Sheila Cameron QC CBE *Chairman* Rt Revd Christopher Hill *Secretary* Mr Howard Dellar *Deputy Secretary* Mr Stephen Borton, 1 The Sanctuary, London, SW1P 3JT
T: 020 7222 5381
E: info@ecclawsoc.org.uk
W: www.ecclawsoc.org.uk

Ecclesiological Society

For those who love churches. Studies the arts, architecture and liturgy of the Christian Church through meetings, tours and publications. *President* David Stancliffe *Chairman of the Council* Trevor Cooper *Hon Secretary* Becky Payne, Hillside Cottage, Burpham, Arundel, BN18 9RR
T: 01903 885349
E: admin@ecclsoc.org
W: www.ecclsoc.org

Ecumenical Council for Corporate Responsibility (ECCR)

ECCR, founded in 1989, is a church-based investor coalition and membership organization working for economic justice, human rights, environmental stewardship, and corporate and investor responsibility. It undertakes research, advocacy and dialogue with companies and investors and seeks to influence company policy and practice and to raise awareness of corporate and investor responsibility issues among the British and Irish churches, the investor community and the general public.

It is a Body in Association with Churches Together in Britain and Ireland and a company limited by guarantee, registered in England and Wales. *Executive Director* John Arnold *Administrator and Finance Officer* Mary Frazer, 1 Deepdene Park Road, Dorking, RH5 4AL

T: 07880 437131
E: info@eccr.org.uk
W: www.eccr.org.uk

Ecumenical Society of the Blessed Virgin Mary

Founded in London in 1967, 'to advance the study at various levels of the place of the Blessed Virgin Mary in the Church under Christ and to promote ecumenical devotion'. Patrons include Cardinal Kurt Koch (President of the Pontifical Council for Promoting Christian Unity), The Rt Revd Don Bolen, Bishop of Saskatoon, the Revd Dr Frances Young, Bishop Angaelos of the Coptic Orthodox Church of Alexandria, Archbishop Gregorios of Thyateira, The Most Revd and Rt Hon Justin Welby, the Archbishop of Canterbury, The Rt Revd Richard Chartres, Bishop Emeritus of London, The Rt Revd Christopher Hill, Bishop Emeritus of Guildford, and the Rt Revd Alan Williams, Bishop of Brentwood. *Hon General Secretary* Father Bill OSM *Hon Treasurer acting pro tem* Mr Kevin Gate *Membership Secretary* Mr Bradley Smith *Constitution Secretary* Mrs Lucia Barbato, SS Peter and Paul Presbytery, 112 Entry Hill, Combe Down, Bath, BA2 5LS

T: 01225 832096
E: gensec@esbvm.com
W: www.esbvm.com

Elizabeth Finn Care

Elizabeth Finn Care gives grants and support to people struggling to cope with sudden or unexpected changes in their circumstances. We provide a financial and supportive safety net for people from over 120 occupations. Elizabeth Finn Care helps by providing both one-off and ongoing financial help, tailored to individual circumstances, as well as emotional support through our experienced caseworkers and national volunteer network.

In 2007 we founded Turn2us, a charity offering website and helpline services designed to help people in financial need, and those who support them, access the welfare benefits and grants available to them. Turn2us and EFC joined together as a single charity with effect from October 2009. *Chief Exec*

Matthew Sykes *Director of Income Generation and Communications* Malcolm Tyndall, Hythe House, 200 Shepherds Bush Rd, London, W6 7NL

T: 020 8834 9200
0800 413 220 (helpline)
E: info@elizabethfinn.org.uk
W: www.elizabethfinncare.org.uk /
www.turn2us.org.uk

Elland Society Ordination Fund

Grants are made to applicants who are evangelical in conviction and who are in either residential or non-residential training for ordination in the Church of England. Priority is given to ordinands who are sponsored by dioceses in the Province of York or who intend to serve their title in that Province. Grants are usually to help those with unexpected or special financial needs which were not included in their main Church grant (if any). *Secretary/ Treasurer* The Revd Colin Judd, 57 Grosvenor Road, Shipley, BD18 4RB

T: 01274 584775
E: elland@saltsvillage.co.uk
W: www.ellandsocietygrants.co.uk

English Churches Housing Group

In 2006 ECHG merged with Riverside Housing to become their specialist provider of sheltered and supported housing services. ECHG has gone on to win national awards for its work and each year provides housing and support for over 10,000 people across 170 local authorities. *Chair* Mr Philip Raw *Managing Director* Derek Caren, 2 Estuary Boulevard, Estuary Commerce Park, Liverpool, L24 8RF

T: 0345 111 000
E: info@riverside.org.uk
W: www.riverside.org.uk

English Clergy Association

Founded in 1938, the Association seeks to sustain in fellowship all Clerks in Holy Orders in their vocation and ministry within the Church of England, promoting in every available way the good of English parish and cathedral life and the welfare of clergy. Related Trustees give discretionary clergy holiday grants upon application to the Hon Almoner.

The Association seeks to foster the independence within the Established Church of all clergy whether in freehold office or not, and broadly supports the patronage system. The magazine *Parson and Parish* magazine is published twice-yearly. Lay members may be admitted. Subscription £10 p.a. (£5 retired/ ordinands). *Patron* The Bishop of London *Chairman* Revd John Masding *Deputy Chairman* Dr Peter Smith, Office Address: The Old School, Norton Hawkfield, Bristol, BS39 4HB

T: 01275 830017
01983 565953
E: benoporto-eca@yahoo.co.uk
W: www.clergyassoc.co.uk

Evangelical Alliance
Founded in 1846 as a representative body with denominational, congregational, organizational and individual supporters, its vision is to unite evangelicals and to provide an evangelical voice in the public square. It also aims to encourage action among evangelicals leading to spiritual and social transformation in the UK. The EA Operates in England, Northern Ireland, Scotland and Wales. *General Director* Mr Steve Clifford *Executive Director – England and Churches in Mission* Dr Krish Kandiah *Executive Director – Finance and Services* Emrys Jones *Advocacy Director* Dr David Landrum, 176 Copenhagen Street, London, N1 0ST   *T:* 020 7520 3830
E: info@eauk.org
W: www.eauk.org

Faith and Thought
Founded in 1865 to enquire into the relationship between the Christian revelation and modern scientific research. Publishes *Faith and Thought new series* in succession to *The Journal of the Transactions of the Victoria Institute* (JTVI); from 1958 *Faith and Thought*; from 1989 *Faith&Thought Bulletin*. Jointly with Christians in Science, since 1989 it sponsors the publication of *Science and Christian Belief*.
    Charity Registration no. 285871. *President* Professor Sir Colin J. Humphreys CBE *Chairman* Revd Dr Robert Allaway *Hon. Treasurer and Membership Secretary* Revd John Buxton *Editor and Meetings Secretary* Reginald S. Luhman, 110 Flemming Avenue, Leigh on Sea, SS9 3AX
    T: 01279 422661 (Hon Treas and Membership Secretary)
01702 475110 (Editor and Meeting Secretary)
E: drapkerry@gmail.com
W: www.faithandthought.org.uk

Family Action
Family Action has been the leading provider of services to disadvantaged and socially isolated families since its foundation in 1869. We work with over 45,000 children and families a year by providing practical, emotional and financial support through over 100 services based in communities across England.
    Family Action works with the whole family and helps to tackle some of the most complex and difficult issues facing families today – including domestic abuse, mental health problems, learning disabilities and severe financial hardship.501–505 Kingsland Rd, Dalston, London, E8 4AU   *T:* 020 7241 6251
E: info@family-action.org.uk
W: www.family-action.org.uk

Farnham Castle International Briefing and Conference Centre
Farnham Castle, the former palace of the bishops of Winchester, offers a unique and special location for church weekend retreats. Several London churches are regular visitors. The castle has 31 en suite bedrooms, including some family rooms, all with television. Facilities include two historic consecrated chapels, a wide choice of conference rooms and five acres of beautifully maintained gardens.
    Farnham Castle has an excellent dining room and bar. It overlooks the town of Farnham and is only seven minutes by taxi from the railway station. Farnham is 30 miles west of London, with good rail connections to Waterloo station (55 minutes). Special weekend rates are available for groups of over 30 adults.
    Please contact Teresa Clue, Events Manager, for further information. A video tour is available on the website. *Chief Executive* Mr James Twiss *Director of Marketing & Client Services* Mr Jeff Toms *Conference Manager* Mrs Barbara Milam *Events Manager* Teresa Clue, Farnham Castle, Farnham, GU9 0AG
    T: 01252 721194
E: info@farnhamcastle.com
W: www.farnhamcastle.com

Federation of Catholic Priests
A federation of priests in communion with the See of Canterbury who have undertaken to live in accordance with Catholic doctrine and practice. It exists for mutual support in propagating, maintaining and defending such doctrine and practice and for the deepening of the spiritual life of members. *Chairman* Canon James Southward *Secretary General* Fr Peter Walsh, 2 LIngdale Road, West Kirby, CH48 5DQ   *T:* 0151 632 4728
E: revpeterwalsh@btconnect.com
W: www.priests.org.uk

Feed the Minds
Feed the Minds believes that education saves lives, reduces poverty and builds community. Working in partnership worldwide, Feed the Minds funds a wide variety of innovative, indigenous educational projects. By improving access to knowledge and learning, Feed the Minds helps give people the opportunity to experience life in all its fullness.
    Registered Charity no. 291333 in England and Wales, and in Scotland, No SC041999. *President* Revd David Cornick *Chair of Trustees* Dr David Goodbourn *Director* Ms Josephine Carlsson, Feed the Minds, Park Place, 12 Lawn Lane, London, SW8 1UD   *T:* 08451 21 21 02
+44 (0)20 7582 3535 (International)
E: info@feedtheminds.org
W: www.feedtheminds.org

Fellowship of St Alban and St Sergius
Founded 1928. An unofficial body which fosters understanding and friendship between Eastern Orthodox and Western Christians.

Patrons: Archbishop Gregorios of Thyateira and Great Britain; Lord Williams of Oystermouth; Archbishop Elisey of Sourozh; Metropolitan Kallistros of Diokleia; Archbishop Job of Telemessos; Bishop Angaelos (Coptic Orthodox Church); Dr Sebastian Brock
      1 Canterbury Road, Oxford, OX2 6LU
                      T: 01865 552991
            E: gensec@sobornost.org
            W: www.sobornost.org

Fellowship of St Nicholas (FSN)
FSN uses its resources to offset the disadvantage, deprivation and abuse of children in need in Sussex. Our current services include two centre-based family support and day care services including mobile and outreach, UK online centres, youth clubs, nurseries, a children's bereavement project and family support. *Chairman* Mrs Mollie Green *Chief Executive* Ms Christine Unsworth, The St Nicholas Centre, 66 London Rd, St Leonards-on-Sea, TN37 6AS   *T:* 01424 423683
                      01424 855222
        E: cbrosnan@fsncharity.co.uk
        W: www.fsncharity.co.uk

Fellowship of Word and Spirit
An Anglican evangelical organization comprising 300 clergy and lay people committed to empowering, equipping and encouraging evangelicals through the development of thoughtful biblical theology for the 21st century using publications, conferences and a network of supportive fellowship. *Honorary President* The Rt Revd Wallace Benn *Chairman* The Revd Rob Munro, c/o 86 All Hallows Rd, Bispham, Blackpool, FY2 0AY   *E:* admin@fows.org
              W: www.fows.org

Forward in Faith
Founded in November 1992, Forward in Faith exists to proclaim the catholic faith and uphold catholic order and the catholic doctrine of the sacraments. Through a national and local network it supports all who in conscience are unable to accept the ordination of women to the priesthood or the episcopate. It is working, through the Society under the patronage of St Wilfrid and St Hilda, for an ecclesial structure with a ministry and sacraments in which its members can have confidence, so that they can flourish within the Church of England and make their full contribution to its life and mission.

It is governed by a council elected by the members of its National Assembly, which meets annually. It publishes the monthly journal *New Directions* and the catechetical weekly Pew Sheet *Forward!* and, with other leading catholic societies, a quarterly newspaper. *Chairman* The Rt Revd Tony Robinson ssc *Director* Dr Colin Podmore, 2A The Cloisters, Gordon Square, London, WC1H 0AG   *T:* 020 7388 3588
      E: FiF.UK@forwardinfaith.com
      W: www.forwardinfaith.com

Foundation for Church Leadership
The Foundation for Church Leadership (FCL) is an endowed charitable trust: its aims are to facilitate the support and development of emerging and senior church leaders, faith representatives and organizations for the benefit of leadership across the church. The Foundation primarily delivers its objectives through the provision of a series of consultancy and research initiatives. *Chair* Dame Janet Trotter *Director* Julie Farrar, 16 Sycamore Business Park, Copt Hewick, Ripon, HG4 5DF
                    T: 01765 609167
 E: director@churchleadershipfoundation.org
  W: www.churchleadershipfoundation.org

Foundation of St Matthias
Considers applications for personal and corporate grants with preference given to higher and further education applicants from the dioceses of Bath and Wells, Bristol and Gloucester. This does not preclude applicants from elsewhere.

Applications should show how the chosen subject will contribute to the advancement of the Church of England. Examples of personal study not considered: medicine, veterinary science, engineering, law. Corporate applications should promote projects for the educational training of others and show how the Church's contribution to higher and further education will be enhanced. Closing dates for applications: 31 May and 30 September each year. The Trust is a member of the Association of Church College Trusts (see separate entry). *Correspondent* Mrs K. Prescott, Hillside House, First Floor, 1500 Parkway North Newbrick Road, Stoke Gifford Bristol, BS34 8YU   *T:* 0117 906 0100
    E: stmatthiastrust@bristoldiocese.org
      W: www.stmatthiastrust.org.uk

Frances Ashton Charity
Supports serving or retired members of the Church of England clergy, or the widows/widowers thereof, who are in need. The trustees will consider almost any kind of financial hardship so long as the applicant falls within these categories. Where the applicant has an exceptional and urgent need, the trustees will consider applications quickly and at any time.

Any urgent applications should be discussed with the adminstrator before applying. For holiday applications the deadline is 1 March of the year in which the holiday is to be taken. All other applications are ongoing throughout the year. Please seek

the new applicant form from the administrator or from the website. *Administrator* Georgina Fowle, Beech House, Woolston North Cadbury, Somerset, BA22 7BJ
T: 07775 717 606
E: francesashton@hotmail.co.uk
W: www.francesashton.co.uk

Fresh Expressions
Fresh Expressions encourages new forms of church for a fast-changing world, working with Christians from a variety of denominations and traditions. It was initiated by the Archbishops of Canterbury and York with the Methodist Council and now includes the United Reformed Church, Church of Scotland, The Salvation Army, CWM, Congregational Federation, Ground Level Network, Church Army, CMS, ACPI and 24/7 Prayer as formal partners. The initiative has resulted in hundreds of new congregations being formed alongside more traditional churches.

Names and contact details for team members can be found on the website. *Archbishops' Missioner and Team Leader* Canon Phil Potter
T: 0300 3650563
E: contact@freshexpressions.org.uk
W: www.freshexpressions.org.uk

Friends of Friendless Churches
Founded in 1957 to preserve churches and chapels of architectural or historic interest. Now owns 52 redundant places of worship, half in England and half in Wales. Also administers the Cottam Will Trust, which gives grants for the introduction of works of art into ancient Gothic churches. *President* The Marquess of Salisbury *Chairman* Mr Roger Evans *Director* Mr Matthew Saunders, St Ann's Vestry Hall, 2 Church Entry, London, EC4V 5HB   T: 020 7236 3934
E: office@friendsoffriendlesschurches.org.uk
W: www.friendsoffriendlesschurches.org.uk

Friends of Julian of Norwich
The cell of Julian of Norwich, a chapel attached to St Julian's Church, Norwich, stands on the site where the 14th-century anchoress wrote her book *Revelations of Divine Love*. The Julian Centre, beside the church, houses a small bookshop and a library of works on Julian and spirituality and welcomes visitors and pilgrims (open Monday to Saturday 10.30 a.m. to 3.30 p.m.).

Large parties should book in advance (office hours as above). Accommodation is often available in the small convent beside the church. Quiet days can be arranged. Please contact the Sister in Charge, All Hallows House. The Julian Centre, Rouen Rd, Norwich, NR1 1QT   T: 01603 767380 (group bookings)
01603 624738 (accommodation, quiet days)
E: centre@friendsofjulian.org.uk
W: www.friendsofjulian.org.uk

Friends of Little Gidding, The
Little Gidding is rightly called a 'thin place'. From the seventeenth-century Ferrar family community to T. S. Eliot's visit in 1936 and up to the present time, many have experienced the presence of God at Little Gidding. The Friends (founded in 1947) take a practical and active involvement in the care of the historic church and the old farmhouse, now a retreat centre. It co-ordinates, with the T. S. Eliot Society, an annual Eliot Festival; arranges an annual pilgrimage in May; commemorates Nicholas Ferrar's life on his feast day, 4 December; and supports the provision of accommodation and hospitality for visitors and pilgrims. *Chair* Canon Simon Kershaw *Secretary* Mark Holman, c/o Ferrar House, Little Gidding, Huntingdon, PE28 5RJ   T: 01832 275343
E: friends@littlegidding.org.uk
W: www.littlegidding.org.uk

Friends of the Clergy Corporation
See Sons & Friends of the Clergy

Friends of the Elderly
Friends of the Elderly has been helping older people since 1905. Our vision is that all older people should retain their independence, dignity and peace of mind. We offer high quality residential and nursing care in 14 care homes, some with dementia units. We support older people to stay living in their own homes with a range of community services including welfare grants for those in financial need, day care, home support, home visiting and telephone befriending.

Registered Charity no. 226064 *Patron* HM The Queen *Chief Executive* Richard Furze, 40–42 Ebury St, London, SW1W 0LZ
T: 020 7730 8263
E: enquiries@fote.co.uk
W: www.fote.org.uk

Frontier Youth Trust
Frontier Youth Trust believes that another world is possible – a world that is better for young people. We want all young people, especially young people at risk, to have access to great youth work, so we provide direct training and coaching, create opportunities for sharing ideas and highlight inspiring practice.

We know that working on the margins can be isolating and workers can quickly feel unsupported, so we offer a home for pioneer workers to belong, to be resourced, renewed and sustained. Together, we are a growing movement of people who are advocating for positive change, speaking up for young people, challenging injustice and building church on the margins. *Deputy CEO* Debbie Garden, 434 Forest Road, London, E17 4PY
T: 0121 771 2328
E: info@fyt.org.uk
W: www.fyt.org.uk

Fulcrum

A network for evangelical clergy and laity. Launched in 2003 at the National Evangelical Anglican Congress in Blackpool, Fulcrum seeks to renew the evangelical centre by giving a voice to a nourishing orthodoxy. It provides support, theological exploration and encouragement for evangelical Anglicans and creates a space in which genuine debate can take place in a spirit of non-defensiveness and gracious disagreement, acknowledging that the clash of ideas can be creative and worthwhile. It has a website with regularly updated articles from leading evangelical theologians. *President* Dr Elaine Storkey *Chair* Revd John Watson *Theological Secretary* Rt Revd Graham Kings *General Secretary* Revd Rachel Marszalek, All Saints Vicarage, Elm Grove Road, Ealing London, W5 3JH

     E: admin@fulcrum-anglican.org.uk
     W: www.fulcrum-anglican.org.uk

Germinate: The Arthur Rank Centre

We help rural communities flourish by encouraging and equipping local churches from all denominations. We offer a vast range of resources online covering many aspects of church life, mission and training. Our Germinate suite includes learning communities for rural multi-church ministry; creative and entrepreneurial leadership training; a rural business start-up community franchise; and our national Germinate conference.

The Diocesan Rural Officers meet annually with the Church of England National Rural Officer, a member of staff at Germinate, and with those in equivalent roles in other denominations. We publish the magazine *Country Way* and a free monthly e-newsletter with information on the latest resources and funding for rural churches. *CEO* Jerry Marshall *National Rural Officer, Mission and Public Affairs Division, Abps' Council* Canon Dr Jill Hopkinson, The Arthur Rank Centre, Stoneleigh Park, Warwickshire, CV8 2LG

     T: 024 7685 3060
     E: info@germinate.net
     W: www.germinate.net

Girlguiding UK

Founded in 1910. Open to all girls and women between 5 and 65 years regardless of race, faith or any other circumstance. Its purpose is to enable girls to mature into confident, capable and caring women determined, as individuals, to realize their potential in their career, home and personal life, and willing as citizens to contribute to their community and the wider world.

- Rainbows age 5–7;
- Brownies age 7–10;
- Guides age 10–14;
- Senior Section age 14–25;
- Leaders age 18 plus.

Chief Guide Gill Slocombe *Chief Executive* Julie Bentley, 17/19 Buckingham Palace Rd, London, SW1W 0PT   *T:* 0800 169 5901
     020 7834 6242
     E: join.us@girlguiding.org.uk
     W: www.girlguiding.org.uk

Girls' Brigade England and Wales

Girls' Bridge (GB) works with churches and schools to develop tailored outreach groups which enable children and young people to belong, achieve and discover Jesus. GB is an international, interdenominational children's and youth organization. *National Director* Miss Ruth Gilson, Cliff College, Calver, Hope Valley Derbyshire, S32 3XG   *T:* 01246 582322
     E: gbco@gb-ministries.org
     W: www.girlsb.org

Girls Friendly Society in England and Wales, The (Campaign name GFS Platform)

Established in 1875, GFS Platform works with girls and young women aged 7+. The work focuses on two specific areas, namely four community projects that work with young women between the ages of 14 and 25 who are either pregnant or who have children, and 40 parish-based youth work branches throughout England and Wales that run voluntary youth groups for girls and young women aged 7+.

Main activities include reducing social exclusion and building self-esteem by providing social, formal educational and health awareness sessions and generic support in a single gender and non-judgemental environment. GFS Platform offers young women and girls the opportunity to explore their own personal and social development. This enables them to acquire new skills and knowledge, gain confidence, make informed choices and take responsibility for their own lives. *Director* Joy Lauezzari, Unit 2 Angel Gate, 326 City Rd, London, EC1V 2PT

     T: 020 7837 9669
     E: annualreport@gfsplatform.org.uk
     W: www.gfsplatform.org.uk

Greater Churches Network

The Greater Churches Group (now 'Network') was founded in 1991 as an informal association of non-cathedral churches, which, by virtue of their great age, size and of their historical, architectural or ecclesiastical importance, display many of the characteristics of a cathedral and also fulfil a role which is additional to that of a normal parish church.

Its aims are to provide help and mutual support in dealing with the special challenges of running a 'cathedral-like' church within the organizational and financial structure of a

OTHER ORGANIZATIONS

parish church; to enhance the quality of parish worship in such churches; and to promote wider recognition of the unique position and needs of churches in this category. The group also serves as a channel of communication for other organizations wishing to have contact with churches of this type. *Secretary* Mr Ian Penny, The Parish Office, Priory House, Quay Road, Christchurch, BH23 1BX   *T:* 01202 485804 (option 6)
E: prioryhouse@christchurchpriory.org

Greenbelt Festivals
Greenbelt Festival takes place annually over the August Bank Holiday weekend, gathering together artists, musicians, speakers and performers, alongside 14,000 festivalgoers at Boughton House near Kettering. Its 41-year history is firmly rooted within a Christian tradition which is politically and culturally engaged. The festival is a family-friendly celebration, inclusive and accepting of all, regardless of ethnicity, gender, sexuality, background or belief. *Chair* Andy Turner *CEO* Beccie D'Cunha, Greenbelt Festivals Ltd, 1B Snowhill Court, London, EC1A 2EJ
T: 020 7374 2755 (office)
020 7874 2760 (ticket line)
E: info@greenbelt.org.uk
W: www.greenbelt.org.uk

Guild of All Souls
Founded in 1873 as an intercessory guild, caring for the dying, the dead and the bereaved. Open to members of the Church of England and Churches in communion with her and any who share the objects of the Guild.

Chantry chapel at Walsingham and at St Stephen's Church, Gloucester Road, London W8 5PU. Patron of forty-one livings of the Catholic tradition. *President* The Bishop of Richborough *General Secretary* David Llewelyn Morgan *Warden* Louis A. Lewis *Hon Treasurer* Revd Paul E. Jones, St Alban's Centre, 18 Brooke Street, London, EC1N 7RD
T: 0207 404 8422
E: contact@guildofallsouls.org.uk
W: www.guildofallsouls.org.uk

Guild of Church Braillists
The Guild consists of a group of people who give their services to help blind readers by transcribing a variety of religious literature into Braille. Requests are welcome from individual readers for books, special services, etc. All other productions are sent to the National Library for the Blind or the Library of the RNIB. For further details contact the Secretary. *Secretary* Mary Hazlewood, Farthings, Pennymoor, Tiverton Devon, EX16 8LF
T: 01727 845183
E: info@gocb.org
W: www.gocb.org

Guild of Church Musicians
Founded in 1888, since 1961 the Guild has administered the Archbishops' Certificate in Church Music (ACert.CM) on behalf of the Archbishops of Canterbury and Westminster. This Certificate is a minimum qualification for church organists, choir trainers, cantors, choristers and leaders of instrumental groups and is fully ecumenical.

The Archbishops' Award in Church Music is available for those who wish to be examined in practical skills only and the Guild's Preliminary Certificate in Church Music is aimed at young people and those starting in church music. Since 2002 the new qualification of Archbishops' Certificate in Public Worship (ACert.PW), for all who lead public worship, both clerical and lay, has been established. There is also a Fellowship examination (FGCM).

Patrons: The Archbishop of Canterbury; the Archbishop of Westminster. *President* Dame Mary Archer *Warden* Revd Canon Dr Jeremy Haselock *Registrar and General Secretary* Mrs June Williams *Chairman of Academic Board* Dr Hugh Benham, Tally Ho, Toys Hill, Westerham Kent, TN16 1QG
E: barryandjune@blueyonder.co.uk
W: www.churchmusicians.org

Guild of Health and St Raphael
The Guild of Health and St Raphael is an ecumenical Christian society serving the Healing Ministry which was founded (in 1904) to bring together doctors and clergy, in the first instance, to work together for health and wellbeing.

Originally one organization, the Guild of Health and the Guild of St Raphael separated in 1915, but in the twenty-first century it now seems right for these two complementary ministries to come together once again.

For further information please contact us or visit our website. *Director and Company Secretary* The Revd Dr Gilliam Strainer, c/o St Marylebone Parish Church, 17 Marylebone Rd, London, NW1 5LT   *T:* 020 7563 1389
E: guildofhealth@stmarylebone.org
enquiries@gohealth.org.uk (membership)
W: www.gohealth.org.uk

Guild of Pastoral Psychology
The Guild offers a meeting ground for all interested in the relationship between religion and depth psychology, particularly the work of C. G. Jung and his followers. Depth psychology has contributed many new insights into the meaning of religion and its symbols and their relevance to everyday life.

The Guild has monthly lectures in central London, a day conference in London in the spring and a three-day summer conference at Oxford. Further information and details of membership available from the Administrator. *Administrator* Val Nurse, KVT BusinessCare, GPP Administration, Unit 1, Chapleton Lodge, East Winch Road, Blackborough End, Kings Lynn, PE32 1SF

E: administration@
guildofpastoralpsychology.org
W: www.guildofpastoralpsychology.org.uk

Guild of Servants of the Sanctuary

Founded in 1898 to raise the spiritual standard of Servers, to promote friendship among them and to encourage attendance at Holy Communion in addition to times of duty. *Warden* Fr Darren Smith *Secretary General* Mr Terry Doughty, 52 Cherryleas Drive, Leicester, LE3 0LS   *T:* 0116 431 2592
E: secretary@gssonline.org.uk
W: www.gssonline.org.uk

Guild of St Leonard

The Guild was founded by the Revd John Sankey. Its object is to pray for all prisoners, those on licence or probation and for all who care for them. The Guild publishes a quarterly Intercession Paper. *Warden* Rt Revd Lloyd Rees *Secretary* Revd Andrew Nichols, The Chaplain's Office, HMP Ford, Arundel, BN18 0BX
T: 01903 663000

Harnhill Centre of Christian Healing

A retreat centre for the ministry of Christian Healing through prayer ministry, prayer, quiet days, teaching courses and Christian Healing Services. The Centre provides residential accommodation. *Chairman* Dr David Wells *Director* Revd Kate Picot, Harnhill Manor, Cirencester, GL7 5PX   *T:* 01285 850283
E: office@harnhillcentre.org.uk
W: www.harnhillcentre.org.uk

Henry Bradshaw Society

Founded in 1890 for printing liturgical texts from manuscripts and rare editions of service books, etc. For available texts, please consult the Society's website. *Secretary* Dr Nicolas Bell, Music Collections, The British Library, 96 Euston Rd, London, NW1 2DB
E: nicolas.bell@bl.uk
W: www.henrybradshawsociety.org

Highbury Centre

Christian guesthouse on quiet private road with ample free on-street parking. Reductions for missionaries/clergy. *Manager* Mrs S. Scalora, 20–26 Aberdeen Park, Highbury, London, N5 2BJ   *T:* 020 7226 2663
E: enquiries@thehighburycentre.org
W: www.thehighburycentre.org

Hockerill Educational Foundation

The Foundation makes personal awards to teachers, intending teachers and others in further or higher education, with a priority for the teaching of Religious Education in our schools. It does not make awards to those training for ordination, mission, social work or counselling, or to children at school.

The Foundation makes corporate grants to support the development of religious education, particularly in the Dioceses of Chelmsford and St Albans. Full details of eligibility for awards can be found on our website at www.hockerillfoundation.org.uk. The applications deadline is 31 March each year.

Working with NATRE it provides the Hockerill NATRE Prize for Innovation in the teaching of Religious Education. Available in both the Primary and Secondary sectors, this annual award gives a monetary prize to the school and an educational bursary to the teacher. It is a member of the Association of Church College Trusts (see separate entry), and the RE Council, and it part funds the APPG on Religious Education as well as the RE Quality Mark. *Correspondent/Secretary* Mr Derek J. Humphrey, 3 The Swallows, Harlow, Essex, CM17 0AR   *T:* 01279 420855
E: info@hockerillfoundation.org.uk
W: www.hockerillfoundation.org.uk

Holy Rood House, Centre for Health and Pastoral Care

Opened in 1993, the Centre is a friendly house with a residential community. The house offers a gentle and holistic approach in a Christian environment where individuals or groups, of all ages and backgrounds, can work towards their own healing and explore their spiritual journey within an atmosphere of acceptance, love and openness.

Professional counsellors and therapists, working closely with the medical profession, offer support at times of bereavement, abuse, addiction, relationship breakdown or illness, and creative arts and stress management play an important role in the healing process.

Holy Rood House ministers within an awareness of justice and peace to daily or residential guests, and is also the home of the Centre for the Study of Theology and Health. *Patrons* Lord Williams of Oystermouth; Prof Mary Grey *Executive Director* Revd Elizabeth Baxter *Director, Therapeutic Care* Jane Younger *Director of Mission* Revd Stanley Baxter, Holy Rood House 10 Sowerby Rd, Sowerby, Thirsk, YO7 1HX   *T:* 01845 522580
01845 522004
E: enquiries@holyroodhouse.org.uk
W: www.holyroodhouse.freeuk.com

Homes for Retired Clergy

See separate entries for Beauchamp Community and College of St Barnabas.

OTHER ORGANIZATIONS

Hospice Movement

The word 'Hospice' was first used from the fourth century onwards when Christian orders welcomed travellers, the sick and those in need. It was first applied to the care of dying patients by Mme Jeanne Garnier who founded the Dames de Calvaire in Lyon, France in 1842. The modern hospice movement, however, with its twin emphases on medical and psychosocial intervention, dates from the founding of St Christopher's Hospice by Dame Cicely Saunders in 1967.

Since 1967, 'hospice' has become a worldwide philosophy adapting to the needs of different cultures and settings – hospital, hospice and community – and is established in six continents. Hospice and palliative care is the active, total care of patients whose disease no longer responds to curative treatment, and for whom the goal must be the best quality of life for them and their families.

Palliative medicine is now a distinct medical speciality in the UK. It focuses on controlling pain and other symptoms, easing suffering and enhancing the life that remains. It integrates the psychological and spiritual aspects of care, to enable patients to live out their lives with dignity. It also offers support to families, both during the patient's illness and their bereavement. It offers a unique combination of care in hospices and at home.

Hospice and palliative care services mostly help people with cancer, although increasingly patients with other life-threatening illnesses may also be supported; this includes HIV/AIDS, motor neurone disease, heart failure and kidney disease. Hospice and palliative care is free of charge to the patient regardless of whether it is provided by an independent charitable hospice, Macmillan Service, Marie Curie Cancer Care, Sue Ryder Palliative Care Centre or by an NHS service. The criteria for admission are based on medical, social and emotional need.

Referral to a hospice or palliative care service (including inpatient and home care nursing services) is normally arranged by the patient's own GP or hospital doctor. Further information about hospice care in the UK and overseas, including the facility to find your local hospice and resources for health professionals, is available from The Hospice Information Service. This is a partnership between Help the Hospices and St Christopher's Hospice and provides an enquiry service for the public and professionals. Publications include UK and International Directories of Hospice and Palliative Care.

> *E:* info@helpthehospices.org.uk
> *W:* www.helpthehospices.org.uk

Hulme Trustees

A Trust holding the Rights of Presentation to a number of benefices. *Secretary* Mr Jonathan Shelmardine, 31 Middlewich Road, Sandback, CW11 1HW   *T:* 01270 762521

Hymn Society of Great Britain and Ireland

Founded in 1936 to encourage study and research into hymns, both words and music; to promote good standards of hymn singing and to encourage the discerning use of hymns and songs in worship. The Society publishes a quarterly magazine and there is a three-day annual conference. Further information and details of membership from the Secretary. *Secretary* Revd Robert A. Canham, Windrush, Braithwaite, Keswick, CA12 5SZ

> *T:* 01768 778054
> *E:* robcanham.causeypike@gmail.com
> *W:* www.hymnsocietygbi.org.uk

Hyndman's (Miss) Trustees

Patronage Trust Varied churchmanship. *Executive Officer* Mrs Ann Brown, 6 Angerford Avenue, Sheffield, S8 9BG   *T:* 0114 255 8522

> *E:* ann.brown@hyndmans.org.uk
> *W:* www.hyndmans.org.uk

Industrial Christian Fellowship

Founded in 1918 as a successor to the Navvy Mission (1877) and incorporating the Christian Social Union, ICF is a nationwide ecumenical network that provides support for Christians who want to apply their faith in fresh and creative ways in the everyday working world. A recent new initiative to make links between the local church and working life is the 'Take your Minister to Work' project.

ICF provides resources, including liturgy and prayers for personal and corporate use, reflections and services related to work; a newsletter and occasional papers; and the quarterly journal *Faith in Business* (in association with the Ridley Hall Foundation). Close links with other groups and agencies involved with faith and work are maintained. Membership is open to individuals and organizations. *Chair* Revd Phil Jump *Secretary* Mrs Ann Wright *Treasurer* Revd Jeremy Brown, PO Box 414, Horley, RH6 8WL

> *T:* 01293 821322
> *E:* admin@icf-online.org
> *W:* www.icf-online.org

Industrial Mission Association

The Industrial Mission Association (IMA) is a national and ecumenical association, mainly, though not exclusively, comprised of chaplains appointed to places of work throughout the UK. *Moderator* Randell Moll,

Penn Cottage, Green End, Granborough, MK18 3NT   *E:* info@industrialmission.org.uk
W: www.industrialmission.org.uk

INFORM

Inform is an independent charity founded in 1988 with funding from the British Home Office and mainstream Churches with the aim of obtaining and making available accurate, balanced and up-to-date information about alternative spirituality and new religious movements or 'cults'.

It has a large collection of data on computer and in various other forms (books, articles, cuttings, videos and cassettes), and is in touch with an international network of scholars and other specialists. People with questions or concerns about new religious movements or alternative spirituality should contact the Inform office, which is based at the London School of Economics, between 10 a.m. and 4.30 p.m., Mondays to Fridays. *Chair of the Board of Governors* Dr Marat Shterin *Honorary Acting Director* Professor Eileen Barker *Senior Research Officer* Sarah J. Harvey *Research Officers* Dr Susannah Crockford, Dr Shanon Shah, Dr Catherine Loy and Silke Steidinger, LSE, Houghton St, London, WC2A 2AE
T: 020 7955 7654 (Information line)
E: INFORM@LSE.ac.uk
W: www.inform.ac

Inter Faith Network for the UK

Established in 1987 to encourage contact and dialogue between different faith communities in the United Kingdom, the Inter Faith Network aims to advance public knowledge and mutual understanding of the teaching, traditions and practices of the different faith communities in Britain, including an awareness of their distinctive features and of their common ground, and to promote good relations between persons of different faiths.

Its member organizations include national faith community representative bodies; national, regional and local inter faith bodies; and academic institutions and educational bodies concerned with inter faith issues. *Executive Director* Dr Harriet Crabtree *Co-Chairs* Rt Revd Richard Atkinson and Mr Jatinder Singh Birdi, 2 Grosvenor Gardens, London, SW1W 0DH   *T:* 020 7730 0410
E: ifnet@interfaith.org.uk
W: www.interfaith.org.uk

Intercontinental Church Society

Founded in 1823, ICS is an Anglican mission agency ministering to English-speaking people worldwide; it is engaged in church planting, growth and outreach to tourists and is a patronage society (nominating chaplains for international Anglican churches abroad). *President* Viscount Brentford *Mission Director* The Revd Richard Bromley, Unit 11, Ensign Business Centre, Westwood Way, Westwood Business Park, Coventry, CV4 8JA
T: 024 7646 3940
E: enquiries@ics-uk.org
W: www.ics-uk.org

International Ecumenical Fellowship – British Region

IEF is a community of Christians both lay and ordained, with regional groups in Belgium, Czech Republic, France, Germany, Great Britain, Hungary, Poland, Romania, Slovak Republic and Spain. It also has individual members in various other countries.

Through annual international gatherings and smaller regional groups, Christians from Catholic, Orthodox and Protestant traditions meet to worship, pray, study and enjoy fellowship together. IEF tries to strengthen the spirit of ecumenism and international friendship. IEF practises eucharistic hospitality as far as church discipline and individual conscience permit. *President of British Region* The Revd Richard Hill *Secretary* Mrs Kate Grand *Treasurer* Mr G. Morton,
E: kategrand@tiscali.co.uk
W: www.ief-oecumenica.org

Interserve

Interserve is an interdenominational, evangelical mission agency with over 800 full-time Christian professionals working across Asia, the Arab World, and among ethnic groups in England and Wales. Interservers work in many different ministries, seeking to share the love of Christ through everything they say and do.

All Christians with a burden to respond to Jesus' commission and make disciples of all nations are welcomed for both long and short term periods of service, with the aim of seeing lives and communities transformed through encounter with Jesus Christ. *National Director* Steve Bell, 5/6 Walker Avenue, Wolverton Mills, Milton Keynes, MK12 5TW
T: 01908 552700
E: info@interserve.org.uk
W: www.interserve.org.uk

Journeying

Journeying is an ecumenical organization comprising a team of people who take small groups to beautiful and often remote locations in Britain and Ireland in the spirit of pilgrimage. Formerly known as Pilgrim Adventure, the team has been doing this quietly and unobtrusively for 30 years. Its origins lie in Celtic spirituality and that element is never far away, though there is no heavy religiosity at all – and people of any faith, denomination or none are welcomed openly. *Patron* The Rt Revd John Pritchard, Bishop of Oxford *Directors* Steve Evemy, Iain

Tweedale, Susan Fogarty, Phil Craine and David Gleed, 45 Devonshire Road, Southampton, SO15 2GL   T: 0191 469 9432
E: info@journeying.co.uk
W: www.journeying.co.uk

Jubilate Group
An association of authors and musicians formed in 1974 for the purpose of publishing material for contemporary worship: *Hymns for Today's Church, Church Family Worship, Carols for Today, Carol Praise, Let's Praise!* 1 and 2, *Prayers for the People, Psalms for Today, Songs from the Psalms, The Dramatised Bible, The Wedding Book, Hymns for the People, World Praise* 1 and 2 and *Sing Glory. Chairman* Dr Noel Tredinnick *Secretary* David Peacock *Copyright Manager* Michèle Spear *Editorial Coordinator* Mr Roger Peach,
T: 01803 200132
E: admin@jubilate.co.uk
roger@jubilate.co.uk /
joelresound@gmail.com
W: www.jubilate.co.uk

Julian Meetings, The
A network of Christian contemplative prayer groups, begun in Britain in 1973. There are now about 350 groups in Great Britain and some in Australia, Canada, Ireland, Southern Africa and the USA. Ecumenical. Magazine three times a year. *Contact* Deidre Morris, 263 Park Lodge Lane, Wakefield, WF1 4HY
T: 01924 369437
E: gb@julianmeetings.org
W: www.julianmeetings.org

Keswick Convention
The Keswick Convention is the main event organized annually by Keswick Ministries and has been taking place since 1875. It offers something for everyone – life-changing Bible teaching, uplifting worship and great fellowship combined with the chance to relax and enjoy a holiday in the wonderful setting of the Lake District. *Chairman* Mr John Risbridger *General Director* Mr David Bradley *Operations Manager* Mr Simon Overend, Keswick Convention Trust, Skiddaw St, Keswick, CA12 4BY   T: 01768 780075
E: info@keswickministries.org
W: www.keswickministries.org

Keswick Hall Trust Charity
The Keswick Hall Trust supports the promotion of Religious Education by providing financial support to the Diocesan Education Department in the Anglican dioceses of Ely, Norwich and St Edmundsbury & Ipswich. KHT no longer provided grants for individuals or organizations. KHT is a member of the Association of Church College Trusts. *Executive Officer* Malcolm Green,

Keswick Hall Trust, PO Box 307, Woodbridge, IP13 6WL
T: 07760 433 409
E: admin@keswickhalltrust.org.uk
W: www.keswickhalltrust.org.uk

Keychange Charity (formerly Christian Alliance)
Established in 1920. Offers care, acceptance and Christian community to people in need through the provision of residential care for frail elderly people and supported accommodation for young homeless people. *Chief Executive* Graham Waters, 5 St George's Mews, 43 Westminster Bridge Rd, London, SE1 7JB
T: 020 7633 0533
E: info@keychange.org.uk
W: www.keychange.org.uk

Korean Mission Partnership
Founded in 1889 by Edward White Benson, Archbishop of Canterbury, as the Church of England Mission to Korea, the name was changed in 1993 when the Province of Korea was inaugurated. The name reflects the two-way nature of our mission today. Support goes to Korea by way of prayer, interest and funding. The Province has sent a priest from Seoul to run the Korean Chaplaincy in the Diocese of London, ministering to Korean people who live mainly in and around the Home Counties. *President* The Primate of Korea *Chairman* Revd Mark Williams *Hon Admin Secretary* Revd Martin Fletcher *Hon Treasurer* Mrs Lucille West, St John the Divine Vicarage, 92 Vassall Road, London, SW9 6JA   T: 020 7735 9340
E: fr_mark@yahoo.com
W: www.koreanmission.org

Langley House Trust
Founded in 1958, the Langley House Trust is a national Christian charity that provides support and care to offenders (and those at risk of offending), enabling individuals to live independent and crime-free lives. Langley enables offenders to address their needs, including support for mental health and substance misuse issues and the provision of a safe and stable home. Langley currently runs a number of residential projects across England, including care homes and projects for women. Langley works with a wide variety of people, with the belief that no one's history should define their destiny, achieving an exceptional reoffending rate of just 3 per cent. Langley bases its services on Christian beliefs and values but is open to men and women of any or no faith. *Chair of Trustees* Malcolm N. Hayes *Chief Exec* Tracy Wild *Corporate Operations Director* Pamela Leonce *Corporate Services*

Director David Reynolds, PO Box 6364, Coventry, CV6 9LL   *T:* 03330 035 025
       E: info@langleyhousetrust.org
       W: www.langleyhousetrust.org

Latimer Trust
The Latimer Trust is dedicated to providing a biblical and considered response to the issues facing today's Anglican Communion. Through a range of resources it is continuing and developing the work of Latimer House, founded in Oxford in the 1960s.
    Registered Charity no. 1084337. *Chairman of the Council* Revd Dr Mark Burkill *Director of Research* Revd Dr Gerald Bray, c/o Oak Hill College, Chase Side, London, N14 4PS
       T: 020 8449 0467 ext. 227
       E: administrator@latimertrust.org
       W: www.latimertrust.org

Lee Abbey Household Communities
There are two household communities based in Urban Priority Areas in Birmingham and Bristol. Community members live under a common rule of life and seek to be involved in their local community and church. *Contact* Gill Arbuthnot, 101 Dorridge Rd, Dorridge, Solihull, B93 8BS   *T:* 0121 327 0095
       01567 776558
     W: www.leeabbey.org.uk/households/

Lee Abbey International Students' Club
Founded in 1964 by the Lee Abbey Fellowship as a ministry to students of all nationalities, the Club provides long- and short-term hostel accommodation for students of all faiths or none and is served by a Christian community, which consists of young people from all over the world. Applications are invited from anyone interested in joining the community, residing as a student or staying as a holiday-maker. *Warden* Canon Trevor Hubble, 57–67 Lexham Gardens, London, W8 6JJ
       T: 020 7373 7242
     E: personnel@leeabbeylondon.com
     accommodation@leeabbeylondon.com
       W: www.leeabbeylondon.com

Leprosy Mission, The
We are an international Christian development organization. Inspired by our Christian values, we work in equal partnership with people affected by leprosy and with other stakeholders. As partners, together we transform lives through advocacy and the enablement of physical, social, economic and spiritual development of individuals and communities affected by leprosy and other disabilities. *National Director* Peter A. Walker, Goldhay Way, Orton Goldhay, Peterborough, PE2 5GZ   *T:* 01733 370505
       E: post@tlmew.org.uk
       W: www.leprosymission.org.uk

Lesbian and Gay Christian Movement
LGCM has four principal aims:

1. to encourage fellowship, friendship and support among lesbian and gay Christians through prayer, study and action;
2. to help the whole Church examine its understanding of human sexuality and to work for positive acceptance of gay relationships;
3. to encourage members to witness to their Christian faith within the gay community and to their convictions about human sexuality within the Church; and
4. to maintain and strengthen links with other lesbian and gay Christian groups both in Britain and elsewhere.

An extensive network of local groups exists and a wide range of resources are available. *Chief Executive* Revd Richard Kirker, Oxford House, Derbyshire St, Bethnal Green, London, E2 6HG   *T:* 020 7739 1249
    020 7613 1095 (Christian Homophobia Hotline)
       E: lgcm@lgcm.org.uk
       W: www.lgcm.org.uk

Li Tim-Oi Foundation
The Foundation bears the name of the first ordained woman in the Anglican Communion. Florence Li Tim-Oi was ordained priest in Hong Kong (for ministry in China) on 25 January 1944. The Li Tim-Oi Foundation began its work in 2007, the centenary of the birth of Florence Li Tim-Oi.
    The purpose of the Li Tim-Oi Foundation is to encourage and support financially women training for ministry in the global south/majority world. Most of the women applying come from Anglican/Episcopal churches in Africa, though we have also supported women from South America, Asia and Oceania. The women supported through the Foundation have gone on to become agents for change in church and society.
    The Foundation relies on donations and legacies. Regular donors are particularly welcome, as are donations to mark particular occasions, e.g as a thanksgiving for one's own priesting or anniversary of priesting.
    Patrons: The Most Revd Paul Kwong, Archbishop of Hong Kong; The Rt Revd Libby Lane, Bishop of Stockport; Baroness Perry of Southwark; The Rt Revd Victoria Matthews, Bishop of Christchurch; Dr Jane Williams, Lord Williams of Oystermouth. *Executive Secretary* Sue Parks, 8 Trews Weir Court, Exeter, EX2 4JS   *T:* 07976 414619
       E: litimoi@btinternet.com
     W: http://.ittakesonewoman.org

Liddon Trust
See Society of the Faith (Incorporated).

OTHER ORGANIZATIONS

Lincoln Theological Institute

Inaugurated in 1997 and based at the University of Manchester, the Institute's primary aim is to undertake, promote and support theological enquiry into contemporary society and thereby to practise theology in the fullest sense. It focuses on postgraduate and postdoctoral research, working closely with colleagues in the Department of Religions and Theology.

Core areas for research include:

1. place, locality, habitation and ecology;
2. global threats and powers;
3. religion and civil society;
4. technology, limits and transformation;
5. power and institutions (including the church);
6. liberation, political, ecological and public theologies;
7. culture – including religious cultures – and resources of hope; and
8. theologies of education.

Students wishing to study under the auspices of the Institute may enrol through the University of Manchester for Masters and Doctoral degree programmes. Formal and informal enquiries from prospective students are encouraged.

The Lincoln Theological Institute originated from Lincoln Theological College, founded in 1874 as an ordination training college. Since 2003 the Institute has been a fully integrated research unit within the University of Manchester. For further information please contact the Director. *Director* Prof Peter M. Scott *Research Associate* Dr Scott Midson, School of Arts, Histories and Cultures, University of Manchester, Oxford Rd, Manchester, M13 9PL   *T:* 0161 275 3064
0161 275 3736
E: peter.scott@manchester.ac.uk
W: http://www.lincolntheologicalinstitute.com

Livability (formerly know as the Shaftesbury Society)

Livability is a new charity, formed by the merger of the Shaftesbury Society and John Grooms. Livability creates choices for disabled people and brings life to local communities. We offer a wide range of services to around 8,000 disabled people and their families, including residential care, supported living, education and accessible holidays. We also provide community organizations with the resources, advice and confidence to transform their neighbourhoods. *Chief Executive* Mary Bishop, 50 Scrutton St, London, EC2A 4XQ
T: 020 7452 2000
E: info@livability.org.uk
W: www.livability.org.uk

Liverpool Seafarers Centre

See Mersey Mission to Seafarers, The.

Living Stones (formerly Church and Community Trust)

An independent charitable trust offering friendly guidance and support at both diocesan and individual church level on building a future by making the most effective use of resources – buildings, money, people – for worshipping God and serving the community. *Administrator* Roger Munday, Cally Hall, Blackshawhead, Hebden Bridge, HX7 7JP   *T:* 07971 378 533
E: info@living-stones.org.uk
W: www.living-stones.org.uk

London City Mission

For over 175 years, LCM has been working with churches to bring the Christian message to the people of London. Today, in the workplace, out on the streets and in the various communities of London, over 300 workers and volunteers are actively seeking to bring Christian values and hope to those they meet. *Chairman* Mark Harding *Chief Executive* Revd Dr John Nicholls, Nasmith House, 175 Tower Bridge Rd, London, SE1 2AH   *T:* 020 7407 7585
E: enquiries@lcm.org.uk
W: www.lcm.org.uk

Lord Wharton's Charity

Lord Wharton's Charity gives Bibles to children and young people through clergy, churches and schools. Applications are made using the form downloadable from the website. This Charity was formed in 1696 to give Bibles to children of all denominations across the whole of Great Britain. *Clerk to the Trustees* The Revd Peter Sheasby, 50 Hallcroft Road, Retford, DN22 7LB   *T:* 01777 702573
E: info@lordwhartonbibles.org.uk
W: www.lordwhartonbibles.org.uk

Marshall's Charity

Founded in 1627. Makes grants for:

1. building, purchasing or modernizing parsonages of the Church of England or the Church in Wales
2. repairs to churches in Kent, Surrey and Lincolnshire.

Clerk to the Trustees Catherine de Cintra, Marshall House, 66 Newcomen St, London, SE1 1YT   *T:* 020 7407 2979
E: grantoffice@marshalls.org.uk
W: www.marshalls.org.uk

Martyrs Memorial and Church of England Trust

A Trust holding Rights of Presentation to a number of benefices. Administered by the

Church Pastoral Aid Society. *Secretary* The Revd John Fisher, CPAS, Unit 3, Sovereign Court One, Sir William Lyons Road, Coventry, CV4 7EZ *T:* 0300 123 0780 extn 4387/4388
E: jfisher@cpas.org.uk
patronage@cpas.org.uk

Mediawatch-UK (formerly the National Viewers' and Listeners' Association)

Mediawatch-UK is a voluntary association which campaigns for family values in the media. We believe that the media we consume inevitably shapes the moral, ethical, social and political values of our culture and we champion the rights of the public to socially responsible broadcasting. Our campaigns include fighting for meaningful protection for children from premature sexualization by the media and from potentially harmful material online.

The organization was founded in 1965 by Mary Whitehouse and her associates who were concerned that that television was attacking and undermining family life. Benefits of membership include representation at the highest levels, regular newsletters and updates and assistance to enable members to make their voices heard. *Director* Miss Vivienne Pattison, 3 Willow House, Kennington Rd, Ashford, TN24 0NR
T: 01233 633936
E: info@mediawatchuk.org
W: www.mediawatchuk.org

Melanesian Mission

The Melanesian Mission is an Anglican mission agency that provides support to the Anglican Church of Melanesia (ACoM), through prayer, people and giving. *Chairman* The Rt Revd Mark Rylands *Hon. Treasurer* Mrs Sue Clayton *Executive Officer* Mrs Katie Drew, 21 The Burlands, Feniton, Honiton, Devon, EX14 3UN *E:* mission@mmuk.net
W: http://www.mmuk.net

Mersey Mission to Seafarers, The

Founded 1856 to 'promote the spiritual and temporal welfare of seafarers' from around the world who visit the ports of the River Mersey, Manchester Ship Canal and the Isle of Man. We will also respond to any emergency within the geographical area, Holyhead to Scottish Borders. *Chairman* Mrs Pamela Brown MBE, JP, DL *Chief Executive* John P. Wilson, Liverpool Seafarers Centre, 20 Crosby Rd South, Liverpool, L22 1RQ *T:* 0300 800 8080
07973 824154 (Mobile)
E: admin@liverpoolseafarerscentre.org
W: www.liverpoolseafarerscentre.org

Mid-Africa Ministry (CMS)

Mid-Africa Ministry (MAM), founded in 1921, now forms part of the Church Mission Society.

Mirfield Centre

Events and study days are arranged by the Centre team and information about upcoming courses are available on the website. Offers a meeting place for up to 60 people. Residential conferences are also available. *Director* The Revd June Lawson *Centre Administrator* Mrs Beth Harper *Centre Brothers* Father Dennis Berk, Brother Jacob Pallett, The Mirfield Centre, Stocks Bank Road, Mirfield, WF14 0BW
T: 01924 481920
E: centre@mirfield.org.uk
W: http://www.mirfield.org.uk

Mission to Seafarers, The

Founded in 1856, and entirely funded by voluntary donations, today's Mission to Seafarers offers emergency assistance, practical support, advocacy services, access to legal advice and family liaison to seafarers in need in over 200 ports in 50 countries around the world through its global network of chaplains and volunteers who offer a warm Christian welcome. In many ports it works in close cooperation with Christian societies of other denominations, and it is a member of the International Christian Maritime Association. *President* HRH The Princess Royal *Secretary General* The Revd Canon Andrew Wright, St Michael Paternoster Royal, College Hill, London, EC4R 2RL *T:* 020 7248 5202
E: info@missiontoseafarers.org
W: www.missiontoseafarers.org

MODEM

MODEM is a network/association whose mission is to lead and enable authentic dialogue between exponents of Christian leadership, management and organization, and spirituality, theology and ministry. MODEM is an ecumenical membership organization, open to all Christians irrespective of age, gender, race, culture or nationality, and welcoming dialogue with all comers of all faiths.

In association with SCM/Canterbury Press, MODEM has published three ground-breaking books, *Management and Ministry: appreciating contemporary issues*; *Leading, Managing, Ministering: challenging questions for church and society*; and *Creative Church Leadership: on the challenge of making a difference through leadership*, the latter edited by Dr John Adair and John Nelson. *How to Become a Creative Leader*, was published in February 2008, and is essentially the 'how to' book following the previous three, and a fifth book, *101 Great Ideas for Growing Healthy Churches*, was published in 2012. See website for further information on conferences and book reviews. *Chairman* David Sims *Secretary* Derek McAuley *Treasurer* Tony Berry *Membership Secretary*

Jonathan Emptage, CTBI, 39 Eccleston Square, London, SW1V 1BX   *T:* 020 7901 4890
E: info@modem-uk.org
membership@modem-uk.org
W: www.modem-uk.org

Modern Church (formerly Modern Churchpeople's Union)

Modern Church promotes liberal theology and offers Christian debate and discussion on religious issues. It embraces the spirit of freedom and informed enquiry and seeks to involve the Christian faith in an ongoing search for truth by interpreting traditional doctrine in the light of present day understanding.

It was founded at the end of the nineteenth century as a Church of England society but now welcomes all who share its ethos. It holds an annual conference on contemporary issues. Membership includes subscription to the journal *Modern Believing*. *Administrator* Diane Kutar, 22 The Kiln, Burgess Hill, West Sussex, RH15 0LU   *T:* 0845 345 1909
E: office@modernchurch.org.uk
W: www.modernchurch.org.uk

Montgomery Trust Lectures

This endowment by Sir Alexander Montgomery of Albury, Surrey supports public lectures particularly for theological societies and religious education teachers on the results of modern scholarship on the Bible, with an emphasis on Christian apologetics. Hosts include:

- University departments;
- Further Education colleges;
- organizations providing ministerial support;
- ordinand and preacher training;
- theological societies;
- local groupings of Religious Education teachers;
- Standing Advisory Councils for Religious Education, and
- churches and cathedrals.

Host organizations should contact the Administrator to identify a lecturer/theme. An interactive catalogue is available on our website: http://www.montgomerytrust.org.uk/ Printed copies of the catalogue are available by post. The Administrator arranges the booking with an available lecturer. The host organization gathers an audience in excess of 30 people and provides the venue. After the Lecture the host organization completes and returns to the Trust a straightforward report pro forma. Then the Trust provides the Lecturer direct with an honorarium and reimburses their travel expenses.

The Advisory committee meets in the summer when, among other duties, they approve new additions to the list of Montgomery Lecturers. Suggestions for new additions to this list are invited to our Administrator. *Advisers* Revd Prof Richard Burridge, Dean of King's College London, Very Revd David Ison, Dean of St Paul's Cathedral and Very Revd Dr John Hall, Dean of Westminster *Administrator* Springers, The Street, Coney Weston, Bury St Edmunds, IP31 1HG   *T:* 01359 221600
E: admin@montgomerytrust.org.uk
W: http://www.montgomerytrust.org.uk

Morse-Boycott Bursary Fund (formerly St Mary-of-the-Angels Song School Trust)

Founded in 1932 originally as a parochial Choir School but from 1935 to 1970 served the Church at large. Now provides financial assistance to the parents of boy choristers at cathedral choir schools throughout the UK. The Fund depends entirely on donations and legacies to build the capital from which bursaries can be provided to the needy. *Trustees* Dean and Chapter of Chichester *Administrator* The Communar, The Royal Chantry, Cathedral Cloisters, Chichester, PO19 1PX   *T:* 01243 782595
01243 812 92
E: admin@chichestercathedral.org.uk
W: www.chichestercathedral.org.uk

Mothers' Union

A Christian organization devoted to promoting marriage and the well-being of families worldwide. The Vision of Mothers' Union is 'A world where God's love is shown through loving, respectful and flourishing relationships'. This means that Mothers' Union invests in relationship. Through programmes, policy work, community outreach, Christian fellowship and prayer, Mothers' Union supports and nurtures relationships in the belief that this brings about stable families and benefits society. To do this, Mothers' Union takes positives steps to encourage marriage and family life.

Projects tackle the most urgent needs threatening relationships and communities, and work towards fostering strong families and independent, cohesive communities. Mothers' Union is not a mission-sending organization, or a development charity, although mission and development are strong characteristics of its work. Rather, it is a network of 3.6 million people, each serving Christ in their local community at the grassroots level. It has a subscribers magazine, *Families First* and a magazine for members, *Families Worldwide* which includes the prayer diary material. Further information and resources are available from the charity's website. *Worldwide President* Mrs Lynne Tembey *Chief Executive* Mrs Beverley Jullien, Mary Sumner House, 24 Tufton Street, London, SW1P 3RB   *T:* 020 7222 5533
E: mu@themothersunion.org
W: www.themothersunion.org

Mozambique and Angola Anglican Association (MANNA)

Founded by 1906, MANNA was formed to support the Diocese of Lebombo in southern Mozambique; it has now developed into supporting work within both the former Portuguese Territories, which are among the poorest in the world. While two world wars and lengthy civil wars hindered the work, since peace was established in both countries the church is growing at a great rate, predominantly through indigenous clergy who need support for their work. There are now three dioceses with well over 200 clergy.

Registered Charity no. 262818. *Chair* Ven Christopher Cunliffe, Archdeacon of Derby *General Secretary* Elizabeth Thomas, 1 The Green, Marcham, Oxfordshire, OX13 6NE
T: 07801 523461
E: elizabeth@maninga.org
W: www.manna-anglican.org

National Archdeacons' Forum

The Forum was founded in the early 1990s to offer support, training and development for archdeacons in the Church of England and the Church in Wales, including the deans of the Channel Islands and the archdeacons of HM Forces. The Forum also keeps in touch with Church of Scotland Presbytery Clerks on matters of common concern.

The Forum consists of representatives from each of the archdeacons' regional meetings and, over the years, has developed a provision both for new archdeacons, and for the continuing development of those who are archdeacons. In particular, it arranges a National Archdeacons' Conference every two years, and a New Archdeacons' Conference every nine months. *Chair* The Very Revd Tim Barker *National Executive Officer* The Revd Canon Norman Boakes *Administrator* Jackie Freestone
T: 020 7898 1407
E: jackie.freestone@churchofengland.org

National Archives, The

Records of central government and courts of law from the Norman Conquest (Domesday Book) to the recent past (for example, the Suez Campaign). Kew, Richmond-upon-Thames, TW9 4DU
T: 020 8876 3444
W: www.nationalarchives.gov.uk

National Association of Diocesan Advisers in Women's Ministry

NADAWM is a national network of diocesan advisers, appointed by their Bishop, for the purpose of advising in relation to the ministry of ordained women in the Church of England. This work involves monitoring the culture in which women clergy exercise their roles, consultng with those women, supporting them in their work, celebrating their ministry, acting as advocates of ordained women in a wide range of ways and contexts and advising bishops accordingly. *Chair* The Ven Rosemary Lain-Priestly *Treasurer* The Revd Hilary Jones *Secretary* The Revd Robbin Clark, 15b College Green, Worcester, WR1 2LH
E: rclark@glosdioc.org.uk

National Churches Trust

The National Churches Trust is the only national independent charity dedicated to promoting and supporting church buildings of historic, architectural and community value across the UK. The successor to the Historic Churches Preservation Trust (HCPT), the Trust offers grants mainly for structural repairs, new facilities and improved access, promotes the benefit to communities of church buildings and inspires everyone to value and enjoy them.

Registered charity no. 1119845. *Patron* HM The Queen *Chairman of Trustees* Luke March *Chief Executive* Claire Walker *Grants Manager* Alison Pollard, 7 Tufton Street, London, SW1P 3QB
T: 020 7222 0605
E: info@nationalchurchestrust.org
W: www.nationalchurchestrust.org

National Council for Social Concern

The charity (also known by the short titles 'Concern' and 'Social Concern') has promoted a wide range of activities in connection with the Church of England, but in recent years has had a particular interest in aspects of the criminal justice system and in issues arising from addictions. It works closely with the Church of England Board for Social Responsibility. Details from the Secretary. *Presidents* The Archbishops of Canterbury and York *Chairman* The Rt Revd Ian Brackley *Secretary* Mr Francis MacNamara, 3 Vinson Road, Liss, GU33 7NE
T: 01730 300974
07958 425927
E: info@socialconcern.org.uk
W: www.socialconcern.org.uk

New England Company

A charity founded 1649. It is the senior English missionary society. *Governor* Mr T. C. Stephenson *Treasurer* D. M. F. Scott *Secretary* Nikki Johnson, Flinders Cottage, The Street, Bolney, West Sussex, RH17 5QW
T: 01444 882898
E: johnsonnikki@yahoo.co.uk
W: www.newenglandcompany.org

Newton's Trust

Established to provide financial assistance to needy widows, widowers, separated or divorced spouses and unmarried children of deceased clergy and to divorced or separated spouses of clergy of the Church of England, the Church in Wales and the Scottish Episcopal Church. Applications are considered by the Trustees, and one-off cash grants are

OTHER ORGANIZATIONS

made at their discretion. The Trustees meet four times a year in March, June, September and December. *Chairman* The Ven George Frost *Treasurer* Mr John Allen *Secretary* Mr D. E. Wallington, The Secretary to Newton's Trust, St Mary's House, The Close, Lichfield, WS13 7LD   *T:* 01543 302924 (Evenings)
E: newtonslichfield@gmail.com

Nikaean Club
Founded in 1925 as an association of Anglican clergy and laity. It provides the ecumenical ministry of the Archbishop of Canterbury with a network of ecumenical expertise and the capacity to offer hospitality to visiting Christian leaders, heads of non-Anglican churches and international ecumenical bodies. *Chair* Mr Richard Austen *Guestmaster* The Revd Dr Will Adam *Hon Secretary* Mrs Elspeth Coke *Hon Treasurer* Revd Martin Macdonald, Lambeth Palace, London, SE1 7JU   *W:* nikaeanclub.org.uk

Nikaean Ecumenical Trust
Founded in 1992 and relaunched in 2002, the Trust exists to support ecumenical links between the Church of England and Christian churches overseas. It acts as the charitable wing of the Nikaean Club (see separate entry) and receives support from its members as well as from other Anglican bodies and individuals. It has also acquired the assets of the former Harold Buxton Trust, thanks to the generous co-operation of the SPCK.
    The Trust's principal activity at present is to provide grants to scholars from needy, non-Anglican Churches overseas (particularly the Orthodox and Oriental Orthodox Churches) who wish to study at colleges in the UK which are specifically Anglican or have strong Anglican connections. As the funds are still relatively modest, donations towards the work of the Trust are welcome. *Chair* Vacancy *Hon Secretary* Mrs Margery Roberts, 7 Nunnery Stables, St Albans, AL1 2AS
          T: 01727 856626
E: robertssopwellnunnery@btopenworld.com

Number 1 Trust Fund
Founded in 1909 for holding property and investments for the promotion of catholic practice and teaching within the Church of England, reformed by the Fidelity Trust Act 1977, and incorporated by the Charity Commissioners in 1996. One trustee is appointed by each of the Abbot of Elmore, the Superior of the Community of the Resurrection, the President of the Church Union, the President of the Society for the Maintenance of the Faith, the Master of the Guardians of the Shrine at Walsingham, the Principal of Pusey House, Oxford and the Principal of St Stephen's House, Oxford.

Chairman The Revd Canon R. Ward *Trustees* The Rt Revd J. M. R. Baker, The Revd A. A. Mayoss, Mr J. D. Hebblethwaite, the Rt Revd P. J. North, Dr B. J. T. Hanson, Canon Dr P. E. Ursell, 7 Hampstead Square, London, NW3 1AB   *T:* 07821 108769
E: william.davage@stx.ox.ac.uk

Office of Communications (Ofcom)
Ofcom is the independent regulator and competition authority for the UK communications industries, with responsibilities across television, video-on-demand programme services, radio, telecommunications, postal services and the airwaves over which wireless devices operate. Ofcom, Riverside House, 2a Southwark Bridge Road, London, SE1 9HA
          Textphone: 020 7981 3043
          E: contact@ofcom.org.uk
          W: www.ofcom.org.uk

OMF International (UK) (formerly China Inland Mission)
We serve the church and seek to bring the gospel to all the peoples of East Asia. We help place Christians with professional skills in China and other Asian countries, and share the love of Christ with East Asians worldwide. *National Directors* Peter and Christine Rowan, Station Approach, Borough Green, Sevenoaks, TN15 8BG   *T:* 01732 887299
          E: omf@omf.org.uk
          W: www.omf.org.uk

Open Synod Group
The Open Synod Group provides a safe space in which Christians of all persuasions can meet and discuss any issues without fear of censure. The meetings are a mixture of interactive meetings about matters of concern and social events to foster friendships. The magazine attracts articles from a wide range of contributors of all shades of churchmanship. *President* Rt Revd Trevor Willmott *Chairman* Mrs Caroline Spencer *Secretary* Mrs Debbie McIsaac *Treasurer and Membership Secretary* Mr John Freeman, 11 Orchard Way, Wymeswold, LE12 6SW   *E:* stephen4747@live.co.uk
          W: www.opensynodgroup.org.uk

Ordinands' Association
The Ordinands' Association exists to support and represent all those in training for ordination – whether part-time or full-time, in a college or on a course. It represents the needs and views of ordinands to the Church of England's Ministry Division via a network of elected representatives, who meet together every term. Its aim is that all ordinands receive the best possible training for ministry. OA represents all those sponsored by an Anglican Bishop for ordained ministry in

England, Ireland, Scotland and Wales, as well as those training as evangelists with the Church Army. Prior to 2015, OA was known as The Association of Ordinands and Candidates for Ministry (AOCM).

OA holds three meetings a year, and every training course (both residential and non-residential) is encouraged to send an elected representative. At the meetings, we consider issues relating to the training and support of current ordinands, and longer-term questions which have a bearing on the way ordinands will be trained and supported in future. Representatives from Church House and General Synod are often invited to these meetings to aid communication and accountability. Alongside this, the Ordinands' Association provides a forum for members of different colleges to support each other through prayer and the building of relationships.   *E:* chair@ordinands.org.uk
W: www.ordinands.org.uk

Ordination Candidate Funds (General)
See separate entries for Anglo-Catholic Ordination Candidates' Fund, Bristol Clerical Education Society, Church Pastoral Aid Society Ministers in Training Fund, Cleaver Ordination Candidates' Fund, Elland Society Ordination Fund,

Overseas Bishoprics' Fund
Founded in 1841 to assist towards the endowment and maintenance of bishoprics in any part of the world and to act as trustees of episcopal endowment funds. *Chairman* Dr Charles Mynors *Secretary* Mr Stephen Lyon
T: 020 7898 1571
E: stephenplyon@gmail.com

Oxford Mission
Founded in 1880, the Oxford Mission consists of two Religious Communities, the Brotherhood of St Paul and the Christa Sevika Sangha. It has houses in India and Bangladesh. Their work is pastoral, medical and educational and is carried on in the Dioceses of Kolkata and Dhaka. India: Col Subir Ghosh (Administrator); Bangladesh: Father Francis Pande SPB, Sister Superior, Sister Jharna *General Secretary* Mrs Mary K. Marsh, 18 Market Place, Romsey, SO51 8NA
T: 01794 515004
E: oxfordmission@aol.com
W: www.oxford-mission.org

Papua New Guinea Church Partnership
PNGCP is the voluntary agency through which the Anglican Church of Papua New Guinea and the Church of England relate to each other. In 2007 ACPNG celebrated 30 years as an independent province in the Anglican Communion. Registered as a charity in 1960, the New Guinea Mission was founded in 1891 to give support to the then Diocese of New Guinea in prayer, by sending staff and raising money.

In 1977, when the Province was inaugurated with five dioceses, the agency name was changed to Papua New Guinea Church Partnership in order to reflect the reciprocal nature of the work: giving and receiving. ACPNG continues to request people with skills and experience for governmentally approved support posts, mainly in health and administration. Most years see a steady trickle of 'gap year' students and medical and nursing electives travelling to PNG to gain never-to-be-forgotten experience in the poorest, most populous Pacific nation. An annual grant goes to the provincial budget, money is raised for provincially approved projects, and audited accounts are sent to the UK. *President* The Rt Revd Peter Ramsden *Chairman* The Revd Paul Bagott *General Secretary* Miss Louise Ewington
T: 020 7313 3918
E: pngcpoffice@gmail.com
W: www.pngcp.com

Paradox Ministries
Paradox Ministries encourages Christians to understand and pray about the Israeli – Palestinian Conflict, seeing it through the eyes of both people groups involved, and taking the needs, fear and pain of both sides seriously. Its director, who was Rector of a church in the Old City of Jerusalem for a number of years, circulates a free email newsletter, speaks at seminars and encourages support of indigenous reconciliation ministry in Jerusalem. The website contains background material, advice to clergy and regular news updates, together with a blog. *Directors (Chairman)* Revd Tony Higton *(Executive)* Mrs Patricia Higton, 2 Heggerscale Cottages, Kaber, Kirkby Stephen, CA17 4HZ   *T:* 01768 372159
E: tony@higton.info
W: www.prayerforpeace.org.uk

Peache Trustees
A Trust holding the Rights of Presentation to a number of benefices. Evangelical tradition. *Secretary* Canon Roger Salisbury, 6 Church Street, Widcombe, Bath, BA2 6AZ
T: 01225 489076
E: patronage@btinternet.com

Philip Usher Memorial Fund
Founded in 1948. Grants annual scholarships to Anglican priests, deacons or ordinands, preferably under 35 years of age, to study in a predominantly Orthodox country. *Chairman* Vacancy *Administrator* Mr Tobi Lyanda, The Parish Office, St John's Church, Lansdowne Crescent, London, W11 2NN
T: 020 7727 4752
E: officemanager@stjohnsnottinghill.com

Pilgrim Trust, The

The Pilgrim Trust considers applications from charities and exempt public bodies. The Trust operates two programmes: Social Welfare and Preservation and Scholarship. More details on the programme themes can be found in the Trust's guidelines which are available on the website.

The Pilgrim Trust makes large annual block grants to the Church Buildings Council and the National Churches Trust. Church of England churches seeking grants for the conservation of items of church furniture e.g. repairs to bells/organs/monuments etc. should apply directly to the Church Buildings Council. Applications for repairs to the fabric of a building should be directed towards the National Churches Trust. *Director* Miss Georgina Nayler, Clutha House, 10 Storeys Gate, London, SW1P 3AY   *T:* 020 7222 4723
E: info@thepilgrimtrust.org.uk
W: www.thepilgrimtrust.org.uk

Pilsdon at Malling Community

The Pilsdon Community in Dorset established a new community in 2004, taking over the former Ewell Monastery site next to St Mary's Abbey, West Malling, Kent. The community is dedicated to the same ideals of the Christian Gospel as the original community in Dorset, offering community living, sustainable self-sufficient lifestyle and open hospitality, particularly to those who are homeless, recovering from addiction, mental illness or breakdown.

The community consists of four to five community members (leadership) and resident volunteers, up to twelve long-stay resident guests and up to two visitors and wayfarers/asylum seekers. The six acres of land and two large glasshouses are used for livestock and horticulture. The 16th-century barn chapel is used for daily offices, and the Eucharist is celebrated twice weekly.

Enquiries are always welcome. Please see our website for more details and also the Pilsdon Community entry.

Registered Charity no. 1123682. Company no. 6218667. *Guardian* The Revd Viv Ashworth *Treasurer* Mr Albert Granville *Admissions* The Guardian *Enquiries* Any community member, 27 Water Lane, West Malling, ME19 6HH
T: 01732 870279
E: pilsdon@pilsdonatmalling.org.uk
W: www.pilsdonatmalling.org.uk

Pilsdon Community

The Pilsdon Community is dedicated to the ideals of the Christian gospel in the context of community living and open hospitality. The Community at any one time will comprise between five to seven community members (leadership) and their children, about twenty guests (staying from one month to several years), up to six visitors (staying one day to a week) and up to ten wayfarers (staying up to three days). Many of the guests have experienced a crisis in their lives (e.g. mental breakdown, alcoholism, drug addiction, marital breakdown, abuse, homelessness, prison, etc.).

Pilsdon provides an environment of communal living, manual work, creative opportunities (pottery, art, crafts, music, etc.) recreation, worship and pastoral care, to rebuild people's lives, self-respect, confidence and faith. Founded in 1958 by an Anglican priest, the Community occupies an Elizabethan manor house and its outbuildings and smallholding of thirteen acres, seven miles from the sea near Bridport.

The community life is inspired by the monastic tradition and the Little Gidding Community. The worship and spirituality is Anglican at its root and sacramental, but ecumenical in its practice. Pilsdon welcomes guests of all faiths and none as well as all races and cultures. are welcome.

Membership enquiries should be made to the Warden, enquiries from guests and respite visitors should be directed to the Admissions Officer. More information and application forms are available on our website. *Warden* Revd Michael Deegan *Administrator* Alan Frost, Pilsdon Manor, Pilsdon, Bridport, DT6 5NZ
T: 01308 868308
E: pilsdon@btconnect.com
W: www.pilsdon.org.uk

Plainsong and Medieval Music Society

The Plainsong and Medieval Music Society, founded in 1888, exists to promote the performance and study of liturgical chant and medieval polyphony, through the publication of editions, facsimiles and scholarly articles, and through educational and liaison events. New members are always welcome and membership includes a subscription to the Society's twice-yearly journal, *Plainsong and Medieval Music*, invitations to the Society's events and discounts on many of the Society's publications. *Chair* Dr Emma Hornby *Administrator* Emma Hembry, School of Music, Bangor University College Road, Bangor Gwynedd, LL57 2DG
E: admin@plainsong.org.uk
W: www.plainsong.org.uk

Praxis

Founded in 1990, Praxis is sponsored by the Liturgical Commission, the Alcuin Club and the Grove Group for the Renewal of Worship. Its aims are:

- to enrich the practice and understanding of worship in the Church of England;
- to serve congregations and clergy in their exploration of God's call to worship; and

- to provide a forum in which different worshipping traditions can meet and interact.

Praxis events include day meetings on a whole variety of subjects related to liturgy. Full details are always available on the website. *Chair* The Revd Jo Spreadbury *Secretary* Revd Richard Curtis *Administrator* The Revd Peter Furber, 3 Ravenswood, 23 Wimborne Road, Bournemouth, BH2 6LZ *T:* 01202 296886
E: praxis@praxisworship.org.uk
W: www.praxisworship.org.uk

Prayer Book Society
The Prayer Book Society exists to promote the use of the Book of Common Prayer and to defend the worship and doctrine contained therein. Diocesan branches provide members with regular meetings, Prayer Book services and advice on church matters. It runs the yearly Cranmer Awards for young people.

It has a popular mail order book company stocking a wide range of religious books and Christmas cards. Donations and memberships are appreciated and needed. Membership form from 0118 984 2582 or from any Secretary shown on the website. *Patron* HRH The Prince of Wales *Ecclesiastical Patron* The Bishop of London *Chairman* Miss Prudence Dailey, The Studio, Copyhold Farm, Goring Heath, RG8 7RT *T:* 0118 984 2582
E: pbs.admin@pbs.org.uk
W: www.pbs.org.uk

Pusey House, Oxford
Chaplaincy and library founded in 1884 to continue the work of Dr Pusey, academic and pastoral, in Oxford. *Principal* The Revd Dr George Westhaver *Chaplain* The Revd Mark Stafford *Librarian* Anna James, Pusey House, St Giles, Oxford, OX1 3LZ
T: 01865 278415 (Office)
01865 288024 (Library)
E: pusey.office@stx.ox.ac.uk
pusey.librarian@stx.ox.ac.uk
W: www.puseyhouse.org.uk

Pyncombe Charity
Income about £10,000 p.a. applied to assist needy serving ordained clergy in financial difficulties due to illness, or occasionally other special circumstances, within the immediate family. Applications must be made through the diocesan bishop. *Secretary* Mrs Rita Butterworth, Wingletye, Hagleys Green Crowcombe, Taunton, TA4 4AQ
E: joeandrita@waitrose.com

Queen Victoria Clergy Fund
Founded in 1897 to raise money towards the support of Church of England parochial clergy. All the Fund's income is disbursed annually in block grants to dioceses specifically for the help of the clergy. Requests for assistance should be directed to the diocese. *Chairman* John Booth *Secretary* Chris Palmer CBE, Church House, Great Smith St, London, SW1P 3AZ *T:* 020 7898 1311
E: chris.palmer@churchofengland.org

Radius
Founded in 1929 to promote drama which throws light on the human condition and to support people who create and use drama as a means of Christian understanding. Organizes training events, publishes a magazine and a small number of plays, offers a playwrights' assessment service and holds a collection of photocopiable typescripts suitable for use in churches and by church groups. *Patrons* Dame Judi Dench, Lord Williams of Oystermouth *Patron Magazine/General Enquiries/Council Vice-Chair* Margaret Hunt, 7 Lenton Road, The Park, Nottingham, NG7 1DP *T:* 0115 941 3922
E: office@radius.org.uk
W: www.radiusdrama.org.uk

RE Today Services
RE Today Services is wholly owned by the charity Christian Education, and is committed to the teaching of the major world faiths in religious education, and to an accurate and fair representation of their beliefs, values and practices in all its teaching materials. It carries forward the work of the Christian Education Movement (CEM). *Chief Executive* Zoe Keens, 5–6 Imperial Court, Sovereign Road, Birmingham, B30 3FH *T:* 0121 458 1131
E: admin@retoday.org.uk
W: www.retoday.org.uk

Reader Missionary Studentship Association
Founded in 1904 to offer financial assistance to Readers training as priests for service in the Church overseas. *Chairman* Mr G. E. Crowley *Hon Treasurer* Mr Ron Edinborough *Hon Secretary* Dr Ann Whitfield, 30 Balmoral Drive, Methley, Leeds, LS26 9LE *T:* 01977 602176
E: secretary@rmsa.org.uk
W: www.rmsa.org.uk

Rebecca Hussey's Book Charity
Established in 1714 to give grants of religious and useful books to institutions in the United Kingdom. *Clerk to the Trustees* Elizabeth LeMoine, 29 Hearnshaw Street, London, E14 7BU *E:* elizabethlemoine@gmail.com

Reform
Established in 1993, Reform is a network of individuals and churches within the Church of England. Reform is committed to reforming the Church of England from within according to the Holy Scriptures. *Chairman* The Revd Mark Burkill *Director* Susie Leafe *Administrators*

Jonathan Lockwood, PO Box 1183, Sheffield, S10 3YA   *T:* 0114 230 9256
    E: administrator@reform.org.uk
    W: www.reform.org.uk

Relate
Relate is the country's largest relationship counselling organization, providing help and support for couples, singles, families and in schools. Also the national organisation for sex therapy and a leading source of information and advice online. Help is available at around 600 locations nationwide and by calling 0300 100 1234 or visit the website: www.relate.org.uk *Chief Executive Officer* Ruth Sutherland, Premier House, Lakeside, Doncaster, DN4 5RA
    T: 0300 100 1234 (Helpline)
    W: www.relate.org.uk

Religious Education Council of England and Wales
The Religious Education Council of England and Wales seeks to represent the collective interests of a wide variety of organizations and communities in deepening and strengthening provision for religious education in schools and colleges. The Council was formed in 1973 and is open to national organizations which have a special interest in the teaching of religious education.

The present membership of more than 60 organizations includes representation from the main Christian denominations, the world faiths, Humanists UK and the main educational bodies with professional and academic RE interests. *Chair* Professor Trevor Cooling *Deputy Chair* Dave Francis *Chief Executive Officer* Rudolf Elliott Lockhart *Company Secretary* Peter Ward, CAN Mezzanine, 49–51 East Road, London, N1 6AN   *T:* 020 7250 8166
    E: info@religiouseducationcouncil.org.uk
    W: www.religiouseducationcouncil.org.uk

Retired Clergy Association
Founded in 1927 to act as a bond of friendship in prayer and mutual help to retired clergy. Membership at 31 July 2017 was 3,578. The Association works closely with Bishops and Diocesan Retirement Officers throughout the Church of England to encourage local groups of retired clergy for fellowship and support. It is often consulted by the Church of England Pensions Board on housing issues and other matters of mutual concern. Its officers also meet regularly with the Ministry Division of the Church of England to discuss matters of particular concern to retired clergy.

Registered Charity number 1172186 *President* The Rt Revd Ian Brackley *Chairman* Rt Revd David Jennings *Secretary and Treasurer*

Revd David Phypers, 15 Albert Road, Chaddesden, Derby, DE21 6SL
    T: 01332 239134
    E: secretary@rcacoe.org
    W: www.rcacoe.org

Retreat Association
The Association comprises these Christian retreat groups:

* Association for Promoting Retreats
* Baptist Union Retreat Group
* Catholic Network for Retreats and Spirituality
* Reflect (Methodists supporting spirituality and retreats)
* Affiliates of the Retreat Association

It offers information and resources about retreats to both would-be and seasoned retreatants, facilitates spiritual direction, promotes the work of retreat houses and coordinates training opportunities and regional activity. *Retreats*, an ecumenical journal listing retreat houses and their programmes in the UK and beyond, is published annually (2017 edition £11.00 incl p+p). Other literature available; send for publications list. *Director* Alison MacTier, Clare Charity Centre, Wycombe Road, Saunderton, Bucks, HP14 4BF   *T:* 01494 569056
    E: info@retreats.org.uk
    W: www.retreats.org.uk

Revd Dr George Richards' Charity
Founded in 1837 to provide financial assistance to clergy of the Church of England forced to retire early owing to ill-health. Widows, widowers and dependants can also apply for assistance. *Secretary* Dr P. D. Simmons, 96 Thomas More House, Barbican, London, EC2Y 8BU   *T:* 020 7588 5583

Richmond Fellowship
Established in 1959, Richmond Fellowship (RF) currently operates over 100 services for people with mental health problems throughout England. These include supported housing, registered care homes and care homes with nursing support, employment and training services, individual self-directed packages of care and community and day services. For further information contact us or visit our website. *Chief Executive* Derek Caren *PA to Chief Executive* Marise Willis, 80 Holloway Rd, London, N7 8JG   *T:* 020 7697 3300
    E: communications@ richmondfellowship.org.uk
    W: www.richmondfellowship.org.uk

RNIB (Royal National Institute of Blind People)
RNIB (Royal National Institute of Blind People) is a charity which supports blind and partially sighted people in remaining independent by:

- giving free advice about eye conditions, benefit entitlement and specialist and local support;
- providing employment services and practical help for children and their families;
- suggesting ideas on continuing to enjoy hobbies and leisure time;
- recommending everyday items and gadgets to make life easier; and
- offering a listening ear.

President Dame Gail Ronson DBE *Chairman* Kevin Carey *Chief Executive* Lesley-Anne Alexander, 105 Judd St, London, WC1H 9NE
T: 0303 123 9999 (Helpline)
020 7388 1266
E: helpline@rnib.org.uk
W: www.rnib.org.uk

Royal Alexandra and Albert School
A large coeducational state boarding school for pupils aged 7–18, situated in 260 acres of park on Reigate Hill just outside the M25.

Bursaries are available for applicants who are without one or both parents or who would benefit from boarding education because of their home circumstances. Bursaries of two-thirds of the fees are also available for children of clergy. In exceptional circumstances, further bursary support can be provided.

The school has excellent boarding and sports facilities and a successful Sixth Form of almost 200 pupils. Contact the Headmaster for further details. *Patron* HM the Queen *President* HRH the Duchess of Gloucester *Headmaster* Paul D. Spencer Ellis *Foundation Secretary* Diana Bromley, Gatton Park, Reigate, RH2 0TW   *T:* 01737 649001
E: headmaster@gatton-park.org.uk
W: www.raa-school.co.uk

Royal Asylum of St Ann's Society
The Society, founded in 1702, offers grants towards the expenses of educating children, from the age of 11, at boarding or day schools. Most, but not all, of those aided are children of clergy of the Church of England; however, in the first instance clergy should approach the Corporation of the Sons of the Clergy. The Society welcomes collections, donations and legacies towards this purpose. *President* The Dean of Westminster *Chairman* Mr Peter Ashby *Secretary* Mr David Hanson, King Edward's School, Witley, Petworth Rd, Wormley, GU8 5SG

Royal College of Organists
Founded in 1864 and incorporated by Royal Charter 1893 'to promote the art of organ-playing and choir training'. Holds lectures, recitals and master-classes nationwide. Examinations for Certificate, Associateship, Fellowship, Licentiateship in Teaching and Diploma in Choral Directing. Holds a large specialist library and archive, and publishes a scholarly journal every year. Membership open to all who take an interest in the work and profession of the organist and in organ music. *Patron* HM The Queen *President* James O'Donnell *General Manager* Kim Gilbert, PO Box 56357, London, SE16 7XL   *T:* 05600 767208
E: admin@rco.org.uk
W: www.rco.org.uk

Royal Martyr Church Union
Founded in 1906:

- Ever to cherish the sacred remembrance of Charles the First, King and Martyr, both in public worship and private devotion, and to this end to promote the restoration of his name to its proper place in the calendar of the worldwide Anglican Communion, and the observance of 30 January, the day of his martyrdom, by suitable services in the Book of Common Prayer and elsewhere.
- To maintain the principles of faith, loyalty and liberty for which the King died – the faith of the Church, loyalty to the Crown, and the ancient liberties of the people. Holds annual commemorative eucharists in London and Edinburgh. Subscription £15.00 p.a.to include *Royal Martyr Annual.*

Chairman Tom Kerr *Hon Secretary and Treasurer* David Roberts, 7 Nunnery Stables, St Albans, AL1 2AS   *T:* 01727 856626

Royal School of Church Music
The Royal School of Church Music (RSCM) is the leading organization promoting and supporting church music. It is an educational charity dedicated to raising standards and promoting the best use of music in every style of Christian worship and in every denomination. It is funded through membership subscriptions, publication sales, course fees and the charitable support of individuals and institutions.

It provides musical and educational resources to train, develop and inspire clergy, music leaders, musicians, singers and congregations. Its *Voice for Life* programme is a training scheme for singers of all ages that can be used by individual churches and schools, and *Church Music Skills* provides practical training for those leading music in worship. These programmes are complemented by workshops, festivals and short residential courses, and a network of volunteers runs events to meet local needs in the UK and five overseas branches.

The RSCM publishes music through the RSCM Press, including musical resources for Common Worship, and RSCM Music Direct provides a fast and efficient mail-order service for music from all publishers. Affiliated

churches and schools and individual members receive *Church Music Quarterly*, a highly informative and interesting magazine for all those concerned with church music, and *Sunday by Sunday*, an essential liturgy planner aiding those who plan and lead worship to enhance it through music appropriate to the day. Appointed the official music agency for the Church of England from April 1996. *President* The Archbishop of Canterbury *Chairman* Lord Brian Gill *Director* Vacancy, 19 The Close, Salisbury, SP1 2EB 			*T:* 01722 424848
			01722 424841 (membership)
				E: enquiries@rscm.com
				W: www.rscm.com

Rural Theology Association

Founded in 1981 to provide a forum for the rural churches and to focus for the Church at large the distinctive ways, needs and contributions of the rural. Its aims are to study the gospel and develop theology in a rural setting, to encourage the development of patterns of ministry and mission appropriate to the countryside today, and to discover ways of living in the countryside which embody a Christian response to the world. It publishes the journal *Rural Theology*. *President* Revd Prof Leslie Francis *Chairman* Rt Revd Mark Rylands *Secretary* Canon Stephen Cope *Treasurer* Revd Dr Christine Brewster, Vicarage, 28 Park Ave, Withernsea, HU19 2JU
				T: 01964 611426
		E: secretary@rural-theology.org.uk
		W: www.rural-theology.org.uk

Saint George's Trust

The Trust exists to give grants to individuals to further the work of the Church of England. The Fellowship of Saint John (UK) Trust Association is the sole trustee. The funds at the Trust's disposal do not permit large grants for restoration projects, or any long-term financial support. The wide remit enables it to help a large number of individuals for sabbaticals, gap years and the like to a maximum of £350. All applications should be sent, together with a stamped addressed envelope, to the Trust with as much supporting documentation as possible. St Edward's House, 22 Great College St, London, SW1P 3QA

Samaritans

Samaritans is an organization available round the clock, every single day of the year, to those struggling to cope. People can talk to them any time they like, in their own way, about whatever's getting to them. They do not have to be suicidal to get in touch. *Chief Exec* Ms Ruth Sutherland, The Upper Mill, Kingston Road, Ewell, Surrey, KT17 2AF
			T: 020 8394 8300 (admin)
				E: admin@samaritans.org
				W: www.samaritans.org

Sandford St Martin (Church of England) Trust

Established in 1978, the Trust's initial purpose was to recognize and promote excellence in religious broadcasting, and to encourage Christian involvement in television and radio at both national and local levels. Founded through the vision of the late Sir David Wills, its origins were Anglican, but reflecting the multi-faith nature of contemporary Britain, it currently seeks not only to promote high-quality programmes inspired by any of the major world religions but to develop a higher profile in advocating the importance of religious broadcasting. The Trust holds an annual broadcast media awards ceremony at Lambeth Palace: for details see: http://sandfordawards.org.uk/ Room 202, Church House, Great Smith Street, London, SW1P 3AZ
	E: SandfordSMT@churchofengland.org.uk
			W: http://sandfordawards.org.uk/

Sarum College

Sarum College is a Christian study and research centre based in Salisbury's Cathedral Close. Our courses, conferences, and facilities are open to people of all faiths and no faith. Founded in 1995, the College is based in historic grade I listed buildings with a heritage of theological education stretching back more than 150 years in Salisbury's Cathedral Close.

Our educational programme is organised in seven Sarum Centres of Learning. These Centres offer a variety of courses within our specialist areas of Contemporary Spirituality, Theology, Imagination and Culture, Formation in Ministry, Liturgy and Worship, Human Flourishing, Encountering the Bible and Leadership Learning. Postgraduate programmes are validated by the University of Winchester and can lead to a postgraduate certificate, postgraduate diploma or an MA degree. Some places are set aside for those who wish to attend postgraduate modules without seeking a qualification. Short courses range from short evening lectures to four-day residentials and plenty in between. The content also ranges widely, from academic to experimental to leisurely.

We also offer a range of ministry training programmes validated by Durham University and students can choose full-time, part-time or practice-based study and training. These courses create opportunities for all to learn, to think, to speak and to act with greater theological confidence.

Within the college is a Christian bookshop with specialist and general titles in stock for browsing and mail order facility and a library with an outstanding collection of more than 40,000 books covering all denominations. Sarum College's education, accommodation and services are available to all, whether you're

studying on one of our courses, staying the night as a bed and breakfast guest, hiring one of our meeting rooms or just popping in to enjoy one of our fresh home-made meals. *Principal* The Revd Canon Professor James Woodward *Bursar/Deputy Principal* Mr Mark Manterfield *Director of Learning Resources* Jenny Monds *Residential Services Manager* Linda Cooper, 19 The Close, Salisbury, SP1 2EE *T:* 01722 424800
E: info@sarum.ac.uk
W: www.sarum.ac.uk

Sarum St Michael Educational Charity
Personal grants may be awarded for further or higher education, to those who live, work or study within the Salisbury or adjacent dioceses (also to former students of the college). Bursaries may be awarded to those who live or study within the Salisbury diocese or adjacent dioceses, who intend to train to teach RE.

Grants may be made to local schools, mainly for RE and worship resources. Grants may be made to parishes within the Salisbury diocese, for work with children and young people. Corporate grants may be made, where funds permit, to certain projects within the Salisbury diocese and adjacent dioceses. The governors meet four times a year to consider applications. Grants are not awarded retrospectively. Please consult our website for closing dates for applications, and to download application forms. Member of the Association of Church College Trusts (see separate entry). *Clerk to the Governors*, First Floor, 27A Castle St, Salisbury, SP1 1TT *T:* 01722 422296
E: clerk@sarumstmichael.org
W: www.sarumstmichael.org

SASRA (The Soldiers' and Airmen's Scripture Readers Association)
Founded in 1838 to present the claims of Christ to the men and women serving in the Army and later the RAF, to promote interdenominational Christian fellowship among them and to encourage individual serving Christians to witness to their comrades. *Chairman* Brigadier Ian Dobbie *General Secretary* Sqdn Ldr Colin Woodland, Havelock House, Barrack Rd, Aldershot, GU11 3NP *T:* 01252 310033
E: admin@sasra.org.uk
W: www.sasra.org.uk

SCALA (School Chaplains and Leaders Association) (formerly the Bloxham Project/School Chaplains Assocation
Founded in 1967, charged with developing an understanding of Christian faith and values in education. SCALA offers:

- a spiritual, inspirational and practical resource for schools and educators, helping

to develop spirituality, pastoral care, Christian leadership and ethos and values
- a forum for debate and the exchange of best practice
- consultancy services and tailor-made training, day events, regional meetings, a termly publication and some other materials.
- a network of schools across denominations and sectors
- a resource for headteachers, leadership teams, chaplains, teaching and pastoral staff.

Chair of Trustees Dr Priscilla Chadwick *Director* Revd Gordon Parry *Administrator* Paul Hansford, SCALA, University of Chichester, Bognor Regis Campus, Upper Bognor Road, Bognor Regis, West Sussex, PO21 1HR
T: 01243 812134
E: admin@scala.uk.net
W: www.scala.uk.net

Scout Association, The
Scouting exists to actively engage and support young people in their personal development, empowering them to make a positive contribution to society. Scouting is open to all from six years onwards. Membership 500,000. *Chief Scout* Lt Cdr (Hons) Bear Grylls RN *Chief Executive* Matt Hyde, Gilwell Park, Bury Rd, Chingford, London, E4 7QW
T: 0845 300 1818
0208 433 7100
E: info.centre@scouts.org.uk
W: www.scouts.org.uk

Scripture Union
Scripture Union seeks to make the Christian faith known to children, young people and families and to support the Church through resources, Bible reading and training. SU's work in Britain includes schools work, Bible ministries, digital and conventional publishing, training, evangelism, holidays, missions and family ministry. Scripture Union is active in more than 100 countries. *National Director* Revd Tim Hastie-Smith *Development Director* Mr Terry Clutterham *Managing Director* Mr David Thorpe, 207–209 Queensway, Bletchley, Milton Keynes, MK2 2EB *T:* 01908 856000
E: info@scriptureunion.org.uk
W: www.scriptureunion.org.uk

Seamen's Friendly Society of St Paul
Trust administered by Alton Abbey, able to offer financial assistance to merchant sailors. *Contact* Rt Revd Dom Giles Hill OSB, Alton Abbey, Abbey Rd, Beech, Alton, Hampshire, GU34 4AP *T:* 01420 562145
01420 563575
E: giles@altonabbey.org.uk

Servants of Christ the King

Founded in 1942 by Canon Roger Lloyd of Winchester. A movement of groups or 'Companies' of Christians who seek to develop a corporate life by praying together in silence, with disciplined discussion. They actively wait upon God to be led by the Holy Spirit, and undertake to do together any work which they are given by him to do. *Enquirers' Correspondent* Dr Pauline Waters, Swallowfield, Wheelers Lane, Linton, Maidstone, ME17 4BN

T: 01622 743392

W: www.sck.org.uk

SGM Lifewords (formerly Scripture Gift Mission)

SGM Lifewords creates Bible resources to help people communicate God's word to today's generation. A new, research-based range uses up-to-date Bible versions and contemporary graphics. SGM publishes materials in over 200 languages for use worldwide. 1A The Chandlery, 50 Westminster Bridge Road, London, SE1 7QY

T: 020 7730 2155

E: uk@sgmlifewords.com

W: www.sgmlifewords.com

Shaftesbury Young People

Founded in 1843 to house and educate homeless children in London, the charity is now the leading voluntary sector provider of residential care for children in London. In London and Suffolk the charity also provides services for young people leaving care, and supported housing for the young homeless. Personal development is promoted through venture activities at the Arethusa Venture Centre on the Medway. *Chairman*, 34 High Street, Bromley, Kent, BR1 1EA

T: 020 8875 1555

E: info@shaftesburyoungpeople.org

W: www.shaftesburyyoungpeople.org

Sharing of Ministries Abroad (SOMA)

Founded in 1978 to serve the renewal of the Church throughout the world, particularly in the Anglican Communion, SOMA has eleven centres across the world. SOMA works for the transformation of individuals and churches, and the healing of communities and their lands through the renewing power of the Holy Spirit by intercession and sending and receiving teams worldwide on short-term mission across the Anglican Communion. A newsletter, *Sharing*, is published three times a year. *SOMA International Chairman* Most Revd Ben Kwashi *SOMA UK National Director* Revd Stephen Dinsmore *SOMA UK Finance Administrator* Steve Fincher *SOMA UK Administrator* Zena Durrant, PO Box 69, Merriott, TA18 9AP

T: 01460 279737

E: info@somauk.org

W: www.somauk.org

Sheldon (Society of Mary and Martha)

An independent ecumenical charity run by a mixed lay community providing confidential support for clergy and/or spouses, especially at times of stress, crisis, burnout or breakdown. Resources exclusively for people in ministry include the famous 12,000-mile Service weeks, Family Holiday week, and Linhay Lodges: well-appointed, self-contained accommodation for private retreats, sabbaticals, safe place, emergency bolt-hole or battery re-charge.

Programme events open to everyone include retreat and training resources for personal and spiritual growth. Hen Runs and Pig Pens available for private retreats, open to everyone. The Sheldon Centre is a beautifully converted farm with lovely views across the Teign Valley, just ten miles from the M5 and main line railway at Exeter. Fully en-suite. Facilities include Art Shed, Labyrinth, Chapels, Library and 45 acres of fields and woodlands. Good local walking. Also ideal for residential groups looking to go deeper together.

Sheldon also has a secure online mutual support, listings and reference site for people in ministry: The Sheldon Hub – doing healthy ministry together. www.sheldonhub.org *Warden* Sarah Horsman *Lay Chaplain* Sarah Horsman *Administrator* Hilary Todd, Sheldon, Dunsford, Exeter, EX6 7LE   T: 01647 252752

E: smm@sheldon.uk.com

W: www.sheldon.uk.com

Simeon's Trustees

Holds and administers the patronage of those livings in the Church of England which belong to the Trust on the principles laid down in Charles Simeon's Charge.

Executive Officer Mrs Ann Brown, 6 Angerford Avenue, Sheffield, S8   T: 0114 255 8522

E: ann.brown@simeons.org.uk

W: www.simeons.org.uk

Social Responsibility Network, The

The Network (developed from the Anglican Association for Social Responsibility) aims to share good practice, ideas and information on a wide range of issues and provide peer support and encouragement for Christian practitioners in social responsibility and related fields in England and Wales. We do this by meeting together in local and regional groups, holding an annual conference on key issues, making resources available to one another, and sharing ideas, needs and resources via our discussion e-net. Open to all Christian practitioners. *Chair* The Revd Dr David Primrose *Treasurer* Tony Oakden *Secretary* Mrs Ann Wright *Episcopal Link* The Rt Revd Dr Michael Ipgrave OBE, PO Box 414, Horley, RH6 8WL

E: wright@btinternet.com

W: www.srnet.org.uk

Society for Liturgical Study
Founded in 1978, this ecumenical society for the UK and Ireland promotes liturgical study and research, particularly amongst younger scholars. The society works through postgraduate study days and a biennial conference, and through its peer-reviewed journal, *Anaphora*, published twice a year. Membership of the Society is open to anyone, lay and ordained, with a scholarly interest in the history, development and practice of Christian worship in all its various and diverse forms. *Secretary* Mr Harvey Howlett, 88 Gainsborough Road, New Malden, KT3 5NX
E: secretary@studyliturgy.org.uk
W: www.studyliturgy.org.uk

Society for Old Testament Study
Founded in 1917 as a society for OT/HB scholars in Britain and Ireland. Scholars not resident in the British Isles may also become members. Two meetings to hear and discuss papers are arranged annually. The Society also publishes its annual Book List and is involved in other publishing activities. It maintains links with OT/HB scholars throughout the world, particularly the Dutch-Flemish OT Society with which it holds joint meetings every three years. Candidates for membership must be proficient in biblical Hebrew and be proposed by two existing members. *Hon Secretary* Dr David Shepherd, Assistant Professor of Hebrew Bible/Old Testament, Loyola Institute, Sch of Religions, Theology & Ecumenics, Old Physiology Building Trinity College, Dublin 2 Ireland *T:* 00 353 (0)1 896 4796
E: shepherd@tcd.ie
W: www.sots.ac.uk

Society for Promoting Christian Knowledge
SPCK was founded in 1698 to help people to understand – and to grow in – the Christian faith. It works to support and develop the knowledge of Christians and to interest and inform others.
Throughout its history SPCK has been associated with the spread of education and informative literature in all its forms. It is an Anglican foundation but supports a diversity of Christian traditions. The Society has been involved in publishing since its foundation, and currently publishes around 100 new titles each year. Its output includes Christian books, websites and digital items across a broad spectrum of church traditions for a wide readership from the most popular level to the highly academic. The range includes liturgy, theology, science and religion, biblical studies and spirituality, with resources for clergy, parishes and study groups.
SPCK Worldwide's International Study Guides programme is aimed particularly at those training for ministry in the global south, including many for whom English is not a first language. It depends entirely upon donations from individuals, churches and charitable trusts.
The Assemblies website (www.assemblies. org.uk) provides teachers with regularly updated materials for school assemblies which they can download free of charge. SPCK's Diffusion programme aims to make fruitful contact with those who are searching for meaning but find Christian vocabulary or churches unfamiliar, difficult or off-putting, through projects that seek to reach out to a wider audience. *President* The Archbishop of Canterbury *Chairman of the Governing Body* Rt Revd John Pritchard *Chief Executive* Mr Sam Richardson *Executive Administrator* Mrs Pat Phillips, 36 Causton St, London, SW1P 4ST
T: 020 7592 3900
E: spck@spck.org.uk
W: www.spck.org.uk / www.assemblies.org.uk

Society for the Maintenance of the Faith
Founded in 1873, the society presents, or shares in the presentation of, priests to over 90 benefices. As well as its work as a patronage body the society aims to promote Catholic teaching and practice in the Church of England at large. *President* Dr Brian Hanson *General Secretary* The Revd John Hanks, c/o The Revd John Hanks, 20 Ogleforth, York, YO1 7JG *E:* secretary@smftrust.org.uk
W: www.smftrust.org.uk

Society for the Relief of Poor Clergy (SRPC)
The committee of trustees, which conducts the society's affairs, may consider applications for assistance from:

• evangelical clergy of the Church of England, the Church in Wales, the Church of Ireland and the Scottish Episcopal Church;
• evangelical Accredited Lay workers (those who have been nationally selected, trained and licensed for Anglican ministry; Church Army Officers who have been commissioned and hold the Bishop's licence);
• widows and widowers of the above.

Grants are made to help meet the following categories of need, and the Committee has the discretionary power to consider other circumstances, but only where these are giving rise to exceptional hardship. The Society's resources are limited and grants may therefore have to be refused, even where the required conditions may have been fulfilled:

• bereavement;
• illness;

293

- removals;
- family support to enable young people to participate in a 'ministry experience' during a gap year before university;
- family support to enable children/young people of evangelical ministers to attend Christian camps, for their spiritual benefit and to develop leadership potential;
- other special needs (at the Committee's discretion).

For further details, including an application form, please contact the Secretary. *Secretary* Mrs Pauline Walden, c/o CPAS Sovereign Court One (Unit 3), Sir William Lyons Road, Coventry, CV4 7EZ   *T:* 07962 227959
E: secretary@srpc-aid.com
W: www.srpc-aid.com

Society of Archbishop Justus Ltd
The society, named after the fourth Archbishop of Canterbury, was formed in 1996 and incorporated in 1997 as a non-profit corporation in New York, USA for the purpose of using the Internet to foster and further unity among Christians, especially Anglicans. It focuses on internet information services: web and email servers that help Anglicans to be one body. Members help install, operate and maintain the computers and networks that enable online communication, and help educate the Anglican public about how best to use those computers.

Directors include both Church of England and ECUSA members. The Society sponsors the Anglicans Online website and, on behalf of the International Anglican Domain Committee, administers the anglican.org internet domain. More information is available on the website. *Director* Simon Sarmiento, 22 Rodney Avenue, St Albans, AL1 5SX
E: directors@justus.anglican.org
W: www.justus.anglican.org/soaj.html

Society of Catholic Priests
Founded in 1994, with around 700 members in the UK and Ireland, an inclusive society of priests who 'believe in one, holy, catholic and apostolic church ordaining men and women to serve as deacons, priests and bishops in the Church of God'. The objects of the Society are to promote the formation and support of priestly spirituality and catholic evangelism. *Rector General* The Revd Kevin Maddy *Secretary General* The Revd Michael Skinner, 16 Ambleside Gardens, South Croydon CR2 8SF
E: membership@scp.org.uk
W: www.scp.org.uk

Society of King Charles the Martyr
Founded 1894 in to promote observance of January 30, the day of the martyrdom of King Charles I in 1649, and uphold the traditional Anglican Catholic principles for which he died. Publishes various material including the journal *Church and King. Chairman* Mr Robin Davies, 22 Tyning Rd, Winsley, Bradford on Avon, BA15 2JJ   *T:* 01225 862965
E: robinjbdavies@talktalk.net
W: www.skcm.org

Society of Mary
Founded in 1931 to promote devotion to Our Lady. Originally an Anglican society and now an ecumenical society welcoming all practising Catholics. Organizes pilgrimages to Marian Shrines, in particular Lourdes and Nettuno. *Superior General* Rt Revd Robert Ladds *Chaplain General* Revd G. C. Rowlands *Secretary* Mrs Celia Bush, 169 Humber Doucy Lane, Ipswich, IP4 3PA   *T:* 01473 423750
E: secretary@societyofmary.net
W: www.societyofmary.net

Society of Ordained Scientists
Founded in 1987. A dispersed order for ordained scientists, men and women. Members aim to offer to God, in their ordained role, the work of science in the exploration and stewardship of creation, to express the commitment of the Church to the scientific enterprise and their concern for its impact on the world, and to support each other in their vocation. Associate membership is available to those who are not ordained but are interested in the work of the Society. *Visitor* Rt Revd David Walker, Bishop of Manchester *Secretary* Revd Colin Brockie *Warden* Revd Dr Keith Suckling,
T: 01563 559960
E: revcol@revcol.demon.co.uk
W: www.ordainedscientists.org

Society of Retreat Conductors
Founded in 1923 for the training of retreat conductors, the running of retreat houses and the conducting of retreats. *Chairman* Revd A.Walker *Company Secretary* Mrs Kathryn Redington, c/o St Mary Woolnoth Vestry, Lombard St, London, EC3V 9AN
T: 07979 157603
E: admin.src@btconnect.com

Society of Royal Cumberland Youths
Bell-ringing society founded in 1747. Its headquarters are at St Martin-in-the-Fields and the Society is responsible for ringing at a number of London churches. The society has a worldwide membership, promoting high standards among proficient change-ringers. *Master* Mr Alan Regin *Secretary* Mr John Ford, 28 Villiers Street, Hertford, SG13 7BW
T: 01992 550280
E: secretary@srcy.org.uk
W: www.srcy.org.uk

Society of St Willibrord
Founded in 1908 to promote friendly relations between the Anglican and Old Catholic Churches, including the fullest use of the full Communion established between them in 1931. Membership of the society is open to members of churches in full communion with Canterbury and/or Utrecht. *President* The Rt Revd David Hamid *Patrons* The Archbishops of Canterbury and Utrecht *Hon Secretary* The Revd Markus Duenskofer *Chairman* The Rt Revd Michael Burrows, Bishop of Cashel and Ossory, 1 Ainslie Place, Edinburgh, EH3 6AR
T: 0131 229 7565
E: honsecssw@gmail.com
W: http://willibrord.org.uk

Society of the Faith (Incorporated)
The objects of the society are to act as an association of Christians in communion with the See of Canterbury for mutual assistance in the work of Christ's Church and for the furtherance of charitable undertakings, especially for the popularization of the Catholic Faith.

We have occupied Faith House in Westminster since 1935 and formerly ran the Faith Press and Faithcraft. We manage Faith House as a resource for the Church, promote charitable activities, hold the annual Liddon Lecture and sponsor publications which promote the Society's objects. The restricted Liddon Fund provides two or three grants per year for young Anglicans (under 25 years old) who are engaged in advanced theological study, for example for a second degree. *Principal* Dr Julian Litten *Vice-principal* Canon Robert Gage, Faith House, 7 Tufton St, London, SW1P 3QB   T: 01727 856626
W: www.societyofthefaith.org.uk

Society of the Holy Cross (SSC)
Founded in 1855 for priests (1100 members) 'to maintain and extend the Catholic faith and discipline and to form a special bond of union between Catholic clergy'. Provinces: European Union, Australasia, Canada, Africa, USA. *Master General* Preb Dr David Houlding SSC *Provincial Master (for England)* Fr Nicolas Spicer SSC *Secretary General* Fr Colin Ames SSC *Treasurer General* Fr David Lawson SSC, All Hallows House, 52 Courthope Rd, London, NW3 2LD   T: 020 7267 7833 (Home)
020 7263 6317 (Office)
E: sscmaster@lineone.net

Sons & Friends of the Clergy
The Sons & Friends of the Clergy is an Anglican clergy support charity registered in England with origins dating back to 1655. Our purpose is to promote, sustain and renew the wellbeing of Anglican clergy, whether serving or retired, and their dependants, so that they can flourish and be fruitful as they seek to serve God's people. We do this primarily by providing financial grants to eligible clergy households in times of hardship. Our grants are made to address financial hardship and can be used for any reasonable purpose. We can also provide support for special medical or educational hardship cases. We occasionally provide special purpose gifts for the following: accessibility modifications; bereavement; debt relief; legal fees on buying a first property (clergy who are approaching retirement); nursing home fees; relationship counselling; school fees (where there is a compelling and proven educational need for a child to attend an independent school). *President* The Archbishop of Canterbury *Chair of Trustees* The Rt Revd David Rossdale *Chief Executive* Jeremy Moodey, 1 Dean Trench Street, Westminster, London, SW1P 3HB   T: 020 7799 3696
E: enquiries@sonsandfriends.org.uk
W: www.sonsandfriends.org.uk

South American Mission Society
Merged in 2010 with the Church Mission Society. See Church Mission Society.

Southern Africa Church Development Trust
Founded in 1960 to inform, encourage concern for and involvement in the Church in Southern Africa. Supports churches, community centres and schools, primary and secondary education through scholarships, clergy and lay training, and medical work. Publishes a quarterly bulletin of information and projects which is sent to all subscribers and supporters. *President* Mr Martin Kenyon *Director* Dr Jack Mulder *Chairperson* Canon David Cook *Hon Treasurer* Stuart Barley, 43 Cranham Avenue, Billingshurst, RH14 9EN
T: 01403 581066
E: director@sacdtrust.org
W: www.sacdtrust.org

St Christopher's Educational Trust
Small grants to promote Christian religious education by improving practice in teaching, by developing new programmes of education and nurture for adults and young people and by support for individual study or research. The Trustees meet twice a year. Member of the Association of Church College Trusts (see separate entry). *Clerk to the Trustees* Mrs Lindsey Anderson-Gear, 5 Windmill Avenue, Bicester, Oxon, OX26 3DX
E: stchristopherstrust@hotmail.co.uk
W: www.churchofengland.org/education

St Christopher's Fellowship
St Christopher's is a charity and housing association providing care, accommodation, education, training and support to children,

young people and vulnerable adults. We run children's homes, fostering services, supported housing and hostels, along with education, employment and outreach services. *Chairman* Mr Anthony Hickinbotham *Chief Exec* Mr Jonathan Farrow, 1 Putney High St, London, SW15 1SZ   *T:* 020 8780 7800
E: info@stchris.org.uk
W: www.stchris.org.uk

St George's College, Jerusalem
St George's College is a unique centre of continuing education in the Anglican Communion, offering short-term courses as well as facilities for individual reflection and study. It is open to both clergy and laity.

Since its founding in 1962, the College has hosted participants from 92 countries and 96 Christian traditions. Course members engage with a wide range of biblical texts in the context of the land; encounter Jewish, Christian and Muslim faith as it is exercised today; and come to appreciate anew the rich fabric of faith and spirituality that this environment offers to the pilgrim.

The College is situated 500 metres north of the Damascus Gate of the Old City of Jerusalem, and set in its own grounds adjacent to the Anglican Cathedral of St George the Martyr. Full details of courses can be obtained from the website or the Secretary of the British Regional Committee. *Secretary of the British Regional Committee* Revd Paul Conder, St George's College Jerusalem, Post Office Box 1248, Jerusalem 91000, Israel
T: 1 972 2 626 4704
E: genia@sgcjerusalem.org
W: www.sgcjerusalem.org

St George's House, Windsor Castle
Founded in 1966. A residential consultation centre within Windsor Castle, and part of the fourteenth-century College of St George. Apart from ecumenical clergy conferences, the House also hosts a range of other consultations. Some are internally organized, while others are instigated by external groups under the guidance of House staff. The range of themes is wide but all share a concern for greater human well-being. Accommodation for up to 33 people. *Chairman, Board of Trustees and Council* Rt Revd David J. Conner, Dean of Windsor *Warden* Revd Canon Dr Hueston Finlay *Programme Director* Mr Gary McKeone *Clergy Consultation Administrator* Mrs Patricia Birdseye, St George's House, Windsor Castle, Windsor, SL4 1NJ   *T:* 01753 848848
E: jenna.tyer@stgeorgeshouse.org
W: www.stgeorgeshouse.org

St Hild and St Bede Trust
The Trust's annual income is restricted to the advancement of higher and further education in the Dioceses of Durham and Newcastle, and is presently committed to supporting the North East Religious Learning Resources Centre based in the City of Durham and in Newcastle, the chaplaincies of the College of St Hild and St Bede and of the University of Newcastle. The Trust gives scholarships for theology and music within the colleges of St Hild and St Bede and supports aided status Church of England Schools in both dioceses. Member of the Association of Church College Trusts (see separate entry). *Correspondent* Mr W. Hurworth *Home* 16 Tempest Court, Wynyard Park, Billingham TS22 5TD, c/o College of St Hild and St Bede, Pelaw Leazes Lane, Durham, DH1 1SZ   *T:* 01740 644 274
E: w.hurworth@btinternet.com

St John's Guild
Founded in 1919 to assist the spiritual well-being of blind people, as well as to ease the isolation and loneliness in which some of them lived. Since that time both needs and society have changed. St John's Guild has developed to meet those changes. The Guild supports ten branches, which are located in different parts of the country and meet to provide worship, fellowship and friendship. Regular publications in Braille and audio are produced and widely distributed. *Chairman* Mrs Judith Dunk *Finance Officer* Mrs Patricia Richards, Sovereign House, 11–14 Warwick Street, Coventry, CV5 6ET   *T:* 024 7671 4241
E: info@stjohnsguild.org
W: www.stjohnsguild.org

St Luke's College Foundation
The Foundation's object is the advancement of further and higher education in religious education and theology. Grants are awarded to individuals for research and taught postgraduate qualifications in these fields; and to eligible organizations for related initiatives and facilities. The Foundation does not finance buildings, or provide bursaries for institutions to administer; and it is precluded from the direct support of schools (although it supports teachers who are taking eligible studies). Member of the Association of Church College Trusts (see separate entry). *Director* Dr David Benzie, 15 St Maryhaye, Tavistock, Devon, PL19 8LR
E: director@st-lukes-foundation.org.uk
W: www.st-lukes-foundation.org.uk

St Luke's Healthcare for the Clergy
Providing appropriate physical and psychological healthcare services to the clergy, their spouses, widows, and dependent children, monks and nuns, deaconesses, ordinands, Church Army staff, and overseas missionaries. To find out more or to access these services please contact the Medical Secretary at the

address provided. *President* The Archbishop of Canterbury *Chairman* Mr Edward Martineau *Chief Executive* Dr Claire Walker, Room 201, Church House, Great Smith Street, London, SW1P 3AZ   *T:* 020 7898 1700
     E: medical@stlukeshealthcare.org.uk
     W: www.stlukeshealthcare.org.uk

St Mary's College Trust

The Trust's annual income is normally committed to supporting the Welsh National Centre for Religious Education, WNCRE at Gladstone's Library, Hawarden, Flint, and the Anglican Chaplaincy at the University of Wales, Bangor. As a result, grants to individuals and other institutions are only awarded in very exceptional circumstances. Member of the Association of Church College Trusts. *Clerk to the Trustees,* St Mary's College Trust, Eifionudd, Normal Site (UWB), Holyhead Road, Bangor, LL57 2PX   *T:* 01248 382934

St Michael's Fellowship

Runs four residential family assessment centres and one community assessment service in South London, working in partnership with parents to enable them to meet the needs of their child. Works with adolescent mothers, one- or two-parent families where parents may have learning disabilities, psychiatric illness, a history of abuse, domestic violence and where there are child protection concerns. Offers assessed and supervised contact in a child-friendly 'homely' environment. Runs one supported housing scheme for vulnerable families, with self-contained flats and low support. Through Sure Start Children's Centres, offers community support to teenage parents and young fathers in the Borough of Lambeth. *Director* Mrs Sue Pettigrew, 136 Streatham High Road, London, SW16 1BW
                  T: 020 8835 9570
   E: admin@stmichaelsfellowship.org.uk
   W: www.stmichaelsfellowship.org.uk

St Pancras and Humanist Housing Association

Founded in 1924 by the Revd Basil Jellicoe, this charitable association provides housing and support for families, single people and those with special needs in nearly 4,500 flats and houses in North London and Hertfordshire. c/o Origin Housing, St Richards, 110 Eversholt St, London, NW1 1BS   *T:* 020 7209 9287
     E: enquiries@originhousing.org.uk
          W: www.sph.org.uk

St Peter's Saltley Trust

The Trust's annual income is committed to supporting, developing and evaluating creative, innovative, locally-based project work in adult Christian learning and discipleship, the churches' work in further education and religious education in schools. The Trust's area of benefit comprises the region covered by the Anglican dioceses of Birmingham, Coventry, Hereford, Lichfield and Worcester. The Trust does not make grants towards capital projects or ongoing core costs (e.g., to fund building works or subsidize ongoing staff salaries) or to individuals for personal research or continuing education purposes. Member of the Association of Church College Trusts (see separate entry). *Director* Dr Ian Jones *Bursar and Clerk to the Trustees* Mrs Lin Brown, Grays Court, 3 Nursery Rd, Edgbaston, Birmingham, B15 3JX
                  T: 0121 427 6800
     E: director@saltleytrust.org.uk
      W: www.saltleytrust.org.uk

Student Christian Movement

SCM is a student-led movement inspired by Jesus to act for justice and show God's love in the world. As a community we come together to pray, worship and explore faith in an open and non-judgemental environment.

The movement is made up of a network of groups and individual members across Britain, as well as link churches and affiliated chaplaincies. As a national movement we come together at regional and national events to learn more about our faith and spend time as a community.

We take action on issues of social justice chosen by our members. Visit our website to find out more about our current campaign.

SCM provides resources and training to student groups, churches and chaplaincies on student outreach and engagement, leadership and social action.

The British SCM is part of the World Student Christian Federation which brings together more than two million Christian students around the world. *National Coordinator* Hilary Topp *National Coordinator (maternity cover until May 2018)* Simon Densham *Links Worker* Rosie Venner *Operations Manager* Lisa Murphy, Grays Court, 3 Nursery Road, Edgbaston, Birmingham, B15 3JX
                  T: 0121 426 4918
         E: scm@movement.org.uk
        W: www.movement.org.uk

Summer Biblical Study in Cambridge

Summer Biblical Study in Cambridge is a residential Summer School run by the Vacation Term for Biblical Study (Registered Charity no. 1125494) which takes place at Robinson College, Cambridge, during the first two weeks in August. It is particularly suitable for theology students and any ordained and lay people with an interest in critical biblical study.

Participants can take part for one or both weeks; non-residents are also welcome.

Lectures are given by professional biblical scholars, specializing in Old and New Testament studies and related subjects. There is also the opportunity (optional) for tuition in biblical Greek or Hebrew at absolute beginner, intermediate or advanced level. Participants have time to enjoy the attractions of Cambridge and the surrounding countryside. A limited number of bursaries towards the cost of accommodation are available.

The programme and application form are available from the website from about mid-January. Contact the Treasurer for further details. *Chairman* Professor Keith Elliott *Secretary* Miss Gillian Glenn *Treasurer* Mr Richard Garner, 45 Souldern Street, Watford, Hertfordshire, WD18 0EU   *T:* 01923 229306
E: jrmgarner@btinternet.com
W: www.vtbs.org.uk

Tearfund
Tearfund is an evangelical Christian relief and development charity working with the local church around the world to bring physical, emotional and spiritual transformation to people living in poverty. Responding to natural disasters and emergencies, engaging in longer-term community development and speaking out to challenge injustice, Tearfund aims to make the fullness of life promised by Christ a reality for people in need. With support from individuals and churches in the UK and Ireland, Tearfund is in active partnership with local Christians in more than 60 countries. *Chief Executive* Mr Matthew Frost, 100 Church Rd, Teddington, TW11 8QE
T: 0845 355 8355
E: enquiry@tearfund.org
W: www.tearfund.org

The Smallwood Trust
Founded by the late Miss Edith Smallwood in 1886. Assistance is given to ladies living alone in their own home (either owned or rented) on a low income and domiciled in the United Kingdom, irrespective of age or social status. Registered Charity no. 205798. Enquiries welcome by telephone (calls cost the same as to a number beginning 01 or 02). Donations and legacies gratefully received. *Patron* HM The Queen *Apply* The Secretary, Lancaster House, 25 Hornyold Road, Malvern, WR14 1QQ   *T:* 0300 365 1886 (helpline)
01684 574645 (office)
E: fionaharper@smallwoodtrust.org.uk
W: www.smallwoodtrust.org.uk

Third Province Movement
The object of the Third Province Movement, which was started in November 1992, is to advocate, and eventually secure, the establishment within the Church of England of an autonomous province for all those, whatever their churchmanship, who in conscience cannot accept the ordination of women to the priesthood, the episcopate and other liberal developments. It also advocates a realignment on the same principle within the whole Anglican Communion. *Chairman* Mrs Margaret Brown, Luckhurst, Mayfield, TN20 6TY   *T:* 01435 873007
W: www.thirdprovince.org.uk

Together (Mental After Care Association, formerly MACA)
Together is a leading national charity providing a wide range of quality community- and hospital-based services for people with mental health needs and their carers, including: advocacy, assertive outreach schemes, community support, employment schemes, forensic services, helplines/ information, respite for carers, social clubs, supported accommodation with 24-hour care. *Chief Executive* Liz Felton, 12 Old Street, London, EC1V 9BE   *T:* 020 7780 7300
E: contact-us@together-uk.org
W: www.together-uk.org

Together for Short Lives
Together for Short Lives is the leading UK charity for all children with life-threatening and life-limiting conditions and all those who support, love and care for them. We support families, professionals and services, including children's hospices. Our work helps to ensure that children can get the best possible care, wherever and whenever they need it. From the moment of diagnosis, for whatever life holds, we help to ensure that families make the most of their precious time together.

There are an estimated 49,000 children and young people in the UK living with a life-threatening or life-limiting condition that may require palliative care services. We are there for every single one of these children, and their families, so they know where to go for help and are aware of the support available to them. With the right kind of information, it can become easier to access care and support, as well as practical and emotional help for the whole family when it's needed most. We help families get this information so they know what to expect at different stages throughout their journey.

We also work closely with the organizations and professionals that provide an important lifeline to children and families. We raise funds for children's hospices and a range of other voluntary organizations to enable them to sustain the vital work they do. We offer resources and training to help them maintain consistent, high quality care from the moment a child is diagnosed until their eventual death, and to continue supporting families for as long as they need it.

Our work also involves campaigning for equal coverage of specialized services for children with life-threatening and life-limiting conditions and families across the UK; and better co-ordination of health, social care and education. By working nationally we give a powerful voice to children, families and the organizations that support them, ensuring their views are heard by the government and that they influence policy. Our three-year strategy (2015–18) is designed to lead lasting change for children's palliative care. The strategy – Quality of life, quality of death: Leading change for children's palliative care aims to enable children, young people and their families in the UK to have as fulfilling lives as possible the best care at the end of life. The five strategy priorities are:

- Information and support for families – so families can find the support they need locally and make informed choices about their child's care.
- Quality of life, quality of death – so families receive high quality care through life and at end of life and supporting professionals and services to understand and meet the needs of more children and families in their diverse communities.
- Commissioning and sustainability – influencing local and national children's palliative acre commissioning in all four UK countries and raising vital funds for children's palliative care voluntary sector providers.
- Transition – improve young people's transition from children's to adult services and access to appropriate services and support
- Community engagement and volunteering – improve understanding of childhood death and dying and encouraging the sector to explore a community approach to children's palliative care and invest in volunteering.

Our free Together for Families Helpline provides information and support for families, carers and professionals who look after a child with a life-threatening or life-limiting condition. Lines are open 10am until 4pm, Monday to Friday. Outside of these hours and on Bank Holidays there is an answerphone service and calls will be returned as soon as possible.

Together for Families Helpline
Telephone: 0808 8088 100
Together for Short Lives general enquiries
Telephone: 0117 989 7820
E: info@togetherforshortlives.org.uk
W: www.togetherforshortlives.org.uk

Traditional Choir Trust, The
The Traditional Choir Trust was started in 2002 by Dr John Sanders in Gloucester to: 'give grants, bursaries and scholarships to boys otherwise unable to attend recognized choir schools. To encourage and financially assist choir schools, cathedrals, Chapels Royal, collegiate churches, university chapels, parish churches and other choral foundations to maintain the ancient tradition of the all male choir.' Upon Dr Sanders' death in 2003, the Trusteeship was handed over to the Dean and Chapter of Chichester Cathedral. The Trust relies solely upon donations and legacies to build capital from which bursaries can be provided. *Trustees* Dean and Chapter of Chichester *Patron* Very Revd Michael Tavinor, Dean of Hereford *Administrator* The Communar, The Royal Chantry, Cathedral Cloisters, Chichester, West Sussex, PO19 1PX
T: 01243 782595
01243 812492
E: admin@chichestercathedral.org.uk
W: www.chichestercathedral.org.uk

Trinitarian Bible Society
Founded in 1831 for the circulation of Protestant or uncorrupted versions of the Word of God. The Society will only circulate the Authorized Version in English, and foreign language scriptures translated from the same Greek and Hebrew texts with comparable accuracy. *Office Manager* Mr J. M. Wilson, Tyndale House, Dorset Rd, London, SW19 3NN   *T:* 020 8543 7857
E: tbs@trinitarianbiblesociety.org
W: www.trinitarianbiblesociety.org

True Freedom Trust
An interdenominational support and teaching ministry for people struggling with same-sex attraction and related issues, and for their church leaders, families and friends. It supports people who experience same-sex attraction but who choose not to embrace a gay identity or be involved in same-sex relationships because of convictions of faith. It supplies resources, speakers and organizes conferences to help the Church overcome fear and prejudice and act with understanding and love in a biblical and Christlike way. *Chairman of Trustees* Mr Stefan Cantore *Director* Mr Jonathan Berry, 75 Albion Street, Birkenhead, CH41 5LS *T:* 0151 653 0773
E: info@truefreedomtrust.co.uk
W: www.truefreedomtrust.co.uk

Unitas – The Catholic League
Founded in 1913, the special objects of this ecumenical society are the reunion of all Christians with the See of Rome, the spread of the Catholic faith, the promotion of fellowship among Catholics and the deepening of the spiritual life. It is governed by a Priest Director and six elected members. Further details from

OTHER ORGANIZATIONS

the Secretary. *The Secretary* Mr David Chapman, Lower Flat, 293 Ordnance Road, Enfield, EN3 6HB   *T:* 01992 763 893
E: nomadyane@btinternet.com
W: www.unitas.org.uk

Unite Clergy and Faith Workers

Unite Faith Workers is the union for those who work for religious organizations as ministers, clergy and lay staff. Membership is open to all faiths and denominations. Set up in 1994, it is now part of Unite, which has more than 1.5 million members, following the merger of Amicus with TGWU.

Unite Faith Workers provides its members with a professional association of their own, with access to all the facilities and support of a modern union. Unite is recognized by the Church of England for staff in the National Church Institutions, and by some of the largest church-related charities, including Action for Children and The Children's Society. A growing number of diocesan office staff and others working for church organizations and agencies are members.

Unite Faith Workers has its own Executive, and a national network of local representatives providing support for members, and belongs to the specialist Community, Youth Workers and Non-Profit Sector within Unite, in partnership with a number of national agencies, professional associations and charities. It works to bring about fairness and dignity at work for all its members, whatever their situation, and is currently leading the campaign for modern conditions of service for those who serve as ministers.

A wide range of benefits is provided for members in good standing, including legal representation and professional advice on many issues affecting work and pensions, equal opportunities, harassment and bullying at work, and much more. *Chair of Church of England Section* Revd Pete Hobson *Unite National Officer* Sally Kosky *Communications* Maureen German, Unite the Union, Unite House, 128 Theobald's Road London, WC1X 8TN   *T:* 020 337 2028
0333 123 0021 (Faith Workers' Helpline)
E: maureen.german@unitetheunion.org
W: www.unitetheunion.org

United Learning (formerly the United Church Schools Trust)

Founded as an educational charity in 1883 to create schools that offer pupils a good academic education based on Christian principles with particular reference to the Church of England. The Company's council has developed the concept of offering a broad and challenging education. To achieve this it has invested in the provision of excellent buildings and facilities including extensive ICT at each school. This ideal of strong schools embraces not just academic learning to high standards, but also the development of skills that will be essential throughout life both at work and socially. Teamwork, leadership, an enthusiastic response to challenge and an active concern for others are all attributes which are valued. Schools at Blackpool, Guildford, Surbiton, Caterham, Ashford, Hampshire near Romsey, Hull, Lincoln, Sunderland, Bournemouth and Claygate. Clergy bursaries available. A subsidiary charity, the United Learning Trust, was founded in 2002 to manage a number of City Academies spread across the country. Twenty Academies and one City Technology College are currently open, mainly in inner city areas, with more to be added. *Chairman* Mr Richard Greenhalgh, Worldwide House, Thorpe Wood, Peterborough, PE3 6SB
T: 01832 864444
E: enquiries@unitedlearning.org.uk
W: www.unitedlearning.org.uk

United Nations Association of Great Britain and Northern Ireland (UNA-UK)

The UNA-UK is the UK's leading source of independent information and analysis on the United Nations, and a UK-wide grassroots movement. UNA-UK is committed to a strong, credible and effective UN. We believe that a strengthened UN is in the UK's national interest. We advocate strong government support for the UN, and seek to demonstrate why the UN matters to people everywhere. *Executive Director* Natalie Samarasinghe *Administration and Policy Support Officer* Natalie Saad, 3 Whitehall Court, London, SW1A 2EL
T: 020 7766 3454
E: rsaad@una.org.uk
W: www.una.org.uk

Universities and Colleges Christian Fellowship

UCCF: The Christian Unions exists to give every student in Great Britain an opportunity to hear and respond to the gospel of Jesus. We are full time staff, volunteers, supporters and students all working together to make disciples of Christ in the student world. Visit www.uccf.org.uk to find out more. UCCF: The Christian Unions, Blue Boar House 5 Blue Boar Street, Oxford, OX1 4EE   *T:* 01865 253678
E: email@uccf.org.uk
W: www.uccf.org.uk

Urban Saints

Since 1906 Urban Saints (formerly known as Crusaders) has been reaching out to children and young people with the good news of Jesus Christ. We are passionate about working with all children and young people, helping them to realize their full God-given potential as

they journey from childhood to adulthood. Young people (aged 5 to 18+) connect with the movement in a variety of ways, including weekly youth groups, special events, holidays, community projects and training programmes. These activities are led by thousands of volunteers who are comprehensively trained and supported in order to help them work effectively and achieve the highest possible standards of youth work practice. Whilst much of our work is in the UK and Ireland, increasingly we are helping indigenous churches within countries in the developing world to set up and run outreach work among un-churched children and young people. *Exec Director* Matt Summerfield *Volunteers Director* Mark Arnold *Marketing and Income Development Director* Lorne Campbell *Ministry Development Director* John Fudge, Kestin House, 45 Crescent Rd, Luton, LU2 0AH   *T:* 01582 589850
E: email@urbansaints.org
W: www.urbansaints.org /
www.crusadersreunited.org.uk /
www.urbansaints.org/energize

Urban Theology Unit
Ecumenical educational charity offering academic programmes engaging with contextual theology, ministerial practice, and urban realities. Academic programmes include Foundation Degree, MA in Theology and Ministry and MA in Urban Theology (York St John University), and M Phil/Ph D in Contextual, Urban and Liberation Theology and Ministerial Practice (University of Birmingham). There are UTU publications on British Liberation Theology, urban ministry, and contextual Bible readings. *Chairperson* Revd Eileen Sanderson *Acting Director* Revd Dr Ian K. Duffield *Support Services Manager* Mrs Kate Thompson, 210 Abbeyfield Rd, Sheffield, S4 7AZ   *T:* 0114 243 5342
E: office@utusheffield.org.uk
W: www.utusheffield.org.uk

USPG (United Society Partners in the Gospel)
USPG is an Anglican mission agency supporting churches around the world in their mission to bring fullness of life to the communities they serve. Theologically, practically and financially, we encourage and enable churches in the Anglican Communion to act as the hands and feet of Christ. In relationship with our local and global partners, we work to enliven faith, unlock potential, strengthen relationships and promote justice, so churches and communities are empowered to improve peace, livelihoods, education, health and their preparedness for disaster.

We are partner-informed, mission-driven and people-centred. We believe that God's chosen way of participating in the world is primarily through relationships that are built on mutual responsibility and inter-dependence in the Body of Christ. In theological terms, these relationships are an incarnational expression of God's love, and it is through such relationships that people are best able to renew hope, unlock their potential, and experience life in its fullness.

All our work is founded upon solid relationships and rooted in prayer. Our partnerships are about long-term presence, accompanying churches to achieve well-being and justice for all, especially those on the edges of society who live in poverty or face other forms of injustice. We also work closely with the Churches in Britain and Ireland, inviting people to share in our mission through friendship, prayer and financial support, and encouraging congregations to receive the riches that the global church offers. One of our key aims is to inspire churches and Christians in Britain and Ireland to enjoy closer connections with their brothers and sisters around the world through friendship, prayer and financial support.

Our work in more detail:

1. We support church-based development programmes that empower people and communities to draw upon their faith, skills and resources to tackle poverty and speak out for justice. We want to see lives transformed through healthier living, better education, greater food security, safety for children, an end to gender-based violence, justice for all, and freedom to worship.
2. We support programmes that train leaders and build the capacity of churches so they are better equipped to reach out to local communities.
3. We support the long-term relief and rehabilitation work of Anglican churches in response to emergencies and natural disasters.
4. We provide opportunities for volunteers from Britain and Ireland to take up placements with the world church, including a special programme for clergy and ordinands. We also produce a range of publications for readers in Britain and Ireland, including a magazine, prayer diary and a range of free resources for study and worship at Advent, Lent and Harvest.

We were founded in 1701 as the Society for the Propagation of the Gospel in Foreign Parts (SPG), making us one of the oldest Anglican mission agencies. In 1965 we merged with the Universities' Mission to Central Africa (UMCA) and then with the Cambridge Mission to Delhi

OTHER ORGANIZATIONS

to become USPG. *President* The Archbishop of Canterbury *Chair* Revd Canon Chris Chivers *Chief Executive (from 1/1/18)* The Revd Duncan Dormor, Harling House, 47–51 Great Suffolk Street, London, SE1 0BS   *T:* 020 7921 2200
E: info@uspg.org.uk
W: www.uspg.org.uk

Vergers, Church of England Guild of
Founded in 1932 to promote Christian fellowship and spiritual guidance among the vergers of the cathedrals and parish churches of England. The Guild is divided into branches which meet locally every month and nationally several times throughout the year. The Guild provides a comprehensive training course which students can study from home with the help of an area tutor and mentor. The course works alongside the well-established Annual Training Conference. The Guild Diploma is awarded to successful students. Advice concerning appointments, job descriptions and contracts is available through the Welfare Officer. Contact can be made through the General Secretary. *General Secretary* Stephen Stokes, 3 Benians Court, Cambridge, CB3 0DN   *T:* 01223 322860
E: cegvgensec@gmail.com
W: www.cofegv.org.uk

Walsingham, Shrine of Our Lady of
Founded in 1061 in response to a vision, destroyed in 1538, restored in 1922 by Revd A. Hope Patten, Vicar of Walsingham. Since 1931, when it was moved from the parish church, the Shrine has contained the image of Our Lady of Walsingham together with the Holy House, representing the house of the Annunciation and the home in Nazareth of the Holy Family. Nowadays Walsingham is England's premier place of pilgrimage. It is administered by a College of Guardians. Special facilities include accommodation for people of all ages and those with special needs, an Education Department for school visits, and retreat and conference facilities. Information is available from the Administrator. *Priest Administrator* The Revd Kevin Smith *Shrine Priest* The Revd Andreas Wenzel, The College, Walsingham, NR22 6EF   *T:* 01328 824204
E: pr.adm@olw-shrine.org.uk
W: www.walsingham.org.uk

WATCH (Women and the Church)
Founded in 1996, WATCH promotes the ministry of women in the Church of England. It is based on a vision of the Church as a community of God's people where justice and equality prevail, regardless of gender. WATCH works for an inclusive church in which women and men work together as laypeople, deacons, priests and bishops. Other priorities shaping our work are to achieve honesty and openness in church appointments and better

support for women in ministry, and to challenge barriers which impede the full expression of a woman's vocation and gifts. The ministry of both lay and ordained women is fostered through local diocesan WATCH branches, and members receive the magazine Outlook. *Chair* The Revd Canon Dr Emma Percy, St John's Church, Waterloo Rd, London, SE1 8TY   01993 832514
E: admin@womenandthechurch.org
chair@womenandthechurch.org
W: www.womenandthechurch.org

William Temple Foundation
Founded in 1947, as a research organization focusing on the links between theology, the economy and urban mission practice. The Foundation's current programme reflects theologically and strategically on the evolving relationship between religion and public space, including the mission and identity of the church in postsecular society, urban societies and the contribution of Christianity and other religions to current wellbeing and happiness agendas, public policy and social welfare. This agenda also encompasses mapping and analyzing the ongoing contribution of religion to ethics and economics, including the regulation of business and financial institutions.

The Foundation continues its research into the work and identity of faith-based organizations in civil society across the UK, using the concept of religious and spiritual capital, and completed a major Leverhulme Trust programme in this area (2007–10). The Foundation works with a wide variety of partners including several community and grassroots organizations in the UK and across Europe.

Emerging from this research, the Foundation is contributing teaching at post-doctoral level at the University of Chester, with whom it has signed a research partnership, including the creation of a Centre for Faiths and Public Policy. The Centre produces research, publications and offers MA and doctoral level opportunities in the field. Its most recent project is a partnership with the University of Liverpool entitled *Philosophy and Religious Practice (2013–14)* which explores the ongoing impact of religious and philosophical ideas on public life and policy. *Director of Research* Dr Chris Baker, Centre for Faiths and Public Policy, University of Chester, Parkgate Road, Chester, CH1 4BJ
T: 01244 511074
E: chris.baker@wtf.org.uk
W: www.wtf.org.uk

William Temple House
William Temple House is a residence for 49/50 students from overseas and the United Kingdom in full-time education. The male and female students are of all faiths and

nationalities. The House is under the management of The International Students' Club (C of E) Ltd, a registered charity. Enquiries to the Warden. *The Warden*, International Students Club (C of E) Ltd, William Temple House, 29 Trebovir Rd, London, SW5 9NQ
T: 020 7373 6962!
E: office@williamtemplehouse.co.uk
W: www.williamtemplehouse.co.uk

Womenaid International

A humanitarian aid and development agency run by volunteers in the UK, which provides relief and assistance to women and children suffering distress caused by war, disasters or poverty. It seeks to empower women through education, training, provision of credit, and also campaigns against violations of women's human rights. An implementing partner of the European Community Humanitarian Office (ECHO), the British Government and several UN agencies, it has provided over 30,000 tonnes of food, medical supplies and clothing to more than 1.5 million refugees in the former Yugoslavia, the Caucasus and Central Asia. Development assistance globally has ranged from building and repairing schools, supporting rescue centres for street children, repairing hospitals and providing medical equipment/supplies to micro-credit support and water/sanitation projects. *Founder* Ms Pida Ripley, 3 Whitehall Court, London, SW1A 2EL   *T:* 020 7839 1790
E: womenaid@womenaid.org
W: www.womenaid.org

Women's World Day of Prayer

Founded in America in 1887 (Britain 1930–34) to unite Christian women in prayer by means of services held on the first Friday in March each year, by fostering local interdenominational prayer groups meeting throughout the year and to give financial support to Christian charities throughout the world. *President* Mrs Kathleen Skinner *Chairperson* Dr Elizabeth Burroughs *Administrator* Mrs Mary Judd, WWDP, Commercial Road, Tunbridge Wells, TN1 2RR
T: 01892 541411
E: office@wwdp.org.uk
W: www.wwdp.org.uk

Woodard Schools

Founded by Canon Nathaniel Woodard in 1848 to promote Christian education informed by the doctrines and principles of the Church of England. Woodard now owns some sixteen schools and a further twenty schools are linked to Woodard through formal agreements of affiliation or association. Woodard also sponsors six academies. *President* The Rt Revd Dr John Inge (Bishop of Worcester) *Senior Provost* Canon Brendan Clover *Chairman* Mr Richard Morse *Director of*

Education Mr Christopher Wright, High St, Abbots Bromley, Rugeley, WS15 3BW
T: 01283 840120
E: jillshorthose@woodard.co.uk
W: www.woodard.co.uk

World Association for Christian Communication (WACC)

WACC is an organization of corporate and individual members who wish to give high priority to Christian values in the world's communication and development needs. It is not a council or federation of churches. The majority of members are communication professionals from all walks of life. Others include partners in different communication activities, and representatives of churches and agencies. It funds communication activities that reflect regional interests, and encourages ecumenical unity among communicators.

As a professional organization, WACC serves the wider ecumenical movement by offering guidance on communication policies, interpreting developments in communications worldwide, discussing the consequences that such developments have for churches and communities everywhere but especially in the global South. WACC publishes Media Development, an online quarterly journal; Media and Gender Monitor, a bi-annual bulletin; and occasional publications. It has 1600 members and partners in 120 countries. UK members and affiliates include the Anglican Communion Office, Leeds Trinity University College, Feed the Minds, and SPCK. Contact: WACC UK, 16 Tavistock Crescent, London, W11 1AP
E: info@waccglobal.org

World Congress of Faiths

Founded in 1936 to promote mutual understanding and a spirit of fellowship between people of different religious traditions. WCF works to explain and reconcile religious conflict and the tensions between the different communities. Conferences and lectures are arranged. The journal Interreligious Insight is published two or three times a year, jointly with the Interreligious Engagement Project, and has its own website. *President* Revd Marcus Braybrooke and Rabbi Jacqueline Tabick *Chairman* Revd Dr Alan Race *Hon Treasurer* Pejman Khojasteh *Administrator* Tony Reese, Collaboration House, 77–79 Charlotte Street, London W1T 4PW   *T:* 01935 864055
E: enquiries@worldfaiths.org
W: www.worldfaiths.org

World Vision

Formed in London in 1979, World Vision UK is part of the international World Vision partnership and is a major UK relief and

development agency. World Vision is at work in over 100 countries in Africa, Asia, Eastern Europe, Latin America and the Middle East. It is involved in partnering churches and other non-governmental organizations in projects which range from relief work in Africa to income generation projects in Bangladesh. *Chief Exec Officer* Charles Badenoch *Church Relations Manager* Alistair Metcalfe, World Vision House, Opal Drive, Fox Milne, Milton Keynes, MK15 0ZR   *T:* 01908 841000
E: church@worldvision.org.uk
W: www.worldvision.org.uk/church

YMCA
Founded 1844 to promote the physical, intellectual and spiritual well-being of young people. *President* The Archbishop of York *Chief Executive* Denise Hatton, YMCA England, 29–35 Farringdon Road, London, EC1M 3JF
T: 020 7186 9500
E: enquiries@ymca.org.uk
W: www.ymca.org.uk

York Glaziers' Trust
Established 1967 by the Dean and Chapter of York and the Pilgrim Trust

(1) to conserve and restore the stained glass of York Minster;
(2) to conserve, restore and advise on all stained glass or glazing of historic or artistic importance, in any building whether religious or secular, public or private;
(3) to establish and maintain within the City of York a stained glass workshop dedicated

to the training and employment of conservators and craftsmen specializing in the preservation of glass of historic and artistic importance; and
(4) to encourage public interest in the preservation of stained glass, to collaborate with educational institutions and to assist with scientific and art historical research into stained and painted glass.

Advice should always be sought when considering treatment of glass of artistic or historic value. The Trust welcomes enquiries from all sources. It offers a full advisory service and will compile comprehensive condition reports. *Director* Mrs Sarah E. Brown FSA *Senior Conservator* Nick Teed MA *Business Manager* Trevor Lawson MRICS, MAPM, 6 Deangate, York, YO1 7JB
T: 01904 557228
E: info@yorkglazierstrust.org
W: www.yorkglazierstrust.org

Young Womens' Trust
The Young Womens' Trust is a force for change for women facing discrimination and inequalities of all kinds. Our principal aims are to enable young women who are experiencing particular disadvantage to identify and realize their full potential, to influence public policy in order to achieve equality and social justice for young women, and to provide opportunities for participation in a worldwide women's movement. 7–8 Newbury Street, London, EC1A 7HU   *T:* 020 7250 8339
E: info@youngwomenstrust.org
W: www.youngwomenstrust.org

Anglican and Porvoo Communions

PART 4

THE ANGLICAN COMMUNION

AN INTRODUCTION TO THE ANGLICAN COMMUNION

The Anglican Communion comprises 38 self-governing Member Churches or Provinces that share several things in common including doctrine, ways of worshipping, mission, and a focus of unity in the Archbishop of Canterbury. Formal mechanisms for meeting include the Lambeth Conference, the Anglican Consultative Council, and the Primates' Meeting, together with the Archbishop, known as the Instruments of Communion .

Most Communion life, however, is found in the relationships between Anglicans at all levels of church life and work around the globe; dioceses linked with dioceses, parishes with parishes, people with people, all working to further God's mission. There are around 85 million people on six continents who call themselves Anglican (or Episcopalian), in more than 165 countries. These Christian brothers and sisters share prayer, resources, support and knowledge across geographical and cultural boundaries.

As with any family, the Anglican Communion's members have a range of differing opinions. The Anglican Christian tradition has long valued its diversity, and has never been afraid to tackle publicly the hard questions of life and faith.

HISTORY

In continuity with the ancient Celtic and Saxon churches of the British Isles, and Britain's place within Catholic Europe, Anglicanism found its distinctive identity in the sixteenth and seventeenth centuries. At the Reformation national Churches emerged in England, Ireland and Scotland. With the American Revolution an autonomous Episcopal Church was founded in the United States and later Anglican or Episcopal Churches were founded across the globe as a result of the missionary movements of the eighteenth and nineteenth centuries. Many of these Churches became autonomous Provinces in the course of the nineteenth and twentieth centuries. In South Asia, the United Churches formed between Anglican and Protestant denominations joined the Anglican Communion, as did Churches elsewhere such as the Spanish Episcopal Reformed Church and the Lusitanian Church of Portugal.

OFFICIAL STRUCTURES

It was in 1867 that Lambeth Palace hosted the first conference for Anglican bishops from around the world. From 1948 each Archbishop of Canterbury has called a Lambeth Conference every ten years. The last, in 2008, saw more than 800 bishops from around the world invited to Canterbury. The Conference has no authority of itself: rather it is a chance for bishops to meet and explore aspects of Anglican Communion life and ministry.

Bishops attending the 1968 Lambeth Conference called for a body representative of all sections of the churches – laity, clergy and bishops – to co-ordinate aspects of international Anglican ecumenical and mission work. The resulting body was the Anglican Consultative Council. This council, comprising elected and appointed members from around the globe, meets approximately every three years.

Since 1979 the Archbishop of Canterbury has also regularly invited the chief bishops of the Provinces (known as *Primates*) to join him in a meeting for consultation, prayer and reflection on theological, social and international matters. These Primates' Meetings take place approximately every two years. The last Primates' Meeting took place in 2016, and it was there proposed that the next Lambeth Conference should be called in 2020.

These Instruments of Communion are served by a secretariat with staff based at the Anglican Communion Office in London, England, as well as in New York, Geneva and Lusaka (see page 309 for more information on the Anglican Communion Office).

BELIEFS

There can be many differences between individual Anglican churches, but all uphold and proclaim the Catholic and Apostolic faith, proclaimed in the Scriptures, interpreted in the light of tradition and reason. Anglicans hold these things in common:

- the Holy Bible, comprising the Old and New Testaments, as a basis of our faith;
- the Nicene and Apostles' Creeds as the basic statements of Christian belief;
- recognition of the Sacraments of Baptism and Holy Communion; and
- the Historic Episcopate – ours is a Christian tradition with bishops.

This quadrilateral, drawn up in the nineteenth century, is one of the definitions of Anglican faith and ministry. Another is a style of worship which has its roots in the Book of Common

Prayer and the Services of Ordination (the Ordinal). Anglicans also celebrate the Eucharist (also known as the Holy Communion, the Lord's Supper or the Mass), the Sacrament of Baptism and other rites including Confirmation, Reconciliation, Marriage, Anointing of the Sick and Ordination.

Anglicanism rests on the three pillars of Scripture, Tradition and Reason as it seeks to chart 'a middle way' among the other Christian traditions.

MISSION

Following the teachings of Jesus Christ, Anglicans are committed to proclaiming the good news of the gospel to all creation as expressed in the Marks of Mission:

- to proclaim the Good News of the Kingdom;
- to teach, baptize and nurture new believers;
- to respond to human need by loving service;
- to seek to transform unjust structures of society, to challenge violence of every kind and to pursue peace and reconciliation; and
- to strive to safeguard the integrity of creation and sustain and renew the life of the earth.

These Marks are to be expressed in all areas of a Christian's life: their words and their actions. Therefore, members of the Anglican Communion around the world are involved with a range of life-changing activities that include evangelism and church growth; providing food, shelter and clothing to those in need; speaking out with and for the oppressed; and setting up schools, hospitals, clinics and universities.

PROVINCES

The Anglican Church in Aotearoa, New Zealand and Polynesia
The Anglican Church of Australia
The Church of Bangladesh
Igreja Episcopal Anglicana do Brasil
The Anglican Church of Burundi
The Anglican Church of Canada
The Church of the Province of Central Africa
Iglesia Anglicana de la Region Central de America
Province de L'Eglise Anglicane Du Congo
The Church of England
Hong Kong Sheng Kung Hui
The Church of the Province of the Indian Ocean

The Church of Ireland
The Nippon Sei Ko Kai (The Anglican Communion in Japan)
The Episcopal Church in Jerusalem and The Middle East
The Anglican Church of Kenya
The Anglican Church of Korea
The Anglican Church of Melanesia
La Iglesia Anglicana de Mexico
The Church of the Province of Myanmar (Burma)
The Church of Nigeria (Anglican Communion)
The Church of North India (United)
The Church of Pakistan (United)
The Anglican Church of Papua New Guinea
The Episcopal Church in the Philippines
L'Eglise Episcopal au Rwanda
The Scottish Episcopal Church
Church of the Province of South East Asia
The Church of South India (United)
The Anglican Church of Southern Africa
Iglesia Anglicana del Cono Sur de America
Province of the Episcopal Church of South Sudan
Province of the Episcopal Church of Sudan
The Anglican Church of Tanzania
The Church of the Province of Uganda
The Episcopal Church *(Founded in the USA, it includes overseas dioceses in Taiwan, Haiti, Columbia, Honduras, Dominican Republic, Ecuador and continental Europe)*
The Church in Wales
The Church of the Province of West Africa
The Church in the Province of the West Indies

EXTRA-PROVINCIAL CHURCHES AND OTHER DIOCESES

The Church of Ceylon (Extra-Provincial to Canterbury)
Iglesia Episcopal de Cuba
Bermuda (Extra-Provincial to Canterbury)
The Lusitanian Church (Extra-Provincial to Canterbury)
The Reformed Episcopal Church of Spain (Extra-Provincial to Canterbury)
The Falkland Islands (Extra-Provincial to Canterbury)

CHURCHES IN COMMUNION

The Mar Thoma Syrian Church
The Old Catholic Churches of the Union of Utrecht
The Philippine Independent Church
NB: Anglicans/Episcopalians in certain parts of the Communion are in full communion with some Lutheran Churches.

The Anglican Communion Office

The permanent secretariat (the Anglican Communion Office) serves the Anglican Communion and is responsible for facilitating all meetings of the conciliar Instruments of Communion as well as the commissions, working groups and networks of the Communion. Office staff from countries including Canada, Zambia, Colombia and Wales also maintain the Anglican Communion website where visitors can find the official prayer cycle (daily prayer intentions for the dioceses of the Communion), vast amounts of official information and documentation about the Anglican Communion's Instruments and its ministries, plus the very latest news from around the Anglican world via the Anglican Communion News Service. Most of the funding for the work of the office comes from the Inter-Anglican budget supported by all Member Churches according to their means. The Secretary General of the Anglican Communion is The Most Revd Dr Josiah Atkins Idowu-Fearon.

Anglican Communion Office: St Andrew's House, 16 Tavistock Crescent, London W11 1AP
T: +44 (0)207 313 3900
F: +44 (0)207 313 3999
E: aco@anglicancommunion.org
W: www.anglicancommunion.org

The Anglican Centre in Rome

Promoting Christian unity in a divided world

President The Archbishop of Canterbury

Archbishop Bernard Ntahoturi is the Director of the Anglican Centre in Rome and the Archbishop of Canterbury's Personal Representative to the Holy See. He liaises between Pope Francis and Archbishop Welby and works with Anglican Communion and Vatican bodies on joint projects for education, ecumenism, and shared mission. Bernard Ntahoturi is also co-chair of the Anglican-Roman Catholic International Commission, the official dialogue between the two Communions.

An Anglican Presence

The Anglican Centre in Rome was established in March 1966 following the historic meeting between Archbishop Michael Ramsey and Pope Paul VI and is the Anglican Communion's permanent presence in Rome. It is the living reality of our Communion's commitment to the full visible unity of the Church, working collaboratively with all Christians for justice and peace in the world.

The Centre was integral to the establishment of a multi-faith anti-slavery network, working to combat human trafficking, engaging with churches and agencies in Italy. In 2016 the Centre received a Lampedusa Cross, made from a boat which sank off Lampedusa island in the Mediterranean, which lies on the altar of our chapel reminding us of people who are displaced. The Centre works closely with the Catholic lay community of St Egidio in Rome, who minister to the poor and disadvantaged, and is helping facilitate a similar mission in England.

Hospitality

The Centre provides a meeting place where laity and clergy may come together for discussion, worship and prayer. It is a welcoming reference point for visitors to Rome from member churches of the Anglican Communion. It also offers assistance to visiting Anglican scholars who wish to study in Rome. When possible they can be put in touch with resident scholars in their field. We also encourage choirs from around the Anglican Communion to come to Rome to celebrate the Anglican choral tradition in the Eternal City.

Education

The Centre seeks to bring down barriers of misunderstanding between Anglicans and Catholics; hosting scholars, art exhibitions, creating a space for hospitality and encounter. The Centre is responsible for arranging a number of courses – examples for 2017 include *Power and Politics and the Church; The Francis Effect, Then and Now; The Art of Preaching* and *Women's Leadership in Christian History.* Programmes for visiting groups, theological colleges, parish groups and Friends can be arranged. There is a growing library with over 12,000 books, together with a series of periodicals. *Centro,* the Centre's newsletter, is published online and in paper form twice each year.

Worship

At the heart of the Centre's life is the Chapel. The principal service each week is the

ANGLICAN & PORVOO COMMUNIONS

Eucharist, celebrated on Tuesdays at 1245. Details of celebrant and preacher are available on the website. All are welcome at the Eucharist, including those of different traditions, and to the lunch that follows.

Opening hours – Monday to Friday, 0930am – 1700.

Closed: August; between Christmas and the Epiphany.

Governors

The Rt Revd Stephen Platten *Chair*

The Very Revd Kurt Dunkle, *The American Friends of the Centre*

The Most Revd Dr Josiah Idowu-Fearon, *Secretary General of the Anglican Communion*

The Right Revd David Hamid, *Co-Chair of IARCCUM*

The Most Revd Bolly Lapok, *Former Archbishop of South East Asia*

The Revd Martin Macdonald, *Retired Partner PwC, Treasurer*

The Right Revd Cate Waynick, *Bishop of Indianapolis*

To be appointed, *Representative of the Archbishop of Canterbury*

The Revd Barry Nichols, *Retired Partner Ernst & Young (Secretary)*

Funding

The Anglican Centre survives exclusively on the money we raise ourselves on a year-by-year basis from a variety of sources within the Anglican Communion, including bishops, trusts, and individuals. The Centre is a company limited by guarantee (Company registered in England no 2604444) and a Registered UK Charity – No: 1003666

Staff

Director
Archbishop Bernard Ntahoturi, The Anglican Centre in Rome, Palazzo Doria Pamphilj, Piazza del Collegio di Romano 2, 00186 Rome, Italy   *T:* 39 06 678 0302
F: 39 06 678 0674
E: director@anglicancentre.it

Associate Director
The Revd Marcus Walker
E: associatedirector@anglicancentre.it

Centre Manager
Ms Louise Hettiche
E: administrator@anglicancentre.it

Assistant to Centre Manager and Course Co-ordinator
Mr Luca De Gasperis
E: pa-courses@anglicancentre.it

Development Officer
Catherine Pepinster
E: development@anglicancentre.it

Membership Services Officer
The Revd Jane Ollier
E: acrmembershipuk@gmail.com

UK Friends / 600 Club

The Friends, founded in 1984 and the 600 Club have now come together as the principal UK body to raise interest in the Anglican Centre, to stimulate prayer and prompt financial support. Members receive information twice yearly and a series of events are arranged. Further information and anyone interested in joining should contact the Membership Services Officer. This organization is overseen by the UK Development Committee.

Chairman The Revd Canon Mark Williams, Vicar, St John the Divine, Kennington, 92 Vassall Road, London SW9 6JA
E: fr_mark@yahoo.com

Diocesan Representatives

Each diocese has an ACR Representative to promote interest, promote prayer and promote funding. The full list appears on the Centre website.

Further Information

W: http://www.anglicancentreinrome.org
Facebook: @AnglicanCentre
Twitter: @AnglicanCentre

CHURCHES AND PROVINCES OF THE ANGLICAN COMMUNION

Anglican Church in Aotearoa, New Zealand and Polynesia

Members 469,036

Formerly known as the Church of the Province of New Zealand, the Church covers 168,000 square miles plus 6,835,000 square miles in the Pacific and includes the countries of Aotearoa, New Zealand, Fiji, Tonga, Samoa and the Cook Islands. It was established as an autonomous Church in 1857. A revised constitution adopted in 1992 reflects a commitment to bicultural development that allows freedom and responsibility to implement worship and mission in accordance with the culture and social conditions of the Maori (Tikanga Māori, European (Tikanga Pākehā) and Polynesian (Tikanga Pasefika) membership. The Church has a strong and effective Anglican Missions Board.

Primates/Archbishops

The Most Revd William Brown Turei (*Tikanga Māori*), PO Box 568, Gisborne 4040, New Zealand
T: 64 6 868 7028
F: 64 6 867 8859
E: browntmihi@xtra.co.nz
W: www.anglican.org.nz

The Most Revd Dr Winston Halapua (*Tikanga Pasefika*), PO Box 35, Suva, Fiji Islands
T: 679 330 4716
F: 679 330 2687
E: bishoppolynesia@connect.com.fj
W: www.anglican.org.nz

The Most Revd Philip Richardson (*Tikanga Pākehā*), PO Box 547, New Plymouth 4621, New Zealand
T: 64 6 759 1178
F: 64 6 759 1180
E: bishop@taranakianglican.org.nz
W: www.anglican.org.nz

General Secretary and *Treasurer* The Revd Michael Hughes, PO Box 87188 Meadowbank, Auckland 1742, New Zealand
T: 64 9 521 4439
E: gensec@anglicanchurch.org.nz
W: www.anglican.org.nz

THEOLOGICAL COLLEGES

The College of St John the Evangelist, Private Bag 28907 Remuera, Auckland 1541, New Zealand (serves both Anglicans and Methodists) *Manukura/Principal* The Revd Canon Anthony Gerritsen; *Tikanga Pākehā*

The Revd Karen Kemp; *Tikanga Māori* The Revd Katene Eruera; *Tikanga Polynesia* The Revd Dr Frank Smith
T: 64 9 521 2725
F: 64 9 521 2420
W: www.stjohnscollege.ac.nz

Theology House, PO Box 6728 Upper Riccarton, Christchurch 8442, New Zealand (*Director* The Revd Dr Peter Carrell)
T: 64 3 341 3399
F: 64 3 355 6140
E: director@theologyhouse.ac.nz
W: www.theologyhouse.ac.nz

Selwyn College, 560 Castle St, North Dunedin 9016, New Zealand (*Warden* Dr Neil Rodgers)
T: 64 3 477 3326
E: warden.selwyn@otago.ac.nz
W: www.selwyn.ac.nz

The two last named cater for pre-ordination or post-graduate studies.

AOTEAROA

Bishop of Aotearoa The Most Revd William Brown Turei (*Primate/Archbishop*), PO Box 568, Gisborne 4040, New Zealand
T: 64 6 868 7028
F: 64 6 867 8859
E: browntmihi@xtra.co.nz

Bishop of Te Manawa o Te Wheke The Rt Revd Ngarahu Katene, PO Box 146, Rotorua 3040, New Zealand
T: 64 7 348 4043
F: 64 7 348 4053
E: bishop@motw.org.nz

Bishop of Te Tairawhiti The Most Revd William Brown Turei, PO Box 568, Gisborne 4040, New Zealand
T: 64 6 868 7028
F: 64 6 867 8859
E: browntmihi@xtra.co.nz

Bishop of Te Tai Tokerau The Rt Revd Te Kitohi Wiremu Pikaahu, PO Box 25 Paihia, Bay of Islands 0247, New Zealand   T: 64 9 402 6788
E: tkwp@xtra.co.nz

Bishop of Te Upoko o Te Ika The Rt Revd Muru Walters, 14 Amesbury Drive, Churton Park, Wellington 6037, New Zealand
T: 64 4 478 3549
F: 64 4 472 8863
E: muru.walters@xtra.co.nz

Bishop of Te Waipounamu The Rt Revd Richard Wallace, PO Box 10086, Phillipstown, Christchurch 8145, New Zealand
T: 64 3 389 1683
F: 64 3 389 0912
E: pihopa@waipounamu.org.nz
W: www.waipounamu.org.nz

NEW ZEALAND
Bishop of Auckland The Rt Revd Ross Graham Bay, PO Box 37242, Parnell, Auckland 1151, New Zealand
T: 64 9 302 7201
F: 64 9 302 7217
E: bishop@auckanglican.org.nz
W: www.auckanglican.org.nz

Assistant Bishop of Auckland The Rt Revd James Andrew White, PO Box 37242, Parnell, Auckland 1151, New Zealand
T: 64 9 302 7201
F: 64 9 302 7217
E: jwhite@auckanglican.org.nz
W: www.auckanglican.org.nz

Bishop of Christchurch The Rt Revd Victoria Matthews, PO Box 4438, Christchurch 8140, New Zealand
T: 64 3 348 6701
F: 64 3 379 5954
E: bishop@anglicanlife.org.nz
W: www.anglicanlife.org.nz

Bishop of Dunedin The Rt Revd Dr Kelvin Peter Wright, PO Box 13170, Green Island, Dunedin 9052, New Zealand
T: 64 3 488 0820
F: 64 3 488 2038
E: bishop@calledsouth.org.nz
W: www.calledsouth.org.nz

Bishop of Nelson The Rt Revd Victor Richard Ellena, PO Box 100, Nelson 7040, New Zealand
T: 64 3 548 3124
F: 64 3 548 2125
E: bprichard@nelsonanglican.org.nz
W: www.nelsonanglican.org.nz

Bishop of Waiapu The Rt Revd Andrew Hedge, PO Box 227, Napier 4140, New Zealand
T: 64 6 835 8230
F: 64 6 835 0680
E: bishopandrew@waiapu.com
W: www.waiapu.com

Bishop of Waikato (*until January 2018*) The Rt Revd Dr Helen-Ann Hartley, PO Box 21, Hamilton 3240, New Zealand
T: 64 7 857 0020
F: 64 7 836 9975
E: hah@waikatoanglican.org.nz
W: www.waikatotaranakianglican.org.nz

Bishop of Taranaki The Most Rt Revd Philip Richardson (*Primate/Archbishop*), PO Box 547, Taranaki Mail Centre, New Plymouth 4340, New Zealand
T: 64 6 759 1178
F: 64 6 759 1180
E: bishop@taranakianglican.org.nz
W: www.waikatotaranakianglican.org.nz

Bishop of Wellington The Rt Revd Justin Charles Hopkins Duckworth, PO Box 12046, Wellington 6144, New Zealand
T: 64 4 472 1057
F: 64 4 449 1360
E: justin@wn.ang.org.nz
W: www.wn.anglican.org.nz

POLYNESIA
Bishop of Polynesia The Most Revd Dr Winston Halapua (*Primate/Archbishop*), PO Box 35, Suva, Fiji Islands
T: 679 330 4716
F: 679 330 2152
E: bishoppolynesia@connect.com.fj

Bishop in Viti Levu West and Vanua Levu and Taveuni The Rt Revd Apimeleki Nadoki Qiliho, PO Box 117, Lautoka, Fiji Islands
T: 679 666 0124
E: qiliho@gmail.com

On Study Leave The Rt Revd Gabriel Mahesh Prasad Sharma   E: gabsharma@yahoo.com

Anglican Church of Australia

Members 3,679,688 (2011)
The Church came to Australia in 1788 with the 'First Fleet', which was made up primarily of convicts and military personnel. Free settlers soon followed. A General Synod held in 1872 formed the Australian Board of Missions. The Church became fully autonomous in 1962 and in 1978 published its first prayer book. A second Anglican prayer book was published in 1995. Women were first ordained to the Diaconate in 1985 and to the Priesthood in 1992. The first woman was consecrated Bishop in 2008. There are 22 dioceses forming 5 provinces in the mainland of Australia plus the Diocese of Tasmania. The Anglican Church of Australia is part of the Christian Conference of Asia and of the Council of the Church of East Asia. Links with Churches of New Guinea, Melanesia, and Polynesia are strong, especially through the Anglican Board of Mission – Australia.

Primate of the Anglican Church of Australia The Most Revd Dr Philip Freier (*Archbishop of Melbourne*)

General Secretary of the General Synod Ms Anne Hywood

Hon Treasurer Mr Allan Perryman

General Synod Office Suite 4, Level 5, 189 Kent Street, Sydney, NSW 2000   *T:* 61 2 8267 2700
F: 61 2 8267 2727
E: gsoffice@anglican.org.au
W: www.anglican.org.au

THE ANGLICAN THEOLOGICAL COLLEGES
Moore Theological College, 1 King Street, Newtown, NSW 2042 (*Principal* The Revd Canon Dr Mark Donald Thompson)
T: 61 2 9577 9999
F: 61 2 9577 9988
E: info@moore.edu.au
W: www.moore.edu.au

Nungalinya College, PO Box 40371, Casuarina, NT 0811 (*Principal* Dr Judith Long)
T: 61 8 8920 7500
F: 61 8 8927 2332
E: info@nungalinya.edu.au
W: www.nungalinya.edu.au

Ridley College, 170 The Avenue, Parkville, VIC 3052 (*Principal* Dr Brian Steven Rosner)
T: 61 3 9207 4800
F: 61 3 9387 5099
E: registrar@ridley. edu.au
W: www.ridley. edu.au

St Barnabas Theological College, 18 King William Road, North Adelaide SA 5006 (*Principal* The Revd Dr Matthew Anstey)
T: 61 8 8340 0411
F: 61 8 8416 8450
E: admin@sbtc.org.au
W: www.sbtc.org.au

St Francis Theological College, 233 Milton Road, PO Box 1261, Milton QLD 4064 (*Principal* The Revd Dr Steven Ogden)
T: 61 7 3514 7411
F: 61 7 3369 4691
E: enquiries@ministryeducation.org.au
W: www.stfranciscollege.com.au

St Mark's National Theological Centre, 15 Blackall Street, Barton, ACT 2600 (*Director* The Revd Dr Andrew Cameron)
T: 61 2 6272 6252
F: 61 2 6273 4067
E: stmarksadmin@csu.edu.au
W: www. stmarks.edu.au

Trinity College Theological School, Royal Parade, Parkville, VIC 3052 (*Dean* The Revd Canon Professor Dorothy Lee)
T: 61 3 9348 7127
F: 61 3 9348 7610
E: tcts@trinity.edu.au
W: www.trinity.edu.au/theology

Wollaston Theological College, 5 Wollaston Road, Mt Claremont, WA 6010
T: 61 8 9286 0270
F: 61 8 9385 3364
E: wecadmin@perth.anglican.org
W: www.perth.anglican.org/wollaston

CHURCH NEWSPAPERS
The Adelaide Church Guardian Monthly newspaper containing wide news coverage from the diocese, province and nationally. *Editorial Offices* 18 King William Road, North Adelaide, SA 5006.
E: communications@ adelaideanglicans.com

The Melbourne Anglican Large monthly diocesan newspaper contains extensive news, comment locally and from around the world; with colour pictures. *Director/Editor* The Anglican Centre, 209 Flinders Lane, Melbourne, VIC 3000.
E: editor@melbourneanglican.org.au
W: http://tma.melbourneanglican.org.au

Anglican Encounter Monthly newspaper of Newcastle Diocese, containing diocesan and Australian news. *Editorial Offices* PO Box 817, Newcastle, NSW 2302.
E: editor@newcastleanglican.org.au
W: www.newcastleanglican.org.au

Tasmanian Anglican Monthly small newspaper format, from Tasmania Diocese, containing wide comment. *Editorial Offices* PO Box 748, Hobart, TAS 7001.
E: editor@anglicantas.org.au
W: www.anglicantas.org.au

Southern Cross Large monthly newspaper of Sydney Diocese, containing diocesan, national, world news and comment, Archbishop's letter in both English and Chinese translation. Extensive use of colour. *Editorial Offices* PO Box W185 Parramatta Westfield NSW 2150.
E: info@anglicanmedia.com.au
W: www.anglicanmedia.com.au

Anglican Messenger Monthly newspaper of the Anglican Province of Western Australia, includes news from Perth, North West Australia and Bunbury.
Editorial Offices GPO Box W2067, Perth, WA 6846.   *E:* messenger@perth.anglican.org
W: www.perth.anglican.org/messenger

Focus Monthly newspaper based in Brisbane, containing diocesan and national news. *Editorial Offices* GPO Box 421, Brisbane, QLD 4001.   *E:* focus@anglicanchurchsq.org.au
W: www.anglicanchurchsq.org.au/ discover/focus-magazine

ANGLICAN & PORVOO COMMUNIONS

All diocesan newspapers contain a letter from the Archbishop or Bishop of the Diocese. The Dioceses of Armidale, Ballarat, Bathurst, Bendigo, Canberra and Goulburn, Gippsland, Grafton, Murray, Northern Territory, Riverina, Rockhampton, Wangaratta, and Willochra also produce magazines/Bishop's newsletters, with mainly diocesan and parochial news.

PROVINCE OF NEW SOUTH WALES
Metropolitan The Most Revd Dr Glenn Davies
(Archbishop of Sydney)

ARMIDALE
Bishop The Rt Revd Rick Lewers, PO Box 198, Armidale, NSW 2350   T: 61 2 6772 4491
F: 61 2 6772 9261
E: office@armidaleanglicandiocese.com
W: www.armidaleanglicandiocese.com

BATHURST
Bishop The Rt Revd Ian Palmer, PO Box 23, Bathurst, NSW 2795   T: 61 2 6331 1722
F: 61 2 6332 2772
E: registrar@bathurstanglican.org
W: www.bathurstanglican.org.au

CANBERRA AND GOULBURN
Bishop The Rt Revd Stuart Robinson, GPO Box 1981, Canberra, ACT 2601
T: 61 2 6232 3600
F: 61 2 6245 7199
E: trevor.ament@anglicands.org.au
W: www.anglicancg.org.au

Assistant Bishops
The Rt Revd Dr Matt Brain, GPO Box 1981, Canberra, ACT 2601   T: 61 2 6245 7101
F: 61 2 6245 7199
E: matt.brain@anglicands.org.au

The Rt Revd Trevor W. Edwards, GPO Box 1981, Canberra, ACT 2601   T: 61 2 6245 7101
F: 61 2 6232 3650
E: trevor.edwards@anglicancg.org.au

The Rt Revd Professor Stephen Pickard, 15 Blackall Street, Barton ACT 2600
E: spickard@csu.edu.au

GRAFTON
Bishop The Rt Revd Dr Sarah Macneil, PO Box 4, Grafton, NSW 2460   T: 61 2 6642 4122
F: 61 2 6643 1814
E: admin@graftondiocese.org.au
W: www.graftondiocese.org.au

NEWCASTLE
Bishop The Rt Revd Greg Thompson, PO Box 817, Newcastle, NSW 2300   T: 61 2 4926 3733
F: 61 2 4926 1968
E: reception@newcatleanglican.org.au
W: www. newcastleanglican.org.au

Assistant Bishop The Rt Revd Dr Peter Stuart, PO Box 817, Newcastle, NSW 2300
T: 61 2 4926 3733
F: 02 4926 1968
E: bishoppeter@newcastleanglican.org.au

RIVERINA
Bishop The Rt Revd Rob Gillion, PO Box 10, Narrandera, NSW 2700   T: 61 2 6959 1648
F: 61 2 6959 2903
E: rivdio@bigpond.com
W: www.anglicanriverina.com

SYDNEY
Archbishop The Most Revd Dr Glenn Davies *(Metropolitan of the Province of NSW)*, PO Box Q190, QVB Post Office, NSW 1230
T: 61 2 9265 1555
F: 61 2 9265 1543
E: archbishop@sydney.anglican.asn.au
W: www.sydneyanglicans.net

Assistant Bishops
The Rt Revd Peter Lin *(Bishop of Liverpool & Georges River Region)* *(same address)*
T: 61 2 9823 4244
F: 61 2 9823 4244

The Rt Revd Chris Edwards *(Bishop of Northern Region)* *(same address)*   T: 61 2 9265 1527
F: 61 2 9265 1543

The Rt Revd Dr Michael Stead *(Bishop of South Sydney)* *(same address)*   T: 61 2 9265 1530
F: 61 2 9265 1543
E: mstead@sydney.anglican.asn.au

The Rt Revd Peter L. Hayward *(Bishop of Wollongong)*, 74 Church Street, Wollongong, NSW 2500   T: 61 2 4201 180
F: 61 2 4228 4296
E: phayward@wollongong.anglican.asn.au

The Rt Revd Ivan Yin Lee *(Bishop of Western Sydney)*, PO Box Q190, QVB Post Office NSW 1230   T: 61 2 9265 1574
F: 61 2 9633 3636
E: ilee@sydney.anglican.asn.au

PROVINCE OF QUEENSLAND
Metropolitan The Most Revd Dr Phillip Aspinall *(Archbishop of Brisbane)*

BRISBANE
Archbishop The Most Revd Dr Phillip Aspinall *(Metropolitan of the Province of Queensland)*, GPO Box 421, Brisbane, QLD 4001
T: 61 7 3835 2218
F: 61 7 3832 5030
E: archbishop@anglicansq.org.au
W: www.anglicanchurchsq.org

Assistant Bishops
The Rt Revd Alison Taylor (*Bishop of the Southern Region*) (*same address*)
T: 61 7 3835 2213
F: 61 7 3832 5030
E: amtaylor@anglicanchurchsq.org.au

The Rt Revd Dr Jonathan Holland (*Bishop of the Northern Region*) (*same address*)
T: 61 7 3835 2213
F: 61 7 3832 5030
E: jholland@anglicanchurchsq.org.au

The Rt Revd Cameron Venables (*Bishop of the Western Region*), Box 2600, Toowoomba, QLD 4350
T: 61 7 4639 1875
F: 61 7 4632 6882
E: cvenables@anglicanchurchsq.org.au

NORTH QUEENSLAND
Bishop The Rt Revd William (Bill) Ray, PO Box 1244, Townsville, QLD 4810
T: 61 7 4771 4175
F: 61 7 4721 1756
E: bishopnq@anglicannq.org
W: www.anglicannq.org

THE NORTHERN TERRITORY
Bishop The Rt Revd Dr Gregory Anderson, PO Box 2950, Darwin, NT 0801
T: 61 8 8941 7440
F: 61 8 8941 7446
E: bishop@ntanglican.org.au
W: www. ntanglican.org.au

ROCKHAMPTON
Bishop The Rt Revd David Robinson, PO Box 710, Rockhampton, QLD 4702
T: 61 7 4927 3188
F: 61 7 4927 3188
E: drobinson@anglicanchurchcq.org.au
W: www.anglicanchurchcq.org.au

PROVINCE OF SOUTH AUSTRALIA
Metropolitan The Most Revd Geoff Smith (*Archbishop of Adelaide*)

ADELAIDE
Archbishop The Most Revd Geoff Smith (*Metropolitan of the Province of South Australia*), 18 King William Road, North Adelaide, SA 5006
T: 61 8 8305 9350
F: 61 8 8305 9399
W: www.adelaideanglicans.com
Assistant Bishops
The Rt Revd Dr Timothy Harris (*same address*)
T: 61 8 8305 9350
email: tharris@adelaideanglicans.com

The Rt Revd Christopher McLeod, PO Box 70, Brighton SA 5048
email: cmcleod@adelaideanglicans.com

THE MURRAY
Bishop The Rt Revd John Ford, PO Box 394, Murray Bridge, SA 5253
T: 61 8 8532 2270
F: 61 8 8532 5760
E: bishop@murray.anglican.org
W: www.murray.anglican.org

WILLOCHRA
Bishop The Rt Revd John Stead, PO Box 96, Gladstone, SA 5473
T: 61 8 8662 2249
F: 61 8 8662 2027
E: bishop@diowillochra.org.au
W: www.diowillochra.org.au

PROVINCE OF VICTORIA
Metropolitan The Most Revd Dr Philip Freier (*Archbishop of Melbourne and Primate of the Anglican Church of Australia*)

BALLARAT
Bishop The Rt Revd Garry Weatherill, PO Box 89, Ballarat, VIC 3350
T: 61 3 5331 1183
F: 61 3 5333 2982
E: bishop@ballaratanglican.org.au
W: www.ballaratanglican.org.au

BENDIGO
Bishop The Rt Revd Andrew William Curnow AM, PO Box 2, Bendigo, VIC 3552
T: 61 3 5443 4711
F: 61 3 5441 2173
E: bishop@bendigoanglican.org.au
W: www.bendigoanglican.org.au

GIPPSLAND
Bishop (*until January 2018*) The Rt Revd Kay Goldsworthy, PO Box 928, Sale, VIC 3853
T: 61 3 5144 2044
F: 61 3 5144 7183
E: bishopkay@gippsanglican.org.au
W: www.gippsanglican.org.au

MELBOURNE
Archbishop The Most Revd Dr Philip Freier (*Metropolitan of the Province of Victoria*), The Anglican Centre, 209 Flinders Lane, Melbourne, VIC 3000
T: 61 3 9653 4220
F: 61 3 9653 4268
E: archbishop@melbourneanglican.org.au
W: www.melbourneanglican.org.au

Assistant Bishops
Vacancy (*Bishop of the Southern Region*) (*same address*)
T: 61 3 9653 4220
F: 61 3 9653 4268
E: sthregbishop@melbourneanglican.org.au

The Rt Revd Philip Huggins (*Bishop of the North and Western Region*) (*same address*)
E: bishopphiliphuggins@melbourneanglican.org.au

The Rt Revd Genieve Blackwell (*Bishop of the Eastern Region*) (*same address*)
E: gblackwell@melbourneanglican.org.au

WANGARATTA
Bishop The Rt Revd Anthony John Parkes am, PO Box 457, Wangaratta VIC 3676
T: 61 3 5721 3484
F: 61 3 5722 1427
E: bishop@wangaratta-anglican.org.au
W: www.wangaratta-anglican.org.au

PROVINCE OF WESTERN AUSTRALIA
Metropolitan (from 10/2/18) The Most Revd Kay Goldsworthy (*Archbishop of Perth*)

BUNBURY
Bishop The Rt Revd Allan Ewing, PO Box 15, Bunbury, WA 6231
T: 61 8 9721 2100
F: 61 8 9791 2300
E: bishop@bunbury.org.au
W: www.bunbury.org.au

NORTH WEST AUSTRALIA
Bishop The Rt Revd Gary Nelson, PO Box 2783, Geraldton, WA 6531
T: 61 8 9921 7277
F: 61 8 9964 2220
E: bishop@anglicandnwa.org
W: www.anglicandnwa.org

PERTH
Archbishop (from 10/2/18) The Most Revd Kay Goldsworthy (*Metropolitan of the Province of*

Western Australia), GPO Box W2067, Perth, WA 6846
T: 61 8 9325 7455
F: 61 8 9221 4118
E: archbishop@perth.anglican.org
W: www.perth.anglican.org

Assistant Bishops
The Rt Revd Kate Wilmot (*same address*)
E: kwilmot@perth.anglican.org

The Rt Revd Jeremy James (*same address*)
E: jjames@perth.anglican.org

TASMANIA
Bishop The Rt Revd Dr Richard Condie, GPO 748, Hobart, TAS 7001
T: 61 3 6220 2015
F: 61 3 6223 8968
E: rcondie@anglicantas.org.au
W: www.anglicantas.org.au

DEFENCE FORCE
Bishop The Rt Revd Ian Lambert (*Anglican Bishop to the Australian Defence Force*), Department of Defence, DSG-Duntroon, ACT 2600
T: 61 2 9265 9202
F: 61 2 9265 9959
E: ian.lambert1@defence.gov.au
W: www.defenceanglicans.org.au

The Episcopal Anglican Church of Brazil

(Igreja Episcopal Anglicana do Brasil)

The Episcopal Anglican Church of Brazil is the nineteenth Province of the Anglican Communion, and its work began in 1890 as a result of the missionary work of two north American missionaries in Porto Alegre: James Watson Morris and Lucien Lee Kinsolving. Autonomy from the Episcopal Church in the United States was granted in 1965. The Episcopal Church now has more than a hundred thousand baptized members and a team of more than two hundred clergy, among whom are thirty women priests. It has established communities, and educational and social institutions, in the main urban areas of Brazil. The Brazilian province comprises nine dioceses: Southern, Southwestern, Rio de Janeiro, São Paulo, Recife, Brasília, Pelotas, Curitiba and Amazon. It also has one missionary district: Missionary District West.

Primate The Most Revd Francisco de Assis da Silva (*Bishop of South Western Brazil*)
E: fassis@ieab.org.br / xicoasilva@gmail.com
W: www.ieab.org.br

Provincial Secretary The Revd Arthur Cavalcante

Provincial Offices Praça Olavo Bilac, 63, Campos Elíseos, CEP 01201-050, São Paulo, SP
T: and F: 55 11 3 667 8161
E: acavalcante@leab.org.bs
acavalcante@ieab.org.br
arthurieab@gmail.com

Provincial Treasurer Mrs Silvia Fernandes (*address, etc. as above*)
T: and F: 55 11 3 667 8161
E: silviaieab@gmail.com
tesouraria@ieab.org.br

CHURCH PAPER
Estandarte Cristão, a bimonthly church journal in Portuguese, published since 1893, which contains general articles and news about the life of the Church at local, national and international level. This journal is the main channel of the Communication Department of the Church. Revdo Felix Batista Filho

Editorial Offices: Rua Ferreira Lopez, 401-AP 2302, Casa Amarela, Recife, PE, 52060-02
T: and *F:* 55 81 3267 3926/9488 3194
E: fqbfilho@gmail.com

AMAZON
Bishop The Rt Revd Saulo Maurício de Barros, Av. Sezerdelo Correia, 514, Batista Campos, 66025–240, Belem, PA
T: and *F:* 55 91 3241 9720
E: saulomauricio@gmail.com

BRASÍLIA
Bishop The Rt Revd Maurício José Araújo de Andrade, EQS 309/310, sala 1 – Asa Sul, Caixa Postal 093, 70359–970, Brasília, DF
T: 55 61 3443 4305
F: 55 61 3443 4337
E: brasilia2003@gmail.com
mandrade@ieab.org.br
W: www.dab.ieab.org.br

CURITIBA
Bishop The Rt Revd Naudal Alves Gomes, Rua Sete de Setembro, 3927 – Centro, 80250-010 Curitiba, PR
T: 55 41 3232 0917
E: naudal@yahoo.com.br
naudal321@gmail.com

PELOTAS
Bishop The Rt Revd Renato da Cruz Raatz, Rua Felix da Cunha, 425 – Centro, Caixa Postal 791, 96001–970 Pelotas, RS
T: and *F:* 55 53 3227 7120
E: renatoraatz@terra.com.br
renatoraatz@bol.com.br
rcraatz@ieab.org.br
W: www.dap.ieab.org.br

RECIFE
Bishop The Rt Revd João Câncio Peixoto, Rua Alfredo de Medeiros, 60, Espinheiro – 52021–030 Recife, PE
T: 55 81 3421 1684
E: joao.peixoto1@uol.com.br
W: www.dar.ieab.org.br

RIO DE JANEIRO
Bishop The Rt Revd Filadelfo Oliveira Neto, Rua Fonseca Guimarães, 12 Sta.Teresa, 20240–260, Rio de Janeiro, RJ
T: 55 21 2220 2148
F: 55 21 2252 9686
E: oliveira.ieab@ieab.org.br
W: www.anglicana.com.br

SÃO PAULO
Bishop The Rt Revd Flávio Borges Irala, Rua Borges Lagoa, 172 – Vila Clementino, 04038–030 São Paulo, SP
T: 55 11 5549 9086/5579 9011
F: 55 11 5083 2619
E: flavioirala@ieab.org.br
flavioirala@gmail.com
W: https://www.facebook.com IEAB.DASP? fref–ts

SOUTH WESTERN BRAZIL
Bishop The Most Revd Francisco de Assis da Silva (*Primate of the Episcopal Anglican Church of Brazil*), Av. Rio Branco, 880/Sub-solo – Centro, Caixa Postal 116, 97010–970 Santa Maria, RS
T: and *F:* 55 55 3221 4328
E: fassis@ieab.org.bs
W: www.swbrazil.anglican.org

SOUTHERN BRAZIL
Bishop The Rt Revd Humberto Maiztegui, Avenida Ludolfo Bohel, 278, Baairro Teresópolis, 91720–150, Porto Alegre, RS
T: and *F:* 55 51 3318 6199
E: dmsec@terra.com.br
bispohumberto@ieab.org.br
W: www.dm.ieab.org.br

ANGLICAN & PORVOO COMMUNIONS

Eglise Anglicane du Burundi

(The Province of the Anglican Church of Burundi)

Members 900,000
There are at least 900,000 Anglicans out of an estimated population of just over 9 million in Burundi. An Anglican presence was established through the work of the CMS in the 1930s and grew rapidly as a result of the East African revival. The former Ruanda Mission (now CMS) set up its first mission stations at Buhiga and Matana in 1935, and Buye in 1936. Activities were mainly focused on three pillars : evangelism, education and medical work. Many Christians got baptized and the number grew to the extent that there was a need to make a diocese in Burundi. The

first national bishop was consecrated in 1965 and Buye diocese was created, covering the whole country. The Church of the Province of Burundi now consists of seven dioceses: Buye, Bujumbura, Gitega, Matana, Makamba, Muyinga and Rumonge. It has been an independent province within the Anglican Communion since 1992. Among the Church's main concerns are peace and reconciliation, repatriation of returnees, community development, literacy, education, the reduction of gender-based violence and improvements in healthcare, especially the fight against HIV, AIDS and malaria. It is

committed to mission and evangelism, with
faith in the risen Christ as Lord and Saviour
central to its preaching and teaching. It is
concerned to support theological education
and training for ministry, based on the
authority of Scripture.

Primate The Most Revd Martin
Nyaboho (*Archbishop of Burundi and Bishop of
Makamba*)

Provincial Secretary The Revd Felibien Ndintore,
BP 2098, Avenue de l'Agriculture no 34,
Bujumbura   *T:* 257 22 224 389
                 Direct line: 257 22 229 129
                      E: peab@cbinf.com

Provincial Accountant Christine Niyonkuru

THEOLOGICAL COLLEGES
Matana Theological Institute (Provincial)

Canon Warner Memorial College, EAB Buye,
BP 94 Ngozi

Kosiya Shalita Bible College, EAB Matana,
DS 30, Bujumbura *or* BP 447, Bujumbura

Buhiga Bible College, EAB Gitega, BP 23 Gitega

Makamba College, EAB Makamba, BP 96
Makamba

Muraramvya Bible College, EAB Bujumbura,
BP 1300 Bujumbura

BUHIGA
The Rt Revd Evariste Nijimbere

BUJUMBURA
Bishop The Rt Revd Eraste Bigirimana, BP
1300, Bujumbura   *T:* 257 22 249 104
                    F: it is no longer working
                 E: bigirimanaeraste@yahoo.fr

BUYE
Bishop The Rt Revd Sixbert Macumi, BP 94,
Ngozi   *T:* 257 22 302 210
                             F: 257 22 302 317
                      E: buyedioc@yahoo.fr

GITEGA
Bishop The Rt Revd Jean Nduwayo, BP 23,
Gitega   *T:* 257 22 402 247
                      E: eab.gitega@cbinf.com

MAKAMBA
Bishop The Most Revd Martin Blaise Nyaboho
(*Archbishop of Burundi*), BP 96, Makamba
                             T: 257 22 508 080
                     E: eabdiocmak@yahoo.fr

MATANA
Bishop Seth Ndayirukiye, BP 30, Bujumbura
                             T: 257 79 923 832
                      E: canonseth@gmail.com

MUYINGA
Bishop The Rt Revd Paisible Ndacayisaba, BP
55, Muyinga, Burundi   *T:* 257 79 700 043
                       E: ndacp@yahoo.com

RUMONGE
Bishop The Rt Revd Pedaculi Birakengana
                             T: 257 79 970 926
                     E: birakepeda@yahoo.fr

RUTANA
The Rt Revd Pontien Ribakare

The Anglican Church of Canada

Members 2,035,500 (2001)
The Anglican witness in Canada started in
the eighteenth century with the Church
Missionary Society and the United Society
for the Propagation of the Gospel. The
Eucharist was first celebrated in Frobisher
Bay (now Iqaluit) in 1578; the first church
building was St Paul's, Halifax in 1750. The
Church includes a large number of the
original inhabitants of Canada (First
Nations, Inuit, and Métis) and has been
committed to restoring our relationship
and advocating for Aboriginal rights. A Book
of Alternative Services (BAS) was published
in 1985. The Church has a strong
international role in sustainable development
and humanitarian assistance through the

Primate's World Relief and Development Fund
(PWRDF).

*Offices of the General Synod and of its
Departments* 80 Hayden Street, Toronto, ON
M4Y 3G2   *T:* 1 416 924 9192
                             F: 1 416 968 7983

Primate of The Anglican Church of Canada The
Most Revd Fred J. Hiltz   *T:* 1 416 924 9192
                             F: 1 416 924 0211
                 E: primate@national.anglican.ca
                       W: www.anglican.ca

National Indigenous Anglican Bishop The Rt
Revd Mark L. MacDonald (*same address*)
             E: mmacdonald@national.anglican.ca

General Secretary The Ven Dr Michael J. Thompson
> *E:* mthompson@national.anglican.ca

General Synod Treasurer Ms Hanna Goschy
> *E:* hgoschy@national.anglican.ca

Bishop Ordinary to the Canadian Forces The Rt Revd Peter Coffin,42 Bridle Park Drive, Kanata, ON, K2M 2E2   *T:* 1 613 591 7137
> *Fax:* 1 613 232 3995
> *E:* petercoffin@rogers.com

UNIVERSITIES AND COLLEGES OF THE ANGLICAN CHURCH OF CANADA
*Ecumenical

British Columbia
Vancouver School of Theology*, 6000 Iona Drive, Vancouver, BC, V6T 1L4 (The Revd Dr Richard R. Topping)   *E:* possibilities@vst.edu

Manitoba
Henry Budd College for Ministry, Box 2518, The Pas MB R9A IM3, (*Joint Co-ordinators* Ms Marion Jenkins and The Revd Paul Sodtke)
> *E:* hbcm@mts.net

St John's College, 92 Dysart Road, Winnipeg, MB, R3T 2M5
> *E:* stjohns–college@umanitoba.ca

(*Warden/Vice-Chancellor* Dr Christopher Trott)
> *E:* Christopher.trott@ad.umanitoba.ca

Newfoundland
Queen's College, 210 Prince Philip Drive, Ste 3000, St John's NL, A1B 3R6
> *E:* queens@mun.ca

(*Interim Administrator*) Dr Alex Faseruk
> *E:* afaseruk@mun.ca

Nova Scotia
Atlantic School of Theology*, 660 Francklyn Street, Halifax, NS, B3H 3B5
> *E:* academicoffice@astheology.ns.ca

(*President* Dr Dan O'Brien)
> *E:* dobrien@astheology.ns.ca

University of King's College, 6350 Coburg Road, Halifax, NS, B3H 2A1
> *E:* academicoffice@astheology.ns.ca

(*President* Dr George Cooper)
> *E:* george.cooper@ukings.ca

Nunavut
Arthur Turner Training School,*enquiries to* the Diocese of Arctic, Box 190, Yellowknife, NT, X1A 2N2
> *E* (Debra Gill, *Executive Officer* of Diocese of Artic): debra@articnet.org

Ontario
Canterbury College, University of Windsor, 2500 University Ave West, Windsor, ON, N9B 3Y1   *E:* canter@uwindsor.ca

(*Principal* Dr Gordon Drake)
> *E:* gdrake@uwindsor.ca

Huron University College, University of Western Ontario, 1349 Western Road, London, ON, N6G 1H3   *E:* huron@uwo.ca

(*Principal* Dr Stephen McClatchie)
> *E:* smcclatchie@huron.uwo.ca

Renison College, University of Waterloo, 240 Westmount Road N, Waterloo, ON, N2L 3G4 (*Principal* Dr. Glenn Cartwright)
> *E:* glenn.cartwright@
> renison.uwaterloo.ca

Saint Paul University, Anglican Studies Program,223 Main Street, Ottawa, ON, K1S 1C4   *E:* anglicanstudies@ustpaul.ca

(*Director* Kevin Flynn)   *E:* kflynn@ustpaul.ca

Thorneloe University, 935 Ramsey Lake Road, Sudbury, ON, P3E 2C6
> *E:* info@thorneloe.ca

(*Provost* The Revd Dr Robert Derrenbacker)
> *E:* rderrenbacker@laurentian.ca

Toronto School of Theology, 47 Queen's Park Crescent East, Toronto, ON, M5S 2C3
> *E:* inquiries@tst.edu

(*Director* Canon Dr Alan Hayes)
> *E:* alan.hayes@utoronto.ca

Trinity College, University of Toronto, 6 Hoskin Avenue, Toronto, ON, M5S 1H8
> *E:* divinity@trinity.utoronto.ca

(*Dean of Divinity* The Revd Canon Dr David Neelands)   *E:* d.neelands@utoronto.ca

Wycliffe College, University of Toronto, 5 Hoskin Avenue, Toronto, ON, M5S 1H7
> *E:* info@wycliffe.utoronto.ca

(*Principal* Vacancy)

ANGLICAN & PORVOO COMMUNIONS

Quebec
Bishop's University, 2600 College Street, Sherbrooke, QC, J1M 1Z7

(*President* Dr M. Goldbloom/*Registrar* Hans Rouleau)   E: mgoldbloom@ubishop.ca / hrouleau@ubishops.ca

Montreal Diocesan Theological College, 3475 University Street, Montreal, QC, H3A 2A8
E: info@dio.mdtc.ca

(*Principal* Canon Dr John M. Simons)
E: jsimons@montreal.anglican.ca

Saskatchewan
The College of Emmanuel and St Chad, 114 Seminary Crescent, Saskatoon, SK, S7N 0X3
(*Principal* Vacancy *Registrar* Lisa McInnis)
E: emmanuel.stchad@usask.ca

The James Settee College for Ministry, 1308 Fifth Avenue East Prince Albert, SK, S6V 2H7
(*Principal* Mr Gary Graber)
E: minden2@hotmail.com

Centre for Christian Studies (Anglican, United), Woodsworth House, 60 Maryland Street, Winnipeg, MB, R3G 1K7
E: info@ccsonline.ca

(*Principal* The Revd Canon Maylanne Maybee)
E: mmaybee@ccsonline.ca

CHURCH PAPERS
Anglican Journal Tabloid format, national church paper with 22 diocesan publications inserted regionally. The paper is under the management of a committee appointed by General Synod.

Editorial Office: 80 Hayden Street, Toronto, ON, M4Y 3G2
E: anglican.journal@national.anglican.ca
W: www.anglicanjournal.com

PROVINCE OF BRITISH COLUMBIA AND YUKON
Metropolitan of the Ecclesiastical Province of British Columbia and Yukon The Most Revd John E. Privett (*Archbishop of Kootenay*)

BRITISH COLUMBIA
Bishop The Rt Revd Logan McMenamie, 900 Vancouver Street, Victoria, BC, V8V 3V7
T: 1 250 386 7781
F: 1 250 386 4013
E: bishop@bc.anglican.ca

Diocesan email: synod@bc.anglican.ca
W: www.bc.anglican.ca

CALEDONIA
Bishop The Rt Revd William (Bill) J. Anderson, 201–4716 Lazelle Avenue, Terrace, BC, V8G 1T2
T: 1 250 635 6016
F: 1 250 635 6026
E: bishopbill@telus.net

Diocesan email: caledonia@telus.net
W: www.caledonia.anglican.ca

CENTRAL INTERIOR, ANGLICAN PARISHES OF
Bishop The Rt Revd Barbara J. Andrews, 360 Nicola Street, Kamloops, BC, V2C 2P5
T: 1 778 471 5573
F: 1 778 471 5586
E: apcibishop@shaw.ca

Diocesan email: apci@shaw.ca
W: www.apcionline.ca

KOOTENAY
Archbishop The Most Revd John E. Privett, 201–380 Leathead Road, Kelowna, BC, V1X 2H8
T: 1 778 478 8310
F: 1 778 478 8314
E: bishop@kootenay.info

Diocesan email: admin@kootenay.info
W: www.kootenay.anglican.ca

NEW WESTMINSTER
Bishop The Rt Revd Melissa Skelton, 580–410 West Georgia Street, Vancouver, BC, V6B 5A1
T: 1 604 684 6309
F: 1 604 684 7017
E: bishop@vancouver.anglican.ca
W: www.vancouver.anglican.ca

YUKON
Bishop The Rt Revd Larry D. Robertson, PO Box 31136, Whitehorse, YT, Y1A 5P7
T: 1 867 667 7746
F: 1 867 667 6125
E: synodoffice@klondiker.com
W: http://anglican.yukon.net

PROVINCE OF CANADA
Metropolitan of the Ecclesiastical Province of Canada The Most Revd Ronald W. Cutler (*Archbishop of Nova Scotia and Prince Edward Island*)

CENTRAL NEWFOUNDLAND
Bishop The Rt Revd F. David Torraville, 34 Fraser Road, Gander, NL, A1V 2E8
T: 1 709 256 2372
F: 1 709 256 2396
E: bishopcentral@nfld.net
W: www.centraldiocese.org

EASTERN NEWFOUNDLAND AND LABRADOR
Bishop The Rt Revd Geoffrey Peddle, 19 King's Bridge Road, St John's, NL, A1C 3K4
T: 1 709 576 6697
F: 1 709 576 7122
E: geoffpeddle48@gmail.com

Diocesan email: ecrisby@anglicanenl.net
W: www.anglicanenl.net

FREDERICTON
Bishop The Rt Revd David Edwards, 115 Church Street, Fredericton, NB, E3B 4C8
T: 1 506 459 1801
F: 1 506 460 0520
E: edwardsdavid300@gmail.com

Diocesan email: diocese@anglican.nb.ca
W: www.anglican.nb.ca

MONTREAL
Bishop The Rt Revd Mary Irwin-Gibson, 1444 Union Avenue, Montreal, QC, H3A 2B8
T: 1 514 843 9443
F: 1 514 843 3221
E: bishops.office@montreal.anglican.ca
W: www.montreal.anglican.ca

NOVA SCOTIA AND PRINCE EDWARD ISLAND
Archbishop The Most Revd Ronald W. Cutler, 1340 Martello Street, Halifax, NS, B3H 1X3
T: 1 902 420 0717
F: 1 902 425 0717
E: rcutler@nspeidiocese.ca
Diocesan email: office@nspeidiocese.ca
W: www.nspeidiocese.ca

QUEBEC
Bishop The Rt Revd Dennis P. Drainville, 31 rue des Jardins, Quebec, QC, G1R 4L6
T: 1 418 692 3858
F: 1 418 692 3876
E: bishopqc@quebec.anglican.ca
Diocesan email: synodoffice@quebec.anglican.ca
W: www.quebec.anglican.org

WESTERN NEWFOUNDLAND
Archbishop The Most Revd Percy D. Coffin, 25 Main Street, Corner Brook, NL, A2H 1C2
T: 1 709 639 8712
F: 1 709 639 1636
E: bishop_dsown@nf.aibn.com
W: www.westernnewfoundland.anglican.org

PROVINCE OF ONTARIO
Metropolitan of the Ecclesiastical Province of Ontario The Most Revd Colin R. Johnson (*Archbishop of Toronto and Archbishop of Moosonee*)

ALGOMA
Bishop The Rt Revd Dr Stephen G. W. Andrews, Box 1168, Sault Ste Marie, ON, P6A 5N7
T: 1 705 256 5061
F: 1 705 946 1860
E: bishop@dioceseofalgoma.com
Diocesan email: secretary@dioceseofalgoma.com
W: www.dioceseofalgoma.com

HURON
Bishop The Rt Revd Robert (Bob) F. Bennett, 190 Queens Avenue, London, ON N6A 6H7
T: 1 591 434 6893
F: 1 519 673 4151
E: bishops@huron.anglican.ca
W: www.diohuron.org

Suffragan Bishop Vacancy

MOOSONEE (MOOSONEE MISSION AREA)
Archbishop The Most Revd Colin R. Johnson,135 Adelaide Street East, Toronto, ON, M5C 1L8
T: 1 416 363 6021 ext 250
F: 1 416 363 3683
E: cjohnson@toronto.anglican.ca

NIAGARA
Bishop The Rt Revd Michael A. Bird, Cathedral Place 252 James Street North, Hamilton, ON, L8R 2L3
T: 1 905 527 1316 ext 129
F: 1 905 527 1281
E: bishop@niagara.anglican.ca
W: www.niagara.anglican.ca

ONTARIO
Bishop The Rt Revd Michael D. Oulton, 90 Johnson Street, Kingston, ON, K7L 1X7
T: 1 613 544 4774 ext 129
F: 1 613 547 3745
E: moulton@ontario.anglican.ca
Diocesan email: synod@ontario.anglican.ca
W: www.ontario.anglican.ca

OTTAWA
Bishop The Rt Revd John H. Chapman, 71 Bronson Avenue, Ottawa, ON, K1R 6G6
T: 1 613 233 7741
F: 1 613 232 3995
E: bishopsoffice@ottawa.anglican.ca
W: www.ottawa.anglican.ca

TORONTO
Archbishop The Most Revd Colin R. Johnson, 135 Adelaide Street East, Toronto, ON, M5C 1L8
T: 1 416 363 6021 ext 250
F: 1 416 363 3683
E: cjohnson@toronto.anglican.ca
W: www.toronto.anglican.ca

Area Bishops
The Rt Revd Peter D. Fenty (*York-Simcoe*), PO Box 233, King City, ON, L3B 1A5
T: 1 905 833 8327
F: 1 905 833 8329
E: pfenty@toronto.anglican.ca
W: www.anglican.toronto.ca

ANGLICAN & PORVOO COMMUNIONS

The Rt Revd Linda C. Nicholls (*Trent-Durham*), 207–965 Dundas Street West, Whitby, ON, L1P 1G8   *T:* 1 905 668 1558
F: 1 905 668 8216
E: lnicholls@toronto.anglican.ca
W: www.anglican.toronto.ca

The Rt Revd Patrick T. Yu (*York-Scarborough*), 135 Adelaide Street East, Toronto, ON, M5C 1L8   *T:* 1 416 363 6021 ext 253
F: 1 416 363 3683
E: pyu@toronto.anglican.ca
W: www.anglican.toronto.ca

The Rt Revd M. Philip Poole (*York-Credit Valley*), 135 Adelaide Street East, Toronto, ON, M5C 1L8   *T:* 1 416 363 6021 ext 223
F: 1 416 363 3683
E: ppoole@toronto.anglican.ca
W: www.anglican.toronto.ca

PROVINCE OF RUPERT'S LAND

Metropolitan of the Ecclesiastical Province of Rupert's Land The Most Revd Gregory Kerr-Wilson (*Archbishop of Calgary*)

THE ARCTIC

Bishop The Rt Revd David W. Parsons, Box 190, 4910 51st Street, Yellowknife, NT, X1A 2N2
T: 1 867 873 5432
F: 1 867 873 8478
E: arctic@arcticnet.org
W: www.arcticnet.org

Suffragan Bishop The Rt Revd Darren J. McCartney, Box 5,Iqaluit, NU, X0A 0H0
T: 1 867 873 5432
F: 1 867 873 8478
E: darren@arcticnet.org
W: www.arcticnet.org

ATHABASCA

Bishop The Rt Revd Fraser W. Lawton, Box 6868, Peace River, AB, T8S 1S6   *T:* 1 780 624 2767
F: 1 780 624 2365
E: bpath@telusplanet.net
Diocesan email: dioath@telusplanet.net

BRANDON

Bishop The Rt Revd William Cliff
Box 21009, WEPO, Brandon, MB, R7B 3W8
T: 1 204 727 7550
F: 1 204 727 4135
E: bishopbdn@mymts.net
Diocesan email: diobran@mymts.net
W: www.dioceseofbrandon.org

CALGARY

Archbishop The Most Revd Gregory Kerr-Wilson, 1209 59th Ave SE, Calgary, AB, T2H 2P6   *T:* 1 403 243 3673
F: 1 403 243 2182
E: gkerrwilson@calgary.anglican.ca
Diocesan email: diocese@calgary.anglican.ca
W: www.calgary.anglican.ca

EDMONTON

Bishop The Rt Revd Jane Alexander, 1035 Street, Edmonton, AB, T5J 0X5
T: 1 780 439 7344
F: 1 780 439 6549
E: bishop@edmonton.anglican.ca
Diocesan email: churched@ edmonton.anglican.ca
W: www.edmonton.anglican.org

KEEWATIN

Diocese exists but has no parishes under its jurisdiction.

MISHAMIKOWEESH, INDIGENOUS SPIRITUAL MINISTRY OF

Bishop The Rt Revd Lydia Mamakwa, Box 65, Kingfisher Lake, ON, P0V 1Z0
T: 1 807 532 2085
F: 1 807 532 2344
E: lydiam@kingfisherlake.ca

QU'APPELLE

Bishop The Rt Revd Robert Hardwick, 1501 College Avenue, Regina, SK, S4P 1B8
T: 1 306 522 1608
F: 1 306 352 6808
E: bishop.rob@sasktel.net
General email: quappelle@sasktel.net
W: www.quappelle.anglican.ca

RUPERT'S LAND

Bishop The Rt Revd Donald D. Phillips, 935 Nesbitt Bay, Winnipeg, MB, R3T 1W6
T: 1 204 992 4212
F: 1 204 992 4219
E: bishop@rupertsland.ca
Diocesan email: general@rupertsland.ca
W: www.rupertsland.ca

SASKATCHEWAN

Bishop The Rt Revd Michael W. Hawkins, 1308 5th Avenue East, Prince Albert, SK, S6V 2H7
T: 1 306 763 2455
F: 1 306 764 5172
E: bishopmichael@sasktel.net
Diocesan email: synod@sasktel.net
W: www.saskatchewan.anglican.org

Diocesan Indigenous Bishop The Rt Revd Adam Halkett (*as above*)
E: bishopadam@sasktel.net

SASKATOON

Bishop The Rt Revd David M. Irving, 1403 9th Avenue North, Saskatoon, SK, S7K 2Z6
T: 1 306 244 5651
F: 1 306 244 4606
E: bishopdavid@sasktel.net
Diocesan email: anglicansynod@sasktel.net
W: www.saskatoon.anglican.org

The Church of the Province of Central Africa

Members 600,000

The province includes Botswana, Malawi, Zambia and Zimbabwe. The first Anglican missionary to Malawi was Bishop Charles Mackenzie who arrived with David Livingstone in 1861. The province was inaugurated in 1955 and has a movable bishopric. The countries forming the province are very different. Zambia and Botswana suffer the difficulties of rapid industrialization, along with underdevelopment and thinly populated areas. In Malawi 30 per cent of the adult males are away as migrant labourers in other countries at any given time. Zimbabwe is experiencing problems of social adjustment after independence.

Archbishop of the Province The Most Revd Albert C. Chama

Provincial Secretary Vacancy

Provincial Treasurer Mr Evans Mwewa, CPCA, PO Box 22317, Kitwe, Zambia   *T:* 260 351 081
F: 267 351 668

ANGLICAN THEOLOGICAL COLLEGES

Leonard Kamungu (Anglican) Theological College, PO Box 959, Zomba. Malawi (*Dean* Revd Alinafe Kalemba)   *T:* 265 1 525 286
265 8 856 410 (Mobile)

National Anglican Theological College of Zimbabwe (Ecumenical Institute of Theology), 11 Thornburg Avenue, Groom Bridge, Mount Pleasant, Harare, Zimbabwe

St John's Seminary, Mindolo, PO Box 20369, Kitwe, Zambia (*Rector* The Rt Revd John Osmers)   *T:* 260 2 210960
E: josmers@zamnet.zm

CHURCH PAPER

Link Monthly newspaper for the Dioceses of Mashonaland and Matabeleland giving news and views of the dioceses. *Editorial Offices* Link Board of Management, PO Box UA7, Harare City.

BOTSWANA

Bishop The Rt Revd Metlhayotlhe Rawlings Beleme, PO Box 769, Gaborone, Botswana
T: 267 395 3779
F: 267 395 3015
E: angli_diocese@info.bw

CENTRAL ZAMBIA

Bishop The Rt Revd Derek Gary Kamukwamba, PO Box 70172, Ndola, Zambia
T: 260 2 612 431
E: adcznla@zamnet.zm

CENTRAL ZIMBABWE

Bishop The Rt Revd Ishmael Mukuwanda, PO Box 25, Gweru, Zimbabwe
T: 263 54 221 030
F: 263 54 221 097
E: diocent@telconet.co.zw

EASTERN ZAMBIA

Bishop The Rt Revd William Muchombo, PO Box 510154, Chipata, Zambia
T: and *F:* 260 216 221 294
E: dioeastzm@zamnet.zm

HARARE

Bishop The Rt Revd Chad Gandiya, 9 Monmouth Rdoa, Avondale, Harare, Zimbabwe   *T:* 263 4 308 042
E: chadgandiya@gmail.com

LAKE MALAWI

Bishop The Rt Revd Francis Kaulanda, PO Box 30349, Lilongwe 3, Malawi
T: 265 1 797 858 (Office)
F: 265 1 797 548
E: franciskaulanda@yahoo.com

LUAPULA

Bishop The Rt Revd Robert Mumbi, PO Box 710210, Mansa, Luapula, Zambia
T: 260 2 821 680
E: diopula@zamtel.zm

LUSAKA

Bishop The Rt Revd David Njovu, PO Box 30183, Lusaka, Zambia   *T:* 260 1 254 515 (Office)
E: davidnjovu1961@zamnet.zm /
davidnjovu1961@gmail.com

MANICALAND

Bishop The Rt Revd Erick Ruwona, 146 Herbert Chitepo Road, Mutare, Zimbabwe
T: 263 20 8418

MASVINGO

Bishop The Rt Revd Godfrey Tawonezvi, PO Box 1421, Masvingo, Zimbabwe
T: 263 39 362 536
E: bishopgodfreytawonezvi@gmail.com

MATABELELAND

Bishop The Rt Revd Cleophas Lunga, PO Box 2422, Bulaweyo, Zimbabwe
T: 263 09 61 370
F: 263 09 68 353
E: clunga@aol.com

NORTHERN MALAWI

Bishop The Rt Revd Fanuel E. C. Magangani, Box 120, Mzuzu, Malawi, Central Africa
T: 2651312 858
E: magangani@sdup.org.mw

ANGLICAN & PORVOO COMMUNIONS

NORTHERN ZAMBIA
Bishop The Most Revd Albert Chama (*Archbishop of the Province*), PO Box 20798, Kitwe, Zambia   *T:* 260 2 223 264
F: 260 2 224 778
E: chama_albert@yahoo.ca

SOUTHERN MALAWI
Bishop The Rt Revd Alinafe Kalemba, PO Box 30220, Chichiri, Blantyre, 3, Malawi
T: 265 1 641 218
F: 265 1 641 235
E: dean@sdup.org.mw

UPPER SHIRE
Bishop The Rt Revd Brighton Vitta Malasa, Private Bag 1, Chilema, Zomba, Malawi
T: 265 1 539 203
E: malasab@yahoo.com.uk

The Anglican Church of the Central American Region

(Iglesia Anglicana de la Región Central de América)

Members 15,600
This province of the Anglican Communion is made up of the Dioceses of Guatemala, El Salvador, Nicaragua, Costa Rica and Panama. The Church was introduced by the Society for the Propagation of the Gospel when England administered two colonies in Central America, Belize (1783–1982) and Miskitia (1740–1894). In the later years Afro-Antillean people brought their Anglican Christianity with them. The province is multicultural and multiracial and is committed to evangelization, social outreach, and community development.

Primate The Most Revd Sturdie Downs (*Bishop of Nicaragua*)

Provincial Treasurer Mr Harold Charles, Apt R, Balboa, Republic of Panama
T: 507 212 0062
F: 507 262 2097
E: iarcahch@sinfo.net

COSTA RICA
Bishop The Rt Revd Hector Monterroso, Apartado 2773-100, San José, Costa Rica
T: 506 225 0209/253 0790
F: 506 253 8331
E: hmonterroso@episcopalcostarica.org

EL SALVADOR
Bishop The Rt Revd Juan David Alvarado Melgar, 47 Avenida Sur, 723 Col Flor Blanca, Apt Postal (01), 274 San Salvador, El Salvador
T: 503 2223 2252
F: 503 2223 7952
E: es@gmail.com

GUATEMALA
Bishop The Most Revd Armando Román Guerra-Soria, Apt 58A, Avenida La Castellana 40–06, Guatemala City, Zona 8, Guatemala
T: 502 2472 0852
F: 502 2472 0764
E: agepiscopal@yahoo.com

NICARAGUA
Bishop The Rt Revd Sturdie Downs (*Primate of the Anglican Church of the Central American Region*), Apt 1207, Managua, Nicaragua
T: 505 222 5174
F: 505 2545 248
E: secretaria_diocesana@hotmail.com

PANAMA
Bishop The Rt Revd Julio Murray, Box R, Balboa, Republic of Panama
T: 507 212 0062/507 262 2051
F: 507 262 2097
E: bpmurray@hotmail.com
W: www.episcopalpanama.org

The Church of the Province of Congo

Members approximately 500,000
Ugandan evangelist Apolo Kivebulaya established an Anglican presence in the Democratic Republic of Congo (formerly Zaire) in 1896. The Church reached the Katanga (formerly Shaba) region in 1955, but evangelization did not progress on a large scale until the 1970s. Following independence,

the Church expanded and formed dioceses as part of the Province of Uganda, Burundi, Rwanda, and Boga-Zaire. The new province was inaugurated in 1992 and changed its name in 1997. On 17 September 2002 the then Archbishop Njojo and many other Congolese citizens had to flee to Uganda because of internal tribal warfare.

Archbishop The Most Revd Zacharie Masimango Katanda (*Bishop of Kindu*) PO Box 16482 Kinshasa 1 DR Congo
T: 243 998916258
*E:*angkindu@yahoo.fr@yahoo.fr

Provincial Secretary The Ven Anthonio Kibwela Kifwambwa   *T:* 243 995412138
E: anglicancongo@yahoo.com

Provincial Treasurer Mr Alain Batondela
T: 243 810547929
E: albatondel@gmail.com

Liaison Office in Kampala Mr Fréderick Ngadjole Badja, PO Box 25586, Kampala, Uganda   *E:* eac-mags@infocom.co.ug

Provincial Coordinator of Evangelism The Revd Desire Mukanirwa Kadorho
T: 243 99704614
E: peac.evangelisation@gmail.com

THEOLOGICAL COLLEGE
Anglican University of Congo (Universite Anglicane du Congo 'U.A.C.') PO Box 25586, Kampala, Uganda

Rector Mr Amuda Baba Dieu-Merci
T: 43 994074822
E: email: amuda2b@yahoo.com

ARU
Bishop The Rt Revd Dr Georges Titre Ande, PO Box 226, Arua, Uganda
T: 243 81 039 30 71
E: revdande@yahoo.co.uk

BOGA (formerly BOGA-ZAIRE)
Bishop The Rt Revd William Bahemuka Mugenyi, PO Box 25586, Kampala, Uganda
T: 243 99 0668639
E: mugenyiwilliam@yahoo.com

BUKAVU
Bishop the Rt Revd Sylvestre Bahati Bali-Busane, Av. Mgr Ndahura, No. Q/Nyalukemba, C/Ibanda, CAC-Bukavu, BP 2876, Bukavu, Democratic Republic of Congo / PO Box 134, Cyangugu, Rwanda   *T:* 243 99 401 3647
E: bahati_bali@yahoo.fr

KATANGA
Bishop The Rt Revd Corneille Kasima Muno, 1309 Chaussee do Kasenga, Bel-Air, Lubumbashi, PO Box 22037, Kitwe, Zambia
T: and F: 243 81 475 6075
E: kasimamuno@yahoo.fr

Assistant Missionary Bishop from Tanzania based in Kalemie The Rt Revd Elisha Tendwa Lawrence   *T:* 243 824621849

KINDU
Bishop The Rt Revd Zacharie Masimango Katanda, PO Box 5, Gisenyi, Rwanda
T: 243 99 891 6258
E: angkindu@yahoo.fr

KINSHASA
Bishop The Rt Revd Achille Mutshindu, 11 Ave. Basalakala, Quartier Immocongo Commune de Kalamu, Kinshasa 1, PO Box 16482, DR Congo

Assistant Missionary Bishop based in Congo-Brazzaville The Rt Revd Jean Molanga Botola, EAC-Kinshasa, BP 16482, Kinshasa 1, DR Congo   *T:* 243 99 471 3802
E: molanga2k@yahoo.co.uk

KISANGANI
Bishop The Rt Revd Lambert Funga Botolome (*Dean of the Province*), Av. Bowane, No 10, Quartier des Musiciens, C/Makiso, PO Box 86, Kisangani, DR Congo *or* c/o PO Box 25586, Kampala, Uganda
T: 243 997 252 868 (Mobile)
E: lambertfunga@hotmail.com

NORD KIVU
Bishop The Rt Revd Adoplh Muhindo Isesomo, PO Box 322, Butembo, DR Congo *or* PO Box 25586 Kampala, Uganda
T: 243 99 8854 8601

KASAIS
Bishop The Rt Revd Marcel Kapinga Kayibabu wa Ilunga, PO Box 16482, Kinshasa 1, DR Congo   *T:* 243 99 357 0080
E: anglicanekasai2@gmail.com

KAMANGO
Bishop The Rt Revd Daniel Sabiti Tibafa, PO Box 25586, Kampala, Uganda
T: 243 997791013
e-mail: sabititibafa@gmail.com

ANGLICAN & PORVOO
COMMUNIONS

The Church of England

Baptized members 26,000,000

Covering all of England, the Isle of Man and the Channel Islands; Europe except Great Britain and Ireland; Morocco; Turkey; and the Asian countries of the former Soviet Union. The Church of England is the ancient national Church of the land. Its structures emerged from the missionary work of St Augustine, sent from Rome in ad 597, and from the

work of Celtic missionaries in the north. Throughout the Middle Ages, the Church was in communion with the See of Rome, but in the sixteenth century it separated from Rome and rejected the authority of the Pope. The Church of England is the established Church, with its administration governed by a General Synod, which meets twice a year.

Hong Kong Sheng Kung Hui

(Anglican/ Episcopal Church)

Members 30,000

This dynamic province was inaugurated in 1998. The history of the Church in China dates back to the mid-nineteenth century; missionaries were provided by the American Church, the Church of England, the Church of England in Canada, etc. The Province of Chung Hua Sheng Kung Hui (the Holy Catholic Church in China) was established in 1912 of which the Anglican Church in Hong Kong and Macau was an integral part. Chung Hua Sheng Kung Hui ceased to exist in the 1950s and the diocese of Hong Kong and Macau was associated to other dioceses in South East Asia under the custodianship of the Council of Churches of East Asia, until the recent establishment of the diocese as the 38th province of the Anglican Communion. It has parishes in Hong Kong and Macau, which returned to Chinese sovereignty in 1997 and 1999 respectively. It enjoys autonomy and independence as guaranteed by the Basic Law (the mini constitution governing Hong Kong, the Special Administrative Region of China).

Primate The Most Revd Dr Paul Kwong, Provincial Office, 16/F Tung Wai Commercial Building, 109–111 Gloucester Road, Wanchai, Hong Kong SAR   *T:* 852 2526 5355
F: 852 2521 2199
E: office1@hkskh.org
W: www.hkskh.org

Provincial Secretary General The Revd Peter Douglas Koon (*same address*)
E: peter.koon@hkskh.org

Bishop of Hong Kong Island The Most Revd Dr Paul Kwong, 71 Bonham Road, Hong Kong SAR   *T:* 852 2526 5366
F: 852 2523 3344
E: do.dhk@hkskh.org
W: http://dhk.hkskh.org

Bishop of Eastern Kowloon The Rt Revd Dr Timothy Kwok, Diocesan Office, 4/F Holy Trinity Bradbury Centre, 139 Ma Tau Chung Road, Kowloon City, Kowloon, Hong Kong SAR   *T:* 852 2713 9983
F: 852 2711 1609
E: office.dek@hkskh.org
W: http://dek. hkskh.org

Bishop of Western Kowloon The Rt Revd Andrew Chan, Diocesan Office, 11 Pak Po Street, Mongkok, Kowloon, Hong Kong SAR
T: 852 2783 0811
F: 852 2783 0799
E: dwk@hkskh.org
W: http://dwk.hkskh.org

Bishop of Missionary Area of Macau The Most Revd Dr Paul Kwong, 1 andar A, Edf, HuaDu, No. 2 Trav. Do Pato, No. 49–51 Rua do Campo, Macau SAR   *T:* 853 2835 3867
F: 853 2832 5314
E: skhmma@macau.ctm.net
W: www.hkskh.org

The Church of the Province of the Indian Ocean

Members more than 600,000

The Anglican mission was begun in Mauritius in 1812 by the Revd H. Shepherd, and the first Anglican church in the Seychelles was dedicated in January 1856. The first Anglican missionaries went to Madagascar in 1864. The

growth of the church was fostered both by the Society for the Propagation of the Gospel and by the Church Missionary Society. The Diocese of Mauritius was created in 1854. The first three dioceses in Madagascar, Antananarivo, Toamasina and Antsiranana, were created in 1969 and Seychelles was established as a diocese in 1973. The dioceses of Madagascar and Mauritius and Seychelles combined in 1973 to create the province, which now comprises eight dioceses.

Archbishop The Most Revd Ian Gerald James Ernest (*Bishop of Mauritius*), Bishop's House, Mallatamby Road, Phoenix, Mauritius
T: 230 686 5158
E: dioang@intnet.mu

Provincial Secretary The Revd Canon Samitiana Jhonson Razafindralamo, Dupin Street Rectory, St Clement, Curepipe, Mauritius
T: 230 676 22 50
E: indian.ocean.psec@gmail.com

Treasurer Mr Bernard Laure (*same address as the Archbishop*)

Chancellor of the Province Mrs Hilda Yerriah, Chancery House, Port Louis, Mauritius
T: 230 20 80429 (Office)
230 46 75710 (Home)
E: hilda5885@hotmail.com

Dean of the Province The Rt Revd Jean-Claude Andrianjafimanana (*Bishop of Mahajanga*)

THEOLOGICAL COLLEGES
St Paul's College, Ambatohararana, Merimandroso, Ambohidratrimo, Madagascar (*Warden* Prof Michel Razafiarivony)

Diocesan Training Centre, Rose Hill, Mauritius (*Warden* The Rt Revd Joseph Papatoti)

St Philip's Theological College, La Misère, Seychelles (*Diocesan Trainer* The Revd Peter Raath)

CHURCH PAPERS
Newsletters of the Province of the Indian Ocean Support Assn. *Editor* The Revd Philip Harbridge, Chaplain, Christ's College, Cambridge CB2 3BY, UK

Seychelles Diocesan Magazine A quarterly newspaper covering diocesan events and containing articles of theological and other interest.

Magazine du Diocèse de Maurice (Le Cordage) A quarterly newspaper covering diocesan events and containing articles of theological and ecumenical interest.

Provincial e-letters: provincial e-news *Le phare* every two months and provincial cycle of prayer every three months.

ANTANANARIVO
Bishop The Rt Revd Samoela Jaona Ranarivelo, Évêché Anglican, Lot VK57 ter, Ambohimanoro, 101 Antananarivo, Madagascar
T: 261 20 222 0827
F: 261 20 226 1331
E: eemdanta@yahoo.com

ANTSIRANANA
Bishop The Rt Revd Theophile Botomazava Oliver Simon, Évêché Anglican, BP 278, 4 rue Grandidier, 201 Antsiranana, Madagascar
T:261 20 822 2776

FIANARANTSOA
Bishop The Rt Revd Gilbert Rateloson Rakotondravelo, Évêché due Diocese Fianarantsoa, BP 1418 301 Fianarantsoa, Madagascar
T: 261 20 755 15 83
261 33 73 067 81 (Mobile)
E: eemdiofianara@yahoo.fr

MAHAJANGA
Bishop The Rt Revd Jean-Claude Andrianjafimanana, Évêché Anglican, BP 570, 401 Mahajanga, Madagascar
T: 261 62 23611
261 32 04 55143 (Mobile)
E: andrianjajc@yahoo.fr/
eemdmaha@dts.mg

MAURITIUS
Bishop The Most Revd Ian Gerald James Ernest (*Archbishop of the Province*), Bishop's House, Nallatamby Road, Phoenix, Mauritius
T: 230 686 5158
F: 230 697 1096
E: dioang@intnet.mu

SEYCHELLES
Bishop The Rt Revd James Richard Wong Yin Song, PO Box 44, Victoria, Mahé, Seychelles
T: 248 32 1977/32 3879
248 52 7770 (Mobile)
F: 248 22 4043
E: angdio@seychelles.net
W: www.seychelles.anglican.org

TOAMASINA
Bishop Th e Rt Revd Jean Paul Solo, Évêché Anglican, Lot VK57 ter, Ambohimanoro, 101 Antananarivo, Madagascar
T: 261 20 533 1663
261 32 04 55143 (Mobile)
Fax: 261 20 533 1689
E: eemtoam@moov.mg

TOLIARA
Bishop The Rt Revd Todd MacGregor, Eklesia Episkopaly, Malagasy, BP 408601, Toliara, Madagascar
T: 261 33 374 2745
W: peoplereaching.org

ANGLICAN & PORVOO COMMUNIONS

The Church of Ireland

Figures for the Church of Ireland population are based on those stated in the 2011 censuses for the Republic of Ireland (129,039) and Northern Ireland (248,821). Recent censuses indicate an increase in the Church of Ireland population in the Republic of Ireland.

Members 377,860

Tracing its origins to St Patrick and his companions in the fifth century, the Irish Church has been marked by strong missionary efforts. In 1537 the English king was declared head of the Church, but most Irish Christians maintained loyalty to Rome. The Irish Church Act of 1869 provided that the statutory union between the Churches of England and Ireland be dissolved and that the Church of Ireland should cease to be established by law. A General Synod of the Church, established in 1871 and consisting of archbishops, bishops, and representatives of the clergy and laity, has legislative and administrative power. Irish Church leaders have played a key role in the work of reconciliation in the Northern Ireland conflict.

The Primate of All Ireland and Metropolitan The Most Revd Dr Richard Lionel Clarke (*Archbishop of Armagh*)

The Primate of Ireland and Metropolitan The Most Revd Dr Michael Geoffrey St Aubyn Jackson (*Archbishop of Dublin & Bishop of Glendalough*)

Central Office of the Church of Ireland Church of Ireland House, Church Avenue, Rathmines, Dublin 6, Republic of Ireland D06 CF67
T: 353 1 497 8422
F: 353 1 497 8821
E: office@rcbdub.org

Chief Officer and Secretary, Representative Church Body Mr David Ritchie
E: chiefofficer@rcbdub.org

Head of Synod Services and Communications Mrs Janet Maxwell   *E:* comms@rcbdub.org

THEOLOGICAL INSTITUTE
The Church of Ireland Theological Institute, Braemor Park, Churchtown, Dublin 14, D14 KX24 which conducts courses in conjunction with the School of Hebrew, Biblical and Theological Studies, Trinity College, Dublin, Republic of Ireland (*Director* The Revd Canon Dr Maurice Elliott)   *T:* 353 1 492 3506
F: 353 1 492 3082
E: admin@theologicalinstitute.ie
W: http://www.theologicalinstitute.ie

CHURCH PAPER
Church of Ireland Gazette (independent weekly) Deals with items of general interest to the Church of Ireland in a national context and also contains news from the various dioceses and parishes together with articles of a more general nature. *Editor:* The Revd Canon Dr Ian M Ellis
Editorial Offices 3 Wallace Ave, Lisburn, Co Antrim BT27 4AA   *T:* 44 28 9267 5743
F: 44 28 9266 7580
E: gazette@ireland.anglican.org
W. http://www.coigazette.net

PROVINCE OF ARMAGH
ARMAGH
Archbishop of Armagh (Primate of All Ireland and Metropolitan) The Most Revd Dr Richard Lionel Clarke, c/o Church House, 46 Abbey Street, Armagh BT61 7DZ
T: 44 28 3752 7144 (Office)
F: 44 28 3751 0596
E: archbishop@armagh.anglican.org
W: http://armagh.anglican.org

CATHEDRAL CHURCH OF ST PATRICK, Armagh
Dean The Very Revd Gregory John Orchard Dunstan, The Deanery, Library House, 43 Abbey Street, Armagh BT61 7DY
T: 44 28 3752 3142 (Office)
44 28 3751 8447 (Home)
E: dean@armagh.anglican.org
W: http:// www.stpatricks-cathedral.org

CLOGHER
Bishop The Rt Revd Francis John McDowell, The See House, Fivemiletown, Co Tyrone BT75 0QP   *T: and F:* 44 28 8952 2461
E: bishop@clogher.anglican.org
W: http://clogher.anglican.org

CATHEDRAL CHURCHES OF ST MACARTAN, Clogher and ST MACARTIN, Enniskillen
Dean The Very Revd Kenneth Robert James Hall, St Macartin's Deanery, 13 Church Street, Enniskillen, Co Fermanagh BT74 7DW
T: 44 28 6632 2917 (Office)
44 28 6632 2465 (Home)
E: dean@clogher.anglican.org
W: http://enniskillen.clogher.anglican.org

CONNOR
Bishop The Rt Revd Alan Francis Abernethy, Diocesan Office, Church of Ireland House, 61-67 Donegall Street, Belfast BT1 2QH
T: 44 28 9082 8870 (Office)
E: bishop@connor.anglican.org
W: http://connor.anglican.org

CATHEDRAL CHURCH OF CHRIST CHURCH, Lisburn
Dean of Connor The Very Revd William Samuel Wright, Cathedral Rectory, 11D Magheralave Road, Lisburn, Co Antrim BT28 3BE
T: 44 28 9260 2400 (Office)
44 28 9209 0260 (Home)
E: sam.wright@lisburncathedral.org
W: http://www.lisburncathedral.org

CATHEDRAL CHURCH OF ST ANNE, Belfast
Cathedral of the United Dioceses of Down and Dromore and the Diocese of Connor.

Dean The Very Revd John Owen Mann, The Deanery, 5 Deramore Drive, Belfast BT9 5JQ
T: 44 28 9066 0980 (Home)
44 28 9032 8332 (Cathedral)
F: 44 28 9023 8855
E: dean@belfastcathedral.org
W: http://www.belfastcathedral.org

DERRY AND RAPHOE

Bishop The Rt Revd Kenneth Raymond Good, The See House, 112 Culmore Road, Londonderry, Co Derry BT48 8JF
T: 44 28 7126 2440 (Office)
F: 44 28 7137 7013
E: bishop@derry.anglican.org
W: http://derry.anglican.org

CATHEDRAL CHURCH OF ST COLUMB, Derry
Dean The Very Revd Raymond Stewart
W: http://www.stcolumbscathedral.org

CATHEDRAL CHURCH OF ST EUNAN, Raphoe
Dean The Very Revd Kenneth Arthur Lambart Barrett, The Deanery, Raphoe, Lifford, Co Donegal, Republic of Ireland F93 KT21
T: 353 74 914 5226
E: deanarthur@raphoe.anglican.org

DOWN AND DROMORE

Bishop The Rt Revd Harold Creeth Miller, The See House, 32 Knockdene Park South, Belfast BT5 7AB   *T:* 44 28 9082 8850 (Office)
F: 44 28 9023 1902
E: bishop@down.anglican.org
W: http://down.anglican.org

CATHEDRAL CHURCH OF THE HOLY AND UNDIVIDED TRINITY, Down
Dean The Very Revd Thomas Henry Hull, Lecale Rectory, 9 Quoile Road, Downpatrick, Co Down BT30 6SE   *T:* 44 28 4461 3101
F: 44 28 4461 4456
E: henryhull@downcathedral.org
W: http://www.downcathedral.org

CATHEDRAL CHURCH OF CHRIST THE REDEEMER, Dromore
Dean The Very Revd Geoff Wilson, 30 Church Street, Dromore BT25 1AA   *T:* 44 28 9269 3968
E: jill@dromorecathedral.co.uk
W: http://cathedral.dromore.anglican.org
W: http://www.dromorecathedral.co.uk

KILMORE, ELPHIN AND ARDAGH

Bishop The Rt Revd Samuel Ferran Glenfield, The See House, Kilmore, Cavan, Co Cavan, Republic of Ireland   *T:* 353 49 437 1551
E: bishop@kilmore.anglican.org
W: http://kilmore.anglican.org

CATHEDRAL CHURCH OF ST FETHLIMIDH, Kilmore
Dean The Very Revd Nigel Nicholas Crossey, The Deanery, Danesfort, Cavan, Co Cavan, Republic of Ireland   *T:* 353 49 433 1918
E. dean@kilmore.anglican.org

CATHEDRAL CHURCH OF ST MARY THE VIRGIN AND ST JOHN THE BAPTIST, Sligo
Dean The Very Revd Arfon Williams, The Deanery, Strandhill Road, Sligo, Co Sligo, Republic of Ireland   *T:* 353 71 915 7993
E: arvonwilliams@eircom.net
W: http://sligocathedral.elphin.anglican.org

TUAM, KILLALA AND ACHONRY

Bishop The Rt Revd Patrick William Rooke, Bishop's House, Breaffy Woods, Cottage Road, Castlebar, Co Mayo, Republic of Ireland
T: 353 94 903 5703
E: bishop@tuam.anglican.org
W: http://tuam.anglican.org

CATHEDRAL CHURCH OF ST MARY, Tuam
Dean The Very Revd Alistair John Grimason, Deanery Place, Cong, Co Mayo, Republic of Ireland   *T:* 353 94 954 6909
E: deantuam@yahoo.co.uk

CATHEDRAL CHURCH OF ST PATRICK, Killala
Dean The Very Revd Alistair John Grimason, Deanery Place, Cong, Co Mayo, Republic of Ireland   *T:* 353 94 954 6909
E: deantuam@yahoo.co.uk

PROVINCE OF DUBLIN
CASHEL, WATERFORD, LISMORE, OSSORY, FERNS AND LEIGHLIN

Bishop The Rt Revd Michael Andrew James Burrows, Bishop's House, Troysgate, Kilkenny, Republic of Ireland
T: 353 56 77 86633 (Home)
E: cfobishop@gmail.com
W: http://cashel.anglican.org

CATHEDRAL CHURCH OF ST JOHN THE BAPTIST AND ST PATRICK'S ROCK, Cashel
Dean The Very Revd Gerald Gordon Field, The Deanery, Boherclogh Street, Cashel, Co Tipperary, Republic of Ireland
T: 353 62 61232 (Home)
E: dean@cashel.anglican.org

329

CATHEDRAL CHURCH OF THE BLESSED TRINITY (CHRIST CHURCH), Waterford
Dean The Very Revd Maria Patricia Jansson, The Deanery, 41 Grange Park Road, Waterford, Co Waterford, Republic of Ireland
T: 353 51 858 958 (Office)
353 51 874 119 (Home)
E: dean@waterford.anglican.org
W: http://christchurchwaterford.com

CATHEDRAL CHURCH OF ST CARTHAGE, Lismore
Dean The Very Revd Paul Richard Draper, The Deanery, The Mall, Lismore, Co Waterford, Republic of Ireland   *T:* 353 58 54105
E: dean@lismore.anglican.org

CATHEDRAL CHURCH OF ST CANICE, Kilkenny
Dean The Very Revd Katharine Margaret Poulton, The Deanery, Kilkenny, Republic of Ireland   *T:* 353 56 772 1516
E: dean@ossory.anglican.org

CATHEDRAL CHURCH OF ST EDAN, Ferns
Dean The Very Revd Paul Gerard Mooney, The Deanery, Ferns, Enniscorthy, Co Wexford, Republic of Ireland   *T:* 353 53 936 6124
E: dean@ferns.anglican.org

CATHEDRAL CHURCH OF ST LASERIAN, Leighlin
Dean The Very Revd Thomas William Gordon, The Deanery, Old Leighlin, Co Carlow, Republic of Ireland   *T:* 353 59 972 1570
E: dean.leighlin@gmail.com

CORK, CLOYNE AND ROSS
Bishop The Rt Revd Dr William Paul Colton, St Nicholas' House, 14 Cove Street, Cork, Republic of Ireland, T12 RP40
T: 353 21 500 5080 (Office)
E: bishop@corkchurchofireland.com
W: http://cork.anglican.org

CATHEDRAL CHURCH OF ST FIN BARRE, Cork
Dean The Very Revd Nigel Kenneth Dunne, The Deanery, Gilabbey Street, Cork, Republic of Ireland, T12 CK4C   *T:* 353 21 4318073
E: dean@cork.anglican.org
W: http://cathedral.cork.anglican.org

CATHEDRAL CHURCH OF ST COLMAN, Cloyne
Dean The Very Revd Alan Gordon Marley, The Deanery, Midleton, Co Cork, Republic of Ireland, P25 HY61   *T:* 353 21 463 1449
E: dean@cloyne.anglican.org
W: http://cathedral.cloyne.anglican.org

CATHEDRAL CHURCH OF ST FACHTNA, Ross
Dean The Very Revd Christopher Lind Peters, The Deanery, Rosscarbery, Co Cork, Republic of Ireland, P85 HF61   *T:* 353 23 48166
E: candjpeters@eircom.net
W: http://cork.anglican.org/ross-union

DUBLIN AND GLENDALOUGH
Archbishop The Most Revd Dr Michael Geoffrey St Aubyn Jackson, The See House, 17 Temple Road, Dartry, Dublin 6, Republic of Ireland
T: 353 1 4125 663
E: archbishop@dublin.anglican.org
W: http://dublin.anglican.org

CATHEDRAL CHURCH OF THE HOLY TRINITY (COMMONLY CALLED CHRIST CHURCH)
Cathedral of the United Dioceses of Dublin and Glendalough, Metropolitan Cathedral of the United Provinces of Dublin and Cashel

Dean The Very Revd Dermot Patrick Martin Dunne, 19 Mountainview Road, Ranelagh, Dublin 6, Republic of Ireland
T: 353 1 677 8099 (Cathedral)
F: 353 1 679 8991
E: dean@cccdub.ie
W: http://christchurchdublin.ie

THE NATIONAL CATHEDRAL AND COLLEGIATE CHURCH OF ST PATRICK, Dublin
The National Cathedral of the Church of Ireland has a common relation to all the dioceses of Ireland.

Dean and Ordinary The Very Revd William Wright Morton, The Deanery, Upper Kevin Street, Dublin 8, Republic of Ireland
T: 353 1 475 5449 (Home)
353 1 453 9472 (Cathedral)
F: 353 1 454 6374
E: dean@stpatrickscathedral.ie
W: http://www.stpatrickscathedral.ie

LIMERICK, ARDFERT, AGHADOE, KILLALOE, KILFENORA, CLONFERT, KILMACDUAGH AND EMLY
Bishop The Rt Revd Kenneth Arthur Kearon, Rien Roe, Adare, Co Limerick, Republic of Ireland
T: 353 61 396 244
E: bishop@limerick.anglican.org
W: http://limerick.anglican.org

CATHEDRAL CHURCH OF ST MARY, Limerick
Dean The Very Revd Sandra Pragnell, The Deanery, 7 Kilbane, Castleroy, Limerick, Republic of Ireland   *T:* 00 353 61 338 697
E: sandrapragnell@eircom.net
W: http://cathedral.limerick.anglican.org

CATHEDRAL CHURCH OF ST FLANNAN, Killaloe
Dean Very Revd Gary Alexander Paulsen, The Deanery, Abbey Road, Killaloe, Co Clare, Republic of Ireland   *T:* 353 61 374 779
E: abbeydean2@gmail.com

CATHEDRAL CHURCH OF ST BRENDAN, Clonfert
Dean The Very Revd Gary Alexander Paulsen, The Deanery, Abbey Road, Killaloe, Co Clare, Republic of Ireland   *T:* 353 61 374 779
E: abbeydean2@gmail.com

MEATH AND KILDARE

Bishop The Most Revd Patricia Louise (Pat) Storey, Bishop's House, Moyglare, Maynooth, Co Kildare, Republic of Ireland
T: 353 1 629 2163 (Office)
E: bishop@meath.anglican.org
W: http://meath.anglican.org

CATHEDRAL CHURCH OF ST PATRICK, Trim
Dean of Clonmacnoise The Very Revd Paul David Bogle, St Patrick's Deanery, St Loman's Street, Trim, Co Meath, Republic of Ireland
T: 353 46 943 6698
E: pdbogle@gmail.com

CATHEDRAL OF ST BRIGID, Kildare
Dean The Very Revd John Joseph Marsden, The Deanery, Morristown, Newbridge, Co Kildare, Republic of Ireland
T: 353 45 438 158
E: johnmarsden@eircom.net

The Anglican Communion in Japan

(Nippon Sei Ko Kai)

Members 30,355
In 1859 the American Episcopal Church sent two missionaries to Japan, followed some years later by representatives of the Church of England and the Church in Canada. The first Anglican Synod took place in 1887. The first Japanese bishops were consecrated in 1923. The Church remained oppressed during the Second World War and assumed all church leadership after the war.

Primate The Most Revd Nathaniel Makoto Uematsu (*Bishop of Hokkaido*)

Provincial Office Nippon Sei Ko Kai, 65 Yarai-cho, Shinjuku-ku, Tokyo 162–0805 (Please use this address for all correspondence)
T: 81 3 5228 3171
F: 81 3 5228 3175
E: province@nskk.org
W: www.nskk.org

General Secretary The Revd Jesse Shin-ichi Yahagi   *E:* general-sec.po@nskk.org

Provincial Treasurer Mr Matthias Shigeo Ozaki

THEOLOGICAL TRAINING
Central Theological College, 1–12–31 Yoga, Setagaya-ku, Tokyo 158–0097, for clergy and lay workers

Bishop Williams Theological School, Shimotachiuri-agaru, Karasuma Dori, Kamikyo-ku, Kyoto 602–8332

CHURCH NEWSPAPERS
Japanese language Provincial Office newsletter issued monthly, can be downloaded from the official website of NSKK. Each diocese also has its own monthly paper.

NSKK News English-language newsletter. Published quarterly. Available through the Provincial Office and also on the Anglican Communion website.

CHUBU

Bishop The Rt Revd Peter Ichiro Shibusawa, 28–1 Meigetsu-cho, 2-chome, Showa-ku, Nagoya 466–0034   *T:* 81 52 858 1007
F: 81 52 858 1008
E: office.chubu@nskk.org
W: www.nskk.org/chubu

HOKKAIDO

Bishop The Most Revd Nathaniel Makoto Uematsu (*Archbishop of the Province*), Kita 15 jo, Nishi 5-20, Kita-Ku, Sapporo 001-0015
T: 81 11 717 8181
F: 81 11 736 8377
E: office@nskk-hokkaido.jp
W: www.nskk-hokkaido.jp

KITA KANTO

Bishop The Rt Revd Zerubbabel Katsuichi Hirota, 2–172 Sakuragi-cho, Omiya-ku, Saitama-shi, 331–0852   *T:* 81 48 642 2680
F: 81 48 648 0358
E: kitakanto@nskk.org
W: www.nskk-kitakanto.org

KOBE

Bishop The Rt Revd Augustin Naoaki Kobayashi, 5–11–1 Yamatedori, Chuo-ku, Kobe-shi 650–0011   *T:* 81 78 351 5469
F: 81 78 382 1095
E: aao52850@syd.odn.ne.jp
W: www.nskk.org/kobe

KYOTO
Bishop The Rt Revd Stephen Takashi Kochi, 380 Okakuencho, Shimotachiuri-agaru, Karasumadori, Kamikyo-ku, Kyoto 602–8011
T: 81 75 431 7204
F: 81 75 441 4238
E: nskk-kyoto@kvp.biglobe.ne.jp
W: www.nskk.org/kyoto

KYUSHU
Bishop The Rt Revd Luke Ken-ichi Muto, 2–9–22 Kusakae, Chuo-ku, Fukuoka 810–0045
T: 81 92 771 2050
F: 81 92 771 9857
E: d-kyushu@ymt.bbiq.jp
W: http://www1.bbiq.jp/d-kyushu

OKINAWA
Bishop The Rt Revd David Eisho Uehara, 3–5–5 Meada, Urasoe-shi, Okinawa 910-2102
T: 81 98 942 1101
F: 81 98 942 1102
E: namizato@anglican-okinawa.jp
W: http://anglican-okinawa.jp

OSAKA
Bishop The Rt Revd Andrew Haruhisa Iso, 2–1–8 Matsuzaki-cho, Abeno-ku, Osaka 545–0053
T: 81 6 6621 2179
F: 81 6 6621 3097
E: office.osaka@trad.ocn.ne.jp
W: www.nskk.org/osaka

TOHOKU
Bishop The Rt Revd John Msato Yoshida, 2–13–15 Kokubun-cho, Aoba-ku, Sendai 980-0803
T: 81 22 223 2349
F: 81 22 223 2387
E: sec.tohoku@nskk.org
W: www.nskk.org/tohoku

TOKYO
Bishop The Rt Revd Andrew Yoshimichi Ohata, 3–6–18 Shiba Koen, Minato-ku, Tokyo 105-0011
T: 81 3 3433 0987
F: 81 3 3433 8678
E: general-sec.tko@nskk.org
W: www.nskk.org/tokyo

YOKOHAMA
Bishop The Rt Revd Laurence Yutaka Minabe, 14–57 Mitsuzawa Shimo-cho, Kanagawa-ku, Yokohama 221-0852
T: 81 45 321 4988
F: 81 45 321 4978
E: g-sec.yokohama@anglican.jp
W: anglican.jp/yokohama

The Episcopal Church in Jerusalem and the Middle East

Members 10,000
The Church comprises the dioceses of Jerusalem, Iran, Egypt, Cyprus, and the Gulf. The Jerusalem bishopric was founded in 1841 and became an archbishopric in 1957. Reorganization in January 1976 ended the archbishopric and combined the Diocese of Jordan, Lebanon and Syria with the Jerusalem bishopric after a 19-year separation. Around the same time, the new Diocese of Cyprus and the Gulf was formed and the Diocese of Egypt was revived.

THE CENTRAL SYNOD
Archbishop The Most Revd Dr Mouneer Hanna Anis (*Bishop in Egypt with North Africa and the Horn of Africa*)

Provincial Secretary Mrs Georgia Katsantonis, 2 Grigori Afxentiou, PO Box 22075, Nicosia 1517, Cyprus
T: +357 99619176
E: georgia@spidernet.com.cy

Provincial Treasurer The Ven Dr William Schwartz, PO Box 3210, Doha, Qatar
T: + 974 4416 5726
E: archdeacon.bill@cypgulf.org

The Jerusalem and the Middle East Church Association acts in support of the Episcopal Church in Jerusalem and the Middle East, the Central Synod and all four dioceses. *Secretary* Mrs Shirley Eason, 1 Hart House, The Hart, Farnham, Surrey GU9 7HA
T: 01252 726994
F: 01252 735558
E: secretary@jmeca.eclipse.co.uk

CYPRUS AND THE GULF
Bishop in The Rt Revd Michael Augustine Owen Lewis, PO Box 22075, Nicosia 1517, Cyprus
T: 357 22 671220
F: 357 2 22 674553
E: bishop@spidernet.com.cy
W: www.cypgulf.org

EGYPT WITH NORTH AFRICA AND THE HORN OF AFRICA

Bishop in The Most Revd Dr Mouneer Hanna Anis (*Archbishop of the Episcopal Church of Jerusalem and the Middle East*), Diocesan Office, PO Box 87, Zamalek Distribution, 11211, Cairo, Egypt   *T:* 20 2 738 0829
F: 20 2 735 8941
E: bishopmouneer@gmail.com
W: www.dioceseofegypt.org

Suffragan The Rt Revd Grant Lemarquand (*Horn of Africa*) (*same address*)

IRAN

Bishop in The Rt Revd Azad Marshall, St Thomas Center, Raiwind Road, PO Box 688, Lohore, Punjab, 54000, Pakistan
T: 92 42 542 0452
E: bishop@saintthomascenter.org

JERUSALEM

Bishop in The Most Revd Suheil Dawani, St George's Close, PO Box 1278, Jerusalem 91 019, Israel   *T:* 972 2 627 1670
F: 972 2 627 3847
E: bishop@j-diocese.com
W: www.j-diocese.org

The Anglican Church of Kenya

Members 3,500,000

Mombasa saw the arrival of Anglican missionaries in 1844, with the first African ordained to the priesthood in 1885. Mass conversions occurred as early as 1910. The first Kenyan bishops were consecrated in 1955. The Church became part of the Province of East Africa, established in 1960, but by 1970 Kenya and Tanzania were divided into separate provinces.

Primate The Most Revd Dr Jackson N. Ole Sapit (*Bishop of All Saints Cathedral Diocese*) PO Box 40502, 00100 Nairobi
T: 254 2 714 755 or 0734 – 916358
F: 254 2 718 442
E: archoffice@ackenya.org
W: www.ackenya.org

Provincial Secretary The Revd Canon Rosemary Mbogo   *T:* 254 20 271 4753
F: 254 20 271 8442
E: ackpsoffice@ackenya.org

Provincial Treasurer Professor William Ogara
E: wo.ogara@gmailcom

THEOLOGICAL COLLEGES

ACK Language School and Orientation School, PO Box 47429 – 00100, Nairobi
T: 254 2 721893
E: acklanguageschool@ackenya.org

ACK Guest House, PO Box 56292 – 00200, Nairobi   *T:* 254 2 723200/2724780
E: anglicanghnbi@ackguesthouses.com

ACK St Julian's Centre, PO Box 574 – 00621, Village Market
T: 254 2 3594672/0733 785202
or 0722430075
E: ackjulians@ackenya.org

ACK Guest House Mombasa, PO Box 96170, Likoni, Mombasa   *T:* 0723 712588 (*mobile*)
E: info@ackhotelmombasa.com
W: www.ackhotelmombasa.com

Carlile College for Theology & Business Studies, PO Box 72584 – 00200, Nairobi
T: 254 2 5550490/1/2/3
E: info@carlilecollege.org
W: www.carlilecollege.org

St Andrew's College of Theology and Development Kabare, PO Box 6, Kerugoya
T: 254 60 21256
E: ackstakabare@swiftkenya.com

Berea Theological College, PO Box 1945, Nakuru   *T:* 254 51 52493
E: berea-tc@wananchi.com

St Paul's Theological College, Kapsabet, PO Box 18, Kapsabet   *T:* 254 53 52053
E: ackstpck@multitechweb.com

St Philip's Theological College Maseno, PO Box 1, Maseno   *T:* 254 57 51019
Mobile: 0723 763467
E: stpmaseno@swiftkenya.com

Bishop Hannington Institute Mombasa, PO Box 81150 – 80100, Mombasa
T: 254 41 2491396
E: ackbhanning-msa@swiftmombasa.com

ANGLICAN & PORVOO COMMUNIONS

Church Commissioners for Kenya, PO Box
30422, 00100 Nairobi   *T:* 254 20 717106/9
        E: desmond.mtula@churchcom.co.ke

Uzima Press, PO Box,13966 – 00800 Westlands
Nairobi   *T:* 254 20 4440536/7
        E: info@ackuzima.or.ke

ALL SAINTS CATHEDRAL DIOCESE
Bishop The Most Revd Dr Jackson N. Ole Sapit
(*Archbishop of Kenya*), PO Box 40502, 00100
Nairobi   *T:* 254 20 714 755/0734 916358
        F: 254 20 718 442/714 750
        E: archoffice@ackenya.org

BONDO
Bishop The Rt Revd Johannes Otieno Angela,
PO Box 240, 40601 Bondo
        T: Mobile: 0705 213964
        E: bishopjohannes@gmail.com
        bondoack@yahoo.com

BUNGOMA
Bishop The Rt Revd George Wafula Mechumo,
PO Box 2392, 50200 Bungoma
        T: and *F:* 254 337 30481
        Mobile: 0726 400718/0733 680921
        E: georgemechumo@yahoo.com
        ackbungomadiocese@yahoo.com

BUTERE
Bishop The Rt Revd Dr Timothy Wambunya,
PO Box 54, 50101 Butere
        T: 254 20 2447585
        F: 254 53 2062785
        E: tlwambunya@gmail.com
        buterediocese@gmail.com

ELDORET
Bishop The Rt Revd Chrisopher K. Ruto, PO
Box 3404, 30100 Eldoret   *T:* 254 53 2062785
        Mobile: 0710 577545
        E: ackeldoret@africaonline.co.ke

EMBU
Bishop The Rt Revd David Muriithi Ireri, PO
Box 189, 60100 Embu   *T:* 254 68 30614
        F: 254 68 30468
        Mobile: 0728 787403/0737 126276
        E: ackembu@yahoo.com
        W: info@ackembu.org

KAJIADO
Bishop The Rt Revd Gadiel Katanga Lenini, PO
Box 203, 01100 Kajiado
        T: wireless: 254 203513911
        Mobile: 0716 392564
        Mobile: 0715 216610
        E: ackajiado@gmail.com

KAPSABET
Bishop The Rt Revd Paul Korir, PO Box 643,
30300 Kapsabet
        Mobile: 0723 988119/0719 448282
        Mobile (Office): 0792 711277/0732 961710
        E: info@ackkapsabetdiocese.org

KATAKWA
Bishop The Rt Revd Dr Zakayo Iteba Epusi,
PO Box 68, 50244 Amagoro   *T:* 254 55 54079
        E: itebazake@gmail.com

KERICHO
Bishop The Rt Revd Ernest Kiprotich, PO Box
678 – 20200, Kericho
        E: ackkcodioc@yahoo.com

KIRINYAGA
Bishop The Rt Revd Joseph Kibuchwa, PO Box
95, 10304 Kutus
        Tel wireless: 254 0202124416
        F: 254 163 44 020
        E: info@ackirinyaga.org

KITALE
Bishop The Rt Revd Stephen Kewasis Nyorsok,
PO Box 4176, 30200 Kitale
        Tel wireless: 254 0202028911
        T: 254 054 31631
        E: ack.ktl@gmail

KITUI
Bishop The Rt Revd Josephat Mule, PO Box
1054, 90200 Kitui   *T:* 254 04444/22119
        E: ac.kitui09@yahoo.com

MACHAKOS
Bishop The Rt Revd Joseph Mutungi, PO Box
282, 90100 Machakos   *T:* 254 044 21379
        Mobile: 0704 521061/0738 981942
        F: 254 044 20178
        E: ackmachakos@gmail.com

MAKUENI
Bishop The Rt Revd Joseph Kanuku, PO Box
532, 90300 Makueni
        Mobile: 0733 757767/0727 812020/
                0789 393395
        E: ackmakueni@gmail.com

MALINDI
Bishop The Rt Revd Lawrence Dena, PO Box
6110, 80200 Malindi
        Mobile: 0722 536 743/0735 953635
        E: dena_larry@yahoo.
        comackmalindidiocese@gmail.com

MARALAL
Bishop The Rt Revd Jacob A Lesuuda, PO Box
42, 20600 Maralal   *Mobile:* 0722 693 168
        E: bishopjlesuuda@gmail.com

MARSABIT
Bishop The Rt Revd Daniel Qampicha, PO Box 51, 60500 Marsabit *or* c/o MAF Kenya, PO Box 21123, 00505 Nairobi   *Mobile:* 0700319730
E: ackbishopmarsabit@gmail.com

MASENO EAST
Bishop The Rt Revd Joshua Owiti, PO Box 31, 40101 Ahero   *T:* 0714 890166
T: 0791 571720 (Office)
E: ackmasenoeast@gmail.com

MASENO NORTH
Bishop The Rt Revd Simon M. Oketch, PO Box 416, 50100 Kakemega
T: and *F:* 254 056 30729
E: ackmnorth@jambo.co.ke

MASENO SOUTH
Bishop The Rt Revd Dr Francis Mwayi Abiero, PO Box 114, 40100 Kisumu
T: 254 057 2025148
Mobile: 0733 709378/0722 601110
F: 254 35 21009
E: bpfabiero@yahoo.com

MASENO WEST
Bishop The Rt Revd Dr Joseph Otieno Wasonga, PO Box 793, 40600 Siaya
Mobile: 0722 280648

MBEERE
Bishop The Rt Revd Dr Moses Masamba Nthukah, PO Box 122, 60104 Siakago
E: bishopmbeere@gmail.com
bishopmbeere@ackdiocesembeere.org

MERU
Bishop The Rt Revd Charles Mwendwa, PO Box 427, 60200 Meru
Mobile: 0721 270460/0725 558948
E: ackdmeru@yahoo.com

MOMBASA
Bishop The Rt Revd Julius R. K. Kalu, PO Box 80072, 80100 Mombasa   *T:* 254 41 2331365
E: kalunangombo@yahoo.co.uk
diocese@ackmombasa.or.ke

MOUNT KENYA CENTRAL
Bishop The Rt Revd Isaac Ng'ang'a, PO Box 121, 10200 Murang'a   *T:* 254 060 30559
E: ackmkcentral@wananchi.com

Assistant Bishop The Rt Revd Allan Waithaka (*same address*)

MOUNT KENYA SOUTH
Bishop The Rt Revd Timothy Ranji, PO Box 886, 00900 Kiambu   *T:* 254 66 22521
Mobile: 0724 583596/0735 212414
E: info@ack.mtkenya.org
ackdiocesemtkenyasouth@gmail.com

MOUNT KENYA WEST
Bishop The Rt Revd Joseph M. Kagunda, PO Box 229, 10100 Nyeri   *T:* 254 61 203 2281
E: info@ackmtkwest.co.ke

MUMIAS
Bishop The Rt Revd Beneah Justin Okumu Salala, PO Box 213, 50102 Mumias
T: 254 Wireless 020 2442846
E: ackmumiasdiocese@yahoo.com

MURANG'A SOUTH
Bishop The Rt Revd Julius Karanu, PO Box 414, 01020 Kenol, Murang'a
Mobile: 0737 436466/0733 263547
email: ackmurangasouth@gmail.com
juliuskaranu@yahoo.com
E: wbishopjoseph@gmail.com

NAIROBI
Bishop The Rt Revd Joel Waweru, PO Box 40502, 00100 Nairobi
T: PABX 020 4440524/5
Mobile: 0726 610520/0733 226337
F: 254 2 226 259
E: bishop@acknairobidiocese.org

NAKURU
Bishop The Rt Revd Joseph Muchai, PO Box 56, 20100 Nakuru   *T:* 254 051 2212151/5
Mobile: 0707 681 686 or 0729 558423
F: 254 051 2212437
E: acknkudioc@africaonline.co.ke

Suffragan Bishop – Baringo Mission Area The Rt Revd Musa Kamuren

NAMBALE
Bishop The Rt Revd Dr Robert Magina, PO Box 4, 50409 Nambale
T: 254 055 24040 or 0726 592257
E: acknambale@swiftkenya.com
magina12@yahoo.co.uk

NYAHURURU
Bishop The Rt Revd Stephen Kabora, PO Box 926, 20300 Nyahururu   *T:* 254 065 2032179
E: nyahudc@gmail.com

SOUTHERN NYANZA
Bishop The Rt Revd James Kenneth Ochiel, PO Box 65, 40300 Homa Bay   *T:* 254 059 22054
Wireless: 020 2031079
Mobile: 0721 794968
E: jkochiel@yahoo.com
acksnyanza@swiftkenya.com

Bishop, Kisii Mission Area The Rt Revd John Orina Omangi, PO Box 121, 40200 Kisii
Mobile: 0725 534 047

TAITA TAVETA
Bishop The Rt Revd Dr Samson M. Mwaluda,
PO Box 75, 80300 Voi   *T:* 254 043 2030096
                          E: acktaita@ackenya.org

Bishop Co-Adjutor The Rt Revd Liverson
Mng'onda, P O Box 75 – 80300 Voi
                          E: acktaita@ackenya.org

THIKA
Bishop The Rt Revd Julius Wanyoike, PO Box
214, 01000 Thika
                  T: 254 067 31654/067 2328850
                          F: 254 067 31544
                  E: info@ackthikadiocese.org

The Anglican Church of Korea

(Daehan Seong Gong Hoe)

Members 15,543
From the time when Bishop John Charles Corfe
arrived in Korea in 1890 until 1965, the Diocese
of Korea has had English bishops. In 1993, the
Archbishop of Canterbury installed the newly
elected Primate and handed jurisdiction to
him, making the Anglican Church of Korea
a province of the Anglican Communion. The
Province includes three dioceses, Seoul,
DaeJeon, and Pusan. Apart from these dioceses,
there are two major religious orders for men
and women and one international mission
society for Seafarers in the Korean Anglican
Church and as well as an Anglican university.

Primate The Most Revd Paul Keun Sang Kim
(Bishop of Seoul)

Provincial Offices 15 Sejong-daero 21-gil, Jung-
gu, Seoul 100–120   *T:* 82 2 738 8952
                          F: 82 2 737 4210
                  E: anglicankorea@gmail.com

Secretary-General The Revd Stephen Sikyung
Yoo *(same address)*   *T:* 82 2 738 8952
                          F: 82 2 737 4210
                  E: 08skyoo@naver.com
                  W: www.skh.or.kr

ANGLICAN UNIVERSITY
(Sungkonghoe University) 320 Yeondong-ro,
Guro-gu, Seoul 152–716

(President Revd Augustine Jeong Ku Lee)
                          T: 82 2610 4100
                          F: 82 2 737 4210
                          E: jkl@skhu.ac.kr

CHURCH PAPER
Daehan Seonggonghoesinmun
This fortnightly paper of the Anglican Church
of Korea is the joint concern of all three
dioceses. Tabloid format. Printed in Korean.
Contains regular liturgical and doctrinal
features as well as local, national and
international church news.
                          T: 82 2 736 6990
                          F: 82 2 738 1208

PUSAN DIOCESE
Bishop The Rt Revd Onesimus Dongsin Park,
Anglican Diocese of Busan, 5-1 Daecheong-ro
99beon-gil, Jung-gu, Busan 600–092
                          T: 82 51 463 5742
                          F: 82 51 463 5957
                  E: onesimus63@hanmail.net
                  W: skhpusan.onmam.com

DAEJEON DIOCESE
Bishop The Rt Revd Moses Nakjun Yoo,
Anglican Diocese of Daejeon, 53 Dongseo-
daero   1466beon-gil,   Jung-gu,   Daejeon
301–823   *T:* 82 42 256 9987
                          F: 82 42 255 8918
                  E: ynj600@hanmail.net
                  W: www.djdio.or.kr

SEOUL DIOCESE
Bishop The Most Revd Paul Keun Sang Kim
(Presiding Bishop of the Province), Anglican
Diocese of Seoul, 15 Sejong-daero 21-gil,
Jung-gu, Seoul 100–120   *T:* 82 2 735 6157
                          F: 82 2 723 2640
                  E: paulkim7@hitel.net
                  W: www.skhseoul.or.kr

Society of the Holy Cross
15   Sejong-daero   21-gil,   Jung-gu,   Seoul
100–120   *T:* 82 2 735 7832
                          F: 82 2 7 36 5028
                  E: holycross25@hanmail.net
                  W: www.sister.or.kr

Society of Saint Francis
Balsan-ri 156-1, Nam-myeon, Chuncheon-si,
Gangwon-do 200-922   *T:* 82 33 263 4662
                          F: 82 33 263 4048
                  E: kfb1993@kornet.net
                  W: www.francis.or.kr

The Mission to Seafarers
Port Chaplain The Revd Dr Simon C. Ro,
PO Box 793, Busan 600-607 South Korea
                          T: 82 51 627 9188
                          F: 82 51 624 1713
                  E: difference1961@gmail.com

The Church of the Province of Melanesia

Members 250,000

After 118 years of missionary association with the Church of the Province of New Zealand, the Church of the Province of Melanesia was formed in 1975. The province encompasses the Republic of Vanuatu and the Solomon Islands, both sovereign island nations in the South Pacific, and the French Trust Territory of New Caledonia.

Archbishop of the Province The Most Revd George Takeli (*Bishop of Central Melanesia*)

General Secretary Mr Abraham Hauriasi (*same address*)
T: 677 20470
E: hauriasi_a @comphq.org.sb
W: www.acom.org.sb

ANGLICAN THEOLOGICAL COLLEGE
Bishop Patteson Theological College, Kohimarama, PO Box 19, Honiara, Solomon Islands (trains students up to degree standard) (*Principal* The Revd Atkin Zaku)
T: 677 7363271
F: 677 21098
E: bptckohimarama@gmail.com

BANKS AND TORRES
Bishop The Rt Revd Alfred Patteson Worek
T: 678 38520
E: dobtbishop@gmail.com

CENTRAL MELANESIA
Bishop The Most Revd George Takeli (*Archbishop of the Province*), PO Box 19, Honiara, Solomon Islands
T: 677 26101
F: 677 21098
E: g.takeli@comphq.org.sb

CENTRAL SOLOMONS
Bishop The Rt Revd Ben Seka, PO Box 52, Tulagi, CIP, Solomon Islands
T: 677 32006
F: 677 32113
E: bishopseka@gmail.com

GUADALCANAL
Bishop The Rt Revd Nathan Tome, PO Box 19, Honiara, Solomon Islands
T: 677 23337
E: ntome4080@gmail.com

HANUATO'O
Bishop The Rt Revd Alfred Karibongi, PO Box 20, Kira Kira, Makira Province, Solomon Islands
T: 677 50012
E: bishophanuatoo@solomon.com.sb

MALAITA
Bishop The Rt Revd Samuel Sahu, Bishop's House, PO Box 7, Auki Malaita Province, Solomon Islands
T: 677 7458686
E: sam.malaita@gmail.com

TEMOTU
Bishop The Rt Revd George Angus Takeli, Bishop's House, Lata, Santa Cruz, Temotu Province, Solomon Islands
T: 677 53080
E: peace.gtakeli@gmail.com

VANUATU
Bishop The Rt Revd James Marvin Ligo, Bishop's House, PO Box 238, Luganville, Santo, Republic of Vanuatu
T: and F: 678 37065/36631
E: dovbishop@vanuatu.com.vu

YSABEL
Bishop The Rt Revd Richard Naramana, Bishop's House, PO Box 6, Buala, Jejevo, Ysabel Province, Solomon Islands
T: 677 35124
E: episcopal@solomon.com.sb

The Anglican Church of Mexico

Members 21,000

The Mexican Episcopal Church began with the political reform in 1857, which secured freedom of religion, separating the Roman Catholic Church from the government and politics. Some priests organized a National Church and contacted the Episcopal Church in the United States, seeking the ordination of bishops for the new church. They adopted the name 'Mexican Episcopal Church'. The Mexican Church became an autonomous province of the Anglican Communion in 1995 with the name Iglesia Anglicana de Mexico.

Archbishop The Most Revd Francisco Manuel Moreno (*Bishop of Northern Mexico*)
E: primado@mexico-anglican.org

Provincial Secretary The Revd Canon Alfonso Walls, Acatlán 102 Oriente, Col Mitras Centro, Monterrey, Nuevo Leon, 64460
T: 52 81 8333 0992
F: 52 81 8348 7362
E: awalls@mexico-anglican.org

Provincial Treasurer Laura Gracia
E: lgracia@mexico-anglican.org

CUERNAVACA
Bishop The Rt Revd Enrique Treviño Cruz, Calle Minerva No 1, Col. Delicias, CP 62330 Cuernavaca, Morelos
T: 52 777 315 2870 (Office)
52 777 322 2559 (Home)
E: diocesisdecuernavaca@hotmail.com

MEXICO
Bishop The Rt Revd Carlos Touché Porter, Ave San Jerónimo 117, Col. San Ángel, Delegación Álvaro Obregón, 01000 México, D.F.
T: 52 55 5616 3193
F: 52 55 5616 2205
E: diomex@axtel.net

NORTHERN MEXICO
Bishop The Rt Revd Francisco Manuel Moreno (*Archbishop of the Province*), Acatlán 102 Ote,

Col. Mitras Centro, CP 64460, Monterrey, Nuevo Leon
T: 52 81 8333 0992
F: 52 81 8348 7362
E: primado@mexico-anglican.org

SOUTHEASTERN MEXICO
Bishop The Rt Revd Benito Juárez-Martínez, Avenida de Las Américas #73, Col. Aguacatal, 91130 Xalapa, Veracruz
T: 52 228 814 6951
F: 52 228 814 4387
E: obispobenito.49@gmail.com

WESTERN MEXICO
Bishop The Rt Revd Lino Rodríguez-Amaro, Torres Quintero #15, Col. Seattle, 45150 Zapopan, Jalisco
T: 52 33 3560 4726
F: 52 33 3560 4726
E: obispolino@hotmail.com

The Church of the Province of Myanmar (Burma)

Members 60,767
Anglican chaplains and missionaries worked in Myanmar in the early and mid-nineteenth century. The Church of the Province of Myanmar was formed in 1970, nine years after the declaration of Buddhism as the state religion and four years after all foreign missionaries were forced to leave.

Archbishop of the Province The Most Revd Stephen Than Myint Oo (*Bishop of Yangon*)

Provincial Secretary The Revd Dr Paul Myint Htet Htin Ya, PO Box 11191, 140 Pyidaungsu Yeiktha Road, Dagon, Yangon
T: 95 1 395279
95 1 395350
E: myinthtet@gmail.com

Provincial Treasurer Daw Myint Htwe Ye (*same address*)

Secretary and Treasurer, Yangon Diocesan Trust Association Daw Pin Lon Soe (*same address*)

ANGLICAN THEOLOGICAL COLLEGES
Holy Cross Theological College, 104 Inya Road, University PO (11041), Yangon (*Principal* The Revd Dr Samuel San Myat Shwe)

CHURCH NEWSLETTER
The province publishes a monthly 80-page Newsletter. *Editor and Manager* Mr Soe Thein, PO Box 11191, Bishopscourt, 140 Pyidaungsu Yeiktha Road, Dagon, Yangon

HPA-AN
Bishop The Rt Revd Saw Stylo, No (4) Block, Bishop Gone, Diocesan Office, Hpa-an, Kayin State
T: 95 58 21696

MANDALAY
Bishop The Rt Revd David Nyi Nyi Naing, Bishopscourt, 22nd St, 'C' Road (between 85–86 Rd), Mandalay
T: 95 2 34110

MYITKYINA
Bishop The Rt Revd John Zau Li, Diocesan Office, Tha Kin Nat Pe Road, Thida Ya, Myitkyina
T: 95 74 23104

SITTWE
Bishop The Rt Revd Dr James Min Dein, St John's Church, Paletwa, Southern Chin State, Via Sittwe

TOUNGOO
Bishop The Rt Revd Dr Saw (John) Wilme, Diocesan Office, Nat Shin Naung Road, Toungoo
T: 95 54 23 519 (Office)
95 54 24216 (Home)

YANGON
Bishop The Most Revd Stephen Than Myint Oo (*Archbishop of the Province*), PO Box 11191, 140 Pyidaungsu-Yeiktha Road, Dagon, Yangon
T: 95 1 395279/395350 (Office)
95 1 381909 (Home)

Assistant Bishop The Rt Revd Samuel Htan Oak, 44 Pyi Road, Dagon, Yangon
T: 95 1 372300

The Church of Nigeria

(Anglican Communion)

Members 17,500,000

The rebirth of Christianity began with the arrival of Christian freed slaves in Nigeria in the middle of the nineteenth century. The Church Missionary Society established an evangelistic ministry, particularly in the south. The division of the Province of West Africa in 1979 formed the Province of Nigeria and the Province of West Africa. In the 1990s, nine missionary bishops consecrated themselves to evangelism in northern Nigeria. Membership growth has dictated the need for new dioceses year by year. In 1997 the Church of Nigeria was divided into three provinces to enable more effective management. In 1999 another twelve dioceses were created, and in January 2003 the Church was re-organized into ten provinces. There are currently fourteen provinces.

Metropolitan and Primate of All Nigeria The Most Revd Nicholas D. Okoh (*Archbishop of the Province of Abuja and Bishop of Abuja*)

Provincial Secretary Vacancy, Episcopal House, 24 Douala Street, Wuse District, Zone 5, PO Box 212, Abuja, ADCP Garki, Abuja   *T:* 234 9 523 6950
          E: communicator1@anglican-nig.org
                    W: www.anglican-nig.org

Provincial Treasurer Chief O Adekunle, PO Box 78, Lagos   *T:* 234 1 263 3581

THEOLOGICAL COLLEGES

Ezekiel College of Theology, Ujoelen, Ekpoma, Edo State (*Principal* The Ven Dr Williams Aladekugbe)   *T:* 234 08033 859624
          E: Aladeinlly2001@yahoo.com

Vining College, PMB 729, Oke Emeso, Akure, Ondo State (*Principal* The Ven Dr Steve Fagbemi)   *T:* 234 034 243 031

PROVINCE OF ABA

Archbishop The Most Revd Dr Ikechi Nwachukwu Nwosu (*Bishop of Umuahia*)

AROCHUKWU-OHAFIA

Bishop The Rt Revd Johnson Chibueze Onuoha, Bishopscourt, PO Box 193, Arochukwa, Abia State   *T:* 234 802 538 6407 (Mobile)
          E: aroohafia@anglican.ng.org

IKWUANO

Bishop The Rt Revd Chigozirim U. Onyegbule, Bishopscourt, PO Box 5, Ahaba-Oloko, Abia State   *T:* 234 803 085 9319 (Mobile)
          E: ikwuano@anglican-nig.org

ISIALA NGWA

Bishop The Rt Revd Owen Nwankujiobi Aziibuike, Bishopscourt, St George's Cathedral Compound, PNB 2033, Mbawsi, Abia State
          T: 234 805 467 0528 (Mobile)
          E: bpowenazubuike@yahoo.com

ISIALA NGWA SOUTH

Bishop The Rt Revd Isaac Nwaobia, St Peter's Cathedral Compound, PO Box 15, Owerrinta, Abia State   *T:* 234 803 711 9317 (Mobile)
          E: isialangwasouth@anglican-nig.org

ISIUKWUATO

(Missionary diocese) *Bishop* The Rt Revd Manasses Chijiokem Okere, Bishopscourt, PO Box 350, Ovim, Abia State
          T: 234 803 338 6221 (Mobile)
          E: isiukwuato@anglican-nig.org

UKWA

Bishop The Rt Revd Samuel Kelechi Eze, PO Box 20468, Aba, Abia State
          T: 234 803 789 2431 (Mobile)
          E: kelerem53787@yahoo.com

UMUAHIA

Bishop The Most Revd Dr Ikechi Nwachukwu Nwosu (*Archbishop of the Province of Aba*), St Stephen's Cathedral Compound, PO Box 96, Umuahia, Abia State   *T:* 234 88 221 037
                    Fax: 234 803 549 9066
          E: ik_nwosu01@yahoo.com

PROVINCE OF ABUJA

Archbishop The Most Revd Nicholas D. Okoh (*Metropolitan and Primate of All Nigeria and Bishop of Abuja*)

ABUJA

Bishop The Most Revd Nicholas Okoh (*Metropolitan and Primate of All Nigeria and Archbishop of the Province of Abuja*), Episcopal House, 24 Douala Street, Wuse District, Zone 5, PO Box 212, Abuja, ADCP Garki
          T: 234 56 580 682
          E: nickorogodo@yahoo.com

BIDA

Bishop The Rt Revd Jonah Kolo, Bishop's House, St John's Mission Compound, PO Box 14, Bida   *T:* 234 66 461 694
          E: bida@anglican-nig.org

GBOKO

Bishop The Rt Revd Emmanuel Nyitsse

GWAGWALADA
Bishop The Rt Revd Tanimu Samari Aduda, Diocesan Headquarters, Secretariat Road, PO Box 287, Gwagwalada, Abuja
T: 234 9 882 2083
E: anggwag@skannet.com.ng

IDAH
Bishop The Rt Revd Joseph N. Musa, Bishopscourt's, PO Box 25, Idah, Kogi State
E: idah@anglican-nig.org

KAFANCHAN
Bishop The Rt Revd Marcus M. Dogo, PO Box 29, Kafanchan, Kaduna State
T: 234 61 20 634

KUBWA
Bishop The Rt Revd Duke Timothy Akamisoko, Bishop's House, PO Box 67, Kubwa, Abuja FCT, Nigeria
T: 234 0803 451 9437 (Mobile)
E: dukesoko@yahoo.com

KWOI
Bishop The Rt Revd Paul Samuel Zamani, Bishop's Residence, Cathedral Compound, Samban Gide, PO Box 173, Kwoi, Kaduna State
T: 234 080 651 8160 (Mobile)
E: paulzamani@yahoo.com

LAFIA
Bishop The Rt Revd Miller Kangdim Maza, PO Box 560, Lafia, Nasarawa State
T: 234 803 973 5973 (Mobile)
E: anglicandioceseoflafia@yahoo.com

MAKURDI
Bishop The Rt Revd Nathanial Inyom, Bishopscourt, PO Box 1, Makurdi, Benue State
T: 234 44 533 349
F: 234 803 614 5319
E: makurdi@anglican.skannet.com.ng

OTUKPO
Bishop The Rt Revd David K. Bello, Bishopscourt, PO Box 360, Otukpo, Benue State
T: 234 0803 309 1778
E: bishopdkbello@yahoo.com

ZAKI-BIAM
Bishop The Rt Revd Benjamin A. Vager, Bishopscourt, PO Box 600, Yam Market Road, Zaki-Biam, Benue State
T: 234 0803 676 0018
E: rubavia@yahoo.com

ZONKWA (MISSIONARY DIOCESE)
Bishop The Rt Revd Jacob W. Kwashi, Bishop's Residence, PO Box 26, Zonkwa, Kaduna State 802002
T: 234 0803 311 0252
E: zonkwa@anglican-nig.org

PROVINCE OF BENDEL
Archbishop The Most Revd Friday John Imakhai (*Bishop of Esan*)

AKOKO EDO
Bishop The Rt Revd Jolly Oyekpen, Bishopscourt, PO Box 10, Igarra, Edo State
T: 234 803 470 5941 (Mobile)
E: venjollye@yahoo.com

ASABA
Bishop The Rt Revd Justus Nnaemeka Mogekwu, Bishopscourt, PO Box 216, Cable Point, Asaba, Delta State
T: 234 802 819 2980 (Mobile)
E: justusmogekwu@yahoo.com

BENIN
Bishop The Rt Revd Peter O. J. Imasuen, Bishopscourt, PO Box 82, Benin City, Edo State
T: 234 52 250 552

ESAN
Bishop The Most Revd Friday John Imakhai (*Archbishop of Bendel Province and Bishop of Esan*), Bishopscourt, Ojoelen, PO Box 921, Ekpoma, Edo State
T: 234 55 981 079
E: bishopimaekhai@hotmail.com

ETSAKO
Bishop The Rt Revd Jacob O. B. Bada, Bishopscourt, PO Box 11, Jattu, Auchi, Edo State

IKKA
Bishop The Rt Revd Peter Onekpe, St John's Cathedral, PO Box 1063, Agbor, Delta State
T: 234 55 250-14

NDOKWA
Bishop The Rt Revd David Obiosa, Bishopscourt, 151 Old Sapele Road, Obiaruka, Delta Square
T: 234 803 776 9464 (Mobile)
E: dfao1963@yahoo.com

OLEH
Bishop The Rt Revd John Usiwoma Aruakpor, Bishopscourt, PO Box 8, Oleh, Delta State
T: 234 53 701 062
F: 234 802 307 4008
E: angoleh2000@yahoo.com

SABONGIDDA-ORA
Bishop The Rt Revd John Akao, Bishopscourt, PO Box 13, Sabongidda-Ora, Edo State
T: 234 57 54 132
F: 234 806 087 7137
E: akaojohn@yahoo.com

SAPELE
Bishop The Rt Revd Blessing Erifeta, Bishopscourt, PO Box 52, Sapele, Delta State
T: 234 803 662 4282 (Mobile)
E: dioceseofsapele@yahoo.com

UGHELLI
Bishop The Rt Revd Cyril Odutemu, Bishopscourt, Ovurodawanre, PO Box 760, Ughelli, Delta State   *T:* 234 53 600 403
Fax: 234 803 530 7114
E: ughellianglican@yahoo.com

WARRI
Bishop The Rt Revd Christian Esezi Ideh, Bishopscourt, 17 Mabiaku Road, GRA, PO Box 4571, Warri, Delta State   *T:* 234 53 255 857
F: 234 805 102 2680
E: angdioceseofwarri@yahoo.com

WESTERN IZON (MISSIONARY DIOCESE)
Bishop The Rt Revd Edafe Emamezi, Bishopscourt, PO Box 5, Patani, Delta State
T: 234 822 05 6228 (Mobile)
E: anglizon@yahoo.co.uk

PROVINCE OF ENUGU
Archbishop The Most Revd Amos Amankechinelo Madu (*Bishop of Oji River*)

ABAKALIKI
Bishop The Rt Revd Monday C. Nkwoagu, All Saints' Cathedral, PO Box 112, Abakaliki, Ebonyi State   *T:* 234 43 220 762
E: abakaliki@anglican-nig.org

AFIKPO
Bishop The Rt Revd A. Paul Udogu, Bishop's House, Uwana, PO Box 699, Afikpo, Ebonyi State   *E:* udogupaul@yahoo.com

AWGU-ANINRI
Bishop The Rt Revd Emmanuel Ugwu, Bishopscourt, PO Box 305, Awgu, Enugu State
T: 234 803 334 9360 (Mobile)
E: afamnonye@yahoo.com

EHA-AMUFU
Bishop The Rt Revd Daniel Olinya, St Andrew's Cathedral, Bishopscourt, PO Box 85, Eh-Amufu, Enugu State   *T:* 234 803 089 2131
E: dankol@yahoo.com

IKWO
Bishop The Rt Revd Kenneth Ifemene, Bishop's Residence, Agubia Ikwo, PO Box 998, Abakaliki, Ebonyi State
T: 234 805 853 4849 (Mobile)
E: bishopikwoanglican.@yahoo.com

NGBO
Bishop The Rt Revd Christian I. Ebisike, Bishop's House, PO Box 93, Abakaliki, Ebonyi State   *T:* 234 806 779 4899 (Mobile)
E: vendchris@yahoo.com

NIKE
Bishop The Rt Revd Evans Jonathan Ibeagha, Bishopscourt, Trans-Ekulu, PO Box 2416, Enugu, Enugu State
T: 234 803 324 1387 (Mobile)
E: pnibeagha@yahoo.com

NSUKKA
Bishop The Rt Revd Aloysius Agbo, St Cypran's Compound, PO Box 516, Nsukka, Enugu State
T: 234 803 932 7840 (Mobile)
E: nsukka@anglican-nig.org

OJI RIVER
Bishop The Most Revd Amos Amankechinelo Madu (*Archbishop of the Province of Enugu*), PO Box 123, Oji River, Enugu State
T: 234 803 670 4888 (Mobile)
E: amosmadu@yahoo.com

UDI
Bishop The Rt Revd Chioke Augustine Aneke, Bishopscourt, PO Box 30, Udi, Enugu State
T: 234 806 908 9690
E: bpchijiokeudi@yahoo.com

PROVINCE OF IBADAN
Archbishop The Most Revd Joseph O. Akinfenwa (*Bishop of Ibadan*)

AJAYI CROWTHER
Bishop The Rt Revd Olugbenga Oduntan, Bishopscourt, Iseyin, PO Box 430, Iseyin, Oyo State   *T:* 234 803 719 8182 (Mobile)
E: ajayicrowtherdiocese@yahoo.com

ETIKI KWARA
Bishop The Rt Revd Andrew Ajayi
T: 234 803 470 3522 (Mobile)
E: andajayi@yahoo.com

IBADAN
Bishop The Most Revd Joseph O. Akinfenwa (*Archbishop of the Province of Ibadan*), PO Box 3075, Mapo, Ibadan   *T:* 234 2 810 1400
F: 234 2 810 1413
E: ibadan@anglican.skannet.com.ng

IBADAN NORTH
Bishop The Rt Revd Dr Segun Okubadejo, Bishopscourt, Moyede, PO Box 28961, Agodi, Ibadan   *T:* 234 2 8107 482
E: angibn@skannet.com

IBADAN SOUTH
Bishop The Rt Revd Jacob Ademola Ajetunmobi, Bishopscourt, PO Box 166, St David's Compound, Kudeti, Ibadan
T: and *F:* 234 2 231 9141
E: jacajet@skannet.com.ng

IFE

Bishop The Rt Revd Oluwole Odubogun, Bishopscourt, PO Box 312, Ife, Osun State
T: 234 36 2300 46 (Mobile)
E: rantiodubogun@yahoo.com

IFE EAST

Bishop The Rt Revd Oluseyi Oyelade, Bishop's House, PMB 505, Modakeke-Ife, Osun State
T: 234 802 322 4962 (Mobile)
E: seyioyelade@yahoo.com

IJESA NORTH EAST

Bishop The Rt Revd Joseph Alaba Olusola, PO Box 40, Ipetu Ijesha, Ogun State
T: 234 803 942 8275 (Mobile)
E: bpafsola@gmail.com

IJESA NORTH

Bishop The Rt Revd Isaac Oluyamo, Bishopscourt, PO Box 4, Ijebu-Ijesha, Osun State   T: 234 802 344 0333 (Mobile)

ILESA

Bishop The Rt Revd Olubayu Sowale, Diocesan Headquarters, Muroko Road, PO Box 237, Iesha, Osun State   T: 234 36 460 138
E: ilesha@anglican-nig.org

ILESA SOUTH WEST

Bishop The Rt Revd Samuel Egbebunmi, Bishopscourt, Cathedral of the Holy Trinity, Imo Ilesa, Osun State
T: 234 803 307 1876 (Mobile)
E: segbebunmi@yahoo.com

OGBOMOSHO (MISSIONARY DIOCESE)

Bishop The Rt Revd Dr Matthew Osunade, Bishopscourt, St David's Anglican Cathedral, PO Box 1909, Ogbomosho, Osun State
T: 234 805 593 6164 (Mobile)
E: maaosunade@yahoo.com

OKE-OGUN

Bishop The Rt Revd Solomon Amusan, Bishopscourt, PO Box 30, Saki, Oyo State
T: 234 802 323 3365 (Mobile)
E: solomonamusan@yahoo.com

OKE-OSUN

Bishop The Rt Revd Abraham Akinlalu, Bishopscourt, PO Box 251, Gbongan, Osun State   T: 234 803 771 7194
E: abrahamakinlalu@yahoo.com

OSUN

Bishop The Rt Revd James Afolabi Popoola, PO Box 285, Osogbo, Osun State
T: 234 35 240 325
F: 232 803 356 1628
E: folapool@yahoo.com

OSUN NORTH EAST

Bishop The Rt Revd Humphery Olumakaiye, Bishopscourt, PO Box 32, Otan Ayegbaju, Osun State   T: 234 803 388 2678 (Mobile)
E: bamisebi2002@yahoo.co.uk

OYO

Bishop The Rt Revd Jacob Ola Fasipe, Bishopscourt, PO Box 23, Oyo, Oyo State
T: 234 38 240 225
F: 234 803 857 2120
E: oyo@anglican-nig.org

PROVINCE OF JOS

Archbishop The Most Revd Benjamin A. Kwashi
(*Bishop of Jos*)

BAUCHI

Bishop The Rt Revd Musa Tula, Bishop's House, 2 Hospital Road, PO Box 2450, Bauchi
T: 234 77 546 460
E: bauchi@anglican-nig.org

BUKURU

Bishop The Rt Revd Jwan Zhumbes, Bishopscourt, Plot 31, Citrus Estate, New Abuja, Plateau State   T: 803 397 9906
E: jwanbyfaith@yahoo.com

DAMATURU

Bishop The Rt Revd Abiodun Ogunyemi, PO Box 312, Damaturu, Yobe State
T: 234 74 522 142
E: damaturu@anglican-nig.org

GOMBE

Bishop The Rt Revd Henry C. Ndukuba, Cathedral Church of St Peter, PO Box 39, Gombe   T: 234 72 221 212
F: 234 72 221 141
E: gombe@anglican-nig.org

JALINGO

Bishop The Rt Revd Timothy Yahaya, PO Box 4, Magami, Jalingo, Taraba State
T: and F: 234 806 594 4694
E: timothyyahaya@yahoo.com

JOS

Bishop The Most Revd Benjamin A. Kwashi (*Archbishop of the Province of Jos*), Bishopscourt, PO Box 6283, Jos, 930001, Plateau State
T: 234 73 612 2215
E: benkwashi@gmail.com

LANGTANG

Bishop The Rt Revd Stanley Fube, 87 Solomon Lar Road, PO Box 38, Langtang, Plateau State
T: 234 803 605 8767
E: stanleyfube@gmail.com

MAIDUGURI

Bishop The Rt Revd Emmanuel Kana Mani, Bishopscourt, PO Box 1693, Maiduguri, Borno State   *T:* and *F:* 234 76 234 010
E: bishope-45@yahoo.com

PANKSHIN

Bishop The Rt Revd Olumuyiwa Ajayi, Diocesan Secretariat, PO Box 24, Pankshin, Plateau State   *T:* 234 803 344 7318
E: olumijayi@yahoo.com

YOLA

Bishop The Rt Revd Markus A. Ibrahim, PO Box 601, Jimeta-Yola, Adamawa State
T: 234 75 624 303
F: 234 803 045 7576
E: marcusibrahim2002@yahoo.com

PROVINCE OF KADUNA

Archbishop The Most Revd Edmund E. Akanya (*Bishop of Kebbi*)

BARI

Bishop The Rt Revd Idris Zubairu, Bishopscourt, Gidan Mato Bari, Kano State
T: 234 808 559 7183 (Mobile)

DUTSE

Bishop The Rt Revd Yesufu Ibrahim Lumu, PO Box 67, Yadi, Dutse, Jigawa State
T: 234 64 721 379
E: dutse@anglican-nig.org

GUSAU

Bishop The Rt Revd John Garba, PO Box 64, Gusau, Zamfara State   *T:* 234 63 204 747
E: gusau@anglican.skannet.com

IKARA

Bishop The Rt Revd Yusuf Ishaya Janfalan, Bishopscourt, PO Box 23, Ikara, Kaduna State
T: 234 803 679 3865 (Mobile)
E: ikara@anglican-nig.org

KADUNA

Bishop Vacancy, PO Box 72, Kaduna
T: 234 62 240 085
F: 234 62 244 408

KANO

Bishop The Rt Revd Zakka Lalle Nyam, Bishopscourt, PO Box 362, Kano
T: and *F:* 234 64 647 816
E: kano@anglican.skannet.com.ng

KATSINA

Bishop The Rt Revd Jonathan Bamaiyi, Bishop's Lodge, PO Box 904, Katsina
T: 234 65 432 718 (Mobile)
234 803 601 5584 (Mobile)
E: bpjonathanbamaiyi@yahoo.co.uk

KEBBI

Bishop The Most Revd Edmund E. Akanya (*Archbishop of the Province of Kaduna*), Bishop's Residence, PO Box 701, Birnin Kebbi, Kebbi State   *T:* 234 68 321 179
F: 234 803 586 1060
E: eekanya@yahoo.com

SOKOTO

Bishop The Rt Revd Augustine Omole, Bishop's Lodge, 68 Shuni Road, PO Box 3489, Sokoto
T: 234 60 234 639
F: 234 803 542 3765
E: akin_sok@yahoo.com

WUSASA

Bishop The Rt Revd Ali Buba Lamido, PO Box 28, Wusasa, Zaria, Kaduna State
T: 234 69 334 594
E: lamido2sl@aol.co.uk

ZARIA

Bishop The Rt Revd Cornelius Bello, Bishopscourt, PO Box 507, Zaria, Kaduna State
T: 234 802 708 9555
F: 234 803 727 2504
E: cssbello@hotmail.com

PROVINCE OF KWARA

Archbishop The Most Revd Michael Akinyemi (*Bishop of Igbomina*)

IGBOMINA

Bishop The Most Revd Michael Akinyemi (*Archbishop of the Province of Kwara*), Bishopscourt, PO Box 102, Oro, Kwara State
T: 234 803 669 1940 (Mobile)
E: oluakinyemi2000@yahoo.com

IGBOMINA WEST

Bishop The Rt Revd James Olaoti Akinola, Bishop's House, PO Box 32, Oke Osin, Kwara State   *T:* 234 803 392 3720 (Mobile)
E: olaotimuyiwa@yahoo.com

JEBBA

Bishop The Rt Revd Timothy Adewole, Bishopscourt, PO Box 2, Jebba, Kwara State
T: 234 803 572 5298 (Mobile)
E: bishopadewole@yahoo.com

KWARA

Bishop The Rt Revd Olusegun Adeyemi, Bishopscourt, Fate Road, PO Box 1884, Ilorin, Kwara State   *T:* 234 31 220 879
F: 234 803 325 8068
E: bishopolusegun@yahoo.com

NEW BUSA
Bishop The Rt Revd Israel Amoo, Bishopscourt, PO Box 208, New Bussa, Niger State
T: 234 803 677 3839 (Mobile)
E: bishopamoo@yahoo.com

OFFA
Bishop The Rt Revd Akintunde Popoola, Bishop's House, 78–80 Ibrahim Road, PO Box 21, Offa, Kwara State
T: 234 805 925 0011 (Mobile)
E: tpopoola@anglican-nig.org

OMU-ARAN
Bishop The Rt Revd Philip Adeyemo, Bishop's House, PO Box 244, Omu-Aran, Kwara State
T: 234 806 592 4891 (Mobile)
E: rtrevadeyemo@yahoo.com

PROVINCE OF LAGOS
Archbishop The Most Revd Ephraim Adebola Ademowo (*Bishop of Lagos*)

AWORI
Bishop The Rt Revd Johnson Akinwamide Atere, Bishopscourt, PO Box 10, Ota, Ogun State   T: 234 803 553 7284 (Mobile)
E: dioceseofawori@yahoo.com

BADAGRY (MISSIONARY DIOCESE)
Bishop The Rt Revd Joseph Babatunde Adeyemi, Bishopscourt, PO Box 7, Badagry, Lagos State   T: 234 1 773 5546
Mobile: 234 803 306 4601
E: badagry@anglican-nig.org

EGBA
Bishop The Rt Revd Emmanuel O. Adekunle, Bishopscourt, Cathedral of St Peter, PO Box 46, Ile-oluji, Ondo State
E: egba@anglican-nig.org
mowadayo@yahoo.com

EGBA WEST
Bishop The Rt Revd Samuel Ajani, Bishopscourt, Oke-Ata Housing Estate, PO Box 6204, Sapon, Abeokuta   T: 234 805 518 4822
E: samuelajani@yahoo.com

IFO
Bishop The Rt Revd Nathaniel Oladejo Ogundipe, Bishopscourt, Trinity House KM1, Ibogun Road, PO Box 104, Ifo, Ogun State
T: 234 802 778 4377
E: jaodejide@yahoo.com

IJEBU
Bishop The Rt Revd Ezekiel Awosoga, Bishopscourt, Ejinrin Road, PO Box 112, Ijebu-Ode   T: 234 37 432 886
E: ijebu@anglican-nig.org
bishop@ang-ijebudiocese.com

IJEBU NORTH
Bishop The Rt Revd Solomon Kuponu, Bishopscourt, Oke-Sopen, Ijebu-Igbo, Ogun State   T: 234 803 741 9372 (Mobile)
E: dioceseofijebunorth@yahoo.com

LAGOS
Bishop The Most Revd Ephraim Adebola Ademowo (*Archbishop of the Province of Lagos*), 29 Marina, PO Box 13, Lagos
T: 234 1 263 6026
E: adebolaademowo@dioceseoflagos.org

LAGOS MAINLAND
Bishop The Rt Revd Adebayo Akinde, Bishop's House, PO Box 849, Ebute, Lagos
T: 234 703 390 5522
E: adakinde@gmail.com

LAGOS WEST
Bishop The Rt Revd James O. Odedeji, Vining House, 3rd Floor, Archbishop Vining Memorial Cathedral, Oba Akinjobi Road, GRA Ikeja   T: 234 1 493 7333
F: 234 2 493 7337
E: dioceseoflagoswest@yahoo.com

REMO
Bishop The Rt Revd Michael O. Fape, Bishopscourt, Ewusi Street, PO Box 522, Sagamu, Ogun State   T: 234 37 640 598
E: remo@anglican-nig.org

YEWA
Bishop The Rt Revd Michael Adebayo Oluwarohunbi, Bishopscourt, PO Box 484, Ilaro, Ogun State   T: 234 39 440 695

PROVINCE OF LOKOJA
Archbishop The Most Revd Emmanuel Sokowamju Egbunu (*Bishop of Lokoja*)

DOKO
Bishop The Rt Revd Uriah Kolo, PO Box 1513, Bida, Niger State
T: 234 803 590 6327 (Mobile)
E: uriahkolo@gmail.com

IJUMU
Bishop The Rt Revd Ezekiel Ikupolati, Bishopscourt, PO Box 90, Iyara-Ijumi Kogi State   T: 234 807 500 8780
E: efikupolati@yahoo.com

KABBA
Bishop The Rt Revd Steven Akobe, Bishopscourt, Obara Way, PO Box 62, Kabba, Kogi State
T: 234 58 300 633
F: 234 803 471 4759

KONTAGORA
Bishop The Rt Revd Jonah Ibrahim, Bishop's House, GPA PO Box 1, Kontagora, Niger State
T: 234 803 625 2032 (Mobile)
E: jonahibrahim@yahoo.co.uk

KUTIGI
Bishop The Rt Revd Jeremiah Ndana Kolo, Bishop's House, St John's Mission Compound, PO Box 14, Bida
T: 234 803 625 2032 (Mobile)
E: bishopkolo@yahoo.com

LOKOJA
Bishop The Most Revd Emmanuel Sokowamju Egbunu (*Archbishop of the Province of Lokoja*) Bishopscourt, PO Box 11, Bethany, Lokoja, Koji State
T: 234 58 220 588
E: emmanuelegbunu@yahoo.co.uk

MINNA
Bishop The Rt Revd Daniel Abu Yisa, Bishopscourt, Dutsen Kura, PO Box 2469, Minna
T: 234 803 588 6552 (Mobile)
E: danyisa2007@yahoo.com

OGORI-MAGONGO
Bishop The Rt Revd Festus Davies, Bishop's House, St Peter's Cathedral, Ogori, Kogi State
T: 234 803 451 0378 (Mobile)
E: fessyoladiran@yahoo.com

OKENE
Bishop The Rt Revd Emmanuel Bayo Ajulo, Bishopscourt, PO Box 43, Okene, Kogi State
T: 234 803 700 0016 (Mobile)
E: okenediocese@yahoo.com

PROVINCE OF THE NIGER
Archbishop The Most Revd Christian Ogochukwo Efobi (*Bishop of Aguata*)

AGUATA
Bishop The Most Revd Christian Ogochukwo Efobi (*Archbishop of the Province of the Niger*), Bishopscourt, PO Box 1128, Ekwulobia, Anambra State
T: 234 803 750 1077 (Mobile)
E: christianefobi@yahoo.com

AMICHI
Bishop The Rt Revd Ephraim Ikeakor, Bishopscourt, PO Box 13, Amichi, Anambra State
T: 234 803 317 0916 (Mobile)
E: eoikeakor@yahoo.com

AWKA
Bishop The Rt Revd Alexander Ibezim, Bishopscourt, PO Box 130, Awka, Anambra State
T: 234 48 550 058
E: chioma1560@aol.com

ENUGU
Bishop The Rt Revd Dr Emmanuel O. Chukwuma, Bishop's House, PO Box 418, Enugu, Enugu State
T: 234 42 453 804
F: 234 42 259 808
E: enugu@anglican-nig.org

IHIALA
Bishop The Rt Revd Ralph Okafor, Bishopscourt, St Silas Cathedral, PO Box 11, Ihiala, Anambra State
T: 234 803 711 2408 (Mobile)
E: raphoka@yahoo.com

MBAMILI
Bishop The Rt Revd Henry Okeke, Bishopscourt, PO Box 2653, Onitsha, Anambra State
T: 234 803 644 9780 (Mobile)
E: bishopokeke@yahoo.com

NIGER WEST
Bishop The Rt Revd Johnson Ekwe, Bishop's House, Anambra, Anambra State
T: 234 803 384 3339 (Mobile)

NNEWI
Bishop The Rt Revd Dr Godwin Izundu Nmezinwa Okpala, Bishopscourt, PO Box 2630, Uruagu-Nnewi, Anambra State
F: 234 803 348 5714
T: 234 803 348 5714 (Mobile)
E: okpalagodwin@yahoo.co.uk

OGBARU
Bishop The Rt Revd Samuel Ezeofor, Bishopscourt, PO Box 46, Atani, Anambra State
E: ezechukwunyere@yahoo.com

ON THE NIGER
Bishop The Rt Revd Owen Chidozie Nwokolo, Bishopscourt, Ozala Road, Onitsha, Anambra State
T: 234 803 726 0548 (Mobile)
E: owenelsie@yahoo.com

PROVINCE OF NIGER DELTA
Archbishop The Most Revd Ignatius C. O. Kattey (*Bishop of Niger Delta North*)

ABA
Bishop The Rt Revd Ugochukwa Ezuoke, Bishopscourt, 70–72 St Michael's Road, PO Box 212, Aba, Abia State
T: 234 82 227 666
E: aba@anglican-nig.org

ABA NGWA NORTH
Bishop The Rt Revd Nathan C. Kanu, Bishopscourt, All Saints Cathedral, Abayi-Umuocham 1610165, Owerri Road, PO Box 43, Aba, Abia State
T: 234 803 822 4623 (Mobile)
E: odinathnfe@sbcglobal.net

ANGLICAN & PORVOO COMMUNIONS

AHOADA
Bishop The Rt Revd Clement Nathan Ekpeye, Bishopscourt, St Paul's Cathedral, PO Box 4, Ahoada East L.G.A., Rivers State
T: 234 806 356 6242
E: ahoada@anglican-nig.org

CALABAR
Bishop The Rt Revd Tunde Adeleye, Bishopscourt, PO Box 74, Calabar, Cross River State
T: 234 87 232 812
F: 234 88 220 835
E: calabar@anglican-nig.org

ENUGU NORTH
Bishop The Rt Revd Sosthenes Eze, Bishopscourt, St Mary's Cathedral, Ngwo-Enugu
T: 234 803 870 9362 (Mobile)
E: bishopsieze@yahoo.com

ETCHE
Bishop The Rt Revd Precious Nwala, Bishopscourt, PO Box 89, Okehi, Etche Rivers State
T: 234 807 525 2842 (Mobile)
E: etchediocese@yahoo.com
precious_model5@yahoo.com

EVO
Bishop The Rt Revd Innocent Ordu, Bishopscourt, PO Box 3576, Port Harcourt, Rivers State
T: 234 803 715 2706
E: innocent-ordu@yahoo.com

IKWERRE
Bishop The Rt Revd Blessing Enyindah, Bishopscourt, St Peter's Cathedral, PO Box 14229, Port Harcourt, Rivers State
T: 234 802 321 2824 (Mobile)
E: blessingenyindah@yahoo.com

NIGER DELTA
Bishop The Rt Revd Ralph Ebirien, PO Box 115, Port Harcourt, Rivers State
T: 234 708 427 9095 (Mobile)
E: revpalph_ebirien@yahoo.com

NIGER DELTA NORTH
Bishop The Most Revd Ignatius C. O. Kattey (*Archbishop of the Province of Niger Delta*), PO Box 53, Diobu, Port Harcourt, Rivers State
T: 234 803 309 4331 (Mobile)
E: bishopicokattey@yahoo.com

NIGER DELTA WEST
Bishop The Rt Revd Emmanuel O. Oko-Jaja, Bishopscourt, PO Box 10, Yenagoa, Bayelsa State
T: 234 803 870 2099 (Mobile)
E: niger-delta-west@anglican-nig.org

NORTHERN IZON
Bishop The Rt Revd Fred Nyanabo, Bishopscourt, PO Box 705, Yenagoa, Bayelsa State
T: 234 803 316 0938 (Mobile)
E: fred_nyanabo@yahoo.co.uk

OGBIA
Bishop The Rt Revd James Oruwori, Bishop's House, 10 Queens Street, Ogbia town, Bayelsea State
T: 234 803 73 4746
E: jaoruwori@yahoo.com

OGONI (Missionary diocese)
Bishop The Rt Revd Solomon S. Gberegbara, Bishopscourt, PO Box 73, Bori-Ogoni, Rivers State
T: 234 803 339 2545
E: ogoni@anglican-nig.org

OKRIKA
Bishop The Rt Revd Tubokosemie Abere, Bishopscourt, PO Box 11, Okrika, Rivers State
T: 234 803 312 5226 (Mobile)
E: dioceseofokrika@yahoo.com

UYO
Bishop Prince Asuko Antai, Bishopscourt, PO Box 70, Uyo, Akwa Ibom State
T: 234 802 916 2305
E: uyo@anglican-nig.org

PROVINCE OF ONDO
Archbishop The Most Revd Samuel Abe (*Bishop of Ekiti*)

AKOKO
Bishop The Rt Revd Gabriel Akinbiyi, PO Box 572, Ikare-Akoko, Ondo State
T: 31 801 011
E: bishopgabrielakinbiyi@yahoo.com

AKURE
Bishop The Rt Revd Simeon O. Borokini, Bishopscourt, PO Box 1622, Akure, Ondo State
T: and *F:* 234 241 572

DIOCESE ON THE COAST (*Formerly IKALE-ILAJE*)
Bishop The Rt Revd Joshua Ogunele, Bishopscourt, Ikoya Road, PMB 3, Ilutitun-Osooro, Ondo State
T: 234 803 467 1879 (Mobile)
E: joshuaonthecoast@yahoo.ca

EKITI
Bishop The Most Revd Samuel Abe (*Archbishop of the Province of Ondo*), Bishopscourt, PO Box 12, Okesa St, Ado-Ekiti, Ekiti State
T: 234 30 250 305
E: adedayoekiti@yahoo.com

EKITI-OKE
Bishop The Rt Revd Isaac O. Olubowale, Bishopscourt, PO Box 207, Usi-Ekiti, Ekiti State
T: 234 803 600 9582 (Mobile)
E: ekitioke@anglican-nig.org

EKITI WEST
Bishop The Rt Revd Samuel O. Oke, Bishop's Residence, 6 Ifaki St, PO Box 477, Ijero-Ekiti
T: 234 30 850 314
E: ekitiwest@anglican-nig.org

IDOANI
Bishop The Rt Revd Ezekiel Dahunsi, Bishopscourt, PO Box 100 Idoani, Ondo State
T: 234 803 384 4029 (Mobile)
E: bolaezek@yahoo.com

ILAJE
Bishop The Rt Revd Fredrick Olugbemi, Bishopscourt, PO Box 146, Igbokoda, Ondo State   *T:* 234 806 624 8662 (Mobile)
E: forogbemi@yahoo.com

ILE-OLUJI
Bishop The Rt Revd Samson Adekunle, Bishopscourt, Cathedral of St Peter, PO Box 46, Ile-Oluji, Ondo State
T: 234 803 454 1236 (Mobile)
E: adkulesamson86@yahoo.co.uk

IRELE-ESEODO
Bishop The Rt Revd Felix O. Akinbuluma, Bishopscourt, Sabomi Road, Ode Irele, Ondo State   *T:* 234 805 671 2653
F: 234 803 472 1813
E: felixgoke@yahoo.com

ONDO
Bishop The Rt Revd George L. Lasebikan, Bishopscourt, College Rd, PO Box 265, Ondo
T: 234 34 610 718
E: ondoanglican@yahoo.co.uk

OWO
Bishop The Rt Revd James Adedayo Oladunjoye, Bishopscourt, PO Box 472, Owo, Ondo State
T: 234 51 241 463
F: 234 803 475 4291
E: bishopoladunjoye@yahoo.co.uk

PROVINCE OF OWERRI
Archbishop The Most Revd Bennett C. I. Okoro (*Bishop of Orlu*)

EGBU
Bishop The Rt Revd Geoffrey E. Okorafor, All Saints' Cathedral, PO Box 1967, Owerri, Imo State   *T:* 234 83 231 797
E: egbu@anglican-nig.org

IDEATO
Bishop The Rt Revd Caleb A. Maduomo, Bishopscourt, PO Box 2, Ndizuogu, Imo State
T: 234 803 745 4503 (Mobile)
E: bpomacal@hotmail.com

IKEDURU
Bishop The Rt Revd Emmanuel C. Maduwike, Bishop's House, PO Box 56, Atta, Imo State
T: 234 803 704 4686 (Mobile)
E: emmamaduwike@yahoo.com

MBAISE
Bishop The Rt Chamberlain Chinedu Ogunedo, Bishopscourt, PO Box 10, Ife, Ezinihitte Mbaise, Imo State
T: 234 803 336 9836 (Mobile)
E: ogunedochi@yahoo.com

OHAJI-EGBEMA
Bishop The Rt Revd Chidi Collins Oparaojiaku, Bishop's House, PO box 8026, New Owerri, Imo State   *T:* 234 803 312 1063 (Mobile)
E: chidioparachiaku@yahoo.com

OKIGWE
Bishop The Rt Revd Edward Osuegbu, Bishopscourt, PO Box 156, Okigwe, Imo State
T: 234 803 724 6374 (Mobile)
E: edchuc@justice.com

OKIGWE NORTH
Bishop The Rt Revd Godson Udochukwu Ukanwa, PO Box 127, Anara, Imo State
T: 234 803 672 4314 (Mobile)
E: venukanwa@yahoo.com

OKIGWE SOUTH
Bishop The Rt Revd David Onuoha, Bishopscourt, Ezeoke Nsu, PO Box 235, Nsu, Ehime Mbano LGA, Imo State
E: okisouth@yahoo.com

ON THE LAKE
Bishop The Rt Revd Chijioke Oti, Bishopscourt, PO Box 36, Oguta, Imo State, Nigeria
T: 234 802 788 8738 (Mobile)
E: chijiokeoti72@yahoo.com

ORLU
Bishop The Most Revd Bennett C. I. Okoro (*Archbishop of the Province of Owerri*), Bishopscourt, PO Box 260, Nkwerre, Imo State
T: 234 82 440 538
E: anglicannaorlu@yahoo.com

ORU
Bishop The Rt Revd Geoffrey Chukwunenye, PO Box 91, Mgbidi, Imo State
T: 234 803 308 1270 (Mobile)
E: geoinlagos@yahoo.com

OWERRI
Bishop The Rt Revd Dr Cyril C. Chukwunonyerem Okorocha, Bishop's Bourne, PMB 1063, Owerri, Imo State
T: 234 83 230 784
F: 234 803 338 9344
E: owerri_anglican@yahoo.com

The Anglican Church of Papua New Guinea

Members 200,000

The Anglican Church functions mostly in rural areas where mountains and rainforest provide natural barriers to travel. Some 60 per cent of the funding is raised internally; most of the balance comes from grants from Australia, New Zealand, Canada and the UK-based Papua New Guinea Church Partnership. The Church had played an active role in the development of this country, and has a long history of more than a century (120 years, from 1891 to 2011) of providing service throughout its five established Dioceses in PNG (Dogura, Popondota, Port Moresby, Aipo Rongo and New Guinea Islands). The Church's work has expanded over the years into establishing and operating Social Welfare, Education, Health and Economic Development programmes for the most disadvantaged and rural sectors of our communities. The Anglican Church will continue to do this in the years ahead.

Archbishop The Most Revd Allan Migi (*Primate of ACPNG*)   *E:* archbishopmigi95@gmail.com

General Secretary Mr Dennis Kabekabe, PO Box 673, Lae, Morobe Province 411
T: 675 472 4111
F: 675 472 1852
E: dpk07jan@gmail.com

Provincial Cellenger Justice Bernard Sakora, Chamber of Justice, Supreme and National Courts of Justice, PO Box 7018, Boroko, NCD, PNG   *T:* 675 324 5734

Provincial Registrar Mr Goodwin Poole, PO Box 389, Port Moresby, Level 5 Defence House, Crn Hunter St & Champion Pde, National Capital District   *T:* 675 308 8300
Digicel: 675 720 88300
F: 675 308 8399
W: www.obriens.com.pg

THEOLOGICAL COLLEGE
Newton Theological College, PO Box 162, Popondetta, Oro Province (*Principal* The Revd Peter Moi)   *Tel (Digicel):* 675 713 95018
E: fr.petermoi@gmail.com

CHURCH PAPER
Family Magazine. Published three times a year. *Editor* The Most Revd Joseph Kopapa, PO Box 673, Lae, Morobe Province 411
T: 675 472 4111
F: 675 472 1852
E: joekopapa@gmail.com

AIPO RONGO
Bishop The Rt Revd Nathan Ingen, PO Box 893, Mt Hagen, Western Highlands Province
T: 675 542 1131
F: 675 542 1181
E: bishopnathan2@gmail.com

DOGURA
Bishop The Rt Revd Tennyson Bogar, PO Box 19, Dogura via Alotau, Milne Bay Province
T: 675 641 1530
F: 675 983 5120

NEW GUINEA ISLANDS
Bishop Vacancy, Bishop's House, PO Box 806, Kimbe, West New Britain Province
T: and F: 675 983 5120
E: AllanRirmeMigi@gmail.com

POPONDOTA
Bishop The Rt Revd Lindsley Ihove, Bishop's House, PO Box 26, Popondetta, Oro Province
T: 675 629 7194
F: 675 629 7476
E: bplindsleyihove@gmail.com

PORT MORESBY
Bishop The Rt Revd Denny Bray Guka, PO Box 6491, Boroko, NCD   *T:* 675 323 2489
F: 675 323 2493
E: acpngpom@global.net.pg

The Episcopal Church in the Philippines

Members 170,000

The Philippines is the only Christian nation in Asia. Its 100,000,000 or so population is composed of 75 per cent Roman Catholics while the other 25 per cent are Muslims and other Christian bodies including the Episcopal Church in the Philippines (ECP), which now has seven dioceses. The ECP was first established by the Protestant Episcopal Church in the USA (PECUSA) in 1901 and

became an autonomous province of the Anglican Communion in 1990. It continues to maintain a close relationship with PECUSA. Its ministry after gaining autonomy is focused not only in the nurture of the faith of the believers and doing evangelism. It is actively involved in peace and social justice advocacy and community development projects to help eradicate poverty which is hounding the lives of millions of Filipinos today.

National Office The ECP Mission Center, 275 E Rodriguez Sr Avenue, 1102 Quezon City

(Postal address) PO Box 10321, Broadway Centrum, 1112 Quezon City
T: 63 2 722 8481
F: 63 2 721 1923
E: ecpnational@yahoo.com.ph

Prime Bishop The Most Revd Joel Atiwag Pachao *(same address)*
E: bpjoelpachao@yahoo.com

Provincial Secretary Floyd P. Lalwet *(same address)*
E: flaw997@gmail.com

Corporate Secretary Ms Laura S. Ocampo *(same address)*
E: lbso2@yahoo.com

National Finance Officer Ms Bridget T. Lacdao
E: bbalitog@yahoo.com

CENTRAL PHILIPPINES
Bishop The Rt Revd Dixie C. Taclobao, 281 E. Rodriguez Sr Ave, 1102 Quezon City
T: 63 2 412 8561
F: 63 2 724 2143
E: taclobaodixie@yahoo.com.ph

DAVAO
Bishop The Rt Revd Jonathan L. Casimina, Km. 3 McArthur Highway, Matina, Davao City 8000
T: 63 82 299 1511
F: 63 82 296 9629
E: episcopaldioceseofdavao@yahoo.com

NORTH CENTRAL PHILIPPINES
Bishop The Most Revd Joel A. Pachao (*Prime Bishop*), 358 Magsaysay Ave, 2600 Baguio City
T: 63 74 443 7705
E: bpjoelpachao@yahoo.com

NORTHERN LUZON
Bishop The Rt Revd Esteban G. Sabawil, Bulanao, 3800 Tabuk City, Kalinga
M: 63 946 089 2136
E: esteban.sabawil@yahoo.com.ph

NORTHERN PHILIPPINES
Bishop The Rt Revd Brent Harry W. Alawas, 2616 Bontoc, Mountain Province
T & F: 63 74 602 1026
E: ednpbrent@yahoo.com

SANTIAGO
Bishop The Rt Revd Alexander A. Wandag, Maharlika Highway, 3311 Divisoria Santiago City, Isabela
T: 63 78 662 1561
E: alexanderwandag@rocketmail.com

SOUTHERN PHILIPPINES
Bishop The Rt Revd Danilo Labacanacruz Bustamante, 186 Sinsuat Ave, 9600 Cotabato City
T: 63 64 421 2960
F: 63 64 421 1703
E: edsp_ecp@yahoo.com

ANGLICAN & PORVOO COMMUNIONS

The Church of the Province of Rwanda

Members 1,200,000
In just over 10,170 square miles there are more than one million Anglicans among a fast-growing population, currently 9.5 million. The former Rwanda Mission (now CMS) established its first station at Gahini in 1925 and grew through the revival of the 1930s and 1940s, with the first Rwandan bishop appointed in 1965. Nine dioceses have up to 306 parishes and 379 clergy, organized in 96 deaconries. Like all strata of Rwandan society, the Church suffered, on many levels, through the genocide, and it is a major priority of the Church to replace clergy through training. The Church has a role as a healing ministry to the many traumatized people in Rwanda and to reconciliation, restoration, and rehabilitation. The Church has also been involved in rural development, medical work, vocational training, and education.

Archbishop The Most Revd Dr Onesphore Rwaje (*Bishop of Gasabo*)

Provincial Secretary The Revd Francis Karemera, BP 2487, Kigali
T: 250 514 160
F: 250 516 162
E: egapeer@yahoo.com

Provincial Treasurer Vacancy (*same address*)

BUTARE
Bishop The Rt Revd Nathan Gasatura, BP 225, Butare
T: and F: 250 30 710
E: nathangasatura@gmail.com

BYUMBA
Bishop The Rt Revd Emmanuel Ngendahayo, BP 17, Byumba
T: and F: 250 64 242
E: engendahayo@gmail.com

CYANGUGU
Bishop The Rt Revd Nathan Amooti Rusengo, BP 52, Cyangugu
T: 250 788 409 061
E: nathanamooti@gmail.com

GAHINI
Bishop The Rt Revd Alexis Bilindabagabo,
BP 22, Kigali   *T:* 250 67 422
                                 F: 250 77 831
        E: abilindabagabo@gmail.com

GASABO
Bishop The Most Revd Dr Onesphore Rwaje
(*Archbishop of the Province*), PO Box 2487,
Kigali, Rwanda   *F:* 250 64 242
        E: onesphorerwaje@yahoo.fr

KIBUNGO
Bishop The Rt Revd Emmanuel Ntazinda, EER
Kibungo Diocese, BP 719, Kibungo
                T: and *F:* 250 566 194
        E: emmanuelntazinda@ymail.com

KIGALI
Bishop The Rt Revd Louis A. Muvunyi, EER/
DK, BP 61, Kigali   *T:* 250 576 340
        E: louismuvunyi@hotmail.com

KIGEME
Bishop The Rt Revd Augustin Mvunabandi,
BP 67, Gikongoro   *T:* 250 535 086 (Office)
                        250 535 088 (Secretary)
                        250 535 087 (Home)
        E: dkigemeear@yahoo.fr

KIVU
Bishop The Rt Revd Augustin Ahimana, BP 166
Gisenyi   *T:* 250 788 350 119
        E: aamurekezi@gmail.com

SHYIRA
Bishop The Rt Revd Laurent Mbanda, EER
Shyira Diocese, BP 52, Ruhengeri
                        T: 250 466 02
                        F: 250 546 449
        E: mbandalaurent@gmail.com

SHYOGWE
Bishop The Rt Revd Jéred Kalimba, BP 27,
Gitarama   *T:* 250 62 372
                        F: 250 62 460
        E: kalimbaj60@yahoo.fr

The Scottish Episcopal Church

Members 31,656
The roots of Scottish Christianity go back to St Ninian in the fourth century and St Columba in the sixth. After the Reformation, the Episcopal Church was the established Church of Scotland. It was however replaced as the established Church by the Presbyterians at the Revolution in 1689. Penal statutes in force from 1746 to 1792 weakened the Church, although many congregations remained and the bishops maintained continuity. In 1784 in Aberdeen, the Scottish Church initiated the world-wide Anglican Communion with the consecration of the first bishop of the American Church.

Primus The Most Revd Mark J. Strange (*Bishop of Moray, Ross and Caithness*)
        E: bishop@moray.anglican.org
W: http://www.morayepiscopalchurch.scot

Secretary General Mr John Stuart, 21 Grosvenor Crescent, Edinburgh EH12 5EE
                T: 0131 225 6357
        E: secgen@scotland.anglican.org
        W: www.scotland.anglican.org

The Scottish Episcopal Institute, 21 Grosvenor Crescent, Edinburgh EH12 5EE
                T: 0131 225 6357
        E: institute@scotland.anglican.org

ABERDEEN AND ORKNEY
Bishop Vacancy, Diocesan Office, St Clement's Church House, Mastrick Drive, Aberdeen AB16 6UF   *T:* 01224 662247
        E: office@aberdeen.anglican.org
        W: www.aberdeen.anglican.org

Dean The Very Revd Dr A. E. Nimmo, St Margaret's Clergy House, Gallowgate, Aberdeen AB25 JEA   *T:* 01224 644969
        E: alexander306@btinternet.com

CATHEDRAL CHURCH OF ST ANDREW, Aberdeen
Provost The Very Revd Dr Isaac Poobalan, St Andrew's Cathedral, 28 King Street, Aberdeen AB24 5AX   *T:* 01224 640119
        E: provost@aberdeen.anglican.org

ARGYLL AND THE ISLES
Bishop The Rt Revd Kevin Pearson, St Moluag's Diocesan Centre, Croft Avenue, Oban, Argyll PA34 5JJ   *T:* 01631 570 870
        E: office@argyll.anglican.org
        W: www.argyllandtheisles.org.uk

Dean The Very Revd A. Swift, Holy Trinity Rectory, 55 Kilbride Road, Dunoon PA23 7LN
        E: dean@argyll.anglican.org

ST JOHN THE DIVINE CATHEDRAL, Oban
(The Cathedral of Argyll)
Provost Vacancy, The Rectory, Ardconnel Terrace, Oban PA34 5DJ   *T:* 01631 562323
        E: ProvostOban@argyll.anglican.org

CATHEDRAL OF THE ISLES AND COLLEGIATE CHURCH OF THE HOLY SPIRIT, Millport, Cumbrae
Provost The Rt Revd Kevin Pearson, St Moluag's Diocesan Centre, Croft Road Avenue, Oban PA34 5JJ   *T:* 01475 530353
          E: cathedral_cumbrae@btconnect.com

BRECHIN
Bishop Vacancy, Diocesan Office. Unit 14 Prospect III, Technology Park, Gemini Crescent, Dundee DD2 1SW
          T: 01382 459569
          E: office@brechin.anglican.org
          W: www.thedioceseofbrechin.org

Dean The Very Revd Dr F. Bridger, 3 Wyvis Place, Broughty Ferry DD5 3SX
          T: 01382 562244
          E: office@brechin.anglican.org

ST PAUL'S CATHEDRAL, Dundee
Provost The Very Revd Jeremy Auld, St Paul's Cathedral, Castle Hill, 1 High Street, Dundee DD1 1TD   *T:* 01382 224486
          E: provost@saintpaulscathedral.net

EDINBURGH
Bishop The Rt Revd Dr John Armes, Diocesan Centre, 21a Grosvenor Crescent, Edinburgh EH12 5EL   *T:* 0131 538 7044
          E: office@edinburgh.anglican.org
          W: www.edinburgh.anglican.org

Dean The Very Revd Frances Burberry, 163 Craigleith Road, Edinburgh EH4 2EB
          T: 0131 315 0404
          E: Dean@dioceseofedinburgh.org

CATHEDRAL CHURCH OF ST MARY, Edinburgh
Provost The Very Revd John Conway, Cathedral Office, Palmerston Place, Edinburgh EH12 5AW   *T:* 0131 225 6293
          E: provost@cathedral.net

GLASGOW AND GALLOWAY
Bishop The Rt Revd Dr Gregor Duncan, Diocesan Centre, 5 St Vincent Place, Glasgow G1 2DH   *T:* 0141 221 6911
          E: bishop@glasgow.anglican.org
          W: www.glasgow.anglican.org

Dean The Very Revd Ian Barcroft, The Rectory, 4c Auchingramont Road, Hamilton ML3 6JT
          T: 01698 429895
          E: dean@glasgow.anglican.org

ST MARY'S CATHEDRAL, Glasgow
Provost The Very Revd Kelvin Holdsworth, St Mary's Cathedral, 300 Great Western Road, Glasgow G4 9JB   *T:* 0141 339 6691
          E: provost@thecathedral.org.uk

MORAY, ROSS AND CAITHNESS
Bishop (Primus) The Most Revd Mark Strange, Bishop's House, St Duthac's Centre, Arpafeelie, North Kessock IV1 3XD   *T:* 01463 819900
          E: bishop@moray.anglican.org
          W: https://www.morayepiscoplachurch.scot

Dean The Very Revd Alison Simpson, The New Rectory, 3 Queen Street, Nairn IV12 4AA
          T: 01667 452458
          E: dean@moray.anglican.org

ST ANDREW'S CATHEDRAL, Inverness
Provost Bishop The Most Revd Mark Strange, Bishop's House, St Duthac's Centre, Arpafeelie, North Kessock IV1 3XD   *T:* 01463 819900
          E: bishop@moray.anglican.org

ST ANDREWS, DUNKELD AND DUNBLANE
Bishop Vacancy, Diocesan Centre, 28a Balhousie Street, Perth PH1 5HJ
          T: 01738 580426
          E: bishop@standrews.anglican.org
          W: www.standrews.anglican.org

Dean The Very Revd Kenneth Rathband, 10 Rosemount Park, Blairgowrie PH10 6TZ
          T: 01250 874 583
          E: abcsaints@btinternet.com

ST NINIAN'S CATHEDRAL, Perth
Provost The Very Revd Hunter Farquharson, St Ninian's Cathedral, North Methven Street, Perth PH1 5PP   *T:* 01738 632 053
          E: provost@perthcathedral.co.uk
          W: http://www.perthcathedral.co.uk

ANGLICAN & PORVOO COMMUNIONS

The Anglican Church of South America

(Iglesia Anglicana de Sudamérica)

Members 22,490

British immigrants brought Anglicanism to South America in the nineteenth century. The Church Missionary Society (previously the South American Missionary Society) continues to work effectively among indigenous peoples and today actively supports diocesan initiatives. In 1974 the Archbishop of Canterbury gave over his metropolitical authority for the dioceses of the Southern Cone, and in 1981 the new province was formed. It includes Argentina, Bolivia, Chile, Northern Argentina, Paraguay, Peru and Uruguay.

Presiding Bishop The Most Revd Gregory James Venables (*Bishop of Argentina*)

Provincial Secretary Mrs Cristina Daly
E: cristindaly@gmail.com

Provincial Treasurer Miss Elisa Aguilar Rojas, Victoria Subercaseux 41 oficina 301, Santiago, Chile   *T:* 56 02 2638 3009
E: eaguilar@iach.cl

Personal Assistant to the Bishop Mrs Pamela Santibañez, Victoria Subercaseaux 41 oficina 301, Santiago, Chile   *T:* 56 02 2638 3009
E: psantibanez@iach.cl

THEOLOGICAL EDUCATION

Planned and carried out by a Theological Education Commission which selects candidates, applies grants and sets courses of study, some of which are led by clergy of the diocese. Some students follow courses of theological training 'by extension' and others attend ecumenical seminaries.

ARGENTINA

Bishop The Most Revd Gregory James Venables (*Presiding Bishop of the Province*), 25 de Mayo 282, Capital Federal, Buenos Aires 1001, Argentina   *T:* 54 11 4342 4618
F: 54 11 4784 1277
E: diocesisanglicue@fibertel.cam.ar

BOLIVIA

Bishop The Rt Revd Raphael Samuel, Iglesia Anglicana Episcopal de Bolivia, Casilla 848 Cochabamba, Bolivia
T: and *F:* 591 4 440 1168
E: raphaelsamuel@gmail.com
W: www.bolivia.anglican.org

CHILE

Bishop The Most Revd Héctor Zavala Muñoz, Casilla 50675, Correo Central, Santiago, Chile
T: 56 2 638 3009
F: 56 2 639 4581
E: tzavala@iach.cl
W: www.iach.cl

Suffragan Bishop The Rt Revd Abelino Manuel Apeleo, Pasaje Viña Poniente 4593, Puente Alto, Santiago, Chile
T: and *F:* 56 2 638 3009
E: aapeleo@gmail.com

NORTHERN ARGENTINA

Bishop The Rt Revd Nicholas Drayson, Iglesia Anglicana, Casilla 187, Salta 4400, Argentina
T: 54 387 431 1718
F: 54 371 142 0100
E: nicobispo@gmail.com

PARAGUAY

Bishop The Rt Revd Peter John Henry Bartlett, Iglesia Anglicana de Paraguaya, Casilla de Correo 1124, Asunción, Paraguay
T: 595 21 200 933
F: 595 21 214 328
E: peterparaguay@gmail.com

PERU

Bishop The Rt Revd Harold William Godfrey, Calle Doña María 141, Los Rosales, Surco, Lima 33, Peru   *T:* 51 1 449 0600
E: hwgodfrey@gmail.com
W: www.peru.anglican.org

Suffragan Bishop The Rt Revd Michael Chapman (*same address*)
E: thwmac@juno.com

URUGUAY

Bishop The Rt Revd Michele Pollesel, Reconquista 522, Montevideo 11000, Uruguay 11300   *T:* 598 2 9159627
F: 598 2 916 2519
E: iglesiaau@gmail.com
W: https://www.facebook.com/ Iglesia.Anglicana.del.Uruguay

Suffragan Bishop The Rt Revd Gilberto Obdulio Porcal Martinez (*same address*)
E: gilbertoporcal@hotmail.com

The Province of the Anglican Church in South East Asia

Members 224,200

The Anglican Church in South East Asia was originally under the jurisdiction of the Bishop of Calcutta. The first chaplaincy was formed in West Malaysia in 1805; the first bishop was consecrated in 1855. The Diocese of Labuan, Sarawak and Singapore was formed in 1881. From it the Diocese of Borneo and the Diocese of Singapore (later Malaya was added) was formed in 1909. In 1962 the Diocese of Jesselton, later renamed Sabah, and the Diocese of Kuching were formed from the former Diocese of Borneo. In 1970 the Diocese of West Malaysia was formed from what had been the Diocese of Malaya and Singapore. Until the inauguration of the Church of the Province of South East Asia in 1996, the four dioceses (Kuching, Sabah, Singapore, and West Malaysia) were under the jurisdiction of the Archbishop of Canterbury. Although the province exists under certain social constraints, the Church has experienced much spiritual renewal and has sent out its own mission partners to various parts of the world, especially neighbouring Indonesia, Cambodia, Thailand, Nepal, Laos, Vietnam and Myanmar.

Primate The Most Revd Datuk Ng Moon Hing (*Bishop of West Malaysia*)

Provincial Secretary The Revd Kenneth Thien Su Yin, Desert Stream Anglican Church, Lot 2, 4, & 6, Block A, Wisma Leven, Lorong Margosa 2, Luyang Phase 8, 88300 Kota Kinabalu, Sabah, Malaysia   *Office:* 60 88 270 246
F: 60 88 270 280
E: kenneththien@gmail.com

Provincial Treasurer Mr Keith Chua, 35 Ford Avenue, Singapore 268714, Singapore
E: keithchu@singnet.com.sg

Provincial Chancellor Mr Andrew Khoo, Messrs Andrew Khoo & Daniel Lo (Advocates & Solicitors), 26, Lorong Abang Haji Openg 1, Taman Tun Dr. Ismail, 60000 Kuala Lumpur, Malaysia   T: 60 377268496
E: andrew_khoo@akdl.com

Provincial Registrar Dato' Benedict Bujang Tembak, Hardin & Co., Advocates, 25, Jalan Tabuan, PO Box 103, 93700 Kuching, Sarawak, Malaysia   T: 60 82 252 599
F: 60 82 429041
E: hardintembak@gmail.com

THEOLOGICAL COLLEGES
House of the Epiphany, PO Box No 347, 93704 Kuching, Sarawak, Malaysia (*Warden* The Revd Canon Michael S. Woods)

Trinity Theological College, 490 Upper Bukit Timah Road, Singapore 678093 (interdenominational)

St Peter's Hall, residential hostel for Anglican students at Trinity Theological College, Singapore (*Warden* The Revd Joseph Goh)

Seminari Theoloji Malaysia (STM), Lot 3011, Taman South East, Jalan Tampin Lama, Batu 3, 70100 Seremban, Negeri Sembilan, Malaysia (*Principal* The Revd Dr Philip Siew)
T: 606 6322815/6
F: 606 6329766
W: www.stm.edu.my

KUCHING

Bishop The Rt Revd Datuk Bolly Anak Lapok, Bishop's House, PO Box 347, 93704 Kuching, Sarawak, Malaysia   T: 60 82 240 187
F: 60 82 426 488
E: bpofkuching@gmail.com

Assistant Bishops
The Rt Revd Aeries Sumping Jingan, PO Box 347, 93704 Kuching, Sarawak, Malaysia
T: 60 82 429755
F: 60 82 426488
E: aersumjin@gmail.com

The Rt Revd Solomon Cheong Sung Voon, St Columba's Church, PO Box 233, 98007 Miri, Sarawak, Malaysia   T: 60 85 417 284
F: 60 85 43 370
E: solomon.cheong@gmail.com

SABAH

Bishop The Rt Revd Melter Jiki Tais, PO Box 10811, 88809 Kota Kinabalu, Sabah, Malaysia
T: 60 88 245 846
F: 60 88 261 422
E: uskupmjtais@gmail.com

Assistant Bishop
The Rt Revd John Yeo, 201, Jalan Dunlop, 91000 Tawau   T: 60 89 772 212
F: 60 89 761 451
E: ad.johnyeo@gmail.com

SINGAPORE

Bishop The Rt Revd Rennis Ponniah, St. Andrews Village, No. 1, Francis Thomas Drive, #01–01, Singapore 359340   T: 65 62 887 585
F: 65 62 885 574
E: rennis@anglican.org.sg

Assistant Bishops
The Rt Revd Low Jee King, St Andrew's Village, No. 1, Francis Thomas Drive, #01–01, Singapore 359340   T: 65 62 888 944
F: 65 62 885 574
E: lowjeeking@gmail.com

The Rt Revd Kuan Kim Seng, Chapel of the Resurrection, 1 Francis Thomas Drive #02-17, Singapore 359340   *T:* 65 62 888 944
F: 65 62 885 574
E: kuanks@cor.org.sg

WEST MALAYSIA
Archbishop The Most Revd Datuk Ng Moon Hing, No. 214 Jalan Pahang, 53000 Kuala Lumpur, Malaysia   *T:* 60 3 4024 3213
F: 60 3 4032 3225
E: canonmoon@gmail.com

Assistant Bishops
The Rt Revd Dr Jason Selvaraj, Christ Church, 48, Jalan Gereja, 75000 Melaka, Malaysia
T: 60 62 848804
F: 60 62 848 804
E: jasondaphne101@gmail.com

The Rt Revd Charles K. Samuel, St George's Church, 1 Lebuh Farquhar, 10200 Penang, Malaysia   *T:* 60 64 2612 739
F: 60 64 2642 292
E: vencan.cs@gmail.com

The Anglican Church of Southern Africa

Members 2,600,000
The province is the oldest in Africa. British Anglicans met for worship in Cape Town after 1806, with the first bishop appointed in 1847. The twenty-eight dioceses of the province extend beyond the Republic of South Africa and include the Foreign and Commonwealth Office (St Helena and Tristan da Cunha), Mozambique (Lebombo and Niassa), the Republic of Namibia, the Kingdom of Lesotho, and the Kingdom of Swaziland. This Church and its leaders played a significant role in the abolition of apartheid in South Africa and in peace keeping in Mozambique and Angola. A mission diocese was inaugurated in August 2002 in Angola. The Diocese of Ukhahlamba (renamed Khahlamba) was inaugurated in October 2009 and the Diocese of Mbashe was inaugurated in July 2010.

Primate The Most Revd Dr Thabo Makgoba (*Archbishop of Cape Town and Metropolitan of the Anglican Church of Southern Africa*)

Provincial Executive Officer The Ven Horace Arenz, 20 Bishopscourt Drive, Bishopscourt, Claremont, Western Cape 7708, South Africa
T: 27 21 763 1300
F: 27 21 797 1329
E: peo@anglicanchurchsa.org.za
W: www.anglicanchurchsa.org

Provincial Treasurer Mr Rob S. Rogerson, PO Box 53014, Kenilworth, 7745, South Africa
T: 27 21 763 1300
F: 27 21 797 8319
E: rogerson@anglicanchurchsa.org.za

THEOLOGICAL COLLEGE
The College of the Transfiguration, PO Box 77, Grahamstown 6140   *T:* 27 46 622 3332
F: 27 46 622 3877
E: office@cott.co.za

ANGOLA (Missionary diocese)
Bishop The Rt Revd Andre Soares, Av. Lenini, Travessa D. Antonia Saldanha N.134, CP 10 341, Luanda, Angola   *T:* 244 2 395 792
F: 244 2 396 794
E: anglicanangola@yahoo.com
bispo-Soares@hotmail.com

CAPE TOWN
Archbishop The Most Revd Dr Thabo Makgoba (*Metropolitan of Southern Africa*), 20 Bishopscourt Drive, Bishopscourt, Claremont, Cape Town 7708, Western Cape, South Africa
T: 27 21 763 1300
F: 27 21 797 1298/761 4193
E: archpa@anglicanchurchsa.org.za
W: www.anglicanchurchsa.org

Bishop Suffragan
The Rt Revd Garth Counsell (*Bishop of Table Bay*), PO Box 1932, Cape Town 8000
T: 27 21 469 3760
F: 27 21 465 1571
E: tablebay@ctdiocese.org.za
bishopsuffragan@ctdiocese.org.za

CHRIST THE KING
Bishop The Rt Revd Peter Lee, PO Box 1653, Rosettenville 2130, South Africa
T: 27 11 435 0097
F: 27 11 435 2868
E: bishop@ctkdiocese.org

FALSE BAY
Bishop The Rt Revd Margaret Brenda Vertue, PO Box 2804, Somerset West 7129, South Africa   *T:* 27 21 852 5243
F: 27 21 852 9430
E: bishopm@falsebaydiocese.org.za

GEORGE
Bishop The Rt Revd Brian Melvyn Marajh, PO Box 227, George 6530, Cape Province, South Africa   *T:* 27 44 873 5680
F: 27 44 873 5680
E: bishopbrian@georgediocese.org.za

GRAHAMSTOWN
Bishop The Rt Revd Ebenezer St Mark Ntlali, PO Box 181, Grahamstown 6140, Cape Province, South Africa   *T:* 27 46 636 1996
F: 27 46 622 5231
E: bishop@grahamstowndiocese.org.za

HIGHVELD
Bishop The Rt Revd Charles May, PO Box 17462, Benoni West 1503, South Africa
T: 27 11 422 2231
F: 27 11 420 1336
E: bishophveld@iafrica.com

JOHANNESBURG
Bishop The Rt Revd Stephen Mosimanegape Moreo, PO Box 39, Westhoven, 2142 Gauteng, South Africa   *T:* 27 11 375 2700
F: 27 11 486 1015
E: steve.moreo@anglicanjoburg.org.za

KHAHLAMBA
Bishop The Rt Revd Mazwi Ernest Tisani, PO Box 1673 Queenstown, 5320 South Africa
T: 27 45 858 8673
F: 27 45 858 8675
E: bishopmazwi@mweb.co.za

KIMBERLEY AND KURUMAN
Bishop The Rt Revd Oswald Peter Patrick Swartz, PO Box 45, Kimberley 8300, South Africa   *T:* 27 53 833 2433
F: 27 53 831 2730
E: oppswartz@onetel.com/
Kkdiocese.bishop@telkomsa.net

LEBOMBO
Bishop The Rt Revd Carlos Matsinhe, CP 120, Maputo, Mozambique
T: 258 1 404 364/405 885
F: 258 1 401 093
E: carlosmatsinhe@rocketmail.com

LESOTHO
Bishop The Rt Revd Adam Andrease Mallane Taaso, PO Box 87, Maseru 100, Lesotho
T: 266 22 31 1974
F: 266 22 31 0161
E: dioceselesotho@ecoweb.co.ls

MATLOSANE
Bishop The Rt Revd Stephen Molopi Diseko, PO Box 11417, Klerksdorp 2570, South Africa
T: 27 18 464 2260
F: 27 18 462 4939
E: bishopstephen@diocesematlosane.co.za
E: mikeomoipinmoye@yahoo.com

MBASHE
Bishop The Rt Revd Elliot Sebenzile Williams, PO Box 1184, Butterworth, 4960, South Africa
T: 27 47 491 8030
F: 27 43 740 4766
E: dioceseofmbashe@telkomsa.net

MPUMALANGA
Bishop The Rt Revd Daniel Malasela Kgomosotho, PO Box 4327, White River 1240
T: 27 13 751 1960
F: 27 13 751 3638
E: diompu@telkomsa.net

MTHATHA
Bishop The Rt Revd Dr Sitembele Tobela Mzamane, PO Box 25, Umtata, Transkei 5100, South Africa   *T:* 27 47 532 4450
F: 27 47 532 4191
E: anglicbspmthatha@intekom.co.za

NAMIBIA
Bishop The Rt Revd Luke Pato, PO Box 57, Windhoek, Namibia   *T:* 264 61 238 920
F: 264 61 225 903
E: bishop@anglicanchurchnamibia.com

NATAL
Bishop The Rt Revd Dino Gabriel, PO Box 47439, Greyville, 4023 South Africa
T: 27 31 309 2066
F: 27 31 308 9316
E: bishop@dionatal.org.za

Bishops Suffragan The Rt Revd Dr Hummingfield Charles Nkosinathi Ndwandwe (*Suffragan Bishop of the South Episcopal Area*) (*same address*)   *T:* 27 33 394 1560
E: bishopndwandwe@dionatal.org.za

The Rt Revd Tsietse Edward Seleoane (*Suffragan Bishop of the North West Episcopal Area*), PO Box 463, Ladysmith 3370, South Africa
T: 27 36 631 4650
F: 27 86 547 1882
E: bishopseleoane@dionatal.org.za

NIASSA
Bishop The Rt Revd Vicente Msossa, CP 264, Lichinga, Niassa, Mozambique
T: and F: 258 712 0735
E: bishop.niassa@gmail.com

Bishop Suffragan The Rt Revd Manuel Ernesto, CP 264, Lichinga, Niassa, Mozambique
T: and F: 258 712 0735
E: mernesto.diocese.niassa@gmail.com

PORT ELIZABETH
Bishop The Rt Revd Nceba Bethlehem Nopece, PO Box 7109, Newton Park 6055, South Africa
T: 27 41 365 1387
F: 27 41 365 2049
E: bpsec@pediocese.org.za
bishop@pediocese.org.za

PRETORIA
Bishop The Rt Revd Allan John Kannemeyer, 802 Pretorius Street, Arcadia 0083, PO Box 1032, Pretoria 0001, South Africa
T: 27 12 430 2345
F: 27 12 430 2224
E: ptabish@dioceseofpretoria.org

ANGLICAN & PORVOO COMMUNIONS

SALDANHA BAY
Bishop The Rt Revd Raphael Bernard Viburt Hess, PO Box 420, Malmesbury 7299, South Africa   *T:* 27 22 487 3885
                                   F: 27 22 487 3886
    E: bishop@dioceseofsaldanhabay.org.za
         lizel@dioceseofsaldanhabay.org.za

ST HELENA
Bishop The Rt Revd Dr Richard David Fenwick, PO Box 62, Island of St Helena, South Atlantic
                                        T: 290 4471
                                        F: 290 4728
    E: richard.d.fenwick@googlemail.com

ST MARK THE EVANGELIST
Bishop The Rt Revd Martin Andre Breytenbach, PO Box 643, Polokwane 0700, South Africa
                                    T: 27 15 297 3297
                                    F: 27 15 297 0408
         E: martin@stmark.org.za

SWAZILAND
Bishop The Rt Revd Ellinah Ntfombi Wamukoya, Bishop's House, Muir Street, Mbabane, Swaziland
                                    T: 268 404 3624
                                    F: 268 404 6759
    E: bishopen@swazilanddiocese.org.sz

THE FREE STATE
Bishop The Rt Revd Dintoe Stephen Letloenyane, PO Box 411, Bloemfontein, 9300, South Africa   *T:* 27 51 447 6053
                                   F: 27 51 447 5874
         E: bishopdintoe@dsc.co.za
         W: www.cpsa.org.za/bloemfontein

UMZIMVUBU
Bishop The Rt Revd Mlibo Mteteleli Ngewu, PO Box 644, Kokstad 4700, South Africa
                        T: and *F:* 27 39 727 4117
         E: mzimvubu@futurenet.co.za

ZULULAND
Bishop The Rt Revd Monument Makhanya, PO Box 147, Eshowe 3815, South Africa
                        T: and *F:* 27 354 742 047
         E: bishopzld@netactive.co.za

The Church of the Province of South Sudan

Members 5,000,000
The Church Missionary Society began work in 1899 in Omdurman; Christianity spread rapidly among black Africans of the southern region. Until 1974, the diocese of Sudan was part of the Jerusalem archbishopric. It reverted to the jurisdiction of the Archbishop of Canterbury until the new province, consisting of four new dioceses, was established in 1976. In 1986 the number of dioceses increased to 11 and in 1992 to 24 dioceses. The doubling of the number of dioceses by 1992 was partly due to leadership crises in the Church and partly due to church growth. Civil and religious strife and a constant flow of refugees have challenged the Church. Its heroic witness to faith in Christ continues to inspire the Anglican Communion and its people.

Archbishop and Primate The Most Revd Dr Daniel Deng Bul Yak (*Bishop of Juba*)

Provincial Secretary John Augustino Lumori, PO Box 110, Juba, South Sudan
                        E: provincialsecretary@
                                 sudan.anglican.org

Honorary Provincial Treasurer Mr Evans Sokiri
                        E: sokirik@yahoo.co.uk

THEOLOGICAL COLLEGES
Bishop Gwynne College, PO Box 110, Juba, Sudan (*Acting Principal* The Revd David V. Bako)   *T:* 249 9124 54933 (Mobile)
                        E: davidbako7@hotmail.com

Bishop Alison Theological College, PO Box 1076, Arua, Uganda (*Principal* Dr Oliver Duku)
                                    T: 254 77 685 554
                        E: bat_college@yahoo.com

Shokai Bible Training Institute, PO Box 65, Omdurman, 135 Khartoum, Sudan (*Principal* The Revd Musa Elgadi)   *T:* 249 187 564944
                        E: sbti70@yahoo.com

Renk Bible School, PO Box 1532, Khartoum North, Sudan (*Acting Principal* The Revd Abraham Noon Jiel)
                        T: 249 918 068 125 (Mobile)
                        E: joseph_atem@yahoo.com

Bishop Ngalamu Theological College, PO Box 3364, Khartoum, Sudan (*Principal* The Revd Paul Issa)   *E:* leyeonon@hotmail.com

AKOT
The Rt Revd Isaac Dhieu Ater
T: 00211 928 122 065
E: bishop@akot.anglican.org

ATOOCH
The Rt Revd Moses Anur Ayom
T: 00211 956 602 346
E: mosesanurayom@yahoo.com

AWEIL
The Rt Revd Abraham Yel Nhial
T: 00211 955 621 584
E: bishop@aweil.anglican.org

AWERIAL
The Rt Revd David Akau Kuol
T: 00211 955 526 396
E: bishop.awerila@yirol.anglican.org

BOR
The Rt Revd Ruben Akurdid
T: 00211 955 309 767
E: bishop.akurdid@gmail.com

CUEIBET
The Rt Revd Elijah Matueny
T: 00211 921 192 138
E: bishop@cueibet.anglican.org

DUK
The Rt Revd Daniel Deng Abot
T: 00211 955 523 896
E: danieldengabot@gmail.com

EZO
The Rt Revd John Zawo
T: 00211 954 745 046
E: bishop@ezo.anglican.org

IBBA
The Rt Revd Wilson Elisa Kamani
T: 00211 956 438 805
E: bishop@ibba.anglican.org

JUBA
The Most Revd Daniel Deng Bul Yak,
(Archbishop), PO Box 110, Juba, South Sudan
T: 00211 912 299 275
E: archbishop@sudan.anglican.org

(Assistant) The Rt Revd Fraser Yugu Elias
T: 00211 956 143 577
E: ass.bishop@juba.anglican.org

KAJO-KEJI
The Rt Revd Emmanuel Murye, c/o ECS PO
Box 10, Juba, South Sudan
T: 00211 956 697 429
E: bishopkk@gmail.com

KONGOR
The Rt Revd Gabriel Thuch Agot
E: gabrielthuchagot@yahoo.com

LAINYA
The Rt Revd Elioba Lako Obede
T: 00211 956 009 774
E: bishop@lainya.anglican.org

LOMEGA
The Rt Revd Paul Yugusuk
T: 00211 955 681 468
E: lomegarea@yahoo.com

LUI
The Rt Revd Stephen Dokolo Ismael
T: 00211 917 704 534
E: bishop@lui.anglican.org

MALAKAL
The Rt Revd Hilary Garang, PO Box 114,
Malakal, South Sudan
T: 00211 913 333 333
E: bishop@malakal.anglican.org

MALEK
The Rt Revd Peter Joh Abraham Mayom
T: 00211 977 435 602
E: johabraham@yahoo.com

MALEK RUP
The Rt Revd Peter Marial Agok
T: 00211 955 263 347

MARIDI
The Rt Revd Justin Badi Arama
T: 00211 927 012 719
E: ecsmaridi@hotmail.com

MUNDRI
The Rt Revd Bismark Monday Avokaya
T: 00211 927 602 751
E: bishop@mundri.anglican.org

NZARA
The Rt Revd Samuel Enosa Peni
T: 00211 955 511 555
E: bishop@nzara.anglican.org

OLO
The Rt Revd Tandema Obede
T: 00211 928 403 619
E: bishopolo65@gmail.com

PACONG
The Rt Revd Joseph Maker Atot
T: 00211 929 154 246
E: ecs.pacongdiocese@yahoo.com

REJAF
The Rt Revd Enoch Tombe
T: 00211 955 673 779
E: bishop@rejaf.anglican.org

ANGLICAN & PORVOO
COMMUNIONS

RENK
The Rt Revd Joseph Garang Atem
T: 00211 912 197 051
E: josephatem@gmail.com

ROKON
The Rt Revd Francis Loyo
T: 00211 928 122 065
E: bployo@yahoo.co.uk

RUMBEK
The Rt Revd Alapayo Manyang Kuctiel
T: 00211 955 288 730
E: bishop@rumbek.anglican.org

TEREKEKA
The Rt Revd Paul Modi Farjala
T: 00211 954 125 968
E: bishop@terekaka.anglican.org

TORIT
The Rt Revd Bernard Oringa Balmoi
T: 00211 955 210 268
E: bishop@torit.anglican.org

TWIK EAST
The Rt Revd Ezekiel Diing
T: 00211 955 099 182
E: malangajang@gmail.com

WAU
The Rt Revd Moses Deng Bol
T: 00211 926 954 187
E: bishop@wau.anglican.org

WONDURBA
The Rt Revd Matthew Taban Peter
T: 00211 911 225 000
E: bplmatthewpeter@gmail.com

YAMBIO
The Rt Revd Peter Munde Yacoub
T: 00211 955 805 007
E: yambio2002@yahoo.com

YEI
The Rt Revd Hilary Luate Adeba, PO Box 588,
Arua, Uganda
T: (00256) (756) 561 175
E: hill_shepherd@yahoo.com

YERI
The Rt Revd John Abraham Nyari
T: 00211 923 149 110
E: yeridioceses@gmail.com

YIROL
The Rt Revd Simon Adut Yuang
T: 00211 927 277 975
E: ecsyiroldiocese@yahoo.com

The Church of the Province of Sudan

This newly-created province was inaugurated on 30 July 2017 at a service attended by the Archbishop of Canterbury.

Archbishop of the Province of Sudan and Bishop of Khartoum The Most Revd Ezekiel Kumir Kondo

Provincial Secretary The Revd Musa Abujam

EL-OBEID
Bishop The Rt Revd Ismail Gabriel Abudigin, PO Box 211, El Obeid
W: www.elobeid.anglican.org

KADUGLI AND NUBA MOUNTAINS
Bishop The Rt Revd Andudu Adam Einail
T: 00211 912 230 250
E: bishop@kadugli.anglican.org
W: kadugli.anglican.org

KHARTOUM
Bishop The Most Revd Ezekiel Kumir Kondo *(Archbishop of the Province)*, PO Box 65, Omdurman
E: bishop@khartoum.anglican.org
W: www.khartoum.anglican.org

PORT SUDAN
Bishop The Rt Revd Abdu Elnur Kodi, PO Box 278, Red Sea State
T: 249 31 212 24
E: bunukaa@live.com
W: www.portsudan.anglican.org

WAD MEDANI
Bishop The Rt Revd Sama Farajalla Mahdi
E: bishop@wadmedani.anglican.org
W: www.wadmedani.anglican.org

The Anglican Church of Tanzania

Members over 3,000,000

The Universities Mission to Central Africa and the Church Missionary Society began work in 1863 and 1876 in Zanzibar and at Mpwapwa respectively. The province was inaugurated in 1970 following the division of the Province of East Africa into the Province of Kenya and the Province of Tanzania. The 27 dioceses represent both evangelical and Anglo-Catholic Churches.

Archbishop The Most Revd Dr Jacob Erasto Chimeledya (*Bishop of Mpwapwa*)

Dean The Rt Revd Oscar Mnung'a (*Bishop of Newala*)

Provincial Secretary The Revd Canon Captain Johnson Japheth Chinyong'ole, PO Box 899, Dodoma   *T:* 255 26 232 4574
      F: 255 26 232 4565
      E: chinyongole@anglican.or.tz
      W: www.anglican.or.tz

Provincial Treasurer The Rt Revd Dr Maimbo William Mndolwa (*Bishop of Tanga*)

Provincial Registrar Prof. Palamagamba John Kabudi, Faculty of Law, University of Dar es Salaam, PO Box 35093 Dar es Salaam
      T: 255 022 211 5418
      E: pjkabudi@gmail.com

ACT INSTITUTIONS (COLLEGES/UNIVERSITY)

St Philip's Theological College, PO Box 26, Kongwa (*Principal* The Revd Captain Agrippa Ndatila)   *T:* 255 26 232 0096
      E: stphilipstz@yahoo.com

St Mark's Theological College (Centre of St John's University of Tanzania), PO Box 25017, Dar es Salaam (*Director* Dr Naomi Katunzi)
      T: 255 22 286 3014

Msalato Theological College (Centre of St John's University of Tanzania), Box 264, Dodoma, (*Director* The Revd Canon Kabia)
      T: 255262304180
      E: mtcdctsjut@gmail.com

St John's University of Tanzania, PO Box 47, Dodoma (*Vice Chancellor*) The Revd Prof. Emmanuel D. Mbennah)   *T:* 255 26 239 0044
      F: 255 26 239 0025
      E: vca@sjut.ac.tz
      W: http://www.sjut.ac.tz

CHURCH NEWSLETTER

ACT Forum is issued three times a year (April, August, December) in English containing diocesan, provincial and world church news. *Editor* Vacancy

CENTRAL TANGANYIKA

Bishop The Rt Revd Dr. Dickson Chilongani
PO Box 15, Dodoma   *T:* 255 26 232 1714
      F: 255 26 232 4518
      E: Chilongani@anglican.or.tz

DAR ES SALAAM

Bishop The Rt Revd Dr Valentino Mokiwa PO Box 25016, Ilala, Dar-es-Salaam
      T: 255 22 286 4426
      E: mokiwa–valentine@hotmail.com

KAGERA

Bishop The Rt Revd Dr Aaron Kijanjali, PO Box 18, Ngara   *T:* 255 28 222 3624
      F: 255 28 222 2518
      E: dkagera@googlemail.com

KIBONDO

Bishop The Rt Revd Dr Sospeter Ndenza, P. O. Box 15 Kibondo   *T:* 255 75 469 6846
      E: sndenzas@yahoo.co.uk

KITETO

Bishop The Rt Revd Isaiah Chambala, PO Box 74, Kibaya, Kiteto   *T:* 255 27 255 2106
      E: bishopofkiteto@yahoo.com

KONDOA

Bishop The Rt Revd Dr Given Gaula, PO Box 7, Kondoa   *T:* 255 26 236 0312
      F: 255 26 236 0304 / 0324
      E: givenmgaula@gmail.com

LAKE RUKWA

Bishop The Rt Revd Mathayo Kasagara, PO Box 14, Mpanda   *E:* kasagarajr@gmail.com

LWERU

Bishop The Rt Revd Jackton Yeremiah Lugumira, PO Box 12, Muleba
      T: 255 713 274 085
      E: jact@bukobaonline.com

MARA

Bishop The Rt Revd George Okoth PO Box 131, Musoma   *T:* 255 28 262 2376
      F: 255 28 262 2414

MASASI

Bishop The Rt Revd Dr James Almasi, Private Bag, PO Masasi, Mtwara   *T:* 255 23 251 0016
      F: 255 23 251 0351
      E: jamesalmasi@yahoo.com

MOROGORO

Bishop The Rt Revd Godfrey Sehaba, PO Box 320, Morogoro   *T: and F:* 255 23 260 4602
      E: bishopgsehaba@yahoo.com

ANGLICAN & PORVOO COMMUNIONS

MOUNT KILIMANJARO
Bishop The Rt Revd Stanley Elilekia Hotay, PO
Box 1057, Arusha   T: 255 27 254 8396
                          F: 255 27 254 4187
          E: hotaystanley@yahoo.com

MPWAPWA
Bishop The Most Revd Dr Jacob Erasto
Chimeledya (*Archbishop of the Province*), PO
Box 2, Mpwapwa   T: 255 26 232 0017 / 0825
                          F: 255 26 232 0063
          E: jacobchimeledya@hotmail.com

NEWALA
Bishop The Rt Revd Oscar Mnung'a, PO Box
92, Newala   T: 255 78 233 8822
          E: rtrevonewala@gmail.com

RIFT VALLEY
Bishop The Rt Revd John Lupaa, PO Box 16,
Manyoni   T: 255 26 254 0013
                          F: 255 26 250 3014
          E: act-drv@maf.or.tz

RORYA
Bishop The Rt Revd John Adiema, P. O. Box 38,
Musoma   T: 255 75 289 3957

RUAHA
Bishop The Rt Revd Dr Joseph Mgomi, PO Box
1028, Iringa   T: 255 26 270 1211
                          F: 255 26 270 2479
          E: actruaha@gmail.com

RUVUMA
Bishop Maternus Kapinga, PO Box 1357,
Songea, Ruvuma   T: 255 25 260 0090
                          F: 255 25 260 2987
          E: matemask@gmail.com

SHINYANGA
Bishop The Rt Revd Charles Kija Ngusa, PO Box
421, Shinyanga   T: 255 028 276 3584
          E: ckngusa@yahoo.com

SOUTHERN HIGHLANDS
Bishop The Rt Revd John Mwela, PO Box 198,
Mbeya   T: 255 754 266 668 (Mobile)
          E: mwelajohn@yahoo.co.uk

SOUTH-WEST TANGANYIKA
Bishop The Rt Revd Matthew Mhagama,
PO Box 32, Njombe   T: 255 26 278 2010
                          F: 255 26 278 2403
          E: dswt@africaonline.co.tz

TABORA
Bishop The Rt Revd Elias Chakupewa, PO Box
1408, Tabora   T: 255 26 260 4124
                          F: 255 26 260 4899
          E: chakupewalucy@yahoo.com

TANGA
Bishop The Rt Revd Dr Maimbo Mndolwa,
PO Box 35, Korogwe, Tanga T: 255 27 264 0631
                          F: 255 27 264 0568
          E: imba612@yahoo.com

TARIME
Bishop The Rt Revd Mwita Akiri, P.O. Box 410,
Tarime   T: 255 78 817 7400
          E: bishop.tarime@gmail.com

VICTORIA NYANZA
Bishop The Rt Revd Boniface Kwangu, PO Box
278, Mwanza   T: 255 28 250 0627
                          F: 255 28 250 0676
          E: bandmkwangu@yahoo.co.uk

WESTERN TANGANYIKA
Bishop The Rt Revd Sadock Makaya, PO Box
13, Kasulu   T: 255 28 281 0321
                          F: 255 28 281 0706
          E: smakaya1@yahoo.co.uk

ZANZIBAR
Bishop The Rt Revd Michael Hafidh PO Box 5,
Mkunazini, Zanzibar   T: 255 24 223 5348
                          F: 255 24 223 6772
          E: mhhafidh@gmail.com
          E: anglicanrorya@yahoo.com

The Church of the Province of Uganda

Members 12,000,000
After its founding in 1877 by the Church
Missionary Society, the Church grew through
the evangelization of Africa by Africans. The
first Ugandan clergy were ordained in 1893
and the Church of Uganda, Rwanda and
Burundi became an independent province in
1961. The history of the Church in Uganda
has been marked by civil strife and
martyrdom. In May 1980 the new Province of
Burundi, Rwanda and Zaire was inaugurated;
the Province of Uganda has since grown from
17 to 34 dioceses.

Archbishop of the Province The Most Revd
Stanley Ntagali (*Bishop of Kampala*)

Primatial and Provincial Secretariat PO Box
14123, Kampala   T: 256 414 270 218
          E: couoffice@gmail.com

Provincial Secretary The Revd Amos Magezi
(*same address*)
          E: pschurchofuganda@gmail.com

Provincial Treasurer Mr Richard Obura (*same
address*)   T: 256 414 270 218
          E: richardobura@gmail.com

THEOLOGICAL COLLEGES
Uganda Christian University, Mukono, PO Box 4, Mukono (*Vice-Chancellor* The Revd Canon Dr John Senyonyi)

Bishop Balya College, PO Box 368, Fort-Portal (*Principal* The Revd Y. Kule)

Bishop Barham University College (constituent college of Uganda Christian university, Mukono), PO Box 613, Kabale (*Principal* The Revd Dr Manual Muranga)

Archbishop Janani Luwum Theological College, PO Box 232, Gulu (*Principal* The Revd Sandra Earixson)

Mityana Theological Training College, PO Box 102, Mityana (*Principal* The Revd Mukasa-Mutambuze)

Ngora Diocesan Theological College, PO Box 1, Ngora (*Principal* The Revd S. Amuret)

Uganda Martyrs Seminary Namugongo, PO Box 31149, Kampala (*Principal* The Revd Canon Henry Segawa)

Aduku Diocesan Theological College, PO Aduku, Lira (*Principal* The Revd S. O. Obura)

Kabwohe College, PO Kabwohe, Mbarara (*Principal* The Revd Y. R. Buremu)

St Paul's Theological College Ringili, PO Box 358, Arua (*Principal* Canon Dr Milton Anguyo)

Bishop Usher Wilson, Buwalasi, Mbale (*Principal* The Revd Naphtah Opwata)

Uganda Bible Institute, Mbarara (*Director* The Revd Canon Johnson Twinomujuni)

Bishop McAllister College, Kyogyera (*Principal* The Revd Paul Jefferees)

Diocesan Training Centre, Duhaga, Hoima (*Principal* The Revd Cindy Larsen)

ANKOLE
Bishop The Rt Revd Sheldon Mwesigwa, PO Box 14, Mbarara, Ankole   *T:* 256 787 084 301
E: ruharu@utiouline.co.ug

BUKEDI
Bishop The Rt Revd Samuel Egesa, PO Box 170, Tororo   *T:* 256 772542 164 (Mobile)
E: bukedidiocese@yahoo.com

BUNYORO-KITARA
Bishop The Rt Revd Nathan Kyamanywa, PO Box 20, Hoima   *T:* 256 464 40 128
256 0776 648 232 (Mobile)
E: nathan.kyamanywa@gmail.com

BUSOGA
Bishop The Rt Revd Dr Michael Kyomya, PO Box 1568, Jinja   *T:* 256 752 649 102 (Mobile)
F: 256 43 20 547
E: busogadiocese@gmail.com

CENTRAL BUGANDA
Bishop The Rt Revd Jackson Matovu, PO Box 1200, Kinoni-Gomba, Mpigi
T: 256 772 475 640 (Mobile)
F: 256 772 242 742
E: mapetoruvusi@yahoo.com

EAST RUWENZORI
Bishop The Rt Revd Edward Bamucwanira, PO Box 1439, Kamwenge   *T:* 256 772 906 236
E: edward_bamu@yahoo.com

KAMPALA
Bishop The Most Revd Stanley Ntagali (*Archbishop of Uganda*), PO Box 335, Kampala
T: 256 414 279 218
F: 256 414 251 925
E: abpcou@gmail.com

Assistant Bishop The Rt Revd Hannington Mutebi, PO Box 335, Kampala
T: 256 414 290 231
F: 256 414 342 601
E: mutebihanning@yahoo.com

KARAMOJA
Bishop The Rt Revd Joseph Abura, PO Box 44, Moroto   *T:* 256 782 658 502
E: loukomoru@gmail.com

KIGEZI
Bishop The Rt Revd George Bagamuhunda, PO Box 3, Kabale   *T:* 256 772 450 019
F: 256 486 22 802
E: bishopkigezi@infocom.co.ug

KINKIZI
Bishop The Rt Revd Dan Zoreka, PO Box 77, Kanungu   *T:* 256 772 507 163 (Mobile)
E: zorekadan@yahoo.com

KITGUM
Bishop The Most Revd Stanley Ntagali, PO Box 187, Kitgum   *T:* 256 772 959 924 (Mobile)
E: abpcou@gmail.com

KUMI
Bishop The Rt Revd Thomas Edison Irigei, PO Box 18, Kumi *T:* 256 772 659 460 (Mobile)
E: kumimothersunion@yahoo.com

LANGO
Bishop The Rt Revd John Charles Odurkami, PO Box 6, Lira   *T:* 256 772 614 000 (Mobile)
E: bishoplango@yahoo.com

ANGLICAN & PORVOO COMMUNIONS

LUWERO
Bishop The Rt Revd Eridard Kironde Nsubuga, PO Box 125, Luwero
T: 256 772 349 669 (Mobile)
E: eridard.nsugua@gmail.com

MADI / WEST NILE
Bishop The Rt Revd Joel Obetia, PO Box 370, Arua   T: 256 751 625 414 (Mobile)
E: jobetia@yahoo.com

MASINDI-KITARA
Bishop The Rt Revd George Kasangaki, PO Box 515, Masindi   T: 256 772 618 822
E: georgewakasa@gmail.com

MBALE
Bishop The Rt Revd Patrick Gidudu, Bishop's House, PO Box 473, Mbale   T: 256 45 33 533
256 782 625 619 (Mobile)
E: patrickhgidudu@yahoo.com

MITYANA
Bishop The Rt Revd Stephen Samuel Kaziimba, PO Box 102, Mityana   T: 256 772 512 175
E: sakazimba@yahoo.com

MUHABURA
Bishop The Rt Revd Cranmer Mugisha, PO Box 22, Kisoro   T: 256 486 30 014/058
256 712 195 891 (Mobile)
F: 256 486 30 059
E: cranhopmu@yahoo.co.uk

MUKONO
Bishop The Rt Revd William James Ssebaggala, PO Box 39, Mukono   T: 256 41 290 229
256 712 860 742 (Mobile)
E: Jamesebagala@yahoo.co.uk

NAMIREMBE
Bishop The Rt Revd Wilberforce Kityo Luwalira, PO Box 14297, Kampala
T: 256 414 271 682
256 712 942 161 (Mobile)
E: omulabirizi@gmail.com

NEBBI
Bishop The Rt Revd Alphonse Watho-Kudi, PO Box 27, Nebbi T: 256 772 650 032 (Mobile
E: bpalphonse@ekk.org

NORTH ANKOLE
Bishop The Rt Revd Stephen Namanya, c/o PO Box 14, Rushere-Kiruhura
T: 256 772 622 116(Mobile)
E: nadsrushere@yahoo.com

NORTH KARAMOJA
Bishop The Rt Revd James Nasak, PO Box 26, Kotido   T: 256 772 660 228
E: jnasak@yahoo.com

NORTH KIGEZI
Bishop The Rt Revd Patrick Tugume-Tusingwire, PO Box 23, Rukungiri
T: 256 777 912 010
E: earfchairman@yahoo.com

NORTH MBALE
Bishop The Rt Revd Samuel Gidudu, PO Box 2357, Mbale   T: 256 782 853 094
F: 256 752 655 225
E: revsamgidudu@yahoo.com

NORTHERN UGANDA
Bishop The Rt Revd Johnson Gakumba, PO Box 232, Gulu   T: 256 772 601 421 (Mobile)
E: johnson.gakumba@gmail.com

RUWENZORI
Bishop The Rt Revd Reuben Kisembo, Bishop's House, PO Box 37, Fort Portal
T: 256 772 838 193
E: reubenkisembo@gmail.com

SEBEI
Bishop The Rt Revd Paul Kiptoo Masaba, PO Box 23, Kapchorwa
T: 256 772 312 502 (Mobile)
E: repkmasaba@yahoo.co.uk

SOROTI
Bishop The Rt Revd George Erwau, PO Box 107, Soroti   T: 256 772 565 607 (Mobile)
E: georgeerwau@yahoo.com

SOUTH ANKOLE
Bishop The Rt Revd Nathan Ahimbisibwe, PO Box 39, Ntungamo   T: 256 772 660 636
E: revnathan2000@yahoo.com

SOUTH RUWENZORI
Bishop The Rt Revd Jackson T. Nzerebende, PO Box 142, Kasese
T: 256 772 713 736 (Mobile)
F: 256 483 44 450
E: srdiocese@gmail.com

WEST ANKOLE
Bishop The Rt Revd Yona Katoneene, PO Box 140, Bushenyi   T: 256 752 377 192 (Mobile)
E: yona.katoneene@yahoo.com

WEST BUGANDA
Bishop The Rt Revd Jackson Matovu, PO Box 242, Masaka   T: 256 772 475 640 (Mobile)
E: mapetoruvusi@yahoo.com

The Protestant Episcopal Church in the United States of America

(also known as The Episcopal Church)

Members 2,400,000

Anglicanism was brought to the New World by explorers and colonists with the first celebration of the Holy Eucharist in Jamestown, Virginia in 1607. The need for clergy in the colonies was acute and English missionaries provided temporary relief. Though the Bishop of London was responsible for maintaining the church in the colonies, there was no resident bishop for nearly two hundred years, which meant that colonists had to travel to England to be ordained; this caused difficulties when many of the colonial clergy sided with the Crown during the American Revolution. In 1784 the first American bishop (Samuel Seabury of Connecticut) was consecrated in Scotland, and three years later bishops were consecrated in England for the Dioceses of Pennsylvania and New York. In 1785 the first General Convention was held; in 1821 the Domestic and Foreign Missionary Society was formed; and in 1835, by resolution of General Convention, all members of The Episcopal Church were made members of the Missionary Society.

The Episcopal Church today maintains 100 dioceses within the United States plus 10 overseas dioceses (Colombia, the Dominican Republic, Central Ecuador, Litoral Ecuador, Haiti, Honduras, Puerto Rico, Taiwan, Venezuela and the Virgin Islands), the Mission Territory of Micronesia (Guam), the Convocation of American Churches in Europe, and, together with the Anglican Church of Canada and the Church in the Province of the West Indies, is a partner in the Metropolitan Council which oversees the Episcopal Church of Cuba; it is governed by the triennial General Convention consisting of a House of Clergy and Lay Deputies, and a House of Bishops, which includes all serving diocesan, suffragan, coadjutor and assisting bishops. Between General Conventions, church affairs are managed by the Executive Council, whose members are elected in part by the two Houses and in part by the nine regional provinces. The Executive Council meets three times each year (except twice during a General Convention year). The province is a strong base of support to the Anglican Communion and has a significant crisis ministry through Episcopal Relief and Development. Episcopalians are also very active in the areas of social justice and ecumenical and interfaith relations, and witness to their faith in all walks of national life.

Presiding Bishop and Primate The Most Revd Michael Bruce Curry

Offices of the Episcopal Church and its departments Episcopal Church Center, 815 Second Avenue, New York, NY 10017, USA
T: 1 212 716 6000
E: via website
W: www.episcopalchurch.org

President of the House of Deputies The Revd Gay C. Jennings (*same address*)　*T:* 1 212 922 5183
E: via website

Executive Officer of the General Convention The Revd Canon Michael Barlowe (*same address*)
T: 1 212 922 5184
E: via website

Bishop Suffragan for Armed Services and Federal Ministries The Rt Revd James Magness, 3504 Woodley Road NW, Washington DC, 20016, USA
T: 1 646 434 0275
E: via website

Bishop of the Office of Pastoral Development The Rt Revd F. Clayton Matthews, 2857 Trent Road, New Bern, NC 28562, USA
T: 1 252 635 5004
E: via website

Treasurer and Chief Financial Officer Mr N. Kurt Barnes, Episcopal Church Center, 815 Second Avenue, New York, NY 10017, USA
T: 1 212 922 5296
E: via website
W: www.episcopalchurch.org

THEOLOGICAL SEMINARIES
California
Church Divinity School of the Pacific, 2451 Ridge Road, Berkeley, CA 94709-1211, USA (*President and Dean* The Very Revd Dr W. Mark Richardson)　*W:* www.cdsp.edu

Connecticut
Berkeley Divinity School at Yale University, 409 Prospect Sreett, New Haven, CT 06511, USA (*Dean and President* The Very Revd Andrew McGowan)
W: www.berkeleydivinity.net

Illinois
Bexley Seabury, 8785 W Higgins Road, Chicago, IL 60631, USA (*President* The Revd Dr Roger Ferlo)　*W:* www.bexleyseabury.edu

Massachusetts
Episcopal Divinity School, 99 Brattle Street, Cambridge, MA 02138, USA (*President and Dean* The Very Revd Dr Katherine Hancock Ragsdale)   *W*: www.eds.edu

New York
The General Theological Seminary of The Episcopal Church in the United States, 440 West 21st Street, New York, NY 10011, USA (*Dean and President* The Very Revd Kurt H. Dunkle)   *W*: www.gts.edu

Ohio
Bexley Seabury, 583 Sheridan Avenue, Columbus, OH 43209 (*President* The Revd Dr Roger Ferlo)   *W*: www.bexleyseabury.edu

Pennsylvania
Trinity School for Ministry, 311 Eleventh Street, Ambridge, PA 15003, USA (*Dean and President* The Very Revd Dr Justyn Terry)
                    W: www.tsm.edu

Tennessee
The School of Theology, Sewanee, The University of the South, 335 Tennessee Avenue, Sewanee, TN 37383–0001, USA (*Dean* The Rt Revd J. Neil Alexander)
                    W: www.theology.sewanee.edu

Texas
Seminary of the Southwest, 501 E 32nd Street, Austin, TX 78768, USA (*Dean* The Very Revd Cynthia Briggs Kittredge)   *W*: www.ssw.edu

Virginia
Virginia Thelogical, Seminary, 3737 Seminary Road, Alexandria, VA 22304, USA (*Dean and President* The Very Revd Dr Ian S. Markham)
                    W: www.vts.edu

Wisconsin
Nashotah House, 2777 Mission Road, Nashotah, WI 53058, USA (*Dean* The Rt Revd Edward L. Salmon Jr)   *W*: www.nashotah.edu

CHURCH PAPERS
Episcopal Life An independently edited, officially sponsored monthly newspaper published by the Episcopal Church, 815 Second Avenue, New York, NY 10017, USA, upon authority of the General Convention of the Protestant Episcopal Church in the USA. Also see *episcopallife online*, our electronic news service
                    W: www.episcopalchurch.org/
                    episcopal_life.htm

The Living Church Weekly magazine. *Editorial and Business Offices* PO Box 514036, Milwaukee, WI 53203, USA. Contains news and features about Christianity in general and the Episcopal Church in particular.

ALABAMA (Province IV)
Bishop The Rt Revd John McKee Sloan, Carpenter House, 521 N 20th Street, Birmingham, AL 35203–2611, USA
                    T: 1 205 715 2060
                    F: 1 205 715 2066
                    E: ksloan@dioala.org
                    W: www.dioala.org

ALASKA (Province VIII)
Bishop The Rt Revd Mark Lattime, 1205 Denali Way, Fairbanks, Alaska 99701–4137, USA
                    T: 1 907 452 3040
                    F: 1 907 456 6552
                    E: mlattime@gci.net
                    W: www.episcopalak.org

ALBANY (Province II)
Bishop The Rt Revd William Howard Love, 580 Burton Road, Greenwich, NY 12834, USA
                    T: 1 518 962 3350
                    F: 1 518 692 3352
                    E: via website
                    W: www.albanyepiscopaldiocese.org

ARIZONA (Province VIII)
Bishop The Rt Revd Kirk Stevan Smith, 114 West Roosevelt Street, Phoenix, AZ 85003–1406, USA   *T*: 1 602 254 0976
                    F: 1 602 495 6603
                    E: bishop@azdiocese.org
                    W: http://azdiocese.org

ARKANSAS (Province VII)
Bishop The Rt Revd Larry R. Benfield, 310 West 17 th Street, Little Rock, AR 72216–4668, USA
T: 1 501 372 2168   *F*: 1 501 372 2147
                    E: bishopbenfield@mac.com
                    W: http://episcopalarkansas.org

ATLANTA (Province IV)
Bishop The Rt Revd Robert Wright, 2744 Peachtree Road, Atlanta, GA 30305, USA
                    T: 1 404 601 5320
                    F: 1 404 601 5330
                    E: bishopwright@episcopalatlanta.org
                    W: www.episcopalatlanta.org

Assistant Bishop The Rt Revd Keith Bernard Whitmore (*same address*)
                    E: bishopkeith@episcopalatlanta.org

BETHLEHEM (Province III)
Bishop The Rt Revd Sean Rowe, 333 Wyandotte Street, Bethlehem, PA 18015–1527, USA
                    T: 1 610 691 5655
                    F: 1 610 691 1682
                    E: seanrowe@diobeth.org
                    W: www.diobeth.org

CALIFORNIA (Province VIII)
Bishop The Rt Revd Marc Handley Andrus, 1055 Taylor Street, San Francisco, CA 94108, USA   *T:* 1 415 673 5015
F: 1 415 673 9268
E: bishopmarc@diocal.org
W: www.diocal.org

CENTRAL ECUADOR (Province IX)
Bishop The Rt Revd Victor Scantlebury, Calle Hernando, Francisco Sarmiento N 39–54 y Portete, Sector El Batán, Quito, Ecuador
T: 2 254 1735

CENTRAL FLORIDA (Province IV)
Bishop The Rt Revd Gregory O. Brewer, Diocesan Office, 1017 E Robinson Street, Orlando, FL 32801, USA   *T:* 1 407 423 3567
F: 1 407 872 0006
E: bpbrewer@cfdiocese.org
W: www.cfdiocese.org

CENTRAL GULF COAST (Province IV)
Bishop The Rt Revd James Russell Kendrick, 201 N Baylen Street, Pensacola, FL 32502, USA
T: 1 850 434 7337
F: 1 850 434 8577
E: bishopkendrick@diocgc.org
W: www.diocgc.org

CENTRAL NEW YORK (Province II)
Bishop The Rt Revd Gladstone (Skip) Adams, 1020 North Street, Liverpool, NY 13088, USA
T: 1 315 474 6596
F: 1 315 478 1632
E: bishop@cnyepiscopal.org
W: www.cnyepiscopal.org

CENTRAL PENNSYLVANIA (Province III)
Bishop The Rt Revd Audrey Scanlan, 101 Pine Street, Harrisburg, PA 17101, USA
T: 1 717 236 5959
F: 1 717 236 6448
E: ascanlan@diocesecpa.org
W: www.diocesecpa.org

CHICAGO (Province V)
Bishop The Rt Revd Jeffery Lee, 65 East Huron Street, Chicago, IL 60611, USA
T: 1 312 751 4200
F: 1 312 787 4534
E: bishop@episcopalchicago.org
W: www.episcopalchicago.org

Assisting Bishop The Rt Revd C. Christopher Epting (*same address*)   *E:* ccepting@aol.com

COLOMBIA (Province IX)
Bishop The Rt Revd Francisco José Duque Gomez, Cra6 no 49–85 Piso 2, Bogotá DC, Colombia   *T:* 57 1 288 3167
F: 57 1 288 3248
E: obispoduque@hotmail.com
W: www.iglesiaepiscopal.org.co

COLORADO (Province VI)
Bishop The Rt Revd Robert John O'Neill, 1300 Washington Street, Denver, CO 80203, USA
T: 1 303 837 1173
F: 1 303 837 1311
E: bishoponeill@coloradodiocese.org
W: www.coloradodiocese.org

CONNECTICUT (Province I)
Bishop The Rt Revd Ian Theodore Douglas, 290 Pratt Street, Meriden, CT 061450, USA
T: 1 203 639 3501
F: 1 203 235 1008
E: itdouglas@episcopalct.org
W: www.episcopalct.org

Bishop Suffragan The Rt Revd Laura Ahrens (*same address*)   *E:* lahrens@episcopalct.org

DALLAS (Province VII)
Bishop The Rt Revd George Sumner, 1630 North Garrett Avenue, Dallas, TX 75206, USA
T: 1 214 826 8310
F: 1 214 826 5968
E: gsumner@edod.org
W: http://edod.org

Bishop Suffragan The Rt Revd Paul Emil Lambert (*same address*)
E: plambert@edod.org

DELAWARE (Province III)
Bishop The Rt Revd Wayne Parker Wright, 913 Wilson Road, Wilmington, DE 19803-4012, USA   *T:* 1 302 256 0374
F: 1 302 543 8084
E: bishop@dioceseofdelaware.net
W: www.dioceseofdelaware.net

DOMINICAN REPUBLIC (Province IX)
Bishop The Rt Revd Julio Cesar Holguin, Apartado 764, Calle Santiago No 114, Gazcue, Santo Domingo, Dominican Republic
T: 1 809 688 7493
F: 1 809 688 6344
E: iglepidom@codetel.net.do
W: www.episcopaldominican.org

EAST CAROLINA (Province IV)
Bishop The Rt Revd Robert Stuart Skirving, 705 Doctors Drive, Kinston, NC 28501, USA
T: 1 252 522 0885
F: 1 252 523 5272
E: rskirving@diocese-eastcarolina.org
W: www.diocese-eastcarolina.org

EAST TENNESSEE (Province IV)
Bishop The Rt Revd George Dibrell Young III, 814 Episcopal School Way, Knoxville, TN 37932, USA   *T:* 1 865 966 2110
F: 1 865 966 2535
E: gyoung@dioet.lorg
W: http://dioet.org

ANGLICAN & PORVOO COMMUNIONS

EASTERN MICHIGAN (Province V)
Bishop The Rt Revd Steven Todd Ousley, 924 North Niagara Street, Saginaw, MI 48602, USA
T: 1 989 752 6020
F: 1 989 752 6120
E: tousley@eastmich.org
W: http://eastmich.org

EASTERN OREGON (Province VIII)
Bishop The Rt Revd Bavi Edna (Nedi) Rivera, 1104 Church Stret, Cove, OR 97824, USA
T: 1 541 568 4514
F: 1 541 568 5000
E: nrivera@episdioeo.org
W: www.episdioeo.org

EASTON (Province III)
Bishop The Rt Revd Henry Nutt Parsley, 314 North Street, Easton, MD 21601, USA
T: 1 410 822 1919
F: 1 410 763 8259
E: hparsley@dioceseofeaston.org
W: http://dioceseofeaston.org

EAU CLAIRE (Province V)
Bishop The Rt Revd William J. Lambert, 510 South Farwell St, Eau Claire, WI 54701, USA
T: 1 715 835 3331
F: 1 715 835 9212
E: bishop1075@icloud.com
W: www.dioec.net

EL CAMINO REAL (Province VIII)
Bishop The Rt Revd Mary Gray-Reeves, 154 Central Avenue, Salinas, CA 93901, USA
T: 1 831 394 4465
F: 1 831 394 7133
E: info@realepiscopal.org
W: www.realepiscopal.org

EUROPE, CONVOCATION OF EPISCOPAL CHURCHES IN
Bishop in Charge The Rt Revd Pierre Welté Whalon, American Cathedral of the Holy Trinity, 23 Avenue George V, F-75008 Paris, France
T: 33 1 53 23 84 06
F: 33 1 49 52 96 85
E: bishop@tec-europe.org
W: www.tec-europe.org

FLORIDA (Province IV)
Bishop The Rt Revd Samuel Johnson Howard, 325 North Market Street, Jacksonville, FL 32202-2796, USA
T: 1 904 356 1328
F: 1 904 355 1934
E: jhoward @diocesefl.org
W: www.diocesefl.org

FOND DU LAC (Province V)
Bishop The Rt Revd Matthew Alan Gunter, 1051 North Lynndale Drive, Suite 1B, Appleton, WI 54914-3094, USA
T: 1 920 830 8866
F: 1 920 830 8761
E: mgunter@diofdl.org
W: www.episcopalfonddulac.org

FORT WORTH (Province VII)
Bishop The Rt Revd James Scott Mayer, 4301 Meadowbank Drive, Fort Worth, TX 76103, USA
T: 1 817 534 9000
F: 1 817 534 1904
E: contact@edfw.org
W: http://episcopaldiocesefortworth.org

GEORGIA (Province IV)
Bishop The Rt Revd Scott Anson Benhase, 611 East Bay Street, Savannah, GA 31401, USA
T: 1 912 236 4279
F: 1 912 236 2007
E: bishop@gaepiscopal.org
W: http://georgia.anglican.org

HAITI (Province II)
Bishop The Rt Revd Jean Zaché Duracin, BP 1309, Port-au-Prince, Haiti   T: 509 257 1624
E: epihaiti@egliseepiscopaledhaiti.org
W: egliseepiscopaledhaiti.org

HAWAII (Province VIII)
Bishop The Rt Revd Robert LeRoy Fitzpatrick, Diocesan Office, 229 Queen Emma Square, Honolulu, HI 96813–2304, USA
T: 1 808 536 7776
F: 1 808 538 7194
E: rlfitzpatrick@episcopalhawaii.org
W: www.episcopalhawaii.org

HONDURAS (Province IX)
Bishop The Rt Revd Lloyd Emmanuel Allen, 23 Ave C. 21 St Colony Trejo, San Pedro Sula, Honduras 21105   T: 504 556 6155
F: 504 566 6467
W: http://honduras.fedigitalis.org

IDAHO (Province VIII)
Bishop The Rt Revd Brian James Thom, 1858 Judith Lane, Boise, ID 83705, USA
T: 1 208 345 4440
F: 1 208 345 9735
E: bthom@idahodiocese.org
W: www.episcopalidaho.org

INDIANAPOLIS (Province V)
Bishop The Rt Revd Catherine Elizabeth Maples Waynick, 1100 West 42nd Street, Indianapolis, IN 46208, USA
T: 1 317 926 5454
F: 1 317 926 5456
E: bishop@indydio.org
W: http://indydio.org

IOWA (Province VI)
Bishop The Rt Revd Alan Scarfe, 225 37th Street, Des Moines, IA 50312–4305, USA
T: 1 515 277 6165
F: 1 515 277 0273
E: ascarfe@iowaepiscopal.org
W: www.iowaepiscopal.org

KANSAS (Province VII)
Bishop The Rt Revd Dean Eliott Wolfe, 835 SW Polk Street, Topeka, KS 66612–1688, USA
T: 1 785 235 9255
F: 1 785 235 2449
E: dwolfe@episcopal-ks.org
W: www.episcopal-ks.org

KENTUCKY (Province IV)
Bishop The Rt Revd Terry Allen White, 425 S 2nd Street, Louisville, KY 40202, USA
T: 1 502 584 7148
F: 1 502 587 8123
E: bishopwhite@episcopalky.org
W: www.episcopalky.org

LEXINGTON (Province IV)
Bishop The Rt Revd Douglas Hahn, 203 East 4th Street, Lexington, KY 40508, USA
T: 1 859 252 6527
F: 1 859 231 9077
E: dhahn@diolex.org
W: http://diolex.org

LITORAL ECUADOR (Province IX)
Bishop The Rt Revd Alfredo Morante, Box 0901–5250, Calle Amarilis Fuentes 603 entre Avenida José Vincento Trujillo y la Calle 'D', Barrio Centenario, Guayaquil, Ecuador
T: 593 4 244 6699
F: 593 4 244 3088
E: info@litoralepiscopal.org
W: www.litoralepispcopal.org

LONG ISLAND (Province II)
Bishop The Rt Revd Lawrence C. Provenzano, 36 Cathedral Avenue, Garden City, NY 11530–0510, USA
T: 1 516 248 4800
F: 1 516 248 1616
E: lprovenzano@dioceseli.org
W: www.diocesceolongisland.org

LOS ANGELES (Province VIII)
Bishop The Rt Revd Joseph Jon Bruno, 840 Echo Park Avenue, Box 512164, Los Angeles, CA 90051, USA
T: 1 213 482 2040
F: 1 213 482 5304
E: bishop@ladiocese.org
W: www.ladiocese.org

Bishops Suffragan
The Rt Revd Diane M. Jardine Bruce (*same address*)
E: djbsuffragan@ladiocese.org

The Rt Revd Mary Douglas Glasspool (*same address*)
E: mdgsuffragan@ladiocese.org

LOUISIANA (Province IV)
Bishop The Rt Revd Morris K. Thompson, 1623 7th Street, New Orleans, LA 70115, USA
T: 1 504 895 6634
F: 1 504 895 6637
E: mthompson@edola.org
W: www.edola.org

MAINE (Province I)
Bishop The Rt Revd Stephen Taylor Lane, Loring House, 143 State Street, Portland, ME 04101–3799, USA
T: 1 207 772 1953
F: 1 207 773 0095
E: slane@episcopalmaine.org
W: http://episcopalmaine.org

MARYLAND (Province III)
Bishop The Rt Revd Eugene Taylor Sutton, 4 East University Parkway, Baltimore, MD 21218, USA
T: 1 410 467 1399
F: 1 410 554 6387
E: esutton@episcopalmaryland.org
W: www.episcopalmaryland.org

MASSACHUSETTS (Province I)
Bishop The Rt Revd Alan McIntosh Gates, 138 Tremont Street, Boston, MA 02111–1318, USA
T: 1 617 482 5800
F: 1 617 482 8431
E: dianep@diomass.org
W: www.diomass.org

Bishop Suffragan
The Rt Revd Gayle Elizabeth Harris (*same address*)
E: mscarle@diomass.org

MICHIGAN (Province V)
Bishop The Rt Revd Wendell Nathaniel Gibbs Jr, 4800 Woodward Avenue, Detroit, MI 48201, USA
T: 1 313 833 4000
F: 1 313 831 0259
E: bishop@edomi.org
W: www.edomi.org

MILWAUKEE (Province V)
Bishop The Rt Revd Steven Andrew Miller, 804 E Juneau Avenue, Milwaukee, WI 53202–2798, USA
T: 1 414 272 3028
E: bishop@diomil.org
W: www.diomil.org

MINNESOTA (Province VI)
Bishop The Rt Revd Brian N. Prior, 1730 Clifton Place, Suite 201, Minneapolis, MN 55403–3242, USA
T: 1 612 871 5311
F: 1 612 871 0552
E: info@episcopalmn.org
W: http://episcopalmn.org

MISSISSIPPI (Province IV)
Bishop The Rt Revd Brian R. Seage, 118 N Congress Street, Jackson, MS 39225–3107, USA
T: 1 601 948 5954
F: 1 601 354 3401
E: brseage@dioms.org
W: www.dioms.org

MISSOURI (Province V)
Bishop The Rt Revd George Wayne Smith, 1210 Locust Street, St Louis, MO 63103, USA
T: 1 314 231 1220
F: 1 314 231 3373
E: bishop@diocesemo.org
W: www.diocesemo.org

ANGLICAN & PORVOO COMMUNIONS

MONTANA (Province VI)
Bishop The Rt Revd Charles Franklin Brookhart Jr, 515 N Park Avenue, Helena, MT 59601–8135, USA
T: 1 406 442 2230
F: 1 406 442 2238
E: cfbmt@qwestoffice.net
W: http://diomontana.com

NAVAJOLAND AREA MISSION (Province VIII)
Bishop The Rt Revd David Earle Bailey, 1227 Mission Avenue, Farmington, NM 87499–0720, USA
T: 1 505 326 7194
F: 1 505 327 6904
E: via website
W: http://navajoland.org

NEBRASKA (Province VI)
Bishop The Rt Revd J. Scott Barker, 109 N 18th St, Omaha, NE 68102–4903, USA
T: 1 402 341 5373
F: 1 402 341 8683
E: sbarker@episcopal-ne.org
W: www.episcopal-ne.org

NEVADA (Province VIII)
Bishop The Rt Revd Dan T. Edwards, 9480 S Eastern Avenue, Suite 236, Las Vegas, NV 89123–8037, USA
T: 1 702 737 9190
F: 1 702 737 6488
E: dan@episcopalnevada.org
W: www.episcopalnevada.org

NEW HAMPSHIRE (Province I)
Bishop The Rt Revd A. Robert Hirschfeld, 63 Green Street, Concord, NH 03301, USA
T: 1 603 224 1914
F: 1 603 225 7884
E: arh@nhepiscopal.org
W: www.nhepiscopal.org

NEW JERSEY (Province II)
Bishop The Rt Revd William H. (Chip) Stokes, 808 West State Street, Trenton, NJ 08618–5326, USA
T: 1 609 394 5281
F: 1 609 394 9546
E: wstokes@dioceseofnj.org
W: www.dioceseofnj.org

NEW YORK (Province II)
Bishop The Rt Revd Andrew M. L. Dietsche, Synod House, 1047 Amsterdam Avenue, New York, NY 10025, USA
T: 1 212 316 7400
F: 1 212 316 7405
E: via website
W: www.dioceseny.org

Bishop Suffragan The Rt Revd Allen K. Shin (*same address*)
E: via website

NEWARK (Province II)
Bishop The Rt Revd Mark Beckwith, 31 Mulberry Street, Newark, NJ 07102, USA
T: 1 923 430 9900
F: 1 923 622 3503
E: mbeckwith@dioceseofnewark.org
W: www.dioceseofnewark.org

NORTH CAROLINA (Province IV)
Bishop The Rt Revd Sam Rodman, 200 West Morgan Street, Suite 300, Raleigh, NC 27601, USA
T: 1 919 834 7474
F: 1 919 834 754
E: sam.rodman@episdionc.org
W: http://episdionc.org

Bishop Suffragan The Rt Revd Anne Hodges-Copple, 301 N Elm Street, Suite 308-C, Greenboro, NC 27401, USA
T: 1 336 273 5770
F: 1 336 273 5770
E: bishopanne@episdionc.org

NORTH DAKOTA (Province VI)
Bishop The Rt Revd Michael Gene Smith, 3600 S. 25th Street, Fargo, ND 58104–6861, USA
T: 1 701 235 6688
F: 1 701 232 3077
E: BpNoDak@aol.com
W: www.ndepiscopal.org

NORTHERN CALIFORNIA (Province VIII)
Bishop The Rt Revd Barry Leigh Beisner, 350 University Avenue, Suite 280, Sacramento, CA 95816, USA
T: 1 916 442 6918
F: 1 916 442 6927
E: barry@norcalepiscopal.org
W: www.norcalepiscopal.org

NORTHERN INDIANA (Province V)
Bishop The Rt Revd Edward Stuart Little II, 117 N Lafayette Boulevard, South Bend, Indiana 46601, USA
T: 1 574 233 6489
F: 1 574 287 7914
E: bishop@ednin.org
W: www.ednin.org

NORTHERN MICHIGAN (Province V)
Bishop The Rt Revd Rayford J. Ray, 131 E Ridge Street, Marquette, MI 49855, USA
T: 1 906 228 7160
F: 1 906 228 7171
E: rayfordray@upepiscopal.org
W: www.upepiscopal.org

NORTHWEST TEXAS (Province VII)
Bishop The Rt Revd James Scott Mayer, 1802 Broadway Avenue, Lubbock, TX 79401, USA
T: 1 806 763 1370
F: 1 806 472 0641
E: bishopmayer@nwtdiocese.org
W: www.nwtdiocese.org

NORTHWESTERN PENNSYLVANIA (Province III)
Bishop The Rt Revd Sean W. Rowe, 145 W 6th Street, Erie, PA 16501, USA
T: 1 814 456 4203
F: 1 814 454 8703
E: seanrowe@dionwpa.org
W: www.dionwpa.org

OHIO (Province V)
Bishop The Rt Revd Mark Hollingsworth Jr, 2230 Euclid Avenue, Cleveland, OH 44115–2499, USA
T: 1 216 771 4815
F: 1 216 623 0735
E: mh@dohio.org
W: www.dohio.org

Assisting Bishops
The Rt Revd William Dailey Persell (*same address*)

The Rt Revd Arthur Williams (*same address*)

OKLAHOMA (Province VII)
Bishop The Rt Revd Edward Joseph Konieczny, 924 N Robinson, Oklahoma City, OK 73102, USA
T: 1 405 232 4820
E: bishoped@epiok.org
W: www.epiok.org

OLYMPIA (Province VIII)
Bishop The Rt Revd Gregory H. Rickel, 1551 10th Avenue, Seattle, WA 98102, USA
T: 1 206 325 4200
F: 1 206 325 4631
E: grickel@ecww.org
W: www.ecww.org

OREGON (Province VIII)
Bishop The Rt Revd Michael Joseph Hanley, 11800 SW Military Lane, Portland, OR 97219, USA
T: 1 503 636 5613
F: 1 503 636 5616
E: bishop@episcopaldioceseoregon.org
W: www.dioceseoregon.org

PENNSYLVANIA (Province III)
Bishop The Rt Revd Clifton Daniel, 3717 Chestnut Street, Suite 300, Philadelphia, PA 19104, USA
T: 1 215 627 6434
F: 1 215 900 2928
E: cdaniel@diopa.org
W: www.diopa.org

Assisting Bishops
The Rt Revd Rodney Rae Michel
E: rodneym@diopa.org

The Rt Revd Edward L. Lee
E: bpedwardlee@yahoo.com

PITTSBURGH (Province III)
Bishop The Rt Revd Dorsey W. M. McConnell, 325 Oliver Avenue, Suite 300, Pittsburgh PA 15222-2406, USA
T: 1 412 721 0853
F: 1 412 232 6408
E: dmcconnell@episcopalpgh.org
W: ibwww.epsicopalpgh.org

PUERTO RICO (Province IX)
Bishop The Rt Revd Wilfredo Ramos Orench, Carr. 848 Km. 1.1 Bo, St Just, Trujillo Alto 00978, Puerto Rico
T: 1 787 761 9800
F: 1 787 761 0320
E: iep@episcopalpr.org
W: www.episcopalpr.org

RHODE ISLAND (Province I)
Bishop The Rt Revd W. Nicholas Knisely, 275 N Main Street, Providence, RI 02903–1298, USA
T: 1 401 274 4500
F: 1 401 331 9430
E: nicholas@episcopalri.org
W: www.episcopalri.org

RIO GRANDE (Province VII)
Bishop The Rt Revd Michael Louis Vono, 6400 Coors Boulevard North West, Albuquerque, NM 87107–4811, USA
T: 1 505 881 0636
F: 1 505 883 9048
E: bp.michael@dioceserg.org
W: www.dioceserg.org

ROCHESTER (Province II)
Bishop The Rt Revd Prince Grenville Singh, 935 East Avenue, Rochester, NY 14607, USA
T: 1 585 473 2977
F: 1 585 473 3195
E: prince@episcopaldioceseofrochester.org
W: http://episcopalrochester.org

SAN DIEGO (Province VIII)
Bishop The Rt Revd James Robert Mathes, 2083 Sunset Cliffs Boulevard, San Diego, CA 92107, USA
T: 1 619 291 5947
F: 1 619 291 8362
E: bishopmathes@edsd.org
W: www.edsd.org

SAN JOAQUIN (Province VIII)
Provisional Bishop The Rt Revd David C. Rice, 1528 Oakdale Road, Modesto, CA 95355, USA
T: 1 209 576 0104
F: 1 209 576 0114
E: bishopdavid@diosanjoaquin.org
W: www.diosanjoaquin.org

SOUTH CAROLINA (Province IV)
Bishop The Rt Revd Charles vonRosenberg, 98 Wentworth Street, Charleston, SC 29413, USA
T: 1 843 259 2016
F: 1 843 723 7628
E: bishop@episcopalchurchsc.org
W: www.episcopalchurchsc.org

ANGLICAN & PORVOO COMMUNIONS

SOUTH DAKOTA (Province VI)
Bishop The Rt Revd John Thomas Tarrant, 500 S Main Avenue, Sioux Falls, SD 57104–6814, USA
T: 1 605 338 9751
F: 1 605 336 6243
E: bishop.diocese@midconetwork.com
W: www.diocesesd.org

SOUTHEAST FLORIDA (Province IV)
Bishop The Rt Revd Peter Eaton, 525 NE 15 Street, Miami, FL 33132, USA
T: 1 305 373 0881
F: 1 305 375 8054
E: info@diosef.org
W: www.diosef.org

SOUTHERN OHIO (Province V)
Bishop The Rt Revd Thomas Edward Breidenthal, 412 Sycamore Street, Cincinnati, OH 45202, USA
T: 1 513 421 0311
F: 1 513 421 0315
E: tbreidenthal@diosohio.org
W: www.episcopal-dso.org

SOUTHERN VIRGINIA (Province III)
Bishop The Rt Revd Herman (Holly) Hollerith IV, 11827 Canon Boulevard, Suite 101, Newport News, VA 23606, USA
T: 1 757 423 8287
F: 1 757 440 5354
E: bishop@diosova.org
W: www.diosova.org

SOUTHWEST FLORIDA (Province IV)
Bishop The Rt Revd Dabney T. Smith, 8005 25th Street East, Parrish, FL 34219–9405, USA
T: 1 941 556 0315
F: 1 941 556 0321
E: dsmith@episcopalswfl.org
W: www.episcopalswfl.org

Assisting Bishops
The Rt Revd J. Michael Garrison
The Rt Revd Barry R. Howe

SOUTHWESTERN VIRGINIA (Province III)
Bishop The Rt Revd Mark Allen Bourlakas, 1002 1st Street, Roanoke, VA 24016, USA
T: 1 757 423 8287
F: 1 757 440 5354
E: bishopmark@dioswva.org
W: www.dioswva.org

SPOKANE (Province VIII)
Bishop The Rt Revd James Edward Waggoner Jr, 245 E 13th Avenue, Spokane, WA 99202–1114, USA
T: 1 509 624 3191
F: 1 509 747 0049
E: jimw@spokanediocese.org
W: www.spokanediocese.org

SPRINGFIELD (Province V)
Bishop The Rt Revd Daniel Hayden Martins, 821 S 2nd Street, Springfield, IL 62704, USA
T: 1 217 525 1876
F: 1 217 525 1877
E: bishop@episcopalspringfield.org
W: www.episcopalspringfield.org

TAIWAN (Province VIII)
Bishop The Rt Revd David Jung-Hsin Lai, 10060 Hangzhou South Road, Taipei City, Taiwan, Republic of China
T: 886 2 2341 1265
F: 2396 2014
E: skh.tpe@msa.hinet.net
W: www.episcopaldiotaiwan.org

TENNESSEE (Province IV)
Bishop The Rt Revd John Crawford Bauerschmidt, 3700 Woodmont Boulevard, Nashville, TN 37215, USA
T: 1 615 251 3322
F: 1 615 251 8010
E: info@edtn.org
W: http://edtn.org

TEXAS (Province VII)
Bishop The Rt Revd Charles Andrew Doyle, 1225 Texas Avenue, Houston, TX 77002–3504, USA
T: 1 713 353 2100
F: 1 713 520 5723
E: adoyle@epicenter.org
W: www.epicenter.org

Bishop Suffragan The Rt Revd Dena A. Harrison, 510 Rathervue Place, PO Box 2247, Austin, TX 78768–2247, USA
T: 1 512 478 0580
F: 1 512 478 5615
E: dharrison@epicenter.org

UPPER SOUTH CAROLINA (Province IV)
Bishop The Rt Revd W. Andrew Waldo, 1115 Marion Street, Columbia, SC 29201, USA
T: 1 803 771 7800
F: 1 803 799 5119
E: bishopwaldo@edusc.org
W: www.edusc.org

UTAH (Province VIII)
Bishop The Rt Revd Scott B. Hayashi, 75 South 200 East Street, Salt Lake City, UT 84110–2147, USA
T: 1 801 322 4131
F: 1 801 322 5096
E: shayashi@episcopal-ut.org
W: www.episcopal-ut.org

VENEZUELA (Province IX)
Bishop The Rt Revd Orlando Guerrero, Colinas de Bello Monte, Avenida Caroní, Caracas, Venezuela
T: 58 212 751 3046

VERMONT (Province I)
Bishop The Rt Revd Thomas Clark Ely, 5 Rock Point Rd, Burlington, VT 05401, USA
T: 1 802 863 3431
F: 1 802 860 1562
E: tely@dioceseofvermont.org
W: www.dioceseofvermont.org

VIRGIN ISLANDS (Province II)
Bishop The Rt Revd Edward Ambrose Gumbs, 13 Commandant Gade, Charlotte Amaille, St Thomas, VI 00801, USA   *T:* 1 340 776 1797
F: 1 340 777 8485
E: bpambrosegumbs@yahoo.com

VIRGINIA (Province III)
Bishop The Rt Revd Shannon Sherwood Johnston, 110 W Franklin Street, Richmond, VA 23220, USA   *T:* 1 804 643 8451
F: 1 804 644 6928
E: sjohnston@thediocese.net
W: www.thediocese.net

Bishop Suffragan The Rt Revd Susan Ellyn Goff (*same address*)   *E:* sgoff@thediocese.net

Assistant Bishop
The Rt Revd Edwin F. (Ted) Gulick, 115 E Fairfax Street, Falls Church, VA 22046, USA
T: 1 703 241 0441
E: tgulick@thediocese.net

WASHINGTON DC (Province III)
Bishop The Rt Revd Mariann Edgar Budde, Mount St Alban, Washington, DC 20016–5094, USA   *T:* 1 202 537 6555
F: 1 202 364 6605
E: mebudde@edow.org
W: www.edow.org

WEST MISSOURI (Province VII)
Bishop The Rt Revd Martin Scott Field, 420 W 14th Street, Kansas City, MO 64105–3227, USA   *T:* 1 816 471 6161
F: 1 816 471 0379
E: bishopfield@diowestmo.org
W: http://diowestmo.org

WEST TENNESSEE (Province IV)
Bishop The Rt Revd Don Edward Johnson, 692 Poplar Avenue, Memphis, TN 38105, USA
T: 1 901 526 0023
F: 1 901 526 1555
E: bishopjohnson@episwtn.org
W: www.episwtn.org

WEST TEXAS (Province VII)
Bishop The Rt Revd Gary Richard Lillibridge, 111 Torcido Drive, San Antonio, TX 78209, USA   *T:* 1 210 824 5387
F: 1 210 824 2164
E: gary.lillibridge@dwtx.org
W: http://dwtx.org

Bishop Suffragan The Rt Revd David Reed (*same address*)   *E:* david.reed@dwtx.org

WEST VIRGINIA (Province III)
Bishop The Rt Revd William Michie Klusmeyer, 1608 Virginia Street East, Charleston, WV 25311, USA   *T:* 1 304 344 3597
F: 1 304 343 3295
E: mklusmeyer@wvdiocese.org
W: www.wvdiocese.org

WESTERN KANSAS (Province VII)
Bishop Rt Revd Michael P. Milliken, 2 Hyde Park, Hutchinson, KS 67502, USA
T: 1 620 662 0011
F: 1 620 662 2930
E: tec.wks2011@gmail.com
W: http://diowks.org

WESTERN LOUISIANA (Province VII)
Bishop The Rt Revd Jacob W. Owensby, 335 Main St, Pineville,LA 71360, USA
T: 1 318 422 1304
F: 1 318 442 8712
E: bishopjake@diocesewla.org
W: www.diocesewla.org

WESTERN MASSACHUSETTS (Province I)
Bishop The Rt Revd Douglas John Fisher, 37 Chestnut Street, Springfield, MA 01103, USA
T: 1 413 737 4786
F: 1 413 746 9873
E: communications@diocesewma.org
W: www.diocesewma.org

WESTERN MICHIGAN (Province V)
Bishop The Rt Revd Robert R Gepert, Episcopal Center, 5355 Burdick Street, Suite 1, Kalamazoo, MI 49007, USA   *T:* 1 269 381 2710
F: 1 269 381 7067
E: diowestmi@edwm.org
W: www.edwm.org

WESTERN NEW YORK (Province II)
Bishop The Rt Revd R. William Franklin, 1064 Brighton Road, Tonawanda, NY 14150, USA
T: 1 716 881 0660
F: 1 716 881 1724
E: rwfranklin@episcopalwny.org
W: http://episcopalwny.org

WESTERN NORTH CAROLINA (Province IV)
Bishop The Rt Revd Granville Porter Taylor, 900B Center Park Drive, Asheville, NC 28805, USA   *T:* 1 828 225 6656
F: 1 828 225 6657
E: bishop@diocesewnc.org
W: www.diocesewnc.org

WYOMING (Province VI)
Bishop The Rt Revd John S. Smylie, 123 South Durbin Street, Casper WY 82601, USA
T: 1 307 265 5200
F: 1 307 577 9939
E: bishopsmylie@wyomingdiocese.org
W: www.diowy.org

ANGLICAN & PORVOO COMMUNIONS

The Church in Wales

Members 46,604

The Church in Wales has been an independent province since its disestablishment and separation from the Church of England in 1920. It is practically coterminous with Wales and is the largest denomination in the country. The major policy-forming body is the Governing Body and the Church's inherited assets, including buildings, are held in trust by the Representative Body.

Archbishop The Most Revd John Davies (*Bishop of Swansea and Brecon*)   *T:* 029 2056 2400
F: 029 2056 8410
E: archbishop@churchinwales.org.uk

Provincial Secretary and Archbishop's Registrar Mr Simon Lloyd, 39 Cathedral Road, Cardiff CF11 9XF   *T:* 029 2034 8218
F: 029 2038 7835
E: information@churchinwales.org.uk
W: www.churchinwales.org.uk

Archbishop's Media Officer Anna Morrell (*same address*)   *T:* 029 2034 8208

THEOLOGICAL COLLEGE
St Padarn's Institute (*Principal* The Revd Dr Jeremy Duff), 54 Cardiff Road, Llandaff, Cardiff CF5 2YJ   *T:* 029 2056 2279
E: kathryndelderfield@stpadarns.ac.uk

BANGOR
Bishop The Rt Revd Andrew Thomas Griffith John, Ty'r Esgob, Ffordd Garth Uchaf, Bangor, Gwynedd LL57 2SS   *T:* 01248 362895
F: 01248 372454
E: bishop.bangor@churchinwales.org.uk
W: www.churchinwales.org.uk/bangor

CATHEDRAL CHURCH OF ST DEINIOL, Bangor, Gwynedd
Dean The Very Revd Kathy Jones, The Deanery, Cathedral Precinct, Bangor LL57 1LH
T: 01248 355530
E: sjones1234jones@btinternet.com

LLANDAFF
Bishop The Rt Revd June Osborne, Llys Esgob, The Cathedral Green, Llandaff, Cardiff CF5 2YE
T: 029 2056 2400
F: 029 2056 8410
E: bishop.llandaff@churchinwales.org.uk
W: www.churchinwales.org.uk/llandaff

CATHEDRAL CHURCH OF ST PETER AND ST PAUL, Llandaff, Cardiff
Dean The Very Revd Gerwyn Huw Capon, The Deanery, The Cathedral Green, Llandaff, Cardiff CF5 2YF   *T:* 02920 561545
E: thedean@llandaffcathedral.org.uk

MONMOUTH
Bishop The Rt Revd R. E. Pain, Bishopstow, Stow Hill, Newport NP20 4EA
T: 01633 263510
E: bishop.monmouth@churchinwales.org.uk
W: www.churchinwales.org.uk/monmouth

CATHEDRAL CHURCH OF ST WOOLOS, Newport
Dean The Very Revd Lister Tonge, The Deanery, Stow Hill, Newport NP20 4ED
T: 01633 259627
E: listertonge@gmail.com

ST ASAPH
Bishop The Rt Revd Gregory Kenneth Cameron, Esgobty, Upper Denbigh Road, St Asaph LL17 0TW   *T:* 01745 583503
F: 01745 584301
E: bishop.stasaph@churchinwales.org.uk
W: www.churchinwales.org.uk/asaph

CATHEDRAL CHURCH OF ST ASAPH, St Asaph, Denbighshire
Dean The Very Revd Nigel Howard Williams, The Deanery, Upper Denbigh Road, St Asaph LL17 0RL   *T:* 01745 583597
E: nigelwilliams@churchinwales.org.uk

ST DAVIDS
Bishop The Rt Revd Joanna Susan Penberthy, Llys Esgob, Abergwili, Carmarthen SA31 2JG
T: 01267 236597
F: 01267 243381
E: bishop.stdavids@churchinwales.org.uk
W: www.churchinwales.org.uk/david

CATHEDRAL CHURCH OF ST DAVID AND ST ANDREW, St Davids, Pembrokeshire
Dean The Very Revd David Jonathan Rees Lean, The Deanery, St Davids, Haverfordwest SA62 6RH   *T:* 01437 720456
F: 01437 721885

SWANSEA AND BRECON
Bishop The Most Revd John David Edward Davies (*Archbishop of the Province*), Ely Tower, Castle Square, Brecon LD3 9DJ
T: 01874 622008
F: 01874 610927
E: bishop.swanbrec@churchinwales.org.uk
W: www.churchinwales.org.uk/swanbrec

CATHEDRAL CHURCH OF ST JOHN THE EVANGELIST, Brecon, Powys
Dean The Very Revd Dr Paul Albert Shackerley, The Deanery, Cathedral Close, Brecon LD3 9DP   *T:* 01874 623344
E: admin@breconcathedral.org.uk

The Church of the Province of West Africa

Members 1,565,000

Church work began in Ghana as early as 1752 and in the Gambia, Guinea, Liberia and Sierra Leone in the nineteenth century. The Province of West Africa was founded in 1951 and was divided to form the Province of Nigeria and the Province of West Africa in 1979.

In September 2012, the Province amended its constitution to create two internal provinces to be headed by two Archbishops, with one of them to be the Primate. The Church exists in an atmosphere of civil strife and Christians remain a minority.

Archbishop and Primate of the Province of West Africa The Most Revd Dr Daniel Yinkah Sarfo (*Bishop of Kumasi and Archbishop of the internal province of Ghana*)

Dean of the Province of West Africa The Most Revd Dr Jonathan B. B. Hart (*Bishop of Liberia and Archbishop of the internal province of West Africa*)

Episcopal Secretary of the Province of West Africa The Rt Revd Matthias K. Medadues-Badohu (*Bishop of Ho*)

Provincial Secretary The Revd Canon Anthony M. Eiwuley, PO Box Lt 226, Lartebiokorshie, Accra, Ghana   *T:* 233 26 218 0675
233 27 720 1538 (Mobile)
E: cpwa2014@gmail.com
morkeiwuley@gmail.com

Provincial Treasurer The Revd Canon Andrew N .A. Torgbor (*same address*)
T: 233 30 266 2292
233 20 823 7424 (Mobile)
E: ayorkor33@yahoo.com

THEOLOGICAL COLLEGES
Ghana
Trinity Theological Seminary (Ecumenical), PO Box 48, Legon, Ghana

St Nicholas Anglican Theological Seminary, PO Box A 162, Cape Coast, Ghana

Liberia
Cuttington University College, Suacoco, PO Box 10–0277, 1000 Monrovia 10, Liberia

Sierra Leone
Theological Hall and Church Training Centre, PO Box 128, Freetown, Sierra Leone

ACCRA
Bishop The Rt Revd Dr Daniel S. M. Torto, Bishopscourt, PO Box 8, Accra, Ghana
T: 233 302 662 292
233 277 496 479 (Mobile)
E: dantorto@yahoo.com
W: www.accraanglican.org

ASANTE MAMPONG
Bishop The Rt Revd Dr Cyril K. Ben-Smith, Anglican Diocese of Asante Mampong, Mampong, Ashanti Region, Ghana
T: 233 24 774 308(Mobile)
E: bishop.mampong@yahoo.co.uk

BO
Bishop The Rt Revd Emmanuel Josie Samuel Tucker, PO Box 21, Bo, Southern Province, Sierra Leone   *T:* 232 76 677 862 (Mobile)
E: ejstucker@gmail.com

CAMEROON
Bishop The Rt Revd Dibo Thomas-Babyngton Elango, BP 15705, New Bell, Douala, Cameroon   *T:* 237 755 58276
E: revdibo2@yahoo.com

CAPE COAST
Bishop The Rt Revd Dr Victor R. Atta-Baffoe, Bishopscourt, PO Box A 233, Adisadel Estates, Cape Coast, Ghana   *T:* 233 3321 23 502
233 2065 2319 (Mobile)
F: 233 42 32 637
E: victorattabaffoe@yahoo.com

DUNKWA-ON-OFFIN
Bishop The Rt Revd Edmund K. Dawson-Ahmoah, PO Box DW42, Dunkwa-on-Offin
T: 233 24 464 4764 (Mobile)
E: papacy11@yahoo.co.uk

FREETOWN
Bishop The Rt Revd Thomas Arnold Ikunika Wilson, Bishop's Court, PO Box 537, Freetown, Sierra Leone   *T:* 232 22 251 307 (Mobile)
E: vicnold2003@gmail.com

GAMBIA
Bishop The Rt Revd James Allen Yaw Odico, Bishopscourt, PO Box 51, Banjul, The Gambia, West Africa   *T:* 220 770 5915
E: jayawodico@gmail.com
W: www.gambiadiocese.com

GUINEA
Bishop The Rt Revd Jacques Boston, BP 187, Conakry, Guinea
T: 224 63 58 79 38 (Mobile)
E: bostonjacques@yahoo.com

HO
Bishop The Rt Revd Matthias K. Mededues-Badohu, Bishopslodge, PO Box MA 300, Ho, Volta Region, Ghana
T: 233 3620 26644/233 3620 28606
233 208 162 246 (Mobile)
E: matthiaskwab@googlemail.com

KOFORIDUA
Bishop The Rt Revd Francis B. Quashie, PO Box 980, Koforidua, Ghana
T: 233 3420 22 329
F: 233 81 22 060
E: fbquashie@yahoo.com

KUMASI
Bishop The Most Revd Dr Daniel Yinka Sarfo, Bishop's House, PO Box 144, Kumasi, Ghana
T: and F: 233 51 24 117
233 277 890 411 (Mobile)
E: anglicandioceseofkumasi@yahoo.com
dysarfo2000@yahoo.co.uk

LIBERIA
Bishop The Most Revd Dr Jonathan B. B. Hart, PO Box 10–0277, 1000 Monrovia 10, Liberia
T: 231 777 070 418
231 88 651 6343 (Mobile)
E: jbbhart@yahoo.com
bishopecl12@yahoo.com
W: www.liberia.anglican.org

SEKONDI
Bishop The Rt Revd Alexander Kobina Asmah, PO Box 85, Sekondi, Ghana
T: 233 20 837 8295
E: alexasmah@yahoo.com

SUNYANI
Bishop The Rt Revd Dr Festus Yeboah-Asuamah, PO Box 23, Sunyani, Ghana
T: 233 3520 23213
233 208 121 670 (Mobile)
E: fyasuamah@yahoo.com

TAMALE
Bishop The Rt Revd (Hon) Dr Jacob K. Ayeebo, PO Box 110, Tamale, Ghana
T: 233 3720 26639
233 243 419 864 (Mobile)
F: 233 3729 22906
E: bishopea2000@yahoo.com

WIAWSO
Bishop The Rt Revd Abraham Kobina Ackah, PO Box 4, Sefwi, Wiawso, Ghana
T: 233 274 005 952 (Mobile)
E: bishopackah@yahoo.com

The Church in the Province of the West Indies

Members 770,000

The West Indies became a self-governing province of the worldwide Anglican Communion in 1883 because of the Church of England missions in territories that became British colonies. It is made up of two mainland dioceses, Belize and Guyana, and six island dioceses including the Bahamas and Turks and Caicos Islands, Barbados, Jamaica and the Cayman Islands, North Eastern Caribbean and Aruba, Trinidad and Tobago, and the Windward Islands. Great emphasis is being placed on training personnel for an indigenous ministry as the island locations and scattered settlements make pastoral care difficult and costly.

Archbishop of the Province The Most Revd Dr John Walder Dunlop Holder
F: 1 246 426 0871

Provincial Secretary Mrs Elenor Lawrence, Provincial Secretariat, Bamford House, Society Hill, St John, Barbados, West Indies
T: 1246 423 0842/3/8
F: 1 246 423 0855
E: cpwi@caribsurf.com

THEOLOGICAL SEMINARIES
Codrington College, St John, Barbados (*Principal* The Revd Dr Michael Clarke)

United Theological College of the West Indies, PO Box 136, Golding Ave, Kingston 7, Jamaica (*Anglican Warden* The Revd Garth Minott)

BARBADOS
Bishop The Rt Revd Dr John Walder Dunlop Holder (*Archbishop of the Province*), Mandeville House, Collymore Rock, St Michael, Barbados
T: 1 246 426 2761/2
F: 1 246 426 0871
E: jwdh@outlook.com
W: www.anglican.bb

BELIZE
Bishop The Rt Revd Philip Silvin Wright, 25 Bishops Thorpe, PO Box 535, Southern Foreshore, Belize City, Belize, Central America
T: 501 227 3029
F: 501 227 6898
E: bzediocese@btl.net
W: www.belize.anglican.org

GUYANA
Bishop The Rt Revd Charles Alexander Davidson, The Diocesan Office, PO Box 10949, 49 Barrack Street, Georgetown, Guyana, West Indies
T: 592 226 3862
F: 592 227 6091
E: dioofguy@networksgy.com

JAMAICA AND CAYMAN ISLANDS

Bishop The Rt Revd Dr Howard Kingsley Gregory, 2 Caledonia Ave, Kingston 5, Jamaica
T: 1 876 920 2712
F: 1 876 960 1774
E: bishop.jamaica@anglicandiocese.com
W: www.anglicandiocesejamaica.com

Bishops Suffragan
The Rt Revd Robert McLean Thompson (*Bishop of Kingston*), 3 Duke Street, Kingston, Jamaica, West Indies
T: 876 924 9044
F: 876 948 5362
E: bishop.kingston@anglicandiocese.com

Vacancy (*Bishop of Mandeville*), Bishop's Residence, 3 Cotton Tree Road, PO Box 84, Mandeville, Jamaica, West Indies
T: 1 876 625 6818
F: 1 876 625 6819

The Rt Revd Leon Paul Golding (*Bishop of Montego Bay*), PO Box 346, Montego Bay, Jamaica, West Indies
T: 1 876 952 4963
F: 1 876 971 8838

THE BAHAMAS AND THE TURKS AND CAICOS ISLANDS

Bishop The Rt Revd Laish Zane Boyd, Church House, PO Box N-7107, Nassau, Bahamas
T: 1 242 322 3015/6/7
F: 1 242 322 7943
E: bishopboyd@bahamasanglican.org

Assistant Bishop The Most Revd Drexel Wellington Gomez (*New Providence*) (*same address*)
E: dwgomez@coralwave.com

NORTH EASTERN CARIBBEAN AND ARUBA

Bishop The Rt Revd Leroy Errol Brooks, St Mary's Rectory, PO Box 180, The Valley, Anguilla
T: 1 264 497 2235
F: 1 264 497 8555
E: brookx@anguillanet.com

TRINIDAD AND TOBAGO

Bishop The Rt Revd Claude Berkley, Hayes Court, 21 Maraval Road, Port of Spain, Trinidad, Trinidad and Tobago, West Indies
T: 1 868 622 7387
F: 1 868 628 1319
E: dioceset@gmail.com

WINDWARD ISLANDS

Bishop The Rt Revd Calvert Leopold Friday, Bishop's Court, Montrose, PO Box 502, St Vincent, West Indies
T: 1 784 456 1895
F: 1 784 456 2591
E: diocesewi@vincysurf.com

ANGLICAN & PORVOO COMMUNIONS

OTHER CHURCHES AND EXTRA-PROVINCIAL DIOCESES

Bermuda (Anglican Church of Bermuda)

This extra-provincial diocese is under the metropolitical jurisdiction of the Archbishop of Canterbury.

Bishop The Rt Revd Nicholas Dill

Provincial Treasurer Mr Campbell McBeath

Diocesan Office, PO Box HM 769, Hamilton
HM CX, Bermuda
T: 1 441 292 6987
F: 1 441 292 5421
E: diocese@anglican.bm
W: www.anglican.bm

The Church of Ceylon (Sri Lanka)

Members 52,500

The work of the Anglican Church began in Sri Lanka (Ceylon) with the arrival of the British in 1796 and the appointment of the 1st Colonial Chaplain to minister to the British military and civil officials in the colony. Anglican missions in Sri Lanka commenced as far back as 1818 with the arrival of the Church Missionary Society and in 1840, the Society for the Propagation of the Gospel. The Archdeaconry of Colombo was created in 1818 and the Anglicans in Ceylon were initially within the Diocese of Calcutta and Madras until the Diocese of Colombo was established in 1845 by Letters Patent with The Rt Revd James Chapman DD as first Bishop. The Diocese of Colombo was disestablished in 1886 and was placed under the metropolitical care of the Metropolitan of India in Calcutta

In 1930 the Diocese became part of the newly formed Province of India, Pakistan (from 1947), Burma and Ceylon. In 1950 the Diocese of Colombo was bifurcated and the Diocese of Kurunegala was formed with The Rt Revd Lakdasa de Mel as first Bishop. The Province was dissolved in 1970 with the formation of the Churches of North India and Pakistan and the Province of Myanmar (Burma). Since then the Dioceses of Colombo and Kurunegala have been identified in the Anglican Communion as two extra-provincial Dioceses.

In 1998, with the Church of Ceylon (Incorporation) Act passed by the Parliament of Sri Lanka, the Church of Ceylon was legally recognized and classified as a 'National Church' within the Communion. A new Church of Ceylon Constitution was adopted which now governs the Anglican Church in Sri Lanka and has provided for a General Assembly with a Presiding Bishop. The Incorporated Trustees of the Church of Ceylon have responsibility for the financial

management of the various properties and Trust funds owned and set up by the Dioceses over the past 165 years. The Dioceses are managed by the Bishops, Archdeacons and the respective Standing Committees.

At present the Bishops of the Church of Ceylon are: the Bishop of Kurunegala and The Rt Revd Dhiloraj R. Canagasabey (consecrated 2011) the Bishop of Colombo, who as of 2014 is the Presiding Bishop of the Church of Ceylon. Due to the fact that there are only two dioceses the Church of Ceylon is still classified within the Anglican Communion as an extra-provincial church with the Archbishop of Canterbury performing functions as Metropolitan. Representation has been made to the Anglican Consultative Council to explore the possibility of recognizing the Church of Ceylon as a Province, given its unique situation within the Communion.

Clergy, full-time workers and members of the laity are trained at the Ecumenical Theological College of Lanka, Pilimatalawa and at the Cathedral Institute for Education and Formation, Colombo. On the ecumenical journey, both Dioceses remain committed to the goal of a United Church of Lanka and have been members of the National Christian Council of Sri Lanka since 1914 and the Confederation of Christian Churches of Sri Lanka since its formation in 2008. They maintain cordial working relationships with the Roman Catholic Church, the newer Evangelical and Pentecostal churches and other major faith groups prevailing in Sri Lanka. Through a few (11) government approved private Church Schools, the Dioceses are also involved in primary and secondary secular education.

The challenges we face include the training and the empowerment of the people of God for mission and witness in the context of poverty and ethnic and religious tensions within a multi-ethnic and multi-faith context. The Anglican Church in Sri Lanka, in addition to its parochial and evangelistic ministries, is also now engaged in the areas of reconciliation and reconstruction as well as working for peace with justice for all.

THEOLOGICAL COLLEGE
Theological College of Lanka, Pilimatalawa, nr Kandy

COLOMBO
Bishop The Rt Revd Dhiloraj R. Canagasabey, 368/3A Bauddhaloka Mawatha, Colombo 7
T: 94 1 684 810
F: 94 1 684 811
E: anglican@slttalk.net

Secretary Mrs Mary Thanja Peiris (*same address*)
E: sec.diocese.tr@gmail.com

KURUNEGALA
Bishop Vacancy, Bishop's House, Cathedral Close, Kurunegala
T: 94 37 22 191
F: 94 37 26 806
E: bishopkg@sltnet.lk

Secretary Mr Shaantha de Silva, Diocesan Office, 154, D. S. Senanayake Veediya, Kandy
T: and F: 94 081 2222016
E: diokg@sltnet.lk

General Assembly of the Church of Ceylon
Presiding Bishop The Rt Revd Dhiloraj R. Canagasabey

Provincial Secretary Mrs Ramola Sivasunderam c/o the Polytechnic, Galle Road, Colombo 0600, Sri Lanka
T: 94 1 1258 6603
F: 94 777 35 23 73

General Secretary Mrs Barbara Praesoody

The Episcopal Church of Cuba

(Iglesia Episcopal de Cuba)

Members 7,000
The Episcopal Church of Cuba is under a Metropolitan Council in matters of faith and order. Council members include the Primate of Canada, the Archbishop of the West Indies, and the Presiding Bishop of the Episcopal Church of the United States of America or a bishop appointed by the Presiding Bishop.

Diocesan Bishop The Rt Revd Maria Griselda Delgado del Carpio, Calle 6 No.273, Vedado, Plaza de la revolucion, Ciudad de La Habana, CP 10400, Cuba
T: 53 7 833 5760
E: griselda@enet.cu

Diocesan Treasurer Lic. Canónigo José Raúl Ortiz Figueredo (*address as above*)
T: 537 830 1470 (Office)
E: tesorero@enet.cu

Provincial Secretary Mr Francisco de Arazoza, Calle 6 No 273 Vedado, Plaza de la revolucion, Ciudad de la Habana, CP 10400, Cuba
T: 53 7 832 1120
F: 53 7 834 3293
E: episcopal@enet.cu

THEOLOGICAL COLLEGE
Seminario Evangélico de Teología, Matanzas Aptdo. 149, Matanzas (Interdenominational, run in cooperation with the Presbyterian Church)

CHURCH PAPER
Heraldo Episcopal Published three times a year. Contains diocesan, provincial and world news, homiletics, devotional and historical articles.

The Falkland Islands

In 1977 the Archbishop of Canterbury resumed episcopal jurisdiction over the Falkland Islands and South Georgia which had been relinquished in 1974 to the Church of the Southern Cone of America. In 2006 he appointed Bishop Stephen Venner, then the Bishop of Dover, as his commissary, with the title Bishop for the Falkland Islands. The whole parish covers the Falkland Islands, South Georgia, and the South Sandwich Islands and British Antarctic Territory. Christ Church Cathedral is the most southerly cathedral in the world.

Bishop for the Falkland Islands The Rt Revd Tim Thornton (*Bishop at Lambeth and Bishop to HM Forces*), Lambeth Palace, London SE1 7JU
T: 020 7898 1200
E: tim.thornton@lambethpalace.org.uk

Rector Vacancy, The Deanery, PO Box 160, Stanley, Falkland Islands, South Atlantic FIQQ 1ZZ
T: 00 500 21100
F: 00 500 21100
E: christchurch@horizon.co.fk

Associate Minister The Revd Kathy Biles (c/o *same address*)
E: k.biles@horizon.co.fk

The Lusitanian Church

(Portuguese Episcopal Church)

Members 5,000

Founded in 1880 by a group of local Roman Catholic priests and lay people as a reaction to a number of dogmas from the first Vatican Council. The Church consisted of Roman Catholic priests who formed congregations in and around Lisbon using a translation of the 1662 English Prayer Book. Its own first Prayer Book of Common Prayer was issued in 1884. A Lusitanian bishop was consecrated in 1958 and in the early 1960s many provinces of the Anglican Communion established full communion with the Church in Portugal. Full integration occurred in 1980 when the Church became an extra-provincial diocese under the metropolitical authority of the Archbishop of Canterbury. It takes seriously its role in the emerging Europe and has a commitment to helping the poor. It has a strong mission emphasis for the many unchurched people in the country, specially by its two diaconal institutions providing services and help to children and the elderly.

The Church and its leaders cooperate fully with the Diocese in Europe (Church of England) and the Convocation of American Churches in Europe, assisting in each other's congregation and being a united Anglican voice in an increasingly secular Europe. In 1998 the diocesan synod of the Lusitanian Church approved and accepted the Porvoo Declaration, expressing its desire to be involved in the life of the Porvoo Communion and to cooperate, with interchangeable ministries, with the congregations of the Porvoo Churches in Portugal.

Bishop The Rt Revd Dr José Jorge Tavares de Pina Cabral, Diocesan Centre, Rua Afonso de Albuquerque, 86 Mafamude 4430–003 Vila Nova de Gaia, Portugal   *T:* 351 22 375 4018
F: 351 22 375 2016
E: bispopinacabral@igreja-lusitana.org
W: www.igreja-lusitana.org

Treasurer The Revd Sérgio Filipe de Pinho Alves, Tesouraria Diocesana (*same address*)

The Spanish Episcopal Reformed Church

Members 5,000

Parishes: 32 self supported, plus a similar number of congregations.

The Spanish Church covers the whole country and is divided into three archdiaconates, with three archdeacons:

Archdiaconate I: Catalonia, Valencia and Balearic islands

Archdiaconate II: Andalusia and Canary islands

Archdiaconate III: Central and Northern Spain

Under the leadership of some former Roman Catholic priests, in 1868 the Spanish Reformed Episcopal Church was established in Gibraltar and was for some years under the pastoral care of the Church of Ireland. The first Bishop was appointed in 1880 and consecrated in 1894 by the Bishop of Meath along with two other Bishops, and the Church of Ireland accepted metropolitan authority. The same year the Church adopted the Mozarabic Liturgy, which was the liturgy of the early Spanish Church. The Church was fully integrated into the Anglican Communion in 1980 under the metropolitical authority of the Archbishop of Canterbury. It has a strong evangelistic and mission commitment and it is organized into departments: youth, women, ecumenism, Christian education, mission and evangelization. The Church also has a very important social programme for immigrants, which was established in many parishes by helping with clothes and food for over 26,000 people per year. The history of the Church has been one of persecution and difficulties, especially during Franco's dictatorship, but it is firm in its cooperation with the Diocese in Europe and the Convocation of American Churches in Europe for a stronger Anglican presence throughout Europe.

Bishop The Rt Revd Carlos López Lozano (*Bishop of Madrid*), Spanish Reformed Episcopal Church, Calle Beneficencia 18, 28004 Madrid   *T:* 34 91 445 2560
F: 34 91 594 4572
E: eclesiae@arrakis.es
W: www.anglicanos.org

Treasurer Señor Jose Antonio Rodriguez (*same address*)

REGIONAL COUNCILS

Council of the Anglican Provinces of Africa

The Council of Anglican Provinces of Africa (CAPA) was established in 1979 in Chilema, Malawi, by Anglican Primates in Africa who saw the need to form a coordinating body that would help to bring the Anglican Communion in Africa together and to articulate issues affecting the Church. The organization was set up with the following aims and objectives:

- to help the Anglican churches in Africa develop beneficial relationships between themselves and with the wider Anglican Communion;
- to provide a forum for the Church in Africa to share experiences, consult and support each other;
- to confer about common responsibilities on the African continent;
- to establish opportunities for collaboration and joint activities;
- to maintain and develop relationships between the Anglican Church in Africa, partners, other denominations, fellowships, national and regional councils.

Today CAPA works with 12 Anglican provinces in Africa and the Diocese of Egypt. These provinces include Nigeria, West Africa, Sudan, Kenya, Uganda, Tanzania, Congo, Rwanda, Burundi, Central Africa, Southern Africa and Indian Ocean.

Chairman The Most Revd Albert Chama (*Archbishop of Central Africa*)

General Secretary The Rev Canon Grace Kaiso, PO Box 10329, 00100 Nairobi, Kenya
T: 254 20 3873 283/700
F: 254 20 3870 876
E: Generalsec@capa-hq.org
W: www.capa-hq.org

Administrative Officer Mrs Elizabeth Gichovi (*same address*) *E:* info@capa-hq.org

HIV/AIDS TB & Malaria Programme Coordinator Mr Emmanuel Olatunji (*same address*)
E: olatunji@capa-hq.org/otunuel@yahoo.com

The Council of the Churches of East Asia

This Council, whose history began in 1954, has gone through an evolution. With most of the dioceses forming into provinces, the Council is now a fellowship for common action. Its membership includes dioceses in the Province of South East Asia, the Church of Korea, the Philippine Episcopal Church, Hong Kong Sheng Kung Hui, the Diocese of Taiwan (which is associated with the Episcopal Church of the USA), the Province of Myanmar, Nippon Sei Ko Kai (the Holy Catholic Church in Japan), the Philippine Independent Church and the Anglican Church of Australia who are members as a national Church or province.

Chairman The Most Revd Dr Paul Kwong, Hong Kong Sheng Kung Hui. Provincial office: 16/F, Tung Wai Commercial Building,

No.109–111 Gloucester Road, Wanchai, Hong Kong SAR
T: 852 2526 5355
F: 852 2521 2199
E: Office1@hkskh.org
www.hkskh.org

Bishop The Rt Revd John Alexander Ellison, Iglesia Anglicana de Paraguay, Casilla de Correo 1124, Asunción, Paraguay
T: 595 21 214 328
E: jellison@pla.net.py
W: www.paraguay.anglican.org
F: 595 21 214 328

Bishop The Rt Revd Peter Bartlett, Casilla de Correo 1124, Asunción, Paraguay
T: 595 21 200 933
E: peterparaguay@gmail.com

UNITED CHURCHES IN FULL COMMUNION

The Church of Bangladesh

Members 20,139
Congregations/Pastorates 103

Situated between Burma and India, with the Bay of Bengal in the south, is the small country of Bangladesh. Originally part of India, it gained independence from Britain in 1947, becoming East Pakistan. On 16 December 1971, Bangladesh achieved its sovereign independence, under the leadership of Bangabondhu Sheik Mujibur Rahman, after a bloody liberation war against the Pakistani Army from 26 March in the same year.

The Church of Bangladesh is a church of the Anglican Communion in Bangladesh. It is a united church formed by the union of various Christian churches in the region, principally Anglican and Presbyterian. The Church of Bangladesh came into being as the outcome of the separation from Pakistan. This started as a movement which focused on language and took shape through the liberation war in 1971, which created an independent Bangladesh. The Synod of the Church of Pakistan on 30 April 1974 declared and endorsed a free and independent status for the Church of Bangladesh. The Church of Bangladesh brings together the Anglican and English Presbyterian Churches.

Moderator The Rt Revd Paul S. Saker (*Bishop of Dhaka*)

Deputy Moderator The Rt Revd Samuel S. Mankhin (*Bishop of Kushtia*)

Hon Synod Secretary Mr Joseph Sudhin Mondal

Hon Treasurer Mr Avijit Raksam

Church of Bangladesh, 54/1 Barobag, Mirpur 2, Dhaka   *T:* 880 2 9025876
                                              F: 880 2 8053729
            E: cobsynod@churchofbangladesh.org

THEOLOGICAL COLLEGE
St Andrew's Theological College, 54 Johnson Road, Dhaka – 1100, Bangladesh (*Principal* The Revd Dr Albert Walters)   *T:* 880 2 802 0876

DHAKA
Bishop The Rt Revd Paul S. Saker (*Moderator of the Church of Bangladesh*), Church of Bangladesh, 54/1 Barobag, Mirpur 2, Dhaka 1216

KUSHTIA
Bishop The Rt Revd Samuel S. Mankhin (*Deputy Moderator of the Church of Bangladesh*), 94 N. S. Road, Thanapara, Kushtia
            T: and *F:* 880 71 54618
            E: bishop_mankhin@yahoo.com

The Church of North India

Members approx 1.5 million

The Church of North India is part of the One Holy, Catholic and Apostolic Church, the Body of Christ which He is building up out of persons of all generations and races. The Church of North India is what it is as a Church by reason of what is has received from God in Christ through bringing together into one life the several traditions of the Churches that have united to constitute it. This heritage is the fruit of the continuous working of God's Spirit in His Church in all ages from apostolic times through the Reformation and down to our own day.

The Churches which united to constitute the Church of North India were all linked with the Church of apostolic times by an essential continuity of doctrine, of experience and allegiance to the Lord Jesus Christ, and by a fellowship in the continued proclaiming of the gospel of salvation through him. In different ways, they had all sought to maintain continuity with the early Church in all matters of order.

The six Churches which united on 29 November 1970 in Nagpur to form the Church of North India were:

* The Council of Baptist Churches in Northern India
* The Church of the Brethren in India
* The Disciples of Christ
* The Church of India (formerly known as the Church of India, Pakistan, Burma and Ceylon)
* The Methodist Church (British and Australasian Conferences)
* The United Church of Northern India.

The Church of North India as a united and uniting church together is committed to announcing the Good News of the reign of God inaugurated through the death and resurrection of Jesus Christ in proclamation, and to demonstrating in actions the restoration of the integrity of God's creation through continuous struggle against the demonic powers by breaking down the barriers of caste, class, gender, economic inequality and exploitation of nature.

Moderator The Most Revd P. K. Samantaroy (*Bishop of Amritsar*)

Deputy Moderator The Rt Revd Dr P. C. Singh (*Bishop of Jabalpur*)

General Secretary Mr Alwan Masih, CNI Bhavan, 16 Pandit Pant Marg, New Delhi 110 001　　　　　　*T:* 91 114 321 4000
E: alwanmasih@cnisynod.org
W: www.cnisynod.org

Hon Treasurer Mr Prem Masih (*same address and telephone number*)　*E:* cnitr@cnisynod.org

CHURCH PAPER
The North India Church Review The official monthly magazine of the CNI. Contains articles, reports, diocesan news, world news and letters. *Editor/Editorial Office* (*same address*) Mr Alwan Masih (*Editor in Chief*), Ms Sushma Ramswami (*Managing Editor*)

AGRA
Bishop The Rt Revd Dr Prem Prakash Habil, Bishop's House, 4/116-B Church Road, Civil Lines, Agra 282 002, Uttar Pradesh
T: 91 562 285 4845 / 285 1481
Mobile: 91 941 272 2501
F: 91 562 252 0074
E: doacni@gmail.com
bishopofagra@gmail.com

AMRITSAR
Bishop The Most Revd Pradeep Kumar Samantaroy, 26 R. B. Prakash Chand Road, Opp Police Ground, Amritsar 143 001, Punjab
T: and *F:* 91 183 222 2910/
91 183 256 2010
Mobile: 91 981 546 2121
E: bunu13@rediffmail.com

ANDAMAN AND NICOBAR ISLANDS
Bishop The Rt Revd Christopher Paul, Cathedral Church Compound, MUS, Car Nicobar 744301 / Post Box No 19, Port Blair 744 101, Andaman and Nicobar Islands
Mobile: 91 947 601 6029
E: cniportblair@yahoo.co.in

BARRACKPORE
Moderator's Episcopal Commissary The Rt Revd Ashoke Biswas, Bishop's Lodge, 86 Middle Road, Barrackpore, Kolkata 700120, West Bengal　　　*Telefax:* 91 332 593 1852
Mobile: 91 974 845 6981
F: 91 332 592 0147
E: ashoke.biswas@vsnl.net

BHOPAL
Moderator's Episcopal Commissary The Rt Revd Dr P. C. Singh, Masihi Kanya Hr. Sec. School Campus, 9 Boundary Road, Indore 452 001 Madhya Pradesh　　　*T:* 91 731 249 2789
Mobile: 91 942 515 5379
E: bishoppcsingh@yahoo.co.in
bhopal_diocese@yahoo.com

CHANDIGARH
Bishop The Rt Revd Younas Massey, Bishop's House, Mission Compound, Brown Road, Ludhiana 141 001, Punjab
T: and *F:* 91 161 222 5706
Mobile: 91 991 564 1109
E: bishopdoc2000@yahoo.com
W: chandigarhdiocesecni.org

CHHATTISHARH
Bishop The Rt Revd Robert Ali, Opp. Raj Bhavan, Gate No. 1, Civil Lines, Raipur 492 001, Chhattisgarh
T: and *F:* 91 771 221 0015
Mobile: 91 992 618 6636
E: bishop.robertali@gmail.com

CHOTANAGPUR
Bishop The Rt Revd B. B. Baskey, Bishop's Lodge, PO Box 1, Church Road, Ranchi 834 001, Jharkhand　　　*T:* 91 651 235 0281
F: 91 651 235 1184
Mobile: 91 947 019 3053, 91 754 911 3206
E: rch_cndta@sancharnet.in
chotanagpurdiocese@gmail.com

CUTTACK
Bishop The Rt. Revd S. K. Nanda, Bishop's House, Mission Road, Cuttack 753 001, Orissa
T: 91 671 230 0102
Mobile: 91 943 732 3975
E: sknanda62@gmail.com

DELHI
Bishop The Rt Revd Warris Masih, Bishop's House, 1 Church Lane, Off North Avenue, New Delhi 110 001
T: 91 112 371 7471/91 991 010 3520/
91 112 335 8006
Mobile: 91 800 360 2000
E: wkmasih@yahoo.co.in
W: www.delhidiocese.org

DURGAPUR
Bishop The Rt Revd Probal Kanto Dutta, Diocesan Bhavan, Aldrin Path, Bidhan Nagar, Dugapur 713 212, Dist. Burdwan, West Bengal
T: and *F:* 91 343 253 4552 / 91 343 253 6220
E: probaldutta@ymail.com

EASTERN HIMALAYA
Moderator's Commissary The Most Revd Dr P. P. Marandih, CNI Diocesan Centre, Gandhi Road, PO Box 4, Darjeeling 734 101, West Bengal   *Mobile:* 91 943 121 3138
E: easternhimalaya2010@yahoo.co.in

GUJARAT
Bishop The Rt Revd Silvans S. Christian, Bishop's House, I.P. Mission Compound, Ellisbridge, Ahmedabad 380 006, Gujarat
T: and *F:* 91 792 656 1950
Mobile: 91 740 522 7086
E: gujdio@yahoo.co.in
christiansilvans@yahoo.com

JABALPUR
Bishop The Rt Revd Dr Prem Chand Singh, Bishop's House, 2131 Napier Town, Jabalpur 482 001, Madhya Pradesh
T: 91 761 2622 109 / 91 761 262 2692
Mobile: 91 942 515 5379
E: bishoppcsingh@yahoo.co.in

KOLHAPUR
Moderator's Episcopal Commissary The Rt Revd Prakash D. Patole, Bishop's House, EP School Compound, Nagala Park, Kolhapur 416 001, Maharashtra   *T:* and *F:* 91 231 265 4832
Mobile: 91 983 348 0299
E: bishopprakashpatole@gmail.com

KOLKATA
Bishop The Rt Revd Ashoke Biswas, Bishop's House, 51 Chowringhee Rd, Calcutta 700 071, West Bengal   *T:* 91 336 534 7770
Mobile: 91 974 845 6981
F: 91 332 822 6340
E: ashoke.biswas@vsnl.net

LUCKNOW
Bishop The Rt Revd Peter Baldev, 25/11 Mahatma Gandhi Marg, Allahabad 211 011, Uttar Pradesh   *T:* 91 989 790 8072
E: peterbaldev@yahoo.com;
bishopoflucknow@rediffmail.com

MARATHWADA
Bishop The Rt Revd M. U. Kasab, Bungalow 28/A, Mission Compound, Cantonment, Aurangabad 431 002, Maharashtra
T: 91 240 237 3136
Mobile: 91 976 482 2888
E: revmukasab@yahoo.co.in
bishopofmarathwada@rediffmail.com

MUMBAI
Bishop The Rt Revd Prakash Dinkar Patole, 19 Hazarimal Somani Marg Fort, Mumbai 400 001   *T:* 91 222 207 3904
91 983 348 0299 (Mobile)
F: 91 222 206 0248
E: cnibombaydiocese@yahoo.com
bishopprakashpatole@gmail.com

NAGPUR
Bishop The Rt Revd Paul Dupare, Cathedral House, Opp. Indian Coffee House, Sadar, Nagpur 440 001, Maharashtra
T: and *F:* 91 712 255 3351
Mobile: 91 982 335 4614
E: nagpurdiocese@rediffmail.com

NASIK
Bishop The Rt Revd Pradip Lemuel Kamble, Bishop's House, 1 Outram Road, Tarakpur, Ahmednagar 414 001, Maharashtra
T: 91 241 241 1806
Mobile: 91 942 109 9721
F: 91 241 242 2314
E: bishopofnasik@rediffmail.com

NORTH EAST INDIA
Bishop The Rt Revd Michael Herenz, Bishop's Kuti, Shillong, Meghalaya 793 000
T: 91 364 222 3155
Mobile: 91 943 554 6652
E: michaelherenz@gmail.com

PATNA
Bishop The Most Revd Dr Philip Phembuar Marandih, Bishop's House, Christ Church Compound, Bhagalpur 812 001, Bihar
T: 91 641 240 0033 / 230 0714
Mobile: 91 943 121 3138 (Mobile)
E: cnipatna@rediffmail.com

PHULBANI
Bishop The Rt Revd Bijay Kumar Nayak, Bishop's House, Mission Compound, Gudripori, Gudaigiri, Phulbani 762 100, Kandhamal, Odisha 762 001
T: 91 684 726 0569
Mobile: 91 943 796 5389
E: bp.bkn@rediffmail.com
W: www.cniphulbanidiocese.org

PUNE
Moderator's Episcopal Commissary The Rt Revd M. U. Kasab, 1A, General Bhagat Marg (Stevely Road), Red Bungalow, Pune 411 001, Maharashtra   *T:* 91 202 633 4374
Mobile: 91 976 482 2888
E: revmukasab@yahoo.co.in
punediocese@yahoo.com

RAJASTHAN
Moderator's Episcopal Commissary The Rt Revd Warris Masih, 2/10 CNI Social Centre, Civil Lines, Opp. Bus Stand, Jaipur Road, Ajmer 305 001   *T:* 91 145 242 0633
Mobile: 91 800 360 2000
F: 91 145 262 1627
E: warrisk.masih@yahoo.in
wkmasih@yahoo.co.in

SAMBALPUR
Bishop The Rt Revd Pinuel Dip, Bishop's House, Mission Compound, Bolangir 767 001, Odisha   *T:* 91 665 223 0625
Mobile: 91 943 833 6476
E: bishoppinueldip@gmail.com

The Church of Pakistan

Members approx 1,900,000
One of four United Churches in the Anglican Communion, the Church of Pakistan comprises the Anglican Church of Pakistan, the Dioceses of Peshawar, Faisalabad, Lahore and Karachi, two conferences of the United Methodist Church, the Scottish Presbyterian Church in Pakistan, and the Pakistan Lutheran Church.

Moderator The Rt Revd Samuel Robert Azariah *(Bishop of Raiwind)*,17 Waris Road, Lahore 3
T: 92 423 758 8950
Mobile: 92 300 841 7982
E: sammyazariah@yahoo.com
moderator@churchofpakistan.org.pk

Deputy Moderator The Rt Revd Sadiq Daniel *(Bishop of Karachi)*, Holy Trinity Church, Fatima Jinnah Road, Karachi 4
T: 92 215 216 843
Mobile: 92 301 822 2003
E: sadiqdaniel@hotmail.com

General Secretary Anthony Aijaz Lamuel
T: 92 42 3723 8537
F: 92 42 3723 8587
E: anthony.lamuel100@gmail.com

Treasurer Mr Irshad Nawab, 113 Qasim Road, PO Box 204, Multan Cantt
T: 92 61 458 3694
Mobile: 92 340 640 9867

Women's Synodical Co-ordinator Ms Shunila Ruth, 596-Pak Arab Housing Society, Ferozepur Road, Lahore   *Mobile:* 92 300 402 0193

Synod Coordination Office The Rt Revd Mano Rumalshah *(Co-ordinator)*, 17 Waris Road, Lahore   *T:* 92 423 629 9547
Mobile: 92 300 859 3725
E: cop.co@outlook.com

FAISALABAD
Bishop The Rt Revd John Samuel, Bishop's House, PO Box 27, Mission Road, Gojra, Distt Toba Tek Sing   *T:* 92 46 351 4689
Mobile: 92 300 655 0074
E: jsamuel@brain.net.pk

HYDERABAD
Bishop The Rt Revd Kaleem John, 27 Liaquat Road, Civil Lines, Hyderabad 71000, Sindh
T: 92 22 278 0221
Mobile: 92 301 244 5690
E: kaleemjohn@aol.com

KARACHI
Bishop The Rt Revd Sadiq Daniel *(Deputy Moderator, CoP)*, Holy Trinity Cathedral, Fatima Jinnah Road, Karachi 75530
T: 92 21 521 6843
Mobile: 92 301 822 2003
E: sadiqdaniel@hotmail.com

LAHORE
Bishop The Rt Revd Irfan Jamil, Bishopsbourne, Cathedral Close, The Mall, Lahore 54000
T: 92 42 723 3560 (Office)
92 42 7120 766 (Home)
Mobile: 92 333 475 6730
F: 92 42 722 1270
E: 9 thbishopofl ahore@gmail.com

MULTAN
Bishop The Rt Revd Leo Rodrick Paul, 113 Qasim Road, PO Box 204, Multan Cantt
T: 92 61 458 3694
Mobile: 92 300 630 2101
E: bishop_mdcop@bain.net.pk

PESHAWAR
Bishop The Rt Revd Humphrey Sarfaraz Peters, Diocesan Centre, 1 Sir Syed Road, Peshawar Cantt 2500   *T:* 92 91 527 9094
Mobile: 92 300 858 0325
F: 92 91 527 7499
E: bishopdop@hotmail.com

ANGLICAN & PORVOO COMMUNIONS

RAIWIND
Bishop The Rt Revd Samuel Azariah, (*Moderator of COP*) 17 Waris Road, PO Box 2319, Lahore 3
T: 92 42 758 8950
Mobile: 92 300 841 7982
F: 92 42 757 7255
E: sammyazariah@yahoo.com

SIALKOT
Bishop The Rt Revd Alwin Samuel, Lal Kothi, Barah Patthar, Sialkot 2, Punjab
T: 92 432 264 895
Mobile: 92 305 730 2201
F: 92 432 264 828
E: chs_sialkot@yahoo.com

The Church of South India

Members 4,000,000
The Church was inaugurated in 1947 by the union of the South India United Church (itself a union of Congregational and Presbyterian/ Reformed traditions), the southern Anglican dioceses of the Church of India, and Burma, and the Methodist Church in South India. It is one of the four United Churches in the Anglican Communion. Church of South India has 24 dioceses, 15,000 congregations, 3000 Presbyters, and around 3000 missionaries. It also has around 1500 Primary Schools, 200 Higher Secondary Schools, 100 Institutes/ Colleges of Higher Education including Medical and Technical and Engineering Colleges. For more information visit www. csisynod.com. CSI LIFE Online: http://www. csisynod.com/csilife.php

Moderator The Most Revd Thomas K. Oommen (*Bishop in Madhya Kerala*)

General Secretary The Revd Dr D. R. Sadananda, CSI Centre, 5 Whites Road, Royapettah, Chennai 600 014, India
T: 91 44 2852 1566/4166 (Office)
2852 3763 (Home)
F: 91 44 2852 3528
E: synodcsi@gmail.com,
csisynod@gmail.com

Honorary Treasurer Adv. C. Robert Bruce, Star Cottage, Saralvilai, Kattathurai, Kanyakumari District, 629 158, India
T: 91 44 2852 4166 (Office)
F: 91 44 2858 4163
E: treasurercsisynod@gmail.com

OFFICIAL MAGAZINE
CSI Life English Monthly Magazine. Contains articles, reports and news from the dioceses. *Editor:* The General Secretary CSI; published by Dept of Communication on behalf of CSI, 5 Whites Road, Royapettah, Chennai 600 014; Yearly subscription Rs.150/- (£25 in UK, $30 in USA, $35 in Australia, $35 in New Zealand, sent by Air Mail).

COCHIN (previously NORTH KERALA)
Bishop in The Rt Revd Baker Ninan Fenn, CSI Diocesan Office, PO Box 104, Shoranur 679 121, Palakkad District, Kerala
T: 91 46 6222 2545 (Office)
91 46 6222 2426 (Home)
F: 91 46 6222 2545
E: csicochindiocese@gmail.com
revbnfenn@gmail.com

COIMBATORE
Bishop in The Rt Revd Timothy Ravinder, Diocesan Office, 256 Race Course Road, Coimbatore 641 018, Tamil Nadu
T: 91 42 222 3605/222 1655 (Office)
F: 91 42 222 3369
E: csi.bpcbe@gmail.com

DORNAKAL
Bishop in The Rt Revd Dr Vadapalli Prasada Rao, Diocesan Office, Epiphany Cathedral Compound, Dornakal 506 381, Warangal Dist., Telangana   *T:* 91 8719 227 752 (Home)
91 8719 227 535 (Office)
*E:*dkbpoff@hotmail.com
bshvadapallidornakal@hotmail.com

EAST KERALA
Bishop in The Rt Revd Dr K. G. Daniel, CSI Diocesan Office, Melukavumattom, Kottayam 686 652, Kerala State
T: 91 4822 219 026/
91 4822 220 001 (Office)
F: 91 4822 219 044
*E:*csiekd@gmail.com
bishopkgdaniel@rediffmail.com

JAFFNA
Bishop in The Rt Revd Daniel S. Thiagarajah, Bishop's office in Colombo, 17, Frances Road, Colombo 6, Sri Lanka
T: 94 21 225 0827/0826 (Office)
F: 94 11 258 2015
E: bishopthiagarajah@gmail.com

KANYAKUMARI
Bishop in The Rt Revd Dr G. Devakadasham, CSI Diocesan Office, 71A Dennis Street, Nagercoil 629 001, Kanyakumari District, Tamil Nadu   *T:* 91 4652 278 920 (Home)
91 4652 231 539 (Office)
F: 91 4652 226 560
E: csikkd@bsnl.in

KARIMNAGAR
Bishop in The Rt Revd Dr K. Reuben Mark, CSI Diocesan Office, 2–8–95 CVRN Road, PO Box 40, Mukarampura Post, Karimnagar 505 001,Telangana   *T:* 91 878 226 2229 (Office)
          97 878 226 2971 (Home)
          F: 91 878 226 2971
          E: reubenmark@hotmail.com

KARNATAKA CENTRAL
Bishop in The Rt Revd Dr Prasanna Kumar Samuel, CSI Diocesan Office, 20 Third Cross, CSI Compound, Bangalore 560 027, Karnataka
     T: 91 80 2222 3766/2222 4941 (Office)
          E: bishop@csikcd.in
          revpksamuel@gmail.com

KARNATAKA NORTHERN
Bishop in The Rt Revd Ravikumar J. Niranjan, CSI Diocesan Office, All Saints' Church Compound, Haliyal Road, Dharwad 580 008, Karnataka   *T:* 91 836 244 7733
          F: 91 836 274 5461
          E: haradoni.rn@gmail.com

KARNATAKA SOUTHERN
Bishop in The Rt Revd Mohan Manoraj, CSI Diocesan Office, Balmatta, Mangalore 575 002, Karnataka   *T:* 91 824 243 2657 (Office)
          F: 91 824 243 2363
          E: csiksd2014@gmail.com
          mohhanrraj@gmail.com

KRISHNA-GODAVARI
Bishop in The Most Revd Dr G. Dyvasirvadam (*Moderator*), CSI Diocesan Office, CSI TA Bass Complex, Gopala Reddy Road, Governorpet, Vijayawada 520 002, Andhra Pradesh
          T: 91 866 2573673 (Office)
          F: 91 866 2573673
          E: bishopkrishna@yahoo.com

KOLLAM KOTTARAKARA (NEWLY SEPARATED FROM SOUTH KERALA)
Bishop in The Rt Revd A. Dharmaraja Rasalam, Moderator's Commissary, Diocesan Office, Kollam Kottarakara, N.H. 208, Chinnakada, Kollam 691 001, Kerala
     E: csikollamkottarakaradiocese@gmail.com

MADHYA KERALA
Bishop in The Most Revd Thomas K. Oommen (*Moderator*), CSI Bishop's office, Cathedral Road, Kottayam 686 001, Kerala
          T: 91 481 25667274
          91 481 2566 531 (Home)
          F: 91 481 256 6536
          E: csimkdbishopsoffice@gmail.com

MADRAS
Bishop in The Rt Revd Dr J. George Stephen, Diocesan Office, PO Box 4914, 226 Cathedral Road, Chennai 600 086, Tamil Nadu
          T: 91 44 2811 3929/3933/7629
          F: 91 44 2811 0608

MADURAI-RAMNAD
Bishop in The Rt Revd Dr M. Joseph, 'Rev. Grub's Garden', No.5 Bhulabai Desai Road, Chokkikulam, Madurai 625 002, Tamil Nadu
          T: 91 452 2338222 (Office)
          F: 91 452 2339888
          *E:*bishopmjoseph@gmail.com

MALABAR (previously North Kerala)
Bishop in The Rt Revd Dr Royce Manoj Kumar Victor, CSI Diocesan Office, Bank Road, Calicut 673 001, Kerala   *T:* 91 495 272 1748
          E: csimalabardiocese@gmail.com

MEDAK
Bishop in Vacancy, *contact* The Most Revd Dr G. Dyvasirvadam (*Moderator/Bishop-in-charge*), Diocesan Office, 10–3–165, Church House, Golden Jubilee Bhavan, Old Lancer Lane, Secunderabad 500 025, Telangana
     T: 91 40 2783 3151/2782 2189 (Office)
          F: 91 40 27820543

NANDYAL
Bishop in The Rt Revd E. Pushpalalitha, CSI Diocesan Office, Nandyal RS 518 502, Kurnool Dist., Andhra Pradesh
          T: 91 8514 222 477 (Office)
          E: csibishopnandyal@gmail.com
          rt.rev.pushpalalitha@gmail.com

RAYALASEEMA
Bishop in The Rt Revd Dr B. D. Prasada Rao, CSI Diocesan Office, R.S.Road, Kadapa, Andhra Pradesh   *T:* 91 8562 325 320 (Office)
          91 8562 275 200 (Home)
          F: 91 8562 275 200
          E: lbd_prasad@yahoo.co.in

SOUTH KERALA
Bishop in The Rt Revd A. Dharmaraj Rasalam, CSI Diocesan office, LMS Compound, Trivandrum 695 033, Kerala State
          T: 91 471 231 8662; 231 5490
          F: 91 471 231 6439
          *E:*bishoprasalam@yahoo.com

THOOTHUKUDI-NAZARETH
Moderator's Commissary The Revd D. Jesusagayam, Diocesan Office, Caldwell Hr. Sec. School Campus, Beach Road, Thoothukudi 628 001   *T:* 91 461 232 9408 (Office)
          F: 91 461 232 8408
          *E:*csitnd@bsnl.in
          sagayam08@rediffmail.com

TIRUNELVELI
Bishop in The Rt Revd Dr J. J. Christdoss, CSI Diocesan Office, PO Box 116, 16, No. 5 Punithavathiyar Street, Palayamkottai, North High Ground Road, Tirunelveli 627 002, Tamil Nadu   *T:* 91 462 257 8744
          F: 91 462 257 4525
          E: bishopcsitirunelveli@gmail.com

ANGLICAN & PORVOO COMMUNIONS

TRICHY-TANJORE

Bishop in The Rt Revd Dr G. Paul Vasanthakumar, CSI Diocesan Office, Allithurai Road, Puthur, Tiruchiarapalli 620 017, Tamil Nadu

T: 91 431 241 1102 (Home)
91 431 277 0172/277 1254 (Office)
F: 91 431 241 8485 / 277 0172
E: csittd@rediffmail.com

VELLORE

Bishop in The Rt Revd Dr A. Rajavelu, CSI Diocesan Office, 3/1, Anna Salai, Vellore 632 001, Tamil Nadu

T: 91 416 223 2160 (Office)
91 416 221 6324 (Home)
F: 91 416 222 3835
E: bishoprajavelu@gmail.com

THE HOLY CATHOLIC CHURCH IN CHINA

(Chung Hua Sheng Kung Hui)

The Chung Hua Sheng Kung Hui was an important denomination in China and its history dates back to the mid-nineteenth century. Today the CHSKU, as a separate denomination, no longer exists in the People's Republic of China, except for Hong Kong which returned to Chinese sovereignty on 1 July 1997. Under the formula 'one country – two systems' Hong Kong keeps its autonomy for 50 years, including its religious regulations. The same applies to Macao which was returned by Portugal to China at the end of 1999. On the Chinese mainland the denominational Protestant Churches entered into a post-denominational phase under the Three Self Patriotic Movement/China Christian Council in 1953. A united Church is still in the process of being formed and Christians of Anglican inspiration have very much been a part of this process. The most prominent of these, Bishop K. H. Ting, died in December 2012, and his passing marks the end of an era for the China Christian Council and the Nanjing Union Theological Seminary.

Although the CHSKU is no longer in existence, many former Anglicans still share a strong spiritual affinity with other Anglican Churches on matters of belief and liturgical tradition. As the Chinese Protestant Church develops its own ecclesiology and forms of worship, the Anglican traditions are contributing to a richer synthesis.

Relations between the Church in China and the Churches in Britain are facilitated by the World Programmes Desk of Churches Together in Britain and Ireland (CTBI). It provides advice to government, churches and media, and publishes the *China Study Journal*, a documentary review of Chinese religions and government policy. The World Programmes Desk offers the continuity for the ecumenical China Study Project which was established in 1972 by the leading missionary societies, including Anglican organizations such as the CMS, USPG and the Archbishop's China Appeal Fund.

The Friends of the Church in China, an ecumenical association which works closely with the World Programmes Desk of CTBI, takes a more grass-roots approach in relation to Christians in China. It publishes a popular newsletter on China and organizes visits to Chinese churches.

Contact: Christine Elliott, CTBI World Programmes, 39 Eccleston Square, London SW1V 1BX, *E:* christine.elliott@ctbi.org
Friends of the Church in China (Chairperson, Ms Maggi Whyte)
W: thefcc.org.uk

OTHER CHURCHES IN COMMUNION WITH THE CHURCH OF ENGLAND

Old Catholic Churches of the Union of Utrecht

The Old Catholic Churches are a family of nationally organized churches which bound themselves together in the Union of Utrecht in 1889. Most of them owe their origin to Roman Catholics who were unable to accept the decrees of the First Vatican Council in 1870 and left the communion of that Church. The Archbishopric of Utrecht, however (from which the other Old Catholic Churches derived their episcopal orders), has been independent of Rome since the eighteenth century following a complex dispute involving papal and capitular rights of nomination and accusations of Jansenism (until 1910 in the Netherlands only). The Latin Mass continued in use, though all the Old Catholic Churches now worship in the vernacular. Their rites stand within the Western tradition, with various 'Eastern' features.

By the acceptance of the Bonn Agreement on 20 and 22 January 1932, the Convocation of Canterbury established full communion with the Old Catholic Churches by means of the following resolutions:

'That this House approves of the following statements agreed on between the representatives of the Old Catholic Churches and the Churches of the Anglican Communion at a Conference held at Bonn on 2 July 1931:

- Each Communion recognises the catholicity and independence of the other and maintains its own.
- Each Communion agrees to admit members of the other Communion to participate in the sacraments.
- Intercommunion does not require from either Communion the acceptance of all doctrinal opinion, sacramental devotion, or liturgical practice characteristic of the other, but implies that each believes the other to hold all the essentials of the Christian Faith.

'And this House agrees to the establishment of Intercommunion between the Church of England and the Old Catholics on these terms.'

An Anglican–Old Catholic International Coordinating Council was established in 1998.

AUSTRIA
Bishop The Rt Revd Dr Heinz Lederleitner, Schottenring 17/ 1/3/12, A–1010 Vienna
E: bischof@altkatholiken.at
W: www.altkatholiken.at

CROATIA
Bishop Vacancy, *under the care of* The Rt Revd Dr John Ekemezie Okoro, Schottenring 17/1/3/12, 1010 Vienna
E: bischof.okoro@altkatholiken.at

CZECH REPUBLIC
Bishop The Rt Revd Pavel Benedikt Stránský, Na Bateriich 27, CZ–162 00 Prague 6
E: stkat@starokatolici.cz
W: www.starokatolici.cz

FRANCE
Bishop Delegate The Most Revd Dr Joris Vercammen (*Archbishop of Utrecht*), Kon Wilhelminalaan 3, NL-3818 HN Amersfoort
E: abvu@okkn.nl
W: www.vieux-catholique-alsace.com

GERMANY
Bishop The Rt Revd Dr Matthias Ring, Gregor–Mendel-Strasse 28, 53115 Bonn, Germany
E: ordinariat@alt-katholisch.de
W: www.alt-katholisch.de

NETHERLANDS
Archbishop The Most Revd Dr Joris Vercammen (*Archbishop of Utrecht and President of the International Bishops' Conference*), Kon Wilhelminalaan, 3, NL–3818 HN Amersfoort
E: buro@okkn.nl
W: www.okkn.nl/welkom

Bishop of Haarlem The Rt Revd Dr Dirk Jan Schoon, Ruysdaelstraat 37, NL-1071 XA Amsterdam
E: djschoon@planet.nl

POLAND (The Polish National Catholic Church)
Prime Bishop The Most Revd Prof Dr Wiktor Wysoczanski, ul. Wilcza 31/16c, PL–002–544 Warsaw   *E:* polskokatolicki@pnet.pl
           W: www.polskokatolicki.pl

SWEDEN AND DENMARK
Bishop Delegate The Rt Revd Dr Dirk Jan Schoon, Ruysdaelstraat 37, NL–1070 XA Amsterdam, Netherlands
           E: djschoon@planet.nl

SWITZERLAND
Bishop The Rt Revd PD Dr Harald Rein, Willadingweg 39, CH–3006 Bern
           E: bischof@christkath.ch
           W: www.christkath.ch

Philippine Independent Church

The Philippine Independent Church is in part the result of the Philippine revolution against Spain in 1896 for religious emancipation and Filipino identity. It was formally established in 1902, declaring its independence from the Roman Catholic Church but seeking to remain loyal to the Catholic Faith. It now derives its succession from the Protestant Episcopal Church in the United States of America (and therefore from Anglican sources), with which full communion was established in September 1961. It has a membership of approximately seven million followers, 34 dioceses with 50 bishops, 600 regular church buildings and 2,000 village chapels served by about 600 priests.

Following the report of a Commission appointed by the Archbishop of Canterbury, full communion on the basis of the Bonn Agreement was established between the Church of England and the Philippine Independent Church in 1963 by the Convocations of Canterbury and York. It is in full communion with all the member Churches in the Anglican Communion.

The Philippine Independent Church is very active in its ecumenical relations. It is the most senior member in the National Council of the Churches in the Philippines, a member of the Council of Churches in East Asia, a member of the Christian Churches in Asia, and an active member of the World Council of Churches.

Supreme Bishop (Obisbo Maximo) The Most Revd Tomas A. Millamena, 1500 Taft Avenue, Ermita, Manila, Philippines 2801
           T: 63 2 523 72 42
           F: 63 2 521 39 32
           E: ifiphil@hotmail.com

Mar Thoma Syrian Church of Malabar

The Christian community in South India is very ancient and is believed by its members to have been founded by the Apostle Thomas (Mar Thoma). Over the centuries contact with Christian bodies from outside India has led to the fragmentation of the original community into a number of jurisdictions. During the latter part of the nineteenth century the Christians of the West Syrian (Syrian Orthodox) tradition divided into two over the issue of the removal of non-biblical features from teaching and worship of the Church. The influence of Anglican missionaries of the Church Missionary Society who had been working in Malabar since the beginning of the nineteenth century accelerated the new stance in the Church. The larger section (which itself has subsequently divided into the Indian Orthodox and Jacobite Churches) chose closer links with Antioch and remained 'unreformed'; the smaller group, which eventually adopted the name of Mar Thoma Syrian Church of Malabar, undertook a conservative revision of its rites, removing elements (such as the invocation of saints and prayers for the dead) that were not scriptural practices but had given room for misunderstanding of the gospel. The general form of Mar Thoma worship remains eastern. Its episcopal succession derives from the Patriarchate of Antioch.

The former CIPBC (Church of India, Pakistan, Burma and Ceylon) had partial intercommunion with the Mar Thoma Church from 1937 until 1961 when a Concordat of Full Communion was established. The Mar Thoma Syrian Church of Malabar is now in full communion with the Churches of South India and North India. The union of these three churches is now known as the Communion of Churches in India (CCI), which fosters

ANGLICAN & PORVOO COMMUNIONS

cooperation in mission, theological training, and formulations and involvement in social issues.

The Mar Thoma Church has stated its desire to preserve its eastern traditions and is not willing to merge with the two Western United Churches. A number of Anglican Provinces are in full communion with the Mar Thoma Church, the Church of England having become so in 1974.

The Malabar Independent Syrian Church of Thozhiyoor occupies a unique position in the complex history of the Church in South India. At various times in the past its bishops have consecrated bishops for both the Orthodox and Mar Thoma Churches when the episcopal succession in those churches has died out. The MISC is fully Orthodox in rite and faith. It is in communion with the Mar Thoma Church and its current practice is to extend eucharistic hospitality to Christians of other traditions. The former Metropolitan was an ecumenical participant at the 1998 Lambeth Conference.

THE MAR THOMA SYRIAN CHURCH OF MALABAR

Metropolitan The Most Revd Dr Joseph Mar Thoma, Poolatheen, Tiruvalla 689 101, Kerala, South India   *T:* 91 469 263 0313
    E: metropolitan@marthoma.in

Sabha Secretary The Revd Oommen Philip, Mar Thoma Church Headquarters, Sabha Office, SCS Campus, Tiruvalla 689 101, Kerala, South India   *T:* 91 469 263 0449
    F: 91 469 263 0327
    E: sabhaoffice@marthoma.in

THE MALABAR INDEPENDENT SYRIAN CHURCH

The Most Revd Cyril Mar Basilios, St George's Cathedral, Thozhiyoor, Thrissur Dt 680 520, Kerala, South India

THE COMMUNION OF PORVOO CHURCHES

An Introduction to the Porvoo Communion

In October 1992 representatives of the four British and Irish Anglican Churches, the five Nordic Lutheran Churches and the three Baltic Lutheran Churches met in Finland for the fourth and final plenary session of their formal Conversations, which had commenced in 1989. They agreed *The Porvoo Common Statement*, named after Porvoo Cathedral, in which they had celebrated the Eucharist together.

The Common Statement recommended that the participating churches jointly make the Porvoo Declaration, bringing them into communion with each other. This involves common membership, a single, interchangeable ministry and structures to enable the Churches to consult each other on significant matters of faith and order, life and work. The implementation of the commitments contained in the Declaration is coordinated by the Porvoo Agreement Contact Group. The Porvoo Panel of the Church of England was established in 2000 to monitor and develop the implementation of the Porvoo commitments in dioceses and sector ministries.

In 1994 and 1995 the Declaration was approved by the four Anglican Churches, four of the Nordic Lutheran Churches and two of the Baltic Lutheran Churches. The General Synod's final approval of the Declaration in July 1995, following a reference to the diocesan synods, was by overwhelming majorities in each House. The Declaration was signed in the autumn of 1996 at services in Trondheim (Norway), Tallinn (Estonia) and Westminster Abbey.

In 1980 the Lusitanian Church (Portuguese Episcopal Church) became an extra-provincial diocese under the metropolitical authority of the Archbishop of Canterbury and in 1998 the diocesan synod of the Lusitanian Church approved and accepted the Porvoo Declaration. Furthermore in 1980 the Spanish Reformed Episcopal Church fully integrated into the Anglican Communion also coming under the metropolitical authority of the Archbishop of Canterbury. Both churches by virtue of coming under the Archbishop of Canterbury's metropolitical authority and accepting the Porvoo Declaration were integrated into the Porvoo Communion.

The Evangelical Lutheran Chuch in Denmark signed the Porvoo Declaration in December 2009 and in 2010 the Estonian Evangelical Lutheran Church Abroad and the Estonian Evangelical Lutheran Church Abroad united.

The Evangelical–Lutheran Church of Latvia has not yet decided to sign the Porvoo Declaration, but continues to participate as an observer.

In October 2010 during the Porvoo Contact Group Meeting in Madrid, the decision was taken to invite the Latvian Evangelical Lutheran Church Abroad and the Lutheran Church in Great Britain as observers to the Porvoo Communion. At the Porvoo Primates meeting in Reykjavik, Iceland in October 2013, the Primates unanimously agreed to both the Latvian Evangelical Lutheran Church Abroad and the Lutheran Church in Great Britain becoming full members of the Porvoo Communion of Churches. These two churches have followed the process for membership agreed by the Porvoo Primates. Their ecclesiology and polity are along the lines of the Porvoo Agreement. They are committed to a theology of episcopacy and their bishops are being consecrated in historic succession. Both Churches signed the Porvoo Declaration in September 2014 during the Church Leaders Consultation in York.

The Nordic Lutheran Churches are the historic national Churches of their respective countries. At the Reformation, when they adhered to Lutheranism, they continued to be episcopally ordered, retaining the historic sees. In Sweden and Finland the succession of the laying on of hands at episcopal consecration was unbroken, whereas in Denmark, Norway and Iceland this was not the case. The Estonian and Latvian Lutheran Churches are similarly their countries' historic national Churches, which became Lutheran at the Reformation. Only in the northern part of Estonia was episcopacy retained, and there only until 1710, but it was restored in both Estonia and Latvia in the twentieth century, the bishops being consecrated in the historic succession. The Lithuanian Lutheran Church, which is now a small minority Church, adopted episcopacy in historic succession in 1976.

The Porvoo Agreement supersedes earlier separate agreements dating from the 1920s, 1930s and 1950s with the Churches concerned (except the Lithuanian Lutheran Church). These provided for mutual eucharistic hospitality and (with the Swedish, Finnish, Estonian and Latvian Churches) mutual participation in episcopal consecrations. Because of the Soviet occupation of the Baltic States, however, it was only in 1989 and 1992 respectively that it was possible for an Anglican bishop to participate in a Latvian and an Estonian consecration for the first time.

The Porvoo Declaration commits the signatory Churches 'to regard baptized members of all of our Churches as members of our own'. It also means that clergy ordained by bishops of the signatory Churches are placed in the same position with regard to ministry in the Church of England as those ordained by Anglican bishops overseas.

Further information can be found on the Porvoo website: www.porvoocommunion.org, or is available from the European Secretary at the Council for Christian Unity at Church House, Westminster.

The Porvoo Agreement Contact Group
Co-Chairmen
The Most Revd Dr Michael Jackson (*Archbishop of Dublin*)   *T:* 353 1 497 7849
E: archbishop@dublin.anglican.org

The Rt Revd Peter Skov-Jacobsen (*Bishop of Copenhagen*)   *T:* 45 33 47 65 00
E: kmkbh@km.dk

Co-Secretaries
Ms Beate Fagerli (Nordic and Baltic Churches)
E: beate.fagerli@kirken.no

The Revd Dr William Adam (Church of England Council for Christian Unity)
E: william.adam@lambethpalace.org.uk

Porvoo Chaplains in England
Denmark
The Revd Flemming Kloster Poulsen, 4 St Katharine's Precinct, Regent's Park, London NW1 4HH   *T:* 020 7935 1723

Estonia
The Very Revd Lagle Heinla, Estonian House, 18 Chepstow Villas, London W11 2RB
T: 020 7229 6700

Finland
The Revd Teemu Hälli, The Finnish Church in London, 33 Albion Street, London SE16 7JG
T: 020 7237 1261

Iceland
Chaplaincy being carried out by visits at regular intervals from the Revd Adda Björnsdottie

Norway
The Revd Torbjørn Holt, 1 St Olav's Square, Albion Street, London SE16 7JB
T: 020 7740 3900

The Revd Thomas Wagle (*same address*)

The Revd Ingrid Ims, Student Chaplain (*same address*)

Sweden
The Very Revd Eric Muhl, 6 Harcourt Street, London W1H 2BD   *T:* 020 7723 5681

NORDIC LUTHERAN CHURCHES

The Evangelical Lutheran Church in Denmark

The Evangelical Lutheran Church in Denmark (ELCD) is the national church in Denmark, with approx. 2000 congregations divided into 10 dioceses, each presided over by a bishop. A bishop is elected by parish council members and pastors in the respective diocese. The role of the bishop is to oversee ministers and congregations in the diocese. The bishop of Copenhagen holds a specific position of honour as *primus inter pares*. There is no office of archbishop. Since 1948 the office has consequently been open to both men and women. In 2017 75.9 per cent of the Danish population (numbering 5.2 million) were members of the ELCD. A vast majority enter into membership as children when they are baptized.

In Denmark there is a strong relationship between the national church and the state. The ELCD is regarded as 'the church of the people' as well as an official national church since the institution of the Danish Constitution of 1849 in which it is particularly mentioned. Every parish council has had its own rights to decide on activities in its local context and to select the pastor of the parish. Thus the local congregation is the cornerstone of the church structure. The queen or king of Denmark is the supreme authority when it comes to organization, liturgy etc. whereas the national parliament (Folketinget) is the *de facto* deciding body with regard to church legislation. Thus, the ELCD is not regulated by a synod, a national church council, as is seen in most other Lutheran churches. The main part of the church budget comes from a membership fee collected by the national tax authorities and ear-marked grants from the state budget. In this way the state contributes to the administration of the church.

The ELCD signed the Porvoo Declaration at a ceremony in Copenhagen Cathedral on 3 October 2010.

General Secretary
Dr Joergen Skov Soerensen, Council on International Relations of the Evangelical Lutheran Church in Denmark, Peter Bangs Vej 1, DK-2000 Frederiksberg   *T:* 45 33 11 44 88
F: 45 33 11 95 88
E: interchurch@interchurch.dk
W: www.interchurch.dk

AALBORG
Bishop The Rt Revd Henning Toft Bro, Thulebakken 1, 9000 Aalborg
T: 45 98 18 80 88
E: kmaal@km.dk

AARHUS
Bishop The Rt Revd Henrik Wigh-Poulsen, Dalgas Avenue 46, 8000 Aarhus C
T: 45 86 14 51 00
E: kmaar@km.dk

FYENS
Bishop The Rt Revd Tine Lindhardt, Klingenberg 2, 5000 Odense C
T: 45 66 12 30 24
F: 45 66 12 35 24
E: kmfyn@km.dk

HADERSLEV
Bishop The Rt Revd Marianne Christiansen, Ribe Landevej 37, 6100 Haderslev
T: 45 74 52 20 25
F: 45 74 53 36 06
E: kmhad@km.dk

HELSINGØR
Bishop The Rt Revd Lise-Lotte Rebel, Vor Frue Kloster, Hestemøllestræde 3 A, DK-3000 Helsingør
T: 45 49 21 35 00
F: 45 49 21 35 16
E: llr@km.dk

KØBENHAVNS
Bishop The Rt Revd Peter Skov-Jakobsen, Nørregade 11, DK-1165, København K
T: 45 33 47 65 00
E: kmkbh@km.dk

LOLLAND-FALSTERS
Bishop The Rt Revd Marianne Gaarden, Bispegården, Østre Allé 2, 4800 Nykøbing F
T: 45 54 85 02 11
E: lfstift@km.dk

RIBE
Bishop The Rt Revd Elisabeth Dons Christensen, Korsbrødregade 7, 6760 Ribe
T: 45 75 42 18 00
E: elch@km.dk

ANGLICAN & PORVOO COMMUNIONS

ROSKILDE
Bishop The Rt Revd Peter Fischer-Møller, Palæet, Stændertorvet 3A, 4000 Roskilde
T: 45 46 38 19 20
E: pfm@km.dk

VIBORG
Bishop The Rt Revd Henrik Stubkjaer, Domkirkestræde 1, 8800 Viborg
T: 45 86 62 09 11
E: kmvib@km.dk

The Evangelical Lutheran Church of Finland

The first bishop in the Finnish Church was St Henrik, the Apostle of Finland. According to tradition, St Henrik was an Englishman who accompanied King Erik II of Sweden on a military expedition to south-western Finland in 1155 and was martyred there the following year. From the middle of the thirteenth century until 1809 Finland was part of Sweden, and until the Reformation it formed a single diocese (Turku) in the Province of Uppsala.

In 1554 the Swedish king appointed the Finnish Lutheran Reformer Mikael Agricola (d. 1557) as Bishop of Turku, at the same time founding a second Finnish see, Viipuri (eventually transferred to Tampere). In addition to translating the New Testament and parts of the Old into Finnish, Mikael Agricola compiled the first catechism, liturgy and ritual in Finnish. He is regarded as the father of Finnish as a written language.

A wave of revivals, beginning in the eighteenth century, gave rise in the nineteenth to four mass movements. These remained within the Church of Finland and are still influential on its life today.

In 1809 Finland was annexed by Russia. As a result, the Finnish Church became entirely independent of the Church of Sweden, and from 1817 the Bishop of Turku was styled Archbishop. Finland finally gained its independence in 1917.

Today, roughly 73 per cent of Finns are members of the Evangelical Lutheran Church of Finland, while only 4 per cent are members of other registered Christian Churches. The ELCF is a 'folk church' (as is the Orthodox Church). The framework for its life is set by the Ecclesiastical Act. Amendments to this state law can only be proposed by the Synod, and Parliament can accept or reject but not amend such proposals. The Church is governed by the Synod, the Church Council and the Bishops' Conference. Although the Archbishop is only *primus inter pares* of the Finnish bishops, he is the President of the Synod and chairs both the Bishops' Conference and the Church Council.

The Church is organized in nine dioceses, one of which consists of the Swedish-speaking parishes (Porvoo).

Porvoo Agreement Contact Chief Secretary for Ecumenical Relations and Theology, The Revd Dr Tomi Karttunen, Department for International Relations, Eteläranta 8, P.O. Box 210, FI-00131 Helsinki
T: 358 50 5941 713
F: 358 9 1802 350
E: tomi.karttunen@evl.fi
W: evl.fi/english

ESPOO
Bishop The Rt Revd Dr Tapio Luoma, Diocesan Chapter, PO Box 203, FI-02771 Espoo
T: 358 9 8050 80
F: 358 9 855 4020
E: tapio.luoma@evl.fi
Web: www.espoonhiippakunta.evl.fi

HELSINKI
Bishop The Rt Revd Irja Askola, Diocesan Chapter, PO Box 142, FI-00121 Helsinki
T: 358 9 2340 3000
F: 358 9 2340 3050
E: irja.askola@evl.fi
W: www.helsinginhiippakunta.evl.fi

KUOPIO
Bishop The Rt Revd Dr Jari Jolkkonen, Diocesan Chapter, PO Box 42, FI-70101 Kuopio
T: 358 17 288 8400
F: 358 17 288 8420
E: jari.jolkkonen@evl.fi
W: www.kuopionhiippakunta.fi

LAPUA
Bishop The Rt Revd Dr Simo Peura, Diocesan Chapter, PO Box 160, FI-60101 Seinäjoki
T: 358 207 630 910
F: 358 207 630 911
E: simo.peura@evl.fi
W: www.lapuanhiippakunta.fi

MIKKELI
Bishop The Rt Revd Dr Seppo Häkkinen, Diocesan Chapter, PO Box 122, FI-50101 Mikkeli
T: 358 15 3216 00
F: 358 15 3216 016
E: seppo.hakkinen@evl.fi
W: www.mikkelinhiippakunta.evl.fi

OULU
Bishop The Rt Revd Dr Samuel Salmi, Diocesan Chapter, PO Box 85, FI-90101 Oulu
T: 358 8 5358 510
F: 358 8 5358 533
E: samuel.salmi@evl.fi
W: www.oulunhiippakunta.evl.fi

PORVOO

(The Diocese of Porvoo (Borgå) is a non-geographical Swedish-language diocese.)

Bishop The Rt Revd Dr Björn Vikström, Diocesan Chapter, PO Box 30, FI-06101 Borgå
T: 358 40 142 5213
F: 358 19 585 705
E: bjorn.vikstrom@evl.fi
W: www.borgastift.fi

TAMPERE

Bishop The Rt Revd Dr Matti Repo, Diocesan Chapter, Eteläpuisto 2C, FI-33200 Tampere
T: 358 3 238 1130
F: 358 3 238 1150
E: matti.repo@evl.fi
W: www.tampereenhiippakunta.fi

TURKU

Archbishop of Turku and Finland The Most Revd Kari Mäkinen, Diocesan Chapter, PO Box 60, FI-20501 Turku
T: 358 2 279 7031
F: 358 2 279 7002
E: arkkipiispa@evl.fi
W: www.arkkipiispa.fi/en/

Bishop of Turku The Rt Revd Kaarlo Kalliala (*same address*)
T: 358 2 279 7033
Fax: 358 2 2797 001
E: kaarlo.kalliala@evl.fi
W: www.arkkihiippakunta.fi

The Evangelical Lutheran Church of Iceland

Christianity was adopted at Thingvellir by decree of the legislature in the year 1000. The ancient Icelandic sees of Skálholt and Hólar were founded in 1055 and 1106 respectively. Having previously been under the jurisdiction of Bremen and Lund, from 1153 Iceland belonged to the Province of Nidaros (Trondheim). Part of the Kingdom of Norway from 1262, Iceland eventually came under Danish rule. The Lutheran Reformation was introduced in 1541. From this time onwards until 1908 (with one exception in the late eighteenth century), Icelandic bishops were consecrated by the Bishops of Sealand (Copenhagen).

The two Icelandic sees were united in 1801, but in 1909 they were revived as suffragan sees. Iceland gained its independence from Denmark in 1918, becoming a republic in 1944.

A new Church law came into effect on 1 January 1998, granting the Church considerable autonomy from the state. The Church Assembly is the highest organ of the Church. Today, around 75 per cent of the Icelandic population are members of the Church of Iceland.

Porvoo Agreement Contact The Revd Sigurdur Arni Thordarson, Hallgrimskirkja, 101 Reykjavík
T: 354 510 1000
F: 354 51 1010
E: s@hallgrimskirkja.is

The Church of Iceland comprises a single diocese, with two suffragan bishops in the ancient sees of Hólar and Skálholt.

Bishop of Iceland The Rt Revd Agnes M. Sigurdardottir, Laugavegi 31, 150 Reykjavík
T: 354 528 4000
F: 354 528 4098
E: agnes.m.sigurdardottir@kirkjan.is

Bishop of Skálholt The Rt Revd Kristjan Valur Ingolfsson, Skálholt, Biskupshús, Skálholti, 801 Selfoss
T: 354 486 8972
F: 354 486 8975
E: kristjan.valur.ingolfsson@kirkjan.is

Bishop of Hólar The Rt Revd Solveig Lára Gudmundsdottir, Biskupssetur, Hólar, 551 Saudárkrókur
T: 354 453 6300
F: 354 453 6301
E: holarbiskup@kirkjan.is

Contact for ecumenical affairs The Revd Thorvaldur Vidisson, Bishops Secretary and Ecumenical Secretary, Bishop's Office, Laugavegur 31, 150 Reykjavík
T: 354 528 4000
F: 354 528 4099
E: biskupsritari@kirkjan.is

Chairman of committee for ecumenical affairs The Revd Hulda Hronn Helgardottir, Bishop's Office, Laugavegur 31, 150 Reykjavík
T: 354 528 4000
F: 354 528 409964 4201
E: hulda.hronn.helgadottir@kirkjan.is

ANGLICAN & PORVOO COMMUNIONS

The Church of Norway

From around AD 1000 Christianity was brought to Norway by missionaries both from the British Isles and from Germany. Central to the Christianizing of Norway was King Olav Haraldsson. After his death in 1030 he was venerated as St Olav, and his shrine in Nidaros Cathedral (Trondheim) was a centre of pilgrimage. Episcopal sees were established in Nidaros, Bergen, Oslo (by 1100), and in Stavanger (1125) and Hamar (1153). Part of the Province of Lund from 1103, Norway became a separate province when Nidaros was raised to an archiepiscopal see in 1153. In addition to the five Norwegian sees, the Province of Nidaros also included six further dioceses covering Iceland, the Faeroes, Greenland, the Shetland and Orkney Islands, the Hebrides and the Isle of Man. Under Olav IV (1380–87) Norway was united with Denmark.

The Norwegian Reformation of 1537 was imposed by the new King of Denmark, Christian III, with little evidence of popular enthusiasm. New bishops ('superintendents') were ordained to the sees of Nidaros, Bergen and Stavanger by Johannes Bugenhagen, the Superintendent of Wittenberg, in 1537, and Bugenhagen's Danish Church Order was extended to Norway in 1539. Of the pre-Reformation bishops, Bishop Hans Rev of Oslo alone accepted the Reformation, and returned to his see (to which that of Hamar had been united) as Superintendent in 1541. The diocesan structure had been retained, with four of the five historic sees, and the term 'bishop' soon replaced its Latin synonym 'superintendent', but until recent years neither Bishop Rev nor any other bishop consecrated in the historic succession of the laying on of hands participated in the consecration of future bishops. Nidaros ceased to be an archiepiscopal see.

In the eighteenth and nineteenth centuries, pietist movements became influential, but they remained within the Church of Norway, the membership of which still amounts to 77 per cent of the population.

The Church of Norway has an 116-member General Synod, consisting of the members of the eleven diocesan councils (including the bishops), three members representing clergy, laity and lay employees, the moderators of the Sami Church Council and the Council on Ecumenical and International Relations, and three non-voting representatives of the theological faculties. Its executive is the 15-member National Council, which has a lay chair person. Related central bodies include the Bishops' Conference, the Council on Ecumenical and International Relations and the Sámi Church Council.

On 21 May 2012, the Norwegian Parliament passed a constitutional amendment that granted the Church of Norway increased autonomy.

The Parliament's recent decisions loosen historical ties between institutions of State and the majority Lutheran Church, which date back to the sixteenth century. One major consequence is that the responsibility for the appointment of bishops of Church of Norway shifted from the state to the church. A 500-year state-church tradition of the King/the Government appointing bishops has ended. The 116-member General Synod comprising bishops, pastors and lay church members adopted the new order for appointing bishops on 12–17 April 2012. The first bishop appointment following the new order was made by the board of the National Council (15 members elected by the General Synod) in 2012. On 27 January 2013, Bishop Stein Reinertsen was consecrated as bishop of the diocese of Agder and Telemark.

Porvoo Agreement Contact Ms Beate Fagerli, Council on Ecumenical and International Relations, PB 799 – Sentrum, N-0106 Oslo
T: 47 23 08 12 74
F: 47 23 08 12 01
E: beate.fagerli@kirken.no

Presiding Bishop The Rt Revd Helga Haugland Byfuglien, Diocesan Centre, Archbishop's House, N-7013 Trondheim
T: 47 73 53 91 00
Or:

Church of Norway Bishop's Conference, PB 799 – Sentrum, N-0106 Oslo
T: 47 23 08 13 90
F: 47 23 08 12 01
E: bispemotet@kirken.no

AGDER AND TELEMARK
Bishop The Rt Revd Stein Reinertsen, Diocesan Centre, PB 208, 4662 Krisitansand S
T: 47 38 10 52 20
F: 47 38 10 51 21
E: agder.biskop@kirken.no

BJØRGVIN
Bishop The Rt Revd Halvor Nordhaug, Diocesan Centre, Strandgt 198, PB. 1960, Nordnes, 5018 Bergen
T: 47 55 30 64 70
F: 47 55 30 64 85
E: bjoergvin.biskop@kirken.no

BORG
Bishop The Rt Revd Atle Sommerfeldt, Diocesan Centre, Bjarne Aas gt 9, PB 403, N-1601 Fredrikstad
T: 47 69 30 79 00
F: 47 69 30 79 01
E: borg.bdr@kirken.no

HAMAR

Bishop The Rt Revd Solveig Fiske, Diocesan Centre, Folkestadgate 52, PB 172, N-2302 Hamar   *T:* 47 62 55 03 50
          F: 47 62 55 03 51
          E: hamar.bdr@kirken.no

MØRE

Bishop The Rt Revd Ingeborg Synøve Midtømme, Diocesan Centre, Moldetrappa 1, N-6415 Molde   *T:* 47 71 25 06 70
          F: 47 71 25 06 71
          E: moere.bdr@kirken.no

NIDAROS

Bishop The Rt Revd Tor Singsaas, Diocesan Centre, Archbishop's House, N-7013 Trondheim   *T:* 47 73 53 91 00
          F: 47 73 53 91 11
          E: nidaros.bdr@kirken.no

NORD-HÅLOGALAND

Bishop The Rt Revd Per Oskar Kjølaas, Diocesan Centre, Conrad Holmboesvei 20, PB 790, N-9258 Tromsø   *T:* 47 77 60 39 60/61
          F: 47 77 60 39 70
          E: nord-haalogaland.bdr@kirken.no

OSLO

Bishop The Rt Revd Ole Chr. M. Kvarme, Diocesan Centre, St Halvards plass 3, PB 9307, Gronland, N-0135 Oslo   *T:* 47 23 30 11 60
          F: 47 23 30 11 99
          E: oslo.bdr@kirken.no

SØR-HÅLOGALAND

Bishop The Rt Revd Tor Berger Jørgensen, Diocesan Centre, Tolder Holmersvei 11, N-8003 Bodø   *T:* 47 75 54 85 50
          F: 47 75 54 85 60
        E: soer-haalogaland.bdr@kirken.no

STAVANGER

Bishop The Rt Revd Erling J. Pettersen, Diocesan Centre, Domkirkeplassen 2, PB 629, N-4003 Stavanger   *T:* 47 51 84 62 70
          F: 47 51 84 62 71
          E: stavanger.bdr@kirken.no

TUNSBERG

Bishop The Rt Revd Laila Riksaasen Dahl, Diocesan Centre, Håkon 5.s gt, PB 1253, N-3105   *T:* 47 33 35 43 00
          F: 47 33 35 43 01
          E: tunsberg.bdr@kirken.no

ANGLICAN & PORVOO COMMUNIONS

The Church of Sweden

The first to preach the gospel in Sweden was St Ansgar (801–65), the first Archbishop of Hamburg-Bremen, but it was in the eleventh century that the systematic conversion of Sweden was begun, largely by missionaries from England. From 1104 the new Swedish dioceses formed part of the Nordic Province of Lund (which was Danish until 1658), but only until 1164, when Uppsala was raised to an archiepiscopal see. The most celebrated figure of the medieval Swedish Church is St Birgitta of Vadstena (1303–73), foundress of the Brigittine Order.

Under the Lutheran Reformers Olaus Petri (1493–1552) and his brother Laurentius (d. 1573), who became the first Lutheran archbishop in 1531, the Swedish Reformation was gradual, and moderate in character. The Augsburg Confession was adopted in 1593.

The eighteenth and nineteenth centuries saw both latitudinarian and pietist movements, and in the early twentieth century a strong high-church movement developed. Archbishop Nathan Söderblom (1866–1931), one of the leading figures of the Ecumenical Movement, used the concept of 'evangelical catholicity' to describe the Church of Sweden's position. The Conference of Bishops of the Anglican Communion adopted a resolution of altar and pulpit fellowship with the Church of Sweden in 1920. In 1997 Christina Odenberg became the Church of Sweden's first woman bishop, when she was appointed Bishop of Lund.

The Church of Sweden is governed by a General Synod with 251 members and a 15-member Central Board (chaired by the archbishop), together with the Bishops' Conference. The bishops attend the Synod, but are not members of it, although they have all the rights of members except the right to vote. They are *ex-officio* members of the Synod Committee on Church Doctrine.

A separation of Church and State was effected in the year 2000, a year which also was marked by the 1000-year celebration of Christian faith in Sweden at the well of Husaby in the Diocese of Skara.

Porvoo Agreement Contact The Revd Jenny Sjögreen, Chief Ecumenical Officer, Church of Sweden, S-751 70 Uppsala
          T: 46 18 16 95 20
       46 70 693 17 10 (Mobile)
          F: 46 18 16 95 38
       E: jenny.sjogreen@svenskakyrkan.se

(**Note:** *The dioceses here are arranged alphabetically. The order traditionally used in Sweden reflects the chronological seniority of the Swedish dioceses.*)

GÖTEBORG
Bishop The Rt Revd Dr Per Eckerdal, Stiftskansliet, Box 11937, SE-404 39 Göteborg
T: 46 31 771 30 00
F: 46 31 771 30 30
E: per.eckerdal@svenskakyrkan.se

HÄRNÖSAND
Bishop The Rt Revd Eva Nordung, Stiftskansliet, Box 94, SE-871 22 Härnösand
T: 46 611 254 00
F: 46 611 134 75
E: eva.nordung@svenskakyrkan.se

KARLSTAD
Bishop The Rt Revd Dr Sören Dalevi, Stiftskansliet, Box 186, SE-651 05 Karlstad
T: 46 54 17 24 00
F: 46 54 17 24 70
E: soren.dalevi@svenskakyrkan.se

LINKÖPING
Bishop The Rt Revd Dr Martin Modéus, Stiftskansliet, Box 1367, SE-581 31 Linköping
T: 46 13 24 26 00
F: 46 13 14 90 95
E: biskopen.linkoping@svenskakyrkan.se

LULEÅ
Bishop The Rt Revd Hans Stiglund, Stiftskansliet, Stationsgatan 40, SE-972 32 Luleå
T: 46 920 26 47 00
F: 46 920 26 47 21
E: hans.stiglund@svenskakyrkan.se

LUND
Bishop The Rt Revd Johan Tyrberg, Stiftskansliet, Box 32, SE-221 00 Lund
T: 46 46 35 87 00
F: 46 46 18 49 48
E: johan.tyrberg@svenskakyrkan.se

SKARA
Bishop The Rt Revd Åke Bonnier, Malmgatan 14, SE-532 32 Skara
T: 46 511 262 00
F: 46 511 262 70
E: ake.bonnier@svenskakyrkan.se

STOCKHOLM
Bishop The Rt Revd Eva Brunne, Stiftskansliet, Box 16306, SE-103 25 Stockholm
T: 46 8 508 940 00
F: 46 8 24 75 75
E: eva.brunne@svenskakyrkan.se

STRÄNGNÄS
Bishop The Rt Revd Dr Johan Dalman, Stiftskansliet, Box 84, SE-645 22 Strängnäs
T: 46 152 234 00
F: 46 152 234 56
E: strangnas.biskop@svenskakyrkan.se

UPPSALA
Archbishop The Most Revd Dr Antje Jackelén, SE-751 70 Uppsala
T: 46 18 16 95 00
F: 46 18 16 96 25
E: archbishop@svenskakyrkan.se

Bishop The Rt Revd Dr Ragnar Persenius, Box 1314, SE-751 43 Uppsala
T: 46 18 68 07 00
F: 46 18 12 87 62
E: ragnar.persenius@svenskakyrkan.se

VÄSTERÅS
Bishop The Rt Revd Dr Mikael Mogren, Stiftskansliet, V Kyrkogatan 9, SE-722 15 Västerås
T: 46 21 17 85 00
F: 46 21 12 93 10
E: mikael.mogren@svenskakyrkan.se

VÄXJÖ
Bishop The Rt Revd Dr Fredrik Modéus, Box 527, SE-351 06 Växjö
T: 46 470 77 38 00
F: 46 470 72 95 50
E: biskop.vaxjostift@svenskakyrkan.se

VISBY
Bishop The Rt Revd Sven-Bernhard Fast, Stiftskansliet, Box 1334, SE-621 24 Visby
T: 46 498 40 49 00
F: 46 498 21 01 03
E: sven-bernhard.fast@svenskakyrkan.se

BALTIC LUTHERAN CHURCHES

The Estonian Evangelical Lutheran Church

The conversion of Estonia to Christianity began at the end of the tenth century, and the first known bishop was consecrated in 1165. The mission was prosecuted by the Brethren of the Sword, an order founded in 1202 which merged with the Teutonic Order in 1237. In 1219 the Danes conquered the northern area and founded the capital Reval (Tallinn), which became an episcopal see within the Province of Lund. Further sees were established at Dorpat (Tartu) in 1224 and Hapsal (Saare-Lääne) in 1227, within the Province of Riga, the capital of Livonia, which included the southern part of modern Estonia. In some areas secular authority was in the hands of the bishops, while in others the Teutonic Order held sway. The entire area was very much under German dominance.

The Lutheran movement reached Estonia in 1523, and as early as the following year an assembly in Reval decided to adhere to the Reformation. Later in the century, however, the twin provinces of Estonia and Livonia became divided between neighbouring powers. Most of Estonia placed itself under Swedish rule in 1561, but Denmark ruled the island of Oesel (Saarema) from 1560 to 1645 and Livonia was annexed by Poland from 1561 to 1621. In Swedish Estonia, the Church was governed by a bishop and consistory, but Danish ecclesiastical law was introduced in Oesel, while Livonia came under the influence of the Counter-Reformation. Superintendents, rather than bishops, were appointed for these areas after they came under Swedish rule (in 1621 and 1645).

In 1710 both provinces came under Russian rule. In Estonia the office of bishop was replaced with that of superintendent. The consistories were chaired by laymen. In 1832 the Lutheran Churches of all three Baltic provinces were united with Russia's German-speaking Lutheran Church into a Russian Lutheran Church, with a General Consistory in St Petersburg. Each province (and – until 1890 – Reval, Oesel and Riga separately) had its own general superintendent and consistory. The University of Dorpat (Tartu), originally founded in 1632, was refounded in 1802. As the only Protestant theological faculty in the Russian Empire, it was of great importance. Throughout the period up to 1918 the clergy were German, like the ruling elite. The Moravian Church, which was active in Estonia and Livonia from 1736, enjoyed considerable influence over the Estonian peasantry, and by 1854 there were 276 Moravian prayer halls. However, the Moravian authorities blocked the development of this movement into a separate Moravian Church, and the Moravians' adherents remained within the Lutheran Church.

In 1918 Estonia and the Estonian northern part of Livonia became an independent state. The Church too became independent. It remained united, having both German and Estonian clergy and members. The office of bishop was immediately restored, the first bishop being consecrated in 1921 by the Archbishop of Uppsala and a Finnish bishop.

Estonia's independent existence lasted little more than 20 years, however. In 1940 it was occupied by the Red Army. German occupation followed, but Soviet rule was restored in 1944. Archbishop Kópp, who had remained unconsecrated because the war prevented bishops from other countries travelling to Estonia, went into exile with 70 other clergy and tens of thousands of church members. As a result of this the Estonian Evangelical Lutheran Church Abroad was born. Of the clergy who remained, one-third were eventually deported to Siberia. Not until 1968 was it possible for an archbishop to be consecrated, although the first post-war Archbishop had already been elected in 1949.

In 1988, Estonia began to move towards independence, which was achieved in 1991. This was accompanied by a remarkable blossoming of church life. The Theological Faculty at Tartu, which had been dissolved by the Soviet authorities, was reopened. The Theological Institute of the EELC in Tallinn, which was set up after the war, also continues its work.

The Estonian Evangelical Lutheran Church still forms one diocese with 167 parishes and congregations, headed by an Archbishop and three Suffragan Bishops. It is governed by a General Synod, the executive organ of which is the nine-member Consistory.

Porvoo Agreement Contact The Revd Tauno Teder, Nikolai 22, 80010 Pärnu
T: 372 56 335 750
E: tauno.teder@eelk.ee

Archbishop of Estonia The Most Revd Urmas Viilma, Consistory of the EELC, Kirikuplats 3, 10130 Tallinn
T: 372 6 27 73 50
F: 372 6 27 73 52
E: konsistoorium@eelk.ee
W: www.eelk.ee

The Evangelical Lutheran Church of Lithuania

Not until 1387 was an episcopal see established in Vilnius, following the baptism the previous year of Grand Duke Jogaila (whose coronation as King of Poland inaugurated a union lasting until 1795), and it was 1418 before the inhabitants of German-dominated Samogitia (covering much of present-day Lithuania) were forced to accept baptism.

A Lutheran congregation was founded in Vilnius as early as 1521, but persecution forced the Lithuanian Reformer Martin Mazvydas to flee to Königsberg. In time the Lithuanian nobility established the Reformed faith on their estates, while the numerous German merchants and craftsmen established Lutheran congregations in the towns from the 1550s. Until the early nineteenth century, the Lutheran Church continued to be a German and urban minority Church.

Sigismund Vasa (1587–1632) successfully restored Roman Catholicism as the religion of the people, and subsequent anti-Protestant policies meant that by 1775, when religious freedom was granted, just 30 Reformed and five Lutheran congregations remained (except those in Prussian-ruled Tauragé/Tauroggen).

In 1795 most of Lithuania was ceded to Russia, and Lithuania's Lutheran congregations were placed under the Consistory of Courland (now southern Latvia). Immigration of Lutheran Letts, Germans and Lithuanians from East Prussia produced new Lutheran congregations, especially in the countryside. The pastors (only nine in 1918) were all Germans.

At independence in 1918, Lithuania's population included 75,000 Lutherans, of whom roughly 30,000 were Germans, 30,000 Lithuanians and 15,000 Letts. In 1920 separate synods had to be formed for the three linguistic groups, and for much of the inter-war period tension between them paralysed the Lutheran Church. By 1939, however, there were 55 congregations with 33 pastors. To these should be added the separate Lutheran Church of the Prussian *Memelgebiet*, which Lithuania annexed in 1923. By 1939 this had 135,000 members (the majority German) in 32 parishes, served by 39 pastors.

Lithuanian Lutheranism was soon to be decimated. In 1941, following the 1940 Soviet annexation of Lithuania, most of the German population, together with a large number of Lithuanian Lutherans, emigrated to Germany. In Memelland and the Vilnius area, both reintegrated into Lithuania and thus the Soviet Union in 1945, the picture was even more stark. All but 30,000 inhabitants fled, while the pastor of the historic Lutheran church in Vilnius emigrated with his entire congregation.

A provisional Lutheran Consistory found itself responsible for 20,000 Lithuanians and Letts in Lithuania proper, together with just 15,000 Lithuanians in Klaipéda (Memelland). There were no pastors in Klaipéda and only six in the rest of the country, three of whom were soon banished to Siberia. After Stalin's death in 1953 and a first post-war synod in 1955, the structures of church life were gradually restored, but several thousand more Protestants emigrated between 1957 and 1965. At a second synod in 1970, Jonas Kalvanas, the only pastor left who had studied theology at university (he was ordained in 1940), was elected to chair the Consistory. It was with his consecration as Bishop by the Archbishop of Estonia in 1976 that his church gained the historic episcopate. He was succeeded in 1995 by his son and namesake, whose early death in 2003 left the see vacant until the consecration in June 2004 of Bishop Mindaugas Sebutis.

In 2014 the Lutheran Church had 56 congregations, with about 20,000 communicant members and twenty-nine clergy.

Porvoo Agreement Contact The Revd Jonas Liorancas   *E:* jliorancas@yahoo.com

Bishop of the Evangelical Lutheran Church of Lithuania The Rt Revd Mindaugas Sabutis, Vokieciu 20, LT-01130 Vilnius

T: +370 687 95417;
+370 5 2626745 (office)
F: +370 5 2123792
E: konsistorija@lelb.lt
W: http://www.liuteronai.lt/eng

The Latvian Evangelical Lutheran Church Abroad

This church began work in 1945 when the first Archbishop of the Evangelical Lutheran Church of Latvia, Prof. Teodors Grinbergs, with nearly all the members of the Church council and half of the pastors and about 200,000 Latvian refugees were living in Western and Northern Europe. After 1990 a close relationship between the Latvian Evangelical Lutheran Church Abroad (LELCA) and the existing Church in Latvia was established. Nevertheless, both Churches are independent, mostly due to different positions in some areas of theology, for example on the ordination of women. Half of the 70 pastors of LELCA, serving 120 congregations with over 25,000 members, are female, and the bylaws of Church say, that all duties can be fulfilled by male or female.

The Archbishop at the time of signing of the Porvoo Declaration was The Most Revd Elmars Ernsts Rozitis, consecrated in 1994 in historic succession by Bishop Henrik Svennungsson of the Stockholm diocese of the Church of Sweden. The current Archbishop is The Most Revd Lauma Zuševics. Due to the difficult economic situation in Latvia many Latvians now are emigrating to Western Europe. This represents a huge challenge for church. The work of providing support for Latvians abroad is done in close cooperation with the embassies and consulates of the Republic of Latvia.

LELCA is a founding member of the Lutheran World Federation and a member of WCC and CEC. The archbishop is assisted by an 18-member Church council with equal numbers of clergy and lay members, which has executive powers.

The Lutheran Church in Great Britain

The Lutheran Church in Great Britain (LCiGB) is a very diverse church, worshipping in seven languages (English, Polish, Tigrinya, Amharic, Swahili, Mandarin and Cantonese). The LCiGB has a long history of serving immigrant communities in the UK often offering a 'home away from home'. In serving a variety of cultures and traditions, LCiGB member churches have been able to conduct worship services that include everything from Swahili and *a cappella* choirs to Bach organ preludes. The rich diversity of the LCiGB has created strong connections with national Lutheran churches around the world such as the Evangelical Lutheran Church in Tanzania and the Evangelical Lutheran Church in America.

In 2009, the LCiGB had the honour of installing the first woman bishop to serve in a British church, The Rt Revd Jana Jeruma-Grinberga. In 2013 The Rt Revd Martin Lind replaced Bishop Jana.

ANGLICAN & PORVOO COMMUNIONS

NON-SIGNATORY CHURCHES

The Evangelical Lutheran Church of Latvia

The Church of Latvia has not yet voted on the Porvoo Declaration.

Archbishop of Riga and Latvia The Most Revd Janis Vanags, M.Pils 4, LV 1050, Riga
T: 371 6722 5406
E: lelb@lelb.lv / arhibiskaps@lelb.lv

Porvoo Agreement Contact The Revd Ainars Rendors, M.Pils 4, Riga, LV 1050, Latvia
E: ainars.rendors@lelb.lv

Ecumenical   PART 5

ECUMENICAL

INTRODUCTION

The Church of England is committed to the search for the full, visible unity of the Christian Church, and to the bodies which promote this at the local, intermediate, national, European and world levels. The Council for Christian Unity advises the General Synod and the Archbishops' Council on inter-church relations and acts as the principal channel of communication between the General Synod and the churches and ecumenical bodies, at the national and international levels. The CCU engages in informal ecumenical dialogue and implements any decisions of the General Synod regarding formal conversations.

ECUMENICAL CANONS

Canon B 43 (Of Relations with Other Churches) and Canon B 44 (Of Local Ecumenical Projects) make provision for sharing in worship and ministry with other churches. Full background information is given in *The Ecumenical Relations Code of Practice* (Church House, 1989). This paper, with its supplements, is now available electronically from http://www.churchof england.org/about-us/work-other-churches/ resources/the-ecumenical-canons.aspx or by contacting cu@churchofengland.org. A range of useful introductory resource papers is also available from the same address.

CHURCHES DESIGNATED UNDER THE ECUMENICAL RELATIONS MEASURE

The Church of England's legal office maintains the list of the churches that have been designated by the Archbishops of Canterbury and York as churches to which the Church of England (Ecumenical Relations) Measure, and thus Canons B 43 and B 44, apply. An up-to-

date list is maintained on the Church of England web site at https://www. churchofengland.org/about-us/structure/ churchlawlegis/canons/supplementary- material.aspx. The following are currently listed:

The Baptist Union
The Methodist Church
The Moravian Church
The Roman Catholic Church in England and Wales
The United Reformed Church
The Congregational Federation
The International Ministerial Council of Great Britain
The Lutheran Council of Great Britain
The Greek Orthodox Archdiocese of Thyateira and Great Britain (Ecumenical Patriarchate)
The Council of African and Afro-Caribbean Churches
The Free Church of England
The Southam Road Evangelical Church Banbury
Member Churches of the Evangelical Church in Germany (EKD)
The Assemblies of God in Great Britain and Ireland
The New Testament Church of God
The Russian Patriarchal Church of Great Britain being the Orthodox Diocese of Sourozh (Moscow Patriarchate)
The Independent Methodist Churches
The Reformed Church of Alsace and Lorraine
The Reformed Church of France
The Council of Oriental Orthodox Churches of Great Britain and the Republic of Ireland
The Church of the Nazarene British Isles South District
The Church of Scotland

Churches Together in England

Churches Together in England is in association with Churches Together in Britain and Ireland. Its basis is as follows:

Churches Together in England unites in pilgrimage those Churches in England which, acknowledging God's revelation in Christ, confess the Lord Jesus Christ as God and Saviour according to the Scriptures, and, in obedience to God's will and in the power of the Holy Spirit, commit themselves:

– to seek a deepening of their communion with Christ and with one another in the Church, which is his body; and
– to fulfil their mission to proclaim the Gospel by common witness and service in the world to the glory of the one God, Father, Son and Holy Spirit.

The Presidents of Churches Together in England are: The Archbishop of Canterbury, the Archbishop of Westminster and The

Revd Michael Heaney; Archbishop Gregorios (Oecumenical Patriarchate, Archdiocese of Thyateira and GB), who meet together quarterly.

It has forty-two Member Churches:

Antiochian Orthodox Church
Apostolic Pastoral Congress
Armenian Orthodox Church
Assemblies of God
Baptist Union of Great Britain
Cherubim and Seraphim Council of Churches
Church of England
Church of God of Prophecy
Church of Scotland (in England)
Churches in Communities International
Congregational Federation
Coptic Orthodox Church
Council for African and Caribbean Churches
Council of Oriental Orthodox Christian Churches
Council of Lutheran Churches
Elim Pentecostal Church
Evangelical Lutheran Churches
Exarchate of Orthodox Parishes of the Russian Tradition (Ecumenical Partriarchate)
Free Church of England
Ground Level
Ichthus Christian Fellowship
Indian Orthodox Church
Evangelische Synod Deutscher Sprache in Grossbritannien
Independent Methodist Churches
International Ministerial Council of Great Britain
Joint Council for Anglo-Caribbean Churches
Malankara Orthodox Syrian Church (Indian Orthodox)
Mar Thoma Church
Methodist Church
Moravian Church
New Testament Assembly
New Testament Church of God
Oecumenical Patriarchate (Archdiocese of Thyateira and GB)
Pioneer
Redeemed Christian Church of God
Religious Society of Friends
Roman Catholic Church
Russian Orthodox Church
Salvation Army
Seventh Day Adventists (observer)
Transatlantic and Pacific Alliance of Churches,
United Reformed Church
Wesleyan Holiness Church

The Religious Society of Friends has membership under a clause designed for 'any Church or Association of Churches which on principle has no credal statements in its tradition'.

All substantive decisions are taken by these Member Churches.

Churches Together in England encourages its Member Churches to work together nationally, and provides various means for this purpose. There is an *Enabling Group*, which meets two times a year. Its Convenor is Bishop Christopher Foster and its Deputy Convenor Ruth Bottoms. There is a *Forum* of 300 members, which meets every three years. Its Moderator is Bishop Doyé Agama and its Deputy Moderator Ruth Gee.

- There are 6 *Coordinating Groups* (*see below*).
- There are also a large number of informal or as yet not formally recognized groups and networks.
- Churches Together in England encourages its Member Churches to work together locally. To enable this most counties and metropolitan areas have established ecumenical councils and officers, whose task is to foster and encourage all sorts of ecumenical work locally within their areas. The main task of the two Field Officers (*see below*) is to support those working in counties and metropolitan areas.
- Churches Together in England publishes an ecumenical e-news monthly.

General Secretary The Revd Dr David Cornick, Churches Together in England, 27 Tavistock Square, London WC1H 9HH
Tel: 020 7529 8131
Web: www.cte.org.uk
email: firstname.surname@cte.org.uk

Finance Officer Mr Stephen Cutler (*same address*)

Education Officer Ms Sarah Lane Cawte (*same address*)

Training, Resourcing and Events Jenny Bond (*same address*)   *Tel:* 07708 929022

Pentecostal and Multicultural Relations Bishop Joe Aldred (*same address*)   *Tel:* 07775 632288

Evangelisation, Mission and Media Captain Jim Currin (*same address*)   *Tel:* 07837 973214

Inter Faith Relations Celia Blackden (*same address*)   *Tel:* 07926 666218

Administrator Lorraine Shannon (*same address*)
Tel: 020 7529 8131

COORDINATING GROUPS
GROUP FOR EVANGELIZATION
Secretary Captain Jim Currin (*address see above*)
Tel: 07837 973214
email: jim.currin@cte.org.uk

CHURCHES COMMITTEE FOR HOSPITAL CHAPLAINCY
Secretary The Revd Debbie Hodge
Tel: 020 3651 8337
email: debbie.hodge@freechurches.org.uk

CHURCHES COMMUNITY WORK ALLIANCE
Secretary Nils Chittenden, St Chad's College, North Bailey, Durham DH1 3RH
Tel: 0191 374 7342
email: nilsc@ccwa.org.uk

ECUMENICAL LIAISON GROUP FOR MINISTERIAL EDUCATION
Secretary The Revd Fiona Thomas, United Reformed Church, 86 Tavistock Place, London WC1H 9RT
email: fiona.thomas@urc.org.uk

THEOLOGY AND UNITY GROUP
Secretary The Revd Dr David Cornick (*CTE address see above*)
Tel: 020 7529 8131
email: david.cornick@cte.org.uk

CHURCHES RURAL GROUP
Convenor Barry Osborne
email: barry@ruralmissions.org.uk

There are also three *Agencies*:

CHRISTIAN ENQUIRY AGENCY
Administrator Patricia Flynn, Christian Enquiry Agency, Freepost WC2947, South Croydon CR2 8UZ
Tel: 020 8144 7177
email: cea@deogloria.co.uk

CHRISTIAN AID
PO Box 100, London SE1 7RL
Tel: 020 7620 4444
email: info@christian-aid.org

CAFOD
Director Mr Chris Bain, 2 Romero Close, Stockwell Road, London SW9 9TY
Tel: 020 7733 7900
email: hqcafod@cafod.org.uk

The following are *Bodies in Association* with Churches Together in England:

Action by Christians Against Torture
Association of Inter-Church Families
Bible Society
Christian Council on Ageing
Christian Council on Approaches to Defence and Disarmament
Christian Education
Christians Aware
Church Action on Poverty
Churches Alert to Sex Trafficking Across Europe (CHASTE)
Churches Community Work Alliance (CCWA)
Churches East–West Europe Relations Network (CEWERN)
Churches for All
College of Preachers
Community of Aidan and Hilda
Corrymeela Community
Ecumenical Council for Corporate Responsibility
Ecumenical Society of the Blessed Virgin Mary
Faith in Europe
Feed the Minds
Fellowship of St Alban and St Sergius
Fellowship of Reconciliation
Focolare Movement
Housing Justice
Industrial Mission Association
International Ecumenical Fellowship
Iona Community
Irish School of Ecumenics
L'Arche
Living Stones
MODEM
Oikocredit
Retreat Association
Society for Ecumenical Studies
Student Christian Movement
William Temple Foundation
Women's World Day of Prayer
Young Men's Christian Association
Y Care International

ECUMENICAL

Intermediate County Bodies and Area Ecumenical Councils

BEDFORDSHIRE
CHURCHES TOGETHER IN BEDFORDSHIRE
Anita Nancollas   email: ct.beds@gmail.com

BERKSHIRE
CHURCHES TOGETHER IN BERKSHIRE
Louise Cole, 14 Hertford Close, Woose Hill, Wokingham, Berkshire, RG41 3BH
Tel: 0118 977 6437
email: ctberks@sky.com

BIRMINGHAM (*see also* **West Midlands**)
BIRMINGHAM CHURCHES TOGETHER
The Revd Dr Colin Marsh, St George's Community Hub, Great Hampton Row, Newtown, Birmingham, B19 3JG
Tel: 0121 236 3966
email: office@birminghamchurches.org.uk

BLACK COUNTRY (*see also* **Staffordshire**)
BLACK COUNTRY CHURCHES ENGAGED (BCCE)
Graham Sim
email: graham_sim1@ btinternet.com

BRISTOL
GREATER CHURCHES TOGETHER IN GREATER BRISTOL
Jon Doble, 162 Pennywell Lane, Bristol BS5 0TX
Tel: 0117 955 7430
email: jon@ccisr.org.uk

BUCKINGHAMSHIRE
CHURCHES TOGETHER IN BUCKINGHAMSHIRE (EXCEPT MILTON KEYNES)
Barrie Cheetham   email: barrie@bern
Web: wodeforest.org.uk

CAMBRIDGESHIRE
CAMBRIDGESHIRE ECUMENICAL COUNCIL
Mrs Priscilla Barlow, Silverlands, Church St, Litlington, Royston, Herts, SG8 0QB
Tel: 01763 852841
email: priscilla.barlow@keme.co.uk

CHESHIRE
CHURCHES TOGETHER IN CHESHIRE
Andrew Taylor   email: ceo.ctic@gmail.com

CORNWALL
CHURCHES TOGETHER IN CORNWALL
David Smith, Chyreene Warra, Rosehill, Marazion, Cornwall, TR17 0HB
Tel: 01736 719 432
email: ses.dhs@hotmail.co.uk

COVENTRY
See **Warwickshire**

CUMBRIA
CHURCHES TOGETHER IN CUMBRIA
Helen Boothroyd   email: htctic@tiscali.co.uk

Ruth Harvey, Croslands, Beacon Street, Penrith, CA11 7TZ   Tel: 074 0363 8339
email: rctic@phoencoop.coop

DERBYSHIRE AND NOTTINGHAMSHIRE
CHURCHES TOGETHER IN DERBYSHIRE AND NOTTINGHAMSHIRE
Vacancy

DEVON
CHURCHES TOGETHER IN DEVON
Sue Macbeth
email: churchestogetherdevon@gmail.com

DORSET
CHURCHES TOGETHER IN DORSET
Katja Babei   email: ctdorset@clara.net

DURHAM
See **North-East England**

Bill Offler, 42 John Street North, Meadowfield, Durham, DH7 8RS   Tel: 0191 378 2883
email: william.offler@virgin.net

ESSEX AND LONDON, EAST
CHURCHES TOGETHER IN ESSEX AND EAST LONDON CLG
Vacancy

GLOUCESTERSHIRE
GLOUCESTERSHIRE CHURCHES TOGETHER
The Revd Dr Alison Evans, Britannia Cottage, High Street, Kings Stanley, Stonehouse, GL10 3JD   Tel: 01453 824034
email: malcolm.alison@btinternet.com

GUERNSEY
CHURCHES TOGETHER IN GUERNSEY
Mr Roy Sarre, Le Campère, Les Villets, Forest, Guernsey, Channel Islands, GY8 0HP
Tel: 01481 263930

HAMPSHIRE AND ISLE OF WIGHT
CHURCHES TOGETHER IN HAMPSHIRE AND THE ISLE OF WIGHT
Andrew Wood, 4 The Chase, Thornbury Wood, Chandler's Ford, Eastleigh, Hants, SO53 5AZ
email: Andrew.wood4@btopenworld.com

HEREFORDSHIRE
CHURCHES TOGETHER IN HEREFORDSHIRE
Anna Nugent
email: herefordshireceo@gmail.com

HERTFORDSHIRE
CHURCHES TOGETHER IN HERTFORDSHIRE
Callan Slippe, 138 Parkway, Welwyn Garden City, Herts AL8 6HP   Tel: 01707 339 242
email: facilitator@ctherts.org.uk

ISLE OF MAN
CHURCHES TOGETHER IN MAN
Mrs Mavis Matthewman, Tarnalforn, 12 Ballagarey Road, Glen Vine, Isle of Man, IM4 4EA   *Tel:* 01624 851693

ISLE OF WIGHT
see **Hampshire**

JERSEY
CHRISTIANS TOGETHER IN JERSEY
Martin Dryden, Monte Urbe House, La Rue de la Blinerie, St Clements, Jersey JE2 6QT
email: martin@mont-ube.net

KENT
CHURCHES TOGETHER IN KENT
Chris Ruddle
email: CTKentHub@yahoo.co.uk

LANCASHIRE
CHURCHES TOGETHER IN LANCASHIRE
Anton Muller
email: antonmuller@ ctlancashire.org.uk

The Revd Steven Hughes (Inter Faith Officer), 69 Liverpool Old Road, Much Hoole, Preston, Lancs, PR4 4RB   *Tel:* 01772 612267
email: steven.hughes@ctlancashire.org.uk

LEICESTERSHIRE
CHURCHES TOGETHER IN LEICESTERSHIRE
Vic Allsop, c/o 14 Church Lane, Hoby, Melton Mowbray, Leicestershire, LE14 3DR
Tel: 01664 434 697
email: cedo.ctil@fsmail.net

LINCOLNSHIRE
CHURCHES TOGETHER IN ALL LINCOLNSHIRE
Mel Parkin (administrator), c/o Church House, The Old Palace, Lincoln, LN2 1PU
Tel: 01522 504071
email: ctal@lincoln.anglican.org

LONDON, EAST
See **Essex**
EAST LONDON CHURCH LEADERS GROUP
Vacancy

LONDON, NORTH
See **North Thames**

LONDON, NORTH THAMES
CHURCHES TOGETHER NORTH THAMES
Wendie Heywood   *email:* office@ctnt.org.uk

LONDON, SOUTH
CHURCHES TOGETHER IN SOUTH LONDON
John Richardson, c/o St John's Vicarage, Secker Street, London, SE1 9UF
Tel: 01462 422502
email: john@ctslondon.org.uk

LONDON, WEST
Vacancy

MANCHESTER, GREATER
GREATER MANCHESTER CHURCHES TOGETHER
St John's Rectory, Railton Terrace, Moston, Manchester, M9 4WE   *Tel:* 0161 205 8838

Bishop Doyé Agama (Acting GMCT contact)
email: doye@hotmail.com

Seifa Afiesimama (Administrator)
email: admin@apostolicpastors.info

MERSEYSIDE
CHURCHES TOGETHER IN THE MERSEYSIDE REGION
The Revd Ian Smith, Quaker Meeting House, 22 School Lane, Liverpool, L1 3BT
Tel: 0151 709 0125
email: office@ctmr.org.uk

MILTON KEYNES
MISSION PARTNERSHIP OF THE MILTON KEYNES CHRISTIAN COUNCIL
John Robertson, c/o Christian Foundation, The Square, Aylesbury Street, Wolverton, MK12 5HX   *Tel:* 01908 311310
email: admin@missionpartnership.org.uk

NORFOLK
NORFOLK AND WAVENEY CHURCHES TOGETHER
Simon Wilson, The Rectory, Guist Road, Foulsham, Norfolk, NR20 5RZ
Tel: 01352 683 275
email: simon.wilson@norwich.anglican.org

NORTH-EAST ENGLAND
NORTH EAST CHRISTIAN CHURCHES TOGETHER (NECCT)
Bill Offler, 42 John Street North, Meadowfield, Durham, DH7 8RS   *Tel:* 01865 723 801
email: william.offler@virgin.net

NOTTINGHAMSHIRE
See **Derbyshire**

OXFORDSHIRE
CHURCHES TOGETHER IN OXFORDSHIRE
The Revd Peter Ball, c/o Cowley Road Methodist Church, Jeune Street, Oxford, OX4 1BN   *Tel:* 01865 723801
email: ctoshire@gmail.com

PETERBOROUGH
see **Shire and Soke**

SHIRE AND SOKE
CHURCHES TOGETHER IN NORTHAMPTONSHIRE & PETERBOROUGH
Gill Crow (Northamptonshire)
email: gillcrow@shireandsoke.org.uk

Philip Hutchinson (Peterborough)
email: philiphutchinson@ shireandsoke.org.uk

ECUMENICAL

SHROPSHIRE (*Except* Telford)
CHURCHES TOGETHER IN SHROPSHIRE
Mr Ged Cliffe, Fern Villa, Four Crosses, Llanymynech, Powys SY22 6PR
Tel: 01691 831374
email: gerard.cliffe@btinternet.com

SOMERSET
SOMERSET CHURCHES TOGETHER
Gabrielle Grace, 3 Champford Mews, Wellington, TA21 8JW   *Tel:* 07811 108 218
email: sctogether@phonecoop.coop

STAFFORDSHIRE
CHURCHES LINKED ACROSS STAFFS & THE POTTERIES (CLASP) (AS BLACK COUNTRY)
Graham Sim
email: graham_sim1@btinternet.com

SUFFOLK
CHURCHES TOGETHER IN SUFFOLK
Julie Mansfield, Applegarth, Wilmslow Avenue, Woodbridge, Suffolk, IP12 4HW
Tel: 01394 384370
email: jmmansfield@ homecall.co.uk

SURREY
CHURCHES TOGETHER IN SURREY
The Revd Susan Loveday, 10 Abbey Gardens, Chertsey, Surrey, KT16 8RQ
Tel: 01932 566920
email: sue.loveday.ctsurrey@lineone.net

SUSSEX
CHURCHES TOGETHER IN SUSSEX
Mr Ian Chisnall, 85 Hollingbury Rise, Brighton, BN1 7HH
Tel: 07976 811654 (Mobile)
email: ianpchisnall@aol.com

SWINDON
SWINDON CHURCHES TOGETHER
Vacancy

TELFORD
TELFORD CHRISTIAN COUNCIL
Andy Smith, Meeting Point House, Southwater Square, Town Centre, Telford, TF3 4HS
Tel: 01952 291904
email: andysmith@ telfordchristiancouncil.co.uk

WARWICKSHIRE
CHURCHES TOGETHER IN COVENTRY & WARWICKSHIRE
Christine Craven, 310 Holyhead Road, Coventry, Warwickshire, CV5 8JP
Tel: 02476 599454
email: christine.craven9@btinternet.com

WAVENEY
See **Norfolk**

WILTSHIRE
WILTSHIRE CHURCHES TOGETHER
Liz Overthrow
email: liz.overthrow@btinternet.com

WORCESTERSHIRE
CHURCHES TOGETHER IN WORCESTERSHIRE
The Revd David Ryan, 4 Daty Croft, Home Meadow, Worcester, WR4 0JB
Tel: 01905 616109
email: dpryangb@aol.com

YORKSHIRE, EAST AND HULL
KINGSTON UPON HULL & EAST YORKSHIRE CHURCHES TOGETHER
Vacancy, Key Churches Together, Methodist Central Hall, King Edward Street, Hull, HU1 3SQ
Tel: 01482 328196

YORKSHIRE, NORTH YORK MOORS
NORTH YORK MOORS CHURCHES TOGETHER
Barbara Burke, York & Hull District Office, 28 The Green, Acomb, York, YO26 5LR
email: northyorkschurch@hotmail.co.uk

YORKSHIRE, SOUTH
CHURCHES TOGETHER IN SOUTH YORKSHIRE
Erica Dunmow, CTSY Office, C/O SCEC, Montgomery Hall, Surrey Street, Sheffield, S1 2LG   *email:* emdo@ctsy.yahoo.co.uk

YORKSHIRE, VALE OF YORK
ENVOY (ECUMENICAL NETWORK IN THE VALE OF YORK)
Nigel Currey, 17 Mayfield Drive, Brayton, Selby, North Yorkshire, YO8 9JZ
Tel: 01757 704892
email: ncurrey1@talktalk.net

YORKSHIRE, WEST
WEST YORKSHIRE ECUMENICAL COUNCIL
Clive Barrett, Hinsley Hall, 62 Headingley Lane, Leeds, LS6 2BX   *Tel:* 0113 261 8053
Fax: 0113 261 8054
email: clivebarrett@wyec.co.uk

Churches Together in Britain and Ireland

Churches Together in Britain and Ireland (CTBI) is an umbrella body through which the Churches co-operate on common issues. It works closely with the other 'Churches Together' bodies, which focus separately on England, Wales, Scotland and Ireland. Together they have an important role to witness to the essential unity of the Christian movement. CTBI's core tasks are providing 'structured ecumenical space' for meeting and encounter, facilitating shared study on common issues and fostering relationships – among the Churches and between the Churches and the wider world.

Churches Together in Britain and Ireland (formerly the Council of Churches for Britain and Ireland and the direct successor of the British Council of Churches) was established by its member Churches to enable them to work together for the advancement of the Christian religion, the relief of poverty, the advancement of education and any other charitable purpose. It seeks to further these objects by providing opportunities for representatives of the Churches from the four nations to meet together and to share some of their resources in the pursuance of jointly agreed activities.

Following a review of its work, Churches Together in Britain and Ireland has become an agency serving the churches through the four National Ecumenical Instruments. As a separate charitable company, limited by guarantee, CTBI now relates to the churches, as members, through the ecumenical structures of the nations. It is now more relational and its focus is on working agreed common themes across the different work areas described below. The current themes are:

  – environment/climate change
  – migration and the movements of people
  – culture, identity and the public space

Our principal activities and Networks are:

- Witnessing to and working towards the visible unity of the Christian Churches and providing opportunities for representatives of the Churches to meet and to plan their work together. A **Senior Representatives Forum**, attended by delegates from all member churches and bodies in association, is held in the spring of each year. An annual **Networking Conference** brings together the various Networks which comprise members of the member Churches, Agencies and Bodies in Association.

- Working on the Churches' behalf on issues of racial justice through the **Churches Racial Justice Network** (formerly known as CCRJ, the Churches' Commission for Racial Justice). The Racial Justice Network is a major vehicle for the Churches' engagement with the complex work of racial justice throughout Ireland, Scotland, Wales and England. Central to the work is the Racial Justice Fund, which supports a wide range of grassroots organizations. These funded groups are invited into a dynamic partnership designed to build their capacity for effective action and to provide first rate information and experience for use in education, lobbying and campaigning. **Racial Justice Sunday**, celebrated ecumenically on the second Sunday in September, gives an opportunity for vital educational work with churches and congregations and raises the media profile of the work of racial justice. Other projects include Capacity Building for Black Churches, the Bail Circle and the Peers project. The recent publication of *Migration Principles*, which in turn is building on the work of *Asylum Principles*, seeks to promote an active discussion and programme around the complex issue of migration. Working with other departments within CTBI, the Racial Justice team are taking forward Migration as a major theme.

- Through the **Churches Network for Mission (CNM)**, seeking to serve and assist churches, agencies and the four national ecumenical instruments in our common task of participating in God's mission in the world. GMN is a key point of contact with world ecumenical mission bodies, particularly the World Council of Churches and the Council of European Churches. GMN's current projects include:

  – **Mission Theology Advisory Group**, offering expertise from around the four nations in Mission theology. Publications and web resources are being produced to support the ongoing work of the churches' mission in new contexts.
  – **China** – the China Desk provides a dedicated expert centre maintaining a wide range of relationships in China and undertaking research and analysis on Chinese affairs. It co-ordinates the work of the China Forum which acts as a bridge to Chinese Christians, both Catholic and Protestant, with partnership maintained through a variety of on-going projects.

ECUMENICAL

- Through the **Churches Inter Religious Network**, working with the Churches to engage effectively in relations and dialogue with other faiths in Britain and Ireland. The Network is a point of reference for the Churches which facilitates an exchange of information and experience among Christians about inter faith relations, whilst enabling critical reflection on the religiously and socially plural society of the four nations. In Scotland, it works through the Churches' Agency for Inter Faith Relations in Scotland. The Network seeks to fulfil its aims by responding to requests by the Churches on inter faith issues, monitoring inter faith relations in the four nations, nurturing links between Christians working in this field, pooling the theological resources of the Churches for ministry and witness in this area, and producing appropriate written or other material to help the Churches. In addition CTBI is a member body, on behalf of the Churches, of the Inter Faith Network for the United Kingdom, which provides a national forum for people from the main faith communities to meet, discuss and share.
- Through the **Churches International Student Network**, supporting international students by networking, education and communication among the Churches and between them, government and other agencies specializing in international students' affairs. The Network seeks to link the varied work of the many church agencies among students and supports the Churches in their response to the needs of international students. It initiated and maintains co-funding from the Foreign Office for denominational and ecumenical scholarships, administers World Council of Churches scholarships in Britain and Ireland and operates a hardship fund for international students for which it raises funding.
- Developing and publishing for the Churches **resources for study and prayer**. This includes printed and web based materials for the Week of Prayer for Christian Unity, which is observed each year from 18 to 25 January, as well as a Lent study programme.
- Through the **Church and Public Issues Network**, supporting and resourcing the Churches in their work on political, social and ethical issues, paying particular attention to:

  - public policy agendas of Westminster, and also Cardiff, Edinburgh, Belfast, Dublin and Brussels
  - the churches' engagement with contemporary social issues

  - moral/ethical issues, especially where there is a distinctive Christian contribution to be made

The Church and Society Forum takes a lead in networking those who work on church and society issues across the four nations, and in sharing and disseminating information and expertise. It represents the Churches jointly, where appropriate, to Government bodies, other agencies and elsewhere. It has one main residential meeting each year, with others as the need arises.

Office 39 Eccleston Square, London SW1V 1BX
Tel: 020 3794 2288
Fax: 020 7901 4894
email: info@ctbi.org.uk
Web: www.ctbi.org.uk

STAFF
Canon Robert Fyffe, *General Secretary*
The Revd Peter Colwell, *Deputy General Secretary*
Christine Elliott *Director of International Programmes*
Mr Dave Chadwick, *Web Manager*

CTBI MEMBER CHURCHES AND BODIES OF CHURCHES
ANTIOCHIAN ORTHODOX CHURCH
email: fathergeorge@macace.net

BAPTIST UNION OF GREAT BRITAIN
The Revd Jonathan Edwards *General Secretary*
Baptist House, 129 Broadway, Didcot OX11 8RT
Tel: 01235 517700
Fax: 01235 517715
email: info@baptist.org.uk
Web: www.baptist.org.uk

CATHOLIC BISHOPS' CONFERENCE OF ENGLAND AND WALES
The Revd Christopher Thomas *General Secretary*
39 Eccleston Square, London SW1V 1BX
Tel: 020 7630 8220
Fax: 020 7901 4821
email: secretariat@cbcew.org.uk
Web: www.cbcew.org.uk

CATHOLIC BISHOPS' CONFERENCE OF SCOTLAND
The Revd Paul Conroy *General Secretary*
64 Aitken Street, Airdrie ML6 6LT
Tel: 01236 764061
Fax: 01236 762489
email: GenSec@BpsConfScot.com
Web: www.scmo.org/_titles/bishops_conference.htm

CHURCH IN WALES
Simon Lloyd *Provincial Secretary*
39 Cathedral Road, Cardiff CF11 9XF
Tel: 029 2034 8200
Fax: 029 2038 7835
email: information@churchinwales.org.uk
Web: www.churchinwales.org.uk

CHURCH OF ENGLAND
Mr William Nye *Secretary General of the General Synod and the Archbishops' Council*
Church House, Great Smith Street, London SW1P 3AZ　　　　　*Tel:* 020 7898 1000
　　　　　　　　　　　Fax: 020 7898 1369
email: cofe.comms@churchofengland.org
Web: www.churchofengland.org

CHURCH OF GOD OF PROPHECY
Bishop Wilton R. Powell *National Overseer*
6 Beacon Court, Birmingham Road, Great Barr, Birmingham B43 6NN　　*Tel:* 0121 358 2231
　　　　　　　　　　　Fax: 0121 358 8617
email: admin@cogop.org.uk
Web: www.cogop.org.uk

CHURCH OF IRELAND
Mrs Janet Maxwell *Head of Synod Services and Communications*
Church of Ireland House, Church Avenue, Rathmines, Dublin 6, RoI
　　　　　　Tel: ++ 353 (0)1 4125621
　　　　　　Fax: ++ 353 (0)1 4978821
email: janet.maxwell@rcbdub.org
Web: www.ireland.anglican.org

CHURCH OF SCOTLAND
The Revd John Chalmers *Principal Clerk*
Principal Clerk's Office, 121 George Street, Edinburgh EH2 4YN　　*Tel:* 0131 240 2240
　　　　　　　　　　　Fax: 0131 240 2239
email: pracproc@cofscotland.org.uk
Web: www.churchofscotland.org.uk

CONGREGATIONAL FEDERATION
The Revd Michael Heaney *General Secretary*
8 Castle Gate, Nottingham NG1 7AS
　　　　　　　　　　　Tel: 0115 911 1460
　　　　　　　　　　　Fax: 0115 911 1462
email: admin@congregational.org.uk
Web: www.congregational.org.uk

COPTIC ORTHODOX CHURCH
Bishop Angaelos
Coptic Orthodox Church Centre, Shephalbury Manor, Broadhall Way, Stevenage SG2 8RH
　　　　　　　　　　　Tel: 01438 745232
　　　　　　　　　　　Fax: 01438 313879
email: admin@CopticCentre.com
Web: www.CopticCentre.com

COUNCIL OF ORIENTAL ORTHODOX CHURCHES
Bishop Angaelos *President*
c/o Coptic Orthodox Church Centre (*as above*)
email: admin@CopticCentre.com

GERMAN-SPEAKING CONGREGATION
Mr Georg Staab
Council for German Church Work, 35 Craven Terrace, London W2 3EL　　*Tel:* 020 7706 8589
　　　　　　　　　　　Fax: 020 7706 2870
email: office@ev-synode.org.uk
Web: www.ev-synode.org.uk

INDEPENDENT METHODIST CHURCHES
Mr William Gabb *General Secretary*
Independent Methodist Resource Centre & Registered Office, Fleet St, Pemberton, Wigan WN5 0DS　　　　　　*Tel:* 01942 223526
　　　　　　　　　　　Fax: 01942 227768
email: resourcecentre@imcgb.org.uk
Web: www.imcgb.org.uk

INTERNATIONAL MINISTERIAL COUNCIL OF GREAT BRITAIN (IMCGB)
Bishop Onye Obika
217 Langhedge Lane, London N18 2TG
　　　　　　　　　　　Tel: 020 8345 5376
email: imcgb@aol.com
Web: www.imcgb.com

JOINT COUNCIL FOR ANGLO AND AFRICAN-CARIBBEAN CHURCHES
The Revd Esme Beswick *President*
141 Railton Road, London SE24 0LT
　　　　　　Tel and Fax: 020 7737 6542

LUTHERAN COUNCIL OF GREAT BRITAIN
The Revd Thomas Bruch *General Secretary*
30 Thanet Street, London WC1H 9QH
　　　　　　　　　　　Tel: 020 7554 2900
　　　　　　　　　　　Fax: 020 7383 3081
email: enquiries@lutheran.org.uk
Web: www.lutheran.org.uk

MAR THOMA CHURCH
Dr Zac Varghese *Ecumenical Officer*
3 Rose Garden Close, Edgware, London HA8 7RF　　　　　　*Tel:* 020 8951 5273
email: zacvarghese@aol.co.uk

METHODIST CHURCH
The Revd Dr Martin Atkins *General Secretary*
25 Marylebone Road, London NW1 5JR
　　　　　　　　　　　Tel: 020 7467 5143
　　　　　　　　　　　Fax: 020 7467 5226
email: generalsecretary@methodistchurch.org.uk
Web: www.methodist.org.uk

METHODIST CHURCH IN IRELAND
The Revd Donald Ker *General Secretary*
1 Fountainville Ave, Belfast BT9 6AN
　　　　　　　　　　　Tel: 028 9032 4554
　　　　　　　　　　　Fax: 028 9023 9467
email: secretary@irishmethodist.org
Web: www.irishmethodist.org

MORAVIAN CHURCH
Jackie Morten
Moravian Church House, 5 Muswell Hill, London N10 3TJ　　　*Tel:* 020 8883 3409
　　　　　　　　　　　Fax: 020 8365 3371
email: office@moravian.org.uk
Web: www.moravian.org.uk

ECUMENICAL

NEW TESTAMENT ASSEMBLY
The Revd Nezlin Sterling *General Secretary*
5 Woodstock Ave, London W13 9UQ
Tel: 020 8579 3841
Fax: 020 8537 9253
email: njsterlnta@aol.com

NEW TESTAMENT CHURCH OF GOD
Bishop Donald Bolt
3 Cheyne Walk, Northampton NN1 5PT
Tel: 01604 643311
Fax: 01604 790254
email: bigmove@ntcg.org.uk
Web: www.ntcg.org.uk

OECUMENICAL PATRIARCHATE (ARCHDIOCESE OF THYATEIRA AND GREAT BRITAIN)
His Eminence Archbishop Gregorios
5 Craven Hill, London W2 3EN
Tel: 020 7723 4787
Fax: 020 7224 9301
email: thyateiragb@yahoo.com
Web: www.nostos.com/church/

PRESBYTERIAN CHURCH OF WALES
The Revd Ifan Roberts *General Secretary*
Tabernacle Chapel, 81 Merthyr Road, Whitchurch, Cardiff CF14 1DD
Tel: 029 2062 7465
Fax: 029 2061 6188
email: swyddfa.office@ebcpcw.org.uk
Web: www.ebcpcw.org.uk

RELIGIOUS SOCIETY OF FRIENDS
Gillian Ashmore *Chief Recording Clerk*
Friends House, 173 Euston Road, London NW1 2BJ
Tel: 020 7663 1000
Fax: 020 7663 1001
email: enquiries@quaker.org.uk
Web: www.quaker.org.uk

RELIGIOUS SOCIETY OF FRIENDS IN IRELAND
Mr Ian Woods
40 Castle Grove, Swords, Co Dublin

RUSSIAN ORTHODOX CHURCH (ECUMENICAL PATRIARCHATE)
Mrs Gillian Crow
6 Maiden Place, London NW5 1HZ
email: gillian@crow.co.uk
Web: www.exarchate-uk.org

SALVATION ARMY
Commissioner John Matear *Territorial Commander UK and RoI*
101 Newington Causeway, London SE1 6BN
Tel: 020 7367 4500
Fax: 020 7367 4728
email: info@salvationarmy.org.uk
Web: www.salvationarmy.org.uk

SCOTTISH EPISCOPAL CHURCH
Mr John Stuart *Secretary General for Synod Office*
21 Grosvenor Crescent, Edinburgh EH12 5EE
Tel: 0131 225 6357
Fax: 0131 346 7247
email: office@scotland.anglican.org
Web: www.scottishepiscopal.com

TRANS-ATLANTIC & PACIFIC ALLIANCE OF CHURCHES
Archbishop Paul Hackman *President*
281-283 Rye Lane, London SE15 4UA
Tel and Fax: 020 7639 4058
email: tapacglobal@aol.com

UNDEB YR ANNIBYNWYR CYMRAEG/UNION OF WELSH INDEPENDENTS
The Revd Dr Geraint Tudor *General Secretary*
The John Penri, 5 Axis Court, Riverside Business Park, Swansea Vale, Swansea SA7 0AJ
Tel: 01792 795888
Fax: 01792 795376
email: Undeb@annibynwyr.org
Web: www.annibynwyr.org

UNITED FREE CHURCH OF SCOTLAND
The Revd Andrew McMillan
11 Newton Place, Glasgow G3 7PR
Tel: 0141 332 3435
Fax: 0141 333 1973
email: office@ufcos.org.uk
Web: www.ufcos.org.uk

UNITED REFORMED CHURCH
The Revd Roberta Rominger *General Secretary*
86 Tavistock Place, London WC1H 9RT
Tel: 020 7916 2020
Fax: 020 7916 2021
email: urc@urc.org.uk
Web: www.urc.org.uk

ASSOCIATE MEMBER
ROMAN CATHOLIC CHURCH OF IRELAND
The Revd Aidan O'Boyle *Executive Secretary*
The Irish Episcopal Conference, Columba Centre, Maynooth, Co Kildare, Republic of Ireland
Tel: 00 353 1 505 3020
Fax: 00 353 1 629 2360
email: ex.sec@iecon.ie
Father George Hackney

Little Portion, Back Lane, Barnby, Newark NG24 2SD
Tel: 01636 626417

BODIES IN ASSOCIATION
ACTION BY CHRISTIANS AGAINST TORTURE
Chas Raws, 38 The Mount, Heswello, Wirrall CH60 4RA
email: uk.acat@googlemail.com
Web: www.acatuk.org.uk

ASSOCIATION OF INTER-CHURCH FAMILIES
Mr Keith Lander (*Executive Officer*), 27 Tavistock Square, London WC1H 9HH
Tel: 020 7529 8131
Fax: 020 7529 8134
email: info@interchurchfamilies.org.uk
Web: www.interchurchfamilies.org.uk

BIBLE READING FELLOWSHIP
Richard Fisher, 15 The Chambers, Vineyard, Abingdon OX14 3FE   *Tel:* 01865 319 700
email: enquiries@brf.org.uk
Web: www.brf.org.uk

BIBLE SOCIETY
Paul Williams (*Chief Executive*), Stonehill Green, Westlea, Swindon SN5 7DG
Tel: 01793 418 100
Web: www.biblesociety.org.uk

CHRISTIAN COUNCIL ON AGEING
Mrs Christine Hodgson, 6 The Ridgeway, Market Harborough LE16 7HQ
Tel: 01858 432771
email: info@ccoa.org.uk
Web: www.ccoa.org.uk

CHRISTIAN EDUCATION
Peter Fishpool (*Chief Executive*), 5/6 Imperial Court, 12 Sovereign Road, Birmingham B30 3FH   *Tel:* 0121 472 4242
Fax: 0121 472 7575
email: admin@christianeducation.org.uk
Web: www.christianeducation.org.uk

CHRISTIANS AWARE
Mrs Barbara Butler, 2 Saxby Street, Leicester LE2 0ND   *Tel* and *Fax:* 0116 254 0770
email: barbarabutler@christiansaware.co.uk
Web: www.christiansaware.co.uk

CHURCH ACTION ON POVERTY
Mr Niall Cooper (*National Coordinator*), Dale House, 35 Dale Street, Manchester M1 2HF
Tel: 0161 236 9321
Fax: 0161 237 5359
email: info@church-poverty.org.uk
Web: www.church-poverty.org.uk

CHURCHES' ALERT TO SEX TRAFFICKING ACROSS EUROPE
Angela Deavall (*Chief Executive*), PO Box 983, Cambridge CB3 8WY   *Tel:* 0845 456 9335
email: contact@chaste.org.uk
Web: www.chaste.org.uk

COLLEGE OF PREACHERS
Ms Marfa Jones (*Administrator*), Chester House, Pages Lane, Muswell Hill, London N10 1PR
Tel: 020 8883 7850
email: administrator@
collegeofpreachers.org.uk
Web: www.collegeofpreachers.org.uk

COMMUNITY OF AIDAN AND HILDA
Lindisfarne Retreat, The Open Gate, Holy Island, Berwick-upon-Tweed TD15 2SD
Tel: 01289 389222
email: ca-and-h@demon.co.uk
Web: www.aidanandhilda.org.uk

CORRYMEELA COMMUNITY
Corrymeela House, 8 Upper Crescent, Belfast BT7 1NT   *Tel:* 028 9050 8080
Fax: 028 9050 8070
email: annemcdonagh@corrymeela.org
Web: www.corrymeela.org

ECUMENICAL COUNCIL FOR CORPORATE RESPONSIBILITY
Miles Litvinoff (*Coordinator*), PO Box 500, Oxford OX1 1ZL   *Tel:* 020 8965 9682
email: info@eccr.org.uk
Web: www.eccr.org.uk

ECUMENICAL SOCIETY OF THE BLESSED VIRGIN MARY
Father Bill OSM, Ss Peter and Paul Presbytery, 112 Entry Hill, Combe Down, Bath BA2 5LS
Tel: 01225 832096
email: gensec@esbvm.com
Web: http://www.esbvm.com

FAITH IN EUROPE
Dr Philip Walters (*General Secretary*), 81 Thorney Leys, Witney OX28 5BY
Tel: 01993 771778
email: philip.walters@waltfam.freeserve.co.uk
Web: www.faithineurope.org.uk

FEED THE MINDS
Josephine Carlssen (*Director*), Park Place, 12 Lawn Lane, London SW8 1UD
Tel: 020 7592 3900
Fax: 020 7592 3939
email: info@feedtheminds.org.uk
Web: www.feedtheminds.org

FELLOWSHIP OF RECONCILIATION
The Revd John Johansen-Berg (*Director*), St James' Church Centre, Beauchamp Lane, Oxford OX4 3LF   *Tel:* 01865 748796
email: office@for.org.uk
Web: www.for.org.uk

FELLOWSHIP OF ST ALBAN AND ST SERGIUS
The Revd Stephen Platt, 1 Canterbury Road, Oxford OX2 6LU   *Tel:* 01865 52991
Fax: 01865 316700
email: gensec@sobornost.org
Web: www.sobornost.org

FOCOLARE MOVEMENT
Celia Blackden, 11 Drummond Avenue, Leeds LS16 5JZ
email: celiablackden@yahoo.co.uk
Web: www.focolare.org.uk

ECUMENICAL

HOUSING JUSTICE
Ms Alison Gelder (*Chief Executive*), 209 Old Marylebone Road, London NW1 5QT
Tel: 020 7723 7273
Fax: 020 7723 5943
email: info@housingjustice.org.uk
Web: www.housingjustice.org.uk

INDUSTRIAL MISSION ASSOCIATION
The Revd Stephen Hazlett, Northumbrian Industrial Mission, 14 The Oaks West, Sunderland SR2 8HZ   *Tel:* 07900 231360
Web: www.industrialmission.org.uk

INTERNATIONAL ECUMENICAL FELLOWSHIP
David Hardiman, 59 Old Street, Headington, Oxford OX3 9HT   *Tel:* 0191 4566 1643
email: davidhardiman@blueyonder.com
Web: www.uk-ief.co.uk

IONA COMMUNITY
The Revd Peter Macdonald, 4th Floor, Savoy House, 140 Sauchiehall Street, Glasgow G2 3DH
Tel: 0141 332 6343
Fax: 0141 332 1090
email: admin@iona.org.uk
Web: www.iona.org.uk

IRISH SCHOOL OF ECUMENICS
Prof Linda Hogan, 683 Antrim Road, Belfast BT15 4EG *and* Bea House, Milltown Park, Dublin 6, RoI   *Tel:* +44 (0) 28 9077 5010
Fax: +44 (0) 28 9037 3986
email: lhogan2@tcd.ie
Web: www.tcd.ie/ise

L'ARCHE
Ms Lal Keenan, L'Arche Community, 15 Northwood High Street, London SE27 9JU
Tel: 020 8670 6714
Fax: 020 8670 0818
email: info@larche.org.uk
Web: www.larche.org.uk

LIVING STONES
Dr Aziz Nour, 77 Exeter Road, Southgate, London N14 5JU
Web: www.livingstonesonline.org.uk

MAGNET RESOURCES
Lynne Ling, PO Box 10378, Bishop's Stortford CM23 9FT   *Tel:* 0844 7362524
Web: www.ourmagnet.co.uk

MODEM
Mr John Nelson (*National Secretary and Publications Editor*), 24 Rostron Crescent, Formby L37 2ET   *Tel:* 01704 873973
Fax: 01704 871273
email: jrn24rcf2003@yahoo.co.uk
Web: www.modem.uk.com

OIKOCREDIT, ECUMENICAL DEVELOPMENT COOPERATIVE SOCIETY
Patrick Hynes, UK Support Office, PO Box 809, Garstang, Preston PR3 1TU
Web: www.oikocredit.org

OPERATION NOAH
Anne Pettifor, Grayston Centre, 28 Charles Square, London N1 6HT   *Tel:* 0207 324 4761
email: admin@operationnoah.org
Web: www.operationnoah.org

PRISON FELLOWSHIP ENGLAND AND WALES
Tim Diaper, PO Box 945, Maldon, Essex CM9 4EW   *Tel:* 01621 843232
Web: www.prisonfellowship.org

RETREAT ASSOCIATION
Alison MacTier, The Central Hall, 256 Bermondsey Street, London SE1 3UJ
Tel: 020 7357 7736
Fax: 020 7357 7724
email: info@retreats.org.uk
Web: www.retreats.org.uk

SOCIETY OF ECUMENICAL STUDIES
The Revd Mark Woodruff (*Secretary*), 26 Daysbrook Road, London SW2 3TD
Tel: 020 8678 8195
email: ecumenicalstudies@btinternet.com
Web: www.ecumenicalstudies.org.uk

STUDENT CHRISTIAN MOVEMENT
The Revd Martin Thompson, Unit 308F, The Big Peg, 120 Vyse St, Jewellery Quarter, Birmingham B18 6NF   *Tel:* 0121 200 3355
email: co@movement.org.uk
Web: www.movement.org.uk

Jean Hackett, National Office, Commercial Road, Tunbridge Wells TN1 2RR
Tel: 01892 541411

WOMEN'S WORLD DAY OF PRAYER MOVEMENT
Fax: 01892 541745
email: office@wwdp-natcomm.org
Web: www.wwdp-natcomm.org

YOUNG MEN'S CHRISTIAN ASSOCIATION (YMCA)
Ms Helen Dennis (*Policy and Parliamentary Officer*), 53 Parker Street, London WC2B 5PT
Tel: 0845 873 6633
email: enquiries@ymca.org.uk
Web: www.ymca.org.uk

Scotland, Wales and Ireland

ACTS SCOTLAND

ACTS is the national ecumenical body for Scotland, the expression of the Churches' commitment to cooperation with one another in the service of Christ. ACTS works closely with its partners in England, Wales and Ireland. Its principal body is the Members' Meeting, composed of representatives from the member churches. Further information is available on the ACTS website: www.acts-scotland.org

Member Churches Church of Scotland, Congregational Federation, Methodist Church, Religious Society of Friends, Roman Catholic Church, Salvation Army, Scottish Episcopal Church, United Free Church, United Reformed Church.

Office Jubilee House, Forthside Way, Stirling FK8 1QZ   *Tel:* 01259 216980
    email: ecumenical@acts-scotland.org

General Secretary The Revd Matthew Z. Ross

Convenor of the Trustees and ACTS Members' Meeting The Revd John Butterfield

CYTÛN: EGLWYSI YNGHYD YNG NGHYMRU CHURCHES TOGETHER IN WALES
Cytûn's Basis and Commitment:

CYTÛN unites in pilgrimage those churches in Wales which, acknowledging God's revelation in Christ, confess the Lord Jesus Christ as God and Saviour according to the Scriptures; and, in obedience to God's will and in the power of the Holy Spirit, commit themselves to seek a deepening of their communion with Christ and with one another in the Church, which is his body, and to fulfil their mission to proclaim the gospel by common witness and service in the world, to the glory of the one God Father, Son and Holy Spirit.

Member Denominations The Baptist Union of Wales, the Roman Catholic Church, the Church in Wales, the Congregational Federation, the Covenanted Baptist Churches, the German-speaking Lutheran Church, Indian Orthodox Churches, The Methodist Church, the Presbyterian Church of Wales, the Quakers, the Salvation Army, the Union of Welsh Independents, the United Reformed Church and the South Wales Baptist Association.

Aligned Groupings
The Covenanted Churches in Wales, the Free Church Council of Wales.
    Cytûn also works in close collaboration with the Commission of the Covenanted Church in Wales and the Free Church Council of Wales.

Office 58 Richmond Road, Cardiff, South Wales CF24
    Tel (main office): 029 2046 4204
    Web: www.cytun.org.uk

Chief Executive The Revd Canon Aled Edwards OBE   *Tel:* 029 2046 4375
    email: aled@cytun.org.uk

Bilingual Office Administrator to the Chief Executive
Mrs Sasha Perriam   *Tel:* 029 2046 4204
    email: post@cytun.org.uk

Policy Officer
The Revd Gethin Rhys   *Tel:* 029 2046 4378
    email: gethin@cytun.org.uk

Witness and Publications Officer
Mr Ynyr Roberts   *Tel:* 029 2046 4371
    email: ynyr@cytun.org.uk

ECUMENICAL

IRISH COUNCIL OF CHURCHES

From 1906 the Presbyterian and Methodist Churches had a joint committee for united efforts. In 1910 the General Assembly of the Presbyterian Church invited other evangelical Churches to set up similar joint committees with it. The Church of Ireland accepted and by 1911 the joint committee of these two Churches was in action. Following a recommendation of the 1920 Lambeth Conference, these joint committees developed in 1922 into the United Council of Christian Churches and Religious Communions in Ireland including six of the present member churches. In 1966 the United Council changed its name to the Irish Council of Churches. The Council employed its first full-time secretary in April 1972.

Aims The Irish Council of Churches is constituted by Christian Communions in Ireland willing to join in united efforts to promote the spiritual, physical, moral and social welfare of the people and the extension of the rule of Christ among all nations and over every region of life.

Member Churches
Antiochian Orthodox Church in Ireland
Greek Orthodox Church
Lutheran Church in Ireland
Methodist Church in Ireland
Irish District of the Moravian Church
Non-Subscribing Presbyterian Church of Ireland
Presbyterian Church in Ireland
Religious Society of Friends in Ireland
Cherubim and Seraphim Church
Redeemed Christian Church of God
Romanian Orthodox Church in Ireland
Russian Orthodox Church in Ireland
Salvation Army (Ireland Division).

Structure The Council consists of 83 members appointed by the member Churches, together with the Heads of the member Churches and up to ten co-opted members, the Executive Secretary, Treasurer and immediate Past President of the Council. There is an Annual Meeting and occasional gatherings. The member Churches appoint an Executive Committee, which meets quarterly and is responsible for the oversight of the work of the Council.

The Council continues to serve both jurisdictions (Northern Ireland and the Republic of Ireland) and comprises 14 member churches (see above). It is an associate member of Churches Together in Britain and Ireland and the Conference of European Churches and has links with the World Council of Churches.

It is currently re-assessing its purpose and direction in the rapidly changing contexts both sides of the border; its ecumenical witness across the island and relationships between and beyond its member churches, and its international links through its Board of Overseas Affairs.

- It meets quarterly with the Roman Catholic Church in Ireland through the Irish Inter-Church Committee and every 18 months as the Irish Inter-Church Meeting. The last Meeting was held in Dublin in in October 2010, taking the focus of Baptism.
- The Inter-Church Committee on Social Issues (ICCSI), a forum of the Irish Inter-Church Committee, currently employs a Project Officer to working on a parish-based integration programme in the Republic.
- It is represented on various regional, national and CTBI bodies concerned with regional equality panels, inter-faith, international, mission, overseas aid, racial justice and TV and radio affairs, and the Week of Prayer for Christian Unity.
- It is currently serviced by 3 staff based in the Belfast office (Executive Officer, Administrator and Communications and Administration Assistant).

More information about the Council's work can be obtained from www.irishchurches.org which includes the most recent Annual Report.

Inter-Church Centre, 48 Elmwood Avenue, Belfast BT9 6AZ   *Tel:* 028 9066 3145
Fax: 028 9066 4160
email: info@irishchurches.org
Web: www.irishchurches.org

President The Rt Revd John McDowell

Vice-President The Revd Brian Anderson

Hon Treasurer Mr Jonathan Wilson

General Secretary Dr Nicola Brady

Meissen Agreement with the Evangelical Church in Germany

The Evangelical Church in Germany (Evangelische Kirche in Deutschland – EKD) is a Communion of 20 member churches (mostly *Landeskirchen* or territorial churches). Of these, seven are members of the United Evangelical Lutheran Church of Germany – VELKD (eight Lutheran churches were founding members of VELKD). One church in the EKD is purely Reformed, one is predominantly Reformed and twelve today form the Evangelical Church of the Union – UEK (seven churches were founding members of the UEK). One Church (the Evangelische Kirche in Mitteldeutschland) is a member of both VELKD and the UEK. In many of the United churches the Lutheran tradition predominates.

In November 1988 the General Synod welcomed the Meissen Common Statement, *On the Way to Visible Unity*, which called for a closer relationship between the Church of England and the German Evangelical Churches. The Meissen Declaration, which it recommended, was approved by the General Synod in July 1990 without dissent, and solemnly affirmed and proclaimed an Act of Synod on 29 January 1991. The Meissen Declaration makes provision for the Church of England and the Evangelical Church in Germany to live in closer fellowship with one another (though not yet with interchangeable ministries) and commits them to work towards the goal of full visible unity. The member churches of the EKD have been designated as churches to which the Ecumenical Canons apply (*see* **Ecumenical Canons**).

The Meissen Commission (the Sponsoring Body for the Church of England–EKD Relations) exists to oversee and encourage relationships (*see* Council for Christian Unity). Fuller information is contained in *The German Evangelical Churches* (CCU Occasional Paper No 1 £2.95 + 35p p&p) and *Anglo-German Ecumenical Links: An Information Pack* (£1 inc. p&p).   The text of the Meissen Agreement can be found in *The Meissen Agreement: Texts* (CCU Occasional Paper No 2 £2.10 inc. p&p). These are all available from the Council for Christian Unity. Most of this material is downloadable from the CCU web site at www.cofe.anglican.org/info/ccu.

Co-Chairmen of the Meissen Commission Bishop Dr Friedrich Weber (*EKD*), The Rt Revd Nicholas Baines (*Church of England*)

English Co-Secretary of the Meissen Commission Vacancy, Council for Christian Unity, Church House, Great Smith Street, London SW1P 3AZ
Tel: 020 7898 1474

German Co-Secretary of the Meissen Commission OKR Christoph Ernst, EKD Kirchenamt, Postfach 21 02 20, D – 30402 Hannover, Germany   *Tel:* 00 49 511 2796 127
Fax: 00 49 511 2796 725
email: christoph.ernst@ekd.de
Web: www.ekd.de

The Reuilly Common Statement

Encouraged by the positive reception of the Meissen and Porvoo Agreements, the Anglican Churches of Britain and Ireland engaged in dialogue with the French Reformed and Lutheran Churches, with formal conversations beginning in 1994. These Churches had signalled their desire to enter into closer fellowship with Anglican Churches on the model of the Meissen Agreement, which the Church of England had concluded with the Evangelical Church in Germany (EKD).

The relations between the Anglican and French Churches are steeped in history. Contacts go back to the Middle Ages and took on a new character through the impetus of the Reformation. In later years, at times of turbulence and persecution, churches on both sides of the Channel welcomed those persecuted for their faith.

The conversations involved four participating churches from each side: the four Anglican Churches of the British Isles (the Church of England, the Church of Ireland, the Scottish Episcopal Church and the Church in Wales) and the four French Churches of the Lutheran and Reformed traditions (the Church of the Augsburg Confession of Alsace and Lorraine, the Evangelical Lutheran Church of France, the Reformed Church of Alsace and Lorraine and the Reformed Church of France).

The Reuilly Common Statement which forms the outcome of these conversations takes its name from a community of deaconesses, committed to prayer and meditation. The Statement was approved by the General Synod of the Church of England in November 1999, and the Statement was signed by the

ECUMENICAL

participatory Churches in Canterbury and Paris during the summer of 2001.

In common with other ecumenical statements, the Reuilly document first sets the scene, with the history and present context of the participants, and then moves on to current theological issues: the Church as Sign, Instrument and Foretaste of the Kingdom of God; the Church as Communion (*koinonia*); Growth towards Visible Unity; Agreement in Faith and the Apostolicity of the Church and its Ministry.

The Churches declare that they have found a high degree of unity and faith, and outline three areas of future work together: common efforts in witness and service; continuing theological work, particularly on questions of oversight, authority, eucharistic ministry and formally uniting ministries; the practical consequences of the Agreement: prayer, sharing of worship, partnership, and joint ventures across a range of areas.

Within France there have been conversations for greater unity and closer fellowship. The Evangelical Lutheran Church of France (EELF) and the Reformed Church of France (ERF) united in 2013 forming the United Protestant Church of France. The EELF and ERF's move toward unity followed a similar process by the Church of the Augsburg Confession of Alsace and Lorraine (ECAAL) and the Reformed Church of Alsace and Lorraine (ERAL), which in 2004 formed the Union of Protestant Churches in Alsace and Lorraine (UEPAL).

The implementation of the Agreement is coordinated by a Contact Group. The Anglican Co-Chairman is the Bishop of Warwick, the Rt Revd John Stroyan and the French Co-Chairman is Revd Joel Dautheville, President, Communion Protestant Luthéro-Réformée de France.

For information on current links and initiatives, contact: The Council for Christian Unity, Church House, Great Smith Street, London SW1P 3AZ (tel. 020 7898 1474).

The full text of the Reuilly Declaration, together with background articles on the theological issues and the participating Churches, can be found in *Called to Witness and Service*, Church House Publishing (1999), ISBN 0 7151 5757 4.

Conference of European Churches

Born in the era of the 'cold war' 53 years ago, CEC emerged into a fragmented and divided continent. Thus it was that Churches of Eastern and Western Europe felt one priority of their work to be promoting international understanding – building bridges. This CEC has consistently tried to do, always insisting that no 'iron curtain' exists among the Churches.

The supreme governing body of the Conference is the Assembly. Here all 114 member Churches are represented. The first Assembly was in 1959 and further Assemblies were held in 1960, 1962, 1964, 1967, 1971, 1974, 1979, 1986, 1992, 1997, 2003, 2009 and 2013.

CEC initiated the European Ecumenical Assembly 'Peace with Justice' held in Basel in May 1989, co-sponsored with the Council of European Bishops' Conferences (CCEE, Roman Catholic). A second European Ecumenical Assembly was held in Graz, Austria, in 1997 with the theme 'Reconciliation: Gift of God and Source of New Life'. In 2001, CEC and CCEE launched the 'Charta Oecumenica – guidelines for the growing cooperation among the Churches in Europe'. A third European Ecumenical Assembly was held in Sibiu, Romania, in 2007 with the theme 'The light of Christ shines upon all – Hope for renewal and unity in Europe'.

The twenty-member Governing Board oversees the implementation of the decisions of the Assembly.

Since 1 January 1999 the European Ecumenical Commission on Church and Society (EECCS) with offices in Brussels and Strasbourg integrated with CEC, and, together with CEC's existing work, created the new Church and Society Commission of the CEC. A merger is also planned between CEC and the Brussels-based Churches' Commission for Migrants in Europe (CCME).

The Secretariat in Geneva and offices in Brussels and Strasbourg ensure the continuity of the activities.

In July 2013 at its fourteenth General Assembly in Budapest (theme: 'And now what are you waiting for? CEC and its Mission in a Changing Europe'), CEC adopted a renewed and reformulated constitution which included a new vision and mission statement as well as directions for the move of the headquarters from Geneva to Brussels. The Rt Revd Christopher Hill was elected as President of CEC.

General Secretary Fr Heikki Huttenen, Ecumenical Centre, Rue Joseph II 174, 1000 Brussels, Belgium   *Tel:* 32 2 230 17 32 or 33 3 88 15 27 60 (Strasbourg Office)
Fax: 32 2 231 14 13
email: gensecretariat@cec-kek.org
Web: ceceurope.org

World Council of Churches

The Church of England has taken its full share in the international ecumenical movement since the Edinburgh Conference of 1910. In 2009 the General Synod made a grant of £108,000 to the General Budget of the World Council of Churches.

The World Council of Churches was brought into formal existence by a resolution of its first Assembly at Amsterdam in 1948.

Member Churches agree to the following basis:

The World Council of Churches is a fellowship of churches which confess the Lord Jesus Christ as God and Saviour according to the Scriptures and therefore seek to fulfil together their common calling to the glory of the one God, Father, Son and Holy Spirit.

Extract from the Constitution

The primary purpose of the fellowship of churches in the WCC is to call one another to visible unity in one faith and in one eucharistic fellowship, expressed in worship and common life in Christ, through witness and service to the world, and to advance towards that unity in order that the world may believe.

In seeking *koinonia* in faith and life, witness and service, the churches through the Council will:

- promote the prayerful search for forgiveness and reconciliation in a spirit of mutual accountability, the development of deeper relationships through theological dialogue, and the sharing of human, spiritual and material resources with one another;
- facilitate common witness in each place and in all places, and support each other in their work for mission and evangelism;
- express their commitment to *diakonia* in serving human need, breaking down barriers between people, promoting one human family in justice and peace, and upholding the integrity of creation, so that all may experience the fullness of life;
- nurture the growth of an ecumenical consciousness through processes of education and a vision of life in community rooted in each particular cultural context;
- assist each other in their relationships to and with people of other faith communities;
- foster renewal and growth in unity, worship, mission and service.

In order to strengthen the one ecumenical movement, the Council will:

- nurture relations with and among churches, especially within but also beyond its membership;
- establish and maintain relations with national councils, regional conferences of churches, organizations of Christian World Communions and other ecumenical bodies;
- support ecumenical initiatives at regional, national and local levels;
- facilitate the creation of networks among ecumenical organizations;
- work towards maintaining the coherence of the one ecumenical movement in its diverse manifestations.

The World Council shall offer counsel and provide opportunity for united action in matters of common interest. It may take action on behalf of constituent churches only in such matters as one or more of them may commit to it and only on behalf of such churches.

The World Council shall not legislate for the churches; nor shall it act for them in any manner except as indicated or as may hereafter be specified by the constituent churches.

The WCC is governed by an Assembly of Member Churches, a Central Committee, and by an Executive Committee and other subordinate bodies as may be established. Assemblies are held every six to eight years and have been as follows:

- AMSTERDAM, 1948 – theme: 'Man's Disorder and God's Design'
- EVANSTON, 1954 – theme: 'Christ the Hope of the World'
- NEW DELHI, 1961– theme: 'Jesus Christ, the Light of the World'
- UPPSALA, 1968 – theme: 'Behold, I Make All Things New'
- NAIROBI, 1975 – theme: 'Jesus Christ Frees and Unites'
- VANCOUVER, 1983 – theme: 'Jesus Christ the Life of the World'
- CANBERRA, 1991– theme: 'Come, Holy Spirit – Renew the Whole Creation'
- HARARE 1998 – theme: 'Turn to God – Rejoice in Hope'
- PORTO ALEGRE 2006 – theme: 'God, in your grace, transform the world'
- BUSAN 2013 - theme: 'God of life, lead us to justice and peace'

The WCC has 349 member churches, including 38 which are associated. Almost every Church of the Anglican Communion is included, together with most of the Orthodox Churches and all the main Protestant

ECUMENICAL

traditions. The Roman Catholic Church is not a member but has sent official observers to all main WCC meetings since 1960. It is a full member of the Faith and Order Commission of the WCC.

Presidium The Revd Dr Mary-Anne Plaatjis van Huffel (United Reforming Church in Southern Africa; The Revd Professor Dr Sang Chang (Presbyterian Church in the Republic of Korea); The Most Revd Anders Wejryd (Church of Sweden); The Revd Gloria Nohemy Ulloa Alvarado (Presbyterian Church in Colombia); The Rt Revd Mark MacDonald (Anglican Church of Canada); The Revd Dr Mele'ana Puloka (Free Wesleyan Church of Tonga); HB John X (Patriarch of the Greek Orthodox Church of Antioch and All the East); HH Karekin II (Supreme Patriarch and Catholicos of All Armenians)

Moderator of Central Committee Dr Agnes Abuom (Anglican Church of Kenya)

Vice-Moderators

Metropolitan Prof Dr Gennadios of Sassima (Limouris) (Ecumenical Patriarchate of Constantinople)

The Rt Revd Mary Anne Swenson (United Methodist Church, USA)

General Secretary The Revd Dr Olav Fykse Tveit (Church of Norway)

Office PO Box 2100, 150 route de Ferney, 1211 Geneva 2, Switzerland

Tel: 00 41 22 791 61 11
Fax: 00 41 22 791 03 61
Web: www.oikoumene.com
Cable: Oikoumene Geneva
email: infowcc@wcc-coe.org

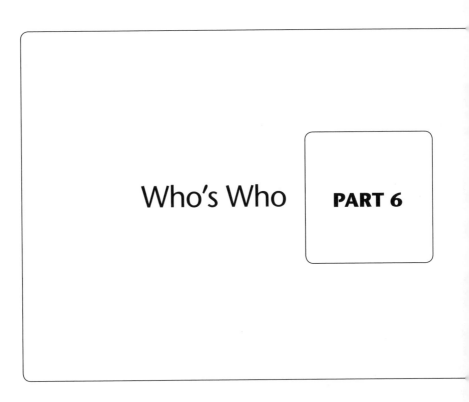

Who's Who

PART 6

Whole Who PART 6

Abbreviations used in the biographies

ABIST .... Associate, British Institute of Surgical Technology
ACA ..... Associate, Institute of Chartered Accountants
ACE........... Associateship of the College of Education, Member, Association of Conference Executives
ACGI.............................Associate, City and Guilds of London Institute
ACIB ....Associate, Chartered Institute of Bankers (formerly AIB)
ACII ....Associate, Chartered Insurance Institute
ACIS........................ Associate, Institute of Chartered Secretaries and Administrators
ACMA...................... Associate, Chartered Institute of Management Accountants (formerly ACWA)
ACP.......................... Associate, College of Preceptors
ACertCM ....Archbishop of Canterbury's Certificate in Church Music
ADipR .... Archbishop's Diploma for Readers
AIA...............................Associate, Institute of Actuaries
AKC ....Associate, King's College London
ALA............................. Associate, Library Association
ALCD..............Associate, London College of Divinity
ALCM ....Associate, London College of Music
ARCM .... Associate, Royal College of Music
ARCO................Associate, Royal College of Organists
ARCO(CHM) .....Associate, Royal College of Organists with Diploma in Choir Training
ARCS.................... Associate, Royal College of Science
ARMIT ....Associate, Royal Melbourne Institute of Technology
ATCL........Associate, Trinity College of Music London
ATII.............. Associate Member, Institute of Taxation
AdDipEd .... Advanced Diploma in Education
BA .... Bachelor of Arts
BCh or BChir................................Bachelor of Surgery (also see BS and ChB)
BD.. Bachelor of Divinity
BDS....................................Bachelor of Dental Surgery
BEd .... Bachelor of Education
BLitt.. Bachelor of Letters
Bmet .... Bachelor of Metallurgy
BMus .... Bachelor of Music (also see MusB or MusBac)
BS..........................Bachelor of Science (also see BSc), Bachelor of Surgery (also see BCh, BChir and ChB)
BSc .... Bachelor of Science (also see BS)
BSocSc ....Bachelor of Social Science (also see BSSc)
BTh Btheol .... Bachelor of Theology (also see STB)
BVM&S ....Bachelor of Veterinary Medicine and Surgery
BVSc .... Bachelor of Veterinary Science
CA.......................Institute of Chartered Accountants of Scotland
CB............................. Companion, Order of the Bath
CBE............Commander, Order of the British Empire
CCYW ....Certificate in Community Youth Work
CD ....Canadian Forces Decoration
CERT TH................................. Certificate in Theology
CJGS ....Community of the Companions of Jesus the Good Shepherd
CPA.................................... Chartered Patent Attorney
CPC .... Certificate of Professional Competence (Road Transport)
CQSW........Certificate of Qualification in Social Work

CR............ Community of the Resurrection (Mirfield)
CSC..............Community of the Servants of the Cross
CSEM ....Certificate in Special Education Management
CSWG..................Community of the Servants of the Will of God
CTH .... Certificate in Theology
CTM ....Certificate in Theology for Ministry
CYCW .....Certificate in Youth and Community Work
Cchem ....Certified/Chartered Chemist
CdipAF ....Certified Diploma in Accounting and Finance
Ceng..Chartered Engineer
Cert CT.................Certificate in Ceramic Technology
CertEd....................................Certificate of Education
CertMBiol........................Certificate of Microbiology
ChB....................... Bachelor of Surgery (also see BCh, BChir and BS)
Cmaths............................ Chartered Mathematician
Cphys ....Chartered Physicist of the Institute of Physics
Cstat .... Chartered Statistician
DAC........................... Diploma in Adult Counselling
DCH ....Diploma in Child Health
DCL ....Doctor of Civil Law
DD .... Doctor of Divinity
DDS ....Doctor of Dental Surgery
DHSM .... Diploma in Health Service Management
DIC ....Diploma of Membership of Imperial College London
DL..Deputy Lieutenant
DLC ....Diploma of Loughborough College
DMS........................Diploma in Management Studies
DN.......................................Diploma in Nursing
DPA......................Diploma in Public Administration
DPS ....Diploma in Pastoral Studies
DMin ....Doctor of Ministry
DPhil ....Doctor of Philosophy (also see PhD)
DProf ....Doctor in Professional Studies
DSPT .... Diploma in Social and Pastoral Theology
DSS ....Diploma in Social Studies
DSc .... Doctor of Science (also see ScD)
DTS .... Diploma in Theological Studies
DTh ....Doctor of Theology (also see ThD)
DUniv....................................Doctor of the University
Dip.. Diploma
DipAdEd .... Diploma in Advanced Education
DipBA .... Diploma in Business Administration
DipC .... Diploma in Counselling
DipChemEng.........Diploma in Chemical Engineering
DipEd....................................... Diploma in Education
DipHE......................... Diploma in Higher Education
DipLA ....Diploma in Liturgy and Architecture
DipLRM ....Diploma in Leadership, Renewal and Mission Studies
DipMin ....Diploma in Ministry
DipN......................................Diploma in Nursing
DipPallMed ....Diploma in Palliative Medicine
DipRJ ....Diploma in Retail Jewellery
DipSE........................... Diploma in Special Education
DipSW ....Diploma in Social Work
DipSocSc...........................Diploma in Social Sciences
DipTh ....Diploma in Theology
Dip UEM........Diploma in Urban Estate Management
Dr .... Doctor
EPA .... European Patent Attorney
EurIng...European Engineer
Eur Phys ....European Physicist

FASC ....Fellow, Academy of St Cecilia
FBA .... Fellow, British Academy
FBCS .... Fellow, British Computer Society
FCA..........Fellow, Institute of Chartered Accountants
FCAA ....Fellow, Cyprus Association of Actuaries
FCCA ....Fellow, Chartered Association of Certified
                Accountants (formerly FACCA)
FCEM............Fellow, College of Emergency Medicine
FCIM............ Fellow, Chartered Institute of Marketing
                      (formerly FInstM)
FC INST M .... Fellow, Chartered Institute
                       of Marketing
FCIOB............. Fellow, Chartered Institute of Building
FCIPD ....Fellow, Chartered Institute of Personnel
            and Development (formerly FIPD)
FCP ....Fellow, College of Preceptors
FDSRCS......... Fellow in Dental Surgery, Royal College
                of Surgeons of England
FGMS..............Fellow, Guild of Musicians and Singers
FIA .... Fellow, Institute of Actuaries
FIBMS ....Fellow, Institute of Biomedical Sciences
FIHT.......... Fellow of the Institution of Highways and
                       Transportation
FIMA................. Fellow, Institute of Mathematics and
                     its Applications
FIMgt ....Fellow, Institute of Management
FJMU ....Fellow, Liverpool John Moores University
FKC.............................. Fellow, King's College London
FPMI ....Fellow, Pensions Management Institute
FRAI ....Fellow, Royal Anthropological Institute
FRAeS....................Fellow, Royal Aeronautical Society
FRAS ....Fellow, Royal Astronomical Society
FRCO .... Fellow, Royal College of Organists
FRCOG ..... Fellow, Royal College of Obstetricians and
                    Gynaecologists
FRCOphth ....Fellow, Royal College of
                     Ophthalmologists
FRCS .... Fellow, Royal College of Physicians and
                Surgeons of England
FRCSE or FRCSEd ....Fellow, Royal College of
                Surgeons of Edinburgh
FRHistS ....Fellow, Royal Historical Society
FRICS ....Fellow, Royal Institution of Chartered
            Surveyors (formerly FLAS and FSI)
FRIPHH..........Fellow, Royal Institute of Public Health
                    and Hygiene
FRGS ....Fellow, Royal Geographical Society
FRS... Fellow, Royal Society
FRSA ....Fellow, Royal Society of Arts
FRSC .... Fellow, Royal Society of Chemistry
                     (formerly FRIC)
FRSL...................... Fellow, Royal Society of Literature
FRSM .... Fellow, Royal Society of Medicine
FSA.............................Fellow, Society of Antiquaries
FSCA ....Fellow, Royal Society of Company and
              Commercial Accountants
FTII ....Fellow, Institute of Taxation
Fell(s).............................. Fellow(s), Fellowship
HDipEd........................ Higher Diploma in Education
HNC .... Higher National Certificate
HND ....Higher National Diploma
Hon ....Honorary, Honourable
IDC ....Inter-Diocesan Certificate
JP ....Justice of the Peace
KA................. Knight of St Andrew, Order of Barbados
KCVO ....Knight Commander, Royal
                     Victorian Order
KHS................................Knight of the Holy Sepulchre
LDSRCS(Eng)...................Licentiate in Dental Surgery
            of the Royal College of Surgeons
                     (of England)

LICeram...................Licenciate, Institute of Ceramics
LLAM...............Licentiate, London Academy of Music
                    and Dramatic Art
LLB ....Bachelor of Laws
LLD..Doctor of Laws
LLM .... Master of Laws
LRAM................. Licentiate, Royal Academy of Music
LRCP..............Licentiate, Royal College of Physicians
LRPS...............Licentiate, Royal Photographic Society
LRSC .... Licentiate, Royal Society of Chemistry
LTCL......Licentiate, Trinity College of Music, London
LTh .... Licentiate in Theology (also see LST)
LVO .... Lieutenant, Royal Victorian Order
Lic..Licentiate
M..Member
MA...Master of Arts
MB,BS &MB,ChB........ Conjoint degree of Bachelor of
          Medicine, Bachelor of Surgery
MBCS................... Member, British Computer Society
MBE ....Member, Order of the British Empire
MCIH............Corporate Member, Chartered Institute
                    of Housing
MCIJ ....Member, Chartered Institute of Journalists
MCIM .... Member, Chartered Institute of Marketing
                     (formerly MInstM)
MCIPD........................Member, Chartered Institute of
            Personnel and Development
                    (formerly MIPD)
MCLIP .... Member, Chartered Institute of Library
            and Information Professionals
MCS.................................. Master of Christian Studies
MCSP..........................Member, Chartered Society of
                    Physiotherapy
MCST..............Member, College of Speech Therapists
MCT .... Member, Association of Corporate
                     Treasurers
MDCT.......................Manager's Diploma in Ceramic
                     Technology
MDiv ....Master of Divinity
MEd ....Master of Education
MIBC .... Member, Institute of Business
                     Counsellors
MICE ....Member, Institution of Civil Engineers
                    (formerly AMICE)
MIChemE ....Member, Institution of Chemical
                     Engineers
MIEE........Member, Institution of Electrical Engineers
             (formerly AMIEE MIERE)
MIMA ....Member, Institute of Management
                     Accountants
MIMgt ....Member, Institute of Management
MIOT .... Member, Institute of Operating Theatre
                     Technicians
MIPD ....Member, Institute of Personnel
            and Development (now see MCIPD)
MIPR................Member, Institute of Public Relations
MIStructE .... Member, Institute of Structural
                     Engineers
MInstD .... Member, Institute of Directors
MInstGA............ Member, Institute of Group Analysis
MInstP....................... Member, Institute of Physics
MLitt... Master of Letters
MP ....Member of Parliament
MPhil..Master of Philosophy
MRCGP.................Member, Royal College of General
                     Practitioners
MRCS....................................Member, Royal College
                     of Surgeons
MRCVS ....Member, Royal College of
                Veterinary Surgeons
MRSC................ Member, Royal Society of Chemistry

MSc.. Master of Science
MTech.. Master of Technology
MTh or MTheol............................ Master of Theology
                                (also see STM and ThM)
MusB or MusBac............................ Bachelor of Music
                                        (also see BMus)
NCA....................... National Certificate in Agriculture
NDA.........................National Diploma in Agriculture
NDD ....National Diploma in Design
OAM .... Order of Australia Medal
OBE..................... Officer, Order of the British Empire
OGS ....Oratory of the Good Shepherd
ONC ....Ordinary National Certificate
OStJ ....Officer, Most Venerable Order of
                    the Hospital of St John of Jerusalem
PACTA .... Professional Associate, Clinical
                                    Theology Association
PGCE ....Postgraduate Certificate in Education
PhD..................Doctor of Philosophy (also see DPhil)
Preb .... Prebendary
Prof..Professor
QC .... Queen's Counsel
QHC ....Queen's Honorary Chaplain
RAMcC .... Royal Army Medical Corp
RAF ....Royal Air Force
RCO ....Royal College of Organists
RD.............................Royal Navy Reserve Decoration
RGN......................................Registered General Nurse
RIBA............................... (Member) Royal Institute of
                British Architects (formerly ARIBA)

RICS................ Royal Institute of Chartered Surveyors
RM .... Registered Midwife
RMN ....Registered Mental Nurse
RN...Royal Navy
RSA ....Royal Society of Arts
Revd... Reverend
Rt ....Right
Rtd or rtd..Retired
SCM ....State Certified Midwife
SRN...State Registered Nurse
SRP............................State Registered Physiotherapist
SSC ....Secretarial Studies Certificate,
                                Societas Sanctae Crucis
                            (Society of the Holy Cross)
SSF .... Society of St Francis
SSM...............................Society of the Sacred Mission
STB.....................Bachelor of Theology (also see BTh)
STh ....Scholar in Theology (also see ThSchol)
STL.............. Reader (or Professor) of Sacred Theology
STM ....Master of Theology
                (also see MTh or MTheol and ThM)
ScD .... Doctor of Science (also see DSc)
TCert ....Teacher's Certificate
TEFL............Teacher of English as a Foreign Language
Tdip ....Teacher's Diploma
ThD ....Doctorate in Theology (also see DTh)
ThM......Master of Theology (also see MTh or MTheol
                                        and STM)
Ven .... Venerable

WHO'S WHO

WHO'S WHO

A Directory of General Synod members, together with those suffragan bishops, deans and archdeacons who are not members of General Synod, and principal staff members of the General Synod, the Archbishops' Council, the Church Commissioners, the Pensions Board and Lambeth Palace, and Church Commissioners who are not members of General Synod. General Synod members are distinguished by the date of their membership, printed at the end of their entry, following the letters GS. Current membership of the General Synod is denoted by the lack of a closing date. The information contained here is supplied by the individuals concerned and no warranty is given as to its accuracy.

ADAMS, Canon Peter George Michelmore MA, MSc
c/o St Mary's Church Church Street Luton LU1 3JF [ST ALBANS] *educ* The Skinners School, Tunbridge Wells, Pembroke College Oxford; University College, London *CV* Missionary, Youth with a Mission 1981–2002; Intercultural Relations Training and Consultancy (self employed) 2002–07; Interfaith and Intercultural Peacebuilding consultancy 2007–16; Director, St Mary's Centre for Peace and Reconciliation from 2016
GS 2015–   *T:* 01582 721 867
                                        07979 510 709
                            E: pgmadams@gmail.com
                        W: www.ReconciliationTalk.org
                            Twitter: @PeterGMAdams

ADCOCK, Mrs Isabel Ruth *LLB*
47 East Street Tollesbury Maldon CM9 8QD [CHELMSFORD] *b* 1955 *educ* Gillingham School; Mid-Essex Technical College, Inns of Court School *CV* Barrister 1975–81; Sixth-form teacher 1996–99; Teacher 1999–2000; Lecturer in Legal Practice 2000–13; Legal Aid Committee 2000–05, from 2010
GS 2005–10, 2010–15, 2015–
                                      T: 01621 860326
                        E: adcocki@hotmail.co.uk

ADENEY, Mrs Susan Margaret Eliza *BEd, BLitt, DipPS*
The Villa Gilberts End Worcester Worcestershire WR8 0AS [WORCESTER] *b* 1955 *educ* St Brides School, Helensburgh, Dartford College of Education, UniversIty of London Institute of Education & University of Birmingham *CV* Teacher of Physical Education Malvern Girls College 1977–79; Head of Department 1979–86; Diploma in Pastoral Studies at Birminham University 1986–87; Deputy Headteacher Lawnside School, Malvern 1987–91; Education Officer at Worcester Cathedral 1998–16; Authorized Lay Minister Worcester Diocese
GS 2015–   *T:* 01684 310440
                        E: sadeney@metronet.co.uk

AINSCOUGH, Miss Rhian
56 Blackwell End Potterspury Northampton NN12 7QE [LEICESTER] *b* 1996 *educ* St Mary's RC High School, Chesterfield, The University of Leicester
GS 2015–   *E:* rhian.ainscough@yahoo.com

ALDERTON-FORD, The Revd Jonathan Laurence *BTh*
Church Office Christ Church Moreton Hall Symonds Rd Bury St Edmunds IP32 7EW [ST EDMUNDSBURY AND IPSWICH] *b* 1957 *CV* Curate St Faith Gaywood Norwich 1985–87; Curate St Andrew Herne Bay 1987–90; Minister Christ Chuch Local Ecumenical Partnership Moreton Hall from 1990; Canon St Edmundsbury Cathedral from 2008; Broadcaster for Premier Christian Radio; Vice Chair Diocesan Synod from 2012
GS 1999–   *T:* 01284 769956 (Home)
                                    01284 725391 (Office)
                            E: minister@ccmh.org.uk
                                      F: 01284 725391

ALDRED, Bishop Dr Joseph Daniel *PhD*
3 Shakespear Crescent Birmingham B18 5BT [GENERAL SYNOD ECUMENICAL REPRESENTATIVE – BLACK-LED CHURCHES] *b* 1952 *educ* Sheffield University Urban Theology Unit *CV* Secretary Pentecostal and Multicultural Relations, Churches Together in England from 2003; Honorary Research Fellow Roehampton University; Bishop in Church of God of Prophecy from 1989
GS 2010–   *T:* 0207 529 8131
                                        07775 632288
                            E: joe.aldred@cte.org.uk

ALEXANDER, Mrs April Rosemary *BA, CertEd*
59 High Street Bletchingley Redhill RH1 4PB [SOUTHWARK] *b* 1949 *educ* Royal Masonic School Rickmansworth; Open University; Homerton College Cambridge *CV* Various teaching posts 1964–84; Financial Services Industry 1984–92; Financial Services Authority (formerly Securities and Investments Board) 1992–1999; Executive Director Occupations Pensions Regulatory Authority 1999–2005; Head of Trustee Education The Pensions Regulator 2005–2007; Consultant The Pensions Regulator and Pensions Industry 2007; Lay Chair Diocesan Synod 1996–2006; Member

Deployment, Remuneration and Conditions of Service Committee; Member General Synod Legislative Committee; Member Church Commission Board of Governors 2009; Member Audit Committee of Church Commissioners; Member Steering Committee Clergy Terms of Service 2007; Member Review Committee Bishops and Priests (Consecration and Ordination of Women) Measure 2009
GS 2000–   *T:* 01883 743421
                          E: april@abalexander.co.uk
                          M: 07867 977823

ALI, Canon Linda *BA, MA*
51 Thief Lane York YO10 3HQ [YORK] *b* 1943 *educ* Bishop Abstey Grammar School Trinidad; University of York *CV* Trade Marks Co-ordinator, Colgate Palmolive Europe 1970–89; Trade Marks Manager Unilever Plc UK 1989–97; Researcher/writer, National Archives, London 2003–3; Set All Free-Churches Together in England 2004–8; Retired; Member York Forum for Racial Concerns; Member Committee for Minority Ethnic Anglican Concerns from 2006; Chair of Trustees United Society for the Propagation of the Gospel: Anglicans in World Mission from 2009; Member Derwent Deanery Synod; Member Society Responsibility Council, North Yorkshire; Lay Chair of Heslington Church (LEP)
GS 2005–   *T:* 01904 413698
                          E: linda@jj26.fsnet.co.uk
                          M: 07966 363721 (Mobile)

ALLAIN CHAPMAN, The Ven Dr Justine Penelope Heathcote *BA, AKC, PGCE, DThMin, MDiv*
Archdeacon's House Castle Hill Welbourn Lincoln LN5 0NF [ARCHDEACON OF BOSTON; LINCOLN] *educ* Kings College London; Nottingham University; Lincoln Theological College *CV* Head of Religious Studies, South Hampstead High School 1989–91; Curate Christ Church with St Paul, Forest Hill 1993–96; Team Vicar St Paul Clapham 1996–2001; Vicar St Paul Clapham 2002–04; Director of Mission and Pastoral Studies South East Institute for Theological Education 2004–13, Vice Principal 2007–13; Priest Vicar Rochester Cathedral 2005–13; Archdeacon of Boston from 2013; General Synod Representative Churches' Commission on Mission 2001–3; Southwark Diocesan Liturgical Committee 1994–2004; Vocations Advisory Panel Ministry Division 2003–06; Bishop's Inspector for Theological Education from 2010
GS 2000–04, 2015–   *T:* 01400 273335
              E: archdeacon.boston@lincoln.anglican.org
                          M: 07715 077993 (Mobile)
                          Twitter: @JustinePHAC

ALLAIN CHAPMAN, Dr Thomas Joseph *BA, MA, PhD*
Church House Great Smith Street London SW1P 3AZ [PUBLISHING MANAGER, ARCHBISHOPS' COUNCIL]

b 1969 *educ* Mount St Mary's College Sheffield; King's College London *CV* Freelance writer and editor 1994–5; Editor HarperCollins Religious 1995–97; Assistant Commissioning Editor, Collins Education 1997–2000, Commissioning Editor 2000, Publishing Manager 2000–5; Head of Publishing, Church House Publishing 2005–09; Director ROOTS for Churches Ltd from 2006; Publishing Manager Archbishops' Council from 2009   *T:* 020 7898 1450
                          E: thomas.allain-chapman@
                          churchofengland.org

ALLBERRY, The Revd Samuel *BA, BTh*
St Mary's Church St Mary's Close 14 High Street Maidenhead Berkshire SL61YY [OXFORD] *b* 1949 *educ* Judd School, Tonbridge, Chichester Institute of Higher Education *CV* Curate, St Ebbe's Oxford, 2003–08; Associate Vicar, St Mary's Maidenhead, from 2008
GS 2015–   *T:* 01628 638866
                          E: samallberry@gmail.com
                          W: www.livingout.org
                          Twitter: @SamAllberry

ALLDREAD, Mrs Katherine Christian *BA, JD*
6 Woodland Grove Old Tupton Chesterfield S42 6JQ [DERBY] *b* 1972 *educ* Fenton High School, DePaul University, University of Michigan Law School *CV* Attorney, Law Offices of Dean T Yeotis, 1998–2001; Owner and Manager, Curves for Women Fitness Centre 2002–05; Parent/Carer 2005–10; Church Administrator, St Bartholomew, Clay Cross and St Barnabas, Danesmoor 2010–14; Office Manager and PA to the Diocesan Secretary, Derby Diocese from 2014
GS 2015–   *T:* 01246 865187
              E: kat@theorderoftheblacksheep.com

ALLEN, Mrs (Penelope) Penny *Teaching Cert*
12 Cranbrook Grove Perton Wolverhampton WV6 7RY [LICHFIELD] *b* 1949 *educ* Education Kibworth Beauchamp Grammar; Oadby Beauchamp Upper School; Leicester City College of Education *CV* Teacher 1971–2009 in Leicestershire, Wolverhampton, Staffordshire; Head of Religious Education and PSHCE; Member South Staffordshire District Council from 1987; Member Ecumenical Church Council Perton; Member Trysull Deanery; Member Lichfield Diocesan Finance Committee; Member Bishop's Council; Member Patronage Board
GS 2010–   *T:* 01902 756125
                          E: mrspennyallen@yahoo.co.uk
                          W: Online diary for GS: httyp://
                          pennyatgeneralsynod.weebly.com

ALLISTER, The Rt Revd Donald Spargo *MA, DTh (Hon)*
Bishop's Lodging The Palace Peterborough PE1 1YA [BISHOP OF PETERBOROUGH] *b* 1952 *educ*

WHO'S WHO

Birkenhead School; Peterhouse Cambridge; Trinity Theological College Bristol *CV* Curate St George Hyde, Chester 1976–79; Curate St Nicholas Sevenoaks, Rochester 1979–83; Vicar Christ Church Birkenhead, Chester 1983–89; Chaplain Arrow Park Hospital 1983–85; Rector St Mary Cheadle 1992–2002; Archdeacon of Chester 2002–10; Bishop of Peterborough from 2010; Council for Christian Unity from 2006, Chair from 2013; Archbishops' Council Finance Committee 2011–13; Faith and Order Commission from 2014
GS 2005–   *T:* 01733 562492
        E: bishop@peterborough-diocese.org.uk
                                    F: 01733 890077

ALLWOOD, Canon Tony (Anthony Robert) *BSc*
29 Warren Hill Road Woodbridge Suffolk IP12 4DU [ST EDMUNDSBURY AND IPSWICH] *b* 1949 *educ* The King's School, Chester, Durham University *CV* Professional Engineer then Manager with British Telecom 1974–2000; Management Consultant 2000–04; Operational Manager at St John's Church, Woodbridge 2004–12; Retired
GS 2015–   *T:* 01394 384575
        E: tony_allwood@btopenworld.com

ANGAELOS, His Grace Bishop
The Coptic Church Centre Shepalbury Manor Broadhall Way Stevenage SG2 8NP [ECUMENICAL REPRESENTATIVE (COPTIC ORTHODOX CHURCH)] *b* 1967 *CV* Coptic Orthodox monk, Monastery of Saint Bishoy, Wadi-El-Natroun, from 1990; papal secretary to His Holiness Pope Shenouda III, Monastery of Saint Bishoy 1990–95; Parish Priest, Coptic Orthodox Church Centre, Stevenage 1995–99; General Bishop, Coptic Orthodox Church in the UK from 1999; Moderator of Churches Together in Britain and Ireland; President of Churches Together in England; Chair of the Council of the Oriental Orthodox Churches in the United Kingdom and the Republic of Ireland; Co-chair of the Anglican-Oriental Orthodox Regional Forum; Member of the Anglican-Oriental Orthodox International Commission; Co-founder and Co-chair of the Catholic-Oriental Orthodox Regional Forum; Co-founder and Co-chair of the Lausanne-Orthodox Initiative; Moderator of the Churches' Inter-Religious Network for Churches Together in Britain and Ireland; Ecumenical participant of the Church of England General Synod; Member of the Global Council of the United Bible Society; Member of the Coptic Delegation to the World Council of Churches; Chair of Christians Aware; Member of Christian Solidarity Worldwide Board of Reference; Scholar-Consultant on the Christian-Muslim Forum;

Chair and Founder of Foundations for Hope (FFH); Patron: Christians Aware; The Ecumenical Society of the Blessed Virgin Mary; The Apostolic Order of St Hadrian of Canterbury; The SAT 7 Trust UK; British Egyptian Public Affairs Committee; Embrace The Middle East; Awareness Foundation
GS 2013–   *T:* 020 7993 9001
                                    01438 745232
                E: admin@copticcentre.com
                W: www.copticcentre.com
                Twitter: @BishopAngaelos

ANGUS, Dr Christopher John *MA, PhD*
Burtholme East Lanercost Brampton CA8 2HH [CARLISLE] *b* 1967 *educ* Hampton School; Trinity Hall Cambridge; Newcastle University *CV* Senior Systems Analyst, ICL 1970–75; Consultant, Mancos 1975–78; Application Development Manager, CADCentre, Cambridge 1978–83; Technical Director, Prosys Technology 1983–89; Director, Angus Association 1989–2000; Software Architect, Shell 2000–03; Chief Architect, Kalido 2003–13; Member Bishop's Council 2006; Member Archdeaconry Mapping Committee from 2001; Member Rule Committee from 2012; Member Steering and Revision Committeess draft Care of Churches and Ecclesiastical Jurisdiction Measure 2013–14; Lay Chair Carlisle Diocese from 2015; Member Steering and Revision Committees Draft Mission and Pastoral (Amendment) Measure 2016–17; Member Steering and Revision Committees Draft Church Representation, Ecumenical Relations and Minister Measure from 2016; Member of Appeal Panel under Rule 44(8) of Church Representation Rules from 2015
GS 2010–   *T:* 01697 741504
        E: chris.angus@btinternet.com

ANNAS, The Rt Revd Geoff
Ash Garth Broughton Crescent Barlaston Stoke-on-Trent ST12 9DD [AREA BISHOP OF STAFFORD; LICHFIELD] *b* 1953 *educ* Sarum & Wells Theological College *CV* Curate Holy Trinity with St Matthew Southwark 1983–1987; Team Vicar St Peter Walworth 1987–1994; Warden, Pembroke Missionary College Walworth 1987–1994; Vicar St Christopher Thornhill 1994–2010; Honorary Canon Winchester Cathedral 2007–2010; Area Bishop of Stafford from 2010   *T:* 01782 373308
        E: bishop.stafford@lichfield.anglican.org

APPLEBY, Dr John Christopher *MA, PhD*
38 Beech Grove Whitley Bay NE26 3PL [NEWCASTLE] *b* 1956 *educ* Chace School, Enfield; Enfield Grammar School, Jesus College Cambridge, Leeds University *CV* Research Fellow, Leeds University, 1981–84; Lecturer/

Senior Lecturer, Newcastle University, 1984–2003; Head of School of Mechanical and Systems Engineering, Newcastle University 2003–17; Senior Lecturer in Engineering Mathematics from 2017
GS 2015–   *T:* 0774 273 1766
                          E: johncappleby@gmail.com

ARCHER, Mr Anthony William *LLB*
Barn Cottage Little Gaddesden Berkhamsted Herts HP4 1PH [ST ALBANS] *b* 1953 *educ* St Edward's School, Oxford, University of Birmingham *CV* Partner Odgers Berndtson 1995–2010; Partner, JWA Governance Services LLP from 2012; Managing Partner Bridgewater Leadership Advisory from 2010; Member Dioceses Commission from 2016; Member Crown Nominations Commission from 2017
GS 1993–2010, 2015–   *T:* 01442 842397
                                       07721 504125
     E: anthony.archer@bridgewaterassociates.
                                       co.uk

ARDRON, Canon (Yvonne) Shayne *BSc*
93 Letchworth Road Leicester LE3 6FN [LEICESTER] *b* 1958 *educ* Laurence Jackson School; Prior Pursglove College; Leicester Polytech *CV* Quality Control Tester 1988–95; Lay Reader from 2005; Mother of 4; Reader and co-leader play group Church of the Martyrs Leicester; Member Bishop's Council Leicester; Member Growth Fund Leicester; Member Bishop's Youth Council Leicester; Member Liturgical Commission
GS 2010–   *T:* 0116 254 1560
          E: shayne.ardron.gs@gmail.com
                          Twitter: @piglets4mum

ASHCROFT, The Rt Revd Mark David *BA, MA*
Bishop's Lodge Walkden Road Worsley Manchester M28 2WH [SUFFRAGAN BISHOP OF BOLTON] *b* 1954 *educ* Rugby; Worcester College Oxford Cambridge; Ridley Hall *CV* Assistant Curate Burnage St Margaret 1982–85; Tutor St Paul School of Divinity Kapsabet Kenya 1986–90; Principal St Paul Theological College Kapsabet Kenya 1990–95; Rector Christ Church Harpurhey, Manchester 1996–2009; Area Dean North Manchester 2000–2006; Archdeacon of Manchester 2009–16, Bishop of Bolton from 2016   *T:* 0161 790 8289
     E: bishopbolton@manchester.anglican.org

ASHE, The Ven (Francis) John *BMet, Cert Th*
Holly Tree House Whitwell Road Sparham Norwich NR9 5PN [ARCHDEACON OF LYNN; NORWICH] *b* 1953 *educ* Christ's Hospital; Sheffield University; Ridley Hall Cambridge *CV* Curate Ashtead, Guild 1979–82; Priest in Charge St Faith Plumstead, Cape Town 1982–87; Rector Wisley-with-Pyrford, Guild

1987–93; Vicar Godalming, Guild 1993–2001; Rural Dean Godalming 1996–2002; Team Rector Godalming 2001–09; Member Bishop's Council; Bishop's Advisory Panel 2002–2009; Honorary Canon Guildford Cathedral 2003–2009; Warden of Readers, Norwich 2009–16; Archdeacon of Lynn from 2009
GS 2003–09   *T:* 01362 688032
     E: archdeacon.lynn@dioceseofnorwich.org

ASHTON, Mr David
2 Manor Drive Battyeford Mirfield WF14 0ER [LEEDS] *b* 1941 *educ* Warwick Road Junior School; Dewsbury and Batley Tech School; Kitson English College *CV* British Telecom Integrity Manager; Member General Synod Standing Orders Committee; Member Bishop's Council
GS 1972–   *T:* 01924 497996
          E: david_ashton@hotmail.com

ASTIN, The Ven Moira Anne Elizabeth *MA, MA*
Croydon Episcopal Area Office 100 George Street Croydon CR0 1PJ [ARCHDEACON OF REIGATE; SOUTHWARK] *b* 1965 *educ* City of London Girls School; Sir William Perkins School, Chertsey; Clare College Cambridge; Wycliffe Hall Oxford *CV* Assistant Curate Newbury 1995–99; Team Vicar Thatcham 1999–2005; Team Vicar Southlake St James Woodley 2005–09; Vicar Southlake St James 2009–11; Diocesan Ecumenical Officer Oxford 2010–12; Priest-in-charge Frodingham and New Brumby 2011–16; Archdeacon of Reigate from 2016; Board of Mission 2000–02; Mission Shaped Church Working Party 2002–04; Standing Committee House of Clergy 2005–12
GS 2000–12   *T:* 020 8256 9630
     E: Moira.astin@southwark.anglican.org
                          Twitter: @MoiraAstin

ASTON, Dr Nigel Roy *BA*
36 Butt Lane South Luffenham Oakham LE15 8JN [PETERBOROUGH] *educ* Allerton Grange School; University of Durham; University of Oxford *CV* Reader in Early Modern History, University of Leicester from 2001; Peterborough Diocesan Synod; Patronage Committee
GS 2015–   *T:* 01780 721458
                          E: nra1710@gmail.com
                          M: 07792 490077

ATHERSTONE, The Revd Dr Andrew Castell *MA, MSt, DPhil*
Wycliffe Hall 54 Banbury Road Oxford OX2 6PW [OXFORD] *b* 1949 *educ* The King's School, Ely; The Skinners' School, Tunbridge Wells, University of Cambridge; University of Oxford *CV* Curate of Christ Church, Abingdon

2001–05; Associate Minister of Eynsham and Cassington from 2005; Research Fellow of the Latimer Trust from 2005; Tutor at Wycliffe Hall from 2007
GS 2015–   *T:* 01865 274589
E: andrew.atherstone@wycliffe.ox.ac.uk

ATKINSON, The Very Revd Peter Gordon *MA, Hon DLitt, FRSA*
The Deanery 10 College Green Worcester WR1 2LH [DEAN OF WORCESTER] *b* 1952 *educ* Maidstone Grammar School; St John College Oxford; Westcott House Cambridge *CV* Curate Clapham Old Town Team 1979–83; Priest in Charge Tatsfield 1983–90; Rector Holy Trinity Bath 1990–91; Principal Chichester Theological College 1991–94; Bursalis Prebendary Chichester Cathedral 1991–97; Rector Lavant 1994–97; Chancellor Chichester Cathedral 1997–2007; Dean of Worcester from 2007; Master St Oswald's Hospital Worcester from 2007
GS 2000–05   *T:* 01905 732909 (Office)
                       01905 732939 (Study)
E: peteratkinson@worcestercathedral.org.uk

ATKINSON, The Rt Revd Richard William Bryant *MA, MA, OBE*
Bishop's Lodge Bedford Road Cardington Bedford MK44 3SS [SUFFRAGAN BISHOP OF BEDFORD; ST ALBANS] *b* 1958 *educ* St Paul's School London; Magdalene College Cambridge; Cuddesdon Theological College; Birmingham University *CV* Curate Abingdon with Shippon 1984–87; Team Vicar Sheffield Manor Parish 1987–91; Honorary Member of Staff Cuddesdon Theological College 1987–92; Team Rector Sheffield Manor Parish 1991–96; Vicar All Saints Rotherham 1996–2002; Honorary Canon Sheffield Cathedral 1998–2002; Archdeacon of Leicester 2002–12; Bishop of Bedford from 2012; Member Churches Together England and Churches Together Britain and Ireland 1997–2002; Church Commissioner 2001–08; Member Central Church Fund Committee 1997–2002; Church Urban Fund Trustee 2003–08; Deputy Chair Places for People 1997–2005; Chair Phoenix Enterprises (Rotherham) Ltd 1998–2002; Chair Braunstone New Deal for Communities Programme 2003–06; Chair St Philip's Centre for Study and Engagement in Multi Faith Society 2005–12; Chair Launde Abbey Management Committee 2002–08; Member Carnegie Trust UK Enquiry into the Future of Civil Society in Britain and Ireland 2007–10; Member Presence and Engagement Task Group; Co-Chair National Hindu Christian Forum 2010–16; Near Neighbours Trustee from 2011; Vice-Chair MPA from 2012; Chair St Albans Diocesan Board of Education from 2013; Co-Chair Inter Faith Network UK from 2014; Chair Eastern Region Ministry Course

from 2014; Chair St Albans Diocesan Mission and Pastoral Committee from 2016
GS 1991–2012   *T:* 01234 831432
E: bishopbedford@stalbans.anglican.org

ATTWOOD, The Revd Andrew *BEd, BA*
St John's Vicarage Clarke's Avenue Kenilworth CV81HX [COVENTRY] *b* 1949 *CV* Primary School Teacher, Derby 1991–96; Youth and Student Worker, St Alkmund, Derby 1996–2000; Curate and Associate Leader, St Mary, Leamington Spa 2002–10; Vicar St. John, Kenilworth from 2010
GS 2015–   *T:* 07884 136816
E: andrew@stjohnschurchkenilworth.org.uk

ATWELL, The Rt Revd Robert Ronald *BA (Hons), MLitt*
The Palace Exeter EX1 1HY [BISHOP OF EXETER] *b* 1954 *educ* Wanstead High School; St John's College Durham; Westcott House Cambridge *CV* Asst Curate John Keble Church Mill Hill 1978–81; Chaplain Trinity College Cambridge 1981–87; Benedictine Monk Burford Priory 1987–98; Vicar Parish of St Mary-the-Virgin Primrose Hill 1998–2008; Bishop Stockport 2008–14; Bishop of Exeter from 2014; Chair Ministry Committee Chester Diocese; Trustee SNWTP; Member Working Group on Discipline in relation to matters of Doctrine, Ritual and Ceremonial; Chair Liturgical Commission from 2014
GS 2014   *T:* 01392 272362
E: bishop.of.exeter@exeter.anglican.org

AYERS, The Ven Paul Nicholas *MA*
Church House 17–19 York Place Leeds LS1 2EX [LEEDS] *b* 1967 *educ* Bradford Grammar School; St Peter College Oxford; Trinity College Bristol *CV* Curate St John Baptist Clayton 1985–88; Curate St Andrew Keighley 1988–91; Vicar St Cuthbert Wrose 1991–97; Vicar St Lawrence and St Paul Pudsey 1997–2017; Archdeacon of Leeds from 2017
GS 1995–   *T:* 07539 873940
E: paul.ayers@leeds.anglican.org

BACK, Mr Robin Philip *AIB, FRSA*
The Old Manse Church Lane Guestwick NR20 5QJ [NORWICH] *educ* Uppingham; Geneva University *CV* Standard Chartered Bank in Middle East, India, Indonesia, Thailand and USA 1967–88; MD Backs Electronic Publishing Ltd 1989–16; Prime Warden, Worshipful Company of Dyers of City of London 2002–03; Member Bishop's Council 2003–15; Lay Chair, Diocesan Synod 2003–09; Lay Chair, Sparham Deanery Synod 1996–2001; Member Diocesan Board of Finance from 2003; Chair Friends of Scott Polar Research Institute, University of Cambridge 2007–10; Director Wispire Ltd (diocesan trading company)

2009–16; Director Spire Property Services Ltd (diocesan trading company) from 2009
GS 2005–   *T:* 01362 683281
                                     01362 683835
                                E: robin@bepl.co.uk
                                M: 07802 244619

BACON, Mr Nigel *MA*
10 The Meadows Market Deeping Peterborough PE6 8PE [LINCOLN] *educ* Bolton School; Stamford School, Churchill College, University of Cambridge *CV* Professional Trainee, Perkins Engines Co Ltd 1973–77; Research and Development Engineer, Perkins Engines Co Ltd 1977–84; Applications Engineer, Perkins Engines Co Ltd 1984–86; Marketing and Business Planning Manager, Perkins Technology Ltd 1986–90; Projects Engineering Manager, Perkins Engines Co Ltd 1990–94; Product Engineering Manager, Perkins Engines Co Ltd 1994–2000; Engine Test Operations Manager, Technical Centre, Caterpillar Inc USA-based 2000–04; Technical Manager, Mining and Construction Products Division, Caterpillar Inc USA-based 2004–6; Engineering Manager, Industrial Power Systems Division, Caterpillar Inc 2006–10; Strategy Manager, Industrial Power Systems Division, Caterpillar Inc 2010–13; Business Improvement Manager, Industrial Power Systems Division, Caterpillar Inc. from 2013
GS 2015–   *T:* 01778 342737
                          E: nandjbacn@btinternet.com

BAGG, Mrs Emily Rachel *BA(Hons)*
56 Castle Road Newport Isle of Wight PO30 1DP [PORTSMOUTH] *educ* Hayesfield Girls School, Bath, University of Winchester *CV* Chaplaincy Assistant, Univesity of Winchester 2008–10; Learning Support Advisor, Prison Officer's Assocation 2011–12; Special educational needs teacher 2010–14
GS 2015–   *T:* 07446 093930
                                     01983 718908
                          E: emily.bagg@hotmail.co.uk

BAIN, The Ven (John) Stuart *BA*
St Nicholas' Vicarage Hedworth Lane Boldon Colliery NE35 9JA [ARCHDEACON OF SUNDERLAND; DURHAM] *educ* Blaydon Secondary School; Durham University; Westcott House Cambridge *CV* Curate Holy Trinity Washington 1980–84; Curate St Nicholas Dunston 1984–86; Vicar St Oswald Shiney Row and St Aidan Herrington 1986–92; Priest in Charge St Paul Spennymoor and Whitworth 1992–97; Priest in Charge St John Merrington 1994–97; Area Dean Auckland 1996–2002; Honorary Canon Durham 1998; Vicar St Paul Spennymoor, Whitworth and St John Merrington 1997–2002; Chair DFW Adoption from 1999; Assistant Priest St Nicolas from 1999; Assistant Priest St Nicolas Hedworth 2002; Priest in Charge St Nicholas Hedworth from 2003; Priest in Charge St George East Boldon from 2009; Priest in Charge St Nicholas Boldon from 2010; Archdeacon of Sunderland from 2002
                                T: 0191 536 2300
                    E: Archdeacon.of.Sunderland@durham.
                                     anglican.org
                                F: 0191 519 3369

BAINES, The Rt Revd Nicholas *BA (Hons)*
Hollin House Weetwood Avenue Leeds LS16 5NG [BISHOP OF LEEDS] *b* 1958 *educ* Holt Comprehensive School Liverpool; Bradford University; Trinity College Bristol *CV* Curate St Thomas Kendal 1987–91; Curate Holy Trinity Leicester 1991–92; Vicar Rothley 1992–2000; Rural Dean Goscote 1995–2000; Archdeacon of Lambeth 2000–03; Broadcaster; Director EIG 2002–10; Bishop of Croydon 2003–10; Anglican Co-Chair Meissen Community; Chair Sandford St Margaret Trust from 2009; Bishop of Bradford 2011–14; Bishop of Leeds from 2014; House of Lords from 2014
GS 1995–2003, 2004–05, 2011–
                                T: 0113 284 4300
                    E: bishop.nick@leeds.anglican.org
                        W: nickbaines.wordpress.com
                                Twitter: @nickbaines

BAKER, The Rt Revd Jonathan Mark Richard *MA, M Phil, Hon DD*
The Vicarage 5 St Andrew Street London EC4A 3AF [SUFFRAGAN BISHOP OF FULHAM; LONDON] *educ* Merchant Taylors' School Northwood; St John College Oxford; St Stephen's House Theological College *CV* Curate All Saints Ascot Heath 1993–96; Curate, St Mark Reading, Oxford 1996; Priest in Charge St Mark and Holy Trinity Reading 1996–99; Vicar St Mark and Holy Trinity Reading 1999–2002; Principal Pusey House, Oxford 2003–13; Honorary Curate, St Thomas the Martyr Oxford 2008–13; Bishop of Ebbsfleet 2011–13; Honorary Assistant Bishop, Oxford 2011–2013; Assistant Bishop, Bath and Wells 2011–2013; Bishop of Fulham from 2013
GS 2000–11   *T:* 020 7932 1130
                    E: bishop.fulham@london.anglican.org
                                M: 07881 522669 (Mobile)

BALDRY, Sir Tony Brian *MA, LLB*
Dovecote House Church Street Bloxham Banbury Oxfordshire OX15 4ET [OXFORD] *b* 1967 *CV* Barrister at Lincoln's Inn from 1975; Chair of the Church Buildings Council
GS 2010–   *T:* 07798 840570
                          E: sirtonybaldry@gmail.com
                            W: www.tonybaldry.co.uk

BALL, Mr John Peter *MA (Oxon), MSc*
53 New Street Chelmsford CM1 1AT [DIOCESAN SECRETARY; CHELMSFORD] *educ* Keble College,

University of Oxford, University of Westminster *CV* Senior Executive Transport for London 1999–2011; Chief Executive and Diocesan Secretary, Diocese of Chelmsford from 2011 *T:* 01245 294409
E: jball@chelmsford.anglican.org

BANKS, The Rt Revd Norman *MA (Oxon)*, *PGCE*
Parkside House Abbey Mill Lane St Albans AL3 4HE [BISHOP OF RICHBOROUGH] *educ* Wallsend Grammar; Oriel College Oxford; Oxford Department Education; St Stephen's House *CV* Curate Christ Church with St Ann Newcastle 1982–84; Cleric in Charge St Ann 1984–87; Priest in Charge Christ Church with St Ann 1987–1990; Vicar Tynemouth St Paul Cullercoats 1990–2000; Vicar Walsingham, Houghton and the Barshams 2000–11; Rural Dean Burnham and Walsingham 2008–11, Chaplain to HM the Queen 2008–11; Chaplain to High Sheriff of Norfolk 2010–11; Bishop of Richborough from 2011; Member Council North East Ordination course 1993–2000; Advisory Board of Ministry Selector 1993–2000; Inspector of Theological Colleges and Courses 1995–2000
GS 1990–2000, 2010– *T:* 01727 836358
E: bishop@richborough.org.uk

BARKER, The Revd Mark *BTh*
St Stephen's Vicarage 6 Brook Street Tonbridge Kent TN9 2PJ [ROCHESTER] *educ* Stowe School, University of Nottingham *CV* Barclays Bank 1980–1992; Assistant Curate St. Margaret's Barking 1995–1998; Assistant Curate St Luke's Cranham 1998–2004; Vicar St Stephen's Tonbridge from 2004
GS 2013– *T:* 01732 353079
E: mark.barker@ststephenstonbridge.org

BARKER, The Very Revd Timothy Reed *MA*
St Andrew's Rectory Route de St Andre St Andrew Guernsey GY6 8XN [DEAN OF GUERNSEY] *educ* Manchester Grammar School; Queens' College Cambridge; Westcott House *CV* Curate Nantwich 1980–83; Vicar Norton St Berteline and St Christopher 1983–88; Vicar Runcorn All Saints 1988–94; Urban Officer Chester 1990–98; Bishop of Chester's Chaplain 1994–98; Priest Associate, Chester Cathedral 1994–98; Vicar Spalding St Mary and Nicholas 1998–2009; Rural Dean Elloe West 2000–09; Member Lincoln Cathedral Chaplain 2000–09; Canon and Prebendary of Lincoln from 2003; Rural Dean Elloe East 2008–09; Priest in Charge Spalding St Paul 2007–09; Member Deployment, Renumeration and Conditions of Service Committee 2001–05; Member Continuing Ministerial Education Panel 2003–06; Member Clergy Terms of Service Implementation Group 2005–07; Member Marriage Law Working Party 2006; Member

Marriage (Amendment) Measure Steering Committee; Member Diocesan Synod 1999–2015; Trustee Alcuin Club from 1990; Archdeacon of Lincoln 2009–15; Dean of Guernsey from 2015; Rector St Andre de la Pommeraye Guernsey from 2015; Priest-in-charge Sark from 2015; Honorary Canon Winchester Cathedral from 2015; Member Church Buildings Council from 2011; Chair National Archdeacons' Forum from 2015
GS 2000–05; 2008– *T:* 01481 238568
E: deanofguernsey@gmail.com
M: 07781 166095 (Mobile)

BARON, Ms Christina Murray *BSc*
The Old Vicarage St Thomas Street Wells Somerset BA5 2UZ [BATH AND WELLS] *educ* St Leonard's School, St Andrews, Fife, City University, London *CV* Mayor of Wells, 1980–81; Research Fellow, University of Bath, 1984–86; lecturer, SOAS, University of London, 1986–99; Teaching Fellow, University of Bath, 1999–2015; Chair, Somerset Partnership NHS and Social Care Trust, 1997–2004; Interim Chair, North Somerset PCT, 2004–05; Council Member, Nursing and Midwifery Council, 2007–10; Independent member of selection panels, Judicial Appointments Commission from 2004; Chair House of Laity Bath and Wells 2009–15; Tribunal Member, Medical Practitioners' Tribunal Service from 2014; Crown Nominations Commission from 2017
GS 2013– *T:* 01749 675071
07745 423253
E: baron.christina@gmail.com
Twitter: @baron.christina

BARRON, Mrs Enid Monica *MA, Dip*
110 The Avenue Ealing London W13 8JX [LONDON] *b* 1945 *educ* Wakefield Girls High School; St Anne's College Oxford; York University; Oxford Brookes University *CV* School Care Organizer, Inner London Education Authority 1968–69; Civil Service Environment Department Assistant Principal, Principal 1969–99; Gwilym Gibbon Fellow, Nuffield College Oxford; Royal Commission on Environmental Pollution, Assistant Secretary; Reader 2010–
GS 2015– *T:* 0208 9971958
E: enid@enidmbarron.waitrose.com
F: 07850 261307

BASHFORTH, The Revd Canon Alan George *MA, BTh*
Four Winds Green Lane Truro TR1 2HP [TRURO] *educ* Humphrey Davy Grammar School; Oxford University; Exeter University; Ripon College Cuddesdon *CV* Police officer, South Yorkshire Police 1983–90; nursing auxiliary 1990–93; Curate Calstock, Truro 1996–98; Curate St Ives, Truro 1998–2001; Vicar St Agnes and Mithian with Mount Hawke from 2001;

Bishop's Council, Diocesan Board of Education from 2003; Trustee South West Ministry Training Course from 2005; Rural Dean Powder 2004–13; Member Diocesan Pastoral Committee; Chair House of Clergy from 2009; Honorary Canon Truro Cathedral from 2013; Canon Chancellor Truro Cathedral from 2014
GS 2005–   *T:* 01872 276782
    E: alanbashforth@trurocathedral.org.uk

BATTYE, The Revd Canon Lisa *BN, DipC, MA, MTh, M.Prof*
1 Moorside Road Kersal Salford M7 3PJ [MANCHESTER] *b* 1954 *educ* Holy Family Convent High School, Rock Ferry; Manchester Polytechnic; Chester University *CV* Midwife, St Mary's Hospital, Manchester, 1978–79; Carer for Holocaust victims, Jerusalem, 1979–80; Staff Nurse, Christie Hospital, Manchester, 1981–82; District Nurse, Burnage, Manchester, 1982–85; Geriatric Health Visitor, Chorlton, Manchester, 1985–86; Independent Advisor, Univite Ltd, 1983–98; Buying and managing rented properties, from 1984; Assistant curate, Clifton, Manchester, 1999–2002; Rector, Parish of St Paul, Kersal Moor and St Andrew, Carr Clough 2002–17; Area Dean of Salford 2012–17; Canon Manchester Cathedral from 2016; Team Vicar St James and Emmanuel Didsbury from 2017
GS 2015–   *T:* 0161 792 5362
                                      07539 775483
    E: lisabattye@stpaulsparish.org.uk
    W: www.stpaulsparish.org.uk
                            Twitter: @lisabattye

BAYES, The Rt Revd Paul *BA, DipTheol*
Bishop's Lodge Woolton Park Woolton Liverpool L25 6DT [BISHOP OF LIVERPOOL] *b* 1953 *educ* Belle Vue Boys' School, Bradford; University Birmingham; Queen's College Birmingham *CV* Curate Tynemouth Cullercoats St Paul Newcastle 1979–82; Chaplain Queen Elizabeth College London 1982–87; Chaplain Chelsea College 1985–87; Team Vicar High Wycombe 1987–90; Team Rector 1990–94; Team Rector Totton Winchester 1995–04; Area Dean Lyndhurst 2000–04; National Mission and Evangelism Advisory Archbishop's Council 2004–10; Honorary Canon Worcester Cathedral 2007–10; Bishop of Hertford 2010–14; Bishop of Liverpool from 2014   *T:* 0151 421 0831
    E: bishopslodge@liverpool.anglican.org

BAYNES, Mr Simon Henry Crews *BSc, CEng, FBCS*
4 Pilgrim Close St Albans AL2 2JD [ST ALBANS] *educ* Orange Hill Boys' Grammar School, Edgware, Middlesex; Sheffield University *CV* Logica 1979–2009, Director Simon Baynes Ltd from 2009; Client Director, Capital Cranfield Trustees Ltd from 2009; Member CofE

Pensions Board from 2009; Chair, Pension Trustees, Logica 1997–2012; Trustee Cambridge University Press Senior Staff Pension Scheme from 2008; Member National Audit Office Panel of Pensions Experts from 2011; Trustee, Life Academy (The Pre-Retirement Assoc) 2007–14; Chartered Engineer from 1990; Member St Albans Diocesan Synod from 2003; Member St Albans Diocesan Board of Finance from 2003; Member Deanery Synod from 2001; Member St Albans Cathedral Finance Committee 1997–2007 and from 2010; Member Inter-Diocesan Finance Forum from 2005; Member Bishop's Council from 2007; Member Crown Nominations Commission (St Albans Vacancy-in-See) 2008–09; Founder and vice-chair St Albans Diocesan Penal Affairs Group from 2008; Chair National Conference Standing Group 'Engaging Churches in Rehabilitation' 2014
GS 2005–   *T:* 01727 875524 (Home)
                          01727 875537 (Office)
    E: simon@simonbaynes.fsnet.co.uk
        M: 07860 828711 (Mobile)

BECK, Mrs Joan Culberson
The Orchard St Martins Avenue Bawtry DN10 6NH [SOUTHWELL AND NOTTINGHAM] *educ* Selly Oak College, now University of Birmingham, University of Westminster *CV* Director of Adults, Doncaster Council 2007–11; Director Adults and Communities, Doncaster Council 2011–14; Semi-retired/Independent from 2014
GS 2015–   *T:* 01302 711334
    E: joan.beck@outlook.com
                            Twitter: @BeckJoan

BELCHER, Dr William Peter Argent *BSc, PhD*
39 Redgrove Park Cheltenham Gloucestershire GL51 6QY [GLOUCESTER] *educ* Framlingham College, Suffolk; Leeds University; Cambridge University *CV* Post-doctoral Fellowship, UK Atomic Energy Authority (Harwell) 1976–79; Metallurgist, National Nuclear Corporation (Whetstone) 1979–87; Metallurgist, Central Electricity Generating Board (Knutsford) 1987–90; Metallurgist, Nuclear Electric plc (Knutsford) 1990–95; Metallurgist, British Energy Generation (Gloucester) 1995–2006; Metallurgist, Structural Integrity Services, EDF Energy (Gloucester) from 2007; Vacancy-in-See Committee, Gloucester
GS 2010–   *T:* 01242 228690
    E: williambelcher@btinternet.com
        M: 07813 344759

BELL, Dr Andrew Robert *MA, PhD*
Gerrards Cross Gerrards Cross SL9 7LG [OXFORD] *educ* The High School, Newcastle under Lyme, Clare College, Cambridge *CV* Medicinal Chemist, Wellcome Research Labs 1981–86; Clinical Research Scientist, Wellcome/

GlaxoWellcome 1986–95; Clinical Operations Director, GlaxoSmithKline 1995–2015; Retired from 2015; Churchwarden St James Gerrards Cross, from 2015

GS 2015–   T: 01753 893942
                               07876 391382
                               E: andrew@bell.uk.com
                               Twitter: @andrewbell137

BELL, Mrs Rachel Louise *BA*
10 Brecon Close Long Eaton NG10 4JW [DERBY] *educ* Regent's Park Christian Community High School, Sydney; Littleover Community School, Derby; The Millennium Centre, Derby *CV* Children and Youth leader, The Oakes Holiday Centre 2009–10; Administrative Staff, Village Primary School Normanton 2010–11; Teaching Assistant, Village Primary School Normanton 2011; Shop Assistant, The Craft Studio from 2014; 10Parties Ambassador, 10ofThose from 2014

GS 2015–   T: 0115 998 9566
                               07717 461911
                               E: rachel@bell.uk.com

BELLAMY, The Revd Dr (John) Stephen *MA, DipTh, PhD*
11 Beechways Durham DH1 4LG [DURHAM] *educ* Rhyl High School, Jesus College, Oxford; Liverpool University *CV* Pharmaceutical Production Manager (Boots Co) 1977–81; Curate of All Hallows, Allerton, Liverpool 1984–87; Curate of Christ Church, Southport 1987–89; Personal Chaplain and Press Officer to the Bishop of Liverpool 1989–91; Vicar of St James, Birkdale 1991–2008; Vicar of St Nicholas, Durham from 2008

GS 2015–   T: 0191 384 6066
                               E: vicar@stnics.org.uk
                               Twitter: @BellamyStephen

BENFIELD, The Revd Paul John *LLB, BTh, Barrister*
St Nicholas Vicarage Highbury Ave Fleetwood FY7 7DJ [BLACKBURN] *b* 1967 *educ* Cambridge Grammar School for Boys; Newcastle University; College of Law, Chancery Lane, Lonond; Chichester Theology College *CV* Chancery barrister 1978–86; Curate Shiremoor Newcastle 1989–92; Curate Hexham Newcastle 1992–93; Team Vicar All Saints, St Anne, St Michael and St Thomas Lewes 1993–97; Rector Pulborough 1997–2000; Vicar St Nicholas Fleetwood from 2000; Member Legal Aid Commission from 2006; Member Revision Committee Draft Vacancies in Suffragan Sees and Other Ecclesiastical Offices Measure 2008; Member Revision Committee Draft Crown Benefices (Parish Representatives) Measure 2008; Member Revision Committee Draft Pastoral and Mission Measure 2009; Member Steering Committee Draft Care of Cathedrals Measure 2009; Member Fleetwood

Town Council 2009–11; Member Dioceses Commission from 2010, Vice-Chair from 2014; Member C of E Pensions Board from 2011; Chair Steering Committee Church of England (Miscellaneous Provisions) Measure 2014; Member Steering Committee Bishops and Priests (Consecration and Ordination of Women) Measure 2014; Member Legal Advisory Commission from 2016; Member Legislative Committee from 2016; Deputy Prolocutor of the Convocation of York from 2016; Synodal Secretary of the Convocation of York from 2017

GS 2005–   T: 01253 874402
                               E: benfield@btinternet.com

BENSON, The Ven Paddy (George Patrick) *MA, BD, MPhil*
3 Hatterall Close Hereford HR1 1GA [ARCHDEACON OF HEREFORD] *b* 1967 *educ* Benrose School Derby, Leighton Park School Reading; Christ Church Oxford; Trinity College Bristol; All Nations Christian College Ware; St John's College Nottingham *CV* Director Academic Studies St Andrew's Institute, Kabare, Kenya 1978–87; Acting Director Communications, Diocese Mount Kenya East 1987–89; Assistant Curate St Mary Upton, Chester 1991–5; Vicar Christ Church Barnston, Chester 1995–2010; Canon Emeritus Chester 2010; Archdeacon of Hereford from 2011   T: 01432 265659
                               E: archdeacon@hereford.anglican.org
                               M: 07946 565697

BETTS, The Ven Steven James *BSc, CertTh*
8 Boulton Road Norwich NR7 0DF [ARCHDEACON OF NORFOLK: NORWICH] *b* 1958 *educ* Nottingham Bluecoat Grammar School; York University; Cuddesdon Theological College *CV* Curate Bearsted with Thurnham 1990–94; Chaplain to Bishop of Norwich 1994–97; Vicar Old Catton Norwich 1997–2005; Rural Dean Norwich North 2001–05; Member Diocesan Commission 2001–09; Chair Diocesan House of Clergy 2003–12; Member Bishop's Council from 2003; Member Diocesan Board of Finance Executive from 2003; Bishop's Officer for Ordination and Initial Training 2005–12; Honorary Canon Norwich Cathedral from 2008; Archdeacon of Norfolk from 2012; Member Diocesan Board of Education from 2012; Diocesan Advisory Committee from 2012; Diocesan Board of Patronage from 2012; Diocesan Glebe Committee from 2012, Diocesan Investment Policy Group from 2012; Diocesan Asset Management Committee from 2012; Diocesan Property Committee from 2012; Director Spire Services from 2012; Chair Norwich Diocesan Deceased Clergy Dependants Fund from 2012; Chair Norwich Diocesan Churches Trust from 2014

GS 2000–15   T: 01603 559199
E: archdeacon.norfolk@dioceseofnorwich.org

BEYNON, The Revd (Vincent) Wyn Beynon
MA, STh, DipTheol, CertEd
The Rectory Fish House Lane Stoke Prior
Bromsgrove Worcestershire B60 4JT [WORCESTER]
educ Sir Henry Floyd School, Aylesbury;
Hockerill College of Education, Bishops
Stortford; St Michael's College, Archbishop's
Examination in Theology, Llandaff; Cambridge
Theological Federation *CV* Assistant Curate
Llantrisant Llandaff 1981–83; Assistant Curate,
Caerphilly 1983–85; Rector Gelligaer 1985–88;
Team Vicar, Greater Corsham Bristol 1988–99;
Rural Dean Biggleswade St Albans 2002–07;
Rector of Potton with Sutton and Cockayne
Hatley 1997–08; Priest in Charge United Parish
of Stoke Prior, Wychbold and Upton Warren
from 2012; Associate Priest Bowbrook Group
from 2014; Chair House of Clergy Worcester
from 2015
GS 2015–
T: 01527 832501
07595 313035
E: wynbeynon@gmail.com
W: www.wynbeynon.co.uk
Twitter: @WynBeynon

BIJL, Mr (Arend, Cornelis) Tjeerd *MA*
Zaanstraat 30 Leiden The Netherlands 2314 XE
[EUROPE] *educ* Thomas More College, Leiden
University *CV* Waiting staff member at
Restaurant 'Eethuis Den Dieje' 1999–2008;
Member of Timetable Department at
Hogeschool Leiden (University of applied
sciences) from 2008
GS 2015–
T: +31(0)622707012
E: tjeerd.bijl@gmail.com

BIRD, Mrs (Liz) Elizabeth Ann *Dip*
37 Avondale Road Bridgnorth Shropshire WV16
5DJ [HEREFORD] *b* 1967 *educ* Rawlins Upper
School, Moorlands College *CV* Administration/
Pastoral Torchbearers Trust 1990; Invigilator
Bridgnorth Endowed School 2010; Bridgnorth
Food Bank and Volunteer Coordinator from
2013; Chair of Bridgnorth Food Bank
Committee from 2017
GS 2015–
T: 01746 767510
07595 440555
E: libuffb@btinternet.com

BISHOP, The Ven Ian Gregory *BA, BSc*
ARICS
57A Sandbach Road Congleton Cheshire CW12
4LH [ARCHDEACON OF MACCLESFIELD; CHESTER] *educ*
Devizes School; Portsmouth Polytechnic; Oak
Hill Theology College *CV* Surveyor Croydon
Council 1984–86; Estate Manager Gatwick
Airport 1986–88; Curate Christ Church Purley
Southwark 1991–95; Rector Tas Valley Team
Ministry 1995–2001; Rector Middlewich and
Byley 2001–10; Rural Dean of Middlewich
2004–10; Archdeacon of Macclesfield from 2011
GS 2010–
T: 01260 272875
E: ian.bishop@chester.anglican.org
M: 07715 102519

BLACK, Mrs Heather B *BA*
The Vicarage James Street North Ormesby
Middlesbrough TS3 6LD [YORK] *educ* Belper High
School, Hull University *CV* Staff Nurse burns
and plastic surgery 1987–89; Staff Nurse
medicine and haematology 1989–90; Staff
Nurse/Sister colo-rectal surgery 1990–91;
Specialist stoma care nurse 1991–95;
Development Officer Search (York Diocese)
1999–2003; Development Officer Holy Trinity
Church & Trinity Centre 2007–12; Development
Officer Together Middlesborough and
Cleveland (Church Urban Fund) from 2012
GS 2013–15
T: 01642 271814
07446 908451
E: heather.black@trinitycentre.org
Twitter: @HeatherCUF

BLACKBURN, The Rt Revd Richard Finn
BA, MA
34 Central Avenue Eccleston Park Prescot
Merseyside L34 2QP [BISHOP OF WARRINGTON;
LIVERPOOL] *educ* Aysgarth School; Eastbourne
College; St John College Durham; Hull
University; Westcott House Theology College
CV NatWest Bank 1976–81; Curate St Dunstan
and All Saints Stepney 1983–87; Priest in
Charge St John Baptist Isleworth 1987–92;
Vicar St Mark Mosborough with Emmanuel
Waterthorpe 1992–99; Rural Dean Attercliffe
1996–99; Honorary Canon Sheffield Cathedral
1998–99; Canon Residential Sheffield
Cathedral 1999–2005; Member Pensions
Board 2004–09, Vice-Chair from 2006;
Archdeacon of Sheffield and Rotherham
1999–2009; Bishop of Warrington from 2009
GS 2000–05
T: 0151 426 1897 (Home)
0151 705 2140 (Office)
E: bishopofwarrington@
liverpool.anglican.org
M: 07887 905970

BLINKHORN, Mr Phillip Steel *BA*
1 Blundell Close Unsworth Bury BL9 8LH
[MANCHESTER] *educ* Salford Grammar School,
University of Durham *CV* Burne Phillips,
Chartered Accountants 1972–76; Ingersoll-
Rand Co: 1976–2011; CFO, Industrial
Solutions EMEA 2005–09; Director of Business
Development IS EMEAI 2009–11; Chairman,
Manchester Diocesan Board of Finance from
2011
GS 2012–
T: 0161 766 6301
07770 683532
E: blinkhorn@talk21.com
Twitter: @BlinkhornPS

BODDINGTON, Canon Caroline Elizabeth
MA (Oxon), MCIPD
Church House Great Smith Street London SW1P
3AZ [ARCHBISHOPS' SECRETARY FOR APPOINTMENTS]
educ Malvern Girls' College; Keble College
Oxford *CV* BG Group 1986–2003: HR Strategy

and Development Manager 1997–99, Head of Learning and Development 2000, Head of HR Operations 2001–03; Archbishops' Secretary for Appointments from 2004
T: 020 7898 1876
020 7898 1877
E: caroline.boddington@churchofengland.org

BONNEY, The Very Revd Mark Philip John *MA(Cantab), MA (Oxon), PGCE*
The Deanery The College Ely CB7 2DN [DEAN OF ELY] *educ* Northgate Grammar School for Boys, Ipswich; St Catharine's College Cambridge; St Stephen's House *CV* Assistant Curate St Peter's Stockton-on-Tees 1985–88; Chaplain, St Albans Abbey 1988–90; Precentor, St Albans Abbey 1990–92; Vicar Eaton Bray with Edlesborough 1992–96; Rector Great Berkhamsted 1996–2004; Rural Dean Berkhamsted 2002–04; Treasurer and Canon Residential Salisbury Cathedral 2004–12; Dean of Ely from 2012; General Synod Representative Royal School of Church Music 1998–2001, 2005–10; Chaplain to General Synod 2001–05; Member Westcott House Council 2002–05; Member Liturgical Commission 2002–05; Chair Salisbury Diocesan Advisory Committee 2007–12
GS 2015–   T: 01353 660316
E: m.bonney@elycathedral.org
M: 07811 466517

BOOKER, The Revd Alison Susan Wray *BA (Hons), MA*
The Vicarage Gaulby Road Billesdon Leicestershire LE7 9AG [LEICESTER] *educ* Dorcan School, Swindon, New College Swindon, Worcester College of Higher Education *CV* Evangelist with the Sheffield Centre, Church Army national post 2000–02; Assistant Minister, Wigston Magna, Leicester Diocese 2002–08; Assistant Curate, Countesthorpe with Foston, Leicester Diocese 2008–11; Vicar, The Coplow Benefice, Leicester Diocese from 2011
GS 2015–   T: 0116 2596321
E: revdaswb@mybtinternet.com

BOOKER, The Revd Canon Michael Paul Montague *BA, MA, PGCE*
92 Swaynes Lane Comberton Cambridge CB23 7EF [ELY] *educ* Cambridgeshire County High School; Jesus College, Oxford; Bristol University; Trinity College, Bristol *CV* Teacher, Purley Boys' High School 1980–84; Curate, St Mary Bredin, Canterbury 1987–91; Vicar, St Mary, Leamington Priors 1991–96; Director of Mission and Pastoral Studies, Ridley Hall, Cambridge 1996–2005; Priest in Charge, Comberton and Toft 2005–10; Team Rector, Lordsbridge Team Ministry from 2010; Chair Diocesan Children's Council 2006–2010
GS 2010–   T: 01223 260095
E: mikebooker@elydiocese.org

BOOYS, The Revd Canon Sue (Susan) Elizabeth *BA, Cert Th, PGCE, MA*
Rectory Manor Farm Rd Dorchester-on-Thames Wallingford OX10 7HZ [OXFORD] *educ* Harrow County Girls' School; Bristol University; Oxford Ministry Course; Heythrop, London University *CV* Curate Kidlington Team Oxford 1995–99; Team Vicar Dorchester Team Oxford from 1999, Team Rector from 2005; Member Bishop's Council; Member General Synod Business Committee; Governor Ripon College Cuddesdon 2006–14; Area Dean Aston and Cuddesdon 2007–12; Chair of General Synod Business Committee; Chair of Oxford Diocese House of Clergy
GS 2002–   T: 01865 340007
E: rector@dorchester-abbey.org.uk
F: 01865 340007
M: 07815 609602 (Mobile)

BOUGHTON, The Revd Paul Henry *BSc, ACA*
The Vicarage Manor Road Goring Reading RG8 9DR [TRUSTEE MEMBER, CHURCH OF ENGLAND PENSIONS BOARD] *educ* Guildford; Imperial College London; Ridley Hall Cambridge *CV* Coopers & Lybrand (now PwC) 1977–81; various posts with SGS UK and Swiss head office leading to Chief Financial Officer SGS, UK 1981–9; Assistant Curate Christ Church, Guildford 1991–96; Rector Fetcham from 1996; voluntary member local authority Standards Committee 2000–05, Vice-Chair 2005–12; Member Diocesan Worship Committee from 2001; Member Diocesan Synod from 2009; Clergy representative C of E Pensions Board 2010–16; Pensions Board representation on EIAG from 2012; Chair C of E Pensions Board Audit and Risk Committee from 2016   E: boughtonfamily@yahoo.com

BOURNE, The Revd Nigel Irvine *MA(Oxon), MBA, BA*
The Vicarage 2A Vicarage Lane Chalk Gravesend DA12 4TF [TRUSTEE MEMBER, CHURCH OF ENGLAND PENSIONS BOARD] *b* 1955 *educ* The Vyne Comprehensive School Basingstoke; Queen Mary's VI Form College Basingstoke; St John's College Oxford; Trinity College Bristol; Open University *CV* Royal Naval Engineer Officer 1979–89; Royal Naval Reserve Engineer Officer 1989–92; Curate St Thomas Bedhampton 1992–94; Curate St John Newport Isle of Wight 1994–98; Vicar St Mary Chalk (Diocese of Rochester) from 1998; Member Diocesan Synod from 1998; Member Finance Committee Bishop's Council 2003–06 and 2014–16; Trustee Hands of Compassion (Zambia school charity) 2008–17; Member C of E Pensions Board from 2009; Member of Pensions Board Housing Committee from 2009; Member of PB Board Development Committee from 2016; Vice-President of

Churches' Mutual Credit Union (CMCU) and prior steering group from 2012

T: 01474 567906
E: vicarofchalk@hotmail.com

BOYALL, Mr Stephen John *BSc (Hons)*
273 Lancaster Road North Preston PR1 2SQ
[BLACKBURN] *educ* Solihull School, Alcester Grammar School, Oxford Brookes University *CV* Ministry Trainee, St Marks Church Chester Diocese, 2008–09; Sampler, Severn Trent Water, 2009–10; Process Operator, United Utilities, 2010–14; Process Controller, United Utilities, from January 2015
GS 2015– *T:* 01772 933125
0 7729 454251
E: s_boyall@hotmail.com

BOYD-LEE, Mr Paul Winston Michael *BA, Dip Th*
Manor Barn Horsington Templecombe BA8 0ET
[SALISBURY] *educ* Brighton College; Open University; Exeter University *CV* Theatre Manager Rank Organization 1963–66; Credit Controller International Factors Ltd 1966–72; Director Bible Truth Publishers from 1972; a Director of Church Army 1999–2011; Member Church Army Investment and Remuneration Committees; Member Archbishops' Council 2005–16; Member Audit Committee 2006–16; Member Ethical Investment Advisory Group 2006–16
GS 1991– *T:* 01963 371137
E: paulbl@btinternet.com
M: 07710 604777

BOYLING, The Very Revd Mark Christopher *MA*
The Deanery Carlisle CA3 8TZ [DEAN OF CARLISLE] *educ* King James Grammar School Almondbury, West Yorkshire; Keble College Oxford; Cuddesdon Theological College *CV* Curate St Mark Northwood, Kirkby 1977–79; Team Vicar 1979–85; Chaplain to Bishop of Liverpool 1985–89; Vicar St Peter Formby, Liverpool 1989–94; Canon Residential and Precentor Liverpool Cathedral 1994–2004; Dean of Carlisle from 2004
GS 2010–15 *T:* 01228 523335
E: dean@carlislecathedral.org.uk

BRADLEY, The Very Revd Peter Edward *MA*
Sheffield Cathedral Church St Sheffield S1 1HA
[DEAN OF SHEFFIELD] *b* 1964 *educ* Royal Belfast Academical Institute; Trinity Hall Cambridge; Ripon College Cuddesdon *CV* Curate St Michael and All Angels with St Edmund Northampton 1988–90; Chaplain Gonville and Caius College Cambridge 1990–95; Team Vicar St Michael Abingdon 1995–98; Team Vicar All Saints High Wycombe 1998–2003, Team Rector 2003; Dean of Sheffield from 2003; Fellow College of Preachers, Washington

DC from 2006; Chair, Church and Community Fund from 2013 *T:* 0114 275 3434
0114 263 6063
E: dean@sheffield-cathedral.org.uk
deanpeterbradley@gmail.com
F: 0114 279 7412
W: www.sheffield-cathedral.org.uk

BRAND, The Ven Richard Harold Guthrie *BA*
22 St John's Street Winchester SO23 0HF
[ARCHDEACON OF WINCHESTER] *b* 1967 *educ* Sherborne, Durham University *CV* Assistant Curate, St Margaret's, King's Lynn 1989–93; Senior Curate, Croydon Parish Church 1993–96; Companion Team Priest, St Barnabas Fendalton, Christchurch, New Zealand 1996–98; Priest in Charge of St Peter and St Paul, Hambledon, Portsmouth, 1998–2006; Diocesan Director of Ordinands Portsmouth 1998–2006; Team Rector of The Harborough Anglican Team, Leicester Diocese 2006–16; Area Dean of Gartree I & II Deaneries 2013–16; Archdeacon of Winchester from 2016
T: 01962 710961
E: richard.brand@winchester.anglican.org

BRANDON, The Revd Dr Beatrice *DD, MA, DMS, FRSA, FRSM*
Clopton Manor Clopton Northants NN14 3DZ
[ARCHBISHOPS' ADVISER FOR THE HEALING MINISTRY] *b* 1954 *educ* Heythrop College London *CV* Member Diocesan Pastoral Committee 1992–2005; Member Archbishops' Millenium Advisory Group 1996–2000; Diocesan Vacancy-in-See Committee 1996–2003; Member Folllow-up Steering Group to Archbishops' Commission on the Reorganization of the National Institutions 1996–98; Chair House Laity and Lay Vice Chair Diocesan Synod Peterborough 1997–2003; Convener House Bishops Healing Ministry Steering Group 2000–07; Member Cathedral Council Peterborough Cathedral 2001–05; Chair Churches Together for Healing 2004–08; Member Peterborough Diocesan Board of Patronage from 2006; Trustee Archbishop of York Youth Trust 2008–11; Archbishops' Adviser for Healing Ministry from 2007; Doctor of Divinity (Lambeth Degree) 2012; Archbishop's Adviser and Adviser to the Bench of Bishops for the Ministry of Deliverance and the Healing Ministry in the Church in Wales from 2016; Member Spiritual Abuse Task and Finish Group, CofE National Safeguarding Team from 2016
GS 1995–2005 *T:* 01832 720346
E: beatrice@healingministry.org.uk

BRECKWOLDT, The Revd Peter Hans *BA, BA*
15 St John's Hill Wimborne Dorset BH21 1BX
[SALISBURY] *educ* Hulme Hall School; Macclesfield College of Further Education;

Manchester Polytechnic; Oak Hill Theological College *CV* Curate St John's Knutsford 1988–1992; St Peter and St Paul Moulton 1992–2011; Vicar New Borough and Leigh St John 2011– GS 2015– *T:* 01202 886551 *E:* pbreckwoldt@stjohnswimborne.org.uk

BREEN, Miss Susan Colette *LLB*
6 Hertford Road London N2 9BU [LONDON] *educ* University College London; Chester College of Law *CV* Solicitor in private practice in Manchester 1989–2002, in London 2002–13; Solicitor at Collyer Bristow LLP from 2013
GS 2015– *T:* 07961 009234
E: ladybreen@gmail.com

BREWER, Mrs Rosalind Patricia Anne *BA, RGN*
37 Greenstead Road Newby Scarborough YO12 6HN [YORK] *b* 1967 *CV* Qualified Registered General Nurse 1968; Staff Nurse 1968–70; Night Sister 1972–78; Practice Nursing Sister 1982–90; Family Planning Sister 1984–2006; Senior Practice Nursing Sister/Manager 1990–2006; Cytology Advisor to Primary Care Trust 1995–2006; Nurse Tutor and Assessor 1998–2006; Diocesan Property Sub Committee from 2010; Archbishops' Council from 2006; Patronage Board from 2006; Vice Chair Diocesan Pastoral and Mission Sub Committee from 2004; York Diocesan Synod from 2006; Lay Chair Scarborough Deanery Synod from 2005; Lay Dean of Scarborough from 2017
GS 2010– *T:* 01723 369731
E: rosbrewer47@gmail.com

BREWSTER, Mrs Lucinda Anne Morrine *GLCM*
66 Berlin Road Edgeley Stockport Cheshire SK3 9QF [CHESTER] *educ* Bishop Stopford C of E Secondary; London College of Music; All Saints Centre for Mission and Ministry *CV* Peripatetic Music Teacher 1990–99; Primary School Governor 2005–15; Primary School Teaching Assistant 2007–12; Higher Level Teaching Assistant 2013–15; Teaching Assistant from 2015
GS 2015– *T:* 0161 480 5896
E: lucybrewster@talktalk.net
F: 07436 017841

BRIDEN, Rt Worshipful Timothy John *MA, LLB*
Lamb Chambers Lamb Building Temple London EC4Y 7AS [GENERAL SYNOD EX OFFICIO] *b* 1951 *educ* Ipswich School; Downing College Cambridge *CV* Chancellor of Diocese of Bath and Wells from 1993; Chancellor of Diocese of Truro from 1998; Vicar-General of Canterbury from 2005; Member Legal Advisory Commission
GS 2005– *T:* 020 7797 8300
E: info@lambchambers.co.uk
F: 020 7797 8308

BRINDLEY, The Very Revd David Charles *BD, MTh, MPhil, AKC*
The Deanery 13 Pembroke Rd Portsmouth PO1 2NS [DEAN OF PORTSMOUTH] *b* 1953 *educ* Wednesfield Grammar School; King's College London *CV* Curate Epping, Chelmsford 1976–79; Lecturer, College of St Paul and St Mary, Cheltenham 1979–82; Vicar Quorn and Director of Clergy Training, Leicester 1982–86; Principal West of England Ministerial Training Course 1987–94; Team Rector Warwick 1994–2002; Dean of Portsmouth from 2002; Chair Portsmouth Diocesan Advisory Committee from 2003; Decretary and Treasurer Association of English Cathedrals 2005–09
GS 1985–87, 2004–2005, 2011–
T: 023 9282 4400 (Home)
023 9234 7605 (Office)
E: david.brindley@ portsmouthcathedral.org.uk
F: 023 9229 5480

BROADBENT, The Rt Revd Pete (Peter Alan) *MA*
173 Willesden Lane Brondesbury London NW6 7YN [AREA BISHOP OF WILLESDEN; LONDON] *b* 1958 *educ* Merchant Taylors School Northwood; Jesus College Cambridge; St John College Nottingham *CV* Curate St Nicholas Durham City 1977–80; Curate Emmanuel Holloway 1980–83; Chaplain to North London Polytechnic and Honorary Curate St Mary Islington 1983–89; Bishop's Chaplain for Mission in Stepney 1980–89; Councillor and Chair of Planning London Borough of Islington 1982–89; Vicar Trinity St Michael Harrow 1989–95; Area Dean Harrow 1994; Archdeacon of Northolt 1995–2001; Bishop of Willesden from 2001; Member Dioceses Commission 1989–92; Member Panel of Chairmen General Synod 1990–92, 2009–14; Member C of E Evangelical Council 1984–95, from 2006; Chair Vacancy-in-See Committee Regulation Working Party 1991–93; Member General Synod Standing Orders Committee 1991–95; Member Appointments Sub-Committee 1992–95; Member Central Board of Finance 1991–98; Member General Synod Standing Committee 1992–98; Chair General Synod Business Sub-Committee 1996–98; Chair Elections Review Group 1996–2000; Chair London Diocesan Board for Schools 1996–2006; Chair Essential Christian Board (Spring Harvest/ICC); Chair Business Committee 1999–2000; M AC 1999–2000; Member City Parochial Foundation 1999–2003; Trustee Church Urban Fund 2002–11; Chair Council St John College Nottingham 2002–10; President YMCA West London from 2004; Chair Standards Committee, London Borough Harrow 2006–2010; Vice President Church Pastoral Aid Society from 2009; Acting Bishop of Stepney 2010–11; Chair of Simplification Group from

2014; Acting Bishop of Edmonton 2015–16; Acting Bishop of London from 2017
GS 1985–2001; 2004–   *T:* 020 8451 0189
E: bishop.willesden@btinternet.com
F: 020 8451 4606
W: Http://bishopofwillesden.blogspot.co.uk
Facebook: Pete Broadbent
M: 07950 299685 (Mobile)
Twitter: @petespurs

BROOKE, The Revd David Martin *MA, PGCE*
6 Brent Court Billingham TS23 1PT [DURHAM] *b* 1958 *educ* Ferryhill Comprehensive School; Selwyn College Cambridge; ULIE; SAOMC *CV* Assistant Master, Bedford School 1981–85; Marketing Manager, Epson UK 1985–92; Marketing Manager, Dell UK 1992–99; Curate Luton Lewsey St Hugh St Alban 1999–00; Non Stipendiary Minister Sunnyside with Bourne End 2000–02; Curate 2002–04 Vicar Bishopton with Great Stainton Durham 2004–13; Rector Redmarshall 2004–13; Rector Grindon, Stillington and Wolviston 2004–13; Priest in Charge Billingham St Mary 2010–13; Area Dean Stockton 2007–16; Rector Stockton 2014–16; Honorary Canon Durham Cathedral from 2016; Lead Mission Support Partner from 2016
GS 2010–   *T:* 07967 326085
E: david.brooke@durham.anglican.org

BROOM, The Ven Andrew (Andy) Clifford
27 Molescroft Road Beverley HU17 7DX [ARCHDEACON OF THE EAST RIDING] *CV* Assistant Curate All Saints Wellington with St Catherine's Eyton 1992–96; Assistant Curate St Thomas Brampton 1996–2000; Vicar St John's Walton 2000–09; Director of Mission and Ministry Derby Diocese 2009–14; Archdeacon of the East Riding from 2014
GS 2015–   *T:* 01482 881659
E: ader@yorkdiocese.org

BROOMHEAD, The Revd Mark Roger
BSc Hons, MA
35 Whitecotes Park Walton Chesterfield Derbyshire S40 3RT [DERBY] *b* 1971 *educ* St Mary Redcliffe and Temple School, The University of Nottingham *CV* Recording/touring Musician 1990–96; Director, Embryo Industries Limited 1999–2010; Learning and Behavioural Support, Eastwood Grange 2000–02; Student Support Coordinator, Teacher of Design Technology, Hasland Hall 2002–04; Teacher of Design Technology, The Long Eaton School 2004–06; Assistant Pioneer Curate, St Bartholomew's Clay Cross, St Barnabas Danesmoor and St Thomas Brampton, Derby Diocese 2006–11; Ordained Pioneer Minister, The Order of the Black Sheep, Derby Diocese from 2011
GS 2015–   *T:* 01246 555988
E: mark@theorderoftheblacksheep.com
Twitter: @MarkBroomhead

BROWN, The Ven Andrew *BA, MA*
St George's Vicarage 16 Devonshire Rd Douglas Isle of Man IM2 3RB [ARCHDEACON OF MAN; SODOR AND MAN] *educ* Ashmole Comprehensive School; South Bank Poly *CV* Curate St Peter's Burnley 1980–83; Priest-in-charge St Francis Brandlesholme 1983–86; Vicar St Peter's Ashton-under-Lyne 1986–96; Vicar St Luke's Halliwell 1986–2003; Canon Theologian Derby Cathedral and Diocesan Continuing Ministerial Education Adviser 2003–11; Archdeacon of Man and Vicar of St George's Douglas from 2011
GS 2013–   *T:* 01624 675430
E: archdeacon@sodorandman.im
M: 07624 228100

BROWN, Mr Andrew Charles *BSc, FRICS*
Church House Great Smith St London SW1P 3AZ [SECRETARY, CHURCH COMMISSIONERS] *b* 1958 *educ* Ashmole Comprehensive School; South Bank Polytechnic *CV* Healey & Baker 1981–84; St Quintin 1984–94; Deputy Secretary and Chief Surveyor Church Commissioners 1994–2003, Secretary from 2003; Member Finance and Investment Committee, Lionheart from 2007; Member Allchurches Trust from 2008; Trustee and Chair the 2:67 project 2007–10; Trustee William Leech (Foundation) and Director William Leech (Investment) from 2007; CEDR Accredited Mediator from 2012; Chair Church Mission Society Pensions Trust from 2013; PCC member St Paul's Church St Albans 2013–17; Trustee, Mediation Hertfordshire from 2015   *T:* 020 7898 1785
E: andrew.brown@churchofengland.org

BROWN, The Revd Canon Anne *BA*
The Rectory 52 Trelinnoe Gardens South Petherwin Launceston Cornwall PL15 7TH [TRURO] *CV* 2009–12 Assistant Curate Probus Team; from 2012 Priest in charge Three Rivers Team
GS 2015–   *T:* 01566 770649
E: threeriversteam@btinternet.com
Twitter: @AnneBrown30

BROWN, The Revd Dr Malcolm Arthur *MA, PhD, FHEA, FRSA*
Church House Great Smith St London SW1P 3AZ [DIRECTOR, MISSION AND PUBLIC AFFAIRS DIVISION, ARCHBISHOPS' COUNCIL] *b* 1954 *educ* Eltham College; Oriel College Oxford; Manchester University; Westcott House Cambridge *CV* Curate Riverhead with Dunton Green, Rochester 1979–83; Team Vicar and Industry Missioner, Southern City Centre, Winchester 1983–91; Executive Secretary William Temple Foundation 1991–2000; Honorary Curate St Paul Heaton Moor, Manchester 1993–2000; Principal East Anglian Ministerial Training College 2000–05; Principal Easter Region Ministerial Course 2005–07; Director Mission

and Public Affairs from 2007; Member Board of Social Responsibility Industry and Economic Affairs Committee 1987–91; Member Board of Social Responsibility Society, Economic and Industry Affairs Committee 1997–2002; Theology Consultant Review of Diocesan, Pastoral and Related Measures 2001–04; Member Ministry Division Theology Education and Training Committee 2003–07; member Ministry Division Finance Panel 2006–07; Licensed to Diocese of Ely from 2011   *T:* 020 7898 1468
E: malcolm.brown@churchofengland.org

BRUINVELS, Canon Peter Nigel Edward
LLB, FRSA, FCIM, MCIJ, MCIPR
4 Dunkeld Place Roman Road Dorking RH4 3EU [GUILDFORD] *educ* St John School Leatherhead; London University; Inns of Court School of Law *CV* Member of Parliament Leicester East 1983–87; Party Candidate The Wrekin 1997; Principal Peter Bruinvels Associates, Media Management and Public Affairs Consultants; Member Diocesan Synod and Dorking Deanery Synod from 1974; Freeman of City of London 1980; Member Dioceses Commission 1991–96; Member Legislative Committee 1991–96 and from 2000, Deputy Chair from 2010; News Broadcaster, Political Commentator and Freelance Journalist; Church Commissioner from 1992, Mission and Pastoral Committee from 1992, Governor Church Commissioners from 1992; Management Advisory Committee 1999–2009; Ofsted and Section 48 SIAS RE School Inspector from 1994; Member Department Social Security Child Support and Society Security Appeals Tribunal 1994–99; Managing Editor Bruinvels News & Media, Press and Broadcasting Agents; Member Diocesan Board of Education from 1994; Member General Synod Board of Education 1996–2006; Co-opted Member Surrey Local Education Authority 1997–2007; Governor University of York St John 1999–2007; Director Church Army and Chair Remuneration Committee 1999–2004; Independent Lay Chair NHS Complaints (SE) Tribunal 1999–2004; Member Clergy Discipline Review Group 1999–2010; Chair Surrey Schools Organisation Committee 2000–07; Court Member University of Sussex 2000–08; Member Dearing Implementation Group 2001–10; County Field Officer (Surrey and Sussex) Royal British Legion 2002–12; Director East Elmbridge and Mid Surrey Primary Care Trust 2002–07; Member Management Advisory Committee 1999–2009; Lay Canon Guildford Cathedral from 2002; Vice-President and Chair House of Laity, Diocesan Synod 2003–13; Guild Crown Nominations Commission from 2003; Member South East Veterans and War Pensions Committee from 2003, Deputy Chair 2013–17, Chair from 2017; Chair Surrey Joint Services Charities Committee from 2004; Chair Guildford Diocesan Board of Education 2005–08, Vice Chair from 2008; Honorary Secretary Surrey County Military Appeals Committee from 2002; Member Guildford College of Canons from 2002; Member Cathedrals Fabric Commission for England 2006–16; Member Guildford Cathedral Council from 2006; Governor Whitelands College (Roehampton University) from 2007, Chair 2009–12; Deputy Chair Nominations and Governance Committee (Church Commissioners) 2009–12; Member Surrey SACRE from 2013; Regional Fundraiser South East ABF The Soldiers' Charity from 2013; Director Guildford Diocesan Education Trust (GDET) from 2012; Chief Executive Surrey Civilian-Military Partnership Board from 2013; Deputy Chairman Mission and Pastoral Committee The Church Commissioners from 2015; Project Officer for National Armed Forces Day Guildford 2015; Surrey CC Liaison Adviser Civilian-Military Partnership Board from 2012; Kent CC Liaison Adviser and Military Expert Civilian-Military Kent and Medway Partnership Board from 2016; Armed Forces Champion Church of England from 2016; Armed Forces Champion 11 Infantry Brigade SE from 2016; awarded The Canterbury Cross by the Archbishop of Canterbury 2017
GS 1985–   *T:* 01306 887082 (Home)
               01306 887680 (Office)
E: canonpeterbruinvels@talk21.com
canonbruinvels@gmail.com
M: 07721 411688; 07535 396188
Twitter: @canonbruinvels

BRUSH, The Revd Dr Sarah Louise *PhD,*
MA, MA, BA
89 Stourbridge Road Halesowen West Midlands B63 3UA [WORCESTER] *b* 1953 *educ* Wycombe High School for Girls, University of Reading, Queens Foundation for Ecumenical Theological Education Birmingham *CV* Temporary Lecturer in Latin and Medieval History, University of Reading, 1996–2002; Roger Vere Youth Worker & Licensed Youth Minister, All Saints Church, High Wycombe, 2002–08; Diocesan Youth Officer, Worcester Diocese 2008–14; Curate in the Halas Team, Worcester Diocese from 2014
GS 2015–   *T:* 07804 648598
               07986 284157
E: sarah@halasteam.org.uk
Twitter: @DocBrush

BRYANT, The Rt Revd Mark Watts *BA*
Bishop's House 25 Ivy Lane Gateshead NE9 6QD [SUFFRAGAN BISHOP OF JARROW; DURHAM] *educ* St John School Leatherhead; St John College Durham; Cuddesdon Theological College *CV*

Curate Addlestone 1975–79; Curate St John Studley, Trowbridge 1979–83, Vicar 1983–88; Chaplain Trowbridge College of Further Education 1979–83; Diocesan Director of Ordinands and Director Vocations and Training, Coventry 1988–96; Honorary Canon Coventry Cathedral 1993–2001; Team Rector Coventry Caludon 1996–2001; Archdeacon Coventry East 1999–2001; Archdeacon of Coventry 2001–07; Canon Residential Coventry Cathedral 2006–07; Bishop of Jarrow from 2007
GS 1998–2008   *T:* 0191 491 0917
     E: bishop.of.jarrow@durham.anglican.org
               Twitter: @BishopMark1

BRYDON, Mr Andrew Edward *LLB*
57 Grandison Road London SW11 6LT [LONDON] *b* 1973 *educ* Nottingham High School, Bristol University *CV* Solicitor from 2000
GS 2015–   *T:* 020 7490 6364
                    07725 368006
          E: andrew.brydon@btinternet.com

BUCKNALL, Mary Catherine *BA, BA*
The Post Office Flat Bishops Caundle Sherborne DT9 5ND [GENERAL SYNOD REPRESENTATIVE: DEAF ANGLICANS TOGETHER] *b* 1952 *educ* St Michael's Burton Park, Petworth; Somerville College Oxford; London School of Theology *CV* Executive Officer (Programmer) Inland Revenue, Electronic Data Systems Ltd and Capgemini UK Plc 1987–2005; Canterbury Deaf and Disability Ministry Co-ordinator Church in Society, Kent 2007–10; Project Officer Deaf Services Kent County Council 2010–11; Quality Management System Administrator 2012–13; Data Quality Administrative Assistant 2013–15
          T: 07787 872070 (SMS only)
          E: mary.bucknall@yahoo.co.uk

BUGGS, Miss Debbie (Deborah Ruth) *BSc*
Flat 10 4 Violet Road London E3 3QH [LONDON] *educ* Tonbridge Girls' Grammar School, University of Kent at Canterbury *CV* Trainee accountant Neville Russell (now Mazars) 1993–96; various accounting posts 1996–2002; Accountant, Global Aerospace Underwriting Managers from 2002; Trustee, Kingham Hill Trust 2007–17; Trustee CPAS from 2017
GS 2015–   *T:* 020 7369 2829 (work)
                    020 7538 3534 (home)
          E: drbuggs@tiscali.co.uk
          M: 07729 589461

BULL, The Revd Canon Dr Timothy *MA, PhD, MA, PhD, FRSA*
43 Holywell Hill St Albans AL1 1HD [ST ALBANS] *educ* Bradford Grammar School, Worcester College, Oxford; Durham University; Fitzwilliam College, Cambridge; King's College Lond *CV* Member of the Lee Abbey Community,

Devon, 1987–89; Computer Software Engineer, DSE Ltd., 1989–95; Lecturer in Computer Science, Durham University, 1995–96; Curate, Walcot, Bath and Wells Diocese, 1999–2003; Priest-in-Charge, Langham with Boxted, Chelmsford Diocese, 2003–13; Colchester Area CMD Adviser, Chelmsford Diocese, 2003–13; Residentiary Canon, St Albans Cathedral from 2013; Director of Ministry, St Albans Diocese from 2013
GS 2010–   *T:* 01727 818179
                    01727 818151
     E: dom@stalbans.anglican.org
               Twitter: @Ministry_Tim

BULLOCK, The Ven Sarah Ruth *BA(Hons), BA(Hons), PGCert Theol*
1 New Lane Huntington York YO32 9NU [ARCHDEACON OF YORK] *educ* Fallowfield C of E School; University of Surrey; Cranmer Hall, St John's College, Durham *CV* English Teacher, Cheadle Hulme School 1986–90; Assistant Diocesan Youth Officer, Manchester 1986–90; Assistant Curate St Paul, Kersal Moor with St Andrew, Manchester, 1993–98; Priest in Charge St Edmund, Whalley Range 1998–2004; St James' with St Clement, Moss Side, 1999–2004; Rector United Benefice of St Edmund, Whalley Range and St James' with St Clement, Manchester 2004–13; Honorary Canon Manchester Cathedral from 2007; Bishops' Advisor Women's Ministry, Manchester 2009–13; Dean City and Borough Manchester 2010–13; Member Manchester Urban Regeneration Commission Urban Life & Faith, 1999–2009; Member Bishops Advisory Group Sexuality 2004; Chair Discipleship and Ministry Training Committee, Manchester, 2005–13; Bishops Advisor Women's Ministry, Manchester 2009–13; Member Manchester Synod and Diocesan Board of Finance 2009–13; Member Bishop's Council 2010; Member Ministry Development Review Team, Manchester, 2010–13; Archdeacon of York from 2013
GS 2010–13   *T:* 01904 758241
          E: adyk@yorkdiocese.org
          M: 07432 289895

BURROWS, The Rt Revd Peter *BTh*
Doncaster House Church Lane Fishlake Doncaster DN7 5JW [SUFFRAGAN BISHOP OF DONCASTER; SHEFFIELD] *educ* Spondon House Secondary School; Derby College of Further Education; Sarum and Wells Theological College *CV* Curate Baildon 1983–87; Rector Broughton Astley 1993–93; Priest in Charge Stoney Stanton with Croft 1993–95; Team Rector Broughton Astley and Croft with Stoney Stanton 1995–2000; Rural Dean Guthlaxton I 1994–2000; Diocesan Director Ordinands and Parish Development Officer 1996–2000; Member Diocesan Synod; Member Vacancy-in-See

Committee; Member Diocesan Advisory Committee; Coordinator Diocesan Team Forum; Member Bishop's Council; Honorary Canon Leicester Cathedral; Deputy Director Ministry from 2002; Director Ministry 2003–05; Archdeacon of Leeds 2005–11; Honorary Canon Ripon Cathedral 2005–11; Bishop of Doncaster from 2012; Chair Ministry and Training Development Group; Chair One City Projects and Oastler Centre; Trustee Children's International Summer Villages; Member Institute of Directors
GS 2010–12   *T:* 01302 846610
   E: bishoppeter@bishopofdoncaster.org.uk

BURTON-JONES, The Ven Simon David *MA (Hons), BTh, MA*
The Archdeaconry Kings Orchard The Precinct Rochester Kent ME1 1TG [ARCHDEACON OF ROCHESTER] *educ* Fleetwood High School; Emmanuel College Cambridge; St John's College Nottingham *CV* Team Curate St Peter's Darwen with St Paul's Hoddlesdon 1993–96; Curate St Mark's Biggin Hill 1996–98; Vicar St Mary's Bromley 1998–2005; Rector St Nicholas Chislehurst 2005–10; Archdeacon of Rochester from 2010   *T:* 01634 813533 (Home)
                01634 560000 (Office)
                E: archdeacon.rochester@
                       rochester.anglican.org
             W: www.simonburton-jones.com

BUSH, The Very Revd Roger Charles *BA*
14 St Mary's Street Truro TR1 2AF [DEAN OF TRURO] *b* 1967 *educ* Fakenham Grammar School; King's College London; College of the Resurrection, Mirfield *CV* Curate Newbold, Derby 1986–90; Team Vicar Parish of the Resurrection, Leicester 1990–94; Team Rector Redruth with Lanner and Treleigh, Truro 1994–2004; Canon Chancellor, Truro Cathedral 2004–06; Archdeacon of Cornwall 2006–12; Dean of Truro from 2012
GS 2001–15   *T:* 01872 276782
         E: dean@trurocathedral.org.uk

BUTCHERS, The Ven Dr Mark Andrew *MA, MTh, PhD*
Stage Cross Sanders Lane Bishop's Tawton Barnstaple EX32 0BE [ARCHDEACON OF BARNSTAPLE: EXETER] *CV* Curate, St Luke's and Christ Church, Chelsea 1987–90; Curate, St Peter and St Paul, Mitcham 1990–93; Rector, North Tawton, Sampford Courtenay, Bondleigh and Honeychurch 1993–99; Chaplain and Director of Studies in Theology, Keble College, Oxford 1999–2005; Vicar, St Peter's Wolvercote 2005–15 and All Saints, Wytham 2011–15; Area Dean of Oxford 2012–15; Archdeacon of Barnstaple from 2015
                               T: 01271 375475
             E: archdeacon.of.barnstaple@
                       exeter.anglican.org

BUTLER, The Rt Revd Paul Roger *BA (Jt Hons), BA Oxon*
Auckland Castle Bishop Auckland DL14 7NR [BISHOP OF DURHAM] *b* 1967 *educ* Kingston Grammar School; Nottingham University; Wycliffe Hall *CV* All Saints with Holy Trinity, Wandsworth 1983–87; Scripture Union Inner London Evangelism 1987–92; Deputy Head of Mission 1992–94; Non-Stipendiary Minister St Paul's, East Ham (Chelmsford) 1988–94; Priest in Charge St Mary with St Stephen Walthamstow (Chelmsford) 1994–97; St Luke, Walthamstow 1994–97; Team Rector of Walthamstow 1997–2004; Archdeacon Waltham Forest 2000–04; Canon St Paul's Byumba, Rwanda from 2001; Bishop of Southampton 2004–09; Bishop of Southwell and Nottingham 2009–13; Chair of Church Mission Society 2008–10; Joint Chair Churches Safeguarding Advisory Committee 2011–14; President Scripture Union 2011–17; Bishop of Durham from 2013; Chair National Safeguarding Panel 2014–16
GS 2009–   *T:* 01388 602576
   E: bishop.of.durham@durham.anglican.org
      W: bishoppaulbutler.wordpress.com
                               M: 07939 213795
                 Twitter: @bishoppaulb

BUTLER, Mr Richard Michael *BA, MEd, PhD*
109 Dereham Road Easton Norfolk NR9 5ES [DIOCESAN SECRETARY; NORWICH] *educ* University of Durham University of Canbridge, University of East Anglia *CV* Chief Executive, Mobilise 2008–09; Director of Finance and Business, The Benjamin Foundation 2003–08; Director of Operations, The Wootton Estates, 1998–2003; Diocesan Secretary/Chief Executive from 2009   *T:* 01603 880853
      E: richard.butler@dioceseofnorwich.org
                 Twitter: @RichardMBE

BUTLER, The Revd Canon Simon *BSc, DTS, MA*
St Mary's Vicarage 32 Vicarage Crescent London SW11 3LD [SOUTHWARK] *b* 1958 *educ* Bournemouth School; University of East Anglia; Britannia Royal Naval College; St John College Nottingham *CV* Curate Chandler's Ford, Winchester 1992–94; Curate St Joseph Worker Northolt, London 1994–97; Vicar Immanuel and St Andrew Streatham, Southwark 1997–2004; Rural Dean Streatham 2001–04; Priest in Charge and acting Team Rector Sanderstead Team Ministry 2004–06; Team Rector 2006–11; Honorary Canon Southwark Cathedral from 2006; Chair Southwark Diocesan Liturgical Committee 2009–12; Vice-Chair SEITE Council 2008–13; Vicar St Mary Battersea from 2011; Chair Southwark Diocesan Liturgical Committee;

Prolocutor of the Lower House of the Convocation of Canterbury from 2015
GS 2005–   *T:* 020 7228 8141
        E: Vicar@stmarysbattersea.org.uk
                    M: 07941 552407

BUTTERY, The Revd Graeme *BA, MA*
St Oswald's Clergy House Brougham Terrace Hartlepool TS24 8EY [DURHAM] *educ* Dame Allan's Boys School Newcastle; York University; Newcastle University; St Stephen's House Theological College *CV* Curate Peterlee 1988–91; Curate Sunderland, Team Minister 1991–92; Team Vicar Sunderland, Team Minister 1992–94; Vicar St Lawrence the Martyr Horsley Hill 1994–2005; Vicar St Oswald Hartlepool from 2005; Canon Durham Cathedral from 2010
GS 1995–   *T:* 01429 273201
                    E: G_BUTTERY@sky.com

BUXTON, The Revd Alyson Christina *BA, MA*
The Rectory Wormgate Boston PE21 6NP [LINCOLN] *educ* Bridlington High School; York School of Nursing; St John's Nottingham *CV* Assistant Curate Sleaford 2002–05; Diocesan Synod 2002–12; Vocation Advisor Selection Panellist 2012–13; Lay Ministry Co-ordinator and Priest-Vicar Lincoln Cathedral 2005–08; Diocesan Safeguarding Committee 2005–08; Rector of Horncastle 2008–10; Diocesan Council 2008–11; Rector of the South Wolds Group Benefice of Asterby, Horncastle, Hemingby 2010–13; Reviewer Diocesan MDR Steering Committee; Director of Ministry 2013–14; Diocesan Advisory Committee from 2014; Team Rector Boston from 2014
GS 2015–   *T:* 01205 354670
                    E: alybux@mac.com

CAMPBELL, Dr (John) Graham *PhD, BSc, FCA*
18 Eaglesfield Hartford Northwich CW8 1NQ [CHESTER] *b* 1942 *educ* Manchester Grammar School, Birmingham University *CV* Birmingham University Research Chemist Imperial Chemical Industries 1966–71; Student Accountant Worth & Co 1971–74; Audit Senior Spicer & Pegler 1974–76; Accountant then Commercial Manager British Nuclear Fuels plc 1976–2003; Member Bishop's Council from 1998; Member Diocesan Finance and Central Services Committee from 1997; Member Foxhill Diocesan Conference Centre Council 1998–15; Member C of E Pensions Board 2004–15; Treasurer C of E Evangelical Council 2005–10
GS 2000–   *T:* 01606 75849
        E: j.graham.campbell@gmail.com

CANNINGS-JURD, Miss Fenella Katherine Margaret
50 Wavendon Avenue Barton on Sea New Milton Hampshire BH25 7LS [SALISBURY] *educ* The Arnewood School, Durham University *CV* Healthcare Advisor at Boots UK, 2012–14; Paralegal Assistant at Leonard and Co, Solicitors, from 2013; Full-time Student at Durham University 2014–17
GS 2015–   *T:* 07894 216962
        E: fenella1995@yahoo.co.uk
                    Twitter: @fenellaCJ

CARTWRIGHT, The Revd Paul *BA, PGCE, MA, MSET*
St Peter's Vicarage 1 Osborne Mews Barnsley S70 1UU [LEEDS] *educ* Hemsworth High School; Leeds Metropolitan University; University of Huddersfield; Leeds University; College of the Resurrection, Mirfield *CV* Police Officer, West Yorkshire Police, 1990–2006; Major Incident/Crime Family Liasion Officer, West Yorkshire Police 2002–06; Equalities and Diversity Trainer, West Yorkshire Police 2003–06; Assistant Convenor Wakefield Fellowship of Vocation from 2008; Barnsley Deanery Vocations Offocer from 2010; Assistant Curate St Helen's Church, Athersley 2008–10; Assistant Curate St John the Evangelist, Carlton 2010–11; Priest in Charge St Peter the Apostle and St John the Baptist, Barnsley from 2011; Chaplain to Further Education and Higher Education, Barnsley from 2011; Police Chaplain to West Yorkshire Police from 2010; General Synod Representative on Committee for Minority Ethnic Anglican Concerns from 2011
GS 2010–   *T:* 01226 282220
        E: fr.paul.cartwright@gmail.com
                    M: 07852 174303

CARY, Mr James *BA*
Yeovil Somerset [BATH AND WELLS] *b* 1975 *educ* Monton Combe School; Durham University *CV* Freelance comedy writer 1999–
GS 2015–   *E:* jamesedwardcary@gmail.com
        W: www.inpursuitoftheobvious.com
                    Twitter: @thatjamescary

CAWDELL, The Revd Preb Simon Howard *BA, MA CTM*
The Rectory 16 East Castle Street Bridgnorth WV16 4AL [HEREFORD] *educ* Kings School, Worcester; University College Durham; Kings College, London; Ridley Hall, Cambridge *CV* Investment Analyst; Coast Securities Ltd, London 1987–91; Curate St Philip, Cheam Common Southwark 1994–98; Vicar Claverley and Tuck Hill 1998–2010; Team Rector Bridgnorth and Priest in Charge Morville with Aston Ayre, Acton Round and Monkhopton with Upton Cresset from 2010; Rural Dean of Bridgnorth 2009–13; Diocesan Synod from 2000–06, from 2009; Chair House Clergy from 2012; Bishop's Council from 2012; Diocesan Board Finance from 1999 (Executive Member 2007–10), Vice Chair Benefice Buildings Committee 2001–07,

Chair Diocesan Investment Committee 2007–10
GS 2010–   T: 01746 761573
             E: s.h.cawdell@btinternet.com
             W: www.bridgnorthteamministry.org.uk

CAWDRON, Mr Keith William *BA*
Baringo 61 Burbo Bank Road Blundellsands Liverpool L23 6YQ [LIVERPOOL] *educ* Stockport Grammar School, Durham University *CV* Civil Servant Department of Education and Science 1977–87; Admin and Research Officer, Lambeth Palace 1985–87; Diocesan Secretary, Diocese of Liverpool 1987–2001; Director of Corporate Affairs, Liverpool Health Authority 2001–02; Chief Executive, St Joseph's Hospice Association, Liverpool from 2002; Retired
GS 1995–2000, 2015–   T: 0151 931 2098
                        07974 759564
             E: kmarcawdron@btinternet.com

CHAFFEY, The Ven Jonathan Paul Michael *BA, MA, QHC*
Chaplaincy Services (RAF) HQ Air Command RAF High Wycombe Bucks HP14 4UE [ARCHDEACON FOR THE ROYAL AIR FORCE] *b* 1962 *educ* Worksop College; Durham University; Cranmer Hall Theological College *CV* Assistant Curate St Stephen's Gateacre, Liverpool 1987–1990; RAF Chaplain 1990–2014; Chaplain in Chief RAF 2014–
                        T: 01494 493802
             E: airchapservs-chaplaininchief@mod.uk
                jonathan.chaffey350@mod.uk

CHAMBERLAIN, The Ven Malcolm Leslie *BA, BTh, MPhil*
34 Wilson Road Sheffield South Yorkshire S11 8RN [ARCHDEACON OF SHEFFIELD AND ROTHERHAM; SHEFFIELD] *b* 1967 *educ* Oadby Beauchamp College, University of York; Liverpool Hope University *CV* Mission Partner (CMS) in Peshawar, Pakistan 1992–93; Curate, St John's Pleck and Bescot Walsall 1996–99; Associate Anglican Chaplain University of Liverpool 1999–2002; Curate St Matthew and St James Mossley Hill 1999–2002; Anglican Chaplain University of Liverpool 2002–07; Diocesan Emerging Church Consultant (initially 19–30s Adviser) Liverpool 2002–07; Module Tutor (Mission in Britain Today)SNWRTP 2007–14; Rector (initially Priest in Charge) of St Mary's Wavertree 2008–14; Toxteth and Wavertree Deanery Pioneer Minister 2008–14; Area Dean Toxteth and Wavertree 2012–14; Archdeacon of Sheffield and Rotherham from 2014; Mission and Public Affairs Council from 2016
GS 2015–   T: 01709 309110
             0114 418 3917
             E: malcolm.chamberlain@
                sheffield.anglican.org
             Twitter: @malchamb

CHAMBERLAIN, The Rt Revd Dr Nicholas
The Old Palace Lincoln LN2 1PU [SUFFRAGAN BISHOP OF GRANTHAM; LINCOLN]
                        T: 01552 504092
             E: bishop.grantham@lincoln.anglican.org

CHANDLER, The Ven Ian Nigel *BD, AKC, CMTh*
St Mark's House 46a Cambridge Road Ford Plymouth PL2 1PU [ARCHDEACON OF PLYMOUTH; EXETER] *educ* Bishopsgarth School Stockton-on-Tees; Stockton Sixth Form College; King's College London; Chichester Theological College *CV* Curate All Saints Hove 1992–96; Domestic Chaplain to Bishop of Chichester 1996–2000; Vicar St Richard Haywards Heath 2000–10; Rural Dean Cuckfield 2004–06; Member Diocesan Synod from 2000; Member Diocesan Finance Committee 2004–07; Archdeacon of Plymouth from 2010
                        T: 01752 202401
             E: archdeacon.of.plymouth@
                exeter.anglican.org

CHAPMAN, The Revd Mark David *MA, DipTh, DPhil*
1 Church Close Cuddesdon Oxford OX44 9HD [OXFORD] *b* 1960 *educ* St Bartholomew's School, Newbury; Trinity College Oxford; Munich University; OMC *CV* Sir Henry Stephenson Fellow, University Sheffield 1989–91; Non-Stipendiary Minister Dorchester Team Ministry, 1994–99; Lecturer Systematic Theology Ripon College Cuddesdon from 1992; Vice- Principal, Ripon College Cuddesdon from 2001; Visiting Professor, Oxford Brookes University from 2009; Reader Modern Theology, Oxford University from 2008; Non-Stipendiary Minister Associate Priest Wheatley Team Ministry with special responsibility Cuddesdon, Garsington and Horspath 1999–2014; Associate Priest Garsington, Cuddesdon and Horspath from 2014; Professor of the History of Modern Theology, University of Oxford from 2015; Canon Theologican Truro Cathedral from 2016
GS 2010–   T: 01865 874310
             01865 877405
             E: mark.chapman@rcc.ac.uk
             M: 07790 524494

CHAPMAN, Mrs Mary Madeline *BA, CHARTERED DIR, DIP CIM*
22 Addison Grove London W4 1ER [ARCHBISHOPS' COUNCIL] *educ* Sutton High School; University Bristol *CV* Marketing Executive, British Tourist Authority; Division Director Nicholas Kiwi; Marketing Director L'Oreal UK; Director Biotherm; Director Helena Rubenstein; Director Personnel Operations and Management Development L'Oreal UK 1990–93; Chief Executive Investors in People 1993–98; Chief Executive CMI 1998–2008; Member

Council Girls' Day School Trust from 2004; Non-exec Director Royal Mint from 2008; Commissioner National Lottery from 2008; Chair Institute Customer Service from 2009; member Council Brunel University from 2009; Member Ministry Council
T: 020 8994 4934
E: mary@marychapman.org
M: 07919 415994

CHARMAN, Canon Jane Ellen Elizabeth *MA*
4 The Sidings Downton Salisbury SP5 3QZ [SALISBURY] *b* 1960 *educ* Newstead Wood School, Orpington; St John's College Durham; Selwyn College Cambridge; Westcott House Theological College *CV* Curate, St George's Tuffley with St Margaret's Whaddon, Gloucester, 1985–90; Chaplain, Clare College Cambridge, 1990–95; Rector Duxford St Peter and Vicar St Mary and St John Hinxton and St Mary Magdalene Ickleton, Ely, 1995–2004; Rural Dean Shelford Deanery, Ely, 2003–04; Director Learning for Discipleship and Ministry, Salisbury, from 2004; Diocesan Representative South Central Regional Training Partnership Management Board from 2006; Chair South Central Regional Training Partnership CMD Coordinator Group from 2006; Chair South Central Regional Training Partnership Pioneer Ministry Coordinator Group from 2008; Member National CMD panel from 2009; Member Southern Theological Education and Training College Board of Studies from 2009; Bishop's Advisor for selection of candidates for ordination from 2012
GS 2010–   *T:* 01725 512620
E: jane.charman@salisbury.anglican.org
M: 07814 899657
Twitter: @janeeecharman

CHEETHAM, The Rt Revd Richard Ian *MA, PGCE, Cert Theol, PhD*
Kingston Episcopal Area Office 620 Kingston Road Raynes Park SW20 8DN [AREA BISHOP OF KINGSTON; SOUTHWARK] *educ* Kingston Grammar School; Christ Church College Oxford; Ripon College Cuddesdon; King's College London *CV* Curate Holy Cross Fenham 1987–90; Vicar St Augustine of Canterbury Limbury, Luton 1990–99; Rural Dean Luton 1995–98; Archdeacon of St Albans 1999–2002; Bishop of Kingston from 2002; President YMCA (London South West) from 2002; Chair Southwark Diocesan Board of Education 2002–15; Member Roehampton University Council 2006–12; Chair C of E Continuing Ministerial Development Panel 2007–12; Co-Chair Christian Muslim Forum 2008–12; Anglican President 2012–16; Honorary Research Fellow, King's College London from 2011; Chair British Regional Committee of St George's College Jerusalem from 2013; Member, Foundation and Executive,

St George's College Jerusalem from 2013; Whitelands Professorial Fellow in Christian Theology and Contemporary Issues, University of Roehampton from 2013; Patron, Curriculum for Cohesion from 2013; Co-Leader of project 'Equipping Christian Leadership in an Age of Science' (Durham University) from 2015; Member, Church of England's Working Group on the Environment from 2015; Patron Fircroft Trust   *T:* 020 8545 2443
E: bishop.richard@southwark.anglican.org
W: www.bishoprichardcheetham.com

CHEGWIN HALL, The Revd Canon Elaine *MTh*
17 Frewland Avenue Davenport Stockport SK3 8TZ [CHESTER] *educ* Wintringham Grammar School, Liverpool University; Chester College *CV* Staff Nurse Fazakerley Hospital 1982–83; Ward Sister Fazakerley Hospital 1983–85; District Nurse training Liverpool Royal Hospital 1985–86; District Nursing Sister South Sefton Health Authority 1986–91; School Nursing Sister Wirral Health Authority 1991–97; Assistant Curate (Stipendiary) at Frankby with Greasby 1997–2001; Vicar at St Matthew's, Stretton and St Cross, Appleton Thorn 2001–13; Rural Dean of Great Budworth 2003–10; Vicar of St George, Stockport with St Gabriel's Adswood from 2013; Honorary Canon of Chester Cathedral from 2012; Chaplain to Air Training Corps from 2014; Chaplain to Fleet Air Arm Association (Manchester Branch) from 2002
GS 2015–   *T:* 0161 456 9382
E: vicar@stgeorgestockport.org.uk

CHESSUN, The Rt Revd Christopher Thomas James *MA*
Trinity House 4 Chapel Court Borough High Street London SE1 1HW [BISHOP OF SOUTHWARK] *educ* Hampton Grammar School; University College Oxford; Westcott House Cambridge *CV* Assistant Curate St Michael and All Angels Sandhurst 1983–87; Senior Curate St Mary Portsea 1987–99; Chaplain and Minor Canon St Paul's Cathedral 1989–93; Rector Stepney, St Dunstan and All Saints 1993–2001; Area Dean Tower Hamlets 1997–2001; Archdeacon of Northolt 2001–05; Member Diocesan Synod 2001–05; Bishop of Woolwich 2005–11; Bishop for Urban Life and Faith 2010–13; Bishop of Southwark from 2011; House of Lords from 2014   *T:* 020 7939 9420 (Office)
020 8769 3256 (Home)
E: bishop.christopher@
southwark.anglican.org
F: 0843 2906 894

CLACK, Mr Jeremy William James *MMATH, FIA*
198 Rugby Road Leamington Spa CV32 6DU [TRUSTEE MEMBER OF CHURCH OF ENGLAND PENSIONS

BOARD] *b* 1981 *educ* King Edward VI School Southampton; University of Warwick *CV* Actuarial consultant; Church Commisioner from 2012: Member C of E Pensions Board from 2012 *E:* jwjclack@gmail.com
M: 07779 639381

CLARK, The Rt Revd Jonathan Dunnett
BA, MLitt, MA
St Matthew's House 100 George Street Croydon CR0 1PE [AREA BISHOP OF CROYDON; SOUTHWARK] *educ* Exeter University; Bristol University; Southern University; Trinity College Bristol *CV* Curate Stanwix 1988–92; Chaplain Bristol University 1992–93; Director of Studies Southern Dioceses Ministerial Training Scheme 1994–97; Chaplain London Metropolitan University 1997–2003; Area Dean Islington 1999–2003; Rector St Mary Stoke Newington 2003–12; Priest in Charge Brownswood Park 2004–11; Area Bishop of Croydon from 2012
GS 2005–2010 *T:* 020 8256 9630
020 8686 1822
E: bishop.jonathan@southwark.anglican.org
F: 020 8256 9631
W: http://clarkinholyorders.wordpress.com
M: 07968 845698 (Mobile)
Twitter: @bishopofcroydon

CLARK, The Revd Jonathan Jackson *MA*
St George's Church Great George Street Leeds LS1 3BR [LEEDS] *educ* St Peters School, York; Lincoln College, Oxford; Ridley, Cambridge *CV* Curate, St Lukes, Princess Drive, Liverpool 1984–87; Curate, St John and St Mark, Clacton-on-Sea 1987–92; Vicar St Simon, Shepherds Bush, London 1993–2003; Area Dean, Hammersmith and Fulham 1996–2001; Rector St George's Leeds from 2003; Chair of St George's Crypt Trustees from 2005
GS 2010– *T:* 0113 243 8498
E: jonathan.clark@stgeorgesleeds.org.uk

CLARKE, Canon Professor Michael Gilbert
CBE, DL, BA, MA, DLitt, D Univ
Millington House 15 Lansdowne Crescent Worcester WR3 8JE [WORCESTER] *b* 1944 *educ* Queen Elizabeth Grammar School Wakefield; Sussex University *CV* Lecturer in Politics Edinburgh University 1969–75; Deputy Director Policy Planning Lothian Regional Council 1975–81; Director Local Government Trade Board 1981–90; Chief Executive Local Government Management Board 1990–93; Head of School of Public Policy Birmingham University 1993–98; Pro-Vice Chancellor Birmingham University from 1998, Vice-Principal 2003–08; Lay Canon and Chapter Member Worcester Cathedral 2001–10; Canon Emeritus 2010; Member Diocese Commission from 2008, Chair from 2011; Member Panel of Chairs from 2009
GS 1990–93-, 1995– *T:* 01905 617634
E: michael.clarkeinworcester@btinternet.com

CLEVERLY, The Revd Canon Charles St George (Charlie) *MA Oxon, PGCE*
Holy Trinity House 19 Turn Again Lane Oxford OX11QL [OXFORD] *b* 1951 *educ* Radley College, St John's College Oxford; Goldsmith's College, London, *CV* Curate then Incumbent St Luke's Cranham Park 1982–92; Pasteur Eglise Reformée de Paris-Belleville 1992–2002; Rector of St Aldate's Oxford from 2002
GS 2015– *T:* 01865 24802
E: charlie.cleverly@staldates.org.uk
W: www.staldates.org.uk

CLIFT, Dr Simon *MB, BS, MSc, MRCGP, DTM&H, MFTM, RCPS, MFOM*
Baraka 25 Harland Crescent Southampton SO15 7QB [WINCHESTER] *educ* Colchester Royal Grammar School; Guy's Hospital Medical School University of London; All Nations Christian College *CV* Mission Partner with Crosslinks 1996–2002; Churchwarden Shirley Parish Church within Southampton Deanery 2008–14; Director of Health Services, Interhealth Worldwide 2014–
GS 2015– *T:* 07753 291964
E: simon.clift@interhealth.org.uk

COCKETT, The Ven Elwin Wesley *BA*
86 Aldersbrook Rd Manor Park London E12 5DH [ARCHDEACON OF WEST HAM; CHELMSFORD] *b* 1959 *educ* St Paul's Cathedral Choir School; Forest School, Snaresbrook; Aston Training Scheme; Oak Hill College *CV* Curate St Chad, Chadwell Heath 1991–94; Curate in Charge St Paul, Harold Hill 1994–95, Priest in Charge 1995–97, Vicar 1997–2000; Team Rector Billericay and Little Burstead Team Minister 2000–07; Rural Dean Basildon 2004–07; Archdeacon of West Ham from 2007; Club Chaplain West Ham United Football Club 1992–2011
T: 020 8989 8557
E: a.westham@chelmsford.anglican.org
F: 020 8530 1311

COCKSWORTH, The Rt Revd Dr Christopher John *BA (Hons), PhD, PGCE, Hon DD*
Bishop's House 23 Davenport Rd Coventry CV5 6PW [BISHOP OF COVENTRY] *educ* Forest School for Boys, Horsham; University of Manchester; Didsbury School of Education; St John College, Nottingham *CV* Assistant Curate Christ Church Epsom 1988–92; Chaplain Royal Holloway University of London 1992–96; Director Southern Theological Education and Training Scheme 1996–2001; Principal Ridley Hall Cambridge 2001–08; Bishop of Coventry from 2008
GS 2008– *T:* 024 7667 2244
E: bishop@bishop-coventry.org
F: 024 7610 0535
W: www.dioceseofcoventry.org

COLES, Mr Peter
5 Romsey Way High Wycombe HP11 1QP
[DIOCESAN SECRETARY; GUILDFORD] *b* 1958 *educ*
Oxford University Said Business School;
Henley Management College; The Open
University *CV* Programme Director Journalism
Production Tools, BBC 2008–10; Technology
Controller Journalism, BBC 2009–13; Chief
Technology Officer BBC 2013–2015; Diocesan
Secretary Guildford from 2015; Diocesan
Synod; Bishop's Council; Board of Education;
Parish Share Working Group
              T: 01483 790300
    E: peter.coles@cofeguildford.org.uk
    W: http://www.cofeguildford.org.uk/

COLLIER, Rt Worshipful Peter Neville *MA*, QC
*Leeds Crown Court The Courthouse 1 Oxford Row
Leeds LS1 3BG* [GENERAL SYNOD EX OFFICIO] *educ*
Hymers College, Hull; Selwyn College
Cambridge *CV* Chancelor Wakefield 1992–
2006; Chancellor Lincoln 1998–2006; Lay
Canon, York Minster from 2001; Chair York
Minster Council from 2005; Chancellor York
from 2006; Senior Circuit Judge and Honorary
Recorder of Leeds from 2007; Legal Advisory
Commission from 2008; Vicar General
Province of York from 2008
GS 2008–   *T:* 0113 306 2800

COLLINS, The Ven Gavin Andrew *MA*, *MA*
*Victoria Lodge 36 Osborn Road Fareham PO16
7DS* [ARCHDEACON OF THE MEON; PORTSMOUTH]
b 1954 *educ* Sackville School East Grinstead;
Trinity Hall Cambridge; College Law
Guildford; Trinity College Bristol *CV* Assistant
Curate St Barnabas Cambridge 1997–2002;
Vicar Christ Church Chorleywood 2002–11;
Rural Dean Rickmansworth 2006–11;
Honorary Canon St Alban Cathedral 2009–11;
Archdeacon of the Meon from 2011; Diocesan
Warden of Readers from 2014
GS 2013–   *T:* 01329 608895
   E: gavin.collins@portsmouth.anglican.org

CONALTY, The Ven Julie Anne *BA*, *MA*
*c/o Diocesan Office St Nicholas Church Boley Hill
Rochester ME1 1SL* [ARCHDEACON OF TONBRIDGE;
ROCHESTER] *educ* Ormskirk Grammar School,
University of Sheffield, Middlesex Polytechnic,
University of Kent Canterbury *CV* Night shelter
manager, 1985–86; Community Service Officer
1986–88; Probation Officer 1990–99; Probation
Service Education, Training and Employment
Development Manager, 1999–2002; Curate
(SSM) 1999–2004; Education, Training and
Resettlement Policy Advisor for The Youth
Justice Board, 2002–03; Associate Priest (SSM)
2004–10; self employed consultant 2003–2005;
National Manager of RESET project 2005–06;
Specialist Youth Services Manager 2006–08;
Partner in Sustainable Change Consulting LLP
2008–10; Associate Priest (stipendiary)

Plumstead Common United Benefice, 2010–12;
Vicar of Christ Church Erith 2012–17; Area
Dean of Erith 2014–17; Bishop's Advisor for the
Ministry of Ordained Women from 2013;
Archdeacon of Tonbridge from 2017
GS 2013–
        E: archdeacon.tonbridge@
              rochester.anglican.org

CONDRY, The Rt Revd Dr Edward Francis *BA*, *BLitt*, *DPhil*, *MBA*
*White Lodge 22 Westbury Road Warminster
Wilts BA12 0AW* [SUFFRAGAN BISHOP OF RAMSBURY;
SALISBURY] *b* 1954 *educ* Latymer Upper School
Hammersmith; University of East Anglia;
Exeter College, Oxford; Unversity of
Nottingham; Lincoln Theological College;
Open University *CV* Assistant Curate Weston
Favell, Peterborough 1982–85; Vicar Bloxham,
Milcombe and South Newington, Oxford
1985–1993; Team Rector, Rugby Team
Ministry, Coventry 1993–2002; Canon
Residential Canterbury Cathedral 2002–12;
Canon Librarian 2002–3; Director IME 4–7
Canterbury Diocese 2002–07; Canon
Treasurer and Director of Education 2006–12;
Bishop of Ramsbury from 2012
             T: 01722 438662
  E: edward.condry@salisbury.anglican.org

CONNER, The Rt Revd David John *MA*, KCVO
The Deanery Windsor Castle Windsor SL4 1NJ
[DEAN OF WINDSOR] *educ* Exeter College Oxford;
St Stephen's House Theological College *CV*
Honorary Curate Summertown Oxford 1971–
76; Assistant Chaplain St Edward's School
Oxford 1971–73; Chaplain 1973–80; Team
Vicar Wolvercote with Summertown 1976–80;
Chaplain Winchester College 1980–87; Vicar
Great St Mary with St Michael Cambridge
1987–94; Rural Dean Cambridge 1989–94;
Bishop of Lynn 1994–98; Dean of Windsor
from 1998; Bishop to HM Forces 2001–09
            T: 01753 865561
  E: david.conner@stgeorges-windsor.org
            F: 01753 819002

CONWAY, The Rt Revd Stephen David *MA*, *MA*
*The Bishop's House Ely Cambridgeshire CB7
4DW* [BISHOP OF ELY] *b* 1967 *educ* Archbishop
Tenison's Grammar School London; Keble
College Oxford; Selwyn College Cambridge;
Westcott House *CV* Curate St Mary Heworth
1986–89; Curate St Michael and All Angels
Bishopwearmouth 1989–90; Diocesan
Director of Ordinands 1989–94; Honorary
Curate St Margaret Durham 1990–94; Priest in
Charge then Vicar St Mary Cockerton 1994–
98; Senior Chaplain to Bishop of Durham and
Diocesan Communications Officer 1998–
2002; Archdeacon of Durham and Canon
Residential Durham Cathedral 2002–06; Area

Bishop of Ramsbury 2006–10; Member Bishops Inspector of Theological Colleges and Courses 1997–2006; Chair of Mental Health Matters 2004–2010; GS 1995–2000; Chair Diocesan Learning, Discipleship and Ministry Council 2006–10; Warden of Lay Ministry from 2006–2010; Trustee Affirming Catholicism 2001–08, Vice-President from 2008; Bishop for L'Arche UK from 2007, Church Leaders's Group, L'Arche International from 2012; Bishop of Ely from 2010; Member of the Faith and Order Commission, World Council of Churches from 2014; House of Lords from 2014; Member of the Archbishops' Council from 2015; Chair of Council of National Society; Visitor of Jesus College, Peterhouse College and St John's College Cambridge; Honorary Fellow, Harris Manchester College Oxford from 2017; House of Bishops Standing Committee from 2017
GS 1995–2000   T: 01353 662749
                          E: bishop@elydiocese.org
                          Twitter: @bishop_s_conway

COOMBEY, Mrs Wendy
1 Minster Court Leominster Herefordshire HR6 8LJ [HEREFORD] *educ* Leominster Minster School, Hereford Colege of Technology, Worcester Colleges *CV* Halifax Building Society 1984–94; Mencap 1994–96; Herefordshire Council for Voluntary Services 1995–98; Herefordshire Council 1998–2001; Community Partnership and Funding Officer, Diocese of Hereford 2001
GS 2015–   T: 01584 871088
                                      07738 226625
          E: w.coombey@hereford.anglican.org

COOPER, The Ven Annette Joy *BA, CQSW, Dip RS, MA*
63 Powers Hall End Witham CM8 1NH [ARCHDEACON OF COLCHESTER; CHELMSFORD] *b* 1967 *educ* Lilley and Stone Newark Girls High School; Open University; London University Extra-mural Department; Southwark Ordination Course; St John's College, Durham *CV* Local Authority Social Worker; Assistant Chaplain Tunbridge Wells Health Authority 1988–91; Non-Stipendiary Minister Deacon St Peter Pembury 1988; Chaplain Bassetlaw Hospital and Community Services NHS Trust 1991–96; Chaplain to Center Parcs Sherwood Village 1996–99; Chaplain to Southwell Diocesan Mothers Union 1996–99; Priest in Charge Edwinstowe 1996–2004; Governor St Mary's C of E (Aided) Primary School 1996–2004; Area Dean Worksop 1999–2004; Honorary Canon Southwell Minster 2002–04; Member Diocesan Board of Education 1994–97; Member Bishop's Council 1999–2004; Vice-President/Chair Diocesan House of Clergy 2001–04; Member General Synod Panel of Chairmen 2003–04, 2006–11; Member Discipline Commission

2003–13; Archdeacon of Colchester from 2004; Chelmsford Diocesan Board of Finance from 2004; Trustee Dedham Lectureship Trust from 2004; Trustee Lovibond Almshouses from 2004; Member National Stewardship Committee 2007–10; Director All Churches Trust from 2008; Member Appointments Committee 2011–15; Member Archbishops' Council Finance Committee 2011–15; Member Clergy Discipline (Amendment) Measure Steering Committee 2011; Chair George Richards Charity from 2012; Elected Representative (Eastern Region) House of Bishops 2013–16; Member Development Advisory Group 2014–16; Member National Safeguarding Panel from 2014
GS 2000–04; 2005–10; 2010–15
                                      T: 01376 513130
          E: a.colchester@chelmsford.anglican.org
                                      F: 01376 500789
                              Twitter: @AnnetteAcooper

COOPER, The Revd Canon Robert (Bob) Gerard *B.D. Hons*
St Giles Vicarage 9 The Mount Pontefract W Yorks. WF8 1NE [LEEDS] *educ* The Bluecoat School Oldham, University of Wales, Aberystwyth *CV* Assistant Curate Whitkirk Leeds 1993–6; Assistant Priest Richmond Hill Parish, Leeds 1996–7; School Chaplain, Agnes Stewart High School Leeds 1996–7; School Chaplain Chigwell School, Essex 1997–8; Vicar Lightcliffe, Halifax 1998–2005; Chaplain Halifax RLFC 2000–2005; Vicar Pontefract from 2005; Area Dean Pontefract from 2006; Canon Wakefield Cathedral from 2008; Canon Musoma Cathedral, Diocese of Mara, Tanzania from 2017
GS 2009–10, 2015   T: 01977 706803
                                      07931 565516
                          E: Robert_Cooper@msn.com

CORNES, Canon Andrew Charles Julian *MA*
12 Cavendish Avenue Eastbourne BN22 8EN [CHICHESTER] *b* 1949 *educ* Eton, Corpus Christi College, Oxford *CV* Curate, St Michael-le-Belfrey, York 1973–76; Director of Training, All Souls, Langham Place, London 1976–85; Principal, All Souls College of Applied Theology 1981–85; Rector, Church of the Ascension, Pittsburgh, Pennsylvania, USA 1985–88; Vicar, All Saints, Crowborough 1989–2015; Rural Dean of Rotherfield 1997–2003; Canon of Chichester Cathedral 2000–15, Canon Emeritus from 2015; Retired with PTO
GS 2015–   T: 07583498845
                                      07967862419
                          E: andrewcjcornes@hotmail.com

CORTEEN, Mrs Christine
21 Hillside Road Wool Wareham BH20 6DY [SALISBURY] *educ* Merchant Taylors' School,

Liverpool; Liverpool University *CV* Local Government Officer from 1977; Income and Payments Manager, Poole Borough Council from 1990; Council Mission, Sarum; St Aldhelm's Mission Fund, Sarum; Learning for Discipleship and Ministry, Sarum
GS 2010–   *T:* 01929 462642
                    E: chriscorteen@gmail.com

COTTON, Canon Robert Lloyd *MA, DipTh*
Holy Trinity Rectory 9 Eastgate Gardens Guildford GU1 4AZ [GUILDFORD] *b* 1958 *educ* Uppingham; Merton College Oxford; Westcott House Cambridge *CV* Curate St Mary Bromley 1983–85; Curate Bisley and West End 1987–89; Priest in Charge St Paul East Molesey 1989–96; Principal Guildford Diocesan Ministry Course 1989–96; Rector Holy Trinity and St Mary Guildford from 1996; Chair House of Clergy 2004–11; Canon Diocese of Highveld, South Africa from 2006; Canon Guildford Cathedral from 2010; Archbishop's Council from 2010
GS 2004–   *T:* 01483 575489
        E: rector@holytrinityguildford.org.uk
        W: www.holytrinityguildford.org.uk/blog
                              M: 07710 757248

COTTRELL, The Rt Revd Stephen Geoffrey *BA*
Bishopscourt Main Road Margaretting Ingatestone CM4 0HD [BISHOP OF CHELMSFORD] *educ* Belfairs High School for Boys; Polytechnic of Central London; St Stephen's House *CV* Curate Christ Church and St Paul Forest Hill, Southwark 1984–88; Priest in Charge St Wilfred Parklands, Chichester and Assistant Director of Pastoral Studies, Chichester Theological College 1988–93; Diocesan Missioner, Wakefield 1993–98; Springboard Missioner 1998–2001; Canon Pastor Peterborough Cathedral 2001–04; Bishop of Reading 2004–10; Bishop of Chelmsford from 2010
GS 2010–   *T:* 01277 352001
        E: bishopscourt@chelmsford.anglican.org
                              F: 01277 355374

COULSTON, Mr David Jack *BSc (Hons), MSc*
161 Ashworth Park Knutsford Cheshire WA16 9DJ [EUROPE] *b* 1947 *educ* King Edward VI Grammar School, Spilsby Lincolnshire; Lincoln College of Technology, The University of Hull, The University of Salford *CV* Member of Health & Safety Commission 1996–99 (concurrent with BNFL employment); Retired; Justice of the Peace in Cheshire; Director of Environment, Health & Safety, British Nuclear Fuels Limited 1992–2000; Interim Manager, The National Probation Directorate 2003–06; Interim Manager The City of York 2006–07
GS 2015–   *T:* 07740 779446
                    E: davidjcoulston@gmail.com

COULTER, Mrs Alison Jane (Alison) *MA, MSc*
The Square House St Cross Road Winchester Hampshire SO23 9RX [WINCHESTER] *b* 1964 *educ* Haberdashers' Aske's Girls' School, Gonville and Caius College Cambridge, London School of Hygiene and Tropical Medicine *CV* Physiotherapist 1986–95; Lecturer at Southampton University 1997–98; NHS Manager 1999–2007; Director of Artesian Transformational Leadership Ltd from 2007
GS 2015–   *T:* 07946 873105
        E: alison.coulter@artesiangroup.co.uk
                    Twitter: @AlisonCoulter1

COURT, The Rt Revd Dr David Eric *PhD, BSc, BA*
The Old Palace Minster Yard Lincoln LN2 1PU [BISHOP OF GRIMSBY; LINCOLN] *educ* Heartsease Comprehensive, Norwich, Southampton University *CV* Teacher of Science, Prince William School, Oundle, 1984–88; Assistant Curate St Botolph's, Barton Seagrave, 1991–93; Assistant Curate, St Andrew's, Kinson, 1993–97; Vicar, St Catherine's, Mile Cross, 1997–2003; Vicar, Cromer, 2003–14; Bishop of Grimsby from 2014   *T:* 01522 504090
        E: bishop.grimsby@lincoln.anglican.org

COX, The Revd Alison *BTh, MHort*
St Mark's Vicarage 2 Church Square Railway Street Dukinfield SK16 4PX [CHESTER] *b* 1963 *educ* Westville Girls' School; Weymouth Grammar School; Pershore College Horticulture; Ripon College Cuddesdon *CV* Assistant Garden Centre Manager; Journalist; Curate St Mary's & St Nicolas, Spalding 2003–07; Priest in Charge St Mark's Dukinfield from 2007; Rural Dean Mottram from 2012
GS 2010–   *T:* 0161 330 2783
                    E: alisoncox19@hotmail.com

CROFT, The Rt Revd Dr Steven John Lindsey
Bishop's Lodge 43 Mill Street Kidlington Oxford OX5 2EE [BISHOP OF OXFORD] *educ* Heath School Halifax; Worcester College Oxford; Cranmer Hall, St John College Durham *CV* Curate St Andrew Enfield 1983–1987; Vicar St George's Ovenden 1987–1996; Warden Cranmer Hall 1996–2004; Archbishops' Missioner and Team Leader of Fresh Expressions 2004–09; Bishop of Sheffield 2009–16; Archbishops' Council from 2011; House of Bishops' Standing Committee from 2011; Ministry Council from 2011, Chair from 2012; Bishop of Oxford from 2016
GS 2009–   *T:* 01865 208222
                    E: bishop.oxford@oxford.anglican.org
                              Twitter: @Steven_Croft

CRYER, Mr Jonathan Patrick *LLB, AKC*
4 Honeybourne Close Oadby Leicester LE2 5PJ [LEICESTER] *educ* The College Marlborough Wiltshire; King's College London *CV*

Resources Adviser Diocese of Winchester 1980; Assistant Diocesan Secretary Diocese of Chichester 1984; Diocesan Secretary Diocese of Leicester 1989; Diocesan Secretary Diocese of Durham 1998–2004; National Church Fundraiser Church Urban Fund 2005–09; Senior Fundraiser Action Homeless Leicester 2009–12; Registrar of Births, Deaths and Marriages, Leicestershire 2013–

T: 0116 271 9712
07854 580364
E: cryerjonathan@gmail.com

CUNLIFFE, The Ven Dr Christopher John
MA, DPhil, MA, A R Hist S
Derby Church House Full St Derby DE1 3DR
[ARCHDEACON OF DERBY] *educ* Charterhouse; Christ Church Oxford; Trinity College Cambridge; Westcott House Cambridge *CV* Curate Chesterfield Parish Church 1983–85; Chaplain and Junior Research Fellow, Lincoln College Oxford 1985–89; Chaplain City University and Guildhall School of Music and Drama 1989–91; Selection Secretary and Vocations Officer, Advisory Board of Ministry 1991–96; Bishop of London's Advisor for Ordained Minstry 1996–2003; Clerk, All Saints Education Trust 2004; Chaplain to Bishop of Bradwell 2004–06; Archdeacon of Derby from 2006; Canon Residentiary Derby Cathedral 2006–08; Commissary to Bishop of Angola from 2015			*T:* 01332 388676
E: archderby@derby.anglican.org
F: 01332 292969

CUTTING, The Ven Alastair Murray BEd,
MA, LTh, DPS
Woolwich Episcopal Area Office Trinity House 4 Chapel Court Borough High Street London SE1 1HW [ARCHDEACON OF LEWISHAM AND GREENWICH; SOUTHWARK] *b* 1954 *educ* George Watson's College Edinburgh; Lushington (Hebron) School Ooty, South India; Watford Boy's Grammar School; Westhill College Birmingham; St John's College Nottingham; Heythrop College London *CV* Curate All Saints Woodlands, Sheffield 1987–88; Curate Wadsley, Sheffield 1989–91; Chaplain to The Nave and Town Centre, Uxbridge, London 1991–96; Vicar Copthorne, Chichester 1996–2010; Vicar Henfield, Rector Sharmanbury and Woodmancote 2010–13; Archdeacon of Lewisham and Greenwich from 2013; Member Bishop's Council Chichester 1998–2013; Assistant Rural Dean East Grinstead 2002–10; Chair House of Clergy Chichester 2009–13; Pro-Prolocutor Province of Canterbury 2011–13
GS 2005–13				*T:* 020 7979 9408
E: alastair.cutting@southwark.anglican.org
F: 020 7939 9465
W: www.acutting.org
M: 07736 676106
Twitter: @AlCutting

DAILEY, Miss Prudence Mary Prior MA
9 Spring Lane Littlemore Oxford OX4 6LF
[OXFORD] *educ* Simon Langton Grammar School for Girls Canterbury; King's School Canterbury; Merton College Oxford *CV* NHS General Management Trainee and various admin posts in NHS 1988–97; Oxford City Councillor 1992–96; Senior Business Systems Analyst, Toys 'R' Us 1998–2009; Chairman Prayer Book Society from 2007
GS 2000–					*T:* 01865 236124
E: prudence.dailey@gmail.com
M: 07730 516620

DAKIN, The Rt Revd Timothy John BA,
MTh
Wolvesey Winchester SO23 9ND [BISHOP OF WINCHESTER] *b* 1958 *educ* Priory School Shrewsbury; St Mary's School Nairobi; Henley Sixth Form College; St Mark's and St John College Plymouth; King College London; Christ Church Oxford; Carlile College Nairobi *CV* Principal Carlile College, Nairobi 1993–2000; Honorary Curate Nairobi Cathedral 1994–2000; General Secretary Christian Mission Society 2000–11; Canon Theologian Coventry Cathedral 2001–11; Associate Priest St James Ruscombe and St Marys Twyford 2000–11; Member Mission and Public Affairs Council; Member Partnership for World Mission Panel, Bishop of Winchester from 2011
GS 2005–					*T:* 01962 854050
E: bishop.tim@winchester.anglican.org
W: www.winchester.anglican.org

DALLISTON, The Very Revd Christopher Charles MA
The Deanery 26 Mitchell Avenue Newcastle upon Tyne NE2 3LA [DEAN OF NEWCASTLE] *educ* Diss Grammar School; Peterhouse Cambridge; St Stephen's House Oxford *CV* Curate St Andrew Halsead with Holy Trinity and Greenstead Green 1984–87; Domestic Chaplain to Bishop of Chelmsford 1987–91; Vicar St Edmund Forest Gate, Chelmsford 1991–95; Vicar St Botolph with St Christopher Boston 1995–2003; Dean of Newcastle 2003–17; Dean of Peterborough from 2018
T: 0191 281 6554
0191 232 1939
E: dean@stnicnewcastle.co.uk

DALLOW, The Revd Gillian Margaret BA,
MEd, PGCE, CEM
26 Baron's Court Road Penylan Cardiff CF23 9DF
[SYNODICAL SECRETARY, CONVOCATION OF CANTERBURY] *b* 1967 *educ* Cathays High School Cardiff; University of North Wales Bangor; Bristol University; Oak Hill Theological College; West of England University *CV*

Teacher Mill St Secondary School Pontypridd 1968–70; Head of RE Hereford High School for Girls 1970–73; Head of RE and Student Counselling Hereford Sixth Form College 1973–74; Scripture Union Schools Worker South West and Wales 1974–79; Head of RE Colston's Girls School Bristol; Education Advisor Bath and Wells 1985–91; Director Training London Bible College 1991–98; Advisor for Children's Ministry and Priest in Charge St Giles Barlestone 1999–2018; Diocesan Director Under 25s Training from 2002; General Synod Board of Education 200–05; Synodical Secretary, Convocation of Canterbury from 2006; Member C of E Evangelical Council from 2006; Secretary Eggs (Evangelicals on General Synod) from 2009; Permission to Officiate: Diocese of London and Diocese of Llandaff; Cardiff Bay Chaplain to Welsh Assembly Government from 2009; Associate Priest St Mark's Gabalfa and St Philip's Community Church Tremorfa Cardiff from 2009
GS 2000–05   *T:* 0292 0463754
              E: g.dallow@btinternet.com
                          M: 07801 650187

DALTON, The Revd Laura Michelle
41 Innage Lane Bridgnorth Shropshire WV16 4HS [HEREFORD] *educ* South Craven School, New College Bromsgrove *CV* Playleader (part-time), Malvern Special Families, 1989–95; Childcare Assistant, Safe Hands After School Club, Droitwich, September 1994–95; Nanny, The Killington Family, Droitwich, September 1994–95; Full-time Homemaker/Parent, 1995–2003; Student Support Worker (Inclusion), The Lord Silkin School, Telford, 2003–04; Learning Mentor, Brookside Primary School, Telford, 2005; Full-time Homemaker/Parent, 2005–06; Pupil Support Manager, Lickhill Middle School, Stourport, 2006–07; Student Support Manager (KS3), Stourport High School, 2007; Full-time Homemaker/Parent, 2007–10; Assistant Curate, Bridgnorth Team Ministry, Diocese of Hereford, from 2012
GS 2015–   *T:* 01746768027
                                   07540066785
              E: revlaura72@icloud.com

DAVENPORT, Miss Laura Elizabeth *BA, MA*
8 Ashfield Avenue Union Mills Isle of Man IM4 4LN [SODOR AND MAN] *b* 1988 *educ* Queen Elizabeth II High School, Isle of Man; Cambridge University; Durham University *CV* Diocesan Youth Advisor from 2010; Youth Leader, Braddan Church from 2010; Business Analyst, Barclays Wealth from 2010; Diocesan Communication Forum from 2010
GS 2010–   *T:* 01624852167
    E: laura.elizabeth.davenport@gmail.com
                          M: 07624467232

DAVIES, The Very Revd Dr John Harverd *MA, MPhil, PhD*
The Dean's Lodging 25 The Liberty Wells BA5 2SZ [DEAN OF WELLS] *educ* Brentwood School; Keble College Oxford; Corpus Christi College Cambridge; Lancaster University; Westcott House *CV* Curate Liverpool Parish Church 1984–87; Curate Peterborough Parish Church and Minor Canon Peterborough Cathedral 1987–90; Vicar St Margaret Anfield, Liverpool 1990–94; Chaplain, Fellow and Director of Studies in Theology, Keble College Oxford 1994–99; Vicar Melbourne and Diocesan Director of Ordinands Derby Diocese 1999–2009; Dean of Derby 2010–16; Member Derby Diocesan Board for Ministry; Member Diocesan Synod; Member General Synod Theological Education and Training Committee 2006–07; Chair Industrial Mission in Derbyshire 2009–16; Dean of Wells from 2016   *T:* 01749 670278
    E: deanchaptersec@wellscathedral.uk.net
                          F: 01332 203991

DAVIES, The Rt Revd Mark *BA, Cert PS*
The Hollies Manchester Rd Rochdale OL11 3QY [SUFFRAGAN BISHOP OF MIDDLETON; MANCHESTER] *b* 1962 *educ* Hanley High School; Stoke-on-Trent Sixth Form College; University College of Ripon and York St John; Mirfield Theological College *CV* Curate St Mary Barnsley 1989–92; Priest in Charge St Paul Old Town Barnsley 1992–95; Rector Hemsworth from 1995; Assistant Diocesan Director of Ordinands from 1998; Rural Dean Pontefract from 2000; Honorary Canon Wakefield Cathedral 2002–06; Archdeacon of Rochdale 2006–08; Bishop of Middleton from 2008
GS 2000–06   *T:* 01706 358550
    E: bishopmark@manchester.anglican.org

DAWTRY, The Ven Dr Anne Frances *BA(Hons), PhD, Dip Min*
2 Vicarage Gardens Brighouse West Yorkshire HD6 3HD [ARCHDEACON OF HALIFAX; LEEDS] *b* 1967 *CV* Curate Corfe Mullen 1993–96; Curate Parkstone St Peter with Branksea and St Osmund 1996–97; Chaplain Bournemouth University and Bournemouth and Poole College of Further Education 1997–99; Principal Ordained Local Ministry and Integrated Training 1999–2003; Director Training and Principal Diocesan Ordained Local Ministry Scheme Manchester 2003–06; Course Director Southern North West Training Partnership 2006–08; Curate Chorlton-cum-Hardy St Werburgh 2006–08; Priest-in-charge 2008–09; Rector 2009–11; Hon Canon Manchester Cathedral 2006–11; Archdeacon of Halifax from 2011; Warden of Readers from 2012: Consultant Liturgical Commission 2000–05; Member Liturgical Commission

2005–15; Member Church Buildings Council from 2016 *T:* 01484 714553
E: archdeacon.halifax@leeds.anglican.org
W: www.leeds.anglican.org
M: 07980 751902

DE BERRY, The Revd Barnabas John Delatour *BA*
57 Nunnery Fields Canterbury CT1 3JN [CANTERBURY] *b* 1975 *educ* Stowe, Heythrop College, University of London *CV* Curate St Alkmund's Derby 2001–04; Associate Vicar, Holy Trinity Cambridge 2004–10; Vicar, St Mary Bredin, Canterbury from 2010
GS 2015–   *T:* 01227 453777
07968 728840
E: vicar@smb.org.uk
Twitter: @Barney_deBerry

DE BERRY, Mrs Gill (Gillian Patricia) *BEd*
27 Cossor Road Pewsey Wiltshire SN9 5HX [SALISBURY] *b* 1967 *educ* Bradford Girls' Grammar School, Dartford College of PE (University of London) *CV* Assistant PE teacher; Wyke Manor Grammar School, Bradford 1969–70; Teso College, Aloet, Uganda 1972–73; Sheffield High School 1980–83; North London Collegiate School, Edgware 1986–88; St Paul's Girls' School, London 1989–2008; Retired from 2008
GS 2015–   *T:* 01672562907
E: gilldeberry18@gmail.com

DETTMER, The Ven Douglas James *BA, MDiv*
Blue Hills Bradley Road Bovey Tracey Newton Abbot Devon TQ13 9EU [ARCHDEACON OF TOTNES; EXETER] *educ* Council Grove High School, University of Kansas; Yale University *CV* Curate, Ilfracombe Team Ministry 1990–94; Domestic Chaplain to the Bishop of Exeter 1994–98; Priest-in-Charge, Raddon Team Ministry 1998–2010; Priest-in-Charge, Stoke Canon Benefice 2006–10; Rural Dean of Cadbury 2006–13; Rector, Netherexe Parishes 2010–15; Prebendary of Exeter Cathedral 2012–15; Archdeacon of Totnes from 2015
GS 2012–15   *T:* 01626 832064
E: archdeacon.of.totnes@exeter.anglican.org

DOBBIE, Brigadier William Ian Cotter *OBE, BSc*
5 Richmond Court White Lodge Close Hitchen Hatch Lane Sevenoaks TN13 3BF [ROCHESTER] *educ* Wellington College; Royal Military Academy Sandhurst; Royal Military College of Science; Army Staff College; Royal Air Force Staff College *CV* Reg Officer 1958–1992; Deputy Chief of Staff 3 Armoured Division 1986–88; Comd Engineer HQ BAOR 1988–92; Project Director and Adminstrator St Nicholas, Sevenoaks 1992–95; General Secretary Council of Voluntary Welfare Work 1995;

Chair Soldiers' and Airmens' Scripture Readers Associate, 1991; Rochester Diocesan Board of Patronage
GS 2000–   *T:* 01732 465109
E: gensec@cvww.org.uk

DOBSON, The Very Red John Richard *BTh, CertTh*
Minster House Bedern Bank Ripon HG4 1PE [DEAN OF RIPON: LEEDS] *educ* Garforth Comprehensive; Durham University; Ripon College Cuddesdon Theological College *CV* Curate Benfieldside 1989–92; Curate Darlington St Cuthbert 1992–96; Curate-in-charge All Saints and Salutation Blackwell 1996–98; Vicar All Saints and Salutation Blackwell 1998–2014; Priest-in-charge Coniscliffe 2004–14; Area Dean of Darlington 2001–14; Dean of Ripon from 2014; Diocesan Board of Leeds *T:* 01765 602609
E: deanjohn@riponcathedral.org.uk

DOCHERTY, Mrs Lucy Clare *BA*
33 Southampton Road Fareham Hampshire PO16 7DZ [PORTSMOUTH] *educ* Tavistock School; Nottingham University *CV* Commercial retail and marketing posts 1977–83; Non-executive Director and Chair NCT Publishing Ltd 1996–99; Member and one-time Chair Christians Together in Fareham since 1996; Lay Board Member Fareham Primary Care Group 1999–2002; Vice Chair National Association of Lay People in Primary Care 2000–03; Chair Fareham and Gosport Primary Care Trust 2002–06; Non Executive Director Hampshire Probation Trust 2007–14; Elected Governor Portsmouth Hospital Foundation Trust 2007–16; Chair Governors 6th Form College 2010–17; Chair Rainbow Centre for Conductive Education 2012–16, Chair House of Laity Portsmouth 2006–15; Chair Portsmouth Diocese Council for Social Responsibility from 2006; Executive Member Churches Together in Hampshire, 2000–09; Member Council Church House from 2010; Lay Canon Portsmouth Cathedral from 2013; Member Churches Together England Enabling Group; Lay Board Member Fareham and Gosport CCG from 2016
GS 2007–   *T:* 01329 233602
E: lucy@docherty1.co.uk

DOE, The Rt Revd Michael David *BA, LLD (Hon)*
405 West Carriage House Royal Carriage Mews Royal Arsenal Woolwich SE18 6GA [PREACHER, GRAY'S INN; HONORARY ASSISTANT BISHOP OF SOUTHWARK] *b* 1952 *educ* Brockenhurst Grammar School; Durham University; Ripon Hall Theological College *CV* Curate St Peter St Helier Morden 1972–76, Honorary Curate 1976–81; Youth Secretary British Council of Churches 1976–81; Vicar Blackbird Leys Local Ecumenical Partnership Oxford 1981–89; Rural Dean Cowley 1987–89; Society Responsibility

Advisor Portsmouth 1989–94; Canon Residential Portsmouth Cathedral 1989–94; Bishop of Swindon 1994–2004; Convenor Churches Together England 1999–2003; General Secretary USPG 2004–11; Assistant Bishop Southwark from 2004; Preacher Gray's Inn from 2011
GS 1990–94, 2000–04   *T:* 020 3259 3841
E: michaeldd@btinternet.com
W: http://www.graysinn.info/
index.php/chapel
Twitter: @GraysInnChapel

DOHERTY, The Revd Dr Sean *BA, MPhil, DPhil*
50 Wayneflete Square London W10 6UD [LONDON] *b* 1980 *CV* Donor Care Assistant, USPG, 2003–04; Curate, St Gabriel, Cricklewood, 2007–10; Tutor and Lecturer in Ethics, St Mellitus College from 2010; Director of Assessment, 2012–2014; Director of Studies from 2014
GS 2015–   *T:* 07710 515800
E: Dohertysw@gmail.com
Twitter: @swdoherty

DORAGH, The Revd Sonya Jacqueline *BA, DipFr, MA*
Christ Church Vicarage 34 Church Lane Eccleston St Helens WA10 5AD [LIVERPOOL] *b* 1967 *educ* Aylesbury High School, Oxford Brookes University, L'école supérieure de commerce La Rochelle *CV* Public Relations and Prayer Mobilisation Manager Viva 1995–2000; Latin American Regional Centre Establishment Team Viva Costa Rica 2001; Feeding and Literacy Centre Project Manager Hijos Del Nuevo Pacto Guatemala 2000–01; Youth and Community Worker Hull Youth for Christ 2001–02; Full time Foster Carer 2002–04; Classroom Support Assistant and Cover Supervisor for French Stepney Primary School 2004–05; Pastoral Assistant Anfield Infant School 2005–06; Vocations Initiative Administrator Liverpool 2007–08; Urban Discipleship Development Worker Unlock Liverpool 2008–10; Curate St Peter's Woolton also serving All Saints and St Aidan's Speke 2012–16; Vicar Christ Church Eccleston from 2016
GS 2015–   *T:* 01744 22698
E: sonya@doragh.co.uk
W: thepursuitofwisdom.co.uk
Twitter: @Sonya_Doragh

DORBER, The Very Revd Adrian John *BA, MTh*
The Deanery 16 The Close Lichfield WS13 7LD [DEAN OF LICHFIELD] *educ* St John College, Durham University; King's College London; Westcott House Cambridge *CV* Curate Easthampstead, Bracknell, Oxford 1979–85; Deanery Youth Officer 1982–85; Priest in Charge St Barn Emmer Green 1985–88;

Chaplain Portsmouth Polytechnic 1988–92, Lecturer 1991–97, Senior Chaplain, Public Orator Portsmouth University 1992–97; Honorary Chaplain Portsmouth Cathedral 1992–97; Priest in Charge Brancepeth, Durham 1997–2001; Director Ministry and Training 1997–2005; Honorary Canon Durham Cathedral 1997–2005; Dean of Lichfield from 2005; Member Diocesan Synod and Bishop's Council; Member Executive Committee Association English Cathedrals; Chair Cathedrals Research Project; Chair of Governors, Lichfield Cathedral School; Trustee Lichfield Festival   *T:* 01543 306294 (Home)
01543 306250 (Office)
E: adrian.dorber@lichfield-cathedral.org
bernice.alexander@lichfield-cathedral.org
F: 01543 306109
W: www.lichfield-cathedral.org

DORGU, The Rt Revd Dr Woyin (Karowei) *MB, BS, BA*
Woolwich Episcopal Area Office Trinity House 4 Chapel Court Borough High Street London SE1 1HW [AREA BISHOP OF WOOLWICH; SOUTHWARK] *b* 1958 *educ* College of Medicine, University of Lagos; All Nations Christian College; London Bible College, Oak Hill Theological College *CV* 1995–1998 Curate St Mark Tollington; 1998–2000 Curate St John the Evangelist Upper Holloway; Team Vicar 2000–12; Vicar 2012–17; Prebendary, St Paul's Cathedral 2016–17; Area Bishop of Woolwich from 2017
T: 020 7939 9405
E: bishop.karowei@southwark.anglican.org

DOTCHIN, The Revd Andrew Steward *Dip Th (Hons), PG Pstl Th*
The New Vicarage 54 Princes Road Felixstowe IP11 7PL [ST EDMUNDSBURY AND IPSWICH] *educ* Royal Hospital School, Ipswich; Witwatersrand Technikon, Johannesburg; FedTheo Seminary, Imbali; Anglia Ruskin University *CV* Curate and Priest in Charge, Parish of Standerton with Evander, Johannesburg 1985–87; Assistant Priest St Martin's in the Veld, Rosebank, Johannesburg 1987–88; Rector St John the Divine, Belgravia Johannesburg, 1989–94; Chaplain St Martin's School, Rosettenville, Christ the King 1994–2000; Team Vicar: Blyth Valley Team Ministry, Diocese St Edmundsbury and Ipswich 2000–04; Editor Third Order Chronicle, Europe Province Third Order Society St Francis, 2003–10; Member House of Clergy, Synod Anglican Church of South Africa 1980–2000; Member Provisions Elective Assembly Committee of ACSA, 1993–2000; Member ACSA Pub Committee, 1998–2000; Member Executive Committee Scripture Union Independent School, 1997–2000; Member Diocesan HIV/AIDS Committee, Diocese Johannesburg, 1990–94; Rector Parish of Whitton with Thurleston and Akenham

2004–15; Member Diocesan Synod from 2002; Member Diocesan Board Education from 2006; Member Diocesan Board Patronage from 2006; Member Vacancy in See Committee from 2006; Diocesan Chaplain to Mothers' Union from 2010; Chaplain 188 (Ipswich) Squadron Air Training Corps from 2005; Chaplain Wolsey District Scouts 2012–15; Chaplain RBL Ipswich 2013–15; Chaplain Merchant Navy Association Ipswich from 2012; Voluntary Chaplain Suffolk Police from 2014; Vicar Felixstowe, St John the Baptish with St Edmund, St Edmundsbury and Ipswich from 2015; Rural Dean of Colneys,St Edmundsbury and Ipswich from 2015
GS 2010–   T: 01473 741 389
E: revdotchin@gmail.com
M: 07814 949828

DOWLER, The Ven Dr (Robert) Edward Mackenzie *MA PhD*
Beechmount Beacon Road Crowborough TN6 1UQ [ARCHDEACON OF HASTINGS; CHICHESTER] *b* 1967 *educ* Harrow School; University of Oxford; University of Cambridge; Durham University; Westcott House *CV* Assistant Curate Christ Church Southgate 1994–97; Assistant Curate St Mary's Somers Town 1997–2001; St Stephen's House Oxford 2001–09, Vice-Principal from 2004; Assistant Chaplain Malvern College 2009; Vicar St John and St Luke Clay Hill 2010–16; Archdeacon of Hastings from 2016   T: 01273 425044
E: archhastings@chichester.anglican.org

DOYLE-BRETT, The Revd (Jackie) Jacqueline Margaret *MA, BA(Hons)*
79 Burton Stone Lane York North Yorkshire YO30 6BZ educ Withernsea High School, Hull University, York St John *CV* Civil Servant 1979–83; Retail Manager 1983–87; Parent at Home 1987–2000; Teacher Hull 2000–13; Curate from 2013–16; Vicar St Luke's York from 2016; Assistant Diocesan Advisor Young Vocations 2016
GS 2015–   T: 01904 628337
07793 545755
E: jackiemdb@gmail.com

DUDLEY-SMITH, The Revd James *BA, MA, BTh*
The Rectory 41 The Park Yeovil BA20 1DG [BATH AND WELLS] *b* 1966 *educ* Fitzwilliam College Cambridge; Wycliffe Hall Oxford *CV* Curate New Borough and Leigh Sarum 1997–2001; Curate Hove Bishop Hannington Memorial Church Chichester 2001–06; Rector Yeovil with Kingston Pitney Bath and Wells from 2006; Rural Dean of Yeovil from 2015
GS 2010–   T: 01935 475352
E: jamesds@tesco.net

DUNNETT, The Revd John Frederick *MA, MSc, BA, CQSW*
39 Crescent Rd Warley Brentwood CM14 5JR [CHELMSFORD] *educ* King Edward School Edgbaston; Sidney Sussex College Cambridge; Worcester College Oxford; Trinity College Bristol *CV* Research Assistant and Press Officer to Bishop of Bath and Wells 1987–88; Curate Kirkheaton Parish Church 1988–93; Vicar St Luke Cranham Park 1993–2006; General Director Church Pastoral Aid Society from 2006
GS 2005–   T: 01277 221419
E: jd@johndunnett.co.uk

DURLACHER, Mrs Mary Caroline
Archendines Chappel Road Fordham Colchester CO6 3LT [CHELMSFORD] *educ* Cranborne Chase School; Kent University; Moore College *CV* Churchwarden, All Saints Fordham and Eight Ash Green 1999–2005; Foundation Governor, C o E All Saints Fordham Primary School from 2005; Member Cathedrals Fabric Commission from 2011; Member Bishop's Council Chelmsford from 2013
GS 2010–   T: 01206 240627
E: marydurlacher@hotmail.com

DZIEGIEL, Mrs Julie Patricia *MA(Hons)*
239 Chartridge Lane Chesham Bucks HP5 2SF [OXFORD] *b* 1963 *educ* Pynton County High School; Newham College, Cambridge *CV* Arthur Andersen, Chartered Accountants, 1984–88; Chartered Accountant 1988–94; Accountant & Company Secretary from 1994; Church Treasurer from 2002
GS 2010–   T: 01494 773713
E: julie@stronglg.demon.co.uk

EAGLES, The Rt Revd Peter Andrew *BA, AKC, BA, MTh*
Thie yn Aspick 4 The Falls Douglas Isle of Man IM4 4PZ [BISHOP OF SODOR AND MAN] *educ* RGS Guildford; School Slavonic Studies London; University Heidelberg; St Stephen's House *CV* Teacher and translator 1982–86; Curate St Martin's Ruislip 1989–92; Rector Army Chaplains Department from 1992; Assistant Chaplain General from 2008; Director Training and Continuing Ministerial Education from 2011; Archdeacon for the Army 2011–17; Royal College Defence Studies 2013–17; Bishop of Sodor and Man from 2017
GS 2011–   T: 01624 622108
E: bishop@sodorandman.im

EDMONDSON, The Very Revd Canon Dr John James William *BA, Cert Th, MA, PhD*
The Deanery Caldbec Hill Battle TN33 0JY [DEAN OF BATTLE] *b* 1967 *educ* Strode's School, Egham; Durham University; Cranmer Hall, Durham *CV* Curate Gee Cross, Chester 1983–86; Curate St Paul Camberley, Guildford 1986–88, Team

Vicar 1988–90; Chaplain Elmhurst Ballet School, Camberley 1986–90; Vicar Foxton with Gumley and Laughton and Lubenham, Leicester 1990–94; Rector St Mark Bexhill, Chichester 1994–2005; Chichester Diocesan Vocations Advisor 1998–2002; Assistant Diocesan Director of Ordinands, Chichester 2002–05; Dean of Battle, Vicar Battle, Chichester from 2005; Priest in Charge Sedlescombe and Whatlington, Chichester 2005–07; Assistant Rural Dean Battle and Bexhill 2010–13; Member Diocesan Finance Committee 2013–15; Rural Dean Battle and Bexhill, Chichester 2013–15; Prebendary and Honorary Canon of Chichester Cathedral from 2015   *T:* 01424 772693
E: dean@johnedmondson.org
F: 01424 772693

EDWARDS, Canon (Diana) Clare *BTh*
22 The Precincts Canterbury CT1 2EP [CANTERBURY] *b* 1956 *educ* Nottingham University; Lincoln Theological College *CV* Deaconess South Wimbledon Holy Trinity and St Peters Southwark 1986–90; Parish Deacon 1987–90; Parish Deacon Lingfield and Crowhurst 1990–94; Curate 1994–94; Chaplain St Piers Hospital School Lingfield 1990–95; Rector Bletchingley Southwark 1995–2004; Rural Dean Godstone 1998–2004; Honorary Canon Southwark Cathedral 2001–04; Dean of Women's Ministry 2003–04; Canon Residential Canterbury Cathedral from 2004
GS 2010–   *T:* 01227 865227
E: canonclare@canterbury-cathedral.org

EDWARDS, Mr Bob (Robert)
Stubbers Adventure Centre Ockendon Road Upminster Essex RM14 2TY [CHELMSFORD] *educ* Colbayns Comprehensive, University of Hertfordshire *CV* Centre Manager, Stubbers Adventure Centre 1996; Director, Activities Industry Mutual 2007; Governor, Gaynes Secondary School from 2009
GS 2015–   *T:* 01708 256700
E: bob@stubbers.co.uk

ELCOCK, Dr Martin *BA, MB, ChB*
The Cottage 3 Digbeth Lane Claverley Wolverhampton WV5 7BP [HEREFORD] *educ* Oldbury Wells Comprehensive School Bridgnorth; Bristol University; Manchester University *CV* General Practitioner; Chair Good Shepherd Trust (homelessness and social inclusion charity in West Midlands/Derbys); primary school governor; Member Hospital Chaplains Council 2006–10
GS 2000–   *T:* 01746 710423
E: m.elcock@btinternet.com
M: 07971 784639 (Mobile)

ELKINGTON, The Ven Audrey Anne *BA, PhD, MA*
4 Park Drive Bodmin Cornwall PL31 2QF [ARCHDEACON OF BODMIN; TRURO] *b* 1957 *educ* King Edward's School Witley; St Catherine's Oxford; University of East Anglia; Durham; St John's Nottingham; EA Ministry Training Course *CV* Deaconess St Mary Monkseaton 1988–91; Assistant Curate St Mary Ponteland 1991–93; Assistant Curate St Mary Magdalene Prudhoe 1993–2002; Advisor Women's Ministry 2001–11; Bishop's Chaplain and Diocesan Director of Ordinands 2002–11; Archdeacon of Bodmin from 2011
T: 01208 892811
E: audrey@truro.anglican.org
M: 07766 822872

ELLIS, Mr Ashley
Church House 17–19 York Place Leeds LS1 2EX [JOINT DIOCESAN SECRETARY; LEEDS] *b* 1961 *CV* Diocesan Secretary Wakefield 2000–14; Joint Diocesan Secretary Leeds from 2014
T: 0113 2000 340
E: ashley.ellis@leeds.anglican.org
W: http://www.leeds.anglican.org

EMERTON, The Revd Dr (Andy) Andrew Neil *BSc, BTh, MA, DPhil,*
18 Collingham Road London SW5 0LX [LONDON] *b* 1967 *educ* Upton-by-Chester County High School Chester, University of York; Queens College Oxford; Ridley Hall Cambridge; King's College London *CV* Industrial DPhil sponsor, Schlumberger Cambridge Research, Cambridge 1993–96; Scientific Consultant, Smith System Engineering Ltd (now Detica), Guildford, Surrey 1996–98; Youth Pastor, St Saviours Church, Guildford 1998–2002; Curate, Holy Trinity Brompton, 2005–07; Assistant Dean St Mellitus College 2008–15; Dean St Mellitus College and Principal St Paul's Theological Centre from 2015
GS 2015–   *T:* 020 7052 0577
07815 498162
E: andrew.emerton@stmellitus.ac.uk
Twitter: @andyemerton

EMERTON, Mr Mark Simon *MA, LLM*
c/o Church of The Resurrection Penrhyn Avenue Drayton Portsmouth PO6 2AP [PORTSMOUTH] *b* 1954 *educ* Perse School Cambridge; Britannia Royal Naval College Dartmouth; St Peter's College Oxford; City University; Inns of Court School of Law; London South Bank University; Portsmouth University; Cardiff University *CV* Naval Officer 1979–2002, Commissioner at Criminal Cases Review Commission 2002–09; Employment Judge from 2009; Barrister: Called to the Bar by Gray's Inn 1991, elected Bencher of Gray's Inn 2017; Previous part-time roles include: Royal Navy Judge Advocate, First Tier Tribunal Judge (Immigration and

Asylum Chamber), Chair of Investigating Committee at General Dental Council, Legal Assessor at General Medical Council, National Medico-Legal Adviser at St John Ambulance, Board Member at the Office of the Independent Adjudicator for Higher Education, Independent Drug Testing Scrutiny Panel Member at UK Sport, Parking Adjudicator at Traffic Penalty Tribunal, Governor of Solent Infant School Portsmouth
GS 2015–
    E: mark.emerton.generalsynod@yahoo.com

EVANS, Mr Paul Lawson *MA*
Bishops Woodford House Ely Cambridgeshire CB7 4DX [DIOCESAN SECRETARY; ELY] *educ* Trinity College Cambridge *CV* Royal Navy HM Diplomatic Service 1982–2001; HM Customs & Excise 2001–06; Serious Organized Crime Agency 2006–11; KPMG 2011–14; Diocesan Secretary Ely from 2014   *T:* 01353 652700

EVERITT, The Ven Michael John *BD, AKC*
6 Eton Park Preston PR2 9NL [ARCHDEACON OF LANCASTER; BLACKBURN] *b* 1968 *educ* Warriner School, Bloxham; Banbury Upper School; King's College London; Gregorian University Rome; Queen's College Birmingham; Venerable English College Rome *CV* Assistant Curate Cleveleys St Andrew 1992–95; South Africa 1995–98; Succentor Bloemfontein Cathedral 1995–96, Precentor 1996–98; Anglican Chaplain National Hospital Bloemfontein 1995–98; Anglican Chaplain and Lecturer in Theology, University of the Orange Free State 1996–98; Senior College Chaplain; St Martin's College Lancaster 1998–2002; Assistant Director of Ordinands, Blackburn Diocese 2000–02; Rector Standish St Wilfrid 2002–11; Area Dean Chorley Deanery 2005–11; Priest in Charge Appley Bridge All Saints 2006–10; Honorary Canon Blackburn Cathedral 2010–11; Archdeacon of Lancaster from 2011
    T: 01772 700331
    E: michael.everitt@blackburn.anglican.org

FARMBROUGH, Miss Catherine Mary
2 Pinewood Crescent Farnborough GU14 9TP [GUILDFORD] *educ* Mary Hare School; Kingsway College; Farnborough College of Technology *CV* Domestic Assistant 1976–78; Clerical Assistant 1978–82; Nursery Assistant 1992–93; Personal Assistant 2005–06; Police Support Volunteer from 2010
GS 2015–   *T:* 01252 504144
    07796 776759 text only
    E: cmfarmbrough@hotmail.com

FAULL, The Very Revd Vivienne Frances *MA, BA, MBA*
Church House 10–14 Ogleforth York YO1 7JN [DEAN OF YORK] *b* 1967 *educ* Queen School

Chester; St Hilda's College Oxford; Nottingham University; Open University Business School; St John's College Nottingham *CV* Deaconess St Matthew and St James Mossley Hill 1982–85; Chaplain Clare College Cambridge 1985–90; Fellow Clare College Cambridge from 1986; Chaplain Gloucester Cathedral 1990–94; Canon Pastor Coventry Cathedral 1994–2000; Vice Provost Coventry Cathedral 1995–2000; Provost of Leicester 2000–02; Dean of Leicester 2002–12; Chair Associations of English Cathedrals 2009–15; Dean of York from 2012; Chair National Deans' Conference from 2015
GS 1987–90, 2004–12   *T:* 01904 557202
    E: dean@yorkminster.org
    F: 01904 557204
    W: www.yorkminster.org

FEENEY, The Revd Damian Prescott Anthony *MA, BTh, BA, ALCM, PGCE*
Holy Trinity Vicarage Farrington Road Wolverhampton WV4 6QH [LICHFIELD] *b* 1962 *educ* St Joseph's College, Blackpool, Grey College, University of Durham *CV* Assistant Teacher, Cheltenham Burnside School 1984–88; Director of Music, Marling School, Stroud 1988–91; Theological College 1991–94; Assistant Curate, Harrogate, St Wilfrid and St Luke 1994–96; Assistant Priest, Preston, St John & St George the Martyr, 1996–99; The Bishop of Blackburn's Mission Priest to Longsands, 1999–2001; Team Rector of Ribbleton 2001–04; Vicar of Woodplumpton and Assistant Diocesan Missioner 2004–09; Vice-Principal and Charles Marriott Director of Pastoral Studies, St Stephen's House, Oxford 2009–15; Vicar, Ettingshall Holy Trinity; Mission Advisor to Catholic Parishes in Lichfield Diocese from 2015
GS 2015–   *T:* 01902 478679
    07949 570387
    E: damian.feeney@lichfield.anglican.org
    W: https://damianfeeney.wordpress.com
    Twitter: @damianfeeney

FELIX, The Revd David Rhys *LLB, CertTh*
Vicarage Daresbury Warrington WA4 4AE [CHESTER] *b* 1955 *educ* Calday Grange County Grammar School; University of Wales; Ripon College, Cuddesdon *CV* Curate St Barnabas Bromborough 1986–89; Vicar St Andrew Grange, Runcorn 1989–99; Chaplain Halton General Hospital 1995–99; Priest in Charge Holy Trinity Runcorn 1996–99; Rural Dean Frodsham 1998–99; Industry Missioner, Halton 1998–99; Vicar All Saints Daresbury from 1999; Senior Industry Missioner Chester Diocese 2000–08; Member Diocesan Advisory Board for Ministry 1988–90; Member Diocesan Adoption Services Committee 1990–92; Deanery Ordination Chaplain 1990–96;

Member Diocesan Pastoral Group 1994–95; Member Diocesan Synod from 1994; Director Diocesan Board of Finance and Member Bishop's Council from 1995; Member Diocesan Board of Education and Schools Committee 1997–2003; Member Archidiaconal Pastoral Committee 1992–94 and from 1998; Member Ecclesiastical Law Society from 1987 and of General Committee from 2002; Member Diocesan Committee for Mission and Unity 2001–08; Honorary Canon Chester Cathedral 2006; Trustee, Southern North West Training from 2010
GS 2002–   T: 01925 740348
          E: david.felix@btinternet.com
                 M: 07778 859935 (Mobile)

FENDER, Mr Carl David BA, LLM
45 St John's Close Ryhall Stamford Lincolnshire PE9 4HS [LINCOLN] *educ* Stockport School, Universities of Kent and Leicester *CV* Member of PCC at St George's Church, Stamford, Lincolnshire; Call to the Bar of England and Wales in 1994
GS 2015–   T: 01780480461
                             07740766561
          E: carlfender@icloud.com

FERGUSON, Mrs Linda Ann BA(Hons), ILM L7 Cert
Church House Great Smith Street London SW1P 3PS [CHURCH OF ENGLAND PENSIONS BOARD] *educ* Burnham Grammar School, University of Birmingham *CV* Inland Revenue 1985–2005; HM Revenue and Customs Senior Policy Advisor 2005–08; Head of Complaints Policy 2008–11; Senior Customer and Strategy Advisor 2011–12; Director Customer Insight and Strategy C of E Pensions Board from 2012; Trusteee The Grange Centre for People with Disabilities from 2015   T: 020 7898 1833
       E: linda.ferguson@churchofengland.org

FERGUSON, The Rt Revd Paul John MA, FRCO (CHM), PGCE
21 Thornton Road Stainton Middlesborough TS8 9DS [SUFFRAGAN BISHOP OF WHITBY; YORK] *educ* Birkenhead School; New College Oxford; Westminster College Oxford; King's College Cambridge; Westcott House Theological College *CV* Curate St Mary Chester 1985–88; Chaplain and Sacrist Westminster Abbey 1988–92; Precentor Westminster Abbey 1992–95; Precentor and Residential Canon York Minster 1995–2001; Archdeacon of Cleveland 2001–14; Warden of Readers 2004–14; Secretary House Bishops' Theology Group 1992–2001; Member Porvoo Panel from 2009; Bishop of Whitby from 2014
GS 2010–14   T: 01642 593273
          E: bishopofwhitby@yorkdiocese.org
                     M: 07770 592746

FIDDES, The Revd Professor Paul MA, DPhil, DD
Regent's Park College Pusey St Oxford OX1 2LB [ECUMENICAL REPRESENTATIVE] *educ* St Peter College, Oxford; Regent's Park College, Oxford *CV* Principal, Regent's Park College, Oxford; Prof of Systematic Theology, Oxford University; Minister of Baptist Union of Great Britain
GS 2005–   T: 01865 288134
          E: paul.fiddes@regents.ox.ac.uk
                     F: 01865 288121

FINCH, Mrs Sarah Rosemary Ann BA
14 Pensioner's Court Sutton's Hospital in Charterhouse Charterhouse Square London EC1M 6AU [LONDON] *educ* Godolphin School Sarum; Durham University; Oxford University *CV* Editor Barrie and Jenkins 1972–75; Trustee British Foreign and Bible Study 1978–2005; Chair Executive Committee British Foreign and Bible Study 1991–94; Freelance Non-Fiction Editor from 1986; Governor Sir John Cass's Foundation Primary School (C of E) 1996–2014; Member Church of England Evangelical Council 2000–14; Council Member Latimer Trust from 2003; Member Revision Committee, Common Worship Ordinal; elected Member Appointments Committee from 2005; Council Member Oak Hill Theological College from 2006; Member Anglican Mainstream Steering Committee from 2006; Trustee Latimer Trust from 2007; Deputy Chair Latimer Trust Committee from 2009; Member Finance and General Purposes Committee of Oak Hill Theological College from 2009; Member Liturgical Commission 2011–15; GS rep to Council Oak Hill Theological College from 2011
GS 2000–   T: 020 7336 0682
          E: sarahrafinch@yahoo.co.uk

FISHER, Ms Alison CQSW, CMI
[LEEDS] *b* 1959 *educ* King Edward VI, Devon; Leeds University; University College Cardiff *CV* Probation Officer 1981–90, Senior Probation Officer from 1990; Non Executive Director Calderdale and Huddersfield Foundation Trust from 2005; General Teaching Council, Lay member from 2007; Diversity Manager, West Yorkshire Probation Trust from 2008
GS 2010–   E: alison.fisher1@ntlworld.com

FITZSIMONS, Canon Kathryn Anne CertTh, Cert Ed; MA
227 Beech Lane Leeds LS9 6SW [LEEDS] *educ* Richmond School; Bedford College of Higher Education; North East Oecumenical Course; University of Leeds *CV* Non-Stipendiary Minister Curate St John Bilton, Harrogate 1990–2002; Society Responsibility Officer

1992–99; Diocesan Urban Officer from 1999; Honorary Canon Ripon Cathedral from 2004; President Diaconal Association of the C of E 2003–10; Officer, Mission Resourcing Team; Member Diocesan Board of Finance; Priest-in-charge Church of the Epiphany, Gipton 2014–16; Priest-in-Charge Roundhay 2015–16; Area Dean Allerton from 2016; Vicar Gipton from 2016
GS 2004– *T:* 0113 225 6702
E: kathrynfitzsimons@hotmail.com
Twitter: @CanonKathryn

FLACH, Canon Deborah Mary *Dip HE, Dip*
7 rue Leonard de Vinci 59700 Marcq en Baroeul France [EUROPE] *educ* Beckenham Convent School; Trinity College Bristol; Salisbury and Wells Theological College *CV* Curate St Peter Chantilly, France 1994–96; Curate Holy Trinity Maisons-Laffitte, France 1996–2004, Assistant Chaplain 2004–07; Member Diocesan Synod from 1994; Assistant Director of Ordinands (France) 1997–2010; Priest in Charge Christ Church, Lille (Europe) from 2007; Chair House of Clergy from 2007; Bishop's Council from 2007; Area Dean Northern France from 2014
GS 2005– *T:* +33 3 28526636
E: chaplain@christchurchlille.fr

FLETCHER, The Rt Revd Colin William *MA, OBE*
Church House Oxford Langford Lane Kidlington OX5 1GF [AREA BISHOP OF DORCHESTER; OXFORD] *educ* Marlborough College; Trinity College Oxford; Wycliffe Hall Theological College *CV* Curate St Peter Shipley 1975–79; Tutor Wycliffe Hall and Curate St Andrew Oxford 1979–84; Vicar Holy Trinity Margate 1984–93; Rural Dean Thanet 1989–93; Domestic Chaplain to Archbishop of Canterbury 1993–2000; Canon Dallas Cathedral 1993–2000; Bishop of Dorchester from 2000 *T:* 01865 208218
E: bishopdorchester@oxford.anglican.org

FOREMAN, Mrs (Antoinette Joan) Anne *CCYW*
5 St Leonards Road Exeter Devon EX2 4LA [EXETER] *educ* Teignmouth Grammar School; Bradford & Ilkley Community College *CV* Youth and Community Worker, Sutton 1983–85; Senior Youth and Community Worker, Kingston 1985–88; Assistant Principal Youth Officer, Sutton 1988–91; National Youth Officer General Synod Board Education 1991–95; Church House; Member General Synod Board Mission 2001–03; Lay Chair Okehampton Deanery; 2007–12; Member Diocesan Synod; Member Bishop's Council; Vice Chair Diocesan Mission and Pastoral Committee; Chair Vacancy in See Committee; Bishop's Advisor from 2008; External Exam

Bachelor of Education Fieldwork Placements St Martins College Lancaster 1992–94; Member Advisory Council Community and Youth Work Course Goldsmiths College 1991–94; Director and Trustee Guildford Young Men's Christian Association 2002–05; Member Council Management University St Mark and St John 2006–10; Elected Member General Synod Business Committee
GS 1999–2005; 2010– *T:* 01392 279859
01392 217020
E: anne@anneforeman.co.uk

FORSTER, The Rt Revd Dr Peter Robert *MA, BD, PhD*
Bishop's House Abbey Square Chester CH1 2JD [BISHOP OF CHESTER] *educ* Tudor Grange Grammar School Solihull; Merton College Oxford; Edinburgh University; Edinburgh Theological College *CV* Curate St Matthew and St James Mossley Hill Liverpool 1980–82; Senior Tutor St John College Durham 1983–91; Vicar Beverley Minster 1991–96; Bishop of Chester from 1996; Church Commissioner 1999–2004, from 2009
GS 1985–91,1996– *T:* 01244 350864
E: bpchester@chester.anglican.org

FORWARD, Miss Emma Joy *BA, PGCE*
24 Whitchurch Ave Exeter EX2 5NT [EXETER] *b* 1984 *educ* St Peter C of E High School Exeter; St Hugh's College Oxford *CV* Trainee teacher from 2005; full time teacher from 2006
GS 2005– *T:* 01392 251617
E: emmaforward@yahoo.co.uk

FOSTER, The Rt Revd Christopher Richard James *BA, MA, MA, HonDLitt*
Bishopsgrove 26 Osborn Rd Fareham PO16 7DQ [BISHOP OF PORTSMOUTH] *educ* Royal Grammar School Guildford; Durham University; Manchester University; Trinity Hall Cambridge, Wescott House Cambridge *CV* Lecturer in Economics University of Durham 1976–77; Assistant Curate Tettenhall Regis Team Ministry Wolverhampton 1980–82; Chaplain Wadham College Oxford and Assistant Priest St Mary with St Cross and St Peter in the East Oxford 1982–86; Vicar Christ Church Southgate 1986–94; Continuing Ministerial Education Director Edmonton Area 1988–94; Sub Dean and Residential Canon St Albans 1994–2001; Bishop of Hertford 2001–10; Bishop of Portsmouth from 2010
T: 01329 280247
E: bishop@portsmouth.anglican.org
F: 01329 231538

FRANCIS-DEHQANI, The Rt Revd Dr (Guli) Gulnar Eleanor Francis-Dehqani *BA, MA, PhD*
[BISHOP OF LOUGHBOROUGH; LEICESTER] *b* 1967 *educ* University School, Isfahan, Iran and Clarendon

School, Haynes, Bedfordshire, University of Nottingham and University of Bristol *CV* Studio Manager BBC World Service Radio 1989–91; Producer Religious Department BBC Domestic Radio 1991–92; Research Assistant University of Bristol 1994–95; Curate Southwark Diocese 1998–2002; Chaplain Royal Academy of Music and St Marylebone Church of England Secondary School 2002–04; Inter faith Research Assistant Multifaith Chaplaincy Northampton University 2009–10; Diocesan Curate Training Officer (IME Phase 2) Peterborough 2011–17; Adviser for Women's Ministry 2012–17; Honorary Canon Peterborough Cathedral from 2016; Bishop of Loughborough from 2017
GS 2013–17
E: bishop.loughborough@leccofe.org

FRANKS, Mr Benjamin Thomas *BA, Assoc. CIPD*
89 Turchill Avenue Walmley Sutton Coldfield B76 1SG [BIRMINGHAM] *b* 1984 *educ* Ripley St Thomas CE High School and Sixth Form, Lancaster; University College Birmingham; Chartered Institute of Personnel and Develoment *CV* Retail Management 2005–12; Liturgy Officer, Birmingham Cathedral 2012–15; HR Officer Diocese of Birmingham from 2016
GS 2015–   *T:* 0121 238 6817
                                              07722 556494
E: benjamin.franks@me.com
Twitter: @b3njaminfranks

FREEMAN, Mr John Jeremy Collier *Eur Ing, DLC, BSc, MIChemE, Ceng*
Stable Court 20a Leigh Way Weaverham Northwich CW8 3PR [CHESTER] *educ* Embley Park School; Loughborough University *CV* Graduate Chemical Engineer ICI 1961–94 including Assistant to General Manager Magadi Soda Co, Kenya 1975–77; retired 1994, now very active in voluntary sector; Member Local Agenda 21 Forum; Parish Council from 1980; School Governor from 1980; Member Diocesan Finance and Central Services Committee from 1994; Member Executive Churches Together in Cheshire from 1995; Chair Diocesan Partnership for World Mission Committee; Member Diocesan Council for Social Responsibility Committee; Christian Aid activist; Secretary Diocesan Justice and Development Education Group; Member Bishop's Council; Member Diocesan Synod; Diocesan World Development Advisor; Member Core Group Anglican World Development Advisors; Treasurer Open Synod Group; Companion of the Melanesian Brotherhood
GS 2000–   *T:* 01606 852872
E: jjcfreeman@talktalk.net
F: 01606 854140

FREEMAN, The Rt Revd Robert John *BSc, MA*
Holmcroft 13 Castle Road Kendal LA9 7AU [SUFFRAGAN BISHOP OF PENRITH; CARLISLE] *b* 1954 *educ* Cambridgeshire High School; St John College Durham; Fitzwilliam College Cambridge; Ridley Hall Cambridge *CV* Curate St John Blackpool 1977–81; Team Vicar St Winifred Chigwell 1981–85; Vicar Church of the Martyrs Leicester 1985–99; Rural Dean Christianity South (Leicester) 1994–98; Honorary Canon Leicester 1994–2003; National Evangelical Advisory, Archbishops' Council from 1999; Chair Agenda and Support Committee of Group for Evangelization (Churches Together England) 2000–03; Secretary Mission, Evangelism and Renewal in England Committee, Board of Mission, Archbishops' Council 1999–2003; Chair rejesus.co.uk 2000–16; Director Just Fairtrade Ltd 2000–03; Archdeacon of Halifax 2003–11; Member Churches Regional Commission for Yorkshire and Humberside 2004; Chair Christian Enquiry Agency 2006–10; Trustee Simeon and Hyndman's 2007–10; Chair Wakefield Diocesan Board of Finance 2008–11, Bishop of Penrith from 2011
GS 1997–99, 2008–11   *T:* 01539 727836
E: bishop.penrith@carlislediocese.org.uk
M: 07584 684308
Twitter: @BpRobInCumbria

FRENCH, The Ven Judith Karen *BA, MA*
11 Broad Field Road Yarnton Kidlington Oxford OX5 1UL [ARCHDEACON OF DORCHESTER; OXFORD] *educ* Wentworth Milton Mount, Bournemouth, Lampeter St David's University College *CV* Fund Bookkeeper, Schroder Life Assurance Ltd, Portsmouth 1981–86; Parish Deacon, Botley All Saints, 1991–94; Assistant Curate, Bilton St Mark's, Rugby 1994–97; Incumbent, Charlbury with Shorthampton 1997–2014; Area Dean, Chipping Norton 2007–12; Archdeacon of Dorchester from 2014
                                              T: 01865 208245
E: archdeacon.dorchester@
                                    oxford.anglican.org

FRENCH, Mr Philip Colin *MA, MMath, MIET*
Arden Five Oak Green Rd Five Oak Green Tonbridge TN12 6TJ [ROCHESTER] *educ* Royal Grammar School Newcastle; British School Brussels; Churchill College Cambridge *CV* Research Assistant, University College London 1984–87; Overseas Career Service Officer, British Council 1987–96; (First Secretary (Education and Science), Calcutta 1988–91); Senior Consultant, Hewlett-Packard Ltd 1996–99; Technical Director, Software.com, later Openwave Systems Inc 1999–2003; IT Management posts in HM Prison Service and

National Offender Management Service 2003–09; Chief Technology Officer, Ministry of Justice 2009–12; Non-Executive Director and trustee, Eduserv from 2011; Chair of Trustees from 2012; Business Engagement Director, Steria 2012–14; IS Strategy Consultant to Alzheimer's Society, PCC treasurer, URC elder; Lay Chair Rochester Diocesan Synod from 2012; Trustee, Hands of Compassion (supporting education in Zambia) from 2011; Chief Technology Officer, Shared Services Connected Ltd (from 2015)
GS 1985–88, 2005–

T: 01892 838713 (Home)
E: philip.c.french@btinternet.com
W: uk.linkedin.com/in/philipfrench
M: 07952 273253 (Mobile)

FRITH, The Rt Revd Richard Michael Cokayne *MA*
The Bishop's House Hereford HR4 9BN [BISHOP OF HEREFORD] *educ* Marlborough College; Fitzwilliam College Cambridge; St John College Nottingham *CV* Curate Mortlake with East Sheen 1974–78; Team Vicar Thamesmead 1978–83; Team Rector Keynsham 1983–92; Archdeacon of Taunton 1992–98; Bishop of Hull 1998–2014; Bishop of Hereford from 2014
GS 1995–98

T: 01432 373355
E: bishop@hereford.anglican.org
F: 01432 373346

FROST, The Rt Revd Dr Jonathan Hugh *BD, MTh, DUniv, MSSTh, FRSA*
Bishop's House St Mary's Church Close Wessex Lane Southampton SO18 2ST [SUFFRAGAN BISHOP OF SOUTHAMPTON; WINCHESTER] *b* 1964 *educ* KCS Wimbledon; Aberdeen University; Nottingham University; Surrey University; Ridley Hall Cambridge *CV* Curate West Bridgford St Giles 1993–97; Police Chaplain Trent Division, Nottinghamshire Constabulary 1994–97; Rector Ash St Peter 1997–2002; Canon Residential Guildford Cathedral 2002–10; Anglican Chaplain University of Surrey 2002–10; Bishop's Advisor for Inter-Faith Relations 2007–10; Co-ordinator Chaplain University of Surrey 2007–10; Tutor Christian Doctrine Local Ministry Course 1999–2010; Bishop of Southampton from 2010
GS 2009–10

T: 023 8067 2684

E: bishop.jonathan@winchester.anglican.org

W: www.winchester.anglican.org

FROUDE, The Ven Christine Ann *Dip; ACIB*
1 Orchard Close Winterbourne Bristol BS36 1BF [ARCHDEACON OF MALMESBURY AND ACTING ARCHDEACON OF BRISTOL] *educ* Llwyn Y Bryn Girls Grammar Swansea; Salisbury and Wells *CV* Curate St Mary Magdalene Stoke Bishop 1995–99; Chaplain University Hospitals

Bristol NHS Foundation Children's Directorate 1999–2001; Director of Women's Ministry 2001–11; Honorary Canon Bristol Cathedral 2001–11; Archdeacon Malmesbury from 2011; Diocesan Pastoral Management Committee; Diocesan Housing and Glebe Committee; Diocesan Advisory Committee; Diocesan Mission and Pastoral Committee; Diocesan Finance Committee; Acting Archdeacon Bristol from 2012

T: 01454 778366
E: christine.froude@bristoldiocese.org

FROUDE, Canon David Colin *ACIB*
1 Orchard Close Winterbourne Bristol BS36 1BF [BRISTOL] *educ* Colston's School, Bristol *CV* HSBC Bank (formerly Midland) 1967–2004 retiring as Senior Manager; Parish Clerk, St Mary's, Shirehampton, Bristol 2001–11; Member Bristol Cathedral Council 2002–13; Member Provincial Panel Clergy Discipline Measure from 2003; Chair Bristol Diocesan Board Finance Ltd 2004–11; Chair Bristol Diocesan Board of Finance Finance Committee 2004–11; Chair Bristol Diocesan Board Finance Budget Committee 2004–11; Chair Bristol Diocesan Board Finance Remuneration Committee 2004–11; Member Diocesan Board Finance Audit Committee 2004–11; Member Bristol Diocesan Synod Agenda Committee 2004–11; Member Bishop's Council 2004–11; Chair Trustees Bristol Diocesan Board Finance Staff Retirement Benefit Scheme 2004–11; South West Region Diocesan Board Finance Chair, Member 2004–11, Convenor 2006–11; C of E Consultative Group of Diocesan Board of Finance Chairs and Diocesan Secretaries, Member 2006–11, Chair 2009–11; Member C of E National Procurement Group 2007–11; Member Bishop of Bristol Senior Staff 2007–11; Member Bristol Diocesan Strategic Policy Group 2007–09; Member C of E Pensions Board 2009–17; Lay Canon Bristol Cathedral from 2010; Chair C of E Pensions Board Audit Committee 2011–16; Chair Steering Committee Draft Diocesan Europe Measure 2012; Lay Chair Bristol Diocesan Synod 2012–18; Member Bristol Bishop's Council 2012–18; Member Bristol Diocesan Synod Agenda Committee from 2012; Joint Chair Bristol Diocesan Appointments Committee from 2012; Member Bristol Vacancy in See Committee from 2012; Member Bristol HR and Remuneration Committee from 2014; Member Remuneration and Conditions of Service Committee (Pensions Board Nominee) 2014–17; Member C of E Pensions Board Housing Committee 2016–17; Council Member Queen Victoria Fund from 2016
GS 2010–

T: 01454 778366
E: davidcfroude@gmail.com
M: 07768 958704

FRY, Mrs Christine Ann *BA, PGDip*
25 St Leonards Avenue Chineham Basingstoke RG24 8RD [WINCHESTER] *educ* Arden School; Solihull Sixth Form College; Southampton University; Middlesex Poly *CV* Probation Service Officer, Middlesex Probation Area, 1986–88; Trainee Probation Officer, Middlesex Probation Area 1988–90; Probation Officer, Hampshire Probation Area 1990–93; Youth and Community Worker, St Mary's Church, Eastrop, Basingstoke 1993–95; Court Welfare Officer, Hampshire Probation Area 1995–98; Probation Officer, Hampshire Probation Area, 1998–2001; Senior Probation Officer, Hampshire Probation Area 2001–08; Area Manager, Hampshire Probation Area 2008–09; Business Change Manager, Hampshire Probation Trust from 2010; Operations Manager, Hampshire Probation Trust from 2013
GS 1995–2000; 2010–　　　*T:* 01256 474466
　　　　　　　E: chrisfry001@gmail.com

FUTCHER, The Ven Christopher David *BD, MTh, MA*
Emmanuel House Station Road Ide Exeter EX2 9RS [ARCHDEACON OF EXETER] *b* 1958 *educ* Strode's Grammar School, Egham, Surrey; University of Edingburgh; Heythrop College University of London; King's College London; Westcott House *CV* Assistant Curate Borehamwood Team Ministry 1982–85; Assistant Curate All Saints Pin Green Stevenage 1985–88; Vicar All Saints Pin Green Stevenage 1988–96; Vicar St Stephen's St Albans 1996–2000; Rector Harpenden 2000–12; Diocesan Ecumenical Officer 2004–12; Archdeacon of Exeter from 2012　　　　　　　　*T:* 01392 425577
　E: archdeacon.of.exeter@exeter.anglican.org

FYFE, The Revd Stewart John *BSc, PGPip, MA*
The Vicarage Morland Penrith Cumbria CA10 3AX [CARLISLE] *b* 1969 *educ* British School of Brussels; Berkhamsted School, City University; College of Law; University of Cumbria *CV* Assistant Curate, Benefice of the Barony of Burgh, Carlisle Diocese 2005–10; Priest-in-Charge, Leith Lyvennet Parishes, Carlisle Diocese 2010–17; Rural Dean of Appleby from 2012; Assistant Diocesan Director of Ordinands from 2016; Rector North Westmorland Parishes from 2017
GS 2015–　　　　　　　　　*T:* 01931 714620
　　　　　　　E: stewart.fyfe@btinternet.com

GAINSBOROUGH, The Revd Canon Professor (Jonathan) Martin *BA, MA, MSc, MA, PhD*
21 Cotham Lawn Road Bristol BS6 6DS [BRISTOL] *b* 1966 *educ* Dulwich College, University of Bristol, School of Oriental and African Studies, *CV* Research Assistant, BBC Monitoring, Caversham, Reading 1991–92; Asia-Pacific Editor, Oxford Analytica (business

consultancy company) 1992–94; Doctoral candidate Department of Political Studies, School of Oriental and African Studies, University of London 1995–2001; Teaching Assistant Department of Political Studies, School of Oriental and African Studies, University of London 2000–01; British Academy Postdoctoral Research Fellow Department of Politics and International Studies, University of Warwick 2001–03; Lecturer in South East Asian Politics Department of Political Studies, School of Oriental and African Studies, University of London 2003–04; Senior Technical Advisor, United Nations Development Programme, Hanoi, Vietnam/Visiting Research Fellow, Vietnam Academy of Social Sciences (on leave of absence from University of Bristol) 2005–06; Lecturer in Development Politics, University of Bristol 2005–08; Reader in Development Politics University of Bristol 2008–12; Curate, St Luke's Barton Hill, Bristol 2010–13; Professor of Development Politics, University of Bristol from 2012; Priest in charge, St Luke's Barton Hill, Bristol from 2013; Royal Navy Reserve Chaplain from 2014; Canon Theologian and Chapter Member Bristol Cathedral from 2016
GS 2015–　　　　　　　　　*T:* 07726 346142
　　E: martin.gainsborough@virgin.net
　W: http://dbms.ilrt.bris.ac.uk/spais/people/
　　　person/martin-m-gainsborough/

GALLOWAY, Mrs Karen *MTh, MSocSCI, Dip*
4 Gorsehayes Ipswich IP2 9AU [ST EDMUNDSBURY AND IPSWICH] *b* 1962 *educ* Fairfield High School for Girls; University of St Andrews; University of Birmingham *CV* Assistant Warden in a Greater Manchester Probation Hostel 1986–1992; Various roles for Suffolk and Norfolk Probation 1994–; Senior Probation Officer 2014–　　　　　　　　*T:* 07778 264281
　　　　　E: kgalloway230@gmail.com

GARTON, Ms Kashmir Ruth *BA, MA*
Woodbrooke 27 Feckenham Road Headless Cross Redditch Worcestershire B97 5AS [WORCESTER] *b* 1961 *educ* Handsworth New Road, Birmingham, Birmingham University, Keele University, Selly Oak College, Bournville College *CV* Social Worker, Birmingham 1986–89; Probation Officer and Middle Manager, West Midlands 1989–2006; District Manager, West Midlands 2006–09; Assistant Chief Officer, East Midlands 2009–10; Deputy Head of Birmingham, Birmingham 2010–14; Head of Service, Midlands from 2014
GS 2015–　　　　　　　　　*T:* 07596 134540
　　　E: kashmirgarton1@blueyonder.co.uk

GATES, The Ven Simon Philip *MA, BA*
7 Hoadly Road Streatham London SW16 1AE [ARCHDEACON OF LAMBETH; SOUTHWARK] *educ*

Merchant Taylor's School, Crosby, Liverpool; University St Andrews; Cranmer Hall; St John's College, Durham; *CV* Curate St John's Southall 1987–91; Associate Minister, St Andrew's Kowloon, Hong Kong 1991–95; Vicar St Stephen's Clapham Park 1996–2006; Vicar St Thomas with St Stephen Telford Park 2006–13; Area Dean Lambeth South 2006–13; Archdeacon of Lambeth from 2013
T: 020 8545 2440
E: simon.gates@southwark.anglican.org

GAUNT, The Revd Adam *BA, MA*
The Rectory 11 Micklow Lane Loftus-in-Cleveland Saltburn-by-the-Sea North Yorkshire TS13 4JE [YORK] *b* 1979 *educ* Warsett Secondary School, Brotton and The Prior Pursglove College, Guisborough, St John's College, University of Durham *CV* Assistant Curate, The Ascension Middlesbrough 2005–09; Rector of Loftus-in-Cleveland and Carlin How with Skinningrove from 2009
GS 2015–   *T:* 01287 644047
E: AdamGaunt@btinternet.com

GAZE, The Revd Canon Sally (Ann) *MA, MPhil*
The Rectory Church Road Newton Flotman Norwich Norfolk NR15 1QB [NORWICH] *educ* Lynn Grove High School, Gorleston; East Norfolk Sixth Form College; Sidney Sussex College Cambridge; Birmingham University *CV* Voluntary Evangelist, London City Mission 1987–88; Teacher, Head of RE, Haybridge High School, Hagley 1992–94; Assistant Curate, Martley, Wichenford, Knightwick with Doddenham, Broadwas and Cotheridge Diocese of Worcester 1996–2000; Associate Minister, Crickhowell, Cwmdu and Tretower, Diocese of Swansea and Brecon 2000–02; Team Rector, Tas Valley Team Ministry, Diocese of Norwich from 2002; Diocesan Facilitator for Fresh Expressions of Church (.25) from 2009
GS 2015–   *T:* 01508 470762
E: sally@tasvalley.org

GELDARD, Mr Philip *DPSN*
Flat 8 Summerville 65 Daisy Bank Road Victoria Park Manchester M14 5QL [MANCHESTER] *educ* University of Manchester *CV* Charge Nurse, Manchester Royal Infirmary from 2003
GS 2015–   *T:* 0161 224 7864
E: philipgeldard@hotmail.com

GEORGE, The Rt Worshipful Charles Richard *MA, QC*
Francis Taylor Building Inner Temple London EC4Y 7BY [GENERAL SYNOD – EX OFFICIO] *educ* Bradfield College Magdalen College Oxford; Corpus Christi College Cambridge *CV* Assistant Master Eton College 1967–72; Barrister, Francis Taylor Building, Inner Temple (formerly 2 Harcourt Buildings) from 1975; Chancellor Diocese of

Southwark 1996–2009; Member of Panel of Chairmen of Bishops' Disciplinary Tribunals for Provinces of Canterbury and York 2007–09; Member of House Council, St Stephen's House, Oxford 1999–2012; Visiting Lecturer in Environmental Law, King's College London from 2006; Dean of the Arches, Auditor of the Chancery Court of York, Master of the Faculties from 2009; Deputy High Court Judge from 2010; Chairman, Sevenoaks Conservation Council from 2014
GS 2009–   *T:* 020 7353 8415
E: charles.george@ukgateway.net
F: 020 73537622

GIBBS, The Rt Revd Jonathan Robert *MA PhD*
Stone Royd 9 Valley Head Huddersfield HD2 2DH [AREA BISHOP OF HUDDERSFIELD; LEEDS] *b* 1967 *educ* The King's School, Chester; Jesus College Oxford; Jesus College, Cambridge; Ridley Hall, Cambridge *CV* Assistant Curate Stalybridge, Holy Trinity 1989–92; Chaplain, Basel, Switzerland with Freiburg, Germany 1992–98; Rector, Heswall 1998–2014; Member Bishop's Council 1999–14; Member Finance and Central Services Committee 1999–14; Chair of House of Clergy, Diocesan Synod 2006–14; Chair Diocesan Clergy Chairs Forum 2011–14; Member Standing Committee House of Clergy 2011–14; Member Council British Funeral Services 2012–14; Member Meissen Committee from 2012; Area Bishop of Huddersfield from 2014; Member, National Safeguarding Steering Group from 2017
GS 1995–98; 2010–14, 2015–
T: 01484 900656
01484 471801
E: bishop.jonathan@leeds.anglican.org

GIBBS, The Revd William John Morris *BSc (Hons), BTh*
The Vicarage 49 Church End Redbourn St Albans Herts AL3 7DU [ST ALBANS] *b* 1971 *educ* Fosters Grammar School, Wellington School, University of Birmingham, Oxford University *CV* Assistant Curate, St Mary and St Peter, Staines 2000–03; Assistant Curate, St Mary Abbots with St George and Christ Church, Kensington 2003–06; Rural Dean of Wheathampstead 2010–15; Vicar of Redbourn from 2006
GS 2015–   *T:* 01582 791669
E: will@stmarysredbourn.org

GILBERT, Canon Mark (Philip Mark) *BA*
The Rectory Rectory Lane Petworth Chichester GU28 0DB [CHICHESTER] *educ* Bury Grammar School, Liverpool University *CV* Curate St Laurence Frodsham 1987–89; Curate Stockton Heath 1989–92; Rector of Tangmere and Oving 1992–2001; Rector of Graffham and Chaplain to Seaford College 2001–09; Vicar of

St Wilfrid's Chichester 2009–15; Rural Dean of Chichester 2011–15; Rector of Petworth and Egdean from 2015; Canon and Prebendary Chichester Cathedral from 2015; Rural Dean Petworth from 2016
GS 2014–　　　　　　　　　*T:* 01798 345278
　　　　　　　　　　　　　　　07810 004062
　　　　　　　　　E: frmarkssc@msn.com
　　　　　　　　　　　F: 01798 345278
　　　　　　　　　Twitter: @FRMARKSSC

GILBERTSON, The Ven Dr Michael Robert MA, BA, PhD
Church House 5500 Daresbury Park Daresbury Warrington WA4 4GE [ARCHDEACON OF CHESTER] *b* 1967 *educ* Stockport Grammar School; New College Oxford; Cranmer Hall Durham *CV* Department of Trade and Industry 1982–1991; Curate St Matthew's Surbiton 1997–2000; Vicar All Saints Stranton 2000–10; Area Dean of Hartlepool 2002–10; Honorary Canon Durham Cathedral 2008–10; Archdeacon of Chester from 2010; Member Chester Cathedral Chapter from 2017
GS 2015–　　　　　　　　　*T:* 01928 718834
　　　　　　　　　　　　　01244 405253 (Home)
　　E: michael.gilbertson@chester.anglican.org

GILL, Mr Chris (Christopher)
16 Rugby Close Newcastle-under-Lyme ST5 3JN [LICHFIELD] *educ* Abbeydale Grange, Sheffield, *CV* Trainee Accountant, Sheffield Twist Drill and Steel Company Limited 1977–81; Finance Assistant, Trent Regional Health Authority 1981–84; Accountant, Sheffield City Council 1984–88; Accountant/Principal Accountant, Staffordshire City Council 1988–2015; Senior Finance Business Partner, Staffordshire County Council from 2015; Lay Chair, Newcastle-under-Lyme Deanery Synod from 2009
GS 2015–　　　　　　　　　*T:* 01782 625924
　　　　　　　　　　E: chris.gill@tesco.net

GILLIES, The Revd Jenny (Jennifer Susan) FdA, BEd(Hons), MA
The Rectory Mark Rake Bromborough CH62 2DH [CHESTER] *b* 1963 *educ* Marist Convent Barnstaple, Bideford College, Westminster College Oxford, University of Chester *CV* Teacher of English and Music, Longridge High School, 1985–89; Teacher of English and Media Studies (second in Department), Eccles Church of England High School, 1989–93; Head of English, St James' Church of England School, Farnworth, 1993–97; English Teacher, 1998–2005; West Houghton High School, Head of Personal, Social, Health and Citizenship Education, West Houghton High School 2002–05; Family Life Officer, Diocese of Chester and The Mothers' Union, 2005–10; Assistant Curate, St Oswald's Bidston, Diocese of Chester, 2010–13; Rector, St Barnabas with St Matthew, Bromborough, from 2013;

Diocesan foundations for ministry course leader, Chester Archdeaconry from 2012
GS 2015–　　　　　　　　　*T:* 0151 201 9002
　　　　　　　　　　　　　　07935 859605
　　　　E: revdjennygillies@gmail.com
　　　　　　　　Twitter: @revjennyg

GODDARD, Canon Giles William *MA (Cantab), MA, MA*
St John's Vicarage 1 Secker Street London SE1 8UF [SOUTHWARK] *b* 1954 *educ* Lancing College Sussex; Clare College Cambridge; King's College London; Southwark Ordination Course; Goldsmiths College London *CV* Assistant Buyer John Lewis Partnership 1984–87; Housing Corporation 1987–88; Director Development ASRA Housing Association 1988–91; Director Southwark Diocesan Housing Association 1991–95; Curate St Faith's North Dulwich 1995–98; Rector St Peter's Walworth 1998–2009; Area Dean Southwark and Newington 2001–06; Chair Inclusive Church 2006–11; Honorary Canon Southwark Cathedral from 2008; Vicar St John's Waterloo; Appointments Committee; Chair Church of England Environment Working Group; Chair General Synod Human Sexuality Group
GS 2008　　　　　　　　　*T:* 07762 373674
　　　　　　E: giles@stjohnswaterloo.org

GODDARD, Mrs Vivienne *BA, PGCE*
39 Kearsley Ave Tarleton Preston PR4 6BP [BLACKBURN] *b* 1948 *educ* Roch Girls' Grammar School; Durham University *CV* Religious Education Teacher, Cleveland Girls Grammar School 1970–74 Supply Teacher 1974–76; Director Cleveland Lay Training and Foundation Scheme for York Diocese; Religious Education Teacher Bydales School, Marske, 1984–88; Acting Head of Department, 1988–92; Publishing Manager, Rutherford House, Edinburgh, 1994–95; Religious Education Teacher 1996–97; Local Non-Stipendiary Ministry Officer, Blackburn 1998; Ordained Local Ministry Officer, Blackburn 2004; Bishop's Officer for LM 1996–2007
GS 1980–88; 2000–　　　　*T:* 01772 812532
　　　　　E: viviennegoddard@gmail.com
　　　　　　　M: 07779 786141 (Mobile)

GODFREY, The Very Revd Nigel Philip *BA, MA, MBA, MSc, MRTPI*
The Deanery Albany Road Peel Isle of Man IM5 1JS [DEAN OF SODOR AND MAN] *educ* Ripon College Cuddesdon; London Guildhall University; King's College London *CV* Curate Kennington St John with St James Southwark 1979–89; Community of Christ the Servant 1984–93; Vicar Brixton Road Christ Church Southwark 1989–2001; Principal Ordained Local Ministry Scheme 2001–07; Chaplain Southwark Cathedral 2002–07; Vicar German Sodor and

Man from 2007; Priest in Charge Patrick from 2011; Vice-Dean St German's Cathedral from 2007; Dean St Germans Cathedral from 2011
T: 01624 844830
E: dean@cathedral.im
W: www.cathedral.im

GODSALL, The Revd Andrew Paul *BA*
20 Newport Way Exeter Devon EX1 7SA [EXETER] *b* 1959 *educ* Tudor Grange Grammar School; Birmingham University; Ripon College Cuddesdon *CV* BBC Studio Manager 1981–86; BBC Radio Producer 1984–86; Assistant Curate, St John's Great Stanmore, 1988–91; Associate Vicar, All Saints Ealing Community, 1991–94; Vicar, All Saints Hillingdon, 1994–2001; Diocesan Director of Ordinands, Willesden Area, London, 1999–2001; Assistant and Chaplain Bishop Exeter, 2001–06; Director, Council Worship and Ministry, 2006; Canon Chancellor, Exeter Cathedral, 2006; Chair, Willesden Area Litt Resources Group, 1995–99; Sec, Patterns of Ministry Working party, Exeter, 2002–03
GS 2010–   *T:* 01392 294920
E: andrew.godsall@exeter.anglican.org

GOLDSMITH, The Rt Revd Christopher David (Chris) *BA, DPhil*
Lis Escop Feock Truro TR3 6QQ [SUFFRAGAN BISHOP OF ST GERMANS; TRURO] *educ* Dartford Grammar School; York University; North Thames Ministry Training Course *CV* Assistant Curate Pitsea with Nevendon 2000–04; Vicar Warley and Great Warley 2004–13; Bishop of St Germans from 2013
E: bishopofstgermans@truro.anglican.org

GOODALL, The Rt Revd Jonathan Michael *BMus*
Hill House Tree Tops The Mount Caversham RG4 7RE [BISHOP OF EBBSFLEET] *b* 1961 *educ* Pudsey Grammar School; Royal Holloway College University of London; Wycliffe Hall *CV* Macmillan Publishers 1983–86; freelance editor from 1983; freelance singer 1983–89; Assistant Curate Bicester with Bucknell, Caversfield and Launton 1989–1992; Assistant Chaplain, HM Prison Bullingdon 1990–92; Minor Canon, Chaplain and Sacrist Westminster Abbey 1992–98; Bishop's Chaplain, Research Assistant and Diocesan Liturgical Officer Europe 1998–05; Archbishop's Chaplain and Ecumenical Officer 2005–09; Archbishop's Personal Chaplain and Ecumenical Secretary 2009–13; Priest Vicar, Westminster Abbey from 2004; Honorary Canon, Gibraltar Cathedral from 2005; Honorary Canon, Canterbury Cathedral from 2014; Bishop of Ebbsfleet from 2013; Honorary Assistant Bishop: Diocese of Oxford from 2013; Diocese of Lichfield from 2013; Diocese of

Worcester from 2013; Diocese of Exeter from 2014; Diocese of Coventry from 2014; Diocese of Bristol from 2015; Diocese of Bath and Wells from 2016; Diocese of Truro from 2016; Diocese of Birmingham from 2017; Member of the Porvoo Panel 1999–2006; Council for Christian Unity 2005–13; Faith and Order Advisory Group 2005–10; Consultant House of Bishops Theological Group 2005–10; Faith and Order Commission 2010–13; House of Bishops from 2013; Working Group of Communion and Diversity 2015–16; Member Inter-Anglican Standing Committee on Ecumenical Relations 2005–08; Consultant, Inter-Anglican Standing Commission for Unity, Faith and Order, 2010–13; International Commission for Anglican-Orthodox Theological Dialogue (IV) 2009–13; ARCIC (III) 2010–13; Anglican-Roman Catholic Joint Ordinariate Liaison Group 2011–13; International Commission for Anglican-Oriental Orthodox Dialogue (IV) 2013; Archbishop of Canterbury's Representative to the Orthodox Church from 2016
T: 0118 948 1038
E: office@ebbsfleet.org.uk

GOODE, The Revd Timothy *BA Hons Mus, BTh Hons, PGCE*
The Vicarage 8 Whyteleafe Hill Whyteleafe Surrey CR3 0AA [SOUTHWARK] *educ* Ellesmere College, Huddersfield University, Roehampton Institute *CV* Music Teacher, St Philomena's School, Carshalton, Surrey 1991–95; Director of Music, Homefield Preparatory School, Sutton 1995–2007; Associate Curate, Croydon Minster 2009–12; Team Vicar of Whyteleafe and Chaldon from 2012; Disability Advisor for the Southwark Diocese from 2013
GS 2015–   *T:* 020 8660 4015
                                    07832 730124
E: revtimgoode@gmail.com
Twitter: @musicgoode

GORICK, The Ven Martin Charles William *MA(Cantab)*
Archdeacon's Lodgings Christ Church Oxford OX1 1DP [ARCHDEACON OF OXFORD] *b* 1967 *educ* West Bridgeford Comprehensive; Selwyn College Cambridge; Ripon College Cuddesdon *CV* Curate Birtley, Durham 1987–91; Bishop's Chaplain, Oxford 1991–4; Vicar Smethwick, Birmingham 1994–2001; Area Dean Warley 1996–2001; Vicar Stratford-upon-Avon; 2001–13; Archdeacon of Oxford from 2013
GS 2011–13, 2016–   *T:* 01865 208263
E: archdeacon.oxford@oxford.anglican.org
W: www.oxford.anglican.org

GORMAN, Miss Lucy
34 Nordham North Cave Brough East Yorkshire HU15 2LT [YORK] *b* 1989 *educ* South Hunsley, *CV* Kantar Operations 2007–10; Hull Daily

Mail 2010–13; Activation Executive at ITV from 2013
GS 2015–   *T:* 07825 187494
            E: Lucy.gorman@hotmail.co.uk
            Twitter: @lucy25

GOUDIE, Dr (Richard) Angus *MB, BChir, MRCGP*
197 Gilesgate Durham DH1 1QN [DURHAM] *b* 1954 *educ* Barnard Castle School; St John's College Cambridge; King's College Hospital London; Newcastle General Practitioner Vocational Training Scheme *CV* General Practitioner, Cartington Terrace Medical Group, Newcastle 1982–1991; General Practitioner, Kepier Medical Practice, Tyne and Wear, 1991–2016; PCC Member St Nicholas Church Durham and Durham Deanery Synod Member from 1996; Member Durham Diocesan Synod from 2006; Member Durham Diocesan Synod Mission Committee 2006–10; Member Durham Bishop's Council 2010
GS 2010–   *T:* 0191 384 0013
            E: angus.goudie@btinternet.com
            F: 0191 584 9493

GOUGH, Mr Richard Edward *MA*
London Diocesan House 36 Causton Street London SW1P 4AU [DIOCESAN SECRETARY; LONDON] *b* 1963 *educ* Haileybury, Oxford *CV* Audit roles at PwC 1984–88; Investment Manager at 3i plc 1988–92; Financial Controller, and Corporate Finance Manager at BTplc 1992–98; Finance and Trading Director of Tearfund 1998–2010; Managing Director and Finance Director of Perrett Laver 2011–12; Finance Director of Woodard Academies Trust 2013–14; Finance Director of Diocese of London 2014–15; General Secretary of Diocese of London from 2015
            T: 020 7932 1248
            E: richard.gough@london.anglican.org

GOVENDER, The Very Revd Rogers Morgan *BTh, DipTh*
Manchester Cathedral Cathedral Yard Victoria Street Manchester M3 1SX [DEAN OF MANCHESTER] *educ* Glenover High School, Durban, South Africa; University of Natal (Pietermaritzburg), South Africa; St Paul's College, Grahamstown, South Africa *CV* Curate Christ Church Overport, South Africa 1985–87; Rector St Mary Greyville, Durban, South Africa 1988–92; Rector St Matthew Hayfields, Pietermaritzburg, South Africa 1993–99; Archdeacon of Pietermaritzburg 1997–99; Rector St Thomas Berea, Durban 1999–2000; Priest in Charge Christ Church Didsbury, Manchester 2001–05; Priest in Charge St Chris Withington, Manchester 2003–05; Area Dean Withington 2003–05; Dean of Manchester

from 2006; Member Diocesan Synod; Member Bishop's Council; Member Archbishops Council Committee for Minority Ethnic Anglican Concerns from 2006; Member Archbishops' Council Liturgical Commission 2006; Chair Diocesan Pastoral Committee
GS 2008–2010   *T:* 0161 833 2220
            0161 792 2801 (Home)
            E: dean@manchestercathedral.org
            F: 0161 839 6218
            M: 07983 978346 (Mobile)

GRAHAM, Mrs Carolyn Jane *LLB, BSc*
Granby Merrow Street Guildford GU4 7AT [GUILDFORD] *b* 1965 *educ* Merchant Taylors' Girls' School, University of Sheffield; College of Law; Open University *CV* Solicitor (formerly trainee) Victor Lissack & Roscoe 1987–91; Crown Prosecutor at the Crown Prosecution Service 1991–2004; Temp Branch Crown Prosecutor at the Crown Prosecution Service 2004–05; Crown Advocate for the Crown Prosecution Service 2006–11; Advice Session Supervisor/Adviser Citizens Advice Bureau 2012–14; Lawyer at the Electoral Commission 2014–16; Employment Lawyer in the Government Legal Department from 2016. Voluntary work: Volunteer on Saneline the mental health helpline 1990s; Street Angel 2009; Churchwarden 2009–12; Co-founder and organizer Trinity Folk Festival from 2013
GS 2015–   *T:* 07867 520795
            01483 459510
            E: carolynjanegraham@yahoo.co.uk
            Twitter: @carolyngraham07

GRAHAM, The Ven Olivia Josephine *BA*
Foxglove House Love Lane Newbury RG14 2JG [ARCHDEACON OF BERKSHIRE; OXFORD] *educ* Cobham Hall, Stake Farm, University of East Anglia *CV* Teacher 1973–81; Overseas relief and development worker 1984–93; Curate in training 1997–2000; Vicar 2000–07; Diocesan Parish Development Adviser 2007–13; Archdeacon of Berkshire from 2013
            T: 01635 552820
            E: archdber@oxford.anglican.org
            Twitter: @LiviJGraham

GRAY, Mr Andrew (Philip John) *MA Cantab*
36 Sarah West Close Norwich Norfolk NR2 2TE [NORWICH] *b* 1980 *educ* St Joseph's College Ipswich, Churchill College Cambridge *CV* Freelance TV Researcher 2003–05; MD of Independent Studios 2005–12 (Documentary production and distribution); MD of Beauforts Ltd (Media and Tech Start-up) from 2012; Partner in Westbury Consultants from 2012
GS 2015–   *T:* 07882 804398
            E: andrew.gray@cantab.net
            W: www.thehungercode.com

WHO'S WHO

GREEN, The Ven Duncan
9 Sheridan Gardens Harrow HA3 0JT
[ARCHDEACON OF NORTHOLT; LONDON] *b* 1952 *CV*
Archdeacon of Northolt from 2013
T: 020 7932 1274
E: archdeacon.northolt@london.anglican.org

GREEN, The Revd Fleur Estelle *BD*
St Peter's Rectory 2 St Peter's Close Darwen BB3 2EA [BLACKBURN] *b* 1972 *educ* St Michael's CE School Chorley, University College of Wales Bangor *CV* Curate St John's Blackpool 1997–2000; Senior Curate Lancaster Priory 2000–03; Incumbent of St Luke with St Philip's and St Mark's Witton 2003–12; Assistant DDO 2005–11; Incumbent of St Peter's Darwen from 2012; Bishop's Advisor for Women's Ministry (Blackburn) from 2011
GS 2015–   T: 01254 702411
E: chauntry1@live.co.uk

GREENE, Ms Jay (Judith) Mary-Clare *BA, MPhil, HND*
3 Hillside Close West Dean Salisbury SP5 1EX [WINCHESTER] *educ* Convent of St Louis, Bury St Edmunds, Warwick University, University of York, Hartpury College UWE *CV* Guardian ad litem Buckinghamshire 1984–87; Guardian ad litem Wiltshire 1987–90; Freelance community and environmental projects 1990–93; Hospital Social Worker Frenchay, Bristol 1993–96; Freelance project work 1996–2000; Hospital Social Worker Bath 2000–02; Hospital Social Worker Romsey 2002–04; Skills for Care Manager Hampshire and Isle of Wight 2004–07; Project Manager/Change Manager Hampshire County Council 2007–11; Freelance project work from 2012
GS 2015–   T: 01794 342377
E: jaygreene101@btinternet.com

GREENER, The Very Revd Jonathan Desmond Francis *MA*
The Deanery 10 Cathedral Close Exeter EX1 1EZ [DEAN OF EXETER] *b* 1961 *educ* Reigate Grammar School; Trinity College Cambridge; College of Resurrection Mirfield *CV* Curate Holy Trinity with St Matthew, Southwark 1991–94; Domestic Chaplain to Bishop of Truro 1994–96; Vicar Church of Good Shepherd, Brighton 1996–2003; Archdeacon of Pontefract 2003–07; Dean of Wakefield 2007–17; Church Commissioner from 2011; Dean of Exeter from 2017
GS 2003–07   T: 01392 285979
E: dean@exeter-cathedral.org.uk

GREENWOOD, Mr Adrian Douglas Crispin *MA, MCIH*
91 Lynton Rd Bermondsey London SE1 5QT [SOUTHWARK] *educ* Judd School Tonbridge; Jesus College Cambridge; College of Law London *CV* Churchwarden St James Bermondsey 1983–92, 1995–2004; Lay Chair St James Bermondsey 1982; Chief Executive Gateway Housing Association (formerly Bethnal Green and Victoria Park Housing Association Ltd) 1992–2010; Trustee Salmon Youth Centre Bermondsey 2000–10, Chair from 2010; Trustee Isle of Dogs Community Foundation 1998; Member Diocesan Synod 1994, Lay Chair 2006; Member Tower Hamlets Local Strategic Partnership 2002–10; Lay Chair Bermondsey Deanery Synod 2004; Chair Southwark Churches Care from 2011
GS 2000–   *E:* amgreenwood@tiscali.co.uk

GREGORY, The Rt Revd Clive Malcolm *BA, MA*
61 Richmond Road Wolverhampton WV3 9JH [AREA BISHOP OF WOLVERHAMPTON; LICHFIELD] *educ* Sevenoaks School; Lancaster University; Queen College Cambridge Westcott House Cambridge *CV* Curate St John Baptist Margate 1988–92; Senior Chaplain University of Warwick 1992–98; Team Rector Coventry East 1998–2007; Honorary Master of Arts, University of Warwick 1999; Associate Diocesan Director of Ordinands Coventry 2001–07; Area Bishop of Wolverhampton from 2007   T: 01902 824503
E: bishop.wolverhampton@lichfield.anglican.org
F: 01902 824504

GRENFELL, The Ven Dr Joanne Woolway *BA, MA, MSt, MA, DPhil*
313 Havant Road Farlington Portsmouth PO6 1DD [ARCHDEACON OF PORTSDOWN; PORTSMOUTH] *b* 1972 *educ* Egglescliffe Comprehensive School; Oriel College Oxford; University British Columbia; Westcott House *CV* Adviser to Women Students, Oriel College Oxford 1995–98, Lecturer Engineering 1997–98; Curate Kirkby Team Ministry 2000–03; Priest in Charge Sheffield Manor 2003–06; Diocesan Director of Ordinands and Residential Canon Sheffield 2007–13; Dean of Women's Ministry Sheffield 2009–13; Archdeacon of Portsdown from 2013   T: 07936 043945
E: joanne.grenfell@portsmouth.anglican.org
W: http://joannegrenfell.wordpress.com/

GRIFFITHS, The Revd Canon Dr Tudor Francis Lloyd *MA (Oxon), PhD*
35 St Mary's Square Gloucester GL1 2QT [GLOUCESTER] *b* 1967 *educ* Penlan Comprehensive School Swansea; Jesus College Oxford; Leeds University; Wycliffe Hall Oxford *CV* Minor Canon Brecon Cathedral, Curate Brecon 1979–81; Curate Swansea St James 1981–83; Rector Llangattock and Llangynidr 1983–88; Church Mission Society

Mission Partner and Tutor at Bishop Tucker Theological College, Uganda 1989–95; Diocesan Missioner Monmouth 1996–2003; Rector Hawarden 2003–11; Rector and Area Dean Cheltenham 2011–17; Senior Interim Minister Gloucester from 2017
GS 2013– *E:* tgriffiths@glosdioc.org
M: 07718 906066

GRIVELL, Mrs Hannah Rebecca *BA Hons*
44 Applewood Close Belper Derbyshire DE56 1TH [DERBY] *b* 1958 *educ* Lees Brook Community Sports College, Heanor Gate Science College, University of Northampton *CV* Customer Advisor, Boots Customer Care 2014–15; Customer Manager, Boots Customer Care 2015–16; Tour Consultant Venture Abroad from 2016
GS 2010–12 *T:* 07533443407
E: hanpag@hotmail.co.uk
Twitter: @hanpag

GROARKE, The Ven Nikki (Nicola) Jane *BA Hons*
15 Worcester Road Droitwich Worcs WR9 8AA [ARCHDEACON OF DUDLEY; WORCESTER] *educ* Pershore High School, University of Lancaster *CV* Senior Marketing Manager, Elsevier Science Publishers 1985–95; Bereavement Services Co-ordinator, Sobell House Hospice 1985–88; Curate/Associate Vicar Ascension Balham Hill (Southwark) 2000–08; Vicar St Stephen's Canonbury (London) 2008–13; Archdeacon of Dudley from 2014
GS 2015– *T:* 01905 773301
07764 685818
E: NGroarke@cofe-worcester.org.uk
Twitter: @NikkiGroarke

GROOM, The Ven Sue (Susan) Anne *BA, MPhil, DipHE, MA, MPhil, PGCATE*
Southbroom House London Road Devizes SN10 1LT [ARCHDEACON OF WILTS; SALISBURY] *educ* Chosen Hill, Churchdown, University College of North Wales, University of Cambridge, London Bible College, Durham University *CV* Assistant Curate of St Mary the Virgin, Harefield and part-time Chaplain to Harefield Hospital 1996–99; Assistant Curate of St Lawrence, Eastcote 1999–2001; Priest-in-Charge of St Matthew, Yiewsley 2001–03; Vicar of St Matthew, Yiewsley 2003–07; Director of Deanery Licensed Ministers, Kensington Episcopal Area and Core Member of Staff of STETS 2007–09; Assistant Diocesan Director of Ordinands St Albans and Priest-in-Charge of Henlow and Langford 2009–10; Acting Diocesan Director of Ordinands St Albans and Priest-in-Charge of Henlow and Langford 2010–11; Diocesan Director of Ordinands St Albans and Priest-in-Charge of Henlow and Langford 2011–16; Archdeacon

of Wilts from 2016; Canon and Prebendary Salisbury Cathedral from 2016
GS 2015–16 *T:* 01722 438662
E: adwilts@salisbury.anglican.org

GRYLLS, The Revd Catherine Anne *MA, MTh, PGCE*
18 Pineapple Grove Birmingham B30 2TJ [BIRMINGHAM] *b* 1954 *educ* John Hanson School, Andover; Marlborough College; Cambridge University, Birmingham University, Oxford University; Ripon College Cuddesdon *CV* Team Minister Southwark Diocesan Retreat House 1991–92; Maths and RE Teacher, Saltley School, Birmingham, 1993–95; Maths Teacher, Holyhead School, Birmingham, 1995–97; Assistant Curate, St Peter's Hall Green Birmingham 2000–04; Priest in Charge St Paul Balsall Heath and St Mary and St Ambrose Edgbaston, Birmingham 2004–05; Priest in Charge, Balsall Heath and Edgbaston (Saints Mary and Ambrose), Birmingham 2006–08; Incumbent, Balsall Heath and Edgbaston, Birmingham 2008–17; Area Dean Moseley, Birmingham 2013–17; Honorary Canon Birmingham Cathedral from 2015; Incumbent Stirchley The Ascension from 2017
GS 2010– *T:* 0121 443 1371
E: gryllsc@btinternet.com

GWILLIAMS, The Very Revd Dianna Lynn *BA, MA, Dip RS*
The Deanery Cathedral Close Guildford GU2 7TL [DEAN GUILDFORD] *b* 1957 *educ* Villa Park High School; California State University; King's College London; Southwark Ordination Course *CV* Assistant Curate Peckham St Saviours' (Copleston Centre Church) 1992–97; Assistant Curate Dulwich St Barnabas 1997–99; Vicar Dulwich St Barnabas 1999–2013; Foundation Chaplain Alleyn's College of God's Gift Dulwich 1999–2013; Area Dean Dulwich 2005–12; Honorary Canon Southwark Cathedral 2006–13; Priest-in-Charge, Peckham St Saviour 2007–11; Dean of Women's Ministry, Southwark 2009–12; Acting Archdeacon of Southwark 2012–13; Dean of Guildford from 2013
T: 01483 565 258
E: dean@guildford-cathedral.org

HALL, The Very Revd John Robert *BA, Hon DD, Hon DTheol, Hon DLitt, FSA, FRSA, FCT*
The Deanery Westminster London SW1P 3PA [DEAN OF WESTMINSTER] *b* 1955 *educ* St Dunstan's College Catford; St Chad's College Durham; Cuddesdon Theological College *CV* Head of RE Malet Lambert High School Hull 1971–73; Curate St John Divine Kennington 1975–78; Priest in Charge All Saints South Wimbledon 1978–84; Vicar St Peter Streatham 1984–92;

Examining Chaplain to Bishop of Southwark 1988–92; Member General Synod Board of Education 1991–92; Chair FCP 1990–93; Diocesan Director of Education Blackburn 1992–98; Fellow Woodard Corporation from 1992; Member Governing Body, St Martin College Lancaster 1992–98; Honorary Canon Blackburn Cathedral 1992–94 and 1998–2000; Residentiary Canon Blackburn Cathedral 1994–98; Canon Emeritus from 2000; Member National Social Council 1997–98; Trustee St Gabriel Trust 1998–2006; Member Governing Body Canterbury Christ Church University College 1999–2006; Trustee Urban Learning Foundation 1999–2002; Member General Teaching Council 2000–04; General Secretary Board of Education and National Society 1998–2002; CEO, Education Division and General Secretary National Society 2003–06; Honorary Assistant Curate St Alban South Norwood 2003–06; Governor St Dunstan's College 2003–11; Chair of Governors Westminster School from 2006; Honorary Fellow Canterbury Christ Church University; Honorary Fellow College of Teachers from 2009; Honorary Fellow St Chad's College, Durham from 2009; Dean of Westminster from 2006; Dean of the Order of the Bath from 2006; Pro-Chancellor, Roehampton University from 2011; Chair of Governors Harris Westminster Sixth Form from 2014; Chair Commission on Religious Education from 2016

GS 1984–92   *T:* 020 7654 4801
                            020 7654 4803
        E: john.hall@westminster-abbey.org
                    F: 020 7654 4883
       W: www.westminster-abbey.org
         M: 07973 418859 (Mobile)
       Twitter: @deanwestminster

HALLARD, Ms Valerie Jean *BSc*
56 High Street Workington Cumbria CA14 4EU [CARLISLE] *educ* Henley on Thames Grammar School, Universities of Lancaster, Northumbria and Cumbria, *CV* Careers Adviser and Adult Guidance Coordinator, Cumbria Careers Ltd 1979–99; Teacher Secondary RE, St Joseph's Catholic High School, 2000–02; 14–19 Adviser, Learning and Skills Council, Cumbria 2002–03; 14–19 Development Manager, Cumbria County Council 2003–11; Company Secretary, Hallard Associates Lt. from 2011
GS 2015–   *T:* 01900 66469
         E: v.j.hallard@gmail.com

HALLIDAY, Canon Malcolm Keith
8 Malham Court Silsden Keighley BD20 0QB [LEEDS] *educ* Rutlish School, Merton *CV* Inland Revenue 1963–1985; Bradford Diocesan Secretary 1985–2010; Bradford Diocesan Director Education 1999–2003; Reader from 1979; Lay Canon Bradford Cathedral 1999–

2010; Lay Canon Emeritus Bradford Cathedral from 2010
GS 2010–   *T:* 01535 656777
      E: malcolm.halliday@btinternet.com
                  M: 07949 605093

HALSTEAD, Mr Andrew William *BSc*
1 Colmore Row Birmingham B3 2BJ [DIOCESAN SECRETARY; BIRMINGHAM] *b* 1958 *educ* King Edward's School, Birmingham, Durham University *CV* 1980–84 Triad Computing (Project Leader); 1984–89 3i plc (Regional Manager); 1990–94 Kone Corporation (General Manager); 1994–96 WPP plc (IT Director); 1996–99 Saatchi & Saatchi plc (IT Director EMEA); 2000–01 Blue Circle Industries plc (Global Head of Knowledge Management); 2001–08 The Football Association (Director of Operations); Diocesan Secretary from 2011   *T:* 0121 426 0400
       E: AndrewH@cofebirmingham.com

HALSTEAD, The Revd Stuart
St Alban's Vicarage 99 Albert Road Ilford Essex IG1 1HS [CHELMSFORD] *educ* North Thames Ministerial Training Course *CV* Assistant Curate All Saints Houghton Regis 2005–08; Assistant Curate St Augustine Kilburn, London 2008–10; Vicar St Alban Great Ilford 2010–
GS 2015–   *T:* 020 8478 2031
       E: stuart.halstead@btinternet.com

HAMID, The Rt Revd David *BSc, MDiv, DD*
14 Tufton St London SW1P 3QZ [SUFFRAGAN BISHOP IN EUROPE] *b* 1954 *educ* Nelson High School, Burlington, Canada; McMaster University Canada; University of Trinity College, Toronto, Canada *CV* Curate St Christopher Burlington Canada 1981–83; Rector St John Burlington Canada 1983–87; Mission Coordinator for Latin America/Caribbean, General Synod of Anglican Church of Canada 1987–96; Director of Ecumenical Affairs and Studies, Anglican Consultative Council 1996–2002; Suffragan Bishop in Europe from 2002; ex officio Member Faith and Order Advisory Group (C of E) 1996–2002; Co-Secretary Anglican-Roman Catholic International Commission 1996–2002; Co-Secretary Anglican-Orthodox Theological Dialogue 1996–2002; Co-Secretary Anglican-Lutheran International Working Group 1999–2002; Co-Secretary Anglican-Roman Catholic Commission on Unity and Mission 2001–02; Co-Secretary Anglican-Baptist International Conversations 1999–2002; Co-Secretary Anglican-Old Catholic International Co-ordination Council 1998–2002; Co-Secretary Anglican-Oriental Orthodox Dialogue 2001–02; Secretary Inter-Anglican Theological and Doctrinal Commission 2001–02; Secretary Inter-

Anglican Standing Committee on Ecumenical Relations 2000–02; Consultant to Joint Working Group of World Council of Churches and Roman Catholic Church 2000–06; Consultant to Anglican-Roman Catholic Commission on Unity and Mission 2002–12; Member Anglican-Old Catholic International Co-ordination Council from 2005; Co-Chair Anglican-Roman Catholic Commission on Unity and Mission from 2012; Chair Porvoo Panel; Governor of the Anglican Centre in Rome from 2014; Trustee Churches Together in Britain and Ireland from 2014; Member Malines Conservation Group from 2016
T: 020 7898 1160
E: david.hamid@churchofengland.org
F: 020 7898 1166
W: www.eurobishop.blogspot.com
M: 07801 449113
Twitter: @eurobishop

HAMILTON, The Revd (William) Graham MA
The Vicarage Coombe Cross Bovey Tracey Newton Abbot Devon TQ13 9EP [EXETER] *b* 1963 *educ* Liverpool College, Lit Hum, New College, Oxford *CV* Assistant Curate, Ivybridge 1995–99; Vicar, PPT Bovey Tracey with St Mary's Hennock 1999–2015
GS 2015–   *T:* 01626 833813
E: pptbovey@mac.com
Twitter: @pptvicar

HAMMOND, Canon Robert Ian BA, MA, AIWS, FRSA
22 South Primrose Hill Chelmsford CM1 2RG [CHELMSFORD] *educ* Hylands School Chelmsford; Open University; Heythrop College, London University *CV* NatWest Bank 1985–87; HM Customs and Excise 1987–2005; HM Revenue and Customs from 2005; Assistant Director – Head of Location Design; Freelance Wine and Spirit Educator and Judge from 2009; Chelmsford Diocesan Synod from 1996; Member Bishop's Council from 2003; Member Chelmsford Cathedral Council from 2003; Member Mission and Public Affairs Council 2006–11; Member Diocesan Board of Patronage 2007–10; Member Diocesan Pastoral Committee 2007–10; Member C of E (Ecclesiastical Fees) Measure: Steering Committee 2008–10; Member Dioceses Commission from 2011; Chair of Governors Cathedral School Chelmsford
GS 2000–   *T:* 01245 269105
E: rihammond@me.com
M: 07711 672308 (Mobile)
Twitter: @ChelmsRob

HANCE, The Very Revd Dr Stephen DMin, MA, BTh, BSc
27a Penny Long Lane Derby DE22 1AX [DEAN OF DERBY] *b* 1958 *educ* Westwood St. Thomas' School, Salisbury, Portsmouth University

CV Assistant Curate, St. Jude's Southsea (Portsmouth) 1993–96; Team Vicar, Tollington Team (London) 1996–99; Vicar, The Ascension Balham Hill (Southwark) 1999–2012; Canon Missioner, Southwark Cathedral, and Director of Mission and Evangelism, Southwark Diocese 2013–17; Dean of Derby from 2017
GS 2015–   *T:* 01322 341201
E: dean@derbycathedral.org
Twitter: @StephenHance1

HANCOCK, The Rt Revd Peter MA, BA
The Palace Wells Somerset BA5 2PD [BISHOP OF BATH AND WELLS] *b* 1954 *educ* Price's School Fareham; Selwyn College Cambridge; Oak Hill Theological College; St John College Nottingham *CV* Curate Christ Church Portsdown 1980–83; Curate Radipole and Melcombe Regis Team Ministry 1983–87; Vicar St Wilfrid Cowplain 1987–99; Rural Dean Havant 1993–98; Honorary Canon Portsmouth Cathedral 1997–99; Archdeacon of The Meon 1999–2010; Bishop of Basingstoke 2010–14; Acting Warden of Readers 1999–2000; Acting Rural Dean Gosport 2002–03; Director of Mission Portsmouth 1999–2006; Chair Church Pastoral Aid Society Trustees 2004–10; Bishop of Bath and Wells from 2014; Partners in World Mission; Churches Together in Britain and Ireland
GS 2005–10, 2014–15   *T:* 01749 672341
E: bishop@bathwells.anglican.org
W: https://bathwellschap.wordpress.com/
Twitter: @bathwellsbish

HARBORD, Canon (Paul) Geoffrey MA, LLM
4 Clarke Drive Sheffield S10 2NS [SHEFFIELD] *b* 1956 *educ* Thornbridge Grammar School Sheffield; Keble College Oxford; Chichester Theological College; Cardiff University *CV* Curate Rawmarsh with Parkgate 1983–86; Curate St George Doncaster 1986–90; Priest in Charge St Edmund Sprotbrough 1990–95; Vicar Masbrough 1995–2003; Justice of the Peace from 1999; Member Legal Aid Commission; Member Diocesan Advisory Committee; Member Diocesan Worship and Liturgical Committee; Domestic Chaplain to Bishop of Sheffield from 2003; Member Council College of Resurrection, Mirfield; Member Clergy Discipline Committee 2003–06; Honorary Canon Sheffield Cathedral 2007; Member Steering Committee Misc Provisions Measure 2013
GS 2000–   *T:* 0114 266 1932
0114 230 2170
E: geoffrey@bishopofsheffield.org.uk
F: 0114 263 0110

HARDEN, Canon Rachel BA
Church House Great Smith Street London [DEPUTY DIRECTOR OF COMMUNICATIONS; ARCHBISHOPS' COUNCIL] *b* 1962 *educ* Putney High School;

Warwick University *CV* Freelance journalist; Church Times 2000–08; BBC campaigns 2004–08; Senior Media Officer Archbishops' Council 2008–13; Deputy Director of Communications Archbishops' Council from 2013   *T:* 020 7898 1464
E: rachel.harden@churchofengland.org

HARDING, Mr Nick (Nicholas) Andrew *BEd*
8 Belmont Close Mansfield Woodhouse NG19 9GD [SOUTHWELL AND NOTTINGHAM] *b* 1964 *educ* St Philip's Roman Catholic College Birmingham; Exeter University *CV* Primary School Teacher 1985–88; Director ICIS Trust 1989–94; Education Officer, Southwell Minster 1995–2002; Southwell Diocesan Children's Officer from 2002; Member General Synod Board of Education Children's Panel; Member Diocesan Liturgical Committee, Board of Education, Lay Ministry Group; magistrate
GS 2005–   *T:* 01636 817234 (Work)
E: nick@southwell.anglican.org
F: 01623 622272
M: 07827 291694 (Mobile)

HARDMAN, The Rt Revd Christine Elizabeth *BSc, MTh*
Bishop's House 29 Moor Road South Gosforth Newcastle upon Tyne NE3 1PA [BISHOP OF NEWCASTLE] *educ* Queen Elizabeth Girls' Grammar School Barnet; City of London Polytechnic; Westminster College Oxford; St Alban Diocesan Ministerial Training Scheme *CV* Deaconess St John the Baptist Markyate 1984–87; Curate 1987–88; Course Director St Alban Ministerial Training Scheme 1988–96; Vicar Holy Trinity Stevenage from 1996; Rural Dean Stevenage from 1999; Archdeacon of Lewisham and Greenwich 2001–12; Non-stipendiary minister, Southwark Cathedral 2012–15; Permission to officiate, St Albans 2013–15; Bishop of Newcastle from 2015; Member Diocesan Synod; Member Bishop's Council; Prolocutor Lower House Convocation Canterbury from 2011; Member Archbishops' Council from 2011; Member Appointments Committee from 2011; Member LAC from 2011
GS 1998–2001, 2004–   *T:* 0191 285 2220
E: bishop@newcastle.anglican.org
F: 0191 284 6933
M: 07812 078048

HARGREAVES-SMITH, Mr Aiden Richard *MA, LLM, FRSA*
23 Battlebridge Court Wharfdale Rd London N1 9UA [LONDON] *educ* Batley Grammar School; University of Manchester; Europeenne de Formation Professionnelle, Paris; University of Westminster; Manchester Metropolitan University College of Law *CV* Civil Service

1992–95; Tutor, St Anselm Hall, University of Manchester 1991–93, Senior Tutor 1993–98; Trainee Solicitor, Winckworth and Pemberton, Solicitors and Parliamentary Agents 1998–2000; Solicitor, Winckworth Sherwood from 2000, Partner from 2007, Head of Ecclesiastical Education and Charities Dept from 2010; Registrar of Diocese in Europe and Bishop's Legal Secretary from 2009; Registrar of Diocese of Chelmsford and Bishop's Legal Secretary from 2012; Memberships: St Anselm Hall SCR from 1991, Hall Management Council from 1996; Ecclesiastical Law Society from 2002, General Committee (2005–11); Steering Committee, Church of England (Miscellaneous Provisions) Measure 2002–04; Society for the Maintenance of the Faith from 2002; Council, Queen Victoria Clergy Fund from 2003; Governor and Trustee, Pusey House Oxford from 2003; Fellow, Royal Society of Arts from 2003; Revision Committee, Pastoral (Amendment) Measure 2004–05; Charity Law Association from 2004; Ecumenical Council for Corporate Responsibility from 2005; Senior Appointments Review Group (Pilling Commission) 2005–07; Fees Advisory Commission (appointed by the President of the Law Society) 2005–11; Appointments Committee of the Church of England 2005–15; Standing Committee of the House of Laity of the General Synod 2005–15; Pastoral Measure Appeals Panel from 2005; Crown Nominations Commission 2007–17; Ecclesiastical Law Association from 2008, Executive Committee 2012–15; Bishops'/Archbishops' advisory groups for six vacancies in Suffragan Sees 2009–13; Trustee, Clergy Rest Fund from 2011; Legal Aid Commission from 2011; Panel of Chairmen of General Synod from 2012; Consultant Registrar, Revision Committee, Legislative Reform Measure, Statute Law (Repeals) Measure and Pensions (Pre-Consolidation) Measure 2016–17
GS 2000–   *T:* 020 7833 9182 (Home)
020 7593 5064 (Office
E: arhs1@tiscali.co.uk

HARPER, The Revd Canon (Rosemary Elizabeth) Rosie *BA, MA LRAM, DipRAM*
The Rectory Church Street Amersham Bucks HP7 0DB [OXFORD] *educ* Blyth Grammar School; Birmingham University; Royal Academy of Music, London; Heythrop College; North Thames Ministerial Training Course *CV* Singer and lecturer vocal studies; Chaplain High Sheriff of Buckingham 2009–10; Acting Priest in Charge St Leonard's Chesham Bois, 2002–03; Assistant Curate St Mary's with Coleshill, Amersham, 1990–2002; Vicar Great Missenden with Ballinger and Little Hampden 2003; Chaplain Bishop Buckingham 2005; Bishop's Council 2006; Diocesan Board

Patronage 2006; Honorary Canon Christ Church from 2011

GS 2010–
T: 01494 728988
E: rosie51619@aol.com
M: 07743 679651

HARRIS, Mr Adrian William *BSc (Hons)*
Church House Great Smith Street London SW1P 3AZ [HEAD OF DIGITAL COMMUNICATIONS; THE ARCHBISHOPS' COUNCIL] *b* 1984 *educ* Longsands College; Canterbury Christ Church University *CV* Digital Communications team The Conservative Party 2008–11; Digital Communications Manager Tesco Plc 2011–13; Head of Digital Communications Tesco Plc, 2013–15; Head of Digital Communications Bupa 2015–16; Head of Digital Communications; The Archbishops' Council from 2016; Churchwarden and Non-Executive Director St Martin-in-the-Fields Trafalgar Square from 2016
T: 07823 883353
E: adrian.harris@churchofengland.org
Twitter: @AdrianHarris

HARRIS, Mr Jeremy James *MA (Oxon)*
16 Westfield Road Cheadle Hulme Stockport Cheshire SK86EH [CHESTER] *educ* Helsby County Grammar School for Boys, St Peter's College, Oxford *CV* Legal officer, Engineering Employers' Federation 1987–89; Solicitor, Turner Kenneth Brown 1989–92; Solicitor, Halliwell Landau 1992–94; Solicitor, DLA Piper UK LLP 1994–96; Associate, DLA Piper 1996–99; Partner, DLA Piper UK LLP from 1999
GS 2015–
T: 0161 235 4222
07971 142356
E: jeremy.harris@dlapiper.com

HARRISON, Dr Jamie (James Herbert) *MB, BS, FRCGP, MA*
5 Dunelm Court South St Durham DH1 4QX [DURHAM] *b* 1967 *educ* Stockport Grammar School; Magdalen College Oxford; King's College Hospital Medical School London *CV* GP March 1983–90; GP Durham 1990–2013; GP Advisor, Department of Health 2001–06; Sir William Leech Fellow in Applied Christian Theology Durham University 2012–13; Vice President Council St John's College Durham from 2015; Reader from 1984; Lay Chair Durham Diocesan Syod 2009–15; Chair, General Synod House of Laity from 2015; Member Archbishops' Council from 2015; Member Women in the Episcopate Steering Committee 2013–14; Member Clergy Discipline Commission from 2014; Member National Safeguarding Steering Group from 2016; Diocesan Peer Reviewer from 2016; Member Strategic Investment Board from 2017; Member Pastoral Advisory Group from 2017
GS 1995–
T: 0191 384 8643
E: dunelm5@btinternet.com
M: 07799 411512

HARRISON, The Rt Revd Mike *BA, STM, PhD*
Robin Hall Chapel Road Mendlesham Stowmarket IP14 5SQ [BISHOP OF DUNWICH; ST EDMUNDSBURY AND IPSWICH] *b* 1963 *educ* Leamington College; Selwyn College Cambridge; Union Theological Seminary New York; King's College London; Ripon College Cuddesdon *CV* Curate St Anne and All Saints 1990–93; Chaplain Bradford University and BICC 1994–98; Vicar Holy Trinity Eltham 1998–2006; Director of Mission and Ministry Leicester 2006–16; Bishop of Dunwich from 2016
T: 01473 252829
E: bishop.mike@cofesuffolk.org
Twitter: @Bishop_Dunwich

HART, Mr Peter David *CertEd*
10 Ashbank Place Crewe Cheshire CW1 3FR [CHESTER] *b* 1949 *educ* Crewe Grammar School; Madeley College of Education *CV* Primary School Teacher 1971–2004; Lay Chair Nantwich Deanery Synod; Member Archdiaconal Mission and Pastoral Committee; Lay Chair Forward in Faith Chester Diocese
GS 2010–
T: 01270 216248
E: peter.hart03@talktalk.net
M: 07857 500115

HATTON, Mr Thomas Brian *BA*
St Stephen's Vicarage Cressingham Road London SE13 5AG [SOUTHWARK] *b* 1992 *educ* Alder Community High School; Warwick University *CV* Banker 2013–
GS 2015–
T: 07527 911584
E: tomhatton1@hotmail.com
Twitter: @tomhatton1

HAWKINS, The Revd (Patricia Sally) Pat *MA, BPhil, BTh, CQSW*
The Vicarage Lymer Road Oxley WV10 6AA [LICHFIELD] *educ* Wygeston Girls Grammar School, Leicester; Lady Margaret Hall, Oxford; Exeter University; St Stephen's House Theological College *CV* Residential Social worker with adolescents 1980–83; LA Social Worker, Devon 1985–86; Member Community of St Francis 1986–99; Curate, Parish of Stafford 2001–04; Incumbent, Parish of Oxley 2004; Area Dean, Wolverhampton 2008; Member Lichfield Diocesan Synod 2003–04, from 2006; Prebendary Lichfield Cathedral from 2009; Rural Dean Wulfrun from 2011
GS 2010–
T: 01902 783342
E: pathawkins@btinternet.com

HAWKINS, The Ven John Edward Inskipp *BD*
13 Kingscroft Road London NW2 3QE [ARCHDEACON OF HAMPSTEAD; LONDON] *b* 1963 *educ* Aldenham School; King's College London; Batchelor of Divinity, King's College London *CV* Assistant Curate Holy Trinity Birchfield

1988–92; Team Vicar All Saints Poplar 1992–99; Vicar St John West Hendon 1992–2015; Area Dean West Barnet London 2004–10; Priest in charge St Matthias Colindale 2007–15; Prebendary St Paul Cathedral 2012–15; Bishop's Missioner for Kings Cross 2013–14; Archdeacon of Hampstead from 2015

T: 07961 272915
E: archdeacon.hampstead@
london.anglican.org

HEATHFIELD, The Ven Simon David *BMus, BThMin*
1 Colmore Row Birmingham B3 2BJ [ARCHDEACON OF ASTON; BIRMINGHAM] *educ* The Judd School, Tonbridge, University of Birmingham *CV* Assistant Curate, Heswall, 1999–2002; Leadership and Vocations Officer, Church Pastoral Aid Society, 2002–05; Team Rector, The Parish of Walthamstow, 2005–14; Area Dean of Waltham Forest 2012–14; Archdeacon of Aston from 2014
GS 2015–   *T:* 0121 426 0428
                                 07769 187435
                    E: simonh@cofebirmingham.com

HEDGES, The Very Revd Jane Barbara *BA (Hons), Hon PhD*
The Deanery The Close Norwich NR1 4EG [DEAN OF NORWICH] *b* 1955 *educ* Sarisbury Secondary School; St John's College Durham; Cranmer Hall Durham *CV* Deacon Holy Trinity with St Columba, Fareham 1980–83; Team Vicar Southampton City Centre 1983–88; Stewardship Advisor Portsmouth Diocese 1988–93; Residential Canon Portsmouth Cathedral 1993–2001; Team Rector Honiton 2001–06; Canon Steward/Archdeacon of Westminster 2006–14; Dean of Norwich from 2014; Member Board of Finance Portsmouth; Member Board of Education Portsmouth; Chair Adult Learning Group Portsmouth
                                 T: 01603 218300
                       E: dean@cathedral.org.uk

HEMING, The Revd Zoe Norah *BA, MA*
28 Burntwood View Loggerheads Staffordshire TF9 4GZ [LICHFIELD] *b* 1967 *educ* Wolgarston High, University of Bradford *CV* International Leprosy Association Project Officer 1999–2000; Homeless Client Training Centre assistant 2000–01; Aromatherapist and Consultant to NHS anti-natal preparation (Self Employed) 2003–10; On-Call Hospital Chaplain, UHNS 2012–14; Deanery Curate, Hodnet Deanery, Shrewsbury Episcopal Area 2014–17; Priest-in-charge St Andrew's Aston from 2017; Lichfield Diocese Enabling Church Adviser from 2017
GS 2015–   *T:* 01630 657972
                                 07926 805886
                    E: hemingzoe@yahoo.co.uk
                         Twitter: @ZoeHeming

HENDERSON, The Rt Revd Julian Tudor *MA*
Bishop's House Ribchester Road Clayton-le-Dale Blackburn BB1 9EF [BISHOP OF BLACKBURN] *educ* Radley College; Keble College Oxford; Ridley Hall Cambridge *CV* Curate St Mary Islington 1979–83; Vicar Emmanuel and St Mary in the Castle, Hastings 1983–92; Vicar Holy Trinity Claygate 1992–2005; Rural Dean 1996–2001; Chair Diocesan Evangelical Fellowship 1997–2001; Honorary Canon Guildford Cathedral 2002; Tutor Diocesan Ministry Course 2003–12; Archdeacon of Dorking 2005–13; Chair Intercontinental Church Society 2011–16; Chair Business Committee from 2012; Bishop of Blackburn from 2013; President of Church of England Evangelical Council from 2015: Chair of Wycliffe Hall Council from 2016
GS 2004–   *T:* 01254 248234
              E: bishop@bishopofblackburn.org.uk

HENSHALL, The Very Revd Nicholas James *MA (Oxon)*
The Dean's House 3 Harlings Grove Waterloo Lane Chelmsford CM1 1YQ [DEAN OF CHELMSFORD] *educ* Manchester Grammar School; British School of Archaeology, Athens; Wadham College Oxford; Ripon College Cuddesdon *CV* Curate St Mary's Blyth 1988–92; Vicar St Margaret's Scotswood 1992–2002; Canon Precentor Derby Cathedral 2002–08; presenter BBC Radio Derby 2003–08; Vicar Christ Church Harrogate 2008–14; Acting Archdeacon Richmond 2013–14; Dean of Chelmsford from 2014; Member Bishop's Council from 2014   *T:* 01245 294492
                    E: nicholas.henshall@
                    chelmsfordcathedral.org.uk
              W: www.chelmsfordcathedral.org.uk
                         Twitter: @CCathedral

HEPPLESTON, Mr Michael
Turnpike House 1 Turnpike Newchurch Lancashire BB4 9DU [MANCHESTER] *b* 1957 *CV* Manchester Diocesan Synod; Manchester Ministry and Pastoral Committee; Organist and Music Director St Michael and All Angels Peek Green; Regional Operations Manager, Media on the Move from 2005
GS 2010–   *T:* 01706 220349
                    E: mheppleston@mediaotm.com

HERBERT, Mrs Caroline Elizabeth *BA, MA (Cantab), MPhil, MA*
18 Vicarage Road Cromer NR27 9DQ [NORWICH] *b* 1958 *educ* Pembroke College, University of Cambridge; University College, London *CV* Graduate Library Trainee, Newnham College, Cambridge 2004–05; Archives Assistant, Churchill Archives Centre, Cambridge, 2005–11; Content and Metadata Officer, Wellcome Trust, 2011–13; Freelance book cataloguer from 2015
GS 2014–   *T:* 01263 514990
                    E: caroline.herbert@yahoo.co.uk

HERKLOTS, Mrs Lucinda Jane Denise *BA*
Diocesan Office Church House 99 Crane Street Salisbury Wiltshire SP1 2QB [DIOCESAN SECRETARY; SALISBURY] *b* 1958 *educ* School of St Helen's and St Katherine's, Abingdon, Lady Margaret Hall, Oxford University *CV* Electronics Development Engineer, Racal Transcom Ltd 1981–92; Product Development Manager, Racal Transcom Ltd 1992–99; Strategic Marketing Manager, then Director Racal Transcom Ltd then Thales e-Transactions plc 1999–2004; Dioceses Commission 2007–15; Chairman Diocesan Secretaries Liaison Group 2008–12; Diocesan Secretary, Diocese of Salisbury from 2004   *T:* 01722 411922
       E: lucinda.herklots@salisbury.anglican.org
                                 F: 01722 411990

HERRICK, The Ven Vanessa Anne *BA, MA, LTCL*
Glebe House Church Lane Sheering Bishop's Stortford CM22 7NR [ARCHDEACON OF HARLOW; CHELMSFORD] *b* 1958 *educ* Grey Coat Hospital, Westminster; University of York; St John's College, Nottingham; Ridley Hall, Cambridge; Anglia Ruskin University *CV* Assistant Curate St Edmundsbury Cathedral 1996–99; Chaplain and Fellow Fitzwilliam College Cambridge 1999–2002; Tutor in Pastoral Theology Ridley Hall Cambridge 1999–2002; Director of Ministry and Director of Ordinands Ely 2003–11; Rector Wimborne Minster 2012–17 and also of the Northern Villages from 2015; Archdeacon of Harlow from 2017; Member of the Ministry Council of the Archbishops' Council 2008–16
                                 T: 01279 734524
          E: a.harlow@chelmsford.anglican.org
                                 M: 07590 929951
                              Twitter: @Cuthberga2

HIGGINS, Miss Gabrielle Margaret *MA (Oxon)*
Diocesan Church House 211 New Church Road Hove BN3 4ED [DIOCESAN SECRETARY; CHICHESTER] *b* 1955 *educ* Bolton School Girls Division; Perse School for Girls, Cambridge; Merton College, Oxford; City University, London *CV* Barrister, Maitland Chambers, Lincoln's Inn 2002–14; Diocesan Secretary, Diocese of Chichester from 2015   *T:* 01273 421021
    E: gabrielle.higgins@chichester.anglican.org

HILL, The Revd Barry *BTh*
The Rectory Rectory Lane Market Harborough LE16 8AS [LEICESTER] *b* 1955 *educ* Cardinal Newman School, Hove, Cardinal Newman Sixth Form College, Hove *CV* Youth and Pastoral Assistant, St Andrew's, Burgess Hill 1997–98; SEOS Displays Ltd (later SEOS Ltd) Customer Services Manager (UK), 1998–2002 (formally Customer Services Administrator and Customer Services Co-ordinator); Assistant Curate, Parish of Emmanuel, Loughborough (and St Mary-in-Charnwood, Nanpantan), 2005–09; Diocesan Mission Enabler 2009–17; Team Rector Market Harborough Resource Church Team from 2017; Diocesan Resource Church Enabler Leicester from 2017
GS 2015–   *T:* 01858 468461
       E: barry@harborough.anglican.org.uk
    W: www.harborough-anglican.org; http://
       www.leicester.anglican.org/shaped-by-God/
                              Twitter: @revbarryhill

HILL, Professor Joyce Margaret *BA, DPhil, DUniv, FEA, FRSA*
35 Church Lane Adel Leeds LS16 8DQ [LEEDS] *educ* Barnstaple Girls' Grammar; King's College London; University of York *CV* Diocesan Board of Education 1986–90, 1992–4; Quatercentenary Fellow Emmanuel College Cambridge 1993; Bishop's Advisory Panels from 1995; Professor Leeds University 1995, Emeritus from 2008; Pro-Vice Chancellor Leeds University 1995–8; Director of UK-wide policy unit for Higher Education 2001–05; Visiting professorships in USA and Italy; Head of School; Director of Centre; Sundry National and International Advisory roles; Retired; Diocesan Trustee on Leeds Universities Chaplaincy Trust 2009–17; Lay Capitular Canon Ripon Cathedral from 2011; Member Candidates Panel from 2013; Member Theological Educators Panel from 2013; Member Cathedrals Fabric Commission for England from 2016; Member Governing Council Eastern Region Ministry Course from 2016
GS 2015–   *T:* 0113 267 4433
                     E: hill383@btinternet.com
                                 M: 07739 556279

HILL, The Rt Revd Peter *BSc, PGCE, MTh*
Barking Lodge 35A Verulam Avenue London E17 8ES [AREA BISHOP OF BARKING; CHELMSFORD] *b* 1958 *educ* Manchester University; Nottingham University; Wycliffe Hall, Oxford *CV* Schoolteacher 1973–81; Curate Porchester 1983–86; Vicar Huthwaite 1986–95; Priest in Charge Calverton 1995–2004; Rural Dean Southwell 1997–2001; Chair Diocesan Board of Education 2001–04 and 2013–14; Diocesan Chief Executive 2003–07; Honorary Canon Southwell Minster from 2001; Archdeacon of Nottingham 2007–14; Member Dearing Commission Church Schools 1999–2001; Member Convocation Commission on Guidelines for the Professional Conduct of the Clergy 2000–03 and 2012–13; Faiths Advocate Nottingham City Strategic Partnership 2010–14; Vice Chair Diocesan Commission 2011–14; Bishop of Barking from 2014
GS 1993–2004, 2010–14
                          T: 020 8509 7377 (Office)
        E: b.barking@chelmsford.anglican.org
    W: http://www.chelmsford.anglican.org/areas
       -and-bishops/area-bishops/bishop-of-barking

WHO'S WHO

HILLS, Canon Julian James *BSc*
Diocesan House Lady Wootton's Green Canterbury Kent CT1 1NQ [DIOCESAN SECRETARY; CANTERBURY] *educ* Queen Elizabeth's School, Faversham, Royal Holloway College, University of London *CV* Executive Officer, District Audit Service 1978–83; Internal Auditor, Pfizer Ltd 1983–89; Pharmaceutical Business Finance Manager, Pfizer Ltd 1989–2002; Director of Finance Canterbury Diocese 2002–07; Diocesan Secretary from 2007
T: 01227459401
E: jhills@diocant.org

HIND, Mr Timothy Charles *MA, FCII*
Plowman's Corner The Square Westbury-sub-Mendip Wells BA5 1HJ [BATH AND WELLS] *b* 1954 *educ* Watford Boys Grammar School; St John's College Cambridge *CV* Various posts at Sun Life (now AXA) 1972–13, retired 2013; Quality Manager, AXA UK; Chartered Insurer; Member Bishop's Council; Chair Diocesan Vacancy-in-See Committee 1996–98; Member Diocesan Board of Education 1995–97; Member Board of Educations C of E Pensions Board 1996–2010; Member C of E Pensions Board Investment and Finance Committee 1996–97; Member Advisory Board of Ministry 1998; Member Deployment, Remunerations and Conditions of Service Committee 1999–2008; Lay Vice-Chair Diocesan Synod from 1999–2009; Lay Chair Axbridge Deanery Synod 1984–91; Member Diocesan Board of Patronage 1986–94; Vice-Chair Board of Governors Kings of Wessex Comprehensive School 1996–99; Churchwarden St John the Baptist Axbridge 2001–05; Secretary OSG 2001–04; Chair OSG 2004–11; Vice Chair C of E Pensions Board 2010–11; Vice Chair House of Laity 2011–15; Legislative Committee 2011–15; Standing Orders Committee 2011–15; Diocesan Board of Finance Investment Committee from 2017
GS 1995–2000, 2001–
T: 01749 870356 (Home)
E: tim@hind.org.uk
M: 07977 580374

HINE, Mr Peter Geoffrey *BA*
Chapel Howe Sour Nook Sebergham Carlisle CA5 7DY [CARLISLE] *educ* Wallasey Tech Grammar School; Durham University *CV* Various posts with Financial Services sector 1972–98; Voluntary Church and Education worker 1998–2002; Trustee C of E Pension Scheme 1998–2001; Trustee and Director Worldshare from 1999; Finance Resources Officer Diocese Carlisle from 2002
GS 2010–
T: 01228 815401
E: phine999@btinternet.com
F: 01228 815400
M: 07584 684297

HODDER, The Revd Dr Chris *BTh (Hons), MRes, BA (Hons), PhD*
St Paul's House Boundary Road West Bridgford Nottingham NG2 7DB [SOUTHWELL AND NOTTINGHAM] *b* 1958 *educ* Arthur Mellows Village College, Glinton, University of Huddersfield; University of Nottingham; University of Derby *CV* Youthworker Eire 1996–97; Assistant Portfolio Manager Barclays Stockbrokers 1997–98; Curate at Emmanuel and St Mary's Loughborough 2001–05; Anglican Chaplain and Pastoral Services Co-ordinator at the University of Derby and Chaplain to Derby Cathedral 2005–10; Vicar of St Paul's Wilford Hill from 2010
GS 2015–
T: 07505 701640
E: revdchris.hodder@outlook.com

HOGG, Mr Stephen William *BA (Hons), MBA, FCMA, CGMA*
Crag Leith Green Head Lane Settle North Yorkshire BD24 9HG [LEEDS] *educ* Shawlands Academy, Glasgow, University of Newcastle upon Tyne, Durham University *CV* Previous appointments with PricewaterhouseCoopers, Letts Educational, Polygram, English Heritage, Procter and Gamble; Finance Manager, National Crime Squad, CEOP, SOCA, 2003–2006; Head of Management Accounting, Ofsted, 2007–08; Head of Estates Finance, Her Majesty's Courts Service, 2009–10; Finance Manager, Oasis Academies, 2012–13; Senior Finance Business Partner, HS2 Ltd 2013–14; Retired since 2014; Vice Chair Archbishops' Council Audit Committee
GS 2015–
T: 01729823765
E: swhogg@outlook.com
M: 07966 208465
Twitter: @stephenhogg11

HOLBROOK, The Rt Revd John Edward *MA*
Orchard Acre 11 North Street Mears Ashby Northampton NN6 0DW [SUFFRAGAN BISHOP OF BRIXWORTH; PETERBOROUGH] *b* 1962 *educ* Bristol Cathedral School; St Peter College Oxford; Ridley Hall Cambridge *CV* Curate Barnes St Mary Southwark 86–89; Curate Bletchley 1989–93; Curate North Bletchley Conventional District 1989–93; Vicar Adderbury with Milton 1993–2002; Rural Dean Deddington 2000–02; Rector Wimborne Minster 2002–11; Priest in Charge Witchampton, Stanbridge and Long Crichel etc 2002–11; Priest in Charge Horton, Chalbury, Hinton Martel and Holt St James 2006–11; Rural Dean Wimborne 2004–11; Chaplain South and East Dorset Primary Care Trust 2002–11; Canon and Prebendary Salisbury Cathedral 2006–11; Suffragan Bishop of Brixworth Peterborough from 2011; Canon Peterborough Cathedral from 2011
T: 01733 562492
01604 812318
E: bishop.brixworth@peterborough-diocese.org.uk

HOLDSWORTH, Canon Liz *MA(Oxon), PGCE*
St Mary's Vicarage Abbey Road Northampton
NN4 8E2 [PETERBOROUGH] *educ* Wolfreton
School Hull; Somerville College Oxford;
Chester College *CV* History Teacher Bancroft's
School Woodford Green 1982–86; Director of
Ashbee Jewellers 1990–2000; Licensed
Evangelist Diocese of Peterborough 2002–;
Ministry Partnership Development Officer
Peterborough Diocese 2004–11; Director of
Training Peterborough Diocese 2011–17;
Bishop's Leadership Team Peterborough
Diocese 2011; General Synod Economics and
Ethics Committee 2014; National Continuing
Ministerial Development Panel 2015–17;
Director of Mission and Training Peterborough
from 2017
GS 2013–   *T:* 01604 887070
                                 E: liz.holdsworth@
                          peterborough-diocese.org.uk

**HOLLINGHURST, The Rt Revd Anne
Elizabeth** *BA(Hons), MSt*
1 Colmore Row Birmingham B3 2BJ [BISHOP OF
ASTON; BIRMINGHAM] *educ* Range High School
and Sixth Form, Formby; University Bristol;
University Cambridge *CV* Youth worker St
Stephen Hyson Green and St Leodegarius Old
Basford 1990–93; Assistant Curate St Saviour
Nottingham 1996–99; Chaplain University
Derby 1999–2005; Chaplain 1999–2005;
Chaplain Bishop of Manchester 2005–10;
Residential Canon Manchester Cathedral
2005–10; Vicar St Peter's St Albans 2010–15;
Bishop of Aston from 2015
GS 2011–   *T:* 0121 4260400
       E: bishopofaston@cofebirmingham.com

HOLLOWOOD, The Revd Graham *MA,
Dip Min.*
*The Vicarage 1 Skipton Street Oldham Lancashire
OL8 2JF* [MANCHESTER] *b* 1954 *educ* Heysham
High School; Centre for the Study of Jewish
Christian Relations Cambridge; St Stephen's
House Oxford *CV* Trainee, Borough of
Darlington Transport, Management Trainee
1975–78; Traffic Assistant, Borough of
Darlington Transport 1978–79; Chief Traffic
Officer, Merseyside Passenger Transport
Executive, St Helens Division 1980–83;
Divisional Traffic Superintendent, Merseyside
Passenger Transport Executive, Southport
Division, 1983–85; Area Manager, National
Welsh Omnibus Services, Cardiff, 1985–92;
Managing Director, Pedigree Travel, Abertillery
1992–94; Commercial Manager, Cardiff
Bluebird, Cardiff, 1993–96; Marketing Manager,
Phil Anslow Travel Group, Pontypool, 1996–97;
Assistant Curate, Parish of St Julian's, Newport,
1999–2002; Chaplain to 210Sq (1st Mon) ATC.
2001–08; Incumbent, Parish of All Saints,
Newport 2002–08; Part-time Chaplain,
University of Wales, Newport, 2004–08; Wing

Chaplain, East Lancashire Wing Air Training
Corps 2008–11; Incumbent, St Mark with
Christchurch, Glodwick, Oldham from 2008;
Area Dean, Oldham East from 2014
GS 2015–   *T:* 0161 624 4964
           E: graham.hollowood@gmail.com
                               Twitter: @FrGraham1

HOLLYWELL, The Revd Julian Francis
BSc(hons) MA
*St Werburgh's Vicarage Gascoigne Drive Spondon
Derbyshire DE21 7GL* [DERBY] *educ* Ysgol
Uwchradd y Drenewydd, Liverpool University.
University of Westminster. Leeds University
CV Urban Priority Area Officer, Liverpool
Diocese 1996–98; Parish Resources Officer and
Church Urban Fund Officer, Manchester
Diocese 1998–2006; Curate of Christ Church
West Didsbury and St Christopher Withington
2006–08; Vicar of Spondon from 2008; Rural
Dean of Derby North from 2009; Diocesan
Chaplain for Mothers' Union from 2013
GS 2015–   *T:* 01332 673573
               E: fatherjulian@btinternet.com
                                Twitter: @RevJFH

HOLMES, Miss (Millie) Camilla *BSc*
29 Bankfield Terrace Leeds LS4 2RE [LEEDS] *educ*
Hadleigh High School, Colchester County
High School for Girls, University of
Southampton *CV* Intern at St George's
Church, Leeds 2014–15; Lighthouse Pioneer
Pastor in training from 2015
GS 2015–   *T:* 07411 333781
           E: millie.holmes@stgeorgesleeds.org.uk
                              Twitter: @milsholmes

HOLTAM, The Rt Revd Nicholas Roderick
BA, MA, Hon DCL, BD, FKC
*South Canonry 71 The Close Salisbury Wilts SP1
2ER* [BISHOP OF SALISBURY] *educ* Latymer
Grammar School Edmonton; Collingwood
College, Durham; King's College London;
Westcott House Cambridge *CV* Assistant
Curate St Dunstan and All Saints Stepney
1979–83; Tutor Lincoln Theological College
1983–87; Vicar Christ and St John's with St
Luke's Isle of Dogs 1988–95; Vicar St Martin-in
the-Fields 1995–2011; Bishop of Salisbury
from 2011; Trustee National Churches Trust
from 2008; Vice-President Royal School of
Church Music from 2012; Chair Committee
for Ministry of and among Deaf and Disabled
People from 2013
GS 2011–   *T:* 01722 334031
     E: bishop.salisbury@salisbury.anglican.org
                                 F: 01722 4113112

HOME, Mr Oliver Charles Bouverie *MA
(Cantab)*
*c/o Diocese of Bristol 1500 Parkway North
Newbrick Road Bristol BS34 8YU* [DIOCESAN
SECRETARY; BRISTOL] *b* 1979 *educ* University of

Cambridge, Harvard University *CV* Strategic Development Adviser, Diocese of Bristol, 2005–09; Bishop's Chief of Staff, Diocese of Bristol, 2010–14; Diocesan Secretary, Diocese of Bristol from 2014   *T:* 01179060100
          E: oliver.home@bristoldiocese.org

HOWARTH, The Rt Revd Toby Matthew
BA, MA, PhD
47 Kirkgate Shipley BD18 3EH [BISHOP OF BRADFORD; LEEDS] *b* 1962 *educ* Haverstock Comprehensive School, London; Yale University; University of Birmingham; Free University of Amsterdam; Wycliffe Hall, Oxford *CV* Secretary for Inter-religious Affairs for the Archbishop of Canterbury 2011–14; Bishop of Birmingham's Advisor on Inter-faith relations; Bishop of Bradford from 2014
          T: 0113 353 0290
          E: bishop.toby@leeds.anglican.org
          M: 07811 467999
          Twitter: @toby_howarth

HOWELL-JONES, The Very Revd Peter
BMus, PGCE, Dip MM, MA
The Deanery Cathedral Close Blackburn BB1 5AA [DEAN OF BLACKBURN] *b* 1962 *educ* Hillfoot Hey Comprehensive School Liverpool; Huddersfield School of Music; Bretton Hall College; St John's College Nottingham *CV* Assistant Curate St Matthew's Walsall 1993–98; Vicar St Michael's Church Boldmere 1998–2004; Director for Mission and Evangelism and Canon Missioner Birmingham Cathedral 2005–11; Vice Dean Chester Cathedral 2011–17; Dean of Blackburn from 2017; UK Coordinator for Medic Malawi from 2017
          T: 01254 277430
          E: dean@blackburncathedral.co.uk
          M: 07866 778791
          Twitter: @PHJBlackburn

HOYLE, The Very Revd Dr David Michael
MA, PhD
Bristol Cathedral College Green Bristol BS1 5TJ [DEAN OF BRISTOL] *educ* Watford Boys Grammar School; Corpus Christi College Cambridge; Ripon College Cuddesdon *CV* Assistant Curate Good Shepherd Cambridge 1986–1988; Chaplain and Fellow Magdalene College Cambridge 1988–1991; Dean and Fellow Magdalene College Cambridge 1991–1995; Director of Studies Magdalene College Cambridge from 1995; Vicar Christ Church Southgate 1995–2002; Director Post Ordination Training Edmonton Area 2000–2002; Director of Ministry Diocese of Gloucester and Canon Residential Gloucester Cathedral 2002–2010; Dean of Bristol Cathedral from 2010; Secretary House of Bishops Theological Group 2002–2007   *T:* 0117 926 4879
          E: dean@bristol-cathedral.co.uk
          F: 0117 925 3678

HUBBARD, The Revd Julian Richard Hawes
MA (Cantab, Oxon)
Church House Westminster London SW1P 3AZ [DIRECTOR OF MINISTRY, ARCHBISHOPS' COUNCIL] *educ* King Edward VI Grammar School Chelmsford; Emmanuel College Cambridge; Wycliffe Hall Oxford *CV* Curate St Dionis Parsons Green London 1981–84; Chaplain Jesus College Oxford 1984–89; Tutor Wycliffe Hall Oxford 1984–89; Selection Secretary Advisory Council for the Church's Ministry 1989–91; Senior Selection Secretary Advisory Board of Ministry 1991–93; Vicar St Thomas on the Bourne Guildford 1993–99; Rural Dean Farnham 1996–99; Guildford Diocesan Further Education Officer 1993–97; Director Ministerial Training Guildford Diocese 1999–2005; Residential Canon Guildford Cathedral 1999–2005; Archdeacon Oxford and Residential Canon Christ Church 2005–11; Director of Ministry, Archbishops' Council from 2011   *T:* 020 7898 1390
          E: julian.hubbard@churchofengland.org

HUGHES, The Ven Dr Alexander James
MA, PhD
1a Summerfield Cambridge CB3 9HE [ARCHDEACON OF CAMBRIDGE; ELY] *b* 1975 *educ* Priory School, Lewes; Eton College, Greyfriars, Oxford; St Edmund's Cambridge *CV* Assistant Curate, Headington Quarry, Oxford 2000–03; Bishop's Chaplain, Portsmouth 2003–08; Priest-in-Charge, St Luke's Southsea and St Peter's Southsea 2008–14; Archdeacon of Cambridge from 2014   *T:* 01223 355013
                                            01353 652719
          E: archdeacon.cambridge@elydiocese.org

HUGHES, Mr Carl David *MA (Oxon)*
20 Rusholme Road Putney London SW15 3JZ [SOUTHWARK] *b* 1958 *educ* Birkenhead School, St Peter's College, Oxford *CV* Arthur Andersen London 1983; Secondment to Arthur Andersen Melbourne 1987–88; Secondment to BP Exploration/Andersen Consulting 1990–91; Admitted to Arthur Andersen UK partnership 1993; Group Head, Energy, Infrastructure and Utilities, Audit 1996–98; Division Head Commercial Markets Division, Audit 1998–2002; UK Industry Leader Energy, Infrastructure and Utilities 1999–2002; Arthur Andersen UK 1983–2002; UK Industry Leader Energy and Resources, Deloitte UK 2002–11; Global Industry Leader,Energy and Resources, DTTL 2011–15; Member of the Board Deloitte CIS (Russia) 2012–15; Vice Chairman Deloitte UK 2013–15; Senior Audit Partner, Deloitte LLP, UK 2002–15; Senior independent Energy and Resources industry professional and adviser from 2015; Member Council UK Energy Institute from 2015; Member Development Board St Peter's College, Oxford from 2015; Member Diocesan

Synod Southwark; Trustee Southwark Diocesan Council of Trustees; Vice-Chairman Diocesan Board of Finance; Member of Policy and Finance, Audit and Governance and Investment Committees 2015–16; Member Finance Committee Archbishops' Council from 2016; Led Visitation of Peterborough Cathedral on behalf of the Bishop of Peterborough 2016; Non-executive Director and Chairman Audit Committee EnQuest plc from 2016; Member Archbishops' Cathedrals Working Group from 2017
GS 2015–   *T:* 07836 697816
                                  020 8788 0217
            E: cdhughes999@gmail.com

HUGHES, The Ven Paul Vernon *Dip UEM,*
Cert Theol *Oxon*
17 Lansdowne Rd Luton LU3 1EE [ARCHDEACON OF BEDFORD; ST ALBANS] *educ* Pocklington School, East Yorkshire; Polytechnic Central London; Ripon College Cuddesdon *CV* Residential Property Surveyor, Chestertons 1974–79; Curate Chipping Barnet with Arkley 1982–86; Team Vicar Dunstable Team Ministry 1986–93; Vicar Boxmoor 1993–2003; Rural Dean Hemel Hempstead 1996–2003; Archdeacon of Bedford from 2003; Member Diocesan Board of Finance Committees, Diocescan Advisory Committee, Diocesan Pastoral and Mission Committee, Closed Churches Uses Committee, Board for Church and Society, New Development Areas, Bishop's Staff, Bishop's Staff Deployment Group
                                  T: 01582 730722
        E: archdbedf@stalbans.anglican.org
                                  F: 01582 877354

HUMPHREYS, Mrs Jennifer Ann *BA*
34 Riverside Banwell North Somerset BS29 6EE [BATH AND WELLS] *b* 1967 *educ* Wesley College Bristol *CV* World Mission Adviser Bath and Wells 1998–16; Honorary Canon Lusaka Cathedral Zambia
GS 2010–   *T:* 01934 822052
                                  01749 670777
         E: jenny@humphreys.eclipse.co.uk
    jenny.humphreys@bathwells.anglican.org

HUNTER, Lt Col Jane Fiona *BA, MSc,*
PGCE(FE)
SO1 Education Sandhurst Group HQ The Royal Military Academy Sandhurst Camberley GU15 4PQ [ARMED FORCES SYNOD] *b* 1954 *educ* King Edward VI Lichfield, Abbots Bromley School, College of Ripon and York St John, Royal Military College of Science (Cranfield); studying for PhD *CV* Commissioned into the Army 1992; Junior officer jobs based in Germany and the UK included a tour with the UN to Bosnia 1992–96; Adjutant at the Defence School of Languages and then staff jobs 1997–2002; Full time Masters programme

2002–03; Officer in Charge/Officer Tutor (Cyprus) 2003–06; Staff Jobs in HQ 2006–09; Chief Instructor Army Foundation College 2009–11; Commander Education 2011–14; Staff Officer 1 – Assurance Army Headquarters
GS 2014   *T:* 01276 412322
            E: jane.hunter161@mod.gov.uk

HUTCHINSON, The Revd (Andrew) Paul
MA, BTh
The Rectory Leven Close Stokesley North Yorkshire TS9 5AP [YORK] *educ* Durham School, Trinity Hall Cambridge; College of Law, Chester; Ripon College, Cuddesdon *CV* Solicitor 1990–4; Curate Stanley 1997–99; Chaplain Sunderland University and Curate/Team Vicar Sunderland 1999–2002; Team Vicar Penrith etc and Chaplain Newton Rigg Campus 2002–09; Rector Stokesley with Seamer from 2009; Ecumenical Adviser, Cleveland Archdeaconry 2012–17
GS 2013–   *T:* 01642 710405
        E: paul.hutchinson5@btinternet.com
                       Twitter: @PaulHutch5

HUTCHINSON, The Ven Karen Elizabeth
MA (Oxon), MA, Ox Dip Min
31 Bracondale Norwich NR1 2AT [ARCHDEACON OF NORWICH] *educ* Surbiton High School; Lady Margaret Hall Oxford; Guildford College of Law; University of Kent; Wycliffe Hall Oxford *CV* Curate St Lawrence Alton 2001–06; Vicar Crondall and Ewshot 2006–12; Vicar United Benefice of The Bourne and Tilford 2012–16; Honorary Canon Guildford Cathedral 2013–16; Diocesan Advisor in Women's Ministry 2010–16, Archdeacon of Norwich from 2016; Warden of Readers from 2016
GS 2013–   *T:* 01603 620007
              E: archdeacon.norwich@
                   dioceseofnorwich.org

INGE, The Rt Revd Dr John Geoffrey *BSc,*
PGCE, MA, PhD, Hon DLitt
Bishop's Office The Old Palace Deansway Worcester WR1 2JE [BISHOP OF WORCESTER] *educ* Kent College Canterbury; Durham University; Keble College Oxford; College of the Resurrection Mirfield *CV* Assistant Chaplain Lancing College 1984–86; Junior Chaplain Harrow School 1986–89; Senior Chaplain 1989–90; Vicar Wallsend St Luke, Newcastle 1990–96; Residential Canon Ely Cathedral 1996–2003, Vice Dean 1999–2003; Bishop of Huntingdon 2003–07; Member Council Ridley Hall from 2004; Trustee, Common Purpose from 2005, Trust Protector from 2011; Bishop of Worcester from 2007; Visitor, Community of the Holy Name from 2007; Visitor Mucknell Community from 2009; Chair College of Evangelists from 2010; Member Faith and Order Commission from 2010; Honorary Doctor of Letters University

Worcester 2011; Chair Council Archbishops' Examination in Theology from 2012
$\qquad$ *T:* 01905 731599
$\qquad$ *E:* bishop.worcester@cofe-worcester.org.uk
$\qquad$ *F:* 01905 739382

INNES, The Rt Revd Dr Robert Neil *MA, BA, PhD*
47 rue Capitaine Crespel boite 49 1050 Brussels Belgium 1050 [BISHOP OF THE DIOCESE IN EUROPE] *educ* Royal Grammar School Guildford, King's College Cambridge University, St John's College Durham University *CV* Curate St Cuthbert's Durham 1995–97; Lecturer St John's College Durham 1995–99; Curate Sherburn with Pittington Durham 1997–99; Priest in Charge Belmont, Durham 1999–2000; Vicar 2000–05; Senior Chaplain and Chancellor Pro-Cathedral of Holy Trinity Brussels 2005–14; Bishop of the Diocese in Europe from 2014
GS 2014 $\qquad$ *T:* ++32 (0)2 213 7480
$\qquad$ ++32 (0)2 351 2635
$\qquad$ *E:* bishop.europe@churchofengland.org
$\qquad$ *W:* www.europe.anglican.org

IPGRAVE, The Rt Revd Michael Geoffrey *PhD, MA, OBE*
Bishop's House 22 The Close LIchfield WS13 7LG [BISHOP OF LICHFIELD] *b* 1952 *educ* Magdalen College School, Brackley; Oriel College Oxford; St Chad's College Durham; School of Oriental and African Studies, London University; Ripon College Cuddesdon *CV* Deacon 1982; Priest 1983 (Peterborough); Curate All Saints Oakham with Hambleton and Egleton, and Braunston with Brooke, Peterborough 1982–85; Assistant Priest The Resurrection, Chiba, Yokohama, Japan 1985–87; Team Vicar The Ascension, Leicester 1987–90; Team Vicar The Holy Spirit, Leicester 1990–94; Priest in Charge St Mary de Castro, Leicester 1994–95; Team Rector The Holy Spirit, Leicester 1995–99; Diocesan Advisor on Inter Faith Relations 1990–99; Bishop's Chaplain 1990–99; Honorary Assistant Priest The Presentation, Leicester 1999–2004; Honorary Canon Leicester Cathedral 1994–2004; Inter Faith Relations Advisor, Archbishops Council 1999–2004; Secretary Churches Commission on Inter Faith Relations 1999–2004; Archdeacon of Southwark 2004–12; Canon Missioner Southwark Cathedral 2010–12; Bishop of Woolwich 2012–16; Bishop of Lichfield from 2016 $\qquad$ *T:* 01543 306001
$\qquad$ *E:* bishop.michael@lichfield.anglican.org
$\qquad$ *F:* 01543 306009

IRELAND, The Ven Mark Campbell *MTheol, MA*
19 Clarence Park Blackburn BB2 7FA [ARCHDEACON OF BLACKBURN] *b* 1960 *educ* St Andrew's University; Sheffield University; Wycliffe Hall

Oxford *CV* Curate Blackburn 1984–7; Curate Lancaster 1987–89; Vicar Baxenden 1989–97, Lichfield Diocese 1998–2016, Blackburn Diocese from 2016; Archdeacon of Blackburn from 2016
GS 1995–98 and 2005–2015
$\qquad$ *T:* 01254 262571/01254 958836
$\qquad$ *E:* mark.ireland@blackburn.anglican.org
$\qquad$ *W:* https://markcireland.com
$\qquad$ *M:* 07866 778791
$\qquad$ *Twitter:* @Markcireland

ISON, The Very Revd David John *BA, PhD, DPS, FKC*
The Chapter House St Paul's Churchyard London EC4M 8AD [DEAN OF ST PAUL'S; LONDON] *educ* Brentwood School; Leicester University; Nottingham University; St John College Nottingham; King's College London; *CV* Curate St Nicholas with St Luke Deptford, Southwark 1979–85; Tutor, Church Army Training College 1985–88; Vicar St Philip Potters Green, Coventry 1988–93; Diocesan Officer for Continuing Ministerial Education, Exeter 1993–2005; Residential Canon Exeter 1995–2005; Dean of Bradford 2005–12; Dean of St Paul's from 2012; Member of Crown Nominations Commission from 2017
GS 1990–93, 2010–12, 2013–
$\qquad$ *T:* 020 7246 8360
$\qquad$ *E:* dean@stpaulscathedral.org.uk
$\qquad$ *W:* www.stpauls.co.uk

JACKSON, The Rt Revd Richard Charles *MA, MSc, DipHE*
Ebenezer House Kingston Ridge Kingston Lewes BN7 3JU [AREA BISHOP OF LEWES; CHICHESTER] *educ* Latymer Upper School; Christ Church, Oxford; Cranfield University; Trinity College Bristol *CV* Senior Agronomist, Cleanacres Ltd 1985–92; Curate All Saints, Lindfield 1994–98; Vicar Rudgwick 1998–2009; Diocesan Readers Committee 1999–2004; Archdeaconry Warden of Readers 1999–2004; Rural Dean of Horsham, 2004–09; Diocesan Advisor Mission and Renewal 2009–14; Bishop of Lewes from 2014
GS 2010–14 $\qquad$ *T:* 01273 425009
$\qquad$ *E:* bishop.lewes@chichester.anglican.org
$\qquad$ *W:* www.chichester.anglican.org

JAGGER, The Ven Ian *MA, MA*
15 The College Durham DH1 3EQ [ARCHDEACON OF DURHAM] *b* 1967 *educ* Huddersfield New College; King's College Cambridge; St John's College Durham *CV* Curate St Mary Virgin Twickenham London 1982–85; Priest in Charge Willen, Milton Keynes Oxford 1985–87; Team Vicar Willen, Stantonbury Local Ecumenical Project 1987–94; Chaplain Willen Hospice 1985–94; Director Milton Keynes Christian Training Scheme 1986–94; Team Rector Fareham Holy Trinity Portsmouth

1994–98; Ecumenical Officer Portsmouth Diocese 1994–96; Rural Dean Fareham 1996–98; Canon Residential Portsmouth Cathedral and Diocesan Missioner 1998–2001; Archdeaon of Auckland 2001–06; Archdeacon of Durham and Canon Residential Durham Cathedral from 2006
GS 2002–   *T:* 0191 384 7534
                    E: archdeacon.of.durham@
                    durham.anglican.org

JAMES, The Rt Revd Graham Richard *BA*
Bishop's House Norwich NR3 1SB [BISHOP OF NORWICH] *educ* Northampton Grammar School; Lancaster University; Cuddesdon Theological College *CV* Curate Christ Carpenter Peterborough 1975–78; Curate Digswell 1978–82; Team Rector Digswell 1982–83; Selection Secretary and Secretary for Continuing Ministerial Education Advisory Council for the Church's Ministry 1983–85; Senior Selection Secretary 1985–87; Chaplain to Archbishop of Canterbury 1987–93; Bishop of St Germans 1993–99; Bishop of Norwich from 1999; Member Board of Countryside Agency 2001–06; Chair Rural Bishops Panel 2001–06; Chair Central Religious Advisory Committee, BBC and Ofcom 2004–08; Member Archbishops' Council from 2006; Chair Ministry Division 2006–12; Chair Standing Conference on Religion and Belief, BBC 2009–11; Member HoL Selection Committee on Communications from 2011
GS 1995–   *T:* 01603 629001
                    E: bishop@dioceseofnorwich.org
                    F: 01603 761613
                    W: www.dioceseofnorwich.org

JAMES, Mr Philip John *B SocSc*
Church House Great Smith St London SW1P 3AZ [HEAD OF (RESOURCE) STRATEGY AND DEVELOPMENT UNIT, CHURCH COMMISSIONERS AND ARCHBISHOPS' COUNCIL] *b* 1967 *educ* Bristol Grammar School; Birmingham University *CV* On staff of Church Commissioners from 1988; Head of Policy Unit from 1999; Head of (Resource) Strategy and Development Unit, Church Commissioners and Archbishops' Council from 2009   *T:* 020 7898 1671
                    E: philip.james@churchofengland.org

JEANS, The Ven Alan Paul *BTh, MIAS, MIBC, MA*
Herbert House 118 Lower Rd Salisbury SP2 9NW [ARCHDEACON OF SARUM; SALISBURY] *b* 1954 *educ* Bournemouth School; Dorset Institute of Higher Education; Southampton University; Sarum and Wells Theological College; University Wales Lampeter *CV* Curate Parkstone Team 1989–93; Priest in Charge Bishop Cannings, All Cannings and Etchilhampton 1993–98; Diocesan Advisor for Parish Development 1998–2005; Member

Diocesan Advisory Committee; Archdeacon of Sarum from 2003; Assistant Diocesan Director of Ordinands 2005–07; Rural Dean Alderbury 2005–07; Diocesan Director of Ordinands 2007–13; Chair of Diocesan Council for Mission from 2015
GS 2000–05, 2010–15, 2015–
                    T: 01722 438662 (Office)
                    E: adsarum@salisbury.anglican.org
                    F: 01722 411990
                    W: www.salisbury.anglican.org
                    Twitter: @alanpjeans

JENKINS, The Ven Dr David Harold *MA, PhD*
Sudbury Lodge Stanningfield Road Bury St Edmunds IP30 0TL [ARCHDEACON OF SUDBURY; ST EDMUNDSBURY AND IPSWICH] *educ* Belfast Royal Academy; Sidney Sussex College Cambridge; Ripon College Cuddesdon; University Wales: Lampeter *CV* Assistant Curate Good Shepherd Cambridge 1989–1991; Assistant Curate St Peter's Earley Reading 1991–1994; Vicar St Michael and All Angels Blackpool 1994–1999; Vicar St John Baptist Broughton Preston 1999–2004; Diocesan Director of Education Carlisle 2004–10; Residential Canon Carlisle Cathedral 2004–10; Archdeacon of Sudbury from 2010   *T:* 01284 386942
                    E: archdeacon.david@cofesuffolk.org

JENKINS, Canon Gary John *BA, PGCE, BA, MTh*
4 Thurland Road London SE16 4AA [SOUTHWARK] *educ* Sir Walter St John's School, Battersea University of York Oak Hill *CV* Curate St Luke's, West Norwood 1989–94; Vicar St Peter's, St Helier, 1994–2001; Vicar, Holy Trinity, Redhill 2001–12; Member Southwark Theology Issues Group, 2005–10; Member Southwark Diocesan Synod from 2001; Area Dean Reigate 2012; Vicar St James and St Anne, Bermondsey from 2012
GS 2010–   *T:* 020 7394 6449
                    E: garyjjenkins@outlook.com

JEPSON, Dr Rachel Margaret Elizabeth *BEd (Hons), MA, PhD, TEFL, FIMA*
56a Upland Rd Selly Park Birmingham B29 7JS [BIRMINGHAM] *educ* Edgbaston CE College for Girls; University College of St Martin Lancaster; University of Gloucestershire with Trinity College Bristol; St John's College Durham *CV* Teacher Grove School Handsworth 1993–98; Residential Tutor St John College Durham 1998–2002; Member Diocesan Board of Education to 2006; General Synod Representative, Churches Together in England Forum and Churches Together in Britain and Ireland Assembly; Appointment Member Revision Committee Care of Cathedrals Measure 2002; Appointment Member Additional Collects Revision Committee 2003;

Member Birmingham Diocesan Bishop's Council; Member Birmingham Standing Advisory Council for Religious Education; Teacher (Phase Leader, RE Co-ordinator), Rookery School, Handsworth from 2007; Appointment Revision Committee C of E (Misc Provisions) Measure 2008; Vice-Chair PCC St Martin in the Bull Ring Birmingham Parish Church 2008–11; Appointment Member Governing Body Queen's Foundation Birmingham 2012; Council for Christian Unity 2013; Member Steering Committee Clergy Discipline and Safeguarding Measure 2013
GS 2000–   *T:* 0121 472 2064
E: rachel.jepson@tiscali.co.uk

JOHN, The Very Revd Jeffrey Philip Hywel *MA, DPhil, DLitt*
The Deanery Sumpter Yard St Albans AL1 1BY [DEAN OF ST ALBANS] *educ* Tonyrefail Grammar School; Hertford College Oxford; Brasenose College Oxford; Magdalen College Oxford; St Stephen's House *CV* Curate St Augustine Penarth 1978–80; Assistant Chaplain Magdalen College Oxford 1980–82; Chaplain and lecturer Brasenose College Oxford 1982–84; Fellow and Dean of Divinity Magdalen College Oxford 1984–91; Vicar Holy Trinity Eltham 1991–97; Director of Training Southwark Diocese and Canon Theologian and Chancellor Southwark Cathedral 1997–2004; Member General Synod Standing Committee 1996–2000; Member General Synod Appointments Committee 1995–2000; Member Southwark Diocesan Synod, Bishop's Council 1997–2004; Dean of St Albans from 2004; Hon DLitt University of Hertfordshire 2015   *T:* 01727 890202
E: dean@stalbanscathedral.org
F: 01727 890227

JOHNSON, Mrs Carolyn Ann *LLB*
Brook House Bilsborrow Preston PR3 0RD [BLACKBURN] *b* 1952 *educ* Elmslie C of E Girls Grammar School; Manchester University *CV* Barrister-at-law from 1974; Chairman Preston Acute Hospitals NHS Trust 1994–97; Governor Myerscough College; Director Cidari Blackburn Diocese Multi Academy Trist 2014–
GS 2015–   *T:* 07939 579257
E: carolyn_johnson@talk21.com

JOHNSTON, The Revd Canon Geoffrey Stanley *MBA, DipTh*
29 Little Fallows Milford Belper Derbyshire DE56 0RY [ARCHDEACON OF GIBRALTAR; EUROPE] *educ* Gillingham Grammar School, Wolverhampton University, Aston University *CV* Assistant Curate Christ Church Blakenall Heath, Walsall 1968–75; Assistant Curate St Stephen Willenhall 1975–76; Lecturer, West Bromwich College of Commerce and Technology 1978–82; Industrial Chaplain in BCUIM and Team Vicar in Halesowen 1982–94; Information

Officer for MEP (Also NSM St Francis Dudley) 1994–99; Priest in Charge St Francis, Dudley 1999–2008; Priest in Charge, Anglican Parish of Nerja and Almunecar, Spain 2008–2014; Archdeacon of Gibraltar from 2014
T: 01773 270972
07507 391297
E: vengeoffrey@gmail.com

JOLLEY, The Ven Andy *PhD, MBA, BTh, BSc*
1 Selborne Grove Bradford BD9 4NL [ARCHDEACON OF BRADFORD; LEEDS] *b* 1956 *educ* Loughborough Grammar School; University of Nottingham; Warwick Business School; St John's Nottingham *CV* Ford Motor Company 1983–1987; Deloitte Haskins & Sells/Coopers & Lybrand 1988–95; Curate St John's Sparkhill 1998–2002, Vicar Aston 2002–08, Priest in charge St Matthew Nechells and St James Aston 2005–08, Vicar Aston and Nechells 2008–16, Area Dean Aston 2005–12, Honorary Canon Birmingham Cathedral 2015–16; Archdeacon of Bradford from 2016; Diocesan Synod Birmingham 1999–2016; Crown Nominations Commission 2006, Member of Bishop's Council Birmingham 2007–16, Chair of Mission Apprentice Scheme Birmingham 2011–16, Birmingham Cathedral Council 2011–12; Vice Chair Diocesan Board of Education Leeds from 2016
T: 0113 353 0290
E: andy.jolley@leeds.anglican.org
M: 07973 458403
Twitter: @AndyJolley1

JONES, Mrs (Helen) Mary *BSc, MA, PGCE, DEd*
108 Church Road Gateshead NE9 5XE [DURHAM] *b* 1956 *educ* Astley Grammar School Dukinfield; Salford University; Manchester University; Newcastle University *CV* Headteacher Beacon Mill School Wallsend
GS 2015–   *T:* 07505 105184
E: djnell026@blueyonder.co.uk
Twitter: @helengateshead

JONES, Canon Joyce Rosemary *MA*
Oakfield 206 Barnsley Road Denby Dale Huddersfield HD8 8TS [LEEDS] *educ* King Edward VI High School Birmingham; Cambridge University; Newnham College; NOC *CV* Assistant Curate All Saints Pontefract 1997–2000; Vocations Advisor, Assistant Chaplain Kirkwood Hospice and Assistant Curate Cumberworth Denby and Denby Dale 2000–01; Priest in Charge Shelley and Shepley 2001–16; Bishop's Advisor for Prayer and Spirituality 2005–11; Rural Dean Kirkburton from 2011; Vicar Cumberworth, Denby, Denby Dale and Shepley from 2016
GS 2010–   *T:* 01484 862350
E: joycerjones@aol.com
F: 01484 862350

JONES, Canon Julie *BSc*
St Marys House The Close Lichfield WS13 7LD
[DIOCESAN SECRETARY; LICHFIELD] *educ* Stafford
Girls' High School, University of Bath *CV*
British Aerospace, Personnel Manager 1984–
89; KPMG, Executive Consultant 1989–94;
Barkers Advertising, HR Director 1994–2001;
Mission Aviation Fellowship, HR Director
2002–09; Chief Executive Officer and
Diocesan Secretary from 2009
                    T: 01543 306291
                        07803 127319
    E: julie.jones@lichfield.anglican.org

JONES, The Ven Robert George *BA, MA*
Archdeacon's House Walkers Lane Whittington
Worcester WR5 2RE [ARCHDEACON OF WORCESTER]
b 1967 *educ* King Edward's, Birmingham;
Hatfield College, Durham; Ripon College
Cuddesdon; Oxford University Ecumenical
Institute, Bossey, Geneva *CV* Assistant Curate,
Kidderminster Holy Innocents 1980–84;
Vicar, Dudley St Francis 1984–92; Team Rector
Worcester St Barnabas with Christ Church
1992–2008; Rural Dean Worcester East 2001–
07; Diocesan Director of Development 2008–
14; Archdeacon of Worcester from 2014
GS 1995–2005   *T:* 01905 773301
        E: archdeacon.worcester@
            cofe-worcester.org.uk

JONES, Canon Sharon Ann *BA, CertTh*
St Andrew's Vicarage Arm Road Dearnley OL15
8NJ [MANCHESTER] *b* 1960 *educ* St Katherine
College Liverpool; Cranmer Hall Durham *CV*
Department of Social Security 1985; Rubery
Birmingham 1985–89; Parish Deacon 1987–
89; Curate in Charge Chelmsley Wood St
Augustine Conventional District 1989–92;
Permission to Officiate Newcastle 1992–93;
Chaplain HM Prison Acklington 1993–97;
Chaplain HM Young Offenders Institute
Castington 1997–2000; Chaplain HM Prison
Forest Bank 2000–06; Priest in Charge
Dearnley Manchester from 2006; Area Dean
Salford 2003–06; Area Dean Rochdale 2006–15
GS 2010–   *T:* 01706 378466
    E: dearnleyvicarage@yahoo.com
                    M: 07738 96627

KAVANAGH, The Ven Michael (Mike)
Lowther *BA, BA, MSc*
National Offender Management Service Chaplaincy
HQ Post Point 4.08 Clive House 70 Petty France
London SW1H 9EX [GENERAL SYNOD EX-OFFICIO]
educ Beverley Grammar School; Acklam 6th
Form College; York University; Leeds
University; Newcastle University; Mirfield
College of the Resurrection *CV* Curate Boston
Spa and Chaplain Martin House Hospice 1987–
91; Curate St Luke Clifford 1989–91; Vicar
Beverley St Nicholas and Archbishop's Advisor
in Spiritual Direction 1991–97; Rural Dean

Beverley 1995–97; Archbishop of York's
Domestic Chaplain and Diocesan Director of
Ordinands 1997–2005; Prison Chaplain Full
Sutton 2005–8; Anglican Advisor to HM Prison
Service 2008–13; Acting Head of Chaplaincy
2012–13; Head of NOMS Chaplaincy and Faith
Services from 2013; Archdeacon to Prisons
from 2014
GS 2014–   *T:* 07807 509720
    E: michael.kavanagh@noms.gsi.gov.uk

KAY, The Revd Peter Richard *BA, MA*
The Vicarage Thurleigh Road Milton Ernest
Bedfordshire MK44 1RF [ST ALBANS] *b* 1972 *educ*
De Aston School, Market Rasen, Lincolnshire,
St Catharine's College, Cambridge *CV* Credit
Analyst, Phillips Petroleum 1997–2001; Credit
Analyst, Leaseplan UK Ltd 2002–05;
Accountancy Lecturer, FTC Ltd 2005–06;
Chartered Management Accountant, Mouchel
PLC 2007–09; Priest-in-Charge of the Benefice
of Milton Ernest, Pavenham and Thurleigh
from 2014
GS 2015–   *T:* 01234 918027
                        07718 201449
    E: rev.peter.kay@outlook.com

KELLY, Mr Declan Gerard *MSc, BSc, MCLIP*
Church House Great Smith St London SW1P 3AZ
[DIRECTOR OF LIBRARIES AND ARCHIVES, CHURCH
COMMISSIONERS] *b* 1960 *educ* St Hugh's College
Nottingham; Queen Mary College London;
Sheffield University *CV* Research Centre
Manager, BBC World Service 1993–97; Intake
and Acquisitions Manager, BBC Archives
1997–99, Research Services Manager 2000–03;
Output Services Manager 2003–05; Director
of Libraries, Archives and IT, Church
Commissioners from 2005
                    T: 020 7898 1432
    E: declan.kelly@churchofengland.org
        W: www.lambethpalacelibrary.org

KEMP, Mr David Stephen
11 Ham Shades Lane Whitstable Kent CT5 1NT
[CANTERBURY] *educ* Simon Langton Grammar
School, Canterbury *CV* Secretary Herne Bay
Building Society 1978–86; Deputy CEO, Kent
Reliance Building Society 1986–90; Diocesan
Secretary, Canterbury 1990–2007; Governor
Canterbury Christ Church University 2006;
Chair Canterbury Diocese Child Protection
Management Group from 2007
GS 2010–   *T:* 01227 272470
    E: kemps11@btinternet.com

KENNAUGH, Mrs Susan
Beaulieu 2 Upper Dukes Road Douglas Isle of Man
IM2 4BA [SODOR AND MAN] *b* 1954 *educ* St
Ninian's High School Douglas *CV* Church
Commissioners Sodor and Man; Trustee
Mothers' Union Sodor and Man; Bishop's

Representative Council of the United Society; Pensions Consultant Boal & Co 2007
T: 07624 432278
E: mskennaugh@manx.net

KERRY, Mr Jonathan William MA, BD
St Martins House 7 Peacock Lane Leicester LE1 1SY [DIOCESAN SECRETARY; LEICESTER] *b* 1956 *educ* Strode's School, Egham, Surrey, University of Cambridge, University of Manchester, Open University, University of Warwick *CV* Traffic Manager, British Rail 1977–1981; Administrative Officer, Methodist Association of Youth Clubs 1981–1985; Circuit Minister, Methodist Church 1988–2001; Coordinating Secretary, Methodist Church Connexional Team 2001–08; Director, Guy Chester Centre, London 2009–11; Chief Executive, Diocesan Secretary and Cathedral Administrator, Leicester from 2011
T: 0116 261 5326
E: jonathan.kerry@leccofe.org

KIDDLE, The Ven John MA, MTh
620 Kingston Road Raynes Park London SW20 8DN [ARCHDEACON OF WANDSWORTH; SOUTHWARK] *educ* Monkton Combe School; Queens' College Cambridge; Heythrop College, University of London; Ridley Hall, Cambridge *CV* Assistant Curate, Ormskirk Parish Church, 1982–86; Vicar, St Gabriel's Church Huyton Quarry, 1986–91; Vicar, St Luke's Church Watford, 1991–08; Rural Dean of Watford, 1999–04; Honorary Canon St Albans Cathedral 2005–10; Officer Mission and Development, St Albans from 2008; Residential Canon St Albans Cathedral from 2010; Director Mission St Albans 2011–15; Archdeacon of Wandsworth from 2015; Member Diocesan Synod 1986–89; Secretary Board Mission and Unity 1986–89; Member Diocesan Synod 1997–2000; Member Diocesan Pastoral Committee 1997–2000; Member Bedford Deanery Review 1999–2000; Chair Luton Deanery Review Group 2003–04; Chair Diocesan Vision for Action Group 2004–06; Executive Officer Board Church and Society from 2008
GS 2010–15
T: 020 8545 2440
E: john.kiddle@southwark.anglican.org
F: 020 8545 2441
M: 07590 636966

KING, The Ven Robin Lucas Colin MA
The House The Street Bradwell Braintree CM77 8EL [ARCHDEACON OF STANSTED; CHELMSFORD] *educ* King's School Canterbury; Dundee University; Ridley Hall *CV* Curate St Augustines, Ipswich 1989–92; Vicar Bures with Assington and Little Cornard 1992–2013; Rural Dean Sudbury 2006–13; Honorary Canon St Edmundsbury Cathedral 2009–13; Archdeacon of Stansted from 2013
T: 01376 563662
E: a.stansted@chelmsford.anglican.org

KINGSTON, Mr (William) Martin LLB
Kemble House Kemble Cirencester Gloucestershire GL7 6AD [GLOUCESTER] *b* 1949 *educ* Middlewich Secondary Modern, Liverpool University *CV* Asstistant Recorder 1987–91; Recorder 1991–2000; Asstistant Parliamentary Boundary Commissioner from 1992; Deputy Chairman Agricultural Lands Tribunal; Queens Counsel from 1992
GS 2015–
T: 01285 771133
01285 771040
E: mk@no5.com
Twitter: @kingstonwm

KIRK, The Ven Gavin John BTh, MA
Edward King House The Old Palace Lincoln LN2 1PU [ARCHDEACON OF LINCOLN] *CV* Assistant Curate, Seaford-cum-Sutton 1986–89; Succentor Rochester Cathedral 1989–91; Head of Classics and Assistant Chaplain, The King's School, Rochester, 1991–98; Canon Residential and Precentor Portsmouth Cathedral 1998–2003; Canon Residential and Precentor, Lincoln Cathedral from 2003; Chair Portsmouth Bishop's Advisory Group for Worship 1998–2003; Trustee NTMTS 2001–03; Warden Community Holy Cross from 2006; Chair Lincoln Diocesan Liturgy Committee from 2008; Church Bishop's Advisory Group for Prayer and Spirituality from 2011; Archdeacon of Lincoln from 2016
GS 2000–03; 2010–
T: 01522 504039
E: archdeacon.lincoln@lincoln.anglican.org

KUTAR, Mrs Diane Leslie BSc (Hons), MA
22 The Kiln Burgess Hill West Sussex RH15 0LU [CHICHESTER] *b* 1968 *educ* Selwyn Jones High School, University of Bradford/University of Brighton *CV* Credit Officer, HSBC 1991–94; Senior Business Banking Officer, HSBC 1994–95; Account Manager, HSBC 1995–97; Branch Manager, Barnoldswick, HSBC 1997–99; Senior Credit Officer, HSBC 1999–2000; Branch Manager, South Shields, HSBC 2000–01; Commercial Banking Manager, Newcastle, HSBC 2001–05; PGCE training, Brighton 2005–06; NQT Teacher, UCTC 2006–07; Head of Department, Oakmeeds Community College, 2007–13; Finance Manager St Andrew's Pre-school from 2013; Site Co-ordinator St Andrew's Church from 2013
GS 2015–
T: 01444 870509
07887 992257
E: diane@dkutar.com

LAIN-PRIESTLY, The Ven Rosemary Jane BA, MA
London Diocesan House 36 Causton Street London SW1P 4AU [ARCHDEACON OF THE TWO CITIES; LONDON] *b* 1967 *educ* Park High School Colne; University of Kent at Canterbury; Carlisle Diocesan Training Institute *CV* Curate St Paul's Scotforth 1996–98; Assistant Priest, St-Martin-in-the-Fields 1998–2002, Associate

Vicar 2002–06; Dean of Women's Ministry, Two Cities Area 2006–16; Archdeacon of the Two Cities from 2016; Trustee Sandford St Martin's Trust 2006–11; Trustee SPCK 2008–15; Chair National Association of Diocesan Advisers in Women's Ministry 2011–15; Member Transformations Steering Group from 2011; Council Member St Augustine's College of Theology from 2016; Member Archbishops' Project Review Group from 2016
T: 020 3837 5205
E: archdeacon.twocities@london.anglican.org
W: https://rosemarylainpriestley.com
Twitter: @Rose44Lain

LAKE, The Very Revd Stephen David *BTh, MA*
The Deanery 1 Miller's Green Gloucester GL1 2BP [DEAN OF GLOUCESTER] *b* 1952 *educ* Homefield School Dorset; Chichester Theological College *CV* Curate Sherborne Abbey 1988–92; Vicar St Aldhelm Branksome 1992–2001; Rural Dean Poole 2000–01; Canon Residential and Sub Dean St Albans Cathedral 2001–11; Dean of Gloucester from 2011; Member National Safeguarding Steering Group
GS 2003–10   *T:* 01452 524167
E: dean@gloucestercathedral.org.uk
W: www.gloucestercathedral.org.uk
M: 07900 988646

LAMMING, Mr David John *LLB, LLM*
20 Holbrook Barn Road Boxford Sudbury Suffolk CO10 5HU [ST EDMUNDSBURY AND IPSWICH] *b* 1947 *educ* Christ's College Finchley, University College London *CV* Lecturer/Senior Lecturer in Law, Mid-Essex Technical College and School of Art (now Anglia Ruskin University) 1969–74; Barrister in private practice at Cornerstone Barristers, from 1975
GS 2015–   *T:* 01787 210360
        07968 791135
E: djlamming@hotmail.com
F: 01787 329770

LAND, Dr Nick (Nicholas Mark) *MA, MB BS, FRCPsych*
Low Farm House Ingleby Greenhow Great Ayton North Yorkshire TS9 6RG [YORK] *b* 1955 *educ* Thurston Upper School, Cambridge University and Newcastle University *CV* Training Posts in Psychiatry 1987–94; Newcastle City Councillor 1988–94; Programme Director LD Psychiatry Higher Training Scheme – Northern Deanery 2000–09; Clinical Director Forensic and Learning Disability Psychiatry TEWV NHS FT 2007–09; Consultant Psychiatrist TEWV NHSFT from 1994; Executive Medical Director TEWV NHSFT from 2010; Responsible Officer (NHS England/GMC) for TEWV NHS FT from 2012; Chair House of Laity York Diocesan Synod from 2012
GS 2015–   *T:* 01642 778076
E: drnickland@aol.com

LANE, The Rt Revd Libby (Elizabeth) Jane Holden *MA (Oxon)*
Bishop's Lodge Back Lane Dunham Town Altrincham WA14 4SG [BISHOP OF STOCKPORT; CHESTER] *educ* Manchester High School For Girls, St Peter's, Oxford *CV* Assistant Curate, Diocese of Blackburn, 1993–96; Family Life Officer, CSR, Diocese of Chester, 2000–03; Team Vicar, Stockport Southwest, Diocese of Chester, 2003–07; Assistant Diocesan Director of Ordinands, Diocese of Chester, 2005–07; Vicar of Hale and Ashley, Diocese of Chester, 2007–15; Dean of Women in Ministry, Diocese of Chester, 2010–15; Bishop of Stockport from 2015
T: 0161 928 5611
E: bpstockport@chester.anglican.org

LANGHAM, The Revd Paul Jonathan *BA, DipTh., MA*
9 Leigh Road Clifton Bristol BS8 2DA [BRISTOL] *b* 1954 *educ* Queen Elizabeth Grammar, Kirkby Lonsdale, The University of Exeter, The University of Cambridge *CV* Curate, All Saints Weston, Bath, 1987–91; Chaplain, St Catharine's College, Cambridge 1991–96; Vicar, Holy Trinity, Combe Down with St Michael and All Angels, Monkton Combe and St James the Great, South Stoke, 1996–2010; Deputy Rural Dean of Bath, 2003–10; Vicar, Christ Church Clifton, Bristol from 2010
GS 2005–10, 2015–   *T:* 0117 973 6524
E: paul.langham@ccweb.org.uk

LANGSTAFF, The Rt Revd James Henry *MA (Oxon), BA*
Bishopscourt St Margaret's Street Rochester ME1 1TS [BISHOP OF ROCHESTER] *educ* Cheltenham College; Oxford University; Nottingham University; St John's College Nottingham *CV* Curate St Peter Farnborough, Guildford 1981–86, Priest in Charge 1985–86; Priest in Charge St Matthew Duddeston and St Clement Nechells, Birmingham 1986, Vicar 1987–96; Rural Dean Birmingham City 1995–96; Chaplain to Bishop of Birmingham 1996–2000; Rector Holy Trinity Sutton Coldfield, Birmingham 2000–04; Area Dean of Sutton Coldfield 2002–04; Bishop of Lynn 2004–10; Bishop of Rochester from 2010; Chair Flagship Housing Group 2006–10; Member E of England Regional Assembly 2007–10; Chair Housing Justice from 2008; Bishop to HM Prisons from 2013
GS 2010–   *T:* 01634 842721
E: bishop.rochester@rochester.anglican.org
M: 07551 007560

LAWES, Dr Mike (Michael) Robert *MA, MB, BS*
Ashdown House 11 Hungershall Park Tunbridge Wells Kent TN4 8NE [ROCHESTER] *b* 1954 *educ* Price's School, Fareham, Selwyn College, Cambridge. King's College Hospital Medical School, London *CV* House Surgeon, Tunbridge

Wells 1979; House Physician, Whipp's Cross 1979–80; Casualty Officer, Whipp's Cross 1980; GP Vocational Training Scheme, Tunbridge Wells 1980–83; Senior Partner, Rusthall Medical Centre, Tunbridge Wells from 1984; GP Trainer from 1989; GP Appraiser from 2004; Director Crossways Community, Tunbridge Wells (Mental Health) GS 2015–   *T:* 01892 549260
                                                        07818 048321
                        E: mikerlawes@btinternet.com
                                        Twitter: @mikelawes

LAZZ-ONYENOBI, Canon Dr Adanna *BA*, *MEd*, *PhD*
113 Westminster Road Urmston Manchester M41 ORQ [MANCHESTER] *educ* University of Manchester *CV* University of Manchester Lecturer in Community and Youth Work 1992–2014; Retired; Diocese of Manchester member of Bishop's Council, Diocesan Board of Education
GS 2013–2015   *T:* 0161 202 9130
                                                        07736 686417
                            E: addylazz@yahoo.com

LEAFE, Mrs Susannah Mary *BSc*, *PGCE*
6 Troy Court Daglands Road Fowey PL23 1JX [TRURO] *educ* Wimbledon High School; Bristol University; Nottingham University *CV* Head of Geography, Clifton High 1996–2008; Teacher Geography, Queen Elizabeth's Hospital 2008; FLAME Co-ordinator, Truro Diocese 2009–10; Women's Ministry Facilitator, Fowey Parish Church 2008–13; Director of Reform from 2013
GS 2010–   *T:* 01726 832413
                            E: ds.leafe@gmail.com
                                        M: 07753 690120

LEBEY, Captain Nicholas *FdES*
9 Marathon Way Thamesmead London SE28 0JJ [SOUTHWARK] *b* 1982 *educ* Government Technical Training Centre, Accra, Ghana, York St John University, Belfast Bible College, University of the Nations *CV* Youth Coordinator, Praise Chapel Christian Fellowship, Ghana 2000–04; Itinerant Missionary, South Africa 2006–07; Parish Ethnic Minority Outreach Worker and Youth Worker, Willowfield Parish Church, Belfast 2007–09; Church Army Trainee Evangelist, Sorted Youth Church, Bradford Diocese 2009–13; Church Army Pioneer Youth Evangelist, Thamesmead Team Ministry, Southwark Diocese from 2013; Church Army Pioneer Youth Evangelist, Thamesmead Team Ministry, Southwark Diocese from 2013
GS 2015–   *T:* 020 3673 5201
                                                        07933 785179
                        E: n.lebey@churcharmy.org.uk
                                Twitter: @NicholasLebey

LEE, Mr James Alexander *BA*, *MA*
58 Fairfax Road Farnborough Hampshire GU14 8JR [GUILDFORD] *educ* The Cornerstone School, Reigate College, University of Warwick, King's College London *CV* Relay Worker, UCCF, 2008–09; Administrative Officer, Oxfordshire County Council, 2009–10; Operations Assistant/Digital Communications Officer, CARE, 2010–13; Parliamentary Officer, Bible Society, from 2013
GS 2015–   *T:* 01252 548883
                            E: jimmylee42@gmail.com
                                        Twitter: @JamesLee42

LEONARD, The Revd Canon Peter Philip *BA* (hons), *PGCE*
32 Woodville Drive Portsmouth PO1 2TG [PORTSMOUTH] *educ* Winston Churchhill Secondary School, Woking, Woking Sixth Form College, Brooklands Technical College *CV* Heathrow Airport Ltd, Heathrow, Various Roles 1988–92; Woods Car Rental, Southern England, Corporate Sales Manager 1992–93; Cornhill Insurance, Guildford, Market Researcher 1993–94; Trinity College, Bristol, Ordinand 1994–97; Parish Church, Haslemere, Surrey, Curate 1997–2001; Priest-in-Charge St Michael's Church, Sheerwater, Surrey, 2001–07; Classteacher, PE Manager, IT Manager and Member of Senior Management Team Pirbright Village Primary School 2007–10; Deputy Headteacher Mill Hill Primary School 2010–12; Head of School Mill Hill Primary School 2012–14; Canon Chancellor, Portsmouth Cathedral from 2014
GS 2015–   *T:* 023 9282 3300
E: peter.leonard@portsmouthcathedral.org.uk
                    W: https://canonhashtag.com
                                    Twitter: @peterpleonard

LEPINE, The Very Revd Jeremy John (Jerry) *BA*
The Deanery 1 Cathedral Close Bradford BD1 4EG [DEAN OF BRADFORD; LEEDS] *b* 1956 *educ* KCS Wimbledon; Kingston Polytechnic; St John's Nottingham *CV* Curate Trinity St Michael Harrow 1984–88; Team Vicar St Wilfrid's Horley 1988–95; Southwark Diocesan Adviser in Evangelism 1995–02; Rector St Leonard's Wollaton 2002–13; Dean of Bradford from 2013   *T:* 01274 777720
                E: jerry.lepine@bradfordcathedral.org

LESLIE, Mr Keith John *BSc*, *MBA*
2 Hilltop Way Salisbury SP1 3QY [SALISBURY] *b* 1949
GS 2015–   *T:* 07734 919457
                        E: keithj.leslie@btinternet.com

LEWIS, Mr Paul *BA*, *Postgrad Dip*
Church House Great Smith St London SW1P 3AZ [PASTORAL AND CLOSED CHURCHES SECRETARY, BISHOPRICS AND CATHEDRALS SECRETARY, CHURCH

COMMISSIONERS] *b* 1952 *educ* Cantonian High School, Cardiff; Liverpool University *CV* Assistant Planner Chorley Borough Council 1974–85; Appeals Officer Monmouth Borough Council 1985–91; Assistant Borough Planning Officer Hastings Borough Council 1991–95, Borough Planning Officer/Chief Planner 1995–2004; Pastoral and Closed Churches Secretary Church Commissioners from 2004; Bishoprics and Cathedrals Secretary Church Commissioners from 2009

T: 020 7898 1741
E: paul.lewis@churchofengland.org
F: 020 7898 1873
M: 07894 930474

LLOYD WILLIAMS, The Ven Martin Clifford *BA*
12 Walsingham Road Hove BN3 4FF [ARCHDEACON OF BRIGHTON AND LEWES; CHICHESTER] *educ* Kingswood School, Bath, Westminster College *CV* Curate, Bath Walcot 1993–97; Rector Bath St Michael with St Paul 1997–2015; Rural Dean of Bath 2010–15; Archdeacon of Brighton and Lewes from 2015

T: 01273 425691
E: Archbandl@chichester.anglican.org

LODGE, The Revd Sally Nicole *BA, BA, MA*
The Rectory 7 Chippingdell Witham Essex CM8 2JX [CHELMSFORD] *educ* Kingsbridge School, Kingsbridge, South Devon; Guilsborough County School, Guilsborough, Northampton-shire, University of Keele; Leeds Metropolitan University; University of Durham; Anglia Ruskin University *CV* Executive Officer, Treasury Solicitor's Department, Westminster 1983–86; Senior Legal Assistant, Leeds City Council 1986–89; Assistant Solicitor, Kirby's, Harrogate 1991–2002; Parish Administrator, St Wilfrid's Parish Church, Harrogate 2002–07; Assistant Curate, Halstead Area Team Ministry, 2009–12; Team Rector (designate), Witham Team Ministry 2012–14; Team Rector, Witham and Villages Team Ministry from 2014
GS 2015–   *T:* 01376 514190
E: sally.lodge@btinternet.com
Twitter: @RevSallyLodge

LOWSON, The Rt Revd Christopher *MTh, STM, LLM, AKC*
Bishop's Office The Old Palace Minster Yard Lincoln LN2 1PU [BISHOP OF LINCOLN] *educ* Newcastle Cathedral School; Consett Grammar School; King's College London; St Augustine College Canterbury; Pacific School of Religion Berkeley California (World Council of Churches Scholar); Heyt *CV* Curate St Mary Richmond 1977–82; Priest in Charge Holy Trinity Eltham 1982–83, Vicar 1983–91; Chaplain Avery Hill College 1982–85; Chaplain Thames Polytechnic 1985–91; Vicar Petersfield and Rector Buriton 1991–99; Rural Dean Petersfield 1995–99;

Visiting Lecturer Portsmouth University 1998–2006; Archdeacon of Portsmouth 1999–2006; Chair Board of Ministry; Bishop of Portsmouth's Advisor to Hospital Chaplaincy; Diocesan Representative on Inter-Diocesan Finance Forum 1999–2006; Director of Ministry, Archbishops' Council 2006–11; Priest Vicar Westminster Abbey 2006–11; Bishop of Lincoln from 2011
GS 2000–05, 2011–   *T:* 01522 504090
                                     01522 504050
E: bishop.lincoln@lincoln.anglican.org
W: www.lincoln.anglican.org

LUCAS, The Revd Mark Wesley *BSc, BA*
The Rectory St Botolph's Road Barton Seagrave Kettering Northants NN15 6SR [PETERBOROUGH] *b* 1962 *educ* Sir John Deane's Grammar School, Northwich, University of Manchester *CV* Computer Programmer and System Analyst, 1983–91; Assistant Curate, St Peter's Church, Harold Wood, 1994–98; Director of 'The Oast Houses' Christian Conference Centre, East Sussex, 1998–2000; Assistant Adult Education Advisor for Chichester Diocese (East), 1998–2000; Vicar of St John's Church, Polegate and St Wilfrid's Chgurch, Lower Willingdon, Eastbourne, 2000–10; Rector of St Botolph's Church Barton Seagrave and St Edmund's Warkton, Kettering
GS 2015–   *T:* 01536628501
                                     07788100757
E: rector@stbots.org.uk
Twitter: @revmlucas

LUND, The Ven Karen Belinda *BA*
14 Moorgate Avenue Withington Manchester M20 1HE [ARCHDEACON OF MANCHESTER] *b* 1962 *educ* Elthorne High School; Hounslow Borough College; Canterbury Christ Church College; The Queen's College, Birmingham *CV* Assistant Curate St John Southall 1994–97; Associate Vicar St Barnabas Northolt Park 1997–2000, Vicar St Barnabas Gillingham 2000–08, Lay Discipleship Advisor Chelmsford 2008–14; Priest in Charge St Michael and All Angels Roxwell 2008–14, Team Vicar Christ Church and St Andrew Bromley Cross 2014–17; Archdeacon of Manchester from 2017
                                 T: 0161 448 1976
E: archmanchester@manchester.anglican.org

LUNN, Councillor Robin Christopher *BA*
Little Hambledon 10 Malthouse Crescent Inkberrow WR7 4EF [WORCESTER] *b* 1954 *educ* Ditcham Park School; University of Kent *CV* Business Development Manager from 2005; County Councillor for Redditch North from 2005; partner, Independent Financial Advice business, Worcestershire from 2017
GS 2004–   *T:* 01386 792073
E: rlunn47@gmail.com
F: 01386 791531
M: 07785 305849 (Mobile)

LYNAS, The Revd Preb Stephen Brian
BTh, MBE, PGCE
Bishops' Office The Palace Wells BA5 2PD [BATH
AND WELLS] *educ* Borden Grammar School,
Kent; St John College Nottingham; Trinity
Hall Cambridge *CV* Curate Penn, Lichfield
1978–81; Religious Programme Organiser BBC
Radio Stoke-on-Trent 1981–84; Curate Hanley
1981–82; Curate Edensor 1982–84; Religious
Programme Producer BBC Bristol 1985–88;
Religious Programme Senior Producer BBC
South and West England 1988–91; Head
Religious Programmes TV South 1991–92;
Community and Religious Affairs Editor
Westcountry TV from 1992; Archbishops'
Officer for Millennium 1996–2001; Priest
Resources Advisor, Bath and Wells Diocese
2001–07; Senior Chaplain and Advisor to
Bishop of Bath and Wells and Taunton from
2007; Member House of Clergy Standing
Committee from 2010; pro-Prolocutor
Canterbury from 2013
GS 2005–   *T:* 01749 672341
         E: chaplain@bathwells.anglican.org
                              F: 01749 679355
         W: http://bathwellschap.wordpress.com
                        Twitter: @bathwellschap

LYON, Mrs Rosemary Jane *BA, MA, PGCE*
13 New Acres Newburgh Wigan WN8 7TU
[BLACKBURN] *b* 1967 *educ* Ormskirk Grammar
School; St Aidan's College Durham University;
York University; London University *CV*
Teacher Cardinal Vaughan Memorial School
1985–88; Voluntary Pastoral Assistant Diocese
Argentina 1988–89; Cowley High School
1989–90; Chester Catholic High School
1990–92; Tarporley County School 1992–93;
Ormskirk Grammar School 1993–94;
Maricourt Catholic High School from 2002;
St Mary's Catholic Primary School from
2010; Member World Development Group
Blackburn; Observer on Mothers' Union
Worldwide Council from 2014; General Synod
Member National Society Council from 2015
GS 2010–   *T:* 01257 464541
                        E: rosie.jl46@yahoo.co.uk

MacLEAY, The Revd Canon Angus Murdo
MA, MPhil
*St Nicholas Rectory Rectory Lane Sevenoaks TN13
1JA* [ROCHESTER] *b* 1959 *educ* The Vyne
Basingstoke; Queen Mary's Sixth Form College
Basingstoke; University College Oxford;
Wycliffe Hall Oxford *CV* Curate Holy Trinity
Platt, Manchester 1988–92; Vicar St John
Houghton with St Peter Kingmoor, Carlisle
1992–2001; Rector St Nicholas Sevenoaks
from 2001; Member Anglican-Methodist
Formal Conversations 1998–2001; Member
Diocesan Synod; Member Revision Committee
for Consecration and Ordination of Women
Measure; Member House of Bishop's Code of

Practice Working Group Concerning Women
Bishops; Honorary Canon Rochester Cathedral
GS 1995–2001; 2005–   *T:* 01732 740340
    E: angus.macleay@stnicholas-sevenoaks.org
                              F: 01732 742810

MacROW-WOOD, The Ven Antony Charles
MA (Cantab)
28 Merriefield Drive Broadstone Dorset BH18 8BP
[ARCHDEACON OF DORSET; SALISBURY] *educ* Bishop
Wordsworth Grammar School, York and
Cambridge Universities *CV* Assistant Curate,
Parish of Parks and Walcot, Swindon, 1992–
96; Team Vicar, United Benefice of Preston
with Sutton Poyntz and Osmington with
Poxwell, 1996–2004; Salisbury Diocesan UPA
Link Officer 1997–2004; Team Rector, North
Poole Ecumenical Team, 2004–15; Archdeacon
of Dorset from 2015   *T:* 01202 659427
                                      07775 574971
         E: addorset@salisbury.anglican.org
                              F: 01202 891418
                        Twitter: @MacRowWood

MAGOWAN, The Rt Revd Alistair James
BSc, Dip HE, MTh (Oxon)
*Bishop's House Corvedale Road Craven Arms SY7
9BT* [SUFFRAGAN BISHOP OF LUDLOW AND
ARCHDEACON OF LUDLOW; HEREFORD] *educ* King
School Worcester; Leeds University; Trinity
College Bristol; Westminster College Oxford
CV Curate St John Baptist Owlerton 1981–84;
Curate St Nicholas Durham 1984–89;
Chaplain St Aiden College Durham 1984–89;
Vicar St John Baptist Egham 1989–2000;
Rural Dean Runnymede 1993–2000; Chair
Guildford Diocesan Board of Education
1996–2000; Archdeacon of Dorset 2000–09;
Suffragan Bishop of Ludlow from 2009;
Archdeacon of Ludlow from 2009; Chair
Salisbury Diocesan Board of Finance 2004–09
GS 1995–2000, 2004–10   *T:* 01588 673571
                    E: office@bishopofludlow.co.uk

MAKIPAA, The Revd Tuomas
Brysselinkatu 6 D 70 Helsinki Finland 560
[EUROPE] *b* 1978 *CV* Curate, St Nicholas,
Helsinki 2005–12; Chaplain of St Nicholas,
Helsinki from 2012
GS 2015–   *T:* 0358503099132
              E: tuomas.makipaa@anglican.fi
                              Twitter: @tmakipaa

MALLARD, Canon Zahida Revd *Dip, PG Dip*
17 The Crescent Crossflatts Bingley BD16 2EU
[LEEDS] *educ* Westborough High School
Dewsbury; Dewsbury and Batley Technology
and Art College; Wulfrun College
Wolverhampton; Wolverhampton
Polytechnic; Bradford University; Queen's
Birmingham Theological College *CV* Welfare

Rights Officer Bradford Council from 1992, Welfare Rights Manager 2000–09, Interpreting and Translation Service Manager 2006, Development Officer: Equalities and Diversity 2009; Member Diocesan Board of Education; Member Diocesan Board for Church in Society; Diocesan Link Person to Committee for Minority Ethnic Anglican Concerns; Member Mission and Public Affairs Council; Member Bradford Community Legal Services Advice Partnership Board; Common Purpose Graduate; Bishop's Council Bradford from 2003; Board of Education 2006–09; Lay Canon from 2010; Trustee Board of Social Aid and Bradford Hate Crime Alliance
GS 2000–   T: 01274 562640 (Home)
                          01274 435174 (Office)
                   E: zahidamallard@yahoo.co.uk
                        M: 07931 761202 (Mobile)

MALLETT, The Revd Canon Dr Marlene Rosemarie *BA, PhD*
St John's Vicarage 49 Wiltshire Road London SW9 7NE [SOUTHWARK] *b* 1967 *educ* Foxford Comprehensive School; Sussex University; Warwick University; South East Institute for Theological Education *CV* Assistant Curate Christ Church North Brixton 2004–07; Curate Executive Officer, Brent Mental Health Consortium 200204; Research Sociologist, Medical Research Council 1991–2002; Academic Co-ordinator, Centre for Caribbean Medicine, Guys, Kings and St Thomas' Medical School, 2001–02; Honorary Lecturer Department of Legal, Political and Social Sciences, South Bank University 1995–97; Research Fellow Institute of Social and Economic Research, University of the West Indies, Cave Hill Campus, 1989–90; Research Consultant, Swedish International Development Agency, Addis Ababa 1988; Project Admininstrator Research Co-op Advisory Group, 1987–88; Research Consultant Women and Development Project, Commonwealth Secretary HQ, 1986–87; Research Assistant, Institute of Development Studies, 1985–86; Research Administrator, Institute of Development Studies, 1983–85; Researcher/Admininstrator Eastern and Southern African Universities Research Project, ESAURP, University of Dar es Salaam, 1982–83; Priest in Charge St John the Evangelist, Angell Town from 2007; Member Diocesan Synod from 2005; Convenor of Kingston Area Minority Ethnic Anglican Concerns Committee 2006; Member Diocesan Minority Ethnic Anglican Concerns Committee 2006; Member Kingston Area Forum 2007; Member Diocesan Liturgical Committee from 2008; Member Liturgical Commission from 2011; Member Southwark Cathedral Chapter from 2012; Honorary Canon Southwark Cathedral from 2013; Vicar St John the Evangelist Angell Town from 2013; Director Department of Justice, Peace and the Integrity of Creation Southwark from 2016
GS 2010–   T: 020 7733 0585
                    E: rosemarie.mallett@gmail.com
               W: Http://about.me/rosemarie.mallett
                         Twitter: @rosemariemallet

MANDELBROTE, Mr Giles Howard *MA, FSA*
Lambeth Palace Library London SE1 7JU [LIBRARIAN AND ARCHIVIST, LAMBETH PALACE LIBRARY] *educ* Eton College; St John's College Oxford *CV* Editor Quiller Press (publishers) 1989–92; Curatorial Officer, Royal Commission on Historical Manuscripts 1992–95; Curator, British Collections 1501–1800, British Library 1995–2010; Librarian and Archivist, Lambeth Palace Library from 2010
                               T: 020 7898 1266
           E: giles.mandelbrote@churchofengland.org
                               F: 020 7898 7932
                 W: www.lambethpalacelibrary.org
               lambethpalacelibrary.wordpress.com

MANTLE, Dr Richard John *DMus (Hon), FRSA,*
21 Treesdale Road Harrogate HG2 0LX [LEEDS] *educ* Tiffin School; Ealing College of Higher Education *CV* Deputy Managing Director, ENO 1979–85; Managing Director Scottish Opera 1985–91; General Director Edmonton Opera Canada, 1991–94; Guardian of the Holy House, Shrine of Our Lady of Walsingham from 1999; Treasurer, College of Guardians, Director WCTA Ltd; General Director Opera North from 1994; Director and Trustee, National Opera Studio from 1995; Member Council College of the Resurrection Mirfield from 2010; Member Archbishops' Council Finance Committee from 2011; Member Advisory Board, Music Department University York from 2012; Deputy Lieutenant West Yorkshire
GS 2010–   T: 01423 81592
              E: richard.mantle@operanorth.co.uk

MARGRAVE, Councillor Samuel John *MA, CertHE, IOD*
50 Leyland Road Nuneaton Attleborough CV11 4RP [COVENTRY] *educ* Warwick University; Staffordshire University; Coventry University *CV* Politician; Company Director; Bishop's Council
GS 2010–   T: 07985 151669
                       E: sammargrave@gmail.com
                          W: sammargrave.co.uk

MARSH, Mr Geoffrey Richard
Diocesan Office Boley Hill Rochester ME1 1SL [DIOCESAN SECRETARY; ROCHESTER] *CV* Diocesan Secretary from 2014   T: 01634 560002
             E: geoff.marsh@rochester.anglican.org

MARSHALL, Mr Lee *BSc, MBA, FRSA*
Church House Great Smith Street London SW1P
3PS [CHIEF OF STAFF, CHURCH OF ENGLAND PENSIONS
BOARD] *educ* Tunbridge Wells Grammar School
for Boys; University of Lancaster; University of
Manchester (Business School) *CV* On staff of
National Church administrative bodies from
1983, holding various posts including SAP
Project Business Change Manager; currently
Chief of Staff, Church of England Pensions
Board from 2009; Co-founder, Stonewall
1989; Director, Stonewall 1989–1998; Trustee,
Children with Aids Charity 2010–2014;
Trustee, the Ben Cohen StandUp Foundation
from 2012, Chair from 2016; Trustee, Ditch
the Label from 2016, Chair from 2017
                                T: 020 7898 1681
          E: lee.marshall@churchofengland.org

MARTIN, Miss Ruth Alicia *BA, MA,*
ChFCIPD, MCMI, Aff.CISI
Cuzalath Cottage 6 Fisherman Close Ham
Richmond Surrey TW10 7YP [DIOCESAN SECRETARY;
SOUTHWARK] *educ* Falmouth School; Birbeck
London University; Middlesex University *CV*
Managing Director, Chartered Institute of
Securities and Investment (CISI) 2004–2014;
Diocesan Secretary Southwark Diocese;
Governor Canterbury Christ Church University
(Archbishops' Council Representative); Senior
Visiting Fellow, Henley Business School
(Reading University)
                                T: 020 7939 9442
                                F: 020 7939 9468
                      Twitter: @ruthmar58532305

MARTLEW, Dr David *BSc(Hons), Cert Ed,*
MSc, PhD, CSci, C.Chem, MRSC, FiMMM,
HonFSGT
15 Cecil Drive Eccleston St Helens Lancashire
WA10 5DF [LIVERPOOL] *b* 1958 *educ* Prescot
Grammar School, University of Manchester,
Byron Street Technical College, University of
Sheffield *CV* Chemical Analyst Pilkington plc
1966–71; Glass Technologist (various job
titles) Pilkington plc 1971–2007; Consultant
Glass Technologist World of Glass 1998–2000;
Clerk to School Governing Bodies St Helens
MBC 2007–13; retired from 2013; Reader
Christ Church Eccleston 1975–89; Reader
Tutor Liverpool 1978–2008; Reader St Thomas
Eccleston 1978–2010; Reader St James the
Great Haydock from 2010
GS 2015–   *T:* 01 744 24159
                  E: David.Martlew@gmail.com

MASON, Canon Dr John Philip *MA, PhD,*
CChem, FRSC
Willington Mill Weetwood Tarporley CW6 0NQ
[CHESTER] *b* 1959 *educ* King George V School;
Christ College Cambridge; Birmingham
University *CV* Research Scientist, Harwell
Laboratory 1980–85; Research and Business

Manager, AEA Technology 1986–94;
Programme/Business Manager, Laboratory of
the Government Chemist (LGC) 1994–2002;
Director LGC Group Holdings plc 2002–06;
Diocesan Secretary, Chester 2006–10; Secretary
Historic Cheshire Churches Preservation Trust
2010–13; Diocesan Chair House of Laity from
2012; Director NanoFlex Ltd from 2013
GS 2010–   *T:* 01829 733971
                      E: johnpmason@gmail.com

MAY, Mr Nicholas Guy *BA, MBA, FCA*
15 Collett Avenue Shepton Mallet Somerset BA4
5PL [DIOCESAN SECRETARY; BATH AND WELLS]
b 1960 *educ* Kingston Grammar School;
University of Kent; Kingston University; Ernst
& Whinney *CV* Chartered Accountant 1986;
Finance departments in various commercial
companies including as Financial Director and
Company Secretary 1986–2008; Diocesan
Accountant Diocesan Board of Finance Bath
and Wells 2008, later Director of Finance;
Diocesan Secretary from 2014; Member Bishop's
Staff, Principal Officers' Group; Attendance
at Audit Group, Bishop's Council, Common
Fund Working Group, Closed Churches Group,
Diocesan Synod, Finance Group, Fund for
Church Growth   *T:* 01749 685109
          E: nick.may@bathwells.anglican.org
                                F: 01749 674240

McCURDY, The Ven Hugh Kyle *BA(Hons)*
Whitgift House The College Ely CB7 4DL
[ARCHDEACON OF HUNTINGDON AND WISBECH;
ELY] *educ* George Abbot School Guildford;
Portsmouth Polytechnic; Cardiff University;
Trinity College Bristol *CV* Curate St John
Egham 1985–88; Curate St John Woking
1988–91; Vicar St Andrew Histon 1991–2005;
Priest in Charge St Andrew Impington 1998–
2005; Rural Dean North Stowe 1994–2005;
Archdeacon of Huntingdon and Wisbech
from 2005; Member Diocesan Advisory
Committee, Pastoral Committee, Bishop's
Council; Trustee Cambridgeshire ACRE;
Governor Wisbech Grammar School; Member
Cambridge Theological Federation Council;
Member Council Ridley Hall Theological
College; President Huntingdonshire Society
for the Blind; Trustee Bedfordshire and
Cambridgeshire Rural Support Group
GS 2010–   *T:* 01353 658404
                          01353 652709 (Office)
          E: archdeacon.handw@elydiocese.org

McDONALD-BOOTH, Miss Isabella *PG*
Cert, BA Hons
13 Laburnum Avenue Newcastle upon Tyne
NE6 4PP [NEWCASTLE] *educ* Cirencester Deer
Park School, University of Sunderland,
Northumbria University *CV* Branch Manager
and various other posts, Waterstone's

Booksellers 1996–2006; Craft and Design, Retail Manager from 2006
GS 2015–   T: 01916 708176
                                 07803 590542
              E: isabella298@btinternet.com
                           Twitter: @izzy1MB

McFARLANE, The Rt Revd Janet (Jan) Elizabeth *BMed Sci, BA, Dip Min Std*
Repton House 39 Hickton Road Swanwick Alfreton DE55 1AF [BISHOP OF REPTON; DERBY] *b* 1958 *educ* Blythe Bridge High School Stoke-on-Trent; Sheffield University; Durham University; Cranmer Hall Durham *CV* Speech therapist 1987–90; Curate Stafford Team Ministry, Lichfield 1993–96; Chaplain and Minor Canon, Ely Cathedral 1996–99; Norwich Diocesan Communications Officer 1999–2009; Chaplain to Bishop of Norwich 2001–09; Honorary Priest Vicar Norwich Cathedral 2000–09; Member Bishop's Council, Diocesan Synod; Archdeacon of Norwich 2009–16; Diocesan Director of Communications 2009–16; Warden of Readers 2015–16; Bishop of Repton from 2016
GS 2005–16   T: 01332 650583
       E: bishopofrepton@derby.anglican.org
                 W: www.derby.anglican.org

McGREGOR, The Revd and Worshipful Alexander Scott *MA*
Legal Office Church House Great Smith Strett London SW1P 3AZ [DEPUTY OFFICIAL SOLICITOR TO THE CHURCH COMMISSIONERS AND DEPUTY HEAD OF THE LEGAL OFFICE OF THE NATIONAL CHURCH INSTITUTIONS] *b* 1958 *educ* John Lyon School Harrow; Christ Church Oxford; College of Law; Inns of Court School of Law; St Albans and Oxford Ministry Course *CV* Barrister in independent practice 1996–2005; Legal Adviser in the Legal Office of the NCIs 2006–08; Deputy Legal Adviser to the Archbishops' Council and the General Synod from 2009; Member The Honourable Society of Lincoln's Inn from 1994; Member Dacorum Borough Council 1999–2007; Assistant Curate (Non-Stipendiary Minister) St Mary Harrow 2006–09; Assistant Curate (Non-Stipendiary Minister) St Barnabas Pimlico 2009–15; Assistant Curate (Non-Stipendiary Minister) Our Most Holy Redeemer Clerkenwell from 2015; Deputy Chancellor Diocese of Oxford 2007–13; Chancellor Diocese of Oxford from 2013; Deputy Official Solicitor to the Church Commissioners and Deputy Head of the Legal Office of the National Church Institutions from 2017   T: 020 7898 1748
    E: alexander.mcgregor@churchofengland.org

MCHAFFIE, The Revd Alistair *DipHE*
St John's Vicarage Leyland Lane Leyland Lancs PR25 1XB [BLACKBURN] *b* 1957 *educ* Marr College, Troon, *CV* Royal Army Medical Corps 1976–1988; Financial Advisor, Allied Dunbar 1988–89; Medical Representative, Lipha Pharmaceuticals 1989–92; Ordinand, Oak Hill College 1992–94; Curate, St Michael's, Braintree, Chelmsford Diocese 1994–98; Rector of the Falkland Islands 1998–2003; Vicar, St John's, Leyland from 2003; Area Dean of Leyland from 2011
GS 2015–   T: 01772 621646
                                 07896 787878
                      E: alistair@mchaffie.com

McISAAC, Mrs Debrah *BA, LLB/D. Jur.*
Parsonage Farm House White Way Pitton SP5 1DT [SALISBURY] *b* 1953 *educ* Marian High School, Saskatchewan; Canada University of Regina; University of Saskatchewan, Canada; Osgoode Hall, York University, Canada; Wycliffe Hall; Ripon College Cuddesdon *CV* Advisor, Office of the Ombudsman, Province of Saskatchewan 1973; Special Advisor Minister of Justice, Ottawa 1975; Barrister and Solicitor, Edmonton, Alberta, Canada admitted 1976; Barrister and Solicitor, Law Society of Upper Canada admitted 1983; Solicitor, Law Society of England and Wales admitted 1985; Solicitor Durrant Piesse, London 1985–86; Solicitor, Freshfields, London 1986–88; Director Professional Development, Lovells, London 1989–2000; Chief Monitor, Training Contracts, Law Society of England and Wales 2000–06; Principal, D Ball Consulting 2000–10; Legal Education and Training Group: Treasurer, 1994–96; Chair, 1996–98; Lord Chancellor's Advisory Committee Education and Conduct Standing Conference 1994–99; Advocacy Sub-Committee of Law Society's Training Committee 1998–2008; Council of the Law Society of England and Wales: Council Member 2005–08; Chair, Education & Training Committee 2005–08; Member Regulatory Affairs Group 2005–07; Member Regulatory Affairs Board 2007–08; Governor, Old Sarum School 2012; Member Diocesan Synod Sarum from 2009; Member Sarum Archdeaconry Mission and Pastoral Committee from 2010; Lay Chair, Alderbury Deanery Synod from 2010; Alderbury Deanery Standing and Pastoral Committee from 2005; Lay Chair Clarendon Team from 2011; Member Bishop's Council Salisbury from 2013
GS 2010–   T: 01722 712758
                                 01722 712940
                       E: debbie@dball.com
                         M: 07879 662188

McKEE, The Revd Nicholas John *BTh, MEng*
St Paul's Vicarage Sweetloves Lane Bolton BL1 7ET [MANCHESTER] *educ* Portora Royal School, University of Nottingham; University of Cambridge *CV* 1994–2005 Range of positions within the ExxonMobil group of companies; Assistant Curate St James and Emmanuel,

Manchester Diocese 2008–11; Vicar of St Paul's Astley Bridge from 2011
GS 2015–   *T:* 01204 304119
                                  E: rev.nick@live.co.uk
                                  Twitter: @nickjmckee

McKINNEL, The Rt Revd Nicholas Howard Paul *MA(Cantab), MA(Oxon), Hon DD*
108 Molesworth Road Stoke Plymouth PL3 4AQ [SUFFRAGAN BISHOP OF PLYMOUTH; EXETER] *educ* Marlborough College; Queens' College Cambridge; Wycliffe Hall Oxford *CV* Curate St Mary's, West Kensington 1980–83; Anglican Chaplain Liverpool University 1983–87; Rector Hatherleigh, Meeth, Exbourne and Jacobstowe 1987–94; Team Rector St Andrew's Plymouth and St Paul's, Stonehouse 1994–2012; Prebendary Exeter Cathedral 2002; Bishop of Crediton 2012–15; Bishop of Plymouth from 2015   *T:* 01752 500059
        E: bishop.of.plymouth@exeter.anglican.org

McKITTRICK, The Ven Douglas Henry *BTh*
2 Yorklands Dyke Rd Avenue Hove BN3 6RW [ARCHDEACON OF CHICHESTER] *educ* John Marley Comprehensive School, Newcastle-upon-Tyne; St Stephen's House Oxford *CV* Curate St Paul Deptford, Southwark 1977–80; Curate St John Tuebrook, Liverpool 1980–81; Team Vicar St Stephen Grove Street Liverpool 1981–89; Vicar St Agnes Toxteth Park, Liverpool 1989–97; Vicar St Peter with Chapel Royal Brighton, Chichester 1997–2002; Rural Dean of Brighton 1998–2002; Canon and Prebendary of Chichester Cathedral 1998–2002; Archdeacon of Chichester from 2002; Member Diocesan Advisory Committee, Diocesan Board of Education, Diocean Board of Finance, Pastoral Committee, Parsonages Committee; Bishop's Advisor Hospital Chaplaincy; Council Member Additional Curates Society 2005; Member Hospital Chaplain Council 2006; Bishop's Advisor on Ecumenism; Member Ecclesiastical Law Society; Member Nikaean Club
GS 2004–   *T:* 01273 505330 (Home)
                      01273 421021 (Office)
      E: archchichester@chichester.anglican.org
                      F: 01273 421041

McLEAN, The Revd Canon (Margaret Anne) Maggie *MA*
Battyeford Vicarage 107A Stocks Bank Road Mirfield WF14 9QT [LEEDS] *educ* Greenhead Grammar School; Birmingham University; Heythrop College; Cranmer Hall Durham *CV* Curate All Saints, Bedford 1991–94; Chaplain St Alban's High School for Girls 1994–98; Associate Priest St Alban's Abbey; Assistant Social Responsibility Advisor 1998–99; Anglican Chaplain, University of Huddersfield 1999–2002; Priest in Charge St Philip and St James, Scholes and St Luke and Whitechapel, Cleckheaton 2002–09; Christ the King,

Battyeford from 2009; Diocesan Training Officer; Canon Wakefield Cathedral from 2011
GS 2010–   *T:* 01924 493277
                    E: MA.mclean@btinternet.com
        W: www.christthekingbattyeford.org
                                  M: 07484 296 571
                                  Twitter: @CTKMaggie

McPHATE, The Very RevdProf Gordon Ferguson *BA, MA, M Th, M Sc, MB, Ch B, MD, FRCP*
The Deanery 7 Abbey St Chester CH1 2JF [DEAN OF CHESTER] *educ* Perth Grammar School; Cambridge University; Aberd University; Edinburgh University; Surrey University; Westcott House Cambridge *CV* Lecturer in Physiology, Guy's Hospital London 1979–84; Honorary Curate Sanderstead, Southwark 1978–80; Honorary Priest Vicar and Sacrist, Southwark Cathedral 1980–86; Registrar in Chemical Pathology, Guildford Hospitals 1984–86; Lecturer and Senior Lecturer in Pathology, University of St Andrew 1986–2002; Honorary Anglican Chaplain University of St Andrew 1986–2002; Consultant Chemical Pathologist, Fife Hospitals 1993–2002; Dean of Chester from 2002; Visiting Professor of Theology, University of Chester from 2003
GS 2004–05   *T:* 01244 500971
            E: dean@chestercathedral.com

McPHERSON, Mrs Katherine *MBA, BA*
59 Mycenae Rd London SE3 7SE [APPOINTED MEMBER, ARCHBISHOPS' COUNCIL] *educ* P. L. Meth Girls' School Singapore; Temasek Junior College Singapore; National University of Singapore; University of Kent *CV* Executive Consultant, Ernst and Young Singapore 1987–92; Senior Manager, Ernst and Young London 1992–95; London Head of Sales and Marketing (Media and Resources), Ernst and Young 1996–98; National Head of Sales and Marketing (Telecoms, Media & Entertainment), Ernst and Young 1998–99; Project Director (secondment) BBC 1999; Managing Consultant, Cap Gemini Ernst and Young 1999–2001; Operations Director, YMCA Lambeth, Lewisham and Southwark 2001–2002; Director Business Development and Marketing, EMEA, White and Case 2002–04; Appointed Member Archbishops' Council 2003–09; Head of Business Development, Corporate Division, Herbert Smith 2004–05; Head of Business Development, Europe, Herbert Smith 2005–07; Head Winning Business, Global Markets, KPMG 2007–10; Director Global Markets, KMPG 2010–13
GS 2003–10   *T:* 020 8858 1856 (Home)
            E: mcpherson.katherine@gmail.com
                  mcpehrson.katherine@gmail.com
                                  M: 07984 046149 (Mobile)

MEYRICK, The Rt Revd (Cyril) Jonathan
MA (Oxon), DEd(Hon)
The Old Vicarage Castle Acre King's Lynn PE32 2AA [SUFFRAGAN BISHOP OF LYNN; NORWICH] *educ* Lancing College; St John College Oxford; Salisbury and Wells Theological College *CV* Curate Bicester, Oxford 1976–78; Bishop's Chaplain, Oxford 1978–81; Old Testament tutor, Codrington College, Barbados 1981–84; Team Vicar Burnham Team, Oxford 1984–90; Team Rector Tisbury, Salisbury 1990–98; Rural Dean Chalke, Sarum 1997–98; Residentiary Canon Rochester 1998–2005; Acting Dean of Rochester 2002–04; Dean of Exeter 2005–2011; Chair Council for Mission and Unity 2005–2011; Bishop of Lynn from 2011 GS 2013–   *T:* 01760 755553
                                        01760 755085
        E: bishop.lynn@norwich.anglican.org
            W: www.norwich.anglican.org

MICKLEFIELD, The Revd Andrew Mark
BEd (Hons)
St Lawrence Vicarage Church Street Alton Hampshire GU34 2BW [WINCHESTER] *b* 1971 *educ* Poole Grammar School, King Alfred's College, Winchester *CV* Primary School Teacher (Hampshire) 1993–2001; Youth and Children's Work Development Officer – Wessex Synod URC 2001–04; Assistant Curate, St Lawrence, Alton 2006–10; Rector of The Itchen Valley 2010–14; Vicar of The Parish of the Resurrection, Alton from 2014
GS 2015–   *T:* 01420 88794
                                   07749 483407
        E: andrewmicklefield@gmail.com

MILLAR, Canon Dr Sandra Doreen *BA, MA, PhD, DipTh, DipMin*
Church House Great Smith Street London SW1P 3AZ [HEAD OF LIFE EVENTS, ARCHBISHOPS' COUNCIL] *b* 1967 *educ* Rugby High School for Girls; University College, Cardiff; Warwick University; Ripon College, Cuddesdon *CV* Product Manager, Boots Company, 1979–84; Product Manager, Coop 1984–88; Sales/Marketing Manager, Windsor Foods 1989–91; Sales/Marketing Manager, SU 1991–93; National Director King's Kids England 1994–98; Assistant Curate, Chipping Barnet with Arkley 2000–03; Team Vicar, Dorchester Team and Tutor at Ripon College Cuddesdon 2003–07; Children's Officer, Gloucester from 2007; Board for Christian Development, St Albans 2000–03; Diocesan Synod, St Albans 2000–03; Governor of St Albans and Oxford Ministry Course 2001–06; Member Mission Initiatives Group from 2007; Member Bishop's Worship, Prayer and Spirituality Group from 2007; Head of Projects and Developments, Archbishops' Council from 2013; Head of Life Events from 2017
GS 2010–13   *T:* 020 7898 100
        E: sandra.millar@churchofengland.org

MILLER, The Ven Geoff (Geoffrey Vincent)
BEd, MA
80 Moorside North Fenham Newcastle-upon-Tyne NE4 9DU [ARCHDEACON OF NORTHUMBERLAND; NEWCASTLE] *b* 1958 *educ* Sharston High School, Manchester; Durham University; St John's College Nottingham; Newcastle University *CV* Curate Jarrow 1983–86; Team Vicar St Aidan Billingham 1986–92; Diocesan Urban Development Officer 1991–99; Community Chaplain Stockton-on-Tees 1992–94; Priest in Charge St Cuthbert Darlington 1994–96; Vicar 1996–99; Diocesan Urban Officer and Residentiary Canon Newcastle Cathedral 1999–2005; Archdeacon of Northumberland from 2005; Member Diocesan Advisory Committee; Member Diocesan Pastoral Committee; Member Finance, Pastoral, Parsonages Committees and Strategy Development Group Bishop's Council; Member Diocesan Safeguarding Committee; Member Shepherd's Dene, Sons of Clergy, Church Institute, Hospital of God at Greatham, Lord Crewe Trust; Chair British Committee of French Protestant Industrial Mission; Chair Strategic Development Group Bishop's Council; Special Trustee Newcastle Healthcare Charity; Newcastle Fairness Commission 2012   *T:* 0191 273 8245
        E: g.miller@newcastle.anglican.org
                           F: 0191 226 0286

MILLER, Ms Loraine *BA (Hons)*
Church House Great Smith Street London SW1P 3PS [HEAD OF HOUSING, CHURCH OF ENGLAND PENSIONS BOARD] *educ* The Skinners' Company's School for Girls; Queen Mary College *CV* National Training Manager, English Church Housing Group 1984–89; Supported Housing Business Manager, English Church Housing Group 1989–2007; Deputy Housing Manager C of E Pensions Board 2007–09; Head of Housing, C of E Pensions Board from 2009
                              T: 020 7898 1852
        E: loraine.miller@churchofengland.org

MILLER, The Ven Luke Jonathan *MA (Cantab), MA (Oxon)*
St Andrew's House 35 St Andrew's Hill London EC4V 5DE [ARCHDEACON OF LONDON] *educ* Haileybury School; Sidney Sussex College Cambridge; St Stephen's House *CV* Assistant Curate St Matthew Oxhey 1991–94; Assistant Curate St Mary the Virgin Tottenham 1994–95; Vicar St Mary the Virgin Tottenham 1995–2011; Area Dean East Haringay 2005–11; Acting Archdeacon of Hampstead 2009–10; Archdeacon of Hampstead 2011–15; Priest-in-charge Saint Andrew by the Wardrobe (London) 2015, Rector from 2016; Archdeacon of London from 2016; Diocesan Synod 1998–2005 and from 2009; Member Edmonton Area Council from 2005; Member Diocesan

Strategic Planning Committee from 2008; Member St Stephen's House Council from 2008 and Chair Finance and General Purposes Committee 2008–17; Chair Area Finance Committee from 2011; Diocesan Advisory Committee   T: 020 7932 1133
E: archdeacon.london@london.anglican.org
M: 07742 104065
Twitter: @ArchdeaconLuke

MILLS, Mr David John *MBE*
51 Greenways Over Kellet Carnforth LA6 1DE [CARLISLE] *CV* Senior Probation Officer, retired; Reader; Bishop's Advisory Clergy Discipline Commission; Member Diocesan Board of Education
GS 1985–   T: 01524 732194
E: david.j.mills@btinternet.com

MINICHIELLO WILLIAMS, Mrs Andrea Rose
4 Lucas Grange Haywards Heath West Sussex RH16 1JS [CHICHESTER] *b* 1965 *educ* Weymouth Grammar School; University of Wales Cardiff; University of Pisa Italy; Inns of Court School of Law *CV* Barrister Bolt Court Chambers 1988–95; Lawyers Christian Fellowship Student Officer 1992–97, Policy Officer 1997–2008; CEO Christian Legal Centre 2008–; CEO Christian Concern 2008–
GS 2010–   T: 07712 591164
E: andrea.williams@christianconcern.com
W: www.christianconcern.com
Twitter: @A_Minichiello

MITCHELL, The Revd Canon Richard John Anthony *BA (Hons), Cert Th, PGCE*
The Vicarage School Lane Shurdington Cheltenham GL51 4TF [GLOUCESTER] *b* 1964 *educ* Trinity Comprehensive School Carlisle; St Martin's College; University of Lancaster; Salisbury and Wells Theological College *CV* Assistant Curate Holy Trinity Kendal 1991–95; Team Vicar Kirkby Lonsdale Team Ministry 1995–2003; Area Dean Gloucester North 2004–09; Vicar Badgeworth, Shurdington and Witcombe with Bentham from 2004; Area Dean Severn Vale from 2009; Chair House of Clergy Gloucester from 2011; Member Carlisle Diocesan Board of Education 2001–03; Member Gloucester Diocesan Board of Education from 2006; Member Bishop's Council Gloucester from 2011
GS 2013–   T: 01242 702911
E: richard.mitchell@talk21.com
W: www.bswbchurches.co.uk

MOIR, The Revd Canon Nick (Nicholas Ian) *MA, MTh*
10 Lynfield Lane Cambridge CB4 1DR [ELY] *b* 1961 *educ* King's College School, Wimbledon; Gonville and Caius College, Cambridge *CV* Curate, St Andrew's Enfield 1987–78; Chaplain to the Bishop of St Albans 1991–94; Chaplain, St John's College, Cambridge 1994–94; Vicar of Waterbeach, Rector of Landbeach 1998–2007; Vicar of St Andrew's Chesterton from 2007
GS 2015–   T: 01223 303469
E: nicholas.moir@standrews-chesterton.org

MONTEITH, The Very Revd David Robert Malvern *BSC, BTh, MA, LLD*
St Martins House 7 Peacock Lane Leicester LE1 5PZ [DEAN OF LEICESTER] *educ* Portora Royal School, Enniskillen; St John's College Durham; St John's College Nottingham *CV* Assistant Curate All Saints Kings Heath, Birmingham 1993–97; Assistant Curate St Martin-in-the-Fields 1997–2002; Priest in Charge Holy Trinity, South Wimbledon 2002–09; Area Dean Merton 2004–07; Team Rector Merton Priory Team Ministry, Southwark 2009; Canon Chancellor, Leicester Cathedral 2009–13; Dean of Leicester from 2013
T: 0116 261 5356
E: david.monteith@leccofe.org
W: www.leicestercathedral.org

MOORE, Mrs Lucy Bridget *MA*
2 Maldon Close Bishopstoke Eastleigh Hants SO50 6BD [WINCHESTER] *b* 1966 *educ* Boston High School, University of Oxford *CV* Teacher 1988–92; Parent from 1992; Barnabas Team Member and author for The Bible Reading Fellowship (BRF) 2001–08; Messy Church Team Leader at The Bible Reading Fellowship (BRF) from 2008
GS 2015–   T: 023 8065 0824
07885 704366
E: Lucy.moore@brf.org.uk
W: www.messychurch.org.uk
Twitter: @messylucy

MORGAN, The Ven Ian David John *BAHons, LTCL*
The Archdeaconry Church Road Marlesford Woodbridge IP13 0AT [ARCHDEACON OF SUFFOLK; ST EDMUNDSBURY AND IPSWICH] *educ* Wallingford School; University of Hull; Ripon College Cuddesdon *CV* Curate Holy Trinity Hereford 1983–86; Curate St Nicolas and St Mary de Haura, Shoreham by Sea 1986–88; Presenter, Producer, Senior Producer BBC Network and Local Radio 1988–92; Vicar All Hallows Ipswich 1992–95; Rector South West Ipswich Team Ministry 1995–2012; Church Urban Fund Link Officer from 2006; Rural Dean Ipswich 2008–12; Honorary Canon, St Edmundsbury Cathedral from 2009; Archdeacon of Suffolk from 2012
E: archdeacon.ian@
stedmundsbury.anglican.org
W: www.stedmundsbury.anglican.org
M: 07919 916143

MORGAN, Mr Richard Gareth Llewelyn
23 Merivale Way Ely CB7 4GQ [ELY] *b* 1966 *educ* The Kings' School, Ely *CV* Administrator Silver

Fitzgerald Cambridge 2006–16; Manager Tesco Plc Cambridge from 2016; Churchwarden Thaxted 2001–04; Saffron Walden Deanery Synod 1996–06; Chelmsford Diocesan Synod 2003–06; Bishop's Council 2003–06; Governor Cottenham Academy 2007–11, Chairman, Site and Facilities Management 2009–11; Cambridge South Deanery Synod from 2009, Lay Chairman from 2017; Ely Diocesan Synod from 2009, Bishop's Council 2009–12; Member Diocesan Houses Subcommittee from 2006; Member Diocesan Patronage Board from 2011
GS 2017–ㅤㅤㅤㅤㅤ*T:* 01353 667905
ㅤㅤㅤㅤㅤ*E:* rimo@gmx.co.uk
ㅤㅤㅤㅤㅤ*M:* 07771 984848

MORRIS, The Revd Jane Elizabeth *BA, MSc, PGCE*
156 Anson Road London NW2 6BH [LONDON] *b* 1960 *educ* Ealing Grammar School; York University; North East Oecumenical Course *CV* Teacher, Science at Tadcaster Grammar School 1972–74; Head of Science at the Mount School, York 1974–92; Head of Science and Chaplain, Queen Margaret's School, Escrick 1992–95; Assistant Curate St Michael-le-Belfrey Church, York 1992–95; Associate Vicar St George's Church, Leeds 1995–2005; Board of Studies, North East Oecumenical Course 1998–2002; Leader West Yorkshire New Wine Network 2003–05; Member New Wine North Leadership 2003–05; Vicar St Gabriel's, Cricklewood from 2005; Healing Ministry Advisor in the Willesden Episcopal Area until 2013; Member New Wine Leadership Team for London and the South East 2005–10; Resource Church Leader for the Alpha Course
GS 2010–ㅤㅤㅤㅤ*T:* 020 8452 6305
ㅤㅤㅤㅤ*E:* jane.morris@st-gabriels.org

MORRIS, The Rt Revd Roger Anthony Brett *BSc (Hons), ARCS, MA (Cantab)*
1 Fitzwalter Road Colchester CO3 3SS [AREA BISHOP OF COLCHESTER; CHELMSFORD] *educ* Chipping Sodbury School; Filton Tech College; Imperial College London; Trinity College Cambridge; Ridley Hall Cambridge *CV* Assistant Curate of Northleach, with Hampnett and Farmington, Cold Aston, with Notgrove and Turkdean 1993–96; Rector of Sevenhampton with Charlton Abbotts, Hawling and Whittington, Dowdeswell with Andoversford, The Shiptons and Salperton, and Withington 1996–2003; Director Parish Development and Evangelism, Coventry 2003–08; Archdeacon of Worcester 2008–14; Area Bishop of Colchester from 2014
ㅤㅤㅤㅤ*T:* 01206 576648
ㅤㅤ*E:* b.colchester@chelmsford.anglican.org

MORRIS, The Revd Shaun Anthony *BSocSc*
76 Church Lane Hanford Stoke-on-Trent ST4 4QD [LICHFIELD] *b* 1954 *educ* Stamford School, University of Keele *CV* Chartered Accountant,

Deloitte Haskins & Sells, London, 1985–90; Partner, Dean Statham, Stafford, 1992–2004; Deputy Chief Executive, Stafford Railway Building Society, 1993–2004; Assistant Curate, St Andrew's, Newcastle-under-Lyme, 2006–10; Resident Minister, St Matthias Church, Hanford 2010–17; Associate Minister, St Mary's Church, Trentham 2010–17; Priest in Charge, St Matthias Church, Hanford from 2017
GS 2015–ㅤㅤㅤㅤ*T:* 01782 657848
ㅤㅤㅤㅤ*E:* morris.shaun@btinternet.com

MOUNTFORD, Mr Roger Philip *BSc(Econ), MS*
Hookstile House Byers Lane Godstone Surrey RH9 8JH [TRUSTEE MEMBER, CHURCH OF ENGLAND PENSIONS BOARD] *b* 1948 *educ* Kingston Grammar School; London School Economics; Stanford Business School *CV* Merchant banker 1971–2000, followed by various directorships; Governor London School Economics; Member C of E Pensions Board *T:* 01342 893198
ㅤㅤㅤ*E:* mountford.roger@btinternet.com
ㅤㅤㅤㅤ*M:* 07799 662601

MULLALLY, The Rt Revd Dame Sarah Elisabeth
32 The Avenue Tiverton Devon EX16 4HW [SUFFRAGAN BISHOP OF CREDITON; EXETER]
ㅤㅤㅤㅤㅤ*T:* 01884 250002
ㅤ*E:* bishop.of.crediton@exeter.anglican.org

MUMFORD, Mr Adrian *MA, MMus, ARCM, FLCM*
14 Tufton Street London SW1P 3QZ [DIOCESAN SECRETARY; EUROPE] *educ* Latymer Upper School; Surrey University; Kingston University *CV* Career in Internal Auditing 1979–94; Diocesan Secretary, Diocese of Gibraltar in Europe from 1995ㅤㅤㅤㅤ*T:* 020 7898 1155
ㅤㅤㅤㅤㅤ07984 257782
ㅤ*E:* adrian.mumford@churchofengland.org

MUNRO, Ms Josile Wenus *BSc*
89 Brougham Road London E8 4PB [LONDON] *educ* Haggerston Girls School, Kingsway Princeton College Southbank University, London Metropolitan University *CV* Local Government Officer 1985–2003; Local Government Manager 2003–08; Senior Local Government Manager 2008–12; Local Government Officer from 2012
GS 1994–2000, 2015–ㅤㅤ*T:* 020 7254 5577
ㅤㅤㅤㅤ*E:* josile.munro@btinternet.com

MUNRO, The Revd Dr Robert Speight *BSc, BA, Dip Ap Th, PGCE, DMin*
Rectory 1 Depleach Rd Cheadle SK8 1DZ [CHESTER] *b* 1963 *educ* William Hulme's Grammar School Manchester; Bristol University; All Souls College London; Manchester University; Oak Hill Theological College; Reformed Theological Seminary US *CV* Teacher Math and PE Hazel Grove HS 1987–1990; Curate St John Baptist

Hartford 1993–97; Rector St Wilfred Davenham 1997–2003; Rector St Mary Cheadle from 2003; Member Bishop's Council from 2000; Chair House of Clergy Chester from 2014; Rural Dean Cheadle from 2016
GS 2005–   *T:* 0161 428 3440
0161 428 8050
E: rob@munro.org.uk
F: 0161 428 3440
0161 428 8050

MURPHY, The Revd Dr Rosalyn Frances Thomas *BA, Mdiv, MThR, PhD*
The Vicarage 80 Devonshire Road Blackpool Lancashire FY3 8AE [MEMBER, ARCHBISHOPS' COUNCIL] *b* 1953 *educ* Rufus King International High School, Milwaukee, WI (USA); Marquette University, USA; Union Theological Seminary (UTS), USA; Durham University *CV* Public Relations Officer Milwaukee County Airports Division Mitchell International Airport, Milwaukee (USA) 1983–86; Vice-Present Operations and Government Accounts PRO, Inc., Richmond (USA) 1986–92; Senior Vice President Marketing and Fund Development Metropolitan Chamber of Commerce Richmond (USA) 1992–95; Teaching Assistant, Dean of Religious Studies, Virginia Commonwealth University Richmond (USA) 1998–99; Curate St Nicholas Church Durham 2005–08; Vicar St Thomas Church Blackpool from 2008; Archbishops' Council from 2010; Council Member St John's College Nottingham from 2010; TUTV Task Group Archbishops' Council from 2010; Resourcing Ministerial Education, Ministry and Missions Division from 2014; Appointments Committee, General Synod from 2013; Faith and Order Commission from 2016; Church Commissioners Bishropics and Cathedrals Committee from 2017
GS 2010–2015   *T:* 01253 392 544
01253 399 276
E: stthomasvicar@btinternet.com

MYERS, Ms Caroline Mary *BA, MA*
15 Ormonde Court Upper Richmond Road Putney London SW15 6TW [SOUTHWARK] *b* 1967 *educ* Nottingham Girls' High School, Durham University *CV* International Events Coordinator, Girlguiding, December 2010–13; Project Coordinator, Girlguiding, 2008–10; Postgraduate Admissions Secretary, 2007–08; Youth Advocate, Christian Aid, 2002–03; Volunteering Manager USPG 2013–16; Head of Volunteering MS Society from 2017; Reader, Parish of Putney from 2013
GS 2015–   *T:* 07977512813
E: carrie.m.myers@gmail.com

NAGEL, Mrs Mary Philippa *BEd*
Aldwick Vicarage 25 Gossamer Lane Bognor Regis PO21 3AT [CHICHESTER] *b* 1954 *educ* Worthing High School; London University *CV* Section 23 Inspector of Schools until 2005
GS 1990–   *T:* 01243 262049
E: mary@nagel.me.uk
M: 07947 145962

NAY, Mrs Tina (Janet Christina) *BA(Hons)*
34 Baldwin Ave Eastbourne East Sussex BN21 1UP [CHICHESTER] *educ* Nottingham High School for Girls, Leicester University, Canley College of Education *CV* English teacher at Hucknall National School, Nottinghamshire 1972–73; English teacher at Guthlaxton Upper School Leicester 1973–76; English tutor Open University, Eastern region 1980–2000; English teacher South East Essex Sixth Form College 1984–2001; Humanities Team Leader at Southend Adult Community College 2001–07; Community Adult and Community Education Manager at Cambridgeshire County Council 2007–09; Essex Branch Organizer, WEA, Eastern Region 2009–11; Area Learning Manager, WEA Eastern Region 2011–12; Retired from 2013
GS 2015–   *T:* 01323 735115
07846124 755
E: tinafamilynay@gmail.com

NAYLOR, Mr John Thomas
50 Kestrel Drive Loggerheads Market Drayton TF9 2QT [LICHFIELD] *educ* Durham Cathedral Chorister School; Rossall School; St John's College, Cambridge; Emmanuel College, Cambridge *CV* Various Industry Businesses including roles as Marketing Director, Head of Group Strategic Planning, Managing Director 1969–91; Various singing roles in cathedrals and professional choirs 1957–2011; Conductor of The Lydian Singers from 1980; Chief Executive Campbell & Armstrong plc 1991–96; Managing Director and major shareholder NDI Ltd 1997–2001; Conductor Newport and District MVC 2004–09; Chairman, The Big Bird Company Ltd 2004–08; Lay Chair Hodnet Deanery 2004–12; Music Director Nantwich Choral Society from 2005; Conductor The Phoenix Singers 2009–11; Music Director Open University Chapel Choir from 2012; Chairman Lichfield Diocesan Board of Finance from 2012; Lichfield Bishop's Council; Lichfield Diocesan Synod; Chairman Lichfield Finance and Central Services Committee; Lay Chair Cheswardine PCC; Numerous Lichfield Diocesan Committees
GS 2015–   *T:* 01630 672248
E: j.t.naylor@btinternet.com
M: 07957 175425

NEIL-SMITH, Mr (Noel) Jonathan *MA*
Church House Great Smith St London SW1P 3AZ [ADMINISTRATIVE SECRETARY, CENTRAL SECRETARIAT] *educ* Marlborough College; St John College

Cambridge *CV* On staff of Church Commissioners from 1981; Bishoprics Officer 1994–96; Seconded to General Synod from 1997; Assistant Secretary House of Bishops 1997–98; Secretary House of Bishops 1998–2011; Secretary Dioceses Commission from 2011; Secretary House of Clergy from 2011; Honorary Lay Canon Guildford Cathedral 2002–17; Secretary to the Appointments Committee from 2017   *T:* 020 7898 1373
    E: jonathan.neil-smith@churchofengland.org
            F: 020 7898 1369

NEVILLE, Mr Paul
59 East End Crescent Royston Barnsley South Yorkshire S71 4AW [LEEDS] *educ* Royston Comprehensive School, Barnsley VI Form College, Preston College *CV* Civil Servant in the Department of Employment 1988; West Yorkshire Police Administrative Officer 1989; Local Government Officer from 1990
GS 2010–2015   *T:* 07977 838162
       E: pneville@clara.co.uk

NEWCOMBE, Dr Lindsay Kathleen *BEng, PhD*
Holy Trinity Vicarage 3 Bletchley Street London N1 7QG [LONDON] *educ* Purbeck School, Wareham; University College London *CV* Research Fellow, Department of Mechanical Engineering, University College London 2001–06, Doctor of Philosophy research in bioengineering 2006–09; Technical Specialist (Orthopaedics), British Standards Institute from 2009
GS 2010–   *T:* 020 7253 4796
       E: lindsaynewcombe@gmail.com

NEWCOME, The Rt Revd James William Scobie *MA*
Bishop's House Ambleside Road Keswick CA12 4DD [BISHOP OF CARLISLE] *educ* Marlborough College; Trinity College Oxford; Selwyn College Cambridge; Ridley Hall Theological College *CV* Curate All Saints Leavesden 1978–82; Minister Bar Hill Local Ecumenical Project Ely 1982–94; Tutor Ridley Hall Cambridge 1983–88; Vicar Dry Drayton 1990–94; Rural Dean North Stowe 1993–94; Diocesan Director of Ordinands Chester 1994–2000; Residentiary Canon Chester Cathedral 1994–2002; Diocesan Director of Ministry 1996–2002; Suffragan Bishop of Penrith 2002–09; Bishop of Carlisle from 2009; Member Bishops Continuing Ministerial Education Committee; Chair National Stewardship Committee; Member SAGE Group; Lead Bishop on Health and Social Care; Director University of Cumbria; Lead Bishop for United Reformed Church; President St John's College Durham; Clerk of the Closet from 2014; National Chaplain Royal British Legion from 2016;

Member, DAG; Deputy Lieutenant of Cumbria; Chair of Rose Castle Foundation; Member of the House of Lords Select Committee on the Long-term Sustainability of the NHS 2017
GS 2000–02   *T:* 01768 773430
       E: bishop.carlisle@carlislediocese.org.uk

NEWLANDS, The Revd Chris (Christopher William) *BA*
Priory Vicarage Priory Close Lancaster LA1 1YZ [BLACKBURN] *educ* The King's School, Pontefract, University of Bristol *CV* Pastoral Assistant, Holy Trinity, Algiers (Egypt and North Africa) 1979–80; Assistant Curate, Bishop's Waltham with Upham 1984–87; Precentor, Sacrist and Minor Canon, Durham Cathedral 1987–92; Anglican Chaplain in Bucharest and Sofia (Europe) 1992–96; Vicar of Shrub End, Colchester 1996–2004; Chaplain to The Bishop of Chelmsford 2004–10; Vicar of Lancaster from 2010
GS 2000   *T:* 01524 63200
            07802 733254
       E: chris@lancasterpriory.org
       Twitter: @ChrisTheVic

NEWMAN, The Rt Revd Adrian *BSc, Dip Th, MPhil, Doctor of Civil Law*
63 Coborn Road London E3 2DB [AREA BISHOP OF STEPNEY; LONDON] *b* 1958 *educ* Rickmansworth Comprehensive School; Bristol University; Trinity College Bristol *CV* Curate St Mark Forest Gate 1985–89; Vicar Hillsborough and Wadsley Bridge, Sheffield 1989–96; Rector St Martin in the Bull Ring, Birmingham 1996–2004; Dean of Rochester 2005–11; Bishop of Stepney from 2011; Honorary Fellow Canterbury Christ Church University
       T: 0207 932 1140
       E: bishop.stepney@london.anglican.org
       M: 07805 213319

NEWTON, Canon Sandra Clare *MSc, BSc, BA*
50 Broomgrove Road Sheffield South Yorkshire S10 2NA [VICE CHAIR AND TRUSTEE MEMBER, CHURCH OF ENGLAND PENSIONS BOARD] *b* 1967 *educ* Minchenden Grammar School; London School Economics; Open University *CV* Honorary Canon Sheffield Cathedral from 2006; Chair Sheffield Diocesan Board of Finance 2008–15; Member C of E Pensions Board from 2010; Member Archbishops' Council Finance Committee 2011–16
       T: 0114 266 1079
       E: sandracnewton@aol.com

NORTH, The Rt Revd Philip John *MA*
Dean House 449 Padiham Road Burnley BB12 6TE [SUFFRAGAN BISHOP OF BURNLEY: BLACKBURN] *b* 1967 *educ* The Latymer School, Edmonton; York University; St Stephen's House, Oxford *CV* Assistant Curate St Mary and St Peter,

Sunderland 1992–96; Vicar Holy Trinity, Hartlepool 1996–2002; Area Dean of Hartlepool 2000–02; Priest Administrator of the Shrine of Our Lady of Walsingham 2002–08; Team Rector of the Parish of Old St Pancras 2008–15; Bishop of Burnley from 2015
GS 2010–15   *T:* 01254 503087
    E: bishop.burnley@blackburn.anglican.org
                        Twitter: @BpBurnley

NUNN, The Very Revd Andrew Peter *BA, BA*
Southwark Cathedral London Bridge London SE1 9DA [DEAN OF SOUTHWARK] *b* 1958 *educ* Guthlaxton Upper School Wigston, Leicester; Leicester Polytechnic; Leeds University; College of Resurrection Mirfield *CV* Curate St James Manston, Ripon 1983–87; Curate Leeds Richmond Hill 1987–91, Vicar 1991–95; Chaplain Agnes Stewart C of E High School, Leeds 1987–95; Personal Assistant to Bishop of Southwark 1995–99; Vice-Provost, Precentor and Canon Residentiary Southwark Cathedral 1999–2000; Sub-Dean, Precentor and Canon Residentiary Southwark Cathedral 2000–11; Dean of Southwark from 2012; Member Diocesan Synod; Crown Nominations Commission 2011–17
GS 2005–   *T:* 020 7367 6727
    E: andrew.nunn@southwark.anglican.org
                        F: 020 7367 6725
        W: www.southwarkcathedral.org
                        M: 07961 332051
                Twitter: @deansouthwark

NYE, Mr William *LVO*
Church House Great Smith Street London SW1P 3AZ [SECRETARY GENERAL OF THE GENERAL SYNOD] *educ* Christ's Hospital, Horsham; BA Economics Cambridge University; MA Economics Yale University *CV* Head of Arts policy at the Department of Culture Media and Sport 1998–2000; Head of Defence, Diplomacy and Intelligence at the Treasury 2001–02; Director of Performance and Finance at the Home Office 2002–05; Director of Counter-Terrorism and Intelligence at the Home Office 2005–07; Director, Law, Security and International at the Home Office 2007–08; Director in the National Security Secretariat at the Cabinet Office 2008–11; Principal Private Secretary to The Prince of Wales and Duchess of Cornwall 2011–15; Secretary General of the General Synod from 2015   *T:* 020 7898 1361
    E: william.nye@churchofengland.org

OGLE, The Very Revd Catherine *BA, MPhil, MA, MA*
9 The Close Winchester SO23 9LS [DEAN OF WINCHESTER] *b* 1958 *educ* Perse School for Girls, Cambridge; University of Leeds; Fitzwilliam College Cambridge; Westcott House Cambridge; University Leeds *CV* Assistant Curate St Mary Middleton, Leeds 1988–91; Religious Programmes Editor BBC Leeds 1991–95; Non-Stipendiary Minister St Margaret and All Hallows, Leeds 1991–95; Priest in Charge Woolley with West Bretton 1995–2001; Editor Wakefield Diocesan Magazine 1995–2001; Vicar Huddersfield 2001–2010; Member Wakefield Diocesan Liturgy Group, Communications Group, Diocesan Synod; Member Council College of the Resurrection, Mirfield 2008–10; Honorary Canon Wakefield Cathedral 2008–10; Dean of Birmingham 2010–17; Dean of Winchester from 2017   *T:* 01962 857205
    E: dean@winchester-cathedral.org.uk
        W: www.winchester-cathedral.org.uk

OLDHAM, Mr Gavin David Redvers *MA (Cantab)*
Ashfield House St Leonards Tring HP23 6NP [OXFORD] *educ* Eton; Trinity College Cambridge *CV* Wedd Durlacher Mordaunt 1975–86, Partner 1984–86; Secretariat Barclays De Zoete Wedd (BZW) 1984–88; Chief Executive Barclayshare Ltd 1986–89, Chair 1989–90; Chair/Chief Executive The Share Centre Ltd from 1990; Chief Executive Share plc from 2000; Chair The Share Foundation from 2005; Church Commissioner from 1999; Member Finance Committee Archbishops' Council from 2001; Member Ethical Investment Advisory Group from 1999
GS 1995–   *T:* 01494 758348 (Home)
                        01296 439100 (Office)
                    E: gdro@btconnect.com
                        F: 01296 414410
                        W: www.gdro.net
                    M: 07767 337696 (Mobile)

OLIVIER, The Revd Bertrand Maurice Daniel *BA*
All Hallows by the Tower Byward Street EC3R 5BJ [LONDON] *b* 1962 *educ* College Notre Dame des Dunes, Lycée Français de Londres, EDC Business School Paris, Heythrop College *CV* Account Executive, Campbell Dalgleish Associates PR 1986–87; Account Executive, Hill and Knowlton PR 1987–89; Senior Vice President Europe, Ruder Finn PR 1989–93; Managing Director, Complete Pharma PR, 1993–96; Assistant Curate, St John's Walworth 1996–2000; Vicar, St Barnabas Southfields 2000–05; Area Dean of Wandsworth, 2002–05; Vicar of All Hallows by the Tower from 2005
GS 2015–   *T:* 020 7481 2928
                    E: bertrand@ahbtt.org.uk
                        Twitter: @bdo2006

ORMSTON, The Ven Richard Jeremy *BA, MTh*
Westbrook 11 The Drive Northampton NN1 4RZ [ARCHDEACON OF NORTHAMPTON; PETERBOROUGH] *b* 1961 *educ* Stamford School; Roehampton

Institute; Oak Hill Theological College *CV* Assistant Curate Rodbourne Cheney, Swindon 1987–91; Rector Collingtree with Courteenhall and Milton Malsor 1991–2001; Rural Dean Wootton 1996–2011; Vicar Oundle with Ashton and Benefield with Glapthorn 2001–14; Rural Dean Oundle 2002–13; Archdeacon of Northampton from 2014
　　　　　　　　　　　T: 01604 714015
　E: archdeacon.northampton@peterborough-
　　　　　　　　　　　diocese.org.uk
　　　　　　　　　　　F: 01604 792016
　W: www.peterborough-diocese.org.uk

OSBORNE, Canon Emma Charlotte *MA*
Lawn Farm Milton Lilbourne Pewsey SN9 5LQ [CHURCH COMMISSIONER] *educ* Redland High School, Bristol; Christ Church Oxford *CV* County NatWest 1985–89; Lloyds Investment Managers 1989–91; Credit Suisse/CSFB 1991–97; Investment Manager, Chubb Insurance from 1997　　　　　*T:* 01672 563459
　　　　　　　　　　　020 7956 5362
　E: emma.osborne@lawnfarm.co.uk

OSBORNE, The Ven Hayward John *MA, PGCE*
Church of England Birmingham 1 Colmore Row Birmingham B3 2BJ [ARCHDEACON OF BIRMINGHAM] *CV* Curate St Peter and St Paul Bromley 1973–77; Curate Halesowen 1977–80, Team Vicar 1980–83; Team Rector St Barnabas Worcester 1983–88; Vicar St Mary Moseley 1988–2001; Area Dean Moseley 1994–2001; Honorary Canon Birmingham Cathedral from 2000; Archdeacon of Birmingham from 2001
GS 1998–2015　　　*T:* 0121 426 0441 (Office)
　E: hayward@cofebirmingham.com

OZANNE, Ms Jayne Margaret *MA (Cantab)*
Campion Cottage Railway Lane Oxford OX4 4PY [OXFORD] *educ* The Ladies' College, Guernsey, St John's College, University of Cambridge; Magdalen College, University of Oxford *CV* Brand Management, Procter & Gamble 1990–93; Brand Management, Kimberly Clark 1993–96; Head of Marketing, BBC Television 1996–97; Founder, Ozanne Consultancy Services 1998–2006; Advisory Board, International Centre for Reconciliation, Coventry Cathedral 2001–04; Council and Standing Committee, Trinity Theological College 2002–06; Board Member, Church of England Newspaper 2004–06; Foreign Service Programme, University of Oxford 2006–07; Visiting Research Fellow, Department of International Development, University of Oxford 2007–08; Director of Fund Development, World Association of Girl Guides and Girl Scouts 2010–11; Head of Fundraising Partnerships, Oxfam GB 2011; Director of Fundraising, Tony Blair Faith Foundation 2012; Founder, Generosity 2013;

Director of Fundraising, Oxford Radcliffe Hospitals Charitable Funds from 2014
GS 1999–2004, 2015–　　　*T:* 01865 772989
　　　　　　E: jayne@jayneozanne.com
　　　　　　W: www.jayneozanne.com
　　　　　　Twitter: @JayneOzanne

PADDOCK, The Very Revd Dr John Allan Barnes *BA, MA, PhD, PGCE, FRSA*
The Deanery Bomb House Lane Gibraltar [DEAN OF GIBRALTAR; EUROPE] *b* 1951 *CV* Dean of Gibraltar from 2008　　　*T:* 00350 200 78377
　　　　　　E: deangib@gibraltar.gi
　　　　　　F: 00350 78463

PARKER, The Ven Matthew John *BA, BA*
39 The Brackens Clayton Newcastle under Lyme ST5 4JL [ARCHDEACON OF STOKE-UPON-TRENT; LICHFIELD] *educ* Bishop Wand C of E Secondary School Sunbury-on-Thames; Manchester University; Cambridge University; Ridley Hall Cambridge *CV* Assistant Curate St Mary's Twickenham 1988–91; Assistant Curate St George's Stockport 1991–93; Chaplain Stockport Grammar School 1991–94; Priest in Charge St Mark's Edgeley, Stockport 1993–95; Team Vicar Stockport South West 1995–2000; Team Curate Leek and Meerbrook Team Ministry 2000–13; Rural Dean Leek 2007–13; Archdeacon of Stoke-upon-Trent from 2013; Deputy Chair Lichfield Diocesan Board of Finance; Member Lichfield Diocesan Board of Education　　　　　*T:* 01782 663066
　E: archdeacon.stoke@lichfield.anglican.org

PARR, Dr Graham Duncan *BSc, PhD*
Mel Boracis Cottage 8 The Crofts Main Street Ulrome YO25 8UE [CHICHESTER] *b* 1955 *educ* Batley Grammar School, Robert Gordon University, Aberdeen and University of Bradford *CV* Lecturer in Pharmaceutics, University of Nottingham 1979–86; Group Head Pharmaceutical Research and Development, Reckitt & Colman Pharmaceuticals 1986–92; Director of Product Development, Whitehall International, 1992–98; Director of Pharmaceutical Development, Wyeth Consumer Healthcare 1998–2004; Assistant Vice-President Research and Development, Wyeth Consumer Healthcare 2004–08; Assistant Vice-President Research and Development, Pfizer Consumer Healthcare, 2008–11; Independent Consultant, Pharmaceutical Research and Development from 2011
GS 2014–　　　　　　　*T:* 01403 700793
　　　　　　　　　　　07774 271598
　E: graham.d.parr@hotmail.co.uk

PARRETT, Miss Margaret Anne *MSc*
22 Wiltshire Road Chadderton Oldham Lancs OL9 7RY [MANCHESTER] *educ* Windsor Girls' School (BFES Germany; Penhill Junior High School, Swindon; Headlands Senior High

School, Swindon, Portsmouth Polytechnic; Manchester University/UMIST *CV* Occupational Hygienist/Health, Safety and Environmental Manager, Chloride Industrial Batteries/ Chloride Motive Power 1978–89; Regional Manager/Consultancy Manager Thomson Laboratories/Thomson-MTS/NOHS Ltd. 1989– 93; Director/Health, Safety, Environmental & Quality Manager, Environmental Evaluation Limited, 1993–2015; Retired
GS 2015–   T: 0161 620 5115
                                    07976 204635
                           E: marjdit@btinternet.com

PATTERSON, Miss Jane Elizabeth *BSc (Hons), MB ChB (Hons)*
Fulwood Lodge 46 Chorley Road Sheffield S10 3RJ [SHEFFIELD] *educ* St Edmund's College, Liverpool, University of Liverpool *CV* Consultant Surgeon Kingsmill Hospital, Sherwood Forest Hospitals NHS Foundation Trust from 1998; Associate Clinical Sub Dean from 2007; Honorary Associate Clinical Professor from 2012
GS 2010–   T: 0114 2302994
                           E: janeepatterson@aol.com

PATTERSON, The Revd Neil Sydney *MA, BD*
Diocesan Office (Ludlow) The Business Quarter Ludlow Eco Park Sheet Road Ludlow SY8 1FD [HEREFORD] *b* 1954 *educ* Haberdashers' Aske's Boys School, Brasenose College Oxford; Ripon College Cuddesdon *CV* Curate Cleobury Mortimer with Hopton Wafers etc, 2004–08; Rector Ariconium 2008–15; Member Bishop's Council Hereford from 2012; Diocesan Director of Vocations and Ordinands from 2015
GS 2012–   T: 01584 871085
                           E: pattersonneil@hotmail.com

PAVER, Canon Elizabeth Caroline *FRSA*
113 Warning Tongue Lane Bessacar Doncaster DN4 6TB [SHEFFIELD] *educ* Doncaster Girls High School; St Mary's College Cheltenham *CV* In Primary Education 28 years; Head Teacher Crags Road Nursery/Infant School 1976–80; Head Teacher Askern Nursery/Infant School Littlemoor 1980–86; Head Teacher Intake Nursery and First School Doncaster from 1986; Member National Council National Association of Head Teachers from 1991; Centenary National President 1997–97; National Association of Head Teachers Appointee to General Teaching Council from 2000; past Member Panel of Chairmen General Synod; Lay Chair Diocesan Synod; Member Bishop's Council; Member Diocesan Board of Education Training Committee; Appointed Member Archbishops' Council 1999–2002; Lay Canon Sheffield Cathedral from 2000; Church Commissioner from 2004
GS 1991–   T: 01302 530706
                           E: johnpaver@btinternet.com
                                    F: 01302 360811

PERRETT, Canon Janet Rosemary *BA*
38 Beachampstead Road Great Staughton St Neots Cambridgeshire PE19 5DX [ELY] *b* 1942 *educ* Ely High School; Bedford College London University *CV* The Abbey Malvern Wells 1963–66; Milham Ford School Oxford 1966– 1971; Chichele School Rushden 1976–81; Stanground College, Peterborough 1981–95; Retired 95; Lay Chair of Ely Diocesan Synod; ADMPC, Board of Education; Cathedral Council; Bishop's Council; Safeguarding; Education Advisor for BAPs
GS 2010–   T: 01480 860703
                           E: jrperrett@talktalk.net

PERUMBALATH, The Ven Dr John *MA, MTh, PhD*
11 Bridgefields Close Hornchurch RM11 1GQ [ARCHDEACON OF BARKING; CHELMSFORD] *b* 1953 *educ* Calicut University; Osmania University; North West University; Serampore Theological College *CV* Lecturer in New Testament, Serampore College 1993–95; Vicar St James, Calcutta 1995–2000; Vicar St Thomas, Calcutta 2000–01; Assistant Priest St George, Beckenham 2002–05; Team Vicar Northfleet and Rosherville 2005–08; Vicar All Saints, Gravesend 2008–13; Diocesan Urban Officer 2008–13; Member Bishop's Council from 2007; Member Advisory Council for Ministry and Training 2007–10; Tutor, College of Preachers from 2008; Trustee United Society for the Propagation of the Gospel from 2009; Archdeacon of Barking from 2013; Member, Appointments Committee of the Church of England from 2015; Chair, London Churches Refugee Network from 2015; Chair, Committee for Minority Ethnic Anglican Concerns (CMEAC) from 2016; Member Mission and Public Affairs Council from 2016
GS 2010–   T: 01708 474951
                           E: a.barking@chelmsford.anglican.org

PHILIPS, Dr Jacqui (Jacqueline Louise) *MA(Cantab), MA(Durham), DPhil (Oxon)*
Church House Great Smith Street London SW1P 3AZ [CLERK TO THE SYNOD AND DIRECTOR OF CENTRAL SECRETARIAT] *b* 1971
                                    T: 0207 898 1385
                           E: jacqui.philips@churchofengland.org

PICKEN, The Ven David Anthony *BA(Hons), MA, PGCE*
22 Rufford Road Edwinstowe Notts NG21 9HY [ARCHDEACON OF NEWARK; SOUTHWELL] *b* 1963 *educ* Kingsmead; London and Nottingham Universities; Christ Church Canterbury; Lincoln Theological College *CV* Assistant Curate Worth Team Ministry 1990–93; Team Vicar St Clare's and Hospital Chaplain 1993– 97; Team Rector Wordsley 1997–2004; Area Dean Kingswinford 2001–04; Team Rector High Wycombe 2004–11; Area Dean Wycombe 2008–11; Archdeacon of Newark from 2012;

Member Bishop's Council; Chair Liturgical Committee; Member Diocesan Advisory Committee; Member Finance Committee; Member Church closure working group; Member Design Team for 2020 planning; Bishops Advisory Panel adviser; Diocesan Listening Process Convenor
T: 01636 817206
E: archdeacon-newark@ southwell.anglican.org
M: 07917 690576

PICKFORD, The Revd Catherine Ruth BA, MA
The Vicarage Beachlea Stannington Northumberland NE61 6HL [NEWCASTLE] *educ* All Saints RC, Sheffield, Stainburn School, Workington, Cockermouth School, Cockermouth, Nottingham University *CV* Curate of All Saints Gosforth, Newcastle Upon Tyne 2000–04; Team Vicar of the Venerable Bede Church, Benwell, Newcastle Upon Tyne 2004–09; Team Rector of St James' Benwell 2009–15; Continuing Ministerial Development Officer and Priest in Charge of St Marys Stannington, Northumberland 2015 GS 2015–　　　　　　　　*T:* 01670 785 606
　　　　　　　　　　　　　　07758 704780
E: catherine_pickford@yahoo.co.uk

PILGRIM, The Revd (Colin) Mark BA, MA, CertEs
St Peter's Vicarage 17 The Drive Henleaze Bristol BS9 4LD [BRISTOL] *b* 1956 *educ* St John's School, Leatherhead; Kingston Polytechnic; Geneva University; West of England University; Westcott House Theological College *CV* Curate, Chorlton-cum-Hardy, Manchester 1984–87; Curate, Ecumenical Priest Whitchurch, 1987–89; Vicar, St Oswald's, Bedminster Down 1989–95; Diocesan Child and Youth Officer, Bristol 1995–2001; Vicar, St Peter, Henleaze from 2001; Area Dean, Bristol West Deanery from 2006; Chair Diocesan Liturgical and Worcester Committee 2004–08; Member Bishop's Council from 2010 GS 2009–　　　　　　　　*T:* 0117 962 0636
E: markpilgrimis@aol.com

PITKIN, The Revd James Mark BSc, BA
The Vicarage Romsey Road Lockerley Romsey Hampshire SO51 0JF [WINCHESTER] *b* 1962 *educ* Berkhamsted School, Manchester University, University of Gloucestershire *CV* Royal Air Force Engineering Officer 1980–99; Assistant Curate in Chilworth and North Baddesley (Winchester) 1999–2003; Air Training Corps Wing Chaplain 2000–2015; Corps Chaplain of the Air Training Corps from 2015; Vicar of Lockerley and East Dean with East and West Tytherley from 2003 GS 2015–　　　　　　　　*T:* 01794340635
E: jamespitkin@priest.com
Twitter: @RevJamesPitkin

PLAYLE, Mrs Kathleen (Kathy)
136 Abbs Cross Lane Hornchurch Essex RM12 4XT [CHELMSFORD] *b* 1950　　*T:* 01708 442211
E: kathyplayle@btconnect.com

PORTER, The Rt Revd Anthony MA (Oxon), MA (Cantab)
Dunham House 8 Westgate Southwell NG25 0JL [SUFFRAGAN BISHOP OF SHERWOOD; SOUTHWELL AND NOTTINGHAM] *b* 1967 *educ* Aire Borough Grammar School; Don Valley High School; Gravesend School for Boys; Hertford College Oxford; Ridley Hall Cambridge *CV* Curate Edgware, London 1977–80; Curate St Mary Haughton, Manchester 1980–83; Priest in Charge Christ Church Bacup 1983–87, Vicar 1987–91; Rector Rusholme 1991–2006; Bishop of Sherwood from 2006; Member Diocesan Synod, Bishop's Council; Member College of Evangelists from 2009; Archbishops' Sport Ambassador from 2015; Director, Christians in Sport from 2015
　　　　　　　　　　　　　　T: 01636 819133
E: bishopsherwood@southwell.anglican.org

PORTER, Canon David
Lambeth Palace London SE1 7JU b 1954 *educ* RBAI; London School of Theology; University of Ulster *CV* Executive Secretary BMMF 1982–86; Northern Ireland Director Interserve 1986–90; International Co-ordinator (On Track) Interserve 1990–92; Cross Community Co-ordinator, City of Belfast YMCA 1993–94; Director, ECONI Evangelical Contribution on Northern Ireland 1994–2005; Director, Centre for Contemporary Christianity in Ireland 2005–08; Canon Director for Reconciliation Ministry at Coventry Cathedral 2008–13; Archbishop of Canterbury's Director for Reconciliation 2013–16; Archbishop of Canterbury's Chief of Staff and Strategy from 2016
　　　　　　　　　　　　　　T: 020 7898 1223
E: david.porter@lambethpalace.org.uk

PRATLEY, Mr Sam (Samuel) Robin MSc Management Sciences
The Palace Palace Yard Hereford HR4 9BL [DIOCESAN SECRETARY; HEREFORD] *b* 1980 *educ* Bishop Perowne High School; Loughborough University *CV* Hourly Paid Lecturer Worcester University (Social Welfare and Youth and Communities Studies) from 2004; Head of Supported Housing for Young People Project 2007–10; Director of Business Excellence and IT WM Housing Group 2010–13, Managing Director West Mercia Homes 2013–16; Diocesan Secretary Hereford from 2016
　　　　　　　　　　　　　　T: 01432 373300
E: s.pratley@hereford.anglican.org
Twitter: @sampratley

PRATT, The Ven Richard David *MA (Oxon),*
BCS, PhD (Birmingham)
50 Stainburn Road Workington Cumbria
CA14 1SN [ARCHDEACON OF WEST CUMBERLAND;
CARLISLE] *educ* Ranelagh School, Bracknell;
Lincoln College, Oxford; Nottingham
University; Lincoln Theological College;
Birmingham University *CV* Curate All
Hallows Wellingborough 1984–87; Team
Vicar Kingsthorpe 1987–92; Vicar
St Benedict's Hunsbury 1992–97, Priest in
Charge St Cuthbert's Carlisle and Diocesan
Communications Officers Carlisle Diocese
1997–2008; Archdeacon West Cumberland
from 2009   *T:* 01900 66190
        E: archdeacon.west@carlislediocese.org.uk
                                  M: 07788 728508

PRESLAND, Mr Andrew Roy *BSc*
58 Harborough Rd Rushden NN10 0LP
[PETERBOROUGH] *educ* Rushden Boys' School;
Leicester University *CV* Assistant Statistician,
Department of the Environment 1989–95;
Statistician Department of the Environment,
later DETR 1995–99; Senior Library Clerk
(Statistics), House of Commons Library
(secondment) 1999–2001; Statistician, Office of
Deputy Prime Minister (local government
finance) 2001–06, DCLG 2006–11 (strategy
and performance), and from 2011 (homelessness
statistics); Lay Chair, Higham Deanery Synod;
Treasurer East Northants Faith Group from
2005; Member Bishop's Council from 2006;
Member Archbishops' Council Finance
Committee 2006–11; Member Diocesan Board
of Finance 2006–08; Governor Whitefriars
Junior School Rushden from 2012
GS 2003–   *T:* 01933 316927
        E: andrewpresland@harboroughroad58.
                                     freeserve.co.uk
                W: www.dirtyhands.co.uk
                Twitter: @AndrewPresland

PRESTON, Dr John Philip Harry *BSc, PHD*
Church House Great Smith St London SW1P 3AZ
[NATIONAL STEWARDSHIP AND RESOURCES OFFICER,
ARCHBISHOPS' COUNCIL] *b* 1954 *educ* Lakes
School; Exmouth School; Lancaster University
CV Marketing Manager Procter and Gamble
1989–2000; Group Marketing Director South
Staffordshire Group 2000–02; Marketing,
Sales and NPD Manager, Freshway Foods
2002–05; National Stewardship and Resources
Officer from 2005   *T:* 020 7898 1540
        E: john.preston@churchofengland.org

PROUD, The Rt Revd Andrew John *BD, MA,*
AKC
Bishop's House Tidmarsh Lane Tidmarsh Reading
RG8 8HA [AREA BISHOP OF READING; OXFORD] *educ*
King's College London; School of Oriental
and African Studies; Lincoln Theological

College *CV* Curate Stansted Mountfitchet
Chelmsford 1980–83; Team Vicar
Borehamwood St Albans 1983–90; Curate
Bishop's Hatfield 1990–92; Rector East Barnet
1992–2001; Chaplain Addis Ababa St Matthew
Ethiopia 2002–07; Area Bishop Ethiopia and
Horn of Africa 2007–11; Area Bishop of
Reading from 2011   *T:* 0118 984 1216
        E: bishopreading@oxford.anglican.org
                                  F: 0118 984 1218

PYE, Mr Christopher Charles *BA, MSc*
140 Hinckley Rd St Helens WA11 9JY [LIVERPOOL]
educ Grange Park School St Helens; Open
University; Manchester University *CV*
Technologist in Glass Industry from 1963;
Retired Occupational Hygiene Manager; Lay
Chair St Helens Deanery Synod from 1986;
Lay Chair Diocesan Synod 1991–2003; Reader
GS 1985–90, 1992–   *T:* 01744 609506
        E: chrispye@blueyonder.co.uk

RALPH, The Revd Caroline Susan *BA(Hons)*
LLM, MA
The Rectory Church Lane Carhampton TA24 6NT
[BATH AND WELLS] *b* 1960 *educ* Bromley High
School; University of Birmingham; University
of the West of England; Nottingham Trent
University; Westcott House *CV* Solicitor
1987–90; Barrister 1990–2004; Assistant
Priest Crediton 2006–10; Vicar St Peter
Harborne 2010–13; Rector Dunster; Rural
Dean Exmoor; Member Ecclesiastical Fees
Measure Committee 2010
GS GS 2008–10, 2017–   *T:* 01643 821812
        E: caroline@249ralph.eclipse.co.uk

RATCLIFFE HOLMES, Mrs Madeleine
Le Peladis Rte Pommier 24350 Lisle Dordogne
France [EUROPE] *educ* Knutsford Secondary
School; Wimslow Evening Class; St John's,
Nottingham *CV* Fashion Model 1976–80;
Admin/Direct Mail copywriting and PR
Perferap Ltd, High Wycombe 1980–86; Sales
and Production Co-ordinator Communications
Direct High Wycombe, 1985–86; PA and PR
customers of Software House, Actiontech Ltd,
High Wycombe, 1987; PA to Director General
Royal Institute of Public Administration 1989–
91; Odgers & Co London PA to Management
Consultant 1989–97; Reader 2006; Diocesan
Synod Representative 2006–09; Contributor
Chaplaincy Bishop's Council 2006–09; Local
Radio Programme for Chaplaincy 2007–12;
Archdeaconry sub-committee 'Building
Together in France' 2007; Prayer Chain
Co-ordinator Chaplain from 2008; Diocesan
Environment Officer from 2010; Member
Mission and Public Affairs Team
GS 2010–   *T:* 00 33 553 04 85 44
        E: madeleine@peladis.plus.com
                madeleine.holmes13@gmail.com

RAYFIELD, The Rt Revd Dr Lee Stephen *BSc (Hons), PhD, CTM*
Mark House Field Rise Swindon SN1 4HP [SUFFRAGAN BISHOP OF SWINDON; BRISTOL] *educ* Thomas Bennett Comprehensive School, Crawley; Crawley College of Technology; Southampton University; St Mary's Hospital Medical School, London University; Ridley Hall, Cambridge *CV* Curate All Saints with St Andrew Woodford Wells, Chelmsford 1993–97; Priest in Charge St Peter with St Mark Hospital Church Furze Platt, Oxford 1997–2004, Vicar 2004–05; Area Dean Maidenhead and Windsor, Oxford 2000–05; Bishop of Swindon from 2005; Member UK Gene Therapy Advisory Committee 2000–09; Member Society of Ordained Scientists from 1995; Member Fellow of Parish Evangelism from 1995; Council Member Evangelical Alliance from 2007; Member House of Bishops Continuing Ministerial Education Committee from 2007; Continuing Ministerial Development Committee from 2012; Member Ethical Investment Advisory Group from 2007; Member Human Embryology and Fertilisation Authority from 2012   *T:* 01793 538654
E: bishop.swindon@bristoldiocese.org
F: 01793 525181
W: www.bristol.anglican.org/news/microblog

READ, The Revd Charles William
42 Heigham Road Norwich NR2 3AU [NORWICH] *educ* King Edward VI School, Lichfield; Manchester University; Manchester Polytechnic; St John's College, Nottingham *CV* Head of Religious Studies, Audenshaw High School 1982–86; Curate Oldham Team Ministry, 1988–90; Curate St Clement Urmston 1990–93; Goodshaw and Crawshawbooth 1993–94; Priest in Charge and Team Vicar Broughton Team Ministry 1994–99; Lecturer Liturgy and Doctrine, Cranmer Hall, Durham 1999–2006; Vice-Principal and Director Studies Norwich Diocesan Ministry Course from 2007; Eucharistic Prayers Steering Committee 1998–2000; Theological Education and Training Committee 2005–06
GS 1997–2000; 2005–06; 2010–
T: 01603 729813
E: charlesread@norwich.anglican.org

REDFERN, The Rt Revd Dr Alastair Llewellyn John *MA, MA, PhD*
The Bishop's House 6 King St Duffield Belper DE56 4EU [BISHOP OF DERBY] *b* 1958 *educ* Bicester School; Christ Church Oxford; Trinity College Cambridge; Westcott House Theological College; Bristol University *CV* Curate Tettenhall 1976–79; Lecturer in Church History, Director of Pastoral Studies and Vice-Principal Cuddesdon Theological College 1979–87; Curate All Saints Cuddesdon 1983–

87; Canon Residentiary Bristol Cathedral 1987–97; Canon Theologian and Director of Training 1987–97; Moderator of Parish Resource Team Ministry 1995–97; Member Advisory Board of Ministry Initial Ministerial Education Committee; Moderator Archbishops' Diploma for Readers; Bishop of Grantham 1997–2005; Dean of Stamford 1998–2005; Member Board Trustees Christian Aid 2015; Chair Finance Panel, Ministry Division; Member Theology, Education and Training Committee; Member Bishop's Committee for Ministry; Member Bishop's Continuing Ministerial Education Committee; Member Legal Aid Commission; Bishop of Derby from 2005; Member House of Bishops Theology Group; Co-chair Intern Faith Network for the UK 2010–13; Member Board of Trustees Christian Aid 2012–15; Chair of the Churches Legislation Advisory Committee from 2013; Vice-Chair Anglican Alliance from 2016
GS 2005–   *T:* 01332 840132
E: bishop@bishopofderby.org

REES, Canon (Vivian) John (Howard) *MA, LLB, MPhil*
16 Beaumont St Oxford OX1 2LZ [JOINT REGISTRAR, PROVINCE OF CANTERBURY] *b* 1951 *educ* Skinners' School Tunbridge Wells; Southampton University; Oxford University; Leeds University; Wycliffe Hall, Oxford *CV* Solicitor and Ecclesiastical Notary (Admitted 1975); Curate Moor Allerton Team Ministry 1979–82; Chaplain and Tutor Sierra Leone Theological Hall, Freetown 1983–86; Partner Winckworth Sherwood Solicitors from 1986; Treasurer Ecclesiastical Law Society 1995–2015, Chair from 2015; Registrar Oxford Diocese from 1998; Legal Adviser Anglican Consultative Council from 1998; Joint Registrar Province of Canterbury from 2000; Registrar, Court of Arches from 2000; Vice-Chair Legal Advisory Commission from 2001; Provincial Canon Canterbury Cathedral from 2001; Registrar, Clergy Discipline Tribunals Province of Canterbury from 2006; Chaplain to the Queen from 2014; Honorary Canon Christ Church Oxford from 2017
GS 1995–2000   *T:* 01865 297200 (Office)
01865 865875 (Home)
E: jrees@wslaw.co.uk
vjhrees@btinternet.com
F: 0207 593 0309
W: www.wslaw.co.uk
M: 07973 327417 (Mobile)

RENSHAW, Canon Elizabeth *MBE, Adv Dip Bus Man & Admin Man*
82 Ennisdale Drive West Kirby Wirral CH48 9UA [CHESTER] *CV* Business Management 1991–2008; Project Co-ordinator 2008–11; Church Commissioners; Bishoprics and Cathedrals

503

Committee; Lay Canon Chester Cathedral; Parish Giving Advisor; Secondary School Governor; Trustee Educational Trust; Member Archbishops' Council Finance Committee; Chair and Director Chester Diocesan Academies Trust; Director Chester Diocesan Board of Education
GS 2010–   T: 0151 625 5044
                  E: betty.renshaw@gmail.com

RIGBY, Miss Judith *BEd(dist)*
5 Easole Street Nonington Dover Kent CT15 4EU [WINCHESTER] *educ* Upton Hall Convent, Manchester University *CV* Teacher at St Aloysius Junior School, London 1984–92; Teacher at St Peter's Junior School Yateley 1992–97; Headteacher at Stimson House School and Therapeutic Community, Margate 1997–98; Education Consultant 1999; Head of Primary at Bradstow Special School Special Educational Needs/Autism 1999–2003; Self Employed Training, Consultancy and Clerking from 2003; Semi Retired; Clerk for Education Appeals for KCC Schools from 2003 and Academies from 2012; Safeguarding Trainer for Canterbury Diocese from 2005; Independent Autism and Safeguarding Trainer from 2003
GS 2015–   T: 01304 841046
                                    07930 536950
                        E: Judithrigby@sky.com
                        Twitter: @judith_rigby

ROBERTSHAW, The Revd Eleanor Elizabeth Mary *BA(hons), MA, MTh*
The Orchard Pontefract Road Snaith Goole DN14 9JS [SHEFFIELD] *educ* Maltby Comprehensive School; Bangor University; Leeds University *CV* 2000–04 Teacher of Religious Education, Brinsworth Comprehensive School; 2004–10 I/C KS4 Religious Education, Brinsworth Comprehensive School; 2010–13 Assistant Curate, St Mary's Stainforth, Diocese of Sheffield; Team Rector Parish of Great Snaith, Diocese of Sheffield from 2013
GS 2015–   T: 01405 860866
                                    07718 123138
                     E: eleanorbox@yahoo.co.uk
                        Twitter: @eleanorbox

ROBILLIARD, Mr David John
Le Petit Gree Torteval Guernsey GY8 0RD [WINCHESTER (CHANNEL ISLANDS)] *b* 1952 *educ* Guernsey Grammar School for Boys *CV* Clearing and International Banking 1969–82; HM Dep Greffier 1982–87; Principal Assistant Chief Executive Guernsey Civil Service 1987–94; Head of Constitutional Affairs States of Guernsey 1994–2007; Principal Officer States Assembly and Constitution Committee 2008–13; Deputy Clerk Guernsey States of Deliberation from 2010; Private Secretary to Bailiff of Guernsey from 2013; Treasurer

and Trustee Guernsey Deanery Synod; Churchwarden of Torteval
GS 1998–   T: 01481 264344 (Home)
                                  01481 749507 (Office)
                              E: villula@cwgsy.net
                                   F: 01481 713861
                          M: 07781 164344 (Mobile)

ROBINSON, Canon Andrew Ronald *BA (Hons), MSc*
Old Alresford Place Old Alresford SO29 9DH [DIOCESAN SECRETARY; WINCHESTER] *b* 1974 *educ* Bishop Luffa, Canterbury Christ Church College, Portsmouth University, Joint Services Defence College *CV* Business Administrator, Portsmouth City Council 1995–97; DAC and Pastoral Secretary, Diocese of Chichester 1997–99; Assistant Diocesan Secretary, Winchester Diocese 1999–2001; Deputy Diocesan Secretary, Portsmouth Diocese 2001–09; Royal Naval Reserve from 2000; Equerry to HRH Prince Michael of Kent, GCVO, Royal Household from 2013; Chief Executive, Diocese of Winchester from 2009
                                        T: 01962 737305
     E: andrew.robinson@winchester.anglican.org
              W: www.winchester.anglican.org

ROBINSON, The Rt Revd Anthony William *Cert Ed*
Pontefract House 181a Manygates Lane Wakefield WF2 7DR [AREA BISHOP OF WAKEFIELD; LEEDS] *b* 1958 *educ* Bedford Modern School; Bedford College of Higher Education; Sarum and Wells Theological College *CV* Curate St Paul Tottenham 1982–85; Team Vicar Resurrection Leicester 1985–89, Team Rector 1989–97; Rural Dean Christianity North 1992–97; Honorary Canon Leicester Cathedral from 1994; Member Central Board of Finance 1995–97; Member Committee for Minority Ethnic Anglican Concerns 1996–97; Archdeacon of Pontefract 1997–2003; Bishop of Pontefract 2002–14; Member Advisory Council for Religious Communities from 2010; Chair of Presence and Engagement Task Group from 2011; Bishop for the Area of Wakefield and Acting Bishop of Huddersfield 2014; Bishop for the Area of Wakefield from 2014; Area Bishop of Wakefield from 2015
GS 1995–97, 2000–02   T: 01924 250781
            E: bishop.tony@leeds.anglican.org

ROBINSON, The Revd Christopher *BEng, DipTH, PGDip*
The Rectory High Street Rattlesden IP30 0RA [ST EDMUNDSBURY] *b* 1983 *educ* Sevenoaks School, Warwick University *CV* Pastoral Lay Assistant at St Margaret's Church Whitnash 2004–05; Student Minister at Coventry Cathedral 2005–06; Assistant Curate of the South Hartismere Benefice 2009–12; Rector of

Rattlesden, Hitcham, Brettenham and Thorpe Morieux from 2012
GS 2015–　　　　　　　　T: 01449 737197
　　　　　　　　　　　　　07789 772024
　　　　　E: tifferrobinson@gmail.com
　　　　　　　　　Twitter: @tifferrobinson

ROBINSON, Professor Muriel Anita
PhD, MA, BEd
49 Broadway Lincoln LN2 1SG [LINCOLN] *b* 1954
educ West Norfolk and King's Lynn High School, University of London Institute of Education, Furzedown College of Education *CV* Junior classroom teacher 1976–77 Reay Primary School, London (ILEA); Haselrigge JM School, London (ILEA) – junior classroom teacher 1977–80; Immanuel Primary School, London (ILEA) – junior classroom teacher with Scale 2 responsibility for Science 1980–85; Seconded to Avery Hill College as a Teacher Fellow 1984–85; Brighton Polytechnic, Lecturer 2, English in Education 1985–87; Brighton Polytechnic/University of Brighton, Senior Lecturer, English in Education 1987–93; University of Brighton, Principal Lecturer 1993–98; Deputy Head, School of Education, University of Brighton 1998–2000; Vice Principal (Academic Quality), Newman College of Higher Education 2000–03; Principal, Bishop Grosseteste University College Lincoln 2003–12; Vice Chancellor, Bishop Grosseteste University 2012–13; Retired from 2013
GS 2015–　　　　　　　　T: 01522 512969
　　　　　　　　　　　　　07484 103433
　　　　　E: murielr@btopenworld.com

ROBINSON, The Ven Peter John Alan
BA, MA, PhD
4 Acomb Close Morpeth NE61 2YH [ARCHDEACON OF LINDISFARNE; NEWCASTLE] *b* 1961 *educ* St John's College Cambridge; St John's College Durham *CV* Curate North Shields 1995–99; Director Urban Ministry and Theology Project, Newcastle East Deanery; Priest in Charge Byker St Martin 1999–2008; Priest in Charge Byker St Michael with St Lawrence 2001–08; Honorary Canon Newcastle Cathedral 2007–08; Archdeacon of Lindisfarne from 2008; Chair William Temple Foundation from 2009
　　　　　　　　　　　　　T: 01670 503810
　　　　E: p.robinson@newcastle.anglican.org
　　　　　　　　　　　　　F: 01670 503 469
　　　　　　　　　　　　　M: 07786 642124

ROBINSON, Dr Sam (Samuel) *BA, MEd, PhD.*
Bank House 21 Bude Street Appledore Bideford EX39 1PS [EXETER] *educ* Letterkenny Technical College, Bolton Street Dublin College of Technology, Pembroke Technical Institute, University College Dublin, Trinity College Dublin *CV* Teacher, Head of Department, Dean of Discipline, Emmet Road Vocational School, Dublin, 1966–78; Teacher, Bluecoat (Sixth

Form House) Housemaster, The King's Hospital, Dublin, 1978–96; Headmaster, Dundalk Grammar School, Dundalk, Ireland, 1996–2001; Teacher, Housemaster, Longfield and Carisbrook Houses, Edgehill College, Bideford, 2001–06; Councillor Torridge District Council, 2006–11; Northam Town Council, 2007–11; Devon County Council, 2009–13; Councillor Torridge District Council; Bideford Town Council, both from 2015
GS 2015–　　　　　　　　T: 01237 474413
　　　　　E: sande.bhouse@outlook.com

RODHAM, The Ven Morris *MA, PGCE, BA, DipHE*
3 The Gardens Thurlaston Rugby CV23 9LS [ARCHDEACON MISSIONER, DIOCESE OF COVENTRY] *b* 1959 *educ* RGS Newcastle; Durham University Hatfield College; Bristol University; Trinity College Bristol *CV* Regular Army (Royal Artillery) 1978, 1981–84; Teacher Warwick School (Classics, CCF, Hockey) 1985–90; Curate St Mark's Leamington 1993–1997; Vicar St Mary's Leamington 1997–2010; Rural Dean Warwick and Leamington 2006–10; Archdeacon Missioner from 2010
　　　　　　　　　　　　　T: 02476 521337
　　　　　E: morris.rodham@covcofe.org

ROSE, The Revd Susan Margaret *B Ed*
25 Wood Close Wells Somerset BA5 2GA [BATH AND WELLS] *educ* Stoud Girls High School; Keswick Grammar School; Westminster College Higher Education; St Albans and Oxford Ministry Course *CV* Teacher, 1981–98; Curate North Petherton with Moorland, 1998–2000; Rector, The Alfred Jewel Benefice, 2000–09; Priest in Charge, Cheddar; Rodney Stoke with Draycott, 2009; Secretary Committee Ministerial Review, 1999–2002; Vocations Chaplain 2002–07; Design team Bishop Course for Readers, 2002–04; Rural Dean Sedgemoor 2007–09; Member Diocesan Patronage Board from 2009–14; County Chaplain Girl Guiding 2007–13; Area Advisor for Women Clergy 2010–15; Diocesan Synod Representative 1999–2015; Bishop's Council Member 2008–10; Director of Vocations and Initial Ministerial Education Phase 2, Bath and Wells; Vocations Team Leader, Ministry for Mission, Bath and Wells
GS 2010–　　　　　　　　T: 01749 685273
　　　　　　　　　　　　　07958 946199
　　　　　E: sue.rose@bathwells.anglican.org

ROSS, The Ven Vernon *MA Missional Leadership, Bsc(Hons) Biology*
The Vicarage Windermere Road Lindale LA11 6LB [ARCHDEACON OF WESTMORLAND AND FURNESS; CARLISLE] *b* 1957 *educ* St Andrews C of E School Worthing; Portsmouth Polytechnic; Trinity College Bristol *CV* Staff Nurse St Mary's Hospital Portsmouth 1986–87; Research Nurse

Countess Mountbatten Hospice, Southampton 1987–89; Curate St Johns Fareham 1991–94; Priest in Charge Witheridge et al 1994–2000; Team Rector Barnstaple 2000–08; Mission and Ministry Adviser Barking Episcopal Area and Priest in Charge of Fyfield et al 2008–14; Mission and Ministry Adviser Barking Episcopal Area 2014–17; Archdeacon of Westmorland and Furness from 2017; Chair of Schools Committee Exeter Diocese 2000–08; Board of Education Member; Board of Finance and Board of Education Member Carlisle Diocese from 2017

T: 01539 534717
E: archdeacon.south@carlislediocese.org.uk
M: 07388 377105
Twitter: @Barkingmission

ROUCH, The Ven Dr Peter Bradford
MA (Oxon); MA (Cantab); PhD (Manch)
22 Bellflower Way Chandler's Ford Hampshire SO53 4HN [ARCHDEACON OF BOURNEMOUTH; WINCHESTER] *educ* Sir Joseph Williamson's Mathematical School Rochester; Brasenose College Oxford; Peterhouse Cambridge; Manchester University; Westcott House Theological College *CV* Curate St John the Evangelist, East Dulwich 1999–2002; Junior Research Fellow, St Stephen's House Oxford 2002–04; Chaplain St John's College Oxford 2003–04; Priest-in-charge Apostles' Manchester with St Cuthbert Miles Platting Manchester 2005–11; Honorary Research Fellow Manchester University 2007–11; Archdeacon of Bournemouth from 2011
GS 2013– T: 01962 710962
02380 260955
E: peter.rouch@winchester.anglican.org

RUSHTON, The Ven Samantha Jayne
MA (Oxon), BA
48 Langbaurgh Rd Hutton Rudby Yarm North Yorkshire TS15 0HL [ARCHDEACON OF CLEVELAND; YORK] *educ* Lichfield Friary Grange, St Hilda's College, Oxford *CV* Various roles from Graduate Trainee to Head of Process Re-engineering, Business Banking, Lloyds TSB Plc 1987–2002; Curate, Highworth with Hannington, Sevenhampton, Inglesham and Broad Blunsdon 2005–08; Diocesan Adviser for Licensed Ministry, Bristol 2008–15 (including Warden of Readers from 2010); Assistant Minister, North Chippenham Group of Churches 2008–15; Area Dean, Chippenham Deanery 2013–15; Archdeacon of Cleveland and Warden of Readers, Diocese of York from 2015 T: 01642 706 095
E: adcl@yorkdiocese.org

RUSSELL, Canon Mark Kenneth *LLB, FRSA*
Church Army Wilson Carlile Centre 50 Cavendish Street Sheffield S3 7RZ [ELECTED MEMBER, ARCHBISHOPS' COUNCIL] *educ* Portadown College,

The Queen's University of Belfast *CV* Project Executive WD Irwin Ltd 1995–97; Youth Pastor, Lurgan Methodist Church 1997–2000; Youth Minister Christ Church Chorleywood 2000–06; Chief Executive and Community Leader Church Army from 2006; Member Archbishops' College of Evangelists from 2009; Chair Church Army International Leaders Group from 2011; Honorary Canon Worcester Cathedral from 2012; Member of Archbishops' Evangelism Task Group from 2013; Member of Archbishops' Council elected by laity from 2015; Member General Synod Business Committee from 2015
GS 2004– T: 0300 123 2113
E: mark.russell@churcharmy.org
W: www.churcharmy.org/ceo
Twitter: @markrusselluk

RYLANDS, The Rt Revd Mark James *MA*
Athlone House 68 London Road Shrewsbury SY2 6PG [AREA BISHOP OF SHREWSBURY; LICHFIELD] *CV* Area Bishop of Shrewsbury from 2009
T: 01743 235867
E: bishop.shrewsbury@lichfield.anglican.org
Twitter: @shrewsbishop

SALISBURY, Dr Matthew R. C. *MSt DPhil (Oxon), FRHistS, FHEA*
Church House Great Smith Street London SW1P 3AZ [NATIONAL LITURGY AND WORSHIP ADVISER] *educ* Worcester College Oxford *CV* Lecturer in Music, Worcester College Oxford 2010–11, from 2015; Lecturer in Music, University College Oxford from 2012; National Liturgy and Worship Adviser from 2015; Assistant Chaplain Worcester College from 2017
T: 020 7898 1765
E: matthew.salisbury@churchofengland.org
Twitter: @cofe_worship

SARGENT, The Revd Dr Benjamin Charles *BA, MA, MTh, DPhil, AKC*
The Vicarage Ringwood Road Bransgore Hampshire. BH23 8JH [WINCHESTER] *educ* The Petersfield School, University of Oxford *CV* Youth Minister, St John the Evangelist, Penge 2004–06; Chaplaincy Assistant, King's College London 2006–07; Assistant Curate, Warblington with Emsworth 2009–13; Research Fellow, Wycliffe Hall 2011–13; Priest in Charge of Bransgore and Hinton Admiral from 2013
GS 2015– T: 01425 672850
07990 695830
E: vicar@bransgore.org

SCHOFIELD, The Revd Preb Sarah *BA, PGCert, MPhil*
The Vicarage 27 Adelaide Walk Wolverhampton WV2 1DX [LICHFIELD] *educ* Carlton Le Willows, University of Manchester, Urban Theology Unit, University of Birmingham *CV* Assistant

Curate St Luke Longsight Manchester 1997–2002; Priest in Charge St Mary Oranjemund 1999; Tutor to Westcott House Manchester project 2000–04; Priest in Charge St Philip Gorton Manchester 2002–06; Priest in Charge St George Abbey Hey Manchester, 2004–06; Team Vicar Central Wolverhampton from 2006; Prebendary of Weeford (Lichfield Cathedral)
GS 2015–   *T:* 07500 780494
                                E: Revsarah@hotmail.co.uk
                                Twitter: @urbankindness

SCOTT, Mrs Angela Mary *MTh, Cert Ed*
The Stead Willow Grove Chislehurst BR7 5BU [ROCHESTER] *educ* Portsmouth High School; Bedford College of Physical Education; Spurgeon's Theological College *CV* Teacher, Stratford House School, Kent 1972–75; Home Maker 1975–99; Part-time Teacher, Marjory McClure School, Kent 1984–87; Supply Teaching, Bromley 1987–92; Church Administrator 1992–98; Diocesan Pastoral Assistant from 2000; Diocesan Tutor, 2000–08
GS 2000–05; 2010–   *T:* 020 8467 3589
                        E: a@5scotts.freeserve.co.uk
                                    M: 07809 438737

SCOWEN, Mr Clive Richard *LLB*
69 Brooke Ave Harrow HA2 0ND [LONDON] *educ* John Lyon School Harrow; Bristol University; Inns of Court School of Law *CV* Called to bar (Inner Temple) 1981; law reporter, Incorporated Council of Law Reporting 1983–90; Deputy Editor Weekly Law Reports 1990–2000; Joint Editor, Law Reports Consolidated Index from 2000; Managing Editor, Weekly Law Reports 2006–07; Editor Law Reports and Weekly Law Reports from 2008; Councillor, London Borough of Harrow 1990–2002; Reader from 1991; Member Bristol University Court from 1980; Director Glencoe Trust Ltd; Director Soul Survivor Harrow; Trustee, Charles Gardner Memorial Fund; Trustee, Maseno Project Trust; Member Mission and Public Affairs Council; Member General Synod Standing Orders Committee; Member London Diocesan Bishop's Council; Director London Diocesan Fund; Member Willesden Area Council; Member Bishop of London Mission Fund Board; Member Harrow Deanery Standing Committee
GS 2005–   *T:* 020 8422 1329
                            E: clivescowen@onetel.com
                                M: 07771 780805 (Mobile)

SEARLE, The Ven Jacqueline Ann *MA, BEd, Dip Th*
9 College Green Gloucester GL1 2LY [ARCHDEACON OF GLOUCESTER] *educ* Talbot Heath, Bournemouth; Whitelands College, London; Trinity College Bristol *CV* Teacher 1982–90; Curate Christ Church Roxeth 1992–94; Curate St Stephen's Ealing 1994–96; Tutor Applied

Theology and Dean of Women Trinity College Bristol 1996–2003; Dean of Women's Ministry Derby 2007–10; Vicar St Peter's, Littleover, Derby 2003–12; Rural Dean Derby South 2010–12; Archdeacon of Gloucester from 2012; Canon Residentiary Gloucester Cathedral from 2012
GS 2010–12   *T:* 01452 835583
                            E: archdglos@glosdioc.org.uk
                                Twitter: @jackiesearle09

SEDDON, Mr (William Trevor) Bill *BSc, ASIP*
20 Carpenters Wood Drive Chorleywood Rickmansworth WD3 5RJ [ST ALBANS] *educ* Grove Park Boys' Grammar School, Wrexham; University College London *CV* Trainee Investment Manager Central Board of Finance C of E 1973–75; Assistant Investment Manager White Weld 1975–77; Investment Asset Manager Paine Webber 1977–80; Manager Dominion Insurance 1980–85; Assistant Investment Manager, Central Finance Board Methodist Church 1985–87; Investment Manager and Chief Executive, Central Finance Board Methodist Church and Epworth Investment Management Ltd 1987–2017, retired 2017; Council Member and Treasurer Queen Victoria Clergy Fund
GS 2010–   *T:* 01923 285727
        E: bill.seddon@cfbmethodistchurch.org.uk
                                        F: 0207 496 3631

SENTAMU, The Most Revd and Rt Hon Dr John Tucker Mugabi *LLB, MA, Ph D, LLD (Hon), DD (Hon), FRSA, Privy Co*
Bishopthorpe Palace Bishopthorpe York YO23 2GE [ARCHBISHOP OF YORK] *educ* Makerere University Kampala; Selwyn College Cambridge; Ridley Hall Theological College *CV* Assistant Chaplain Selwyn College Cambridge 1979; Chaplain HM Remand Centre Latchmere House 1979–82; Curate St Andrew Ham 1979–82; Curate St Paul Herne Hill 1982–83; Priest in Charge Holy Trinity Tulse Hill 1983–84; Parish Priest St Matthias 1983–84; Vicar Holy Trinity and St Matthias Tulse Hill 1985–96; Priest in Charge St Saviour Brixton 1987–89; Honorary Canon; Southwark Cathedral 1993–96; Bishop of Stepney 1996–2002; Member National Association for the Care and Rehabillitation of Offenders Young Offenders Committee 1986–95; Member Archbishop's Advisory Group on Urban Priority Areass 1986–92; Member Advisory Board of Ministry Council 1985–1990; Member Standing Committee General Synod House of Clergy 1985–96; Member General Synod Standing Committee 1988–96; Member Family Action (formerly Family Welfare Association) 1989–96; Member General Synod Policy Committee 1990–96; Chair Diocesan House of Clergy 1992–96; Member Decade of Evangelism

Steering Group and Springboard Executive 1991–96; Member Turnbull Proposals Steering Group 1995; Member Steering Group Women (Priests) Ordination Measure; Pro-Prolocutor Convocation of Canterbury 1990–94; Chair Committee Minority Ethnic Anglican Concerns 1990–99; Prolocutor Convocation of Canterbury 1994–96; Member The Stephen Lawrence Judicial Inquiry 1997–99; President and Chair London Marriage Guidance Council 2000–04; Chair Damilola Taylor Murder Review 2002; Fellow University College Christ Church Canterbury 2001; Fellow Queen Mary College University of London 2001; Honorary Doctor Open University 2001; Doctor of Philosophy (Honorary) University of Gloucester 2002; Doctor of Divinity (Honorary) University of Birmingham 2003; Chair ECI NDC 2002–04; Chair NHS Sickle Cell and Thalassaemia Screening Programme 2001–13; Trustee, Smith Institute 2002–11; Member, Birmingham Hospitals NHS Trust 2002; Bishop of Birmingham 2002–05; Midlander of the Year 2003; Vice-Chair Commission on Urban Life and Faith 2004–06; President Youth for Christ from 2004 and Young Men's Christian Association England from 2005; Archbishop of York from 2005; Doctor of Letters (Honorary), University of Leicester 2005; Honorary Fellow Selwyn College Cambridge 2005; Chancellor York St John University from 2006; Freeman City of London 2000; Doctor of Divinity (Honorary) University of Hull 2007; Doctor of Laws (Honorary) University of Sheffield 2007; Yorkshire Man of the Year 2007; Speaker of the Year 2007; Master Bencher (Honorary) Gray's Inn 2007; Freeman City of Montego Bay 2007; Doctor of Letters (Honorary) University of the West Indies 2007; Chancellor University of Cumbria from 2007; Honorary Doctor Birmingham City University 2008; Doctor of Divinity (Honorary) University of Cambridge 2008; Doctor of Civil Law (Honorary) Northumbria University 2008; Doctor of Divinity (Honorary) University of Nottingham 2008; Doctor of Divinity (Honorary) Wycliffe College Toronto 2009; Doctor of Letters (Honorary) Teesside University 2009; Doctor of Theology DTh (Honorary) University of Chester 2009; (Honorary) Dr University of York 2010; Doctor of Letters (Honorary) University of Leeds 2010; Doctor of Divinity (Honorary) Sewanee (University of the South) Tennessee 2010; Doctor of Divinity (Honorary) University of London 2010; Visit York's 'Tourism Ambassador' 2010; Sponsor York Fairness Commission 2011–12; Doctor of Divinity (Honorary) Huron University College, London Ontario 2013; Doctor of Divinity (Honorary) Aberdeen University 2013; Chair Living Wage Commission 2013–14; Honorary Fellow St Margaret's College Dunedin 2014;

Harold Turner Visiting Fellow, University of Otago 2014
GS 1985–96; 2002–ㅤㅤㅤㅤ*T:* 01904 707021
ㅤㅤㅤㅤ*E:* office@archbishopofyork.org
ㅤㅤㅤㅤ*F:* 01904 772389
ㅤㅤㅤㅤ*W:* www.archbishopofyork.org

SEWELL, Mr Martin David *LLB*
Appleshaw Close Gravesend Kent DA11 7PB [ROCHESTER] *educ* Gravesend Grammar School for Boys, Kingston Polytechnic *CV* Solicitor 1975–2014; Reader from 1987; Retired
GS 2014–ㅤㅤㅤㅤ*T:* 01474 745443
ㅤㅤㅤㅤ*E:* martin.sewell@me.com
ㅤㅤㅤㅤ*W:* BrotherIvo.com
ㅤㅤㅤㅤ*Twitter:* @BrotherIvo

SHARPLES, The Ven David John
2 The Walled Gardens Ewhurst Avenue Swinton M7 0FR [ARCHDEACON OF SALFORD; MANCHESTER] *b* 1954 *CV* Archdeacon of Salford from 2010; Residentiary Canon Manchester Cathedral from 2017ㅤㅤㅤㅤ*T:* 0161 794 2331
ㅤㅤㅤㅤ0161 708 9366
ㅤㅤㅤㅤ*E:* archsalford@manchester.anglican.org

SHAW, Mr Edward (Ed) Jonathan James *BA*
65 Strathmore Road Bristol BS7 9QH [BRISTOL] *educ* Monkton Combe School, St John's College, Durham *CV* Associate for Students, St Nic's, Durham, 1998–99; Youth and Student Worker, St Luke's, Hampstead, 1999–2001; Student Minister and Ministry Assistant Trainer, Christ Church, Clifton, 2001–07; Associate Pastor, Emmanuel, Bristol, from 2009; Pastor, Emmanuel, City Centre, from 2014
GS 2015–ㅤㅤㅤㅤ*T:* 01179513556
ㅤㅤㅤㅤ01179513556
ㅤㅤㅤㅤ*E:* ed@emmanuelbristol.org.uk

SHEATHER, Mrs Margaret Eleanor *BA, MSc (Oxon)*
2 Old School Close Nailsworth Stroud GL6 0NY [GLOUCESTER] *b* 1952 *educ* Exeter University; Oxford University *CV* Social worker/senior social worker, Berkshire County Council 1978–87; Assistant Divisional Director/Locality Manager/Senior Assistant Director, Berkshire County Council 1987–97; Assistant Director, Operations, Buckinghamshire County Council 1997–2000; Director of Social Services/Group Director Community and Adult Care, Gloucestershire County Council 2000–10; Freelance Social Care Consultant and Knowledge Transfer Fellow, Oxford Brookes University from 2012
GS 2015–ㅤㅤㅤㅤ*T:* 01453 834961
ㅤㅤㅤㅤ*E:* m.sheather@btinternet.com

SHELLEY, Dr (John Richard) Jack *MA, MB BChir, MRCGP, MA*
Shobrooke Park Crediton Devon EX17 1DG [EXETER] *b* 1958 *educ* King's School, Cambridge

University; St Mary's University; Exeter University; SWMTC Reader Certificate *CV* Medical Practitioner 1967; Chair Devon Local Medical Committee 1999–2002; Partner South Molton Health Centre 1974–2003; Farmer from 1974; Member Exeter Diocesan Synod from 2002; Member Council Worship and Ministry Exeter from 2003; Reader Exeter 2009, PTO from 2013
GS 2009–   *T:* 01363 775153
              E: jack@shobrookepark.com
                    M: 07971 136901

SHUTTLEWORTH, Mr Geoffrey Kenneth
23 Ledbury Way Walmley Sutton Coldfield West Midlands B76 1EH [BIRMINGHAM] *educ* King Edward VI Grammar School Aston, Birmingham, University College of Wales, Aberystwyth *CV* Manager HM Customs and Excise 1967–2006; Church Warden and PCC Treasurer, 1999–2008; Magistrate, Birmingham and Solihull Bench from 1999; Voluntary youth worker, The Scout Association from 1970
GS 2014–   *T:* 0121 351 3615
              E: Patatwalmley@aol.com

SIMS, The Ven Vickie Lela *BA, BTh,*
Post-graduate Diploma in Practical
Theology
c/o All Saints' Anglican Church Via Solferino 17 Milano 20121 Italy [ARCHDEACON OF ITALY AND MALTA; DIOCESE IN EUROPE] *b* 1956 *educ* Ames High School; Iowa State University BA; Ripon College Cuddesdon, BTh, Cambridge Theological Federation, Post-Graduate Diploma in Practical Theology *CV* Assistant Curate St Wulfram's Grantham 2002–05; Priest in charge, Vicar St Andrew's Coulsdon 2005–14; Assistant Director of Post-Ordination Training (Croydon Episcopal Area) 2008–14; All Saints' Anglican Church, Milan from 2014, with oversight for Genoa, Lake Como, Varese; Archdeacon of Italy and Malta from 2016; Diocesan Board of Finance Southwark 2006–14; Diocesan Safeguarding Advisory Group Europe from 2016; Diocesan Strategy Group Europe from 2016   *T:* +39 02 655 2258
          E: vickie.sims@europe.anglican.org
                    M: +39 345 583 5978

SINCLAIR, The Rt Revd (Gordon) Keith
MA, BA
Bishop's Lodge 67 Bidston Rd Prenton CH43 6TR [SUFFRAGAN BISHOP OF BIRKENHEAD; CHESTER] *b* 1952 *educ* Trinity School Croydon; Christ Church Oxford; Cranmer Hall Durham *CV* Curate Christ Church Summerfield 1984–88; Part-time Chaplain, Children's Hospital Birmingham; Vicar Saints Peter and Paul Aston juxta Birmingham 1988–2001; Area Dean Aston 2000–01; Vicar Holy Trinity Coventry 2001–06; Bishop of Birkenhead

from 2007; Member Bishop's Council and Diocesan Synod, Chester; Trustee/Chair Chester Diocesan Board of Education; Governor Bishop's High School Chester; Trustee Historic Cheshire Churches Preservation Trust; Trustee Churches Together in Merseyside; Chair Governor Body for Bishop's High School; Chair Church Patoral Aid Society Council of Reference; Trustee, Five Talents; Council of Reference True Freedom Trust
                    T: 0151 652 2741
          E: bpbirkenhead@chester.anglican.org
                    F: 0151 651 2330

SINCLAIR, The Revd John Robert
16 Towers Avenue Jesmond Newcastle NE2 3QE [NEWCASTLE] *educ* Walbottle High School; Oak Hill Theological College *CV* Curate Ponteland St Mary Newcastle 1992–96; Vicar Longbenton St Mary Magdalene Newcastle 1996–2001; Vicar Newburn St Michael and All Angels Newcastle from 2001; Area Dean Newcastle West from 2007; Honorary Canon Newcastle Cathedral from 2008; Chair House of Clergy from 2009; Member Evangelism Task Group 2001; Member Diocesan Finance Strategy Group 2009
GS 2010–   *T:* 0191 281 9375
              E: johnsinclair247@aol.com
                    M: 07746 743857

SKILTON, The Ven Christopher John *MA,*
Cert Theol, MA
St Matthew's House 100 George Street Croydon CR0 1PE [ARCHDEACON OF CROYDON; SOUTHWARK] *b* 1955 *educ* Latymer Upper School Hammersmith; Magdalene College Cambridge; Wycliffe Hall Oxford *CV* Curate St Mary Ealing 1980–84; Curate Newborough with Leigh St John Wimborne 1984–88; Team Vicar St Paul Great Baddow 1988–95; Team Rector Sanderstead 1995–2003; Rural Dean Croydon South 2000–03; Archdeacon of Lambeth 2004–13; Archdeacon of Croydon from 2013
                    T: 020 8256 9633
          E: chris.skilton@southwark.anglican.org
                    M: 07903 704506

SKRINE, The Revd (Charlie) Charles Walter
Douglas *BA*
73 Victoria Park Road London E9 7NA [LONDON] *b* 1958 *educ* Marlborough College, Queen's, Oxford *CV* Pastoral Assistant, Emmanuel Wimbledon 1997–99; Project Assistant, Spitalfields Crypt Trust 1999–2000; Curate/Associate Rector St Helen's Bishopsgate from 2003; Priest in Charge St Michael Cornhill from 2017; Assistant Diocesan Director of Ordinands Two Cities Area from 2017
GS 2015–   *T:* 020 7283 2231
                    07986 088851
              E: c.skrine@st-helens.org.uk

SLACK, Mr Stephen *MA*
Church House Great Smith Street London SW1P 3AZ [REGISTRAR AND CHIEF LEGAL ADVISER TO THE GENERAL SYNOD, JOINT REGISTRAR OF THE PROVINCES OF CANTERBURY AND YORK, CHIEF LEGAL ADVISER TO THE ARCHBISHOPS' COUNCIL] *educ* Aylesbury Grammar School; Christ Church Oxford *CV* Solicitor in private practice 1979–84; Senior Lawyer Charity Commission Liverpool 1984–89; Head Legal Section Charity Commission Taunton 1989–2001; Head Legal Office and Chief Legal Advisor to Archbishops' Council and General Synod from 2001, Registrar General Synod, Joint Registrar Provinces Canterbury and York, Member Legal Advisory Commission from 2001; Official Solicitor to Church Commissioners from 2009
T: 020 7898 1366
E: stephen.slack@churchofengland.org
F: 020 7898 1718

SLATER, Mr Colin Stuart *MBE, MA (Hon)*
11 Muriel Rd Beeston Nottingham NG9 2HH [SOUTHWELL AND NOTTINGHAM] *educ* Belle Vue Grammar School Bradford *CV* Chief PRO Nottinghamshire County Council 1969–87; Severn Trent Water 1987–89, Nottinghamshire County Cricket Club 1989–95; Chair BBC Radio Nottingham Advisory Council 1975–79; former Chair Society of Public Relations Officers and Institute of Public Relations Local Government Group; Member Council Institute of Public Relations 1986–90; Justice of the Peace 1977–2004; Chair Nottingham Magistrates 2003 and 2004; Chair Nottinghamshire Courts Board 2005–07; Chair Nottinghamshire-Derbyshire Courts Board 2007–12; PR Consultant and freelance broadcaster from 1995; member Bishop's Council, Finance Committee; Vice-Chair Christian Stewardship Committee of Archbishops' Council 1999–2012; Member Council St John (Nottingham) College from 2006 and its Standing Committee from 2008, Vice Chair from 2010; awarded Freedom of Borough of Broxtowe (Nottinghamshire) 2010
GS 1990–
T: 0115 925 7532
E: colinslater@mac.com
F: 0115 925 7532
M: 07919 008788 (Mobile)

SLATER, The Rt Revd Paul John *MA, BA*
Church House 17–19 York Place Leeds LS1 2EX [BISHOP OF RICHMOND; LEEDS] *b* 1967 *educ* Bradford Grammar School; Corpus Christi Oxford; St John's College Durham *CV* Curate St Andrew Keighley 1984–88; Priest in Charge St John Cullingworth 1988–93; Director Lay Training Foundation Course 1988–93; PA to Bishop of Bradford 1993–95; Warden of Readers 1992–96; Rector St Michael Haworth

1995–2001; Bishop's Officer for Ministry 2001–14; Archdeacon of Craven from 2005–14; Archdeacon of Richmond and Craven 2014–15; Bishop of Richmond from 2015
GS 2013–15
T: 0113 353 0252
E: bishop.paul@leeds.anglican.org

SLATER, Mrs Susan Gay *Cert Ed, DGA, BA(Hons)*
3 Church Street Spalding PE11 2PB [LINCOLN] *b* 1953 *educ* Oxford High School; Homerton College Cambridge; Lincoln School of Theology, University of Lincoln *CV* Admin trainee/Higher Executive Officer, DHSS 1967–74; domestic admin and voluntary work 1974–94; PA to National Director Leprosy Mission England and Wales 1994–2005; Retired 2005; General Advisor South Holland Citizens Advice Bureau 2005–12; Member Lincoln Diocesan HR Committee 2005–10; Secretary Elloe West Deanery Synod 2005–10; Member Church and Community Fund Committee 2005–10; Chair South Holland Fairtrade Steering Group 2008–10; Reader in Training, Lincoln Theological School 2010–13, Reader from 2013, with PTO from 2014; Lay Chair Elloe West Deanery from 2016; Area Secretary Elloe Readers from 2017
GS 2005–
T: 01775 768286
E: sueslater@d-lweb.net

SMITH, The Rt Revd Dr Alan Gregory Clayton *BA, MA, Ph D, Hon DD (Birm)*
Abbey Gate House Abbey Mill Lane St Albans AL3 4HD [BISHOP OF ST ALBANS] *b* 1958 *educ* Trowbridge High School for Boys; Birmingham University; Wycliffe Hall Theological College; University of Wales, Bangor *CV* Curate St Lawrence Pudsey 1981–82, with St Paul 82–84; Chaplain Lee Abbey 1984–90; Diocesan Missioner and Executive Secretary Lichfield Diocesan Board of Mission and Unity 1990–97; Team Vicar St Matthew Walsall 1990–97; Archdeacon of Stoke-upon-Trent 1997–2001; Canon of Lichfield Cathedral, 1997–2009; Bishop of Shrewsbury 2001–09; Chair Shropshire Strategic Partnership 2006–09; Member Rural Bishops Panel from 2006–09; Joint Chair Anglican Methodist Working Party on the Ecclesiology of Emerging Expressions of Church from 2009; Vice Chair Mission and Public Affairs Council from 2016; President of the Rural Coalition from 2016; Bishop of St Albans from 2009
GS 1999–2001, 2009–
T: 01727 853305
E: bishop@stalbans.anglican.org
F: 01727 846715

SMITH, Mr Bradley Francis *BA*
St Mary's Anchorhold Church Lane Barnham West Sussex PO22 0BP [CHICHESTER] *b* 1983 *educ* Lady Lumley's School, Pickering, North Yorkshire, University College Chichester *CV*

Churchwarden, St Mary the Virgin Barnham 2008–15; Manager, St Olav Trust Chichester from 2009
GS 2015–   *T:* 01243 554734
                  07931 527724
         E: bradley.smith4@gmail.com

SMITH, The Revd Christopher Matthew
BA(Oxon), MA(Oxon), BA, LLB, LLM
The Clergy House 18 Brooke Street London EC1N 7RD [LONDON] *b* 1954 *educ* New College Oxford, St Stephen's House Oxford, College of Law/Open University, Cardiff University *CV* Curate, St Peter and St Paul Wantage, Diocese of Oxford, 1995–99; Bishop's Chaplain, Bishop of Horsham, Diocese of Chichester, 1999–2001; Vicar, St Michael and All Angels, Beckenham, Diocese of Rochester, 2001–11; Vicar, St Alban the Martyr Holborn Diocese of London, from 2011; Church Commissioner from 2017
GS 2015–   *T:* 020 7405 1831
                  020 7430 2551
         E: fathercsmith@gmail.com

SMITH, Mrs Helen Margaret *BSc Hons Community Health Nursing*
30 St Cuthberts Way Sherburn Village Durham DH6 1RH [DURHAM] *b* 1964 *educ* Dame Allan's Girls School, New College Durham *CV* Anaesthetic nurse 1987–2001 Freeman Hospital/University Hospital of North Durham; School Nurse from 2001
GS 2015–   *T:* 0191 372 3499
         E: Helenm.smith6@googlemail.com

SMITH, The Ven Jonathan Peter
6 Sopwell Lane St Albans Herts AL1 1RR [ARCHDEACON OF ST ALBANS] *CV* Assistant Curate All Saints Gosforth 1980–82; Assistant Curate Waltham Abbey 1982–85; Chaplain The City University 1985–88; Rector Harrold and Carlton with Chellington 1988–97; Vicar St John's Harpenden 1997–2008; Rural Dean Wheathampstead 1999–2008; Archdeacon of St Albans from 2008; St Albans Bishop's Council; St Albans Board of Patronage; St Albans Board of Finance; St Albans Mission and Pastoral Committee; St Albans Board of Education; St Albans Advisory Committee; St Albans Urban Forum; Residentiary Canon St Albans Cathedral
GS 2010–   *T:* 01727 818121
         E: archdstalbans@stalbans.anglican.org
                  F: 01727 844469

SNOW, The Rt Revd Martyn James *BSc, BTh, MA*
12 Springfield Road Leicester LE2 3BD [BISHOP OF LEICESTER] *educ* Newcastle Royal Grammar; Sheffield University; Wycliffe Hall Oxford; St John's Durham *CV* Curate St Andrew Brinsworth with St Mary's Catcliffe 1995–98; 1999–2001 Church Mission Society Mission

Partner Diocese Guinea; 2001–10 Vicar Christ Church Pitsmoor; Archdeacon of Sheffield and Rotherham 2010–13; Bishop of Tewkesbury 2013–16; Bishop of Leicester from 2016; Chair Central Readers' Council from 2016
                  T: 0116 270 8985
         E: bishop.leicester@leccofe.org

SOWERBY, The Rt Revd Mark Crispin Rake *BD, AKC, MA*
Bishop's House 21 Guildford Road Horsham RH12 1LU [AREA BISHOP OF HORSHAM; CHICHESTER] *b* 1958 *educ* Barnard Castle School; St Aidan and St John Fisher's United Sixth Form Harrogate; King's College London; Lancaster University, College of the Resurrection, Mirfield *CV* Curate Knaresborough 1987–90; Curate St Cuthbert Darwen with St Stephen Tockholes 1990–92; Vicar St Mary Magdalene Accrington 1992–97; Chaplain St Christopher's CE High School Accrington 1992–97; Chaplain Accrington Victoria Hospital 1992–97; Assistant Diocesan Director of Ordinands Blackburn 1993–96; Member Blackburn Diocesan Synod; Selection Secretary/Vocations Officer Advisory Board of Ministry/Ministry Division of Archbishops'Council 1997–2001; Secretary Vocations Advisory Sub-Committee (Advisory Board of Ministry) then Vocation Panel (Ministry Division); Staff Member Vocations, Recruitment and Selection Committee and Candidates Committee/Panel 1997–2001; Vicar St Wilfred Harrogate 2001–04, Team Rector from 2004; Member Ripon Diocesan Synod 2001–09; Assistant Diocesan Director of Ordinands Ripon 2005–09; Diocesan Ministerial Review Advisor from 2008; Member Mirfield/NOC Joint Monitoring Body 2001–09; Bishop's Inspection of Colleges and Courses; Member Council College of Resurrection, Mirfield; Frere Trustee (Mirfield); Member Vocations, Recruitment and Selection Committee 2006–07; Member Ministry Council from 2008; Team Rector St Wilfrid's Harrogate; Member Ripon Diocesan Deanery 2002–09; Member Mirfield/NOC Joint Monitoring Body 2001–09; Member Council College of Resurrection Mirfield 2005–09; Suffragan Bishop of Horsham from 2009
GS 2005–09   *T:* 01403 211139
         E: bishop.horsham@chichester.anglican.org

SPELMAN, The Rt Hon Caroline *BA*
c/o Parliamentary Unit Church House Great Smith Street London SW1P 3AZ [SECOND CHURCH ESTATES COMMISSIONER] *CV* Sugar Beet Advisor, NFU, 1981–84; Deputy Director, European Confederation of Sugar Beet Growers, Paris, 1984–89; Director, Spelman, Cormack and Associates (food and biotechnology consultancy), 1989–2009. MP for the Meriden Constituency from 1997; Shadow Secretary of State for International Development,

2001–03; for Environment 2003–04; for local and devolved government affairs, 2004–05; DCLG, 2006–07; Shadow Minister: for women, 2001–04; ODPM, 2005–06; Chair Conservative Party, 2007–09; Shadow Secretary of State for Communities and Local Government 2009–10; Secretary of State for Environment Food and Rural Affairs, 2010–12; Second Church Estates Commissioner from 2015; Member: Environmental Audit Committee, 2013–15; Joint Committee on Modern Slavery Bill, 2014. Parliament Chair 2013–15; Vice-President Tearfund from 2013
T: 020 7898 1478
E: caroline@carolinespelman.com
W: https://churchofengland.org/our-views/the-church-in-parliament/second-church-estates-commissioner
Twitter: @spelmanc

SPENCER, Dr Jonathan Page *CB, MA, DPhil*
Little Eggarton Eggarton Lane Godmersham Canterbury CT4 7DY [GENERAL SYNOD EX OFFICIO] *educ* Bournemouth School; University of Cambridge; University of Oxford *CV* Department of Trade and Industry 1974–2002 (Principal Private Secretary 1982–3, Director Insurance 1991–97, Director General 1997–2002); LCD/DCA 2002–05 (Director General Policy); Chair C of E Pensions Board from 2009; Deputy Chair, East Kent Hospitals Trust 2007–15; Member Gibraltar Finance Services Commission 2011, Chair from 2016; Member Solicitors Regulatory Authority 2005–09; company director from 2006
GS 2009–   *T:* 01227 731170
E: jspencer1688@gmail.com

SPIERS, The Ven Peter Hendry *BA, CertTh*
2A Monfa Road Bootle Liverpool L20 6BQ [ARCHDEACON OF KNOWSLEY AND SEFTON; LIVERPOOL] *educ* Liverpool College; St John College Durham; Ridley Hall Theological College *CV* Curate St Luke Princess Drive 1986–90; Team Vicar St Peter Everton 1990–95; Vicar St George Everton 1995–2005; Priest in Charge St Luke's Great Crosby 2005–13; Vicar St Luke' Great Crosby from 2013; Archdeacon of Knowsley and Sefton from 2009
GS 2000–   *T:* 0151 709 9722
E: peter.spiers@liverpool.anglican.org
M: 07590 690780

SPRINGETT, The Rt Revd Robert Wilfred *BTh, MA*
Bishop's House 3 Hill Road Gloucester GL4 6ST [SUFFRAGAN BISHOP OF TEWKESBURY; GLOUCESTER] *b* 1958 *educ* Brentwood School; Nottingham University; King's College London; Lincoln Theological College *CV* Curate St James Colchester 1989–92; Curate St Martin Basildon 1992–94; Priest in Charge South Ockendon and Belhus Park 1994–2001; Area Dean

Thurrock 1998–2001; Rector Wanstead 2001–10; Area Dean of Redbridge 2008–10; Archdeacon Cheltenham 2010–16; Member Diocesan Advisory Committee; Board of Education 2010–16, Chair from 2017; Diocesan Pastoral Group from 2017; Bishop of Tewkesbury from 2016
T: 01452 835563 (office)
E: btewkesbury@glosdioc.org.uk
M: 07962 273544

SPUFFORD, Mr Francis Peter *BA, MA*
Powchers Hall The College Ely CB7 4DL [ELY] *b* 1958 *educ* Westminster School, Trinity Hall, University of Cambridge *CV* Publisher's Reader, Chatto & Windus 1986–90; Self-employed writer from 1990; (Author of 'I May Be Some Time', 1995; 'The Child That Books Built', 2003; 'Backroom Boys', 2004; 'Red Plenty', 2010; 'Unapologetic', 2012; 'Golden Hill', 2016); Royal Literary Fund Writing Fellow, Anglia Ruskin University 2005–07; Senior Lecturer, Department of English and Comparative Literature, Goldsmiths College from 2007
GS 2015–   *T:* 01223 503340
E: fspufford@gmail.com

STACEY, The Revd Kate *BTh, MA*
The Vicarage Church Street Shipton under Wychwood Oxon OX7 6BP [OXFORD] *b* 1967 *educ* Bromsgrove School, Camberwell Art College, College of St Mark and St John, London Bible College, Ripon College Cuddesdon *CV* Placements Manager, Hill Homes, London 1996–98; Mother with various part time jobs/lay ministry 1998–2005; Curate, West Berkshire, 2008–11; Vicar, Wychwood Benefice from 2011
GS 2015–   *T:* 01993 832514
E: kate@wychwoodbenefice.org.uk

STAMPER (NÉE WHITESIDE), Mrs Jacqueline Mary *MA (Oxon), PG Dipl, PG Cert*
7 Oakwood Gardens Lancaster LA1 4PF [BLACKBURN] *b* 1950 *educ* Chelmsford High School for Girls, University of Oxford, Universiteit Twente (Netherlands), Lancaster University *CV* Assistant Librarian, British Library of Political and Economic Science, London School of Economics, 1975–81; Sub-Librarian, British Library of Political and Economic Science, London School of Economics, 1981–88; Deputy Librarian, University College London, 1986–88; Freelance translator (Dutch/English) 1989–92; Self-Employed Management Consultancy, Semiotica (MEASUR) [Enschede, Netherlands] 1992–94; University Librarian, Lancaster University 1994–2009; Director of the Centre for North-West Regional Studies, Lancaster University 1999–2009; Retired; Archbishops'

Council, Ministry Division, Bishops' Reviewer of Ministerial Training from 2014
GS 2015–   *T:* 01524 64083
         07808 765364
         E: j.stamper@btinternet.com

STEADMAN, The Ven Mark John *LLB, MA*
Edward King House Minster Yard Lincoln LN2 1PU [ARCHDEACON OF STOW AND LINDSEY; LINCOLN] *educ* Horndean Community School; University of Southampton; Inns of Court School of Law; Cambridge University; Westcott House Theological College *CV* Assistant Curate St Mary's Portsea 2002–05; Priest in Charge St Philip with St Mark Camberwell 2005–11; Area Dean Bermondsey 2008–11; Acting Area Dean Camberwell 2009–11; Chaplain to Bishop of Southwark 2011–15; Member Diocesan IME Staff Team from 2005–15; Member Legal Advisory Commission 2011–15; Member Porvoo Panel 2012; Archdeacon of Stow and Lindsey from 2015
GS 2010–   *T:* 01522 504050
     E: archdeacon.stow@lincoln.anglican.org
         M: 07870 266553

STEELE, The Ven Gordon John *MA*
The Diocesan Office The Palace Peterborough PE1 1YB [ARCHDEACON OF OAKHAM; PETERBOROUGH] *b* 1955 *educ* Owen's Grammar School London, University Kent, Worcester College Oxford, College of the Resurrection, Mirfield *CV* Diocesan Treasurer, Tanzania 1977–80; Curate St John the Baptist, Greenhill, Harrow 1984–88; part-time Chaplain to Bishop of Willesden 1987–92; Team Vicar, St Andrew, Uxbridge 1988–94; Vicar St Alban's, Northampton 1994–2001; Vicar St John the Baptist, Peterborough 2001–12; Rural Dean Peterborough 2004–10; Honorary Canon Peterborough Cathedral from 2004; Archdeacon of Oakham from 2012
         T: 01733 887017
     E: archdeacon.oakham@
       peterborough-diocese.org.uk
         F: 01733 555271
     W: www.peterborough-diocese.org.uk

STEEN, The Ven Dr Jane Elizabeth *MA, PhD*
2 Harmsworth Mews West Square London SE11 4SQ [ARCHDEACON OF SOUTHWARK] *educ* The Old Palace; University of Cambridge; Westcott House *CV* Assistant Curate Chipping Barnet with Arkley, St Albans 1996–99; Domestic Chaplain, Bishop of Southwark 1999–2005; Honorary Senior Lecturer, Canterbury Christ Church University 2006–11; Canon Chancellor, Southwark Cathedral; Canon Theologian and DME, Southwark 2005–13; Archdeacon of Southwark from 2013; Member Joint Implementation Committee, Anglican-Methodist Covenant from 2012
         T: 020 7939 9400
     E: jane.steen@southwark.anglican.org

STOKER, The Revd Canon Howard Charles *BTh*
The Rectory Church Street Holt Norfolk NR25 6BB [NORWICH] *educ* Barlby High School, *CV* Assistant Curate Hessle, All Saints 1993–96; Assistant Curate Richmond, St Mary 1996–99; Curate-in-charge Marske, St Edmund and Downholme, St Michael and All Angels 1996–99; Rural Dean Holt 2005–11; Guardian of the Shrine of Our Lady of Walsingham from 2011; Honorary Canon of Norwich Cathedral from 2013; Rector of Holt St Andrew with High Kelling All Saints from 1999
GS 2015–   *T:* 01263 712048
     E: holtrectory@tiscali.co.uk

STRATFORD, The Ven Dr Timothy Richard *BSc, PhD*
St Martins House 7 Peacock Lane Leicester LE1 5PZ [ARCHDEACON OF LEICESTER] *educ* Knowsley Hey Comprehensive School; York University; Wycliffe Hall Theological College; University of Sheffield *CV* Curate Mossley Hill 1986–89; Curate St Helens St Helen 1989–91; Chaplain to Bishop of Liverpool 1991–94; Vicar Good Shepherd West Derby 1994–2003; Team Rector Kirkby and Team Vicar St Chad Kirkby 2003–12; Member Liturgical Commission 2006–15; Archdeacon of Leicester from 2012
GS 2000–13, 2015–   *T:* 0116 261 5309
         0116 270 4441
     E: tim.stratford@leccofe.org
         F: 0116 261 5220
     W: www.leicester.anglican.org

STROYAN, The Rt Revd John Ronald Angus *MTheol, MA*
Warwick House School Hill Offchurch Leamington Spa CV33 9AL [SUFFRAGAN BISHOP OF WARWICK; COVENTRY] *educ* Harrow School; St Andrew University; Queen College Birmingham; Ecumenical Institute, Bossey, Switzerland; University of Wales *CV* Curate St Peter Hillfields, Coventry East Team 1983–87; Vicar St Matthew with St Chad Smethwick, Birmingham 1987–94; Vicar Bloxham, Milcombe and South Newington, Oxford 1994–2005; Area Dean Deddington, Oxford 2002–05; Bishop of Warwick from 2005; President Community of the Cross of Nails UK from 2007; Secretary West Midlands Regional Group 2008–15; Member Rural Bishop's Panel 2009; Co-Moderator Churches Together in Coventry and Warwickshire 2009–12; Member International Commission for Anglican-Orthodox Theological Dialogue 2009–15; member House of Bishops Working Group on Human Sexuality 2012–14; Co-Chair of the Reuilly Contact Group from 2013; President of the Association for Promoting Retreats from 2017
         T: 01926 427465
     E: bishop.warwick@CovCofE.org

STUART-WHITE, The Ven Bill (William Robert) MA(Oxon), BA
10 The Hayes Bodmin Road Truro TR1 1FY [ARCHDEACON OF CORNWALL; TRURO] b 1959 educ Winchester College; Merton College Oxford; Trinity College Bristol CV Assistant Curate Upper Armley 1986–91; Priest in Charge Austrey 1991–92; Priest in Charge Warton 1991–92; Vicar Austrey and Warton 1992–98; Rector Camborne 1998–2006; Priest in Charge Stoke Climsland 2006–09; Priest in Charge Linkinhorne 2006–09; Priest in Charge St Breoke and Egloshayle 2009–12; Rural Link Officer 2006–12; Archdeacon of Cornwall from 2012				T: 01872 242374
				E: bill@truro.anglican.org

SULLIVAN, The Very Revd Nicola Ann BTh, SRN, RM
The Residence Vicars Court Church Street Southwell NG25 0HP [DEAN OF SOUTHWELL] b 1953 educ Ipswich Convent of Jesus and Mary; Mills Grammar School, Framlingham; St Bart's Hospital; Bristol Maternity Hospital; Wycliffe Hall Oxford CV Curate St Anne Earlham, Norwich 1995–99; Associate Vicar Bath Abbey 1999–2002; Sub-Dean Wells Cathedral 2003–07; Bishop's Chaplain and Pastoral Assistant 2002–07; Archdeacon of Wells and Residentiary Canon Wells Cathedral 2007–11; Member Norwich Diocesan Synod 1997–99; Member Bath and Wells Diocesan Synod, Bishop's Council, Diocesan Board of Finance 2007–16; Participating Observer in the House of Bishops 2013–16; Dean of Southwell from 2016				T: 01749 685147
				E: dean@southwellminster.org.uk

SUTTON, The Ven Peter Allerton BA
5 The Boltons Wootton Bridge Ryde Isle of Wight PO33 4PB [ARCHDEACON OF THE ISLE OF WIGHT; PORTSMOUTH] b 1954 educ Exeter University CV Curate Holy Trinity Fareham 1987–90; Curate St Mary's Alverstoke and Chaplain Haslar Prison 1990–93; Vicar of St Faith's, Lee-on-the-Solent 1993–2012; Archdeacon Isle of Wight and Initial Ministerial Education 4–7 Officer from 2012				T: 01983 884432
				E: adiow@portsmouth.anglican.org

SWINSON, Mrs Margaret Anne MA, ACA, CTA
46 Glenmore Ave Liverpool L18 4QF [LIVERPOOL] b 1957 educ Alice Ottley School Worcester; Liverpool University CV Accountant (Tax Specialist); member (Vice-Chair) Council for Christina Unity from 2006; Moderator Churches Together Britain and Ireland from 2006; Member Anglican Consultative Council from 2012; General Synod Standing Committee 1991–97; Member Board of Social Responsibility 1990–95; Chair Race and Community Relations Committee 1990–95;

Trustee Church Urban Fund 1987–97; Member Churches Together Britain and Ireland; C of E Delegate to World Council of Churches Canberra 1991; Member Central Board of Finance 1996–98; Member Board of Mission 2001–03; Member Council for Christian Unity from 2006; Moderator Churches Together Britain and Ireland from 2006
GS 1985–				T: 0151 724 3533
				E: maggie@swinsonfamily.net

SYKES, Mr John Nicholas MA
Tower Place West London EC3R 5BU [CHURCH COMMISSIONER] b 1959 educ Bradford Grammar School; Jesus College Oxford CV Investment Consultant; Baillie, Gifford & Co Ltd 1980–84; Baring Asset Management 1984–97; Senior Consultant William M Mercer Investment from 1997; Church Commissioner from 2001; member Assets Committee and Securities Group				T: 020 7178 3268
				E: nick.sykes@mercer.com
				F: 020 7178 3268

TACKIE, Miss Michelle MEng
c/o St Nicholas Parish Church 208 Long Road Canvey Island SS8 0JR [CHELMSFORD] b 1986 educ University of Bristol
GS 2015–		E: michelletackie@gmail.com

TALBOTT, The Revd Simon John BD
The Vicarage 12 Church Street Great Shelford Cambridge CB22 5EL [ELY] b 1967 educ St Benedict's Catholic VA High School, Bury St Edmunds, All Hallows College, Dublin and Pontifical University of Maynooth, Dublin CV Assistant Curate St George's RC Parish Norwich 1982–85; Senior Assistant Curate St John's RC Cathedral Norwich 1985–87; RC Chaplain Norfolk and Norwich Hospital 1985–87; Received into the communion of the Church of England 1987; Assistant Curate St Michael and All Angels Headingly 1987–91; Vicar of Great and Little Ouseburn with Marton-cum-Grafton 1991–97; Chaplain, Queen Ethelburga's College York 1991–97; Area Dean of Ripon 1997–2001; Priest-in-charge of Markington with South Stainley and Bishop Thornton 1997–2001; Vicar of St Martin of Tours, Epsom 2001–13; Member of the Church Commissioners Church Buildings (Uses and Disposals) Committee from 2009; Ecumenical chaplain to the University of Creative Arts (Epsom Campus) 2002–10; Priest-in-charge of Great Shelford from 2013; Priest-in-charge of Stapleford from 2015; Area Dean of Granta from 2016
GS 2015–				T: 01223 847068
				07740 665210
				E: simon@thetalbotts.co.uk

TAN, Dr Chik Kaw BPharm, MSc, PhD, MRPharmS, PGCMedEd
12 Montfort Place Westlands Newcastle-under-Lyme ST5 2HE [LICHFIELD] educ Anglo-Chinese

School, Ipoh, Malaysia; Bath University; Aston University; Keele University *CV* President Bath University Christian Union 1979–80; Advisor Bristol Chinese Church Fellowship 1981–86; Prayer Group leader, Newcastle-under-Lyme Overseas Missionary Fellowship Prayer Group 1986–95; Member Overseas Missionary Fellowship International 1996–2002; Associate Pastor, Surabaya (Indonesia) International Christian Fellowship 2001–02; Member Preaching Team, St James Audley from 1987; Honorary Senior Lecturer Keele University from 2005; Member Newcastle Deanery Synod; Member Lichfield Diocesan Synod; Member North Staffs Local Research Ethics Committee 2002–08
GS 2005–   *T:* 01782 441604
       E: ck11x@yahoo.ie

TANNER, The Rt Revd Mark Simon Austin
MA (Oxon), BA (Hons), MTh
Berwick House Longhirst Road Pegswood Morpeth NE61 6XF [SUFFRAGAN BISHOP OF BERWICK; NEWCASTLE] *educ* Loughborough Grammar, Christ Church Oxford, St John's College Durham (Cranmer Hall), University of Liverpool (Chester College) *CV* Youth Worker, Holy Trinity, Coventry 1992–95; Assistant Curate St Mary's, Upton 1998–2001; Vicar St Mary's, Wheatley, Doncaster 2001–07; Vicar Holy Trinity, Ripon 2007–11; Area Dean Ripon 2009–11; Officiating Chaplain to Military 2009–13; Warden of Cranmer Hall and Vice-Principal of St John's College, Durham 2011–16, Bishop of Berwick from 2016
GS 2015–16   *T:* 01670 519000
    E: bishopofberwick@newcastle.anglican.org
       Twitter: @tanner_mark

TATTERSALL, Worshipful Canon Geoffrey Frank *MA, QC*
2 The Woodlands Lostock Bolton BL6 4JD [MANCHESTER] *educ* Manchester Grammar School; Christ Church Oxford *CV* Barrister; Called to Bar Lincoln's Inn 1970; Bencher 1997; In practice Northern Circuit from 1970; Recorder Crown Court from 1989; QC from 1992; Called to Bar New South Wales 1992; SC from 1995; Judge of Appeal IOM from 1997; Deputy High Court Judge from 2003; Lay Chair Bolton Deanery Synod 1993–2002; Chair House of Laity Diocesan Synod 1994–2003; Member Fees Advisory Commission from 1995; Member Steering Committee Bishop's Council; Member Diocesan Board of Finance and Trust and Finance Committee till 2004; Chair Standing Orders Committee General Synod from 1999; Panel of Chairmen of General Synod from 2011; Chancellor of Carlisle Diocese from 2003; Honorary Lay Canon Manchester Cathedral 2003; Chancellor Manchester Diocese from 2004; Deputy Vicar-General Sodor and Man 2004–

08; External Reviewer of decisions of Director of Fair Access 2005–13; Chair Disciplinary Tribunals, Clergy Discipline Measure from 2006; Chair Revision Committee, draft C of E Marriage Measure 2006–07; Chair Revision Committee, draft Ecclesiastical Officer (Terms of Service) Measure 2007–08; Member Steering and Revisions Committee for draft C of E Bishops and Priests (Consecration and Ordination of Women) Measure 2009–12; Member Worshipful Company of Parish Clerks from 2009; Parish Clerk St George-in-the-East
GS 1995–   *T:* 01204 846265
       E: gftqc@hotmail.co.uk
       F: 01204 849863

TAVINOR, The Very Revd Michael Edward
MA, MMus, MTh, ARCO, PGCE
The Deanery College Cloisters Cathedral Close Hereford HR1 2NG [DEAN OF HEREFORD] *educ* Bishopshalt School Hillingdon, Middlesex; University College Durham; Emmanuel College Cambridge; King's College London; Ripon College Cuddesdon; University Wales: Lampeter *CV* Curate St Peter Ealing London 1982–85; Precentor, Sacrist and Minor Canon Ely Cathedral 1985–90; Priest in Charge Stuntney Ely 1987–90; Vicar Tewkesbury with Walton Cardiff Gloucester 1990–2002; Vicar Twyning Gloucestershire 1999–2002; Honorary Canon Gloucester Cathedral 1997–2002; Dean of Hereford from 2002; Member Diocesan Synod from 2002; President Church Music Society 2005; Honorary Fellow Guild of Church Musicians from 2006
       T: 01432 374203
    E: dean@herefordcathedral.org
       F: 01432 374220

TAYLOR, The Revd Martyn Andrew Nicholas
16 St George's Square Stamford PE9 2BN b 1966 *educ* Bournemouth School for Boys; Liverpool University; Goldsmiths PGCE; Oak Hill Theological College *CV* Theological Educator, Uganda Martyrs Seminary 1995–96; St George's Stamford Curate 1996–2000, Associate Rector 2000–02, Rector 2003–
GS 2015–   *T:* 01780 481800
       01780 757343
       E: rector@stgeorgeschurch.net

TAYLOR, The Ven Paul Stanley *BEd, MTh*
Aldhelm House Rectory Lane West Stafford Dorchester DT2 8AB [ARCHDEACON OF SHERBORNE; SALISBURY] *educ* Lodge Farm County Secondary School; Redditch County High School; Westminster College Oxford; Westcott House Cambridge *CV* Curate St Stephen Bush Hill Park 1984–88; Vicar St Andrew Southgate 1988–97; Assistant Director Post Ordination Training 1987–94, Director 1994–2000, 2002–04; Vicar

St Mary and Christ Church Hendon 1997–2004; Area Dean West Barnet 2000–04; Associate Tutor North Thames Ministerial Training Course 2001–04; Archdeacon of Sherborne from 2004 		*T:* 01305 269074
E: adsherborne@salisbury.anglican.org
F: 01305 269074
M: 07796 691203

TAYLOR, The Ven Stephen Ronald *MA*
4 Redcliffe Lane Maidstone ME14 2AG [ARCHDEACON OF MAIDSTONE; CANTERBURY] *b* 1955 *educ* Durham; Honorary Fellow Sunderland University; Cranmer Hall St John's Durham *CV* Curate Chester le Street 1983–87; Vicar Newbottle 1987–92; Vicar Stranton Hartlepool 1992–2000; Provost of Sunderland 2000–11 (Team Rector 2000–07); Hon Canon Diocese of the Rift Valley from 2000; Archdeacon of Maidstone from 2011 		*T:* 01622 200221
E: stephen.taylor@archdeacmaid.org
M: 07944 680855
Twitter: @revcan

TEBBUTT, The Revd Christopher Michael *BA*
The Rectory Canford Magna Wimborne Dorset BH21 3AF [SALISBURY] *CV* Trainee Chartered Accountant, Thornton Baker, 1975–79; Chartered Accountant, Ernst & Young, 1979–81; Finance Professional and Manager, 1981–94; St John's College Nottingham, Theological education, 1994–96; Assistant Curate, Catherington and Clanfield, Portsmouth Diocese, 1996–2000; Priest in charge and Vicar, St James Southbroom, Devizes, Salisbury Diocese, 2000–09; Team Rector, Canford Magna Team Ministry, from 2009; Rural Dean of Wimborne, from 2011
GS 2015– 		*T:* 01202 882270
07917 190307
E: rector@canfordparish.org
Twitter: @chris_tebbutt

THOMAS, The Ven Paul Wyndham *BA, MA, BA, CertTh*
Archdeacon's House The Vicarage Tong Shifnal TF11 8PW [ARCHDEACON OF SALOP; LICHFIELD] *educ* Cardiff High School; Oriel College Oxford; Wycliffe Hall Oxford *CV* Curate Llangynwyd with Maesteg 1979–85; Team Vicar Langport Area churches 1985–90; Priest in Charge Thorp Arch West Walton and Clergy Training Officer York 1990–93 Vicar Nether with Upper Poppleton 1993–2004; Doxey and Parish Development Advisor 2004–11; Archdeacon of Salop from 2011; Diocesan Advisory Committee; Buildings and Benefices Committee; Glebe Committee; Bishop's Council; Diocesan Synod
		T: 01902 372622
E: archdeacon.salop@lichfield.anglican.org
F: 01902 374060

THOMAS, The Rt Revd Rod (Roderick Charles Howell) *BSc, CertTh*
28 St John's Meadow Blindley Heath Lingfield RH7 6JU [SUFFRAGAN BISHOP OF MAIDSTONE] *b* 1967 *educ* Ealing Grammar School for Boys; London School of Economics and Political Science; Wycliffe Hall Theological College *CV* Director Employment Affairs Confederation of British Industry 1987–91; Curate St Paul Stonehouse Plymouth 1993–95; Curate St Andrew Plymouth 1995–99; Priest in Charge St Matthew Elburton 1999–2005, Vicar 2005–12, Prebendary 2012–15; Chair Reform 2007–15; Member Board of Mission 2001–03; Member Working Party on Senior Church Appointments 2005–07; Member Church Pastoral Aid Society Council of Reference 2005–14; Member Standing Committee on Women in the Episcopate Legislation 2013–14; Bishop of Maidstone from 2015; Member Bishops' Reflection Group on Sexuality 2016–17
GS 2000– 		*T:* 01342 834140
E: admin@bishopofmaidstone.org

THOMPSON, The Very Revd Matthew *MA MPhil*
Birmingham Cathedral Colmore Row Birmingham B3 2QB [DEAN OF BIRMINGHAM] *b* 1968 *educ* Queen Mary's Grammar School, Walsall; Corpus Christi College, Cambridge; Ridley Hall Cambridge *CV* Curate The Ascension Hulme 1994–97; Curate Langley and Parkfield Team 1997–98; Team Vicar Langley and Parkfield Team 1998–2000; Priest-in-Charge St Cross Clayton 2000–08; Area Dean of Ardwick 2003–08; Priest-in-Charge St Peter Bolton-le-Moors 2008–11; Vicar, St Peter with St Philip, Bolton-le-Moors 2011–17; Borough Dean of Bolton 2010–17; Honorary Canon, Manchester Cathedral 2012–17; Dean of Birmingham from 2017; Diocesan Board of Ministry 1997–2000; Diocesan CME Committee 1997–2002; Diocesan Board of Finance 2000–03; Diocesan Synod 2000–08, 2010–17; Examining Chaplain 2001–17; Diocesan Pastoral Committee 2003–08; Bishop's Council 2010–17; Diocesan Board of Education 2013–17; Chair of the House of Clergy, Diocese of Manchester 2015–17
		T: 0121 262 1840
E: dean@birminghamcathedral.com

THOMSON, The Rt Revd David *MA, DPhil, FSA, FRHistS*
14 Lynn Road Ely CB6 1DA [SUFFRAGAN BISHOP OF HUNTINGDON] *b* 1954 *educ* King Edward VII School Sheffield; Keble College Oxford; Selwyn College Cambridge; Westcott House Cambridge *CV* Curate Maltby 1981–84; Team Vicar Banbury 1984–94; Team Rector Cockermouth 1994–2002; Chair Diocesan Children and Young People's Committee;

Bishop's Advisor for Healthcare Chaplain, Team and Group Ministries and Deliverance Ministry; Archdeacon of Carlisle and Canon Residentiary Carlisle Cathedral 2002–08; Bishop Huntingdon from 2008; Honorary Canon Ely Cathedral from 2008; Interim Bishop of St Edmundsbury and Ipswich 2013–2015   *T:* 01353 662137
E: bishop.huntingdon@elydiocese.org
F: 01353 669357
W: bpdt.wordpress.com
M: 07771 864550 (Mobile)

THOMSON, The Rt Revd Dr John Bromilow BA (Hons) York, MA Oxon, PhD
Bishop's House York Road Barlby Selby YO8 5JP [BISHOP OF SELBY; YORK] *b* 1959 *educ* The Edinburgh Academy; The Haberdashers' Aske's Boys' School, University of York; University of Oxford; University of Nottingham *CV* Assistant Curate and Youth Chaplain, All Saints, Ecclesall, Diocese of Sheffield 1985–89; Tutor, St Paul's College, Grahamstown, South Africa 1989–92; Assistant Lecturer, Rhodes University, Grahamstown, South Africa 1991–92; Vicar, St Mary Wheatley, Doncaster, Diocese of Sheffield 1993–2001; Director of Ministry, Diocese of Sheffield 2001–14; Bishop of Selby, Diocese of York from 2014;   *T:* 01757 429 982
E: bishopofselby@yorkdiocese.org
W: http://jjbthomson.wordpress.com
Twitter: @john59thomson

THORNTON, The Rt Revd Tim (Timothy) Martin BA, MA
Lambeth Palace London SE1 7JU [BISHOP AT LAMBETH] *educ* Devonport High School for Boys; Southampton University; St Stephen's House Oxford; King's College London *CV* Curate Todmorden 1980–82; Priest in Charge Walsden 1982–85; Chaplain 1985–86; Senior Chaplain 1986–87; Bishop's Chaplain Wakefield 1987–91; Diocesan Director of Ordinands Wakefield 1988–91; Bishop's Chaplain London 1991–94; Principal North Thames Ministerial Training Course 1994–98; Vicar Kensington St Mary Abbots with St George; Governor St Mary Abbots C of E Primary School; Chair Campden Charities 1998–2001; Area Dean Kensington 2000–01; King's College Theological Trustee; Area Bishop of Sherborne 2001–08; Bishop of Truro 2009–17; Bishop at Lambeth from 2017; Bishop to the Forces from 2017; Bishop in the Falkland Islands from 2017; Chair The Children's Society   *T:* 020 7898 1200
E: tim.thornton@lambethpalace.org.uk

THURSTON, Mr Andrew
Cuthbert House Stonebridge Durham DH1 3RY [DIOCESAN SECRETARY; DURHAM]
T: 01388 604515
E: diocesan.secretary@durham.anglican.org

TODD, Dr Michael John BA, PhD, PhD
50 Talmena Avenue Wadebridge PL27 7RR [TRURO] *b* 1943 *educ* Bodmin Grammar, Alleyns, Keele, Loughborough, Winchester *CV* British Ship Research Association 1970–81; GEC 1981–91; Trevanion House Ltd 1991–2012 GS 2015–   *T:* 01208 816043
E: mike@mjcmtodd.plus.com

TOMLIN, The Rt Revd Dr Graham Stuart MA, PhD
Dial House Riverside Twickenham TW1 3DT [BISHOP OF KENSINGTON; DIOCESE OF LONDON] *b* 1958 *educ* Bristol Grammar School; Lincoln College Oxford; Wycliffe Hall *CV* Curate St Leonard's Church Exeter 1986–89; Chaplain Jesus College Oxford and part-time Tutor in Church History Wycliffe Hall Oxford 1989–94; Full-time Tutor in Historical Theology and Director of Evangelism and Mission Wycliffe Hall Oxford 1994–98; Vice-Principal Wycliffe Hall, Oxford 1998–2005; Acting Principal Wycliffe Hall 2001, 2004–05; Principal St Paul's Theological Centre Holy Trinity Brompton London 2005; Principal St Mellitus College London 2007–15; Bishop of Kensington from 2015   *T:* 020 3720 7699
E: bishop.kensington@london.anglican.org
W: http://grahamtomlin.blogspot.co.uk
M: 07929 048720
Twitter: @gtomlin

TOWNEND, The Ven Lee Stuart MA
The New Vicarage Plumpton Penrith S32 3YF [ARCHDEACON OF CARLISLE] *b* 1965 *educ* The Henry Fanshawe School; Durham University; Cranmer Hall *CV* Curate Buxton 1998–2001; Vicar Loose 2001–08; Vicar Ilkley 2008–12; Diocesan Missioner, Diocese of Derby 2012–17; Archdeacon of Carlisle from 2017
T: 01768 807772
E: archdeacon.north@carlislediocese.org.uk

TOWNLEY, The Ven Peter Kenneth BA, DSPT
The Vicarage Kirkthorpe Wakefield WF1 5SZ [ARCHDEACON OF PONTEFRACT; LEEDS] *b* 1958 *educ* Moston Brook High School Manchester; Sheffield University; Manchester University; Ridley Hall Theological College *CV* Curate Christ Church Ashton-under-Lyne 1980–83; Priest in Charge St Hugh's CD Oldham 1983–88; Rector All Saints Stretford 1988–96; Vicar St Mary-le-Tower Ipswich 1996–2008; Member Meissen Commission 1991–2001; Member Inter-Diocese Finance Forum 1997–14; Rural Dean of Ipswich from 2001; Honorary Canon from 2003; Member Porvoo Panel from 2003; Archdeacon of Pontefract from 2008; Chair Wakefield Diocesan Board of Education 2008–14; Chair Meissen Library Management Committee in Durham; Chair

Diocesan Academies Trust from 2011; Chair Enhance Academies Trust from 2011
GS 1992–95, 2000–08

T: 01924 434459 (Office)
01924 896327 (Home)
E: peter.townley@leeds.anglican.org
F: 01924 364834 (Office)
01924 896327 (Home)

TREWEEK (nee Montgomery), The Rt Revd Rachel BA, BTh
Bishopscourt Pitt Street Gloucester GL1 2BQ [BISHOP OF GLOUCESTER] *educ* Broxbourne School; Reading University; Wycliffe Hall Oxford *CV* Paediatric Speech and Language Therapist, Gospel Oak Health Centre, Hampstead Health Authority 1985–87; Speech and Language Therapist, Child Development Team, Hampstead Health Authority 1987–89; Clinical Manager for Paediatric Speech and Language Therapists in Health Centres, Bloomsbury, Hampstead and Islington Health Authorities 1989–91; Curate St George Tufnell Park, London 1994–97, Associate Vicar 1997–99; Vicar St James the Less Bethnal Green, London 1999–2006; Archdeacon of Northolt 2006–11; Archdeacon of Hackney from 2011; Continuing Ministerial Education Officer, Stepney Area, London Diocese 1999–2001; Bishop's Visitor, Stepney Area 2004–06; Bishop of Gloucester from 2015
GS 2010–15   T: 01452 835512

TROTT, The Revd Stephen BA, MA, LLM
The Rectory Humfrey Lane Boughton Northampton NN2 8RQ [PETERBOROUGH] *b* 1954 *educ* Bishop Vesey's Grammar School Sutton Coldfield; Hull University; Fitzwilliam College Cambridge; Cardiff University; Westcott House Theological College (Cambridge Federation of Theological Colleges) *CV* Curate Hessle 1984–87; Curate St Alban Hull 1987–88; Rector Pitsford with Boughton from 1988; Secretary Continuing Ministerial Education 1988–93; Visiting Chaplain Pitsford School from 1991, Governor and Director from 2001; Surrogate for Marriage Licences from 2001; Member Diocesan Synod from 1990; Member Vacancy-in-See Committee from 1995; Clerical Vice-President Diocesan Synod and Chair Diocesan House of Clergy 2000–03; Member Peterborough Cathedral Council 2001–04, 2013–16; Member Diocesan Board of Finance and Bishop's Council 2010–16; Chair Church Buildings Committee from 2010; Fellow, Royal Society of Arts 1986; Member Ecclesiastical Law Society from 1988; Member Legislative Committee 1995–2000, 2005–10; Member Legal Advisory Commission 1996–2006; Member Churches Together Britain and Ireland and Churches Together England 1996–99; Member Revision Committee on Calendar, Lectionary and Collects 1996; Church Commissioner from 1997, Board of Governors from 1999; Member

Pastoral Committee 1998–2012; Closed Churches Committee from 2004, Deputy Chair from 2009; Member Nominations and Governance Committee 2009–12; Member Deployment, Remuneration, and Conditions of Service Committee 1999–2001; Member Revision Committee on Clergy Discipline Measure 1999–2000; General Synod Representative on Governing Body of St Albans and Oxford Ministry Course 2001–06; C of E Delegate to Confederation of European Churches, Trondheim, 2003; Member Pastoral (Amendment) Measure Revision Committee from 2004; Member Follow-up Group, Review of Dioceses, Pastoral and Related Measures from 2004; Member Panel of Reference, Anglican Communion from 2005; Member Steering Committee Diocesan Pastoral and Mission Measure 2005–06; Standing Committee, Convocation of Canterbury 2006–10, from 2015; Member Revision Commttee, Ecclesiastical Fees Measure 2011; Synodical Secretary, Convocation of Canterbury from 2010; Member Council of Christians and Jews from 2011; Fees Advisory Commission from 2013; Editor Guidelines for the Professional Conduct of the Clergy 2015; Rural Dean Brixworth Peterborough from 2015; Honorary Canon Theologian of Richmond(British Columbia) from 2015; Chaplain to the Forces (TA) Leicester, Northants and Rutland Army Cadet Force from 2016; Member Northampton Interfaith Forum from 2016
GS 1995–   T: 01604 845655
E: revstephentrott@gmail.com
W: http://laworgospel.wordpress.com
M: 07712 863000
Twitter: @revstrott

TUCKER, Mrs Kathryn Louise Slader
Stetfold Rocks Farm Exford Minehead Somerset TA24 7NZ [BATH AND WELLS] *educ* Tiverton Grammar School, St Mary's College, Cheltenham *CV* Initial Teacher training course 1971–72; Au pair, Belgravia, London 1972–73; Secretary/personal assistant to Fabric Designer, John Heathcoat and Co, Tiverton Devon 1973–76; Marriage, raising family 1976; Farm partner in farm business and separate property lettings business until present day; School Invigilator Farm Business partner from 2013; Separate property lettings business; West Somerset College Invigilator from 2013
GS 2015–   T: 01643 831213
07875 868376
E: stetfoldfarm@gmail.com

URQUHART, The Rt Revd David Andrew BA(Hons), Hon DD, Hon DUniv
Bishop's Croft Old Church Road Harborne Birmingham B17 0BG [BISHOP OF BIRMINGHAM] *educ* Rugby School; Ealing Business School;

Wycliffe Hall Theological College *CV* Curate St Nicholas Hull 1984–87; Team Vicar Drypool Hull 1987–92; Vicar Holy Trinity Coventry 1992–2000; Bishop of Birkenhead 2000–06; Chair Church Mission Society Trustees 1994–2007; Prelate of Order of St Michael and St George from 2005; Archbishop of Canterbury's Episcopal Link with China from 2006; Bishop of Birmingham from 2006; Chair Ridley Hall Council from 2010; Lords Spiritual from 2010
GS 2006–　　　　　　　　*T:* 0121 427 1163
　　　E: bishop@cofebirmingham.com
　　　W: www.cofebirmingham.com
　　　　　　　Twitter: @David_Urq

USHER, The Rt Revd Graham Barham *BSC, BA, MA*
Bishop's House Bishop's Walk Cradley Heath B64 7RH [SUFFRAGAN BISHOP OF DUDLEY: WORCESTER] *educ* Edinburgh University; Corpus Christi Cambridge; Westcott House; St Nicholas Theological College Ghana *CV* Curate Nunthorpe, York 1996–99; Vicar North Ormsby 1999–2004; Rector Hexham Newcastle 2004–14, Area Dean Hexham 2006–11; Bishop of Dudley from 2014; Honorary Canon Kumasi Ghana 2007–14; Board Member Northumberland National Park Authority 2009–13; Chair Forestry Commission Northeast Advisory Committee 2009–14; Board Member Human Tissue Authority from 2016　　*T:* 0121 550 3407
　　E: bishop.dudley@cofe-worcester.org.uk
　　　　　　　　Twitter: @bishopdudley

VANN, The Ven Cherry Elizabeth *GRSM, ARCM, Dip RS, Cert in Counselling, Br Sign L*
57 Melling Road Oldham OL4 1PN [ARCHDEACON OF ROCHDALE; MANCHESTER] *b* 1954 *educ* Lutterworth Upper School; Royal College of Music; Westcott House *CV* Curate St Michael, Flixton 1989–92; Chaplain Bolton College of Higher Education and Further Education and Curate Bolton Parish Church 1992–98; Chaplain among Deaf People and Team Vicar East Farnworth and Kearsley 1998–2004; Team Rector East Farnworth and Kearsley 2004–08; Bishop's Advisor in Women's Ministry 2004–09; Area Dean Farnworth 2005–08; Honorary Canon Manchester Cathedral 2007; Archdeacon Rochdale from 2008; Prolocutor Lower House Convocation York from 2013
GS 2003–　　　　　　　　*T:* 0161 678 1454
　　E: archrochdale@manchester.anglican.org
　　　　　　　　　　M: 07587 132707

VINCE, Mr Jacob Peter *MA, DBA, MRICS*
3 High St Horam Heathfield TN21 0EJ [CHICHESTER] *educ* Latymer Upper School; University of Wales; City University; *CV* Director and Charterer Surveyor from 1996; member Bishop's Council; Church Commissioner;

Member Church Buildings (Uses and Disposals) Committee
GS 2005–　　　　　　　　*T:* 01453 812623
　　　　　　　　　　　　　01435 813700
　　　E: jacob.vince@btconnect.com
　　　　　　　　　　F: 01435 813732

WADDINGTON, The Revd Gary Richard *BSc, BTh, MA*
The Rectory 51B Kent Road Harrogate HG1 2EU [LEEDS] *educ* Ermysted's Grammar School, Skipton, St Chad's College, Durham; Heythrop College, University of London *CV* Pastoral Assistant, All Hallows Gospel Oak, Hampstead, 1991–93; Assistant Curate, Holy Spirit, Southsea 1996–2000; Vicar, Paulsgrove, 2000–10; Succentor, Portsmouth Cathedral, 2000–10; Team Rector, St Wilfrid's Harrogate from 2010
GS 2015–　　　　　　　　*T:* 01423 503259
　　　　　　　　　　　　　07920 464818
　　　　E: Teamrector@stwilfrid.org
　　W: https://thebusypriest.wordpress.com
　　　　　　　Twitter: @GaryWaddington

WADDLE, Canon Shane *MSc*
Church House St John's Terrace North Shields NE29 6HS [DIOCESAN SECRETARY; NEWCASTLE] *b* 1969 *educ* Blyth Tynedale High School; Derby University *CV* Payroll Services Manager, Church of England 2001–13; Diocesan Secretary from 2013　　　*T:* 0191 270 4100
　　E: s.waddle@newcastle.anglican.org
　　　W: www.newcastle.anglican.org
　　　　　　　　　M: 07775 037121
　　　　　　　Twitter: @WaddleShane

WAINE, The Very Revd Stephen
The Royal Chantry Cathedral Cloisters Chichester PO19 1PX [DEAN OF CHICHESTER] *b* 1959 *CV* Archdeacon of Dorset 2010–15; Dean of Chichester from 2015　　　*T:* 01243 782595
　　E: deansec@chichestercathedral.org.uk

WALKER, Mrs (Pauline) Debra *BPharm, MRPharmS*
Willow Lodge Church Lane Lydiate L31 4HL [LIVERPOOL] *b* 1960 *educ* Ormskirk Grammar School; Bradford University *CV* Pharmacist qualified 1982
GS 2010–　　　　　　　　*T:* 0151 520 2496
　　　E: debrawalker@btinternet.com

WALKER, The Rt Revd David Stuart *MA, FRSA*
Bishopscourt Bury New Road Manchester M7 4LE [BISHOP OF MANCHESTER] *educ* Manchester Grammar School; King's College Cambridge; Queen's Theological College Birmingham *CV* Curate Handsworth 1983–86; Team Vicar Maltby 1986–91; Chaplain Maltby 1986–91; Vicar Bramley and Ravenfield 1991–95; Team Rector Bramley and Ravenfield with Hooton Roberts and Braithwell 1995–2000; Honorary Canon Sheffield Cathedral 2000; Bishop of

Dudley from 2000; Member Advisory Council on Relations of Bishops and Religious Communities from 2002, Chair from 2008; Chair Housing Justice 2003–07; Secretary West Midlands Regional Bishops Group 2003–08; Chair Housing Association Charitable Trust 2004–10; Member Bishops' Urban Panel 2004–10; Member NPIA Independent Advisory Panel from 2009; Member C of E Pensions Board from 2006, Deputy Vice Chair 2010–11, Vice Chair from 2011; Member Committee Minority Ethnic Anglican Concerns from 2006; Member Church Urban Fund 2008–15; Member Equality and Diversity Board Advisory Group (Homes and Committeess Agency) from 2009; Chair C of E Pensions Board Housing Committee from 2009; Chair Sandwell Homes from 2011; Bishop of Manchester from 2013; Archbishops' Council Remuneration and Conditions of Service Committee 2010–16, Chair from 2013; Archbishops' Council Ministry Council 2013–16; Church Commissioners Board of Governors from 2013 (Deputy Chair from 2017); Church of England Ethical Investments Advisory Group from 2014; Church Commissioners Pastoral Committee 2014–15; Greater Manchester Police Ethics Committee 2014; Wythenshawe Community Housing Group Board from 2014 (Chair from 2016)
GS 2005–   T: 0161 792 2096
E: bishop.david@manchester.anglican.org

WALKER, The Revd Ruth Elizabeth *BA, PGCE*
The Vicarage 5 Howard Close Bidford-on-Avon B50 4EL [COVENTRY] *educ* Hayes School; St.John's College, Durham; Hughes Hall, Cambridge; St John's College Nottingham *CV* RE Teacher The Embrook School, Wokingham, Berks 1980–83; RE Teacher, Ranelagh School, Bracknell, Berks 1983–86; Parish Deacon St Mary's Princes Risborough with Ilmer 1988–90; Assistant Curate and Congregational Chaplain Bradford Cathedral 1990–93; Assistant Curate West Swindon and the Lydiards 1993–94; Non-Stipendiary Minister West Swindon and the Lydiards 1994–96; Assistant Curate St John the Baptist and St Andrew Parks and Walcot 1996–98; Honorary Permission to Officiate Christ Church Swindon 1999; Associate Minister Keresley with Coundon and Curate in Charge Keresley Village Community Church 1999–2010; Area Dean Coventry North 2004–10; Associate Minister Heart of England Parishes from 2010
GS 2010–   T: 01789 772217
E: ruth@heartparishes.org.uk
F: 01789 772217

WALLACE, The Revd Brenda Claire *MA*
The Forge Nurseries Church Road Rawreth Wickford SS11 8SH [CHELMSFORD] *b* 1952 *educ* Rayleigh Sweyne Grammar School; Mid Essex Technical College; Sarum College; Lincoln Theological College and Southwark Ordination Course *CV* Parish Deaconess Sutton at Hone 1980–83; Parish Deacon Borstal 1983–89; Assistant Chaplain HMP Cookham Wood 1983–89; Assistant Curate Stansted Chelmsford 1989–97; Administrator Diocesan Youth Centre 1993–97; Associate Priest Hutton Chelmsford, 1997–2013; Priest in Charge, Hullbridge and Rettendon Chelmsford and Deanery Mission Adviser 2013–17; Associate Priest, Rawreth, Rettendon and Hullbridge from 2017
GS 2017–   T: 07853 088907
E: brenda.wallace93@outlook.com

WALTERS, Miss Rosemary Anne *BA, MA, MA, PGCE, DipRE*
1 Mary Green Walk Canterbury Kent CT1 1HZ [CANTERBURY] *b* 1954 *educ* Launceston College; University of East Anglia; Liverpool University; Westhill College; Canterbury Christ Church University; University of Kent *CV* Teacher Comprehensive School 1973–1988; Religious Studies Support Teacher 1988–1993; Schools Officer Canterbury Cathedral 1993–2003; Senior Lecturer Primary Religious Education 2003–2015; Sessional Lecturer in Primary Education 2015–16
GS 1985–1993, 2015–   T: 01227 768891
E: ra.walters@btinternet.com

WARD, The Revd Dr Kevin *MA, PhD*
Theology & Religious Studies University of Leeds Leeds LS2 9JT [UNIVERSITIES, NORTHERN] *educ* Pudsey Grammar School; Edinburgh University; Trinity College Cambridge; Bishop Tucker Theological College, Mukono, Uganda *CV* Church Mission Society Mission Partner (Tutor Bishop Tucker Theological College, Church of Uganda) 1975–91; Tutor Queen's College Birmingham 1991; Parish Ministry Halifax, Wakefield Diocese 1991–95; Senior Lecturer in African Studies, School of Theology and Religious Studies, Leeds University from 1995; Non-Stipendiary Minster St Michael Headingley, Ripon Diocese; Member Ripon Diocesan Working Group in Human Sexuality; Trustee Church Mission Society 2003–10; Newsletter Editor, Uganda Church Association from 1993
GS 2003–05; 2005–   T: 0113 343 3641
E: trskw@leeds.ac.uk

WARNER, The Rt Revd Martin Clive *BA, MA, PhD*
The Palace Chichester West Sussex PO19 1PY [BISHOP OF CHICHESTER] *educ* King's School Rochester; Maidstone Grammar School; St Chad's College Durham; St Stephen's House *CV* Curate St Peter Plymouth 1984–88; Team Vicar Resurrection Leicester 1988–93; Priest

Administrator Shrine of Our Lady of Walsingham 1993–2002; Canon Pastor, St Paul's Cathedral from 2003; Treasurer, St Paul's Cathedral 2008–09; Bishop of Whitby 2009–12; Bishop of Chichester from 2012　　　　　　　　*T:* 01243 782161
E: bishop@chichester.anglican.org
F: 01243 531332

WARNER, Dr Meg (Megan Elizabeth)
BTheol
Flat 1 23 Red Lion Street London WC1R 4PS [LONDON] *b* 1966 *educ* Warrnambool High School, Ballarat Grammar School, Methodist Ladies College (Perth), University of Western Australia, Bristol University, University of Divinity *CV* Lecturer in Law, University of Western Australia 1991–99; Associated Lecturer in Biblical Studies, United Faculty of Theology, 2002–06; Executive/Research Assistant to the Primate of the Anglican Province of Australia 2006–09; Lecturer in Biblical Studies, Trinity College Theological School 2010–12; Visiting Lecturer, King's College London 2013–15; Teaching Fellow in Biblical Studies, King's College London from 2015
GS 2015–　　　　　　　　　*T:* 020 7404 6530
E: meg.warner@kcl.ac.uk

WARREN, Dr Yvonne *MA, PhD, UKCP, BACP*
Cornerston 6 Hillview Stratford Upon Avon CV37 9AY [COVENTRY] *educ* Bedford High School *CV* Nurse 1957–61; Relate Supervisor 1980–95; Psychotherapist from 1996; Bishop's Advisor from 1990; Candidates Panel from 1994; Rector from 1996; Bishop's Visitor 1990–2006; Lay Representative General Synod Ridley Hall Theological College 2000–07; Act Diocesan Advisor Pastoral Care and Counselling until 2011; Archbishops' Assessor from 2011
GS 2000–05; 2005–07; 2010–
T: 01789 414255
E: ywarren@hotmail.co.uk

WARRY, Canon Peter John *BSc*
Diocesan House Amy Johnson Way Clifton Moor York YO30 4XT [DIOCESAN SECRETARY; YORK] *b* 1954 *educ* King James's School, Almondbury, Huddersfield, Lancaster University *CV* Operational Research Manager, Nestlé UK 1994–99; Director of European Software Development, Adaytum 1999–2003; Director of Enterprise Planning Software Development (Europe), Cognos 2003–05; Diocesan Secretary from 2006; Lay Canon York Minster from 2008
T: 01904 699503
E: peter.warry@yorkdiocese.org

WATSON, The Rt Revd Andrew John *MA*
Willow Grange Woking Road Guildford GU4 7QS [BISHOP OF GUILDFORD] *b* 1954 *educ* Winchester College; Corpus Christ College Cambridge; Ridley Hall Theological College *CV* Curate St Peter Ipsley 1987–90; Curate St John and St Peter Notting Hill 1990–95; Vicar St Stephen East Twickenham from 1995; Member Bishop's Council; member Mission and Public Affairs Council from 2006; Area Dean Hampton 2003–08; Bishop of Aston from 2008; Member Board Queen's Foundation, Birmingham from 2011; Member Board Archbishops' College of Evangelists from 2011; Chair of Trustees Church Pastoral Aid Society 2013; Chair of Panel for World Mission and the Anglican Communion 2013; Bishop of Guildford from 2014; Chair Ordained Vocations Working Group from 2015
GS 2000–08, 2014　　　　　*T:* 01483 590500
E: bishop.guildford@cofeguildford.org.uk
F: 01483 590501

WEBSTER, The Rt Revd Glyn Hamilton *SRN*
Holy Trinity Rectory Micklegate York YO1 6LE [BISHOP OF BEVERLEY] *educ* Darwen Secondary Tech (Grammar) School; St John College Durham *CV* Curate All Saints Huntington York 1977–81; Vicar St Luke Evangelist York and Senior Chaplain York District Hospital 1981–92; Senior Chaplain York Health Services NHS Trust 1992–99; Canon and Prebendary York Minster 1994–99; Rural Dean York 1997–2004; Canon Residentiary and Treasurer York Minster from 1999; Canon Pastor from 2000; Prolocutor of York from 2000; Member Archbishops' Council from 2000; Chair Diocesan House of Clergy; Chancellor York Minster from 2004; Associate Diocesan Director of Ordinands from 2005; Member General Synod Business Committee from 2005; Member Hospital Chaplain Council from 2005; Bishop of Beverley from 2012
GS 1995–　　　　　　　　　*T:* 01904 628155
E: office@seeofbeverley.org.uk
F: 0

WEBSTER, The Ven Martin Duncan *BSc, DipTh*
Glebe House Church Lane Sheering Bishops Stortford CM22 7NR [ARCHDEACON OF HARLOW; CHELMSFORD] *educ* Dury Falls Secondary Modern School; Abbs Cross Tech High School; Nottingham University; Lincoln Theological College *CV* Curate St Peter and St Michael Thundersley, Chelmsford 1978–81; Team Vicar Canvey Island 1981–86; Vicar All Saints and St Giles Nazeing 1986–99; Area Dean Harlow 1989–99; Non-Stipendiary Minister Officer 1995–99; Team Rector Waltham Abbey 1999–2009; Archdeacon Harlow from 2009
GS 2005–2010　　　　　　　*T:* 01297 734524
E: a.harlow@chelmsford.anglican.org

WELBY, The Most Revd and Rt Hon Justin Portal MA, BA
Lambeth Palace London SE1 7JU [ARCHBISHOP OF CANTERBURY] *educ* Eton College; Trinity College Cambridge; St John College Durham; Cranmer Hall *CV* Manager Project Finance, Society Nationale Elf Aquitaine, Paris 1978–83; Treasurer Elf UK plc, London 1983–84; Group Treasurer Enterprise Oil plc, London 1984–89; Curate All Saints Chilvers Coton and St Mary Virgin, Astley, Nuneaton, Coventry 1992–95; Rector St James Southam and St Michael & All Angels Ufton, Coventry 1995–2002; Director of International Ministry and residentiary Canon Coventry Cathedral 2002–05; Sub-Dean and Canon for Reconciliation Ministry, Coventry Cathedral 2005–07; Priest in Charge Holy Trinity Coventry 2007; Dean of Liverpool 2007–11; Bishop of Durham 2011–12; Archbishop of Canterbury from 2013   *T:* 020 7898 1200
E: contact@lambethpalace.org.uk
W: www.lambethpalace.org.uk

WELCH, The Ven Stephan John BA, DipTheol, MTh
98 Dukes Ave Chiswick London W4 2AF [ARCHDEACON OF MIDDLESEX; LONDON] *b* 1967 *educ* Luton Grammar School; Luton Sixth Form College; Hull University; Birmingham University; Heythrop College, London University; Queen's College Birmingham *CV* Curate Christ Church Waltham Cross, St Albans 1977–80; Priest in Charge and Vicar St Mary Reculver and St Bartholomew Herne Bay, Canterbury 1980–92; Vicar St Mary Hurley and St James the Less Stubbings, Oxford 1992–2000; Vicar St Peter Hammersmith, London 2000–06; Area Dean Hammersmith and Fulham 2001–06; Archdeacon of Middlesex from 2006; Member Diocesan Advisory Committee, Diocesan Board of Finance, Bishop's Council; Trustee All Saints Educational Trust   *T:* 020 8742 8308
E: archdeacon.middlesex@london.anglican.org
M: 07780 704059 (Mobile)

WELLER, The Ven Dr Susan Karen BSc, BA, PhD
The Church of England Diocese of Lichfield The Small Street Centre 1a Small Street Walsall WS1 3PR [ARCHDEACON OF WALSALL; LICHFIELD] *educ* Wolfreton Secondary School, University of Leeds, University of Manchester, University of Liverpool *CV* Higher Scientific Officer, Plymouth Marine Laboratory 1989–93; Pastoral Assistant University College Plymouth St Mark and St John 1993; Curate, St Peter's Caverswall with St Andrew's Weston Coyney and All Saints, Dilhorne June 1996–99; Assistant Minister, Holy Trinity, Wilnecote, with St Catherine's in Two Gates,

Tamworth 2000–05; Christ Church, Rio de Janeiro, Brazil 2005–11; Interim Minister St Augustine and St Chad's Wednesfield 2012–14; Interim Minister All Saints Darlaston and All Saints Moxley 2014–15; Archdeacon of Walsall from 2015   *T:* 01922 707861
E: archdeacon.walsall@lichfield.anglican.org

WELLINGS-THOMAS, Mr Richard Peter John
Wells House 4 Orville Road SW11 3LR [LONDON] *b* 1971 *CV* Independent Entertainment Professional 1992–2010; Food Importer at Unique Fine Foods from 2010
GS 2015–   *T:* 02072237709
E: wellingsthomas@yahoo.com

WELLS, The Rt Revd Dr Jo Bailey MA, MA, BA, PhD
13 Pilgrims Way Guildford GU4 8AD [BISHOP OF DORKING; GUILDFORD] *b* 1965 *educ* Queenswood School; Marlborough College; Corpus Christi College, University of Cambridge; University of Minnesota; Durham University; Cranmer Hall, St John's College, Durham *CV* Youth Pastor Messiah Episcopal Church St Paul Minnesota 1988–90; Chaplain Clare College Cambridge 1994–97; Dean Clare College Cambridge 1997–2001; Lecturer in Old Testament and Biblical Theology Ridley Hall Cambridge 2001–05; Associate Professor of the Practice of Bible and Ministry and Director of the Anglican Episcopal House of Studies Duke University 2005–12; Chaplain to the Archbishop of Canterbury 2013–16; Bishop of Dorking from 2016; Member (and Moderator) of Diocesan Readers' Board Ely 1996–2002; Diocesan Commission on Marriage North Carolina 2006–08; Trustee of Ridley Hall from 2013; Trustee of the Anglican Centre in Rome 2013–16; Member of Bishop's Council Guildford from 2016; Chair Diocesan Board of Education Guildford from 2017
                 T: 01483 570829
E: Bishop.Jo@cofeguildford.org.uk
Twitter: @BishopDorking

WHARTON, The Revd Canon Kate Elizabeth BSc, BTh
St. George's Vicarage 40 Northumberland Terrace Liverpool L5 3QG [LIVERPOOL] *educ* Merchant Taylors' Girls' School, Leeds Metropolitan University *CV* Speech and Language Therapist, Wakefield and Pontefract NHS Trust 2000–01; Pastoral Assistant, St George Leeds 2001–02; Assistant Curate, St Luke West Derby, Liverpool 2005–09; Vicar, St George Everton, Liverpool 2009–17; Area Dean, Liverpool North 2013–17; Vicar St Bartholomew Roby from 2017
GS 2015–   *T:* 0151 263 6005
                        07957 247581
E: katewharton@btinternet.com
W: www.katewharton.blogspot.co.uk
Twitter: @KateWharton27

WHEATLEY, The Ven Ian James *BTh*
Naval Chaplaincy Service Navy Command HQ Mp 1–2 Leach Building Whale Island Portsmouth PO2 8BY [ARCHDEACON FOR THE ROYAL NAVY] *educ* Royal Grammar School Worcester; Chichester Theological College *CV* Royal Navy 1981–91; Curate Braunton 1994–97; Chaplain Royal Navy from 1997; Royal Navy Principal Denominational Chaplain (Anglican) and Deputy Chaplain of the Fleet
GS 2013–   *T:* 023 9262 5193
       E: ian.wheatley928@mod.uk
       F: 023 9262 5134

WHITE, The Rt Revd Alison Mary *BA, MA*
Hullen House Woodfield Lane Hessle HU13 0ES [BISHOP OF HULL; YORK] *b* 1956 *educ* Notting Hill and Ealing High School; University of Durham; University of Leeds; St John's College, Cranmer Hall, Durham *CV* Community theatre 1978–81; Fairtrade worker 1981–83; Curate St Mary and St Cuthbert Chester le Street 1986–89; Diocesan Adviser in Local Mission Durham 1989–93; Director of Mission and Pastoral Studies, Cranmer Hall 1993–98; Director of Ordinands Durham 1998–2000; Archbishops' Springboard Initiative 2000–04; IME 4–7 officer Peterborough 2005–10; Priest in Charge of St James Riding Mill and Diocesan Adviser in Spirituality and Spiritual Direction Newcastle 2011–15; Bishop of Hull from 2015   *T:* 01482 649019
      E: bishopofhull@yorkdiocese.org

WHITE, Canon Bob (Robert Charles) *MA, CertTh*
St Mary's Vicarage Fratton Rd Portsmouth PO1 5PA [PORTSMOUTH] *educ* Portsmouth Grammar School; Mansfield College Oxford; St Stephen's House Oxford *CV* Curate St John Forton 1985–88; Curate St Mark North End with special responsibility for St Francis Hilsea 1988–92; Vicar St Clare Warren Park 1992–2000; Vicar St Francis Leigh Park 1994–2000; Rural Dean Havant 1998–2000; Vicar St Mary Portsea from 2000; Area Dean Portsmouth from 2011; Member Bishop's Council; Diocesan Advisor on Urban Ministry; Church Urban Fund Link Officer; Chair Diocesan House of Clergy
GS 1995–2000, 2004–   *T:* 023 9282 2687
      E: vicar@portseaparish.co.uk

WHITE, Mr David Peter *AMusLCM, BSc, FCMA, DChA, CGMA*
Church House Great Smith St London SW1P 3AZ [HEAD OF FINANCIAL POLICY AND PLANNING, FINANCE AND RESOURCES, NATIONAL CHURCH INSTITUTIONS] *educ* Dartford Grammar School; London School of Economics *CV* On staff of Church Commissioners since 1990, Head of Finance Planning, Church Commissioners 2002–07, Head of Finance Policy and Planning, Archbishops' Council and Church Commissioners 2007–11, Head of Finance Policy and Planning, National Church Instutions from 2011   *T:* 020 7898 1684
      E: david.white@churchofengland.org
      F: 020 7898 1131

WHITE, The Revd Canon Priscilla Audrey *MA*
The Vicarage Church Lane Kingsbury Tamworth B78 2LR [BIRMINGHAM] *b* 1958 *educ* Perse School for Girls, St Hugh's College Oxford *CV* Parish Deacon Church of the Holy Spirit Southway 1989–93; Team Deacon North Sutton Team 1993–94; Priest North Sutton Team 1994–99; Priest-in-Charge St Mary's Abbotskerswell 1999–2005; also Chaplain to Seale Hayne 1999–2004; Bishop's Adviser for Women 2001–05; Priest-in-Charge of St Faith and St Laurence Harborne Birmingham 2005; Vicar from 2010; Area Dean 2010–17
GS 2015–   *T:* 0121 427 2410
      07896 935798
   E: priscillawhite.harborne@btinternet.com
      Twitter: @priscillavicar

WHITEHOUSE, Mr Robin John
25c Bilbrook Road Bilbrook Wolverhampton WV8 1EU [LICHFIELD] *b* 1953 *educ* Tettenhall College, Wolverhampton, Wolverhampton Polytechnic (now University) *CV* Local Government Officer 1969–2014; Retired from 2014; School Governor from 2003; Chair of School Governing Body 2013–17; Member St Stephen's Church of England Multi-Academy Trust Wolverhampton from 2017, Trustee from 2017, Chair of Trust Board from 2017; Reader from 1983
GS 2015–   *T:* 01902 845328
      07960 889605
   E: robin.wh@college-of-readers.org.uk
      Twitter: @robinjwh

WICKHAM, The Rt Revd Robert James *MA, BA,*
27 Thurlow Road Hampstead London NW3 5PP [BISHOP OF EDMONTON; LONDON] *b* 1967 *educ* Hampton School; University of Durham; King's College London *CV* Curate of St Mary's Willesden 1998–2001; Team Vicar in the Parish of Old St Pancras 2001–07; Rector of Hackney 2007–15; Area Dean of Hackney 2014–15; Bishop of Edmonton from 2015
      T: 020 3837 5250
      07971 699218
   E: bishop.edmonton@london.anglican.org
      Twitter: @bpedmonton

WILCOCKSON, The Ven Stephen Anthony *MA(Oxon), BA*
75 Orion Way Balby Doncaster DN4 8AE [ARCHDEACON OF DONCASTER; SHEFFIELD] *educ* Park High School Birkenhead; Nottingham University; Oxford University; Wycliffe Hall *CV* Curate St Lawrence Pudsey 1976–78; Senior

Curate All Saints with Holy Trinity Wandsworth 1978–81; Vicar St Peter Rock Ferry 1981–86; Vicar St Mark, Lache cum Saltney 1986–95; Vicar St Paul, Howell Hill 1995–2009; Rural Dean Epsom 2000–07; Parish Development Officer Chester Diocese 2009–12; Archdeacon of Doncaster from 2012; Diocesan Synod; Mission and Pastoral Committee; Bishop's Council; Diocesan Advisory Committee; Board of Education; Finance and Property Committee; Safeguarding Committee; Communications Group   *T:* 01302 325787
     E: steve.wilcockson@sheffield.anglican.org
                                  M: 01709 309110

WILCOX, The Rt Revd Dr Pete (Peter Jonathan) *BA, MA, DPhil*
Bishopscroft Snaithing Lane Sheffield S10 3LG [BISHOP OF SHEFFIELD] *educ* Worksop College; St John College Durham; Robinson College Cambridge; St John's College Oxford; Ridley Hall Cambridge *CV* Curate All Saints, Preston on Tees 1987–90; Assistant Priest St Margaret's with St Philip and St Giles Oxford 1990–93; Team Vicar St Edmund's Chapel Gateshead and Director Cranmer Hall Urban Mission Centre 1993–98; Priest in Charge St Paul's Church at the Crossing, Walsall 1998–2006; Canon Chancellor Lichfield Cathedral 2006–12; Dean of Liverpool 2012–17, Bishop of Sheffield from 2017   *T:* 0114 230 2170
          E: bishop@sheffield.anglican.org

WILLIAMS, Mr Andrew John *BSc (Hons), MBCS, MIAP, MRI, MiEEE*
PO Box 5118 Coventry CV1 9FN [COVENTRY] *educ* Eastwood High School, Newton Mearns, Glasgow; Denbigh School, Milton Keynes; Coventry University *CV* Technical Support Analyst, Perkins Engines, Peterborough 1996–97; Software Development Engineer, Marconi Communications, Coventry 1998–2001; Analyst Programmer, Milton Keynes Council, Milton Keynes 2002–05; Freelance IT Consultant, AW CompuTech, Coventry 2005–12; PHP Developer, PC Control Systems, Northampton 2012–13; Councillor Bablake Ward, Coventry City Council, Coventry 2000–14 (Chairman, Finance Scrutiny Board 2005–08; Cabinet Member, Neighbourhoods and Community Safety 2008–10; Conservative Chief Whip 2008–12); Member West Midlands Integrated Transport Authority (Centro), Birmingham 2004–12 (Lead Member, Environment 2011–12; Lead Member, Equality and Diversity 2008–11; Chairman, Business Improvement Committee 2007–08; Chairman, Pension Fund Committee 2006–07; Non Executive Director, Coventry Transport Museum, Coventry 2010–12); Trustee, Coventry (Church) Municipal Charities, Coventry 2005–11; Trustee, The Coventry Refugee and Migrant Centre 2009–10; Software

Developer, Fluid7, Coventry 2013–16; Analyst Developer, Harley Medical Group from 2016
GS 2015–   *T:* 024 7625 6079
          E: synod@andrew-williams.com
          W: http://www.andrew-williams.com/
                            Twitter: @a_j_williams

WILLIAMS, The Revd Preb Canon Brian *AKC*
Sneyd Vicarage Hamil Road Burslem ST6 1AP [LICHFIELD] *educ* Birkenhead Institute, King's College London *CV* Assistant Curate St Mary's Kettering 1977–80; Assistant Curate St Gabriel's Fullbrook, Walsall 1980–83; Priest in charge Holy Trinity, Sneyd, Burslem, Stoke on Trent 1983–85, Incumbent from 1985; Vocations Adviser 1990–2004; Rural Dean 1991–96; Surrogate for marriages from 1991
GS 2015–   *T:* 01782 825841
          E: brianluke@talktalk.net

WILLIAMS, The Rt Revd David Grant *BSc Soc Sci*
Bishop's Lodge Old Alresford Place Colden Lane Alresford SO24 9DY [SUFFRAGAN BISHOP OF BASINGSTOKE; WINCHESTER] *educ* Newport Free Grammar School; Bristol University; Crowther Hall, Birmingham; Wycliffe Hall Theological College *CV* Deputy Headteacher (Church Mission Society Mission Partner), Kitui District, Kenya 1983–85; Lay Assistant, Christ Church Clifton, Bristol 1985–86; Assistant Curate Ecclesall, Sheffield Diocese 1989–92; Vicar Christ Church Dore, Sheffield Diocese 1992–2002; Area Dean, Eccesall Deanery, Sheffield Diocese 1997–2002; Chaplain, Aldine House Secure Unit, Sheffield 1998–2002; Vicar Christ Church Winchester 2002–14; Bishop of Basingstoke from 2014; Chair Diocesan Stewardship Group 2000–02; Member Bishops' Council and Diocesan Standing Committee; Trustee of Ridley Hall Cambridge from 2012; Patron of Treloars College from 2014; Governor of Winchester University from 2014; Patron Congo Church Association from 2016; Member of Thy Kingdom Come Leadership Group from 2016; Chair of Perins Multi-Academy Trust from 2017; Governor of Peter Symmonds FE College from 2017; Chair of the National Stewardship Committee from 2017
GS 2010–14   *T:* 01962 737330
                                    01962 737350
     E: bishop.david@winchester.anglican.org
                                  M: 07889 547095

WILLIAMS, The Revd Giles Peter *BA, MA*
2–4 avenue Général Ferrié 06400 Cannes France [EUROPE] *educ* Strodes School Egham, London University Westfield College; London University School of Oriental and African Studies *CV* Curate Greyfriars Church, Reading 1982–85; Missionary with Rwanda Mission

CMS), Kigali, Rwanda 1986–94 Vicar St John he Baptist, Woking 1995–2010; Rural Dean Woking 2008–10; Chaplain, Holy Trinity Church, Cannes, France
GS 2015–   T: 00 33 494 930 456
                              00 33 493 945 461
                         E: gilesp@gmail.com

WILLIAMS, The Rt Revd Paul Gavin *BA*
c/o Jubilee House Westgate Southwell NG25 0JH
[BISHOP OF SOUTHWELL AND NOTTINGHAM] *educ* Court Fields School Wellington; Grey College University Durham; Wycliffe Hall Oxford *CV* Curate St James Muswell Hill 1992–95; Assistant Vicar Christ Church Clifton 1996–99; Rector St James Gerrards Cross with Fulmer 1999–2009; Area Bishop of Kensington 2009–15; Bishop of Southwell and Nottingham from 2015; Chair Trustees Church Pastoral Aid Society from 2011   T: 01636 817996
            E: bishop@southwell.anglican.org

WILLIAMS, The Revd Dr Rowan Clare
St Lawrence Vicarage 11 Newland Park Close York YO10 3HW [YORK] *educ* King's College Cambridge; Jesus College Cambridge; Westcott House Cambridge *CV* Curate Leicester Resurrection 2005–08; Chaplain University Hospitals Leicester NHS Trust 2008–10; Chaplain York University from 2010; Member Board of Education from 2013
GS 2013–   T: 01904 415460
                         E: rcw514@york.ac.uk
                            M: 07919 861912

WILLIS, The Very Revd Robert Andrew *DL*
The Deanery The Precincts Canterbury CT1 2EP
[DEAN OF CANTERBURY] *b* 1947 *educ* Kingswood Grammar School; Warwick University; Worcester College Oxford; Cuddesdon Theological College *CV* Curate St Chad Shrewsbury 1972–75; Vicar Choral Sarum Cathedral 1975–78; Team Rector Tisbury and Rural Dean Chalke 1978–89; Vicar Sherborne 1987–92; Rural Dean Sherborne 1991–92; Dean of Hereford 1992–2001; Dean of Canterbury from 2001; Member Partnership for World Mission Committee 1990–2001; Member Cathedrals Fabric Commission from 1993; Member Liturgical Commission 1994–98; Chair Deans' Confederation from 1999
GS 1985–92, 1994–   T: 01227 762862
                                   01227 865200
            E: dean@canterbury-cathedral.org
                              F: 01227 865222

WILLMOTT, The Rt Revd Trevor *MA*, *Dip Theol*
The Bishop's Office Old Palace Canterbury CT1 2EE [BISHOP OF DOVER AND BISHOP IN CANTERBURY; ASSISTANT BISHOP OF WINCHESTER] *educ* Plymouth College; St Peter College Oxford; Fitzwilliam College Cambridge; Westcott House Theological College *CV* Curate St George Norton 1974–77; Assistant Chaplain Oslo with Trondheim 1978–79; Chaplain Naples with Capri, Bari and Sorrento 1979–83; Rector Ecton and Warden Peterborough Diocese Retreat House 1983–89; Diocesan Director of Ordinands and Director of Post Ordination Training 1986–97; Canon Residentiary and Precentor Peterborough Cathedral 1989–97; Archdeacon of Durham and Canon Residentiary Durham Cathedral 1997–2002; Suffragan Bishop of Basingstoke 2002–10; Bishop of Dover from 2010; Member General Synod Business Sub-committee from 2005; Member House of Bishops Standing Committee from 2005; Trustee Foundation for Christian Leadership; Member Rural Bishops Panel from 2004; Patron Cross Borders YMCA from 2005; Trustee St Michael's College, Llandaff; Visitor to the Sisters of Bethany
GS 2000–   T: 01227 459382
            E: trevor.willmott@bishcant.org
                              F: 01227 784985

WILSON, The Rt Revd Alan Thomas Lawrence *MA, DPhil*
Sheridan Grimms Hill Great Missenden HP16 9BG
[AREA BISHOP OF BUCKINGHAM; OXFORD] *educ* St John College Cambridge; Balliol College Oxford; Wycliffe Hall Oxford *CV* Honorary Curate Eynsham, Oxford 1979–81; Curate 1981–82; Curate Caversham and Mapledurham 1982–89; Vicar St John Caversham 1989–92; Anglican substitute Chaplain, Her Majesty's Prison Reading, 1990–92; Rector Sandhurst 1992–2003; Rural Dean Sonning 1998–2003; Area Bishop of Buckingham from 2003; Member Council, Wycombe Abbey School from 2008; Chair Oxford Diocesan Board of Education from 2010; University of Buckingham Visiting Professor in Theology from 2010; Member Church of England Pensions Board and CEPB Housing Committee from 2016
                               T: 01494 862173
            E: bishopbucks@oxford.anglican.org
                              F: 01494 890508
                            M: 07525 655756

WILSON, Mr Brian Kenneth *MA FIA*
84 Albert Road Epsom Surrey KT17 4EL
[SOUTHWARK] *educ* Lewes Comprehensive School for Boys; University of Oxford *CV* School Master, Dulwich College 1971–74; School Master, King's School Canterbury 1974–76; Assistant Actuary, Bacon and Woodrow 1976–83; Partner, Bacon and Woodrow 1983–2002; Principal, Hewitt Association 2002–10; Principal, Aon Hewitt 2010; Retired 2010; Member C of E Pensions Board from 2011; Member Remuneration and

Conditions of Service Committee of Archbishop's Council from 2011
GS 2010–   *T:* 01372 740155
                    E: brian.k.wilson@btinternet.com

WILSON, The Very Revd Christine Louise *DipTh*
11 Minster Yard Lincoln LN1 1PJ [DEAN OF LINCOLN] *educ* Margaret Hardy School, Brighton; Southern Dioceses Ministerial Training Scheme *CV* Curate Henfield with Shermanbury and Woodmancate, Chichester 1997–2002; Team Vicar Hove 2002–08; Vicar Goring by Sea 2008–10; Archdeacon Chesterfield 2010–16; Chichester Diocese Overseas Committee 2007–09; Advisory Committee, Derby 2010–16; Board of Finance, Derby 2010–16; Board of Education, Derby 2010–16; Pastoral Committee, Derby 2010–16; Parsonages Committee, Derby 2010–16; Chair Peak Centre 2010–16; Glebe Committee, Derby 2010–16; Dean of Lincoln from 2016
GS 2010–16   *T:* 01522 561630
                    E: dean@lincolncathedral.com

WILSON, Mr John *MIH, MIF*
49 Oakhurst Lichfield WS14 9AL [LICHFIELD] *educ* Polytechnic of North London *CV* HM Forces 1961–76; Deputy Area School Meals Advisor, Cambridgeshire County Council 1977–78; Regional Sales and Marketing Manager, Bateman Catering 1978–83; Director of Training, Mantislight Ltd, 1983–87; Director Operations, Deansbury Ltd, 1987–92; Charity Management Consultant, Charity Support Services, 1992–97; National Fundraising and Marketing Advisor, Age Concern England, 1997–2001; Charity Management Consultant, Charity Support Services, 2001–06; Chief Executive, Line Line, 2006–10; Member Diocesan Synod from 1989; Member Diocesan Pastoral Committee from 2000; Member Bishop's Council from 2000; Member Board of Patronage from 2003; Diocesan Chair of House of Laity from 2009; Lay Chair of Lichfield Deanery from 1987; Treasurer Church House Deaneries Group (The National Deaneries Network) from 2003; Chair Board of Directors/Trustees Link Line Community Services from 2010; Managing Director Church Jobs Ltd (www.churchjobfinder.co.uk) from 2010
GS 2005–   *T:* 01543 268678
                    E: charity.services@btclick.com
                                 F: 01543 411685
                                 M: 07785 334077

WINDSOR, The Ven Fiona
20 Langley Lane Ifield Crawley West Sussex RH11 0NA [ARCHDEACON OF HORSHAM; CHICHESTER] *CV* St Peters Chertsey Guildford Diocese 2000–04; Team Vicar Papworth Team Ministry 2004–06; Ely Diocese, Team Rector Papworth

Team Ministry Ely Diocese 2006–14; Archdeacon of Horsham from 2014.
                                 T: 01273 425048
           E: archhorsham@chichester.anglican.org

WINROW, Mrs Kathryn Mary *MA, BEd(hons)*
Pineridge 244a Andover Road Newbury RG14 6PT [OXFORD] *educ* Broadway Grammar School, University of London *CV* Teacher/Senior Teacher, Cranford Community School, Hounslow 1972–82; Deputy Head Teacher, Lampton School, Hounslow 1983–90; Education Inspector 1990–93; Head Teacher, Ranelagh School, Bracknell 1993–2015; Executive Head Teacher, Oxford Diocese
GS 2015–   *T:* 01635 45380
                                     07774 212410
                    E: kwinrow@btinternet.com

WINTER, The Revd Canon Dr Dagmar *Dr Theol*
The Vicarage Kirkwhelpington Newcastle upon Tyne NE19 2RT [NEWCASTLE] *b* 1963 *educ* Gesamtschule Oberursel; Erlangen University; Aberd University; Heidelberg University; Herborn Theological College *CV* Curate St Mark Bromley 1996–99; Associate Vicar and Deaner Training Officer Hexham Abbey 1999–2006; Priest in Chrage Kirkwhelpington with Kirkharle and Kirkheaton, and Cambo and Diocesan Officer for Rural Affairs from 2006; Area Dean of Morpeth from 2010; Honorary Canon Newcastle Cathedral from 2011
GS 2005–   *E:* dagmar.winter@btinternet.com

WINTERTON, Lt Gemma *BA, MA*
72 Osbourne Road Warsash SO31 9GG [ARMED FORCES SYNOD] *educ* Chichester High School for Girls, University of Manchester *CV* HMS King Alfred 2006–11; SO3 PsyOps Production based in Lashka Gah, Afghanistan 2011–12; Britannia Royal Naval College 2013–14; 1Lt Thunderer Squadron, Defence Technical Undergraduate Scheme 2014–15; Officer in the Royal Navy from 2006
GS 2013–   *T:* 01489 482186
                    E: gemma.winterton@gmail.com

WINTON, The Rt Revd Alan Peter *BA, PhD*
Herfast House 5 Vicar Street Wymondham NR18 0PL [SUFFRAGAN BISHOP OF THETFORD; NORWICH] *educ* Chislehurst and Sidcup Grammar School; Trinity College Bristol; University Sheffield; Lincoln Theological College *CV* Assistant Curate Christ Church Southgate 1991–95; Priest in Charge St Paul's Walden with Preston 1995–99; Continuing Ministerial Education Officer Diocese St Albans 1995–99; Rector Welwyn with Ayot St Peter 1999–2005; Team Rector Welwyn 2005–09; Bishop of Thetford

from 2009; Chair Discipleship and Ministry Forum Diocese Norwich; Chair Norwich Diocesan Ministry Course Governing Body

T: 01953 528010
E: bishop.thetford@dioceseofnorwich.org

WITCOMBE, The Very Revd John Julian MA, MPhil
1 Hill Top Coventry CV1 5AB [DEAN OF COVENTRY] educ Bramcote Hills Grammar School; Nottingham High School; Emmanuel College, Cambridge; Nottingham University; St John College, Nottingham CV Curate, St John Birtley, Durham 1984–87; Curate-in-Charge, St Barnabas Inham Nook, Southwell 1987–91; Vicar, St Luke Lodge Moor, Sheffield, 1991–95; Team Rector, Uxbridge, London, 1995–98; Dean, St John College Nottingham, 1998–2005; Ministry Officer and Director of Ordinands, Gloucester, 2005–2010; Director, Department of Discipleship and Ministry, Gloucester 2010–12; Residentiary Canon Gloucester Cathedral 2010–12; Dean of Coventry from 2012
GS 2010–   T: 024 7652 1223
E: john.witcombe@coventrycathedral.org
W: www.coventrycathedral.org.uk

WITTS, Mrs Susan Anne BA
20 Amber Drive Chorley PR6 0LA [BLACKBURN] educ Mather College Manchester; Edge Hill University; Church College Certificate School Work St Martin's Lancaster CV Primary School Teacher 1979–2005; Assistant Director Children's Work, Board of Education; Blackburn Diocese from 2005; Diocese Blackburn Board of Education Liturgical Committee
GS 2010–   T: 01254 503070
E: susan.witts@blackburn.anglican.org

WOLSTENHOLME, Canon Carol OBE, FCIPD
12 Ashleigh Crescent Denton Newcastle upon Tyne NE5 2AE [NEWCASTLE] b 1967 educ Rutherford High School Newcastle CV Department Work and Pensions Human Resources 1960–2003; Management Consultant from 2000 including Croatia, Myers Briggs, Employment Tribunal Service member, coaching individuals, Design and development of Culture and Change Management; Reader 2006; Cathedral Council 2006; Chair Newcastle Diocesan Mission and Pastoral Committee 2006–14; Member Newcastle Diocesan Strategical Development Group from 2007; Bishop's Council from 2007; Chair Deaneries Development Task Group 2009; Trustee Lindisfarne Regional Training Partnership 2012–14; Lay Leadership Newcastle Diocese; Commission for Clergy Discipline 2015; Remuneration and Conditions of Service Committee 2015
GS 2008–   T: 0191 274 5144
E: cawol43@aol.com

WOODHOUSE, The Revd Canon Thomas Mark Bews MA
17a Edward Road Dorchester Dorset DT1 2HL [SALISBURY] educ Robert Smyth School, Market Harborough, Southfields College of Further Education, Leicester; The University of Gloucestershire, Cheltenham CV The Kings Head Hotel, Cirencester, Larder Chef and First Commis 1984–86; General Assistant, 1986–88; Assistant Manager, 1988–90; Senior Assistant Manager 1990; Assistant Warden, Southwark Diocesan Training Centre, September 1990–1992; Ordinand 1992–95; Assistant Curate of St Matthew's, Cainscross with All Saints, Selsley, 1995–98; Vicar of Hardwicke and Elmore with Longney October 1998–2005; Vicar of Royal Wootton Bassett September 2005–14; Team Rector of Dorchester and The Winterbournes February from 2014
GS 2015–   T: 01305 267944
                           07926 082533
E: tmbwoodhouse@gmail.com

WOODS, Miss Deborah (Debbie) Jayne BA, MA
10 South Downs Knutsford Cheshire WA16 8ND [CHESTER] educ Knutsford High School, Hertford College Oxford. CV Articled Clerk and Solicitor with DWF solicitors Manchester 1989–93; Lecturer in Legal Practice at The College of Law Chester 1993–2009; Associate Professor at the University of Law Manchester from 2009
GS 2015–   T: 01565 651099
                           07505 381109
E: debbiewoods@ntlworld.com

WRIGHT, The Ven Dr Paul BD, MTh, DMin, AKC
The Archdeaconry The Glebe Chislehurst BR7 5PX [ARCHDEACON OF BROMLEY AND BEXLEY; ROCHESTER] educ Crayford School; King's College London; Heythrop College London; Ripon College, Cuddesdon; Lampeter University of Wales CV Curate St George Beckenham, Rochester 1979–83; Curate St Mary with St Matthias and St John, Southwark 1983–85; Chaplain Church School Richmond, Southwark 1983–85; Vicar St Augustine Gillingham, Rochester 1985–90; Rector St Paulinus Crayford, Rochester 1990–99; Rural Dean Erith 1993–97; Honorary Canon Rochester Cathedral 1998–2003; Vicar St John Evangelist Sidcup, Rochester 1999–2003; Archdeacon of Bromley and Bexley from 2003; Member Bishop's Council; Member Diocesan Board of Patronage; Chair Advisory Board for Mission and Unity; member Ecclesiastical Law Society; Bishop's Inspector of Theological Colleges   T: 020 8467 8743
E: archdeacon.bromley@
rochester.anglican.org
F: 020 8467 8743
M: 07985 902601

WHO'S WHO

WHO'S WHO

YATES, The Revd Andrew *BA, PGCE*

Hanover House 6A King's Road Penzance TR18 4LG [TRURO] *b* 1953 *educ* King Edward VI School Lichfield, Durham University *CV* Curate St Margaret's Brightside, Sheffield 1980–83; Team Vicar in Haverhill Team Ministry and Industrial Chaplain, Suffolk 1984–90; Vicar of Aylesham and Adisham, Kent 1990–97; Priest-in-charge of St Augustine's, Dudley and Black Country Urban and Industrial Mission Chaplain to Merrt Hill Retail Centre 1997–2003; Priest-in-charge of Tresillian and St Michael Penkivel and Diocese of Truro Social Responsibility Officer 2003–12; Diocese of Truro Social Responsibility Officer from 2003; Priest in Charge of St Pol de Leon, Paul in the Penlee Cluster of Churches from 2012

GS 2015–

T: 01736 367863
07773 088906
E: srotruro@btinternet.com
W: www.penleecluster.org.uk

YEMM, Mr Ian *MA, PGDip, BAHons, LRAM*

33 Horse Street Chipping Sodbury Bristol BS37 6DA [BRISTOL] *educ* The Wakeman School Shrewsbury; Shrewsbury VIth Form College; University of Winchester; Sarum College Salisbury; Royal Academy of Music; University of Surrey; Roehampton *CV* Opera Singer, Welsh National Opera, 2003–09; University Coordinating and Anglican Chaplain, University of the West of England Bristol, from 2010

GS 2012–

T: 01454 318608
07514 139825
E: tenor@ianyemm.co.uk
W: www.ianyemm.co.uk
Twitter: @ianyemm